D0941655

ALSO BY ANATOLE CHUJOY

Ballet (1936)

The Symphonic Ballet (1937)

The New York City Ballet (1953)

Fundamentals of the Classic Dance (1947)
(translator and editor of
Agrippina Vaganova's definitive textbook
on Russian ballet technique)

The Dance Encyclopedia (1949)
(compiler and editor)

Fokine, Memoirs of a Ballet Master (1961)
(editor)

ALSO BY P. W. MANCHESTER

Vic-Wells: A Ballet Progress (1942)

The Rose and the Star (1948)
(with Iris Morley)

The Dance Encyclopedia

REVISED AND ENLARGED EDITION

Compiled and edited by

Anatole Chujoy

and

P. W. Manchester

SIMON AND SCHUSTER
NEW YORK

PUBLISHED BY SIMON AND SCHUSTER
ROCKEFELLER CENTER, 630 FIFTH AVENUE
NEW YORK, NEW YORK 10020

FIRST PRINTING

LIBRARY OF CONGRESS CATALOG CARD NUMBER: 67–28038
DESIGNED BY EVE METZ
MANUFACTURED IN THE UNITED STATES OF AMERICA
LITHOGRAPHED BY THE MURRAY PRINTING CO., FORGE VILLAGE, MASS.
BOUND BY AMERICAN BOOK–STRATFORD PRESS, INC., NEW YORK, N.Y.

ACKNOWLEDGMENTS

IN COMPILING AND EDITING this book we have been assisted in many ways by a number of individuals and publications.

We especially wish to acknowledge our sincere appreciation to the following not only for their articles but also for additional help and advice: Dr. George H. Amberg, George Balanchine, Ann Barzel, Cyril W. Beaumont, Alice Bingham, Esmée Bulnes, George Chaffee, Mary Clarke, Dr. Selma Jeanne Cohen, A. V. Coton, Edwin Denby, Derra de Moroda, Dr. M. Frances Dougherty, Marian Eames, Ann Hutchinson, La Meri, Mr. and Mrs. Reginald Laubin, John Martin, Jacqueline Maskey; Genevieve Oswald, Curator of the Dance Collection of the New York Performing Arts Library and Museum, and her co-workers, Virginia Christ-Janer, Giovanna Gioé, Barbara Goldberg, Isabel Kerr, and Rosalie Stone; Angiola Sartorio, Frederick C. Schang, Dr. Miron Silberstein, Walter Terry, the late Dr. Pierre Tugal, G. B. L. Wilson, Dr. Rachael D. Yocom.

Our grateful appreciation is due Lincoln Kirstein for his Introduction and permission to use material from his published works.

We are indebted to the late Miss Lillian Moore for her articles and for her research in establishing correct dates and, in many instances, proper first names of eighteenth- and early nineteenth-century choreographers, to James Lyons, editor of the *American Record Guide,* for his assistance in music identification, and to the photographers whose names are listed in the Credits in the back of the book.

We acknowledge with grateful thanks the contributions from our foreign collaborators, among them Paula Balma and Nel Roos (The Netherlands); Jaques Corseuil (Brazil); Svend Kragh-Jacobsen and Jeanne Steinmetz (Denmark); Irène Lidova (France); Dr. Max Niehaus (Germany); Natalia Roslavleva (Soviet Union); Anna Greta Ståhle (Sweden); Lauretta Thistle (Canada); Victoria Garcia Victorica (Argentina); Kathrine Sorley Walker (Great Britain and Australia).

Our special thanks go to Charlotte Seitlin, our editor at Simon and Schuster, for her direction and assistance for more than three years, and to Eve Metz for her talent, taste and skill in designing the book.

Introduction

BY LINCOLN KIRSTEIN

WE ARE TOLD that the word "Encyclopedia" derives from a late-Latin or pseudo-Greek term indicating "a circle of learning," a general course in instruction, sources for comprehensive information. Information about the art and science of dancing is doubly difficult to secure. That part, the movement of the human body in space to some aural accompaniment, is based on performances at a certain time, which by their nature are unique, irreplaceable, unrepeatable and ephemeral in memory. What does get itself written is hardly ever authored by dancers, who, most of all, since they possess it in their bodies, know whereof the writing is concerned. The art of dance in performance bears slight reference to words on a printed page, or even pictures, except as jogs to memory. A medical encyclopedia presumably gets closer to the heart of its matter since patterns of health and illness can be mapped through the microscope, and close observations over the years provide materials for continual corroboration. Encyclopedias of art and artists, music and musicians seem superficially even easier—if there is anything easy about the craft of the encyclopedia. But attempts to provide concrete information about the dance must baffle the specialist, dancers and teachers of dancing alike. Fortunately, the generalist comes to the rescue of the specialist. What can be set down as signpost, ground rules, remembrancer or history amounts to no mean memorial. The operation of the ant and bee is full of use and sometimes sweetness. Industry, in itself, is a kind of passion; it inspirits. This book cannot produce dancing or dancers, but it gives them another floor, an intellectual one. This floor can help put their abstractions in order, if they are more than physically inclined. Metaphysics has not occupied many dancers, but those whom it attracts have often found it useful. Facts about dancing help make it more legible.

The date of an encyclopedia tells much of the condition of its subject at the moment. An eighteenth-century work would have included many passages quoting Greek and Latin sources that we no longer feel add up to much for our use. They have more to do with libraries than theatres. And more has happened in theatres for the dance in the last sixty years than in the previous six hundred, as far as audiences today go. Ballet alone, the descent of the classic academic opera-house tradition in the West, has forsaken a small élite public and has been transformed into mass entertainment. It is supported by a huge bibliography of books, pictorial materials and films. The education of dancers, in those centers which establish standards, differs only stylistically. Just as gross anatomy is taught to first-year medical students much the same in America or Japan, only minor differences separate the daily ballet class of widely diffused national institutions. The information supporting such basic training will be found herein. The linking facts amounting to historical development are here, too.

As for national taste—what would be the difference of a similar encyclopedia, edited, for example, in Leningrad, London, Paris or Rome? Traces of native bias might be perceived. Rome might have least to write about, since the Italian audience is far more operatic than balletic. The Russians would naturally stress the Slav contribution, which has at times been preponderant, but more in exile than at home. A xenophobic policy prevents much interest in progressive aims. One can imagine that the French might have more entries about costume, scenery and music than choreography, and more about French theatres than the rest of the world. English and American versions share a common language and an allied and truly international culture. The audiences of both nations have seen much of the same dancing and dancers since World War II.

The present book was projected for use over a large area. It provides source material not easily found in library files. Historically, it is indispensable. It also makes very absorbing reading. Its organization, based on the experience of earlier editions, is exemplary. Its tone is dispassionate. Its authors are responsible; they have laid down limits which are strict, lean and peremptory. They had to; this is an encyclopedia, not a library. They were imbued with a passion for the dance based on half a century of close personal observation in the day-to-day experience of performances. They have written from firsthand inspection as much as, or more than, from researched sources.

Although what one sees on the stage defies description and can only come alive by analogy, there is always, in the dancing of repertories, the aura of past repetitions and earlier performers. It makes a quivering halo of history and tradition around living performances. This encyclopedia provides binoculars to enhance such seeing. There is the sweat of mind and memory, as well as of the body; much of this intangible material, also part of the flesh and blood and bones of dancing, saturates the pages of this generous compendium.

Contents

Principal Articles and Contributors:

A Thousand Times Neigh. See FORD BALLET.

Aakesson, Birgit, contemporary Swedish dancer and choreographer. Studied with Mary Wigman and made her debut in Paris at the Vieux Colombier in 1934; gave recitals in Sweden and in many European countries, appearing in the U.S. at Jacob's Pillow Dance Festival (1955). She has developed her own extremely personal style of movement which remains unique. In 1957 she staged her first ballet for a professionally trained troupe—*Sisyphus,* for the Royal Swedish Ballet. *The Minotaur* followed (1958), then *Rites* (1960), and *Play for Eight* (June 8, 1962, during the Swedish Festival of Music and Ballet). Karl-Birger Blomdahl composed the score for *Play for Eight;* the décor, by Olle Bonnier, an easel artist, was his first for the theater. One scene used only mobiles and lights for the entire movement. All Aakesson's ballets are worked out in collaboration with the Norwegian pianist Kaare Gundersen. She choreographed *Icaros,* premièred May 24, 1963, as a ballet for one dancer, Bjorn Holmgren, on the theme of modern man in space, with music by Sven Erik Back, and décor by Lage Lindell. Since June, 1963, she has been a member of the artistic council (with Antony Tudor and Birgit Cullberg) responsible for the policy of the Royal Swedish Ballet.

Abramova, Anastasia, artist of the RSFSR, ballerina of the Moscow Bolshoi Theatre, b. 1902. Abramova was one of the quartet of ballerinas trained by Alexander Gorsky and Vassily Tikhomirov in the 1920's (the others being Liubov Bank, Valentina Kudriavtseva and Nina Pod-

Birgit Aakesson in Soir Bleu

goretskaya) who became the first Soviet-style leading dancers of the Bolshoi Theatre. Abramova entered the Bolshoi school in 1910 and was graduated in 1917, having also studied with Yekaterina Geltzer and Yekaterina Vazem. Her first ballerina role was Lise in *La Fille Mal Gardée* (1922). She was also particularly successful as Swanilda (*Coppélia*) and Aurora (*The Sleeping Beauty*). In Soviet ballets she danced Jeanne (*Flames of Paris*), Tao-Hoa (*The Red Flower*), Stepmother and Fairy (*Cinderella*). Retired from the Bolshoi in 1948.

Abraxas. Ballet in 5 scenes; chor.: Marcel Luipart; music: Werner Egk; book: Heinrich Heine; décor: Wolfgang Znamenacek. First prod.: Munich Staatsoper, June 6, 1948, with Luipart (Faust), Solange Schwarz (Bellastriga), Irina Kladivova (Archiposa). Egk utilized Heine's dance poem "Doctor Faustus" (1847) for his ballet, the basic premise of which is that anyone who sells himself to the devil for the sake of a life of sensual pleasure perishes as a result of the pact. French choreographer Janine Charrat staged the ballet for the Berlin Städtische Oper, October 8, 1949; the music and theme have also been used by other choreographers.

Abstract Ballet, a ballet composition of pure or absolute dance movements expressed for their own sake, not restricted by plot, definite program or general idea. It is dance for dance's sake usually, but not always motived by the music to which it is performed. Some examples of abstract ballets are: Michel Fokine's *Les Sylphides* (Chopin), Leonide Massine's *Choreartium* (Brahms), George Balanchine's *Concerto Barocco* (J. S. Bach) and *Agon* (Igor Stravinsky), Frederick Ashton's *Symphonic Variations* (César Franck), John Taras' *Designs With Strings* (Tchaikovsky). An example of an abstract ballet danced without music is Jerome Robbins's *Moves*.

Abstract Dance.

1. Generic term for a composition of pure dance movements having no plot and no literal or implied meaning except as movement, choreographed in any of the theatrical dance forms including ballet, modern dance, tap, etc., or combination of these.

2. A type of "pure" dance, popular in Germany ca. 1925, in which the dancer's body was only important functionally as it gave movement to the geometrical costumes which covered it. Oscar Schlemmer, a painter, was a leader in this experimental dance at the Bauhaus in Weimar. He composed his *Triadic Ballet,* a series of twelve abstract dances grouped in threes, for which he used three colors (yellow, pink, black) to express three moods—gay, majestic, and fantastic—indicated by the movement. The dance was subordinated to the costumes which used a contrast of shiny and dull textures against moving spheres, spirals, etc. The idea and its expression in the original forms have been dead for some thirty-five years, but an influence or, at least a trace of this "pure" dance, can be seen in the work of Alwin Nikolais and his pupils Murray Louis, Beverly Schmidt, Dorothy Vislocky, and others, for Henry Street Playhouse, N.Y.

Academic Ballet. See CLASSIC BALLET.

Académie Royale de Danse, L', was established in Paris in 1661 by Louis XIV. Before this time dancing masters had belonged to the Guild of Musicians, but the King felt this Guild unqualified to judge the merits of dancers. The functions of the academicians were to teach dancing to courtiers, prepare ballets for royal fetes, and train ballet masters and choreographers. The charter members of the Académie were thirteen professional masters who taught in a room in the Palace of the Tuileries. They also met for discussions at a tavern called l'Epée de

Bois. In 1672 Louis combined l'Académie de Danse with l'Académie Royale de Music (which had been founded in 1669), appointing Jean Baptiste Lully as director of the organization. Charles Louis Beauchamps was maître de ballet. In 1713 a school was established to prepare dancers for the Opéra, and the Académie was entrusted with directing this school as well as its own. Thus, the organization began to train professional dancers, as well as teachers and ballet masters. Among the outstanding dancers trained by the academicians were Marie Allard, Marie Camargo, Marie Sallé, Madeleine Guimard, Gaetan Vestris, Jean Georges Noverre, Maximilien Gardel, and Jean Lany. In 1760 Noverre attacked the Académie for having published no treatise on either the theory or technique of dancing. He charged that although the academicians were outstanding as individuals, they accomplished nothing as a group. By this time the meetings of the organization were already infrequent. No mention of it is found after 1779. See also ACADÉMIE ROYALE DE MUSIQUE, L'.

Académie Royale de Musique, L', the original name of the Théâtre National de l'Opéra (see PARIS OPÉRA BALLET). L'Académie Royale de Musique acquired its name in 1671, two years after l'Abbé Perrin and the Marquis de Sourdeac had founded the Académie d'Opéra. The change was made when Perrin and Sourdeac staged the first-opera-ballet, *Pomone,* choreographed by Charles Beauchamps to music by Robert Cambert. The Académie underwent various title changes with changes in the French political scene, becoming l'Académie Nationale, reverting briefly to l'Académie Royale, and finally becoming l'Académie Impériale de Musique before acquiring its present name, Théâtre National de l'Opéra in 1871. The first permanent home of the Académie Royale de Musique was the Salle Molière in the old Palais Royal (1673–1763). When this burned down, the Académie was established in the Salle Montansier in the Rue Richelieu (1794–1820). In 1821 it moved to a new location in Rue le Peletier, where it remained until 1873, when this structure also burned down. The present building, familiarly known as the Palais Garnier after its architect, was built between 1861 and 1874. The façade is decorated with statuary, the most notable group being Jean-Baptiste Carpeaux's masterpiece, *La Danse.* The ornate interior is famous for its magnificent marble staircase, the mirrored and chandeliered foyer, and the foyer de danse immediately behind the stage. When opened up, the stage, including the foyer de danse, has a depth of 120 feet. This is done on special occasions, such as state gala performances, when the Théâtre National de l'Opéra stages a défilé in which the entire Paris Opéra Ballet, from petits rats to étoiles, enter, rank by rank, to the march from Hector Berlioz's *Les Troyens à Carthage.* See also ACADÉMIE ROYALE DE DANSE; PARIS OPÉRA BALLET; DÉFILÉ.

Accidents While Dancing.

BY DR. MIRON SILBERSTEIN.

In the practice of their profession dancers may be subject to the following conditions due to accidents: fractures, dislocations, sprains, strains, and bruises. A FRACTURE is a broken bone. Most often it is acquired by a dancer through an unfortunate fall. There are simple and compound fractures. The general symptoms are severe pain at the place of fracture, deformity, and swelling. In a simple fracture there may be no deformity. In cases of fracture the best and actually only thing to do is to leave the extremity in absolute rest, apply cold applications, and call a physician. Do not attempt to treat a fracture yourself. It is a serious accident, but fortunately not a very frequent one.

DISLOCATION is a condition in which a bone gets out of joint. Usually it breaks the capsules (the sac-like structures enclosing the joint) and causes severe pain, swelling, and deformity. It is difficult for a layman to reduce (put back in place) a large dislocated joint, such as a shoulder, hip joint, or knee. Therefore the proper thing to do is to call a physician immediately and not to attempt to reduce the dislocation. While waiting for the physician, the affected joint should be immobilized and cold compresses applied locally. It is much easier to reduce a dislocation of the small bones of the fingers and toes. Generally, it is sufficient to pull upon the dislocated joint in the direction of the axis of the finger or toe until the bone jumps back into place.

SPRAINS are momentary dislocations: the bone is thrown out of its place, but springs back immediately. Wrist and ankle sprains are frequently observed by dancers. They are caused by violent stretches or twists of certain joints. Muscular tension, lifting, or falling are also common causes of sprains. In cases of sprain the joints are usually very painful and present swelling, inability to use the joint and, later, discoloration due to hemorrhage. The first aid for this condition is to elevate the affected part, apply cold applications, cold water, ice-bag, or a wet dressing with lead and opium solution. If the condition improves there is no need to call a physician. If no improvement takes place, a physician should be consulted.

STRAINS are injuries to the muscles and tendons as a result of severe exertion. Dancers who have to lift partners or jump frequently are susceptible to this condition. Local symptoms are stiffness and pain in movement of the injured part. Rest for the injured muscles in the most comfortable position is first aid for this condition. The application of heat brings considerable relief.

BRUISES are caused by blows to some part of the body. These blows usually break the small blood vessels and tissue just under the skin. This explains the blue discoloration, swelling, and pain of the injured place. Treatment unnecessary, but in case of pain and a large area of discoloration, applications of cold water or ice-bags are advised. Almost anyone can recognize the conditions described above. Recognition, however, should not be followed by treatment by a lay person except to alleviate the immediate discomfort of the injured.

Acrobats of God. Modern dance work; chor.: Martha Graham; commissioned music: Carlos Surinach, scored for orchestra and three on-stage mandolinists; décor: Isamu Noguchi; costumes: Martha Graham. First prod.: Martha Graham and Dance Company, 54th St. (formerly Adelphi) Theatre, N.Y., Apr. 27, 1960, with Martha Graham, Helen McGehee, Akiko Kanda, Linda Hodes, Ethel Winter, Mary Hinkson, David Wood, Bertram Ross, Paul Taylor, Robert Powell, Richard Kuch, Dan Wagoner. Says the program note: "This is Martha Graham's fanfare to dance as an art . . . a celebration in honor of the trials and tribulations, the disciplines, denials, stringencies, glories and delights of a dancer's world . . . and of the world of the artist."

Actors Equity Association (Equity). See TRADE UNIONS, THEATRICAL.

Adagio.

1. Any dance or combination of steps done to slow music, as contrasted with allegro.

2. A series of exercises during a ballet lesson designed to develop grace, a sense of line, and balance.

3. Part of the classic pas de deux danced by the ballerina and her partner. French dancers and teachers call it adage, Americans and Russians prefer the Italian term.

Adam, Adolphe Charles (1803–1856), French composer of music for *Giselle* (1841), *Le Corsaire* (1856), and other ballets. Also composed many operas and the well-known Christmas carol "Minuit Chrétien" (O Holy Night). See also ROMANTIC BALLET; GISELLE.

Adam Zero. Ballet in 1 act; chor.: Robert Helpmann; commissioned music: Arthur Bliss; book: Michael Benthall; décor: Roger Furse. First prod.: Sadler's Wells (now Royal) Ballet, Royal Opera House, Covent Garden, London, Apr. 10, 1946, with Robert Helpmann (title role), June Brae, and David Paltenghi in principal roles. Man's life from birth to death symbolized by the creation of a ballet, with the three Fates deciding on his life's span.

Adama, Richard (Richard Adams), American dancer, b. Long Beach, Calif., 1928. Studied with Bronislava Nijinska (Hollywood), Nora Kiss (Paris), Georgia Hiden (Vienna). With Original Ballet Russe in Spain, Portugal, and North Africa, 1948; with Grand Ballet du Marquis de Cuevas (1949–54), becoming soloist (1950), and first soloist (1952). Concert tour as partner of Yvette Chauviré (1954–55). Guest artist with Maurice Béjart company and Janine Charrat Ballet (1955). First soloist, Vienna State Opera Ballet (1955–61), dancing principal roles in *Giselle, Swan Lake, Les Sylphides, Legend of Joseph* (Erika Hanka version), *Le Spectre de la Rose, Hamlet* (Boris Blacher–Yvonne Georgi version), and Iago in *The Moor of Venice* (Blacher-Hanka). Leading dancer, assistant ballet master, and choreographer, Hannover Opera Ballet (1961), revising *Giselle* to follow original Adolphe Adam score, opening cuts and eliminating the Marius Petipa additions. Staged *Spiralen* (Spirals), original ballet to music by Ronnefeld (1962). Appointed director of Bremen (Ger.) State Opera Ballet (fall, 1963). His first major production there was the re-creation of Filippo Taglioni's *La Sylphide,* featuring Elisabeth Paul in the title role and Hans Georg as James, with the original Jean Schneitzhoeffer score (for which he researched in the Paris Opéra archives for a year prior to the ballet's presentation in Dec. 1964); also staged a very successful production of *Giselle* (summer, 1966).

Richard Adama, dancer-choreographer

Adamova, Adela, Argentine ballerina, b. Turin, Italy, 1927, now Argentine citizen. Studied dance with Michel Borovski. Joined Teatro Colón (1942); promoted to soloist (1947); then to ballerina (1948). Her repertoire includes *Sueño de Niña, Evolucion del Movimiento, Hamlet, Les Patineurs, Apollon Musagète, Coppélia, La Boutique Fantasque* (Margaret Wallman version), *The Sleeping Beauty, The Nutcracker,* and others. In 1953 appeared as guest artist at the Paris Opéra, Teatro alla Scala, Milan, Maggio Musicale Fiorentino (May Musical Festival in Florence). Since 1953 appears mostly in musical comedy as dancer and actress; records songs in Spanish, Portuguese, Italian, and English.

Adams, David, Canadian dancer, b. Winnipeg, Manitoba, 1928; m. Lois Smith. Began his dance training with Winnipeg Ballet School in 1938; joined the company (now Royal Winnipeg Ballet) in 1946. Later that year studied in London at Sadler's Wells (now Royal Ballet) School and danced with Sadler's Wells Theatre Ballet; also studied with Vera Volkova, George Gontcharov, and others. Danced with International Ballet and Metropolitan Ballet in England (1946–48), creating one of the two male roles in *Designs with Strings* while with the latter company. Returned to Canada to join National Ballet of Canada at its inception and has been premier danseur ever since except for two leaves of absence (1961–62, 1963) as guest artist with London's Festival Ballet. Adams dances all the principal classic roles, Siegfried (*Swan Lake*), Albrecht (*Giselle*), Franz (*Coppélia*), Sugar Plum Fairy Cavalier (*The Nutcracker*), *Le Spectre de la Rose* and also Lover (*Lilac Garden*), Second Song (*Dark Elegies*), Italian Cavalier (*Gala Performance*), and others. For Festival Ballet he has danced Mizgir (*The Snow Maiden*), title role (*Peer Gynt*), among others. He has also choreographed a number of works, the best known of which is *Barbara Allen*. His brother, Lawrence, is also a dancer with National Ballet of Canada.

Adams, Diana, contemporary American ballerina, b. Stanton, Va. Studied ballet with her stepmother, Mrs. Emily Hadley Adams in Memphis, Tenn., then with Edward Caton and Agnes de Mille in N.Y. Made her debut in the musical *Oklahoma!* (1943); joined Ballet (now American Ballet) Theatre (1944), rising to leading soloist, dancing Helen (*Helen of Troy*), Mother and Medusa (*Undertow*), Queen of the Wilis (*Giselle*); created Mother (*Fall River Legend*), etc. Joined New York City Ballet (1950), of which she was a leading dancer with a large repertoire including important creations in *Caracole* (later *Divertimento No. 15*), *Agon, Episodes, Liebeslieder Walzer* in the George Balanchine repertoire; Iseult in Frederick Ashton's *Picnic at Tintagel.* Her Siren in *Prodigal Son* is an outstanding creation in contemporary ballet. Appeared in Gene Kelly's film *Invitation to the Dance;* was ballerina to Danny Kaye's premier danseur in the ballet in his film *Knock on Wood.* Now retired, teaching at the School of American Ballet, N.Y.

Diana Adams, ballerina, teacher

Addison, Errol (Addison Smith), British dancer, teacher, b. Heaton, 1901. Pupil of Enrico Cecchetti who left him his London school in 1923. Principal dancer with Covent Garden Opera (1918); joined Diaghilev Ballets Russes (1919), the first English male dancer to have position as soloist. Danced in musicals, variety, pantomime (1923–47); was famous for his multiple pirouettes. Principal dancer, International Ballet (1947–53); ballet master, Sadler's Wells Theatre Ballet (1955); teacher to the Royal Ballet and Royal Ballet School (1954–63). Currently teaching at school of Ballet Rambert, London.

Addor, Ady, contemporary Brazilian dancer, b. Rio de Janeiro. Studied at Teatro Municipal school with Maryla Gremo, Tatiana Leskova; later with Aurel Milloss, Igor Schwezoff. Made her debut with Ballet da Juventude (1948). Joined corps de ballet of Teatro Municipal; promoted to soloist (1952). Joined Ballet do IV Centenario (1953) as first dancer. Returned to Teatro Municipal (1956) as ballerina, dancing *Les Sylphides, Swan of Tuonela, Les Présages, Capriccio Espagnol, La Boutique Fantasque, Le Beau Danube, Gaîté Parisienne,* among others. Joined American Ballet Theatre as soloist (1957); worked with Ballet Nacional de Venezuela and toured South America with Alicia Alonso's Ballet de Cuba (1959); rejoined American Ballet Theatre as ballerina (1960), then returned to Brazil. Currently lives in São Paulo and dances with local groups.

Afternoon of a Faun. Ballet in 1 act; chor. and book: Vaslav Nijinsky; music: Claude Debussy's *Prélude à l'après-midi d'un faune;* décor: Leon Bakst. First prod.: Diaghilev Ballets Russes, Théâtre du Châtelet, May 29, 1912, with Nijinsky as the Faun. The Faun, dreaming away a hot afternoon, surprises some nymphs on their way to bathe. As they run from him in fear, one drops her scarf and he takes it with him as he resumes his dreaming. The ballet was formerly in the repertoire of nearly all companies but is now performed infrequently. Notable interpreters of the role of the Faun in addition to its creator have been Serge Lifar, David Lichine, and Jean Babilée.

Afternoon of a Faun. Ballet in 1 act; chor.: Jerome Robbins; music: Claude Debussy's *Prélude à l'après-midi d'un faune;* décor: Jean Rosenthal; costumes: Irene Sharaff. First prod.: New York City Ballet, City Center, N.Y., May 14, 1953, with Tanaquil LeClercq and Francisco Moncion. The scene is an empty ballet studio, the long mirror in which all dancers watch themselves being the fourth wall of stage convention—the audience. The Nymph and Faun are dancers who meet there by chance, and were it not that they are more absorbed in their own images in the mirror than in the reality of their intimate physical contact as they dance together, a romance might have ensued. Robbins is here saying something fundamental about the essential narcissism of dancers. He also staged it for his own company, Ballets: U.S.A., with Wilma Curley and Jay Norman.

AFTRA (American Federation of Television and Radio Artists). See TRADE UNIONS, THEATRICAL.

Age of Anxiety. Ballet in 1 act, 6 scenes; chor.: Jerome Robbins; music: Leonard Bernstein's Symphony No. 2, based on W. H. Auden's poem *The Age of Anxiety;* décor: Oliver Smith; costumes: Irene Sharaff. First prod.: New York City Ballet, City Center, N.Y., Feb. 26, 1950, with Tanaquil LeClercq, Francisco Moncion, Todd Bolender, Jerome Robbins. Following the outline of the poem, Robbins divides his ballet into six sections: The Prologue, The Seven Ages, The Seven Stages, The Dirge, The Masque, The Epilogue. Four strangers meet, each seeking inner security and hoping to find it in companionship but, in the end, accept the essential loneliness of man and go their separate ways. Nora Kaye and Melissa Hayden have also danced the girl's role, and Roy Tobias and Hugh Laing danced the male roles.

Agent, a person representing a dancer in his contacts with an impresario, director of a ballet or opera company, or producer of a musical show; often and more properly called personal representative; also known as personal manager. Also a person commissioned by a producer, or more often proprietor of a night club or similar business, to assemble dancers and other performers for a show. An agent generally performs his duties on a commission basis, the commission usually amounting to five or ten percent of the dancer's salary. Agents are prohibited by law from accepting a commission from dancers in the corps de ballet, ensemble, line or chorus of a musical, etc. To operate legally, agents must be recognized by dancers' trade unions having jurisdiction in the various fields. Although agents or personal representatives are employed by most actors and singers, only a few dancers have representatives to take care of their contract arrangements, etc. Actors' Equity, and other unions recognize the following categories of agents: (1) employment agent, a person who secures a job for a dancer or other performer, may charge no more than five percent of a dancer's salary for a period not to exceed ten weeks; (2) special employment representative, who is required to give more personal service and, in general, more expert service than an employment agent, negotiating in person all details of the dancer's contract; is permitted to charge up to five percent of the dancer's salary for the duration of the contract he negotiated, or the run-of-the-play; (3) personal representative, who is required to guarantee the dancer at least twenty weeks' employment in a season at a salary not less than the dancer's average salary during the preceding three years, and is permitted to charge a commission up to ten percent of the dancer's salary for the period of the engagements he secures for the dancer. See also MANAGER; BOOKING AGENT.

Agitanado, heel work used in the non-Flamenco Spanish dance. Heel work in the Flamenco dance is called taconeo. See SPANISH DANCE.

Aglaë, ou l'Élève de l'Amour. Ballet divertissement in 1 act; chor. and book: Filippo Taglioni; music: Keller. First prod.: St. Petersburg, Jan. 22, 1841, for Maria Taglioni's guest appearance; London première: Her Majesty's Theatre, July 8, 1841, with Maria Taglioni in the title role. The slight story concerns a nymph (the Pupil of Cupid), Cupid, a faun, and a young man. Anton Dolin's ballet *Romantic Age* (1942) is based on *Aglaë*.

AGMA (American Guild of Musical Artists). See TRADE UNIONS, THEATRICAL.

Agoglia, Esmeralda, Argentine ballerina, b. Buenos Aires, 1926. Studied dance with Mercedes Quintana, Michel Borovski and Esmée Bulnes. Joined Teatro Colón (1941); became ballerina (1949). Her repertoire includes David Lichine's *Prodigal Son, Capriccio Espagnol, Apollon Musagète, Firebird, Rouge et Noir, Swan Lake, Les Sylphides, Giselle* (Queen of the Wilis), Vassily Lambrinos' *Interplay,* Tamara Grigorieva's *Concierto Coreografico,* and many others. In 1951, and again in 1958–59, she directed ballet performances on television; appeared on television with Nathalie Krassovska and Igor Youskevitch (1961). Danced Odile in the full-length *Swan Lake* staged by Jack Carter (May 28, 1963).

Agon. Ballet consisting of an introduction and 3 parts; chor.: George Balanchine; commissioned music: Igor Stravinsky. First prod.: New York City Ballet, City Center, N.Y., Nov. 27, 1957, at a special March of Dimes Benefit performance; first public performance: Dec. 1, 1957, with Diana Adams, Melissa Hayden, Barbara Walczak, Barbara Milberg, Todd Bolender, Roy Tobias, Jonathan Watts, Arthur Mitchell, Roberta Lubell, Francia Russell, Dido Sayers, Ruth Sobotka. A series of short dances, ensembles, soli, pas de deux, pas de trois, pas de quatre, as ingenious and intricate as the music. The score was commissioned by the New York City Ballet under a grant from the Rockefeller Foundation and was dedicated by the composer to Lincoln Kirstein and Balanchine. The music has also been used by various European choreographers, the best known version being that of Kenneth MacMillan for the Royal Ballet with décor by Nicholas Georgiadis, premièred at the Royal Opera House, Covent Garden, London, Aug. 20, 1958, with Anya Linden, David Blair, Annette Page, and Pirmin Trecu as principals.

AGVA. See AMERICAN GUILD OF VARIETY ARTISTS.

Ailes de Pigeon (lit. pigeon wings; also known as pistolets), a ballet step. Technique: Start 5th pos. R ft. front, demi-plié on R ft. and raise L ft. to grande seconde; jump off R ft. and beat R calf in back of L, then L in back of R; land on R ft. with L leg in 2nd pos. Repeat to other side.

Ailey, Alvin, dancer, choreographer, teacher, director, b. Rogers, Tex., 1931. Moved to Los Angeles (1942); studied Romance languages at Univ. of California, also two years at State College, San Francisco. Studied dance with Lester Horton, joined his company and remained with it as choreographer after Horton's death. Gave first N.Y. concert in 1957, and not long after formed his own company (American Dance Theater), dancing frequently with Carmen de Lavallade. Sponsored by the U.S. Dept. of State, the company toured in Far East (1962); also toured Europe with Joyce Trisler as guest artist (fall, 1964), with important seasons in Paris and London. Among his works are *Blues Suite* (1958), *Creation of the World, Revelations* and *Knoxville, Summer 1915* (all 1960), *Roots of the Blues* (1961), his long solo to Samuel Barber's *Hermit Songs,* and *Been Here and Gone* (both 1962). He also choreographed *Feast of Ashes* for the Robert Joffrey Ballet (1962). He has appeared in Broadway musicals *House of Flowers, Jamaica,* and on tour as featured dancer in Harry Belafonte's *Sing, Man, Sing.* Has acted leading roles off-Broadway in *Call Me By My Rightful Name,* on Broadway in *Tiger, Tiger Burning Bright.* Co-directed *Jerico-Jim Crow* (song-play by Langston Hughes) off-Broadway (Jan., 1964); in same year staged *Ariadne* for Harkness Ballet. Toured Australia and Europe with his company (spring, 1965). In 1966 again toured Europe. Choreographed *Macumba* to music by Rebekah Harkness for the Harkness Ballet; also choreographed dances for the opera *Antony and Cleopatra* by Samuel Barber which opened the first season of the Metropolitan Opera at its new house in Lincoln Center for the Performing Arts (Sept. 16, 1966).

Alvin Ailey

Air, en l', in ballet a step done off the ground, such as rond de jambe en l'air, tour en l'air, etc. The opposite of en l'air is par terre.

Aitken, Gordon, British dancer, b. Scotland, 1928. Trained by Lillian Mcneile, Glasgow. Gave up school teaching to join Sadler's Wells Ballet (Oct. 1954); transferred to Sadler's Wells Theatre Ballet, (1955); currently soloist, Royal Ballet. Roles include Carabosse (*The Sleeping Beauty*), Dr. Coppelius (*Coppélia*), Hilarion (*Giselle*), The Outcast (*The Burrow*).

Akesson, Birgit. See AAKESSON, BIRGIT.

Albertieri, Luigi (ca. 1860–1930), Italian-born ballet master and teacher. At the age of eight came to the attention of

Enrico Cecchetti, whose foster-son he became. He lived at Cecchetti's home and studied with him for ten years. When Cecchetti was in Russia (1886), Albertieri joined him at the Arcadia Theatre in Moscow, where he danced in the ballet *The Triumph of Love.* He danced in Italy upon his return, substituting for Cecchetti. He also appeared in the Empire Ballets in London with Katti Lanner, Adeline Genée, etc.; came to the U.S. (1895) and later became ballet master of the Chicago Opera and, subsequently, of the Metropolitan Opera, N.Y. He remained with the Metropolitan for fourteen years. In 1915 he opened his own school in N.Y. where he taught until his death, Aug. 25, 1930. Author of a ballet textbook, *The Art of Terpsichore* (1923).

Alcestis. Modern dance work; chor. and costumes: Martha Graham; music: Vivian Fine; décor: Isamu Noguchi. First prod.: Martha Graham and Dance Company, 54th St. (formerly Adelphi) Theatre, N.Y., Apr. 29, 1960, with Martha Graham (Alcestis), Gene McDonald (Admetus), Bertram Ross (Thanatos—figure of death), Paul Taylor (Hercules). Based on the Greek legend of Alcestis journeying to the underworld in her husband's place and her rescue by Hercules. Graham sees it also as a variant of the Persephone legend of vernal rebirth after winter's death.

Aldous, Lucette, British ballerina, b. Auckland, N.Z., 1939; m. concert pianist M. Maurice Fitzmaurice. Studied ballet in Sydney, Australia and at Royal Ballet School (1955–57). Joined Ballet Rambert (1957), becoming soloist and subsequently ballerina (1958–63). Roles included title role (*La Sylphide*), Swanilda (*Coppélia*), title role (*Giselle*), *Coquette* (*Night Shadow*), Kitri (*Don Quixote*). Enjoyed a triumph when this last-named evening-length ballet was premièred by Ballet Rambert July 26, 1962. Joined London's Festival Ballet (1963).

Alegrias, one of the oldest of Spanish Flamenco dances; it is considered the purest, most refined, and dignified of the Spanish repertoire. See SPANISH DANCE.

Aleko. Ballet in 1 act, 4 scenes; chor. and book: Leonide Massine; music: Peter Tchaikovsky's Trio in A minor, orch. by Erno Rapee; décor: Marc Chagall. First prod.: Ballet (now American Ballet) Theatre, Palacio de Bellas Artes, Mexico City, Sept. 8, 1942; N.Y. première: Metropolitan Opera House, Oct. 6, 1942, with George Skibine (Aleko), Alicia Markova (Zemphira), Hugh Laing (Gypsy), Antony Tudor (Zemphira's father), and Rosella Hightower, Maria Karnilova, Annabelle Lyon, Ian Gibson, Yurek Lazowski, Nicolas Orlov, Richard Reed in principal parts. Later Nora Kaye danced Zemphira with notable success and Massine, Anton Dolin and André Eglevsky alternated the title role. The ballet was inspired by the narrative poem *The Gypsies* by the Russian poet Alexander Pushkin. The poem tells of Aleko, a stranger who joins a Gypsy camp because of his love for the Gypsy girl Zemphira. He kills his adversary, the Gypsy boy who is in love with Zemphira, and Zemphira's father banishes him from the camp for his crime.

Alexander, Dorothy (Dorothea), American dancer, teacher, choreographer, cofounder of the Regional Ballet Festival movement in the U.S.A., b. 1904, Atlanta, Ga. Graduated from Atlanta Normal Training School (1925); studied at Univ. of Georgia and Emory Univ.; B.A. (Education), Oglethorpe College (1930). Studied dance during summers with Michel Fokine, Irma Duncan, Yeichi Nimura, Tatiana Chamié, Bronislava Nijinska, Ted Shawn (at Jacob's Pillow School of Dance), Hanya Holm (at Colorado College), and at the Summer Course for Teachers, Sadler's Wells (now Royal) Ballet School, London. Since 1921 has had her own school in Atlanta. In 1927 she

Dorothy Alexander

initiated a creative arts course in the Atlanta public school system. Taught dance in public schools, subsequently becoming Supervisor of Physical Fitness through Dance for the Atlanta public school system. Performed in summer productions in Athens, Ga.; guest artist, Solomonoff-Menzelli Ballet, Lucille Marsh's Concert Group, Hollywood Ballet, Edwin Strawbridge companies. Was leading dancer of the Dorothy Alexander Concert Group, established in 1929 and renamed (1941) the Atlanta Civic Ballet, for which she choreographed most of the repertoire. At the same time her school was renamed the Atlanta Civic Ballet School. After World War II the company was sent by the U.S.O. to dance for the U.S. military personnel in Iceland, Bermuda, the Azores, Korea, and Japan. In 1956 the Atlanta Civic Ballet was the host company for the first Southeastern Regional Ballet Festival (the first ever to be held in the U.S.), with Dorothy Alexander as first president and moving spirit of the entire movement. When the Northeast had its first festival (1959), a Regional Ballet Festival Advisory Board was formed to coordinate the activities of the Regional Festival Associations and Dorothy Alexander was named its president. When the Advisory Board was replaced by the National Regional Ballet Association (1963), Miss Alexander was elected its only permanent director.

Alexander, Rod, American dancer, b. Colo., 1925. Studied dance with Jack Cole, Hanya Holm, Carmalita Maracci, Tatiana Riabouchinska, Elizabeth Anderson-Ivantzova, Lester Horton, Nick Castle, Edna McRae. Worked with Jack Cole at Columbia Pictures Studio (1945–48) and with Jack Cole Dancers (night club tour, 1948–49). First appearance on Broadway was in *Inside U.S.A.* (chor.: Helen Tamiris), as partner of Valerie Bettis (1948). Teamed with Bambi Linn by Tamiris for *Great to be Alive* (1952), they continued as a team in supper clubs. Staged dances and danced with Miss Linn in television's *Your Show of Shows* (1953–55) and later in *Max Liebman Presents.* Choreographed the film version of the musical *Carousel* (1956); a year later staged the dances in the film *The Best Things in Life Are Free.* Choreographed the Broadway production of *Shinbone Alley* (1958) and a number of television shows. Toured U.S. with a company of 20, entitled Rod Alexander's Dance Jubilee (1958–59), under the aegis of Columbia Artists Management; toured the show in the Middle- and Far East for the U.S. State Department Cultural Exchange Program (1959–60). Staged the dances for the Broadway show *Thirteen Daughters* as well as for a number of television programs (1960–61).

Alexandre le Grand. Ballet in prologue, 3 scenes, epilogue; chor. and book: Serge Lifar; music: Philippe Gaubert's symphonic suite *Inscriptions pour les Portes de la Ville;* décor: P. R. Larthe. First prod.: Paris Opéra Ballet, Théâtre de l'Opéra, Paris, June 21, 1937, with Yvette Chauviré and Lifar in the leading roles. Alexander the Great cuts the Gordian knot and captures Jerusalem, but spares the Temple of Solomon. He accepts the title "god and son of Zeus" in an Egyptian oasis from a priest of Zeus, and dies by drinking a poisoned cup of wine proffered by the captured Queen of Babylon.

Alfvén, Hugo (1872–1960), Swedish composer. His rhapsody *Midsommarvaka* (Midsummer Vigil) was used for Jean Börlin's ballet *La Nuit de Saint Jean* (Les Ballets Suédois, 1920) and for Björn Holmgren's *Swedish Rhapsody* (Edinburgh Music Festival, 1958). Börlin's pantomime-ballet *Bergakungen* (Royal Swedish Ballet, 1923) also had a score by Alfvén. His last work for ballet was *The Prodigal Son,* choreographed by Ivó Cramer premièred by the Royal Swedish Ballet (1957). Alfvén collected folk music and used old dances and hymns in his score for this work. His polka for *The Prodigal Son* became a hit tune in Sweden to such an extent that recordings and sheet music were made of it. This popularity delighted the aged composer because his publisher had not liked that particular tune.

Algaroff, Youly, contemporary French dancer, b. Simferopol, Russia; m. Christane Franky. Studied ballet with Eugenia Edouardova, Lubov Egorova, Boris Kniaseff. Made his debut with Egorova's Les Ballets de la Jeunesse, Paris (1937). Was a leading dancer with Les Ballets des Champs-Elysées (1945), creating roles in *La Fiancée du Diable, Jeu de Cartes, La Forêt;* leading dancer, Nouveau Ballet de Monte Carlo, creating principal male role in *Chota Rustaveli* (1946). Returned to Ballets des Champs-Elysées (1948), creating leading role in *Le Peîntre et son Modele* (Leonide Massine–Georges Auric, 1948). Appointed premier danseur étoile of Paris Opéra (1952), where his repertoire includes *Giselle, Symphonie Fantastique, Firebird* (Serge Lifar version, 1954), Harald Lander's *Printemps à Vienne* (1954), and *Suite en Blanc,* among others. Toured Soviet Russia as partner of Yvette Chauviré (1960), appearing in Moscow and Leningrad; makes many guest appearances with European companies. Since 1965 impresario in Paris.

Algeranoff, Harcourt (Harcourt Essex), contemporary English dancer, teacher, ballet master; m. Claudie Leonard (Algeranova). Began his career as a character dancer with Anna Pavlova's company; member of Markova-Dolin company in England; created role of Astrologer in Col. de Basil's Ballets Russes production of Michel Fokine's *Le Coq d'Or* (1937). Character soloist, International Ballet; teacher of character dance at International Ballet School, London, during the mid-1940's. Gave lecture-recitals with Australian Children's Theatre and in Malaya, Indonesia, and Dutch New Guinea (1955–57); ballet master, Borovansky's Australian Ballet (1959). Guest artist, Australian Ballet, under the direction of Peggy Van Praagh (1962–63).

Algeranova, Claudie (Claudie Leonard), English dancer, b. Paris, 1924, of English parentage; m. Harcourt Algeranoff. Studied at Cone-Ripman School in England. Joined International Ballet (1941), dancing under her maiden name of Claudie Leonard until her marriage. Became ballerina, dancing *The Sleeping Beauty, Swan Lake,* and others. Ballerina, Borovansky's Australian Ballet (1954). Gave lecture-recitals with Australian Children's Theatre, and in Malaya, Indonesia, Dutch New Guinea (1955–57). Ballerina, Lucerne Opera, Switzerland (1959).

Algues, Les (Seaweed). Ballet in 1 act, 4 scenes; chor.: Janine Charrat; music: electronic score by Guy Bernard; book and décor: L.-B. Castelli. First prod.: Ballets Janine Charrat, Théâtre des Champs-Elysées, Paris, Apr. 20, 1953, with Janine Charrat and Peter van Dijk. Janine Charrat's most successful ballet. A young man pretends madness in order to rejoin his beloved who has been confined in an asylum. His subterfuge is discovered and he is forced to return to the outside world. The score, which mixes music with sound effects, helped to create an unhappy world of hallucination and terror.

Alhambra Ballets, a name coined by the English writer and publisher Cyril W. Beaumont for the ballet performances given at the Alhambra Theatre, London, between 1871 and 1914 which, with the Empire Ballets, were the only ballet performances in England at that period. The Alhambra Theatre opened in 1871 with programs of farces, pantomimes, light operas, and ballets. Gradually it began to present ballets as the main attraction. It had a permanent corps de ballet and among the famous principal dancers who appeared at one time or another were Pierina Legnani, Carlotta Mossetti and Catherine Geltzer. See "The Alhambra Ballet" by Ivor Guest, *Dance Perspectives* No. 4.

Allan, Maude (1883–1956), dancer, actress, pianist, painter; b. Toronto, Canada. Educated in San Francisco, Vienna, Berlin. Though she was trained as a musician, she wished to revive the Greek classic dance. She usually danced barefoot in a loose Greek gown. She made her debut in Vienna in *The Vision of Salomé* (1903) to Richard Strauss' music and was very successful. She danced in London, Moscow, St. Petersburg (1909), U.S. (1910); toured South Africa, India, Malaya, China, Australia, New Zealand; later toured South America and (1913) Egypt, Gibraltar, Malta. Some of her dances were set to Edvard Grieg's *Peer Gynt Suite,* Felix Mendelssohn's "Spring Song," Johann Strauss's "Beautiful Blue Danube," Rubinstein's "Melody in F," and "Valse Caprice," and Frédéric Chopin's "Funeral March." After she stopped dancing, she taught in England. She was the author of various articles and a book, *My Life and Dancing* (1908).

Maude Allan (ca. 1917) (Courtesy Dance Collection, N.Y. Public Library)

Allard, Marie (1742–1802), French ballerina of the Paris Opéra. Entered the theatre at an early age; her mother died soon thereafter and Marie went from her native Marseille to Lyon. At the age of fourteen she went to Paris where she studied with Gaetan Vestris and made her debut at the Opéra (June, 1760). She was equally good in comic and tragic ballets. One of her outstanding successes was in *Sylvia,* a comic ballet in which she danced the title role. Another success was Jean George Noverre's tragic *Medea.* She was the mistress of Gaetan Vestris and the mother of Auguste Vestris, subsequently one of the greatest male dancers of all time. Allard retired from the Opéra in 1781, having become too fat to dance.

Allegory. Modern dance work; chor.: Alwin Nikolais; music: magnetic tape arranged by Nikolais and Roger Mason; color and costumes: George Constant. First prod. Henry Street Playhouse Dance Company, Henry Street Playhouse, N.Y., Jan. 30, 1959, with Murray Louis, Arlene Laub, Beverly Schmidt, Coral Martindale, Phyllis Lamhut, Ruth Ravon, Dorothy Vislocky, and others. A continuation of the Nikolais experiments which first attracted general attention with *Masks—Props—Mobiles. Allegory* contains the famous sequence (Finials) in which the dancers assume the shapes of column tops, ancient and moss-stained, and engage in a weird formal dance.

Allegro.

1. Any dance or combination of steps done to fast or moderate tempo.
2. Part of ballet lesson which follows adagio.

3. In ballet, all forms of jumps, leaps, turns in the air, are part of allegro.

Allegro Brillante. Ballet in 1 act; chor.: George Balanchine; music: the single movement of Peter Tchaikovsky's unfinished Third Piano Concerto. First prod.: New York City Ballet, City Center, N.Y., Mar. 1, 1956, with Maria Tallchief and Nicholas Magallanes, and an ensemble of four girls and four male dancers. Balanchine staged *Allegro Brillante* at very short notice when the projected revival of Jerome Robbins' *The Guests* fell through, but its alternating lyricism and dazzling virtuosity have shown an unexpected staying power. Melissa Hayden took over the Tallchief part subsequently with great success.

Allemande (Alman), a heavy, 16th century court dance in strains of eight measures, originating in Switzerland and Germany. It was in 2/4 time and a characteristic figure was that in which the gentleman turned the lady under his arm, and vice versa. There is a hint of this in the "allemand" of American square dancing.

Allen, Ivan, contemporary American dancer, b. Detroit. Studied dance with Sandra Severo. Joined American Ballet Theatre, becoming soloist (1960), premier danseur (1961). Dances *Les Patineurs* (Green Skater), *Graduation Ball* (Junior Cadet), *Les Sylphides* and others. Joined the Metropolitan Opera Ballet, N.Y. (summer, 1964).

Allongé, in ballet, an elongated line; usually refers to the arabesque, in which one arm and the body are stretched forward, the other arm extended back.

Alma Mater. Ballet in 1 act; chor.: George Balanchine; commissioned music: Kay Swift; orch.: Morton Gould; book: Edward M. M. Warburg; décor: John Held, Jr. First prod.: The American Ballet, Adelphi (now 54th Street) Theatre, N.Y., Mar. 1, 1935, with a cast headed by Gisella Caccialanza, Heidi Vosseler, William Dollar, Charles Laskey. The ballet was a humorous rendition of the antics of American college boys and their girl friends at football time, complete with cheer leaders, players, raccoon coats, and other paraphernalia. It belongs to that period when Lincoln Kirstein believed that American ballet should reflect the American way of life, its history and mores.

Almaszade, Gamer, People's Artist of the USSR (1959), Azerbaijan prima ballerina and choreographer, b. 1915. Studied at Baku ballet studio and Leningrad Kirov school under Maria Romanova, graduating 1936. Prima ballerina of the Akhundov Opera and Ballet Theatre in Baku since 1936. Since 1953 chief choreographer of the Theatre. Among her ballets are *Maiden's Tower* (A. Badalbeili, 1940), *Gulshen* (S. Gadjibekov, 1950), and her versions of *The Red Flower* (1954) and *Laurencia* (1956). She teaches at Baku ballet school and writes on ballet.

Alonso, Alicia (Alicia Martinez), contemporary ballerina, b. Havana, Cuba; m. Fernando Alonso; studied ballet with Sociedad Pro-Arte Musical, Havana; Alexandra Fedorova, School of American Ballet, Anatole Vilzak, Leon Fokine, N.Y.; Vera Volkova, London. Made her professional debut in musicals *Great Lady, Stars in Your Eyes.* Soloist, Ballet Caravan (1939–40); Ballet (now American) Ballet Theatre (1941). Ballerina, Pro-Arte, Havana (1941–43), dancing *Coppélia, The General's Daughter, Concerto,* etc. With Ballet Theatre (1943–48; 1950–55; 1958–60); with Ballet Russe de Monte Carlo (1955–57). Formed her own company, Ballet Alicia Alonso (1948; renamed *Ballet de Cuba* in 1955), with which she performed in Cuba and on tour in Latin America (1949; spring and summer 1955; and intermittently thereafter). She has

Alicia Alonso, American ballerina

also made numerous guest appearances with both American Ballet Theatre and Ballet Russe de Monte Carlo as well as many concert appearances, usually partnered by Igor Youskevitch (occasionally by André Eglevsky or Royes Fernandez). During the summers of 1957–59 she headed a company which appeared at the Greek Theatre, Los Angeles. Her latest appearance in the U.S. as guest artist with American Ballet Theatre (spring, 1960). Has since danced as ballerina of Ballet de Cuba on tour through Soviet Russia and China (1960–61). Alonso danced a large repertoire including the famous classic pas de deux (*Black Swan, Blue Bird, Don Quixote, The Nutcracker*) and was especially noted for her *Giselle;* created the ballerina role (*Theme and Variations*), the Accused (*Fall River Legend*), Ate (*Undertow*), ballerina (Bronislava Nijinska's *Schumann Concerto*), all for American Ballet Theatre; also danced *Swan Lake, Les Sylphides,* Taglioni (*Pas de Quatre*), Terpsichore (*Apollo*), Italian Ballerina (*Gala Performance*), Juliet (Antony Tudor's *Romeo and Juliet*), Zemphira (*Aleko*), Mother and Sweetheart (*Billy the Kid*), Lise (*La Fille Mal Gardée*) and others; also created leading roles in numerous ballets in Cuba. As a choreographer her works include *La Tinaja* to Maurice Ravel's music for Pro-Arte, 1943; *Ensayos Sinfonicos* (Johannes Brahms' *Variations on a Theme by Haydn*), *Lidia,* and other ballets for Ballet Alicia Alonso. At a special performance given in her honor in Havana, August 5, 1947 the Cuban Government presented her with the Decoration of Carlos Manuel de Cespedes. Alonso was the first ballerina from the Western Hemisphere to be invited by the U.S.S.R. as guest artist (in *Giselle* and *Swan Lake,* winter of 1957–58). Received a Dance Magazine Award (1959). At present limits her activities to Cuba where she continues to head her company, only occasionally making guest appearances in other Latin American countries.

Alonso, Fernando, dancer, teacher, b. Havana, Cuba, 1914; m. Alicia Alonso; studied dance at Sociedad Pro-Arte Musical, Havana; with Mikhail Mordkin, Alexandra Fedorova, School of American Ballet, Anatole Vilzak, N.Y.; with Vera Volkova, London. Made his professional debut with the Mordkin Ballet; danced in musicals, with Ballet Caravan (1939–40); Ballet (now American Ballet) Theatre (1941 and 1943–48), dancing Peter (*Peter and the Wolf*), Mercutio (*Romeo and Juliet*), Devil (*Three Virgins and a Devil*), Faun, Ajax (*Helen of Troy*), among others. Also premier danseur, Pro-Arte, Havana (1941–43). Has chor. *Pelléas and Mélisande* to Debussy's music for Pro-Arte Ballet (1943). Director of Ballet de Cuba since fall, 1948. Currently teaches at Academia de Ballet Alicia Alonso, Havana.

Alternate, a dancer who alternates with another dancer in a given role; not to be confused with an understudy. In ballet companies the regular alternation between principals is called tour de role. In theory each dancer of such a role is of equal importance but, in practice, the dancer who creates the role at the première will almost always be considered the dancer for whom the role was choreographed.

Alton, Robert (1902–57) (Robert Alton Hart), American stage and screen choreographer, b. Bennington, Vt. Studied dance with Mikhail Mordkin and was a leading member of his company. Choreographed and staged musical numbers in a great number of musicals from the mid 1930's until his death, among them *Anything Goes, Panama Hattie, Ziegfeld Follies* of 1936, 1938, 1940 and 1942, *Du Barry Was a Lady, Hellzapoppin', Pal Joey* (1940 and 1951), *Hazel Flagg, Me and Juliet.* His list of Hollywood credits is equally long: *Ziegfeld Follies, Easter Parade, Annie Get Your Gun, Show Boat, Call Me Madam, White Christmas, No Business Like Show Business, Daddy Long Legs,* and many others. He gave their first opportunities to many artists who went on to fame, including Betty Hutton, Vera-Ellen, Betty Grable, Mary Martin, June Allyson, Cyd Charisse, Van Johnson, and Gene Kelly who he suggested for the title role of *Pal Joey* when he was still comparatively unknown.

Amati, Olga, Italian ballerina, b. 1924. Entered the ballet school of the Teatro alla Scala, Milan (1934), and studied with Ettorina Mazzucchelli, Paula Giussani, Vera Volkova, Esmée Bulnes. Became ballerina in 1942, dancing principal roles. At present teaching at the ballet school of Teatro dell'Opera, Rome.

Amaya, Carmen (1913–1963), great Spanish flamenco dancer, b. Barcelona; m. guitarist Juan Antonio Aguero. Daughter and grand-daughter of dancers. Amaya danced publicly from the age of seven, appeared in Paris at age eight, and went on to a career of almost continuous success. She left Spain with her family at the outbreak of the Spanish Civil War (1936), lived in Mexico for some time, and then in Buenos Aires, Argentina, where she was such a sensation that a theatre was named for her. Made her N.Y. debut in 1941, appearing in night clubs and later toured with her group (among whom were her father and two sisters). Returned to Argentina (1945); danced in Europe (1948) and again toured the U.S. (1955). Made her final appearances in U.S. in 1962, mainly in night clubs and for occasional concerts. She also appeared in the motion picture *Los Tarantos,* released in the U.S. in 1964. In the summer of 1963 she began to suffer from a kidney ailment and spent some time in a Barcelona hospital, but left in early Nov. and died at her home in Bagur, Nov. 19. The Spanish Government decorated her with the Medal of Isabela la Catolica a week before her death.

Olga Amati, prima ballerina, Teatro dell'Opera, Rome

Amazon Symphony. Ballet in 1 act; chor. and book: Helba Nogueira; commissioned music: Walter Portoalegre; décor: Arlindo Rodrigues. First prod.: Teatro Municipal, Rio de Janeiro, Brazil, 1961, with Tatiana Leskova in the principal role. Mythical characters of the Amazon legends figure in a complicated story about the birth of the Victoria Regia flower; a Brazilian theme with classic choreography.

Amberg, George H., lecturer, writer, photographer, b. Halle (Saale), Germany, 1901, American citizen since 1946. Studied at universities of Kiel, Munich, Cologne (Ph.D.), specializing in art criticism, history and aesthetics of the theatre; published thesis on art criticism (Heidelberg, 1930). Founded avant-garde theatre Cassette, Cologne (1923); stage director in Cologne, Darmstadt, and at Heidelberg Festivals (1924–28); lecturer and member of Drama Department Univ. of Cologne where he helped organize the Theatre Museum, established and directed its Film Library and Institute (1930–33). Also lectured in Berlin, Frankfurt, Zurich, Basel, etc. Contributing editor on dance to Ullstein and Herder encyclopedias. Photographer in Paris (1933–39); joined French Army at outbreak of World War II. Came to U.S. in 1941. Named curator of Dance Archives, Museum of Modern Art, N.Y. (1943); organized there Department of Dance and Theatre Design, later called Department of Theatre Arts, of which he was also curator; resigned in 1948 when the department became a division of the Music Library of the Museum. Lecturer, Division of General Education, N.Y. Univ. (1948–52); Associate Professor, Univ. of Minn., Minneapolis (1952–56); since 1956 Professor at Univ. of Minnesota and Minneapolis School of Art. Has contributed to *Encyclopedia of Arts, Encyclopedia Americana, Dance Encyclopedia, Dance News,* etc. Edited *Art in Modern Ballet* (N.Y., 1946); author of *Ballet in America* (N.Y., 1949), *Ballet in America* (N.Y., 1950); contributing editor, *Funk and Wagnalls Standard Encyclopedia* (from 1958); author of *The Captive Eye, Theory and Aesthetics of the Motion Picture* (U. Minneapolis, 1960). Has also contributed many important articles on dance to *Graphis, Interiors, Theatre Arts,* and other publications.

Ambrose, Kay, contemporary English artist, designer, b. Surrey. Received scholarship for Fine Arts at Reading Univ.; awards in drama, elocution and dance. Illustrated Arnold L. Haskell's *Ballet* (1938); wrote and illustrated *Ballet–to Poland* (London, 1941); collaborated with Haskell on *Balletomane's Sketch-book* (London and N.Y., 1941); wrote and illustrated *Ballet-Lover's Pocket-Book* (London, 1943; N.Y., 1945), also published in French and Spanish; *Ballet Impromptu* (London, 1943); *Ballet-Lover's Companion* (London and N.Y., 1948); *Classical Dances and Costumes of India* (London, 1950); *Beginners, Please* (London, 1953). Travelled with Ram Gopal and his company as art-director, lecturer, and dancer. Artistic director, National Ballet of Canada (1952–61), designing many of the ballets, including *Swan Lake, Coppélia, Giselle, The Nutcracker,* returning to England to resume her career as author-illustrator.

American Ballet, The. The American Ballet company was founded by Lincoln Kirstein and Edward M. M. Warburg in 1934. Its foundation was laid a year earlier when Messrs. Kirstein and Warburg invited George Balanchine and Vladimir Dimitriew to come to the United States to establish the School of American Ballet. The American Ballet made its initial appearance in Hartford, Conn. in a three-day engagement in December, 1934. Beginning March 1, 1935 the company played a two-week engagement at the Adelphi Theatre, New York. It presented seven ballets, all by George Balanchine: *Alma Mater, Dreams, Reminiscences,*

Serenade, Transcendence, Mozartiana and *Errante*. The company included among others: Leda Anchutina, Ruthanna Boris, Gisella Caccialanza, William Dollar, Charles Laskey, Joseph Levinoff, Eugene Loring, Annabelle Lyon, Kathryn Mullowney, Yvonne Patterson, Elise Reiman, Heidi Vosseler. Tamara Geva and Paúl Haakon were guest artists. In the fall of that year the company was engaged by the Metropolitan Opera in New York as its opera ballet. Almost from the very beginning of this association the management of the Opera was openly dissatisfied with the American Ballet despite the fact that the Metropolitan in all its existence never had a more gifted ballet master nor a finer company. The reason for the dissatisfaction was an artistic one. Balanchine as choreographer of the opera ballets staged the dances in his own way, disregarding opera tradition. The management of the opera house wanted to have simple, traditional material to which the stage directors, singers and audience had been accustomed. The American Ballet, which received a flat monthly fee for its performances, did not spare its own expenses to invite Anatole Vilzak as premier danseur and augment the company with additional dancers, among them: Ruby Asquith, Kyra Blanc, Harold and Lew Christensen, Douglas Coudy, Erick Hawkins, Albia Kavan, Monna Montez, Lillian Moore. Its repertoire included the ballets from its first season and The Bat by Balanchine. The ballets were performed on programs with short operas. In the spring of 1936 Balanchine produced Gluck's *Orfeo ed Euridice* as a ballet, accompanied by singers who sat in the orchestra pit. Pavel Tchelitchev designed the scenery and costumes. It was an ultra modern production which did not appeal to the conservative opera audience. A year later (April 27 and 28, 1937), the American Ballet staged a two-day Stravinsky Festival. It consisted in the presentation of three ballets choreographed by Balanchine to the music of Igor Stravinsky: *Apollon Musagète, The Card Party* and *Le Baiser de la Fée*. The composer conducted both performances which were very successful. In the spring of 1938 the American Ballet and the Metropolitan Opera parted company, the parting being accompanied by much publicity. For nearly three years after its appearances with the Metropolitan Opera the American Ballet did not function as a performing organization. In the spring of 1941 Nelson A. Rockefeller, then head of the United States Office for Coordination of Commercial and Cultural Relations Between the American Republics, commissioned Lincoln Kirstein to organize a ballet company for a good-will tour to Latin American countries that summer. Kirstein assembled dancers and a repertoire from both the American Ballet and *Ballet Caravan,* and the company assumed the name *The American Ballet Caravan*. New works were added and rehearsals began under George Balanchine as Artistic Director. The repertoire listed: *Ballet Imperial, Juke Box, Pastorela, Concerto Barocco, The Bat* (to the overture from *Die Fledermaus*), *Billy the Kid, Charade, Time Table, Filling Station, Errante, Apollon Musagète*. The company included among others: Georgia Hiden, Helen Kramer, Yvonne Patterson, Mary Jane Shea, Beatrice Tompkins, Todd Bolender, Fred Danieli, Charles Dickson, John Kriza, Nicholas Magallanes, David Nillo, Zachary Solov, John Taras. Marie Jeanne and Gisella Caccialanza were the ballerinas, Lew Christensen and William Dollar the premiers danseurs. The Latin American tour lasted from June to October. Upon its return to the United States the American Ballet was disbanded as a performing organization. In spite of its relatively short existence the American Ballet played a most important part in the development of ballet in America; it established the first big ballet school in the United States, the only one approximating in scope the Russian State Schools of Ballet; it introduced to the United States George Balan-

ITY PORTRAIT
horeography by Eugene Loring
Music by Henry Brant
Décor by James Stewart Morcom
Book by Lincoln Kirstein

ièred December 28, 1939, St. James The-
New York. Dancers: Eugene Loring and
company.

merican Ballet Caravan

JUKE BOX
Choreography by William Dollar
Music by Alec Wilder
Costumes and décor by Tom Lee
Book by Lincoln Kirstein

mièred May 28, 1941, Hunter College
yhouse, New York. Principal Dancers:
nne Patterson, Rabana Hasburgh, Lew
ristensen, William Dollar.

PASTORELA
Choreography by Lew Christensen
and José Fernandez
Music by Paul Bowles
Costumes and décor by Alvin Colt
Book by José Martínez

remièred May 28, 1941, Hunter College
layhouse, New York. Principal Dancers:
isella Caccialanza, Beatrice Tompkins, Lew
hristensen, José Fernandez, Todd Bolender,
Nicholas Magallanes, Charles Dickson, José
Martínez.

CONCERTO BAROCCO
Choreography by George Balanchine
Music by Johann Sebastian Bach
(*Double Violin Concerto in D minor*)
Costumes and décor by Eugene Berman

Premièred May 28, 1941, Hunter College
Playhouse, New York. Principal Dancers:
Marie Jeanne, Mary Jane Shea, William
Dollar.

BALLET IMPERIAL
Choreography by George Balanchine
Music by Tchaikovsky (*Piano Concerto in G major*)

Costumes and décor by Msti
Doboujinsky

Premièred May 29, 1941, Hunter Coll
Playhouse, New York. Principal Danc
Marie Jeanne, Gisella Caccialanza, Willi
Dollar, Nicholas Magallanes, Fred Danieli.

TIME TABLE
Choreography by Antony Tudor
Music by Aaron Copland (*Music*
the Theatre)
Costumes and décor by James Stewa
Morcom

Premièred May 29, 1941, Hunter Colle
Playhouse, New York. Principal Dancer
Marie Jeanne, Gisella Caccialanza, Mary Ja
Shea, Beatrice Tompkins, Lew Christense
John Kriza.

4. Ballet Society

THE SPELLBOUND CHILD
Choreography by George Balanchin
Music by Maurice Ravel (*L'Enfan
et les sortilèges*)
Costumes and décor by Aline Bernstein
Poem by Colette

Premièred November 20, 1946, Central High
School of Needle Trades, New York. Principal
Dancers: Gisella Caccialanza, Ruth Gilbert,
Georgia Hiden, Tanaquil LeClercq, Elise Rei
man, Beatrice Tompkins, Paul d'Amboise,
William Dollar.

THE FOUR TEMPERAMENTS
Choreography by George Balanchine
Music by Paul Hindemith
Costumes and décor by Kurt Seligmann

Premièred November 20, 1946, Central High
School of Needle Trades, New York. Principal
Dancers: Gisella Caccialanza, Georgia Hiden,
Rita Karlin, Tanaquil LeClercq, Mary Ellen
Moylan, Elise Reiman, Beatrice Tompkins,
Todd Bolender, Lew Christensen, Fred Danieli, William Dollar, José Martínez, Francisco
Moncion.

chine, one of the greatest choreographers of our time; it developed a number of outstanding American dancers and several young choreographers. Most importantly, it paved the way for the organization of the New York City Ballet.

There follows a complete listing of all ballets created by American Ballet and the companies that succeeded it, up to September, 1966. It seemed both logical and less confusing to have one listing only, rather than separate lists for each of the companies although, naturally, the creations for New York City Ballet now represent the bulk of the achievement.

1. American Ballet, The (*Chronological List of Ballets March, 1935–Dec., 1966*)

SERENADE
Choreography by George Balanchine
Music by Peter Ilyitch Tchaikovsky (*Serenade for Strings in C major*)
Décor by Gaston Longchamp
Costumes by Jean Lurçat

Premièred March 1, 1935, Adelphi Theatre, New York. (Prior to the official première, *Serenade* was presented by the Producing Company of the School of American Ballet, December 6, 1934, in Hartford, Conn.) Principal Dancers: Leda Anchutina, Ruthanna Boris, Gisella Caccialanza, Kathryn Mullowney, William Dollar, Charles Laskey.

ALMA MATER
Choreography by George Balanchine
Music by Kay Swift, arranged by Morton Gould
Décor by Eugene Dunkel
Costumes by John Held, Jr.
Book by Edward M. M. Warburg

Premièred March 1, 1935, Adelphia Theatre, New York. (Prior to the official première, *Alma Mater* was presented by the Producing Company of the School of American Ballet, December 6, 1934, in Hartford, Conn.) Principal Dancers: Leda Anchutina, Ruthanna Boris, Gisella Caccialanza, Kathryn Mullowney, Heidi Vosseler, William Dollar, Charles Laskey, Eugene Loring.

ERRANTE
Choreography by George Balanchine
Music by Franz Schubert (*Wanderer Fantasy* for piano, orchestrated by Charles Koechlin)
Costumes, lighting and dramatic effects by Pavel Tchelitchew

Premièred, March 1, 1935, Adelphi Theatre, New York. (Revival from the repertoire of Les Ballets 1933.) Principal Dancers: Tamara Geva, Charles Laskey, William Dollar.

REMINISCENCE
Choreography by George Balanchine
Music by Benjamin Godard, orchestrated by Henry Brant
Costumes and décor by Sergei Soudeikine

Premièred March 1, 1935, Adelphi Theatre, New York. Principal Dancers: Leda Anchutina, Ruthanna Boris, Gisella Caccialanza, Elena de Rivas, Holly Howard, Annabelle Lyon, Elise Reiman, William Dollar, Paul Haakon, Joseph Levinoff.

MOZARTIANA
Choreography by George Balanchine
Music by Tchaikovsky (*Suite No. 4, Mozartiana*)
Costumes and décor by Christian Berard

Premièred March 1, 1935, Adelphi Theatre, New York. (Revival from Les Ballets 1933. Prior to the official première, *Mozartiana* was presented by the Producing Company of the School of American Ballet, December 6, 1934, in Hartford, Conn.) Principal Dancers: Rabana Hasburgh, Holly Howard, Helen Leitch, Daphne Vane, Heidi Vosseler, Charles Laskey.

TRANSCENDENCE
Choreography by George Balanchine
Music by Franz Liszt, orchestrated by George Antheil
Décor by Gaston Longchamp
Costumes by Franklin Watkins
Book by Lincoln Kirstein

Premièred March 5, 1935, Adelphi Theatre, New York. (Prior to the official première, *Transcendence* was presented by the Producing Company of the School of American Ballet, December 6, 1934, in Hartford, Conn.) Principal Dancers: Elise Reiman, William Dollar.

DREAMS
Choreography by George Balanchine
Music by George Antheil
Book, costumes and décor by André Derain

Premièred March 5, 1935, Adelphi Theatre, New York. (Revival from Les Ballets 1933.) Principal Dancers: Leda Anchutina, Ruthanna Boris, Paul Haakon.

THE BAT
Choreography by George Balanchine
Music by Johann Strauss (Overture to *Die Fledermaus*)
Costumes by Keith Martin
Book by Lincoln Kirstein

Premièred season 1935–6, Metropolitan Opera House, New York. Principal Dancers: Leda Anchutina, Rabana Hasburgh, Annabelle Lyon, Lew Christensen, Charles Laskey.

ORPHEUS AND EURYDICE
Choreography by George Balanchine
Music by Christoph Willibald von Gluck
Costumes and décor by Pavel Tchelitchew

Premièred May 22, 1936, Metropolitan Opera House, New York. Principal Roles: Orpheus, Lew Christensen; Eurydice, Daphne Vane; Angel, William Dollar.

APOLLON MUSAGÈTE (Later called *Apollo,* and *Apollo, Leader of the Muses*)
Choreography by George Balanchine
Music by Igor Stravinsky
Costumes and décor by Stewart Chaney

Premièred April 27, 1937, Metropolitan Opera House, New York. (Revival from the Diaghilev Ballets Russes.) Dancers: Lew Christensen, Daphne Vane, Holly Howard, Elise Reiman, Kyra Blank, Rabana Hasburgh, Jane Burkhalter.

THE CARD PARTY (Later called *Card Game*)
Choreography by George Balanchine
Music by Igor Stravinsky
Costumes and décor by Irene Sharaff
Book by Igor Stravinsky in collaboration with M. Malaieff

Premièred April 27, 1937, Metropolitan Opera House, New York. Principal Roles: The Joker, William Dollar; Aces, Ann Campbell, Jane Burkhalter, Lillian Moore, Vera Volkenau; Kings, Lew Christensen, Joseph Lane, Douglas Coudy, Erick Hawkins; Queens, Annabelle Lyon, Leda Anchutina, Ariel Lang, Hortense Kahrklin; Jacks, Charles Laskey, Joseph Levinoff, Eugene Loring, Serge Temoff.

LE BAISER DE LA FÉE (Later called *The Fairy's Kiss*)
Choreography by George Balanchine
Music by Igor Stravinsky
Costumes and décor by Alice Halicka
Book by Igor Stravinsky, based on a story by Hans Christian Andersen

Premièred April 27, 1937, Metropolitan Opera House, New York. Principal Roles: The Fairy, Kathryn Mullowney; Shadow, Rabana Hasburgh; Bride, Gisella Caccialanza; Friend, Leda Anchutina; Bridegroom, William Dollar; Mother, Annabelle Lyon.

2. The Ballet Caravan

ENCOUNTER
Choreography by Lew Christensen
Music by Mozart (*"Haffner" Serenade*)
Costumes by Forrest Thayr, Jr.

Premièred July 17, 1936, Bennington, Vermont. Principal Dancers: Annabelle Lyon, Ruby Asquith, Charles Laskey, Lew Christensen, Harold Christensen.

HARLEQUIN FOR PRESIDENT (Later called *Harlequin*)
Choreography by Eugene Loring

Music by Domenico Scarlatti, orchestrated by Ariadna Mikeshina
Costumes by Keith Martin
Book by Lincoln Kirstein

Premièred July 17, 1936, Bennington, Vermont. Principal Dancers: Annabelle Lyon, Eugene Loring, Charles Laskey, Harold Christensen, Fred Danieli.

FOLK DANCE
Choreography by Douglas Coudy
Music by Emmanuel Chabrier
Costumes by Charles Rain

Premièred July 17, 1936, Bennington, Vermont. Principal Dancers: Ruthanna Boris, Lew Christensen.

PROMENADE
Choreography by William Dollar
Music by Maurice Ravel (*Valses Nobles et Sentimentales*)
Costumes by Horace Vernet

Premièred July 17, 1936, Bennington, Vermont. Principal Dancers: Annabelle Lyon, Ruthanna Boris, Charles Laskey, Erick Hawkins.

YANKEE CLIPPER
Choreography by Eugene Loring
Music by Paul Bowles
Costumes by Charles Rain
Book by Lincoln Kirstein

Premièred July 12, 1937, Town Hall, Saybrook, Conn. Dancers: Eugene Loring and company.

SHOW PIECE
Choreography by Erick Hawkins
Music by Robert McBride
Costumes by Keith Martin

Premièred August, 1937, Bar Harbor, Maine. Principal Dancers: Marie Jeanne, Annabelle Lyon, Eugene Loring, Fred Danieli, Erick Hawkins.

POCAHONTAS
Choreography by Lew Christensen
Music by Elliott Carter, Jr.
Costumes by Ka
Book by Lincoln

Premièred August 17, 1
Keene, New Hampshir
Ruthanna Boris, Lew
Laskey, Harold Christe

FILLING STATION
Choreography by L
Music by Virgil Th
Costumes and décor
Book by Lincoln Ki

Premièred January 6, 1938
Theatre, Hartford, Conn. I
Jane Deering, Marie Jeanne,
Todd Bolender, Harold C
Christensen, Douglas Coudy
Erick Hawkins, Eugene Lori

BILLY THE KID
Choreography by Euge
Music by Aaron Coplan
Costumes by Jared Frenc
Book by Lincoln Kirstein

Premièred October 16, 1938, C
House. Principal Roles: Billy, Eu
Mother and Sweetheart, Marie
Garrett, Lew Christensen; Alias
lender.

AIR AND VARIATION
Choreography by William
Music by Johann Sebasti
(*Goldberg Variations,* arr.
two pianos by Trude Ritt
Costumes by Walter Gifford

Premièred November, 1938, Athens,
The entire company.

CHARADE, OR THE DEBUTANTE
Choreography by Lew Christen
American melodies, arrange
Trude Rittmann
Costumes by Alvin Colt
Book by Lincoln Kirstein

Premièred December 26, 1939, St. James T
tre, New York. Principal Dancers: Gi
Caccialanza, Lew Christensen, Harold C
tensen.

Renard (*The Fox*)
Choreography by George Balanchine
Music by Igor Stravinsky
Costumes and décor by Esteban Francés
Book by Igor Stravinsky, English text by Harvey Officer

Premièred January 15, 1947, Hunter College Playhouse, New York. Principal Roles: The Fox, Todd Bolender; The Rooster, Lew Christensen; The Cat, Fred Danieli; The Ram, John Taras.

Divertimento
Choreography by George Balanchine
Music by Alexei Haieff

Premièred January 13, 1947, Hunter College Playhouse, New York. Dancers: Gisella Caccialanza, Tanaquil LeClercq, Mary Ellen Moylan, Elise Reiman, Beatrice Tompkins, Todd Bolender, Lew Christensen, Fred Danieli, Francisco Moncion, John Taras.

The Minotaur
Choreography by John Taras
Music by Elliott Carter
Costumes and décor by Joan Junyer
Book by Lincoln Kirstein and Joan Junyer

Premièred March 26, 1947, Central High School of Needle Trades, New York. Principal Roles: Pasiphae, Queen of Crete, Elise Reiman; Minos, King of Crete, Edward Bigelow; Ariadne, Tanaquil LeClercq; Theseus, John Taras; Bulls, Fred Danieli and Paul d'Amboise.

Zodiac
Choreography by Todd Bolender
Music by Rudi Revil
Costumes and décor by Esteban Francés

Premièred March 26, 1947, Central High School of Needle Trades, New York. Principal Dancers: Virginia Barnes, William Dollar, Todd Bolender, Job Sanders, Patricia McBride, Janice Roman, Ruth Sobotka, Jean Reeves, Irma Sandré, Joan Djorup, Marc Beaudet, John Scancarella, Betty Nichols, Gisella Caccialanza, Edward Bigelow, Gerard Leavitt.

Highland Fling
Choreography by William Dollar
Music by Stanley Bate
Costumes and décor by David Ffolkes

Premièred March 26, 1947, Central High School of Needle Trades, New York. Principal Roles: Bride, Gisella Caccialanza; Groom, Todd Bolender; Sylphide, Elise Reiman; Bridesmaids, Tanaquil LeClercq and Beatrice Tompkins; Minister, José Martínez.

The Seasons
Choreography by Merce Cunningham
Music by John Cage
Costumes and décor by Isamu Noguchi

Premièred May 18, 1947, Ziegfeld Theatre, New York. Principal Dancers: Gisella Caccialanza, Tanaquil LeClercq, Beatrice Tompkins, Merce Cunningham.

Blackface
Choreography by Lew Christensen
Music by Carter Harman
Costumes and décor by Robert Drew

Premièred May 18, 1947, Ziegfeld Theatre, New York. Principal Dancers: Betty Nichols, Beatrice Tompkins, Talley Beatty, Marc Beaudet, Fred Danieli, Paul Godkin.

Punch and the Child
Choreography by Fred Danieli
Music by Richard Arnell
Costumes and décor by Horace Armistead

Premièred November 12, 1947, City Center of Music and Drama, New York. Principal Roles: Father and Punch, Herbert Bliss; Mother and Judy, Beatrice Tompkins; the Child, Judith Kursch; Fishwife and Polly, Gisella Caccialanza; Peg Leg and Constable, Charles Laskey; Puppeteer and Devil, Lew Christensen; Musician and Doctor, Edward Bigelow; Street Cleaner and Hangman, Victor Duntiere; Professor, Luis Lopez.

Symphonie Concertante
Choreography by George Balanchine
Music by Mozart (*Symphonie Concertante in E flat,* K. 364)

Costumes and décor by James Stewart Morcom

Premièred November 12, 1947, City Center of Music and Drama, New York. (Prior to première, Symphonie Concertante was presented November 5, 1945, at Carnegie Hall, New York, on a program "Adventure in Ballet" by pupils of the School of American Ballet.) Principal Dancers: Maria Tallchief, Tanaquil LeClercq, Dorothy Dushok, Ruth Gilbert, Georgia Hiden, Rita Karlin, Patricia McBride, Irma Sandré, Todd Bolender.

THE TRIUMPH OF BACCHUS AND ARIADNE (Ballet Cantata)
Choreography by George Balanchine
Music by Vittorio Rieti
Costumes and décor by Corrado Cagli

Premièred February 9, 1948, City Center of Music and Drama, New York. Principal Roles: Major-domo, Lew Christensen; Bacchus, Nicholas Magallanes; Ariadne, Tanaquil LeClercq; First Satyr, Herbert Bliss; First Nymph, Marie Jeanne; Silenus, Charles Laskey; Midas, Francisco Moncion; the Little Girl, Claudia Hall; the Young Girl, Patricia McBride.

CAPRICORN CONCERTO
Choreography by Todd Bolender
Music by Samuel Barber
Costumes and décor by Esteban Francés

Premièred March 22, 1948, City Center of Music and Drama, New York. Principal Dancers: Maria Tallchief, Herbert Bliss, Francisco Moncion.

SYMPHONY IN C
Choreography by George Balanchine
Music by Georges Bizet

Premièred March 22, 1948, City Center of Music and Drama, New York. (First produced for the Paris Opéra under the title *Palais de Cristal,* July 28, 1947.) Principal Dancers: First Movement, Maria Tallchief, Nicholas Magallanes; Second Movement, Tanaquil LeClercq, Francisco Moncion; Third Movement, Beatrice Tompkins, Herbert Bliss; Fourth Movement, Elise Reiman, Lew Christensen.

ELEGIE
Choreography by George Balanchine
Music by Igor Stravinsky

Premièred April 28, 1948, City Center of Music and Drama, New York. (Prior to première, *Elegie* was presented November 5, 1945, at Carnegie Hall, New York, on a program "Adventure in Ballet" by pupils of the School of American Ballet.) Danced by Tanaquil LeClercq and Patricia McBride.

ORPHEUS
Choreography by George Balanchine
Music by Igor Stravinsky
Costumes and décor by Isamu Noguchi

Premièred April 28, 1948, City Center of Music and Drama, New York. Principal Roles: Orpheus, Nicholas Magallanes; Dark Angel, Francisco Moncion; Eurydice, Maria Tallchief; Apollo, Herbert Bliss; Pluto, Edward Bigelow; Satyr, Job Sanders; Leader of the Bacchantes, Tanaquil LeClercq; Leader of the Furies, Beatrice Tompkins.

5. New York City Ballet

MOTHER GOOSE SUITE
Choreography by Todd Bolender
Music by Maurice Ravel

Premièred November 1, 1948, City Center of Music and Drama, New York. (Revival from the American Concert Ballet, 1941.) Principal Roles: Spectator, Beatrice Tompkins; Young Girl, Marie Jeanne; Hop o' My Thumb, Todd Bolender; Bird, Una Kai; Prince, Dick Beard; Beast, Francisco Moncion.

THE GUESTS
Choreography by Jerome Robbins
Music by Marc Blitzstein

Premièred January 20, 1949, City Center of Music and Drama, New York. Principal Dancers: Maria Tallchief, Francisco Moncion, Nicholas Magallanes.

JINX
Choreography by Lew Christensen
Music by Benjamin Britten (Variations on a theme by Frank Bridge)

chine, one of the greatest choreographers of our time; it developed a number of outstanding American dancers and several young choreographers. Most importantly, it paved the way for the organization of the New York City Ballet.

There follows a complete listing of all ballets created by American Ballet and the companies that succeeded it, up to September, 1966. It seemed both logical and less confusing to have one listing only, rather than separate lists for each of the companies although, naturally, the creations for New York City Ballet now represent the bulk of the achievement.

1. American Ballet, The (*Chronological List of Ballets March, 1935–Dec., 1966*)

SERENADE
Choreography by George Balanchine
Music by Peter Ilyitch Tchaikovsky (*Serenade for Strings in C major*)
Décor by Gaston Longchamp
Costumes by Jean Lurçat

Premièred March 1, 1935, Adelphi Theatre, New York. (Prior to the official première, *Serenade* was presented by the Producing Company of the School of American Ballet, December 6, 1934, in Hartford, Conn.) Principal Dancers: Leda Anchutina, Ruthanna Boris, Gisella Caccialanza, Kathryn Mullowney, William Dollar, Charles Laskey.

ALMA MATER
Choreography by George Balanchine
Music by Kay Swift, arranged by Morton Gould
Décor by Eugene Dunkel
Costumes by John Held, Jr.
Book by Edward M. M. Warburg

Premièred March 1, 1935, Adelphia Theatre, New York. (Prior to the official première, *Alma Mater* was presented by the Producing Company of the School of American Ballet, December 6, 1934, in Hartford, Conn.) Principal Dancers: Leda Anchutina, Ruthanna Boris, Gisella Caccialanza, Kathryn Mullowney, Heidi Vosseler, William Dollar, Charles Laskey, Eugene Loring.

ERRANTE
Choreography by George Balanchine
Music by Franz Schubert (*Wanderer Fantasy* for piano, orchestrated by Charles Koechlin)
Costumes, lighting and dramatic effects by Pavel Tchelitchew

Premièred, March 1, 1935, Adelphi Theatre, New York. (Revival from the repertoire of Les Ballets 1933.) Principal Dancers: Tamara Geva, Charles Laskey, William Dollar.

REMINISCENCE
Choreography by George Balanchine
Music by Benjamin Godard, orchestrated by Henry Brant
Costumes and décor by Sergei Soudeikine

Premièred March 1, 1935, Adelphi Theatre, New York. Principal Dancers: Leda Anchutina, Ruthanna Boris, Gisella Caccialanza, Elena de Rivas, Holly Howard, Annabelle Lyon, Elise Reiman, William Dollar, Paul Haakon, Joseph Levinoff.

MOZARTIANA
Choreography by George Balanchine
Music by Tchaikovsky (*Suite No. 4, Mozartiana*)
Costumes and décor by Christian Berard

Premièred March 1, 1935, Adelphi Theatre, New York. (Revival from Les Ballets 1933. Prior to the official première, *Mozartiana* was presented by the Producing Company of the School of American Ballet, December 6, 1934, in Hartford, Conn.) Principal Dancers: Rabana Hasburgh, Holly Howard, Helen Leitch, Daphne Vane, Heidi Vosseler, Charles Laskey.

TRANSCENDENCE
Choreography by George Balanchine
Music by Franz Liszt, orchestrated by George Antheil
Décor by Gaston Longchamp
Costumes by Franklin Watkins
Book by Lincoln Kirstein

Premièred March 5, 1935, Adelphi Theatre, New York. (Prior to the official première, *Transcendence* was presented by the Producing Company of the School of American Ballet, December 6, 1934, in Hartford, Conn.) Principal Dancers: Elise Reiman, William Dollar.

DREAMS
Choreography by George Balanchine
Music by George Antheil
Book, costumes and décor by André Derain

Premièred March 5, 1935, Adelphi Theatre, New York. (Revival from Les Ballets 1933.) Principal Dancers: Leda Anchutina, Ruthanna Boris, Paul Haakon.

THE BAT
Choreography by George Balanchine
Music by Johann Strauss (Overture to *Die Fledermaus*)
Costumes by Keith Martin
Book by Lincoln Kirstein

Premièred season 1935–6, Metropolitan Opera House, New York. Principal Dancers: Leda Anchutina, Rabana Hasburgh, Annabelle Lyon, Lew Christensen, Charles Laskey.

ORPHEUS AND EURYDICE
Choreography by George Balanchine
Music by Christoph Willibald von Gluck
Costumes and décor by Pavel Tchelitchew

Premièred May 22, 1936, Metropolitan Opera House, New York. Principal Roles: Orpheus, Lew Christensen; Eurydice, Daphne Vane; Angel, William Dollar.

APOLLON MUSAGÈTE (Later called *Apollo,* and *Apollo, Leader of the Muses*)
Choreography by George Balanchine
Music by Igor Stravinsky
Costumes and décor by Stewart Chaney

Premièred April 27, 1937, Metropolitan Opera House, New York. (Revival from the Diaghilev Ballets Russes.) Dancers: Lew Christensen, Daphne Vane, Holly Howard, Elise Reiman, Kyra Blank, Rabana Hasburgh, Jane Burkhalter.

THE CARD PARTY (Later called *Card Game*)
Choreography by George Balanchine
Music by Igor Stravinsky
Costumes and décor by Irene Sharaff
Book by Igor Stravinsky in collaboration with M. Malaieff

Premièred April 27, 1937, Metropolitan Opera House, New York. Principal Roles: The Joker, William Dollar; Aces, Ann Campbell, Jane Burkhalter, Lillian Moore, Vera Volkenau; Kings, Lew Christensen, Joseph Lane, Douglas Coudy, Erick Hawkins; Queens, Annabelle Lyon, Leda Anchutina, Ariel Lang, Hortense Kahrklin; Jacks, Charles Laskey, Joseph Levinoff, Eugene Loring, Serge Temoff.

LE BAISER DE LA FÉE (Later called *The Fairy's Kiss*)
Choreography by George Balanchine
Music by Igor Stravinsky
Costumes and décor by Alice Halicka
Book by Igor Stravinsky, based on a story by Hans Christian Andersen

Premièred April 27, 1937, Metropolitan Opera House, New York. Principal Roles: The Fairy, Kathryn Mullowney; Shadow, Rabana Hasburgh; Bride, Gisella Caccialanza; Friend, Leda Anchutina; Bridegroom, William Dollar; Mother, Annabelle Lyon.

2. The Ballet Caravan

ENCOUNTER
Choreography by Lew Christensen
Music by Mozart (*"Haffner" Serenade*)
Costumes by Forrest Thayr, Jr.

Premièred July 17, 1936, Bennington, Vermont. Principal Dancers: Annabelle Lyon, Ruby Asquith, Charles Laskey, Lew Christensen, Harold Christensen.

HARLEQUIN FOR PRESIDENT (Later called *Harlequin*)
Choreography by Eugene Loring

Music by Domenico Scarlatti, orchestrated by Ariadna Mikeshina
Costumes by Keith Martin
Book by Lincoln Kirstein

Premièred July 17, 1936, Bennington, Vermont. Principal Dancers: Annabelle Lyon, Eugene Loring, Charles Laskey, Harold Christensen, Fred Danieli.

FOLK DANCE
Choreography by Douglas Coudy
Music by Emmanuel Chabrier
Costumes by Charles Rain

Premièred July 17, 1936, Bennington, Vermont. Principal Dancers: Ruthanna Boris, Lew Christensen.

PROMENADE
Choreography by William Dollar
Music by Maurice Ravel (*Valses Nobles et Sentimentales*)
Costumes by Horace Vernet

Premièred July 17, 1936, Bennington, Vermont. Principal Dancers: Annabelle Lyon, Ruthanna Boris, Charles Laskey, Erick Hawkins.

YANKEE CLIPPER
Choreography by Eugene Loring
Music by Paul Bowles
Costumes by Charles Rain
Book by Lincoln Kirstein

Premièred July 12, 1937, Town Hall, Saybrook, Conn. Dancers: Eugene Loring and company.

SHOW PIECE
Choreography by Erick Hawkins
Music by Robert McBride
Costumes by Keith Martin

Premièred August, 1937, Bar Harbor, Maine. Principal Dancers: Marie Jeanne, Annabelle Lyon, Eugene Loring, Fred Danieli, Erick Hawkins.

POCAHONTAS
Choreography by Lew Christensen
Music by Elliott Carter, Jr.
Costumes by Karl Free
Book by Lincoln Kirstein

Premièred August 17, 1936, Colonial Theatre, Keene, New Hampshire. Principal Dancers: Ruthanna Boris, Lew Christensen, Charles Laskey, Harold Christensen, Erick Hawkins.

FILLING STATION
Choreography by Lew Christensen
Music by Virgil Thomson
Costumes and décor by Paul Cadmus
Book by Lincoln Kirstein

Premièred January 6, 1938, Avery Memorial Theatre, Hartford, Conn. Principal Dancers: Jane Deering, Marie Jeanne, Marjorie Moore, Todd Bolender, Harold Christensen, Lew Christensen, Douglas Coudy, Fred Danieli, Erick Hawkins, Eugene Loring.

BILLY THE KID
Choreography by Eugene Loring
Music by Aaron Copland
Costumes by Jared French
Book by Lincoln Kirstein

Premièred October 16, 1938, Chicago Opera House. Principal Roles: Billy, Eugene Loring; Mother and Sweetheart, Marie Jeanne; Pat Garrett, Lew Christensen; Alias, Todd Bolender.

AIR AND VARIATION
Choreography by William Dollar
Music by Johann Sebastian Bach (*Goldberg Variations,* arranged for two pianos by Trude Rittmann)
Costumes by Walter Gifford

Premièred November, 1938, Athens, Georgia. The entire company.

CHARADE, OR THE DEBUTANTE
Choreography by Lew Christensen
American melodies, arranged by Trude Rittmann
Costumes by Alvin Colt
Book by Lincoln Kirstein

Premièred December 26, 1939, St. James Theatre, New York. Principal Dancers: Gisella Caccialanza, Lew Christensen, Harold Christensen.

City Portrait
Choreography by Eugene Loring
Music by Henry Brant
Décor by James Stewart Morcom
Book by Lincoln Kirstein

Premièred December 28, 1939, St. James Theatre, New York. Dancers: Eugene Loring and entire company.

3. American Ballet Caravan

Juke Box
Choreography by William Dollar
Music by Alec Wilder
Costumes and décor by Tom Lee
Book by Lincoln Kirstein

Premièred May 28, 1941, Hunter College Playhouse, New York. Principal Dancers: Yvonne Patterson, Rabana Hasburgh, Lew Christensen, William Dollar.

Pastorela
Choreography by Lew Christensen and José Fernandez
Music by Paul Bowles
Costumes and décor by Alvin Colt
Book by José Martínez

Premièred May 28, 1941, Hunter College Playhouse, New York. Principal Dancers: Gisella Caccialanza, Beatrice Tompkins, Lew Christensen, José Fernandez, Todd Bolender, Nicholas Magallanes, Charles Dickson, José Martínez.

Concerto Barocco
Choreography by George Balanchine
Music by Johann Sebastian Bach (*Double Violin Concerto in D minor*)
Costumes and décor by Eugene Berman

Premièred May 28, 1941, Hunter College Playhouse, New York. Principal Dancers: Marie Jeanne, Mary Jane Shea, William Dollar.

Ballet Imperial
Choreography by George Balanchine
Music by Tchaikovsky (*Piano Concerto in G major*)
Costumes and décor by Mstislav Doboujinsky

Premièred May 29, 1941, Hunter College Playhouse, New York. Principal Dancers: Marie Jeanne, Gisella Caccialanza, William Dollar, Nicholas Magallanes, Fred Danieli.

Time Table
Choreography by Antony Tudor
Music by Aaron Copland (*Music for the Theatre*)
Costumes and décor by James Stewart Morcom

Premièred May 29, 1941, Hunter College Playhouse, New York. Principal Dancers: Marie Jeanne, Gisella Caccialanza, Mary Jane Shea, Beatrice Tompkins, Lew Christensen, John Kriza.

4. Ballet Society

The Spellbound Child
Choreography by George Balanchine
Music by Maurice Ravel (*L'Enfant et les sortilèges*)
Costumes and décor by Aline Bernstein
Poem by Colette

Premièred November 20, 1946, Central High School of Needle Trades, New York. Principal Dancers: Gisella Caccialanza, Ruth Gilbert, Georgia Hiden, Tanaquil LeClercq, Elise Reiman, Beatrice Tompkins, Paul d'Amboise, William Dollar.

The Four Temperaments
Choreography by George Balanchine
Music by Paul Hindemith
Costumes and décor by Kurt Seligmann

Premièred November 20, 1946, Central High School of Needle Trades, New York. Principal Dancers: Gisella Caccialanza, Georgia Hiden, Rita Karlin, Tanaquil LeClercq, Mary Ellen Moylan, Elise Reiman, Beatrice Tompkins, Todd Bolender, Lew Christensen, Fred Danieli, William Dollar, José Martínez, Francisco Moncion.

RENARD (*The Fox*)
Choreography by George Balanchine
Music by Igor Stravinsky
Costumes and décor by Esteban Francés
Book by Igor Stravinsky, English text by Harvey Officer

Premièred January 15, 1947, Hunter College Playhouse, New York. Principal Roles: The Fox, Todd Bolender; The Rooster, Lew Christensen; The Cat, Fred Danieli; The Ram, John Taras.

DIVERTIMENTO
Choreography by George Balanchine
Music by Alexei Haieff

Premièred January 13, 1947, Hunter College Playhouse, New York. Dancers: Gisella Caccialanza, Tanaquil LeClercq, Mary Ellen Moylan, Elise Reiman, Beatrice Tompkins, Todd Bolender, Lew Christensen, Fred Danieli, Francisco Moncion, John Taras.

THE MINOTAUR
Choreography by John Taras
Music by Elliott Carter
Costumes and décor by Joan Junyer
Book by Lincoln Kirstein and Joan Junyer

Premièred March 26, 1947, Central High School of Needle Trades, New York. Principal Roles: Pasiphae, Queen of Crete, Elise Reiman; Minos, King of Crete, Edward Bigelow; Ariadne, Tanaquil LeClercq; Theseus, John Taras; Bulls, Fred Danieli and Paul d'Amboise.

ZODIAC
Choreography by Todd Bolender
Music by Rudi Revil
Costumes and décor by Esteban Francés

Premièred March 26, 1947, Central High School of Needle Trades, New York. Principal Dancers: Virginia Barnes, William Dollar, Todd Bolender, Job Sanders, Patricia McBride, Janice Roman, Ruth Sobotka, Jean Reeves, Irma Sandré, Joan Djorup, Marc Beaudet, John Scancarella, Betty Nichols, Gisella Caccialanza, Edward Bigelow, Gerard Leavitt.

HIGHLAND FLING
Choreography by William Dollar
Music by Stanley Bate
Costumes and décor by David Ffolkes

Premièred March 26, 1947, Central High School of Needle Trades, New York. Principal Roles: Bride, Gisella Caccialanza; Groom, Todd Bolender; Sylphide, Elise Reiman; Bridesmaids, Tanaquil LeClercq and Beatrice Tompkins; Minister, José Martínez.

THE SEASONS
Choreography by Merce Cunningham
Music by John Cage
Costumes and décor by Isamu Noguchi

Premièred May 18, 1947, Ziegfeld Theatre, New York. Principal Dancers: Gisella Caccialanza, Tanaquil LeClercq, Beatrice Tompkins, Merce Cunningham.

BLACKFACE
Choreography by Lew Christensen
Music by Carter Harman
Costumes and décor by Robert Drew

Premièred May 18, 1947, Ziegfeld Theatre, New York. Principal Dancers: Betty Nichols, Beatrice Tompkins, Talley Beatty, Marc Beaudet, Fred Danieli, Paul Godkin.

PUNCH AND THE CHILD
Choreography by Fred Danieli
Music by Richard Arnell
Costumes and décor by Horace Armistead

Premièred November 12, 1947, City Center of Music and Drama, New York. Principal Roles: Father and Punch, Herbert Bliss; Mother and Judy, Beatrice Tompkins; the Child, Judith Kursch; Fishwife and Polly, Gisella Caccialanza; Peg Leg and Constable, Charles Laskey; Puppeteer and Devil, Lew Christensen; Musician and Doctor, Edward Bigelow; Street Cleaner and Hangman, Victor Duntiere; Professor, Luis Lopez.

SYMPHONIE CONCERTANTE
Choreography by George Balanchine
Music by Mozart (*Symphonie Concertante in E flat,* K. 364)

Costumes and décor by James Stewart Morcom

Premièred November 12, 1947, City Center of Music and Drama, New York. (Prior to première, Symphonie Concertante was presented November 5, 1945, at Carnegie Hall, New York, on a program "Adventure in Ballet" by pupils of the School of American Ballet.) Principal Dancers: Maria Tallchief, Tanaquil LeClercq, Dorothy Dushok, Ruth Gilbert, Georgia Hiden, Rita Karlin, Patricia McBride, Irma Sandré, Todd Bolender.

THE TRIUMPH OF BACCHUS AND ARIADNE (Ballet Cantata)
Choreography by George Balanchine
Music by Vittorio Rieti
Costumes and décor by Corrado Cagli

Premièred February 9, 1948, City Center of Music and Drama, New York. Principal Roles: Major-domo, Lew Christensen; Bacchus, Nicholas Magallanes; Ariadne, Tanaquil LeClercq; First Satyr, Herbert Bliss; First Nymph, Marie Jeanne; Silenus, Charles Laskey; Midas, Francisco Moncion; the Little Girl, Claudia Hall; the Young Girl, Patricia McBride.

CAPRICORN CONCERTO
Choreography by Todd Bolender
Music by Samuel Barber
Costumes and décor by Esteban Francés

Premièred March 22, 1948, City Center of Music and Drama, New York. Principal Dancers: Maria Tallchief, Herbert Bliss, Francisco Moncion.

SYMPHONY IN C
Choreography by George Balanchine
Music by Georges Bizet

Premièred March 22, 1948, City Center of Music and Drama, New York. (First produced for the Paris Opéra under the title *Palais de Cristal,* July 28, 1947.) Principal Dancers: First Movement, Maria Tallchief, Nicholas Magallanes; Second Movement, Tanaquil LeClercq, Francisco Moncion; Third Movement, Beatrice Tompkins, Herbert Bliss; Fourth Movement, Elise Reiman, Lew Christensen.

ELEGIE
Choreography by George Balanchine
Music by Igor Stravinsky

Premièred April 28, 1948, City Center of Music and Drama, New York. (Prior to première, *Elegie* was presented November 5, 1945, at Carnegie Hall, New York, on a program "Adventure in Ballet" by pupils of the School of American Ballet.) Danced by Tanaquil LeClercq and Patricia McBride.

ORPHEUS
Choreography by George Balanchine
Music by Igor Stravinsky
Costumes and décor by Isamu Noguchi

Premièred April 28, 1948, City Center of Music and Drama, New York. Principal Roles: Orpheus, Nicholas Magallanes; Dark Angel, Francisco Moncion; Eurydice, Maria Tallchief; Apollo, Herbert Bliss; Pluto, Edward Bigelow; Satyr, Job Sanders; Leader of the Bacchantes, Tanaquil LeClercq; Leader of the Furies, Beatrice Tompkins.

5. New York City Ballet

MOTHER GOOSE SUITE
Choreography by Todd Bolender
Music by Maurice Ravel

Premièred November 1, 1948, City Center of Music and Drama, New York. (Revival from the American Concert Ballet, 1941.) Principal Roles: Spectator, Beatrice Tompkins; Young Girl, Marie Jeanne; Hop o' My Thumb, Todd Bolender; Bird, Una Kai; Prince, Dick Beard; Beast, Francisco Moncion.

THE GUESTS
Choreography by Jerome Robbins
Music by Marc Blitzstein

Premièred January 20, 1949, City Center of Music and Drama, New York. Principal Dancers: Maria Tallchief, Francisco Moncion, Nicholas Magallanes.

JINX
Choreography by Lew Christensen
Music by Benjamin Britten (Variations on a theme by Frank Bridge)

Costumes and décor by George Bockman
Story by Lew Christensen

Premièred November 24, 1949, City Center of Music and Drama, New York. (Revived from Dance Players, 1942.) Cast: Jinx, a Clown, Francisco Moncion; Wire-walkers, Janet Reed, Ruth Sobotka, Frank Hobi; Equestrians, Herbert Bliss, Barbara Milberg, Barbara Walczak; Bearded Lady, Beatrice Tompkins; Strong Lady, Georgia Hiden; Tattooed Lady, Dorothy Dushok; Ringmaster, Val Buttignol.

FIREBIRD
Choreography by George Balanchine
Music by Igor Stravinsky
Costumes and décor by Marc Chagall

Premièred November 27, 1949, City Center of Music and Drama, New York. Principal Roles: Firebird, Maria Tallchief; Prince Ivan, Francisco Moncion; Prince's Bride, Patricia McBride; Kastchei, Edward Bigelow.

BOURRÉE FANTASQUE
Choreography by George Balanchine
Music by Emmanuel Chabrier
Costumes by Karinska

Premièred December 1, 1949, City Center of Music and Drama, New York. Principal Dancers: Bourrée Fantasque, Tanaquil LeClercq, Jerome Robbins; Prelude, Maria Tallchief, Nicholas Magallanes, Edwina Fontaine, Yvonne Mounsey; Fête Polonaise, Janet Reed, Herbert Bliss.

ONDINE
Choreography by William Dollar
Music by Antonio Vivaldi (Violin Concertos)
Costumes and décor by Horace Armistead

Premièred December 9, 1949, City Center of Music and Drama, New York. Principal Roles: Ondine, Tanaquil LeClercq; Matteo, Francisco Moncion; Giannina, Melissa Hayden; Hydrola, Yvonne Mounsey.

THE PRODIGAL SON
Choreography by George Balanchine
Music by Serge Prokofiev
Costumes and décor by Georges Rouault

Premièred February 23, 1950, City Center of Music and Drama, New York. (Revival from the Diaghilev Ballets Russes, 1929.) Principal Roles: The Prodigal Son, Jerome Robbins; The Siren, Maria Tallchief; The Father, Michael Arshansky; Servants of the Prodigal Son, Frank Hobi, Herbert Bliss; the Two Sisters, Jillana, Francesca Mosarra.

THE DUEL
Choreography by William Dollar
Music by Raffaello de Banfield
Costumes by Robert Stevenson

Premièred February 24, 1950, City Center of Music and Drama, New York. Dancers: Melissa Hayden, William Dollar, Val Buttignol, Walter Georgov, Shaun O'Brien.

AGE OF ANXIETY
Choreography by Jerome Robbins
Based on the poem of the same name by W. H. Auden
Music by Leonard Bernstein (*Symphony No. 2*)
Décor by Oliver Smith
Costumes by Irene Sharaff

Premièred February 26, 1950, City Center of Music and Drama, New York. Principal Dancers: Tanaquil LeClercq, Todd Bolender, Francisco Moncion, Jerome Robbins, Melissa Hayden, Patricia McBride, Yvonne Mounsey, Beatrice Tompkins, Edward Bigelow, Herbert Bliss.

ILLUMINATIONS
Choreography by Frederick Ashton
Based on poems by Arthur Rimbaud
Music by Benjamin Britten (*Les Illuminations,* for tenor and strings)
Costumes and décor by Cecil Beaton

Premièred March 2, 1950, City Center of Music and Drama, New York. Principal Roles: Poet, Nicholas Magallanes; Sacred Love, Tanaquil LeClercq; Profane Love, Melissa Hayden.

PAS DE DEUX ROMANTIQUE
Choreography by George Balanchine
Music by Carl Maria von Weber (Concerto for Clarinet)
Costumes by Robert Stevenson

Premièred March 3, 1950, City Center of Music and Drama, New York. Dancers: Janet Reed and Herbert Bliss.

JONES BEACH
Choreography by George Balanchine and Jerome Robbins
Music by Juriaan Andriessen (Berkshire Symphonies)

Premièred March 9, 1950, City Center of Music and Drama, New York. Principal Dancers: Melissa Hayden, Tanaquil LeClercq, Yvonne Mounsey, Maria Tallchief, Beatrice Tompkins, Herbert Bliss, Todd Bolender, William Dollar, Frank Hobi, Nicholas Magallanes, Jerome Robbins, Roy Tobias.

THE WITCH
Choreography by John Cranko
Music by Maurice Ravel (Piano Concerto)
Costumes and décor by Dorothea Tanning

Premièred August 18, 1950, Royal Opera House, Covent Garden, London. Principal Dancers: Melissa Hayden, Francisco Moncion.

MAZURKA from A LIFE FOR THE TSAR
Choreography by George Balanchine
Music by Mikhail Glinka

Premièred November 30, 1950, City Center of Music and Drama, New York. Dancers: Janet Reed and Yurek Lazowski; Vida Brown and George Balanchine; Barbara Walczak and Harold Lang; Dorothy Dushok and Frank Hobi.

SYLVIA: PAS DE DEUX
Choreography by George Balanchine
Music by Léo Delibes
Costumes by Karinska

Premièred December 1, 1950, City Center of Music and Drama, New York. Dancers: Maria Tallchief and Nicholas Magallanes.

PAS DE TROIS
Choreography by George Balanchine
Music by Leon Minkus (From *Don Quixote*)
Costumes by Karinska

Premièred February 18, 1951, City Center of Music and Drama, New York. (Revival from Grand Ballet du Marquis de Cuevas, 1948.) Dancers: Maria Tallchief, Nora Kaye, André Eglevsky.

LA VALSE
Choreography by George Balanchine
Music by Maurice Ravel (*Valses Nobles et Sentimentales and La Valse*)
Costumes by Karinska

Premièred February 20, 1951, City Center of Music and Drama, New York. Principal Dancers: Diana Adams, Tanaquil LeClercq, Yvonne Mounsey, Patricia Wilde, Herbert Bliss, Frank Hobi, Nicholas Magallanes, Francisco Moncion.

LADY OF THE CAMELLIAS
Choreography by Antony Tudor
Music by Giuseppe Verdi (selection)
Costumes and décor by Cecil Beaton
Story after the novel by Alexandre Dumas fils.

Premièred February 28, 1951, City Center of Music and Drama, New York. Principal Roles: Prudence, Vida Brown; Marguerite Gautier, Diana Adams; M. le Comte de N., Brooks Jackson; Armand Duval, Hugh Laing; Armand's Father, John Earle (Antony Tudor).

CAPRICCIO BRILLANTE
Choreography by George Balanchine
Music by Felix Mendelssohn
Costumes by Karinska

Premièred June 7, 1951, City Center of Music and Drama, New York. Dancers: Maria Tallchief and André Eglevsky; Barbara Bocher, Constance Garfield, Jillana, Irene Larsson.

CAKEWALK
Choreography by Ruthanna Boris

Music by Louis Moreau Gottschalk, arranged and orchestrated by Hershy Kay
Costumes and décor by Robert Drew

Premièred June 12, 1951, City Center of Music and Drama, New York. Principal Dancers: Tanaquil LeClercq, Yvonne Mounsey, Janet Reed, Beatrice Tompkins, Patricia Wilde, Herbert Bliss, Frank Hobi.

THE CAGE
Choreography by Jerome Robbins
Music by Igor Stravinsky (*String Concerto in D*)
Costumes by Ruth Sobotka

Premièred June 14, 1951, City Center of Music and Drama, New York. Principal Roles: The Novice, Nora Kaye; The Queen, Yvonne Mounsey; The Intruders, Nicholas Magallanes, Michael Maule.

THE MIRACULOUS MANDARIN
Choreography by Todd Bolender
Music by Béla Bartók
Costumes and décor by Alvin Colt
Libretto by Melchior Langyel

Premièred September 6, 1951, City Center of Music and Drama, New York. Cast: The Men, Robert Barnett, Edward Bigelow, Jacques d'Amboise, Walter Georgov, Michael Maule; The Woman, Melissa Hayden; An Old Man, Frank Hobi; A Young Man, Roy Tobias; A Blind Girl, Beatrice Tompkins; The Mandarin, Hugh Laing.

A LA FRANÇAIX
Choreography by George Balanchine
Music by Jean Françaix (*Serenade for Small Orchestra*)

Premièred September 11, 1951, City Center of Music and Drama, New York. Dancers: Janet Reed, Maria Tallchief, André Eglevsky, Frank Hobi, Roy Tobias.

TYL ULENSPIEGEL
Choreography by George Balanchine
Music by Richard Strauss
Costumes and décor by Esteban Francés

Premièred November 14, 1951, City Center of Music and Drama, New York. Principal Roles: Tyl Ulenspiegel as a child, Alberta Grant; Philip II as a child, Susan Kovnat; Tyl Ulenspiegel, Jerome Robbins; Nell, his wife, Ruth Sobotka; Philip II, King of Spain, Brooks Jackson; Duke and Duchess, Frank Hobi and Beatrice Tompkins; Woman, Tomi Wortham.

SWAN LAKE
Choreography by George Balanchine (after Lev Ivanov)
Music by Peter Ilyitch Tchaikovsky
Costumes and décor by Cecil Beaton

Premièred November 20, 1951, City Center of Music and Drama, New York. Principal Roles: Odette, Maria Tallchief; Prince Siegfried, André Eglevsky; Benno, Frank Hobi; Leading Swans, Patricia Wilde and Yvonne Mounsey; Cygnets, Doris Breckenridge, Kaye Sargent, Ruth Sobotka, Gloria Vauges; Von Rothbart, a Sorcerer, Edward Bigelow.

LILAC GARDEN
Choreography by Antony Tudor
Music by Ernest Chausson (*Poème*)
Décor by Horace Armistead
Costumes by Karinska

Premièred November 30, 1951, City Center of Music and Drama, New York. (Revival from Ballet Rambert, 1936, when it was given under the title *Jardin aux Lilas.*) Principal Roles: Caroline, Nora Kaye; Her Lover, Hugh Laing; The Man She Must Marry, Antony Tudor; The Woman in His Past, Tanaquil LeClercq.

THE PIED PIPER
Choreography by Jerome Robbins
Music by Aaron Copland (*Concerto for Clarinet and String Orchestra*)

Premièred December 4, 1951, City Center of Music and Drama, New York. Principal Dancers: Diana Adams, Melissa Hayden, Jillana, Tanaquil LeClercq, Janet Reed, Barbara Bocher, Herbert Bliss, Todd Bolender, Nicholas Magallanes, Jerome Robbins, Roy Tobias.

BALLADE
Choreography by Jerome Robbins

Music by Claude Debussy (*Six Epigraphes Antiques*)
Costumes and décor by Boris Aronson

Premièred February 14, 1952, City Center of Music and Drama, New York. Dancers: Nora Kaye, Tanaquil LeClercq, Janet Reed, Robert Barnett, Brooks Jackson, Louis Johnson, John Mandia, Roy Tobias.

CARACOLE
Choreography by George Balanchine
Music by Mozart (*Divertimento No. 15 in B flat major,* K. 287)
Costumes by Christian Bérard

Premièred February 19, 1952, City Center of Music and Drama, New York. Principal Dancers: Diana Adams, Melissa Hayden, Tanaquil LeClercq, Maria Tallchief, Patricia Wilde, André Eglevsky, Nicholas Magallanes, Jerome Robbins.

BAYOU
Choreography by George Balanchine
Music by Virgil Thomson (*Acadian Songs and Dances*)
Costumes and décor by Dorothea Tanning

Premièred February 21, 1952, City Center of Music and Drama, New York. Principal Roles: Boy of the Bayou, Francisco Moncion; Girl of the Bayou, Doris Breckenridge; Leaves and Flowers, Melissa Hayden, Hugh Laing, Irene Larsson, Barbara Walczak, Walter Georgov, Stanley Zompakos; Starched White People, Diana Adams, Herbert Bliss, Una Kai, Marilyn Poudrier, Brooks Jackson, Shaun O'Brien.

LA GLOIRE
Choreography by Antony Tudor
Music by Beethoven (*Egmont, Coriolanus, Leonora III* overtures)
Décor by Gaston Longchamp
Costumes by Robert Fletcher

Premièred February 26, 1952, City Center of Music and Drama, New York. Principal Roles: La Gloire, Nora Kaye; Sextus Tarquinius and Hamlet's Stepfather, Francisco Moncion; Hippolytus and Laertes, Hugh Laing; Ophelia, Doris Breckenridge; Hamlet's Mother, Beatrice Tompkins; the Dancer in Gray, Diana Adams.

PICNIC AT TINTAGEL
Choreography by Frederick Ashton
Music by Sir Arnold Bax (*The Garden of Fand*)
Costumes and décor by Cecil Beaton

Premièred February 28, 1952, City Center of Music and Drama, New York. Cast: The Husband (King Mark), Francisco Moncion; The Wife (Iseult), Diana Adams; Her Maid (Brangaene), Yvonne Mounsey; Her Lover (Tristram), Jacques d'Amboise; His Rivals (the False Knights), Stanley Zompakos, Brooks Jackson; Her Chauffeur and Footman (Heralds), Alan Baker, John Mandia; The Caretaker (Merlin), Robert Barnett.

SCOTCH SYMPHONY
Choreography by George Balanchine
Music by Felix Mendelssohn (*"Scotch" Symphony;* 2nd, 3rd and 4th movements)
Décor by Horace Armistead
Costumes by Karinska and David Ffolkes

Premièred November 11, 1952, City Center of Music and Drama, New York. Principal Dancers: Maria Tallchief, Patricia Wilde, André Eglevsky, Michael Maule, Frank Hobi.

METAMORPHOSES
Choreography by George Balanchine
Music by Paul Hindemith (*Variations on Themes by Carl Maria von Weber*)
Costumes by Karinska

Premièred November 25, 1952, City Center of Music and Drama, New York. Principal Dancers: Tanaquil LeClercq, Nicholas Magallanes, Todd Bolender.

HARLEQUINADE PAS DE DEUX
Choreography by George Balanchine
Music by Richard Drigo
Costumes by Karinska

Premièred December 16, 1952, City Center of Music and Drama, New York. Dancers: Maria Tallchief and André Eglevsky.

KALEIDOSCOPE
Choreography by Ruthanna Boris
Music by Dimitri Kabalevsky
Costumes by Alvin Colt

Premièred December 18, 1952, City Center of Music and Drama, New York. Dancers: Melissa Hayden, Patricia Wilde, Herbert Bliss, Todd Bolender, Frank Hobi.

INTERPLAY
Choreography by Jerome Robbins
Music by Morton Gould (*American Concertette*)
Costumes and décor by Irene Sharaff

Premièred December 23, 1952, City Center of Music and Drama, New York. (Revival from The Ballet Theatre, 1945.) Dancers: Carolyn George, Jillana, Irene Larsson, Melissa Hayden, Robert Barnett, Shaun O'Brien, Jacques d'Amboise, Michael Maule.

CONCERTINO
Choreography by George Balanchine
Music by Jean Françaix
Costumes by Karinska

Premièred December 30, 1952, City Center of Music and Drama, New York. Dancers: Diana Adams, Tanaquil LeClercq, André Eglevsky.

VALSE FANTAISIE
Choreography by George Balanchine
Music by Mikhail Glinka
Costumes by Karinska

Premièred January 6, 1953, City Center of Music and Drama, New York. Dancers: Tanaquil LeClercq, Diana Adams, Melissa Hayden, Nicholas Magallanes.

WILL O' THE WISP
Choreography by Ruthanna Boris
Music by Virgil Thomson
Costumes and décor by Dorothea Tanning

Premièred January 13, 1953, City Center of Music and Drama, New York. Principal Dancers: Ruthanna Boris, Frank Hobi.

THE FIVE GIFTS
Choreography by William Dollar
Music by Ernest Dohnanyi (*Variations on a Nursery Tune*)
Costumes by Esteban Francés
Based on a story by Mark Twain

Premièred January 20, 1953, City Center of Music and Drama, New York. (Revival from American Concert Ballet, 1943.) Principal Roles: The Youth, Todd Bolender; The Fairy, Melissa Hayden; Pleasure, Carolyn George; Death, Yvonne Mounsey; Fame, Jillana; Riches, Patricia Wilde; Love, Irene Larsson; Another Youth, Jacques d'Amboise.

AFTERNOON OF A FAUN
Choreography by Jerome Robbins
Music by Claude Debussy
Décor by Jean Rosenthal
Costumes by Irene Sharaff

Premièred May 14, 1953, City Center of Music and Drama, New York. Dancers: Tanaquil LeClercq and Francisco Moncion.

THE FILLY (or A STABLEBOY'S DREAM)
Choreography by Todd Bolender
Music by John Colman
Costumes and décor by Peter Larkin

Premièred May 19, 1953, City Center of Music and Drama, New York. Principal Roles: Stableboy, Roy Tobias; The Mare, Diana Adams; The Stallion, Nicholas Magallanes; The Foal, Ellen Gottesman; The Filly, Maria Tallchief.

FANFARE
Choreography by Jerome Robbins
Music by Benjamin Britten (*The Young Person's Guide to the Orchestra*)
Costumes and décor by Irene Sharaff

Premièred June 2, 1953, City Center of Music and Drama, New York. Danced by the company.

CON AMORE
Choreography by Lew Christensen
Music by Gioacchino Rossini (*La Gazza Ladra, Il Signor Bruschino* and *La Scala di Seta* overtures)
Costumes and décor by Esteban Francés
Libretto by James Graham-Lujan

Premièred June 9, 1953, City Center of Music and Drama, New York. (Revival from the San Francisco Ballet, 1953.) Principal Dancers: Sally Bailey, Nancy Johnson, Jacques d'Amboise.

OPUS 34
Choreography by George Balanchine
Music by Arnold Schoenberg (The accompaniment music for a motion picture)
Décor by Jean Rosenthal
Costumes by Esteban Francés

Premièred January 19, 1954, City Center of Music and Drama, New York. Principal Dancers: Diana Adams, Patricia Wilde, Tanaquil LeClercq, Nicholas Magallanes, Francisco Moncion, Herbert Bliss.

THE NUTCRACKER
Choreography by George Balanchine (after Lev Ivanov)
Music by Peter Ilyitch Tchaikovsky
Décor by Horace Armistead
Costumes by Karinska

Premièred February 2, 1954, City Center of Music and Drama, New York. Principal Dancers: Maria Tallchief, Tanaquil LeClercq, Yvonne Mounsey, Janet Reed, Jillana, Irene Larsson, Alberta Grant, Nicholas Magallanes, Herbert Bliss, Francisco Moncion, Robert Barnett, Edward Bigelow, George Li, Michael Arshansky, Paul Nickel.

QUARTET
Choreography by Jerome Robbins
Music by Serge Prokofiev (*String Quartet No. 2, Opus 92*)
Costumes by Karinska

Premièred February 18, 1954, City Center of Music and Drama, New York. Principal Dancers: Patricia Wilde, Jillana, Yvonne Mounsey, Herbert Bliss, Jacques d'Amboise, Todd Bolender.

WESTERN SYMPHONY
Choreography by George Balanchine
Music by Hershy Kay
Décor by John Boyt
Costumes by Karinska

Premièred September 7, 1954, City Center of Music and Drama, New York. Principal Dancers: First Movement, Diana Adams, Herbert Bliss; Second Movement, Janet Reed, Nicholas Magallanes; Third Movement, Patricia Wilde, André Eglevsky; Fourth Movement, Tanaquil LeClercq, Jacques d'Amboise.

IVESIANA
Choreography by George Balanchine
Music by Charles Ives

Premièred September 14, 1954, City Center of Music and Drama, New York. Principal Dancers: Janet Reed, Patricia Wilde, Allegra Kent, Diana Adams, Tanaquil LeClercq, Francisco Moncion, Jacques d'Amboise, Todd Bolender, Herbert Bliss.

ROMA
Choreography by George Balanchine
Music by Georges Bizet
Costumes and décor by Eugene Berman

Premièred February 23, 1955, City Center of Music and Drama, New York. Principal Dancers: Tanaquil LeClercq and André Eglevsky; Barbara Milberg, Barbara Walczak, Roy Tobias, John Mandia.

PAS DE TROIS (II)
Choreography by George Balanchine
Music by Mikhail Glinka
Costumes by Karinska

Premièred March 1, 1955, City Center of Music and Drama, New York. Dancers: Patricia Wilde, Melissa Hayden, André Eglevsky.

PAS DE DIX
Choreography by George Balanchine
Music by Alexander Glazounov (from *Raymonda*)
Costumes by Esteban Francés

Premièred November 9, 1955, City Center of Music and Drama, New York. Dancers: Maria Tallchief and André Eglevsky; Barbara Fallis, Constance Garfield, Jane Mason, Barbara Walczak, Shaun O'Brien, Roy Tobias, Roland Vazquez, Jonathan Watts.

SOUVENIRS
Choreography by Todd Bolender
Music by Samuel Barber
Costumes and décor by Rouben Ter-Arutunian

Premièred November 15, 1955, City Center of Music and Drama, New York. Principal Dancers: Irene Larsson, Jillana, Carolyn George, Todd Bolender, Roy Tobias, Jonathan Watts, John Mandia, Herbert Bliss.

JEUX D'ENFANTS
Choreography by George Balanchine, Barbara Milberg, Francisco Moncion
Music by Georges Bizet
Costumes and décor by Esteban Francés

Premièred November 22, 1955, City Center of Music and Drama, New York. Principal Dancers: Melissa Hayden, Barbara Fallis, Barbara Walczak, Roy Tobias, Robert Barnett, Richard Thomas, Jonathan Watts.

ALLEGRO BRILLANTE
Choreography by George Balanchine
Music by Peter Ilyitch Tchaikovsky (*Third Piano Concerto*)

Premièred March 1, 1956, City Center of Music and Drama, New York. Dancers: Maria Tallchief and Nicholas Magallanes; Barbara Fallis, Carolyn George, Barbara Milberg, Barbara Walczak, Arthur Mitchell, Richard Rapp, Roland Vazquez, Jonathan Watts.

THE CONCERT
Choreography by Jerome Robbins
Music by Frédéric Chopin
Décor by Jean Rosenthal
Costumes by Irene Sharaff

Premièred March 6, 1956, City Center of Music and Drama, New York. Principal Dancers: Tanaquil LeClercq, Yvonne Mounsey, Wilma Curley, Todd Bolender, Robert Barnett, John Mandia, Richard Thomas.

THE STILL POINT
Choreography by Todd Bolender
Music by Claude Debussy, transcribed by Frank Black

Premièred March 13, 1956, City Center of Music and Drama, New York. (Originally arranged for the Emily Frankel-Frank Ryder modern dance group.) Dancers: Melissa Hayden, Irene Larsson, Jillana, Jacques d'Amboise, Roy Tobias, John Mandia.

DIVERTIMENTO NO. 15
Choreography by George Balanchine
Music by Wolfgang Amadeus Mozart (K.V. 287)
Décor by James Stewart Morcom
Costumes by Karinska

Premièred December 19, 1956, City Center of Music and Drama, New York. (Prior to the official première, *Divertimento No. 15* was presented at the Mozart Festival in Stratford, Connecticut, May 31, 1956.) Principal Dancers: Diana Adams, Melissa Hayden, Yvonne Mounsey, Patricia Wilde, Barbara Milberg, Nicholas Magallanes, Roy Tobias, Jonathan Watts.

THE UNICORN, THE GORGON AND THE MANTICORE (A Madrigal Fable)
Choreography by John Butler
Music and libretto by Gian Carlo Menotti
Décor by Jean Rosenthal
Costumes by Robert Fletcher

Premièred January 15, 1957, City Center of Music and Drama, New York. (Commissioned by the Elizabeth Sprague Coolidge Foundation in the Library of Congress and first presented in the Coolidge Auditorium, Washington, D.C., October 21, 1956.) Roles: The Countess, Janet Reed; The Count, Roy Tobias; Man in the Castle (the Poet), Nicholas Magallanes; The Unicorn, Arthur Mitchell; The Gorgon, Eugene Tanner; The Manticore, Richard Thomas; The Mayor and His Wife, John Mandia and Wilma Curley; The Doctor and His Wife, Jonathan Watts and Lee Becker.

THE MASQUERS
Choreography by Todd Bolender
Music by Francis Poulenc
Costumes and décor by David Hays

Premièred January 29, 1957, City Center of Music and Drama, New York. Principal Roles: A Young Woman, Melissa Hayden; A Soldier, Jacques d'Amboise; The Passerby, Yvonne Mounsey; A Friend of the Young Woman, Charlotte Ray; The Boy She Meets, Robert Barnett; Another Soldier, Jonathan Watts.

PASTORALE
Choreography by Francisco Moncion
Music by Charles Turner
Décor by David Hays
Costumes by Ruth Sobotka

Premièred February 14, 1957, City Center of Music and Drama, New York. Dancers: Allegra Kent, Francisco Moncion, Roy Tobias, Geralyn Donald, Barbara Fallis, Ruth Sobotka, Anthony Blum, Richard Rapp, Shaun O'Brien.

SQUARE DANCE
Choreography by George Balanchine
Music by Arcangelo Corelli and Antonio Vivaldi

Premièred November 21, 1957, City Center of Music and Drama, New York. Principal Dancers: Patricia Wilde and Nicholas Magallanes.

AGON
Choreography by George Balanchine
Music by Igor Stravinsky

Premièred November 27, 1957, City Center of Music and Drama, New York. Dancers: Diana Adams, Melissa Hayden, Barbara Milberg, Barbara Walczak, Todd Bolender, Arthur Mitchell, Roy Tobias, Jonathan Watts, Roberta Lubell, Francia Russell, Dido Sayers, Ruth Sobotka.

GOUNOD SYMPHONY
Choreography by George Balanchine
Music by Charles Gounod (*Symphony No. 1 in D major*)
Décor by Horace Armistead
Costumes by Karinska

Premièred January 8, 1958, City Center of Music and Drama, New York. Principal Dancers: Maria Tallchief and Jacques d'Amboise.

STARS AND STRIPES
Choreography by George Balanchine
Music by Hershy Kay (after music by John Philip Sousa)
Décor by David Hays
Costumes by Karinska

Premièred January 17, 1958, City Center of Music and Drama, New York. Principal Dancers: Allegra Kent, Diana Adams, Robert Barnett, Melissa Hayden, Jacques d'Amboise.

WALTZ SCHERZO (Pas de Deux)
Choreography by George Balanchine
Music by Peter Ilyitch Tchaikovsky
Costumes by Karinska

Premièred September 9, 1958, City Center of Music and Drama, New York. Dancers: Patricia Wilde and André Eglevsky.

MEDEA
Choreography by Birgit Cullberg
Music by Bela Bartok, orchestrated by Herbert Sandberg
Costumes by Lewis Brown

Premièred November 26, 1958, City Center of Music and Drama, New York. (Revival from the Royal Swedish Opera Ballet, Stockholm, 1954.) Principal Roles: Medea, Melissa Hayden; Jason, Jacques d'Amboise; Their Children, Delia Peters, Susan Pillersdorf; Creon, King of Corinth, Shaun O'Brien; Creusa, His Daughter, Violette Verdy.

OCTET
Choreography by William Christensen
Music by Igor Stravinsky

Premièred December 2, 1958, City Center of Music and Drama, New York. Dancers: Barbara Walczak, Dido Sayers, Roberta Lubell, Judith Green, Edward Villella, William Weslow, Robert Lindgren, Richard Rapp.

THE SEVEN DEADLY SINS
Choreography by George Balanchine
Music by Kurt Weill
Costumes and décor by Rouben Ter-Arutunian
Lyrics by Berthold Brecht, translated by W. H. Auden and Chester Kallman

Première, new version, December 4, 1958, City Center of Music and Drama, New York. (Originally produced by Les Ballets 1933.) Principal Roles: Anna I (singer), Lotte Lenya; Anna II, Allegra Kent; The Family (singers), Mother, Stanley Carlton, bass; Father, Gene Hollman, bass; Brother I, Frank Porretta, tenor; Brother II, Grant Williams, tenor.

NATIVE DANCERS
Choreography by George Balanchine
Music by Vittorio Rieti (*Symphony No. 5*)
Décor by David Hays
Girls' Costumes by Peter Larkin
Jockey Silks by H. Kauffman & Sons, Saddlery Co.

Premièred January 14, 1959, City Center of Music and Drama, New York. Principal Dancers: Patricia Wilde and Jacques d'Amboise.

EPISODES
Choreography by Martha Graham and George Balanchine
Music by Anton Webern (from his orchestral works)
Décor and lighting by David Hays
Costumes designed and executed by Karinska

Premièred May 14, 1959, City Center of Music and Drama, New York. First Part choreography by Martha Graham, music *Passacaglia, Opus 1;* and *Six Pieces, Opus 6.* Principal Dancers: Martha Graham (Mary, Queen of Scots), Bertram Ross (Bothwell), Sallie Wilson (Elizabeth, Queen of England). Second Part choreography by George Balanchine, music *Symphony, Opus 21; Five Pieces, Opus 10; Concerto, Opus 24; Variations, Opus 30;* Ricercata in six voices from Bach's "Musical Offering." Principal Dancers: Violette Verdy, Jonathan Watts, Diana Adams, Jacques d'Amboise, Allegra Kent, Nicholas Magallanes, Paul Taylor, Melissa Hayden, Francisco Moncion.

THE NIGHT SHADOW (Later called *La Sonnambula*)
Choreography by George Balanchine
Music by Vittorio Rieti, after themes by Bellini
Décor by André Levasseur
Costumes by Esteban Francés

Revived for this company by John Taras (world première by Ballet Russe de Monte Carlo February 27, 1946). Première by this company January 6, 1960 at City Center of Music and Drama. Principal Dancers: Allegra Kent, Erik Bruhn, John Taras.

PAN AMERICA
A series of short works by Latin-American composers Carlos Chavez, Luis Escobar, Alberto Ginastera, Julian Orson, Juan Orrego Salas, Silvestre Revueltas, Hector Tosa, Heitor Villa-Lobos
Choreography by George Balanchine, Gloria Contreras, Jacques d'Amboise, Francisco Moncion, John Taras
Décor and lighting by David Hays
Costumes by Karinska and Esteban Francés

Premièred January 20, 1960 at City Center of Music and Drama. Principal Dancers: Violette Verdy, Erik Bruhn, Patricia Wilde, Jillana, Edward Villella, Diana Adams, Nicholas Magallanes, Francisco Moncion, Maria Tallchief, Arthur Mitchell, Conrad Ludlow, Allegra Kent, Jonathan Watts.

THEME AND VARIATIONS
Choreography by George Balanchine
Music by Peter Ilyitch Tchaikovsky (*Suite No. 3 in G*)

(World première by Ballet Theatre September 27, 1947.) Première by this company February 5, 1960 at City Center of Music and Drama. Principal Dancers: Violette Verdy and Edward Villella.

THE FIGURE IN THE CARPET (ballet in 5 scenes)
Choreography by George Balanchine
Music by George Frederic Handel (Water Music and Fireworks Music)
Scenario by George Lewis
Décor and costumes by Esteban Francés

Premièred April 13, 1960 at City Center of Music and Drama. Principal Dancers: Francisco Moncion, Judith Green, Francia Russell, Nicholas Magallanes, Patricia McBride, Mary Hinkson, Arthur Mitchell, Diana Adams, Deni Lamont, Michael Lland, Richard Rapp, Roy Tobias, Jacques d'Amboise, Melissa Hayden.

MONUMENTUM PRO GESUALDO
Choreography by George Balanchine
Music by Igor Stravinsky (an arrangement for orchestra of three madrigals by Don Carlo Gesualdo)

Premièred November 16, 1960 at City Center of Music and Drama. Principal Dancers: Diana Adams and Conrad Ludlow.

VARIATIONS FROM DON SEBASTIAN (Later called *Donizetti Variations* from fall, 1961)
Choreography by George Balanchine
Music by Gaetano Donizetti

Premièred November 16, 1960 at City Center of Music and Drama. Principal Dancers: Melissa Hayden and Jonathan Watts.

LIEBESLIEDER WALZER
Choreography by George Balanchine
Music by Johannes Brahms (*Op. 52 and 65*). (Two sets of love-song waltzes sung by four singers, accompanied by four-hand piano)
Décor by David Hays
Costumes by Karinska

Premièred November 22, 1960 at City Center of Music and Drama. Dancers: Diana Adams and Bill Carter, Melissa Hayden and Jonathan Watts, Jillana and Conrad Ludlow, Violette Verdy and Nicholas Magallanes.

JAZZ CONCERT, a four-part program including:
Creation of the World
Choreography by Todd Bolender
Music by Darius Milhaud

Dancers: Patricia McBride, Conrad Ludlow, Janet Reed, Lois Bewley, Arthur Mitchell, Edward Villella.

Les Biches
Choreography by Francisco Moncion
Music by Francis Poulenc

Principal Dancers: Sara Leland and Anthony Blum.

Ragtime
Choreography by George Balanchine
Music by Igor Stravinsky

Dancers: Diana Adams and Bill Carter.

Ebony Concerto
Choreography by John Taras
Music by Igor Stravinsky

Dancers: Patricia McBride and Arthur Mitchell.

Premièred December 7, 1960 at City Center of Music and Drama.

MODERN JAZZ: VARIANTS
Choreography by George Balanchine
Music by Gunther Schuller, arranged for orchestra, playing in the pit, and the Modern Jazz Quartet, playing on stage.

Premièred January 4, 1961 at City Center of Music and Drama. Principal Dancers: John Jones (guest artist), Diana Adams, Melissa Hayden, Arthur Mitchell.

ELECTRONICS
Choreography by George Balanchine
Music by Remi Gassmann; electronic work by Oskar Sala and the composer
Décor by David Hays

Premièred March 22, 1961 at City Center for Music and Drama. Principal Dancers: Diana Adams, Violette Verdy, Jacques d'Amboise, Edward Villella.

VALSES ET VARIATIONS (Later called *Raymonda Variations*)
Choreography by George Balanchine
Music by Alexander Glazounov (a score compiled from the ballet *Raymonda*)
Costumes by Karinska

Premièred December 7, 1961 at City Center of Music and Drama. Principal Dancers: Patricia Wilde, Jacques d'Amboise, Victoria Simon, Suki Schorer, Gloria Govrin, Carol Sumner, Patricia Neary, Susan Keniff, Marlene Mesavage, Marnee Morris, Ellen Shire, Bettijane Sills, Lynda Yourth.

A MIDSUMMER NIGHT'S DREAM (ballet in two acts and six scenes, based on the Shakespeare comedy)
Choreography by George Balanchine
Music by Felix Mendelssohn: all incidental music composed for the several productions of the play, among them *Op. 20 and 61, Die Erste Walpurgisnacht* (*op. 60*), the concert overture *Die Schöne Melusine* (*op. 32*), and other orchestral pieces closely related in style
Décor by David Hays
Costumes by Karinska

Premièred January 17, 1962 at City Center of Music and Drama. Principal Dancers: Melissa Hayden (Titania), Conrad Ludlow (Cavalier to Titania), Edward Villella (Oberon), Arthur Mitchell (Puck), Patricia McBride (Hermia), Jillana (Helena), Nicholas Magallanes (Lysander), Bill Carter (Demetrius), Gloria Govrin (Hippolyta), Francisco Moncion (Theseus), Roland Vazquez (Bottom), Violette Verdy and Conrad Ludlow (pas de deux in Act 2).

BUGAKU
Choreography by George Balanchine
Music by Toshiro Mayuzumi
Décor and lighting by David Hays
Costumes by Karinska

Premièred March 20, 1963 at City Center of Music and Drama. Principal dancers: Allegra Kent, Edward Villella.

ARCADE
Choreography by John Taras
Music by Igor Stravinsky (*Concerto for Piano and Wind Instruments*)
Décor by David Hays
Costumes by Ruth Sobotka

Premièred March 28, 1963 at City Center of Music and Drama. Principal dancers: Suzanne Farrell, Arthur Mitchell.

MOVEMENTS FOR PIANO AND ORCHESTRA
Choreography by George Balanchine
Music by Igor Stravinsky of the same name (composed 1958–59)

Premièred April 9, 1963 at City Center of Music and Drama. Principal dancers: Suzanne Farrell, Jacques d'Amboise.

THE CHASE
Choreography by Jacques d'Amboise
Music by Wolfgang Amadeus Mozart (*Horn Concert No. 3*)
Décor by David Hays
Costumes by Karinska

Premièred September 18, 1963 at City Center of Music and Drama. Principal dancers: Allegra Kent (The Fox), André Prokovsky (The Duke), Shaun O'Brien (The Duke's Friend).

FANTASY
Choreography by John Taras

Music by Franz Schubert (*Fantasy Piano Duet, Opus 103,* orchestrated by Felix Mottl)
No décor or costume credit listed in program

Premièred September 24, 1963 at City Center of Music and Drama. Principal dancers: Patricia McBride, Edward Villella, with Carol Sumner, Marlene Mesavage, Robert Rodham, Earle Sieveling.

MEDITATION (Pas de deux)
Choreography by George Balanchine
Music by Peter Ilyitch Tchaikovsky (from *Au Lieu Cher,* a set of three pieces for violin and piano, *Opus 42, No. 1* orchestrated by Alexander Glazounov)
Costumes by Karinska

Premièred December 10, 1963 at City Center of Music and Drama. Dancers: Suzanne Farrell, Jacques d'Amboise.

TARANTELLA (Pas de deux)
Choreography by George Balanchine
Music by Louis Gottschalk (*Grand Tarantelle,* reconstructed and orchestrated by Hershy Kay)

Premièred January 7, 1964 at City Center of Music and Drama. Dancers: Patricia McBride, Edward Villella.

QUATUOR
Choreography by Jacques d'Amboise
Music by Dimitri Shostakovich (*String Quartet No. 1*)

Premièred January 16, 1964 at City Center of Music and Drama. Dancers: Mimi Paul, Jacques d'Amboise, with Roland Vazquez and Frank Ohman.

CLARINADE
Choreography by George Balanchine
Music by Morton Gould (*Derivations for Clarinet and Jazz Band* [1954–55])

Premièred April 29, 1964. Principal dancers: Gloria Govrin and Arthur Mitchell, Suzanne Farrell and Anthony Blum, with Bettijane Sills and Richard Rapp, Carol Sumner and Robert Rodham and corps de ballet. The music, composed for Benny Goodman, was played by him in the orchestra pit on opening night. *Clarinade* was the first new ballet staged at New York State Theater.

DIM LUSTRE
Choreography by Antony Tudor
Music by Richard Strauss (*Burleske for Piano and Orchestra*)
Costumes, Décor and Lighting by Beni Montresor

Premièred May 6, 1964 at the New York State Theater. Principal dancers: Patricia McBride (The Lady with Him), Edward Villella (The Gentleman with Her), Robert Rodham (It Was Spring), Patricia Neary (She Wore Perfume), Richard Rapp (He Wore a White Tie). This ballet was originally created by Tudor for Ballet Theatre, October 20, 1943.

PIÈGE DE LUMIÈRE
Choreography by John Taras
Music by Jean-Michel Damase
Décor by Felix Labisse
Costumes by André Levasseur
Supervision and Lighting by David Hays
Book by Philippe Hériat

Premièred October 1, 1964, New York State Theater. Principal dancers: Maria Tallchief (Queen of the Morphides), André Prokovsky (Iphias), Arthur Mitchell (Young Convict). This ballet was originally created by Taras for Grand Ballet du Marquis de Cuevas, December 23, 1952.

IRISH FANTASY
Choreography by Jacques d'Amboise
Music by Camille Saint-Saëns (from his incidental ballet music for the opera Henry VIII)
Décor and Lighting by David Hays
Costumes by Karinska

Premièred August 12, 1964, Greek Theatre, Los Angeles. New York première, October 8, 1964, New York State Theater. Principal dancers: Melissa Hayden, André Prokovsky, and Anthony Blum, Frank Ohman.

BALLET IMPERIAL
Choreography by George Balanchine
Staged by Frederic Franklin
Music by Peter Ilyitch Tchaikovsky (*Piano Concerto No. 2 in G Major*)
Décor and Lighting by Rouben Ter-Arutunian
Costumes by Karinska

Premièred October 15, 1964, New York State Theater. Principal dancers, Suzanne Farrell, Patricia Neary, Jacques d'Amboise. This ballet was originally created by Balanchine for American Ballet Caravan, May 29, 1941.

PAS DE DEUX AND DIVERTISSEMENT
Choreography by George Balanchine
Music by Léo Delibes (from *Sylvia, La Source,* and *Naïla*)
Costumes by Karinska
Lighting by David Hays

Premièred January 14, 1965, New York State Theater. Principal dancers: Melissa Hayden, André Prokovsky, Suki Schorer.

SHADOW'D GROUND
Choreography by John Taras
Music by Aaron Copland (Dance Panels, 1962)
Libretto by Scott Burton
Production (with photographic projections) designed by John Braden

Premièred January 21, 1965, New York State Theater. Principal dancers: Kay Mazzo, Robert Maiorano, Suki Schorer, Richard Rapp, Jillana, Roland Vazquez.

HARLEQUINADE
Choreography by George Balanchine
Music by Riccardo Drigo
Décor, Costumes and Lighting by Rouben Ter-Arutunian

Premièred February 4, 1965, New York State Theater. Principal dancers: Patricia McBride, Edward Villella, Suki Schorer, Deni Lamont, Gloria Govrin.

DON QUIXOTE
Choreography by George Balanchine
Music by Nicolas Nabokov
Décor and costumes by Esteban Francés
Costumes executed by Karinska

Premièred May 28, 1965, New York State Theater. Principal dancers: Richard Rapp, Suzanne Farrell, Deni Lamont, Mimi Paul, Marnee Morris. (Ballet Society Benefit Preview, May 27, 1965 with George Balanchine in title role for this performance only.)

VARIATIONS
Choreography by George Balanchine
Music by Igor Stravinsky (*Aldous Huxley Variation*—1965)
Lighting by Ronald Bates

Premièred Mar. 31, 1966, New York State Theater. Principal dancer: Suzanne Farrell.

SUMMERSPACE
Choreography by Merce Cunningham
Music by Morton Feldman
Scenery and costumes by Robert Rauschenberg
New York production supervised by John Braden
Lighting by Ronald Bates

Premièred April 14, 1966, New York State Theater. Dancers: Anthony Blum, Kay Mazzo, Patricia Neary, Sara Leland, Deni Lamont, Carol Sumner.

BRAHMS-SCHOENBERG QUARTET
Choreography by George Balanchine
Music by Johannes Brahms (*First Piano Quartet in G Minor,* Opus 25, orchestrated by Arnold Schoenberg)

Scenery by Peter Harvey
Lighting by Ronald Bates
Costumes by Karinska

Gala Benefit Première April 19, 1966, public première, April 22, 1966, New York State Theater. Principal dancers: Melissa Hayden, André Prokovsky, Gloria Govrin, Patricia McBride, Kent Stowell, Allegra Kent, Edward Villella, Suzanne Farrell, Jacques d'Amboise.

DIVERTIMENTO NO. 15
Choreography by George Balanchine
Music by Wolfgang Amadeus Mozart (K.V. 287)
Scenery and lighting by David Hays
Costumes by Karinska

(Revival) Premièred April 27, 1966, New York State Theater. Principal Dancers: Melissa Hayden, Carol Sumner, Sara Leland, Mimi Paul, Suki Schorer, Arthur Mitchell, Richard Rapp, Kent Stowell.

JEUX
Choreography by John Taras
Music by Claude Debussy
Scenery and costumes by Raoul Pène DuBois
Lighting by Jules Fisher
Costumes executed by Karinska

Premièred April 28, 1966, New York State Theater. Dancers: Melissa Hayden, Allegra Kent, Edward Villella.

NARKISSOS
Choreography by Edward Villella
Music by Robert Prince
Scenery, costumes and lighting by John Braden

Premièred July 21, 1966, Saratoga Springs Performing Arts Center. New York première, Nov. 24, 1966, New York State Theater. Principal Dancers: Edward Villella (Narkissos), Patricia McBride (Echo Figure), Michael Steele (Image—Nemesis Figure).

LA GUIRLANDE DE CAMPRA
Choreography by John Taras
Music, *Variations on a Theme* (written in 1717) by André Campra, by Georges Auric, Arthur Honegger, Francis Poulenc, Germaine Tailleferre, Daniel Lesur, Alexis Roland-Manuel, Henri Sauguet)
Scenery by Peter Harvey
Costumes by Peter Harvey and Esteban Francés (the latter some costumes taken from Balanchine's *Figure in the Carpet*)

Premièred Dec. 1, 1966, New York State Theater. (A private benefit performance at the same theatre was presented April 19, 1966.) Principal Dancers: Violette Verdy, Melissa Hayden, Conrad Ludlow, Mimi Paul, Patricia Neary, Marnee Morris, Sara Leland, Suki Schorer, Carol Sumner.

American Ballet Caravan. See BALLET CARAVAN.

American Ballet, School of, a professional school of ballet established in 1934 in New York by Lincoln Kirstein, Edward M. M. Warburg, George Balanchine and Vladimir Dimitriew, as a basis for an academy similar to the Russian Imperial and State Schools. The School, currently headed by Kirstein and Balanchine, with Eugenie Ouroussow as Executive Director, is conducted as a non-profit educational institution incorporated under the laws of the State of New York. It is the official school of the New York City Ballet. See also AMERICAN BALLET; BALLET CARAVAN; BALLET SOCIETY.

American Ballet Theatre, the name officially assumed by Ballet Theatre at the time of its 1956–57 tour of Europe and the Near East. See BALLET THEATRE entry for the company history.

American Concert Ballet, ballet group founded (spring, 1943) and directed by Mary Jane Shea, William Dollar and

Todd Bolender. The group, consisting of sixteen dancers, gave performances in the fall of the same year. The repertoire consisted of George Balanchine's *Concerto Barocco,* Bolender's *Mother Goose Suite,* William Dollar's *Five Boons of Life,* Mary Jane Shea's *Sailor Bar.*

American Dance Festival, the series of modern dance performances held annually as the culmination of the Connecticut College School of Dance summer session. Since the first festival in 1948 many distinguished works have had their premières at these festivals, among them Martha Graham's *Diversion of Angels* (1948, under the title *Wilderness Stair*); José Limón's *The Moor's Pavane* (1949); Sophie Maslow's *The Village I Knew* (1950); Doris Humphrey's *Night Spell* (1951) and *Ruins and Visions* (1953); Limón's *The Traitor* (1954); Ruth Currier's *The Antagonists* and Pauline Koner's *Concertino* (1955); Alwin Nikolais' *Kaleidoscope* (1956), in which year also Birgit Aakesson made one of her rare appearances in the U.S.; Daniel Nagrin's solo *Indeterminate Figure* and Dore Hoyer's U.S. debut (1957); Merce Cunningham's *Antic Meet* (1958); Pearl Lang's *Shirah* and Jack Moore's *Songs Remembered* (1960); Paul Taylor's *Insects and Heroes* (1961); Martha Graham's *Secular Games* (1962). In recent years students of the summer school have appeared in works especially choreographed for them by one of the resident teacher-choreographers and/or an early Doris Humphrey work, taught and rehearsed during the summer school. In 1962 six Saturday evening performances were presented during the regular summer school session in addition to the Dance Festival during the final week of the school. Each Saturday program consisted of works by choreographers not necessarily on the faculty of the summer school and not appearing on the actual Festival programs which, to celebrate the fifteenth year of the Summer School of Dance and the American Dance Festival, were jointly presented by Martha Graham and José Limón with their companies. The Saturday evening performances were continued in 1963. In 1964 the Festival presented a Louis Horst Memorial Program for which Martha Graham revived three of her early works with music by Horst: her solo, *Frontier,* danced by Ethel Winter; *El Penitente,* with Marni Thomas in the choreographer's original role; and *Primitive Mysteries,* danced by Yuriko and ensemble.

American Dance Theatre, The, was organized in Oct., 1964, in N.Y., with the assistance of the New York State Council on the Arts, as a repertory company for modern dance. With José Limón as artistic director, the company gave its initial performances Nov. 18 and 19 at the New York State Theater, Lincoln Center. The program included works by Doris Humphrey, Limón, Donald McKayle, and Anna Sokolow. A second set of performances, under the same aegis, was given Mar. 2–7, 1965, at the same theatre. Choreographers represented were Valerie Bettis, Merce Cunningham, Paul Draper, Lucas Hoving, Doris Humphrey, Pearl Lang, José Limón, Sophie Maslow, Alvin Nikolais, and Anna Sokolow.

American Dancer, The (publication). See PERIODICALS, DANCE (U.S.).

American Document. Modern group dance; chor.: Martha Graham; commissioned music: Ray Green; spoken text selected by Martha Graham; costumes: Edythe Gilfond. First prod.: State Armory, Bennington, Vt., Aug. 6, 1938, with Martha Graham, Erick Hawkins, and Housely Stevens Jr. as Interlocutor. Within the framework of an old minstrel show, the birth and growth of America was depicted in movement. American writings, including quotations from the Declaration of Independence, a letter from Red Jacket of the Seneca Indians, Jonathan Edwards' sermons, Walt Whitman's poems, Lincoln's Gettysburg Address, and the Emancipation Proclamation were spoken by the Interlocutor. This work marked the real beginning of Martha Graham's dance company as opposed to a concert group.

American Federation of Television and Radio Artists (AFTRA). See TRADE UNIONS, THEATRICAL.

American Festival Ballet, American based company performing mainly in Europe. Organized in 1957 as American Concert Ballet by Renzo Raiss, then choreographer of Bremen Opera Ballet, it gave its first performances in Bremen; changed its name to present title the following year. In 1962 its official name was again changed to Festival Ballet of Rhode Island, but it continued to tour outside the U.S. under the old title to which it reverted in 1964. American Festival Ballet made its N.Y. debut with two performances at Fashion Institute of Technology Auditorium, Feb. 28, 29, 1964, at which time Renzo Raiss' *Golden Pagoda,* to a score by Rebekah Harkness was premièred. The company's repertoire includes the basic classic ballets as well as its own contemporary works by Raiss, Walter Gore, Job Sanders, and others. Christine Hennessy is ballerina; guest artists appear from time to time.

American Guild of Musical Artists (AGMA). See TRADE UNIONS, THEATRICAL.

American Indian Dancing.

BY REGINALD AND GLADYS LAUBIN.

Dancing was an extremely important phase of Indian life in the early days. It is difficult for us today to understand this, for many of us regard dancing almost entirely as an entertainment. To the Indian, however, even his good-time dances had religious significance. Indians went to a dance partially for the same reason that we go to church.

Although we are guaranteed religious freedom under the Constitution, it was not granted to the Indian. His dancing was feared as "war dancing" by the whites, which partially led to its suppression. Better informed people realized something of its real significance, and also recommended its suppression. Why?—because thus, at one blow, the entire social, political, and religious life of the Indians could be crushed. Dancing was the most Indian thing about Indians. It was completely interwoven into their daily lives. The government wanted to destroy all tribal organization, everything Indian—to make white men out of Indians—so it did everything possible to exterminate the dancing.

Under the present enlightened policy, inaugurated in 1934, the old bans have been removed. Once more Indians are allowed to dance when and as they please. But the change of heart on the part of the government has come almost too late for many tribes. Much of the art work and most of the old religious and ceremonial dances of the Plains and Woodlands have now passed away and on the few occasions when these people dance at all they do mostly social dances, or "white man's" dances.

Even though today much of the old significance has been lost, a dance still remains an opportunity for a social, political, and religious meeting all in one.

Observation and study of the dance in earlier days might have revealed the very soul of the people, for they were at one and the same time the focal point of all their material culture and the highest expression of their mystical yearnings. The making or doing of any beautiful thing was a kind of prayer, a method of appealing to or communicating with the surrounding spiritual forces, of placing oneself in harmony with the great controlling power of the universe. From this standpoint, all Indian art work might be regarded as sacred. Every act of the day, every event of life, was strung on a sort of invisible chain of prayer, and that prayer was expressed visibly through the designs on the Indian's face, on his costumes and his equipment, and expressed also through his songs, his ceremonies and his dances. The dance, therefore, was the most important of all, the culmination of all his artistic achievement, for the dance combined all other art forms. A dance of men on earth was a dramatization, a pantomime, of the actions of the spirits above. Life was dancing—dancing was life.

Indians had a ceremony for every significant occasion. Practically all of these ceremonies involved dancing. In fact, among some tribes, the words for ceremony and for dance are synonymous. Indians danced for peace and for war, in joy and in sorrow—danced with religious fervor or in joyous abandonment.

We might almost say that every costume, every color and pattern, every step and motion in the dances had meaning. Each dance had its own peculiar ritual associated with it, which included special songs, costumes, face and body paint, ceremonial objects, and frequently certain taboos. Plains Indians often danced to the left, clockwise, "in a Sun circle," following the path of the sun through the sky, for the sun was the highest manifestation of the Great Mystery. On the other hand, the Woodland people usually moved to the right, "with their hearts toward the fire," for to them fire was the all important gift to man and symbolized light and life, truth, renewed strength and vigor, purification and power.

Contrary to popular opinion, Indian dancing is not a mere "hopping up and down" or "crude jumping about." Actually the dances are often extremely difficult and complicated.

Each tribe had definite forms, patterns, traditions, and conventions which were necessarily followed by the dancers. One untrained in understanding these conventions of course misses a great deal when watching Indian dances.

All Indian dancing seems to be characterized by a bent knee position quite different from anything found in either classic or ballroom dancing. Backs are straight and usually erect; arms are not used to a great extent, but there is a great deal of head movement, sometimes comparable to that of the East Indian dancing —movements representing those of graceful birds.

Steps are many and varied. Some students claim that Indians have a duplicate or substitute for almost every known dance step. Sudden, yet subtle, shifts in weight add to the difficulties an outsider has in trying to imitate Indian dancing. The very simplicity with which steps seem to be executed is a compliment to the grace and skill of the performers.

Some Indian dances are among the most vigorous to be found anywhere, but they are never frenzied. The dancing is always dignified and controlled, which immediately separates it from "jitterbugging" and other forms of popular dancing to which the untrained observer has occasionally compared it. The most strenuous Indian dance still leaves the spectator with the impression that the dancer is completely relaxed and using only a portion of his power.

The dancing is accompanied by percussion instruments and singing. Various types of drums and rattles, or sometimes beating on either a rolled or flat dried hide, furnish the rhythm. Often the rhythm of the songs is different from that of the drums. The drum seems to govern the bodily movements whereas the melody of the song expresses the emotion.

The Indian learned much of his dancing by watching the birds and animals, many of which actually dance. Just as in the animal kingdom the male is usually outstanding in appearance, so the Indian man does most of the dancing and usually wears the most spectacular costumes—not necessarily the most beautiful, for among Plains Indians, at any rate, the women were the ones who wore the most clothing. Some of their "party dresses" were elaborately decorated with beadwork, embroidery, and elk teeth. The very weight of these dresses would prohibit them from taking a very active part in the dancing, even had custom permitted it.

Certain distinguished women—women who had gone to war and achieved war honors like men—were allowed to participate in the men's dances. There were very few of these, of course. There were many dances for women, however, even if they were not as spectacular as those of the men. In a number of social dances men, women, and children all took part. Men and women did not dance arm in arm as they now do in the rabbit dance and a few other modern dances definitely patterned after the white man's manner of dancing.

In many dances only warriors were allowed to participate but the so-called "war dance" is largely a white man's invention. It seems rather ironical that fear of war dances was partly responsible for the suppression of Indian dancing, but that when the white man gave the Indian permission to dance he always wanted to see "the war dance."

In a few places, notably the Southwest, the dancing goes on much as it always has. During the 1920's an effort was made to suppress this dancing, too. For the first time since the rebellion against the Spanish in the early 18th century, these Indians became war-like and threatened to fight if molested. Since they inhabited a barren and seemingly worthless country, not coveted to any extent by the white man, it was decided there was really no great necessity for "civilizing" them, so they have been allowed to continue living much as they have for centuries.

Early observers declared that the Plains Indians, and particularly the Sioux, were the finest dancers and had the greatest variety of dances. These people were hunters and warriors, so their dances were naturally quite different in spirit and character from those of their more settled agricultural neighbors in the Southwest, or from those of other areas whose customs and ways of life were different. Without a doubt, many of the dances popular in the Southwest today, as the buffalo and the eagle dances, were originally copied from the Plains tribes. When we realize that the Sioux Indians alone had as many as thirty-five different dances and that today they do not dance even one completely, we can understand something of the great wealth of material which has all but passed away.

The Sioux culture was built around the buffalo. Consequently the disappearance of that animal contributed much toward the discontinuance of many of the dances. The few the Indian kept in his heart to remind him of his golden age were soon restricted. Men under forty years of age were not allowed to dance by the government authorities and those over forty had to have special permission.

The most popular dance remaining among the Plains Indians today is known, depending on the locality, as Grass Dance, Omaha Dance, Dream Dance, Hot Dance, or just Happy Dance, although to please the white people, when talking to them, all call it War Dance. In this dance, as the Sioux do it, one will find many snatches of old-time dances. One dancer may be doing part of an old buffalo dance, another old-timer may re-enact some personal war experience, or still another show that he was a scout or a hunter. At the same time younger dancers may be "just dancing fancy," or with a hoop, or perhaps imitating birds or butterflies. It's every man for himself.

The Plains Indians were individualists in name and in deed and this fact is still reflected in their dancing. The Southwest dances are more of the group type, best comparable, perhaps, to the chorus, or the ballet corps.

Originally the men wore little clothing for dancing. The dancer's body was his instrument and he did not believe in hiding it or in handicapping its movements. Such costumes and decorations as were worn often had as much ceremonial as decorative value. A man could wear only the regalia to which he was entitled. Today, on the Plains, this symbolism is largely lost, and the dancers wear anything they choose.

Not so many years ago the majority of whites in the Indian country were shocked by the nude dancing. This nudity upheld the missionaries' contentions that the dancing was immoral, enforcing the argument for suppression. So, on the few occasions when Indians were given permission to dance, they did the next best thing —they danced in dyed underwear. Although today such bans no longer exist, this recently acquired modesty is still in evidence; dyed underwear is the foundation for the Indian dancer's costume from Oklahoma to Canada.

The general hope for the survival of Indian dancing is somewhat encouraging. People now realize that here is a real American art and that something should be done to preserve it. The Indian himself is being taught to recover his racial pride and this will go a long way toward retaining native characteristics and customs. The dancing goes hand in hand with it.

In some localities the dancing shows a definite revival. The Crows, in Montana, have become interested in the Sun Dance within the last few years. Their own Sun Dance had not been given since 1874. It died out primarily because it failed to meet the changing life of the people. The dance they now do they learned from the Shoshones of Wyoming. It is a much simpler and less involved ritual but they feel that it definitely does meet a present day need. The Crows first did this Sun Dance in August, 1941. The following June it was repeated, this time as a prayer for victory in World War II. They gave it each year since in expectation of victory and after the war, in thanksgiving for the blessings of the previous year. The Crows ascribe the fact that they lost only two boys in the war to their Sun Dance prayers. Neither of these boys was killed in actual combat, although Crow boys participated in some of the severest fighting on battlefields all over the world. In 1946 the Sun Dance was given in celebration and thanksgiving for the final and decisive victory over the enemies of mankind.

In many places the revival of Indian dancing shows growth and development. New costumes, new dances, based on the old and fundamental Indian dance ideas, but changing to fit their changing world, are evolving. Once more the future looks bright for American Indians and they have good reason to dance again.

Some people resent these changes and modern intrusions, but no art lives if it is static. To survive, Indian dancing must fit the lives of the Indian people. It is hoped that it will remain essentially Indian, but that it will continue to grow and to gain strength and eventually become a very conscious part of our American heritage.

American Modern Dance.

BY JOHN MARTIN.

In the literal meaning of the phrase, American modern dance might be construed as referring to the general state of dancing in the Western Hemisphere over a roughly defined period that includes the present. When the combination of words is employed, however, as it most frequently is with the implication of three capital letters instead of one, it has a narrower meaning and indicates a particular artistic movement which came to full flowering during a span of thirty years, chiefly between the two World Wars.

This period, to be sure, does not define its term of life, for its roots are as old as the race itself and as indestructible. To fix limits between dates for any renascence is both arbitrary and controversial, yet something of the sort is demanded if the subject is to be isolated for discussion.

The cycle of American modern dance, then, can be said to have opened with the New York debut of Martha Graham in 1926 and to have closed with the death of Doris Humphrey in 1958. The former date is conveniently precise; the latter is merely a critical assumption on grounds that will appear subsequently.

Neither Graham, however, nor Humphrey "invented" the art. Nor did any of its other acknowledged leaders, who consisted of Helen Tamiris, whose first New York recital was in 1927; Charles Weidman, who made a joint debut with Humphrey and a company in 1928; and later, Hanya Holm, who came to this country from Germany with Mary Wigman in 1931 and remained to become a vital figure in the American scene. The movement itself was a composite of individual inspirations, discoveries and adaptations, frequently divergent and even antagonistic, but all impelled by the exigencies of the times (hence, perhaps, legitimately to be called modern), and rooted in the specific heritage of Isadora Duncan.

Actually there had been no contact by any of these figures with Isadora herself, but all of them knew well the nature of her artistic revolution—how she had bared not only her soul but also, and more startlingly for that day, her body, in order to pour out in unimpeded lyric movement her sensibility to the truths of life. This was the Promethean gesture that had brought fire to all their altars.

But not even Isadora had created a revolution in a vacuum; she was the eager instrument of the Zeitgeist. The world that produced her, and that she helped to produce, was in general one of insurgency and revolution, in many almost ridiculously divergent strata of thinking and behavior including the arts, athletics, psychology, the emancipation of women, sartorially as well as politically. That parallel forces in the art of the dance should have broken through first in America and immediately afterwards in Germany was altogether natural, for the walls of resistance were thinnest where there had never been any dance "establishment."

The only other American dance source besides Isadora that contributed to the development of the new art's independence was Denishawn, including both the school and the performing companies of Ruth St. Denis and Ted Shawn, in which Graham, Humphrey and Weidman all received their training and early experience. To belong to such a continuously active, performance-minded company enriched them permanently in many ways, general and specific, but the aesthetic basis of the organization served them chiefly as something to rebel against. It was deliberately eclectic, and, deliberately or not, tended to use the dance to exhibit the dancer's personality and skills instead of the other way round.

There were also influences, though somewhat more remote, from Germany where the modern dance had achieved wide renown, with the figure of Wigman as a symbol, immediately after World War I. It was in a sense an aesthetic by-product of the nationwide effort toward postwar physical rehabilitation, or at least had found substantial support in that effort. Later, Wigman herself made three tours in America in the early 1930's to enormous acclaim. At the same time Holm entered the local field as head of an official Wigman school, with no expectation of staying on to become, as she did, a naturalized artist in her own right. From all these sources the Wigman analysis of movement, conscious relationship to space, and experimentations in the use and production of music could not have failed to be of influence here.

It is important to note, however, that except for the great central liberation provided by Isadora's revolution, which had animated each of these manifestations, the American modern dance differed from them all, and from Isadora, in character and direction.

Isadora's own dancing dealt in heroic generalities, impassioned romantic affirmations inspired by music of similar character and so dependent upon it as to be utterly shapeless without it. Wigman's dance dealt similarly in large generalities, but they were more philosophical and mystical, frequently concerning death and possession. Far from being an affirmation of individuality, it was a reconciliation of the self with unknown forces, an "acceptance of life," as she described it. The American dancers were not tempted by generalities, but were activated by specific aspects of reality pinpointed in personal experience. Their attitude was not one of acceptance but of affirmation, definite commitment and even challenge. Among them, Graham's world alone recognized the presence of mystic forces. Her relation to them, however, was not one of passive submission but of conflict to the point of foregone defeat and purgation.

But whatever its sources and influences, the new dance in America was both revolutionary and radical: it rejected all traditional schools with their codifications of gesture into standard, selective, authorized vocabularies, their paradigmatic processes of form, and their objective criteria of performance; it returned instead to those animal laws under which the body operated as an instrument of expression and communication, functioning through the emotional and psychological innervations of the musculature.

This approach opened up an area closer to the nucleus of experience than was attainable by a medium of communication dependent upon intellection and verbalization. As for the spectator's capacity for reception, he was equipped by nature to make complementary use of the neuromuscular mechanism, innately attuned to automatic subintellectual inner motor mimicry—in short, to kinesthetic transfer. The entire process, accordingly, operated on the very ground level of contact.

From such a premise the dance becomes inevitably a lyric art; it deals with no literary program, no story-telling involving characterization, no exploitation of either personal charm or technical virtuosity. It is directed solely to the publishing of the artist's immediate revelation of some aspect of his relation to the universe, a flash of insight which he is unable to rationalize or reduce to direct factual statement.

Fundamentally this is a dance closely akin to the dance of ecstasy common to primitive societies, but with one all-transforming difference: its compulsion is toward communication. In the ecstatic dance the effect sought is a mystic or religious experience for the dancer himself; there is no consideration for what effect the movement or its organization and progression may have upon any possible spectator. Composition and choreography are therefore irrelevant.

It was probably not until the poet Arion "ordered" the dithyramb in Lesbos some 2700 years ago that the seeds of such conscious processes were planted. After which, it is to be noted, the dithyramb lost its ecstatic possession, becoming first a ritual with a leader, then adding a second "leader," and a third, who brought with them conflict and personification. The dance had become drama. This sequence is more than a semi-historical record; it is a recurring formula amounting virtually to law.

The compulsion of the new art toward communication made composition and choreography of paramount importance, and for this a fresh grasp of functional form was indispensable. The forms inherited from the immediate past were not useful, having long since lost any direct involvement with motor impulsion.

To the now urgent discovery of essential dance form, music offered both a bridge and a barrier. It had pursued an independent course since it first broke away from its original state as an inseparable aspect of dancing; nevertheless, the breath phrase of the dancer remained perforce the basis of its melodic line and his blood pulse that of its rhythmic life. This very identity of fundamental impulse, however, made music, as it now existed, also a barrier.

Only yesterday, to be sure, Isadora, yielding her entire artistic will to it, had swept the dance into a new dimension. She had, indeed, submitted eagerly to its superior strength and authority, possibly as a fulfilment of her intensely self-conscious womanliness. And in her wake had followed, somewhat weakly, a whole generation of equally feminine "interpretative" dancers. But when the modern dancer, re-inspired by the principles of the basic dance, turned to music as a natural collaborator, he found it instead a tyrant, dictating formal procedures from the throne of long-established dominion. Here was a subjection that had to be broken if dancing was to be emancipated.

In pursuit of this emancipation, the German field—particularly Wigman and her associates, including Holm, both with an earlier training in the eurhythmics of Emil Jaques Dalcroze to draw upon whether positively or negatively—was responsible for the great clearing of the way. The procedure consisted logically of first putting aside all music in order to find the natural architecture of the body's self-impelled manipulation of phrase and pulse; then the addition of simple instruments, such as flutes and percussions, to complement these findings, preferably by means of joint improvisation with sensitive and sympathetic musicians. In this wise it can fairly be said that the substance of dance movement was discovered and related to music at its own level. From there on, the free development of dance forms became the province and the responsibility of the individual dancers.

In the American field the search for a compatible music was quickly diverted to a different procedure, which largely bypassed such experimentations with joint improvisation and moved directly from the inheritance of "interpretation" and "visualization" to the evolving of collaborative scores by composers, with however, the same principles prevailing.

This shortening of method came about through the presence of a composer, in the person of Louis Horst, who had dropped quite fortuitously into the heart of the movement with the requisite qualifications. Formerly musical director of Denishawn, he left that organization along with Graham to serve in the same capacity for her. During the late '20's and early '30's, however, he played the inevitable piano accompaniments for all the major modern dancers' recitals. Besides his responsiveness to the creativity of movement, he possessed a stubborn musical mind, and his instinctive reconciliation of the two produced a demonstrable awareness that music evoked by the urgencies of dance form need not thereby forfeit musical form.

Dancers at this time habitually drafted their compositions without any music at all, except perhaps a drum to set and maintain tempi; they then presented their "counts" (that is, a summary of their metrical requirements) to the composer as a guide. This was substantially the same practice by which hack composers for the old-fashioned ballet had been required to produce: tailored-to-order successions of 8-bar phrases, in duple or triple time as specified. But there was one vital difference: Horst sat in on the creative choreographic sessions from their reasonably early stages, absorbed the substance of the work as it progressed, and came forth eventually with a score that had actually grown out of the process. Other composers emerged to adopt the same approach, and in theory, at least, the music problem was solved.

At this point, roughly in the middle 1930's, the American modern dance attained its peak and enjoyed a creative harvest on the high plateau that had been its first goal. Its own dynamic potentialities, however, made it impossible to rest there, even though pushing onward could only mean the pursuit of a new goal and a descent from the peak. The road, already implicit in Arion's "law," led toward the theatre, with Graham in the van of the march.

Of the five leaders, she had been most completely released by the process of the commissioned score. She was, indeed, dependent upon it, for hers was an unequivocally dramatic talent, stultified when forced into musical parallels, not concerned with "pure" forms, and not wishing (perhaps not able) to take a simple emotionally based motor theme and develop it after the absolute manner of music.

From another direction, also, she was urged toward the theatre, for she possessed a bold and original attitude toward costume and scenery and their collaborative functions. Without being literal in any way, she tied the visual setting of her productions, including the shapes and fabrics in which she clothed herself and her dancers, into the substance of the choreography, much as the music she demanded was tied into it.

The prodigious drive that characterized her career had been leading her always, without her awareness of its destination, not only into the territory of the modern dance, but through it and eventually out of it, to the evolution of a virtually new art. The road was rough and uneven, and led through valleys and over mountains with many artistic climates. After the longest and deepest of her periods of depression, she emerged on certainly the loftiest of her heights in 1958 with a full-evening work, *Clytemnestra,* in which with transparent logic and authority she expanded the original lyric intent of the modern dance once and for all into the full dimensions of a great tragic theatre.

The common theatrical direction of the movement, however, produced a variety of individual results. Tamiris, Weidman, and Holm, widely different though they were from each other, all found themselves engaged in the commercial theatre, partly for economic reasons and partly because of mutations in the dance itself. The Broadway musical comedy had at last awakened to the existence of the modern dance and offered a livelihood to dancers with a theatrical bent and a new challenge to choreographers. To this latter they all responded, if with varying degrees of reluctance.

Both Tamiris and Weidman, in their separate ways, were dramatically rather than musically motivated by nature. Tamiris, though the Broadway musical was by no means the medium of her preference, proved herself admirably equipped to contribute to it artistically in her own characteristic terms. As for Weidman, with his penchant for mimicry and humor, even "show business" found him at home without compromise.

Holm, however, was primarily of musical motivation. She had also a strong, though not primarily dramatic, inclination toward the theatre. It was to the formal, musical, and expressive potentialities of the stage, even the commercial stage, that she was drawn. This was due in part, no doubt, to the superior imaginative range and quality of the theatre in Germany by which her concepts of stagecraft had early been influenced. Thus, though she maintained her always influential teaching activities, both in her New York school and elsewhere, it was in the Broadway area that she found her major creative outlet.

Humphrey, with a drive as strong as Graham's, was, like her, undeviating in her commitment to the dance itself, wherever it might lead. She had early investigated the possibilities of Broadway and rejected them. But the expansiveness provided only by the dimensions of the essential theatre, if not of its commercial simulacrum, exerted a strong artistic appeal. More and more she thought in terms of large ensembles. Also, she was able at will to employ dramatic themes, even involving a degree of characterization, and to reconcile their development with that of the structure of the work in its "pure" aspects. Possessed of a great curiosity of mind, she was outstandingly equipped to explore the full range of the dance without forcing it, as Graham did, across the "sound barrier," so to speak, into another realm.

In her total work there was implicit a formulation of creative method, an impersonal isolation of the orderly processes by which a highly personal nucleus of artistic experience is shaped into communicable form. This is something beyond and above her justly admired classes in composition, which only touched its borders.

With Graham pushing through the boundaries of the modern dance into the creation of perhaps the most significant theatre of our time, and Tamiris, Weidman, and Holm all diverted, however temporarily, to the practice of modern dance as an applied art in the conventional theatre, it is unavoidable to conclude that Humphrey's death marked the end of the era.

Activity in the direct line, however, by no means ended. José Limón, who must be considered as virtually the sixth leader of the movement, never relaxed his dedication or his vigorous manifestation of it. Humphrey had been his first teacher, and long his director in the Humphrey-Weidman company; when her career as a dancer came to an end in 1944 because of arthritis, she became artistic director of his company, creating new works (which remained permanently in his active repertory) and spurring him on to do likewise. In him, then, her principles lived on, adapted and developed by his personal application of them.

In the 1950's, Tamiris, with her Broadway excursion behind her, returned to her original purpose, and with her longtime partner, Daniel Nagrin, now as codirector, organized a concert company to pursue the creative adventure anew. Weidman, even earlier, had resumed his former direction, first in continuation of his association with Humphrey in their joint company, and later on his own.

Nevertheless, the end of a cycle is clearly indicated. The signs of its approach were evident as far back as the "golden days" of the middle 1930's. In that crucial time of re-orientation, destructive economic forces unquestionably hastened, without actually causing, the decline, for a general rise of costs made it impossible any longer to give performances without heavy financial losses, and only a fortunate few were able to do so with the aid of either personal subsidy or institutional sponsorship. But this was an external force, which said nothing about the art itself. The actual decline of the modern dance was strictly in terms of itself.

In its essence the new dance was the externalization of a single individual's intensely personal vision. As such it was necessarily a solo art. When it sought to widen its scope by the inclusion of other dancers, it embarked unwittingly on the route of self-destruction, since joint creativity is obviously impossible where the communication of specific concepts to a spectator is involved. The procedure still demanded the domination of a single creative mind and some sort of uniformity of method to avoid chaos. Once more Arion's precedent prevailed, if now in reversed application.

As a matter of course the type of movement characteristic of the leader was superimposed upon the other dancers, however alien it might be to their own tendencies. Though most of the choreographers allowed as much creative leeway as possible to the members of the company, and even encouraged it, it was circumscribed by the imposition of both a central creative theme and a style of movement. The next step was the growth of objective vocabularies, eventuating in a series of sterile personal "academies," based on somebody else's physical and psychological idiosyncrasies.

Even the leaders themselves fell into the repeated use of their own clichés, and in time an upcoming generation, too young to have participated in the original mystery and too unadventurous to question established practice, arose to take these fossilized residues of somebody else's long forgotten experience as the alphabet of all creation.

At the less ingenuous extreme, the decadent influences ruled out as old-fashioned and bourgeois the concept of inner vision as the invoker of art and substituted chance and happenstance; adding palindromes, interchangeable phrases, and esoteric and contrived mathematical formulas as methods of composition, frequently with every man for himself and no collaboration beyond a hope for no collision. Since the inertias of vocabulary still prevailed, this self-styled advance guard proved only to have led itself into a blind alley in which to play what amounted to cynical games of jackstones with the bones of the prophets.

So much for the dark side of the heritage; there is also a brighter side. For one thing, the concrete image of "theatre" that has emerged is so great that it may justify the destruction of the modern dance manifestation out of which it grew, as the fruit justifies the destruction of the blossom. Also, the principle of that dance is indestructible, and must continue to produce other blossoms, if only in turn to give place to other fruit in a new cycle. Only the who, the how and the when of such a cycle are unpredictable.

Certainly dedication, determination and capacity persist over a broad field of artists whose works demand respect. They range all the way from the evocative lyric fantasies of the altogether original Sybil Shearer, working in the Midwest deliberately apart form the centers of contention, to the opposite extreme of theatrical synthesis in which Alwin Nikolais fuses lights, functional décors, masks, properties, and sound tracks of every sort from Indonesian gamelans to musique concrète, with a highly depersonalized concept of the dancer.

Some of this multifarious activity is undoubtedly the backwash of a receding tide; some of it, however, may contain the substance of the next flowering of the art, awaiting a new Zeitgeist.

Amiel, Josette, contemporary French ballerina. Trained at Conservatoire Français under Jeanne Schwarz and Alexander Volinine, winning first prize after examination. After dancing principal roles at Opéra Comique (1952), entered Paris Opéra corps de ballet (1952); became première danseuse (1955), and étoile (1958). Leading roles included *Oberon* (1954), *La Belle Hélène* (John Cranko, 1955), *Chemin de Lumière* (1957), *Gounod Symphony* (George Balanchine, 1959). Returned to Opéra Comique as principal guest star (1959). In 1961 she danced Odette-Odile in Vladimir Bourmeister's version of the full-length *Swan Lake* at the Paris Opéra. Has been guest artist with Rome Opera Ballet, Royal Danish Ballet, Ruth Page's Chicago Opera Ballet (Jan. 1962).

Josette Amiel, première danseuse, Paris Opéra Ballet.

Amor Brujo, El (Love, the Sorcerer). Ballet in 1 act; chor.: Pastora Imperio; music: Manuel de Falla; book: G. Martinez Sierra. First prod.: Teatro Lara, Madrid, Apr. 15, 1915, with Pastora Imperio as Candelas. The story is Spanish folk lore and takes place in the caves of Granada. Candelas loves Carmelo but always between them is the memory of the dead Gypsy she formerly loved; only magic can break the spell. In the light of a brazier Candelas performs the Ritual Fire Dance and the ghost of her former lover appears. A second Gypsy girl diverts his attention and the two lovers are finally able to exchange a kiss of perfect love. Argentinita staged another version at the Paris Opéra Comique (1928). There have been many versions choreographed by La Meri, Boris Romanoff for Ballets de Monte Carlo, Leon Woizikowski for his own company, Serge Lifar at the Paris Opéra, and by the Spanish dancers Mariemma, Espanita Cortez, and Antonio, among others. The Roberto Ximenez and Manolo Vargas version had its première at the 1963 Jacob's Pillow Dance Festival, with Maria Alba as Candelas. The Ritual Fire Dance is a favorite solo number of nearly all Spanish dancers.

Amour et Son Amour, L'. Ballet in 1 act; chor.: Jean Babilée; music: César Franck's tone poem *Psyché;* décor: Jean Cocteau. First prod.: Les Ballets des Champs-Elysées, Théâtre des Champs-Elysées, Paris, Dec. 13, 1948, with Nathalie Philippart and Babilée. The legend of Cupid and Psyche is told in a mysteriously formalized style. This was Babilée's first ballet. It was briefly in the repertoire of Ballet (now American Ballet) Theatre with the same artists (1951).

Amours de Jupiter, Les. Ballet in 1 act, 5 scenes; chor.: Roland Petit; commissioned music: Jacques Ibert; book: Boris Kochno based on themes from Ovid's *Metamorphoses;* décor: Jean Hugo. First prod.: Ballets des Champs-Elysées, Théâtre des Champs-Elysées, Paris, Mar. 5, 1946, with Roland Petit (Jupiter), Ana Nevada (Juno), Nathalie Philippart (Danae), Irène Skorik (Leda), Ethery Pagava (Ganymede), Jean Babilée (Mercury). The metamorphoses of Jupiter as the Golden Rain visiting Danae, as the Swan with Leda, carrying off Ganymede as an Eagle, and finally returning in his own guise to the faithful Juno. Mercury here is Jupiter's messenger to those on whom the god has decided to bestow his favors.

Amours des Dieux, Les. Ballet by Louis Fuzelier and Mouret in which Marie Sallé made her debut at the Paris Opéra (1727).

Amsterdam Ballet. See HOLLAND, DANCE IN.

Anaya, Dulce (Dulce Esperanza Wohner de Vega), ballerina, b. 1933, Rancho Boyeros, Havana, Cuba. Studied at Sociedad Pro-Arte Musical, Havana, under Georges Milenoff, Alicia and Alberto Alonso; in N.Y. at the School of American Ballet. Began professional career at age fifteen, with Ballet (now American Ballet) Theatre. When activities of the company were temporarily interrupted, returned to Havana where she joined the Ballet de Cuba. Made an extensive Latin-American tour, during which she was promoted to ballerina. In 1951 toured the U.S. again with Ballet Theatre, then returned to Ballet de Cuba for a long South American tour. Danced in Europe for the first time with the Stuttgart Ballet under Nicholas Beriosov. After appearing as guest artist with the Bavarian State Opera Ballet, Munich, on the occasion of the celebration of the 800th anniversary of Munich, she signed with the company to create the title role in *Ondine,* Hans Werner Henze's ballet, choreographed by Alan Carter. She remained with the company until 1963, when she was invited as prima ballerina to the Hamburg State

Dulce Anaya, American ballerina in Giselle, *Act 2*

Opera Ballet. Her principal roles are in *Swan Lake, Giselle, The Sleeping Beauty, Coppélia, Le Beau Danube, Graduation Ball, Coq d'Or, Les Patineurs, Petrouchka, Les Sylphides, The Nutcracker, Le Spectre de la Rose, Gala Performance* and *Paganini*. She returned to Munich in 1964 as ballerina and ballet mistress and at the beginning of the 1964–65 season collaborated with Heinz Rosen, the Bavarian State Opera House director of ballet, to stage *The Sleeping Beauty*.

Ancient Russia. Ballet in 3 scenes; chor. and book: Bronislava Nijinska; music: Peter Tchaikowsky's Piano Concert No. 1 in B flat minor; décor: Nathalie Gontcharova (originally used in *Bogatyri*). First prod.: Ballet Russe de Monte Carlo, Music Hall, Cleveland, Ohio, Oct. 11, 1943; N.Y. première: City Center, Apr. 11, 1944, with a cast headed by Alexandra Danilova, Maria Tallchief, James Starbuck, Igor Youskevitch. The ballet has no clear scenario; it concentrates on old Russian customs and stylized folk dances.

And Daddy Was a Fireman. Modern dance work; chor. and costumes: Charles Weidman; music: Herbert Haufrecht, adapting popular airs (including "Oh, Susanna"); décor: Harnley Perkins. First prod.: Humphrey-Weidman Theatre, N.Y., 1943. Gossiping townswomen read selections from the local newspapers depicting the rise from ordinary fireman to captain of the fire department of the Canal Zone (during the building of the Panama Canal) of the gallant Fireman Weidman, taking in a romance on the way.

And Joy Is My Witness. Modern dance work; chor. and costumes: Pearl Lang; music: John Sebastian Bach's Toccata, Adagio and Fugue in G minor. First prod.: Pearl Lang and Company, Central High School of Needle Trades, N.Y., Dec. 5, 1953, with Pearl Lang, Joan Skinner, Jessica Nooney, Irving Burton, Dale Sehnert, John Coyle, Paul Taylor. A themeless work following the musical line, arranged in the manner of a passacaglia with a series of overlapping entries, the strong movements for the men counterpointing the lightness of the women. At its first performance in 1953 only the fugue was set. The toccata and adagio (a solo for Pearl Lang) were added and the entire work presented at Central High School of Needle Trades, Apr. 3, 1955.

Andersen, Ruth, Danish dancer, b. Randers, 1931; m. Werner Andersen. Entered the Royal Danish Ballet School in 1941; accepted into the company in 1949; made soloist in 1956. Toured the U.S. with the Inge Sand group in 1957. Dances leading roles in *Napoli, Coppélia, Giselle, Night Shadow, Polovetsian Dances from Prince Igor, Les Sylphides, Pas de Quatre, Petrouchka, La Ventana, The Sleeping Beauty, Serenade, Peter and the Wolf,* and *Graduation Ball.*

Andersen, Werner, Danish dancer, b.

Copenhagen, 1930; m. Ruth Andersen. Entered the Royal Danish Ballet School in 1939, graduating into the company; soloist since 1957. Toured the U.S.A. with the Inge Sand group, in 1957. Dances leading roles in *Swan Lake, Coppélia, Moon Reindeer, Cyrano de Bergerac, La Ventana, Napoli, Night Shadow, Giselle, The Sleeping Beauty* and *Miss Julie.*

Anderson, Elisabeth, Russian Ballerina, teacher; b. Moscow; m. Ivan Ivantzov. Studied at Imperial School of Ballet, Moscow. Made her debut as ballerina as Princess Aurora in *The Sleeping Beauty,* Bolshoi Theatre, Moscow, 1917. Staged Igor Stravinsky's *Les Noces,* Metropolitan Opera House, N.Y., April 28, 1929. Opened ballet studio, N.Y. (1937), where she still teaches.

Andersson, Gerd, Swedish dancer, b. Stockholm, 1932. Pupil of Royal Swedish Ballet school and privately of Lilian Karina. Accepted into the company in 1948. Made her debut as Margareta in Janine Charrat's *Abraxas* (1951); became ballerina in 1958. Appeared in television film with Gene Kelly in 1959; the same year was guest artist in the Christmas pantomime *Where the Rainbow Ends* (London). She is particularly successful in such roles as the Glove Seller (*Gaîté Parisienne*), Swanilda (*Coppélia*), etc., but her range includes the Princess of the Copper Mountain in the Royal Swedish Ballet's production of *The Stone Flower,* which she created Feb. 27, 1962. Also created the leading woman's role in Antony Tudor's *Echoes of Trumpets* (1963). In 1966 spent six weeks in N.Y. on a Swedish government fellowship.

Gerd Andersson in Miss Julie

Anderton, Elizabeth, English dancer, b. London, 1938. Studied with Nesta Brooking. Won first Beaumont Scholarship to *Sadler's Wells* (now Royal Ballet) School (1952). Joined Sadler's Wells Opera Ballet (1955); Royal Ballet (1956), becoming soloist (1958). Roles include The Girl (*Solitaire*), The Gypsy (*Les Deux Pigeons*), Johanna (*Sweeney Todd*), and others.

Andrade, Adolfo (Adolfo Pato), Argentine dancer, b. Buenos Aires, Argentina, 1925. Studied in Buenos Aires with Michel Borowski, Esmée Bulnes, Vassili Lambrinos, Otto Werberg; and in Paris with Nora Kiss, Serge Peretti. Soloist with Ballet International du Marquis de Cuevas, the Jean Babilée, Maurice Béjart, Janine Charrat, and Milorad Miscovitch companies, as well as Balletto Europeo de Nervi. Since 1961 has been first soloist of the State Opera in Munich, dancing principal classical and demi-caractère roles. Choreographed for *Orpheus* (Liszt) and *Don Perlimplin* (de Falla) for television.

Andreani, Jean-Paul, premier danseur étoile of Paris Opéra, b. Rouen, 1929. Studied at Paris Opéra school (1939–45) under Gustave Ricaux, Serge Peretti; became premier danseur in 1948, étoile in 1953. Created principal roles in *Blanche Neige* (1951), *Grand Pas* (1953), *Romeo and Juliet* (1955), *Gounod Symphony* (George Balanchine, 1959), full-length *Swan Lake* choreographed for the Paris Opéra by Vladimir Bourmeister (1961), *Pastorale* (1962). Has toured in U.S. and South America with Paris Opéra ballet.

Andrew, Thomas (Edward Thomas Andrulewicz), American dancer and choreographer, b. Mount Carmel, Pa., 1932, of Polish parentage. Studied with Douglas Henkel (Newport News, Va.), Igor Schwezoff, Ballet Theatre School, Metropolitan Opera Ballet (1956–62), can Ballet Center. Began professional activities as dancer and choreographer in the U.S. Army Special Services (1952–54), followed by engagement in the musical *Silk Stockings* as dancer-singer (1955–56). Was dancer and dancer-choreographer with Metropolitan Opera Ballet (1956–62), staging dances in *Martha* (1961) and *Un Ballo in Maschera* (1962). Danced in Central City Opera and Santa Fe (N. Mex.) Opera. Staged for the latter *Clarissa, Invitations,* and *Le Wagon Couvert.* Staged and danced in several operas, among them Igor Stravinsky's *Persephone,* in which he appeared as partner (Mercury) to Vera Zorina (Persephone) at Santa Fe and with that company in West Berlin and Belgrade (1961). Choreographed *Strange Sweet Gestures* and *Rustic Pas de Deux* for Thomas Andrew and Company at Jacob's Pillow Dance Festival (1959). Also appeared in television shows and as guest artist with regional opera companies, dance groups, and symphony orchestras. Danced in *America Dances* presentation by Walter Terry (1963). Director and choreographer Ballet Today, company organized in 1964.

Angélica, Maria (Maria Angélica Braga Faccini), Brazilian dancer, b. Rio de Janeiro, 1933. Began her studies under Yuco Lindberg at Teatro Municipal ballet school (1945); made her debut with Ballet da Juventude under Igor Schwezoff (1947). Came to U.S. in 1948 to study under Schwezoff, also at School of American Ballet. Returned to Rio de Janeiro (1949), and danced as ballerina with Ballet Society under Tatiana Leskova. Joined Teatro Municipal as first dancer (1950). Engaged in 1954 by the Paul Szilard company to tour Japan and Hawaii. Joined American Ballet Theatre in 1955 as first soloist. Has married and is retired from the stage.

Angiolini, Gasparo (1731–1803), Italian dancer and outstanding choreographer of his time who was appointed ballet master of the Vienna Hofoper (1757) when Gluck was the opera's conductor. Among his ballets choreographed to Gluck's music are *Don Juan* (1761) and *Semiramis* (1765). In 1765 he succeeded Hilverding as ballet master of the Imperial Theatre in St. Petersburg, Russia. Throughout his career Angiolini, a true adherent of the Italian style of choreography and dance, was antagonistic to Jean-Georges Noverre and the French style and carried on a lively, and often bitter, controversy with Noverre, ridiculing the fact that he could not tell his complicated story ballets without detailed program notes.

Anguish Sonata. Ballet in 3 movements. Idea and chor.: Aurel Milloss; music: Béla Bártok's Sonata for Two Pianos and Percussion; décor: Darcy Penteado. First prod.: Ballet do IV Centenario, Teatro Municipal, Rio de Janeiro, Brazil, 1954, with Edith Pudelko, Cristian Uboldi, Eduardo Sucena, Ismael Guiser. The ballet has no definite plot. Milloss called it a ballet mystery in three tempi. Under the sign of the Unknown, not even Fantasy can save Poetry, if one does not also accept Anguish as its muse.

Anisimova, Nina, Honored Art Worker, leading Soviet character dancer and choreographer, b. 1909. Studied at the Leningrad ballet school (1919–26) under Maria Romanova, Agrippina Vaganova, and Alexander Shiryayev. Her fiery temperament and great dramatic talent enabled her, not only to perform character dances with great brio and academic virtuosity, but to create many important roles in the dramatic ballets typical of the 1930's. Much of the actual choreographic texture of the role of Therese in Vassily Vainonen's *Flames of Paris* was created by Anisimova. She became one of the first Soviet women choreographers. Among her works are *Gayané* (Leningrad Kirov Theatre, 1945); *The Magic Veil* (S. Zaranek, 1947); *Coppélia* (new version, 1949); *Schéhérazade* (new version, 1950); *Willow Tree* (O. Yevlakhov, 1957), all at the Maly (Little) Opera Theatre, Leningrad, with which she has long been associated, simultaneously occupying the position of leading character dancer at the Kirov. Retired as a dancer in 1957, to devote herself to choreography.

Annabel Lee. Ballet in 1 act; chor. and book based on the poem by Edgar Allan Poe: George Skibine; commissioned music: Byron Schiffmann; décor: André Delfau. First prod. Grand Ballet du Marquis de Cuevas at Deauville Theatre, Aug. 28, 1951, with Marjorie Tallchief and the choreographer as Annabel Lee and her lover. This romantic ballet is accompanied by a singer, and follows the Poe poem in showing two happy lovers and the grief of one as the other (Annabel Lee) dies. Three dancers in black symbolize the tomb in a moving and effective final passage.

Ansermet, Ernest (1883–   ), Swiss conductor. One of Serge Diaghilev's collaborators in the latter's Ballets Russes, and its regular conductor from 1915. A noted interpreter of Igor Stravinsky's ballet music of that period.

Anspannung-Abspannung, the German term developed and formulated by Rudolf von Laban which is translated in America as contraction-release or fall-recovery and in England as tension-relaxation. The term is used in the modern dance.

Antagonists, The. Modern dance work; chor.: Ruth Currier; music: Igor Stravinsky's Concertino and Three Pieces for String Quartet; décor: Thomas de Gaetani. First prod.: Eighth American Dance Festival, Connecticut College, New London, Aug. 20, 1955, with Ruth Currier (Zealot) and Betty Jones (Victim). By sheer force of will the Zealot draws her victim out of the safety of the protective walls she has built around herself; but freedom offers nothing but other fears.

Antheil, George (1900–1959), American composer. His *Ballet Mécanique* introduced non-musical instruments for sound effects. This ballet is not to be confused with A. Mossolov's *Iron Foundry*. He also composed the music for the ballets *Dreams* (George Balanchine, 1935) and *The Capital of the World* (Eugene Loring, 1953), for Ballet (now American Ballet) Theatre, and orchestrated Franz Liszt's Piano Etudes d'Éxécution Transcendante for Balanchine's *Transcendence* (1934).

Anthony, Gordon. See PHOTOGRAPHERS, DANCE (ENGLAND).

Anti-Masques. See MASQUES.

Antic Meet. Modern dance work; chor.: Merce Cunningham; music: John Cage. First prod.: Merce Cunningham Dance Company, eleventh American Dance Festival, Connecticut College, New London, Aug. 14, 1958, with Merce Cunningham, Carolyn Brown, Viola Farber, Marilyn Wood, Judith Dunn, Remy Charlip; N.Y. première: Phoenix Theatre, Feb. 16, 1960. A satirical look at almost everything, but mostly at the little man whose aim in life is to keep up with everybody doing everything.

Antic Spring. Ballet in 1 act; chor.: Grant Strate; music: Jacques Ibert's Divertissement and Three Short Pieces for Wood Wind Quintet; décor: Mark Negin. First prod.: National Ballet of Canada, Palace Theatre, Hamilton, Oct. 26, 1960, with Patrick Hurde (Toby), Jacqueline Ivings, Judie Colpman, Sally Brayley (Flowers), Angela Leigh (Bride), Earl Kraul (Groom). A slight satire on city life in which Toby, a country boy, leaves his flower playmates and is off to the big city where he quickly becomes disillusioned after a brief infatuation with a newly married bride. His flowers rescue him and he returns to the country sadder and wiser.

Antigone. Ballet in 1 act; chor.: John Cranko; commissioned music: Mikis Theodorakis; décor: Rufino Tamayo. First prod.: Royal Ballet at Royal Opera House, Covent Garden, London, Oct. 19, 1959 with Svetlana Beriosova (Antigone), Donald Macleary (Haemon), David Blair (Polynices), Michael Somes (Creon), Gary Burne (Etiocles), Julia Farron (Jocasta), Leslie Edwards (Oedipus). The story is based on the Antigone legend, specifically the play by Sophocles; tells how the usurper Creon forbids honorable burial to the sons of Oedipus, killed in battle. Defying his order, Antigone goes at night to bury her brother Polynices, knowing that it will mean her own death.

Antonia. Ballet in 1 act; chor. and libretto: Walter Gore; music: Jan Sibelius; tone poem *The Bard,* incidental music for *The Tempest* and Festivo from *Scènes Historiques;* décor: Harry Cordwell. First prod.: Ballet Rambert, King's Theatre, Hammersmith, London, Oct. 17, 1949, with Paula Hinton (Antonia), David Paltenghi (Sebastian), Walter Gore (Rafael). The ballet is the drama of a man's disillusionment with his beloved when he discovers that she is unfaithful, and the violence of his revenge.

Antonio (Antonio Ruiz Soler), the outstanding Spanish dancer of his day, b. Seville, Spain, 1922. Studied under Realito; made his debut with his cousin Rosario in Liège, Belgium (1928), and from then until 1953 toured triumphantly all over the world as the team Rosario and Antonio. Made their American debut in 1940, Edinburgh Festival debut in 1950, and London debut the following year. Separated from Rosario in 1953 to form his own company; reunited for N.Y. season and American tour (fall, 1964). In 1966 became the first Spanish artist to appear in the Soviet Union since the Spanish Civil War (the Igor Moiseyev company appeared in Spain on a reciprocal basis). Although his strength lies in his mastery of the many forms of Spanish dance, and particularly in the brilliance of his zapateado, his recent preoccupation has been with the possibilities of wedding the Spanish dance to classic ballet to create a more expressive theatrical dance form than Spanish dance by itself allows. His successes in that direction are still far behind those he achieves as an individual.

Apasionada. Modern dance work; chor.: Pearl Lang; music: Carlos Surinach; costumes: Pearl Lang. First prod.: Pearl Lang and Dance Company, Hunter College Playhouse, N.Y., Jan. 5, 1962, with Pearl Lang, Bruce Marks, Paul Sanasardo, Kevin Carlisle, and company. Pearl Lang uses the corrida as the symbol of life's span with the matador as man accepting death at the last in the knowledge that there is one to take his place, and that, in this continuity, lies our immortality.

Apivor, Dennis, British composer, b. Collinstown, Eire, 1916, of Welsh parentage. Private composition pupil of Prof. Patrick Hadley and Alan Rawsthorne; professional chorister in choirs of Christchurch College, Oxford and Hereford Cathedral. Compositions for ballet include *A Mirror for Witches* (Royal Ballet, 1952), *The Good Man of Paris* (used by Andrée Howard for *Vis-à-Vis,* Walter Gore Ballet, 1953), *Blood Wedding* (Royal Ballet, 1953), *Saudades* (Royal Ballet, 1955). Arranged and orchestrated a Donizetti score for *Veneziana* (Royal Ballet, 1953). Contributed "The Musician's Role in Ballet," (five articles) to *Dancing Times* (1959). Apivor has lived in London, India, and the West Indies. He is opposed to regionalism and likes to think of European composers as being at least European, in the way American composers are American.

Aplomb, in ballet, the ability to hold one's balance; also the balance itself.

Apollo. Ballet in 1 act, 2 scenes; chor.: George Balanchine; music and book: Igor Stravinsky; décor: André Bauchant. First prod.: Diaghilev Ballets Russes, Theatre Sarah Bernhardt, Paris, June 12, 1928, with Serge Lifar (Apollo), Alice Nikitina (alternating with Alexandra Danilova as Terpsichore), Lubov Tchernicheva (Polyhymnia), Felia Doubrovska (Calliope). Apollo, Leader of the Muses, prepares himself for his duties as a god and, supported by the muses, ascends Olympus to drive his sun chariot across the heavens. Revived in décor by Stewart Chaney for American Ballet, Metropolitan Opera House, N.Y., Apr. 27 and 28, 1937, with Lew Christensen (Apollo) and Elise Reiman, Holly Howard, Daphne Vane as the three muses, for the Stravinsky Festival. These productions were given under the title *Apollon Musagète.* Under its present title *Apollo,* it was revived by Ballet (now American Ballet) Theatre, Metropolitan Opera House, Apr. 25, 1943, in décor by Pavel Tchelitchev, with André Eglevsky (Apollo) and Vera Zorina, Nora Kaye, Rosella Hightower as the Muses; Alicia Alonso, Nora Kaye, and Barbara Fallis later danced these roles. Balanchine staged it for New York City Ballet, City Center, N.Y. (Nov. 15, 1951), with André Eglevsky (Apollo), Maria Tallchief (Terpsichore), Tanaquil LeClerq (Polyhymnia), Diana Adams (Calliope). Jacques d'Amboise and Allegra Kent are also notable interpreters of Apollo and Terpsichore. Balanchine has also staged this ballet for the Paris Opéra Ballet, in décor by André Delfau (May 21, 1947) for Alexandre Kalioujny, Maria Tallchief, Jacqueline Moreau, Denise Bourgeois, and for the Royal Danish Ballet (which reverted to the title of *Apollon Musagète*), Copenhagen, Jan. 9, 1957, with Henning Kronstam, Mette Mollerup, Kirsten Simone, Kirsten Petersen. Like the New York City Ballet production, the Danish *Apollo* is performed in practice costume. Balanchine staged *Apollo* for the Royal Ballet, Royal Opera House, Covent Garden, London (Nov. 15, 1966), with Donald MacLeary, Svetlana Beriosova, Georgina Parkinson, Monica Mason. This company reverted to the original title *Apollon Musagète.*

Apollon Musagète (Chor.: George Balanchine.) See APOLLO.

Apollon Musagète. Ballet in 2 scenes; chor.: *Adolph Bolm;* music and book: *Igor Stravinsky*. Commissioned by *Elizabeth Sprague Coolidge.* First prod.: Library of Congress, Washington D.C., Apr. 27, 1928, with Adolph Bolm (Apollo), Ruth Page (Terpsichore), Berenice Holmes (Polyhymnia), Elise Reiman (Calliope).

N.Y.C. Ballet's Apollo: *Edward Villella (Apollo), Suki Schorer, Patricia McBride, Carol Sumner (Muses).*

Appalachian Spring. Modern dance work; chor.: Martha Graham; commissioned music: Aaron Copland; artistic collaboration and décor: Isamu Noguchi; costumes: Edythe Gilfond. First prod.: Library of Congress, Washington, D.C., Oct. 30, 1944. Principal roles danced by Martha Graham, May O'Donnell, Merce Cunningham, Erick Hawkins. *Appalachian Spring* was commissioned by the Coolidge Foundation. The work tells a simple tale about a young American pioneer couple settling in their newly built home. The plot is no more than a canvas upon which is painted one of the great American choreographic creations.

Apparitions. Ballet in prologue, 3 scenes and epilogue; chor.: Frederick Ashton: music: Franz Liszt (Consolation No. 3 for prologue and epilogue; 1st Valse Oubliée, The Christmas Tree [6 pieces], Galop in A Minor, Elegie No. 2, Unstern [Sinister], 3rd Mephisto Valse), selected by Constant Lambert and orch. by Gordon Jacob; book: Constant Lambert, inspired by the synopsis for Hector Berlioz's *Symphonie Fantastique;* décor: Cecil Beaton. First prod.: Vic-Wells (later Sadler's Wells, now Royal) Ballet, Sadler's Wells Theatre, London, Feb. 11, 1936, with Margot Fonteyn (Woman in the Ball Dress), Robert Helpmann (Poet), Harold Turner (Hussar), Maurice Brooke (Monk). The Poet, seeking inspiration in opium, sees in the visions which the drug induces: the tantalizing figure of the woman in a ball dress who leads him on into a fantastic ballroom, to a snowbound landscape, and finally to a saturnalia. He dies as the visions fade. Revived by Sadler's Wells Theatre Ballet (1947), with Anne Heaton (Woman in the Ball Dress) and John Field (Poet).

Applebaum, Louis, Canadian composer, b. Toronto, Ont. 1918. Educated at the Univ. of Toronto (Faculty of Music); studied music in New York with Bernard Wagenaar and Roy Harris. Composed music for *Dark of the Moon* (1953), *Legend of the North* (Janet Baldwin Ballet, 1957), *Barbara Allen* (a revised version of the *Dark of the Moon* score, 1960). Former music director of the Stratford (Ont.) Festival (1953–60), composing incidental music for productions there. Founded and directed Stratford (Ont.) Music Festival (1955–60) and was music director for Tyrone Guthrie's productions of Gilbert and Sullivan operas. He has also composed a great deal of music for film, radio, and television, earning many awards in each category including Canadian Film Award. Is currently music consultant for television, Canadian Broadcasting Corporation.

Appleyard, Beatrice, English dancer, choreographer, teacher, b. Maidenhead, Berks, 1918. Studied ballet with Ninette de Valois, Tamara Karsavina, and Bronislava Nijinska. An original member of the Vic-Wells Ballet (which became Sadler's Wells, and finally Royal Ballet), she was one of the first English dancers to make a name for herself in the early days of English ballet. Soloist, Markova-Dolin Ballet (1935); followed by several years as principal dancer and choreographer, Windmill Theatre, London, and choreographer for several London musicals. Teaching in Turkey since 1951.

Apprenti Sorcier. See SORCERER'S APPRENTICE, THE.

Après-Midi d'un Faune, L'. See AFTERNOON OF A FAUN.

April, Roland, French dancer b. Strasbourg, 1929. Studied with Charlotte April and Jean Combes. First professional engagement was at Théâtre Municipal, Strasbourg (1945–55). Later danced with Janine Charrat company (1955), Bordeaux Opera House (1956–58), and in Basel, Switzerland since 1958. Dances principal roles in classic and modern ballets. Staged dances in opera and operettas, among them *Zar und Zimmermann, Graf von Luxemburg, Gypsy Baron,* and others.

Arabesque, in ballet, pose in which one leg is extended straight in back; positions of arms and body vary. Most common arabesque is one in which opposite arm to leg is extended forward. Weight of supporting leg may be on whole foot, pointe or demi-pointe. Supporting leg may or may not be in plié. Pose may be in croisé, effacé, or en face. Arms may be à deux bras, in second position.

Arbeau, Thoinot (Jehan Tabouret), author of Orchésographie, b. Dijon, 1519. Son of a king's counsellor, he became a priest, canon of Langres. Orchésographie was published at Langres in 1588. It is a record of 16th century dancing, including musical notations. There are descriptions of the volte, courante, allemande, gavotte, morisque and nineteen forms of branles. The book also includes advice on related subjects, including fencing and marriage. The text is written in the form of a dialogue between Arbeau and his young friend Capriol. By means of the system of dance notation the book defines the principles of turned-out legs and feet with the weight equally distributed on both. This principle was the foundation of the five absolute positions of classic dance formulated by Pierre Beauchamp a century or more later. This book was instrumental in establishing France in a position of importance in developing ballet, a position until then held by Italy. A modern translation of Orchésographie has been published by Cyril W. Beaumont (London, 1925), and Kamin Dance Publishers (N.Y., 1948).

Arcade. Ballet in 1 act; chor.: John Taras; music: Igor Stravinsky's Concerto for Piano and Wind instruments; décor: David Hays; costumes: Ruth Sobotka. First prod.: New York City Ballet, City Center, N.Y., Mar. 28, 1963, with Suzanne Farrell and Arthur Mitchell in the leading roles. A ballet of atmosphere and suggestion, without a definitive plot. From among the boys whose costumes suggest a carnival, one is chosen by black clad figures called "Chaperones" to dance with a young girl, but at the end the girl is taken away and all the boys are left, presumably in a room from which they cannot escape. For the winter, 1963, season the costumes were replaced by practice clothes, thereby eliminating both atmosphere and suggestion of plot.

Archives Internationales de la Danse, Les, was founded in Paris June 16, 1931 by Rolf de Maré and Dr. Pierre Tugal in memory of the Ballets Suédois company (1920–25) and their choreographer Jean Börlin. The buildings of the AID housed, besides the offices, a large library of books, magazines, pictures, newspapers, clippings, music, etc., pertaining to the dance, some of them dating back to the 15th century. There was also a large lecture-exhibition hall and a smaller one suited to the exhibition of smaller paintings, engravings, etc. Among the exhibitions held at the AID were: Dance in Painting and Sculpture (works of artists no longer living in 1933, and works of living artists in 1934); Dance and Movement (winter, 1933–34); Ballerines, Coryphées et Funambules (1937); Photographs of the Dance; Dance in Ceramics; Books on the Dance; Pavlova Memorial Exhibition; Marionette Exposition. Exhibitions on folklore included: Dances of the Netherlands Indies by Claire Hold; Japanese Dances Through the Ages; Old Dances of France, etc. In 1937 AID held an exposition, Popular Dances of Europe, in which twenty-two European countries participated. From 1933 to 1935 a series of monographs was published by the Archives. These included articles on the art and on the technique of the dance, interviews with prominent dancers, etc. In 1932 Rolf de Maré, through the Archives Internationales de la Danse, sponsored the first Choreographic Competition in Paris. It was at this competition that Kurt Jooss first won renown: his ballet *The Green Table* received the first prize. Trudi Schoop won second prize with *Fridolin*. During World War II the competitions were discontinued. They were renewed in 1947 when de Maré sponsored a competition in Copenhagen, Denmark. In 1950 the Archives were dissolved. The greater part of the material was transferred to the Musée de l'Opéra, Paris, and the remainder to the Dance Museum of the Royal Swedish Opera House, Stockholm, of which Bengt Haeger is director.

Archives of the Dance (London), was founded under a trust deed on Jan. 9, 1945. The nucleus of the Archives was a collection of books, programs, pictures, etc., acquired by the Ballet Guild (London) over a period of years and presented to the Archives. Since then the Archives has acquired a collection of manuscript ballet scores, printed ballet piano scores, a collection of some six hundred photographs donated by Arnold L. Haskell and a collection of items associated with Maria Taglioni, donated by Margaret Rolfe, a pupil of Taglioni. It is housed by the Imperial Society of Teachers of Dancing, 70 Gloucester Place, London, W.1. The trustees are Dame Adeline Genée, Mr. Cyril W. Beaumont, Sir Bronson Albery, and Mr. Christmas Humphreys.

Ardent Song. Modern dance work; chor.: *Martha Graham;* commissioned music: Alan Hovhaness; costumes: Martha Graham. First prod.: Martha Graham Dance Company, Saville Theatre, London, Mar. 18, 1954; N.Y. première: ANTA Theatre, May 3, 1955, with Yuriko (Moonrise), Helen McGehee (Moonset), Pearl Lang (Dawn), and company. Episodes of nocturnal rites.

Argentina, La (Antonia Mercé) (1888–1936).

BY F. C. SCHANG.

In January, 1916 the Metropolitan Opera Company invited the Spanish composer, Enrique Granados, to attend the world première of his opera *Goyescas,* scheduled for the 26th of that month. Before sailing for New York, the composer cabled his friend, the great Spanish dancer La Argentina, then in Buenos Aires, to meet him in New York to dance the leading role in this opera. Unfortunately he neglected to inform Mr. Gatti-Casazza, General Director of the Metropolitan, of these arrangements. When he arrived in New York he found that the Metropolitan production had been fully rehearsed, with its leading dancer, Rosina Galli, doing the part intended for La Argentina. Thus when the young Spanish dancer arrived, she was met with apologies. The opera was not a success, and is now only remembered for its sparkling intermezzo.

This was the greeting received by Antonia Mercé known as La Argentina, on her first visit to New York. She hastily got a program together and appeared in a matinee at the Maxine Elliot Theatre, attended by no critics and a very sparse public.

She returned to Europe crestfallen, but hardly less so than Granados, the failure of whose opera was climaxed by his own tragic death when the SS Sussex was submarined in the English Channel on March 24th, 1916.

Scarcely less auspicious was La Argentina's second appearance in New York, at the Park Avenue Theatre on November 7, 1919, in a Spanish musical extravaganza by Valverde called *The Land of Joy*. On this occasion she was merely noted as a member of the company.

But nine years later when she returned to New York on November 9, 1928, for the first of six recital tours in this country, she established herself as the greatest

Spanish dancer ever to visit this continent and, indeed, probably the greatest Spanish dancer who ever lived. In fact, no solo dancer was ever so idolized by the American public (in one year alone she gave thirty-eight sold out recitals in New York City), and surely no one so deserved this public esteem, for Argentina was modest to a point of humility about her art, and the generous and kindly nature which shone from her countenance established a great bond of sympathy between her and the public.

Although born in Buenos Aires (hence her surname), La Argentina was of pure European stock: her father, Manuel Mercé, was an Andalusian, and her mother, Josefina Luque, a Castilian, both professional dancers. Under her father's tutelage she started the study of ballet at the age of four, and made her debut at eleven, at the Royal Theatre, Madrid.

Though thoroughly schooled in the classic forms, she nevertheless preferred her native dances, and by the time she was fourteen decided to retire from the ballet and took a sort of post-graduate course with her mother as her sole teacher, her father having died. To her the native dances were brusque, even brutal, and lacking in plastique. They were a crude form of art needing refinement. To this she applied herself, devising a series of programs illustrating the various dances of Spain, with costumes designed by herself, which she presented throughout the world and to world-wide acclaim.

The great dance critic, André Levinson, attributes the renascence of the Spanish dance as an art form solely to Argentina's genius. "She alone," he wrote, "has revived and developed an art form too long debased by the gypsies of the music hall."

More than any predecessor, La Argentina mastered the art of the castanets, continuously experimenting with variations in wood, size and modifications of shape. She declared that the best castanets, producing the greatest variety of tone and the finest nuances, were made from the wood of the pomegranate tree. La Argentina was tireless in mating her castanets. It is the female castanet that is worn on the right hand and gives a delicate sound, while the male on the left hand with its deeper tone plays the role of accompaniment. She succeeded in developing in this humble instrument musical possibilities which became a perfect collaboration to her choreographic art.

In the period 1928 to 1936, Argentina made six transcontinental tours of North America, all presented by the impresario F. C. Coppicus, of the Metropolitan Musical Bureau, and managed by F. C. Schang. Argentina's world representative was her friend and stage manager, Arnold Meckel, of Paris.

After her recital tour of 1935–36, Messrs. Coppicus and Meckel arranged with Columbia Concerts Inc. to present La Argentina with her Ballets Espagnoles and Escudero for an American tour the following winter, in a program which was to include a complete performance of Manuel De Falla's *El Amor Brujo* with orchestra.

Summering at her Villa Miraflores, near Bayonne, France, on July 18, 1936, she motored across the Spanish border to attend a dance festival in a small village. She returned to her home that evening full of zest and enthusiasm for what she had seen. She was demonstrating some new steps to her guests on the veranda, when a sudden spasm seized her, and she sank in a chair.

In that sad second, the noble heart of La Argentina ceased to beat.

Argentinita (Encarnación López) (1898–1945), famous Spanish dancer, was born in Buenos Aires, the daughter of a Castilian Spanish exporter. She was taken to Spain by her parents when she was four and began her training in the Spanish dance. A finished musician, actress, and brilliant technician, she mastered the various types of Spanish classic dancing

Argentinita

to the complete satisfaction of the discriminating Spanish audiences. She made her American debut in the International Revue (1930). Her reception was cold and she soon left the cast, understandably unimpressed with American audiences. She was persuaded to dance again during that same season under the auspices of the Concert Dancers, and this time her dancing was received with great enthusiasm by the press and public alike. In 1932 Argentinita returned to Spain where she and the late Federico García Lorca organized the Madrid Ballet. In 1938 impresario S. Hurok signed Argentinita and her group for a tour of the U.S. and Central and South America. Argentinita and her troupe (which included her sister, Pilar López) appeared all over the U.S. and as guest artists with Ballet (now American Ballet) Theatre during its season at the Metropolitan Opera House, N.Y. Her last appearance on the American stage was with that organization in April, 1945. Argentinita died in New York on Sept. 24, 1945. Her body was taken for burial to Madrid, Spain.

Argyle, Pearl (Pearl Wellman) (1910–47), English ballerina and actress; m. American film producer Curtis Bernhardt. Studied with Marie Rambert. Made her debut with the Ballet Club (later Ballet Rambert) in 1926, quickly rising to leading roles, creating La Fille (*Bar aux Folies-Bergère*), Hebe (*Descent of Hebe*), Wife (*Les Masques*), title roles (Andrée Howard's *Cinderella, Mermaid*) et al. Also danced in the Camargo Society seasons and the London season of Les Ballets 1933. Joined Sadler's Wells (now Royal) Ballet in 1935, dancing *Les Sylphides, Swan Lake,* creating the Queen (*Le Roi Nu*), Fairy (Frederick Ashton's *Baiser de la Fée*), etc. She was an outstanding beauty and was also successful in revues and a number of English films of the time. She lived in the U.S. from the time of her marriage in 1938 until her early death, dancing in several Broadway musicals, among them *One Touch of Venus.* The library of the Royal Ballet School is dedicated to her memory.

Armitage, Merle, author, designer, impresario; b. Mason City, Iowa, 1893. First engaged in civil engineering; later designer of stage settings until 1911. Managed tours of many singers and opera companies (1911–15); publicity director, Diaghilev Ballets Russes (1915); publicity manager, Anna Pavlova. During World War I taught mechanical engineering for the U.S. Army; was Major in

U.S. Air Force in World War II. Has edited numerous books (biography, paintings, photographs, etc.), including *Modern Dance* (1935), *Igor Stravinsky* (1936), *Arnold Schoenberg* (1937), *The Psychologist Looks at Art* (Tanz, 1937), *Martha Graham, Dancer* (1937), *Dance Memoranda* (1946), and others.

Armour, Thomas, dancer, choreographer, teacher, b. Tarpon Springs, Fla., 1909. Started ballet training as a small boy with Ines Noel Armour in Tampa; continued in Paris with Olga Preobrajenska and Lubov Egorova. Made his professional debut with the Ida Rubinstein company in Paris (1928); later toured Europe with Bronislava Nijinska. With the Leon Woizikowski company in Europe (1935–36), afterwards joining Col. de Basil's Ballets Russes de Monte Carlo. Joined the Massine-Blum Ballet Russe de Monte Carlo (1939). Danced major roles in *Les Sylphides, Le Spectre de la Rose, Polovetsian Dances from Prince Igor* (Warrior Chief), *La Boutique Fantasque,* (Tarantella) and many others. During World War II was 1st Lieutenant with Military Intelligence. On his return to civil life opened school in Miami where he is also artistic director and choreographer of Miami Ballet (see REGIONAL BALLET), which was the first of such groups to be invited by Ted Shawn to dance at a Jacob's Pillow Dance Festival (1957).

Arms (in ballet), positions of. There is no universally accepted system of numbering the positions of the arms. There is great flexibility in the adaptation of arm movements and no rigid relationship between arm and foot positions, e.g. when feet are in second position, arms need not necessarily be in second. The arms are slightly curved in all positions. The most commonly used systems are: Cecchetti Method: 1st pos.—both arms hanging down at sides a few inches from body; 2nd pos.—arms extended to sides slightly below shoulder level; 3rd. pos.—one arm at side just below shoulder level; other arm front, crossing body and pointing diagonally down; 4th pos.—en avant, one arm at side slightly below shoulder level, other arm held forward at chest level; en haut, one arm at side slightly below shoulder level, other arm extended upward; 5th pos.—en bas, both arms extended downward and held in front of body; en avant, both arms held forward at chest level; en haut, both arms extended upward. Russian System: 1st pos. —both arms held forward at chest level, 2nd pos.—both arms extended to sides slightly below shoulder level; 3rd pos.—one arm at side slightly below shoulder level, other arm held forward at chest level; 4th pos.—one arm extended to side at slightly below shoulder level, other arm extended upward; 5th pos.—both arms extended upward. Vaganova System: preparatory pos.—both arms extended downward and held in front of body; 1st pos.—both arms held forward at chest level; 2nd pos.—both arms extended to sides at slightly below shoulder level; 3rd pos.—both arms extended upward.

Arnold, Malcolm, English composer, b. 1912. Educated at the Royal College of Music, London. Principal trumpet, London Philharmonic Orchestra (1941–44; 1945–48). Received Mendelssohn Scholarship for study in Italy (1948). His scores for ballets include *Homage to the Queen* (1953), *Rinaldo and Armida* (1955), *Solitaire* (1956), for which he composed a Sarabande and Polka, the remainder of the score being his *Eight English Dances,* and *Electra* (1963).

Arova, Sonia (Sonia Errio), ballerina, b. Sofia, Bulgaria, 1927. Began dance training with Opera Ballet in Sofia and continued when her family moved to Paris when she was nine, studying with Olga Preobrajenska and Serge Lifar; later studied at the Cone-Ripman School in

Sonia Arova

England. Made her debut with the International Ballet (1942); spent two seasons with Ballet Rambert (1946); leading dancer, Metropolitan Ballet (1947–48), with which company she created one of the three leading women's roles in *Designs With Strings* and a leading role in Frank Staff's *Lovers' Gallery*. Created Azucena in Ruth Page's *Revenge* (based on the opera *Il Trovatore*) for Les Ballets des Champs-Élysées (1951); as guest artist with London's Festival Ballet created the title role of *The Merry Widow* (1953), at that time called *Vilia*. Has since danced these roles many times with Ruth Page's Chicago Opera Ballet, of which she has been a guest ballerina for several seasons beginning 1955; also dances Baroness Popoff in the same ballet. Guest artist, Ballet (now American Ballet) Theatre (1954–56); seasons with Nora Kovach, Istvan Rabovsky and Job Sanders (1956–58); returned for a season in 1957 to dance in Japan where she had first danced with the Komaki Ballet in 1951 (the first Western ballerina to dance in Japan after World War II). In Europe with American Festival Ballet (1958–60), for which she created *Bachianos Brasileiros No. 5* (to the music of Heitor Villa-Lobos; chor. by Job Sanders). With Rosella Hightower, Erik Bruhn, and Rudolph Nureyev gave three sensational concert performances in Paris (1962). Was Nureyev's partner when he made his U.S. debut in the *Don Quixote* pas de deux at Brooklyn Academy of Music, N.Y., with Ruth Page's Chicago Opera Ballet (Mar. 10, 1962); later danced *Le Corsaire* pas de deux with him in Chicago. Was guest ballerina with the Royal Ballet of England, dancing the full-length *Swan Lake* with Rudolph Nureyev June 25 and July 3, 1962. Première of Job Sander's *The Taming* (with Glen Tetley) at Jacob's Pillow Dance Festival (summer, 1962). Guest ballerina, Australian Ballet (winter season, 1962–63); ballerina National Ballet (Washington, D.C., fall-winter, 1963–65). Guest artist, American Ballet Theatre, N.Y. State Theater (Mar.–Apr., 1965). Married dancer Thor Sutowski in 1965. Currently (1966) ballerina and ballet mistress of Norwegian State Opera Ballet, Oslo.

Arpino, Gerald, contemporary dancer, choreographer, teacher, b. Staten Island, N.Y. Began dance training with Mary Ann Wells in Seattle, Wash., where he was stationed with the Coast Guard (in which he had enlisted when only sixteen during World War II). Studied modern dance with May O'Donnell, appearing with her company during the early 1950's. A leading member of the Robert Joffrey Ballet from its earliest days, he was particularly outstanding as Colin in this company's production of *La Fille Mal Gardée,* and as the blind young man in Francisco Moncion's *Pastorale*. His first two ballets, *Partita for Four* and *Ropes* (1961), are in the Joffrey repertoire; two others—à pas de deux, *Sea Shadow,* and *Incubus*—were added in 1962, and *Palace* in 1963. Co-director of American Ballet Center, school of the Robert Joffrey Ballet, where he teaches when not on tour. Became assistant director of Robert Joffrey Ballet when it was re-formed in 1965 following receipt of a Ford Foundation Grant; continues in that capacity and as principal choreographer of the re-named City Cen-

Gerald Arpino

ter Joffrey Ballet. His ballets presented during 1965–66 were: *Viva Vivaldi!* (mus.: Antonio Vivaldi's Violin Concerto P. 151, arr. by Rodrigo Riera for Guitar and String Orchestra), *Olympics* (comm. score: Toshiro Mayuzumi), and *Nightwings* (mus.: John La Montaine's Birds of Paradise).

Art for Art's Sake, an aesthetic principle propounded by Théophile Gautier, which sets pure art above realism or utility. George Balanchine has been a follower of this doctrine almost since the beginning of his career as choreographer, but had never stated the fact until he gave an interview to a reporter of the Moscow publication *The Soviet Artist* (October, 1962), while the New York City Ballet was appearing in the U.S.S.R. He stated: "I am an adherent of pure art, or art for art's sake."

Arts Council of Canada. See CANADA COUNCIL.

Arts Council of Great Britain, a nonpolitical, typically British adaptation of the usual European Ministry of Fine Arts. It was a development of C.E.M.A. (Council for the Encouragement of Music and the Arts), a wartime organization formed in 1939, as a committee under the chairmanship of Lord Macmillan. Its aims were to assist the active interest in the arts under wartime conditions. Its original fund of £25,000 was provided by the Pilgrim Trust (of which Lord Macmillan was also chairman), a private body operating a fund set up in 1930 by Stephen Harkness the American railway magnate.

The Board of Education provided an office and a secretary and, in Apr. 1940, Parliament recognized C.E.M.A. by offering to match private funds pound for pound up to £50,000. The committee, slightly enlarged, then became the Council, which was formally appointed by the President of the Board of Education. The funds were used to finance drama and ballet performances, orchestral and solo concerts in factory canteens and camps, travelling picture exhibitions, etc. C.E.M.A. was directly responsible for financing certain of these enterprises, e.g. Ballet Rambert. In other instances, e.g. Sadler's Wells (now Royal) Ballet, it merely guaranteed against loss.

It became obvious that the usefulness of such an organization far exceeded its wartime responsibilities. In 1945, it was established as the Arts Council of Great Britain under a Royal Charter which stated, in part, that it was to develop "a greater knowledge, understanding and practice of the fine arts exclusively, and in particular to increase the accessibility of the fine arts to the public . . . to improve the standard of the execution of the fine arts and to advise and co-operate with Government departments and local authorities and other bodies on matters concerned directly or indirectly with these objects."

The Council, its chairman and executive board are disinterested persons all acting voluntarily in a personal capacity and without salary. Appointments for stated terms are made by the Chancellor of the Exchequer. It was under the chairmanship of Lord Keynes, the famous economist, that the switch to Arts Council from C.E.M.A. was made; he took an active part in drafting the charter.

There are four panels of experts in music, drama, the visual arts, and poetry (also unpaid) with a member of the Council as chairman of each panel; these panels make their suggestions to the Council as to the annual administration of grants.

The money comes from the Treasury, and the Chancellor of the Exchequer answers any questions about the work of the Arts Council which may be raised in the House of Commons. At the same time the Council works quite independently of any government restrictions. Its funds are administered with a degree of independence which would not be possible were it actually a government department.

The total amount of grants for all Arts Council beneficiaries for the year 1960–61 was £1,500,000 ($4,200,000) of which the Royal Opera House, Covent Garden, received £495,000 ($1,386,000) for the opera and ballet (there is no breakdown on how this money is divided but it is generally believed that the opera gets a far larger sum). £350,000 ($980,000) went to other opera and ballet activities, these including the opera and ballet at Sadler's Wells Theatre, Ballet Rambert, and Western Theatre Ballet. The Arts Council grant of £1,500,000 costs the British taxpayer 7d. (approx. 7½ cents) a year.

Present chairman is Lord Cottesloe, who succeeded Sir Kenneth Clark, one of the original C.E.M.A. committee members, in 1960; present Secretary General is Nigel Abercrombie.

Arts Council of New York. See NEW YORK STATE COUNCIL ON THE ARTS.

As I Lay Dying. Modern dance work; chor.: Valerie Bettis; music: Bernardo Segall; costumes: Kim Swados; properties: Eddie Light. First prod.: Valerie Bettis and group, presented by Choreographers' Workshop, Hunter College Playhouse, N.Y., Dec 19, 1948, with Valerie Bettis (Addie Bundren), Beverly Bozeman (Dewey Dell), J. C. McCord (Darl), Boris Runanin (Lafe), Richard Reed, Duncan Noble, and others. An adaptation of parts of the William Faulkner novel, with flash-back episodes of Addie's romance with Lafe, and spoken passages from the book to link the narrative.

Asafiev, Boris (1884–1949), Russian composer and musicologist. He wrote a number of ballets, among them *The Flames of Paris* and *Lost Illusions* (1932), *The Fountain of Bakhchisarai* (1934) and *The Prisoner of the Caucasus* (1938). Asafiev wrote on music under the pen name Igor Glebov.

Ashbridge, Bryan, New Zealand dancer, b. Wellington, 1927; m. Dorothea Zaymes. Studied in Wellington and, from 1939, in Sydney under Helene Kirsova and Edouard Borovansky. Won the Adeline Genée Gold Medal for Male Dancers. Entered Sadler's Wells School (1947); danced in film *The Red Shoes* (1948); joined Sadler's Wells (now Royal) Ballet same year, becoming soloist (1954), principal dancer (1958). His roles included Siegfried (*Swan Lake*), Florimund (*The Sleeping Beauty*), Albrecht (*Giselle*), Orion (*Sylvia*), Prince (*Cinderella*), *Don Quixote* pas de deux. Guest artist (with Beryl Grey) in Romania, Munich, Oslo; (with Svetlana Beriosova) in Finland, India, Australia. Travelled in Australia with Margot Fonteyn Concert Ballet (1962).

Ashton, Sir Frederick, choreographer, dancer, director of Royal Ballet, b. Guayaquil, Ecuador, 1906, of English parentage. Educated in Lima, Peru, and Dover College, England. His interest in the dance began when he saw Anna Pavlova in Lima when he was fourteen, and was intensified a few years later when he saw the Diaghilev Ballets Russes in England. After leaving school he worked for about a year and a half as foreign correspondent for an export merchant in London. In 1924 he began to study dance, first with Leonide Massine and later with Marie Rambert who encouraged him to try to choreograph ballets. His first attempt, *A Tragedy of Fashion,* was presented in a revue, *Riverside Nights,* at the Lyric Theatre, Hammersmith (1926). After spending a year as a member of Ida Rubinstein's company, he returned to Rambert and choreographed many ballets for the Ballet Club (later Ballet Rambert) and also for the Camargo Society. These included *Les Petits Riens, Leda and the Swan,* (1928), *Capriol Suite, The Tartans, Passionate Pavane,* (1930), *Mercury, Lady of Shalott, La Péri* (1931), *Foyer de Danse, Récamier* (1932), *Les Masques,* (1933), *Mephisto Valse* (1934), *Valentine's Eve* (1935) and others, for Ballet Club; *Pomona* (1930), *Façade, The Lord of Burleigh* (1931), *A Day in a Southern Port* (1932; revived as *Rio Grande* for Vic-Wells Ballet, 1935), and others for Camargo Society. He also danced in *Les Sylphides, Swan Lake,* Act 2 (Siegfried), *Carnaval* (Pierrot), in some of his own ballets and in Andrée Howard's *Cinderella* (Prince), Ninette de Valois' *Bar aux Folies-Bergère* (Wainter), among others. Guest artist with Vic-Wells Ballet during most of this period; choreographed *Les Rendez-Vous* for this company (1933). Choreographed Gertrude Stein's *Four Saints in Three Acts* (N.Y., 1933–34). Became permanent member of the Vic-Wells company in 1935 and since then has been chief choreographer of the company that became, successively, Sadler's Wells and now Royal Ballet. Between 1935 and 1939 he choreographed *Le Baiser de la Fée, Nocturne, Apparitions, A Wedding Bouquet, Les Patineurs, Horoscope, The Wise Virgins, Harlequin in the Street, Cupid and Psyche; Dante Sonata* and *The Wanderer* belong to the early war years. While serving as interpreter with the Royal Air Force during World War II, he was granted special leave of absence to create *The Quest.*

Sir Frederick Ashton, choreographer, director, Royal Ballet

He also staged *Façade* adding several numbers and dancing the Gigolo; other dancing roles included The Red King (*Checkmate*), Monsieur Noverre—creation (*The Prospect Before Us*), etc. After the company's move to the Royal Opera House, Covent Garden (1946), he choreographed *Symphonic Variations, Les Sirènes, Scènes de Ballet, Don Juan, Cinderella* (the first full-length ballet by a British choreographer), *Daphnis and Chloe, Tiresias, Sylvia* (also a full-length ballet), *Homage to the Queen* (celebrating the Coronation of H. M. Queen Elizabeth II, 1953), *Rinaldo and Armida, Madame Chrysanthème, Birthday Offering* (for the Gala Performance marking the 25th Anniversary of the company, 1956); *Ondine* (3 acts), *La Fille Mal Gardée* (3 acts), *The Two Pigeons* (2 acts), *Persephone, Marguerite and Armand.* For other companies he has created *Devil's Holiday* (Ballet Russe de Monte Carlo, 1939); *Valses Nobles et Sentimentales* (Sadler's Wells Theatre

Ballet, 1947); Vision of Marguerite (London's Festival Ballet); *Illuminations* and *Picnic at Tintagel* (New York City Ballet); *Romeo and Juliet* (Royal Danish Ballet); *La Valse* (Teatro alla Scalla, Milan). Staged the operas *Manon* (1947) and *Orfeo ed Euridice* (1953), Royal Opera House, Covent Garden. Has also created various soli and pas de deux for gala performances. Choreographer for *A Midsummer Night's Dream* (Old Vic, 1954) and for the film, *The Tales of Hoffmann* (1951), in which he also appeared as *Cochenille.* He created the Elder Ugly Sister in his own *Cinderella* and gave a classic mimetic performance as Carabosse (*The Sleeping Beauty*). An associate director of the Royal Ballet for many years, he took over the position of director on Dame Ninette de Valois' retirement in 1963. Since assuming that position, his duties have inhibited his creative activities, but he has re-staged and partly re-choreographed *Swan Lake* in collaboration with Robert Helpmann and staged *The Dream.* This last was created as part of the special Shakespeare Quatercentenary program presented by the Royal Ballet Apr. 2, 1964, the other two ballets being Kenneth MacMillan's *Images of Love* and Robert Helpmann's *Hamlet.* Another composition is a pas de trois, *Monotones,* to Erik Satie's *Trois Gymnopedies,* for the Royal Ballet Benevolent Fund Gala (1965). Vyvyan Lorayne, Anthony Dowell, and Robert Mead danced the last named. It is Ashton's choreography and his strong classic feeling which, more than any other factors, have developed the Royal Ballet style with its lightness, precision, and lyric qualities. He is noted particularly for his mastery of the art of pas de deux which, in many of his ballets, becomes the equivalent of a love duet. For his services to British ballet he was created C.B.E. (Commander of the Order of the British Empire) in 1950, and knighted in the order of Knights Bachelor (K.B.) in 1962. He has the Légion d'Honneur, and in 1959 received the Royal Academy of Dancing Queen Elizabeth II Coronation Award.

Assemblé, in ballet, a jump which is completed with both feet together, usually in 5th pos. Technique: Assemblé Dessus: start 5th pos., R ft. in back; slide R ft. to side and raise it to demi-seconde, at same time plié on L; jump off L ft., straightening both knees in air and pointing feet downward; land in 5th pos. demi-plié, R ft. front. Assemblé can also be done front, back, dessous, soutenu, en tournant, etc.

Assembly Ball. Ballet in 1 act, four movements; chor. and décor: Andrée Howard; music: Georges Bizet's Symphony in C. First prod.: Sadler's Wells Theatre Ballet, Sadler's Wells Theatre, Apr. 8, 1946, with June Brae, Leo Kersley, Claude Newman heading the cast. Themeless, but the idea of a ball gives the choreographer a chance to hint at attractions and romances, while strongly marked Scottish rhythms in the 3rd movement are echoed in the choreography. Svetlana Beriosova and David Blair later danced the Brae and Kersley roles very successfully. This ballet preceded George Balanchine's *Symphony in C* by just over a year.

Astafieva, Serafima (1876–1934), Russian dancer and teacher. She was graduated from the St. Petersburg Imperial School of Ballet (1895) into the corps de ballet of the Maryinsky Theatre. In 1896 she married Joseph Kchessinsky-Nechui, older brother of ballerina Mathilde Kchessinska. They were divorced in 1905; she resigned from the Theatre the same year. In 1909–11 she was a member of the Diaghilev Ballets Russes, after which she opened a ballet school in London where Alicia Markova and Anton Dolin, among other dancers, received professional training. Margot Fonteyn was also her pupil.

Astaire, Adele (Adele Austerlitz), actress and dancer, b. Omaha, Neb., 1898. First appeared at age eight in a brother and sister act with her brother Fred Astaire. The two continued in vaudeville until they made their successful debut in the Broadway musical *Over the Top* (1916), followed by many others, including *Apple Blossoms, Lady Be Good, For Goodness Sake, Smiles.* In 1932 she married Lord Charles Arthur Francis Cavendish, left the stage and went to live in England. After the death of Lord Cavendish she married Kingman Douglass (1947).

Astaire, Fred (Frederick Austerlitz), dancer and actor, b. Omaha, Neb., 1899. Began to study dance at age five and, with his sister Adele Astaire, appeared in a vaudeville act at seven; began to study tap dancing at eight in N.Y. After nine years on vaudeville circuits, Fred and Adele Astaire made their Broadway debut in the musical Over the Top (1916), followed by *Passing Show of 1916, Apple Blossoms, For Goodness Sake, Lady Be Good* (also in London), *Funny Face* (also in London), *Smiles* and *The Band Wagon* among others. In 1932 Adele married and left the stage. Fred carried on alone successfully in *The Gay Divorcee* (N.Y. and London) and in films. His first picture was *Dancing Lady* with Joan Crawford, followed by *Flying Down to Rio* with Ginger Rogers, which established them as the most successful dance team (probably of all time) in films. Their films included *The Gay Divorcee, Roberta, Top Hat, Follow the Fleet, Swing Time, Shall We Dance?, Carefree, The Story of Vernon and Irene Castle,* and (after going their separate ways for several years) *The Barclays of Broadway*. He made pictures with a number of other partners, best known of whom were Eleanor Powell and Rita Hayworth. He made one of the all-time musical successes, Easter Parade, with Judy Garland. He planned to retire after 1946 but has made occasional films since then, including *Funny Face* with Audrey Hepburn and *On the Beach,* in which he played a serious role. His annual television spectacular "An Evening With Fred Astaire," is always an event. Since 1947 he has given his name to a chain of dance studios.

Astruc (Gabriel)—Diaghilev Archives, an integral part of the Dance Collection of the New York Public Library, acquired in 1959 with the assistance of the Committee for the Dance Collection. It includes more than 1,300 documents relating to the formation and early years of the Diaghilev Russian Opera and Ballet in Paris (1907–1913). This manuscript collection of letters, telegrams, contracts, and other papers, such as production notes, casting and salary schedules, offers detailed information concerning the policy and intimate financial and administrative activities of the company. These were the working files of Gabriel Astruc, impresario who managed the Diaghilev activities. Among those represented by correspondence in the collection are Serge Diaghilev, Baron Dmitri Günzburg, Comtesse de Greffulhe, Claude Debussy, Vaslav Nijinsky, Anna Pavlova, Igor Stravinsky, Renaldo Hahn, Pierre Monteux, Ida Rubinstein, Michel Fokine, Tamara Karsavina, and Feodor Chaliapine.

Atanasoff, Cyril (Cyrille-Ivan Atanasoff), French dancer, b. Puteaux-Seine, 1941; m. Claire Motte. Dance training at Paris Opéra School (1953–57), entering the corps de ballet; when only sixteen, was promoted to coryphé. Was nominated premier danseur at age twenty; became étoile (Jan., 1964). Dances one of the leading male roles in Harald Lander's *Etudes,* pas de quatre in first act of Vladimir Bourmeister's *Swan Lake,* George Skibine's *Danses Brèves* at Opéra Comique, etc. Was one of the Paris Opéra dancers who appeared at Jacob's Pillow (1963).

Atavisms. Suite of three modern group

dances; chor. and costumes: Charles Weidman; commissioned music: Lehman Engel. First prod.: Guild Theatre, N.Y., Jan. 26, 1936. Charles Weidman was the floorwalker unable to cope with the hordes of bargain seekers in *Bargain Counter;* a tycoon in *Stock Exchange,* collapsing and bringing everyone else down with him as Wall Street crashed; and the victim of blood lust in *Lynch Town,* the most substantial work of the three which remained in his repertoire long after the other two had been dropped.

À Terre. See PAR TERRE.

Attitude, in ballet, a pose wherein one leg is raised in back, well-bent at the knee. Usually the same arm as leg is raised. In front attitude the working leg is raised in front, knee slightly bent, opposite arm raised. This pose is supposed to have been invented by Carlo Blasis, who was inspired by the statue of Mercury by Giovanni Bologna. In the Italian style attitude, the knee at the back must be higher than the foot. The Soviet style attitude brings the leg up much higher, with the foot higher than the knee; in its most exaggerated form it resembles an arabesque in which the dancer has not properly straightened her leg.

Auber, François (1782–1871), French composer. He wrote the scores for *Le Dieu et la Bayadère* (Filippo Taglioni, 1830), *Marco Spado* (Joseph Mazilier, 1857), for various operas, etc. The music of his *L'Enfant Prodigue* was arranged by Constant Lambert for *Les Rendezvous* (Frederick Ashton, 1937); selections from his music were also used by Ruthanna Boris for *Quelques Fleurs* (1948).

Augusta, Mlle. (Caroline Augusta Josephine Thérèse Fuchs, Comtesse de Saint-James, 1806–1901), French dancer. She had the greatest successes of her career in the U.S. where she made her debut in *Les Naïades* danced *La Bayadère* (1836). She was first to dance *Giselle* in N.Y. on Feb. 2, 1846, a month after Mary Ann Lee danced the ballet for the first time in the U.S. (in Boston). *La Sylphide,* which she danced in an adapted version in N.Y. (1838), was another successful ballet in her repertoire, as was *La Muette de Portici.*

Auld, John, Australian dancer, b. Melbourne, 1920. Studied with Xenia Borovansky, Marie Rambert, Olga Preobrajenska. Joined Borovansky Ballet (1950, with further seasons 1953 and 1957). Principal dancer in the musical *Paint Your Wagon* (London, 1952); danced in British television (1956–58). Principal dancer, *Lola Montez* (Australia, 1958). Returned to England (1959), dancing in television and appearing with Bristol Old Vic, Windsor Repertory Theatre. With Nora Kaye's and Herbert Ross' Ballet of Two Worlds (1960). Joined London's Festival Ballet (1961). Roles include Dr. Coppelius (*Coppélia*), Preacher (*The Witch Boy*), Showman (*Petrouchka*), Button Moulder (*Peer Gynt*).

Aureole. Modern dance work, chor.: Paul Taylor; music: George Frederick Handel: Concerto Grosso in C (4th movement *Alexander's Feast*); 3rd movement Concerto Grosso in F op. 6, No. 9, Symphony; *Sinfonia Jephthah*). First prod.: Paul Taylor Dance Company, Fifteenth American Dance Festival, Connecticut College, New London, Aug. 4, 1962, with Paul Taylor, Elizabeth Walton, Dan Wagoner, Sharon Kinney, and Renee Kimball. A "white" abstract dance work in modern idiom.

Auric, Georges, French composer, b. Montpellier, 1899. Member of "Les Six." Participated in the composition of the music for *Les Mariés de la Tour Eiffel* for Les Ballets Suédois (1921). The other composers were Arthur Honegger, Darius Milhaud, Francis Poulenc, Germaine Tailleferre. It was a satirical ballet about the middle class Sunday crowd visiting the Eiffel Tower and its environs. For the Diaghilev Ballets Russes Auric composed *Les Facheux* (1924), *Les Matelots* (1925), *Pastorale* (1926); for Ballets Russes de Monte Carlo, *Concurrence* (1932), for Ballets des Champs Elysées, *Le Peintre et son Modèle* (1948); for Paris Opéra, *Phèdre* (1950); for Munich Opera and later Paris Opéra, *Chemin de Lumière* (1957); for England's Royal Ballet, *Le Bal des Voleurs* (1963). Appointed General Administrator of the National Lyric Theatres (Paris Opéra and Opéra Comique), succeeding A. M. Julien (1962).

Aurora's Wedding. See THE SLEEPING BEAUTY.

Australia, Ballet in.

Ballet began to exist in Australia on a permanent basis when Hélène Kirsova settled there after the 1936–37 season of the Ballet Russe de Monte Carlo, in which she had been a soloist. She opened a school in Sydney (1940) and formed a small company made up of her pupils with herself as ballerina. The Kirsova Ballet gave its first professional season in July, 1941, and was so successful that it grew from a group of sixteen to a company of thirty-five dancers, including former soloists of the Ballet Russe Tamara Tchinarova, Valery Shaievsky, and Edouard Sobishevsky. Later the company toured the Australian capital cities with *Les Sylphides, Swan Lake, Les Matelots,* and some of Kirsova's own ballets. During World War II most of the male dancers left to join the army. The company was disbanded and Kirsova returned to Europe (1946). In 1939 Edouard Borovansky, a soloist of Ballet Russe de Monte Carlo who had remained when the company changed its name to Original Ballet Russe, decided to stay in Australia when that company toured there. He and his wife Xenia Nikolaeva opened a school in Melbourne. This school was backed by the Melbourne Ballet Club, which organized a small studio theatre. In 1940 Borovansky produced ballets at the Melbourne Princess Theatre. Each year he and his pupils gave longer seasons, presenting new ballets and some from the classic repertoire. Two of his dancers, Laurel Martyn and Dorothy Stevenson, choreographed for the company as did Borovansky himself. In 1944, with Tamara Tchinarova as ballerina, the troupe became a professional company instead of a group of people with outside jobs who could devote only their evenings to classes and rehearsals. At this time, under the management of J. C. Williamson, Ltd., it made its first tour of Australia and later of New Zealand. This was followed by a number of other tours separated by months, sometimes years, during which the company was in abeyance because the population of Australia, mainly centered in less than half-a-dozen large towns, could not support year-long seasons. The repertoire included ballets by Borovansky, Martyn, and Stevenson, with *Giselle, Le Beau Danube, Carnaval, Coppélia* (2 acts), Les Sylphides, Swan Lake, etc. After the Borovansky Ballet became a professional company, the Melbourne Ballet Club, changing its name to Ballet Guild, revived its activities and engaged Laurel Martyn to form a small company (1946), augmented by members of the Ballet Guild, to give performances of new works and establish a school.

Since 1948 the Australian ballet scene has changed. After every tour by overseas companies, especially Ballet Rambert and Royal Ballet, dancers of repute have decided to stay in Australia or New Zealand and have founded schools or in other ways helped the cause of ballet. The Borovansky Ballet continued to give seasons and, after one of its long periods of inactivity, was on the eve of beginning another tour when Borovansky died suddenly (Dec., 1959). However, it was possible to obtain the services of Peggy van Praagh as artistic director and the season was given. Increasing costs necessitated the disbandment of the company in 1960. Shortly afterwards there took place what may well prove to be the most significant event in the development of ballet in Australia: the establishment of the Australian Ballet Foundation by Dr. H. C. Coombs, Sir Frank Tait, and other directors of the Australian Elizabethan Theatre Trust, and J. C. Williamson Theatres, Ltd. In 1962 it engaged Peggy van Praagh as artistic director of a new company, The Australian Ballet, founded on the old Borovansky Ballet with the addition of young dancers trained in Australia, and guest artists from major European and American companies. Ray Powell, of the Royal Ballet, was engaged for the 1962–63 season as balletmaster. The initial 28-week tour began Nov. 2 in Sydney. Sonia Arova and Erik Bruhn, Soviet dancers Tatiana Zimina and Nikita Dolgushin, and Jonathan Watts were guest artists for varying periods. Caj Selling of the Royal Swedish Ballet was with the company for the entire first season, as was Harcourt Algeranoff; Kathleen Gorham, Marilyn Jones, and Garth Welch headed the regular roster. The ballets presented during this 1962–63 season included the full-length *Swan Lake* and *Coppélia, Les Sylphides, Don Quixote* pas de deux, Frederick Ashton's *Les Rendez-Vous,* John Cranko's *The Lady and the Fool;* Ray Powell's *One in Five* and *Just for Fun* (staged for this company), and *The Night is a Sorceress* and *Melbourne Cup,* both by the Australian choreographer Rex Reid. Among the people taking an active interest in this company or teaching in Australia are Xenia Borovanska, Laurel Martyn, Sally Glimour, Margaret Scott; also Peggy Sager and Paul Hammond, both former members of the Borovansky Ballet. In 1965 the company toured in Europe for the first time, making its debut at the Baalbek Festival, Lebanon (Aug. 12). Further appearances were made in Nice, at the International Dance Festival at the Théâtre des Champs-Elysées (Paris), and in London, Liverpool, Glasgow, and Cardiff (as part of the Commonwealth Art Festival of Great Britain). For this tour Rudolf Nureyev staged *Raymonda* and Robert Helpmann choreographed *The Display* and *Yugen,* both on Australian themes. The latter remained with the company as co-artistic director with Peggy van Praagh.

Autumn Leaves. Ballet in 1 act; chor. and book: Anna Pavlova; music: piano pieces by Frédéric Chopin, principally his Nocturne in D flat major and the middle section of the Fantaisie Impromptu; décor: Konstantin Korovin. First prod.: Rio de Janeiro, Brazil, 1918, with Pavlova, Alexandre Volinine, and Hubert Stowitts. Pavlova was particularly fond of this ballet which, except for an occasional divertissement, was her only achievement as choreographer. The naïve plot tells of a Poet struggling against an Autumn Wind which uproots a Chrysanthemum (Pavlova) and flings her around among falling leaves; the Chrysanthemum expires as the sun sets. The Poet tries to revive her but fails, and finally, with his betrothed departs as the curtain falls.

Aveline, Albert, French dancer, ballet master, teacher, b. Paris, 1883. Entered the Paris Opéra (1894), becoming premier danseur étoile and ballet master (1917). Was partner of Carlotta Zambelli and, in 1924, of Olga Spessivtzeva. Danced most of the principal roles in the repertoire of his period. Choreographed *La Grisi* (1935), *Jeux d'Enfants, Elvire* (1937), *La Grand Jatte* (1950), *Les Santons,* among others. Was director of the opéra ballet school. Is now retired.

Axial Movement, movement around an axis, as arm movement around an individual body; or movement of one group of dancers around another group, or individual, as axis.

Babilée, Jean, French dancer and choreographer, b. Paris, 1923; m. Nathalie Philippart. Had his dance training at the Paris Opéra under Gustave Ricaux. During World War II went to south of France and had success dancing with local Monte Carlo and Cannes companies. Returned to Paris Opéra briefly and then left to join the Resistance Army. First major success was with Roland Petit's Ballets des Champs-Elysées (1945), creating the Joker in *Jeu de Cartes* and dancing in *Le Spectre de la Rose* and *Blue Bird* pas de deux. The role of his life, *Le Jeune Homme et la Mort* (Jean Cocteau-Petit-Georges Wakhevitch), came in 1946; also toured Europe with the company. His first attempt at choreography was *L'Amour et son Amour* (1948), followed by *Til Eulenspiegel* (1949). When the company disbanded, he became guest star with Grand Ballet du Marquis de Cuevas (1950). Danced a single season with Paris Opéra (1953), dancing one performance of *Giselle* and creating *Hop Frog* (Harald Lander). Guest artist at La Scala, Milan, creating *Mario et la Mage* (Leonide Massine, 1956). Formed his own company, Les Ballets Babilée, with a season at the Champs-Elysées Theatre (1956), his own ballets including *Sable, Cameleopard,* and *Balance à Trois,* first given in Monte Carlo in 1955. Other ballets include *La Boucle, Divertimento.* Toured with his company in Europe, Israel, Brazil, etc. Was guest artist with American

Jean Babilée, French dancer, choreographer

Ballet Theatre in U.S. for two seasons, staging *Til Eulenspiegel* for the company. Has acted in motion pictures and on Paris stage in Tennessee Williams' *Orpheus Descending*. Assumed the leading role in the musical show *The Green Queen*, written and staged by Maurice Béjart, in Paris (1963).

Baby Ballerinas, the appellation given to the three young ballerinas, Irina Baronova, Tatiana Riabouchinska, and Tamara Toumanova, who headed the Ballets Russes de Monte Carlo in 1932. Baronova was then thirteen, Riabouchinska fifteen, and Toumanova fourteen. Although the appellation was originally a publicity expedient on the part of the director, Col. de Basil, at a time when the Ballets Russes de Monte Carlo had no box office names, these dancers were true prodigies. Unfortunately their success gave rise to an entirely false impression regarding the merits of sheer youth as apart from talent. This had an adverse effect on ballet in the West for nearly twenty years.

Baccelli, Giovanna (Zanerini), Italian ballerina, b. Venice, ca. 1753, d. London, 1801. Spent most of her career in London and Paris, making her London debut in the King's Theatre, Haymarket, Nov. 19, 1774, in the role of Rose in Jean Lany's *Le Ballet des Fleurs* (probably an entrée in Rameau's opera-ballet *Les Indes Galantes*). Her fame rested as much on her talent as ballerina as on the fact that she was the mistress of the third Duke of Dorset and, after some fifteen years, of the Earl of Pembroke. During her career she danced with Gaetan Vestris and Charles Le Picq. Sir Joshua Reynolds painted Baccelli as a bacchante and Thomas Gainsborough did a full length portrait of her which was included in the Royal Academy exhibition of 1782. For a full account of Baccelli's career see "The Italian Lady of Knole," by Ivor Guest in *The Ballet Annual,* No. 11 (London, 1957).

Bacchanale. Ballet in 1 act; chor.: Leonide Massine; music: Richard Wagner; book and décor: Salvador Dali. First prod.: Ballet Russe de Monte Carlo, Metropolitan Opera House, N.Y., Nov. 9, 1939, with Nathalie Krassovska, Jeanette Lauret, Milada Mladova, Nini Theilade, André Eglevsky, Casimir Kokitch, Marc Platoff, and Christ Volkoff in principal parts. Set to the *Tannhäuser* Bacchanale, it was described by Dali as a "paranoic ballet" and depicted the nightmares of the mad Ludwig II of Bavaria.

Bachiana No. 1. Ballet in 1 act; chor.: Maryla Gremo; music: Heitor Villa-Lobos of the same title; décor: Fernando Pamplona. First prod.: Teatro Municipal, Rio de Janeiro, Brazil, 1954, with Tatiana Leskova, Arthur Ferreira, and Dennis Gray in the principal roles. Life in the camps of the "retirantes"—people who leave their land and homes in the Brazilian Northeast, forced out by the drought. Life is grim during the day, but at night the children sing and dance. The next morning the "retirantes" continue their exodus.

Bailey, Sally, American ballerina, b. Oakland, Calif., 1932. Studied principally with the San Francisco Ballet School, of which she considers herself a product. In 1955 took a three-month leave to study privately with Vera Volkova at the Royal Theatre, Copenhagen, and to take classes with Olga Preobrajenska, Lubov Egorova and Mme. Rousanne in Paris. Became ballerina of the San Francisco Ballet with her first performance of Odette-Odile in *Swan Lake* (1951). Premièred the role of Amazon Captain in *Con Amore* with the New York City Ballet. Toured with San Francisco company under the auspices of the U.S. Department of State Cultural Exchange Program in the Far East (1956), Latin America (1958), Middle East (1959), including command performances before the King and Queen of Greece and Emperor Haile Selassie of

Sally Bailey, ballerina, San Francisco Ballet

Ethiopia, receiving from the latter a gold medal. Currently prima ballerina of the San Francisco Ballet.

Baiser de la Fée, Le. Ballet in 1 act, 4 scenes; chor.: George Balanchine; music and book: Igor Stravinsky (the score, based on Tchaikovsky themes was Stravinsky's "Homage" to the composer); décor: Alice Halicka. First prod.: American Ballet, Metropolitan Opera House, N.Y., Apr. 27, 1937, with Gisella Caccialanza (Girl), William Dollar (Bridegroom), Kathryn Mullowny (Fairy), Leda Anchutina (Friend), Annabelle Lyon (Mother); revived for Ballet Russe de Monte Carlo at Metropolitan Opera House, N.Y., Apr. 10, 1940, with Alexandra Danilova (Bride), André Eglevsky (Bridegroom), Nini Theilade (Mother); again revived by the same company at City Center, N.Y., Feb. 17, 1946, with Danilova, Frederic Franklin (Bridegroom), Maria Tallchief (Fairy), Marie Jeanne (Friend and Mother); also staged by Balanchine for Paris Opéra Ballet (summer, 1948). A considerably revised version was staged by New York City Ballet at City Center, N.Y., Nov. 28, 1950, with Tanaquil LeClercq (Bride), Maria Tallchief (Fairy), Nicholas Magallanes (Bridegroom), Patricia Wilde (Friend), Beatrice Tompkins (Mother). Freely based on Hans Christian Andersen's *The Ice Maiden,* the ballet tells of the Fairy who saves the life of a baby, lost with its mother in a snowstorm. Because she kissed the child, the Fairy may claim him for herself at any time she chooses, and on the day of his wedding she comes for him and leads him away to her own land of immortality. The first production of *Le Baiser de la Fée* was choreographed by Bronislava Nijinska, with décor by Alexandre Benois for the Ida Rubinstein company, Paris Opéra, Nov. 27, 1928. Frederick Ashton's version for Sadler's Wells (now Royal) Ballet at Sadler's Wells Theatre, Nov. 26, 1935 had décor by Sophie Fedorovitch and had Margot Fonteyn as the Bride, (her first-created ballerina role), Pearl Argyle as the Fairy, and Harold Turner as the Bridegroom. Kenneth MacMillan staged his version for the Royal Ballet, with décor by Kenneth Rowell at Royal Opera House, Covent Garden, London, Apr. 12, 1960, with Svetlana Beriosova (the Fairy), Lynn Seymour (the Bride), Donald Macleary (the Bridegroom). As with Fonteyn before her, this was Lynn Seymour's first important created role.

Baker, Josephine, American dancer, b. St. Louis, Mo., 1906. Began her career as chorus girl in a colored revue. Went to Paris with a colored show (1924) and remained there, except for occasional trips to U.S., until the fall of France during World War II, when she left for North Africa. Danced at the Folies-Bergère and night clubs in Paris. Studied ballet with George Balanchine, who later choreographed dances for her. Appeared in *Ziegfeld Follies,* N.Y., co-starring with Harriet Hoctor (1936). Currently living in southwest France where she supports an orphanage. Gave hugely successful benefit performances in Carnegie Hall, N.Y. (Oct. 12) and Philadelphia (Oct. 18, 1963).

Bakhrushin, Yuri, Soviet ballet historian, b. 1898. Son of Alexei Bakhrushin (1865–1929), founder of Bakhrushin Theatre Museum, Moscow. He began writing on ballet in 1918 and his first published article was on Avdotia Istomina, Russian ballerina of the early 19th century mentioned by Alexander Pushkin in his *Eugen Onegin.* Was director and chief of repertoire of the Stanislavsky-Nemirovich-Danchenko Lyric Theatre (1924–39). Collaborated with Karl Waltz, master of scenic illusion and former chief mechanic of the Bolshoi Theatre, on the book *Sixty-Five Years in the Theatre* (1928). Published a fundamental work, "Tchaikovsky's Ballets and Their Stage History," in *Tchaikovsky and the Theatre Almanach* (1940). Author of a biography of Alexander Gorsky (Moscow, 1946); also wrote section on ballet in the *Bolshoi Theatre Almanach* (1947). Author (in Russian) of many articles on the history of Russian ballet and of the book *History of Russian Ballet* (1965), used in state ballet schools of U.S.S.R. Since 1942 has taught history of ballet at Bolshoi School; also lectures on ballet and acts as advisor at Bakhrushin Museum.

Yuri Bakhrushin (Courtesy Mrs. Carolyn Parks)

Bakst, Léon (1866–1924), Russian painter, b. Grodno, Russia. Co-founder with Serge Diaghilev and Alexandre Benois of the society The World of Art, which launched the Diaghilev Ballets Russes. His first ballet décor was done for *The Fairy Doll* (1902), for the Maryinsky Theatre. Member of the Diaghilev organization from its inception; left Russia with the company in 1909, never to return. His greatest works include: *Cléopâtre, Carnaval, Le Spectre de la Rose, Schéhérazade, Thamar, Daphnis and Chloé, The Legend of Joseph, L'Après-Midi d'un Faune, The Good-Humored Ladies, The Sleeping Beauty*—all for the Diaghilev company.

Bal, Le. Ballet in 1 act, 2 scenes; chor.: George Balanchine; commissioned music: Vittorio Rieti; book: Boris Kochno; décor: Giorgio de Chirico. First prod.: Diaghilev Ballets Russes, Monte Carlo, July 5, 1929, with Alexandra Danilova, Alice Nikitina, Lydia Sokolova, Anton Dolin, Serge Lifar. Typical of the final period of the Diaghilev ballet in which the choreography took second place to décor, *Le Bal* has an importance as the final creation of the Diaghilev Ballets Russes. It is a divertissement in which a masked ball is the excuse for a series of entries: Spanish Entry, Italian Entry, pas de deux of lovers, etc. The unmasking at the end shows that the lovely young girl who has enticed the young man is really a raddled old woman—except that this is only another mask. Leonide Massine presented his version of the ballet for

Col. de Basil's Ballet Russe de Monte Carlo (1935), but it was given only a few times. Another version, with choreography by Kurt Jooss and décor by Hein Heckroth, was presented by Jooss Ballets in Essen (1930).

Bal des Blanchisseuses, Le. Ballet in 1 act; chor.: Roland Petit; commissioned music: Vernon Duke; book: Boris Kochno; décor: Stanislas Lepri. First prod.: Ballets des Champs-Elysées, Paris, Dec. 19, 1946, with a cast including Danielle Darmance and Roland Petit. A young apprentice leaves his work to follow a street musician playing a clarinet. He is surrounded by pretty young laundresses (and some not so pretty) and an impromptu ball develops in the street.

Balaban, Emanuel, conductor, b. Brooklyn, N.Y., 1895. Studied in U.S. and Germany. Former conductor, Dresden and Berlin Philharmonic Orchestras and American Opera Company; assistant conductor, Dresden Opera; former head of Opera Depart., Eastman School of Music, Rochester, N.Y.; Musical Director, American Ballet Caravan (South American tour, 1941); Ballet Russe de Monte Carlo (1944–46). Currently conducting symphony orchestras in U.S.

Balakirev, Mily Alexeivich (1837–1910), Russian composer, pianist, conductor. His symphonic poem *Thamar* Michel Fokine used for his ballet of the same name (1912).

Balancé, in ballet, a step performed in place, usually in 3/4 time; a balancing step. Technique: start in 5th pos. R ft. front; step forward on R ft.; bring L ft. behind R in 5th pos. in demi-pointe, rising on R demi-pointe at same time; sink onto R heel. Balancé may also be done back, to the side, en tournant, etc.

Balanchine, George, choreographer, b. Georgi Melitonovitch Balanchivadze, Jan. 9, 1904, in St. Petersburg, Russia. Entered the Imperial School of Ballet at the age of ten; when he graduated in 1921 that institution had already changed its name to the Soviet State School of Ballet.

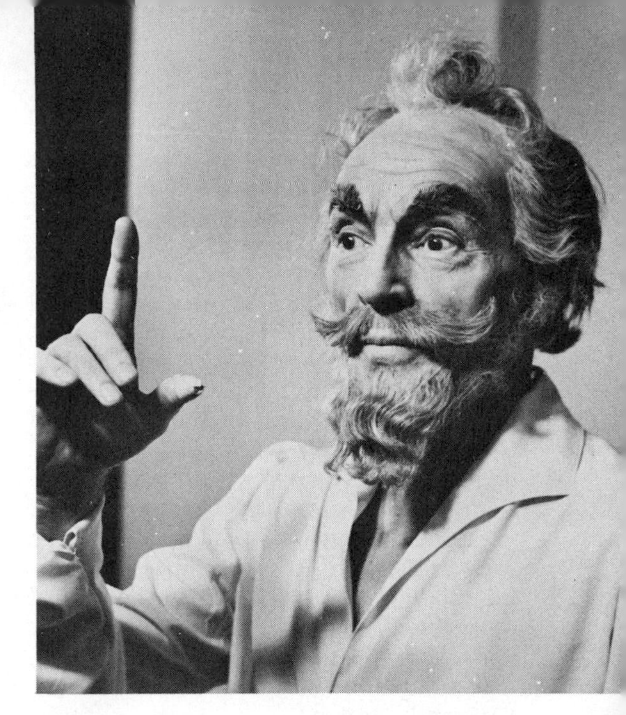

George Balanchine as Don Quixote

The son of the Georgian composer Meliton Balanchivadze, Balanchine studied piano and composition at the Petrograd Conservatory of Music. He soon demonstrated that he was a would-be revolutionary in ballet. His initial work in choreography was with a group of dancers who banded together in 1923 to organize Evenings of Young Ballet in Petrograd. These Evenings were too advanced for Russian spectators.

Then Balanchine, together with Alexandra Danilova, Tamara Geva, and two other dancers, sought permission to tour Germany under the name Soviet State Dancers. After many efforts permission was granted and the troupe left Russia in the spring of 1924. Following a tour of German spas, the company gave a performance in Paris that was seen by Serge Diaghilev, who engaged Danilova, Geva, and Balanchine for his company.

During his four years with Diaghilev, Balanchine choreographed *Barabau, La*

Pastorale (1925), *Jack in the Box, The Triumph of Neptune, The Nightingale* (1926), *La Chatte* (1927), *Apollon Musagète, The Gods Go A-Begging* (1928), *Le Fils Prodigue,* and *Le Bal* (1929).

Three years after Diaghilev's death and the disbanding of his company (1929), Balanchine was the first choreographer to be invited to join the new Ballets Russes de Monte Carlo of René Blum and Col. W. de Basil. For this company he staged *La Concurrence, Cotillon,* and *Le Bourgeois Gentilhomme.* His association with the Ballets Russes lasted only one season. He left it to organize his own Les Ballets 1933, for which he staged *Mozartiana, Errante, Songes, Les Sept Péchés Capitaux* (*The Seven Deadly Sins*). The company disbanded after seasons in Paris and London.

Toward the end of that year Balanchine and Vladimir Dimitriew received an invitation from Lincoln Kirstein and Edward M. M. Warburg to organize the School of American Ballet and the American Ballet Company. For this company Balanchine revived some of his previous works and choreographed new ones including *Alma Mater, Serenade, Baiser de la Fée,* and *Card Party.* In the spring of 1941 he staged two ballets for the American Ballet Caravan's (which see) South American tour, *Concerto Barocco* and *Ballet Imperial.*

In Jan. 1941, he produced for the Original Ballet Russe *Balustrade,* and, in the spring of 1944 he choreographed *Waltz Academy* for Ballet Theatre. Between the fall of 1944 and the spring of 1946 Balanchine staged *Danses Concertantes* and *Night Shadow* for the Ballet Russe de Monte Carlo and also mounted some of his previous works for that company.

In the fall of 1946 Balanchine and Kirstein organized the Ballet Society, with Balanchine as artistic director. For that organization he staged *Four Temperaments, Renard, Orpheus,* and other new ballets, also adding to the repertoire Symphony in C (Bizet), which he had created for the Paris Opéra Ballet in 1947 as *Palais de Cristal.*

In 1948 Ballet Society became the New York City Ballet with Balanchine as artistic director. In the next eighteen years he choreographed some sixty ballets for the company. In addition to the revivals of some of his earlier ballets, there were restagings of classics such as *Firebird* and *Swan Lake.* There were numerous brief and brilliant showpieces—pas de deux and small ensemble pieces for his virtuoso dancers. There were two full-length ballets: Tchaikovsky's *The Nutcracker,* first produced in 1954 and revised in 1964, with new décor by Rouben Ter-Arutunian and costumes by Karinska; and *A Midsummer Night's Dream* to music by Felix Mendelssohn, with décor by David Hays and costumes by Karinska. There were also ballets pervaded by mood or romantic atmosphere, most notably *La Valse, Scotch Symphony,* and *Liebeslieder Waltzer.* Also attention provoking was a series of ballets (their descent traceable to *Four Temperaments*) that used contemporary music as a basis for experimental manipulations of classical technique. Among these were *Opus 34, Ivesiana, Agon, Episodes, Electronics,* and *Bugaku.*

A most important milestone in Balanchine's career came in 1965 with his production of a third full-length ballet for the New York City Ballet, *Don Quixote,* to a commissioned score by Nicolas Nabokov, with décor and costumes by Esteban Francés. There is a mystique about this ballet that transcends the music (which is little more than serviceable) and the scarcity of danced scenes. *Don Quixote* is probably the least "dansant" of all Balanchine's ballets, but also dramatically the most potent. It had its première May 28, 1965, with Richard Rapp as the Don, Suzanne Farrell as Dulcinea, and Deni Lamont as Sancho Panza. There was a gala benefit preview performance the preceding evening at which Balanchine danced the title role. He has since appeared in this role a few times on special occasions.

An earlier 1965 production (premièred Feb. 4), less magnificent than *Don Quixote* but in its own way extremely well choreographed, tongue-in-cheek, and most amusing, was *Harlequinade,* to the Riccardo Drigo score (for the ballet for the Maryinsky Theatre, St. Petersburg), with décor by Ter-Arutunian, adapted by him from the New York City Opera's production of Rossini's *Cenerentola.* Among other ballets of this period were *Ballet Imperial* to Tchaikovsky's Piano Concerto in G major, which had its New York City Ballet première Oct. 15, 1964, which had been originally staged for the American Ballet Caravan (1941), then revived for Ballet Russe de Monte Carlo (1945), and the Royal Ballet (1950); and the *Brahms-Schönberg Quartet* to Brahms's *Quartet in G minor,* premièred April 21, 1966.

In the early 1960's there were demands for Balanchine's ballets from a number of opera houses in central and western Europe. At the outset Balanchine accepted invitations to stage his ballets, but soon realized that he could not spare the time the work required. It was then that he arranged for the New York City Ballet's associate and assistant ballet mistresses, among whom were Vida Brown (subsequently resigned), Una Kai, Francia Russell, and one or two others, to rehearse the companies in the ballets they desired. From time to time he would fly in to tighten up the ballet during the final rehearsals; on occasion ballet master John Taras would go on a special mission for the same purpose.

In this manner Balanchine ballets became part of the repertoire of the Royal Ballet (London), the Royal Danish Ballet, the Paris Opéra Ballet, the ballet of Teatro alla Scala, Milan (staged personally by Balanchine), the Netherlands Ballet, the ballet companies of Hamburg, Cologne, and other West German cities, and in Vienna, Austria, and Oslo. In Stockholm the Royal Swedish Ballet presented an all-Balanchine program (Oct. 16, 1966), which included *Allegro Brillante, La Valse,* and *Symphony in C.* Balanchine flew over to have a look at a rehearsal or two and to attend the première.

In the U.S. Balanchine ballets are danced by the American Ballet Theatre, the National Ballet (Wash., D.C.), the Pennsylvania Ballet (Philadelphia), the Boston Ballet, the Eglevsky Ballet (L.I.), City Center Joffrey Ballet, and a few others.

In 1954 Doubleday and Company (N.Y.) published Balanchine's *Complete Stories of the Great Ballets.* The book also included the chapters "How to Enjoy Ballet," "A Brief History of the Ballet," "Chronology of Significant Events of Ballet (1469–1953)," and an autobiography entitled "How I Became a Dancer and Choreographer." A decade later, the Friedrich Verlag (Hanover, Ger.) published in German Horst Koegler's *Balanchine und das moderne Ballett,* which added much to the popularity of the choreographer in central Europe; regrettably, the book has not yet been translated into English. In 1962 Bernard Taper wrote a book *Balanchine* (Harper & Row, N.Y.). On June 13, 1965, Brandeis Univ., Waltham, Mass., gave Balanchine the honorary degree of Doctor of Humane Letters.

The peak moment in Balanchine's professional life came on Apr. 23, 1964, with the opening of the New York State Theater in Lincoln Center. Its architect Philip Johnson stated publicly on several occasions that he designed the theatre for George Balanchine and his New York City Ballet. In June, 1966, Balanchine directed the filming of his *A Midsummer Night's Dream* as a feature dance film, the first such undertaking in the U.S.

Many writers in many languages have tried to analyze Balanchine's philosophy as a creative artist, but no one has succeeded in presenting it so clearly as Balanchine himself. Balanchine is a staunch believer in the self-sufficiency of ballet; he holds that neither story nor décor and costumes should be allowed to distract the attention of the audience from the chief attraction of a ballet—dancing. When the New York City Ballet was in Moscow (Oct., 1962), Balanchine succinctly stated his opinions in an interview for The Soviet Artist. Noting that he had originally dispensed with scenery and costumes for economic reasons, he explained that "this obligates the artist to execute every movement with maximal purity, and us, the ballet masters, to invent diverse and expressive choreography." He continued to defend his views of pure dance: "The ballet is such a rich art form that it should not be an illustrator of even the most interesting, even the most meaningful literary primary source. The ballet will speak for itself and about itself . . . I am always sorry when an excellent ballerina depicts with her movements only some literary theme. The human body, and in particular the female body, carries in itself true beauty. And one really does not want to know whom this or that ballerina represents but only to see the pure beauty of her body, her movements . . . Yes, if you like, I am an adherent of pure art, or art for art's sake."

Balanchine's use of music has drawn special praise and his collaborations with Igor Stravinsky have produced some of his most important ballets. Balanchine has often remarked that he liked Stravinsky's music because it was "pure and heartless"; it was not the kind of music that encouraged day-dreams in the listener, but rather it was like a rose that could be admired for itself and not for the feelings that it provoked. It is important for Balanchine to find the right music because his choreography is inspired by it. He has remarked that he could not move without a reason, and the reason is music. What he likes in both music and dancing is purity; he wants both sound and movement to be uncluttered with emotional connotations.

Of all the Russian choreographers outside Russia, Balanchine is the only one who did not come under the direct influence of Michel Fokine. When Balanchine entered the Imperial School Fokine had already left the Maryinsky Theatre to work with the Diaghilev company in Western Europe. While the influence of Fokine on methods of teaching was strong in the school, the ballet itself continued to develop in the direction indicated by his predecessor Marius Petipa. When Balanchine joined the Diaghilev company Fokine was in America. Thus, artistically, Balanchine is a direct descendant of Petipa and, if classicism in ballet is to continue, Balanchine is the one who will carry it on.

Balanchine is undoubtedly one of the most brilliant choreographers of our generation and the only one who has a genius for pure ballet. The possessor of a fertile and inventive mind, a musician of great knowledge and distinct talent, Balanchine is far ahead of his contemporaries, both in the audience and in the profession.

Most of Balanchine's ballets are abstractions, either of the music to which they are choreographed or of the themes upon which they are based. The ideas involved, the emotions expressed, even the humor contained in the ballets are presented with such subtlety that on occasion the spectators find it difficult to understand them. However, the oftener one sees Balanchine ballets, the clearer they become and the greater the enjoyment they evoke. It is interesting to note that none of the choreographers since Petipa, not even Michel Fokine, has had so many and so sincere followers as Balanchine. With William Dollar, John Taras, and Todd Bolender as the most talented representatives, one can almost speak of a Balanchine school in choreography.

To George Balanchine, more than to any other choreographer, goes the credit for introducing ballet into Broadway musical comedies. His choreography in the

1930's and 1940's for *On Your Toes, I Married an Angel, Babes in Arms,* and *Louisiana Purchase* actually started the trend of ballet in musicals. His dances in *Rosalinda* (*Die Fledermaus*) and *The Merry Widow* were greatly responsible for the amazing success of these operettas and also of *The Song of Norway,* for which he staged all choral numbers as well as the dances. In 1953 he staged Stravinsky's *The Rake's Progress* for the Metropolitan Opera. Balanchine also staged dances in several motion pictures, among them *The Goldwyn Follies, On Your Toes,* and *I Was an Adventuress.*

As chairman of the faculty at the School of American Ballet (N.Y.), Balanchine has also had a considerable influence on the technical training of ballet dancers in the U.S. Under the sponsorship of the Ford Foundation, he has observed schools throughout the country and has held summer seminars for teachers.

George Balanchine married Vera Zorina Dec. 24, 1938. They were divorced Jan. 17, 1946. On Aug. 16, 1946, Balanchine married Maria Tallchief; they were divorced in 1952. On Jan. 1, 1953, he married Tanaquil LeClercq, his present wife.

Balançoire, in ballet, grand battement executed from 4th position front (or back) en l'air, to 4th position back (or front) en l'air, passing through 1st position; also called battement en cloche.

Balasaraswati, contemporary Hindu dancer, b. Madras, India. She is considered the greatest living exponent of Bharata Natyam. Her abinhaya (mimed passages) have never been equalled for delicacy and intensity of feeling. The demands for her in her own country are so great that she has rarely left India, except once for a tour of Japan, and for her U.S. tour (1962), making her debut at the Jacob's Pillow Dance Festival. Engaged to teach at the new Center for Performing Arts of the Near and Far East, organized by the American Society for Eastern Arts, when it opened in the San Francisco Bay area in 1965.

Bales, William, American modern dancer and teacher, b. Carnegie, Pa., 1910; m. Jo Van Fleet. B.S., Univ. of Pittsburgh; A.B., Carnegie Institute of Technology (Drama Major). Studied ballet in Pittsburgh with Frank Eckl, modern dance in N.Y. with Doris Humphrey and Charles Weidman. A member of the Humphrey-Weidman Dance Company (1936–40), during which period he also danced in the Radio City Music Hall corps de ballet (1937) and appeared in *Straw Hat Revue* (1940). From 1942 to 1954 was a member of the Dudley-Maslow-Bales Trio (with Jane Dudley and Sophie Maslow) and Dance Company as dancer and choreographer. As a teacher, he has been on the faculty of Bennington College, Vt., since 1940; on the faculty of Bennington College School of Dance (1937–41); faculty of Conn. College School of Dance (1947–53, and again since 1961); faculty of N.Y. Univ. (1952); Juilliard School of Music Dance Department (1962). Since 1942 has been on faculty of New Dance Group Studio, N.Y. Is a member of the Dance Panel of International Cultural Exchange Service.

Ball in Old Vienna, A. Ballet in one act; chor.: Kurt Jooss; music: Joseph Lanner, arr. by Fritz Cohen; costumes: Aino Siimola. First prod.: Essen Dance Group, Opera House, Cologne, Germany, Nov. 21, 1932; in repertoire of Jooss Ballet. The ballet has no clear plot but illustrates the niceties of behavior at a formal mid-nineteenth century ball, the dances being heightened to stage proportions.

Ballabile. Ballet in 1 act, 6 scenes; chor.: Roland Petit; music: Emanuel Chabrier: "Three Romantic Waltzes," "Au Bois," "Marche Joyeuse," arr. Constant Lambert, "España," (orch. and partly arr. by Lambert); décor: Antoni Clavé. First prod.: Sadler's Wells (now Royal) Ballet, Royal Opera House, Covent Garden, London, May 5, 1950, with Violetta Elvin, Philip Chatfield, Alexander Grant, Anne Negus, Kenneth Melville in principal roles. A series of sketches, fantastic and atmospheric though without actual plot: an impression of a circus, Sunday on the river, a funeral in the rain, a final romp with a Spanish flavor.

Ballad. Ballet in 1 act; chor.: Grant Strate; music: Harry Somers; décor: Mark Negin. First prod.: National Ballet of Canada, Capitol Theatre, Ottawa, Nov. 4, 1959, with Earl Kraul (Ben, the Stranger), Lilian Jarvis (Rose), Lois Smith (Martha), Jacqueline Ivings (Mother), Donald Mahler (Father). Set in the dry farm belt of the West, the story is centered around the older generation's rejection of the land and the younger generation's happy acceptance. Ben and the two sisters become enmeshed in frustration, jealousy, and hate which is resolved with the violence the land itself demands.

Ballad in a Popular Style. Modern dance solo chor. and danced by Anna Sokolow; commissioned music: Alex North. First prod.: Nov. 14, 1937, Guild Theatre, N.Y. The work is a lyrical jazz journey danced to whistled accompaniment.

Ballerina, a principal female dancer in a ballet company; formerly a definite rank given to an outstanding ballet soloist. The Russian Imperial Ballet companies consisted of ballerinas, premiers danseurs, soloists, coryphées, and corps de ballet. This strict division of members of a ballet company is no longer used, but the titles ballerina, premier danseur, and soloist are still recognized. (For the titles in French ballet companies see SUJET.)

Ballet.

The primary expressions of the art impulses of mankind are considered to be those of dance and building. From the progress and development of dance have evolved music, theater and poetry; from that of building, sculpture, architecture, painting and writing.

The art form we call ballet bears as close a resemblance to architecture as movement can come to immobility. Like architecture, ballet is the result of geometrical, spatial thinking. Ballet uses its instrument—the human body—in the same terms as architecture uses its units. The pure unbroken line is as characteristic of the ballet dance as it is of the temple.

One of the basic laws of the ballet dance is aplomb. Aplomb is perfect balance, an equilibrium which the dancer must have in order to retain stability in any given pose or movement. To gain aplomb is a matter of primary importance to the ballet dancer. Similarly, aplomb is the basic law of architecture. For instance, in its functional essence, totally aside from its artistic value, a colonnade is but a system of pillars which maintains the balance of a beam.

Ballet further resembles architecture in that it is the only form of dance which does not limit itself to the two dimensions of the flat surface of the floor. Figures and movements in the air are as much a characteristic of the ballet dance as poses and steps executed on the ground. A dancer who has no elevation is almost as handicapped as one who has no aplomb.

No definition of a living art can be absolute; however, for our purpose we shall define ballet as classic theatrical dancing. Though simple, this definition stands analysis. Ballet is differentiated from other forms of theatrical dance—such as tap and the modern dance—because its basis is classicism. The dance in ballet may and does change; but the underlying principle of the classic dance—the reduction of human gesture to bare essentials, heightened and developed into meaningful patterns—remains constant. So that this principle may be preserved, the dance in ballet is based on the five classic positions of the feet and must be performed by dancers trained in the classic technique.

The five classic positions, as first formulated by Pierre Beauchamp around 1700, are the only five positions of the feet from which it is convenient and practicable to move in any given direction. There are inverted positions with the toe pointing in, there are intermediate positions (between one position and another), but of comfortable positions there are only five; a sixth cannot be invented. These positions form the base upon which a ballet dancer stands and from which he moves. They are the only ones from which the dancer can exercise stability or aplomb, the basic law of the ballet dance.

The five positions are based on the foundation which underlies the ballet dance, the turn-out. The turn-out is the ability of the dancer to turn out his knees much farther than is natural in everyday life. The anatomical origin of the turn-out is the hip-joint. The importance of the turn-out is so great that it should be explained in some detail.

The normal movements of the legs are very much limited by the structure of the joint between the pelvis and the hip. As the leg is drawn to the side, the hip-neck meets the brim of the acetabulum, and further movement is impossible; but if the leg is turned out, the big trochanter recedes, and the brim of the acetabulum meets the flat side surface of the hip-neck. This allows the dancer to extend the leg so that it forms an angle of 90 degrees or more with the other leg.

The turn-out is not an aesthetic conception but a technical necessity for every ballet dancer. It is the turn-out that makes the difference between a limited number of steps on one plane and the control of all conceivable dance movements in space.

Only dancers trained in the classic technique will have acquired the turn-out, will have mastered the five positions, will possess the aplomb that is necessary to perform intricate ballet steps. Only they will have acquired the fundamentals of the ballet dance; only they will possess line, lightness and elevation, without which there is no ballet.

A ballet dancer need not necessarily go through the known ballet steps and poses when performing, or even use the five positions; but he must be able to execute the steps and positions when required. It should be evident in his dancing that he has had ballet training, that his dance—no matter what it is—is based on ballet technique, because the classic technique is an integral part of the ballet dance.

Ballet technique, like any other technique, is mastery over the instrument of expression. In dancing that instrument is the human body. Dance technique, consequently, is complete control over the muscles of the body. In order to gain that control the ballet dancer must go through a long and arduous period of training, for which there is no substitute. This strenuous training and continuous exercise last as long as the dancer's artistic life. Because of these requirements the ballet dance is one of the few art forms which does not tolerate amateurs and amateurism.

Either you are a dancer or you are not; either you have mastered your instrument of expression or you have not; you possess technique or you do not possess it. "Ballet," said the great French ballet master and theoretician of the 18th century, Jean Georges Noverre, "is an art form which does not admit of mediocrity, it exacts a perfection difficult to acquire." This perfection is the essence of ballet technique and probably the chief attraction ballet holds for the audience, especially that part of the audience which is willing to learn a little in order to derive greater pleasure from a ballet performance. When all the component parts of the ballet—dance, music, story, décor—are accounted for, it is the dance that furnishes the chief attraction for the public. This is because the perfect craftsmanship, deftness, precision, and streamlined quality of the ballet dance find a response in our kinesthetic sense. It is ballet training and technique that furnish the dancer with the ability to execute everything perfectly, that give him his elegance of manner, his accurate craftsmanship, facility, lightness, and quickness.

In order to appreciate ballet fully one should understand why ballet training and technique are so essential to dancing, and the brilliance and style ballet technique can create. This brilliance and style make for eloquence in the language of ballet. This language must not only be articulate in so far as the dancers are concerned, but it must also communicate to the audience. The better we understand the language of ballet, the more pleasure we derive from it. It is not difficult to understand, once we are willing to grant it its conventions and accept the apparent irrationality of the ballet dance. Since we accept this in other art forms there is no reason why we should resist it when it comes to ballet.

The ballet artist creates a new and unknown reality from various known elements. The painter does the same thing in his medium. Canvas, paint, and brush are known materials; his finished picture, which contains these and something we call talent and technique, is a new reality which we must learn to accept.

We often hear that the ballet dance (meaning dancing on pointe) is not natural. The moment the ballet dancer rises on her toes she gets away from natural movements, movements which are habitual, ordinary, mechanical, spontaneous. She frees herself from them, and all her movements become subject to only one thing—perfect control. The movements become interrelated; even muscular reflexes are foreseen and made part of the whole chain of movement. Dancing on toes *is* unnatural, but so too is coloratura singing.

From a technical point of view, dancing on the toes has a far greater significance than the mere execution of steps on toes. Dancing on the toes and continuous exercise on them gives the dancer that precision of movement, that certainty and deftness, that economy and compactness which are characteristic of the ballet style and which no other dance form can claim. These are the qualities which create the virtuoso effect and the impression of ease during the execution of the most difficult steps which every ballet dancer strives to achieve.

When we watch a complicated ballet dance composed of brilliant pirouettes, leaps, and beats, we derive great pleasure from them not only because they are thrilling in themselves, but also because they have the appearance of security, facility, exuberance, and ease. We are not aware of the intricate technique which makes this brilliant execution possible. We do not see the strenuous preparations for them, nor are we forewarned by gestures, spontaneous or voluntary, of the coming feats. Whether simple or difficult, the movement is performed with ease, economy, deftness, and grace. We find that the simplest steps performed on the toes are as beautiful as the most complicated ones; a chain of movements composed of simple steps can transport the spectator as completely as a virtuoso feat.

Although it is true that the moment the ballerina rises to her toes she gets away from natural movements, by this action she gains a wide range of movement impossible to achieve while standing on her soles. In turns, for instance, a comparison of the flat foot, the half-toe (our everyday tip-toe), and the toe as pivots for turning, makes one realize immediately the importance of the toe.

A discussion of dancing on the toes leads naturally to that inherent quality of ballet dancing of which the toes are only part: allegro. The third dimension—height—is then brought in by allegro, for all jumps and leaps are part of allegro. It is not necessary to elaborate on the importance of the third dimension to dancing. It is self-evident that dancing in the air immensely enhances the possibilities of expression for the dancer and choreographer; the toes of the ballerina, her pirouettes and fouettés, the entrechats and cabrioles and all other jumps and leaps of the male dancer are part of allegro. Allegro is as much a part of ballet dancing as the five positions and the turn-out: allegro defines ballet.

It is to the Italian school of dancing that ballet is indebted for allegro. Most of the greatest exponents of allegro throughout the history of ballet in European countries have been of Italian origin. There is no doubt that allegro is more suited to the Italian temperament than to the French. But there is also a sociological explanation for the development of allegro in Italy. Italian ballet emerged from the limited sphere of court dancing and lost its amateur standing sooner than the French. It became the property of professionals as far back as the 17th century. The dancers introduced into ballet choreographic elements taken from different social backgrounds, notably from the peasantry. This influence is reflected in the names of some ballet steps. The entrechat, for instance, is derived from the Italian capra intrecciata—literally "a bound (braided) goat." The entrechat in execution reminds one of the jumps of a goat whose hind legs have been tied so that he cannot run away too far.

The counterpart of allegro is adagio. This form of ballet dancing originated in France, and the French school is responsible for its development up to the 1840's. In this case, too, we find a sociological explanation. It lies in the attachment of ballet to the court ceremonies of the French monarchs. The ladies and gentlemen of the court were the first ballet dancers. Louis XIV, "the Sun King," took lessons from the famous ballet master, Beauchamp, and appeared in ballets for forty-eight years. One could not expect fast movements and virtuoso technique from these aristocratic amateurs. It was enough for them when they managed to give a slow, but graceful ("noble" was the word) performance. It was natural that professional dancers took the line of least resistance and did not try to outdo in technique these socially prominent amateurs. The French temperament did the rest.

Out of this "noble" and graceful dancing arose the adagio—the most beautiful and expressive form of ballet dancing. Adagio (as well as allegro) derives its name from the type of music it employs. On the stage adagio is built on two planes: the relation of the dancers' bodies to each other and the relation of the bodies to space.

In the classic ballet adagio is performed by two dancers, a female and a male. Contemporary modern choreographers, notably Leonide Massine, George Balanchine, Antony Tudor, sometimes use three dancers: one female and two males, or two females and one male. Thus performed, adagio constitutes a love dance and is therefore fundamentally romantic.

Up to the advent of these choreographers, adagio was essentially the dance of the female. The male dancer was subservient to his partner; he was there only to assist and support her, to display her to the audience. This probably explains why most great male dancers are not always the best partners in adagio. Vaslav Nijinsky, for example, excellent dancer though he was, was never a perfect partner. However, all great adagio partners were always outstanding dancers, although not too many of them appear in the history of ballet. From the beginning of our century to this day, the following dancers may be regarded as exceptionally talented partners: Nicolas Legat, Mikhail Mordkin, Pierre Vladimirov, Anatole Vilzak, Anton Dolin, Igor Youskevitch,

André Eglevsky, Paul Petroff, Nicholas Magallanes, Erik Bruhn, Royes Fernandez, and Caj Selling.

In adagio, the arabesque is the most characteristic of ballet poses and the most beautiful. The ballerina stands on the toes of one foot, bending forward; the other leg, with the foot pointing upward, is raised to form an angle of ninety degrees with the supporting leg. The corresponding arm is extended in front of the body, thus forming the longest possible line from the fingertips to the toe of the raised leg.

Another beautiful pose in adagio is the attitude. The ballerina stands on the toes of one foot, the body bending backwards slightly; the other leg is raised to form an angle of ninety degrees and is bent at the knee joint, while the corresponding arm is raised.

Adagio and allegro, as well as other forms of ballet, serve as a framework for the expression of an idea, for the translation of thoughts, emotion, or music into terms of movement.

It is probably correct to say that the essence of ballet lies not in the plot or story, but in the music. The dancer dances not an emotion, or a situation, but the music which expresses an emotion or characterizes a situation. The relation of dance to music is closer than its relation to any of the other arts. Up to the first decade of this century ballet adhered strictly, but probably unconsciously, to Nietzche's idea that there is music in which the spirit dances as opposed to music in which the spirit swims. The latter is the transcendental music, the former is an outward thing suitable to the street and the theatre.

Modern ballet upset this theory. It realized and activated the proposition that ballet is danced not *to* music but *with* music, that the tie between ballet and music is rhythm, the one thing that penetrates the audible music and the visible dance. It is only through rhythm that movement passes into plastic form.

Rhythm, as Wagner said, is the skeleton of sound, the intellect of dance. It is the only limit to the mobile material of the art.

The relation between ballet and music is so close that it is of little importance whether the dance interprets the music, or whether the music explains the dance. Music supplies rhythm that underlies the dance; the dance illuminates the mystery that music conceals. Because of this close relation it is essential that the dance and the music be in perfect harmony, and that there be a contrapuntal and rhythmic justification for every movement and every pose. If this relation is properly carried out, music and dance cease to be separate entities. They become a single unit, a new art form which we call ballet.

This art form is incomplete, however, if the expression of a third great art—painting—is not present. For painting, in the form of scenery and costumes, is an integral part of ballet, as important as dance and music, and, like these two arts, undergoes a basic change when it becomes allied with ballet.

A painting is, by nature, static. It exists on a flat surface and is immobile in time and space. Once it becomes a décor for a ballet, however, it acquires a new dimension. The flat surface of the backdrop ceases to be just that and becomes a background for dancers. The two elements—the immobile background and the constantly moving dancers—form a sculptural, three-dimensional series of pictures. Each grouping is a new foreground set against a different part of the background; as the groupings change, the picture changes. With each change we perceive a new picture, a new sculptural unit.

A picture will remain a picture once painted, music will be music no matter where played, and dance will remain dance wherever performed; but it takes painting, music, and dance to create ballet. Thus, three arts joined to produce a fourth.

See also History of Ballet.

Ballet (definition). 1. From the Italian *ballare,* to dance. 2. *Ballate* were songs to accompany dancing in Tuscany in the 13th and 14th centuries. Later, in the high Renaissance, the Medici princes themselves wrote *canzon a ballo,* or dance-songs; *balleti* is the diminutive, hence ballet. 3. Classic theatrical dancing.

Lincoln Kirstein in his *Ballet Alphabet* gives the following definitions: "Generally speaking, a ballet is a theatrical representation achieved through terms of dancing. Mark Perugini, the author of *A Pageant of Dance and Ballet,* makes his own definition which can stand for our time: A ballet is a series of solo and concerted dances with mimetic actions accompanied by music and scenic accessories, all expressive of a poetic idea or series of ideas, or a dramatic story provided by an author or choreographer. Baltasarini, choreographer of *Le Ballet Comique de la Reine,* stated that a ballet was a geometric combination of several persons dancing together. The Encyclopedia of Diderot and d'Alembert (ca. 1772) tells us that Ballet is action explained by a dance. It goes on to trace the origin of dancing, repeating all earlier errors and confirming the confusion that persists into our own day that dance and ballet are identical. However, if we understand that the dancing is specifically theatrical, spectacular and done to be seen, the subsequent definition, probably by Cahusac, explains the 18th-century conception. A ballet is a picture, or, rather, a series of pictures linked together by the action which makes the subject of the ballet. The stage is, as it were, the canvas on which the composer (choreographer) renders his ideas; the choice of music, scenery and costumes are his colors; the choreographer is the painter. All action, however, is not dancing, and in recent years, the most important developments in ballet have been to transform mimed action or pantomime into dramatic dancing, eliminating dumb-show and elevating the ballet into an independent art form, completely expressive in its own terms." See also BALLET, HISTORY OF BALLET.

Ballet (publication). See PERIODICALS, DANCE (ENGLAND).

Ballet Alicia Alonso. See BALLET DE CUBA.

Ballet Annual, yearbook of ballet, published by A. & C. Black, London. Ballet Annual No. 1 covered the year 1946; the final issue, No. 18, was published in 1964. Editorial board included Arnold L. Haskell, C. W. Swinson (d. 1963), G. B. L. Wilson, Mary Clarke, Ivor Guest. It was a valuable addition to the literature on ballet and useful as a reference book.

Ballet Associates in America, a non-profit corporation organized to foster, encourage, and promote the work of choreographers, composers, and designers in the field of ballet and to cultivate the appreciation of ballet in America. The organization was first formed in 1941 as Ballet Associates, then changed its title and corporate standing in 1944. From its foundation it contributed to and sponsored the production of the ballets *Pillar of Fire, Romantic Age, Romeo and Juliet,* and *Tally-Ho.* It produced on its own *On Stage!* and *Camille.* These were all for Ballet (now American Ballet) Theatre. It also produced *Sebastian* for the Marquis de Cuevas Ballet International. By underwriting a ballet, Ballet Associates in America remained the owner of the production, the performing company being required to pay Ballet Associates in America a royalty for each performance. The organization sponsored four Dinner Dances (1950–1952) at which funds were raised for production costs for the New York City Ballet. John Alden Talbot was responsible for the founding of the organization and was its moving spirit throughout its active period. It has been dormant since the end of 1952.

Ballet Blanc, a ballet performed in white tutus, such as *Les Sylphides, Swan Lake* (Acts 2 and 4), *Giselle* (Act 2), etc.

Ballet Caravan, a performing organization founded by Lincoln Kirstein in the spring of 1936 to furnish an opportunity of expression to American choreographers, dancers, composers, and scenic designers. During the initial season which opened in Bennington, Vt. in July, 1936, the Ballet Caravan presented *Pocahontas* (Lew Christensen–Elliott Carter, Jr.), *Encounter* (Lew Christensen–Mozart), *Harlequin for President* (Eugene Loring–Scarlatti), *Promenade* (William Dollar–Ravel). The next season (summer, 1937) brought *Yankee Clipper* (Loring–Paul Bowles), *Filling Station* (Lew Christensen–Virgil Thompson), and *Show Piece* (Erick Hawkins–Robert McBride). In Oct., 1938, Ballet Caravan mounted its most ambitious production–Eugene Loring's *Billy the Kid,* to Aaron Copland's music, in costumes by Jared French. The first two years Ballet Caravan performed only during the summer, since most of its dancers were members of the American Ballet company. In the fall of 1938 Ballet Caravan changed its name to American Ballet Caravan and embarked on an extended tour. Among the dancers were Ruthanna Boris, Gisella Caccialanza, Jane Deering, Marie Jeanne, Todd Bolender, Lew Christensen, Fred Danieli, William Dollar, Erick Hawkins, and Eugene Loring. In the spring of 1940 the American Ballet Caravan was engaged by the Ford Motor Company to appear in the Ford Pavilion at the N.Y. World's Fair in a ballet entitled *A Thousand Times Neigh,* choreographed by William Dollar. The company, divided into two units, appeared ten times a day in a season lasting six months. In the spring of 1941 American Ballet Caravan merged with the American Ballet company for a Latin-American tour sponsored by the United States Office for Coordination of Commercial and Cultural Relations Between the American Republics. The performing company was disbanded on its return to the United States in Oct., 1941. See also AMERICAN BALLET, THE.

Ballet Club (London). See BALLET RAMBERT.

Ballet Clubs, Association of, a British organization founded by G. B. L. Wilson in 1947 to link ballet clubs and study and further their interests. It organizes an annual production for the member-clubs and a summer school of ballet.

Ballet Comique de la Reine. Ballet by Balthasar de Beaujoyeux (Baldassarino da Belgiojoso), produced Oct. 15, 1581, and considered the first ballet more or less as we understand it today. It was commissioned by the French Queen (Catherine de Medici) on the occasion of the betrothal of her sister, Marguerite de Lorraine, to the Duc de Joyeuse. The verses were written by La Chesnaye, the King's Almoner, and the music composed by Sieur de Beaulieu, a relative of the Queen. The scenery and costumes were designed by Jacques Patin. The spectacle lasted from 10:00 P.M. to 3:30 A.M. The ballet was chiefly concerned with the legend of Circe and part of the set represented the Garden and Castle of Circe. The principal dancers were a group of twelve Naiads, danced by a princess and several duchesses. Characters included Jupiter, Pallas Athene, Pan, Mercury, Dryads, Four Virtues, and Eight Satyrs. Musicians sat in a golden vault, framed by clouds lighted from the inside. Chariots were used as in the Italian "triumphs." The cost of the spectacle was 3,600,000 gold francs. The libretto of the ballet was published in 1582 and was to become one of the first books on ballet. This type of entertainment was much imitated for the next decade in Italy as well as in France.

Ballet d'Action, a ballet having a plot, generally with tragic subject, supposedly introduced by Jean Georges Noverre (1727–1809). Not technical mastery of steps (dancing for the sake of dancing) alone was important, but a flow of action with gestures and facial expression to fit the plot. The corps de ballet, from being mere background for the principals, became an integral part of action. Instead of selecting music and setting steps to it, Noverre looked for a story which would offer opportunities for presenting dances, studied expressions, movements and gestures that would best illustrate the theme, and then had music especially written or adapted to fit each situation in the development of his story. The court costumes gave way to clothing appropriate to and in harmony with the subject.

Ballet d'École. See CLASSIC BALLET.

Ballet de Cuba, a company formed in 1948 by Alicia and Fernando Alonso, originally called Ballet Alicia Alonso; renamed Ballet de Cuba in 1955 after receiving a government subsidy. First performances in Havana, Oct., 1948. Following a season in Havana, it toured through Latin America (1949); Cuba and Mexico (spring-summer, 1950). Since then the company has performed regularly in Havana and throughout Cuba and has made numerous tours through Puerto Rico, Central and South America. Winter 1960–61 toured Soviet Russia, China, among others. Alicia Alonso, prima ballerina, dances frequently with the company. When she was with American Ballet Theatre or Ballet Russe de Monte Carlo, a guest ballerina was generally invited to appear with Ballet de Cuba. Dancers with the company have included ballerinas Melissa Hayden, Carlota Pereyra, Barbara Fallis, Paula Lloyd, Dulce Wohner (Anaya); premiers danseurs Igor Youskevitch, Royes Fernandez, Nicholas Magallanes, Michael Maule, Luis Trápaga, and currently, Rodolfo Rodriguez. Soloists and corps de ballet have included American as well as Cuban dancers, many of the latter trained at Sociedad Pro-Arte Musical, or in the Academia de Ballet Alicia Alonso, Havana. Fernando Alonso has been director of the company since its inception. In addition to the classics, such as the full-length *Swan Lake, Coppélia, Giselle, La Fille Mal Gardée, Pas de Quatre,* and various pas de deux, the company performs original works choreographed by Alicia Alonso, Alberto Alonso, Cuca Martinez del Hoyo, Enrique Martinez, and others.

Ballet de la Nuit. Ballet produced in Paris in 1653. It was concerned with events that happen after sundown. The mythological background had as a primary plot the story of Venus and Endymion. A feature of the production was a fight between robbers and soldiers. The entire ballet lasted thirteen hours. Jean Lully, the composer, danced in *Ballet de la Nuit.*

Ballet der Lage Landen. See HOLLAND, DANCE IN.

Ballet des Polonais, Le. Ballet presented in 1573 before the Polish ambassadors to France. The affair was arranged by Catherine de Medici and danced by sixteen ladies of the court. It was important in the development of ballet, as the dancing itself was the center of attraction and it contained many complete dance figures.

Ballet Foundation. See FOUNDATIONS, PHILANTHROPIC.

Ballet Guild, a non-profit organization founded in N.Y. in 1939 by Mrs. Arne Horlin Eckstrom and Baron Nicholas de Guinzbourg to promote public interest in ballet and to encourage native talent to develop ballet as an American art form. It held a national competition for a new ballet in 1940. The winning libretto was *The Dream of Audubon* by Glenway Westcott; the winning composer was

David Diamond. Due to difficulties with the stage designers' union there was no competition for décor. The ballet was not produced. Ballet Guild has been inactive since 1942.

Ballet Guild (London), an English organization formed in London in 1941 by Christmas Humphreys and Deryck Lynham, presenting performances by a company under the direction of Molly Lake. Its reference library and archives formed the nucleus of the London Archives of the Dance; it also presented lectures, recitals, and exhibitions. The company marked the centenary of *Giselle* with a special performance with Molly Lake in the title role, although 1942 was one of the darkest of all the war years for England. The Ballet Guild was dissolved in 1947.

Ballet Imperial. Ballet in 3 movements; chor.: George Balanchine; music: Peter Tchaikovsky's Piano Concerto No. 2 in G major; décor: Mstislav Doboujinsky. First prod.: American Ballet Caravan, Hunter College Playhouse, N.Y., May 29, 1941, with Marie Jeanne, Gisella Caccialanza, William Dollar. Staged for New Opera Company, Broadway Theatre, N.Y., Nov., 1942, with Mary Ellen Moylan, Gisella Caccialanza, William Dollar. Taken into the repertoire of Ballet Russe de Monte Carlo, City Center, N.Y., Feb. 20, 1945, with Maria Tallchief, Mary Ellen Moylan, Nicholas Magallanes. Balanchine staged the ballet (with a considerably revised second movement) for Sadler's Wells (now Royal) Ballet at Royal Opera House, Covent Garden, London, Apr. 5, 1950, with Margot Fonteyn, Beryl Grey, Michael Somes, in décor by Eugene Berman. The Royal Ballet revived *Ballet Imperial* in décor by Carl Toms, Oct. 18, 1963, with Nadia Nerina, Anya Linden, David Blair. On Oct. 15, 1964, Balanchine revived the ballet, with the help of Frederic Franklin, for the New York City Ballet at New York State Theater, Lincoln Center for the Performing Arts, in décor by Rouben Ter-Arutunian and costumes by Karinska, with Suzanne Farrell, Patricia Neary, Jacques d'Amboise. *Ballet Imperial* is a plotless ballet in the classic tradition. With it Balanchine pays homage to the style of ballet in which he grew up, the Imperial Maryinsky Theatre, St. Petersburg (now the Kirov, Leningrad).

Ballet in America.

BY LILLIAN MOORE.

The history of ballet in the U.S. begins with the visits of European artists and performances of European ballets. Until the 1930's there were comparatively few American dancers trained in the technique of the ballet. American ballets were even more rare. This state of affairs may be blamed directly on the absence of established schools and permanent, state-endowed companies where ballet, an art which requires long, arduous preparation, might be nourished and developed.

America, however, has always been receptive to ballet (except during a period in the second half of the 19th century when everywhere, save in Russia, it was at a very low ebb) and almost all of the great productions of the Romantic ballet were seen here shortly after their creation. Among the dancers who have appeared here were some of the greatest of their time, from Fanny Elssler and Paul Taglioni in the past century to Anna Pavlova and Vaslav Nijinsky in this. In spite of haphazard methods of training, a handful of distinguished American dancers such as Augusta Maywood, Mary Ann Lee, and George Washington Smith, emerged during the Romantic period.

It was probably Henry Holt, an English dancer, who introduced ballet to the American Colonies. In 1735 he appeared in Charleston, S.C., in *The Adventures of Harlequin and Scaramouch,* with *The Burgo'master Trick'd.* Later he gave the same work in N.Y. Dance performances of various types were seen on pre-Revolutionary stages, and harlequinades and pantomimes became fairly common.

The first actual ballet season was probably that presented by Alexandre Placide in N.Y. in 1792. Placide, a former Paris celebrity who was adept at everything from acrobatics and pantomime to classic ballet, had formed a partnership in Santo Domingo with a pretty young French dancer named Suzanne Vaillande, known professionally as Mme. Placide. At their first performance in N.Y. (Jan. 25, 1792) they presented a "Dancing Ballot" (*sic*) called *The Bird Catcher*. In the cast was the first American professional dancer, John Durang. In addition to a number of harlequinades, the Placides during their first N.Y. season produced two more "dancing ballets," *The Return of the Labourers* and *The Two Philosophers, or The Merry Girl*. Later Mme. Placide married the singer Louis Douvillier. For many years she was prima ballerina of the New Orleans theatre, where she staged ballets after Jean-Georges Noverre and Jean Dauberval and created several original works, thus becoming America's first woman choreographer.

One of the earliest American operas, James Hewitt's famous *Tammany* (1794), contained a brief ballet in the form of an Indian dance, executed by Durang and a Mr. Miller. A pantomime ballet called *The Huntress, or Tammany's Frolics*, based on the same theme, was given later in the same year.

The first serious ballet given in this country was *La Forêt Noire*, a French work for which Alexander Reinagle composed new music. It had its première at the New Theatre, Philadelphia, on Apr. 26, 1794. On this occasion Mme. Anna Gardie, a dancer from Santo Domingo who had appeared in Paris, made her American debut. An accomplished artist, noted for her ability as both dancer and mime, she won great popularity in N.Y., Boston and Philadelphia before her tragic death at the hands of her crazed husband a few years later.

Several other elaborate ballet pantomimes, such as *Sophia of Brabant* and *The Danaides*, were given at the old Southwark Theatre, Philadelphia, during the autumn of 1794. A Frenchman named Quesnet was responsible for the choreography of *The Danaides* and possibly of other works as well. *Sophia of Brabant*, when it was given in N.Y. on Dec. 29, 1794, acquired the distinction of being the first serious ballet presented in that city. N.Y. generally lagged behind Philadelphia in things theatrical until well into the 19th century.

Meanwhile, a choreographer named William Francis had been imported from England to stage rustic and comic ballets at the Chestnut St. Theatre, Philadelphia. One of his most popular productions was *The Caledonian Frolic*, which was revived intermittently for many years.

Charleston, S.C., was another center of ballet production in the late 18th century. During the season of 1794–95 Placide, with the aid of a gifted choreographer named Jean Baptiste Francisqui, who had danced at the Paris Opéra, presented no less than 34 different ballets and pantomimes at the Charleston Theatre. Some of these were original works, but others derived from popular Paris productions, including Noverre's *The Whims of Galatea* and Maximilien Gardel's *Le Deserteur Français*. Among the dancers in this company was the child prodigy Louis Duport, who may or may not have been the great virtuoso Louis Antoine Duport, later the bitter rival of Auguste Vestris. (See *Dance Perspectives* 7: "The Duport Mystery," by Lillian Moore.)

In 1796 Francisqui left Placide and came to N.Y. With a small group of French dancers, including Mme. Gardie, Jean Baptiste Val and his wife, and the American John Durang, he produced a number of ballets for the old John St. Theatre. A prolific choreographer, Francisqui staged spectacles ranging from *Pygmalion*, "a lyric scene of celebrated J. J. Rousseau, with musical interludes by the same author," to comic pantomimes like *The Milkmaid, or The Death of the Bear,* and historical pageants like the "Grand Historic and Military Pantomime," *The American Heroine,* which featured Indian dances by Durang and his colleagues.

James Byrne, the famous English dancer and mime who revolutionized the whole conception and presentation of the traditional character of Harlequin, spent four or five years in the U.S. (1796–1800). His first production here (Philadelphia, Nov. 7, 1796) was the "grand serious pantomime," *The Death of Captain Cook,* with native dances of the Hawaiian Islands. Byrne's son Oscar, who later became first dancer at Drury Lane, London, made his stage debut in Philadelphia when he was about three years old, in his father's production, *The Origin of Harlequin.* The Byrne family's success in the U.S. was hindered, however, by the fact that at her American debut Mrs. Byrne was hissed off the stage because her costume was considered inadequate.

During the early years of the 19th century the theatres of N.Y. and Philadelphia presented many pantomimes and ballets, but the actual dancing, usually in what was known as the "English style," seems to have been based upon simple English and Scotch country dances, and social dance forms like the minuet and gavotte. The Durang family continued something of a balletic tradition. Mr. and Mrs. Parker, whose two daughters, Sarah and Jane, later danced with them, and Mr. and Mrs. Edward Conway were among the featured dancers at the Park Theatre, N.Y., during this period. Quaint, delightful prints of these dancers attest to their charm, if not their virtuosity. Mr. Conway was the author of one of the earliest dance text-books to be published in this country, *Le Maitre de Danse, or the art of dancing cotillions.*

In 1821 the Park Theatre engaged a French ballet master, Claude Labasse, who paved the way for the importation of an entire company of highly skilled French dancers six years later. Francisque Hutin, ballerina of this troupe, seems to have introduced classical dancing of an excellence never before seen in this country. Her technical equipment included multiple pirouettes, supported adagio and pointe work, which was then a daring innovation even in the theatrical capitals of Europe. After her debut, the public was no longer satisfied with the simple English dances, but constantly demanded what they called the "new French style of dancing."

Other members of this company, which appeared at the Bowery Theatre, were M. and Mme. Achille (immortalized in an early print), M. Labassé, whom Hutin later married, and Mlle. Celeste, a pupil of the Paris Opéra school, who later became a famous mime, actress, and manager. Among the ballets presented that season was *The Deserter,* "as performed at the Paris Opéra," presumably implying that the choreography followed the original of Gardel.

Charles and Marietta Ronzi Vestris, relatives of the great "Dieu de la Danse," joined the Bowery company in Aug., 1828, and remained in the U.S. for a year. They were by far the most renowned and skillful dancers who had yet appeared here.

Two opera-ballets by Auber, *La Muette de Portici* (*Masaniello, or The Dumb Girl of Genoa*) and *Le Dieu et la Bayadère* (*The Maid of Cashmere*) were popular here as early as the 1830's, serving as vehicles for French artists like Mlle. Celeste, Mme. Augusta, and Mme. Lecomte, and the Americans, Augusta Maywood and Mary Ann Lee. It was Mlle. Celeste who first danced Taglioni's *La Sylphide* in America (1835), one year before August Bournonville staged in Copenhagen the version which survives today.

Lee and Maywood, child prodigies both, made their debuts together as Zoloe and Fatima, respectively, in *The Maid of Cashmere,* at the Chestnut St. Theatre, Philadelphia, Dec. 30, 1837. Augusta Maywood danced *La Sylphide* here before she left for Europe in 1838. She appeared briefly at the Paris Opéra and enjoyed a flourishing career in Italy and Austria, attaining the rank of prima ballerina at Teatro alla Scala, Milan, during the reign of Carlo Blasis there. Mary Ann Lee also studied in Europe, under Coralli, but returned to the United States, where she was first to dance *Giselle* (Boston, Jan. 1, 1846).

During the summer of 1839 Paul Taglioni and his wife Amelie, on leave from the Berlin Opera, danced *La Sylphide, Le Dieu et la Bayadère,* and *Nathalie, La Laitière Suisse,* at the Park Theatre, N.Y. Paul was the brother of the great ballerina Maria Taglioni, creator of *La Sylphide,* whose art epitomized the delicate, spiritual aspects of the Romantic ballet. Her influence is still felt today in such works as Fokine's *Les Sylphides,* the recreated *Pas de Quatre,* and other examples of the ballet blanc. Maria Taglioni never visited this country, although a cousin of hers, Louise Taglioni, danced in N.Y. in 1855.

Marius Petipa, future dictator of the Imperial Russian Ballet, paid a brief visit to the U.S. in 1839 as a young man of twenty, when he danced with his father in the company of Mme. Lecomte.

The Romantic ballet in America reached its pinnacle with the visit of Fanny Elssler, who toured the country for two years (1840–42). Appearing in such ballets as *La Tarentule, Nathalie* and *La Gypsy,* she revealed a mature and brilliant art which captivated the public and won the respect of discriminating intellectuals like Ralph Waldo Emerson and Margaret Fuller. Her colorful "Cachucha" and "Cracovienne" swept the country; shops were filled with lithographs of the dancer; Congress was recessed when she danced in Washington. She was the object of a violent adulation equalled only by the Jenny Lind furore a few years later. Elssler encouraged American dancers, engaging several, such as Julia Turnbull, Henrietta Vallee, and George Washington Smith, for her company. Her partner, the Irish James Sylvain (Sullivan) had a number of American pupils, but he did not remain in the country long enough to establish a permanent school. (In this connection see the entry FANNY ELSSLER IN AMERICA.)

After Elssler's departure ballet continued to enjoy a wave of tremendous popularity, which endured for another decade. Hermine Blangy, who had danced in Paris and Vienna, arrived in 1846 with an extensive repertoire of new productions, including *The Devil's Violin, Le Lac des Fées, La Fille de Marbre, L'Illusion d'un Peintre, La Chatte Metamorphosée en Femme, Le Diable Boiteux,* and other ballets which had been danced on the Continent by Elssler and Fanny Cerito. The Ravel family, a troupe of acrobats and tight-rope performers who toured this country from 1832 to 1866, frequently presented ballets. Leon Espinosa was a member of their company for a season. The Monplaisir Ballet, which arrived in 1847, presented *Esmeralda* and *Le Diable à Quatre.* They traveled as far as California before returning to Italy where Hippolyte Monplaisir later became choreographer at Teatro alla Scala. The Petites Danseuses Viennoises, forty-eight well-drilled children who executed garland dances and military maneuvers, much in the manner of present-day precision dancers, were as successful in America as they had been in Paris and London.

Pupils of the great pedagogue Carlo Blasis flocked to the U.S. Giovanna Ciocca, Gaetano Neri, and Gaetano Morra were among the first Italians to arrive, dancing here in the late 1840's. In 1857 the Ronzani Ballet, which included Cesare and Serafima Cecchetti with their small son Enrico, opened the Academy of Music in Philadelphia. Enrico Cecchetti appeared here, at the age of seven, in the title role of *Il Biricchino di Parigi.* The Ronzani repertoire also included Jules

Perrot's epic *Faust.*

Ballet was a prominent feature of *The Black Crook,* first of a long series of elaborate but rather vulgar musical spectacles which dominated the American theatre during the latter half of the century. Rita Sangalli, who was to create the title role of Delibes' *Sylvia* at the Paris Opéra, was among its original ballerinas. Marie Bonfanti, who established a school in N.Y., was another. Both were products of the academy at La Scala, as was Giuseppina Morlacchi, exquisite artist who won the admiration of Brander Mathews and Philip Hale, but married an Indian scout named Texas Jack, friend of Buffalo Bill!

Katti Lanner, daughter of the composer, and later choreographer of London's Empire Theatre, danced *Giselle* in N.Y. in 1870. The ballet was not seen here again until it was revived by Pavlova and Mikhail Mordkin, forty years later.

With the opening of the Metropolitan Opera House in 1883, one might have expected that ballet would find a permanent home in the U.S., where dancers could be trained and the art might flower and develop along national lines. Such was not the case. The company imported all its dancers and did not establish a school until 1909, when Malvina Cavallazzi, who had been the "Met's" first ballerina, returned from London to teach there. The Metropolitan did not engage its first American-born choreographer, Zachary Solov, until 1951.

The American Opera Company, guided by Theodore Thomas, made an honest effort to present fine ballet. During its unfortunately brief existence (1885–87) it introduced Delibes' *Coppélia* and *Sylvia* and starred first-rate dancers like Maria Giuri, who later danced in Russia. Carlotta Brianza was another Italian virtuoso who toured the U.S. before winning immortality as creator of Marius Petipa's *The Sleeping Beauty* in St. Petersburg (1890).

Except in connection with opera performances at the Metropolitan, where Luigi Albertieri, pupil and protégé of Enrico Cecchetti, was ballet master for a short time, very little ballet was seen in N.Y. until the debut of the Danish dancer Adeline Genée. First in a musical comedy called *The Soul Kiss* (1908) and later as guest artist at the Metropolitan, Genée, with her precise technique and sprightly charm, did much to re-awaken American appreciation of ballet as an art form. Cia Fornaroli, who danced at the Metropolitan from 1910 to 1913, also brought personal artistry of a high order.

In the meantime, Diaghilev's Ballets Russes had burst upon Western Europe. First of the Russians to dance here were Anna Pavlova and Mikhail Mordkin, who appeared at the Metropolitan Opera House on Feb. 28, 1910, in *Coppélia,* supported by the resident ballet corps. Their success was little short of sensational. The Diaghilev company did not reach these shores until six years later, although three Fokine ballets (*Schéhérazade, Cléopâtre,* and *Les Sylphides*) were presented here in unauthorized versions produced by Gertrude Hoffman. When the Diaghilev Ballet finally arrived (1916), it presented several of Fokine's masterpieces, such as *Petrouchka, Schéhérazade,* and *Les Sylphides,* as well as Nijinsky's *L'Après-Midi d'un Faune,* with young Leonide Massine in the principal role. The stunning color and riotous opulence of Léon Bakst's sets and costumes were a revelation no less impressive than Fokine's new use of classic dance forms.

Upon the belated arrival of Vaslav Nijinsky, whose departure from Europe had been delayed by his wartime internment, *Le Spectre de la Rose* was added to the repertoire. Nijinsky, whose transcendental art left a deep impression upon the American theatre despite the brevity of his sojourn, created one ballet in the U.S., *Til Eulenspiegel,* danced to the tone poem of Richard Strauss, with settings and costumes by Robert Edmond Jones.

In 1918 the Metropolitan Opera presented the Fokine-Diaghilev version of

Rimsky-Korsakov's *Le Coq d'Or,* with Rosina Galli as the Queen of Shemakhan. Adolph Bolm staged this production and that of *Petrouchka,* given by the Metropolitan the following year. Two American ballets—Gilbert's *The Dance in Place Congo* (1917), and John Alden Carpenter's *Skyscrapers* (1926)—complete the list of independent ballets given at the opera until George Balanchine's appointment as ballet master in 1935.

During these years Anna Pavlova visited the U.S. almost every season, indefatigably touring the length and breadth of the country and bringing her superb artistry to thousands of persons who had never before seen any sort of ballet performance. Her last appearances here took place in 1925, although she had been scheduled to return in the year of her death (1931).

There were sporadic attempts at ballet production by the Neighborhood Playhouse and the League of Composers, during the 1920's. Michel Fokine, who had been a resident of N.Y. for some time, gave a few independent recitals, and Adolph Bolm formed the Ballet Intime, which flowered briefly. However, between the departure of Anna Pavlova in 1925 and the arrival of the Ballet Russe de Monte Carlo in 1933, there were few professional ballet performances in the U.S.

The subsequent revival of interest in ballet, the tours of the various Russian companies, the emergence of New York City Ballet (which began as the American Ballet), and the foundation of Ballet Theatre, the establishment of permanent professional ballet schools, the development of native American dancers and choreographers, and the present emergence of a national form of an international art, all make up a story too extensive to be chronicled in these brief paragraphs; however, articles devoted to more recent manifestations will be found in this volume under AMERICAN BALLET, BALLET THEATRE, BALLET RUSSE DE MONTE CARLO.

For more detailed information on early American dances and productions see the following issues of *Dance Index* (N.Y.): "American Souvenir Lithographs of the Romantic Ballet," by George Chaffee (Feb., 1942); "The Petipa Family in Europe and America," by Lillian Moore (May, 1942); "John Durang, First American Dancer," by Lillian Moore (Aug.. 1942); "American Music Prints of the Romantic Ballet," by George Chaffee (Dec., 1942); "Augusta Maywood," by Marian Hannah Winter (Jan.–Feb., 1943); "Mary Ann Lee, First American Giselle," by Lillian Moore (May, 1943); "The Black Crook and the White Fawn," by George Freedley (Jan., 1945); "George Washington Smith," by Lillian Moore (June–July–Aug., 1946). Also: *Chronicles of the American Dance,* ed. by Paul Magriel (N.Y., 1948); "Four Centuries of American Dance," by Arthur Todd, *Dance Magazine* (Sept., Nov., 1949; and Jan., Mar., Apr., 1950); *Russian Ballet Master—The Memoirs of Marius Petipa,* ed. by Lillian Moore (A. and C. Black, London; and The Macmillan Company, N.Y., 1958); "The Duport Mystery," by Lillian Moore, *Dance Perspectives* (No. 7, 1960); "New York's First Ballet Season, 1792," by Lillian Moore (The New York Public Library, 1961).

Ballet International, a ballet company founded in N.Y. the summer of 1944 by the Marquis George de Cuevas. The plan for the organization of the company dates back to Nov., 1943 when the Marquis established a trust fund under the title The Ballet Institute with the stated objective of promoting and advancing the art of ballet, the education and instruction of students of ballet, and the development and furtherance of public appreciation of ballet. The Ballet Institute was capitalized at $150,000. In Mar., 1944, the trust fund acquired the Vilzak-Schollar School of Ballet. Auditions for the new company began in May, rehearsals early in June. In mid-June Ballet International leased the

Park Theatre, on New York's Columbus Circle, and renamed it International Theatre. The performing company was headed by Viola Essen, Marie Jeanne, André Eglevsky, William Dollar. Among the choreographers were Leonide Massine, Bronislava Nijinska, Boris Romanoff, Antonia Cobos, Edward Caton, William Dollar, Simon Semenoff. Anatole Vilzak was ballet master. The repertoire included *Brahms Variations, Sentimental Colloquy, Mad Tristan, Memories, The Mute Wife, Pictures at an Exhibition, Sebastian, Constantia, Prince Goudal's Festival,* and a number of revivals of standard ballets. The season opened on Oct. 30 and closed Dec. 23, a financial failure which had cost the Marquis de Cuevas an estimated $800,000. Artistically Ballet International had the distinction of bringing to the fore the choreographic talents of Edward Caton, William Dollar, and Antonia Cobos. The physical properties of the company were added in the summer of 1947 to that of the Grand Ballet de Monte Carlo, directed by the Marquis de Cuevas, which in 1950 became Grand Ballet du Marquis de Cuevas. In 1958 the name reverted to Ballet International, its full title being Ballet International du Marquis de Cuevas. After the Marquis' death in 1961, his widow continued the company under the title Ballet International de la Marquese de Cuevas. The Marquese de Cuevas disbanded the company on June 30, 1962.

Ballet Intime, a small ballet troupe organized by Adolph Bolm with which he toured several seasons in the middle and late 1920's. In addition to Bolm the dancers included Berenice Holmes (première danseuse), Elise Reiman, Boris Volkov; as well as Roshanara, a Hindu, accompanied by Ratan Devi, a Hindu musician; Michio Ito, a Japanese dancer; Rita Zalmani, a former member of Anna Pavlova company; and several others.

Ballet Master, Ballet Mistress, a person in charge of the dancers and ballets in a company whose duty it is to rehearse ballets, assign roles and, usually, give classes to the dancers. In Russian and French literature a person who stages ballets is also called a ballet master. In some European companies it also means director (e.g. Royal Danish Ballet). In American and English usage a person who stages ballets is called choreographer. In the Diaghilev Ballets Russes company and later in the Ballet Russe de Monte Carlo the person exercising the duties of ballet master was designated regisseur-general.

Ballet Mécanique. 1. composition by George Antheil which introduced non-musical instruments for sound effects. 2. name often applied to Mosoloff's *The Iron Foundry,* a ballet (chor. Adolph Bolm, 1932) whose characters represent movements of machinery.

Balletomane, a ballet enthusiast; a ballet fan. The word balletomane was coined in Russia in the first quarter of the 19th century. The suffix -mane is used to indicate a person having a strong liking for something: a musicomane is a person with a strong liking for music, an anglomane for things English. This suffix often takes the place of the suffix -phile, as in francophile, bibliophile, etc. Mane or -phile is contrasted with -phobe, denoting hatred, as francophobe, for instance, a person who hates everything French. Philologically -mane is neither as dignified nor as sound as -phile; it carries the implication of an unreasonable liking for something to the exclusion of everything else. There is no adequate direct translation of the word balletomane.

Balletomania, enthusiasm for ballet. See also BALLETOMANE.

Ballet Premier. Ballet in 1 act; chor.: Arnold Spohr; music: Felix Mendelssohn's Piano Concerto No. 1 in G minor; décor: Grant Marshall. First prod.: Winnipeg (now Royal Winnipeg) Ballet, Playhouse

Theatre, Winnipeg, May 2, 1950; revived Mar. 3, 1958. This ballet was given at the Royal Command Performance before T. R. H. Princess Elizabeth (now H. M. Queen Elizabeth II) and the Duke of Edinburgh, Oct. 16, 1951. The original cast was headed by Jean McKenzie and Arnold Spohr. A themeless ballet inspired by the Imperial Russian style using the classic technique in modern idiom.

Ballet Rambert. Beginning with the presentation of Frederick Ashton's *A Tragedy of Fashion* in the revue *Riverside Nights,* at the Lyric Theatre, Hammersmith (June, 1926), the students of Marie Rambert used to give performances in Mme. Rambert's studio or in various theatres in London. Their own first public performance was given at the Lyric Theatre, Hammersmith, Feb. 25, 1930, a date which marks the beginning of the Ballet Rambert, though at first the company was simply known as The Rambert Dancers. In the fall of 1930 the Ballet Club was founded and the dancers gave performances in the tiny Mercury Theatre which also housed the ballet school. The company also continued to perform in other theatres but the Sunday performances at the Mercury became part of the ballet life of London. During its early seasons the company had Tamara Karsavina and, on a few occasions, Leon Woicikowski as guest artists. From the Rambert school came Pearl Argyle, Diana Gould, Prudence Hyman, Andrée Howard, Elisabeth Schooling, Frederick Ashton, William Chappell, Walter Gore, Harold Turner, Antony Tudor. Alicia Markova was ballerina of the Ballet Club for four years. In 1932 Hugh Laing had his first important role as Laeg in the ballet *Unbowed.* After Markova left the company, Peggy van Praag, Frank Staff, and later Maude Lloyd, Sally Gilmour, Celia Franca, Leo Kersley, and others came into prominence. Early in 1940 Ballet Rambert became associated with the Arts Theatre Club and gave London seasons there. In June of that year the company joined forces with the London Ballet, forming the Rambert-London Ballet, a union which continued until Sept., 1941. Then the Arts Theatre Club discontinued its ballet activities and the company was forced to disband until Mar., 1943, when Ballet Rambert was reorganized under the auspices of the Arts Council of Great Britain, giving performances in wartime factories and camps in addition to the regular theatrical tours. In 1947–48 Ballet Rambert, headed by its founder-director and with a company of thirty-six (which included among the principals Belinda Wright and John Gilpin, teenagers at the time), toured in Australia and New Zealand for eighteen months. Since that time Ballet Rambert has continued to tour widely. It visited China (1947), made its U.S. debut at the Jacob's Pillow Dance Festival (1959), Baalbek and Malta (1960) and Italy (1961), among other places. In 1955 David Ellis, Marie Rambert's son-in-law, became Associate Director. In 1962 the company and Marie Rambert's work was given particular recognition by the award to her of the D.B.E. (Dame of the Order of the British Empire). Since World War II the company has been enlarged and no longer performs in the Mercury Theatre, now entirely given over to the school. The tiny auditorium and stage is now another studio but its former appearance is captured permanently in one of the best scenes in the film *The Red Shoes.* There is also another building which houses the academic educational school. Ballet Rambert now has an annual season at Sadler's Wells Theatre in addition to its tours of Great Britain and abroad. Current leading dancers with the company (1962–63) include Lucette Aldous (who left after the 1963 London season to join London Festival Ballet), June Sandbrook, Anna Truscott, Shirley Dixon, Kenneth Bannerman, John Chesworth, Norman Morrice. Ballet Rambert has always had works produced by young choreographers developed out of its own group. Ashton's early works for this company included *Capriol Suite, Façade* (first done for the Camargo Society, but taken immediately into the Rambert repertoire), *Lady of Shalott, Foyer de Danse, Les Masques, Mephisto Valse,* and others; Antony Tudor's first ballet, *Cross-garter'd,* was presented Nov. 12, 1931 and followed by *Lysistrata, Atalanta of the East, The Planets, The Descent of Hebe, Jardin aux Lilas* (Lilac Garden) and *Dark Elegies.* Concurrently Andrée Howard was staging *Mermaid, Alcina Suite, Rape of the Lock, Cinderella, Death and the Maiden,* and later *Lady Into Fox, The Fugitive, The Sailor's Return,* and others. Ninette de Valois staged one work for Ballet Rambert, Bar Aux Folies-Bergère. After Ashton and Tudor left, Frank Staff and Walter Gore developed as choreographers, Staff's best known works being *Peter and the Wolf, Czernyana, Enigma Variations,* and *Un Songe.* Walter Gore's first ballet *Valse Finale* in 1938 was followed by *Paris-Soir* in 1939. After war service, he returned to create *Simple Symphony, Plaisance, Mr. Punch,* and others. In the post-war years David Paltenghi was both a leading dancer and choreographer (*Prismatic Variations, The Eve of St. Agnes,* and others). Robert Joffrey was invited in 1955 to stage *Persephone and Pas des Déesses,* and John Cranko choreographed *Variations on a Theme* and *La Reja.* Then from the company emerged Norman Morrice with *The Two Brothers, The Wise Monkeys, Hazana, A Place in the Desert, Conflicts, The Travellers,* etc. From its early days Ballet Rambert had versions of the standard classic ballets in its repertoire: *Swan Lake* (Act 2), *Les Sylphides, Carnaval, Le Spectre de la Rose, Afternoon of a Faun.* In 1945 the second act of *Giselle* was staged by Marie Rambert; in 1946 the first act was added to make the whole a triumph of Romantic re-creation. A new production of *Giselle* was premièred July 13, 1965, with a new décor by Peter Farmer and with Alida Belaid and Kenneth Bannerman in the leading roles. Elsa-Marianne von Rosen staged the Bournonville *La Sylphide* in 1960, dancing the first few performances. The Moscow version of the old Petipa ballet *Don Quixote* was reproduced by Witold Borkowski in 1962. In spite of an annual grant from the Arts Council of Great Britain, the company battled with financial difficulties all through the early 1960's. A proposal early in 1964 that it should combine with London's Festival Ballet came to nothing. David Ellis resigned as associate director in the spring of 1966, the company's usual summer season at Sadler's Wells Theatre was cancelled, and it was announced that Ballet Rambert would re-organize completely, reverting to a group of sixteen or so dancers, with Marie Rambert and Norman Morrice as joint directors. The intention was to keep the best of the works created for a small cast and to concentrate on ballets by young choreographers of the new generation both in England and abroad. Rudi van Dantzig from Holland and Paul Taylor were among those asked to stage new works. The re-formed Ballet Rambert began its first London season in Nov., 1966.

Ballet Russe de Monte Carlo. Serge Diaghilev died penniless in 1929. Numerous attempts were made to revive his company but nothing much happened until 1931. That summer an opera company, which called itself L'Opéra Russe à Paris, headed by a Georgian, Prince Zeretelli, gave a season in London. One of the associates of Prince Zeretelli, Colonel W. de Basil, was more interested in ballet than in opera, and when he learned toward the end of 1931 that the director of the Monte Carlo Opera Ballet, René Blum, was forming a separate ballet company, he hastened to the resort. When he arrived, Blum's ballet was already in existence under the name Ballets de Théâtre de Monte Carlo. There was little of a concrete nature that Col. de

Basil could offer Blum, but so strong was the Colonel's personality, so persuasive his manner, that Blum did not hesitate to accept him into partnership and to appoint him co-director of the ballet. The company became the René Blum and Col. de Basil Ballets Russes de Monte Carlo.

With George Balanchine and Leonide Massine as choreographers and Serge Grigorieff as régisseur-general, Blum and de Basil assembled the best Russian dancers available outside Russia, including ballerina Alexandra Danilova and the three so-called "baby ballerinas": Irina Baronova, Tamara Toumanova, and Tatiana Riabouchinska. The repertoire included some of the works of the Diaghilev Ballets Russes and new compositions by Balanchine and Massine, including *La Concurrence, Cotillon, Jeux d'Enfants,* and *Le Beau Danube.* The first season was an artistic success; financially, however, it could have been better.

In 1933, the American impresario S. Hurok booked the company for a U.S. tour. The first season at the St. James Theatre, N.Y., and the tour that followed were, like the first London season, successful artistically but left much to be desired financially. Hurok continued to bring the Ballets Russes to America, however, and with every year the seasons grew longer, the tours more extensive, the audiences more appreciative. By the fall of 1935, the ballet seemed to have gained a foothold in the scheme of cultural life in America, and Hurok—deciding that the New York season should take its glamorous place among the gala events of the city's theatrical and social life—booked the Ballet Russe into the Metropolitan Opera House. The season was a huge success.

These first seasons of the Ballet Russe (it had changed its name to the singular after the second season) were among the most productive and artistically the most satisfying. The revived ballets from the Diaghilev repertoire were still fresh and interesting to the public. The new ballets, most of them by Massine, were among the greatest this choreographer has ever created. They included his symphonic ballets, *Les Présages, Choreartium,* and *Symphonie Fantastique.* René Blum gave up his part of the management in 1934, continuing only as artistic director. Two years later he disassociated himself from the company.

At this time, clashes developed within the organization. The two most forceful personalities in the Ballet Russe, Col. de Basil and Massine, found themselves at odds. Their animosity, fed by factions in the company, resulted in an open breach by the summer of 1937, when Massine announced that he was leaving upon the expiration of his contract. His last appearance with the company took place in Oakland, Calif., on Jan. 30, 1938. Artists of the company still tell of that evening when tears mixed with champagne, corps de ballet girls fainted, and Col. de Basil tactfully absented himself from the scene.

Massine now lost no time in getting to Monte Carlo, where René Blum had once more assembled a ballet company, ostensibly for the Monte Carlo Opera. Again, Blum agreed to a partnership. This time, however, his partner was an American corporation, World Art, Inc. (This name was subsequently changed to Universal Art, Inc.) The corporation included Julius Fleischmann, of the Cincinnati Yeast Fleischmanns (president), and Sergei I. Denham of N.Y. financial circles (vice-president).

When the American season of Col. de Basil's Ballet Russe was over in Feb., 1938, Danilova, Toumanova, Eleanora Marra, Roland Guerard, Marc Platoff, George Zoritch, and a few others left to join Massine. This was a blow to Col. de Basil, who thought he was entitled to a greater display of loyalty. A worse blow came when S. Hurok announced that beginning with the following season he would book the new company and not de Basil's.

With Fleischmann as president, Denham as vice-president and director, René Blum as co-director, Leonide Massine as artistic director (a title he had coveted ever since joining de Basil), Efrem Kurtz as musical director, Hurok as American impresario, and an array of dancers that included (in addition to those mentioned above) Alicia Markova, Serge Lifar, Nathalie Krassovska, Nini Theilade, Igor Youskevitch, Frederic Franklin, and others, the new company offered serious competition to Col. de Basil.

In March came the announcement that both organizations agreed in principle on a merger. By April both sides stated that all that was missing were the signatures of the principals. Fleischmann was mentioned as chairman of the executive committee and president of the corporation, Denham as vice-president, de Basil as member of the board of governors, Massine as head of the artistic council. And then, on June 17, Universal Art, Inc., instituted proceedings to restrain de Basil from "producing, performing, or authorizing the production of certain ballets," which were scheduled for his London season. On June 20th Col. de Basil's company, notwithstanding the suit, opened the season at the Covent Garden Royal Opera House; on July 11 the Massine company opened its season at the Drury Lane Theatre. To make possible the opening of the season, Col. de Basil had to resign his post as director of the company and the ballet took a new name, the Royal Covent Garden Ballet Russe. The directorship of the company went to Victor Dandré, German Sevastianov, and Serge Grigorieff. Col. de Basil was supposed to have retired.

The direct result of this "ballet war" was that Massine's Ballet Russe de Monte Carlo came to America in Oct. 1938, headed by Massine, Danilova, Markova, Toumanova, Mia Slavenska, Youskevitch, André Eglevsky, Franklin, and Lifar. Additions to the repertoire were Massine's *Gaîté Parisienne* and *Seventh Symphony* from the European season and his new *Saint Francis*. The Covent Garden company went to Australia in August with Baronova, Riabouchinska, Anton Dolin, and David Lichine.

The Ballet Russe de Monte Carlo toured the U.S. for two seasons with great success. The Royal Covent Garden Ballet Russe changed its name to Educational Ballets, Ltd., and still later to Original Ballet Russe. Col. de Basil succeeded in regaining the management, if not the ownership, of the Original Ballet Russe and rejoined the company in Australia. *Graduation Ball* was premièred there. In the fall of 1940 the company came to the U.S. from Australia, and Hurok presented the Original Ballet Russe following the Ballet Russe de Monte Carlo at the 51st Street Theatre in the longest ballet season N.Y. had ever witnessed. Of the two companies, the Ballet Russe de Monte Carlo had the advantage of possessing two of the great ballerinas of the time, Danilova and Markova; and three of the great male dancers, Youskevitch, Eglevsky, and Franklin. The Original Ballet Russe evoked a nostalgic feeling by assembling Baronova, Toumanova, and Riabouchinska.

The N.Y. 1940–41 season over, the Ballet Russe de Monte Carlo went on its scheduled tour through the U.S., and the Original Ballet Russe embarked for Central and South America. The beginning of the tour in Mexico was quite successful. The second stop was Havana, Cuba. It also turned out to be the last stop, for no sooner had the company arrived in Cuba than eighteen of the dancers declared a strike against Col. de Basil, alleging breach of contract, underpayment of salaries, and other charges. The result of the strike was that the company failed to sail for South America, and Hurok had to cancel the bookings. The company was stranded in Havana and did not return to the U.S. until the late summer.

Col. de Basil succeeded in acquiring another impresario. This was Fortune Gallo, manager of the San Carlo Opera Company. Under Gallo, the Original Ballet Russe opened its 1941–42 season in Aug. at the Watergate Stadium, Washington, D.C. For two months everything was fine, and then, in Detroit, de Basil and Gallo decided they could no longer cooperate. The Original Ballet Russe was once again left without an impresario.

On Dec. 31, 1941, the company left for Mexico, whence, in March, it sailed for South America. The Latin American sojourn lasted over four years. The company returned to the U.S. in the fall of 1946 and, once more under S. Hurok, danced the fall season at the Metropolitan, went on tour through the U.S., and again appeared at the Metropolitan in the spring of 1947. In the fall, the company toured Europe. It was disbanded in France that winter.

Meanwhile the Ballet Russe de Monte Carlo had a successful 1941–42 season, climaxed by a spring season at the Metropolitan. In the fall the company premièred Agnes de Mille's *Rodeo.* The contract between Ballet Russe de Monte Carlo and S. Hurok expired at the end of Oct. The company then signed with a new impresario, Columbia Concerts, Inc., headed by Messrs. F. C. Coppicus and F. C. Schang. This association lasted only one season. In the spring of 1943 the company appeared at the Broadway Theatre, N.Y.; it had no N.Y. season in the fall.

Beginning with the season 1943–44 David Libidins, formerly company manager of the Ballet Russe, took over the booking direction of the company, a function he continued to perform until fall, 1948. In the spring of 1944, the Ballet Russe de Monte Carlo had its first season at the N.Y. City Center of Music and Drama, where it appeared every fall and mid-winter until the fall of 1948, when it celebrated its 10th anniversary at the Metropolitan Opera House. By that time the company was a nonprofit organization headed by its director, Sergei I. Denham.

Until 1950, the company continued to tour the U.S. and to perform in N.Y., though with diminishing success. Danilova and Franklin continued to head the company, and other soloists in this period were Leon Danielian, Ruthanna Boris, Mary Ellen Moylan, Oleg Tupine, Roman Jasinsky, Gertrude Tyven, Nina Novak, Yvonne Couteau, and Robert Lindgren. After a period of inactivity, the Ballet Russe resumed local touring with a personnel led by Franklin and Maria Tallchief. The ballet was again associated with Columbia Artists Management. In 1957 the Ballet Russe played its first New York season in seven years. Alicia Alonso and Igor Youskevitch were guest artists for the occasion, and the other principals were Novak, Alan Howard, and Irina Borowska. Thereafter, the company made annual tours of the U.S., but played only occasional, isolated performances in the N.Y. area. The Ballet Russe has been inactive as a performing company since 1962–63, but continues to maintain its ballet school in N.Y.

Ballet School. Ballet in 1 act; chor.: Asaf Messerer; music: Liadov, Liapunov, Glazounov and Shostakovitch. First prod.: Bolshoi Ballet, Metropolitan Opera House, N.Y., Sept. 17, 1962, with Maya Plisetskaya, Yekaterina Maximova, Maya Samokhvalova, Margarita Smirnova, Nina Fedorova, Tatiana Popko, Nicolai Fadeyechev, Vladimir Vasiliev, Vladimir Nikonov, Mikhail Lavrovsky, with corps de ballet and six boys and twelve girls from schools in the N.Y. area. The first Soviet ballet ever to be premièred outside the Soviet Union, this work was created at the suggestion of S. Hurok after watching a short ballet *Dance Lessons,* which forms part of the annual graduation exercises at the Bolshoi Theatre Ballet School. Asaf Messerer prepared *Ballet School,* in which he appears briefly as ballet master with the young pupils, as a documentary display of the teaching methods of the school, building into a prodigious demonstration of virtuoso feats by principal members of the company. The score was later changed to music entirely by Shostakovitch.

Ballet Society, The, a non-profit, tax-exempt membership corporation for the encouragement of the lyric theatre by the production of new works; founded by George Balanchine and Lincoln Kirstein, July 15, 1946. The inaugural performance was presented by Ballet Society Nov. 20, 1946, at the Central High School of Needle Trades. It included Maurice Ravel's *The Spellbound Child* and Paul Hindemith's *The Four Temperaments,* both choreographed by George Balanchine. Between that date and Apr. 28, 1948, the brilliant première of the Stravinsky-Balanchine *Orpheus* at the City Center, Ballet Society was mainly a producing organization, offering performances of new ballets four times a year. From time to time the membership was offered other performances, among which Gian-Carlo Menotti's operas *The Medium* and *The Telephone* were probably the most outstanding. Other events sponsored by Ballet Society included lecture demonstrations and exhibitions of dance films. Members also received the Nijinsky, Isadora Duncan, and Anna Pavlova books edited by Paul Magriel, *The Yearbook of Ballet Society,* 1946–47 (only one issue of the Yearbook was published), and subscriptions to the excellent magazine *Dance Index.* When the performing company was invited by Morton Baum, Chairman of the Finance Committee of the New York City Center of Music and Drama to become the New York City Ballet, in Apr., 1948, Ballet Society became a holding company, since the New York City Ballet was not a registered corporation or company. With parts of its activities taken over by the New York City Ballet and the City Center, Ballet Society enlarged the scope of its interests. In 1959 the Ford Foundation (see FOUNDATIONS, PHILANTHROPIC) made a grant of $150,000 to Ballet Society for a number of scholarships to be awarded during three years to talented students (outside N.Y. and San Francisco) to provide them with advanced training at the School of American Ballet, N.Y. or the San Francisco Ballet School, and later, to provide opportunities to perform with the corps de ballet of the New York City Ballet or the San Francisco Ballet. Auditions were held in many schools throughout the country by George Balanchine (Eastern U.S.) and by Lew Christensen, director of the San Francisco Ballet and School (Western U.S.), or their representatives. Taking cognizance of the rapid development of civic ballets in the U.S. and the regional ballet and festival movement, Ballet Society organized a conference on the subject, Ballet—A National Movement, Nov. 25–26, 1960, to which it invited directors of civic and regional ballets, teachers, choreographers, writers, and non-professionals interested in the movement. Some one hundred and fifty guests came to New York to attend the conference to listen to such speakers as Joseph B. Martinson, President, Ballet Society; George Balanchine, Artistic Director of the New York City Ballet and its principal choreographer; Dr. Charles B. Fahs, Director, Division of Humanities, The Rockefeller Foundation (see FOUNDATIONS, PHILANTHROPIC); W. McNeil Lowry, Director, Program in Humanities and the Arts, The Ford Foundation; Morton Baum; Dorothy Alexander, member Advisory Board, Regional Ballet Festival Association; Lucia Chase, Director, American Ballet Theatre; Lew Christensen; Hy Faine, National Executive Secretary, American Guild of Musical Artists (AGMA) and others. The guests also participated in the discussions, and the organizers had a chance to hear and reflect on the opinions of those who did the actual work in the field. Nothing like the conference had ever happened to the dance in America; both the guests and the organizers realized its importance. In fact, the organizers thought that the conference could be made into an annual event, but soon after it ended they realized that this was not feasible because it was too large and too complex an undertaking to be held annually. Instead Ballet Society selected a number of special and unique services which would be of the greatest possible benefit to the dance field, especially to teachers and directors of civic and regional companies, and made them their goal. These services included annual one-week, two-hour-a-day seminars for teachers held in mid-June at the School of American Ballet, instructed by George Balanchine and demonstrated by members of the New York City Ballet (1963 attendance was approx. 70); assistance to out-of-N.Y. schools in diverse ways; staging of Balanchine ballets for regional companies by the choreographer or his assistants; a pool of guest artists for regional companies; free ballet performances for N.Y. high schools during Assembly periods. This last is a special project of Mrs. Nancy Lassalle, a member of the board of Ballet Society. Both Lincoln Kirstein and George Balanchine continue to take a most active interest in all facets of work of the organization.

Ballet Theatre, launched in New York City in the fall of 1939, was an outgrowth of the Mordkin Ballet, which began in 1937 as an outlet for the talents of the students of Mikhail Mordkin's school. In the Mordkin Ballet the soloists were Lucia Chase, Viola Essen, Leon Varkas, Dimitri Romanoff, George Chaffee, and Leon Danielian. The repertoire included *Giselle, La Fille Mal Gardée, Dionysius* (to Glazounov's music), and *The Goldfish,* all choreographed by Mordkin who also appeared in some of the ballets.

The second season of the Mordkin Ballet (1938) brought many additions and a number of changes in the personnel. Richard Pleasant was appointed general manager of the company; Patricia Bowman was engaged as prima ballerina; Nina Stroganova, Karen Conrad, Edward Caton, Vladimir Dokoudovsky, Kari Karnakoski, and Savva Andreeff were new soloists. The repertoire was augmented by *Voices of Spring, Trepak* (Alexander Tcherepnine's music) and what was called a symphonic version of *Swan Lake* (Act 2). It was an open secret that the Mordkin Ballet was financed by Lucia Chase.

By the summer of 1939 Miss Chase and Mr. Pleasant had decided that the Mordkin Ballet was too small an undertaking and they began to formulate plans for a full-fledged company, to be called Ballet Theatre. Pleasant was appointed director of the organization. Only one of Mordkin's ballets, *Voices of Spring,* was retained.

The repertoire of the first season of Ballet Theatre listed Michel Fokine's *Les Sylphides* and *Carnaval;* Adolph Bolm's *Ballet Mécanique* and *Peter and the Wolf;* Mordkin's *Voices of Spring;* Anton Dolin's *Quintet* and his versions of *Giselle* and *Swan Lake;* Antony Tudor's *Dark Elegies, Lilac Garden,* and *Judgment of Paris;* Andrée Howard's *Lady into Fox* and *Death and the Maiden;* Agnes de Mille's *Black Ritual;* Eugene Loring's *The Great American Goof;* José Fernandez' *Goyescas;* Bronislava Nijinska's *La Fille Mal Gardée;* Yurek Shabelevski's *Ode to Glory.*

Among the dancers were Adolph Bolm, Patricia Bowman, Edward Caton, Lucia Chase, Karen Conrad, Leon Danielian, Vladimir Dokoudovsky, Anton Dolin, William Dollar, Viola Essen, Miriam Golden, Nana Gollner (who was announced but did not dance during the first N.Y. season), Kari Karnakoski, Maria Karnilova, Nora Kaye, Andrée Howard, Eugene Loring, Hugh Laing, Annabelle Lyon, Dimitri Romanoff, Donald Saddler, Nina Stroganova, Yurek Shabelevski, Antony Tudor, Leon Varkas.

The first Ballet Theatre season opened Jan. 11, 1940, at the Center Theatre,

N.Y., and lasted four weeks. Between Feb. and Nov. the company gave scattered performances in Philadelphia and at Lewisohn Stadium in N.Y. In Nov. and Dec. it danced in Chicago as the official ballet of the Chicago Opera, giving twelve ballet evenings and appearing in opera ballets.

The second season opened in N.Y. at the Majestic Theatre on Feb. 11, 1941. The company announced some innovations. There would be no division in ranks of the dancers; all were to be divided into two groups: principals and company. The roster of principals included Chase, Conrad, Gollner, Lyon, Katharine Sergava, Stroganova, Caton, Danielian, Dolin, Laing, Loring, Romanoff, and Tudor. Alicia Alonso, Miriam Golden, Nora Kaye, John Kriza, and Jerome Robbins were among "the company."

Another innovation was the absence of a regisseur-general. In lieu of one, Ballet Theatre had choreographers-in-residence, who were regisseurs for separate "wings" of the repertoire. Dolin was regisseur of the Classical wing, Eugene Loring of the American wing, and Antony Tudor of the new English wing. Five ballets new for the company were presented: Dolin's *Capriccioso* and *Pas de Quatre,* Loring's *Billy the Kid;* Tudor's *Gala Performance,* and de Mille's *Three Virgins and a Devil.*

At the close of the four-week season, Richard Pleasant resigned as director of the company. Shortly thereafter, Ballet Theatre began to reorganize. German Sevastianov was invited as director; Charles Payne became executive managing director; Antal Dorati was appointed musical director. Alicia Markova and Irina Baronova were signed as ballerinas.

In June, 1941, Markova and Dolin organized an International Dance Festival at Jacob's Pillow, where most of the company's dancers spent the summer, thus giving an opportunity to some of the choreographers to work on their new productions.

Meanwhile arrangements were made for impresario S. Hurok to book Ballet Theatre beginning Nov., 1941. The company then included, among others: Markova, Baronova, Muriel Bentley, Chase, Conrad, Rosella Hightower, Kaye, Karnilova, Jeannette Lauret, Lyon, Sono Osato, Nina Popova, Rozsika Sabo; Dolin, Charles Dickson, Ian Gibson, Frank Hobi, Kriza, Laing, Yurek Lazowski, Nicolas Orloff, Richard Reed, Jerome Robbins, Romanoff, Borislav Runanin, Donald Saddler, Simon Semenoff, George Skibine, and Tudor.

The company played a season in Mexico City, then opened in N.Y. on Nov. 12th at the 44th Street Theatre. Four new ballets were presented: *Bluebeard* by Fokine, *Beloved* by Nijinska, *Princess Aurora* (another title for *Aurora's Wedding*) by Dolin, *Slavonika* by Vania Psota.

After an American tour, the company returned to N.Y. opening at the Metropolitan Opera House, Apr. 6, 1942. The new works were Michel Fokine's *Russian Soldier* and Tudor's *Pillar of Fire.* Nora Kaye's performance in the latter placed her in the rank of ballerina overnight. Then there was a summer season in Mexico City with Fokine and Leonide Massine as choreographers. There the company rehearsed *Aleko* and *Don Domingo* by Massine; *Romantic Age* by Dolin; *Petrouchka,* restaged by Fokine; as well as revivals of *Billy the Kid* and *Coppélia.* Fokine began work on *Helen of Troy* but did not finish it due to illness. He returned to N.Y. on Aug. 12 and died Aug. 22 of double pneumonia complicated by pleurisy.

The six ballets prepared in Mexico City were presented during the fall season, which opened at the Metropolitan Opera House, Oct. 6. Adolph Bolm had been signed as regisseur-general, Leonide Massine as choreographer and dancer, André Eglevsky as guest artist; Michael Kidd joined the company. On the tour that followed, *Helen of Troy* was choreographed by David Lichine. Irina Baronova left the company late in 1942.

For the N.Y. season (beginning Apr. 1, 1943) at the Metropolitan, Vera Nemchinova, Vera Zorina, and Janet Reed joined the company as guest artists. Additions to the repertoire were *Romeo and Juliet* by Tudor; *Errante* and *Apollo,* revived by George Balanchine. This season J. Alden Talbot became director of the company, replacing Sevastianov who had joined the U.S. Army. For the fall season Zorina was again guest artist; Janet Reed joined the company as soloist, and Alicia Alonso returned as soloist after an absence of two years. The new ballets were *Dim Lustre* by Tudor, *Mam'zelle Angot* by Massine, *Fair at Sorochinsk* by Lichine. Alicia Alonso was given the opportunity to dance *Giselle* (Nov. 2, 1943), which raised her to ballerina status. During the tour that followed, Nana Gollner and Paul Petroff joined the company.

In the spring of 1944, *Tally-Ho* by de Mille and *Fancy Free* by Robbins were added to the repertoire, and in the fall Balanchine's *Waltz Academy*. The guest artists were Tatiana Riabouchinska, Tamara Toumanova, Eglevsky and Lichine; Markova and Dolin had left the company.

Undertow by Tudor was the only important new ballet presented in the spring of 1945. Markova, Dolin, Toumanova, and Eglevsky were back as guests. Talbot resigned as director, and Lucia Chase and Oliver Smith became co-directors, positions they have held ever since. The fall brought five new ballets: *On Stage!* by Kidd; *Gift of the Magi* by Semenoff; *Graziana* by John Taras; *Interplay* by Robbins; and a new version of *Firebird* by Bolm.

After the spring of 1946, the contract between Ballet Theatre and S. Hurok was terminated, and the directors announced a return to the company's 1940 policy of being "American in character" and of building "from within its own ranks." Ballet Theatre played July 4–Aug. 31 at Covent Garden Royal Opera House, London. Eglevsky, Kaye and Alonso were leading soloists. While the company was in England, Keith Lester staged his version of *Pas de Quatre* for it, and Frederick Ashton staged *Les Patineurs.*

The company played a fall season at the Broadway Theatre, N.Y. *Giselle* was restaged by Balanchine, with new scenery and costumes by Eugene Berman, and *Facsimile* was choreographed by Robbins. Igor Youskevitch was invited as premier danseur; newly appointed soloists were Diana Adams, Melissa Hayden, and Ruth Ann Koesun. Tudor was artistic administrator.

The 1946–47 tour was an artistic success, but the company lost money. The N.Y. season at the City Center for Music and Drama (Apr. 28–May 18) was successful artistically and financially. An engagement in Havana, Cuba, closed the season on an optimistic note.

In the spring of 1947, Ballet Theatre Foundation was established as a tax-exempt, non-profit corporation for the purpose of supporting Ballet Theatre as a performing organization.

The fall season, also at the City Center, introduced Balanchine's *Theme and Variations.* Following its 1947–48 tour, the company played a season at the Metropolitan, where it premièred Tudor's *Shadow of the Wind* and de Mille's *Fall River Legend.* There was no fall season, but a short spring tour in 1948 was followed by an engagement at the Metropolitan from Apr. 17 to May 8. Maria Tallchief joined the company.

The spring 1950 season at the City Center, N.Y., was preceded by a national tour. From August 7 to December 10, the company made its first tour of Europe, traveling as the American National Ballet Theatre, sponsored by the State Department. Leading soloists seen in Europe were Alicia Alonso, Nora Kaye, John Kriza, John Taras, Mary Ellen Moylan, and Igor Youskevitch. *Designs with Strings* and *Caprichos* (Herbert Ross) were premièred this season; *Rodeo* was added to the repertoire. In the fall of 1950, Ballet Theatre became the ballet of the Metropolitan Opera. The association only lasted one season. Adams, Kaye, Laing, and Tudor left the company.

In the spring of 1951, the N.Y. season featured Jean Babilée, Colette Marchand, Nathalie Philippart, and Mia Slavenska as guest artists. *Le Jeune Homme et la Mort, Les Demoiselles de la Nuit,* and *L'Amour et son Amour* were given their American premières. Herbert Ross did his *The Thief Who Loved a Ghost* for the company, and Carmalita Maracci created *Circo de España.* In May and June, the company toured South America. Coinciding with a season at the Metropolitan, the Ballet Theatre School opened officially in Dec. A fall season without significant premières was followed by a national tour.

A second European tour, sponsored by the State Dept. occupied Ballet Theatre from May 4 to end of Sept., 1953. Principal soloists were Alonso, Hayden, Kriza, Moylan, and Youskevitch. The following season was devoted largely to touring the U.S. and was also marked by television appearances of the company, notably on the "Omnibus" show for which the Ford Foundation commissioned *Capital of the World* by Eugene Loring.

In the spring of 1955, Ballet Theatre celebrated its fifteenth anniversary with a gala season at the Metropolitan, followed by a South American tour. For the gala, a number of former soloists returned to dance their original roles in revivals of ballets associated with the company.

May 7, 1956 saw the initiation at N.Y.'s Phoenix Theatre of the Ballet Theatre Workshop, formed to provide choreographers with a showcase to try out new works. The first program was praised more for its intention than its attainment. The following year (1957) two Workshop programs featured significant new works, Kenneth MacMillan's *Journey* and Herbert Ross's *Paean.* This Workshop was preceded by a tour of Europe and the Near East. Featured soloists were Erik Bruhn, Scott Douglas, Rosella Hightower, Nora Kaye, John Kriza, and Lupe Serrano.

On the return from Europe the company changed its name from Ballet Theatre to American Ballet Theatre. In the summer of 1957, American Ballet Theatre toured the U.S. The following spring it set out for North Africa and Europe. Violette Verdy and Royes Fernandez were the new principals for this successful tour. The autumn 1958 season at the Metropolitan brought some undistinguished premières, but the addition to the repertoire of *Miss Julie* was an asset. With only scant bookings available for 1959, American Ballet Theatre was forced to suspend its activities for a year.

The spring, 1960 season at the Metropolitan marked the temporary return to the company of Nora Kaye and the moderately successful première of *Lady from the Sea.* Maria Tallchief and Erik Bruhn headed the company that set off for Europe in May. In Sept. American Ballet Theatre became the first American ballet company to dance in the Soviet Union.

A spring tour in the U.S. was made in 1961 and was followed by an autumn season at N.Y.'s 54th Street Theatre with guest artists Mariane Orlando and Caj Selling joining soloists Ivan Allen, Elisabeth Carroll, Fernandez, Kriza, Koesun, Toni Lander, Serrano, Bruce Marks, and Sallie Wilson. Two European ballets were added to the repertoire: *Moon Reindeer* and *Etudes,* the latter with notable success.

In Nov., 1962, Ballet Theatre announced that it was moving its headquarters to Washington, where it would henceforth operate under the auspices of the Washington Ballet Guild. A few performances were given in that city, but in Apr., 1963, the Guild stated that the cost of maintaining the company had run far beyond preliminary estimates. Later the

Guild decided to sponsor Ballet Theatre performances in Washington. Miss Chase and Mr. Smith announced that Ballet Theatre had been disbanded for the summer, but would resume full-scale activity in the fall of 1964, which it did, ending its Washington connection and making N.Y. its home base again.

From mid-Aug. to early Nov., 1964, the company toured South America and Mexico sponsored by the U.S. Dept. of State's Cultural Presentations Program, following this with a brief tour in Texas and the South. During this tour Harald Lander's staging of August Bournonville's *La Sylphide,* with Toni Lander and Royes Fernandez in the principal roles had its première (San Antonio, Nov. 11). American Ballet Theatre celebrated its 25th anniversary with a season (Mar. 16 to Apr. 11, 1965) at the N.Y. State Theater, Lincoln Center. The company was in splendid form and had a resounding success. *La Sylphide* had its N.Y. première and other new works were Agnes de Mille's *The Wind in the Mountains* (Mar. 17), and *The Four Marys* (Mar. 23), the latter with guest artist Carmen de Lavallade in the leading role; Glen Tetley's *Sargasso* (the first major creation for Sallie Wilson, Mar. 24), Bentley Stone's *L'Inconnue* (Apr. 6) and, most importantly, the great Jerome Robbins version of Igor Stravinsky's *Les Noces* (Mar. 30). The season also saw the revival of Antony Tudor's *Dark Elegies* and three new young sailors (Eliot Feld, Edward Verso, William Glassman) in *Fancy Free.* In Sept. the company danced in Hawaii and Alaska. On Nov. 15, 1965, the National Council on the Arts announced an emergency grant of $100,000 to insure the company's immediate survival and an additional $250,000 towards the expenses of a projected tour of the U.S., both grants being on a matching basis. The company's second season at the N.Y. State Theater (Jan. 18 to Feb. 13, 1966) did not produce any new work as distinguished as *Les Noces,* but the revival of Tudor's *Pillar of Fire,* with Sallie Wilson or Veronika Mlakar in the role of Hagar was another triumph. New works were Glen Tetley's *Ricercare* with guest artist Mary Hinkson and Scott Douglas (Jan. 25), Todd Bolender's *Kontraste* (Jan. 28) and Enrique Martinez's *Balladen der Liebe* (Feb. 8). John Kriza gave his final performance with the company (Feb. 3), dancing the Minister in *Fall River Legend,* retiring to become assistant to the directors. During June and July the company toured the Soviet Union for the second time under the auspices of the Cultural Presentations Program and on its return, after a rehearsal period in N.Y., began its most extensive tour of the U.S. and Canada, appearing in nearly one hundred cities. Leading dancers for this tour were listed as Lupe Serrano, Royes Fernandez, Toni Lander, Scott Douglas, Ruth Ann Koesun, Bruce Marks, Sallie Wilson, Eleanor D'Antuono, Gayle Young, Paul Sutherland, Veronika Mlakar. Before the company started on this tour, its third annual season at the N.Y. State Theater was announced for May, 1967.

Ballet Theatre Foundation. See FOUNDATIONS, PHILANTHROPIC.

Ballet Today (publication). See PERIODICALS, DANCE (ENGLAND).

Ballet Workshop, an experimental English ballet organization founded by David Ellis and his wife Angela Ellis (daughter of Marie Rambert) at the Mercury Theatre, London. Its working life (Sunday eve. performances) extended from 1951 to 1955.

Ballets de Cour, Les (Court Ballets), spectacles that were produced from the middle of the 16th to the middle of the 17th centuries. Created to celebrate special occasions, they included verse, vocal music, and danced entrées. The subject matter was pastoral, allegorical, and mythological. The finale was always Le Grand Ballet, in which the entire cast appeared. The dancers were the noble guests, not professionals. The dances included the various court dances of the day and also the Morisco. Although France was the home of the Court Ballets, a number were produced in Italy. The Prince of Savoy appeared in one. Carriages were used drawn by horses and, at times, elephants and camels. Prunières has written in detail of the Ballet de Cour in his *Le Ballet de Cour Avant Lully*.

Ballets de Monte Carlo, new company established in the summer of 1966 by Sergei I. Denham, director of the dormant Ballet Russe de Monte Carlo, to be situated in Monte Carlo under the patronage of Prince Rainier III of Monaco, with the Monte Carlo Opera House as its home. (See also in this connection the Diaghilev Ballet, Ballet Russe de Monte Carlo, Original Ballet Russe.) With Mr. Denham as director of the new organization and Leonide Massine as choreographer and artistic adviser, the company presented its first season during the 1966 Christmas holidays.

Ballets de Paris de Roland Petit, a French company formed by Roland Petit in 1948 after he had left Les Ballets des Champs-Elysées. The new company was supported by the Italian Prince Alessandro Ruspoli. For its first season at the Théâtre Marigny in May, 1948 Petit invited Margot Fonteyn to create the leading role in his new ballet, *Les Demoiselles de la Nuit. L'Oeuf à la Coque, La Croquese de Diamants* and the sensational *Carmen,* premièred in London in 1949, were the principal works of the period. The small company included Renée Jeanmaire, Colette Marchand, Janine Charrat, Nina Vyroubova, Gordon Hamilton, Serge Perrault, Vladimir Skouratoff, and Petit himself. The company disbanded in the U.S. in 1950, following a season in N.Y. and a tour. Re-formed in Paris in 1953, with Violette Verdy, Claire Sombert, Hélène Constantine, José Ferran, Perrault, George Reich, Jean Babilée and Petit, and a new repertoire including *Le Loup, Deuil en 24 Heures, Ciné Bijou, Lady in the Ice*. After seasons in Paris, London, and N.Y. the company again broke up in America in 1954. It had a season in Paris in 1955, with Verdy, Veronika Mlakar, and Petit, and finally, in 1958, seasons at the Alhambra in Paris, and N.Y., the new repertoire being *Centre-Pointe, La Dame dans la Lune, La Rose des Vents*. Dirk (Dick) Sanders was an attractive newcomer, but again the company was disbanded after a short engagement.

Ballets des Champs-Elysées, the first important entirely French company, organized in Paris in 1945 by Roland Petit, Boris Kochno, and Irène Lidova, from the younger generation of French dancers who developed toward the end and immediately after World War II. First season at Théâtre des Champs-Elysées, Oct. 1945, with Petit as principal choreographer, ballet master and leading male dancer. Financial help came from Petit's father, Edmond Petit, and also from the direction of the Théâtre des Champs-Elysées. The freshness and novelty of this company with its very Parisian style made a great impression in France and England, where it had a London season in 1946 (the first foreign company to appear in England after the war), and wherever it traveled. The original talent of the young Petit was a revelation, as were the talents and personalities of such young artists as Jean Babilée, Ana Nevada, Irène Skorik, Ethery Pagava (only thirteen in 1945), Nathalie Philippart and, later, Nina Vyroubova, Youly Algaroff, Christian Foye, Jean Guélis, Danielle Darmance, Violette Verdy (under her family name of Nelly Guillerm), Leslie Caron, and others. The repertoire of the first two years included *Les Forains, Le Rendezvous, Le Déjeuner sur l'Herbe, La Fiancée* *du Diable, Les Amours de Jupiter* (all choreographed by Petit); *Jeu de Cartes* (Janine Charrat), *Caprichos* (Ana Nevada), *Concert de Danse* (Marcel Bergé); *La Sylphide,* choreographed by Victor Gsovsky as a re-creation of the original Filippo Taglioni ballet, based on material in the Paris Opéra Museum; and the striking *Le Jeune Homme et la Mort.* Petit's last works for the company were *Le Bal de Blanchisseuses* (Dec., 1946), and *Treize Danses* (1947). Aurel Milloss was invited to stage *Le Portrait de Don Quichotte,* Nov., 1947. During that year Petit broke with the company and the management of the theatre took over the entire organization, Petit losing even the rights to his own works. Boris Kochno, the administrator Jean Robin and ballet master Victor Govsky kept the company going, inviting David Lichine as choreographer (1948). He staged two works: *Création* (ballet without music) and *La Rencontre, ou Oedipe et la Sphinx,* with Leslie Caron as the Sphinx (in Nov.), while Babilée choreographed *L'Amour et son Amour* (Dec.). This was the end of the company's successful period. By 1949 the enthusiasm was lost. Kochno engaged John Taras who produced some works, including *Devoirs des Vacances,* and Leonide Massine (*Le Peintre et son Modèle*). Christian Bérard, friend and inspirer of the company from the beginning died, and Roland Petit made competition with his Ballets de Paris. Les Ballets des Champs-Elysées was disbanded in 1949 in an atmosphere of confusion. Kochno and Robin, with the collaboration of Ruth Page and Walter Gore tried to revive the company in 1951 with a season at the Théâtre de l'Empire in Oct., bringing together Jacqueline Moreau, Sonja Arova, Hélène Trailine, and as guest artist, the American dancer Leon Danielian. New ballets included *La Revanche* (*The Revenge*) choreographed by Ruth Page, based on the music and story of Verdi's *Il Trovatore;* and Walter Gore's *The Damned.* After a short tour the company was finally disbanded. So ended the career of the Ballets des Champs-Elysées which began so gloriously and which, during its short life span, presented so many leading French dancers and musicians, and such brilliant designers as Antoni Clavé, Jean-Denis Malclès, Stanislas Lepri, Tom Keogh, André Beaurepaire, Georges Wakhevitch, and others.

Ballets Jooss. See Jooss Ballet.

Ballets 1933, Les, a ballet company founded by the English patron of the arts Edward James, choreographer George Balanchine, ballet scenarist Boris Kochno, and manager Vladimir Dimitriev, after they realized the retardative and dominantly commercial aims of Col. W. de Basil, who had organized his Ballets Russes de Monte Carlo a year earlier. In his provocative book *Blast at Ballet* (N.Y., 1938) Lincoln Kirstein says the following about Les Ballets 1933:

"It [the founding of the company] was not an easy task, for after a single season the Monte Carlo company had appropriated unto itself the prestige of the 'true' mantle of [Serge] Diaghilev. However, when the first nights of both companies arrived in June, 1933, the actual hereditary distinction of Diaghilev was found to be resident not in the old Châtelet, the scene of triumph of *Les Sylphides,* (*Prince*) *Igor* and *Petrouchka,* but in the newer Champs-Elysées (where Les Ballets 1933 had its season).

"The creators of Les Ballets 1933 included: [André] Derain, with his marvelous Etruscan decorations and clothes for *Fastes* and *Les Songes,* and the musicians [Henri] Sauguet, and [Darius] Milhaud. Pavel Tchelitchev set his white, hysterical and crystalline stage for *Errante,* with Charles Koechlin's splendid orchestration of Schubert's "Wanderer" fantasy; the active German poet and creator of contemporary epic drama, Bertolt Brecht and his composer-colleague Kurt Weill; the surrealist architect Emilio

Terry; and the brilliant young stage designer Casper Neher.

"Their dozen or so evenings of ballet in Paris and London in the summer of 1933 were, in reality, the swan song of the Diaghilev period. Here was real artistic discovery, real theatrical invention, true collaboration on Diaghilev's own ground, even without him. It could not have been greatly different even had he been alive to supervise the scene, for every new talent of the day, with the possible exception of Sàlvador Dali and the surrealists (who had refused on ideological grounds to be included), was somehow involved.

"Significant and novel ideas in music, dance, poetry and social comment were presented. Nothing as powerful, influential or original as this had happened in the world of theatrical dancing since that time. If the responsibility for the success of Les Ballets 1933 was due to any one person, it was to their choreographer, George Balanchine."

The repertoire of the company included *Errante, Songes (Dreams), Mozartiana, Les Sept Péchés Capitaux (The Seven Deadly Sins,* also called *Anna-Anna), Fastes, Valses by Beethoven, Job,* of which the first three works were made part of the first season (1935) of The American Ballet, and the fourth was restaged by Balanchine for the New York City Ballet and premièred Dec. 4, 1958. The principal dancers in Les Ballets 1933 included Tamara Toumanova, Lubov Rostova, Tilly Losch, Nathalie Krassovska (who danced under her family name of Leslie), Pearl Argyle, Roman Jasinski. Lotte Lenya (wife of composer Kurt Weill) played the singing Anna in *The Seven Deadly Sins,* a role which she repeated twenty-five years later in the New York City Ballet production of the ballet.

Ballets Suédois, Les. See SWEDISH BALLETS.

Ballets: U.S.A., or to give the company its full title Jerome Robbins's Ballets: U.S.A., was founded by Robbins in the spring of 1958 for appearances at the first Festival of Two Worlds, Spoleto, Italy, organized by composer Gian-Carlo Menotti, and in the U.S. Pavilion at the Brussels Exposition. It appeared in both places with notable success, having made its debut June 6 at the Teatro Nuovo in Spoleto with a program consisting of *Concerto* (Todd Bolender–Chopin), *Afternoon of a Faun* (Robbins's version) and *N.Y. Export: Opus Jazz* (Robert Prince–Robbins). In addition to these places the company also danced at the Maggio Musicale Fiorentino, Florence, and in Trieste. Upon its return to the U.S. it played a three-week engagement (Sept. 4–28), at the Alvin Theatre, N.Y. To the touring program Robbins added a short ballet entitled *3x3,* to music by Georges Auric. In the spring of 1959 the company was invited to return to Spoleto for the second Festival of Two Worlds for which Robbins created a new addition to the repertoire, *Moves,* a ballet without music or other sounds. Danced in complete silence —on the stage and in the audience—it established itself as an immediate success. Following the Spoleto engagement the company made a long tour of Europe, a side trip to Israel, and danced in the Edinburgh Festival of Music and Drama, in London and Paris, among other places. The company did not perform in 1960, but in the summer-fall of 1961 it again had a long and very successful tour, sponsored on this occasion by the Rebekah W. Harkness Foundation. It added to the repertoire a new Robbins work, *Events,* to music by Robert Prince, with décor by Ben Shahn, and older works which had been done by other companies: *The Cage* and *Interplay*. The tour began in Spoleto and the high points included Paris, as part of the Théâtre des Nations Festival, Germany, Copenhagen, and London. The long season terminated with a N.Y. season (Oct. 8–28) at the ANTA Theatre. The company has had no public performances since 1962, but on Apr. 10 of that year it danced at the White House on the occasion of a State Dinner given by the President and Mrs. Kennedy for the Shah and Empress of Iran. The command performance, as it were, included *Afternoon of a Faun* and *N.Y. Export: Opus Jazz.*

The philosophy of Ballets: U.S.A. was succinctly stated as follows by Robbins: "The name of the company was chosen, not in any way to represent all of dance in the United States, but to clearly identify to Europeans (since we were beginning our life as a company in Europe) the source and homeground from which the dancers and the choreography emerged. Nor was it meant to suggest 'Americans' in terms of folklore or that it employs only native talent. I feel and believe very strongly that ballet dancing in America, regional and imported product (much as were the forefathers of the people who now dance it), has been completely influenced and drastically changed by this nation and the culture in which it has grown up. We in America dress, eat, think, talk, and walk differently from any other people. We also dance differently, and this brilliant art of our dancers —unmistakably from the U.S.A.—has gained more friends and greater respect abroad than many people realize.

"It was interesting to discover (after the company was assembled) that our talented group was typically American, not only in style, but also in that the individual members represented almost every national trait, strain and background.

"The program of the company was planned to show Europeans the variety of techniques, styles and theatrical approaches that are America's particular development in dance. Its repertory was chosen to extend from the classic ballet danced in tights, tutus, toe shoes to our own current jazz style, most often performed in sneakers and knee guards.

"Ballets: U.S.A. is a distillation of all our efforts."

Balli, in court dances a term for all the livelier dances as differentiated from "low" or basse dances.

Ballo, the name of standard Italian dances and music to them of the 15th and 16th centuries. From its diminutive "balleti" stems the word ballet. See also MUSIC FOR DANCE.

Ballon, in ballet, the ability of a dancer to remain in the air during a jump; part of elevation; also elasticity in jumps.

Balloné, in ballet, a bounding step with round movement. Technique: start in 5th pos., R ft. front; slide R ft. forward to demi-quatrième effacé; jump off L ft., at same time bend R knee and bring R ft. sharply to calf of L leg; land on L ft. in demi-plié. Balloné may also be done back, to side, croisé, etc. A well-known example comes in Giselle's first variation in *Giselle* (Act 1), which she later repeats when dancing with Albrecht.

Ballotté, in ballet, a rocking step. Technique: start 5th pos., R ft. front; demi-plié and jump off both feet, bending both knees in air, and passé R leg forward to grande quatrième en effacé; land on L ft. in plié; bend R knee and bring R leg in sharply, at same time jumping off L ft. and bending L knee in the air, then passé L leg back; land on R ft. Giselle and Albrecht perform a series of ballottés in their first dance together in *Giselle* (Act 1).

Ballroom Dances, social dances, usually performed by couples, at balls, in night clubs, restaurants, and at other social gatherings. Modern ballroom dances include: foxtrot, waltz, tango, rumba, conga, samba, lindy, cha cha, paso doble, merengue, and such evanescent dance crazes as the charleston, the twist and others. In Eastern European countries forms of polka, mazurka, and czardas, basically folk dances, are also danced on ballroom floors.

Ballroom Dancing, Official Board of (England), a committee formed in 1929, consisting of representatives of all the recognized Associations of Teachers of Ballroom Dancing and certain other prominent ballroom teachers. Its duties are to act as a liaison committee between the associations to regulate competitive dancing and govern the amateur or professional status of competitors, to authorize Championships and to look after the general interests of the profession. Among other things it developed the basic technique which now governs the English style. The late P. J. S. Richardson was chairman for its foundation until 1958 when he was succeeded by A. H. Franks (d. 1963).

Balon, Jean, French dancer who first appeared in Paris in 1691. He was connected for many years with the Académie Royale and was often the partner of Françoise Prévost and Marie Subligny. He appeared with Prévost in 1708 in a ballet adopted from Corneille's *Les Horaces,* presented at the Duchess of Maine's chateaux at Sceaux. His most noteworthy characteristic was his exceptional lightness. It is possible but not probable that his name (sometimes spelled Ballon) is now used as the term to designate that attribute of dance.

Balustrade. Ballet in 4 movements; chor.: George Balanchine; music: Igor Stravinsky; décor: Pavel Tchelichev. First prod.: Original Ballet Russe, Fifty-first Street Theatre, N.Y., Jan. 22, 1941, with Tamara Toumanova, Roman Jasinski, Paul Petroff in the main parts. Set to Stravinsky's Concerto for Violin and Orchestra, the ballet gets its title from the décor which was dominated by a white balustrade in perspective in the background.

Banks, Margaret, dancer, b. Vancouver, B.C., Canada, 1924. Studied with June Roper (Vancouver), Ninette de Valois, Ursula Moreton, Nicholas Sergeyev (London), Vilzak-Shollar, Antony Tudor, Anton Dolin (N.Y.). Member Vic-Wells company (1946), Original Ballet Russe (1946–47), Ballet Theatre. Created role of Parassia (*Fair at Sorochinsk*), Competition Dance (*Graduation Ball,* Ballet Theatre revival); also danced Boulotte (*Bluebeard*), variation and pas de trois (*Princess Aurora*), The Innocent (*Tally-Ho*), Mazurka (*Les Sylphides*), Grahn (*Pas de Quatre*), etc. Danced in musicals and supper clubs. Currently in Hollywood where she works with choreographers (Jerome Robbins, Michael Kidd, Gene Kelly, and others) as dance assistant for films (*West Side Story, Can-Can, State Fair,* etc.); also choreographs and stages dances for television.

Bannerman, Kenneth, British dancer, b. Heddington, Scotland, 1936. Studied dance with Marjory Middleton (Edinburgh), and continued at Ballet Rambert school. His studies were interrupted by military service. Joined Ballet Rambert in 1956 and rose to position of leading dancer. Has a wide repertoire of classic and modern roles. Created James in the Ballet Rambert production of *La Sylphide* (1960), and Elder Son in Norman Morrice's *Place in the Desert* (1961); other leading roles include Franz (*Coppélia*), Harlequin and Baron (*Night Shadow*), Popular Song and Yodeling Song (*Façade*), St. Léon (Robert Joffrey's *Pas des Déesses*), 5th Song (*Dark Elegies*), etc. He has also made many television and film appearances.

Bar aux Folies-Bergère. Ballet in 1 act; chor. and book: Ninette de Valois; music: Emmanuel Chabrier's *Dix Pièces Pittoresques;* décor: William Chappell. First prod.: Ballet Rambert, Mercury Theatre, London, May 15, 1934, with Alicia Markova (La Goulue), Pearl Argyle (La Fille au Bar), Diana Gould (Grille d'Egout),

Frederick Ashton (Valentin, waiter), Oliver Reynolds (Le Vieux Marcheur). The ballet opens and closes on a tableau—a reproduction of the famous painting by Edouard Manet—but except for La Fille herself, the characters are from Toulouse-Lautrec. The action involves La Goulue, the Can-Can girls, the waiter, the habitués, the barmaid. La Goulue's solo and the Can-Can were the high points of the ballet, the only work Ninette de Valois choreographed for Ballet Rambert.

Barbara Allen. Ballet in 1 act; chor.: David Adams; music: Louis Applebaum; décor: Kay Ambrose. First prod.: National Ballet of Canada, Palace Theatre, Hamilton, Oct. 26, 1960, with Angela Leigh, (Barbara Allen), David Adams (John, a Stranger). A version of *Dark of the Moon,* it tells of the struggle between John, a stranger, and Marvin, a native, for the love of Barbara Allen. John is aided by two young witches and, in a fight, Barbara is killed by Marvin's knife.

Barber, Samuel, American composer, b. West Chester, Pa., 1910. Graduate of Curtis Institute of Music, Phila.; awarded fellowship at American Academy of Music, Rome, and Pulitzer Prize (both 1935). Composed music for Martha Graham's *Cave of the Heart* (1946), Todd Bolender's *Souvenirs* (1955). Bolender used Barber's *Capricorn Concerto* for the ballet of the same name. The English choreographer Peter Wright used his *Suite of Six Short Dance Movements* for *A Blue Rose* (Royal Ballet, 1957). His orchestral pieces are often used by modern dancers. Alvin Ailey created a solo suite to Barber's *Hermit Songs* (1961) and staged dances for his opera *Antony and Cleopatra,* which opened the first season of the Metropolitan Opera at its new house in Lincoln Center for the Performing Arts (Sept. 16, 1966).

Barberina, La (Barberina Campanini; 1721–1799), dancer, b. Parma, Italy. Studied with Rinaldi Fossano, a Neapolitan comic dancer. In 1739 La Barberina was presented in Paris at the Académie Royale in *Les Fêtes d'Herbe, ou Les Talents Lyriques.* Four special dances were written for her for this occasion by Rameau. She was very successful; her technical skill, particularly her pirouettes and jetés battus were mentioned. The ballet had a run of fifty performances. She next appeared as *Zaide, Reine de Grenade,* and in *Momus Amoureux* in which she danced with Fossano. La Barberina, also captivating in private life, became the mistress in turn of Prince Carignan, Lord Arundel, the Marquis de Thebouville, and the Duc de Durfort. In Dec. 1739 she danced in Dardanus, and a few months later in a special performance at Versailles. The same year she danced at Covent Garden, London, and in 1741 returned to the Académie Royale to dance in *L'Empire de L'Amour* and *Les Fêtes Greques et Romaines,* then returning to Covent Garden. In 1742 she danced in Smock Alley Theatre, Dublin. Frederick the Great engaged her for an appearance in Berlin in 1743, but she fell in love and eloped with Lord Stuart Mackenzie to Venice. Finally, forced to go to Berlin, she became a favorite and stayed four years, commanding an immense salary and dancing in ballets arranged by Metestasio with music by Gruan. Noverre was starting his career at this time, dancing in the corps. In 1749 Barberina married Carlo Luigi Cocceii, son of Frederick the Great's chancellor. They separated in 1759, and in 1788 she retired and divorced Cocceii but kept the title by permission of the king. She was created Comtesse de Campanini and in exchange she endowed an institution for Poor Ladies of Good Birth, became Abbess of the institution and administered it until her death on June 7, 1799.

Bardin, Micheline, French ballerina, b. France, 1926. Studied at Paris Opéra Ballet School from age of twelve, graduating into corps de ballet of the Paris

Opéra Ballet. Became première danseuse étoile in 1948. Among her roles were La Femme (*Les Mirages*), Guignolette (*Guignol et Pandore*), *La Péri* (title role), *Palais de Cristal* (3rd movement), *Suite en blanc, Le Chevalier et la Demoiselle, Divertissement* (Rose Adagio). Has given recitals in Copenhagen, Zurich, and other cities in Europe. Left the Opéra in 1957 and danced in *La Périchole* at the Metropolitan Opera, N.Y. in Nov., 1957. Currently residing in N.Y.

Bari, Tania, Dutch dancer, b. Rotterdam, 1936. Studied with Netty van der Valk (Rotterdam), Nora Kiss and Asaf Messerer (Paris). Has danced since 1955 with Maurice Béjart's Ballet Théâtre de Paris and Ballet du XXme Siècle, Brussels. A classic and modern dancer, her principal roles in Maurice Béjart's repertoire include *Le Sacre du Printemps, Symphonie pour un Homme Seul, Haut Voltage, L'Etranger, Huis-Clos, Orphée* (Euridice).

Barn Dance. Ballet in 1 act; chor. and book: Catherine Littlefield; music: a potpourri of folk tunes by Louis Moreau Gottschalk, David Guion, John Powell; décor: A. Pinto; costumes: S. Pinto. First prod.: Littlefield Ballet Company, Fox Theatre, Phila., Pa., Apr. 23, 1937, with Dorothie Littlefield and Thomas Cannon in principal roles; revived for Ballet Theatre with new décor and costumes, Metropolitan Opera House, N.Y., May 9, 1944, with Dorothie Littlefield and Thomas Cannon as guest artists in their original roles (subsequently taken by Nana Gollner and Paul Petroff). A village barn dance in which apparently the whole village takes part with the exception of the Deacon who tries to maintain his dignity. In the midst of the high time a Light Lady, a former villager who moved to the big city, and her friend, the City Slicker, interrupt the proceedings by making a grand entrance. The newcomers do a dance of their own which delights the assembled, especially the younger element. The ice is broken and general dancing resumes, even the Deacon joining it, albeit reluctantly. This ballet became the "signature" of the Littlefield Ballet.

Barn Dancing, generic term for American folk dancing in rural communities, from the place where such dancing was done. Originating in the early 19th century, it came into vogue again in the early 1930's, probably due to the depression and accompanying lack of funds for more expensive entertainment.

Barnes, Clive, critic and writer on dance, b. London, 1927. Educated at Oxford University, where he was co-editor of quarterly *Arabesque,* published by Oxford Univ. Ballet Club (1950). Joined staff of London magazine *Dance and Dancers* (1950); became assistant editor (1951), associate editor (1956), executive editor (1963). Contributed on ballet to the *New Statesman* (1951). London correspondent for *Dance Magazine* (N.Y.) and ballet critic of the *Daily Express* (1956–65); ballet critic of *The Spectator* (1959–65). Writer on dance subjects for the London *Times* (1961–65). Visited N.Y. in the spring of 1963, after which he became London dance correspondent of *The New York Times* and (since Sept., 1965) its N.Y. dance critic. Publications include *Ballet in Britain Since the War* (1953); "Frederick Ashton and his Ballets" (*Dance Perspectives,* No. 9, Winter, 1961); *Ballet Here and Now* (1961).

Baron. See PHOTOGRAPHERS, DANCE (ENGLAND).

Baronova, Irina, b. Petrograd, Russia, 1919, m. German Sevastianov (divorced), Cecil G. Tennant. Studied at College Victor-Hugo, Paris; ballet with Olga Preobrajenska, Paris. Soloist at Opéra, Paris (1930); Théâtre Mogador (1931). Discovered by George Balanchine at the Preobrajenska school, she became one of

Irina Baronova in Aurora's Wedding

three "baby ballerinas" of the Ballets Russes de Monte Carlo in 1932 (the other two were Tatiana Riabouchinska and Tamara Toumanova) and continued as ballerina of the several Ballet Russe de Monte Carlo companies from 1932 to 1940. In 1941–42 she was ballerina of Ballet Theatre. She also danced with Serge Lifar in France (summer, 1933), starred in the films *Florian* (MGM, 1939) and *Yolanda* (Mexico, 1942); in the musical *Follow the Girls* (1944). With Leonine Massine's Ballet Russe Highlights (1945); was guest artist in Original Ballet Russe (1946); and appeared in the musical *Bullet in the Ballet* and the comedy *Black Eyes* (both in England, 1946). In addition, she created ballerina roles in *The Hundred Kisses* (Princess), *Les Présages* (Passion), *Choreartium, Scuola di Ballo* (Josephina), *Bluebeard* (Boulotte), *Helen of Troy* (Helen), *Le Beau Danube* (First Hand), and others. She danced ballerina roles in *Aurora's Wedding, Swan Lake, Les Sylphides, Coq d'Or* (Queen of Shemakhan), *Coppélia, La Fille Mal Gardée, Petrouchka, Le Spectre de la Rose, Jeux d'Enfants,* and others. Retired from the stage (1946), she now lives with her husband and three children in England. She is a member of the Technical Committee of the Royal Academy of Dancing and teaches mime in the Teacher's Course of the Academy.

Barre (or bar), usually of wood, fastened to the walls of a dance studio or rehearsal room, generally placed three feet six inches from the floor. It serves as a point of support for the dancer in his classroom exercises. See also BARRE EXERCISES.

Barre Exercises, a group of exercises at the barre of a ballet studio with the dancer holding on to the bar to maintain his balance; every ballet lesson begins with these exercises (compare with CENTER PRACTICE).

Bartholin, Birger, Danish dancer, choreographer and teacher, b. 1900. Studied dance in Denmark and with Michel Fokine, Nicholas Legat and Alexander Volinine. Danced with the Ida Rubinstein company; René Blum's Ballets de Monte Carlo; Boris Kniaseff troupe; Nemtchinova-Oboukhov company; as well as in a Cochran revue in London. Was ballet master and choreographer of Ballet de la Jeunesse (Paris, 1937). Choreographed *Classical Symphony* (Prokofiev), *Romeo and Juliet* (Tchaikovsky, 1937), and *Parisian* (1954), which were later added to the repertoire of the Royal Danish Ballet. Was ballet master of the National Opera Ballet, Helsinki (1954), and Oslo (1955). Currently teaching in Copenhagen where he heads very successful International Ballet Seminars (summer 1963–67).

Bartók, Béla (b. Nagy Szent Miklos, 1881, d. N.Y. 1945), great Hungarian composer. Studied at the Budapest Academy and was later appointed to its faculty. He is noted for his extensive research in folk music and for his original musical idiom which emanated from his native folk music. Only two of his compositions were written specifically for the theatrical dance: *The Wooden Prince,* a ballet (1917) and *The Miraculous Mandarin,* a dance pantomime (1926). Many of his other compositions have been and are being used by choreographers and dancers for ballets, modern dance works, and solo dances. (See BARTÓK'S MUSIC USED FOR DANCE.) Bartók was a man of high principles and firm opinions, freely expressed. In 1936 when the Nazis arranged in Düsseldorf an exhibition of "degenerate music," Bartók found enough courage to write a letter of protest to the German Foreign Office asking why his music was not exposed to public derision along with that of Schönberg, Stravinsky, and Milhaud. Shortly after this incident he left Central Europe: he saw no more hope there for the free artist. He settled in the U.S. and for most of his residence here led an austere life because his compositions were not receiving enough public performances to enable him to live in comfortable circumstances. His music began to have a much wider acceptance after his death. Toward the end of his life he suffered acute longing for his fatherland, but refused an invitation from the Communist government of Hungary, which by then had replaced the Nazis, to return to Budapest.

Bartók's Music Used for Dance.

Béla Bartók's music, though not specifically composed for dance, has been used by so many choreographers that a listing, even though incomplete, should be recorded in a dance reference volume. The difficulty of compiling such a listing is due mainly to the reluctance of choreographers to mention the specific composition as well as the composer's name in their programs. The following listing is arranged in alphabetical order by the titles of the musical compositions and in chronological order within the titles; the choreographers' names are in parentheses. (*The Miraculous Mandarin* and the *Wooden Prince,* the only two compositions written by Bartók expressly for dance, are listed separately.)

CONCERTO FOR ORCHESTRA: *Concerto Aux Étoiles* (Harald Lander), Paris Opéra, July 26, 1956.

CONCERTO FOR TWO PIANOS AND PERCUSSION: *Corybantic* (Doris Humphrey), José Limón Co., Connecticut College, Aug. 18, 1948.

CONTRASTS FOR VIOLIN, CLARINET AND PIANO: *Caprichos* (Herbert Ross), Choreographers Workshop, N.Y., Jan. 29, 1950; American Ballet Theatre, Apr., 1950; *The Venus Flower* (Faith Worth), Sunday Ballet Club, London, Jan., 1959; *Theatre for Fools* (Daniel Nagrin) American Dance Festival, Aug., 1959.

DIVERTIMENTO IN THREE MOVEMENTS: *Gypsy* (Doré Hoyer), ca. 1945.

FIRST VIOLIN SONATA (1st and last movements): *Sonata* (Jane Dudley) American Dance Festival, Aug. 12, 1950.

MICROCOSMOS (Vol. 6 #114 and Minor 2nd and Major 7th): *Vagary* (Jane Dudley) for herself, American Dance Festival, Aug. 16, 1949.

MICROCOSMOS (and other piano pieces, arr. by Herbert Sondberg): *Medea* (Birgit Cullberg), Rikstheatern, Gaevle, Sweden, Oct. 31, 1950; Elsa Marianne von Rosen's Swedish Ballet, London, Feb. 12, 1951; Royal Swedish Ballet, Royal Theatre, Stockholm, Apr. 11, 1953; New York City Ballet, N.Y., Nov. 26, 1958; Royal Danish Ballet, Royal Theatre, Copenhagen, Apr. 24, 1959.

MICROCOSMOS (arr. Arthur Oldham): *Concerto Burlesko* (Walter Gore) Ballet Rambert, King's Theatre, Hammersmith, London, Nov. 5, 1956.

MUSIC FOR STRINGS, PERCUSSION AND CE-

LESTE: *Afflicted Children* (Marion Scott) YM-YWHA, N.Y., 1953; *Dance Concerto* (May O'Donnell), May O'Donnell Co., Henry Street Settlement Playhouse, N.Y., Jan. 9, 1954; *Journey* (Kenneth Macmillan), Ballet Theatre Workshop, N.Y., May 6, 1957; *The Prisoners* (Peter Darrell), Western Theatre Ballet, Dartington Hall, Devon, England, June 24, 1957; *Place of Panic* (Joyce Trisler) for her company, Henry Street Settlement Playhouse, N.Y., Dec. 5, 1958.

SONATA FOR TWO PIANOS AND PERCUSSION: *Sonata* (Doré Hoyer), ca. 1945; *Anguish Sonata* (Aurel Milloss), Ballet do IV Centenario, Teatro Municipal, Rio de Janeiro, 1954; *Sonate à Trois* (Maurice Béjart) Ballet Theatre de Maurice Béjart, Paris, June 19, 1957; *Yesterday's Papers* (Dick Sanders) Robert Joffrey Theatre Ballet, 1959; Western Theatre Ballet, Hanley, England, Feb. 16, 1960.

Barzel, Ann, American writer and teacher, b. Chicago, 1913. Ph.D., Univ. of Chicago. Studied dance with Adolph Bolm, Alexandre Volinine, School of American Ballet, N.Y., Vecheslav Swoboda, Berenice Homes, Nicholas Legat, and others. Dance critic, *Chicago Times* (1946–49), and of the *Chicago American* since 1951. Contributor to *Dance Index, Ballet Annual, Dance Encyclopedia;* on the editorial staff of *Dance News, Dance Magazine.* See DANCE PUBLICATIONS.

Bas, in ballet, low. Arms en bas indicates low position of arms.

Basaluda, Hector, Argentine stage designer, b. Pergamino (Buenos Aires), 1894. Studied at the Academia Nacional de Bellas Artes de Buenos Aires and later in Paris with André Lhote and Othon Friesz. Received First Prize and Gold Medal at the Exposition des Arts Decoratifs, Paris, 1936. From 1930 to 1956 was Scenic Director, Teatro Colón, Buenos Aires; during those years designed most of the décor and costumes for opera and ballets presented at the theatre. Has retired from the theatre and devoted his time to painting; has had exhibits in Argentina and Brazil.

Basic Agreement. See CONTRACTS, DANCERS'.

Basic Movement, in ballroom dance, a characteristic figure of a dance which does not change.

Basil, Col. W. de. See DE BASIL, COL. W.

Basse Danse (Ital.: Bassa Danza; Ger.: Hoftanz), a court dance; a steady, dignified low dance from which the minuet is descended.

Battement, in ballet; literally a beating movement. The following are the most generally used forms of battement: 1. battement tendu: start in 5th pos. R ft. front; slide R toe into 4th pos. front; return R ft. to 5th pos. Battements tendus may also be done to the back, to the side (to 2nd pos.), in croisé, effacé, écarté, etc. 2. battement dégagé (also battement tendu jeté): similar to battement tendu to front, side or back, but continuing the movement so that the foot is slightly off the floor before returning to 5th pos. 3. grand battement: start in 5th pos., R ft. front; raise R leg to grande quatrième devant; return to 5th pos. Grand battement is also done to grande seconde and to quatrième derrière, and with varying positions of body; croisé, effacé, écarté, etc. 4. battement en cloche, another name for balançoire (which see). 5. battement fondu: start in 5th pos. R ft. front; move R ft. to sur le cou-de-pied, at same time demi-plié with L leg; open R leg forward, toe pointed, straightening L knee; return R ft. to sur le cou-de-pied front, demi-plié with L leg; open in same manner to 2nd pos.: return to sur le cou-de-pied back, demi-plié, on L leg; open R leg to side, return ft. sur le cou-de-pied front, etc. 6. battement frappé, usually an exercise at the barre: start with R ft. in 2nd pos.; move R ft. to sur le cou-de-pied front, ft. relaxed; with a sharp movement return R ft. to 2nd pos., toe pointed. Accent is on 2nd pos. Battement frappé may also be done to the front and to the back. 7. battement soutenu: start in 5th pos., R ft. front; take R leg out into 2nd pos., at same time demi-plié with L leg; rising on half-toe on L leg, return R leg, both feet meeting in 5th pos. on half-toe. Battement soutenu may also be done to the front and to the back. 8. petits battements sur le coup-de-pied: start with R ft. sur le cou-de-pied front; open R leg halfway in direction of 2nd pos., kneejoint not extended; return R ft. to sur le cou-de-pied back; open again in same manner and return R ft. sur le cou-de-pied front.

Batterie, in ballet, generic term applied to all movements in which the feet beat together or one foot beats against the other. There are two divisions of batterie: petite batterie, which includes entrechat, brisé, assemblé battu, etc.; and grande batterie, which includes cabriole, sissonne battue, temps de poisson, temps de l'ange, ailes de pigeon, etc. See BEATS.

Battu, in ballet, a step into which a beat has been introduced, as jeté battu, assemblé battu, sissonne battue, etc.

Bauer, Margarete (Gretl), Austrian ballerina, b. Vienna, 1927, m. dancer Erwin Pokorny. Studied at the ballet school of the Vienna State Opera, in Salzburg with Derra de Moroda, in Paris and in Switzerland. Accepted into the company of the Vienna State Opera Ballet in 1945; became ballerina in 1951. Danced *Giselle* in the inaugural ballet performance of the reconstructed opera house, Nov. 29, 1955. In 1959 she danced as guest artist with the Moscow Bolshoi Ballet in Moscow. Although a regular member of the Vienna State Opera Ballet, her appearances are rather sporadic.

Bayadère, La (Bayaderka). Ballet in 3 acts; chor.: Marius Petipa; music: Leon Minkus; book by Petipa and Sergei Khudekov after the dramas of the Indian classic *Kalidasa: Sakuntala* and *The Cart of Clay;* décor: (for the old Maryinsky production) K. Ivanov, P. Lambin, O. Allegri and A. Kwapp. First prod.: Maryinsky Theatre, St. Petersburg, Jan. 23, 1877, with Yekaterina Vazem in the title role; revived with the same décor by Agrippina Vaganova at the Kirov Theatre Dec. 13, 1932; revived by Vladimir Ponomaryov with new dances and mise-en-scènes by Vakhtang Chabukiani and same settings, Feb. 10, 1941, with Natalia Dudinskaya as Nikia, the Bayadère, and Chabukiani as Solor. This production is in the current repertoire of the Kirov. The famous Kingdom of Shades scene, in which the Petipa

Margarete Bauer as Kitri in Don Quixote *with Michael Birkmeyer*

choreography is faithfully reproduced, was first seen outside Russia when the Kirov Ballet appeared in London, U.S. and Canada (1961). Rudolf Nureyev staged it (with certain of his own revisions) for England's Royal Ballet (première at Royal Opera House, Covent Garden, London, Nov. 27, 1963) with himself and Margot Fonteyn in the leading roles. The story of the complete version is as follows: Nikia, the bayadère, loves Solor, a warrior who is also loved by Gamzatti, daughter of the Rajah. During the ceremony to celebrate the betrothal of Solor and Gamzatti, the latter sends Nikia a basket of flowers concealing a poisonous snake. Nikia dies and Solor, dreaming of her, sees her in the Kingdom of Shades. The ballet originally ended with an epilogue wherein the temple where Solor was being married to Gamzatti collapsed, burying them under the ruins; in the revivals, this scene is omitted.

Bayaderka. See BAYADÈRE, LA.

Bayanihan Dance Company, a company of Filipino musicians and dancers directed by Lucrecia Reyes Urtula who is also the company's choreographer. It presents a program based on the varied cultural background of the Philippines—Far Eastern, Mohammedan and Spanish; it also reflects recent American influences. It appeared with great success at the Brussels World Fair (1958) and toured Europe; then toured the U.S. (1959), making its N.Y. debut at the Winter Garden Theatre, Oct. 13, 1959. Toured the U.S. again in 1961 and 1964.

Baylis, Lillian (1874–1937) director, London Old Vic and Sadler's Wells Theatre, b. South Africa, d. London. It was Lillian Baylis who invited Ninette de Valois first to stage the opera ballets, then an occasional small ballet, and finally an entire ballet evening at the Old Vic Theatre (May 5, 1931). This was the actual birth of the company which ultimately became the Royal Ballet of England. When an entirely new theatre was built on the old site of Sadler's Wells (1931), Miss Baylis invited de Valois to establish a school there. Early performances which were given on alternate weeks at the Old Vic and Sadler's Wells soon were given entirely at Sadler's Wells; the Old Vic reverted to its great Shakespeare seasons, leaving opera and ballet to flourish at Sadler's Wells.

Beat, in ballet, a beating movement of one leg against the other while in the air; also crossing of legs in the air. Beats bring into the dance the element of brilliance and virtuosity. See BATTERIE.

Beaton, Cecil, English designer, photographer, writer, b. 1904. Designed scenery and costumes for *Apparitions* (1936), *Les Sirènes* (1946), *Marguerite and Armand* (1963) for Sadler's Wells (now Royal) Ballet; *Le Pavillon* (David Lichine, Col. de Basil's Ballet Russe, 1936); *Les Patineurs* and John Taras's *Camille,* both for Ballet (now American Ballet) Theatre (1946); *Illuminations* (1950), George Balanchine's *Swan Lake* (1951), *Picnic at Tintagel* (1952), all for the New York City Ballet; *The Nutcracker* (1951) for Sadler's Wells Theatre Ballet. Among his many publications is *Ballet* (1951). Created C.B.E. (Commander of the Order of the British Empire), 1957.

Beatty, Talley, contemporary American dancer. Studied with Katherine Dunham and began his career in Dunham's first small group (1940), with which he appeared in Chicago and N.Y. In 1942 and later he danced in Dunham's *Tropical Revue.* In N.Y. he danced in the film *Study in Choreography for Camera,* a most successful composition by Maya Deren (1945). He danced the leading part with Pearl Primus in *Showboat,* choreographed by Helen Tamiris (1946). Later the same year he was the leading dancer in the musical *Spring in Brazil,* choreographed by Esther Junger. When Lew Christensen was assembling the cast for *Blackface* (1947), a ballet which he was staging for Ballet Society, he selected Talley Beatty for a featured part. It was in that year that Beatty set out on his career as concert dancer, at first specializing in dances based on Negro sources and later embracing a more general style, closely related, however, to jazz. He has taught, choreographed, and danced in several European countries and in Israel. Among his most notable concert works are *The Road of the Phoebe Snow* (1959), *Come and Get the Beauty of It Hot* (1960), *Concerto for Harpsichord* (1961). Arranged the movement for the off-Broadway production of Jean Gênet's *The Blacks* (1961).

Beau Danube, Le. Ballet in 1 act; chor. and book: Leonide Massine; music: Johann Strauss, principally "Schützen Quadrille," "New Vienna Waltzes," waltz from *Die Fledermaus,* "Vienna Chronicle," "The Beautiful Blue Danube," "Motor Quadrille," and one piece by Josef Lanner: "Der Schönbrunner"; décor: Vladimir and Elizabeth Polunin, after Constantin Guys; costumes: Comte Etienne de Beaumont. First prod.: Comte Etienne de Beaumont at his *Soirées de Paris* (May 17–June 30, 1924), with Lydia Lopoukhova as the Street Dancer. Restaged for Col. de Basil's Ballets Russes de Monte Carlo, Théâtre de Monte Carlo, Apr. 15, 1933, with Alexandra Danilova (Street Dancer), Leonide Massine (Hussar), Tatiana Riabouchinska (Daughter), Irina Baronova (First Hand, or Seamstress), David Lichine (King of the Dandies). When Massine split with Col. de Basil and joined René Blum in the company that became Ballet Russe de Monte Carlo he lost the rights to the décor and costumes (which remained with the de Basil company, Original Ballet Russe) and Comte Etienne de Beaumont designed new décor and costumes. The ballet was given in this décor for its first season at Drury Lane Theatre, June, 1938, and subsequently, Massine has staged *Le Beau Danube* for many companies, notably Royal Danish Ballet and London's Festival Ballet. Alexandra Danilova has always remained the nonpareil of Street Dancers. The scene is a Vienna Public Garden which features a reunion between a Street Dancer and a Hussar, complicated by the presence of a family whose elder Daughter is apparently engaged to the dashing officer and who wins him back after his brief flutter with the Street Dancer (to the strains of "The Beautiful Blue Danube" waltz).

Beauchamp, Pierre (1636–1705), dancer and maître de ballet at the Académie Royale de Musique, Paris. Was superintendent of Court Ballets in 1661, appearing in many ballets with Louis XIV. He was dancing master to the king and in 1671 became maître de ballet at the Académie. As a dancer he was dignified. He introduced technique in the shape of the turnout and added virtuosity with his elevation and turns. He was known as a brilliant performer of pirouettes; descriptions also indicate he performed tours en l'air. He named the five positions of classic ballet (ca. 1700) and laid the basis of technique and virtuosity. He created a shorthand or notation system which he intended to publish. He worked and danced with Lully appearing in the Lully-Molière ballet *Le Mariage Forcé.* He also danced in *Le Triomphe d'Amour.* Retired in 1687.

Beaugrand, Léontine (1842–1925), ballerina of the Paris Opéra. Made her debut in the pas de trois in Maria Taglioni's ballet *Le Papillon* (1860). Had her first great success four years later dancing the lead in the revival of Arthur Saint-Léon's *Diavolino.* She succeeded to the role of Swanilda in *Coppélia* in 1871 when Giuseppina Bozzachi died during the German siege of Paris, and was considered at least the equal if not the superior of its creator. She retired in 1880 after differences with the Opéra management. She was famous for her elevation. In 1867 Nestor Roqueplan wrote about her: "She dances no longer, she flies." A poem dedicated to Beaugrand by the French poet Sully Prudhomme contains a stanza which, freely translated, reads: "You forced thinkers to respect your art, because moved by your noble joy they have understood why the sages of Greece have taken part in the admiration of the dance."

Beaujoyeux, Balthasar de (Baldassarino da Belgiojoso), producer of *Ballet Comique de la Reine* (1581). A violinist, he went from Italy to Paris in 1555 and was introduced by the Duc de Brissac to Catherine de Medici, whose valet de chambre he became. He was the unofficial organizer of court festivals and his ballet gave form to subsequent works as he was extensively imitated. His intention was chiefly to appeal to the eye.

Beaumont, Comte Etienne de (1885–1956), French designer of costumes for *Le Beau Danube* (first presented for his Soirées de Paris, 1924), and décor and costumes for *Scuola di Ballo* (also presented at the Soirées). Both were revived for Col. de Basil's Ballets Russes de Monte Carlo in 1933. He also wrote the book and designed the décor and costumes for *Gaîté Parisienne* (1938). He designed (with Pavel Tchelitchev) *Nobilissima Visione* (St. Francis) in 1938. All these had choreography by Leonide Massine. Two ballets by David Lichine—*Nocturne* (1933) and *Les Imaginaires* (1934)—were also designed by him.

Beaumont, Cyril William, writer and publisher, b. London, England, 1891. Educated at Stationers' Company's School and privately. Antiquarian bookseller specializing in dance. His store in Charing Cross Road, London, "Under the Sign of

Cyril W. Beaumont outside his bookstore

the Harlequin," was a mecca for anyone interested in the theatrical dance, especially ballet. It was also a favorite place for writers in need of sources of research on dance subjects. He closed his store at the expiration of his lease in Sept., 1965, to be able to devote himself to more writing and to care for his invalid wife. He is a prolific writer on dance, particularly classic ballet, an interest which began in 1910 when he saw Anna Pavlova and Mikhail Mordkin dance and was intensified by seeing the Diaghilev Ballets Russes in 1912. Chairman, Honorary Fellow and Examiner, Imperial Society of Teachers of Dancing; chairman, Cecchetti Society Branch of I.S.T.D.; member of Grand Council, Royal Academy of Dancing. Codified Enrico Cecchetti's method of training in classic ballet (1918–22); ballet critic on *Dancing World* (1921–24); editor of *Dance Journal* since 1924; ballet critic of *Sunday Times* (1950–59). Initiated founding of Cecchetti Society (1922), which amalgamated with Imperial Society of Teachers of Dancing (1924). His many honors and awards include: Palmes Académiques (1934), Gold Medal, Institute Historique et Heraldique de France (1934), Gold Medal Reconnaissance Française (1938), Légion d'Honneur (1950), Imperial Society's Imperial Award (1961), Royal Academy of Dancing's Queen Elizabeth II Coronation Award (1962), Knight Officer of the Order of Merit of the Italian Republic (1962), in recognition for his work in recording and propagating the Cecchetti Method of training in classic ballet. For his long service to British Ballet he received the Order of the British Empire (O.B.E.) in 1962. Probably the most erudite English writer on ballet, he has published the following books: *Impressions of the Russian Ballet* (in 12 parts; 1914–21); *The Art of Lydia Lopokova* (1920); *The Art of Lubov Tchernicheva* (1921); *A Manual of the Theory and Practise of Theatrical Dancing* (with Stanislas Idzikowski, 1922); *A Burmese Pwè at Wembley* (1925); *The Art of Stanislas Idzikowski* (1926); *The History of Harlequin* (1926); *Serge Lifar* (1928); *Enrico Cecchetti, a Memoir* (1929); *A Bibliography of Dancing* (1929); *The Theory and Practise of Allegro in Classical Ballet* (with Margaret Craske) (1930); *A History of Ballet in Russia (1613–1881)* (1930); *A French-English Dictionary of Technical Terms Used in Classical Ballet* (1931); *Fanny Elssler* (1931); *Anna Pavlova* (1932); *Vaslav Nijinsky* (1932); *A Short History of Ballet* (1933); *Serge Diaghilev* (1933); *A Miscellany for Dancers* (1934); *Three French Dancers of the 18th Century* (1934); *Three French Dancers of the 19th Century* (1935); *The Monte Carlo Russian Ballet* (1934); *Alicia Markova* (1935); *The Vic-Wells Ballet* (1935); *Michel Fokine and His Ballets* (1935); *A Primer of Classical Ballet for Children* (1935); *Design for the Ballet* (1937); *The Complete Book of Ballets* (1937); *The Romantic Ballet in Lithographs of the Time* (with Sacheverell Sitwell, 1938); *Five Centuries of Ballet Design* (1939); *The Diaghilev Ballet in London* (1940); *A Third Primer of Classical Ballet for Children* (1941); *Supplement to the Complete Book of Ballets* (1942); *The Ballet Called Giselle* (1944); *The Sadler's Wells Ballet* (1946); *The Sleeping Beauty* (1946); *Ballet Design: Past and Present* (*Design for Ballet* and *Five Centuries of Ballet Design* combined into one volume, with additional material, 1946); *Margot Fonteyn* (1948); *Dancers Under My Lens* (1949); *The Swan Lake* (1949); *Antonio* (1952); *The Ballet Called Swan Lake* (1952); *Ballets of Today* (1954); *Ballets Past and Present* (1955); as translator: *Vaslav Nijinsky* by F. de Miomandre (1913); *Orchesography* by Thoinot Arbeau (1925); *Letters on Dancing and Ballets* by J. G. Noverre (1930); *Maria Taglioni* by André Levinson (1930); *The Dancing-Master* by P. Rameau (1931); *The Romantic Ballet as Seen by Théophile Gautier* (1932); *Ballet: Traditional to Modern* by Serge Lifar (1938); *The Dance* by Pierre Tugal (1947); as editor: *Thamar Karsavina* by Valerian Svetlov (1922); *The Continental Method of Scene Painting* by Vladimir Polunin (1927); *New and Curious School of Theatrical Dancing* by Gregorio Lambranzi (1927); *The Csardas and Sor Tanc* by Derra de Moroda (1929); *Some Traditional Scottish Dances* by G. Douglas Taylor (1929); *Rational Limbering* by Zelia Raye (1929); *Some Classic Dances of Japan* by Rikuhei Umemoto (1934).

Beauty and the Beast. Ballet in 1 act; chor.: John Cranko; music: Maurice Ravel (from *Mother Goose Suite*); décor: Margaret Kaye. First prod.: Sadler's Wells Theatre Ballet, Sadler's Wells Theatre, Dec. 20, 1949, with Patricia Miller and David Poole. The famous fairy tale told in pas de deux form. One of the few ballets (*Le Spectre de la Rose, Le Jeune Homme et la Mort,* and Jerome Robbins's *Afternoon of a Faun* are others) which use only two people to tell a complete story.

Beck, Hans (1861–1952), Danish dancer, ballet master and choreographer, b. Copenhagen. Studied in the school of the Royal Danish Ballet. He was one of the greatest dancers Denmark has produced. He became ballet master in 1894 and it is mainly due to his loving care that the Bouronville ballets and the Danish production of *Coppélia* retain such a remarkable degree of preservation both in choreography and style. After his retirement in 1915 he continued, almost up to the time of his death, to oversee rehearsals. He choreographed a number of ballets, the best known being *The Little Mermaid* (1909).

Beckett, Keith, English dancer, b. Bletchley, 1929. Studied at Cone-Ripman School. First appeared as actor in plays (1942–46). Won Adeline Genée Silver Medal, Royal Academy of Dancing (1946). With London's Festival Ballet (1950–59), rising to soloist. An interesting character dancer who danced an outstanding *Petrouchka,* and created Quasimodo (*Esmeralda*), among other roles. Left in 1959 to become producer, Tyne-Tees Television (England).

Beckley, Christine, English dancer, b. Stanmore, 1939. Studied with Phyllis Bedells and at the Royal Academy of Dancing. Entered Sadler's Wells School (1951); joined Royal Ballet (1956), promoted to soloist (1959). Her roles include Black Queen (*Checkmate*), Queen of the Wilis (*Giselle*), Lilac Fairy (*The Sleeping Beauty*), Fairy Winter (*Cinderella*), and others. Toured East Africa, July, 1959, with group of Royal Ballet dancers, dancing The Girl (*Solitaire*), The Lady (*Lady and the Fool*), *Don Quixote* and *Blue Bird* pas de deux.

Bedells, Phyllis, English dancer and teacher, b. Bristol, 1893. Studied with Malvina Cavallazzi, Alexander Genée, Adolph Bolm, Enrico Cecchetti, Anna Pavlova. Made her debut as a child solo dancer at Prince of Wales Theatre, London, Dec. 1906, in *Alice in Wonderland.* Began career at the Empire, Leicester Square, with two solos in *The Debutante* (May, 1907). She became second ballerina to Lydia Kyasht for five years, then prima ballerina, remaining until 1916, after which she appeared in many revues. Also danced for Covent Garden Opera season (1920) and with Laurent Novikov in London (1920). Following more revue work she danced with Anton Dolin at London Coliseum seasons (1926–27) and with her own company (1928). One of the original committee members of The Carmargo Society, appearing on most of its programs. Guest artist Vic-Wells (later Sadler's Wells now Royal) Ballet (1931); performances in South Africa (1933). Farewell performance, London Hippodrome, Nov. 8, 1935. She was born perhaps ten years too soon for the great career in British Ballet which her talents could have brought her. Teaches in own school since 1925. Vice-President, Royal Academy of Dancing; member of the Dramatic Advisory Board of the British Council, representing ballet. Received Queen Elizabeth II Coronation Award of the R.A.D. (1958). Author of *My Dancing Years* (1954).

Beecham, Sir Thomas (1879–1961), English conductor, one of the most eminent of his time. He was genuinely interested in ballet and was frequently guest conductor for the Diaghilev Ballets Russes seasons in both England and the U.S. In his earlier years he was almost better known as an impresario for the Covent Garden Opera seasons than as a conductor. In that capacity was instrumental in bringing the Diaghilev company to London (1911). In 1928 he arranged music of Handel for the score of George Balanchine's *The Gods Go a-Begging,* the same music later being used by both David Lichine and Ninette de Valois. For the latter he also arranged Handel music for *The Origin of Design* (Camargo Society, 1932). He conducted the Offenbach score for the 1951 film version of *The Tales of Hoffmann.* He was knighted in 1916 for his services to British music and succeeded to his father's baronetcy later the same year.

Beef Trust, a line of fleshy, voluptuous English dancers brought to U.S. by Billy Watson in the early 1870's, who appeared in variety theatres and beer gardens. They were the forerunners of Hootchy-Kootchy dancers and other dance groups and individual dancers who specialized in sensual dance numbers, which culminated in the striptease of the late 1920's.

Beelitz, Claus, German dancer, b. Berlin, 1938. Studied with Tatiana Gsovska and a number of other teachers. Was soloist of the Berlin Municipal Opera and National Theatre, Mannheim; soloist of the Berlin German Opera since 1961.

Beethoven, Ludwig van (1770–1827), German composer who wrote two ballet scores: *Das Ritterballett* (Equestrian Ballet) in 1790, but apparently never produced although the score was published in 1872; and *Die Geschöpfe Des Prometheus* (The Creatures of Prometheus) in 1801, which Salvatore Vigano produced on Mar. 28 the same year and restaged in 1811. In the 20th century Serge Lifar produced Beethoven's *Prometheus* for his debut as choreographer of the Paris Opéra (1929), and Ninette de Valois staged a version for Sadler's Wells (now Royal) Ballet (Oct. 1936). Other music by Beethoven used by choreographers includes his Symphony No. 7 for *Seventh Symphony* for Ballet Russe de Monte Carlo (1938) and the "Archduke" Trio for a work entitled *Les Arabesques* for Ballet for America (1946), both by Leonide Massine; and Sonata in F Major ("Spring" Sonata) for *Company at the Manor* by Kurt Jooss for his troupe in 1943.

Beguine, a contemporary ballroom dance of South American origin. It has become a variation of the foxtrot.

Beiswanger, George, American writer, critic and teacher, b. Baltimore, Md., 1902. Studied at Carthage College, Ill. (A.B., 1922), State Univ. of Iowa, Iowa City (M.A., 1927; Ph.D., 1928). Professor of Philosophy, Ohio Wesleyan College, Delaware, O. (1928–1935); Monticello College, Godfrey, Ill. (1935–1939); Georgia State College for Women, Milledgeville, Ga. (1939–1944), Chairman Department of Arts, Philosophy and Religion (1944–1963); since 1963 Professor of Philosophy, Georgia State College, Atlanta, Ga. On summer faculty of Conn. College School of Dance, New London, since 1955. Dance critic *Theatre Arts Monthly* (1939–1944). Contributor of articles and reviews to *Dance News, Dance Observer, Dance Magazine* (see DANCE PUBLICATIONS [U.S.]), *Saturday Review, Journal of Aesthetics and Art Criticism* and others. Contributor to the following books: *Martha Graham, Producing the Play, Twenty-Five Years of American Dance, Theatre Arts Anthology.* Conducted dance seminar at Salzburg Seminar in American Studies (1964).

Béjart, Maurice, French dancer and choreographer, b. Marseilles, 1928. Pupil of the Marseille Opéra Ballet School and dancer of the Opéra ballet until 1945; also studied with Leo Staats in Paris. Toured Europe with Ballets de Roland Petit (1947–49). Principal dancer, International Ballet, London (1949–50); guest artist, Royal Swedish Ballet (1951–52). In 1954 organized Les Ballets de l'Etoile with writer and critic Jean Laurent. For that company he choreographed his major work, *Symphonie Pour Un Homme Seul* to musique concrète by Pierre Schaeffer and Pierre Henry, a ballet typical of his individual style. He choreographs in an expressive style which combines the classic dance with modern, jazz, and acrobatics. Among his other compositions to musique concrète are *Voyage Au Coeur d'Une Enfant* and *Voilà l'Homme.* He also choreographed

Maurice Béjart with actress-dancer Michèle Seigneuret

Haut Voltage, Promethée, Orphée, Sonate a Trois, the last named based on Jean Paul Sartre's *Huis Clos,* staged for Western Theatre Ballet. Changing the name of his company to Ballet Théâtre de Maurice Béjart, he gave two Paris seasons at the Marigny and Théâtre des Champs-Elysées and toured Germany, Spain, Italy, and Belgium. After the success of his version of Igor Stravinsky's *Le Sacre du Printemps* (Dec. 1959) he was appointed ballet director of the Théâtre Royale de la Monnaie, Brussels, where the ballet company assumed the name Les Ballets du XXme Siècle. This company appeared in Paris (1960, 1961), invited by Théatre des Nations, the annual performing arts festival. Béjart still finds time to appear as guest choreographer. In the summer of 1961 he choreographed Salvador Dali's ballet *Gala,* with Ludmilla Tcherina as ballerina, in Venice. Later that year he staged the Bacchanale in *Tannhäuser* at Bayreuth and produced Offenbach's *Tales of Hoffmann* in Brussels, opening up a further career as director of operas. In 1963 his version of the opera *Tales of Hoffmann* was given at the Théâtre des Champs-Elysées (Paris) as part of the theatre's 50th anniversary celebrations. Wrote and staged the musical show *The Green Queen* (music by Pierre Henry), Hérbértot Théâtre, Paris, during his year's leave of absence from Brussels (1963). Staged the Hector Berlioz opera *Damnation of Faust* at Paris Opéra (1964). This production was sent to Greece (summer, 1965) to be performed in the famous Epidaurus amphitheatre. Also in 1964 he staged an enormous production of Beethoven's Ninth Symphony at the Royal Circus in Brussels (prem.: Oct. 27), which he re-created at the Sport Palace, Paris (prem.: June 3, 1966). Presented his versions of *Sacre du Printemps, Le Renard,* and *Les Noces* for a special Stravinsky evening at the Paris Opéra (Apr. 23, 1965). On Nov. 17, 1966 he presented his company in the première of *Romeo and Juliet* to the Berlioz score at the Royal Circus, Brussels. King Baudoin and Queen Fabiola attended the gala performance. The ballet was later performed at the Paris Opéra (Dec. 15) and in Antwerp (Jan. 13–15, 1967).

Belgiojoso, Baldassarino da. See BEAUJOYEUX, BALTHASAR DE.

Belle au Bois Dormant, La. See SLEEPING BEAUTY, THE.

Bells, The. Ballet in 5 episodes; chor. and book: Ruth Page; music: Darius Milhaud; décor: Isamu Noguchi. First prod.: Chicago Univ. Composers' Series, Chicago, Ill., Apr. 26, 1946, with Ruth Page, Jerome Andrews, and Robert Josias in principal roles; N.Y. première: Ballet Russe de Monte Carlo, N.Y. City Center, Sept. 6, 1946, with Ruth Page and Frederick Franklin, subsequent performances with Ruthanna Boris and Franklin in leading roles. Based on the poem of the same title by Edgar Allan Poe, the ballet's five episodes are the development of poet's theme: 1. Silver Bells ("What a world of merriment their melody foretells.") 2. Golden Bells ("Hear the mellow wedding bells.") 3. Brazen Bells ("How they clang and clash and roar.") 4. Iron Bells ("What a world of solemn thought their melody compels.") 5. Dance of the Ghouls ("They are neither brute nor human—they are Ghouls."

Beloved, The. Ballet in 1 act; Bronislava Nijinska; music: Franz Schubert and Franz Liszt, arr. by Darius Milhaud; book and décor: Alexandre Benois. First prod.: Théâtre National de l'Opéra, Paris, Nov. 22, 1928, with Ida Rubinstein (for whom the ballet was written) and Anatole Vilzak in leading parts; revived by Nijinska for the Markova-Dolin Company (1937) with new décor by George Kirsta; and for Ballet Theatre (1941) with décor and costumes by Nicolas de Molas. Alicia Markova and Anton Dolin danced the leading roles in both these companies. A poet, seated at a piano, reminisces about his youth with the help of his Muse with whom he dances. The original French title of the ballet was *La Bien-Aimée*.

Belsky, Igor, Honored Artist of the RSFSR, Soviet character dancer and choreographer, b. 1925; m. Lyudmila Alexeyeva, Kirov Ballet soloist. Graduated from the Leningrad Ballet School in 1943 under Alexander Pisarev (ballet) and Andrei Lopukhov (character dance). He was accepted into the Kirov company as early as 1942 while still at school, when the Kirov theatre was evacuated to Perm. His formal debut on the Kirov stage in Leningrad took place in 1943 when he danced the Chief Warrior in the *Polovetsian Dances from Prince Igor.* Other roles include Tybalt (*Romeo and Juliet*), Izmail (Gayané), Nur-Ali (*The Fountain of Bakhchisarai*), leading Basque (*Flames of Paris*). He created the title role in *Shurale* and of Mako in *Path of Thunder.* His first big choreographic work, *Coast of Hope* (1959), placed him among the most promising Soviet choreographers seeking for a new idiom to interpret contemporary themes. His second ballet, *Seventh Symphony* (*Dimitri Shostakovitch,* 1961), continues in this vein.

Benefit, or Benefit Performance, the custom of giving a dancer or a group of dancers the proceeds of a performance staged in their honor. The custom originated in the English dramatic theatre in the 17th century but received its widest acceptance at the Paris Opéra and the Imperial Russian Theatres where the dancer's contract included a benefit in addition to salary. In pre-revolutionary Russia the receipts of a benefit often equalled a year's salary, and sometimes exceeded it, because tickets for the benefit were sold at a much higher price. Only ballerinas, premiers danseurs, and ballet masters received full benefits; soloists generally were given a half-benefit, i.e. two dancers shared the proceeds of one performance; lesser soloists a quarter-benefit; the corps de ballet were entitled to one common benefit the proceeds of which were divided among its members. A benefit was a gala occasion at which the beneficiary received expensive gifts and flowers from the audience. The practice of benefits disappeared from the Russian stage after the revolution and had petered out in France by the Middle of the 19th century. In the U.S. benefits are given only for charitable causes, and they are regulated by Theatre Authority, a voluntary organization.

Benesh, Rudolf, English painter, b. London, 1916. With his wife, Joan (neé Rothwell, b. Liverpool, 1920), copyrighted a system of dance notation

(1955); published *Introduction to Benesh Dance Notation* (London, 1956). Since 1956 this system has been included in the syllabus of the Royal Academy of Dancing Teachers' Training Course. Completed system of shorthand (1957); founded Institute of Choreology (Examining and Professional Body, 1960); College of Choreology for the training of choreographic notators for ballet companies (1962), of which he and his wife are directors. Is responsible for teaching subject to Royal Ballet School, Ballet Rambert School, and others. Joan Benesh was formerly a member of Sadler's Wells Ballet.

Bennett, Alexander, British dancer, b. Edinburgh, Scotland, 1930. Studied under Marjorie Middleton in Edinburgh and made his debut with the Edinburgh Ballet Club. After military service in World War II, resumed training and joined Ballet Rambert (1951), becoming principal dancer (1953). Left to join Sadler's Wells Theatre Ballet (1956), becoming principal dancer (1957). Principal dancer with Royal Ballet since 1958, with which he has toured South Africa, Far East and Middle East. Roles include Albrecht (*Giselle*), Florimund (*The Sleeping Beauty*), Husband (*The Invitation*), Master of Tregennis (*The Haunted Ballroom*), Franz (*Coppélia*), etc. Rejoined Ballet Rambert (1963).

Bennington School of the Dance. In 1932 the Bennington College and Undergraduate Liberal Arts College for Women opened in Bennington, Vt., including among its possible majors the dance. In the summer of 1934 the Bennington School of the Dance opened and continued each summer thereafter through 1938 with production of new works in the modern dance and a broad program of dance study. The School and the Festivals run by the School offered an opportunity to Martha Graham, Doris Humphrey, Hanya Holm, Charles Weidman, and the younger exponents of the modern dance to work and create under nearly ideal conditions. In the summer of 1939 the Bennington School of the Dance held its session at Mills College, Calif. In 1940 the name of the School was changed to Bennington School of the Arts and that summer and the next it met at Bennington with courses in dance, drama, music, and theatre design. In 1942 the Bennington College Summer Session offered no major work in dance but enlarged its program to include fields other than the arts, such as social studies and literature. Because of World War II and the change of the academic calendar at Bennington College, the summer project was discontinued after that summer. Since then the aim of the Bennington summer sessions has been carried out at Connecticut College School of the Dance, New London, Conn.

Benois, Alexandre, Russian painter, art historian, theatrical worker, b. St. Petersburg, 1870, d. Paris, 1960. Co-founder with Léon Bakst and Serge Diaghilev of the society The World of Art, which launched the Diaghilev Ballets Russes. Made his debut as scenic designer with décor for *Sylvia* (1901) at the Maryinsky Theatre, and for *Cupid's Revenge* there the same year. Created libretto, décor, and costumes for *Le Pavillon d'Armide* (Maryinsky, 1907), Diaghilev Ballets Russes (1909). Designed décor and costumes *Les Sylphides* (1909), *Giselle* (1910), *Petrouchka* (also co-author of the libretto, with Igor Stravinsky, 1911)—all for Diaghilev; décor and costumes, *La Bien-Aimée, Les Noces de Psyche et l'Amour* and *La Valse* (1929) all for the Ida Rubinstein company; décor and costumes, *Graduation Ball* (1940), for Original Ballet Russe; *The Nutcracker,* (1940), *Raymonda* (1946) for Ballet Russe de Monte Carlo; *Enchanted Mill* (1948), for Grand Ballet du Marquis de Cuevas; *Graduation Ball* and *The Nutcracker* (1957), for Lon-

Alexandre Benois, last photo of the artist taken on the occasion of his visit in 1960 on stage of London's Festival Ballet, following Graduation Ball *in his décor and costumes. He also wrote the libretto for the ballet.*

don's Festival Ballet. His published works include *Reminiscences of the Ballet Russe* (London, 1941) and *Memoirs* (London, 1960).

Benois, Nadia, contemporary painter. Niece of Alexandre Benois and mother of actor-director Peter Ustinov. Her designs for ballet include décor for *Dark Elegies* (1937), *Lady Into Fox* (1939), both for Ballet Rambert; *The Sleeping Beauty* for Sadler's Wells Ballet (1939). This was the first version presented by Sadler's Wells (now Royal) Ballet and was called *The Sleeping Princess,* after the Serge Diaghilev production of 1921.

Bensserade, Isaac de, b. in the French village of Lion, near Ruean. Became interested in the theatre while a student and wrote verse for the ballets in which Louis XIV appeared. He wrote other poetry including numerous sonnets. In all he wrote over twenty ballets, in most of which the King took part: *Mascarade en forme de Ballet,* presented at the Palace of the Cardinal and danced by the King (1651); *Ballet de la Nuit* (1653); *Ballet Royal des Noces de Pelée et de Thetis* (1654); *Ballet Royal des Proverbes* (1654); *Ballet Royal des Saisons,* danced at Fontainbleau (1661); *Les Amours Déguisés* (1664); *Le Triomphe d'Amour* (1681), and a number of others for which the complete verses are given in *Les Oeuvres de Monsieur de Bensserade,* published in 1897.

Bentley, Muriel, contemporary American dancer, b. New York City. Studied dance with Vecheslav Swoboda, Leon Fokine, Metropolitan Opera Ballet School,

Ruth St. Denis, Helen Veola, Anton Dolin, et al. Danced as a child in Ruth St. Denis's production of *The Prophetess* (1931). Teamed with José Greco in Spanish dancing (1936–37); Metropolitan Opera Ballet (1938–39); Ballet Theatre (from 1940), dancing important roles in *Fancy Free, Tally-Ho, Capriccio Espagnol, Three Virgins and a Devil, Judgement of Paris, Undertow, Fall River Legend,* and others. Since 1958 has danced with Jerome Robbins' Ballets: U.S.A., with roles in *N.Y. Export: Op. Jazz, The Concert, Moves, Events,* and others.

Bérain, Jean (1638–1711), French designer of costumes and settings, b. Bar le Duc. He went to Paris in 1659 and worked first as an engraver. Later he became a designer of tapestries, embroidery, costumes, and stage properties. He was connected with the Académie Royale from 1673 until his death, at first designing only the costumes; but in 1681, when he designed *Le Triomphe d'Amour,* he also designed the sets. He worked on many of Lully's ballets. The female costumes of Bérain followed the line and general fashion of female court clothes of the day. The men's costumes were for the most part, "à la Romain," or along the lines of the Roman warrior's vestments. Bérain's costumes are characterized by much ornamentation and elegant symbolism. In his sets he simplified the Baroque then in vogue. Bérain designed the costumes worn by Louis XIV in his appearances in a number of ballets.

Bérain II, Jean, French stage designer, son of the great designer of the same name. In 1711 he succeeded his father at the Académie Royale, Paris, and held the position until 1721. His work shows the influence of his father.

Bérard, Christian (1902–1949), French painter and designer. He contributed some of the most imaginative décor and costumes ever devised for contemporary ballet. Among his works are *Cotillon* (1932), *Mozartiana* (1933), *Symphonie Fantastique* (1936), Beethoven's *Seventh Symphony* (1938), *Les Forains* (1945), *La Rencontre* (1948). He was co-founder with Roland Petit and Boris Kochno of Les Ballets des Champs-Elysées (1945).

Bergamasque (Bergamasca, also Bergamask), a rustic dance in 2/4 time of great antiquity, which derives its name from Bergamo, a town in Lombardy, Italy. The dance took its characteristics from the inhabitants of Bergamo who were said to be egotistical and cunning, possessing in a high degree the faults and the virtues of the typical rustic. From these characteristics developed the Harlequin of commedia dell'arte. The dance itself was a round dance of couples, the men moving forward, the women backward, in a circle. With a change in the tune, each couple embraced, performed a few turning steps and began again. In essence it is typical of all courtship dances. It was well known long before the end of the sixteenth century. In Shakespeare's *A Midsummer Night's Dream* (1592), Bottom asks King Theseus at the conclusion of the "tedious brief scene of young Pyramus and his love Thisbe": "Will it please you to see the epilogue, or to hear a Bergamask dance between two of our company?" Theseus tactfully settles for the bergamask. Nearly 250 years later, Mendelssohn included this bergamask in his incidental music to the play.

Bergsma, Deanne, British dancer, b. Harrismith, S. Africa, 1941. Studied with Marjorie Sturman in S. Africa, and at Royal Ballet School, London. Member of the company since 1959; promoted to soloist (1962). Roles include Lilac Fairy (*The Sleeping Beauty*) Prayer (*Coppélia*), Queen of the Wilis (*Giselle*), Fairy Winter (*Cinderella*). For Sunday Ballet Club created the single girl's role in Ray Powell's *One In Five.* Created one of the three Harlots in Kenneth MacMillan's *Romeo and Juliet,* and a variation in *La Bayadère* (both 1965). Dances the Hostess in the revival of *Les Biches* and Josephine in the revival of *A Wedding Bouquet,* all in the Royal Ballet repertoire.

Beriosoff, Nicholas, dancer, ballet master, choreographer, b. Lithuania, 1906, father of ballerina Svetlana Beriosova. Studied in Czechoslovakia and danced with Prague Opera Ballet; then with Lithuanian National Ballet in Kaunas. Joined the René Blum company in Monte Carlo (1935). With Ballet Russe de Monte Carlo (1938); ballet master, Marquis de Cuevas' Ballet International (1944), and his Grand Ballet (1947). Later that year became ballet master of Metropolitan Ballet, England. Ballet master, Teatro alla Scala, Milan (1950–51); London's Festival Ballet (1951–54), staging *Petrouchka, The Nutcracker, Schéhérazade, Prince Igor,* and his own version of *Esmeralda* (1954). Returned to the Marquis de Cuevas company (1956), and again for its final (1961–62) season; between these periods he was ballet director at Württemberg State Opera, Stuttgart. Since 1962, Director of Finnish National Ballet, staging *The Sleeping Beauty, Swan Lake, Les Sylphides, Esmeralda, Le Sacre du Printemps,* and others.

Beriosova, Svetlana, ballerina, b. Lithuania, 1932, daughter of Nicholas Beriosoff; now a British subject. Brought to U.S. in 1940 where she studied ballet with Anatole Vilzak and Ludmila Shollar. Made her debut as guest artist with the Ottawa Ballet Company, dancing *Les Sylphides,* and *The Nutcracker* (Mar. 12, 1947); Grand Ballet de Monte Carlo (1947); ballerina, Metropolitan Ballet (1948–49), dancing *Swan Lake* (Act 2), and others, and creating leading roles in *Designs with Strings* and Frank Staff's *Faniciulla delle Rose.* Joined Sadler's Wells Theatre Ballet as leading dancer (1950), dancing leading roles in *Assembly Ball, Swan Lake, The Nutcracker, Les Sylphides,* and creating leading role in *Trumpet Concerto.* Transferred to Sadler's Wells (now Royal) Ballet, as soloist (1952); ballerina (1955). She dances the ballerina roles in the entire classic repertoire and has created the leading female roles in *The Shadow* (1953), *Rinaldo and Armida* (1955), *The Prince of the Pagodas* (1957), *Antigone* (1959), *Le Baiser de la Fée* (the Fairy, 1960), *Diversions,* and *Persephone* (in which her role involved both speaking and dancing, 1961). Guest artist with state ballet companies in Italy, Germany, Yugoslavia, and other countries. In 1959 she married Dr. Masud Khan, a psychologist.

Berk, Fred, dancer, choreographer, director, b. 1911, Vienna; now an American citizen. He studied at the State Academy of Dance, Vienna, coming to the U.S. in 1942. He devotes his interest to the Jewish dance and tours the U.S., Canada, and Israel. Since 1945 has taught at the Jewish Theological Seminary. In 1950 founded and continues to direct the Jewish Dance Division of Young Men's and Young Women's Hebrew Association, N.Y. (the so-called "92nd Street Y"). Co-founder of the Merry-Go-Rounders dance company for which he choreographed *Holiday in Israel* and *Wedding in Austria.* Headed Stage for Dancing (1949–54), producing modern dance performances at the Brooklyn (N.Y.) Museum. Since 1958 directs his own company, the Hebraica Dancers. Has written many articles and booklets on Israeli folk dance and Jewish dance. He has edited a bibliography entitled *The Jewish Dance* (N.Y., 1959). Received citation for the development of the Jewish Dance (1960).

Svetlana Beriosova, prima ballerina of the Royal Ballet in Swan Lake

Berlioz, Hector (1803–1869), French composer. His *Symphonie Fantastique* (Episodes de la vie d'un artiste) was used by Leonide Massine for his ballet of the same title, staged for the Ballet Russe de Monte Carlo (1936). In 1954 Massine staged a ballet to Berlioz's *Harold in Italy* for Ballet Russe de Monte Carlo. In 1955 George Skibine staged Berlioz' *Romeo and Juliet* for the Grand Ballet du Marquis de Cuevas in Paris, for special performances in Le Cour Carre, the Louvre.

Berman, Eugene, painter and scenic designer, b. St. Petersburg, Russia, 1899; American citizen since 1945. A resident of U.S. since 1937, and for nearly twenty years one of the foremost stage designers for ballet, he considers himself self-taught, although he had studied painting in his youth in Russia (1914–1918). His décors for ballet include *Icare* (Serge Lifar, 1938), *Devil's Holiday* (Frederick Ashton, 1939), *Concerto Barocco* (George Balanchine, 1941), *Romeo and Juliet* (Antony Tudor, 1943), *Danses Concertantes, Le Bourgeois Gentilhomme* (Balanchine, 1944), *Giselle* (new décor for Ballet Theatre, 1946), two versions of Balanchine's *Ballet Imperial* (Sadler's Wells Ballet, London, 1950; Teatro alla Scala, Milan, 1952), *Roma* (Balanchine, 1955). Since 1956 Berman has been devoting himself to painting rather than to stage designing. He considers as the highlight of his career his décor for *Danses Concertantes* for Ballet Russe de Monte Carlo, when he had the inspiring collaboration of Igor Stravinsky and George Balanchine. Despite Berman's eleven-year absence from the theatrical and, especially, ballet scene, he has not been forgotten. In Oct.–Nov., 1966, the Harkness Foundation organized an exhibition of his ballet set and costume designs at the Harkness House for Ballet Arts, N.Y. At the same time his opera and theatre designs were on view at the Forum Gallery, also in N.Y. For further details see "The Theatre of Eugene Berman," by George Amberg (Museum of Modern Art, N.Y., Jan. 1947); also "The Stage and Ballet Designs of Eugene Berman," by Allison Delarue, *Dance Index* (N.Y., Jan. 1948).

Berners, Lord (1883–1950), English composer, stage designer and writer. A diplomat by profession, his ballet scores include *The Triumph of Neptune* for the Diaghilev Ballets Russes (George Balanchine, 1926); Foyer de Danse, for Ballet Rambert (1932); *A Wedding Bouquet* (1937), *Cupid and Psyche* (1939), and *Les Sirènes* (1946), for the Sadler's Wells Ballet, all by Frederick Ashton. He also devised the book, décor, and costumes for *A Wedding Bouquet,* and the book for *Cupid and Psyche.* Parts of his score for *The Triumph of Neptune* were used for *Le Boxing* and *Waterloo and the Crimea* (both by Susan Salaman, Ballet Rambert, 1931).

Bernstein, Harry, American dancer, educator, writer, b. Chicago, Ill. Early dance studies in Chicago with Adolph Bolm, Kurt Graff, Bernice Holmes, Bentley Stone. B.S., Juilliard School of Music; A.M., New York Univ. Studied dance in N.Y. with Margaret Craske, Martha Graham, Hanya Holm, Louis Horst, Doris Humphrey, José Limón, Alwin Nikolais, Helene Platova, and Antony Tudor. Served in U.S. Army Air Corps (1941–46), on active duty in Burma where he received three battle stars and a Presidential Unit Citation. Was a soloist in Graff Concert Ballet before army service. From 1946 to 1954 danced with Chicago Ballet Company, Hanya Holm Dance Company, Doris Humphrey Repertory Company, Ballet Americain, and Henry Street Playhouse Company, among others. Has choreographed for concert stage, ballet, opera, and musical comedy. Editor and critic, *Dance Observer* (1953–64). After teaching at several colleges joined the faculty of Adelphi College (now University) N.Y. (1956), and was appointed

Chairman of the Dance Department and Director of the Summer Dance Workshop with the rank of Associate Professor (1959). Is Chairman of the Dance Committee of the Long Island (N.Y.) Arts Center, Inc., and a member of its Board of Directors and Executive Committee. Is married to Bunty Kelley, former soloist of Sadler's Wells (now Royal) Ballet and the Agnes de Mille Dance Theatre.

Bernstein, Leonard, American pianist, composer, conductor, Musical Director of the N.Y. Philharmonic Orchestra, b. Lawrence, Mass., 1918. Graduated from Boston Latin School (1935); Harvard Univ. (1939); Curtis Institute of Music, Phila. (1941). Composed scores for the ballets *Fancy Free* (1944), and *Facsimile* (1946). His Symphony No. 2 *(Age of Anxiety,* 1949), was used for a ballet of the same title. All his ballet music has been choreographed by Jerome Robbins. His scores for Broadway musicals include *On The Town* (1944), an extension of the subject matter of *Fancy Free* (sailors on leave), *Wonderful Town* (1953), *Candide* (1956), *West Side Story* (1957).

Bertl, Inge, German dancer, b. Munich, 1933. Studied with Victor Gsovsky, Lula von Sachnovsky, Vaslav Orlikovsky, and others. Soloist, Bavarian State Opera, Munich. Among her principal roles are Myrtha *(Giselle)*, Prostitute *(Miraculous Mandarin)*, Lady *(The Lady and the Unicorn)*, Belle Rose *(The Prince of the Pagodas)*, Eurydice *(Orpheus)*.

Beryozka, Soviet State Dance Company, founded in 1948 with Nadezhda Nadezhdina as artistic director. It was organized after a group of dancers from the Kalinin region won the finals of the competition for amateur village artists assembled from all parts of the Russian Federation. It was then that Nadezhdina choreographed the famous *Beryozka* round dance wherein the girls glided effortlessly round the stage with birch-tree branches in their hands, their gliding feet concealed under long red Russian "sarafans," thus creating an illusion of small figures being mechanically propelled in a round. This dance gave its name to the all-girl company that has become known all over the world. It has visited over twenty countries, among them the U.S. (1958) and Latin America (1962). In 1961 Nadezhda Nadezhdina, desiring to extend the range of her choreography, added male character dancers to the company and choreographed such new scenes as *An Autumn Village Fair* and *Near Moscow*. The majority of the dancers are graduates of the Bolshoi School, fully grounded in the classical technique which is still taught every morning at the company class. Currently the troupe is being reorganized into a larger company of the Russian Federation, with the possibility of adding new dances of other peoples of this largest constituent republic of the Soviet Union.

Bessy, Claude, première danseuse étoile of the Paris Opéra. Trained in the Paris Opéra School, she became an étoile in 1956. Created Venus in John Cranko's *La Belle Hélène* (1955), Oceanide in *Les Noces Fantastiques* (1955), 3rd movement—pastorale—*Symphonie Fantastique* (1957), Chloe in *Daphnis and Chloe* (1959), ballerina roles in Gene Kelly's *Pas de Dieux* (1960) and Michel Descombey's *Symphonie Concertante* (1962). Revealed herself as a good comédienne in *L'Atlantide* and *Le Bel Indifférent* (1958). Has been guest star with American Ballet Theatre in N.Y. and on U.S. tour. Guest ballerina, Bolshoi Theatre Ballet, Moscow, dancing *Swan Lake* (1961). Dances all principal roles in the classic repertoire as well as modern ballets.

Bettis, Valerie, American dancer, choreographer, b. Houston, Tex., 1920. Studied at Univ. of Texas; dance training with Rowena Smith and Tina Flade in Houston, and with Hanya Holm in N.Y.

Valerie Bettis

(1937), making her professional debut in *Trend* that summer. Joined the Hanya Holm company the following year, remaining for two years. Appearing in *Railroads on Parade,* N.Y. World's Fair (1939–1940). Gave her first recitals Nov. 27 and 28, 1941, at Carnegie Hall, N.Y. Created her first major solo, *The Desperate Heart* (1943). Organized her own group (1944), beginning with a performance at the YM-YWHA, her best known works for the group being *As I Lay Dying,* and *Domino Furioso.* Choreographed *Virginia Sampler* for Ballet Russe de Monte Carlo (1947) and the following year had a big success on Broadway as Tiger Lily in the musical *Inside U.S.A.,* following this with roles in *Great To Be Alive* and *Bless You All.* A pioneer of dance on television since middle 1940's, she turned to motion pictures in 1951 with two films starring Rita Hayworth. Choreographed a version of Tennessee Williams' play *A Streetcar Named Desire* for the Slavenska-Franklin company (1952), which was also in the repertoire of American Ballet Theatre. Continued to give performances with her group, in television and off-Broadway. Choreographed the movements for the off-Broadway and London productions of *Ulysses in Nighttown* (1958), adapted from James Joyce's *Ulysses,* in which she also appeared. Choreographed *Early Voyagers* for National Ballet, Washington, D.C. (1963). Has taught at Perry-Mansfield School, Connecticut College, etc. Currently teaches in N.Y.

Bewitched, The. Modern dance work; chor.: Joyce Trisler; music: Harry Partch, composed for instruments designed and built by the composer plus clarinet, bass clarinet, and cello; setting design and production coordination: Thomas de Gaetani; costumes: Malcolm McCormack. This work was given two performances, Apr. 10 and 11, 1959, at the Juilliard Concert Hall, N.Y., sponsored by Columbia Univ. Juilliard School of Music Dance Department, and Univ. of Illinois. The score was commissioned by the Fromm Foundation, Chicago, for performance at the Univ. of Illinois' 1957 Festival of Contemporary Arts, when it was played by faculty and student musicians conducted by Prof. John Garvey, with choreography by Alvin Nikolais. The same conductor, again with faculty and student musicians, played for the two N.Y. performances. The strange instruments were arranged at the back of the stage behind a scrim, in front of which the huge figure of the Witch rose out of the ground and disappeared back into the ground after commanding the fantastic series of dance events, all of which had the real-unreal quality of dreams—beautiful as in the passage called Euphoria Descends a Sausalito Stairway, satirically grotesque as in The Cognoscenti are Plunged into a Damoniac Descent While at Cocktails. Although the particular nature of the score and the production has made further performances an impossibility, *The Bewitched* has had a considerable influence on modern dance—musically, scenically, and in costuming. The dancers were Joyce Trisler, John Wilson, Jaime Rogers, Florence Peters, Carol Egan, Penny Frank, Deborah Jowitt, Horst Muller, Baird Searles, and David Wynne.

Bharata Natya. See HINDU DANCE.

Bhaskar, Hindu dancer and choreographer

Bhaskar, Roy Chowdhury (known professionally as Bhaskar), Hindu dancer, choreographer, teacher. He is reputed to be the first Hindu dancer to restore the Tribanga style of dance in the present generation. He has given performances alone, with a partner, and with small and large ensembles, most of which he organized. Has appeared on the stage, screen, and television. His style is frequently acrobatic and is remarkable for his ability to balance in difficult poses on one leg. At present performing, staging, and teaching in the U.S., mainly in N.Y. where he arrived in 1955.

Bibiena, Giuseppe Galli de (1696–1751), Italian designer of sets for ballet, opera, and drama. One of a famous family of designers that influenced the entire trend of theatrical design. Oliver Messel's sets for the Royal Ballet's *The Sleeping Beauty* owe much to the extant designs of Bibiena.

Bibliska Bilder (The Message). Ballet in 1 act; chor.: Ivo Cramèr; music: Handel-Gluck; décor: Alvar Granström. First prod.: the Concert Hall, Stockholm Nov. 16, 1945, with the choreographer as Herod, Per Arne Qvarsebo as Joseph, and Birgit Boman as Maria. The ballet was subsequently produced several times. One of several Cramèr works on biblical themes.

Biches, Les. Ballet in 1 act; chor.: Bronislava Nijinska; commissioned music: Francis Poulenc; curtain, décor, and costumes: Marie Laurencin. First prod.: Diaghilev Ballets Russes, Théâtre de Monte Carlo, Jan. 6, 1924, with Alexandra Danilova, Ninette de Valois, Felia Dubrovska, Natalie Komarova, Vera Nemtchinova, Alice Nikitina, Bronislava Nijinska, Lubov Tchernicheva, Leon Woicikowski, Anatole Vilzak, and Nicholas Zverev in the original cast; revived for the Markova-Dolin Company in England (1937), under the title *The House Party,* with Alicia Markova and Anton Dolin in the Nemtchinova and Vilzak roles; revived for Grand Ballet du Marquis de Cuevas (1947), with Marjorie Tallchief and George Skibine. The ballet deals with a house party populated by a motley crowd of male and female guests, most of them of good looks and somewhat easy morals. It is in effect a biting satire on the behavior of the young men and young women of the 1920s. There is no actual plot but rather a series of meetings between individuals, an occasional glance, a touch, a smile, into which anything can be read. Revived by Nijinska for England's Royal Ballet, Dec. 2, 1964, with Georgina Parkinson as La Garçonne, Svetlana Beriosova as the Hostess, and David Blair, Keith Rosson, and Robert Mead as the Athletes.

Bie, Oscar, German writer and critic,

active chiefly in Berlin. Author of *Gesellschaftstanz der Renaissance* (1903), *Der Tanz als Kunstwerk* (1905), *Das Ballett* (1905), *Der Tanz* (1906), *Tanzmusik* (1907), *Der Moderne Tanz* (1920).

Bien-Aimée, La. See BELOVED, THE.

Big Apple, a form of jitterbug dancing involving groups of people, popular in the middle 1930's.

Big City, The. Ballet in 3 scenes; chor. and book: Kurt Jooss; music: Alexander Tansman (*Sonatine Transatlantique*). First prod.: Jooss Ballet, Opera House, Cologne, Nov. 21, 1932, with Mascha Lidolt, Sigurd Leeder, and Ernst Uthoff in the leading parts. The plot: "In the hurrying throng of a continental city are seen the Young Girl and the Young Workman, her sweetheart, homeward bound after the day's work. The Libertine, in search of new conquests, follows the Young Girl to her home. Dazzled by the promise of adventure she fares forth on his arm to the dance halls, where disillusion awaits her." The role of the Young Workman afterwards became one with which Hans Zullig has always been identified.

Bigottini, Emilie (1784–1858), French dancer at the Paris Opéra. She danced at the Opéra from 1801 until her retirement in 1823, becoming a principal dancer (though more famous for her great talent as a mime). Her chief role was Nina in *Nina, ou La Folle par Amour,* which she created in 1813. She married a millionaire in 1816.

Billboard, weekly theatrical publication, founded 1893, the oldest publication devoted to people and events in the field of amusement. Covers legitimate theatre, vaudeville, night clubs, dance bands, circuses, etc. Among other services is a letter forwarding service, used by countless show people who have no permanent address except c/o *Billboard.*

Billy the Kid. Ballet in 1 act; chor.: Eugene Loring; music: Aaron Copland; book: Lincoln Kirstein; costumes: Jared French. First prod.: Ballet Caravan, Chicago Opera House, Chicago, Oct. 16, 1938, with Eugene Loring in title role, Marie Jeanne (Mother and Sweetheart), Lew Christensen (Pat Garrett), Todd Bolender (Alias); revived for Ballet Theatre, Majestic Theatre, N.Y., Feb. 13, 1941, with Eugene Loring (Billy), Alicia Alonso (Mother and Sweetheart), Richard Reed (Pat Garrett), David Nillo (Alias); in repertoire of Dance Players, National Theatre, N.Y., opening Apr. 21, 1942, with Loring and Christensen in their original roles. Charles Dickson, Ian Gibson, Michael Kidd, and John Kriza have also danced the role of Billy, the last named being especially identified with it. Based on American folklore, it is a story of frontier days, pioneers, and cowboys, and in particular of William Bonney (the Kid), a notorious outlaw who was admired as well as feared and who was finally shot in ambush by his former friend, Sheriff Garrett.

Birds, The. Ballet in 1 act; chor. and libretto: Robert Helpmann; music: Ottorino Respighi's suite *The Birds,* for the Aristophanes play of that title; décor: Chiang Lee. First prod.: Sadler's Wells (now Royal) Ballet, New Theatre, London, Nov. 24, 1942, with Beryl Grey (Nightingale, her first created role), Alexis Rassine (Dove), Moyra Fraser (Hen). A comedy of ornithological loves and jealousies.

Birthday Offering. Ballet in 1 act; chor.: Frederick Ashton; music: from Alexander Glazounov's Valse de Concert No. 1, op. 47; *Scènes de Ballet; The Seasons; Ruses d'Amour;* Prelude and Mazurka No. 3 for piano, op. 25, arr. by Robert Irving. First prod.: Sadler's Wells (now Royal) Ballet, Royal Opera House, Covent Garden, London, May 5, 1956, with seven ballerinas of the company and their partners: Margot Fonteyn, Beryl Grey, Violetta Elvin, Nadia Nerina, Rowena Jackson, Svetlana Beriosova, Elaine Fifield, and Michael Somes, Alexander Grant, Brian Shaw, Philip Chatfield, David Blair, Desmond Doyle, Bryan Ashbridge. A divertissement created to mark the twenty-fifth birthday of the Sadler's Wells Ballet, it was so successful that it has remained in the repertoire.

Bischoff, Egon, German classic dancer, b. Gotha, 1934. He first studied at the modern dance school of Gret Palucca (Dresden); later studied for five years at the Leningrad Ballet Academy. Soloist of the Berlin State Opera; also teaches at the Professional School for the Dance Art, Berlin.

Bizet, Georges (1838–1875), French composer. Though best known for his opera *Carmen,* his music has been often used by choreographers. *Jeux d'Enfants* has been used by Leonide Massine (1932) and George Balanchine (1955); selections from *Carmen* were used by Ruth Page for her Ballet *Guns and Castanets* (1939), and for her ballet version of the opera (1959); also by Roland Petit for his ballet *Carmen.* Bizet's Symphony in C served Andrée Howard as the score for *Assembly Ball* (1946); and Balanchine for *Palais de Cristal* (Paris Opéra, 1947) and *Symphony in C* (revised version, New York City Ballet, 1948).

Bjørnsson, Fredbjørn, soloist of Royal Danish Ballet, b. Copenhagen, 1926, of Icelandic parentage; m. Kirsten Ralov. Entered Royal Danish Ballet school in 1935; graduated into the company and was made soloist in 1949. Dances Franz (*Coppélia*), Gennaro (*Napoli*), Youngest Brother (*Kermesse in Bruges*), second Scottish variation (*La Sylphide*), Junior Cadet (*Graduation Ball*), Tybalt (Frederick Ashton's *Romeo and Juliet*), Magician (*Moon Reindeer*), Blackamoor (*Night Shadow*), Percussion Leader (*Fanfare*), *Flower Festival at Genzano* pas de deux, Thief (*Carmen*), and others. Repeated last named role in Roland Petit's film *Black Tights* (1961). Visited N.Y. on a study grant (1961) and worked with George Balanchine, Jerome Robbins, Martha Graham, Robert Joffrey; also taught at American Ballet Center (school of Robert Joffrey Ballet). Was one of the ten Danish dancers who appeared at Jacob's Pillow (1955). With his wife, staged *Napoli* for the New Zealand Ballet (1962), the first time the complete version has ever been staged outside Denmark. Bjørnsson is one of the great exponents of the August Bournonville style. Created Knight of the Order of Dannebrog (1961). Choreographed *Bag Taeppet* (1954), *Skaelmeri* (Bergensiana) (1957), *Lykke på Rejsen* (1959). In 1965 assumed the role of Dr. Coppelius in *Coppélia.* He has become one of the leading mimes in the great Royal Danish Ballet tradition.

Blacher, Boris, German composer, b. Newchang, China, 1903, of Baltic-German parentage. He studied music in Berlin and later taught in Dresden and Berlin. Since 1953 he has been director of the Berlin Hochschule Für Musik (Musical College). His ballet scores include *Holiday in the South* (1937), *Harlequinade, Chiarina* (1950), *Hamlet* (1950), *Lysistrata* (1951), *The Moor of Venice* (1955). Todd Bolender used his *Orchestral Variations on a Theme of Paganini* for his ballet *Theme and Variations* (première: Cologne Opera Ballet, Dec. 22, 1963).

Black Bottom. See JITTERBUG.

Black Crook, The. A theatrical extravaganza produced in 1866 and which continued in popularity for over forty years. It is said to have created the basis for American music hall, variety theatre, vaudeville, and even musical comedy. It was premièred Sept. 12, 1866, at Niblo's

Garden, N.Y. and ran continuously for sixteen months. Two years later it was revived; subsequent N.Y. revivals followed one another until 1903. On the road it ran almost continuously until 1909. The production came about through one of those fortuitous accidents that happen from time to time in the theatre. Jarrett and Palmer, well-known theatrical managers of the time, had imported from Europe a great deal of scenery and machinery for a production called *La Biche au Bois,* to open at the Academy of Music on East 14th Street in N.Y. The theatre burned down shortly before the première. To avert financial disaster, the enterprising managers sold the scenery and the dancers' contracts to William Wheatley, another impresario, who combined the elaborate production and dance scenes with the melodrama *The Black Crook.* However, the melodrama was little more than a tenuous connection for the ballet numbers and the changes and transformations of the really magnificent scenery. The plot was based on a Faustian theme: an alchemist enters into a pact with Satan to deliver him one soul for each year of his (the alchemist's) life. At the end of the year the alchemist decides to deliver the soul of a poor artist whose beloved was abducted by the count. However, the Fairy Queen saves the artist and unites him with his beloved. According to contemporary reviews, no one paid the slightest attention to the ridiculous story. The spectators filled the theatre nightly to watch the dancers and see the wondrous transformations of the scenery. Some of the outstanding European and American dancers appeared in the various productions of *The Black Crook.* The ballet of the original production was under the direction of David Costa and featured dancers included the ballerinas Maria Bonfanti and Rita Sangalli, as well as a number of lesser lights. When the original production of *The Black Crook* closed, Mr. Wheatley lost no time in following it with another extravaganza, *The White Fawn.* A tongue-in-cheek revival of *The Black Crook* took place in 1929, when Christopher Morley, Cleon Throckmorton, and Henry Wagstaff Gribble presented it in a theatre–beer hall in Hoboken, N.J., across the river from New York City. New Yorkers enjoyed both the spectacle and the illegal beer (prohibition was in full force). Agnes de Mille did the choreography (her first work for a large group) and danced the ballerina part; Warren Leonard and Bentley Stone were the principal male dancers. The troupe included some thirty names, none of which (with the exception of the above) have survived in the dance profession.

Blair, David (David Butterfield), English dancer, b. Halifax, 1932; m. Maryon Lane. Won Royal Academy of Dancing scholarship to enter Sadler's Wells School (1946); joined Sadler's Wells Theatre Ballet (1947), where he was something of an infant prodigy, dancing the Sugar Plum Fairy Cavalier when only sixteen. Among other roles he created were Captain Belaye (*Pineapple Poll*) and Harlequin (*Harlequin in April*). Joined Sadler's Wells (now Royal) Ballet as soloist (1953); promoted to principal dancer (1955). In 1961 he became Margot Fonteyn's official partner, succeeding Michael Somes. His recent creations include Salamander Prince (*The Prince of the Pagodas,* 1957), Polynices (*Antigone* 1959), Colas (*La Fille Mal Gardée* 1960), Orestes (*Elektra* 1963), Mercutio (Macmillan's *Romeo and Juliet,* 1965); also dances Albrecht (*Giselle*), Siegfried (*Swan Lake*), and Florimund (*The Sleeping Beauty*). Guest artist, Teatro alla Scala, Milan (1957); toured in Australia (1958), Turkey, Spain, with Margot Fonteyn Concert Ballet (1959); Australasia (1962). Has frequently appeared on television in England and U.S. Received C.B.E. (Commander of the Order of the British Empire) in the 1963 New Year's Honors List. Staged *Swan Lake*

(1965) and *The Sleeping Beauty* (1966) for Atlanta's (Ga.) Municipal Theater, performed at Chastain Park, with casts composed mainly of selected dancers from regional ballet companies.

Bland, Alexander, pseudonym for Maude Lloyd, former leading English dancer, and her husband Nigel Gosling. Cooperatively, they write some of the best ballet criticism of the day under this name, principally for the London *Observer.* They wrote the introduction to the autobiography of Rudolph Nureyev, *Nureyev* (London, 1962; N.Y. 1963); also authors of *The Dancer's World* (N.Y., 1963).

Blank, Gustav, contemporary German choreographer and teacher. Since Sept. 1962, has been head of the Ballet and National Dance Department of the Blank-Hasting Schools, Munich, in which his partner, Margarete Hasting, heads the Modern Dance Department. Prior to that Blank was instructor, ballet master, and choreographer of the Hamburg State Opera and the Berlin (West) Municipal Opera. As instructor, he has developed a number of excellent dancers appearing as soloists and principals in many of the German ballet companies; as choreographer, his most productive years were the 1950's at the Berlin Municipal Opera, where he staged among other works, *Lysistrata* and the satirical ballet-opera *A Prussian Fairy Tale,* both to the music of Boris Blacher; *Scènes de Ballet* (Stravinsky); *The Emperor's New Clothes* (Jean Françaix); *Princess Turnadot* (Gottfried von Einem), and such standard ballets as *Polovetzian Dances from Prince Igor, Schéhérazade, Firebird,* and others. A rather shy and retiring man, Gustav Blank is practically unknown outside Germany, but he is a talented as well as a conscientious choreographer and teacher who renounces all publicity because he believes that the constant high level of his choreographic work should speak for itself. When the State College for Music, Munich, added a Ballet Department in the summer of 1964, Gustav Blank became principal teacher.

Blasis, Carlo (1795–1878), Italian dancer, choreographer, teacher, and codifier of ballet technique. Trained by Jean Dauberval, he made his stage appearance at the age of twelve. Became premier danseur at Teatro alla Scala, Milan, where he worked with Salvatore Vigano. Soloist and choreographer, King's Theatre, London (1826–30); later danced in St. Petersburg. Appointed director of the Royal Academy of Dance at La Scala (1837). Blasis wrote two textbooks, *The Elementary Treatise* (1820) and *The Code of Terpsichore* (1828). The first edition of the *Code* had a very limited distribution because the publisher failed and most of the copies were destroyed, apparently by his creditors. The book was re-published in London in 1830. His treatise was translated into English by Mary Stewart Evans and published by the Kamin Dance Gallery, New York, in 1944 under its full title, *An Elementary Treatise Upon the Theory and Practice of the Art of Dancing.* After one hundred and thirty years, his method of teaching ballet remains the backbone of the purest traditions of the classic dance.

Bliss, Sir Arthur, English composer, b. London, 1891. Educated at Pembroke College, Cambridge, and Royal College of Music, London; Master of the Queen's Musick since 1953. His compositions for ballet include *Checkmate* (1937), *Miracle in the Gorbals* (1944), *Adam Zero* (1946). A very early work by Ninette de Valois was arranged to his *Rout* (for soprano and chamber orchestra) for which he and Dr. (now Sir) Malcolm Sargent played two pianos in the first performance at de Valois's studio, Jan. 22, 1928. His *Music for Strings* (1935) was used by Kenneth MacMillan for *Diversions* (1961).

Bliss, Herbert (1923–1960), dancer, teacher, b. Kansas City, Mo. Began dance training at Kansas City Conservatory of Music; continued at School of American Ballet, N.Y. (1939). Made his professional debut in musical *Rosalinda* (1942–43). Joined Ballet Russe de Monte Carlo (1944) when that company danced in *Song of Norway,* and remained to dance such roles as Champion Roper (*Rodeo*), Czardas (*Raymonda*), pas de trois (*Ballet Imperial*). Danced with Ballet Society (1947), remaining when the company became New York City Ballet, of which he was a soloist until early 1958, dancing a large repertoire including *Serenade, Four Temperaments* (Melancholic), *La Valse, Orpheus* (Apollo), *Western Symphony* (1st movement), and others. Taught in Cleveland for a time, then left ballet altogether and was living in San Francisco, Calif., when he was killed, Apr. 18, 1960, in an automobile accident.

Blomdahl, Karl-Birger, Swedish composer and professor of the Swedish Academy of Music, b. 1916. Composed scores for Birgit Aakesson's *Sisyphus* (1957), *Minotaur* (1958), *Play for Eight,* all staged for the Royal Swedish Ballet. American modern dancers have used his scores, among them Lucas Hoving (*Aubade,* 1963).

Blood Wedding. Ballet in 1 act, 5 scenes; chor.: Alfred Rodrigues; commissioned music: Denis ApIvor; book: Rodrigues and ApIvor, based on the Federico García Lorca play; décor: Isabel Lambert. First prod.: Sadler's Wells Theatre Ballet, Sadler's Wells Theatre, London, June 5, 1953, with Elaine Fifield (The Wife), David Poole (Leonardo), Pirmin Trecu (The Bridegroom). The ballet, like the Lorca play, deals with love, jealousy, and revenge. The young wife elopes with her lover, Leonardo, immediately after her arranged marriage. They are persued and, betrayed by the Moon, the lover is killed by the bridegroom. The ballet is also in the repertoire of the Royal Danish Ballet and had a single performance in an American Ballet Theatre Workshop presentation at Phoenix Theatre, N.Y., May 6, 1957.

Blue Rose, A. Ballet in 1 act: chor.: Peter Wright; music: Samuel Barber's *Suite of Six Short Dance Movements;* décor: Yolande Sonnabend. First prod.: Royal Ballet, Royal Opera House, Covent Garden, London, Dec. 26, 1957, with Anne Heaton, Susan Alexander, Patricia Cox, Audrey Farriss, Donald Macleary, Michael Boulton, Edward Miller. A divertissement ballet tracing the travels from hand to hand of a blue rose.

Bluebeard. Ballet in 2 prologues, 4 acts, 3 interludes; chor. and book: Michel Fokine; music: Jacques Offenbach, from his opéra-bouffe of the same name; décor: Marcel Vertès. First prod.: Ballet Theatre (now American Ballet Theatre), Palacio de Bellas Artes, Mexico City, Oct. 27, 1941; American première: Forty-Fourth Street Theatre, N.Y., Nov. 12, 1941, with Anton Dolin (Bluebeard), Alicia Markova (Floretta or Princess Hermilia), Irina Baronova (Boulotte), Ian Gibson, alternating with George Skibine (Prince Sapphire), Lucia Chase, Miriam Golden, Rosella Hightower, Maria Karnilova, Nora Kaye, Jeanette Lauret, Annabelle Lyon, Jerome Robbins, Boris Runanin, Simon Semenov, and Antony Tudor. *Bluebeard,* based more or less on the opéra-bouffe of Henri Meilhac and Ludovic Halévy (1866), was one of Fokine's most successful ballets and no choreographer could have wished for a better cast and greater cooperation from the dancers. *Bluebeard* was later shortened by the omission of two of the three interludes. The ballet treats the well-known story of Count Bluebeard and his seven wives in a lighthearted manner, making great fun of the essentially gruesome story. Fokine was at his most inventive when he was creating the ballet, and in its original version it was a brilliant ballet by a great master. After Fokine died each principal took it upon himself to "improve" on Fokine's choreography and pantomime, with the result that the ballet lost almost all its beauty, humor, and even sense.

Blum, René (1884–1944), French ballet impresario. A gentleman of great erudition, culture, and exquisite taste, he was the one person in the European ballet business who was capable of carrying on the modern ballet tradition established by Serge Diaghilev and his collaborators. He gave to ballet everything he possessed in talent, emotion, and worldly goods, receiving very little in return because of his modesty. Contrary to general belief, it was René Blum who founded the René Blum and Col. de Basil Ballets Russes de Monte Carlo (subsequently the Original Ballet Russe) and, later, the present Ballet Russe de Monte Carlo. Soon after Diaghilev's death (1929), the Société des Bains de Mer de Monaco appointed Blum director of the Ballets de l'Opéra de Monte Carlo, a post he held until the Nazi invasion of France and Monaco. René Blum's Monte Carlo Opera Ballet was an active organization when he agreed to join forces with Col. de Basil, the manager of Prince Zeretelli's Paris Russian Opera (1932). The new company became known as the René Blum and Col. de Basil Ballets de Monte Carlo. In 1934 Blum retired from the management of the affairs of the company, continuing as artistic director until 1936. That year he disassociated himself from the company, which then assumed the name Col. de Basil's Ballet Russe de Monte Carlo. He kept his post of director of the Monte Carlo Opera Ballet, however, and in the spring of 1936 founded a new company, the René Blum Ballets Russes de Monte Carlo, with Michel Fokine as first choreographer and ballet master. In the winter of 1938 Leonide Massine left the de Basil company and went to Monte Carlo to ask

René Blum

René Blum to collaborate on World Art, Inc. (subsequently renamed Universal Art, Inc.), which was about to sponsor a ballet company with Massine as artistic director. Blum agreed to the collaboration and his company, with the addition of several dancers from the de Basil company, became the present Ballet Russe de Monte Carlo. Blum remained co-director of this company until 1940. The manuscript of his book, *Memoirs of the Ballet,* which was in the hands of a Paris publisher when the Germans occupied France, was not recovered after the liberation. René Blum died Sept. 28, 1944, in the German concentration camp at Auschwitz.

Bocane (ca. 1640), a sedate dance in 2/4 time for two people. It was named for the teacher Bocan, who was dancing master to Anne of Austria and to Charles I of England.

Bodenweiser, Gertrud, Austrian dancer, teacher, choreographer, b. 1886 Vienna, d. 1959, Sydney, Australia. Beginning in 1919, she was instructor of dance at the Austrian State Academy of Music and the Performing Arts. Formed a dance group which played an important part in developing her style of dance in Central

European countries. Subsequently emigrated to Australia where she opened a school and founded a new group with Australian dancers.

Bogatyri. Ballet in 3 scenes; chor. and book: Leonide Massine; music: Alexander Borodin; excerpts from his 2nd and 3rd Symphonies and Nocturne from his String Quartet; décor: Nathalie Gontcharova. First prod.: Ballet Russe de Monte Carlo, Metropolitan Opera House, N.Y., fall, 1938, with a cast headed by Alexandra Danilova (subsequently Mia Slavenska, alternating), Frederick Franklin, Nathlalie Krassovska, Roland Guerard, Casimir Kokitch, Marc Platoff, Igor Youskevitch, and George Zoritch. In Russian folklore, Bogatyri were the legendary heroes—in another connotation, giants (as the biblical giants)—in the service of the Russian princes who preceded the Russian czars. The theme of the ballet is based on the traditional exploits attributed to the Bogatyri. The ballet was a rather short-lived work, whose décor and costumes were later used for Bronislava Nijinska's ballet *Ancient Russia* (1943), a similarly short-lived work. The reason for the production of either of these ballets was the public success of Michel Fokine's *Le Coq d'Or,* presented by a competing company.

Bogomolova, Liudmila, Honored Artist of the RSFSR, Soviet dancer, b. Moscow, 1932. Entered Bolshoi school in 1945, graduating 1951 with the class of Maria Kozhukhova (who was conducting an experimental six-year course at that time). In spite of Bogomolova not having the full nine years' of study she was accepted into the ballet company and rose to important solo parts after only a few seasons. Her first part of any consequence was that of one of the proposed brides in *Swan Lake.* In 1952 she was given the role of Olia in *Little Stork,* one which requires considerable technical ability. Real recognition came in 1954 when she danced Kitri in *Don Quixote,* a role which requires great technical prowess and the ability to portray three different characters in the course of the three acts. She has since danced in many ballets, being particularly outstanding as the Mistress of the Copper Mountain (*The Stone Flower*), Jeanne (*Flames of Paris*), Sarie (*The Path of Thunder*), Madelon (*Fadette*), Suimbike, the Girl-Bird (*Shurale*). She prefers roles in the heroic and lyric repertoire, though her reputation is connected more with those requiring strength and virtuosity.

Bojangles. See ROBINSON, BILL.

Bolender, Todd, American dancer and choreographer; b. Canton, Ohio, 1919. Began his dance studies in 1936 with Chester Hale, Anatole Vilzak, School of American Ballet. Soloist, Ballet Caravan (1937); the Littlefield Ballet; American Ballet Caravan (for South American tour, 1941). Also danced in several musicals. Founder-member (with Mary Jane Shea and William Dollar) of American Concert Ballet which gave several performances in 1943 and for which he choreographed his first ballet, *Mother Goose Suite.* Member, Ballet (now American Ballet) Theatre for the 1944 season; guest artist Ballet Russe de Monte Carlo (1945), and choreographed *Comedia Balletica.* Member, Ballet Society from its initial season (1946), choreographing *Zodiac* for the company (1947). When Ballet Society became New York City Ballet, he remained as one of the leading male dancers, creating many important roles. His repertoire included *Four Temperaments* (Phlegmatic), *Symphonie Concertante* (only male role) *Age of Anxiety* (one of the three male roles), *Fanfare*

Liudmila Bogomolova with Stanislaw Vlasov of the Moscow Bolshoi Ballet in Spring Water

(Leader of Percussion), *Agon* (one of the four male roles), all of these being creations. Among his ballets choreographed for New York City Ballet are *The Miraculous Mandarin* (1951), *Souvenirs* (1955), *The Still Point* (1956), *Creation of the World* (1960). At the request of the State Department he went to Turkey (1961) and staged for the Devlet Konservatori (the State school and company in Ankara) *The Still Point* and *Creation of the World,* both premièred at the State Opera (May 13 and 14, 1961). He staged the ballet (with Jacques d'Amboise as first dancer) for Franco Zeferelli's production of *Thaïs* for the Dallas (Tex.) opera, Nov. 3 and 12, 1961. On Oct. 12, 1962, he staged the dances in *Die Meistersinger* at the Metropolitan Opera House, N.Y. In 1963–64, Bolender became Director of Ballet at the Cologne Opera House, Germany. He presented his first Ballet Evening Dec. 22, 1963, the program consisting of *The Still Point, Souvenirs,* and two new works: *Serenade No. 9 to* Mozart's Serenade in D Major, K. 320, and *Theme and Variations* to Boris Blacher's *Orchestral Variations on a Theme of Paganini.* He left the Cologne Opera Ballet at the end of 1965–66 season. He is now (1967) Director of Ballet at the Frankfurt Opera House.

Bolero, dance of Moorish-Spanish origin in 3/4 time. See Spanish Dance.

Bolero. Ballet in 1 act; chor.: Bronislava Nijinska; music: Maurice Ravel, commissioned by Ida Rubinstein. First prod.: Ida Rubinstein Company, Paris, 1928, with Ida Rubinstein and Anatole Vilzak in the principal roles. Nijinska staged a second version for her own company (Paris, 1934), with herself and Vilzak. Revived for Ballet International (Marquis de Cuevas Company) Oct. 30, 1944, N.Y., with Viola Essen, Alexander Iolas, David Ahdar. Harald Lander staged *Bolero* for the Royal Danish Ballet (1934); Serge Lifar for the Paris Opéra (1941), among other versions. The ballet is a stylization of the Spanish dance for the ballet stage. There is no actual story. The ballet is charged with emotion—the love between the two principals—which grows in intensity with the hypnotic repetition of the basic theme music. Anton Dolin danced a shortened version as a solo (Sadler's Wells Theatre, Dec. 6, 1932.)

Bolger, Ray, outstanding American tap dancer and actor in musical comedies, revues, and motion pictures, b. Boston, Mass. 1904. Among the productions in which he has appeared are the musicals *On Your Toes,* which included George Balanchine's famous *Slaughter on Tenth Avenue* ballet, with Tamara Geva; *By Jupiter!; Three to Make Ready!; Where's Charley?; All American* (1962); and the motion pictures *The Wizard of Oz* (as the Straw Man), *The Harvey Girls,* and Walt Disney's *Babes in Toyland,* among others.

Bolm, Adolph (1884–1951), dancer and choreographer. He was graduated from the Russian Imperial Ballet School (1904) and accepted into the ballet of the Maryinsky Theatre, St. Petersburg, becoming a soloist (1910). He organized and danced the first tours of Anna Pavlova (1908, 1909). Joined the Diaghilev Ballets Russes in 1908 and danced with it also in 1909 and 1910, his most successful part being that of the Chief Warrior in the *Polovetzian Dances from Prince Igor* and as Pierrot in *Carnaval,* both choreographed by Michel Fokine. In 1911 he resigned from the Maryinsky Theatre and rejoined Diaghilev as premier danseur, choreographer, and ballet master, touring Europe, South America and the U.S. After the second U.S. tour he remained in the U.S. to teach and organized the Adolph Bolm Ballet Intime. He staged *Le Coq d'Or* (1918) and *Petrouchka* (1919) for the Metropolitan Opera; also produced ballets for musical comedies and revues. In 1919 he staged the *Birthday of*

Adolph Bolm, choreographer, teacher

the Infanta, and a year later *Krazy Kat* (both with music by John Alden Carpenter) for the Chicago Grand Opera Ballet. He subsequently became ballet master and premier danseur of the Chicago Civic Opera. In 1924 he helped establish the Chicago Allied Arts, Inc., which aimed to produce modern American ballets. In 1928 Bolm choreographed *Apollon Musagète,* commissioned by Elizabeth Sprague Coolidge, and later staged *Le Coq d'Or, Petrouchka,* and other ballets for the Colón Opera, Buenos Aires, Argentina. Moving to Hollywood, he staged a number of ballets for motion pictures, among them *The Mad Genius, The Men in Her Life, Life of Cellini.* In 1932 he choreographed his *Ballet Mécanique,* to music of Mosolov's *The Iron Foundry,* at the Hollywood Bowl. In 1933 he joined the San Francisco Opera Company as choreographer and ballet master, and established there a ballet school sponsored by the Opera Association. Bolm came to New York in the fall of 1939 to join Ballet (now American Ballet) Theatre, then preparing its initial season of Jan., 1940. For that season he staged Sergei Prokofiev's *Peter and the Wolf,* which is still in the repertoire of the company, and the less successful *Ballet Mécanique.* He also danced with great distinction the role of Pierrot in *Carnaval.* He returned to Ballet Theatre as ballet master and regisseur general (1942–43). His last work for any ballet company was a less successful version of *The Firebird* to Igor Stravinsky's music, staged in 1945 for Ballet Theatre with Alicia Markova and Anton Dolin in the principal roles. He returned to Hollywood where he continued to teach and work on his memoirs until his death.

Bolshoi, in Russian means big or large and, used in connection with the name of a theatre or a ballet company, grand (but never great, as is erroneously used by many English speaking persons). In the case of the Moscow Bolshoi, the word means big. Literally translated, Moscow *Bolshoi Theatre* means the Moscow Big Theatre, as differentiated from the Moscow Maly Theatre, which means the Moscow Little Theatre, the home of the Russian classic drama (actually a large theatre with a seating capacity of some 1,800). Great in Russian is Velikiy, as in Piotr Velikiy—Peter the Great.

Bolshoi Theatre (Moscow), a State (formerly Imperial) opera house, which was opened to the public Jan. 6, 1825. It is the home of the Moscow Bolshoi Ballet and the center of Soviet Ballet activity. See SOVIET BALLET.

Bolshoi Theatre (St. Petersburg), Imperial Russian Theatre, home of the Russian ballet from 1783 to 1889. The theatre opened Sept. 24, 1783, and burned down New Year's Eve, 1811. It was rebuilt the following year. Until 1880 all official ballet performances were given at the Bolshoi Theatre. Beginning in 1880, occasional ballet performances were given at the Maryinsky Theatre. The last ballet performance at the Bolshoi Theatre was given Feb. 19, 1889, when the season closed for Lent. That year the theatre was pronounced unsafe for performances and was closed. The building was remodeled and became the home of the St. Petersburg Conservatory of Music. Beginning

Apr. 12, 1889, all ballet performances were transferred to the Maryinsky Theatre (which see).

Bon, René, French dancer, b. 1924. Pupil of Leo Staats and Nora Kiss. Was soloist of the Opéra Comique and the Opéra (Paris), Grand Ballet du Marquis de Cuevas, Ballet Janine Charrat, Massine's troupe at the Nervi (Italy) Festival (1960), and others. Bon is a sensitive artist and a strong technician; he is well known for his prodigious turns, elevation, and ballon. Most recently active as ballet master and instructor, Vienna State Opera Ballet (1963–66).

Bonfanti, Marietta (also called Maria and Marie) (1847–1921), Italian ballerina. She studied with Carlo Blasis and at the ballet school of Teatro alla Scala, Milan. In 1866 she made her American debut in *The Black Crook,* the extravaganza at Niblo's Garden, N.Y. In 1869 she toured through the U.S. and the following year appeared in a revival of *The Black Crook.* Following this engagement she danced in a number of operettas and the ballet *Sylvia.* In 1884 she became prima ballerina of the Milan Italian Grand Opera (not opera of the Teatro alla Scala), touring the U.S. In 1885–86 she was prima ballerina of the Metropolitan Opera, N.Y. During the years 1888–94 she made several U.S. and European tours. Subsequently she opened a ballet school in N.Y. Ruth St. Denis was one of her pupils. Mme. Bonfanti married George Hoffmann, an American businessman.

Bonne-Bouche. Ballet in 3 scenes; chor. and libretto: John Cranko; commissioned music: Arthur Oldham; décor Osbert Lancaster. First prod.: Sadler's Wells (now Royal) Ballet, Royal Opera House, Covent Garden, London, Apr. 4, 1952, with Pauline Clayden (The Daughter), Pamela May (Mother), Brian Shaw (Lover), Alexander Grant (Cannibal King). A farcical ballet about a matchmaking mother who marries off her daughter to a cannibal king. The setting is Kensington in Edwardian days and the African jungle.

Book, the plot or libretto of a dance production, generally but not always furnished by the choreographer or composer. Although many have tried, few have ever succeeded in selling a choreographer or director of a ballet company a book for a ballet.

Boquet, Louis (Bosquet), designer at the Paris Opéra (1760–1782). He was Jean Georges Noverre's favorite designer and worked with him before either was employed by the Opéra. In 1754 they collaborated on Noverre's *Fêtes Chinoises.* Boquet, like other designers of his day, for the most part exaggerated the fashionable clothes of the day into dance costumes.

Borg, Conny, Swedish dancer, b. 1938. Entered Royal Swedish Ballet school (1947); accepted into the company (1955); promoted to premier danseur (1963). He also studied with Lilian Karina in Stockholm and Anna Northcote (Anna Severskaya) in London. Received the Swedish King's fellowship for study (1961). Shares with Verner Klavsen the role of Danila, the young stonecutter, in the Royal Swedish Ballet's production of *The Stone Flower;* followed his success in Antony Tudor's *Dark Elegies* (1961) by creating the role of the Young Man from the House Opposite in *Pillar of Fire,* and *Romeo and Juliet* (both Dec. 30, 1962) in Tudor's staging of these ballets in Stockholm.

Yvonne Brosset and Conny Borg of the Royal Swedish Ballet in Borg's Enjoy Yourself *(1966) to Paul Hindemith score.*

Ruthanna Boris

Boris, Ruthanna, ballerina, teacher, b. Brooklyn, N.Y., 1918; studied at Professional Children's School, N.Y.; Metropolitan Opera School of Ballet, Helene Veola (Spanish dancing), and Leon Fokine. Member American Ballet (1935). Made her debut as soloist, Metropolitan Opera Ballet, in *Carmen* (1935); première danseuse (1939–1943). Soloist, Ballet Russe de Monte Carlo (from 1943), later being promoted to ballerina. Her repertoire included *Serenade, Frankie and Johnnie, Les Sylphides, Concerto Barocco, Raymonda, Coppélia, Blue Bird* pas de deux, etc. Choreographed *Cirque de Deux* (1947) and *Quelques Fleurs* (1948). After leaving the company, she choreographed *Cakewalk* for New York City Ballet (1951; revived in 1966 by City Center Joffrey Ballet), *Kaleidoscope* (1953), *Will o' the Wisp* (1953). Director of Royal Winnipeg Ballet (1956–57), choreographing several ballets including *The Comedians* and a re-working of *Kaleidoscope,* among others. A hip ailment cut short her dancing career and she currently teaches. Since the fall of 1965, associate professor of Drama and Director of Dance at the Univ. of Wash. (Seattle).

Börlin, Jean (1893–1930), Swedish dancer and choreographer. Studied with Gunhild Rosen of the Theatre Royal, Stockholm (1902); taken into corps de ballet of the opera (1905). In 1911 his interest in ballet was increased by the advent of Michel Fokine who was staging ballets for the Royal Theatre. In 1913 he became second dancer in the company. Left the theatre in 1918 (when he would have been promoted to premier danseur) to study with Fokine in Copenhagen. About this time he met *Rolf de Maré,* and when the latter formed his Ballets Suédois, Börlin was engaged as premier danseur and choreographer. In Mar., 1920, Börlin gave a recital at the Théâtre des Champs Elysées; in Oct., 1920, he presented the new group, Les Ballets Suédois, at the same theatre. Among the ballets he devised as sole choreographer for the company were *Jeux, Nuit de Saint-Jean, Iberia, Le Tombeau de Couperin, Les Vierges Folles* (1920), *L'Homme et son Désir, Les Mariés de la Tour Eiffel* (1921), *Skating Rink* (1922), *La Création du Monde, Within the Quota* (1923), *Le Roseau, La Jarre, Relâche* (1924). The company disbanded in 1925.

Borodin, Alexander Porfirievitch (1834–1887), Russian composer. His opera *Prince Igor,* provided the music for the Polovetzian dances which were used as a separate ballet by Michel Fokine (1909). This ballet, more than any other, created the great success of the first season of the Diaghilev Ballets Russes in Paris. Leonide Massine used excerpts from Borodin's 2nd and 3rd Symphonies and the Nocturne from his String Quartet for his ballet *Bogatyri* (1938).

Borovansky, Edouard, dancer, choreographer, director, b. Prerov, Czechoslovakia, 1902, d. Sydney, Australia, Dec. 18, 1959. Studied at Prague National Theatre School; premier danseur, Prague National Theatre; member, Anna Pavlova company; soloist, Col. de Basil's Ballet Russe de Monte Carlo (1932–39), dancing character roles such as King Dodon (*Coq d'Or*), Eunuch (*Schéhérazade*), Strong

Man (*Le Beau Danube*), etc. Remained in Australia when the Ballet Russe toured there in 1939, establishing his own Ballet Academy (1940) and the Borovansky Ballet Company (1942), for which he restaged many ballets in the standard repertoire and created several, including *Fantasy on Grieg's Concerto in A Minor, Capriccio Italien* (Tchaikovsky), and others. The formation of The Education in Music and Dramatic Arts Society, with the cooperation of J. C. Williamson Theatres Ltd., gave great assistance in the presentation of seasons and enabled the company to invite outstanding guest artists from time to time. However the vast distances and small population of Australia and New Zealand outside the few principal cities made continuous seasons impossible, and long lay-offs meant periodic dispersals of the company. The company was re-formed in 1959, but Borovansky died just before the opening of the season. The company continues as The Australian Ballet (which see).

Borowska, Irina, American ballerina, b. Buenos Aires, Argentina, 1931, of Polish parentage. Studied at Colón Theatre Ballet School and at the Argentine National Conservatory of Music. Her first position was with the company of Teatro Colón (1940–1954). In 1954 she came to the U.S. and joined the Ballet Russe de Monte Carlo, with which she remained until 1959. In 1960 she was ballerina with the Ruth Page Chicago Opera Ballet and in 1961 made a U.S. tour with the Zachary Solov Ensemble. She joined London's Festival Ballet in the spring of 1961, staying on to the beginning of 1962, when she returned to the U.S. In the spring of 1962 she re-joined London's Festival Ballet. Her large and varied repertoire includes, among others, *Les Sylphides, The Lady and the Unicorn, Gaîté Parisienne, Le Beau Danube, Symphonie Fantastique, Rouge et Noir, Capriccio Espagnol, Swan Lake,* (both the standard version and the Stanislavsky-Nemirovich-

Irina Borowska, ballerina

Danchenko Theatre version choreographed by Vladimir Bourmeister), *The Snow Maiden, The Nutcracker, Giselle, Schéhérazade, Ballet Imperial, Le Spectre de la Rose, Apollon Musagète, Don Juan de Zarissa, Sombreros, Bolero, Harold in Italy, Raymonda.* Created The Grey One in Vaslav Orlikovsky's *Peer Gynt* (London's Festival Ballet, 1963). Married Karl Musil, premier danseur of Vienna Staatsoper Ballet, in Vienna (Oct. 8, 1966).

Bortoluzzi, Paolo, Italian dancer, b. Genoa, 1938. Studied with Ugo Dell'Ara, Nora Kiss, Victor Gsovsky, Maurice Béjart, Asaf Messerer. He is a classic dancer who has appeared with the following troupes: Ballets Européens (the Leonide Massine company), Milorad Miskovitch's Ballets des Étoiles, Béjart's Les Ballets du XXme Siècle. Classic ballets in his repertoire include *Coppélia, The Nutcracker, The Sleeping Beauty, Les Sylphides* and *Fantaisie Concertante* (Janine Charrat).

Bosman, Petrus, British dancer, b. South Africa, 1932. Studied with Univ. of Cape Town Ballet Company. After a period with London's Festival Ballet, he returned to Univ. of Cape Town Ballet, staging and dancing in *Petrouchka, The Nutcracker,* and *Les Sylphides.* Coming to England once more, he appeared in revues, summer shows, and then was accepted into the Royal Ballet, the first dancer to be taken into that company with no previous period in its school. Dances Florestan pas de trois (*The Sleeping Beauty*), pas de trois (*Les Rendez-vous*), etc. Also has group which has appeared in Kenya and gives charity performances and performances for students in London.

Boston, a form of slow waltz, originating in U.S., in which the couples turn in circles in several directions.

Boston Ballet, one of the professional companies brought into being under the Ford Foundation grant (Dec., 1963). It is a development of the New England Ballet of Boston, a regional group directed by E. Virginia Williams. It gave its initial performance as a professional company at the Boston Arts Festival, July 29–31, 1964.

Botta, Bergonzio di, arranged the first spectacle that could be called a ballet (1459). The occasion was the marriage of the Duke of Milan and Isabella of Aragon. Each dish at the wedding banquet was presented with appropriate dances. Jason and the Argonauts was the central theme; the characters included Jason, Diana, Mercury, Atalanta, Theseus, Hebe. Each brought in one course assisted by an ensemble. The Gods of the Sea brought in the various fish dishes and executed characteristic dances. Near the end of the feast a ballet with characters such as Hymen, Conjugal Faith, Semiramis, Helen, and Cleopatra suggested the occasion. The ballet ended with Bacchus and his revellers. The importance of this presentation is that it set a fashion which led to the development of balletic productions, of which *Ballet Comique de la Reine,* presented in 1581, was an outstanding example.

Boulton, Michael, English dancer, b. London, 1930; m. Margaret Hill. Studied at Sadler's Wells School (1943); entered Sadler's Wells (now Royal) Ballet (1944); principal dancer Sadler's Wells Theatre Ballet, where he danced The Bridegroom (*Blood Wedding*), lead male role (*Les Rendez-vous*), Harlequin (*Carnaval*), etc.; rejoined Sadler's Wells Ballet (1953, 1955); with Royal Ballet when the two companies combined, usually dancing leading roles for the touring part. Resigned from the company in Dec. 1959, and is no longer in the dance field.

Bourgeois Gentilhomme, Le. Ballet in 2 scenes; chor. and book: George Balanchine; music: Richard Strauss's incidental music for the Molière play; décor: Eugene Berman. First prod.: Ballet Russe de Monte Carlo, New York City Center, Sept. 23, 1944, with Nicholas Magallanes (Cléonte), Michel Katcharov (M. Jourdain), Nathalie Krassovska (His Daughter), with Ruthanna Boris, Maria Tallchief, Leon Danielian, and Nikita Talin in principal roles. The ballet is based on Molière's comedy of the same title. A ballet by the same name was staged by Balanchine for the René Blum Ballets de Monte Carlo (1932).

Bourman, Anatole (1888–1962), outstanding American ballet teacher. A former dancer of the Russian Imperial Maryinsky, he later danced with the Diaghilev Ballets Russes. While in the Diaghilev company he married Leokadia Klementovicz, a soloist of the Warsaw State Opera Ballet before she joined the Diaghilev organization. In 1922 the Bourmans came to the U.S. For nearly six years they were associated with the Strand, and for one year with the Paramount Theatres, both in

N.Y., where Mr. Bourman was ballet master and his wife ballerina. In 1930 the Bourmans opened a ballet school in Springfield, Mass., and later added another in Hartford, Conn. A close friend of Vaslav Nijinsky, Anatole Bourman wrote the book *The Tragedy of Nijinsky* (1936), in collaboration with Dorothy Lyman, then on the staff of *The Springfield Republican*. During World War II Bourman, as part of the national war effort, worked in a munitions plant while his wife ran the school. Mrs. Bourman died in 1960. Anatole Bourman retired from teaching in 1962 and died Nov. 16 of that year.

Bourmeister, Vladimir, Soviet dancer and choreographer, Honored Art Worker of the RSFSR, b. 1904. Pupil of E. Dolinskaya, V. Shelepina and V. Semyonov of the ballet faculty of the Lunacharsky Theatre Technicum, Moscow (1925–29). While in his last year at school, he entered the Dramatic Ballet company headed and founded by Nina Gremina. In 1930 he was invited to the Moscow Art Theatre of Ballet founded by Victorina Krieger, gradually rising to leading soloist rank. This company became in 1933 the Ballet of the Stanislavsky and Nemirovich-Danchenko Lyric Theatre. He became chief choreographer in 1941. The artistic principles of dramatic content in ballet of this theatre were close to his own from the beginning of his career. As a dancer Bourmeister performed mostly character roles and national dances. His debut as a choreographer took place in 1931 when he staged a new version of *Le Corsaire* at the Moscow Art Theatre of Ballet, performing the role of Birbanto, the villain. For the Stanislavsky and Nemirovich-Danchenko theatre he has choreographed *Straussiana* (1941), *Merry Wives of Windsor* (music by V. Oransky, 1942), *Lola* (S. Vasilenko, 1943), *Schéhérazade* (new version, 1944), *Le Carnaval* (new version, 1946), *Happy Coast* (A. Spadaveccia, 1956), *Jeanne d'Arc* (N. Peiko, 1957) and most importantly, *Swan Lake* (1953). In the last named ballet Bourmeister created his own original interpretation of the 1877 Tchaikovsky score. In 1960 the Paris Opéra invited him to stage this version of *Swan Lake*. In 1961 he choreographed *Snow Maiden* for London's Festival Ballet, using Tchaikovsky's incidental music for Ostrovsky's play *Spring Tale,* and his Symphony No. 1. in G. Bourmeister has also choreographed several ballets for the theatre in Tallinn, capital of Estonia.

Bournonville, Antoine (1760–1843), French dancer and choreographer; father of August Bournonville. A pupil of Jean Georges Noverre, he was choreographer of the Royal Danish Ballet and, after the death of Vincenzo Galeotti, became the moving spirit of the organization. He contributed greatly to the development of the Danish ballet.

Bournonville, August (1805–1879), Danish dancer, choreographer, ballet master, teacher. It is to Bournonville that the Royal Danish Ballet owes its particular character and unique style which is the only surviving link with the ballet of the mid-nineteenth century before the Russian dominance began towards the end of the century. He started his ballet studies with his father, Antoine Bournonville, and at the age of eight was accepted into the Royal Danish Ballet School, then headed by Vincenzo Galeotti. At the age of fifteen he was engaged by the Royal Theatre as a dancer and at the same time given a scholarship for advanced study with the famous ballet teachers of Paris, among them Auguste Vestris. On his return to Copenhagen after a few months in Paris, he became an important member of the company; but when his father was dismissed from the Royal Theatre (1823), he again returned to Paris on a two years' leave of absence. At the end of the two years he was accepted into the Paris Opéra company. It was this period in

Paris which gave him the particular style which has continued to be characteristic of the Royal Danish Ballet. Risking the displeasure of the Royal Theatre in Copenhagen and even that of King Frederik VI, Bournonville continued to dance with the Paris Opéra Ballet for two more years, partnering Maria Taglioni, his ideal dancer (1827–28), in a number of ballets. After a tour of European capitals (1829–30), he returned to Copenhagen and signed a contract for 18 years as soloist and choreographer of the Royal Danish Ballet and dancing master to the Court. Speaking of himself as a dancer, Bournonville said in his autobiography *Mit Theaterliv* (My Theatre Life): "As a dancer I possessed strength, lightness, precision and brilliance, and, when my striving for bravura did not carry me away, a natural grace which was developed by an excellent school and inherent musical sense . . . the difficulties which I have worked hard to surmount with only partial success were connected with pirouettes, and to gain the necessary calm in the slow pas and position. My greatest weaknesses were in my wrists and a swaying of the head in the pirouettes, as well as a certain hardness in my elevation. . . . There are dancers who possess greater aplomb, elevation and ability to pirouette, and others who might also dance character parts with more originality, but very few who combine so many of the various branches of dancing as I." This was written in 1848 when Bournonville had given up dancing to devote himself entirely to choreography. His original 18-year contract had been extended to another seven. In 1855 he spent a year with the Court Opera in Vienna, a year full of disappointment for him. He returned to Copenhagen, staying until 1861 when he went to Stockholm for three seasons and, except for a brief visit to Russia, remained until he returned in 1877. In the period from Sept., 1829, when he staged his first ballet, *The Soldier and the Peasant,* until his retirement, he choreographed over fifty works, apart from divertissements for operas and plays. Some of the best known are *Valdemar* (1835), staged for his favorite and greatest pupil, Lucile Grahn; his version of Filippo Taglioni's *La Sylphide,* called *Sylfiden* in Denmark, with a new score by Hermann von Lovenskjold (1836), also for Grahn; *Festival in Albanao* (1839) in honor of the return from Italy of the great Danish sculptor Bertel Thorvaldsen; *Napoli, or The Fisherman and his Bride* (1842); *Konservatoriet eller et Avisfrieri* (The Dancing School, or A Proposal by Advertising, 1849), of which one scene still survives; *Et Folkesagen* (Folk Legend, 1854); *La Ventana* (1856), *Far From Denmark* (1860), *From Siberia to Moscow,* (1876), a reminder of his visit to St. Petersburg to see his former pupil Christian Johansson. For forty years Bournonville carried on a never-ending struggle for the recognition of ballet as an art form and for the dignity of the dancer's profession. With all the means of his great and varied talents and despotic energy he strove to elevate the position of the ballet dancer in the arts as well as society. Bournonville himself was knighted and became a member of the first thousand Danish nobility. Danish ballet became a matter of national pride due to his work. Few people have done more for ballet in their own countries than August Bournonville.

Bourrée. 1. A court dance of the 16th century related to the polka. It originated among the peasants of the Auvergne and consisted of a skipping step. 2. In ballet, see pas de bourrée.

Bourrée Fantasque. Ballet in 3 movements; chor.: George Balanchine; music: Emanuel Chabrier's *Bourrée Fantasque;* Intermezzo from his opera *Gwendoline,* and *Fête Polonaise;* costumes: Barbara Karinska. First prod.: New York City Ballet, City Center, N.Y., Dec. 1, 1949, with Tanaquil LeClercq and Jerome Robbins (Bourrée Fantasque), Maria Tallchief and Nicholas Magallanes (Prelude); Janet Reed and Herbert Bliss (Fête Polonaise). After the introductory *Marche Joyeuse* played as an overture, the three unrelated Chabrier pieces are the musical basis for some satirical choreographic comments on dance in the first and last movements, and for a romantic pas de deux with ensemble in the middle section. Since 1960 the ballet has been in the repertoire of London's Festival Ballet (première: Festival Hall, London, Aug. 18, 1960), with Marilyn Burr, Belinda Wright, Olga Ferri, John Gilpin, and Ronald Emblen. Balanchine staged it for Paris Opéra Ballet, Dec. 18, 1963.

Boutique Fantasque, La. Ballet in 1 act by Léonide Massine; music: Giacomo Rossini, a number of short pieces arr. and orch. by Ottorino Respighi; curtain and décor: André Derain. First produced by the Diaghilev Ballets Russes at the Alhambra Theatre, London, June 5, 1919, with Enrico Cecchetti (Shopkeeper), Lydia Lopoukhova and Léonide Massine (Can-Can Dancers), Lydia Sokolova and Leon Woicikowski (Tarantella Dancers), Stanislas Idzikowski (Snob), Nicholas Zverev (Cossack Chief), Vera Nemtchinova, Lubov Tchernicheva and Serge Grigoriev. The action takes place in the toy shop and the plot deals with two dolls, the can-can dancers, who are in love and unhappy because they are being sold to different families. The toys revolt and as a consequence the lovers are united. The "drama" notwithstanding, the plot permits much excellent and gay dancing. Other ballerinas who danced the can-can with Massine include Tamara Karsavina, Vera Nemtchinova, and Alexandra Danilova. The ballet has been in the repertoire of many companies, among them Col. de Basil's Ballets Russes (1933), Ballet Russe de Monte Carlo (1938), Ballet Theatre (1943), Sadler's Wells (now Royal) Ballet (1947), all revived by Massine.

Boutnikov, Ivan, conductor, b. Russia, 1893; now an American citizen. Studied composition with Sergei Taneyev and conducting with Arthur Nikish. Conductor of symphony orchestras in principal cities of Southern Russia (1918–20); professor of composition and conducting at the Academy of Athens, Greece; principal conductor of the Academy's symphony orchestra and opera company (1922–29); guest conductor of symphony orchestras in Paris, London, Brussels, Berlin, Vienna, Budapest (1929–39). Since 1946 has been conductor of Ballet Russe de Monte Carlo.

Bovt, Violetta, Soviet ballerina, Honored Artist of the RSFSR, b. in the U.S., 1927. Violetta Bovt's parents, Americans of Russian extraction, went to the U.S.S.R. in the 1930's and placed their daughter in the Bolshoi Ballet School (1935). She was graduated in 1944 and invited to the Stanislavsky and Nemirovich-Danchenko Lyric Theatre ballet company for solo roles, making her debut as Anne Page in the Bourmeister-Oransky production of *Merry Wives of Windsor* (1944). Her best roles are Odette-Odile in Vladimir Bourmeister's version of *Swan Lake, Lola* in the ballet of that name by Bourmeister-Vasilenko, *Jeanne d'Arc* in the Bourmeister-Peiko ballet of that name, *Esmeralda,* Medora in *Le Corsaire,* etc. Her brother, George Bovt, is a demi-caractère soloist at the Bolshoi Theatre.

Bowles, Paul, American composer, b. 1909. His scores for ballet include *Yankee Clipper* (Eugene Loring, 1937), *Pastorela* (Lew Christensen, 1941), *Sentimental Colloquy* (André Eglevsky, 1944), *Clowns and Angels* (John Butler, Nervi Dance Festival, 1955), *Brief Encounter,* and *Amusement Park* (John Butler, Festival of Two Worlds, Spoleto, 1959).

Bowman, Patricia, American ballerina and teacher, b. Washington, D.C. Studied with Michel Fokine and Mikhail Mord-

Patricia Bowman, American ballerina

kin, N.Y.; Nicholas Legat, London; Lubov Egorova, Paris; Margaret Wallmann, Berlin. Was ballerina at Roxy Theatre (1937–1939) when Léonide Massine was choreographer and ballet producer, followed by a year at Radio City Music Hall. Ballerina of Mordkin Ballet (1939), and Ballet (now American Ballet) Theatre (1940). Her repertoire included *La Fille Mal Gardée, Swan Lake, Les Sylphides, and Carnaval.* Appeared in vaudeville in most major cities and in many operettas and musicals in U.S., Canada, and in London, also dancing as soloist at Jacob's Pillow Dance Festival. Has taught in N.Y. since 1955, in which year she danced in *Les Sylphides,* partnered by Erik Bruhn, during the 15th Anniversary Season of Ballet Theatre at Metropolitan Opera House. Danced in summer opera and musicals (1955–57).

Bozzacchi, Giuseppina (1853–1870), Italian ballerina of the Paris Opéra. She created the role of Swanilda in *Coppélia* at the age of sixteen. Contemporary critics hailed her as an accomplished dancer and graceful and witty actress. She died on her seventeenth birthday, during the German siege of Paris, of a virulent fever.

Bradley, Lionel (1898–1953), English writer on ballet, b. Manchester. Educated at Manchester Grammar School and Oxford Univ. He was assistant secretary and sub-librarian of the famous London Library. His two great interests in life were ballet and music of all kinds. He rarely missed a performance of ballet or opera, never an important première. Although he was the author of only one book, *Sixteen Years of Ballet Rambert* (Hinrichsen Edition, 1946), he wrote articles for many dance periodicals all over the world and was a regular contributor to the magazine *Ballet.* He was noted, not only for his own accuracy, but for the meticulous care he took to correct the writings of others less accurate than himself. During his lifetime he was chairman of the London Archives of the Dance.

Bradley, Lisa (Rita), American dancer, b. Elizabeth, N.J., 1941. Studied at School of American Ballet, N.Y. Joined Robert Joffrey Ballet (1961) and has created leading roles in Gerald Arpino's *Partita for Four* (the only girl), the pas de deux *Sea Shadow* (with Paul Sutherland), Palace,

Lisa Bradley

Alvin Ailey's *Feast of Ashes,* Robert Joffrey's *Gamelan,* and others. Currently with the City Center Joffrey Ballet, creating the leading role in Arpino's *Nightwings* (1966). Early in 1966 married Michael Uthoff (son of Ernst Uthoff), a member of the same company.

Brae, June (June Bear), English dancer, b. Ringwood, Hampshire, 1917. Studied with George Goncharov in China and Nicholas Legat in London. Made her debut with the Ballet Club (later Ballet Rambert), dancing Caroline (*Lilac Garden*), Mortal under Neptune (*The Planets*), and other roles. Principal dancer, Sadler's Wells (now Royal) Ballet (1936–42), creating Black Queen (*Checkmate*), Rich Girl (*Nocturne*), Josephine (*A Wedding Bouquet*), and dancing many other leading roles including the Lilac Fairy—creation (*The Sleeping Beauty,* first Sadler's Wells version). Retired for several years when she married, returned briefly to create Ballerina (*Adam Zero*) and (during first season of Sadler's Wells Theatre Ballet) leading role in *Assembly Ball,* also dancing Alice (*The Haunted Ballroom*), Bride (*La Fête Etrange*). Now retired.

Brahms, Caryl, contemporary English writer and critic, b. Surrey; editor *Footnotes to the Ballet* (1936); author of *Robert Helpmann, Choreographer* (1943), *A Seat at the Ballet* (1951); co-author with the late S. J. Symons of a number of satirical novels, two of them dealing specifically with Franco-Russian Ballet of the 1930's: *A Bullet in the Ballet* (1937) and *Six Curtains for Stroganova* (called *Six Curtains for Natasha* in U.S., 1945). Member of the Critics' Circle, London.

Brahms, Johannes (1833–1897), German composer. His Fourth Symphony was used by Léonide Massine for his ballet *Choreartium* (1933). Bronislava Nijinska staged the ballet *Brahms Variations* to his *Variations on Themes of Handel and Paganini* (1944). George Balanchine choreographed his ballet *Liebeslieder Walzer* to Brahms' *Liebeslieder Walzer,* op. 52 and op. 55, for four hands; songs for soprano, contralto, tenor and baritone (1960). In addition a number of his Hungarian Dances, are used as separate choreographic compositions, or in groups for longer works.

Branch, Louise, Collection, an integral part of the Dance Collection of the New York Public Library, is relevant to the Dance International, a month-long festival of performances, exhibitions, lectures, and film showings held in N.Y. (1937) and directed by Miss Branch. More than 7,000 items, photographs, letters, programs, and press clippings document every phase of this enterprise, and are a descriptive index to the personalities and companies, both theatrical and ethnic, which were involved.

Brandenburg Concerto. Modern dance work; chor.: Doris Humphrey and Ruth Currier; music: Bach's *Brandenburg Concerto No. 4* in G Major. First prod.: Juilliard Dance Theatre, Juilliard Concert Hall, May 9, 1959. Doris Humphrey's last creation, completed by Ruth Currier who had acted as her assistant and knew the form the choreographer had in mind. It is an abstract work following the musical line.

Branle, 16th century court dance. The name comes from branler, to shake; also known as brawls. Some branles were connected with pantomime and ballets. Several varieties of branles are described in *Orchesography* by Thoinot Arbeau.

Braque, Georges, French artist (1882–1963). One of the great 20th century French painters, he succeeded in combining cubism with traditional classicism. His work for ballet includes Bronislava Nijinska's *Les Facheux,* to music by

Georges Auric for the Diaghilev Ballets Russes (1924); Leonide Massine's *Salade,* to music by Darius Milhaud for Count Etienne de Beaumont's Soirées de Paris (1924); Massine's *Zéphire et Flore,* to music by Vladimir Dukelsky (Vernon Duke), for the Diaghilev company.

Bräuer, Lucia, ballerina of the Vienna State Opera Ballet. Studied at the company's ballet school and with her husband Willy Fränzl, ballet master of the company and teacher of the school. A classic and demi-caractère dancer, she dances in most of the ballets of the company's repertoire. Her ballets include *The Moor of Venice, Joan von Zarissa, Giselle, Swan Lake, Homeric Symphony, Hotel Sacher,* and others.

Brave Song. Ballet in 1 act: chor.: Robert Moulton; music: James Aliferis, based on authentic American Indian tunes; décor: Peter Kaczmarek; costumes: Robert Moulton. First prod.: Royal Winnipeg Ballet, Playhouse Theatre, Winnipeg, Dec. 28, 1959, with Sonia Taverner, David Shields, Jim Clouser, Marina Katronis, Richard Rutherford. Ceremonial dances of the Plains Indians, depicting the pride, terrors, and mysticism of the race.

Brazilian Fantasy. Ballet in 1 act: chor.: Aurel Milloss; music: Souza Lima, commissioned by Ballet do IV Centenário (Brazil); book: Lima and Milloss; décor: Noemia Mourâno. First prod.: Pacaembú, 2nd St. Paulo Ballet do IV Centenário, 1934, with a large cast headed by Edith Pudelko, Lia Dell'Ara, Ady Addor, Juan Giuliano, Raul Severo. A colorful allegory including dances and characters of Brazilian folklore.

Bredow, Erwin, German dancer, choreographer, b. Berlin, ca. 1921. Studied with Tatiana Gsovska and other teachers. Began his career in 1939 and is now character soloist of the Berlin Municipal Opera. Has choreographed for films and television.

Bregvadze, Boris, Soviet dancer, Peoples' Artist of the RSFSR, b. 1926. A Georgian by nationality, Bregvadze was brought up in Saratov and studied at the ballet school of the local opera house (1939–44). Showing great promise, he was sent to Leningrad to study under the well-known teacher Boris Shavrov. He was graduated in 1947 and immediately was entrusted with a leading role as Andrei in *Tatiana* (music: A. Krein; chor.: Vladimir Bourmeister). Shortly thereafter he was transferred to the Kirov Theatre Ballet, Leningrad, where he became one of its leading dancers. His best roles are Solor (*La Bayadère*), Frondozo (*Laurencia*), Batyr (*Shurale*), Lenny (*Path of Thunder*), and title roles in *Othello* and *Spartacus.* He is married to Emma Menchenok, a young soloist of the Kirov company who, like him, studied elsewhere and entered the Kirov ballet school at the age of seventeen, an unusual occurrence.

Brenaa, Hans, Danish dancer and teacher, b. Copenhagen, 1910. Studied in school of Royal Danish Ballet and graduated into the company (1928), becoming solo dancer in 1943. Retired as a dancer in 1955, but continues as tutor and teacher, conducting the school's Bournonville classes.

Brexner, Edeltraud, Austrian prima ballerina, b. Vienna, 1927. Attended the Vienna State Opera Ballet School (1934–44); accepted into the company (1944); promoted to coryphée (1949); to soloist (1953); to prima ballerina (1957). Awarded the Fanny Elssler Ring in 1960 by Prof. Riki Raab, founder of this award. Her first solo roles were Salome Pockerl in *Titus Feuerfuchs* (1950) and Bellastriga in *Abraxas* (1953), both choreographed by Erika Hanka. Ballets in which she dances the principal roles in-

Edeltraud Brexner

clude *The Moor of Venice, The Legend of Joseph, Giselle, Les Sylphides, Hotel Sacher, Joan von Zarissa, Swan Lake, Carmina Catulli, Petrouchka, Symphony in C, Agon, Le Combat, Romeo and Juliet, Turandot, The Seasons, The White Rose.* She has toured with the company in Austria, Germany, Switzerland, Turkey, and Sweden. Miss Brexner possesses the rare quality of being at home in classic and romantic ballets, as well as in the modern compositions of contemporary choreographers. Visited N.Y. in Feb. 1962 and 1963 to dance at the charity-sponsored Vienna Opera Balls with Willy Dirtl as partner.

Briansky, Oleg, premier danseur, b. Brussels, 1929, of Russian parentage; m. Mireille Lefebvre (known professionally as Mireille Briane). Began dance studies privately with Leonide Katchourovsky (1941), then ballet master of Théâtre Royal de la Monnaie, Brussels; later with Victor Gsovsky and Mme. Rousanne Sarkissian, Paris; also with Vera Volkova, London. Presented a performance with five dancers, choreographed and staged by himself, at Palais des Beaux-Arts, Brussels (1945). Joined Les Ballets des Champs-Elysées (1946) and was promoted to leading dancer within one year. Joined Ballets de Paris de Roland Petit (1949), remaining in N.Y. after the company's 1951 season. Danced in the musical *A Tree Grows in Brooklyn;* then joined London's Festival Ballet (1951). His repertoire included the leading male roles in *Swan Lake* (Act 2), *The Nutcracker, Schéhérazade, Polovetsian Dances from Prince Igor, Black Swan* and *Don Quixote* pas de deux, and several creations, including Devil (Frederick Ashton's *Vision of Marguerite*), Gennaro (*Napoli*), Phoebus (*Esmeralda*). Left the company in 1955 after its first American tour to partner Tamara Toumanova in a series of concert performances in South America. With Ruth Page's Chicago Opera Ballet (1955–56 season), dancing Danilo (*The Merry Widow*—with Alicia Markova) and Enrico (*Revanche-Revenge*). During the company's Dec. season in N.Y., he also appeared at the Metropolitan Opera House in Zachary Solov's *Soirée* with Mary Ellen Moylan. Again danced with the Chicago Opera Ballet (1957), having danced in South America with Markova and Nathalie Krassovska between seasons. Partnered Beryl Grey for a five months' tour in South Africa; again returned to Chicago Opera Ballet (1958). Rejoined Festival Ballet (summer, 1958), but sustained a leg injury which kept him from dancing for nearly two years. Choreographed *Pièces Brillantes* to music by Mikhail Glinka in décor by André Levasseur for a gala performance at the Antwerp Opera Mar. 29, 1960, in the presence of Queen Elizabeth of the Belgians; also danced the lead. Staged *Pièces Brillantes* in Munich, Nov., 1960; in Dec. returned to Festival Ballet as premier danseur. He has also choreographed a pas de deux to Tchaikovsky's *Romeo and Juliet* and various other pas de deux. Has partnered Krassovska, Marina Svetlova, Patricia Wilde, Maria Tallchief and Melissa Hayden in various guest artist performances.

Brianza, Carlotta (1867–1930), Italian ballerina. A pupil of Carlo Blasis, she toured the U.S. in 1883. In 1887 she made her debut at the (summer) Arcadia Theatre, St. Petersburg. Her great success forced the direction of the Imperial Theatres to engage her as guest artist of the Maryinsky Theatre (1889), where she made her debut in Lev Ivanov's *Haarlem Tulip*. In 1890 she created the principal ballerina role of Princess Aurora in the Petipa-Tchaikovsky *The Sleeping Beauty*. She left Russia in 1891 and continued to dance and teach in Italy and Paris. Her last appearance as a dancer was as Carabosse in Diaghilev's London production of *The Sleeping Beauty* (1921), called then *The Sleeping Princess*. Brianza was the godmother of Sonia Woicikowska (1919). No definite date of Brianza's death is available. G. B. L. Wilson in his *A Dictionary of Ballet* states that Brianza committed suicide in Paris but gives no authority for the statement, nor the year of her death.

Briggs, Hedley, English dancer, actor, designer, b. King's Norton, 1907. Studied with Phyllis Bedells. Danced with Penelope Spencer (1928–30) and in first ballet evenings at Old Vic and with Camargo Society (1930). Designed décor for the Vic-Wells Ballets *Douanes* (Ninette de Valois, 1932), full-length *The Nutcracker* (1934); also John Cranko's *Tritsch-Tratsch* (1947) for Sadler's Wells Theatre Ballet.

Bring Down the House, an expression used to describe audience reaction when a dancer's performance causes intense and continuous applause. See also OVATION and STOP THE SHOW.

Brinson, Peter, lecturer and writer on ballet, b. Llandudno, North Wales, 1923. Educated at Denstone and Keble College, Oxford. Director of Research Film Centre (1948–53). Arranged first stereoscopic dance film (*The Black Swan* pas de deux with Beryl Grey and John Field, 1952); organizer of ballet films at National Film Theatre. Ballet critic, *The Queen*. Edited *The Ballet in Britain* (Oxford, 1962), a series of lectures originally delivered at the University by Brinson himself, Marie Rambert, Arnold Haskell, William Chappel, and William Cole, D.Mus., with an introduction by Ninette de Valois (which was a paper read in 1957 to the Royal Society of Arts); co-author with Peggy van Praagh of *The Choreographic Art* (N.Y., 1963). In 1966 wrote *Background to European Ballet* (Leyden, A. W. Sijthoff).

Brisé, in ballet, literally a broken movement. Technique: start from 5th pos. R ft. front; slide L leg forward to demi-quatrième en effacé, at same time plié on R leg; jump off floor and beat R leg under L; land on both feet in 5th pos., R ft. front. Swanhilda in *Coppélia* executes two diagonals of brisés at the end of her first act variation.

Brisé Volé, in ballet, literally a flying brisé; a step similar to simple brisé, but landing on one ft. Technique: start 5th pos., R ft. front; slide L leg forward to semi-quatrième devant en effacé, at the same time plié on R leg; jump off floor and beat R leg under L; land on L ft., R leg in demi-quatrième devant en croisé; swing R leg to demi-quatrième derrière and beat L leg under R calf; land on R ft. This is brisé volé en avant et en arrière. The most famous series of brisés volés is that executed by the male dancer in the coda of the *Blue Bird* pas de deux.

British Ballet.

BY KATHRINE SORLEY WALKER.

The impulse toward ballet in England

can be traced to the court masques of the Tudors and Stuarts, but in them dancing played only a slight part. It was emphasized somewhat more at Restoration Whitehall under the strong French cultural influences derived from Charles II's years of exile. But even so it was many years afterward that ballet as a theatrical entertainment for the public can be justly said to have had its beginnings.

British ballet derived directly from French and Italian sources during the late 17th and early 18th centuries. The first British names of importance are those of the Shrewsbury dancing master and writer, John Weaver, and John Rich, whose enormously successful series of Harlequin mimes was produced at the theatre at Lincoln's Inn Fields. Rich played Harlequin (under the name of Lun) from 1717, and among his managerial activities brought Mlle. Sallé and her brother to London in 1725. She was one of many French dancers and ballet masters (including Auguste Vestris and Jean Georges Noverre) who made ballet popular in 18th century London at the King's Theatre or at Drury Lane; an English dancer, Simon Slingsby, reached prominence in the 1780's. The close of the century, which saw the Revolution in France, also saw considerable achievement in the ballet theatres in London.

At the King's Theatre from 1796 to 1800 Charles Didelot was the main influence and his ballets were acclaimed. In 1808 an English ballet master, Louis d'Egville, was engaged and he did his best to introduce English soloists, even founding an Academy of Dancing at the King's Theatre; but this was so unpopular a move that he had only a brief two-years' engagement before a Signor Rossi took over. From 1830 to 1840 Carlo Blasis was ballet master at the King's, and in June 1830 Maria Taglioni made her London debut in Charles Didelot's popular *Flore et Zéphyre*. The 1840's brought London fame as a centre of ballet, particularly through Benjamin Lumley's management of Her Majesty's Theatre (the King's renamed) to which came all the internationally celebrated dancers. From 1842 to 1848 Jules Perrot acted as ballet master. In 1845 a peak of balletic popularity was reached with the *Pas de Quatre* arranged by Perrot for Taglioni, Fanny Cerito, Carlotta Grisi, and Lucile Grahn.

Lumley's retirement from management in 1857 marked an end to such triumphs. During the later years of the 19th century certain foreign dancers were seen and enjoyed, and Katti Lanner (later ballet mistress at the Empire Theatre from 1887, when Enrico Cecchetti made his London debut) came from Vienna about 1872. But the great days of the Romantic Ballet were over, and from 1860 the danseuse travestie replaced the danseur noble. Those great days had of course brought little opportunity for English artists, although Adeline Plunkett, Clara Webster, and James Sullivan (Silvain), who partnered Grisi, Grahn, and Fanny Elssler, had made their names.

In 1872 John Baum took over the Alhambra Theatre, with Georges Jacobi as musical director. Although foreign dancers continued to be the principal draw, English names gradually became more important. From 1884 to 1914 the Empire Theatre rivalled the Alhambra. Adeline Genée made her debut there in 1897 and her golden career belongs to the story of English Ballet. Genée bridged the gap between foreign and English dancers. English principals at the Empire included Kate Vaughan, Dorothy Craske, and Fred Farren, while Topsy Sinden and, later, Phyllis Bedells, became premières danseuses. After this English names crept more and more into the programmes.

The coming of the Russian ballet—first a company led by Anna Pavlova and Mikhail Mordkin with a corps de ballet of eight dancers, at the Palace Theatre, then Tamara Karsavina and Georges Rosay at the Coliseum, and, most importantly, the Diaghilev Ballets Russes in

1911—opened up a new era. They had a great effect on the audiences (who were drawn from the intelligentsia) and also on aspiring talent, and they sounded a death knell for the danseuse travestie. Diaghilev began to engage English dancers, among them Lydia Sokolova (Hilda Munnings), Vera Savina (Clarke), Anton Dolin (Patrick Healey-Kay), Ninette de Valois (Irish, not English—Edris Stannus), Ursula Moreton, and Alicia Markova (Marks). The Pavlova company had Hilda Butsova (Boot), Ruth French, and Molly Lake. English dancers, in turn, began to make a distinct impression abroad.

Diaghilev died in 1929 and Pavlova in 1931. Most of their English dancers turned their attention to their own country. There was already a basis on which to work: the Haines English Ballet existed from 1915; "Sunshine Matinees" had been established in 1919 by P. J. S. Richardson; the Association of Operatic Dancing of Great Britain (Royal Academy of Dancing, 1936) was founded by P. J. S. Richardson and Edouard Espinosa in 1920; the Cecchetti Society in 1921. In 1921 a British Ballet directed by Marian Wilson had given a season at the Kingsway Theatre; in 1926 the Cremorne Company appeared at the Scala. However, neither company was to develop into importance.

1930 saw the beginning of British ballet as we now think of it. The Camargo Society was formed by P. J. S. Richardson, Arnold Haskell, and Edwin Evans, and performed ballets by English choreographers: Ninette de Valois (*Cephalis and Procris, Rout,* and, in particular, *Job*); Frederick Ashton (*Façade, Pomona,* and *Rio Grande*). *Rio Grande* had a score by a young English composer, Constant Lambert, who had composed a ballet on *Romeo and Juliet* for Diaghilev in 1926.

Two mainstreams now become apparent: Marie Rambert's company, known successively as the Marie Rambert Dancers, the Ballet Club, and the Ballet Rambert, based from 1931 at the tiny Mercury Theatre in Nottinghill Gate (capacity 120 persons); and the group of dancers derived from Ninette de Valois' Academy of Choreographic Art, which from 1928 gave support to the operas and plays at the Old Vic and later formed the Vic-Wells Ballet. The two companies are active and flourishing today as the Ballet Rambert and the Royal Ballet.

In the early days talent was frequently interchanged. Dancers appeared at various times with both companies, in particular Alicia Markova, who danced with the Ballet Club and was first ballerina of the Vic-Wells Ballet when this company found a home at the Sadler's Wells Theatre from 1933. Frederick Ashton began his choreographic career with Marie Rambert (*The Tragedy of Fashion, Mars and Venus, Foyer de Danse, Les Masques,* etc.) and then, after an initial guest ballet, *Les Rendez-vous* (1933), for the Vic-Wells, went to them as choreographer on a permanent basis. De Valois mounted one ballet, *Bar aux Folies-Bergère,* for the Ballet Club.

Gradually the companies drew apart as the amount of talent available increased, some of it coming from the Commonwealth. The Ballet Rambert gained Maude Lloyd and Frank Staff from South Africa, the Vic-Wells Ballet Robert Helpmann from Australia. Both companies worked on close budgets, but both gradually built up repertoires of interesting works presented by dancers whose individual personalities left a stamp on the roles they created. Designers emerged also, notably Hugh Stevenson, Sophie Fedorovitch, and William Chappell.

While the Vic-Wells Ballet during its early years depended on Ashton and de Valois for choreography, the Ballet Rambert added to its Ashton works ballets by Antony Tudor and Andrée Howard. In 1935 Markova left the Wells (to be succeeded as ballerina by Margot Fonteyn) and with Dolin led the Markova-Dolin Ballet, a touring company which revived Nijinska works and launched Keith Lester as choreographer. The company ceased performing in 1938 when its two principals joined Ballet Russe companies. In 1937 Antony Tudor left Rambert, and in December, 1938, formed his own London Ballet, a small company based at Toynbee Hall.

When World War II broke out in 1939 the Rambert and Vic-Wells companies were well-established (various full-length classical ballet revivals at the Wells had culminated that year with *The Sleeping Princess*) and Tudor's London Ballet had begun an interesting life. The war naturally interrupted and changed the course of these developments. Tudor went to the U.S.A. and therefore the entire body of his later work became American rather than British. Some of his dancers and ballets from the London Ballet continued with the Arts Theatre Ballet and the Ballet Rambert, giving lunchtime performances at the Arts Theatre in London until September, 1941. The Vic-Wells Ballet found a West End of London home at the New Theatre from 1941.

The war years, however, were remarkable for their artistic achievement in ballet. It was in these days, when enormous dangers and difficulties confronted the two companies, that some of their finest work was done and their fame became much more widely spread. The pre-1939 audience had been relatively small and parochial to London; the war years, with their tours for both companies and their West End of London seasons for the Sadler's Wells (now Royal) Ballet, brought greater recognition in every way. Britain became, at last, justly proud of her balletic prowess.

From 1939 to 1946 the Ballet Rambert rested very much on the fine artistry of such dancers as Sally Gilmour, Walter Gore, and Frank Staff. At this time Gore added a number of ballets to their repertoire (*Simple Symphony, The Fugitive,* etc.) The Sadler's Wells Ballet, held to a high standard by the leadership of Margot Fonteyn and Robert Helpmann, had as well the great strength of Constant Lambert as musical director and conductor. When Ashton went into the R.A.F. in 1941, a new choreographer was found in Helpmann (*Comus, Hamlet, Miracle In the Gorbals*). His ballets, controversial as well as successful, had considerable impact even outside balletomane circles. All this meant that ballet was at last coming into its own as an art with an indigenous life.

The war years also saw the launching of Mona Inglesby's International Ballet, a large touring company that flourished from 1941 to 1953. It produced classical Leonide Massine revivals, and some new ballets by Mona Inglesby and others. It also engaged various foreign dancers as well as employing British talent. The Anglo-Polish Ballet, formed in 1940, brought Polish folk ballets and Fokine revivals, and was led by Alicjia Halama and Czeslaw Konarski. Principal dancers at various times were Helene Wolska, Leo Kersley, Alexis Rassine, and Alexander Walewsky (Gordon Hamilton). A number of smaller companies existed, principally the Ballet Guild, 1941–1947 (also an association giving lectures, etc.) directed by Molly Lake (this company was succeeded by the Embassy Ballet and the Continental Ballet); the Trois Arts Ballet; the Rovi Pavinoff Ballet; the Ballet de la Jeunesse Anglaise of Lydia Kyasht, 1939–1946; the Ambassador Ballet; and the Ballet Group, directed by Pauline Grant.

With the end of the war came the transplantation to the Royal Opera House, Covent Garden, of the Sadler's Wells Ballet (February, 1946). Principal dancers of the time, apart from Fonteyn and Helpmann, included Pamela May, June Brae, Beryl Grey, Moira Shearer, Violetta Elvin, Michael Somes, John Hart, Alexis Rassine. It was the moment for expansion and in April, 1946, a second company, the Sadler's Wells Opera (later Theatre) Ballet, was formed. The Sadler's Wells Ballet School was also more firmly established. From 1946 both the Sadler's Wells Ballet and the Ballet Rambert toured widely overseas, a policy they continue to follow.

The two Sadler's Wells companies were united under a royal charter as the Royal Ballet in 1956. Today their personnel has almost completely changed. They are directed, respectively, by Sir Frederick Ashton and by Dame Marie Rambert, and remain the most important facets of British ballet. Sir Frederick is Principal Choreographer; Assistant Choreographers are Michael Somes, John Hart, and John Field. Dame Marie has her son-in-law, David Ellis, as Associate Director.

In 1950 Festival Ballet was formed out of a touring group led by Markova and Dolin. Its first London season (1950–51) was at the Stoll Theatre. Since then the company has appeared at the Royal Festival Hall and is now known as London's Festival Ballet. It is under the direction of Dr. Julian Braunsweg, and Anton Dolin has now been succeeded as artistic director by John Gilpin. The company has successfully toured overseas. They employ many international stars as guest artists.

The Metropolitan Ballet formed by Cecilia Blatch and Leon Hepner in 1947 continued until 1949. Smaller companies now active include Western Theatre Ballet, directed by Elizabeth West and Peter Darrell; and London Ballet (Walter Gore), which is a successor to the Walter Gore Ballet and the New Ballet, both of which existed for brief periods in the postwar years.

Interest in ballet is widespread in the British Isles. There are many dancing schools which are grouped either according to technique under the Royal Academy of Dancing, the Imperial Society of Teachers of Dancing (founded 1904), or the British Ballet Organization (founded 1930), or exist for some specialized dance style. The Association of Ballet Clubs, founded by G. B. L. Wilson in 1947, has many clubs as members. Some of these are notably active as, for instance, the Harlow Ballet Club (director, Leo Kersley); the Masque Ballet Club (director, Beryl Goldwyn); the Sheffield Ballet Club; or the Edinburgh Ballet Club. There is an annual evening at which ballets by performing clubs are given; the Association has a flourishing Summer School. Other interesting societies in London include the Sunday Ballet Club, at whose occasional performances professional dancers who wish to try choreography get their chance; and the London Ballet Circle, which provides lectures and various other facilities for members.

Ballet criticism in London reaches as high a standard as anywhere: most of the more literary daily or Sunday newspapers, and such weeklies as the Spectator and the New Statesman, give ballet its due space. Three monthly magazines, *Ballet Today, Dance and Dancers,* and, in particular, *The Dancing Times,* all circulate widely on both sides of the footlights. There is a ballet section of the London Critics' Circle; books on ballet are on most publishers' lists. Television ballet (Margaret Dale has made an outstanding career in this medium as producer with the B.B.C.) offers frequent performances by companies and dancers from Great Britain or abroad.

Ballet films made in Great Britain include: *The Red Shoes* (1948); *Steps of the Ballet* (a Crown Film Unit documentary, 1948); *The Little Ballerina; The Black Swan* (a 3-D classical ballet film, 1952); *The Royal Ballet Film* (1959), which Paul Czinner directed with Margot Fonteyn and Michael Somes in *Ondine, Swan Lake* (Act II), and *Firebird;* and *An Evening with the Royal Ballet* (1965), starring Margot Fonteyn and Rudolf Nureyev.

British Ballet Organisation, a teaching and examining organization in Great Britain and the Commonwealth, founded by Edouard Espinosa and his wife in 1930. Its present chairman is Edward Kelland-Espinosa.

Britten, Benjamin, British composer, b. 1913. Although he has only composed music for one ballet, *The Prince of the Pagodas* (1957), his music is often used by choreographers, the best known examples being Jerome Robbins' *Fanfare* to Britten's *Young Person's Guide to the Orchestra;* Frederick Ashton's short-lived ballet to the same music, *Variations on a Theme of Purcell,* for Sadler's Wells (now Royal) Ballet, in décor by Peter Snow (première Jan. 6, 1955), with Nadia Nerina, Rowena Jackson, Elaine Fifield, Alexander Grant; Walter Gore's *Simple Symphony* to the score of that name; Antony Tudor's *Soirée Musicale,* to a suite taken from the Rossini-Britten *Soirées Musicales;* Lew Christensen's *Jinx* to Britten's *Variations on a Theme of Frank Bridge.* This last named appears to have a fascination for choreographers. Ashton used it for *Le Rêve de Léonor* (for Les Ballets de Paris de Roland Petit, 1949), Gore for *Eaters of Darkness,* John Cranko for *Variations on a Theme* (Ballet Rambert, 1954), and Kenneth MacMillan for *Winter's Eve* (American Ballet Theatre, 1957). Zachary Solov's *Soirée* (Metropolitan Opera Ballet, 1956) used both the *Soirées* and the *Matinées Musicales* arranged by Britten from Rossini music.

Britton, Donald, English dancer, b. London, 1929; m. Elaine Thomas. Studied ballet at Maddocks School, Bristol, and Sadler's Wells School, London. Joined Sadler's Wells Theatre Ballet (1946), then Sadler's Wells (now Royal) Ballet (1947). After military service, rejoined Sadler's Wells Theatre Ballet (1951) as principal dancer. Currently principal dancer with the Royal Ballet. His roles include The Rake (*The Rake's Progress*), Boy (*La Fête Etrange*), title role (*Sweeney Todd*), Young Man (*Les Deux Pigeons*), Captain Belaye (*Pineapple Poll*), Blue Skater (*Les Patineurs*). One of his most striking creations is the man who perpetually makes silly jokes in *The Burrow.*

Broken Date. Ballet in 3 acts; chor.: John Taras and Don Lurio; music: Michel Magne; book: Françoise Sagan; décor: Bernard Buffet; costumes: Franco Laurenti. First prod.: Monte Carlo Opera House, Jan. 3, 1958, with Toni Lander, Noelle Adam, Vladimir Skouratoff, William Lundy; Paris première: Théâtre des Champs-Elysées, Jan. 20, 1958; the London première: Dominion Theatre, Feb. 20, 1958, when John Taras had to dance the Skouratoff role at short notice due to a leg injury of the latter. The company, with Adolfo Andrade substituting for Skouratoff, then played Boston (one week beg. May 6, Colonial Theatre) and Philadelphia (one week beg. May 13, at the Schubert), before opening at the Adelphi Theatre, N.Y., May 20, for a run which was more limited than had been intended. The ballet was then taken back to Europe and finally petered out in Sweden. The combination of the fashionable Mlle. Sagan, the fashionable M. Buffet, and the fashionable M. Roger Vadim (first husband of Brigitte Bardot and producer of *Broken Date*), did not blind anyone to the utter meretriciousness of the whole affair. A young student, in love with the French wife of an American, arranges a final rendez-vous with her before she must leave Paris with her husband. He misses the appointment when he is drawn into a beatnik party and commits suicide after a dream in which he dances with his loved one for the last time.

Bronze Horseman, The. Ballet in four acts and 10 scenes; chor.: Rostislav Zakharov; music: Reinhold Glière; book: Pyotr Abolimov; décor: Mikhail Bobyshov. First prod., Kirov Theatre Ballet, Leningrad, Mar. 14, 1949, with Konstantin Sergeyev (Yevgeny) and Natalia Dudinskaya (Parasha). The same version was performed at the Bolshoi Theatre, Moscow, on June 27, 1949, with Mikhail Gabovich and Galina Ulanova. The ballet follows closely the text of Pushkin's poem of the same title: Yevgeny, a poor petty official, is bereft of his beloved Parasha during the historical flood of St. Petersburg in 1824. He loses his reason and believes that the Bronze Horseman—the statue of Peter the Great—is pursuing him because he accused it of ruthlessness.

Brosset, Yvonne, Swedish dancer, b. Stockholm, 1935. Studied at Royal Swedish Ballet school; later studied in Paris and London. Was accepted into the company (1953); promoted to ballerina (1963). Dances leading roles created for her by Birgit Aakesson and Birgit Cullberg, as well as principal parts in the classic repertoire.

Brown, Carolyn, American dancer, b. Fitchburg, Mass., 1927; m. composer Earle Brown. Received her general education at Wheaton College, Norton, Mass. (B.A. cum laude; also designated a Wheaton scholar, member Phi Beta Kappa). Received Denishawn dance training with her mother (Marion Rice) for fourteen years; Dance Department, Juilliard School of Music, under Martha Graham, Louis Horst, Martha Hill, Norman Lloyd; ballet with Antony Tudor and Margaret Craske; modern dance with Merce Cunningham (1952–62). Principal dancer, Merce Cunningham and Dance Company (since 1953), participating in U.S. tours (1955–62); and N.Y. performances; Black Mountain College Summer Institute of the Arts (summer, 1953); Univ. of Illinois Festival of Contemporary Arts (Mar., 1953, 1959); Jacob's Pillow Dance Festival (1955, 1956); American Dance Festival, Connecticut College, New London (1958–61); Boston Dance Festival (July, 1961); Canada Festival, Montreal (Aug., 1961). Danced with Cunningham in duo programs, Europe: 1958 (Royal Opera House, Stockholm; television, Brussels; 'Das Neue Werk', Hamburg); 1960 (Teatro la Fenice, Venice Biennale; Berlin Festival; Munich; Cologne; television, Brussels). Appears in almost the entire repertoire of the Cunningham Dance company, having created nearly all of her roles. She also created her role in the first performance of *Theatre Piece 1960* by John Cage (Circle in the Square Theatre Mar., 1960). Her husband wrote the scores for *Springweather and People, Galaxy,* and *Hand Birds* (a solo work).

Brown, Kelly, dancer, b. Maysville, Ky.; m. Isabel Mirrow. Studied acrobatics with his mother (Sue Brown), in Maysville from age twelve. Began ballet and character dance training in 1946 with Bentley Stone and Walter Camryn, Chicago. Made professional debut with Chicago Civic Opera Ballet under the direction of Ruth Page (1946). Soloist, Ballet (now American Ballet) Theatre (1949–1953), dancing leading roles in *Fancy Free, Interplay, Princess Aurora, The Harvest According* (creation), and Pat Garrett (*Billy the Kid*), Head Wrangler (*Rodeo*), Minister (*Fall River Legend*). Has since appeared in a number of motion pictures including *Seven Brides for Seven Brothers, Oklahoma!, Daddy Long Legs, The Girl Most Likely,* and many Broadway musicals, most recently *Shinbone Alley, Goldilocks, From A to Z, I Can Get It for You Wholesale, A Funny Thing Happened on the Way to the Forum;* also appears frequently on television. Has studied acting and singing, in addition to dance.

Brown, Vida, American dancer and ballet mistress, b. Oak Park, Ill., 1922. Made her professional debut with Chicago Opera Ballet. Member Ballet de la Jeunesse, Paris; member, Ballet Russe de Monte Carlo (1939–48) first in corps de ballet and later as soloist, dancing, among other roles, Flower Girl (*Gaîté Parisienne*), Coquette (*Night Shadow, La Sonnàmbula*), Cowgirl (*Rodeo*), Unidentified Lady on Horseback (*Virginia Sampler*), Fairy (*Le Baiser de la Fée*). In 1949 she left Ballet Russe de Monte Carlo to accept a position as guest ballerina with the Malmö (Sweden) Opera Ballet. In the spring of 1950 she joined the New York City Ballet as a dancer, becoming (1954–55 season) ballet mistress and assistant to George Balanchine, the company's principal choreographer and artistic director. In this capacity she also staged several Balanchine ballets for European ballet companies. She resigned after the company's Far-Eastern tour (1958) and free-lanced until the summer of 1960, when she married Dr. Philip Glotzer. She re-joined the company as ballet mistress for the season 1963–64.

Bruhn, Erik, Danish dancer, b. Copenhagen, 1928. Entered Royal Danish Ballet School (1937); accepted into the company, 1947; became soloist (1949). Recognized as one of the outstanding dancers of his generation, with striking dramatic talent allied to an exceptional classic brilliance and purity of style, he has been guest artist with many companies. For the past several years he has had that status with the Royal Danish Ballet which enables him to accept other engagements, though he continues to dance frequently in Denmark. These guest appearances include seasons with Metropolitan Ballet, London (1947), American Ballet Theatre (1949–51; 1955–58; 1960–61), New York City Ballet (winter seasons 1959–60; 1963–64), England's Royal Ballet (1962), Australian Ballet (1962–63), Royal Swedish Ballet (guest artist and teacher, fall, 1964), Harkness Ballet (first European tour, 1965), and special performances at Paris Opéra, in Stuttgart, etc. Staged August Bournonville's *La Sylphide* (and danced James at première) for National Ballet of Canada (première Dec. 31, 1964, Toronto). Had sensational success with the Royal Danish Ballet during its third U.S. tour (fall, 1965), especially for his James (*La Sylphide*), Jean (*Miss Julie*), and Don José (*Carmen*). As guest artist and choreographer for Rome Opera Ballet staged *Swan Lake* (Act 2), *Romeo and Juliet* (Balcony

Erik Bruhn with Lupe Serrano in Swan Lake, *Act 2*

Scene) and *La Sylphide,* dancing in the first two with Carla Fracci (spring, 1966). In the fall of same year staged his version of full-length *Swan Lake* for National Ballet of Canada. He has made a number of very successful appearances on American television, especially on "The Bell Telephone Hour." Critics and public alike acclaimed him as a supreme artist when he danced in Soviet Russia with American Ballet Theatre (1960). In addition to the ballets mentioned above, he dances *The Sleeping Beauty, Giselle, Le Spectre de la Rose, Etudes, Les Sylphides, Romeo and Juliet* (Frederick Ashton), *Grand Pas-Glazounov* and *La Sonnàmbula* (George Balanchine), *Don Quixote, Nutcracker, Black Swan* pas de deux, etc. Choreographed *Concertette* (1953), *Festa* (1957). Created a Knight of Dannebrog (1963). Appointed Director of Ballet of Royal Swedish Opera House in 1967.

Brushes, in modern dance, an exercise designed to strengthen the ankle and the muscles of the calf and thigh. It may be done either at the bar or in the center. Its nearest ballet equivalent is the beat. The leg is extended straight forward, toe extremely pointed, the leg and foot not turned out. The toe, traveling directly ahead, brushes the floor; on return, the heel brushes the floor. The body weight is supported by the standing leg and is not taken by the active leg on its return to place. The exercise is done alternating between the right and left leg, brushing to three levels: floor, medium height, and waist high. Arms are at the side, carriage is high, erect, hips are tight, buttocks contracted to prevent any buckling at the waist. The knee is kept rigid at all times.

Buckle, Richard, English writer on ballet, b. Warcop, 1916. Educated at Marlborough and Balliol College, Oxford. Founder-editor of magazine *Ballet.* Ballet Critic, *The Observer* (1948–1955) and the Sunday *Times* (since 1959). Organizer of the Diaghilev Exhibition for the Edinburgh Festival (1954), which was afterwards transferred to London. Author of *The Adventures of a Ballet Critic* (1953), *In Search of Diaghilev* (1955), *Modern Ballet Design* (1955); editor, *Dancing for Diaghilev* (the memoirs of Lydia Sokolova, 1960). Member of the Critics' Circle, London.

Buffonata, La. Ballet chanté by Tancred Dorst; chor.: Ilse-Lore Wobke; commissioned music: Wilhelm Killmayer; décor: Frank Schultes; costumes: Haidi Schürmann; choruses by Johannes Zimmermann. First prod.: Städtische Bühne Heidelberg, Apr. 30, 1961. With choreography by Heinz Rosen was produced by the Munich Festwoche des Balletts (1961).

Bugaku (Japanese), a dance performance by Gagaku, the musicians and dancers of the Japanese Imperial Household (which see).

Bugaku. Ballet in 1 act; chor.: George Balanchine; music: Toshiro Mayuzumi; décor and lighting: David Hays; costumes: Barbara Karinska; first prod.: New York City Ballet, City Center, N.Y., Mar. 20, 1963, with Allegra Kent, Edward Vilella (subsequently danced by Mimi Paul and Arthur Mitchell). The music by the Japanese composer is for western instruments; the choreography is based on the technique of ballet. The atmosphere, largely engendered by Hays' beautiful set, is reminiscent of the Japanese court dance, but the acrobatics of the pas de deux are very far from having any connection with the dance art of Japan.

Bulerias, a Spanish flamenco dance not unlike Alegrias in steps, although gayer and faster. See SPANISH DANCE.

Bulnes, Esmée, English dancer and teacher b. Rock Ferry, Cheshire, 1900. Studied ballet with Enrico Cecchetti, Bronislava Nijinska, Lubov Egorova, Yelena Smirnova, Boris Romanov, and others. Began teaching at Colón Theatre, Buenos Aires, Argentina (1931), and acted as assistant to Michel Fokine. Remained at the Colón through 1949. In 1950 joined the Ballet School of the Teatro alla Scala, Milan, as director; remained in that post until 1954 when she was appointed "Direttrice del Ballo" (Director of ballet company and school) of Teatro alla Scala, a post she held until the end of 1962, when she relinquished it to devote herself entirely to the school. In the summer of 1962 she was invited as guest teacher by the School of American Ballet, N.Y.

Bunzel, Gertrude, (née Godwyn), contemporary modern dancer and pedagogue; b. Vienna; now a U.S. citizen. Graduated from Vienna State Academy of

Music; studied with Gertrud Bodenweiser, Gertrud Krauss, Rudolf von Laban; ballet with Hedy Pfundmeyer, Hélène Platova. Danced with Gertrud Krauss group in Max Reinhardt's *The Miracle;* gave recitals in Germany, Austria, Italy, etc. (1929–36); and in N.Y. (1938). Passed Vienna State Examination (1930) and opened own school in rhythmics and dancing; also taught as professor in Lutvak-Patonay Conservatory, Vienna. Returned to U.S. in 1939; since then she has taught in camps and schools and in the Drama Department, Carnegie Institute of Technology (from 1944) and Seton Hall College. After World War II did psychokinetic work with veterans and psychotics. At present teaching in Richmond, Va.

Burchenal, Elizabeth, folk dance authority, b. Richmond, Ind. d. Nov. 20, 1959. B.A., Earlham College, Richmond; Sc.D. (Hon.) Boston Univ. (1943). Founder-president, American Folk Dance Society (1916); later executive chairman and director, Folk Arts Center, Inc. and U.S. member of International Commission on Folk Arts and Folklore. Published many volumes and articles on American folk dances, their sources and music. Beginning 1915 assembled an Archive of American Folk Dance to promote interest in folk dance and folk arts. Gave lectures and demonstrations at universities, colleges, folk art centers, etc., throughout U.S. and in Canada, Germany, Holland, Eire, teaching the folk dances of different nationalities. Was a member of various associations of health and physical education and folk societies in U.S. and abroad.

Burne, Gary, British dancer, b. Bulawayo, South Africa, 1934. Studied with Elaine Archibald, in S. Africa and Ruth French, in London. Joined Sadler's Wells (now Royal) Ballet (1952); became soloist (1956), creating King of the South (*Prince of the Pagodas*), and Etiocles (*Antigone*). Danced in Rhodesia with Merle Park (1956) and in Stuttgart on leave of absence from Royal Ballet (1961).

Burr, Marilyn, Australian dancer, b. Parramatta, New South Wales, 1933; m. Louis Godfrey. Studied at Australian Ballet School under Leon Kellaway. Made her debut in National Ballet Company (1948). Joined London's Festival Ballet as soloist (1953); later promoted to ballerina. Her roles include Queen of the Wilis and title role (*Giselle*), Sugar Plum Fairy (*The Nutcracker*), Kupava (*The Snow Maiden*), Odette (*Swan Lake,* Act 2), Swanilda (*Coppélia*), Zobeide (*Schéhérazade*); created Ingrid in *Peer Gynt* (1963). Since the 1963–64 season has been ballerina of the Hamburg State Opera Ballet.

Burra, Edward, English painter, b. London, 1905. Studied at Chelsea School of Art and Royal College of Art, London. Designs for ballet include *Rio Grande,* (for Camargo Society, 1932; for Vic-Wells Ballet, 1935), *Barabau* (for Sadler's Wells [now Royal] Ballet, 1936), *Miracle in the Gorbals* (1944), *Don Juan* (1948), *Don Quixote* (Ninette de Valois, 1950).

Burrow, The. Ballet in 1 act; chor.: Kenneth MacMillan; commissioned music: Frank Martin; décor: Nicholas Georgiadis; first prod.: Royal Ballet, Royal Opera House, Covent Garden, London, Jan. 2, 1958, with Anne Heaton, Donald Britton, Lynn Seymour, Donald Macleary. The story inevitably is a reminder of *The Diary of Anne Frank,* though the choreographer states that he had neither read nor seen the book, play, or film. The setting is a room in which a number of refugees must live without ever leaving it. Their loves, hates, frustrations, irritations, and terrors are depicted. The ballet ends with the fateful knock at the door which must be the end of hope for all. MacMillan also staged this ballet for Royal Danish Ballet (1962).

Butler, Horacio, Argentine stage designer, b. Buenos Aires, 1897. Studied at Escuela de Bellas Artes, Buenos Aires, and with André Lhote, Othon Friez, and Paquerau in Paris. Member of Academia de Bellas Artes. Has designed décor for numerous ballets in Buenos Aires, Montevideo, Teatro alla Scala, Milan. His latest work is *Variaciones Concertantes,* a ballet by John Taras, to music by Alberto Ginastera, given at the Teatro Colón in 1960. Illustrated *Green Mansions* by W. H. Hudson (New York, 1939).

Butler, John, American dancer and choreographer, b. Memphis, Tenn., 1920. Began his choreographic career with dances for Broadway and off-Broadway shows, among them Gian-Carlo Menotti's *The Consul* (1947). In 1955 he took his John Butler Dance Theatre to the Dance Festival at Nervi (Genoa), Italy, where he presented *Clowns and Angels* (Paul Bowles), *La Cenerentola* (Rossini), *Frontier Ballad* (traditional American folk music). In 1957 he staged *Seven Faces of Love* for the American Ballet Theatre; and the world première of Menotti's *The Unicorn, the Gorgon and the Manticore* at the Library of Congress, Washington, D.C., and later for the New York City Ballet. In 1958 he was appointed Dance Director of the Festival of Two Worlds, Spoleto, Italy, where his company performed *Glory Folk* (American traditional music), *Triad* (Prokofiev, Peggy Glanville-Hicks, Duke Ellington), *Mask of the Wild Man* (Glanville-Hicks), *Unquiet Graves* (Stanley Hollingsworth). In 1959 his company returned to Spoleto to perform *The Sybil* (Carlos Surinach), *Five Senses* (John Lewis), *Brief Encounter* and *Amusement Park* (Paul Bowles). Other dance compositions by Butler include *Three Promenades with the Lord* (traditional music), *Portrait of Billie* (based on the life of Billie Holiday,

John Butler, American choreographer

to recordings of her songs), *Letter from a Beloved* (Ravel), *Malocchio* (Paul Bowles), *Turning Point* (selections from Gil Evans, John Lewis, Ken Hopkins). He staged the world première of Peggy Glanville-Hicks's opera *Nausicaa* at the Athens (Greece) International Festival (1961), and the dances in a number of operas in the U.S. He is also credited with many television productions and two ice shows, as well as several industrial shows. He was choreographer for the New York City Opera Company (1951–54; 1959–61, staging the dances for Aaron Copland's *The Tender Land* and *La Cenerentola* (Rossini), and directing and choreographing Béla Bartók's *Bluebeard's Castle* and Carl Orff's *Carmina Burana.* For the Metropolitan Opera he choreographed the ballet in *Die Fledermaus* (1958) and dances for *The Marriage of Figaro* (1959). Staged his *Carmina Burana* for Nederlands Dans Theater (1962) and for Pennsylvania Ballet (1966). Also for Nederlands Dans Theater choreographed a new work, *Hadrianus,* to a score by Robert Starer (prem.: Rotterdam, Nov. 29, 1962), and his version of *Sebastian* to Gian-Carlo Menotti's score (Oct. 22, 1963). Staged *Sebastian* for the Harkness Ballet (1966); also choreographed a pas de deux *After Eden* to a commissioned score by Lee Hoiby, danced by Lone Isaksen and Lawrence Rhodes, a major success of the company's 1966 European tour.

Butsova, Hilda (Hilda Boot), contemporary British ballerina and teacher, b. Nottingham, England. Began serious dance training at age of eleven at Stedmans Academy, London; later studied with Alexandre Volinine and Enrico Cecchetti. When only thirteen joined Diaghilev Ballets Russes for London season and was seen by Anna Pavlova, who invited her to join her for a tour of Russia. She remained as Pavlova's understudy and was so successful dancing *The Sleeping Beauty* and other Pavlova roles that she was promoted to ballerina, and throughout the remainder of the existence of the company, she was second only to Pavlova in importance, dancing Swanilda (*Coppélia*), Lise (*La Fille Mal Gardée*), *Les Sylphides,* Columbine (*Carnival*), etc. Toured with Mikhail Mordkin in U.S. (1927), then rejoined Pavlova (1928); also danced in concerts with Anton Dolin (1929) and toured with her own company. Returned to U.S. (1930) as ballerina of the Capitol Theatre, N.Y. A very successful teacher for many years after she retired as a dancer, she now teaches only on special occasions, such as at normal schools, conventions, etc.

C

Cabriole, in ballet, a movement in the air, in which the legs are at an angle to the floor and the lower leg beats against the upper leg. Cabriole used to be considered a man's step, but is no longer. The name is supposed to derive from the Italian capriola, meaning gazelle or she-goat. The step resembles the beating of the feet of a gazelle. Technique: Start in 5th pos., R ft. front; step forward on R ft. in demi-plié, bringing L leg to demi-quatrième devant en effacé; jump off R ft., beating calves together, R ft. under L, L leg opening upward slightly after the beat; land on R ft., then put L ft. down in front in 5th pos. This is cabriole fermé. When L leg is left in open position ready to do another step, it is called cabriole ouvert. Cabriole may also be done in back, croisé, etc. A double beat of the calf is called a double cabriole. In character or national dancing, a cabriole is often performed with bent knees, the beat being executed with the feet only.

Caccialanza, Gisella, dancer, b. San Diego, Calif. 1914; m. Lew Christensen. Studied with Enrico Cecchetti (who was her godfather), at the School of American Ballet, N.Y., and the San Francisco Ballet School. Soloist of the American Ballet, Ballet Caravan, Ballet Society, San Francisco Ballet. Now retired and living in

Gisella Caccialanza in Mozartiana

San Francisco, where her husband is director and choreographer of the S.F. Ballet.

Cachucha, a Spanish dance in 3/4 time performed with castanet accompaniment. It is of uncertain origin and was made popular in the middle of the 19th century by Fanny Elssler when she danced it in one of her most successful ballets, *Le Diable Boiteux*. Some traces of the cachucha are to be found in the modern sevillanas.

Cadmus, Paul, painter and illustrator, b. New York City, 1906. Designed the décor and costumes for the ballet *Filling Station* (Lew Christensen, 1938); also illustrated the book *Ballet Alphabet* by Lincoln Kirstein (N.Y., 1939).

Café des Sports. Ballet in 1 act; chor.: Alfred Rodrigues; commissioned music: Antony Hopkins; décor: Jack Taylor. First prod.: Johannesburg, S. Africa, May 24, 1954. London première: perf.: Sadler's Wells Theatre Ballet, Sadler's Wells Theatre, Nov. 18, 1954, with Maryon Lane, Annette Page, David Poole, and Gilbert Vernon. Lively events in a French Mediterranean village during the annual bicycle race.

Cage, John, American composer, b. Los Angeles, Calif., 1912. Studied music with Richard Buhlig, Adolph Weiss, Henry Cowell, and Arnold Schoenberg. Member of the faculty of the Cornish School, Seattle, Wash. (1936–38); moved to N.Y. after a year on the faculty of the School of Design, Chicago. In 1943 directed a concert of percussion music sponsored by the Museum of Modern Art, N.Y., and the League of Composers. Devoting himself to works for the "prepared piano" which he invented in 1938, he received a Guggenheim Fellowship for Creative Work in the Field of Music and an award from the National Academy of Arts and Letters "for having thus extended the boundaries of musical art" (both 1949). Organized a group of musicians and engineers in 1951 for making music directly on magnetic tape, producing works by Christian Wolff, Morton Feldman, Earle Brown, and himself. Teaches composition at the New School for Social Research, N.Y. and since 1943 has been musical director of the Merce Cunningham Dance Company, for which group he has composed many scores. In 1960 was appointed Fellow of the Center for Advanced Studies at Wesleyan University, Middletown, Conn. Co-author (with Kathleen O'Donnell Hoover) of *The Life and Works of Virgil Thomson*. His collected articles and lectures have been published by Wesleyan Univ. Press under the general title *Silence*.

Cage, The. Ballet in 1 act; chor. and book: Jerome Robbins; music: Igor Stravinsky's Concerto in D for Strings (the "Basler"); décor: Jean Rosenthal; costumes: Ruth Sobotka; first prod.: New York City Ballet at City Center, N.Y., June 14, 1951, with Nora Kaye (the Novice), Nicholas Magallanes (Second Intruder), Yvonne Mounsey (Queen), Michael Maule (First Intruder). Among some species of insects the female kills the male, and Robbins makes use of this fact in telling his bitter fable of woman destroying man. The Novice was Nora Kaye's greatest creation outside her repertoire of Antony Tudor ballets.

Cahusac, Louis de (1706–1759), ballet master and historian of the dance. His book *La Danse Ancienne et Moderne* (Paris, 1754) was the most complete history of the art form published up to his time. It contained, among others, a number of chapters that foreshadowed the reforms which Jean Georges Noverre urged in his *Lettres sur la Danse et sur les Ballets*. De Cahusac also produced a number of ballets at the Académie Royale for which Rameau composed the music. These included *Zaïs* (1747), *Naïs* (1749), *La Fête de Pamylie* (1751). Other ballets, upon which he collaborated were *L'Al-*

gérien (1744), *Les Amours de Tempe,* (1752), *Les Fêtes de l'Himen et de l'Amour* (1755), *Les Festes de Polimnie* (1753), and *Zoroastre* (1756).

Cakewalk, a dance of American Negro origin, which reached the height of its popularity at the end of the 19th and the beginning of the 20th century, characterized by fanciful strutting. The name is derived from the custom of giving a piece of pastry as a prize for the most intricate steps performed. It was often used in minstrel shows and vaudeville in U.S. and was adapted by the French for revues and musical comedies.

Cakewalk. Ballet in 1 act; chor.: Ruthanna Boris; music: piano pieces by Louis Moreau Gottschalk, arr. by Hershy Kay; décor: Robert Drew (originally used for Ballet Society's *Blackface*); first prod.: New York City Ballet, City Center, N.Y., June 12, 1951, with Frank Hobi (Mr. Interlocutor), Tanaquil LeClerq and Beatrice Tompkins (End Men), Janet Reed (Wallflower Waltz), Patricia Wilde (Wild Pony, and Leader in Freebee), Yvonne Mounsey (Venus), Janet Reed and Herbert Bliss (Hortense, Queen of the Swamp Lilies, and Harolde, the Young Poet). A good-natured parody on an oldtime minstrel show, presented in dance form, and ending in the cakewalk. Revived by the City Center Joffrey Ballet (Sept. 8, 1966) with Nels Jorgensen (John Jones alternating) as Mr. Interlocutor, Susan Magno and Diana Cartier (End Men), Ivy Clear (Wallflower Waltz and Hortense), Stephania Lee (Wild Pony and Leader in Freebee), Barbara Remington (Venus), Maximiliano Zomosa (Harolde).

Callaghan, Domini, British dancer, b. Leeds, 1923; m. Michel de Lutry Studied at Sadler's Wells (now Royal) Ballet School. Danced with Sadler's Wells Theatre Ballet; soloist with International Ballet, Metropolitan Ballet, and other companies. Has appeared frequently on British television. Now working in Germany (since 1955).

Caller, in the square dance, the man who calls the figures to be performed by the dancers.

Calvocoressi, Michel D., critic and musicologist, b. 1877, France, of Greek parentage. A long time resident of London, his book *Musicians Gallery; music and ballet in Paris and London* (London, 1933), is a vivid report on many aspects of the Diaghilev Ballets Russes. As a specialist in Russian music (and author of the definitive *La Musique Russe*), he severely criticized Michel Fokine for his use of Nicholas Rimsky-Korsakov's score for *Schéhérazade,* a ballet which used a different scenario from the definite program which the composer supplied for this tone poem. His ballet criticisms, published mostly in French magazines, were written from the point of view of a cultured musician who took a serious interest in ballet.

Camargo, Marie (Marie Ann de Cupis de Camargo, 1710–1770), French ballerina, b. in Brussels, of Spanish descent. Daughter of a musician, Marie showed at an early age an aptitude for dancing. She made her debut in Brussels, then went to Rouen and the Paris Opéra, where she studied under Françoise Prévost. Her Paris debut was on May 5, 1726, in the ballet *Les Caractères de la Danse.* She next appeared in *Ajax, Les Amours Déguisés,* and *Le Jugement de Paris.* Though Camargo's career was marked by her rivalry with reformer Marie Sallé, she was herself a reformer: she freed herself and expanded the range of her own technique by shortening the skirt of her stage costume and removing the heels of her dancing slippers. Camargo is credited with making the extreme ninety degree turnout the proper one for ballet dancing and with inventing the entrechat-quatre (ca. 1730).

That entrechats were done long before her time is conceded, but she may have improved on the manner of her execution, and it is known that her petite batterie was brilliant. She was known for several types of jeté and for her pas de basque. Though Jean Georges Noverre wrote that Camargo was "neither pretty, nor tall, nor well formed," the famous painting by Lancret does show her as very attractive. Others wrote that she was not well formed, but moved so swiftly on stage that no one noticed it. Camargo was very popular and set the fashion in shoes, coiffures, etc. In 1735 Camargo retired to live with her protector, the Comte de Clermont. In Dec., 1741, she reappeared in public in *Les Fêtes Grecques et Romaines* and in *Les Talents Lyriques*. She finally retired from the stage on a pension from the French Government (1751). In later years, Charles Lecocq wrote an opera *Camargo,* and Marius Petipa staged a ballet *Camargo,* to music by Minkus. The Camargo Society was formed in London (1930) to sponsor ballets. Escoffier's *Guide to Modern Cookery* describes the following dishes named after Camargo: Bombe Camargo, Filet de Boeuf Camargo, Ris de Veau Grillés Camargo, Soufflé à la Camargo.

Camargo Society, The, a group organized in London in 1930 after the death of Serge Diaghilev and the consequent disbanding of the Ballets Russes, in an attempt to create a national ballet, to revive interest in ballet by performing old works, and to aid English dancers and choreographers to produce new ones. It was first planned by Philip J. S. Richardson and Arnold Haskell in 1929 and had its inaugural meeting in 1930. The original General Committee was under the chairmanship of Edwin Evans, with M. Montagu-Nathan as secretary. Its first performance, before a subscription audience, was Oct. 19, 1930, at the Cambridge Theatre with a program that included a revival of *Robert the Devil* staged by Adeline Genée, a set of *Variations and Coda* to music by Mikhail Glinka arranged by Nicholas Legat, a pas de deux danced by Ninette de Valois and Anton Dolin, and two premières: *Danse Sacrée et Danse Profane* (Ninette de Valois to the Debussy music) and Frederick Ashton's *Pomona,* with the American dancer Anna Ludmila in the title role. Over the next two years the Camargo Society gave a number of performances which included the premières of de Valois' *Job* and *La Création du Monde,* Ashton's *Façade* and a very early Antony Tudor work, *Adam and Eve.* The dancers were recruited mainly from the studios of Marie Rambert and Ninette de Valois, both then in the early stages of creating the companies which afterwards became famous as Ballet Rambert and Sadler's Wells (now Royal) Ballet. Anton Dolin, Alicia Markova, Phyllis Bedells, Lydia Lopoukhova, Ruth French and many others gave their support. In 1932 the Camargo Society gave a two-week public season at the Savoy Theatre, at which Olga Spessivtseva danced in the first British production of *Giselle* and *Swan Lake* (Act 2). The following year the Camargo Society dissolved itself after two special performances at the Royal Opera House, Covent Garden, June 27 and 29, in honor of the World Economic Conference then being held in London. Members of the Royal Family attended the first performance and the Prime Minister and members of the Cabinet the second. By this time both Sadler's Wells Ballet and Rambert were firmly established and the aims of the Camargo Society had been achieved.

Cambert, Robert (1628–1677), Paris-born composer of music of ballets at the Académie Royale. He collaborated with the first director of the Académie (Perrin), and composed the music for the first ballet produced by that institution, *Pomone.* When Lully became director of the Académie, Cambert went to London where his *Ariane* was presented for King Charles II.

Cambré, in ballet, bending back or to the side, as arabesque cambré.

Campra, André, b. Provence, 1660, d. Venice, 1744. Composed the music for a number of ballets for the Académie Royale including *L'Europe Galante, Le Carnaval de Venise, Amaryllis,* etc. He worked at the Paris Opéra for thirty-five years.

Camryn, Walter, American dancer, teacher, choreographer, b. Helena, Mont., 1903. Studied with Adolph Bolm, Alexandra Maximova, Vecheslav Swoboda, Laurent Novikoff, Muriel Stuart. Appeared as premier danseur and choreographer with the Chicago Civic Opera company; first soloist, Page-Stone Ballet; guest-artist and choreographer, Federal Theatre Ballet; guest teacher with various dance teacher associations; teacher, Stone-Camryn School, Chicago. He is the choreographer of some twenty ballets, among them *Roundelay* (Ravel), *Thunder in the Hills* (Foster, 1939), *The Shooting of Dan McGrew* (period music, 1942), *Dr. Eli Duffy's Snakeroot* (period music), *Symphony in C* (Haydn, 1944), *Krazy Kat* (John Alden Carpenter, 1948), *Hansel and Gretel* (Humperdinck, 1954), *Trio Variations* (Schubert, 1956), *In My Landscape* (Aborn, 1960).

Canada, Dance in.

BY LAURETTA THISTLE.

In 1948 Canada had no professional ballet companies; in 1958 it had three—all founded under quite difficult circumstances.

The Royal Winnipeg Ballet is the oldest of the companies. It began as a modest ballet school in 1938, established in Winnipeg by two Englishwomen, Gweneth Lloyd and Betty Farrally. As a performing outlet for its advanced students the school organized a small company which began performing in Winnipeg and its environs. To create a wider scope for itself the company fathered the Canadian Ballet Festival movement in 1948. These annual festivals, bringing together the best non-professional companies, continued through 1954, meeting every spring in different Canadian cities. They played to large, interested audiences and gained a modicum of official recognition. The festivals were discontinued mainly because of the emergence of two professional ballet companies in Canada. These and the establishment of television stations in Toronto and Montreal opened employment possibilities for most of the employable dancers. Since then, however, the lack of opportunity for contact between non-professional directors and choreographers has been keenly felt.

The Winnipeg Ballet became a professional company in 1949. In 1953, on the occasion of the visit to Canada of Queen Elizabeth II and the Duke of Edinburgh, the company was granted the title Royal. The company's repertoire was built around original works, chiefly by Gweneth Lloyd. A fire in 1954 destroyed everything the company owned—sets, scores, costumes. It took nearly five years for the company to re-organize completely. The rebuilt repertoire included works by Canadian choreographers Brian Macdonald, Michel Conte, Arnold Sporh (the company's former premier danseur and current artistic director).

The National Ballet of Canada, with its home base in Toronto, came into being in 1951, backed by a group of people from Eastern Canada who were reluctant to have the Western city of Winnipeg as the ballet capital. Celia Franca, formerly of the Sadler's Wells (now Royal) Ballet of London, was invited as artistic director. The title "National" was assumed, that is, not granted by the state. The repertoire was at first modelled largely on that of the Sadler's Wells Ballet, but choreographers Grant Strate, David Adams, and others were developed within the company.

Les Grands Ballets Canadiens, the third group, began in Montreal in 1952 as a television troupe, directed by Ludmilla Chiriaeff. For its first tentative tours it traveled under the title Ballets Chiriaeff; later, although still a group of fewer than twenty dancers, it took the name Les Grands Ballets Canadiens. The company acquired professional management for tours as the Winnipeg and Toronto companies had done, and extended its tours to the United States, including the Jacob's Pillow Dance Festival in 1959 and 1960. Its repertoire has been built on original ballets, chiefly by Mme. Chiriaeff and Eric Hyrst, but it has also mounted some classics. It was, for instance, the first Canadian group to stage *La Fille Mal Gardée* (1961).

Since all three professional companies were pressing for government support, the Canada Council (a politically independent cultural organization authorized to spend the income from a fixed investment) in 1962 called on experts from outside the country for advice. As a result available funds were apportioned to the National Ballet of Canada, Les Grands Ballets Canadiens, Royal Winnipeg Ballet, and the Classical Ballet Concert Group.

The quick growth of the professional companies and the loss of the Ballet Festivals has resulted in a loss of contact between professionals, semi-professionals, and amateurs. Several schools across Canada have managed to assemble groups capable of local performances and regional tours. One, probably the most outstanding among them, the Classical Ballet Concert Group of Ottawa, directed by Nesta Toumine, has received modest Canada Council grants for the purpose of touring cities and towns within a radius of about 100 miles from Ottawa. This company also has the distinction of being the only foreign company to be invited to participate annually in the Northeastern (U.S.A.) Regional Ballet Festival. The sixth annual Northeastern Festival (1965) was held in Ottawa, hosted by the Ottawa company.

Canada, National Ballet of, a company which began life very modestly with performances in Toronto (fall, 1951), having been organized the previous year by Celia Franca (See also CANADA, DANCE IN). Since this initial season it has grown into a full-scale company which tours all over Canada and the U.S. In 1953 it became the first foreign company ever to be invited to appear at the Jacob's Pillow Dance Festival, Lee, Mass. Kay Ambrose, well-known English artist and writer of many successful books on ballet and dance technique, joined the company as artistic adviser in 1952 and remained through 1961, also designing many of the ballets. In the early years Celia Franca concentrated in establishing a repertoire of standard classics from the Russian and Diaghilev Ballets Russes repertoires, including the full-length *Swan Lake, The Nutcracker* (with many of her own interpretations of the music), *Coppélia, Giselle, Les Sylphides, Le Spectre de la Rose, Carnaval, Polovetsian Dances from Prince Igor,* and *Afternoon of a Faun* (with her own choreography) to which were added a number of the early Antony Tudor ballets: *Lilac Garden, Gala Performance, Dark Elegies.* Tudor also staged *Offenbach in the Underworld* for this company. Other ballets from the British repertoire, such as Frederick Ashton's *Les Rendezvous,* John Cranko's *Pineapple Poll* and Andrée Howard's *The Mermaid* have been added; in 1962 the company staged its first ballet by George Balanchine—*Concerto Barocco.* Over the years National Ballet of Canada has also developed a repertoire by native Canadian choreographies including several by David Adams, who is also premier danseur of the company (*Ballet Behind Us, Pas de Chance, Pas de Six, Pas de Deux Romantique, Barbara Allen*); and Grant Strate (*The Fisherman and his Soul, The Willow, Ballad, Antic Spring, Patterns, House of Atreus*). Ray Powell, character dancer of the Royal Ballet, staged *One in Five* to polkas, mazurkas and galops of Josef and Johann Strauss for the company at Royal Alexandra Theatre, Toronto, Jan. 29, 1962. In addition to being director, Celia Franca was one of the company's ballerinas during the first years, retiring as a dancer early in 1959. She not only directs the company but also the school attached to the company, which in 1962 added an academic education to its dance training. Lois Smith and David Adams have headed the National Ballet of Canada since its beginning; other leading dancers have included Lilian Jarvis, Galina Samtsova, Jocelyn Terelle, Martine Van Hamel, Earl Kraul, Kenneth Melville, Hans Meister.

Canada Council, an instrument of the Canadian Government through which it contributes its support to the arts. The Council functions more or less on the style of the Arts Council of Great Britain. Considering the size of the Canadian population and its national budget, the support, if not lavish, is substantial. Grants made to the three Canadian professional ballet companies for the period 1957–1963 were: National Ballet of Canada, $560,000; Royal Winnipeg Ballet, $207,000; Les Grands Ballets Canadiens, $123,000 (figures for later years are unavailable). In addition, in the season 1961–62 the Council made a grant of $2,000 to the Ottawa Classical Ballet Concert Group, a semi-professional company, to give performances in smaller towns in the province of Quebec. This grant has been repeated annually since 1962. In late summer of 1962 Mrs. Nesta Toumine, the director-choreographer and principal teacher of the Ottawa company, was awarded $1,500 to make a study of methods and procedures in the state (or state-supported) schools of Moscow, Leningrad, Copenhagen, and London.

Canaletto (Bernardo Belotti) (1734–1780), a designer of ballet settings at the Vienna Court Theatre. His best-known work was *Le Turc Généreux*.

Canaries, a spectacular 16th century dance. Its origin has been attributed to Canary Islands, or derived from a ballet or masque in which the dancers were costumed as savages from these islands.

Cancan (also spelled can-can), a rather rowdy social dance of Paris origin which came into vogue about 1830, the main feature of which was high kicks by the dancers. Its popularity as a dance of participation lasted until about 1844. After that year the cancan began to be used as a stage dance in revues and musical comedies, especially in France. Henri de Toulouse-Lautrec immortalized the cancan with his series of paintings and drawings of the dancers at the Moulin Rouge. Music for the most famous cancans was written by Jacques Offenbach. The cancan in Leonide Massine's *Gaîté Parisienne* is an excellent example of its use in ballet.

Cangaceira (The Woman Bandit). Ballet in 1 act; chor.: Aurel Milloss; music Camargo Guarnieri; idea and décor: Flavio de Carvalho. First prod.: Ballet do IV Centenário, Teatro Municipal, Rio de Janeiro, Brazil, 1954, with Edith Pudelko in the title role. A choreographic portrait, daring in many respects, more a stage fantasy than a ballet.

Canticle for Innocent Comedians. Modern dance work; chor. and costumes: Martha Graham; music: Thomas Ribbink; set: Frederick Kiesler. First prod.: Martha Graham Dance Company, Juilliard Concert Hall, N.Y., Apr. 22, 1952, with Pearl Lang, Yuriko, Helen McGehee, Mary Hinkson, Bertram Ross, Stuart Hodes, Robert Cohan, and others. A considerably revised version with new costumes was presented at the Alvin Theatre, Apr. 14, 1953. A hymn to the cycle of life and to the elements, the sun, and the moon.

Capeller, Tamara, Brazilian dancer and teacher, b. Petropolis, Brazil, of Russian parentage. Studied with Maria Olenewa, Yuco Lindberg, and Igor Schwezoff. Made her debut in 1943 at the Teatro Municipal; became soloist in 1945. Left in 1947 to become ballerina of Ballet da Juventude, but returned the following year. Danced nearly all classic, romantic, modern ballets, and pas de deux in the repertoire. Currently teaches at the ballet school of Teatro Municipal.

Capezio Award, The, was established in 1951 by Capezio, Inc., theatrical shoe manufacturers, headed by Ben Sommers, president of the firm, for the purpose of contributing to public awareness of the progress of the dance in the U.S. It is to focus attention on substantial achievements that each year the Capezio Dance Award Committee singles out one person for specific honor. The choice is not limited to the activities of the calendar year. The award takes the form of cash rather than a loving cup or a statuette for the founders of the award consider that money given to an artist or a creative worker inevitably contributes to the art itself. The first committee served through 1956 and included Anatole Chujoy, Martha Hill, John Martin, and Walter Terry. Martin resigned in 1956 and Emily Coleman was co-opted in his stead. The award, which at the beginning was $500, was increased to $1,000 in 1958. The winners of the award have included: Zachary Solov (1952), Lincoln Kirstein (1953), Doris Humphrey (1954), Louis Horst (1955), Genevieve Oswald (1956), Ted Shawn (1957), Alexandra Danilova (1958), S. Hurok (1959), Martha Graham (1961), Barbara Karinska (1962), Donald McKayle (1963), José Limón (1964), Maria Tallchief (1965), Agnes de Mille (1966), Paul Taylor (1967).

Capezio Foundation. See FOUNDATIONS, PHILANTHROPIC.

Capriccio Espagnol. Ballet in 1 act; chor. and book: Leonide Massine, in collaboration with Argentinita; music: Nicholas Rimsky-Korsakov's score of the same title; décor: Mariano Andreù. First prod.: Ballet Russe de Monte Carlo, Théâtre de Monte Carlo, May 4, 1939, with Argentinita (Gypsy Girl), Leonide Massine (Gypsy Youth), Alexandra Danilova (Peasant Girl), Michel Panaieff (Peasant Youth). The ballet follows the score closely in a series of five divertissements. After Argentinita's guest appearances Mia Slavenska and Nathalie Krassovska alternated in the role. Was filmed in technicolor by Warner Brothers under the title *Spanish Fiesta* (1941). In repertoire of Ballet (now American Ballet) Theatre (1943) when Massine was with that company, with Massine and Nora Kaye in the leading roles. Frederic Franklin succeeded Massine in the Ballet Russe de Monte Carlo production. Massine staged *Capriccio Espagnol* for International Ballet in London (1951), dancing in the first few performances.

Caprices du Cupidon, Les. Ballet; chor.: Vincenzo Galeotti; music: Jens Lolle. First prod.: Oct. 31, 1786, Danish Royal Theatre, Copenhagen, where Galeotti was ballet master at the time. The ballet which has a charming quaintness is still in the repertoire of the Royal Danish Ballet. In 1952 Harald Lander lovingly revised the ballet for the Paris Opéra. The plot revolves around Cupid who, as a prank, matches up the wrong boys with the wrong girls. The dancing is mainly a series of national pas de deux. The ballet's interest is chiefly historical, since Galeotti was a teacher of August Bournonville, the creator of what is known as the Danish style of ballet; also, *Les Caprices du Cupidon* belongs to the same year as *La Fille Mal Gardée,* but has remained substantially the same to the present time.

Caprichos. Ballet in 4 episodes and an epilogue; chor.: Herbert Ross; music: Béla Bartók's *Contrasts for Piano, Clarinet and*

Violin; book: Herbert Ross, based on four of Goya's comments to his famous series of etchings of the same name; costumes: Helen Pons. First prod.: Choreographer's Workshop, Hunter College Playhouse, N.Y., Jan. 24, 1950, with Ilona Murai, Emy St. Just, Gina Snyder, Alice Temkin, Dorothy Hill, Frank Glass, Leslie Harris, Herbert Ross, Joseph Stember, Larry Stevens, George Wood. It was immediately taken into the repertoire of Ballet Theatre and premièred Apr. 26, 1950, at City Center, N.Y., with Charlyne Baker and Jenny Workman ("These good girls have seats enough and nothing to do with them better than carry them on their heads"); Nana Gollner, Eric Braun and Peter Gladke ("No one ever escapes who wants to be caught"); Ruth Ann Koesun and John Kriza ("If he were more gallant and less of a bore, she would come to life again"); Mary Burr, Jack Beaber, Scott Douglas (then Jimmy Hicks), Vernon Lusby, Ralph McWilliams ("They are determined to kill this saintly woman. . . . No one can make her ashamed who has nothing to be ashamed of . . ."). As the curtain falls a voice says in Spanish, "The dream of reason produces monsters."

Capriole Suite. Ballet in 1 act; chor.: Frederick Ashton; music: arr. by Peter Warlock from airs from Thoinot Arbeau's *Orchésographie;* décor: William Chappell. First prod.: Rambert Dancers (later Ballet Rambert), Lyric Theatre, Hammersmith, Feb. 25, 1930, with Andrée Howard, Diana Gould, Harold Turner, Frederick Ashton, William Chappell. A suite of old dances—Tordion, Mattachins, Pavane, Pieds en l'air, Branles—done with a mixture of simplicity, style, and invention which marked its youthful choreographer as someone to watch. *Capriole Suite* was for many years in the Rambert repertoire, and for a short while was also danced by Sadler's Wells Theatre Ballet (première Oct. 8, 1948).

Caracole. See DIVERTIMENTO NO. 15.

Caractères de La Danse, Les. Ballet by Rebel, arranged in 1715 for Françoise Prévost. It was a divertissement designed to display virtuosity. Marie Camargo made her first appearance in Paris in this ballet (1726).

Card Game (originally titled *Card Party*). Ballet in 1 act, and 3 hands (or deals); chor.: George Balanchine; music: Igor Stravinsky; book: Stravinsky, in collaboration with M. Malaeiff; décor: Irene Sharaff. First prod.: American Ballet, Metropolitan Opera House, N.Y., Apr. 27 and 28, 1937, with William Dollar as the Joker; revived as *Poker Game* by Ballet Russe de Monte Carlo (1940) with Frederic Franklin as the Joker. A considerably revised version was presented by New York City Ballet, City Center, N.Y., Feb. 15, 1951, with Todd Bolender (the Joker), Janet Reed (Queen of Hearts). Stravinsky, an inveterate poker player, wrote the score and book to have a little balletic joke on the game. The ballet consists of a number of "hands" with the Joker upsetting the playing sequences by his unexpected appearances. See also JEU DE CARTES.

Cardus, Ana, ballerina of the Stuttgart Ballet, b. Mexico City, 1943. Had her initial dance training with Nelsy André and Serge Unger in Mexico City. First professional engagement was with Ballet Concierto de Mexico (1956–60). In 1960 Bronislava Nijinska, at the time ballet mistress of the Grand Ballet du Marquis de Cuevas, saw her in class and engaged her for the company. She danced a number of roles in the repertoire, among them the *Don Quixote* pas de deux with André Prokovsky. She later appeared in the well-known production of *The Sleeping Beauty,* dancing, at one time or another, different variations of the Fairies in the Prologue, and the *Blue Bird* pas de deux (with Georges Govilov and Garth Welch). John Cranko, director of ballet at the Wuertemberg State Opera in Stuttgart, saw her dance and invited her to join the Stuttgart Ballet, which she did in 1962, when the Marquis' company was dissolved. As ballerina she dances principal roles in *Romeo and Juliet* (Juliet), *Swan Lake* (Swan Queen), *The Sleeping Beauty* (Aurora), *Coppélia* (Swanilda), *Firebird* (title role), *Les Sylphides, Eugene Onegin* (Olga), all by Cranko; and *Allegro Brillante* by George Balanchine.

Carmagnole, a wild dance done in public places. It originated in 1789 when the French soldiers drove out the inhabitants of the town of Carmagnole, forcing them to dance. The Carmagnole was danced in the streets of Paris at the fall of the Bastille, and is the prototype of dancing in the streets in modern festivities. The Carmagnole consisted of a galop in the manner of a farandole in a chain. The Soviet ballet *Flames of Paris* (chor.: Vainonen; music: Asafiev) which deals with an episode in the French revolution of 1789 (i.e. when the Carmagnole was invented), includes an excitingly danced and sung Carmagnole.

Carmen. Ballet in 1 act, 5 scenes: chor.: Roland Petit; music: Georges Bizet (arr. from the opera); book based on the libretto of the opera by Henri Meilhac and Ludovic Halévy which, in turn, was inspired by the famous novel of Prosper Mérimée; décor: Antoni Clavé. First prod.: Ballets de Paris de Roland Petit, Prince's Theatre, London, Feb. 21, 1949, with Renée Jeanmaire (Carmen), Roland Petit (José), Serge Perrault (Escamillo). The ballet follows the lines of the opera: the cigarette maker, Carmen, seduces the young soldier, José, and, after leading him to theft and murder, throws him over for a matador. She is strangled by her lover outside the bull ring. The smoky colorings of Clavé's sets and the corset-shaped costume worn by Jeanmaire influenced ballet design for many years. Petit staged Carmen for The Royal Danish Ballet, Copenhagen, Jan. 15, 1960, with Kirsten Simone (Carmen), Flemming Flindt (José), Henning Kronstam (Escamillo). Ruth Page has staged her own version for Chicago Opera Ballet (1959).

Carnaval, Le. Ballet in 1 act; chor. and book: Michel Fokine; music: Robert Schumann's piano pieces of the same name, orch. by Alexander Glazounov, Nicholas Rimsky-Korsakov, Anatole Liadov, Alexander Tcherepnine; décor: Leon Bakst. First prod.: Pavlova Hall, St. Petersburg, for a special charity performance in Lent, 1910, with Tamara Karsavina (Columbine), Leonid Leontiev (Harlequin), Vera Fokina (Chiarina), Ludmila Schollar (Estrella), Bronislava Nijinska (Papillon), Alfred Bekefi (Pantalon), Vasily Kiselev (Florestan), Alexander Shiriaiev (Eusebius), Vsevolod Meyerhold, the famous actor and director (Pierrot). *Carnaval* had its first stage performance by the Diaghilev Ballets Russes on May 20, 1910, Teater des Westens, Berlin, when Tamara Karsavina and Vaslav Nijinsky were the Columbine and Harlequin, the latter becoming one of Nijinsky's most famous roles; Adolph Bolm was the Pierrot. The ballet has no other plot than the gay time a group of masked people are having at a masquerade. It is a delicate work of mood, not commedia dell'arte, the dancers being not characters from commedia dell'arte but guests at a charitable costume ball dressed as characters from commedia dell'arte. Choreographers staging or reviving *Carnaval* often forget this and ruin Fokine's masterpiece. Fokine himself revived it for the first season of Ballet (now American Ballet) Theatre (1940), when Bolm repeated his outstanding performance as Pierrot. Stanislas Idzikowski who succeeded Nijinsky as Harlequin in the Diaghilev company, also danced it during the early days of the Sadler's Wells (now Royal) Ballet. Many companies have had, or continue to have *Carnaval* in their repertoires. In 1963 Tamara Karsavina staged it for Western Theatre Ballet.

Carnival of Animals, orchestral suite composed by Camille Saint-Saëns. The best known movement of the suite is the cello solo, *Le Cygne,* the music used by Michel Fokine for the dance *The Dying Swan,* created by Anna Pavlova (1905). As a ballet, this suite (omitting *Le Cygne*) was given with choreography and décor by Andrée Howard by Ballet Rambert, Mercury Theatre, London, Mar. 26, 1943, with Elisabeth Schooling (Little Girl), Margaret Scott (The Hen), Olivia Sarel (Bantam), Robert Harrold (Personage with Long Ears), Michael Holmes and Nina Shelley (Tortoises), Iris Loraine (Lion), Marguerite Stewart (Kangaroo), Sylvia Hayden and Anne Ashley (Angela Dukes) (Aquarium), Sara Luzita (Cuckoo), Sally Gilmour (Girl with Birds).

Caron, Leslie, dancer, actress, b. Paris, 1931, of French-American parentage; m. English stage director Peter Hall. Her mother was the well-known musical comedy star of the 1920's, Margaret Petit. Leslie Caron studied dance with Jeanne Schwarz at the Paris Conservatoire. Made her debut with Les Ballets des Champs-Elysées (1948) and became an overnight sensation when David Lichine created for her the role of the Sphinx in *La Rencontre.* The same year she also created a leading role in Lichine's music-less, décor-less ballet, *La Création.* Gene Kelly saw her in *La Rencontre* and later engaged her as his leading lady and dance partner for the Academy Award–winning film *An American in Paris.* She went on to star in a number of films, the most notable being *Lili* and *Gigi.* Returned briefly to ballet with Ballets de Paris de Roland Petit, appearing in N.Y. for its 1954 season and dancing the Widow in *Deuil en 24 Heures.* Since 1956 she has mainly concentrated on straight acting roles on the English stage and in films, receiving an Academy Award nomination for her role in *The L-Shaped Room.*

Caroso, Fabritio (da Sermoneta), Florentine dancing master active in Paris ca. 1590. Author of a book, *Il Ballarino* (1581); another notable accomplishment was his *Ballo de Fiore.*

Carpenter, John Alden (1876–1951), American composer of the ballets *The Birthday of the Infanta* (Adolph Bolm, 1919), *Krazy Kat* (Bolm, 1920; Walter Camryn, 1948), *Skyscrapers* (chor. Robert Edmond Jones and Carpenter, assisted by Sammy Lee, 1920; Heinrich Kröller, 1929).

Carroll, Elisabeth (Elisabeth Pfister), American dancer, b. Paris, France, 1937; m. Felix Smith. Educated at a lycée in Paris; began dance training with Julie Sedova and Marika Besobrasova (Monte Carlo). Soloist with Monte Carlo Opera Ballet (1951–53); joined Ballet (now American Ballet) Theatre, Sept. 1954; promoted to soloist (1960); first soloist (1961). Her repertoire includes classic pas de deux (*Graduation Ball*), Prelude (*Les Sylphides*), Girl in Yellow and Romantic Couple (*Les Patineurs*), Bird (*Peter and the Wolf*), Page (*Bluebeard*), Soloist (*Grand Pas-Glazounov*), French Ballerina (*Gala Performance*), and others. She created leading female role in Dania Krupska's *Points on Jazz* (1961). Leading dancer with Hampton Arts Theatre group appearing at Brooklyn College, Lewisohn Stadium and Boston Arts Festival (1961). Joined Robert Joffrey Ballet (1962); Harkness Ballet (1964).

Carrousel de Louis XIV, an outdoor spectacle ballet given in Paris in 1662. Five hundred noblemen on horses took part. The very elaborate costumes were by Henri Gissey.

Carte Blanche. Ballet in 1 act; chor.: Walter Gore; commissioned music: John Addison; décor: Kenneth Rowell. First prod.: Sadler's Wells Theatre Ballet, Empire Theatre, Edinburgh, Sept. 10, 1953; London première, Sadler's Well's Theatre, Oct. 2, 1953, with Margaret Hill (Equestrienne), Pirmin Trecu (Tightrope Walker), Annette Page and Donald Britton (Trapeze Artists), Johaar Mosaval, Stanley Holden. A divertissement based on a series of lighthearted circus scenes.

Carter, Alan, British dancer, choreographer, teacher, ballet master and director, b. London, 1920. Studied with Seraphima Astafieva and Nicholas Legat. Soloist, Sadler's Wells (now Royal) Ballet (1938–40), creating one of the Gemini (*Horoscope*), M. Didelot (*The Prospect Before Us*), and the title role (*Harlequin in the Street*), etc., besides dancing a large repertoire. After service in World War II (1940–46) he returned to the newly-formed Sadler's Wells Theatre Ballet (1946–47), for which he choreographed his first ballet (and danced one of the lead roles), *The Catch,* and created Tramp Lover (Anthony Burke's *The Vagabonds,* 1946). Ballet master and dancer in the film *The Red Shoes* (1947); ballet master, films *Tales of Hoffmann, Invitation to the Dance,* and others (1951–53). Director and choreographer of Arts Council of Great Britain touring company, St. James's Ballet (1948–50). Ballet master and choreographer, Empire Theatre, London (1951–53). Ballet director and choreographer, Bayerische Staatsoper, Munich (1954–59), where he staged a number of works including versions of *The Miraculous Mandarin, Prince of the Pagodas,* and *Ondine.* Guest teacher, Royal Ballet (1962), for which company he choreographed *Toccata* (Bach). Appointed ballet director and resident choreographer of Wuppertal (Germany) Opera, beginning fall of 1964. Has done much television and film work, and in 1961 held an exhibition of his own choreography designs and sketches, with scores of ballets, etc., in the Theatre Art Museum, Munich.

Carter, Bill (William), American dancer, b. Durant, Okla. 1936. Studied dance with Coralane Duane and Carmalita Maracci. Joined American Ballet Theatre (1957–58), dancing First Sailor (*Fancy Free*), Variation (*Interplay*), First Cowboy (*Rodeo*), and others. Danced in musical *First Impressions* (1959); joined New York City Ballet same year; promoted to soloist (1961). His repertoire included Variation (*Interplay*), 4th movement (*Western Symphony*), Dream pas de deux (*Souvenirs*), Ragtime pas de deux with Diana Adams (*Jazz Concert*), 4th movement (*Symphony in C*), *Modern Jazz: Variants;* also created one of four male roles in *Liebeslieder Walzer* and Demetrius in *A Midsummer Night's Dream.* Gave four performances at the 1960 Casals Festival in Puerto Rico for which he choreographed his first work, *Bach Suite* (for unaccompanied cello). With Lois Bewley, Nadine Revene, and Charles Bennett organized the First Chamber Dance Quartet which made its debut Nov. 12, 1961, at the YM–YWHA, N.Y.

Carter, Carlu, Canadian dancer, b. Winnipeg; m. Bill McGrath. Studied at Canadian School of Ballet, Winnipeg, and joined Winnipeg (now Royal Winnipeg) Ballet (1946–51); then went to England to study at Sadler's Wells Ballet School. Joined Sadler's Wells Theatre Ballet (1951), dancing a London season, touring the U.S. and Canada, then returning to London for a further season. Her roles included Young Tregennis (*The Haunted Ballroom*), a Mirliton (*The Nutcracker*), one of the four Little Swans (*Swan Lake*). Rejoined Winnipeg Ballet (1952), creating the role of the Wife in *Shadow on the Prairie.* Was with this company until 1954 and again 1955–56. Has done extensive television work in Toronto with her husband. Currently working in television in Australia.

Carter, Jack, contemporary British dancer and choreographer, b. Shrivenham. Studied dance at Sadler's Wells School (1938), with Vera Volkova and Anna Severskaya (London), Olga Preobrajenska (Paris). Danced in Ballet Guild (1946), then with Original Ballet Russe, Ballet Rambert, London's Festival Ballet. Choreographed in Amsterdam (1954–57) where his best known ballet, *Witch Boy* (1956), was created for Ballet der Lage Landen. Other ballets include *Stagioni* (1950) for Ballet Workshop; *London Morning* (1959) and *Improvisations* (1962) for London's Festival Ballet (which also has mounted his *Witch Boy*); *Señora de Manara* for the Milorad Miskovitch company (1959), etc. Choreographer for the film, *The Life and Loves of Fanny Elssler* (1961). Staged full-length *Swan Lake* for Colón Theatre, Buenos Aires, premièred May 28, 1963, using the complete score as it was originally played for the 1877 Moscow creation. His *Les Invités* (Tchaikovsky's Suite in G), for the Janine Charrat company at the Geneva Opera House, Switzerland, was premièred June 10, 1963.

Carzou, Jean, French theatrical designer, b. 1907. First work for ballet was the Inca scene for *Les Indes Galantes* at the Paris Opéra (1952). His décor for Roland Petit's *Le Loup* (1953) is part of the history of ballet design, though his *Giselle,* for the Paris Opéra (1954) was received with considerable reserve.

Casado, Germinal, dancer, stage and costume designer, b. Casablanca, Morocco, 1934. Studied with Nina Leontieff, Nicholas Zverev, Victor Gsovsky, Asaf Messerer. Danced with the Wuppertaler Bühnen (Germany), Grand Ballet du Marquis de Cuevas. A member since 1957 of Maurice Béjart's Le Ballet Théâtre de Paris and Les Ballets du XXme Siècle, Brussels, where he is now a premier danseur, dancing both classic and demi-caractère roles. Among his stage and costume designs for ballet are *Fanfares, La Mégère Apprivoisée, Jeu de Cartes, Swan Lake, Tales of Hoffmann,* and others.

Cassandre, ballet given in Paris in 1651. Verses were by Bensserade. It was the first ballet in which Louis XIV appeared.

Cassandre, A. M., ballet designer, b. Kharkov, Russia, 1901, of French parentage. Began his career as a poster designer. His first success as stage designer was *Le Chevalier et la Damoiselle* at the Paris Opéra (1941), followed by *Dramma per Musica* (Serge Lifar-Bach) for Nouveau Ballet de Monte Carlo (1946). Other ballets designed by Cassandre are *Les Mirages* (Paris Opéra, 1947), *Coup de Feu* (Aurel Miloss, Grand Ballet du Marquis de Cuevas, 1951), *Chemin de Lumière* (Munich and Paris Operas, 1957). His geometrical style and perfect linear constructions are related to Renaissance architectural art.

Casse Noisette. See NUTCRACKER, THE.

Castanets, a percussion instrument used in the Spanish dance and occasionally in orchestras, consisting of a pair of concave pieces of wood which fit into the palm of the hand, tied together with a cord which passes over the dancer's thumb. The sound is made by clicking the two pieces of wood together. The left hand castanet has a deeper tone than the right hand and represents the male, the right hand castanet representing the female. See also THE SPANISH DANCE and LA ARGENTINA.

Castle, Irene and Vernon, famous exhibition ballroom dancers and teachers of the years preceding World War I. Vernon Castle, born Vernon Blyth in Norwich, England, came to the U.S. and made his debut as an actor (1907). Sometime later he met Irene Foote, a New Rochelle (N.Y.) debutante with stage ambitions. He helped her to get a part in *The Summer Widowers.* They were married in 1911 and, after preparing a number of ballroom dances, left for Paris where a year later their act became a great success at the Café de Paris. Their imaginative choreography and elegant style of dancing earned them a wide reputation in the U.S. and Europe. They popularized ballroom dancing in general and made famous a number of specific dances including the Maxixe, the Castle Walk, the Castle Polka, the Tango, the Hesitation Waltz. At the beginning of World War I Vernon Castle joined a British Air Force unit. After a serious crash he became a flying instructor in the U.S. While flying with a student pilot he was killed in a crash at Fort Worth, Tex., in 1918. Irene Castle discontinued her dancing career after her husband's death, but continued to act on the stage and in films. In 1924 she married Frederic McLaughlin, a Chicago businessman, who died in 1944. In 1946 she married George Einzinger, a Chicago advertising executive. A film based on the life of the Castles was made in 1939 with Fred Astaire and Ginger Rogers playing the stellar parts. The Castles were co-authors of a book on ballroom dancing entitled *The Modern Dance* (1914); Irene Castle herself wrote *My Husband* (1919) and *Castles in the Air* (1958).

Castor et Pollux, ballet with music by Jean Philippe Rameau given at the Académie Royale in 1772 with Gaetan Vestris as Apollo. It was in this ballet that Maximilien Gardel became the first dancer to remove the mask which dancers had always worn. He did it to make sure that the audience knew that he and not Vestris was dancing the role of Apollo. The plot concerned the mild exploits of the twin sons of Leda, who were the protectors of sailors. Antony Tudor staged a ballet under the same title for the Oxford Univ. Opera Club in 1934. In Jan., 1965, Thomas Scherman and his Concert Opera Association presented the U.S. première of *Castor et Pollux* as an opera-ballet at Philharmonic Hall, Lincoln Center, N.Y. Lupe Serrano and Scott Douglas of the American Ballet Theatre headed a ballet troupe of ten.

Castro, Juan José, Argentine composer and conductor, b. Buenos Aires, 1895. Won the Europa Grand Prix in 1914 and left for Europe where he worked for five years under Vincent d'Indy at the Schola Cantorum in Paris and studied piano with Eduardo Risler. Since 1929 he has been conducting nearly all ballet performances at Teatro Colón, where he premièred two of his ballet compositions: *Mekhano,* (1937), with choreography by Paul Petroff, and *Offenbachiana* (1940), with choreography by Margaret Wallman.

Catarina, ou La Fille du Bandit. Ballet in 3 acts, 5 scenes; chor., and book: Jules Perrot; Music: Cesare Pugni; décor: Charles Marshall. First prod.: Her Majesty's Theatre, London, March 3, 1846, with Lucile Grahn and Jules Perrot in principal parts; at La Scala, Milan, Jan. 9, 1847, with Fanny Elssler in the title role; in St. Petersburg Nov. 16, 1849, with Elssler. The ballet was supposedly based on an incident in the life of Salvatore Rosa, famous Italian painter (1615–1673), the role created by Louis Gosselin. It tells the rather confused story of a painter falling in love with Catarina, the leader of the bandits, who is also loved by her lieutenant Diavolino. After many adventures Catarina and Salvatore are united in a happy ending.

Categories of Movement, in ballet, movements are generally divided into seven categories: bending (plié), extending or stretching (développé), rising (élevé or relevé), sliding (glissé), jumping (sauté), darting (jeté or élancé), turning (tourné).

Caton, Edward (Frank), American dancer, teacher and choreographer, b. St. Petersburg, Russia, 1900, of American parentage. Educated at St. Philip de Neri Academy, Moscow. Studied ballet with Lydia Nelidova, Moscow, and at Agrippina Vaganova's private school in Petrograd. Member, Anna Pavlova company (1924–25); Chicago Civic Opera company (1926–29); first dancer, Chicago Opera Ballet (1930–33); Littlefield (later Philadelphia) Ballet (1936–38). Soloist, Mordkin Ballet (1938–39); Ballet Theatre (1940–42). Ballet master, Ballet Russe de Monte Carlo (1943); Ballet Theatre, Marquis de Cuevas Ballet International (1944), to which company he returned several times during the 1950's. His choreography includes *Iphigenia* (Littlefield Ballet); *Sebastian,* to music by Gian-Carlo Menotti (Ballet International, 1944); *Lola Montez* (Ballet for America, 1946), and several musicals. Ballet master, Metropolitan Opera Ballet (1945–46). As a dancer his principal roles included Prince (*Swan Lake*); Prince and Bluebird (*Sleeping Beauty*); Chieftan (*Prince Igor*); Colin, Alain, and Mother Simone (*La Fille Mal Gardée*), and others. At present devotes his time to teaching in the U.S. and Europe.

Cavallazzi, Malvina, Italian dancer. She was the first ballerina of the Metropolitan Opera House when it opened in 1883 and in 1909 came back to found the opera's ballet school. She received her professional training and education at the Teatro alla Scala ballet school in Milan, but spent most of her career in London, where she made her debut in 1879. She danced for a number of years in the ballets of Alhambra and Empire Theatres, usually en travesti, and followed in the succession of renowned ballerinas, among them Rita Sangalli, Emma Besonne, and Pierina Legnani. She was present at the debut and subsequent performances of Adeline Genée, with whom she became very friendly. Cavallazzi was followed in her American sojourn by Maria Giuri, Carlotta Brianza, and Pierina Legnani. In 1909 she was called by the Metropolitan to found the opera's ballet school. Among her pupils in her London school was the English ballerina Phyllis Bedells, who mentions her as a great dancer, famous mime, and excellent teacher in *My Dancing Days* (London, 1954). Malvina Cavallazzi retired in 1914 and died in Ravenna, Italy, in 1924.

Cave of the Heart. Modern dance work; chor.: Martha Graham; commissioned music: Samuel Barber; décor: Isamu Noguchi; costumes: Edythe Gilford. First prod.: Martha Graham Dance Company, Ziegfeld Theatre, N.Y., Feb. 27, 1947, with Martha Graham (Sorceress), Erick Hawkins (Adventurer), Yuriko (Victim), May O'Donnell (Chorus). This dance, commissioned by the Alice M. Ditson Fund of Columbia Univ., was first produced under the title *Serpent's Heart* (McMillin Theatre, N.Y., May 10, 1946), but was radically revised for its presentation as *Cave of the Heart.* The theme is the vengeance of Medea when deserted by Jason and the self-destruction brought about by hate. Like all the early Graham explorations into mythology, the legend itself is only the jumping off point, and *Cave of the Heart* is in no way a choreographic working of the story.

Cébron, Jean, French modern dancer, b. Paris, ca. 1938. He is the son of Mauricette Cébron, soloist (1911–36) and later teacher of the Paris Opéra. His dance education was rather eclectic: he studied ballet, modern, Hindu, Javanese, and other styles. He devoted two years to study at the Sigurd Leeder School, London, which specialized in the Jooss-Leeder technique. He made his debut in London in early 1956 at the Studio Group with a program which included the unaccompanied *Aquatic Vision, Ambiguous Monster* (to musique concrète), and *Horse.* He later

Jean Cébron, French modern dancer

gave recitals in Germany, England, and France, and joined the Jooss Folkwang-ballett for a short time. In the summer of 1957 he studied with Margaret Craske and made his American debut at the Jacob's Pillow Dance Festival with appreciable success. In the autumn of that year he joined Lotte Goslar's troupe for its U.S. and European tours. He returned to Jacob's Pillow in 1958, and again in 1961. That year he choreographed for the Hamburg Opera Ballet and the Jooss group. Currently he tours Europe and other parts of the Eastern Hemisphere with his recital programs. Despite his eclecticism and his apparent limited mastery of the disciplines he uses in his work, he has succeeded in developing a unique style of dance, which more often than not fascinates his spectators and critics. In 1964 Cébron returned to the Jooss Ballet (now called Folkwangballett of Essen) to dance the role of Death in *The Green Table,* the role which Kurt Jooss used to dance in the original cast of the ballet.

Cecchetti, Enrico (1850–1928), Italian dancer and ballet master, b. Rome, d. Milan. He was the son of dancers Cesare Cecchetti and Serafina Casagli, one of a family that produced many dancers. Cecchetti made his first stage appearance at five in *Il Giocatore* in Genoa, and a few years later was with the first Italian ballet company to tour U.S. He studied with Lepri, a pupil of Carlo Blasis, and Coppini. He made his debut at La Scala, Milan in *Gods of Valhalla* (1870), toured Europe as premier danseur, and made his London debut in 1885. He made his debut at the Maryinsky Theatre, St. Petersburg, in *The Tulip of Haarlem* (1887). He became second ballet master of the Imperial Theatre (1890), and instructor at the Imperial School (1892). Many Russian dancers of this time were influenced by Cecchetti and made brilliant technical progress, such as had not been evident in the Russian classrooms until that time. In his classes were such dancers as Pavlova, Preobrajenska, Egorova, Kchessinska, Karsavina, Nijinsky, etc. His success as a teacher was indisputable. However, he seemed to have no faculty for creating ballets; of the many which he choreographed at the Maryinsky, none was successful. Cecchetti resigned in 1902 and became ballet master at the Warsaw Government Ballet School, Warsaw, Poland. He left Poland for Italy (1905), but, dissatisfied with conditions there, he returned to Russia and opened a private school. Then he became the private instructor of Anna Pavlova and accompanied her on her world tour. He became the official instructor for the Diaghilev Ballets Russes (1909). Cecchetti and his wife opened a private school in London in 1918. Among his pupils were Massine, Bolm, Lopoukhova, de Valois, Danilova, Markova, Dolin, Lifar,

Enrico Cecchetti, photo by the late Anatole Burman (1920)

and many other famous dancers. He returned to Italy (1923) and became ballet master at Teatro alla Scala, Milan, (1925). In London the Cecchetti Society was formed (1922) at the instigation of C. W. Beaumont to perpetuate his method of teaching. This method emphasizes a definite program of strict routine in practicing the five positions, seven kinds of movements, etc. of classic ballet. The Cecchetti Society was incorporated into the Imperial Society of Teachers of Dancing (1924). He made the Italian style of dancing popular in England. In the U.S. the Cecchetti Council of America was established (1939) (see also TEACHERS ORGANIZATIONS, U.S.). Some of Cecchetti's roles were the Blue Bird and Carabosse in *The Sleeping Beauty,* the Chief Eunuch in *Schéhérazade,* the Charlatan in *Petrouchka,* all of which he created. His last public appearance was as the Charlatan, in Milan (1926).

Cecchetti Society, British teachers' organization formed in 1922 and incorporated into the Imperial Society of Teachers of Dancing (1924). See also CECCHETTI, ENRICO.

Celeste, Mme. (Celeste Keppler) (1811–82), French dancer. Came to the U.S. in 1827 and danced with great success in N.Y. and on tour; married Henry Elliott, a Baltimore businessman. Went to London in 1830 where she established an excellent reputation. She toured the U.S. again in 1834 when, on her appearance in Washington, D.C., President Jackson introduced her to members of the Congress. In 1835 she came back to the U.S., bringing with her a production of *La Sylphide.* She became the first ballerina to dance this ballet in America. She toured the European continent and danced long seasons in London. In 1843 she and Benjamin Webster, an outstanding English dancer of the time, leased the London Adelphi Theatre and presented there ballets and "ballet-burlesques" for some sixteen years. Retired from the stage (1874) and settled in Paris, her birthplace.

Celli, Vincenzo, contemporary Italian-born ballet teacher. He studied with Enrico Cecchetti and danced at the Teatro alla Scala, Milan in the 1920's. Currently teaches in N.Y.

Censorship, Dance. With the exception of pre-revolutionary Russia, there is no record of the existence of official and legal censorship of dance productions. In Imperial Russia, ballets were subject to the same kind of preliminary censorship as plays and operas. The plot of the ballet *Esmeralda,* for instance, was changed considerably by the "Censorship Committee" before the production was approved. In the U.S., church organizations object occasionally to the presentation of certain ballets. A case on record (Oct., 1946) is the demand of the Temple Baptist Church in Los Angeles (owners of the Philharmonic Auditorium) that *Frankie and Johnny* (Ballet Russe de Monte Carlo) and *Undertow* (Ballet Theatre) not be given in that city. In Sept., 1963, Representative Edna F. Kelly, a Congresswoman for Brooklyn, suggested that some form of censorship should be imposed on theatrical presentations sent abroad under the State Dept. Cultural Programs. This protest was lodged a year after she saw Martha Graham's *Phaedra* in Cologne. Her views had the support of Representative Peter J. Frelinghuysen (N.J.) who also saw the performance. Legislatively, nothing was accomplished, but the publicity stirred up great interest in Martha Graham's Broadway season which was scheduled shortly after the controversy.

Cent Baisers, Les. See HUNDRED KISSES, THE.

Center Practice, a group of exercises during a ballet lesson performed on the floor of the studio, away from the bar (compare with bar exercises).

Central Movements. See EUKINETICS.

Cerito, Fanny (also spelled Cerrito and Cerritto) (1817–1909), famous Italian ballerina of the Romantic period. She made her debut in her birthplace (Naples, 1832) and appeared with great success in Milan, Vienna, London, and Paris. Her most famous ballets were *Alma* (1842), *Ondine* (1843), *Gemma* (which she choreographed, 1854); also created *La Vivandière* (1844), and others. She participated in Perrot's famous *Pas de Quatre* (London, 1845) with Taglioni, Grisi, and Grahn. She was married to Arthur Saint-Léon, the great 19th century choreographer and dancer. She died in Paris just as the Diaghilev Ballets Russes was preparing to open the season which was to change the entire course of ballet history.

Chabrier, Alexis Emmanuel (1841–1894), French composer. His music has been used by several 20th century choreographers for their ballets, among them *Foyer de la Danse* (Adolph Bolm, 1927), *Cotillon* (George Balanchine, 1932), *Bar aux Folies-Bergère* (Ninette de Valois, 1934), *Bourrée Fantasque* (Balanchine, 1949), *Ballabile* (Roland Petit, 1950).

Chabukiani, Vakhtang, premier danseur and choreographer, Peoples' Artist of the USSR, b. Tbilisi, Georgia, 1910. Born into a worker's family, at nine he began making baskets and toys to help support his family. His entire life changed when he was sent to take a box of Christmas-tree toys to the ballet studio of Maria Perrini, the only one at that time in Tbilisi. He was allowed to stay and from that day the boy danced when and where he could. Soon Perrini took him as a scholarship pupil. In her studio he received a fairly firm foundation in Italian technique; however, a visit of the then celebrated Maryinsky dancers, Yelena Lukom and Boris Shavrov to Tbilisi convinced the young dancer that real art was to be found only in Leningrad. In the autumn of 1926 Chabukiani arrived penniless in Leningrad to find that he was much too old for the Choreographic Tekhnikum (form. the Maryinsky School). Despite the slightness of his preliminary training he was accepted for evening courses which were organized in 1923 by the same school to give a chance to talented youngsters older than the required ten to eleven years of age. Within two years Chabukiani was transferred to the regular daytime department and, in the three years he spent at the school he passed the entire syllabus of professional and general education. His exceptional physique, manliness, temperament, personality, and will-power helped him to achieve his goal, and in 1929 he was graduated into the Kirov Ballet. Within two years he had become its premier danseur and the country's greatest classical dancer. Chabukiani has played an outstanding role in the formation of the style of dance in Soviet ballet, introducing many new movements and new ways of execution, full of meaning and athletic energy. His soaring leaps and fast turns have become

Vakhtang Chabukiani, on his visit to New York in 1965, watches a class at the School of American Ballet, taught by André Eglevsky.

legendary. He danced his first *Swan Lake* in his first season at the Kirov, and in the second season (1930–31) danced Basil (*Don Quixote*) and the grand pas classique (*Raymonda*). He danced his first Albrecht (*Giselle*) in 1931. In 1932 he danced the Blue Bird (*The Sleeping Beauty*). Notwithstanding the perfection of his classic dancing, his greatest roles, each connected with an important landmark in Soviet ballet, were in new works: The Sportsman (*Golden Age,* 1931), Jerome (*Flames of Paris,* 1932), Vaclav (*Fountain of Bakhchisarai,* 1934), premier danseur (*Lost Illusions;* chor. Rostislav Zakharov; m.: Boris Asafiev, 1936), Kerim (*Partisan Days;* Vasili Vainonen-Asafiev, 1936–37); also two creations in his own ballets: Gardji in *The Heart of the Hills* (Alexei Balanchivadze, 1938) and Frondozo in *Laurencia* (1939). All these roles were important in the development of the heroic style of male dancing in Soviet ballet as a whole. At the beginning of World War II, Chabukiani moved to Tbilisi where he became principal choreographer, dancer, and teacher at the Paliashvili Theatre of Opera and Ballet. Here he has choreographed outstanding national ballets, dancing leading roles in most of them: *Sinatle* (Georgi Kilzade, 1947); *Gorda* (David Toradze, 1950); *Othello* (1957); *The Daemon,* after the Lermontov poem of the same name (Sulkhan Zinzadze, 1961). He has created his own versions of some of the classic ballets, including *Giselle,* the second act of which he taught to the American Ballet Theatre on its visit to Tbilisi (1960); also choreographed and danced in the Leningrad revival of *La Bayadère* (1947). Currently he still dances but choreographs roles for himself with an accent on acting. Has appeared in the film of his ballet *Othello;* also *Masters of the Georgian Ballet* and with Natalia Dudinskaya in the pas de deux from *La Bayadère,* and others. In 1934 Chabukiani, with Tatiana Vecheslova, toured the U.S. giving some thirty-odd performances, the first Soviet dancers ever to visit America. He came to the U.S. a second time in

Sept.-Oct. 1964 as head of the Soviet troupe Raduga (Rainbow). He danced the pas de deux from *Le Corsaire* (with Vera Tzignadze, ballerina of the Georgian Ballet) with great élan and had a well-deserved success. A detailed biography of the dancer, *Vakhtang Chabukiani* by Vera Krasovskaya, was published in Moscow (1956).

Chaconne, a dance in 3/4 time popular ca. 1750. It may be Spanish in origin, but some authorities consider it Italian, its name deriving from Ciaccono. The Dance of the Seises in the Seville Cathedral was said to be a form of 16th century Chaconne. In the late 19th century and the first decades of the 20th there was a European ballroom dance called Chaconne, which apparently had no connection with the older dances of this name. Chaconne was also the name of a musical composition (17th and 18th centuries) which was often used to conclude a ballet, and the dance done to this music was also called a chaconne.

Chaffee, George, contemporary dancer, teacher, collector, writer; b. Oakland, Calif. Studied with George Balanchine, Anatole Oboukhov, Pierre Vladimirov in the U.S.; with d'Alessandri, Lubov Egorova, Olga Preobrajenska, Victor Gsovsky in Paris; Stanislas Idzikowski in London; Mary Wigman in Dresden. Formerly soloist with Michel Fokine's Ballet, Mordkin Ballet, Ballet Russe de Monte Carlo. Chaffee has a famous collection of lithographs, drawings, painting, sculpture and books on the history and art of ballet embracing five centuries. Has contributed articles to *Dance Index, Dance Magazine, Dance News,* and the *Dance Encyclopedia.* In 1948, on the occasion of the first visit of the Paris Opéra Ballet to America, he arranged an exhibition on French court and opera ballet at the Cultural Division of the French Embassy in N.Y. The French Government awarded Chaffee the Palmes Académiques, a decoration which gave him the title Officier d'Académie. Currently teaches in N.Y.

Chagall, Marc, great Russian painter b. Vitebsk, Russia, 1887, now a citizen of France. His designs for the ballet stage include *Aleko* (1942), the Leonide Massine ballet to Tchaikovsky's Trio in A Minor (orchestrated) for Ballet Theatre; and for Adolph Bolm's version of *The Firebird* for the same company, commissioned by impresario S. Hurok. It was subsequently sold to the New York City Ballet and is now used with certain modifications in the costumes by that company and with choreography by George Balanchine. Chagall was awarded the Order of Légion d'Honneur by the French Government (1962). Created murals for the new Metropolitan Opera House at Lincoln Center for the Performing Arts (1966).

Chaîné, in ballet, a series of short, generally fast, turns done in a straight line, often on the diagonal, such as petits tours, déboulés, etc. See also MANÈGE.

Chalif, Louis H., U.S. ballet teacher, b. Odessa, Russia, 1876, d. N.Y. 1948. Was one of the child-dancers in the ballet *Excelsior* (with ballerina Virginia Zucchi) at the Odessa Municipal Theatre (1887). Studied at the ballet school connected with the Theatre under Alfred Bekefi and Ivan Savitsky, and later under Thomas Nijinsky, father of Vaslav and Bronislava. Was graduated in 1893 and became ballet master of the Theatre in 1897. Served in the Russian army (1899–1902). Became premier danseur in 1903, but left for the U.S. the following year and upon arrival was accepted into the Metropolitan Opera Ballet, with which he danced in the season of 1904–05 under Luigi Albertieri. In the summer of 1905 he was invited to teach at Teachers College of New York Univ. and from that time devoted himself entirely to teaching. In 1907 he opened the Chalif Russian Normal School of Dancing. He published five textbooks on dance technique (the first in 1914), as well as four folk dance books and countless descriptions of ballets and short dances, classical and character, complete with music. During his forty-three year career as teacher and director of his school, he furnished basic dance education to many hundreds of teachers throughout the U.S., Canada, the Latin-American countries and even Europe.

Chamié, Tatiana, Collection, an integral part of the Dance Collection of the New York Public Library, given to the Library in 1953 by the estate of Tatiana Chamié, in memory of the dancer and teacher. It documents the Ballet Russe era from the late Diaghilev period (1923–29) through that of René Blum and the beginning of Col. de Basil, ending with the American epoch of the Ballet Russe de Monte Carlo. Included are more than 600 photographs, 100 programs, clippings, letters, diaries, and other memorabilia that provide valuable information on the works created during the period, the dancers, and the activities of lesser companies, offshoots of the Ballet Russe.

Champion, Gower, dancer, choreographer, director, b. Geneva, Ill. Studied dance at school of Ernest Belcher in Los Angeles, Calif., where he met his future partner and wife Marge (Belcher) Champion. Began career in vaudeville, then teamed with his wife as a nightclub act. Opened at Persian Room, Hotel Plaza, N.Y., 1946, and subsequently danced in numerous nightclubs and hotel supper clubs throughout the U.S. They appeared as a team in Broadway musicals, among them *Streets of Paris* (1939), *Lady Comes Across* (1940), *Count Me In* (1941). He enlisted in U.S. Coast Guard for transport duty in World War II. Toured with the Coast Guard musical *Tars and Spars.* Made screen debut in *Till the Clouds Roll By* (1946), without his wife. In 1950 they were signed by Metro-Goldwyn-Mayer as a team and choreographers, appearing in *Showboat, Lovely to Look At, Everything I Have Is Yours, Give a Girl a Break, Three for the Show, Jupiter's Darling,* as featured artists or co-stars. Appeared frequently as a team in the "Dinah Shore Show," "Telephone Hour," and many other television shows. Co-starred on Broadway and on tour with his wife and Harry Belafonte in *Three For the Show* (1955). Directed television spectaculars (1958–60). Made debut as Broadway musical director-choreographer with *Bye Bye, Birdie* (1960), followed by *Carnival* (1961), *Hello, Dolly!* (1964). Received Tony Award as best director of the year for *Bye Bye, Birdie* (1961) and N.Y. Critics' Circle Award as best director and choreographer for *Carnival.* Director of film *Carnival* and *My Six Loves.* Appointed program adviser for the Theatre-Vision Corp., closed circuit Pay-TV, Hollywood (summer, 1963). Returned briefly to dancing as co-star with Gene Kelly in television spectacular called "New York, New York" (fall, 1965). Directed Jerome Chodorov's comedy, *Funny Game* (winter, 1965); directed musical *I Do! I Do!* (1966).

Champion, Marge (née Belcher), dancer, actress, choreographer, b. Los Angeles, Calif. Studied dance with her father, Ernest Belcher, in Los Angeles and later taught classes in his school. Began career with Los Angeles Light Opera Company as principal dancer and actress in *Blossom Time* and *The Student Prince;* on Broadway in *Dark of the Moon* and *Beggars' Holiday.* In 1946 joined Gower Champion in a nightclub act booked into the Persian Room of the Plaza Hotel, N.Y., as Marge and Gower Champion (they had married the day of the première). Thereafter played leading nightclubs and supper clubs in the U.S. until 1950, when team was signed by Metro-Goldwyn-Mayer as dancers, choreographers, and actors. Her film credits include featured and co-starring roles in

Showboat, Lovely to Look At, Everything I Have Is Yours, Give a Girl a Break, Three for the Show, Jupiter's Darling, Mr. Music. Co-starred (1955) with her husband and Harry Belafonte on tour and on Broadway in *Three for the Show.* In 1958 made television debut in a straight dramatic role in the G.E. Theatre telefilm production of *Mischief at Bandylegs.* Subsequently appeared with Gower Champion on the "Dinah Shore Show," "Telephone Hour," and other television programs. Toured summer theatres as star of *The Great Sebastians* (1960) and in *Invitation to a March* (1961).

Changement de Pieds, in ballet, a jump during which the dancer changes the position of feet. Technique: start 5th pos., R ft. front; demi-plié and jump into the air off both feet, in the air changing the feet to 1st pos.; land on both feet in 5th pos., L ft. front in demi-plié.

Chappell, Annette, dancer, b. Liverpool, England, 1929; m. Igor Barczinsky. Studied with Mona Clague locally, and with Judith Espinosa, Royal Academy of Dancing. Joined Ballet Rambert (1944); principal dancer (1945–49). Her repertoire included *Les Sylphides, Façade* (Polka), *Peter and the Wolf* (Bird), etc. Danced in musicals 1949–55. Ballerina of Munich Staatsoper (since 1955).

Chappell, William, English designer, former dancer, b. 1908. One of the early members of Ballet Rambert (when it was still the Ballet Club), he danced *Le Spectre de la Rose, Afternoon of a Faun* and many other roles in the repertoire of that time, including a number of creations. Created Elihu (*Job*) for Camargo Society (1931); with Vic-Wells (later Sadler's Wells, now Royal) Ballet he created Stranger Player (*The Haunted Ballroom*), Second Red Knight (*Checkmate*), etc., and danced many other roles. He designed décor and costumes for many ballets: *Capriole Suite, Lysistrata, Bar aux Folies-Bergère, Lady of Shalott,* etc., for Ballet Rambert; *Jackdaw and the Pigeons, The Wise and Foolish Virgins, The Jar* (all by Ninette de Valois), several versions of *Les Rendez-vous, Les Patineurs* (both by Frederick Ashton), *Giselle* and *Coppélia,* and others for Sadler's Wells Ballet; *Swan Lake* for International Ballet, etc. Wrote and illustrated *Studies in Ballet* (1948), *Margot Fonteyn* (1951). Currently director of plays and revues.

Character Dance, The. When people speak of the character dance within the framework of ballet they generally have in mind the study of folk dances of various nationalities. Actually, this is not correct. The study of the character dance is not and should not be quite so simple. Had it not been so, the character class would but resemble a simple rehearsal limited to the study and practice of ballet steps characteristic of various dances in national costumes. The authentic ethnic dance, i.e. the non-stylized dance, is outside the art form of ballet and can play only a subsidiary role as material for artistic development. Only in this sense does it have a definite value. The art of ballet cannot be carried into the domain of ethnic research. There is no place in ballet for naturalism and the authentic folk dance, not stylized and heightened to theatrical proportions, would cause only an impoverishment of the art form. The study of the character dance is the study of a special technique in ballet, a technique which is absent in the classic dance and which might be called the technique of syncopated accents. The study and practice of syncopated accents forces those muscles to work which take no part in the movements of the classic dance. Only the study of the character dance technique can bring them to life and develop them to the same degree as the muscles which participate in the movements of the classic dance. In addition, this study communicates to the dancer clarity of movement, sureness of gesture and, most important, a rhythmic feeling which forces the student and dancer to "live" in a musical rhythm. With the technique of the character dance at his command the dancer becomes master of the character dance, whether it be American folk dance, Jazz, Spanish, Russian, Italian, Hungarian, Polish, or any other.

Charisse, Cyd (Tula Ellice Finklea), American dancer, b. Amarillo, Tex., 1923. Studied dance with Adolph Bolm, Nico Charisse (her first husband), and Bronislava Nijinska. Made her debut with Col. de Basil's Ballet Russe (1939) under the name of Felia Sidorova. Her main career, however, has been in film musicals. Since 1946 she has had a long line of successes, among them *The Band Wagon, Singin' in the Rain, Brigadoon, Silk Stockings.* She danced the Widow in *Deuil en Vingt-quatre Heures* (called *A Merry Mourning*) in the film *Black Tights,* made from four ballets by Roland Petit (with *La Croqueuse de Diamants, Cyrano de Bergerac,* and *Carmen*), released in U.S. in 1962. During 1964–65 season toured very successfully in a nightclub act, sometimes with her husband, singer Tony Martin; also appears on television.

Charleston. See JITTERBUG.

Charnley, Michael, English dancer and choreographer, b. Manchester, 1927. Studied with Kurt Jooss. Danced with Sadler's Wells Ballet and Ballets Jooss (1943–47). Choreographer for Ballet Workshop (1951–52), Sunday Ballet Club, London's Festival Ballet, and musicals. Ballets include *Bagatelle* (1951), *Symphony for Fun* (1952), *Alice in Wonderland* (1953), *Hence in Solitude* (1960); musicals include *A Girl Called Jo* (1955), *The Ballad of Dr. Crippen* (1961).

Charrat, Janine, French ballerina, choreographer, director, b. Grenoble, 1924. Daughter of a Commandant Fireman. Her first teachers were Jeanne Ronay and Lubov Egorova. Was the child star of the famous motion picture *La Mort du Cygne* (1937), known in the U.S. as *Ballerina.* A child prodigy, she began her career as a choreographer at the age of fourteen, when she presented herself as a dancer in a program of her own works. Between 1940 and 1944, she gave concerts with Roland Petit in Paris, creating ballets for two (*Orfeo and Eurydice, Paul and Virginia,* etc.). Created *Jeu de Cartes* for Jean Babilée when Roland Petit's Ballets des Champs-Elysées was formed (1945). A ballerina with Nouveau Ballet de Monte Carlo (directed by Eugene Grünberg and Serge Lifar), 1946. Choreographed *Cressida* for this company and danced in *Romeo and Juliet, Passion,* and other Lifar ballets. Choreographer at Opéra Comique and Berlin Opera (1949), where her *Abraxas* (Werner Egk) was a big success. Formed her own company in 1951, choreographing *Le Massacre des Amazones, Herakles, Les Liens* and, her most important work, *Les Algues* (1953), in collaboration with producer Bertrand Castelli and in which she also danced the principal role with great dramatic force. Has toured with her company in Europe, U.S., and Japan. For other companies has choreographed *Adame Miroir,* to a libretto by Jean Gênet (Ballets de Paris de Roland Petit, 1948), *Joueur de Flute* (Colón Theatre, Buenos Aires). In 1959 was associated with Maurice Béjart in reorganizing the company of the Brussels Theatre de la Monnaie, staging and dancing in *Les Algues, Jeu de Cartes,* and creating the chief dancing role in Kurt Weill's *Seven Deadly Sins* (staged by Béjart, 1961). In Dec., 1961, while preparing a new repertoire for her company's second tour of the U.S. (*Zone Interdite, Champagne Party*), her career was interrupted

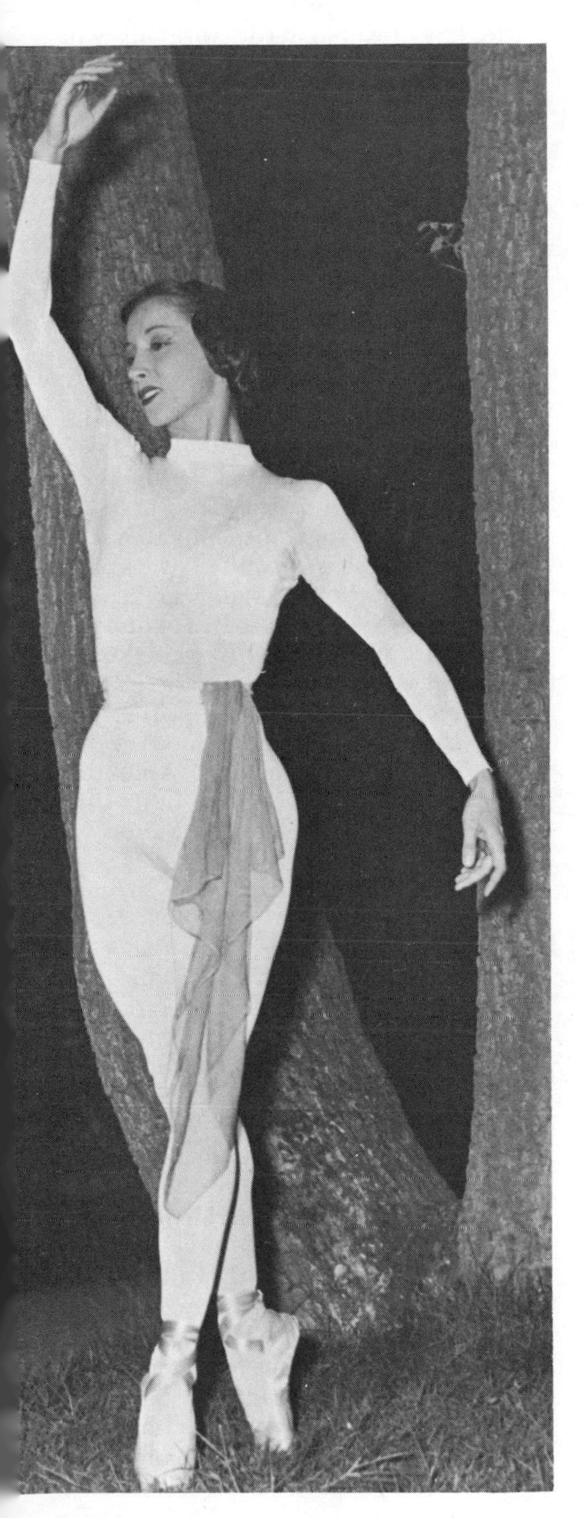

Janine Charrat, French dancer and choreographer

by a terrible accident in a television studio in Paris where she was rehearsing for a television appearance in *Les Algues.* Her dress caught fire and she was burned all over her body, except for her head and neck. On her recovery, she was appointed as director of ballet at Geneva Opéra (1962). As a dancer-choreographer Charrat returned to the stage in June, 1963, when she danced in her own ballet *Tristan and Isolde,* partnered by Viktor Rona, in Geneva.

Chase, Lucia (Mrs. Thomas Ewing), American dancer and ballet director, b. Waterbury, Conn., 1907. Received her Academic education at St. Margaret's School, Waterbury; professional education at the Theatre Guild School (acting), and with Mikhail Mordkin, Michel Fokine, Antony Tudor, Anatole Vilzak, and Bronislava Nijinska (ballet). Ballerina of Mordkin Ballet (1938 and 1939), dancing *Giselle, La Fille Mal Gardée, The Goldfish, Trepak,* and others. Founder-director of Ballet Theatre (1940–45); co-director with Oliver Smith of American Ballet Theatre (beginning 1945). Created following roles for that company: Girl in *Great American Goof;* Minerva in *Judgment of Paris;* The Greedy One in *Three Virgins and the Devil;* Nurse in *Romeo and Juliet;* Oldest Sister in *Pillar of Fire;* Queen in *Bluebeard;* Pallas Athena in *Helen of Troy;* Khivria in *Fair at Sorochinsk;* Innocent in *Tally-Ho; Dark Elegies;* for ten years danced the Step-Mother in *Fall River Legend.* She also danced Ballerina in *Petrouchka,* Prelude in *Les Sylphides,* Cerito in *Pas de Quatre.* In addition to being a most active co-director of the American Ballet Theatre and devoting substantially all her time to managing the affairs of the company, she has contributed a substantial part of her fortune

Lucia Chase, dancer and director of the American Ballet Theatre

to its upkeep without any thought of financial gain or artistic ambition.

Chassé, in ballet, a sliding step, or chasing step, in which one foot displaces the other as if by chasing it. Technique: start 5th pos., R ft. front; demi-plié on L, raising R ft. slightly off floor and stretching the R arch; bound lightly off L ft.; step forward on R half-toe and glide L ft. to 5th pos. in back. Chassé is also done to the side, to the back, and in various poses of the body.

Chatfield, Philip, English dancer, b. Easleigh, 1927; m. Rowena Jackson. Studied at Sadler's Wells School (1939–44), entering Sadler's Wells (now Royal) Ballet (1946) and becoming a principal dancer (1955). He danced all the leading classic roles, creating Titus in *A Mirror for Witches* (1952), the leading male role in *The Shadow* (1953), and was outstanding as the Fool (*The Lady and the Fool*), which he created for the Royal Ballet production (1955). Appeared on television in England, U.S., and Germany. Retired in 1959 to settle with his wife in her native New Zealand. Currently artistic director of United Ballet of New Zealand.

Chatte, La. Ballet in 1 act; chor.: George Balanchine; music: Henri Sauguet; book: Sobeka (Boris Kochno); décor: Naum Gabo and Antoine Pevsner. First prod.: Diaghilev Ballets Russes, Théâtre de Monte Carlo, Apr. 30, 1927, with Olga Spessivtzeva and Serge Lifar in principal roles. Subsequently the part of the Cat was danced by Alice Nikitina, and later by Alicia Markova. It is based on one of Aesop's fables. A Young Man falls in love with a Cat and prays to Aphrodite to change the animal into a girl. The goddess assents, the Cat becomes a Girl and the Young Man wins her affection. However Aphrodite puts the Girl's fidelity to a test: during the Young Man's and Girl's love-making the goddess sends a mouse scampering across the bridal chamber. The Girl forsakes her lover to pursue the mouse. Aphrodite changes the Girl back into a Cat to the distress of the Young Man, who dies.

Chausson, Ernest (1855–1899), French composer. His *Poème* (for violin and orchestra) was used by Antony Tudor for his ballet *Lilac Garden* (Jardin aux Lilas) staged by Ballet Rambert (1936), Ballet Theatre (1940), New York City Ballet (1951). Herbert Ross used his Suite for Violin, Piano and String Quartet for *Paean* (American Ballet Theatre Preview: May 27, 1957, and later taken into the company's repertoire). Chausson was killed in a bicycling accident.

Chauviré, Yvette, French ballerina, b. Paris, 1917. Studied at Paris Opéra School and with Boris Kniaseff. Was already one of the leading dancers of the Paris Opéra Ballet when she appeared as a star of the film *La Mort du Cygne* (1937), known in the U.S. as *Ballerina.* Nominated première danseuse étoile (1941) after her creation of the ballet *Istar,* having earlier danced important roles in Serge Lifar's *David Triomphant* and *Alexandre le Grand.* Became ballerina of Nouveau Ballet de Monte Carlo (directed by Eugène Grünberg and Lifar) in 1946, creating leading roles in *Dramma per Musica, Chota Rustaveli.* Returned to Paris Opéra the following year, while continuing to make guest appearances with other companies, including Ballet Russe de Monte Carlo in U.S. and London's Festival Ballet. Her last major creation at the Opéra was *Mirages* (1947), and her final creation as a regular member of the company was *La Dame aux Camèlias* (chor.: Tatiana Gsovska; music: Henri Sauguet) in 1959. Since that date she has made many guest appearances at the Opéra and also with the Berlin Opera (creating full-length *Romeo and Juliet* in a version by Gsovska, and dancing *Giselle* with Erik Bruhn), Royal Ballet (dancing *Giselle* and *The Sleeping Beauty*), giving concert performances in South America, and appearing in the Soviet Union with Youly Algaroff, where she had an immense success. Guest ballerina with Ballet International de la Marquese de Cuevas (formerly Ballet International du Marquis de Cuevas) in the fall of 1961, dancing *The Sleeping Beauty* and *Giselle* (with Rudolf Nureyev) during tours of Germany and Italy. In 1963 she was appointed director of the Paris Opéra Ballet School; also continues to give special guest appearances at the Opera. Her *Giselle* with Bruhn was another triumph for her in Feb., 1964. Known in Paris as "La Chauviré Nationale," she is one of the most delicate of French dancers, with a pure style and moving romantic feeling.

Yvette Chauviré, French ballerina as Juliet in Romeo and Juliet *at the Paris Opéra*

Chavez, Carlos, Mexican composer, b. 1899. His work for dance includes *H.P.* (Littlefield Ballet, 1932), *Dark Meadow* (Martha Graham, 1946), *Los Cuatro Soles* (José Limón, 1950). Some Chavez music not written expressly for dance has been used with good effect by several choreographers, among them by George Balanchine for part of the Pan-American Program presented by the New York City Ballet (1960).

Checkmate. Ballet in prologue and 1 scene; chor.: Ninette de Valois; commissioned music and book: Arthur Bliss; décor: E. McKnight Kauffer. First prod.: Vic-Wells (later Sadler's Wells, now Royal) Ballet, Théâtre des Champs-Elysées, Paris, June 15, 1937, with June Brae (Black Queen), Pamela May (Red Queen), Robert Helpmann (Red King), Harold Turner (Red Knight), and with Margot Fonteyn, Mary Honer, Frederick Ashton, Alan Carter, William Chappell, Richard Ellis, and Michael Somes also in the cast; London première: Sadler's Wells Theatre, Oct. 15, 1937. The Black Queen, which was June Brae's most successful role, was also a later triumph for Beryl Grey. A plot of love and intrigue is acted out as a game of chess played by Love and Death. The powerful Black Queen first captures the Red Queen, then defeats the Red Knight by simulating love for him, and finally drives the defenseless Red King to his death at the hands of her "army"—the black pawns, castles, and knights. The ballet has been staged also in Vienna and in Ankara, Turkey, by de Valois (1964).

Chesworth, John, English dancer, b. Manchester, 1930. Began training at Rambert School of Ballet (1950) after two years' service in the Royal Air Force. Graduated into the company (1952) where he is one of the leading dancers. His repertoire includes Prince (*Swan Lake,* Act 2), Host (*Laiderette*), 2nd Dance (*Dark Elegies*), Italian Ballerina's Cavalier (*Gala Performance*), Hilarion, (*Giselle*), Gurn (*La Sylphide*), Poet and Baron (*Night Shadow*), Lover and Man She Must Marry (*Lilac Garden*), Popular Song and Tango (*Façade*), etc. Created Elder Brother (*Two Brothers*), The Man (*Hazana*), Patriarch (*A Place in the Desert*), all ballets by Norman Morrice; also title role in Ballet Rambert's *Don Quixote.* He is especially good in ballets requiring genuine characterization.

Chevalier et la Damoiselle, Le. Ballet in 2 acts; chor.: Serge Lifar: commissioned music: Phillipe Gaubert; décor: A. M. Cassandre. First prod.: Paris Opéra Ballet, July 2, 1941, with Lifar and Solange Schwartz in the title roles; revived for the same company, Dec. 8, 1947, with Alexandre Kalioujny and Yvette Chauviré in the title roles. The plot, which stems from an old French legend, concerns a princess who at night is transformed into a hind. A knight-errant watches her at play one night. When she notices his presence she gores him with her antlers. In retaliation (or defense) he stabs her, whereupon she is turned back into a young girl. The knight falls in love with the girl and the girl with him, but at this crucial moment she faints and her squires carry her out. In the second act the princess, hoping to attract the knight, arranges a tournament. The knight, as expected, joins and eventually wins it and the princess. A divertissement in which knights and peasants alike take part concludes the ballet.

Chevtchenko, Tania. See KARINA, TANIA.

Chiarina. Grotesque ballet in 1 act; chor.: Jens Keith; commissioned music: Boris Blacher; book and décor: Paul Strecker. First prod.: Städtische Oper, Berlin, Jan. 22, 1950. The ballet is a burlesque of the daily life and doings of the guests in a spa called Chiarina. It is the third part of a ballet trilogy by the painter Paul Strecker (1898–1950) of which *Her First Ball* and *A Summer Day* are the other parts.

Chiaroscuro. Ballet in 1 act; chor.: Peter Darrell; music: Darius Milhaud's *Saudades do Brasil;* décor: Barry Kay. First prod.: Western Theatre Ballet, Ostend, Belgium, June, 1960, with Hazel Merry and Dennis Griffith. A series of dance impressions of light and shade in human character.

Chicago National Association of Dancing Masters. See TEACHERS' ORGANIZATIONS (U.S.).

Chicago Opera Ballet, a company organized in 1955 by Ruth Page, following the successful appearance of a group of dancers under her direction during the season of the Chicago Lyric Opera. For its opening Nov. 16 performance, Alicia Markova was guest artist in *The Merry Widow,* with Oleg Briansky as Prince Danilo; Vera Zorina also appeared as Venus in Monteverdi's masque *Il Ballo delle Ingrate.* On Nov. 26 the company presented *Revanche* (Revenge), based on Verdi's opera *Il Trovatore,* with Sonia Arova and Oleg Briansky. The troupe, then called Ruth Page Ballets, appeared Dec. 20–24, 1955, at the Broadway Theatre, N.Y., in a program consisting of *Revenge* and *The Merry Widow*. Markova, Arova, Briansky, and Ruth Ann Koesun headed the company. Since that time the company, under its present title, has appeared in Chicago and also toured the U.S. annually. In addition to the artists already mentioned, prominent guest artists both from other American companies and from Europe, have appeared with the company, including Josette Amiel, Melissa Hayden, Kirsten Simone, Maria Tallchief, Marjorie Tallchief, Flemming Flindt, John Kriza, Henning Kronstam, George Skibine, and others. Permanent members of the company include Patricia Klekovic, Ellen Gimpel, Dolores Lipinski, Kenneth Johnson and Orrin Kayan. The repertoire consists for the most part of ballets choreographed by Ruth Page, many of them based on well-known operas, including *Camille, Die Fledermaus,* and *Carmen* (in addition to those already mentioned). Skibine's *Idylle* and Ruth Page's *Concertino pour Trois* (Marius Constant) are also in the current repertoire. Chicago Opera Ballet's performance at Brooklyn Academy of Music, Mar. 10, 1962, was the occasion of Rudolph Nureyev's U.S. debut (apart from a single television performance). As special guest artist, he danced the *Don Quixote* pas de deux with Sonia Arova. The same two dancers were also guest artists in *The Polovetzian Dances from Prince Igor,* especially staged by Ruth Page when the complete opera opened the 1962 Lyric Opera season in Chicago (Oct. 12). They also danced *Le Corsaire* pas de deux, *Flower Festival at Genzano* pas de deux, and the leading roles in *The Merry Widow* at a gala performance of the ballet on Oct. 21. In addition to its performances under its own name, the company supplies dancers for the opera-ballets which Ruth Page stages during the annual Chicago opera season. Because the company's repertoire is gradually changing from opera-inspired works to ballets on a variety of subjects, the name of the company was changed to Ruth Page's International Ballet, beginning with the 1966–67 season. This name was being used for the ballet's touring season; however, appearances of the company in the Chicago Opera season are under the previous name.

Chilean National Ballet, Santiago, Chile, is an outgrowth of the little company Ernst Uthoff and his wife Lola Botka, both soloists of the Jooss Ballet, organized in connection with their school which they had opened in Santiago in 1942. This was the year that the Jooss Ballet made its long tour of Central and South America. After the completion of the tour Kurt Jooss, the company's director, announced that the company would return to England after the N.Y. season and said that those who so desired might remain in the Western Hemisphere. The Uthoffs decided to remain in Santiago. After a few years the school and the little company had grown to such an extent that the government of Chile agreed to accept the company and the school under its sponsorship, and they became a part of Instituto de Extensión Musical of the Univ. of Chile. Uthoff is the principal choreographer and he and Botka are assisted in the school by Rudolf Pescht, another former soloist of the Jooss Ballet. Kurt Jooss visited Santiago in 1948 and staged for the Chilean National Ballet *The Green Table, The Big City, A Ball In Old Vienna,* and *Pavane.* Columbia Artists Management, which booked the Jooss Ballet in the U.S. on its initial tour in 1933 and later, booked the Chilean National Ballet for the 1964–65 season. Mr. and Mrs. Uthoff resigned in 1966.

Chinese Nightingale. Ballet in 4 scenes; chor.: Tatiana Gsovska; music and book: Werner Egk; décor: Helmut Jürgens; costumes: Rosemarie Jakameit. First prod.: May 7, 1953, at the Deutsches Museum, Munich, with Nika Nilanova-Sanftleben

(Nightingale), Natascha Trofimova (Artificial Nightingale), and Dmitry Cheremetev (Little Emperor). The story is based on the famous fairy tale by Hans Christian Andersen of the Emperor who lies sick unto death and can only be consoled by the song of the nightingale which he hears outside the palace. His advisers bring him an artificial nightingale, hoping it will distract him, but he quickly tires of it and, only when the real nightingale is captured and brought to him in a cage, does he begin to grow well. But he realizes that the bird can only pine and die in captivity and he sets her free.

Chiriaeff, Ludmilla, artistic director, Les Grands Ballets Canadiens, b. Riga, Latvia, 1924. Ludmilla Chiriaeff's family established itself in Berlin after the Russian Revolution. Her father, Serge Corny, was a well-known writer. In Berlin she studied dance with Alexandra Nicolaieva, a former member of the Moscow Imperial Ballet. In 1936–37 she danced with Col. de Basil's Ballets Russes and continued her studies under Michel Fokine, Leonide Massine, and others. In 1939 she joined the Berlin Opera Ballet, becoming a soloist and also dancing in operettas and films. World War II interrupted her career. She went to Switzerland at its end and was engaged as première danseuse, choreographer and ballet mistress at the Lausanne Theatre, opening her own school in Geneva (1948). Shortly afterwards she formed her own company, Les Ballets des Arts. She arrived in Montreal in Jan., 1952, and was soon invited to create ballets for Radio-Canada Television, in conjunction with television producer Jean Boisvert. This led to the formation of a company originally called Les Ballets Chiriaeff which gave its first stage performance in 1955 and which, after its successful engagement for the Montreal Festival in 1956, assumed its present name of Les Grands Ballets Canadiens. Ludmilla Chiriaeff has choreographed many ballets, both for her company and specifically for television. Her company ballets include *Etude, Nonagone, Le Concert Royal, Jeu de Cartes, Les Noces,* and others.

Ludmilla Chiriaeff, artistic director, Les Grands Ballets Canadiens

Chirico, Giorgio, di, painter and stage designer, b. Greece, 1888, of Italian parentage. He came to Paris in 1911 and soon found his niche among the avant-garde artists of the period. Rolf de Maré, director of Ballets Suédois, invited him to design the décor for the ballet *La Jarre* (1924), based on a story by Luigi Pirandello, to music by Alfredo Casella, choreographed by Jean Börlin. In 1929 he designed the décor for George Balanchine's *Le Bal* for the Diaghilev Ballets Russes. Subsequently he designed *Pulcinella* (for the Russian Opera Company, Paris, 1930); *Les Bacchantes* and *Bacchus et Ariane* (Paris Opéra, 1938); *Protée* (Col. de Basil's Ballet Russe de Monte Carlo, 1938); *The Legend of Joseph* (Teatro alla Scala, Milan, 1951); *Don Quixote* (Maggio Musicale Fiorentino, 1953).

Chladek, Rosalia, Austrian modern dancer, choreographer, teacher, and since 1952 Chief of Dance Department of the Academy of Music and Dramatic Art, Vienna, b. Brno, Moravia, 1905. Her general

Rosalia Chladek in Women of Trachis

education includes five years gymnasium (high school) and four years women's college; professional education includes "Schule für Rhythmus, Musik und Körperbildung" (School for Rhythm, Music and Physical Education) at Hellerau, near Dresden, Germany, formerly the Dalcroze School (1921–24). Awarded 2nd Prize at the First International Dance Competition for Choreographers, Paris (1932); 2nd Prize at the First International Dance Competition for Solo Dancers, Warsaw (1933). Made her tripartite debut in 1924 as teacher at the Hellerau-Laxenburg School and soloist and choreographer of the Valerie Kratina Dance Group. Her educational activities include Artistic Direction of the Hellerau-Laxenburg School (1930–38), for which she developed her own educational system for modern dance; direction of the training school, "Tanz für Bühne und Lehrfach" (Dance for Stage and as a subject of Study), Vienna Municipal Conservatory (1942–52). Her choreographic activities include a great many works for the stage for her own dance group (1950–59); for festivals in Austria (1947–51) and Greece (1948–52); in opera, musical comedy, motion pictures, and television (1953–61). Her honors include the title Professor, awarded by the Federal President of Austria in consideration of her artistic and pedagogical achievements (1936); Österreichisches Ehrenkreuz für Wissenschaft und Kunst I. Klasse (Austrian Honor Cross for Scholarship and Art, 1st Class, 1960). Professor Chladek was Austrian representative at the International Arts Program, U.S. (1950).

Chopin Concerto. Ballet in 3 movements; chor.: Bronislava Nijinska; music: Frédéric Chopin's Concerto for Piano and Orchestra in E minor; costumes: Alexander Ignatiev. First prod.: Ballet Russe de Monte Carlo, N.Y., Oct. 12, 1942, with Alexandra Danilova, Nathalie Krassovska, Igor Youskevitch, Frederic Franklin, Roland Guerard in leading parts. The ballet was originally presented by the Polish Ballet at the International Exposition, Paris (1937). The ballet has no definite plot, but reflects the mood of the music.

Chopin, Frédéric François (1810–1849), Polish composer of numerous mazurkas, waltzes, preludes, polonaises. His music was used for the ballet *Les Sylphides* (Michel Fokine, 1909), first presented under the title *Chopiniana* (1908). Chopin's music was used for *Autumn Leaves* (Anna Pavlova, 1918); his Concerto in E minor for piano and orchestra was used for a ballet by Bronislava Nijinska (1937); and his Concerto in F minor for *Constantia* (William Dollar, 1944).

Chopiniana. Original title of Michel Fokine's ballet now known as *Les Sylphides* (which see). *Chopiniana* is also the title of this ballet in the Soviet Union and in Denmark.

Choreartium. Ballet in 4 movements; chor.: Leonide Massine; music: Johannes

Brahms' Symphony No. 4 in E minor; décor: Constantine Terechkovich and Eugene Lourie. First prod.: Col. de Basil's Ballet Russe, Alhambra Theatre, London, Oct. 24, 1933, with Irina Baronova, Alexandra Danilova, Tatiana Riabouchinska, Nina Verchinina, Vera Zorina, Roman Jasinski, David Lichine, Paul Petroff, Yurek Shabelevski. *Choreartium* was Massine's second symphonic ballet, the first being *Les Présages.* Nina Verchinina was especially impressive in her role in the Second Movement. Unlike *Les Présages* which preceded it and *Symphonie Fantastique* which followed it, *Choreartium* is completely dictated by the music and has no program.

Choregraphy, old form of the word choreography (which see). It derives from the French root choré rather than the Greek choreo, its justification being that all dance terms are in French.

Choreographer, a composer of dances and ballets; the author of the choreography of a ballet, modern dance, dances in shows, etc. In Russian and French literature a choreographer is often called a ballet master, or maître de ballet. In American and English usage a ballet master is a person in charge of the dancers and ballets in a company, whose duty it is to rehearse ballets, assign roles and, usually, give classes to the dancers. In the Diaghilev Ballets Russes and later in the Ballet Russe de Monte Carlo, the person exercising the duties of ballet master was called regisseur-general. It happens quite often that a choreographer is also ballet master of a company, but the two titles should not be confused, as a ballet master is not necessarily a choreographer. Towards the end of 1963 George Balanchine, artistic director of the New York City Ballet, had decided that he preferred to use the title ballet master rather than artistic director (actually his post in the company). He continues, however, to sign his ballets as choreographer.

Choreographers' Workshop, a nonprofit cooperative organization which functioned in New York between 1946 and 1954. It was founded by Trudy Goth and a small group of dancers for the purpose of providing a means for young, untried choreographers to create experimental dance works using professional dancers as far as possible. Between Nov. 3, 1946 when the first program was presented at the Studio Theatre, N.Y., and Apr. 17, 1954 when its final program was given at Central High School of Needle Trades, Choreographers' Workshop offered two or three performances a season. Each choreographer paid the cost of costumes and scenery (if any) for his own dance work; theatre rental and cost of programs were covered by the sale of tickets, and any profit was divided among the participants. Herbert Ross's first ballet, *Caprichos* (1950), was premièred at the Workshop, as was Robert Joffrey's *Persephone* (1952). Other notable premières were Valerie Bettis' *As I Lay Dying* (1948) and Janet Collins's *Eine Kleine Nachtmusik,* to the Mozart score (1949). Other choreographers who at various times presented new works were Tally Beatty, Tony Charmoli (who became a well-known television choreographer), Jean Erdman, Nina Fonaroff, Louis Johnson, Pauline Koner, Gertrude Lippincott, Iris Mabry, Alwin Nikolais, Marion Scott, Glen Tetley and others. In addition to its creative sponsorship of new works, Choreographers' Workshop also presented programs in collaboration with the Art Students League of N.Y. City, the National Jewish Music Festival, the Dance Series both of Henry Street Settlement Playhouse and Brooklyn Museum of Art, Living Theatre, Inc. It presented a Bach Festival, Dec. 16, 1950, and in April 1951 a group of dancers and choreographers headed by Trudy Goth gave a number of performances in Bermuda under the sponsorship of the Bermuda Arts Festival. A Workshop group appeared at Jacob's Pillow in 1952.

Choreography. 1. The art of composing dances; the science of putting together steps to form a dance and separate dances to form a dance composition or ballet. "In the time of its invention as a dance term (ca. 1700) it meant the notation or stenographic record of dance steps (which is now called dance notation). By corruption and association it has come to signify the design by a dance composer of dance patterns which comprise ballets. It is the most important division of stage-dancing, since it regulates all that the dancers do. Its science is difficult to acquire and its practice, rare. There may be a hundred good dancers to a generation, and but half a dozen choreographers." (Lincoln Kirstein, in *Ballet Alphabet*). 2. All the dances in a ballet or some other dance production; the dance composition as a whole.

Choreography, Notes on.

BY GEORGE BALANCHINE.

We must first realize that dancing is an important independent art, not merely a secondary, accompanying one. I believe that dancing is one of the great arts. Like the music of great musicians, it can be enjoyed and understood without any verbal introduction or explanation.

Nowadays, at concerts of the greatest philharmonic orchestras in the world, the receptivity of the audience is so low that they have to be provided with little stories explaining the action. I have seen row upon row of listeners at a concert following the "plot" in their programs while a symphony is being played: a note on the bassoon—the entrance of the villain; drums—a thunder storm is coming. And at the ballets, some of which, unlike the symphonies, actually cannot be understood without program notes, the audience is constantly referring to the libretto to learn that the two women on the stage are mother and daughter and that the gentleman who enters is the brother-in-law of one of them.

In the times of Saint-Léon and Petipa the things in a ballet which could not be conveyed in simple dance movements were told in pantomime. However, this elaborate art is almost completely neglected now, and has been increasingly replaced by written "plots."

The important thing in ballet is the movement itself, as sound is important in a symphony. A ballet may contain a story, but the visual spectacle, not the story, is the essential element. The choreographer and the dancer must remember that they reach the audience through the eye; the audience, in its turn, must train itself actually to see what is performed upon the stage. It is the illusion created which convinces the audience, much as it is with the work of a magician. If the illusion fails, the ballet fails, no matter how explicit the program note.

Everything cannot be conveyed by ballet, only those things which can be shown on the stage. Dance is not as inclusive an art as literature. Many things, however, can be shown or implied by the simple means of entrances, exits, solo dances, pas de deux, or group movements. Moreover, as in music, the audience should be able to enjoy the movement regardless of the story.

The dance proves that movement is important in itself, for though the other visual arts, such as painting and architecture, are stationary, dance is continually in motion and any single position of a ballet is before the audience's eye for only a fleeting moment.

Perhaps the eye does not see motion, but only these stationary positions, like single frames in a cinema film; memory combines each new image and the ballet is created by the relation of each of these positions, or movements, to those which precede and follow it. This accounts for the fact that action photographs of performances of many ballets have little impact because they catch only attitudes, the flavor and meaning of which depend on the context of a steady progression.

When every emphasis in a ballet is placed on movement it is obvious that a still photograph cannot catch the feeling of it. (It is possible sometimes, however, to succeed by arranging dancers for posed studio photographs.)

The majority of the public may want to relax and make no effort when they go to the theater, but all art requires a certain amount of effort on the part of the audience. To enjoy a ballet of any value necessitates concentration comparable to that necessary for reading a book of value.

Every normal person possesses a certain ability to see, but he often does not make any effort to do so. Some people see more than others, not because they have sharper vision, but because they want to see as much as possible and make the required effort. When someone stares fixedly at a point, his mind is usually wandering and his visual intensity is weakened.

The spectator must be willing to assimilate what is shown on the stage, and possibly to be disturbed by it (for the ballet has spiritual and metaphysical elements, not merely physical ones). He must also retain in his memory the preceding movements which will give significance to the ones that are being performed and the ones which are to follow.

Choreographic movement, used to produce visual sensations, is quite different from the practical movement of everyday life used to execute a task: to walk, to lift an object, to sit down. Choreographic movement is an end in itself, and its only purpose is to create the impression of intensity and beauty. No one intends to produce beautiful movements when rolling barrels or handling trains or elevators. In all these movements, however, there are important visual dynamics if one will look for them.

Choreographic movements are the basic movements which underlie all gesture and action and the choreographer must train himself to discover them. It is necessary for the choreographer to see things which other people do not notice, even though they are before their eyes, and to cultivate his visual sense (it amazes me, for instance, that some people never notice the tops of buildings).

It is natural that these basic movements will at first seem affected and artificial to the body which is accustomed only to the practical movements of everyday life. The object of the dancer's technical training is to enable him to perform with perfect ease choreographic movements unlimited by considerations of practical, daily life.

Without a technical background dancing can only be improvisation. You want to please yourself and others by expressing something, but you don't know how. I often think how wonderfully I could play a certain violin concerto, with what feeling and expression—only, unfortunately, I do not play the violin!

All ballet positions and movements are based on two principles: the horizontal alignment of each movement in space, and the vertical balance of the human figure. The alignment is an invisible horizontal line on which the dance is built; it extends unbroken from the point where the dance begins to where it ends. Upon it the movements of the dancers exist, as upon a thread a string of pearls is held.

The vertical balance of the human figure is the basis of the positions from which every ballet movement originates and in which every ballet movement ends. In the five initial positions the body is balanced on both feet. When a movement is begun with one foot from one of these positions, the body remains balanced on the second, supporting foot, erect, as though an invisible vertical line were drawn from the dancer's head to the floor.

The choreographer frees his mind from the limitations of practical time in much the same way that the dancer has freed his body. He turns, not away from life, but to its source. He uses his technical proficiency to express in movement his essential knowledge.

Talent, inspiration, and personality are not sources which come to an artist in a flash and vanish. They are the accumulated results of all he has felt, thought, seen, and done—the stories he has heard as a child, the art he has enjoyed, his education, and his everyday life—and are always with him, capable of being reached by his technical ability and transformed into dynamic designs of the utmost intensity.

If movement is the main, perhaps the only, means of presenting the art of dancing in its full significance, it is easy to understand the importance of connecting movements one to the other with subtle care, yet at the same time emphasizing by contrast their continuity. For example, very quick, small movements to a fast or slow tempo, in every angle or degree of angle, are developed in relation to following broad, large movements in the identical tempo, and increased from their use by one dancer to their use by many dancers.

A kaleidoscope of such movements lives within the choreographer's brain, not yet, of course, set to any tempo. They are as yet only memories of form. In addition to these memories, the elements of silence, placidity, and immobility are powerful forces, as impressive as rage, delirium, or ecstasy—perhaps even more so.

When the body remains transfixed and immobile, every part of it should be invisibly tense, and even in relaxation there should be an inner muscular control.

The steps which a dancer has learned (after he has studied about ten years with good teachers he should have an impressive vocabulary of movements) are individually devoid of meaning, but they acquire significance when they are coordinated in time and space as parts of a continual, rhythmic flow of the whole.

The student choreographer should at first work out simple technical exercises: for example, fitting eight bars of movement to eight bars of music. Many different interpretations may be given to music, since there is no single meaning behind it which the listener may discover. The choreographic student can fit any number of combinations of movements to the same eight bars of music. On the other hand, he can fit the same combinations of movements to several different pieces of music; or he can fit bars of movement to silence, which has a tempo of its own. If he uses music, however, he must be sure to fit the movements to it completely.

There is a lot of talk about counterpoint in dancing. It is generally believed that counterpoint is based on contrasts. Actually, counterpoint is an accompaniment to a main theme which it serves to enhance, but from whose unity it must not detract.

The only kind of counterpoint that I can see in dancing are the movements of the arms, head, and feet, contrapuntal to the static or vertical position of the body. For instance, in the croisé position the body is vertical, but one arm is raised and the other is horizontal; one foot points forward while the other supports the body; the head is inclined towards one of the shoulders. All this is an accompaniment to the main theme, which is the vertical position of the body.

In dancing one should not strive to achieve counterpoint by contrasting the movements of two dancers or two groups of dancers on the stage. This results not in counterpoint, but in disunity (there is no need to apply musical terms to the dance, but if it is done their meaning must be clearly understood).

The eye can focus perfectly only on objects which are in the center of its field of vision. Those objects which are not head-on are seen clearly only because the observer knows and imagines what they are, while he focuses on the center object.

If some new or different form is placed in the secondary part of a composition, the eye instinctively changes its focus and recognizes the identity of each individual form. And as vision is the channel through which the art of choreography reaches its audience, this inevitably results in confusion, and a loss of attention to the main theme. But the eye can follow the movements of a large group of dancers if these form a harmonious pattern within its central field of vision.

There is very little written about the history and science of choreography. Material on the subject is contained in the following: "Jules Perrot," by Yury Slonimsky, trans. by Anatole Chujoy, *Dance Index,* Dec., 1945; "Marius Petipa," by Yury Slonimsky, trans. by Anatole Chujoy, *Dance Index,* May–June, 1947; "Writings on Lev Ivanov," by Yury Slonimsky, trans. and ed. with annotations by Anatole Chujoy, *Dance Perspectives,* No. 2, Spring, 1959.

Choreutics.

BY ANGIOLA SARTORIO.

Choreutics is the analysis of form in movements. It is a system evolved by Rudolf von Laban (1879–1958) after profound study and exhaustive research. It is not a personal style of a specific dancer, but an impersonal system based on the laws of harmony in space and the laws of movement. As such it touches on the laws of mathematics and philosophy. It applies to all styles of dance.

Choreutics concerns itself with two basic conceptions: space and the dancer. The changing relation of the dancer to space constitutes what is called movement. The twofold movement—incoming and outgoing—is the basis of all existing movement. Actually there is no other movement, for everything else is a variation of these two.

The form of continuous movement is the figure eight. According to Laban this figure is found in the dancing of all races. Laban takes this figure eight and swings it around in three directions: vertical, horizontal, and lateral. In this manner he develops a series of six swings (two in each direction), which are the fundamentals of his future scales.

Each of these swings possesses a typical characteristic, such as lightness or heaviness (strength), narrowness or width (space), swiftness or slowness (speed). These six swings also contain the seeds of the six important types of dance: ballet, modern, primitive, Oriental, Spanish, and the flowing interpretive form.

Laban also developed a scale of movement higher in tension and lighter than the normal six swings. This is based on the inversion of the six swings and is the scale of the high dancer. Many movements in the ballet are similar to these. There exists also a scale lower than the normal six swings, based on the movements of the Dervish dancers, called the Dervish swings.

Laban also developed two more complex scales, called the major and minor, or the active and passive scales. These complement each other in much the same manner as do the major and minor scales in music. Done together and opposite each other they form a sphere. They are based on the twelve directions in space. These directions are inclinations in space, deviations from the true vertical and horizontal. They stay the same wherever they are located and whatever their length and may be compared to the twelve tones of the chromatic scale in music. These tones constitute a certain unchanging vibration regardless of their pitch. Actually, there are many more tones; Hindu music, for example, employs many more tones than the traditional twelve to which the Western scale is confined. This same tonal concept could be applied to dance movement, and we would find that almost all movement fits into these twelve directions plus the pure vertical, horizontal, and lateral movements. It is on this idea that Laban based his system of dance notation.

The twelve directions of movement are based on a fusion of the three directions and the four diagonals of space. The latter are diagonals drawn from the different points of the icosahedron, the crystal form which is nearest to the sphere. And it is in the sphere, the most perfect of forms, that all movement takes place.

The importance of choreutics has not yet been fully realized. It is a forerunner of a trend which will deal less with personalities and more with ideas and currents of force. Choreutics develops a consciousness of space in the dancer and leads the choreographer to consider each dancer, not as an individual and separate entity, but as a single form or member of a group, moving in currents of space. (See also EUKINETICS.)

Chorus Boy or Girl, a member of the dancing or singing ensemble of a musical comedy or revue. These terms have given way in recent years to just dancers and singers, or ensemble.

Chota Rustaveli. Ballet in 4 acts; chor.: Serge Lifar; music: Arthur Honegger, Alexander Tcherepnine and Tibor Harsanyi, each composer being responsible for a different section of the completed work; décor: Chervachidze and Constantine Nepo. First prod.: Nouveau Ballet de Monte Carlo, Monte Carlo, May 5, 1946, with Yvette Chauviré, Sirène Adjemova, Alexander Kalioujny, and Lifar. Based on a Georgian (Caucasian) folk tale by Rustaveli, *A Hero in a Leopard's Skin,* this work has a certain historic interest as being a very early example in contemporary ballet of a full-evening work created outside the Soviet Union. It was also the ballet which first brought Kalioujny into prominence.

Chouteau, Yvonne, American ballerina, b. Fort Worth, Tex., 1929, of Oklahoma Indian descent; m. Miguel Terekhov. Studied dance with Fronie Asher, Adolph Bolm, Veronine Vestoff; in N.Y. (1941–1943) with Anatole Vilzak and Ludmilla Sholler, later winning a scholarship to School of American Ballet. Received her general education at Professional Children's School, N.Y. At age fourteen, joined Ballet Russe de Monte Carlo (1943), rising from corps de ballet to ballerina (1950). Her first solo role was Prayer (*Coppélia,* 1945), followed by Daughter (*Le Beau Danube*), 2nd variation in Grand Pas Hongrois (*Raymonda*), title role (*Paquita*), *Blue Bird* pas de deux, Prelude and pas de deux (*Les Sylphides*), Fanny Cerito (*Pas de Quatre*), Jota (*Capriccio Espagnol*). Her official promotion to ballerina came with the role of Juliette (*Romeo et Juliette,* 1950), followed by Snow Queen (*The Nutcracker,* Act 1), *Don Quixote* pas de deux, Yellow Girl and 2nd movement (Leonide Massine's *Harold In Italy,* 1954), ballerina (*Raymonda,* Act 3), Minkus *Pas de Trois,* Fairy of Goodness (*Harlequinade,* 1957). Went with her husband to Montevideo, Uruguay (1957–1959), and since then they have been artists-in-residence at the Univ. of Oklahoma, Norman. In 1962 a full degree in dance was established at the Univ. for which Yvonne Chouteau and Miguel Terekhov set up the entire curriculum. They also teach in Oklahoma City and make appearances with their own group and as guest artists with various regional ballet groups in the area.

Chrimes, Pamela, South African dancer and teacher, b. Cape Town, 1923. Studied with Univ. of Cape Town Ballet School and danced with Cape Town Ballet during World War II. With Sadler's Wells Theatre Ballet (1945–48). Returned to South Africa; now dances, teaches and stages for Univ. of Cape Town Ballet. The ballets she has staged include *The Haunted Ballroom* (in which she also dances Alicia) and *Coppélia;* also dances Odette-Odile (*Swan Lake*) and title role (*The Firebird*).

Christensen, Harold, contemporary dancer, teacher, b. Brigham City, Utah, of Danish descent, brother of Willam and Lew Christensen, m. Ruby Asquith, dancer. Education: West Point (one

Lew, Willam and Harold Christensen

year), Univ. of Utah (one year). Studied dancing with George Balanchine. Appeared in RKO vaudeville; *The Great Waltz* (1934); Metropolitan Opera Ballet (1934); Ballet Caravan (1936–1940), creating role of Motorist in *Filling Station* (Lew Christensen, 1938); San Francisco Opera Ballet (1942); San Francisco Ballet (1941–46), after which he retired as a dancer. Currently Director of San Francisco Ballet School.

Christensen, Lew, dancer, teacher and choreographer, b. Brigham City, Utah, 1909, brother of Willam and Harold Christensen, m. Gisella Caccialanza. Studied dance with his uncle L. P. Christensen and at School of American Ballet, N.Y. Appeared in vaudeville with his brothers; member American Ballet (1935) with which he danced the title role of *Apollo* in performances at Metropolitan Opera House. Choreographer, ballet master and soloist, Ballet Caravan (1936–1940); soloist, Dance Players (1941–1942); San Francisco Opera Ballet. Served in U.S. Army. Ballet master and dancer, Ballet Society (1946–48); also on faculty of School of American Ballet. Continued until 1955 as ballet master of New York City Ballet, becoming in that year director and principal choreographer of San Francisco Ballet. Choreographed *Charade, Filling Station, Pocahontas, Encounter,* for Ballet Caravan; *Jinx,* for Dance Players; *Blackface,* for Ballet Society; *Con Amore,* full-length *The Nutcracker, Beauty and the Beast* (Tchaikovsky), *Danses Concertantes* (Stravinsky), *Shadows* (Hindemith), *Lady of Shalott* (Arthur Bliss), *Original Sin* (John Lewis), *Jest of Cards* (Krenek), *Sinfonia* (Boccherini), *Divertissement d'Auber* (Auber) and others all for the San Francisco Ballet. He is also ballet master of San Francisco Opera.

Christensen, Willam, American choreographer and teacher, b. 1902, Brigham City, Utah, brother of Lew and Harold Christensen. Education in music and dance: music with father Chris Christensen, a violinist and conductor; ballet with uncle L. P. Christensen, also with Stefano Mascagno, Michel Fokine, Julietta Mendez, and Laurent Novikoff. Toured the U.S. and Canada with quartet of dancers including brother Lew Christensen, Mignon Lee, and Wiore Barrett (1927–32), playing vaudeville and movie houses. In 1932 moved from N.Y. to Portland, Ore. where he opened a school and formed a small company which included Janet Reed and Mattlyn Gavers. Engaged as soloist for the San Francisco Opera ballet (1937); a year later appointed ballet master and choreographer of the S.F. Opera ballet, a position he held for 20 years. At that time he organized the San Francisco Ballet Company with Janet Reed as its first ballerina. Leading dancers from that company who later came to New York to join larger companies include James Starbuck, Zoya Leporska, Peter Nelson, Harold Lang, Scott Douglas, Leo Duggan, Onna White, Carolyn

George, and others. In 1951 Christensen accepted a professorship in Theatre Ballet at the Univ. of Utah, where he established a school of ballet and choreography courses which are offered along with regular academic subjects. In 1955 the full-length *Nutcracker* with guest artists and the Utah Symphony was performed for a week at Kingsbury Hall on the campus. This presentation has continued annually ever since. Also presented each spring is Ballet Gala which runs for a week and includes a varied repertoire. New ballets included: *Concerto* (J. S. Bach Violin Concerto in A minor), *Crown of Joy,* Mendelssohn's Symphony in A "Italian"; *Octet* (Igor Stravinsky); *Caprice de Paris* (Jacques Ibert); *Symphonia* (Mozart "Haffner" Symphony); *La Fille Naïve* (Aubert). Other ballets choreographed by Christensen include *Rumanian Wedding* (Georges Enesco, 1936), *Romeo and Juliet* (Tchaikovsky, 1938), *Coppélia* (1939), *Swan Lake* (1940), *The Nutcracker* (1944), *Pathétique Sonata* (Beethoven's Piano Sonata, Op. 13, in C minor, 1943), *Pyramus and Thisbe* (Fritz Berens, 1945), *Nothing Doing Bar* (Darius Milhaud, 1950), and others. His Utah Ballet, established in 1952 as the result of the interest of local patrons in his work at the Univ. of Utah, was the recipient of a Ford Foundation Grant of $175,000, in Dec. 1963, this grant to be matched over a five-year period by contributions of $100,000. The money is to help support performances and to provide scholarships, thereby helping to maintain a nucleus of professional dancers in Salt Lake City.

Chujoy, Anatole, writer, editor and critic, b. Riga, Latvia, 1894, American citizen since 1931. Graduate Law School, Univ. of Petrograd, 1918. Contributor to *American Dancer* (1935–36); co-founder and managing editor *Dance Magazine* (1936–41); founder and editor-publisher *Dance News* (since 1942). Author of *Ballet* (1936), *Symphonic Ballet* (1937), *The New York City Ballet* (1953), trans. Yury Slonimsky's *Jules Perrot* (1946) and *Marius Petipa* (1947), both for *Dance Index;* and *Lev Ivanov* (1959), for *Dance Perspectives;* trans. Agrippina Vaganova's *Fundamentals of the Classic Dance* (1947); comp. and ed. *Dance Encyclopedia* (1949); co-editor with P. W. Manchester of current edition of the above (1967); ed. *Fokine, Memoirs of a Ballet Master* (1961); contributor to *Grolier's Encyclopedia, Enciclopedia dello Spettacolo, Encyclopedia of Russia and the Soviet Union, The American College Dictionary* (1947 and 1963), Funk and Wagnall's *Standard Dictionary.* Member, Dance Advisory Commission of the High School of Performing Arts, N.Y. Originator of the Regional Ballet Festival Plan in the U.S. (1956). Diploma for Meritorious Research and Fruitful Activities in Realm of Dance from Archives Internationales de la Danse, Paris, 1950. Hon. Overseas Member, The Critics' Circle, London (since 1953).

Church Festival of Delft, The (Die Kirmes von Delft). Ballet in 3 scenes; chor. and book: Sonia Korty; music: Hermann Reutter; décor: Ludwig Sievert. First prod.: Music Festival, Baden Baden, Germany, Mar. 20, 1937, with Sonia Korty (Peregrina), Heinz Denies (Student). At the Church Festival in Delft Peregrina, the daughter of the local clergyman, captivates with her dancing a student who is betrothed to the daughter of the burgomaster. She is taken for a witch, convicted of witchcraft and sentenced to be burned. The student jumps into the bonfire. A snow falls from the summer sky and extinguishes the flames and the rescued lovers run away. The ballet has been performed in many European theatres among them Berlin, Munich, Stuttgart, Amsterdam, Brussels, Vienna, and Warsaw.

Cieplinski, Jan, Polish dancer, choreographer and teacher, b. Warsaw. Upon graduation from the Warsaw Government Ballet School, he was accepted as soloist of the ballet company at the Wielki Theatre. Shortly afterwards he made his debut as choreographer. In 1921 he toured U.S. and Canada with the Anna Pavlova company. After his return to Poland he was ballet master and choreographer for several years, staging during this time ballets to the music of Polish composers Stanislaw Moniuszko, Zygismund Moszkowski, and Mieczyslaw Karlovicz, and to Beethoven's *Prometheus.* After an engagement with the Diaghilev Ballets Russes (1925–27), he became ballet master and choreographer of the Royal Opera House, Stockholm (1927–31), where he staged twelve ballets, among them three by Swedish composers: *Krelantem och Eleeling* (Moses Pergament, 1928), *Per Swinaherde* (Kurt Atterburg, 1929), and *Bergakungen* (Hugo Alfvén, 1931). His other ballets included *The Nutcracker, Coppélia,* and Joseph Bayer's *Die Puppenfee* (The Fairy Doll). In 1932 Cieplinski went to the Budapest Opera House for three years staging there *Hungarian Fantasy* (Franz Liszt), *Fanny Elssler* (M. Nador), *Birthday of the Infanta* (M. Radnai), *Chonger es Tunde* (Leon Weiner), *The Legend of Joseph* (Richard Strauss), and a new production of *Coppélia.* After a year in Warsaw (1934) he went to the Teatro Colón, Buenos Aires (1935, 1936), where he staged *Allelujah* (Carlos Pedrell), *The Wooden Prince* (Béla Bartók) and *La Boite à Joujoux* (Debussy). From Argentina he returned to Budapest and then to Warsaw to stage *Harnasie* (Karol Szymanowski), *Les Danses d'Autrefois* (Ottorino Respighi), *A Fairy Tale* (Stanislaw Moniuszko), and *Cavalier of the Silver Rose* (Richard Strauss). These ballets became part of Ballets Polonais, which toured Europe in 1939 and was also presented at the N.Y. World's Fair the same year. The outbreak of World War II found Cieplinski in Warsaw where he directed a ballet studio. From 1943 to 1948 he was back in Budapest, where he staged *The History of Debreczyn* (Karl Goldmark), *The Emperor Waltz* (Johann Strauss), *L'Amour Sorcier* (de Falla), *Petrouchka* (Stravinsky), and others. In 1948 he went to London as ballet master and choreographer of the Anglo-Polish Ballet. The following year he was engaged for the third time by Teatro Colón, Buenos Aires, where he staged *The Wizard* (Alfredo Pinto). Returning to London in 1950 he dedicated himself to teaching ballet in his own studio and at the Legat School. He is author of *The History of Polish Ballet* (London, 1955). In 1959 Jan Cieplinski settled in N.Y. where he conducts a ballet studio.

Cimarosiana. Ballet divertissement in 1 act; chor.: Leonide Massine; music: Domenico Cimarosa, from his opera *Le Astuzie Femminile;* décor: José Maria Sert. First prod.: Diaghilev Ballets Russes, Monte Carlo, Jan. 8, 1924. This plotless suite of dances was originally part of Diaghilev's revival of *Le Astuzie Femminile,* Paris Opéra, May 27, 1920. *Cimarosiana* was later revived for Col. de Basil's Ballets Russes.

Cinderella. Ballet in 3 acts; chor.: Marius Petipa, Enrico Cecchetti, Lev Ivanov; music: Baron B. Fitinghof-Schell; décor: G. Levogt, M. Shishkov, M. Botcharov; book: Lydia Pashkova. First prod.: Maryinsky Theatre, St. Petersburg, Dec. 5, 1893, with Pierina Legnani in the title role and Paul Gerdt as Prince Charming. The ballet, like all other versions, was based on Perrault's fairy tale. This was the ballet in which Pierina Legnani introduced the famous 32 fouettés for the first time in Russia.

Cinderella. Ballet in 1 act, 3 scenes; chor. and book: Michel Fokine; music: Frederic d'Erlanger; décor: Nathalie Gontcharova. First prod.: Educational Ballets (Col. de Basil), Royal Opera House, Covent Garden, London, July 19,

1938, with Tatiana Riabouchinska (Cinderella), Paul Petroff (Prince Charming). N.Y. première: Fifty-first Street Theatre, Nov. 16, 1940, with Riabouchinska and Petroff.

Cinderella. Ballet in 3 acts and 7 scenes; chor.: Rostislav Zakharov; music, Sergei Prokofiev; book: Nicolai Volkov; décor: Pyotr Williams. First prod.: Bolshoi Theatre, Moscow, Nov. 21, 1945, with Olga Lepeshinskaya (Cinderella) and Mikhail Gabovich (Prince). Another version choreographed by Konstantin Sergeyev was first performed at the Kirov Theatre, Leningrad, Apr. 8, 1946, with Natalia Dudinskaya (Cinderella), and Konstantin Sergeyev (Prince). Both versions include an extended divertissement of the Prince's travels to various countries in search of the owner of the glass slipper. Raisa Stuchkova danced the title role at Royal Opera House, Covent Garden, during the second visit of the Bolshoi Ballet to London (1963) when this version was seen for the first time outside the U.S.S.R.

Cinderella. Ballet in 3 acts; chor. and book: Frederick Ashton; music: Sergei Prokofiev; décor: Jean-Denis Malclès. First prod.: Sadler's Wells (now Royal) Ballet at Royal Opera House, Covent Garden, London, Dec. 23, 1948, with Moira Shearer (Cinderella), Michael Somes (Prince), Pamela May (Fairy Godmother). Frederick Ashton and Robert Helpmann performed the roles of the Ugly Sisters en travesti in the tradition of English pantomime. This version cuts Prokofiev's score by omitting the divertissement of the Prince's travels. It is the first evening-length ballet devised by a British choreographer.

Cinderella. Ballet extravaganza devised by Raymundo de Larrain; chor.: Vaslav Orlikovsky; staging: Orlikovsky and Larrain; music: Serge Prokofiev; décor: Raymundo de Larrain. First prod.: Théâtre des Champs-Elysées, Paris, Dec. 4, 1963, as the final event of the International Dance Festival of that year. Galina Samtsova and the Hungarian dancer Viktor Rona danced Cinderella and the Prince at the première, with Tessa Beaumont, Claire Sombert, Yvonne Meyer, Margo Miklosy and Milenko Banovich (both from Hungary), Paulo Bortoluzzi, and Milorad Miskovitch later appearing in these roles. The ballet ran until Apr. 29, 1964.

Circe. Modern dance work in 1 act; chor.: Martha Graham; commissioned score by Alan Hovhaness; décor: Isamu Noguchi. First prod.: Martha Graham Dance Company, Prince of Wales Theatre, London, Sept. 6, 1963, with Mary Hinkson (Circe), Bertram Ross (Ulysses), Clive Thompson (Helmsman), Robert Powell (Snake), Richard Gain (Lion), Gene McDonald (Deer), Peter Randazzo (Goat). The Helmsman finally succeeds in drawing Ulysses away from the lure of Circe although his sailors, metamorphosed into beasts, aid her in her wiles. This, however, is only the outer shell of the work which Martha Graham sees as "that inner world of bestialities and enchantments where one discovers what it costs to choose to be human." N.Y. première: Oct. 15, 1963, Lunt-Fontanne Theatre, with the same cast. Martha Graham created this work and premièred it in London as a homage to Robin Howard, who undertook the financial risk of a London season after the financial disaster of her first (1954) appearance.

Cirque de Deux. Ballet in 1 act; chor.: Ruthanna Boris; music: Charles Gounod (ballet music from *Faust*); décor: Robert Davison. First prod.: Ballet Russe de Monte Carlo, Hollywood Bowl, Hollywood, Calif., Aug. 1, 1947, with Ruthanna Boris and Leon Danielian in principal roles, Patricia Wilde, Frank Hobi as pages; N.Y. première: City Center, Sept. 10, 1947, with Boris and Hobi in leading roles, Wilde and Stanley Zompakos as pages. Though it has no story, the ballet is gently satirical at the expense of various typical circus acts.

Ciseaux (more correctly, pas ciseaux), in ballet, a jump in which both legs open in a wide 2nd pos. while the dancer is in the air. The jump is done from 5th to 5th pos. and resembles the opening and closing of a scissors' blades, hence the name. Ciseaux often is mistakenly confused with sissone.

City Center Joffrey Ballet. The Robert Joffrey Ballet was renamed City Center Joffrey Ballet when, at the invitation of Morton Baum, chairman of the board of the N.Y. City Center, it became the official resident company at that theatre, with two three-week seasons annually. The invitation came as a result of the company's very successful initial week at City Center (Mar. 30–Apr. 3, 1966). Immediately prior to its first season under its new title (Sept. 6–25, 1966) it was announced that City Center Joffrey Ballet had received a second Ford Foundation Grant of $500,000 over a three-year period, on a matching and supplementary funds basis. See also ROBERT JOFFREY BALLET.

Civic Ballet. See REGIONAL BALLET.

Clarke, Mary, English writer and editor, b. London, 1923. Educated at The Mary Datchelor School, London. Assistant Editor, *The Dancing Times,* London (1954–63), and director of Dancing Times, Ltd; became editor on death of Arthur Franks (1963); Executive Editor, *The Ballet Annual,* London; London Resident Editor, *Dance News* (N.Y.). Author, *The Sadler's Wells Ballet: A History and an Appreciation* (London, 1955); *Shakespeare at the Old Vic* (with Roger Wood and other photographers) in five vols. (1954–58); *Six Great Dancers* (London, 1957); *Presenting People Who Dance* (London, 1961); *Dancers of Mercury: the Story of the Ballet Rambert* (London, 1962).

Classic Ballet. The term classic as applied to ballet is arbitrary. It denotes a style in dance rather than a period. The term academic would be more accurate but has never gained general acceptance. In a broad sense a classic ballet is a ballet based on the classic tradition developed through the centuries of the existence of ballet. Unlike music, drama, or painting, ballet has no permanent record. Its existence continues through direct contact between teacher and student, ballet master and dancer, from generation to generation. This direct contact is the tradition of ballet, its moving spirit, its only means of existence.

We also speak of classic ballet with reference to its technique: the turnout, elevation, beats, turns, the dance on toe. The application of the word classic in this sense is used very often to distinguish a ballet from any other dance form. The word classic here is actually superfluous, but since any dance performance may be called a ballet (and very often is), it does not hurt the ballet to be called classic.

There is yet another application of the word classic: to denote the artistic structure of a ballet which adheres to the definite framework established in the 19th century, a framework which includes the classic pas de deux as a choreographic poem in three verses. The classic pas de deux is as definite in its composition as that of a sonnet in poetry. It consists of the pas de deux proper, otherwise called the adagio, followed by variations, first of the male dancer, and then of the ballerina, concluding with the coda in which both dancers are again together.

The 19th century choreographers Arthur Saint-Léon and Marius Petipa, by strict adherence to and constant repetition of the same principle in the composition of ballets, developed the rules or, more properly, the tradition of the classic ballet.

Classicism in ballet is in no sense a category that can be opposed to romanticism. Classicism applies to style and structure, romanticism to period and content; hence a classic ballet is often romantic (*Swan Lake,* for example) and a romantic ballet is nearly always classic (see ROMANTIC BALLET). Examples of classic ballets in the repertoire of contemporary ballet companies include *The Sleeping Beauty, The Nutcracker, Coppélia, La Fille Mal Gardée, Raymonda.* See also CLASSICISM.

Classicism, in ballet, the accumulation over a period of the past four centuries of the purest in stage tradition of gestures and expressions and of steps based on the five absolute positions of the classic dance (danse d'école). It is a clean and noble style, pure of line and without affectation or mannerisms. Though the Romantic ballet originally was developed as a protest against the restrictions of classicism, today we think of the Romantic ballets (*Giselle, La Sylphide*) and neo-romantic ballets (*Swan Lake, Les Sylphides*) as classic. Carlo Blasis, by his system of bar work and exercises, had enormous influence in spreading the principles of classicism throughout Europe. See also CLASSIC BALLET.

Clavé, Antoni, Spanish painter and ballet designer of the Paris school, b. Barcelona, 1913. Became famous with his décor and costumes for *Carmen* (Ballets de Paris de Roland Petit, 1949) after having first attracted attention with *Caprichos* (Ballets des Champs-Elysées, 1946). His other ballets include *Ballabile* (Sadler's Wells Ballet, 1950), *Revanche* (Ruth Page's Chicago Opera Ballet, 1952), *Deuil en 24 Heures* (Ballets de Paris de Roland Petit, 1953), *La Peur* (Roland Petit Show, 1957). Has designed a number of operas and dramas, but has in the main relinquished work in the theatre in order to devote himself to easel painting.

Clayden, Pauline, English dancer, b. London 1922. Studied at Cone School. Made her debut at Royal Opera House, Covent Garden (opera season, 1938); danced with London Ballet (Arts Theatre, 1939), remaining when it amalgamated with Ballet Rambert (1940). Joined Sadler's Wells (now Royal) Ballet (1942); soloist, then principal dancer until her retirement (Jan. 1956). Her roles included Songbird Fairy, and *Blue Bird* pas de deux (*The Sleeping Beauty*), pas de trois (*Swan Lake*), *Giselle,* Chloë (*Daphnis and Chloë*), Flower Girl (*Nocturne*), Papillon (*Carnaval*), and others. Her creations included Promenade Solo (*Promenade*) The Mayfly (*The Spider's Banquet*), Suicide (*Miracle in the Gorbals*), Autumn (Frederick Ashton's *Cinderella*), and others.

Cléopâtre. Ballet in 1 act; chor. and book: Michel Fokine; music: Anton Arensky and others; décor: Léon Bakst. First prod.: Maryinsky Theatre, St. Petersburg, Mar. 21, 1908, under the title *Une Nuit d'Egypte;* Paris première (with minor changes): Théâtre du Châtelet, June 2, 1909, with Anna Pavlova (Ta-hor, or Berenice), Ida Rubinstein (Cleopatra), Michel Fokine (Amoûn), Tamara Karsavina and Vaslav Nijinsky (Slaves). In this version other music was substituted for Arensky's: Cleopatra arrived to music from Rimsky-Korsakov's *Mlada;* the slaves danced to Danse Orientale from Glinka's *Russlan and Ludmilla;* the final dance was set to Danse Persane from Moussorgsky's *Khovanshchina;* and a new number, the Bacchanale, was set to the Bacchanale from Glazounov's *Les Saisons.* The mime role of Cléopâtre was created especially for Ida Rubinstein and she was a great success in the part. In London Seraphima

Astafieva and Lubov Tchernicheva played the part. Sophie Fedorova as well as Pavlova was successful in the role of Ta-hor. Diaghilev revived the ballet with new décor by Robert Delaunay (1918), but the new set did not convey the mood of the original. The plot of the ballet deals with Amoûn a slave at the court of Cleopatra who loves Ta-hor, a beautiful slave-girl who shares his feelings. However, when Amoûn sees Cleopatra for the first time he falls madly in love with her. He attaches a note to an arrow and shoots the arrow in the direction of the divan upon which Cleopatra reclines. Cleopatra reads the note and commands that Amoûn be brought to her. She is attracted to Amoûn and offers him a night of love for his life. Amoûn accepts. A bacchanale ensues and after it Cleopatra offers him a cup of poison which he drains and then falls dead.

Cloche. See BATTEMENTS.

Clog, a form of tap dance (originating in Ireland and Lancashire, England), in shoes having hard soles (sometimes wooden), and/or having metal taps attached to the toe part of the soles to accentuate the click. An interesting recent balletic use of the clog dance is seen in Mother Simone's dance in Frederick Ashton's *La Fille Mal Gardée.*

Closed Positions, in ballet, 1st, 3rd, and 5th positions of the feet. See POSITIONS OF FEET.

Clouser, James, dancer, b. Rochester, N.Y., 1935. Studied at Ballet Theatre School with Edward Caton, Igor Schwezoff, Anatole Vilzak. Is also a trained musician with a major in composition from Eastman School of Music, Rochester, N.Y. Made his debut as a dancer in summer stock at Beverly, Mass., under Leon Danielian (1956); joined American Ballet Theatre (1957), and Royal Winnipeg Ballet (1958). Was promoted to soloist (1959) and has been a leading dancer with that company ever since. Created Buffalo God (*Brave Song*), Boy (*Un et Un Font Deux*), Oboe (*A Court Occasion*); dances Prince (*Swan Lake,* Act 2), and many roles in the Royal Winnipeg Ballet's contemporary repertoire. Has choreographed many musicals for summer theatres, at Univ. of Manitoba, etc. His ballets *Recurrence* (for which he also wrote the music) and *The Little Emperor* are in the R.W.B. repertoire.

Clustine (more properly, Khlustine), **Ivan,** Russian dancer and ballet master, b. 1862 Moscow, d. 1941, Nice, France. Graduate of the Moscow Bolshoi Ballet School, premier danseur, and ballet master of the Bolshoi, he resigned in 1903 and moved to Paris where he opened a school. Was maître de ballet of the Paris Opéra (1909–1914) for which he choreographed *Roussalka* (1911), *Suite de Danses* and *Les Etoiles* (1913). Left the Opéra to become Anna Pavlova's ballet master (1914–1922), arranging for her company *Snowflakes, The Fairy Doll, Chopiniana, The Last Song, Amarilla, The Sleeping Beauty, Raymonda, La Péri, The Romance of the Mummy, Dionysis,* and others; also a number of solos for Pavlova including the famous *Gavotte,* to music by Paul Linke. After leaving the Pavlova company he retired to Nice, on the French Riviera.

Clytemnestra. Modern dance work in 3 acts; chor. and costumes: Martha Graham; music: Halim El-Dabh; décor: Isamu Noguchi. First prod.: Martha Graham and Dance Company, Adelphi Theatre, Apr. 1, 1958, with Martha Graham (Clytemnestra), Bertram Ross (Agamemnon and Orestes), Paul Taylor (Aegisthus), Gene McDonald (King Hades, Agamemnon's Ghost, Paris), Ethel Winter (Helen), Yuriko (Iphigenia), Linda Hodes (Cassandra), Helen McGehee (Electra), David Wood (Messenger of Death). The Aeschylus trilogy, the

Oresteia, interpreted by Martha Graham in the supreme achievement of her career, as the looking back after death by Clytemnestra as she awaits the decision of the gods about her own eternal fate. It is the first evening-long modern dance work.

Coast of Hope. Ballet in 3 acts; chor.: Igor Belsky; music: Andrei Petrov; book: Yuri Slonimsky; décor: Valery Dorrer. First prod.: Kirov Theatre, Leningrad, June 16, 1959, with Askold Makarov (Fisherman), Alla Osipenko (His Beloved). A Soviet fisherman thrown by the storm on to another coast is, through love for his country and his beloved, able to withstand all trials and return safely home.

Cobos, Antonia (Phyllis Nalte), American dancer and choreographer. Her first ballet, *The Mute Wife* (1944), for Ballet International (U.S.) was a distinct success and was revived for the Original Ballet Russe (1946) and Grand Ballet de Monte Carlo (1948). In 1947 she staged *Madroños* (music by Moszkowski, Yradier, and others) for Ballet Russe de Monte Carlo, and in 1954 *The Mikado* (based on the Gilbert and Sullivan opera), for the same company.

Cocteau, Jean (1889–1963), French poet, novelist and designer, b. Maisons-Lafitte. A modernist who brought a new element of poetry into ballet. As one of the influential members of Serge Diaghilev's circle, he spread propaganda before the seasons of Ballets Russes and helped popularize the ballet. He was a historian of the Diaghilev period and his memoirs are our best source for information about what interested the ballet audience, since he tells us the underlying idea which motivated a ballet and this helps one to understand it better than any picture or description of the ballet. He knew Vaslav Nijinsky, perhaps better than any other living person. He collaborated on many ballets: *Le Dieu Bleu* (Michel Fokine, 1912); with Pablo Picasso and Erik Satie on *Parade* (Leonide Massine, 1917); *Boeuf sur le Toit* (George Balanchine, 1923, as part of the Evenings of Young Ballet in Petrograd); wrote the libretto of *Les Mariés de la Tour Eiffel* (Jean Börlin, *Les Ballets Suédois,* 1921); *Le Train Bleu* (Bronislava Nijinska, 1924); *Roméo et Juliette* (Soirées de Paris, 1924); *Le Jeune Homme et la Mort* (Roland Petit, 1946); Phèdre (Serge Lifar, Paris Opéra, 1950); *La Dame à la Licorne* (Heinz Rosen, Munich Opera and Paris Opéra, 1953). Designed décor and costumes for *L'Amour et Son Amour* (Jean Babilée, 1948), and for *Phèdre* and the Paris Opéra production of *La Dame à la Licorne.* He was an immense influence on French art of the 20th century. Was elected to the Académie Francaise in 1955. He died Oct. 11, 1963, at Milly-la-Forêt, near Paris, after a long illness which followed a heart attack on Apr. 22. The cause of death was heart failure a few hours after he was told of the death of Edith Piaf, a great friend for many years.

Coda. 1. The third part of the classic pas de deux which follows the variations. In it the female and the male dancer are on the stage together. They alternate in their dances, but finish the coda together. 2. The finale of a classic ballet in which all principals appear separately or with their partners, parading, as it were, before the spectators. It used to be followed quite often by an apotheosis. A good example of a coda is the mazurka finale in *The Sleeping Beauty.*

Code of Terpsichore, book written by Carlo Blasis (1830) which contains a history of the dance, the theory and practice of ballet, and an analysis of pantomime. It emphasizes the need for the turnout and plié. It lists three distinct classes of dancers: serious or tragic, demi-caractère, and comic. It was the standard of ballet instruction in Europe and Russia in the 19th century and is still the backbone of classic technique.

Cohan, Robert, American modern dancer, b. New York City, 1925. Studied with Martha Graham and joined her company in 1946, dancing a large repertoire including creations in *Dark Meadow, Deaths and Entrances, Canticle for Innocent Comedians, Diversion of Angels,* and others. Had leading dance roles in the Broadway musicals *Shangri-La* and *Can-Can* (1956). Established his own school in Boston and joined faculty of Harvard's Loeb Drama Center; also formed his own group and gave many performances in his own works with Matt Turney as his partner, best-known being *The Pass* (1960), based on the riddles of the Sphinx. Rejoined the Graham company in 1962, dancing *Acrobats of God, Embattled Garden* (The Stranger—a role which was choreographed on him but which he did not dance at its first performances), and *Phaedra* (Theseus), among other roles.

Cohen, Dr. Frederic (Fritz) **A.,** composer, b. Bonn, Germany, 1904, m. dancer Elsa Kahl. Studied at universities of Bonn, Leipzig, Cologne, Berlin. Pianist for Yvonne Georgi (1924); conductor of opera and ballet and stage director of opera and drama at Münster; (1924–27) Heidelberg Festival, Goettingen Handel Festival, Wuerzburg (1927–28), Essen (where he also taught, 1928–32), Bayreuth Festival (1930). Musical director and artistic co-director, Jooss Ballet (1932–42), for which he composed the scores for *The Green Table, The Prodigal Son, Seven Heroes, The Mirror, Johann Strauss Tonight, Spring Tale, Drums Sound in Hackensack.* When the company returned to Europe after its American tour in 1942, Dr. and Mrs. Cohen remained in the U.S., eventually becoming citizens. He accepted the post of Assistant Professor of Music, Black Mountain College, N.C. (1942–44); transferred to Kenyon College, Gambier, O. (1945), as director of the Music Institute; served as stage director, Opera Department, Berkshire Music Center (1946 and 1954). In 1946 he established a connection with the Juilliard School of Music, N.Y., first as instructor and later as director of the Juilliard Opera Theatre from which he retired July 1, 1963. He was also president of The Music Institute and directed opera productions at the Metropolitan Museum of Art, N.Y.; St. John's College, Annapolis, Md., Opera Society, Washington, D.C., Stanford Univ., Calif.; Univ. of California at Los Angeles, and Conservatoire de la Musique et de l'Art Dramatique, Montreal, Canada. Died in New York on March 9, 1967.

Cohen, Fritz. See COHEN, DR. FREDERIC.

Cohen, Selma Jeanne, American writer, editor and lecturer, b. 1920, Chicago. Ph.D. in English, Univ. of Chicago (1946). Studied dance with Edna L McRae, Eugene Loring, Martha Graham, Hanya Holm, José Limón, Dance Notation Bureau. Instructor in English, Univ. of Chicago, Univ. of California at Los Angeles, Hunter College (1942–53). Lecturer on Dance History at School of Performing Arts, N.Y. (1953–56). Lectured at Mount Holyoke College, Princeton Univ., and others. Has delivered papers at meetings of American Society of Aesthetics and Modern Language Association of America. Staff member, *N.Y. Times* (1955–58). Has had articles and reviews published in *Ballet Annual,* London; *Dance Magazine, Dance News, Dance Observer, Musical America, Theatre Arts, Philological Quarterly, Journal of Aesthetics and Art Criticism* (all U.S.); critical articles in various encyclopedias. Dance editor, Collier's Encyclopedia; editor of catalog of artworks related to the ballets of Igor Stravinsky, for exhibition Stravinsky and the Dance, N.Y., sponsored by the Dance Collection, The New York Public Library (1962).

Co-author with I. K. Fletcher of *Famed for Dance* (The New York Public Library, 1960); forthcoming: *A History of Theatrical Dancing* (N.Y., Collier Books). Grant from the Emily E. F. Skeel Fund of Bibliographical Research (The New York Public Library, 1961) to do analytical bibliography of 19th century ballet librettos in the library collection, to be published by the library. On the staff of Saturday Review (1964–65). Editor and publisher of *Dance Perspectives* since fall of 1965.

Cole, Jack (J. Ewing Cole), American dancer and choreographer, b. New Brunswick, N.J., ca. 1913. Attended Columbia Univ. Studied dance with Ruth St. Denis at Denishawn School, N.Y. Joined company in 1930; also danced with Ted Shawn and His Men Dancers (1933), and later with the Humphrey-Weidman company. From the beginning of his career he became an avid researcher in Orientalism, studying the various forms of the Oriental dance with as many authoritative teachers as he could find. He was the first to conceive the idea of dancing in the Hindu style to American jazz, which he developed with great success in Broadway musicals and night clubs. In 1936–37 he assembled a small group of dancers under the title Ballet Intime for which he choreographed and with which he danced at the elegant Rainbow Room, a night club atop the RCA building in Radio City, N.Y. Prior to that he staged dances for night clubs with Alice Dudley, Anna Austin, Florence Lessing, Beatrice Kraft, and others. Has choreographed for musicals, among them *Magdalena, Alive and Kicking, Carnival in Flanders, Kismet, Jamaica, Foxy, Zenda,* the last named in 1964 with a cast headed by Chita Rivera. He has also choreographed for motion pictures, Hollywood being his headquarters for the past fifteen or twenty years. Among the artists for whom he has choreographed there are Marlene Dietrich, Rita Hayworth, and Danny Kaye. Choreographer of musical *Man of La Mancha* (1965); choreographer and principal dancer of the Zen Buddhist-Hebrew musical *Chu Chem* (1966; closed before its Broadway opening).

Coleman, Emily, contemporary American writer, critic and editor, b. San Antonio, Tex. Educated at American Univ., Washington, D.C. (B.A. 1935; M.A. in Constitutional Law, 1937). Music and dance editor *Newsweek Magazine* (1942–64). Member, Dance Advisory Panel of International Exchange Program of the Department of State; Music Critics Circle, N.Y.; Capezio Dance Award Committee. Author of articles in national publications. Currently free-lancing.

Collins, Janet, American modern dancer, b. New Orleans, La., 1917. Her early dance training was mainly in Calif. with Carmalita Maracci, Adolph Bolm, and Lester Horton. Her first solo concerts were in Los Angeles. Made her N.Y. debut at the YM-YWHA (1949). Continued her studies with Mia Slavenska and Margaret Craske. Principal dancer in the Cole Porter musical *Out of This World,* for which she received the Donaldson Award (1950–51). Taught modern dance at School of American Ballet, N.Y. (1950–52). Première danseuse, Metropolitan Opera Ballet (1951–1954). Between seasons toured in U.S. and Canada in her own programs. Also has made many television appearances. Currently teaching in N.Y.

Colombo, Vera, Italian ballerina, b. Milan, 1931. Entered the ballet school of Teatro alla Scala, Milan, (1940). Was graduated, appeared in her *Passo d'Addio,* and was promoted to soloist (1952); became prima ballerina (1954). Her repertoire includes *Ballet Imperial, Symphony in C, The Nutcracker, Swan Lake,* (Act 2), *Graduation Ball, Les Sylphides, Coppélia, Le Sacre du Printemps,* and others.

Colón, Teatro, famous opera house in Buenos Aires, Argentina, which employs a resident ballet company. Many choreographers have worked at Teatro Colón including Michel Fokine, Bronislava Nijinska, Boris Romanov, George Balanchine, George Skibine, Serge Lifar, Margaret Wallman, Jack Carter, Antony Tudor, and others. Most of the well-known dancers of Europe and the U.S. have appeared at the Colón as guest artists, and many European and several U.S. troupes have danced there.

Colt, Alvin, American costume designer, b. 1916. Designed costumes for *Charade, Pastorela, Serenade* (all Ballet Caravan, 1941); *Saratoga* (Ballet Russe de Monte Carlo, 1941), *Slavonika* (also décor, 1941), *Waltz Academy* (1944), *Graziana* (1945), *On Stage!* (1945) all for Ballet [now American Ballet] Theatre. Currently designs mainly for Broadway.

Columbia Artists Management, Inc. Came into being on Dec. 12, 1930 under its original name, Columbia Concerts Corporation, as a merger of the following concert bureaus: Concert Management Arthur Judson, the Wolfson Musical Bureau, the Metropolitan Musical Bureau, Evans and Salter, Haensel and Jones, Judson Radio Program Corporation (opened by Arthur Judson in 1926, it became the foundation of the Columbia Broadcasting System in 1928), and Community Concerts Corporation, whose function it was to develop and organize concert audiences in the United States and Canada. The new corporation was also affiliated during its early years with the Columbia Broadcasting System. Unlike most mergers, the identity of each division was maintained to assure personal service and individual attention to the artists under its management. Columbia Artists Management continues to maintain its divisions but over the thirty-odd years the divisions themselves have undergone changes in their names, leadership, and personnel. In 1964 the divisions numbered five and included: Schang (a second generation member of the firm, his father, Frederick C. Schang, Jr., being a member of the original corporation), Doulens and Wright; Weinhold and Thompson; Judd, Ries and Dahlgren; André Mertens Division, Nelly Walter, manager; Fox and Wilford. Columbia Artists Management and its predecessors have managed, among others, the following dance attractions and individual artists: Anna Pavlova, Mikhail Mordkin, Diaghilev Ballets Russes, La Argentina, Tatiana Vecheslova and Vakhtang Chabukiani (the first Soviet dancers ever to appear in the U.S.), Jooss Ballet, Takarazuka Dancers, Ballet Russe de Monte Carlo, Angna Enters, Devi Dja and her Java Dancers, Dancers of Bali, La Meri, the Mordkin Ballet, Carmalita Maracci, Mia Slavenska and her Ballet Variant, Korean Dancer Sai Shoki, Marina Svetlova and her group, Paul Draper, Rosario and Antonio, Mata and Hari, Federico Rey and Pilar Gomez, Carola Goya, Royal Danish Ballet, Ruth Page's Chicago Opera Ballet, Bayanihan Philippine Ballet, Kovach and Rabovsky Hungarian Ballet Bihary, Robert Joffrey Ballet, Melissa Hayden and Jacques d'Amboise, Koutev Bulgarian National Ensemble, Rapsodia Romina, Chilean National Ballet, Ximenez and Vargas Ballet Español, Soviet Ballet and Folk Ensemble Raduga, Korean Dancers Arirang, Renée Jeanmaire and Roland Petit's Ballets de Paris, Ballet 64 of San Francisco, The First Chamber Dance Quartet. During 1963 Arthur Judson resigned from Columbia Artists Management. In the same year both André Mertens and Humphrey Doulens died.

Combat, Le. Ballet in 1 act; chor.: William Dollar; music: Rafaello de Banfield; décor: Vicomtesse Marie-Laure de Noailles. First perf.: Ballets de Paris de Roland Petit, Princes Theatre, London, Feb. 24, 1949, with Janine Charrat and Vladimir Skouratoff. The story is that of Tancredi, the Christian knight, and

Clorinda the Saracen girl, from Tasso's *Jerusalem Delivered.* Tancredi unknowingly kills her in combat and only as her helmet falls off, revealing her face and long hair, does he realize what he has done. This version, arranged as a long pas de deux, was premièred in N.Y. at the Winter Garden Theatre, Oct. 6, 1949, with Colette Marchand and Milorad Miskovitch. William Dollar re-staged it with three additional knights for New York City Ballet and it was premièred at City Center, N.Y., Feb. 24, 1950, with costumes by Robert Stevenson. Dollar himself danced Tancredi on opening night with Melissa Hayden as Clorinda. Francisco Moncion took over the leading male role at subsequent performances. The New York City Ballet version is known as *The Duel.* American Ballet Theatre also performs the expanded version, with décor by Georges Wakhevitch (premièred in London, July 23, 1953, with Melissa Hayden and John Kriza); N.Y. première: Metropolitan Opera House, Dec. 27, 1953, had the same dancers. Lupe Serrano has had one of her greatest successes in the role of Clorinda.

Comedians, The. Ballet in 1 act; chor.: Ruthanna Boris; music: Dmitri Kabalevsky's suite *The Comedians;* costumes: Alvin Colt, executed by Barbara Karinska. First prod.: New York City Ballet, City Center, N.Y., Dec. 18, 1952, under the title *Kaleidoscope,* with Patricia Wilde, Melissa Hayden, Todd Bolender, Herbert Bliss, Frank Hobi. Under its present title it was staged for the Winnipeg (now Royal Winnipeg) Ballet June 24, 1959, at the Command Performance in Winnipeg for H.M. Queen Elizabeth II and H.R.H. Prince Philip, Duke of Edinburgh. Travelling players improvise upon themes of everyday life.

Commedia dell'arte, a type of theatrical performance popular in Italy and France from the 16th to 18th centuries—comedies or native farces of particular Italian towns, similar to old Roman Fabulae Atellanae—full of earthy humor, slapstick, and the mimicry inherent in the Latins. An outline of the drama, based on conventional situations, was prepared in advance, but the lines and acting were improvised by professional actors. For this reason it was sometimes called commedia all'improviso. The actors wore masks of characters such as Harlequin, Columbine, Pantalon, etc., which immediately became popular and were soon familiar traditional stock characters. Later dancing was added to the miming. The increasing coarseness, even obscenity, of Commedia dell'arte brought about its decline after the first half of the eighteenth century. The plays of Carlo Goldoni, which utilized the characters but gave them set dialogues and action, were its death blow. The tradition of commedia dell'arte lives on in the famous pantomime theatre in Tivoli Gardens, Copenhagen, where the performances of stylized pantomimes have delighted generations of Danish children. Harlequinades, the English descendant of the commedia dell'arte, became popular in America in the 19th century and national themes were introduced. The traditional Christmas pantomimes in England grew out of the Harlequinades which originally formed the important part of the entertainment, with the play as a very minor appendage. Towards the end of the nineteenth century the Harlequinades declined more and more until they became only short afterpieces to the increasingly elaborate play versions of famous fairy tales; by the early 1900's they had disappeared altogether.

Competitions, Stage Dancing (England). Competitions in stage dancing, as a part of either a dance or musical festival, have proved very popular in England and it is not uncommon for over a thousand entries to be received at an important event. They are in practice limited to young people and as a rule those who have acquired a position on the stage do not compete. The competitors are divided according to age into classes ranging from the Baby Class and those from six to nine to the Senior Class (over eighteen). The classes themselves are divided into styles: classic ballet, character, demi-caractère, natural movement, acrobatic, and revue or cabaret work. The majority of the events are solos, but there are always duets and groups for certain styles. Each dance has a strict time limit of 1½ or 2 minutes for solos, more for duets and groups or in the case of cabaret when a song is also expected. There are generally two or three experienced teachers who act as adjudicators. Though these events are not altogether popular with education authorities if held in term time, they do provide a useful public audition which shows if the candidate has any real aptitude for a stage career. Many well known dancers have been discovered in one of these events.

Comus. Ballet in 2 scenes, after the masque by John Milton; chor.: Robert Helpmann; music: various theatrical works by Henry Purcell, selected and arr. by Constant Lambert; décor: Oliver Messel. First prod.: Sadler's Wells (now Royal) Ballet, New Theatre, London, Jan. 14, 1942, with Robert Helpmann (Comus), Margot Fonteyn (The Lady), John Hart and David Paltenghi (Her Brothers), Margaret Dale (Attendant Spirit), Moyra Fraser (Sabrina). The purity of the Lady is proof (with an assist from the Attendant Spirit) against the evil blandishments of Comus. This was Helpmann's first ballet and in it he spoke two passages from Milton's masque. The entire masque, with long dance sequences, was staged by Leslie French for International Ballet (1946), in décor by Doris Zinkeisen, using the music by Henry Lawes written for the original Milton work and additional music by George Frederick Handel; Mona Inglesby and Harcourt Algeranoff headed the ballet.

Con Amore. Ballet in 1 act, 3 scenes; chor.: Lew Christensen; music: three overtures by Rossini—*La Gazza Ladra, Il Signor Bruschino,* and *La Scala di Seta;* book: James Graham Luján; décor: James Bodrero. First prod.: San Francisco Ballet, Opera House, San Francisco, Mar. 10, 1953, with Sally Bailey (Captain of the Amazons), Nancy Johnson (Lady), Leon Danielian (Bandit). In the first scene the Bandit decides he prefers death to life amongst the Amazons, all of whom, but especially the Captain, have fallen in love with him. In the second scene a faithless wife (the Lady) flees when her husband discovers her with no less than three lovers at once. In the third scene all come together in the forest and Cupid conveniently appears to pair them all off happily. Lew Christensen staged the ballet for New York City Ballet, City Center, N.Y., June 9, 1953, with Sally Bailey and Nancy Johnson repeating their creations, and Jacques d'Amboise as the Bandit. On Mar. 9, 1954, a slightly revised version in décor by Esteban Francés was presented, with Patricia Wilde and Janet Reed as the Captain and the Lady. Yvonne Mounsey, Violette Verdy and Gloria Govrin have also danced the Captain, and Jillana the Lady. Edward Villella and Conrad Ludlow (who took over from guest artist Danielian in the San Francisco production) also dance the Bandit. The ballet is also in the repertoire of the Robert Joffrey Ballet, and National Ballet, Washington, D.C.

Concert, a public performance by a group or organization, either with or without soloists; the opposite of a recital, in which the whole performance is given by one artist. Several individual dancers often band together to appear in a concert. Modern dancers are also called concert dancers.

Concert, The. Ballet in 1 act; chor.: Jerome Robbins; music: various piano pieces by Frédéric Chopin, with orchestral arrangements by Hershy Kay; costumer: Irene Sharaff; First prod.: New York City Ballet, City Center, N.Y., Mar. 6, 1956, with Tanaquil LeClercq, Yvonne Mounsey, Wilma Curley, Todd Bolender, Robert Barnett, Richard Thomas, John Mandia. A series of dance sketches showing the reactions of a group of concert goers as they listen to Chopin (played on stage by Nicholas Kopeikine). To the "Raindrop" Prelude wistful little people walk around with umbrellas; the Prelude, Op. 28, no. 7 (known to all ballet lovers because of *Les Sylphides*) is used for a series of vignettes, including a lady buying a hat and crumpling with dismay when she sees its fellow on the head of a rival; the "Butterfly" Etude serves as a mad mazurka for a faithless butterfly husband and his friends, and so on. A shortened and extensively revised version was staged by Robbins June 8, 1958, for the Spoleto Festival of Two Worlds, with two drop cloths by Saul Steinberg showing two views of the inside of the Spoleto Theatre. This version had its N.Y. première Sept. 4, 1958, at the Alvin Theatre with Betty Waldberg at the piano and Maria Karnilova, Patricia Dunn, and Todd Bolender in leading roles.

Concertino. Modern dance work; chor.: Pauline Koner; music: Pergolesi's Concertino in A major; costumes: Consuelo Gana. First prod.: 8th American Dance Festival, Conn. College, New London, Aug. 20, 1955, with Pauline Koner, Lucy Venable, and Elizabeth Harris. Three dance movements to match the moods of the antique music. Pauline Koner later staged *Concertino* (with a different second movement) for the Chilean National Ballet, directed by Ernst Uthoff.

Concerto. Ballet in 3 movements; chor.: Vassili Lambrinos; music: Edvard Grieg's Piano Concerto in A minor; décor: Francisco Reymundo. First prod.: London's Festival Ballet, Festival Hall, London, July 27, 1953, with Nathalie Krassovska, Noel Rossana, Keith Beckett. A themeless ballet following the development of the concerto.

Concerto. Ballet in 3 movements; chor. and book: George Skibine; music: André Jolivet's Concerto for Piano and Orchestra. First prod.: Opéra Comique, Paris, Mar. 28, 1958, with Marjorie Tallchief, George Skibine, and Michel Rayne in the principal parts. Also in the repertoire of the Teatro Colón, Buenos Aires, Argentina, where it was premièred in 1961 with Marjorie Tallchief, Skibine and Wasil Tupin, and later danced by Esmeralda Agoglia, José Neglia, and Tupin.

Concerto Barocco. Ballet in 3 movements; chor.: George Balanchine; music: J. S. Bach's Concerto for 2 Violins and Orchestra in D minor; décor (for original production): Eugene Berman. First prod.: American Ballet, for its South American tour, 1941; prod. by American Concert Ballet, at YM-YWHA, N.Y., Nov. 14, 1943, with Mary Jane Shea, Lillian Lanese, Francisco Moncion. First perf. by New York City Ballet at City Center, N.Y., Oct. 11, 1948, with Marie Jeanne, Ruth Gilbert, Francisco Moncion. Shortly thereafter both set and costumes were supplanted by a cyclorama and practice costumes. Ballet Russe de Monte Carlo presented this ballet in practice costumes at City Center, N.Y., Sept. 9, 1945, with Marie Jeanne, Patricia Wilde, and Nicholas Magallanes. Other companies which have this ballet in their repertoires include Grand Ballet de Monte Carlo (1948), Royal Danish Ballet, National Ballet of Canada, Paris Opéra Ballet (première, Dec. 18, 1963).

Concerto Brasileiro. Ballet in 3 movements; chor.: Maryla Gremo; music: Heckel Tavares's *Concerto Brasileiro;* book: Accioly Netto; décor: Fernando

Pamplona; costumes: Nelly Laport. First prod.: Ballet Rio de Janeiro, Teatro Municipal, 1960, with a cast headed by Nelly Laport and Raul Severo. A poet once said that the Brazilian soul was born of three sad races: the Portuguese exile, the African slave, and the conquered Indian. The first movement expresses the sadness of the Brazilian people; the second its longing for love; the third the melting of the three sadnesses into a new-born joy.

Concerto Dansant. Abstract ballet in 3 movements; chor.: Igor Schwezoff; music: Camille Saint-Saëns' Concerto No. 2 in G minor for piano and orchestra; décor: S. Castello Branco. First prod.: Teatro Municipal, Rio de Janeiro, Brazil, 1945; revived by Schwezoff in 1956 at Teatro Municipal with Ady Addor, Aldo Lotufo, Beatriz Consuelo, Raul Severo, Tatiana Leskova, Juan Giuliano, Rosemary Brantes, Johnny Franklin, Sandra Dieken, Jaques Chaurand.

Concierto Coreografico (Choreographic Concerto). Ballet in 3 movements; chor.: Tamara Grigorieva; music: Peter Tchaikovsky's Piano Concerto No. 1 in B flat minor; décor: green cyclorama; costumes: Raul Sempol. First prod.: S.O.D.R.E. Ballet Company, Teatro S.O.D.R.E. Montevideo, Uruguay, 1951, with Tamara Grigorieva in the leading part. Since Nov. 10, 1957, in the repertoire of the Teatro Argentino de la Plata, Argentina, with costumes by Darian Rénard. Since Oct. 29, 1961, in the repertoire of the Teatro Colón, Buenos Aires, with costumes by Alvaro Duranona y Vedia; leading dancers Esmeralda Agoglia, Norman Fontenla, Wasil Tupin, Mercedes Serrano, Margarita Fernandes, Rodolfo Fontán, Carlós Schiafino, and corps de ballet. Fernando Emery has defined this ballet as "a perfect visualization of a musical score."

Concurrence, La. Ballet in 1 act; chor.: George Balanchine; music: Georges Auric; book, décor and costumes: André Derain. First prod.: René Blum & Col. de Basil Ballets Russes de Monte Carlo, 1932, with Irina Baronova and Tamara Toumanova alternating in the principal role and Léon Woicikowski as the Tatterdemalion. A competition between two tailoring establishments offers a thin thread for a number of whimsical dances and exquisite scenes. One highlight of the ballet was the dance of the Tatterdemalion who enters one of the shops in rags and is dressed to the teeth when he emerges.

Confessional. Ballet in 1 scene; chor.: Walter Gore; music: Jan Sibelius (Death of Mélisande from the *Pelléas* Suite); décor: Andrée Howard. First prod.: Oxford Ballet Club, May 10, 1941, with Sally Gilmour and Walter Gore. The work was done to the Sibelius music and the narration of the Robert Browning poem of the same name which tells of the despair and bitterness of a girl who has betrayed her lover under the secrecy of the confessional, only to discover that he has been executed by the Inquisition. The work was taken into the repertoire of Ballet Rambert (première, Arts Theatre, London, Aug. 21, 1941). It was never performed by anyone other than Sally Gilmour and was one of her most moving creations.

Conflicts. Ballet in 1 act; chor.: Norman Morrice; music: Ernest Bloch (Quintet for Piano and Strings); realization: Ralph Koltai. First prod.: Ballet Rambert, Sadler's Wells Theatre, July 23, 1962, with Jonathan Taylor (the Choreographer) and a cast led by Gillian Martlew, June Sandbrook, John Chesworth, Kenneth Bannerman. The emotional difficulties encountered as a choreographer rehearses a ballet.

Conga, a ballroom dance of Afro-Cuban origin in 4/4 time in which the dancers step to each of the first three beats of the music and kick to the fourth. The dance is done either by couples or in a conga line formed by alternating men and women placing their outstretched hands on the shoulders of the person in front of them.

Connecticut College School of Dance, a summer school of modern dance, which, with its American Dance Festivals at Conn. College, New London, is an outgrowth of the Bennington School of the Dance. The plans for the project to bring together student and teacher, artist and audience, were initiated in 1948 by Martha Hill (at that time still at New York Univ.), president Rosemary Park, and the late John F. Moore of Conn. College. N.Y.U. and Conn. College were joint sponsors from 1948 to 1951. Martha Hill and Ruth Bloomer were co-directors, Miss Hill gradually withdrawing after the first few years but remaining as a member of the advisory board. Ruth Bloomer remained as director until 1958 when she resigned for reasons of health. She continued as adviser until her death the following year. Jeanette Schlottmann was her successor as director. Dr. Theodora Weisner, a member of the faculty since the early days, took over in 1963. Among the faculty members for the first year were William Bales, Jane Dudley, Martha Graham, Erick Hawkins, Louis Horst, Doris Humphrey, José Limón, Norman Lloyd, Natanya Neumann, Miriam Pandor, and Ethel Winter. From the beginning Doris Humphrey was a guiding spirit and over the years the faculty has continued to list some of the great names in the dance field: Mary Wigman, Valerie Bettis, Pauline Koner, Pearl Lang, Merce Cunningham, Alvin Ailey, Alwin Nikolais, to name but a few. To quote from the brochure issued on the occasion of the Tenth Annual American Dance Festival: "The program offered by the School of the Dance makes possible an integrated study of the whole art, emphasizing active relationships between technique and composition, practice and performance. The session is, in effect, a laboratory for study and experimental production in which the student works for six weeks as apprentice to a group of artists and teachers responsible for the main developments in contemporary dance." Dancers and dance teachers, actors, musicians, composers, painters, sculptors, theatre designers, and writers have all been and continue to be part of this laboratory. Students from all over the U.S. and from more than twenty foreign countries have taken this summer course which, from 1952, has been sponsored by Conn. College for Women as an additional but separate activity from its own regular dance courses. Two Rockefeller Foundation grants, each for three-year periods (1955–57 and 1958–60), were used for various projects: to increase faculty salaries; to make it possible to engage an orchestra for the American Dance Festival performances; to initiate a film notation project; to institute a program of co-operative scholarships with colleges and studios. After these two foundation grants expired, the trustees of Conn. College continued all these projects. The summer school culminates in a series of performances presented in the college's Palmer Auditorium (see American Dance Festival). As a memorial to Doris Humphrey, an award was established in 1960 for a young choreographer to have the opportunity to work at the summer school on a new dance piece to be publicly presented at a later date, probably (though not necessarily) at the American Dance Festival. The first winner was Jack Moore and his work *Songs Remembered,* was premièred at the 1960 Festival.

Conrad, Karen, American dancer and teacher, b. Philadelphia, Pa., 1919; m. Pittman Corry. Studied for ten years with Catherine Littlefield from age eight; then briefly with Lubov Egorova in Paris. Leading dancer with Littlefield (later Philadelphia) Ballet, dancing principal roles in *Barn Dance, Fairy Doll, Snow Queen, The Sleeping Beauty, Aubade, Daphnis*

Karen Conrad, American ballerina and teacher

and Chloë, (1935–1937). Joined Mordkin Ballet (fall, 1937) as soloist, dancing *The Goldfish, Voices of Spring, Giselle.* When this company was taken over in the organization of Ballet (now American Ballet) Theatre (1939), she remained as leading soloist. Created Woman in His Past (*Lilac Garden*), Duck (*Peter and the Wolf*), French Ballerina (*Gala Performance*), and others. She also danced Mazurka (*Les Sylphides*), Ballerina (*Petrouchka*), Lucile Grahn (*Pas de Quatre*), Odette (*Swan Lake,* Act 2), Can-Can Dancer (*La Boutique Fantasque*), Boulotte (*Bluebeard*). Left the company in 1944 upon her marriage to Pittman Corry, and with him established a school in Atlanta, Ga., and the The Southern Ballet of Atlanta (1946), a regional company for which they have choreographed many ballets, and in which she frequently danced leading roles until she retired as a dancer (1959).

Conservatory, or a Proposal of Marriage Through a Newspaper (Konservatoriet eller Et Avisfrieri). Vaudeville-ballet in two acts; chor.: August Bournonville; music: Holger Simon Paulli. First perf.: Royal Danish Ballet, Copenhagen, May 6, 1849. The action takes place in Paris at the dance school of the Conservatory. The ballet is a combination of a merry intrigue with reminiscences of the time the choreographer spent at the Paris Opéra. Currently only the first act (under the title *Konservatoriet*), showing a typical Bournonville class is being performed. Children of the Royal Danish Ballet School appear in this act.

Constantia. Ballet in 3 movements; chor.: William Dollar; music: Frédéric Chopin; décor: Horace Armistead; costumes: Grace Houston. First prod.: Ballet International, International Theatre, N.Y., Oct. 31, 1944, with Marie Jeanne, William Dollar, and Yvonne Patterson in leading roles; revived for Original Ballet Russe, Metropolitan Opera House, N.Y., Oct. 16, 1946, with Rosella Hightower, André Eglevsky, and Yvonne Patterson; also revived summer, 1947, for Grand Ballet de Monte Carlo with the same cast. The ballet gets its name from Constantia Gladowska, Chopin's ideal for whom he composed his Piano Concerto in F Minor, to which the ballet is set. The ballet reflects the mood of the music.

Constantine Collection, an integral part of the Dance Collection of the New York Public Library, is a gift of the well-known dance photographer Constantine (Constantine Hassalevris). Presented in the fall of 1964, it consists of some 1,000 negatives and about 500 prints with their negatives of American ballet and modern dancers active in the 1940's, a period with the least adequate iconographic coverage. The collection thus fills a serious gap in the documentation of the dance in the U.S. The negatives are of the 4x5 and 5x7 in. sizes, all excellently preserved.

Consuelo, Beatriz (Beatriz Consuelo Cardoso), contemporary Brazilian dancer, b. Porto Alegre. Began study under Toni Seitz. Went to Rio de Janeiro in 1947; studied with Nina Verchinina, Tatiana Leskova. Made her debut with Rio Ballet Society (1948). Joined Teatro Municipal as first dancer (1949), dancing *Giselle, Pas de Quatre, Les Sylphides, Aurora's Wedding, Swan Lake* (Act 2), *Masquerade,* and others. Joined Grand Ballet du Marquis de Cuevas (later Ballet International) (1953); promoted to soloist (1954); to première danseuse (1956); to étoile (1958), the first Brazilian dancer to attain this position in an international company. Her ballets include: *Corrida, Le Retour, Gaîté Parisienne, Le Beau Danube, L'Ange Gris, Les Sylphides, The Bridge, Arlequinade, Fiesta, Perlinpinade, Contrepoint d'Amour, Sebastian, Le Forêt Romantique, The Sleeping Beauty.* After the Cuevas company was disbanded she joined Serge Golovine's company.

Conte, Michel, French dancer, choreographer, composer, b. Villeneuve-sur-Lot, 1932. A Bachelor of Arts with a second prize piano and first prize harmony and composition from the Paris Conservatory, he began his dance studies with Alexandre Volinine in Paris (1950); danced in the corps de ballet of both the Strasbourg and Vichy Opera ballets (1951), and with Les Ballets Parisiens (1952). Emigrated to Canada (1955). His ballets *Un et Un Font Deux* (for which he also composed the score) and *Variations for a Lonely Theme* are in the repertoire of the Royal Winnipeg Ballet. He is a television choreographer and director with the Canadian Broadcasting Corporation, Montreal.

Contemporary Dance, Inc., founded as Contemporary Dance Productions (1956) by William Burdick, Doris Rudko, Elizabeth Rockwell, and Marion Scott for the purpose of contributing to the field of modern dance by presenting new works of merit in joint programs. The works are chosen at auditions which are open to all choreographers. Two or three concerts are presented every season and the works of two to five choreographers are shown in each program. The board of directors unanimously selects the works to be performed, arranges the program order and takes care of the production details. Authorities in the dance field join the board of directors in an advisory capacity for several run-through rehearsals which are held before each performance. Concert expenses and profits are shared by the participating choreographers. A separate series for the younger choreographers who have never presented their works before N.Y. critics is also a regular part of the season's activities. These concerts have separate auditions and are presented whenever there is enough suitable material for a program. Contemporary Dance Productions was incorporated as a nonprofit organization as Contemporary Dance, Inc. (1961), to be eligible for grants from foundations so that concerts could be presented without any expense to the choreographers and new works might be commissioned from gifted choreographers. The present board of directors includes Lucas Hoving, Ann Mackenzie, Jack Moore, Elizabeth Rockwell, Doris Rudko, and Marion Scott. Louis Horst was artistic adviser until his death in early 1964.

Contes Russes. Ballet in prologue and 4 scenes; chor.: Leonide Massine; music: Anatole Liadov; décor: Michel Larionov.

First prod. (in its entirety): Serge Diaghilev Ballets Russes, Théâtre du Châtelet, Paris, May 11, 1917, with Lydia Sokolova (Kikimora), Stanislas Idzikowski (Cat), Lubov Tchernicheva (Swan Princess), Leonide Massine (Bova Korolevich), Nicholas Kremnev (Baba-Yaga). The Kikimora episode alone had been given in San Sebastian, Spain (1916). For the 1918 London season, a dance prelude for Leon Woicikowski and a number called The Dragon's Funeral were added. The ballet is based on Russian folklore and was said to be Diaghilev's own favorite ballet. Kikimora was a witch who rocked her cat in a cradle and then chopped off its head. The Swan Princess had a long variation after which the gallant Bova Korolevich galloped on riding a magnificent wooden horse and slew the dragon that held her captive. Baba-Yaga was a wicked demon disguised as an old woman who stumped about on a wooden leg and ate little girls. In later presentations Bronislava Nijinska and Anatole Vilzak often danced the roles of Kikimora and Bova Korolevich, respectively.

Contraction-Release, in modern dance, terms most generally associated with the Martha Graham technique and choreography. Release denotes the moment when the body is in breath, after inhalation, and possesses an aerial quality; contraction, when the breath has been exhaled, and the drive has gone down and out. Both are active states and demand the complete use of the entire body; both are percussive in intent. Compare with FALL-RECOVERY.

Contrary Body Movement, in ballroom dance, leading with the side of the body opposite to the free foot.

Contredanse, originally an English choral dance in which men and women performed, usually in circles or in couples facing each other. Supposedly the word is a Gallic version of "country dance," but the several hundred contredanses collected by John Playford in his book *The English Dancing Master* (1651) show no traces of a rustic origin. In France a number of dances evolved from the contredanse, which was introduced there around 1710, including the cotillon and quadrille.

Contretemps, in ballet, a step in counter time, i.e. off beat. Technique: start 4th pos. L ft. back, toe pointed; demi-plié and jump off R ft., bringing L ft. sur le cou-de-pied back; put L ft. down in 5th pos., front; glissade to R and finish 5th pos., L ft. front.

Controposto, the principle of lateral opposition of arms, body and legs, popularized by the Italian sculptors of the late Renaissance and Baroque and stated with reference to dance by Rameau in his *The Dancing Master*. According to Lincoln Kirstein: "It is the emphasis of the plasticity of the human body as an erect column in space, capable of accentuating its tri-dimensionality by the opposition of arms and legs. This contrast of the upper and lower parts of the body, stressing the free-moving high-relief of arms and legs, contributes enormously to making the static symmetrical human silhouette (two legs supporting a trunk; two arms capped by a head) an interesting, varied and asymmetrical outline."

Conventions, Teachers', annual meetings of teachers' organizations to discuss business, elect officers, and present to the assembled teachers intensive courses of teaching material in the various phases of dance, as well as routines for school performances. Conventions, usually lasting a week, are generally preceded by normal schools during which aspirants and young teachers are given classes in dance and teaching technique. Prominent teachers form the faculties at conventions and normal schools. Shoe, fabric, and other dealers display their wares at these gatherings.

Coolidge, Elizabeth Sprague (1864–1953), American pianist, composer, patron of music. Founder of the Berkshire Chamber Music Festival at Pittsfield, Mass.; sponsor of the Coolidge Foundation at the Library of Congress, Washington, D.C. The first production of Stravinsky's *Apollon Musagète,* choreographed by Adolph Bolm, was commissioned by this foundation (1928). Among other choreographic commissions of the Coolidge foundation are *Herodiade* (Hindemith) and *Appalachian Spring* (Copland) in 1944; *Dark Meadow* (Carlos Chavez) in 1946, all for Martha Graham.

Copland, Aaron, composer, b. Brooklyn, N.Y., 1900. Studied music with his sister, Leopold Wolfson, Victor Wittgenstein, Clarence Adler; theory with Rubin Goldmark (1917–21); with Nadia Boulanger, Ricardo Viñes at Fontainebleau (France) School of Music (1921–24). First composer to be awarded Guggenheim Fellowship (1925–1926). Composed scores for the ballets *Hear Ye! Hear Ye!* (Ruth Page, 1934), *Billy the Kid* (Eugene Loring, 1938), *Rodeo* (Agnes de Mille, 1942). Elected to the National Institute of Arts and Letters (1942). Won the Pulitzer Prize and the New York Music Critics' Award for *Appalachian Spring* (Martha Graham, 1944). His *Music for the Theatre* was used by Antony Tudor for *Time Table* (1941) and his *El Salon Mexico* by Doris Humphrey (1943). Miss Humphrey also used his Piano Sonata for her work *Day on Earth* (1947). Jerome Robbins used Copland's Concerto for Clarinet and String Orchestra for *The Pied Piper* (New York City Ballet, 1951). Pauline Koner choreographed *Dance Symphony* to his work of the same name (première: Jacob's Pillow Dance Festival, 1963). Copland composed the music for Heinz Rosen's *Ballet in Seven Movements,* presented at the first ballet performance of the new Munich National Theatre, Dec. 3, 1963, the composer conducting this performance. A little known fact about Mr. Copland's compositions for dance is that his first composition specifically for this art form was *Grohg* (1925), a ballet in 1 act for one male and three female principals and corps de ballet. The music is in manuscript and the ballet apparently has never been performed.

Copland, Robert, in 1521 published *The Maner of dauncynge of Bace daunces after the use of Fraunce.* These descriptions of the social dances of the day were written as an appendix to a French grammar.

Coppélia, ou La Fille aux Yeux d'Email. Ballet in 3 acts; chor.: Arthur Saint-Léon; music: Léo Delibes; book: Charles Nuitter and Arthur Saint-Léon; décor: Cambon, Despléchin, Lavastre; costumes; Paul Lormier. First prod.: Théâtre Imperial de l'Opéra, Paris, May 25, 1870, with Guiseppina Bozacchi (Swanilda) and Eugénie Fiocre (Franz). The czardas was first introduced into ballet in *Coppélia* and after this numbers based on national and folk dances became very popular. This ballet, taken from Hoffmann's story *Der Sandmann,* was one of the earliest having a doll come to life. A one-act version was staged at the Empire Theatre, London, Nov. 8, 1884. The full version was staged at the same theatre May 14, 1906, and Swanilda provided Adeline Genée with her greatest role. Nicholas Sergeyev revived the ballet in a version based on choreography by Lev Ivanov and Enrico Cecchetti for Vic-Wells (later Sadler's Wells, now Royal) Ballet at Sadler's Wells Theatre, London, Mar. 21, 1933, with Lydia Lopoukhova and Stanley Judson as Swanilda and Franz and Hedley Briggs as Dr. Coppelius. Later Ninette de Valois danced Swanilda in this two-act version. In 1940 the third act divertissement (with the pas de deux in choreography by Sergeyev) was added, new décor was by William Chappell, and Mary Honer, Robert Helpmann, and Claude

Newman were Swanilda, Franz, and Dr. Coppelius, respectively. Later Helpmann's Dr. Coppelius became one of his great comic creations. The current Royal Ballet *Coppélia* (re-staged 1954) has décor by Osbert Lancaster and Swanilda is one of Nadia Nerina's most successful roles. Sadler's Wells Theatre Ballet also had *Coppélia* in its repertoire, with décor by Loudon Sainthill, premièred Sept. 4, 1951, with Elaine Fifield (Swanilda) and David Blair (Franz) and revised, Jan. 16, 1956, in décor by Robert Medley. An unexpectedly delightful Swanilda in this production was Svetlana Beriosova, not normally associated with soubrette roles. A version staged by Nicholas Zverev for René Blum's Ballets de Monte Carlo had Vera Nemtchinova as an outstanding Swanilda. Alexandra Danilova's Swanilda for Ballet Russe de Monte Carlo was one of her greatest triumphs. A shortened version was staged by Simon Semenoff for Ballet (now American Ballet) Theatre at Metropolitan Opera House, N.Y., Oct. 22, 1942, with Irina Baronova (Swanilda), Anton Dolin (Franz), Semenoff (Dr. Coppelius). At the Paris Opéra where Solange Schwarz was a memorable Swanilda, the tradition of a Franz *en travesti* continues, and Paulette Dynalix is famous for her performance. Ballet Rambert staged *Coppélia* (Sadler's Wells Theatre, Aug. 1, 1957) in décor by Mstislav Doboujinsky, with Violette Verdy (Swanilda), Norman Dixon (Franz), Norman Morrice (Dr. Coppelius); Lucette Aldous was later outstanding in this production. The Royal Danish Ballet has a version staged in 1896 by the German choreographer Glasemann and completed by Hans Beck which is almost entirely a folk-character ballet, only Swanilda dancing on point. Margot Lander and then Inge Sand had triumphs in the principal role, and Franz also provided Fredbjørn Bjørnsson with perhaps his most successful role. Harald Lander, who is responsible for its careful preservation—with certain additions of his own—also staged this version for London's Festival Ballet, premièred Aug. 31, 1956, at Festival Hall, London, in décor by Jean-Denis Maillart, with Belinda Wright (Swanilda), John Gilpin (Franz). The story tells of Swanilda taking the place of the mechanical doll in the mysterious workshop of Dr. Coppelius. She fools the old man, wins back her lover Franz, who has been momentarily fascinated by the doll he believes to be real, and all ends happily in a wedding festival which provides an excellent example of a divertissement (which see).

Coq d'Or, Le. Ballet in 3 acts; chor.: Michel Fokine; music: Nicholas Rimsky-Korsakoff; book: V. Bielsky, revised by Alexandre Benois; décor: Nathalie Gontcharova. First prod.: Diaghilev Ballets Russes. Théâtre National de l'Opéra, Paris, May 21, 1914, with Tamara Karsavina (Queen of Shemakhan), Alexis Bulgakov, Enrico Cecchetti. This ballet, based on a narrative poem by Alexander Pushkin, had a double cast, one of which danced and acted the words sung by the second. Fokine revived *Le Coq d'Or* (without singing) for Col. de Basil's Ballet Russe (1937) with Irina Baronova (Queen of Shemakhan) and Tatiana Riabouchinska (The Golden Cockerel). The ballet tells of a mythical Russian Czar of antiquity who acquired from an Astrologer a Golden Cockerel which would sound an alarm—by crowing—at the approach of danger for the country. The precaution notwithstanding, the Czar falls into the clutches of the neighboring beautiful Queen of Shemakhan and loses both his kingdom and the magic Golden Cockerel.

Coralli, Jean (Jean Coralli Peracini) (1779–1854), famous dancer and choreographer, was born in Paris of Bolognese ancestry. He became a student of the ballet school attached to the Paris Opéra and made his debut in 1802. His first choreographic efforts were made at Vienna in 1800, where he produced several ballets.

During 1815 to 1822 he staged a number of ballets at Milan, Lisbon, and Marseilles. He returned to Milan in 1824 and produced *L'Union de Flore et Zéphire* (1824) and *La Statue de Venus* (1825). About 1825 he was appointed ballet master of the Théâtre de la Porte Saint-Martin, Paris, where he composed several ballets, among them *La Neige, Le Mariage de Raison,* and *Les Artistes.* In 1831 he was appointed choreographer of the Opéra, where he produced among other ballets *La Tempête* (1834), *Le Diable Boiteux* (1836), *La Tarentule* (1839), *Giselle* (1841), *La Péri* (1843). Of these *Giselle, La Péri, Le Diable Boiteux,* and *La Tarentule* achieved considerable success, and have been produced by many ballet companies and are often revived. *Giselle,* in the production of which he was helped by Jules Perrot, became a classic example of a Romantic ballet. Little is known of Coralli's characteristics as a person. He died in Paris on May 1, 1854.

Corelli, Juan, French choreographer, b. Barcelona, Spain, 1935. Studied with Josette Izard and Olga Preobrajenska; danced with the Liceo Opera Ballet in Barcelona, Col. de Basil's Original Ballet Russe, and Grand Ballet du Marquis de Cuevas. Began choreographic work at the suggestion of Rosella Hightower, at the time ballerina of the Marquis company. Most of his work is for French television. In 1964 he came to the U.S. at the invitation of Frederic Franklin, artistic director of the National Ballet, Washington, D.C., for which troupe he staged *Othello,* to music by Maurice Thiriet, premièred Nov. 20, at Lisner Auditorium.

Cornazano, Antonio, ca. 1440, Italian dancing master. Author of a book in which are described dances such as saltarello, quarternaria, and basse dances.

Corps de Ballet, all members of a ballet company who do not perform solo dances but appear only in the ensemble. In contemporary ballet companies, members of the corps de ballet occasionally do small solo parts and soloists appear in the ensemble.

Corsaire, Le. Ballet in 3 acts, 5 scenes; chor.: Joseph Mazilier; music: Adolphe Adam and others; book: H. Vernoy de Saint-Georges and Mazilier. First prod.: Theatre Impérial (now National) de l'Opéra, Jan. 23, 1856, with Carolina Rosati (Medora), Mlle. Couqui (Gulnare), Segarelli (Conrad). It was premièred at the Bolshoi Theatre, St. Petersburg, Jan. 24, 1858, with Mme. Fridberg (Medora), Mme. Radina (Gulnare), Lucien Petipa (Conrad). Marius Petipa staged an entirely new version for a benefit performance for Pierina Legnani at the Maryinsky Theatre, Jan. 25 (new style) 1899, and the role of Medora became a favorite with a long line of ballerinas, among them Lubov Roslavleva (1901), Julia Sedova and Marie Grimaldi (both dancing it for the first time in 1902), Anna Pavlova (1904), Tamara Karsavina (1908), Lubov Egorova (1910 and 1913), Olga Preobrajenska (1914), Yelena Smirnova (1915). Vaguely based on the poem *The Corsair* by Lord Byron, the ballet deals with a number of complicated plots and sub-plots. The basic story is the love of the pirate Conrad for a young Greek girl, Medora, sold into slavery. They survive all misfortunes, including a shipwreck, and live happily ever after. The pas de deux for Medora and Conrad is one of the most spectacular in the entire classic repertoire. It caused a sensation when Alla Sizova and Yuri Soloviev danced it during the Kirov Ballet's first U.S. season (1961). Margot Fonteyn and Rudolf Nureyev also dance a highly successful version. The French dancer-choreographer Albert (Ferdinand Albert Decombe) choreographed an earlier version to music by Robert Bochsa, premièred at the King's Theatre, London, June 29, 1837, with himself as Conrad,

Hermine Elssler (a cousin of Fanny) as Medora, and Pauline Duvernay as Gulnare. This was revived Sept. 30, 1844, at Theatre Royal, Drury Lane, London, with Clara Webster as Medora.

Corseuil, Jaques (Ignacio Corseuil Filho), Brazilian dance critic, b. Porto Alegre, 1913. After graduating as a lawyer from Univ. of Brazil (1937), began his journalistic career as a movie critic. Became interested in ballet, studied its history and technique and, since 1940, has been a full time ballet critic and writer in Rio de Janeiro, contributing to many Brazilian magazines and newspapers, and also to publications in Argentina and Chile. Co-founder of Ballet da Juventude (1945). Has a weekly column in Rio's *Correio de Manha* and since 1946 has been correspondent of *Dance News*. Contributor and assistant to a book for local publication on ballet; contributor to *Dance Encyclopedia*.

Coryphé (m) and Coryphée (f), in the Russian Imperial Ballet, members of the company who were not principals but performed in groups of six and eight. Their official position was between soloists and corps de ballet. This classification does not exist in contemporary ballet companies except in the Soviet Union and in France.

Cosi, Liliana, Italian dancer, b. 1941. Entered the ballet school of Teatro alla Scala, Milan, in 1951; was graduated in 1958; appeared in her Passo d'Addio in 1959. Is a key soloist appearing in important roles in most of the repertoire; understudies ballerinas in their roles.

Cotillon, a social dance in which many, and at least four, couples participate. The cotillon consists of many and often complicated figures during the execution of which prizes for best dancing are often distributed. The cotillon belongs to the category of quadrilles and contredanses which were very popular during the 19th century. Cotillon is also often used for ball as name of a formal gathering of people for social dancing, especially in the case of formal balls given for young people.

Cotillon. Ballet in 1 act; chor.: George Balanchine; music: Emmanuel Chabrier ("Menuet Pompeux"—played as an overture), "Tourbillon," "Mauresque," "Scherzo-Valse," "Idylle," "Danse Rustique," and "Valse Romantique"; book: Boris Kochno; décor: Christian Berard. First prod.: Col. de Basil's Ballets Russes, Théâtre de Monte Carlo, Apr. 12, 1932, with Valentina Blinova, Lubov Rostova, Tamara Toumanova, David Lichine, Léon Woicikowski in main parts. Later the parts of Blinova and Toumanova were taken by Tatiana Riabouchinska and Irina Baronova, respectively. It has no definite plot, except that the action takes place at a ball. The imaginative choreography and, here and there, a dramatic episode made this early Balanchine ballet one of his finest creations. Regrettably, it is not in the repertoire of any ballet company and the choreographer alleges that he has forgotten most, if not all, of the choreography.

Coton, A. V., English writer, journalist, broadcaster, and author in all forms of theatre, b. York, 1906. Began writing ballet criticism in 1935. Worked with Antony Tudor in organizing and managing the London Ballet (1938–39), and with Peggy van Praagh and Maude Lloyd when they revived the company (1939–40). Ballet critic *The Daily Telegraph* since 1954; assistant drama critic for same paper since 1957; London correspondent, *Dance News*, N.Y. (1943–56). Author of *A Prejudice for Ballet* (London, 1938) and *The New Ballet: Kurt Jooss and His Work* (London, 1946); part author *Ballet Here and Now* (1961). Visited Russia in 1960 to study ballet in performance and in teaching. Member of the Critics' Circle, London (president, 1961).

Cou-de-Pied, in ballet, the neck of the foot, or ankle. The working leg is placed at one of three positions on supporting leg; knee, calf, or sur le coup-de-pied.

Country Dance, a social dance whose actual name, contredanse, was changed by the English to country dance; it is the source of the 19th century quadrille. Some authorities consider that there is no connection between country dance and contredanse and that country dance, like barn dance, is simply a generic term for social dances in rural communities.

Country Dance Society of America. See FOLK DANCE AND SONG SOCIETY, ENGLISH.

Coupé, literally, cut; in ballet, a step which cuts or displaces one ft. with the other. Technique: Start with L leg in fondu (i.e. demi-plié), R toe pointed in 2nd pos.; slide R ft. towards L, finishing in a demi-plié with a dégagé of L ft. to 2nd pos., toe pointed. There are many other coupés—front, back, etc.

Courante (also Courant and Corranto), 16th-century court dance; name comes from the French "courir," to run; its Italian origin may be "corrente," stream. Dance consisted of short advances and retreats; chief steps were pas glissés.

Couronne, en, in ballet, position of the arms, slightly curved and held above head; also called 5th pos. en haut.

Court Occasion, A. Ballet in 1 act. Chor.: Brian Macdonald; music: J. S. Bach (Brandenburg Concerto No. 2); décor: Robert Prévost. First prod.: Royal Winnipeg Ballet, The Playhouse, Winnipeg, Dec. 26, 1961, with Fredric Strobel, Sonia Taverner, Annemarie, David Holmes, James Clouser, Sheila MacKinnon, Richard Rutherford, Lynette Fry. Originally created for television in 1957, this ballet was re-choreographed and mounted for the Royal Winnipeg Ballet. The choreography follows the trumpet, oboe, violin, and flute lines of the music as four couples dance a command performance.

Couru (pas couru), in ballet, a running step most often used as preparation for a grand jeté, in order to gain force or momentum.

Cova, Fiorella, Italian dancer, b. Milan, 1936. Entered the ballet school of Teatro alla Scala, Milan, in 1946; was graduated in 1954; appeared in her Passo d'Addio in 1955; promoted to soloist in 1958. Her repertoire includes *Serenade, Allegro Brillante, Ballet Imperial, Les Sylphides, La Sylphide* (Effie). She is considered a brilliant technician, excelling in elevation and turns.

Covent Garden, Royal Opera House (London), opened originally as a dramatic theatre in 1732 under the name Covent Garden Theatre. The theatre was destroyed by fire in 1809 and rebuilt the following year. In 1847 the auditorium of the theatre was enlarged and the theatre reopened as an opera house under the name Royal Italian Opera. The opening performance (Apr. 6) was Rossini's *Semiramade,* in which Carlotta Grisi was ballerina. In 1856 the theatre was again destroyed by fire. The existing opera house was built in 1858. Throughout the years it has played host to numerous ballet organizations, among them the Diaghilev Ballets Russes, the Anna Pavlova company, Col. de Basil's Ballets Russes de Monte Carlo and his Original Ballet Russe, Ballet (now American Ballet) Theatre, Grand Ballet du Marquis de Cuevas, New York City Ballet, Bolshoi Ballet, Kirov Ballet, and others. Since Feb. 20, 1946, Covent Garden has been the permanent home of the Sadler's Wells (now Royal) Ballet.

Cox, Patricia, English dancer, b. Edgware, Middlesex, 1936. Studied at Sadler's Wells School from 1946. Entered Sadler's Wells Theatre Ballet (1954); soloist (1956), the title role in *Pineapple Poll* being one of her outstanding roles. To Australia with Royal Ballet (1958); joined Australian Ballet (1960). Currently teaching in Adelaide.

Cramér, Ivo, Swedish choreographer, dancer and director, b. Göteborg, 1921. Studied music and ballet with Vera Alexandrova, Birgit Cullberg, Audrey de Vos, and Vera Volokova. Toured with own group and with Swedish Dance Theatre (1945–47). Ballet master and choreographer of *Verde Gaio* at the San Carlos Opera House, Lisbon (1948–49). Toured England with a Norwegian troupe (1951). Created works for the Norwegian Ballet, Royal Swedish Ballet and companies in Göteborg and Malmö. Resident choreographer of the Bergen Festival (1958, 1959, 1960). Principal works include: Bibliska Bilder, *The Message* (1945), *The Prodigal Son* (1957), *Linden* (1959), *Romantic Suite* and *Bendik and Arolilja* (1959), and *Bluebeard's Nightmare* (1961).

Cranko, John, dancer, choreographer, director, b. Rustenburg, South Africa, 1927. Studied dance at Univ. of Capetown, South Africa, and later at Sadler's Wells (now Royal) Ballet School. Choreographer and dancer, Capetown Ballet Club (1944–45); Sadler's Wells Theatre Ballet (1946–47), creating Pugilist (*Mardi Gras*) and dancing Pierrot (*Carnaval*), Fiancé (*La Fête Etrange*), etc. A frolicking pas de trois *Tritsch-Tratsch* (1946) first brought him to public attention as a promising choreographer and he confirmed his reputation with *Children's Corner,* to the Claude Debussy Suite of that name later the same year, *Sea Change* and *Beauty and the Beast* (both 1949). *Pineapple Poll* and *Harlequin in April* (both 1951) established him as one of the leading British choreographers of the day. All these were for Sadler's Wells Theatre Ballet. For Sadler's Wells (now Royal) Ballet he choreographed *Bonne-Bouche* (1952), *The Shadow* (1953), returning briefly to the Theatre Ballet for *Lady and the Fool* (1954), which was later taken into the repertoire of the Royal Ballet; then in 1957 choreographed the first full-length entirely English ballet, *The Prince of the Pagodas* (Frederick Ashton's *Cinderella* which preceded it had used the Prokofiev score, and his *Sylvia* was a new version of the old French ballet to music by Léo Delibes). Cranko's last ballet for the Royal Ballet was *Antigone* (1960). He choreographed *The Witch* (1950) for New York City Ballet during its first London season but the ballet was withdrawn after a few performances as the Ravel estate refused permission for the use of the Maurice Ravel *Piano Concerto for Two Hands* which had been the score. For Ballet Rambert he choreographed *Variations on a Theme* (1954), *La Reja* (1959); for the Paris Opéra, *La Belle Hélène* (1955); for Teatro alla Scala, Milan, *Romeo and Juliet* (1959). Also author of the revues *Cranks* (1955) and *New Cranks* (1960). Appointed Director of Ballet at Württemberg Staatstheater, Stuttgart, Germany (1961), where his *Romeo and Juliet,* staged in Dec. 1962, had a major success. His Stuttgart company performed at the 1963 Edinburgh Festival. In 1964 he staged *Romeo and Juliet* for the National Ballet of Canada, which also has his *Pineapple Poll,* as has Australian Ballet. In Apr., 1965, he staged *Eugene Onegin* for the Stuttgart Ballet to selected music of Peter Tchaikovsky, excluding the score of the composer's opera of the same name.

Craske, Margaret, contemporary English ballet teacher, a pupil of Enrico Cecchetti. A member for a short time of the Diaghilev Ballets Russes, she also toured with Ninette de Valois in a small group, playing English variety houses during the early 1920's. Taught for many years in London. When Ballet (now American Ballet) Theatre appeared in London for its first season (1946), she was invited to the U.S. as the company's ballet mistress and teacher. When Ballet Theatre and Metropolitan Opera House combined to open a school at the Met (fall, 1950), she remained at the Met to teach, and continued when it became the Metropolitan Opera Ballet School (where she is now assistant director). Has also taught many summers at Jacob's Pillow, Lee, Mass. With C. W. Beaumont wrote *The Theory and Practice of Allegro in Classical Ballet* (1920) and with Derra de Moroda, *The Theory and Practice of Advanced Allegro in Classical Ballet* (London, 1956), both books being expositions of Cecchetti technique.

Creation of the World, The (La Création du Monde). The original version was choreographed by Jean Börlin (1923) for Les Ballets Suédois to a score specially composed by Darius Milhaud on Negro rhythms. Book was by Blaise Cendrars and décor by Fernand Léger. Totemistic deities created a world of trees, animals, birds, insects, until man and woman finally emerged. Ninette de Valois choreographed a new version for the Camargo Society in 1931 in décor by Edward Wolfe, which was taken into the repertoire of Sadler's Wells Ballet (when it was still known as Vic-Wells Ballet) Oct. 30, 1933, at the Old Vic Theatre. The score continues to exercise a fascination and has frequently been used by ballet and modern dance choreographers, recent versions being by Todd Bolender for New York City Ballet (see JAZZ CONCERT) and Alvin Ailey.

Criticism, Dance.

BY EDWIN DENBY.

People interested in dancing as a form of art complain that our dance criticism is poor. Poor it is but not poor in relation to its pay. Anyone who writes intelligently about dancing does so at his own expense. Almost all our dance criticism appears in the form of newspaper reviewing. But almost all papers would rather misinform the public than retain a specialized dance reporter. Even rich ones delight in skimping on costs by sending out a staff music critic who covers ballet as an extra unpaid chore.

In the whole country only two exceptionally well-edited papers make a practice of employing specialized dance critics —*The New York Times* and the *New York Herald Tribune*. Three others, the *Chicago American,* the *Christian Science Monitor,* and the *Washington Post,* are paying dance the compliment of having at least part-time reviewers. The two full-time jobs, the *Times* and the *Tribune,* the best that specialists can hope for, carry an average salary hardly comparable to that of a fair soloist on the ballet stage. If the profit motive is a sacred American right, it is easier to account for miserable performances by our writers than for acceptable ones.

Among the mass of nonsense printed each year about dancing a few specialists and gifted amateurs do produce on their own initiative a trickle of vivid reporting, informed technical discussion, valuable historical research, and striking critical insight. The conditions and the average quality of dance criticism seem to be similar the world over. Ours is no worse than that written elsewhere, except that there is more of it packaged for breakfast.

Most of our criticism is poor but many readers hardly mind how foolish it is; they read it too inattentively to notice. Some of them glance at a review only to see if the verdict on a show is for or against their going. Others, who have opinions of their own, are eager to quote what the paper said either with rage or pride. In their eagerness they often misquote what they read and catch the meaning of written words as vaguely as a playful dog does that of speech. Anyone who writes for a paper is expected to satisfy the canine eagerness of many readers. They love to be bullied and wheedled; to be floored by a wisecrack, excited by gossip, inflamed by appeals to bigotry or popular prejudice; they love a female critic to gasp or fret and a male critic to be opinionated. At this level the difference between good and bad criticism is slight; and if you have to read foolish criticism this is as much fun as you can get out of it.

There are, however, many people who like to find sense even in a dance column. They expect a critic writing as an educated American to give them a clear picture of the event and to place it in its relation to the art of theatre dancing. When good criticism appears in a large newspaper many people welcome and appreciate it. Many all over the country know very well what ballet is about and follow intelligent reviewing not necessarily with agreement but with spontaneous interest. They realize that a good editor can give it to them and that one who doesn't is in this respect slovenly.

To judge a ballet performance as attentively as a work of imagination is judged and by similar standards is nowadays normal enough. To be sure everyone doesn't respond to a high degree of imagination in dancing, and not every intelligent person is convinced that dancing can create the peculiar spell—intimate, sustained and grand—that a work of art does. But in the course of the last two centuries enough intelligent people have been convinced it can, so that now the possibility is normally accepted. Our stage dancing is less abundant an art than our music, painting, or literature; but its claim to serious attention is that it belongs like them to the formal world of civilized fantasy. In recent years ballet has been the liveliest form of poetic theatre we have had.

Dancing that is pleasing and neat, that shows ingenuity and a touch of fancy, is no news in a luxurious city. But dancing that by its sequence of movements and rhythm creates an absorbing imaginative spell is a special attraction a journalist must be able to recognize and describe. The prestige position of a ballet company depends entirely on how well its performances maintain, for people who know what art or poetry is about, a spell as art and a power as poetry. It is these imaginative people who can watch with attention—there are many thousands of them in New York—whose satisfaction stimulates general curiosity and influences wealthy art-patrons to pay the deficits. They go for pleasure, just as they might go to a concert by Gold and Fizdale at Philharmonic Hall or read Stendahl or Jane Bowles at home. Dancing delights them where they see it become an art and it is to see this happen that they like to go. What they want to find out from a review is, did an event of artistic interest take place, and if it did, what particular flavor did it have? And because they are the readers really interested in what only a dance reporter can tell them, it is his business to answer their questions distinctly.

If his report interests them, they will go and see for themselves and incidentally they will notice the sort of news they can rely on him for. If his remarks often turn out to be illuminating, he is judged a good critic; too many foolish or evasive reports on the other hand make him lose his status as a valuable observer. They expect him to recognize and formulate the point at issue in a performance more quickly and sharply than they would themselves. But without considerable experience in several arts and of dancing and its technical basis too, the observer has no standards by which to measure and no practice in disentangling the pretensions of a ballet from its achievements. That is why a newspaper that wants to inform its readers on interesting dance events has to keep a reporter with the particular gift and training needed for the job.

A dance journalist's business is to sketch a lively portrait of the event he is dealing with. His most interesting task is to describe the nature of the dancing—what imaginative spell it aims for, what method it proceeds by and what it achieves. In relation to the performance he describes the gifts or the development of artists, the technical basis of esthetic effects, even the organizational problems that affect artistic production. The more distinctly he expresses himself, the more he exposes himself to refutation and the better he does his job. But beyond this the dance public wants him to be influential in raising the level of dance production in their community; to be enlightening on general questions of theatre dancing, its heritage and its current innovations; and to awaken an interest in dancing among intelligent readers who are not dance fans already.

What awakens the interest of an intelligent reader in a dance column is to find it written in good English. Even if he is not used to thinking about dancing he can follow a discussion that makes its point through a vivid picture of what actually happens on stage. On the other hand he loses interest if a dance column offers him only the same vague clichés he has already read elsewhere in the paper. After reading a movie review or a political commentator he is not thrilled to find that a ballet too is challenging, vital, significant (significant of what? challenging or vital to whom?). When a ballet is called earthy he recognizes the term as a current synonym for commercial-minded. Inappropriate visual images are suggested to him when he reads that a dance is meaty; or that dancers on stage were rooted in the soil and clung bravely to their roots; or that young choreographers are to be admired for their groping. No sensible person can want to watch a dancer brooding over a culture; or filling her old form with a new content; or even being stunningly fertile; or if he wants to, it isn't because of the dancing.

Our unspecialized dance reporters can't in sensible terms tell the public what is interesting and original in current dancing. Since 1942, for instance, strict classic ballet has become widely appreciated and acclimated in this country. It has changed so far from the pre-war Ballet Russe manner that it has now a new and American flavor. But the nation's dance journalists have been notably unenlightening on the subject of classicism, its meaning and its new development (some journalists even confuse classicism with stylized movement). To take another example, in the same period the modern dance has been trying for a new style, a new rhythm and a different sort of theatre appeal than before. Various aspects of the change have been due to Martha Graham's example, to her own shift in technique, to a new supply of male dancers, and to contact with ballet; a new modern style shows particularly in the work of Sybil Shearer and Merce Cunningham. The nation's press knows that something has happened to our dancing in the last fifteen or sixteen years, but it doesn't yet know what.

If only another half-dozen specialized and intelligent dance critics were writing on metropolitan papers, the public all over the country would profit considerably. Not that well-informed critics would agree on all details—far from it—but they could with a sharper authority insist on an improved general level of production.

A special question of dance journalism is its usefulness to the choreographers and dancers who are reviewed. The point concerns few newspaper readers, but those it agitates bitterly. Ignorant criticism is naturally resented by professionals; but intelligent criticism when adverse often is, too. All critics would like very much to be helpful to a good artist. They love the art they review and every one who contributes to it; they know the many risks of the profession. They are constantly trying to help, but the occasions when they are actually helpful seem to be happy accidents.

The professionals of the dance world are of course the most eager readers of dance reviewing, but they do not read their own reviews very rationally. For one thing a poor notice upsets them the way an insult does other people. For another, they argue that it endangers their future jobs. But in the touring repertory system of ballet the critics do not "make and break" a ballet or a dancer; managers do. To a dancer's career a bad notice is a much less serious occupational hazard than a poor figure, laziness, poor hygiene, tactlessness toward fellow-professionals or soloistic megalomania—none of which a dancer who suffers from them complains of nearly so loudly.

A choreographer or a dancer, as he reads his notices, often forgets that they are not addressed to him personally but are a report to the general public. They are a sort of conversation between members of the audience on which the artist eavesdrops at his own emotional risk. What he overhears may make no sense to him; it may shock or intoxicate him; but it is astonishing how rarely it is of any use to him in his actual creative activity. It will sometimes corroborate a guess of his own, but it is generally silent on points he feels are vital. Reviews cannot replace his own conscience, much less driving instinct. A great dancer after twenty years of celebrity cited only two reviews that had been valuable.

In my opinion reading reviews about one's self is a waste of time, like smoking cigarettes. To read reviews of rivals is more likely to be of use. Hardworking artists are refreshed by a rave for their "art," whether it makes sense or not, but blame is exhausting to deal with. Serious professionals often limit the value of reviews to the recognition of good craftsmanship and technical innovations. According to Virgil Thomson—great artist and great critic, too—opinions beyond the recognition of these facts are pure fantasy. But for the audience—to whom the critic reports—the fantasy spell of art is that of conscious device multiplied by unconscious meaning. As long as the critic's fantasy remains intelligible, its forces and its scope are what give the reader a sense of the power and value of the work reviewed.

An intelligent reader learns from a critic not what to think about a piece of art, but how to think about it; he finds a way he hadn't thought of using. The existence of an "authoritative critic" or of a "definitive evaluation" is a fiction like that of a sea serpent. Everybody knows the wild errors of judgment even the best critics of the past have made; it is easier to agree with contemporary judgments but no more likely that they are right. It seems to me that it is not the critics' historic function to have the right opinions but to have interesting ones. He talks but he has nothing to sell. His social value is that of a man standing on a streetcorner talking so intently about his subject that he doesn't realize how peculiar he looks doing it. The intentness of his interest makes people who don't know what he's talking about believe that whatever it is, it must be real somehow—that the art of dancing must be a real thing to some people some of the time. That educates citizens who didn't know it and cheers up those who did.

When people who like dancing say a critic is right they mean he is right enough and that his imaginative descriptions are generally illuminating. He can hardly be illuminating or right enough unless he has a fund of knowledge about his subject. In theory he needs to know the techniques and the historical achievements of dancing, the various ways people have looked at it and written about it, and finally he needs a workable hypothesis of what makes a dance hang together and communicate its images so they are remembered. Experience as a dancer and choreographer is an invaluable help to him.

The best organized and by far the most useful chunk of knowledge a critic has access to is that about the technique and history of classic ballet—in particular, as ballet dancers learn it. Its gymnastic and rhythmic technique is coherent enough to suggest principles of dance logic—as expressive human movement in musical time and architectural space. But so far the best-informed of specialized ballet critics have not formulated these clearly. French ballet criticism as a whole, though it has had for several centuries nearly all the best dancing in the world to look at, though it has had since as far back as 1760 (since Noverre's *Letters*) a brilliant lesson in how to write about dancing, hasn't yet been able to bring order and clarity to the subject. Though they have been writing steadily for two centuries and more—and often writing pleasantly—the Paris critics have left us as reporters no accurate ballet history, as critics no workable theory of dance emphasis, of dance form, or of dance meaning.

The handicap to method in dance criticism has always been that its subject matter—dancing that can fascinate as an art does—is so elusive. Other arts have accumulated numerous wonderfully fascinating examples in many successive styles. Dancing produces few masterpieces and those it does are ephemeral. They can't be stored away; they depend on virtuoso execution, sometimes even on unique interpreters. They exist only in conjunction with music, stage architecture, and decoration in transitory highly expensive performances. It is difficult to see the great dance effects as they happen, to see them accurately, catch them so to speak in flight and hold them fast in memory. It is even more difficult to verbalize them for critical discussion. The particular essence of a performance, its human sweep of articulate rhythm in space and time has no specific terminology to describe it. Unlike criticism of other arts, that of dancing cannot casually refer the student to a rich variety of well-known great effects and it cannot quote passages as illustrations.

This lack of precision, of data and method is not without advantages. It saves everyone a lot of pedantry and academicism, and it invites the lively critic to invent most of the language and logic of his subject. Its disadvantages, however, are that it makes the standards of quality vague, the range of achieved effects uncertain and the classification of their component parts clumsy. Dance esthetics, in English especially, is in a pioneering stage; a pioneer may manage to plant a rose bush in his wilderness next to the rhubarb, but he's not going to win any prizes in the flower show back in Boston.

The esthetics of dancing—that is, a sort of algebra by which the impression a performance makes can be readily itemized, estimated, and communicated to a reader —is vague and clumsy. The dance critic's wits have to be all the sharper; he has to use esthetic common sense to help out. And he has to pull his objectivity out of his hat. The poverty of his dance-critical heritage makes it hard for him to get a good view of his personal blind spots, and develop his special gifts by finding out how he personally reacts to a wide range of much discussed masterpieces. If he is annoyed by Mozart or Vermeer, or even by Picasso and Stravinsky, he can read intelligent opinions different from his own. That way he learns who he is, what he knows and doesn't know. Gaps and crudities of critical technique are of concern to a professional critic; they are questions of his craft.

The earnest craftsman must hope that once a dance-script has become established, once the various hints toward a critical method (including those by modern dance theoreticians or of exotic traditions) have been collected, sifted and codified, dance critics will seem brighter than they do now.

At present a critic has to risk hypothesis. He can try, for instance, to distinguish in the complex total effect of a performance the relationships between dance effect and story effect, between expressive individualized rhythm and neutral structural rhythm, dance impetus and pantomime shock, dance illusion and dance fun, sex appeal and impersonation, gesture which relates to the whole architectural space of the stage and has an effect like singing and gesture which relates to the dancer's own body and so has the effect of a spoken tone. There are, of course, many possible relationships between the dancing and the structure or momentum of the music which, by creating in the visual rhythm illusions of lightness and weight, impediment or support (for instance), affect the meaning of a passage. Dance criticism would be clearer if it found a way to describe these and other relationships in terms of theatrical effect; and to describe just what the dancers' bodies do—the trunk, legs, arms, head, hands and feet—in relation to one another. The expression of a reviewer's personal reaction, no matter how violent or singular, becomes no immodesty when he manages to make distinct to the reader the visible objective action on stage he is reacting to.

Nowadays, however, a critic doesn't screen a dance performance according to such distinctions. What he actually does is to work backwards, so to speak, from the dance image that after the event is over strikes him as a peculiarly fascinating one. He tries to deduce from it a common denominator in what he saw—a coherent principle, that is, among uncertainly remembered, partly intense, partly vague, partly contradictory images. It takes boldness to simplify his impressions so they add up clearly to a forthright opinion; and it sometimes takes a malicious sense of fun, too, to trust to his instinct where he knows he is risking his neck. But the intelligent reader need not be at all sorry that dance criticism is in a rudimentary or pioneering stage. It makes it more inviting to poets than to school teachers; and though its problems and possible discoveries are not colossal ones, still—if it succeeds in attracting poets—it should be for a century or so fun to write and to read.

An intelligent reader expects the critic—in his role of school teacher—to distinguish between good and bad dance technique, to distinguish between good and bad choreographic craftsmanship, to specify technical inventions and specify also the gifts that make a choreographer or a dancer remarkable despite defects in craftsmanship. Here the writer shows his fairness. But what one enjoys most in reading dance criticism is the illusion of being present at a performance, of watching it with an unusually active interest and seeing unexpected possibilities take place. Reading a good critic's description of qualities I have seen, I seem to see them more clearly. If I have not seen them, I try looking for them in performances I remember or try to find them next time I go to the theatre. And when you look for qualities a reviewer has mentioned, you may find something else equally surprising. For your sharpened eye and limberer imagination is still a part of your own identity—not of his—and leads you to discoveries of your own. The fun in reading dance criticism is the discovery of an unexpected aspect of one's own sensibility.

In reading the great ballet critics of the past one is not impressed by their fairness but by their liveliness. In reading Noverre or Théophile Gautier or André Levinson, I find accounts that strike me as so unlikely I interpret them—by analogy to contemporaries—as blind spots, or propaganda and rhetoric; even if some of these accounts are accepted as facts of dance history. But it is not the partisan spirit with which they can blindly propagandize their own esthetic views that differentiates them from lesser critics, it is the vividness of their descriptions that is unique. Gautier, who of the three gives a reader the most immediate sense of the sensuous fluidity and physical presence of ballet, expresses theory in terms of chit-chat and ignores choreographic structure and technical talk. He seems to report wholly from the point of view of a civilized entertainment seeker; the other two from the backstage point of view of the craftsman as well.

Noverre and Levinson advance theories of dance expression which are diametrically opposite. The force with which they are formulated gives their writing an elevation Gautier avoids, but makes them both far easier than he is to misunderstand. Here in a nutshell is the dance critic's problem: the sharper he formulates a theory of the technique of expression, of how dance communicates what it does, the further he gets from the human vivacity of dancing without which it communicates nothing at all. Yet it is difficult to consider the central question of dancing—I mean, the transport and sweep that dance continuity can achieve, the imaginative radiance some moments of dancing are able to keep for years in people's memories, the central question George Balanchine in his illuminating "Notes on Choreography" brings up in speaking of "basic movements"—unless the critic finds some way to generalize and to speak vividly of general as well as of particular dance experience.

I trust the critic of the future will be well-informed enough to discuss such generalized principles of dance expression clearly. He could begin by clarifying our specific ballet tradition—the tradition called classic because its expressive intentions and technical precisions were long ago in some measure modeled on the achievements of ancient classic literature. It seems to me the elements of this theatre dance tradition, if they were vividly appreciated, are various enough to include in one set of critical values both what we call the modern dance and our present classic ballet. It seems to me that a vivid sense of such an inclusive tradition would set the merits of a choreographer or of a dancer in a larger perspective and would offer a way of describing his scope as craftsman and as artist in the light of all the achievements of past theatre dancing.

So I should like to read a critic who could make me appreciate in dancing the magic communal beat of rhythm and the civilized tradition of a personal and measured communication. I expect him to sharpen my perception sometimes to an over-all effect, sometimes to a specific detail. I should not be surprised to find in some of his descriptions general ideas stimulating in themselves, even apart from his immediate subject, nor to find in other descriptions technical terms of dancing, music, painting, or theatre craft. I should like him to place a choreographer or a dancer with his individual derivations and innovations in the perspective of the tradition of theatre dancing. I am far more interested though if a writer is able, in describing dancing in its own terms, to suggest how the flavor or the spell of it is related to aspects of the fantasy world we live in, to our daily experience of culture and of custom; if he can give my imagination a steer about the scope of the meaning it communicates. But as I read I want to see too the sensual brilliance of young girls and boys, of young men and women dancing together and in alternation on stage, the quickness and suavity of their particular bodies, their grace of response, their fervor of imagination, the boldness and innocence of their flying limbs.

A writer is interesting if he can tell what the dancers did, what they communicated, and how remarkable that was. But to give in words the illusion of watching dancers as they create a ballet in action requires a literary gift. An abstruse sentence by Mallarmé, the rhythmic subtlety of a paragraph by Marianne Moore, a witty page-long collage of technical terms by Goncourt can give the reader a sharper sense of what dancing is about than a book by an untalented writer no matter how much better acquainted with his subject he is. Such examples lead to fallacious conclusions, but I am drawing no conclusions, I am stating a fact. A dance critic's education includes dance experience, musical and pictorial experience, a sense of what art in general is about and what people are really like. But all these advantages are not enough unless they meet with an unusual literary gift and discipline.

Now and then in reading dance criticism one comes across a phrase or a sentence that suggests such an ideal possibility. It is to emphasize these passages to people who wonder what good dance criticism is that I am writing. The fact that no criticism is perfect doesn't invalidate its good moments. Granted it is brilliant far less often than the dancing it commemorates; the fact that it is after all occasionally brilliant is what makes it as a form of intellectual activity in a modest way worthwhile. [NOTE: Except for minor changes, the preceding article appears as published in the 1949 edition of *The Dance Encyclopedia.*] Since that time the *N.Y. Herald Tribune* has ceased to exist. As of Sept., 1966, Walter Terry, its dance critic, has filled the same position on the *World Journal Tribune*.

Crofton, Kathleen, Contemporary English dancer, teacher, writer, b. Fyzavad, India. Studied with Laurent Novikov, Olga Preobrajenska, Nicholas Legat, Vera Trefilova. Member of Anna Pavlova's company (1923–27), Chicago Civic Opera Ballet (1929–31). With Bronislava Nijinska's company in Paris and European tour, then joined Col. de Basil's Ballets Russes de Monte Carlo at its inception (1932) travelling with that branch of it which went to Australia directed by Victor Dandré (1934–35). Member of Markova-Dolin Ballet (1935–37). Teaching at her own studio in London since 1951; guest teacher for Royal Ballet since 1960; has also taught as guest in Zurich and Amsterdam. London dance critic for *Christian Science Monitor* since 1958.

Croisé, in ballet, pose of the body, legs and head, in which the dancer stands at an oblique angle to the spectators, with the working leg crossing the line of the body. The pose croisée may be en avant or en arrière.

Croqueuse de Diamants, La (The Diamond Cruncher). Ballet in 1 act, 4 scenes; chor.: Roland Petit; music: Jean-Michel Damase, with lyrics by Raymond Queneau; book: Roland Petit and Alfred Adam; décor: Georges Wakhevitch. First prod.: Ballets de Paris de Roland Petit, Marigny Théâtre, Paris, Sept. 25, 1950, with Renée Jeanmaire (The Diamond Cruncher), Roland Petit (Delivery Boy), Gordon Hamilton (Proprietor of the Bar). In this "ballet-chantant" Jeanmaire sang on the stage for the first time. A girl gangster has a passion for eating the diamonds her associates steal. A delivery boy from the bistro next door to her hideout accidentally discovers both the whereabouts of the gang and her penchant for diamond crunching and capitalizes on both. The ballet had its first N.Y. performance on Oct. 31, 1950, at the National Theatre. It later was the first of the quartet of Petit ballets filmed under the title *Black Tights,* the others being *Carmen, Cyrano de Bergerac* and *Deuil en 24 Heures* (A Merry Mourning).

Crum, George, Musical Director, National Ballet of Canada, b. Providence, R.I., 1926. Studied at Royal Conservatory of Toronto. Chorus master and conductor Canadian Opera Company (1946–52); coach and répétiteur under Leon Furtwängler at the Salzburg Festival (1952). Has conducted Toronto Symphony, CBC Symphony, and other symphony orchestras in Canada and U.S.; has held present position since 1951.

Csardas. See CZARDAS.

Cuadro Flamenco, literally, gypsy picture or gypsy scene. In Spanish dance, a divertissement in which several dancers participate, their dances generally increasing in intensity. The name was originally applied to the dances staged by Spanish gypsies in their caves.

Cucchi, Claudine (1838–1913), Italian ballerina. Danced mostly in Vienna (1857–68), but appeared also in Paris, St. Petersburg, and Warsaw. Made her debut in St. Petersburg in *Catarina* (1866) and also danced *Esmeralda,* these being the ballets for which she was particularly noted.

Cullberg, Birgit, Swedish dancer, choreographer and director, b. Nyköping, 1908. Studied at the Stockholm Univ., attended the Jooss-Leeder School at Dartington Hall, England (1935–39). Returned to Sweden in 1939 and soon formed her own group which appeared in literary revues and gave own performances. Her first ballets were often humorous, psychological studies, animal characterizations, and in *Propaganda* and *Offensive,* satirical. Directed Swedish Dance Theatre with Ivo Cramér (1946–47). Was resident choreographer of Royal Swedish Ballet (1952–57) and is now director and choreographer of Stockholm City Theatre (since 1960). Was awarded the Swedish King's fellowship (1958) and the Order of Vasa (1961). Her outstanding choreographic works are *Miss Julie* (1950), *Medea* (1951), *Romeo and Juliet* (1955), *Moon Reindeer* (1957), *Odysseus* (1959), *The Lady from the Sea* (1960), *Eden* pas de deux (1961) and the television ballet *The Evil Queen* (1961) which won the Prix d'Italia of that year and was shown in U.S. on educational TV (1963, 1964). Birgit Cullberg's ballets are danced by all Scandinavian companies and by American Ballet Theatre (*Miss Julie, Moon Reindeer, Lady from the Sea, Eden*), the New York City Ballet (*Medea*), the Chilean National Ballet, and others. She wrote the book *The Ballet and We* and collaborated on the book *The Ballet School*

Birgit Cullberg, Swedish choreographer

(both in Swedish), and is the author of many articles on dance. Appointed a member of the artistic council to the Royal Swedish Ballet (June, 1963). She staged her own version of *Seven Deadly Sins* (which later went into the repertoire of Royal Swedish Ballet) for performances in twelve open-air theatres in Stockholm during Aug. 1963. During the same month she filmed a special ballet film, including her *Eden* pas de deux. In 1966 she revived *Moon Reindeer* for American Ballet Theatre. In the same year she established a small group of dancers at Stockholm's new City Theatre to perform Sunday and Monday and tour the rest of the week. The Swedish Government made a grant of $100,000 for this purpose.

Cultural Exchange Program. The Cultural Exchange Program of the State Department, as it is now called, was established by the Federal Government in 1954. Its original title was the Performing Arts International Exchange Program. The title has been changed at least a half dozen times, one of the changes being The President's Special International Program of Cultural Presentations. At present the Exchange Program is part of the Bureau of Educational and Cultural Affairs of the Department of State. The Program is made possible by an annual appropriation from the Congress of about $2,400,000.

Soon after the Program was created, the State Department chose the American National Theatre and Academy (ANTA), a Congress-charted, non-profit organization, as the instrumentality through which the Program would be administered. To evaluate the artistic basis of projects requesting State Department assistance for tours abroad, advisory panels were set up in dance, music, and drama.

In the spring of 1963 the State Department assumed full responsibility for managing the presentations. This eliminated the role of ANTA, which had been functioning for an annual fee of $110,000. The panels have continued as before. In 1966 the chairman of the dance panel was Gertrude Macy. In addition to the panels an Advisory Committee on the Arts was created on which Lew Christensen, director and choreographer-in-chief of the San Francisco Ballet, was appointed to represent dance.

The usual procedure is for a company to apply to the State Department for assistance. If the proposed tour is considered to be of possible interest to the State Department, the application is presented to the panel for evaluation of the company, or individual. Occasionally the State Department will assume the initiative of inviting a company or an individual to submit an application for a tour of a part of the world suggested by the State Department.

It has been emphasized from the beginning of the program that the Government assistance will not be in the form of a subvention. The Government will help only to offset unusual costs (such as high travelling expenses) which might otherwise make privately sponsored tours unfeasible. The State Department has noted that "The policy of the Department is that . . . within the limitations of budget, it will send abroad each year the specific attractions that, in the judgment of various specialists in Washington and abroad, will best advance our foreign policy aims, whether they should be dance companies or other attractions."

The Program got into high gear in 1958, when on Jan. 27 the U.S. and the Soviet Union signed an agreement about cultural, educational, technical, and sport exchanges between the two countries. This was the agreement that made possible, among other things, visits of American ballet companies to the Soviet Union and of Soviet ballet companies to the U.S.

The following dance companies and individual dancers have made overseas tours for the State Department: José Limón and Co. (1954, 1957, 1960, 1963); New York City Ballet (1955, 1956, 1958, 1960, 1962, 1965); American Ballet Theatre (1955, 1956, 1958, 1960, 1964, 1966); Maria Tallchief–André Eglevsky (1955); Martha Graham and Co. (1955–56, 1962); Tom Two-Arrows (1956, 1957); San Francisco Ballet (1957, 1958, 1959). Jerome Robbins's Ballets: U.S.A. (1959, 1960); Alvin Ailey–Carmen de Lavallade Dance Theatre (1962); Dance Jubilee (1959–60); Robert Joffrey Ballet (1959–60); Paul Taylor and Co. (1965, 1966 [twice], 1967).

There is no gainsaying the assistance to dance companies that the Program provides, but it also cannot be denied that there exists an intrinsic weakness in the Program insofar as the performing companies are concerned. The Program is not designed to assist performing companies to arrange tours when the companies wish to dance abroad or, occasionally, are forced to because there are not sufficient engagements at home, but to make it possible for the State Department to call on dance companies when the unnamed "specialists in Washington and abroad" decide that a dance company "will best advance our foreign policy aims." In other words, dance companies (and, of course, musical or dramatic companies and individual artists) are in an on-call service of the Government.

Merce Cunningham, American modern dancer

Cunningham, Merce, contemporary American modern dancer, choreographer, b. Centralia, Wash. Studied tap, folk, exhibition ballroom dancing with local teacher, Mrs. J. W. Barrett; two years at Cornish School of Fine and Applied Arts, Seattle. After performing locally in amateur shows and a brief vaudeville and nightclub tour in Ore. and Calif., he danced in Lester Horton's *Conquest,* at Mills College (summer, 1938). Studied at Bennington School of Dance (summer,

1939) and was invited by Martha Graham to join her company in N.Y. Soloist with her company (1940–45), creating Acrobat (*Every Soul Is a Circus*), Christ Figure (*El Penitente*), March (*Letter to the World*), Revivalist (*Appalachian Spring*). During this period studied ballet at School of American Ballet, N.Y. Taught a weekly class in modern dance at this school (1947–48) and choreographed *The Seasons* to music by John Cage (1947) for Ballet Society. He began to choreograph in 1943, at first mainly solos for himself, some of these early works being *The Wind Remains* (1943), *Totem Ancestor, Root of Unfocus, Four Walls* (1944), *Mysterious Adventure, Soliloquy* (1945), *Dream* (1946), *The Monkey Dances* (1948), *16 Dances for Soloist and Company of Three* (1951). Has had his own company since 1952 for which he has choreographed *Suite by Chance, Ragtime Parade* (1952), *Septet, Banjo, Dime a Dance, Fragments* (1953), *Springweather and People* (1955), *Suite for Five, Nocturnes* (1956), *Labarinthine Dances* (1957), *Summerspace, Antic Meet, Night Wandering* (1958), *Rune* (1959), *Crises* (1960) etc., and a few solo dances for himself, *Untitled Solo* (1953), *Lavish Escapade* (1955), *The Changeling* (1957), and *Waka and Handss-Birds,* solos for his leading dancer Carolyn Brown (1960). He has collaborated many times with John Cage and other avant-garde composers, commissioning scores from Earle Brown, Morton Feldman, Alexei Haieff, Lou Harrison, Ben Weber, and others. His *Suite by Chance* was the first dance work with a pure electronic sound score, commissioned from Christian Wolff. His experimental work includes "choreography by chance," of which he says, "Any explicit expressive meaning was left to the continuity as it arose out of the application of the chance elements to the materials. The dancers themselves, as they provide the continuity, provide the expression; the action of movement is expressive, but what it expresses is determined individually." His excerpt (afterwards called *Collage*) from Pierre Schaeffer's *Symphonie Pour Un Homme Seul* in 1952 was the first presentation of musique concrète in the U.S. This was a "chance" work. He teaches in N.Y. and in many American universities and colleges, including Conn. College Summer School of Dance where he and his company have also appeared at many of the American Dance Festivals. In addition to many tours in the U.S. he has appeared with Carolyn Brown, John Cage, and pianist David Tudor in Stockholm, Brussels, and Hamburg (1958); in Venice at the International Festival of Contemporary Music, Berlin, Munich, Brussels, and Cologne (1960). Received Guggenheim Fellowships (1954, 1959) for choreography. In June 1964 Merce Cunningham and company set out on a projected eight-month tour of Europe and the Far-East. The tour was a private undertaking, without Government aid. The first performance was given in Paris, June 12, at Théâtre de l'Est Parisien, to the acclaim of audience and press. Cunningham and his company made a European tour in 1964, appearing in London and Stockholm, among other cities.

Curley's Wife. Modern dance work; chor.: Linda Margolies (Linda Hodes); music: Marc Blitzstein. First prod.: YM–YWHA, N.Y., presented by Dance Theatre, Inc., Dec. 9, 1951, with the choreographer and Stuart Hodes. The idea is taken from John Steinbeck's *Of Mice and Men,* the episode in which the all-but-mindless giant, Lenny, accidentally breaks the neck of the girl, Curley's Wife, who has deliberately incited his passion.

Currier, Ruth (Ruth Miller), American modern dancer, b. Ashland, O., 1926. Educated at Black Mountain College and N.Y. Univ. Studied dance in N.Y., primarily with José Limón; became a member of his company (1949), dancing leading roles in *Invention, Night Spell, The Exiles, Ritmo Jondo, There Is a Time, Missa Brevis,* and many others. She was assistant to Doris Humphrey (1952–58) and was commissioned by her to complete the choreographer's final work, *Brandenburg Concerto No. 4.* Her other choreographic works include *Death's Other Kingdom* (1952), *Threshold* (1953), *Search for an Answer* (1954), *Becoming* (1956), *The Antagonists* (1957), *Quartet* (1958), *Transfigured Season* (1960), *Resonances* (1961). In addition to being a leading member of the Limón company she directs her own group, has taught for Limón, at the Juilliard School of Music Dance Department (1953–58), and is currently on the dance faculty of Bennington College and guest teacher at Sarah Lawrence College.

Curtain Calls, taking bows on the stage with the curtain raised, to acknowledge the applause of the audience. In the Russian Imperial Theatres and the Paris Opéra, certain rules for taking curtain calls and the presentation of flowers were observed, and these have become the custom which is generally followed in ballet companies today, though now they are tradition rather than rules. If the performance is at all successful, the principals with the corps de ballet take three curtain calls; then, if the applause continues, the principals take more calls, often appearing before the curtain, depending on the applause. If flowers are presented, the ballerina is presented with hers first, then the other dancers in order of their importance in the performance. In Russia, France, and Denmark it is customary for both female and male dancers to receive flowers on stage. As a general rule, if there are no flowers for the ballerina, no other dancer is presented with flowers on stage. This tradition, however, is not strictly observed in the U.S. See also APPLAUSE and OVATION.

Cyc. Term used for cyclorama.

Cyclorama, in the theatre, a curved or straight drop of a solid color (generally blue, black, or gray), used instead of scenery. In ballet, the cyclorama is often used for pas de deux and some abstract ballets.

Cydalise et le Chevre-Pied (Cydalise and the Faun). Ballet in 2 acts, 3 scenes; chor.: Leo Staats; music: Gabriel Pierné; book: G. A. de Caillavet and Robert de Flers. First prod.: Théâtre de l'Opéra, Paris, Jan. 15, 1923, with Carlotta Zambelli as Cydalise, Albert Aveline as the Faun. This ballet has probably the silliest plot in a romantic style to which it purports to belong, although created, incredibly, in 1923. Styrax, a Faun, is misbehaving at a music lesson (playing the Pipes of Pan) and is punished by the Satyr who ties him to a tree. When the class leaves, Styrax is forgotten at the tree. One of the Nymphs (who was taking a dance lesson) frees him, but he prefers to remain rather than follow the other fauns. He then hitches a ride in a passing coach which takes him to a garden in Versailles. There dancers are about to rehearse a comedy-ballet, *La Sultane des Indes.* He intrigues Mlle. Cydalise, the ballerina of the piece, with his leaps and jumps. After the rehearsal he manages to get into the ballerina's bedroom where he and his hostess begin to dance. In the morning the Nymphs and Dryads get into the bedroom through the windows and implore him to return to the forest. Blowing a kiss to the sleeping ballerina, he joins the Nymphs and Dryads and leaves for the forest.

Cygne, Le. See DYING SWAN, THE.

Cyrano de Bergerac. Ballet in 3 acts; chor.: Roland Petit; music: Marius Constant; décor: Basarte; costumes: Yves Saint-Laurent. First prod.: Ballets de Paris de Roland Petit, Alhambra Theatre, Paris, Apr. 17, 1959, with Roland Petit (Cyrano), Renée Jeanmaire (Roxane),

George Reich (Christian). Based on the famous play by Edmond Rostand. Cyrano of the great nose loves Roxane, but woos her by proxy for the handsome and inarticulate Christian. Christian dies in battle and Roxane retires to a convent where Cyrano visits her faithfully. Only as he is dying is the story of his lifelong love revealed to her. This was one of the four ballets making up the film *Black Tights,* with Moira Shearer as Roxane.

Czardas, a Hungarian folk dance in 4/4 or 2/4 time consisting of two movements: lassu (slow) and friska (fast); a ballroom dance in Eastern Europe based on the folk dance; a character dance in ballet.

Czernyana. Ballet in 1 act; chor.: Frank Staff; music: arranged from Karl Czerny's piano exercises; décor: Eve Swinstead Smith. First prod.: Ballet Rambert, Duchess Theatre, London, Dec. 5, 1939, with Sally Gilmour, Elisabeth Schooling, Walter Gore and Frank Staff. A "sequel," *Czerny II,* was premièred May 15, 1941, and the version currently in the Ballet Rambert repertoire includes two numbers from this. *Czernyana* is a series of unrelated dances each of which is a satire on various kinds of dance or ballet, particularly of the kind popular in the 1930's.

Dafora, Asadata (John Warner Dafora Horton), dancer, b. Freetown, Sierra Leone, West Africa, 1890. Studied in Sierra Leone and at La Scala, Milan (1910–12). Made his debut as a dancer in 1912, touring several European countries. One of the pioneer exponents of African Negro dance and culture, he formed the Asadata Dafora Dance Group which appeared in N.Y. and on tour in the U.S. Staged the Voodoo scene in Orson Welles's production of Macbeth and a number of shows based on African culture, including *Kyunkor, Zunguru*, and others.

Dalcroze, Emile Jaques (1865–1950), Swiss composer and music teacher who originated the system known as Eurhythmics. Born in Vienna, he studied at the Conservatory in Geneva; also with Léo Delibes in Paris and Anton Bruckner in Vienna. He studied all the arts of the theatre and was director of a theatre in Algiers when about twenty years of age. When he was professor at Geneva, he devised a system intended to help the student of music develop a sense of rhythm—not by specializing in the study of any instrument, but by translating sounds into physical movements. His principles applied to theatrical dance and modern ballet as well as to music and had a definite effect on them. In 1910 a college for the instruction of the Dalcroze method was built in Hellerau, Germany, where in 1913 Serge Diaghilev saw a demonstration by the pupils. He was so impressed that he asked Dalcroze to recommend one of his pupils to instruct the members of his company. Miriam Rambam (now well known as Dame Marie Rambert) was chosen. However, Vaslav Nijinsky was the only one who was much influenced by her; the other Russians, taught in the Imperial schools, felt that they could learn nothing from their young teacher. Nijinsky's *Afternoon of a Faun, Jeux,* and *The Rite of Spring* all showed the result of this contact with Eurhythmics. Mary Wigman, who was first interested in the dance through a demonstration of some Dalcroze pupils, had her earliest training in the dance at the school in Hellerau. Hanya Holm and Uday Shan-Kar were Dalcroze students and Kurt Jooss was also much influenced by Dalcroze. In 1920 the activities of the Hellerau school were transferred to Austria, where Dr. Ernst Ferand and Mrs. Christine Baer-Frissell founded the Hellerau-Laxenburg School near Vienna, to continue the work of the original school. During the life of Hellerau-Laxenburg it graduated some three thousand pupils now scattered in teaching posts all over the world. The school was closed when the Nazis invaded Austria in 1938.

Dr. Ferand came to the U.S. that year and lectured on music in several colleges. Besides the central school in Geneva, where Dalcroze was teaching until his death, there are well established schools of the Dalcroze method in England, Sweden, France, the U.S., and other countries. Dalcroze's books (*Rhythm, Music and Education,* and *Eurhythmics, Art and Education*), originally written in French, have been translated into many languages.

Dale, Margaret (Bolan), English dancer, choreographer and television director, b. Newcastle-upon-Tyne, 1922. Studied with Nellie Potts (Newcastle), and at Sadler's Wells (now Royal) Ballet School. Made debut as the Child in Ninette de Valois' *Le Roi Nu.* As soloist with the company she created Attendant Spirit (*Comus*), Cupid (*The Prospect Before Us*), etc.; was a great success as the simpering Bride in *A Wedding Bouquet,* danced pas de trois in *Swan Lake,* Swanilda (*Coppélia*), and many others. Choreographed *The Great Detective* for Sadler's Wells Theatre Ballet (1953), based on the Sherlock Holmes stories. Left Sadler's Wells Ballet to join British Broadcasting Corporation as ballet producer (1954) and has staged several outstanding productions. One of her early triumphs was to persuade Galina Ulanova to dance *Swan Lake* (Act 2), a role she had long relinquished, when the Bolshoi Ballet paid its first visit to England in 1956. Her partner at that time, Nicolai Fadeyechev, visited England specially to dance *Giselle* with Nadia Nerina (1958), the first time a single dancer from the Soviet Union had been given permission to appear elsewhere. Other important television productions for which she is responsible include Margot Fonteyn and Michael Somes in *The Sleeping Beauty* (1959), London's Festival Ballet in *Graduation Ball* (1960), Kirov Ballet in *The Stone Flower,* Ballet Rambert's *La Sylphide,* Royal Ballet in *The Rake's Progress* (all 1961), *Petrouchka* (1962, also by Royal Ballet). She staged *Giselle* for Santiago (Chile) Ballet in 1961.

Dali, Salvador, Spanish surrealist painter, b. Figueras, 1904. Designed décor for Leonide Massine's ballets *Bacchanale* (Wagner's *Tannhäuser* Overture and Bacchanale, 1939); *Labyrinth* (Schubert's Symphony No. 7, 1941); *Mad Tristan* (excerpts from Wagner's *Tristan and Isolde,* 1944), *Sentimental Colloquy* (Paul Bowles–André Eglevsky, 1944); *Café de Chinitas* (Argentinita, 1944); and *Gala,* to a score by Giulio Confalonieri "à la manière de Scarlatti," with choreography by Maurice Béjart on a theme by Pierre Rhallys, presented at La Fenice Theatre, Venice, Aug., 1961, as part of a "musical-choreographic-pictorial spectacle."

Damase, Jean-Michel, French composer, b. Paris, 1928. Wrote scores for *La Croqueuse de Diamants* (Ballets de Paris de Roland Petit, 1950), *Piège de Lumière* (John Taras, Grand Ballet du Marquis de Cuevas, 1952), *Lady in the Ice* (Ballets de Paris de Roland Petit, 1953), *Balance à Trois* (Jean Balibèe, 1955), *La Tendre Eleonore* (Marseille Opéra, 1962).

D'Amboise, Jacques, American dancer, b. Dedham, Mass., 1934; m. Carolyn George. Studied at School of American Ballet, N.Y. Joined New York City Ballet (1950); was promoted to leading soloist three years later. His first major role was Tristram in *Picnic at Tintagel* (1952). With Mac in the revival of *Filling Station* (1953) he established himself as a popular favorite excelling in happy, extrovert roles in which he personified an ideal all-American boy, as in *Western Symphony, Stars and Stripes,* etc. He has developed year by year and widened his range so that it can include the Princes of George Balanchine's *Swan Lake* (Act 2) and *The Nutcracker;* such ballets as *Apollo, Scotch Symphony, Gounod Symphony, Donizetti*

Variations, A Midsummer Night's Dream (Act 2), *Pas de Dix*. His creations include principal roles in *Episodes, Figure in the Carpet, Movements, Raymonda Variations, Con Amore,* and many others. Has danced leading roles in the films *Seven Brides for Seven Brothers, Best Things in Life Are Free,* and *Carousel,* and is greatly in demand on television. Made a successful Broadway debut as featured dancer in *Shinbone Alley,* a musical based on the Don Marquis *Archy and Mehitabel* stories. His ballet, *The Chase,* to Mozart's Horn Concerto No. 3, was premièred by New York City Ballet, Sept. 18, 1963; and *Quatuor* (Shostakovitch's String Quartet No. 1), Jan. 16, 1964, and *Irish Fantasy* (Saint-Saëns) Aug. 12, 1964.

Dame à La Licorne, La. See LADY AND THE UNICORN, THE.

Dance, the English word, is close to the French danse; deriving from the antique high-German danson, to drag, or stretch. In Middle English danson becomes daunce or dawnce; in Swiss and Dutch dans; in Danish dands; in Spanish and Italian, danza; in Portuguese, dansa; in modern German, by modification of

Jacques d'Amboise, premier danseur of the New York City Ballet in the revival of George Balanchine's Ballet Imperial, *in October, 1964.*

Grimm's phonetic law, tanz. The Russian is close to German. The original Sanskrit root is tan, stretching; the Greek is tenein, and from the Latin teneo come tension, extend, intense, sustain, maintain, etc. "But first," wrote John Weaver in 1721, "it will not be improper to explain what dancing is, and in what it consists. Dancing is an elegant, and regular movement, harmoniously composed of beautiful Attitudes, and contrasted graceful Posture of the Body, and parts thereof." "Dancing, according to the accepted definition of the word, is the art of composing steps with grace, precision and facility to the time and bars given in the music, just as music itself is simply the art of combining sounds and modulations so that they afford pleasure to the ear," wrote J. G. Noverre in 1760. Dancing as defined by Diderot and d'Alembert in the *Encyclopedia* (ca. 1772) is "Ordered movements of the body, leaps and measured steps made to the accompaniment of musical instruments or the voice." Desrat's *Dictionary of Dancing* (1895) says "Dancing is the action of moving the body in harmony with a determined measure, and in allocating a given expression to the movements." Perhaps the most complete contemporary definition is André Levinson's, quoted by Cyril Beaumont in his *Miscellany for Dancers* (1934). "Dancing is the continuous movement of the body traveling in a predetermined space in accordance with a definite rhythm and a conscious mechanism." (*La Danse d'Aujourd'hui,* 1929 and Lincoln Kirstein's *Ballet Alphabet,* N.Y., 1939)

Dance (publication). See PERIODICALS, DANCE (U.S.).

Dance and Dancers (publication). See PERIODICALS, DANCE (ENGLAND).

Dance and Physical Education,
BY M. FRANCES DOUGHERTY, PH.D.

Philosophically and by theoretical affirmation, dance is recognized as a vital part of the total motor learning experiences, to be supported and promoted at all levels of education. Dance has experienced growth in public education within the educational discipline of physical education and under that administration. This is because the learning that takes place is inextricably linked with the physical, the learning environment is prescribed by the nature of the activity, and because a special costume is worn. Authorities in the field of physical education endorse the desirability of including dance in the curricular offerings at every level of the program.

Every current professional publication of physical education that is concerned with aims and principles includes dance as one of the important activities leading toward the realization of values inherent in physical activity. In the eighth edition of *The Principles of Physical Education,* Jesse Fering Williams defines the objectives of dance within the context of physical education: "Physical education should select objectives of dance that aim at vigorous activity, certain skills and controls in poise and movement, appreciation of music, line, rhythm, and design." The leaders in the field are not insensitive to the aesthetic values that dance has to offer, although dance educators have frequently felt this was an incompatibility not to be easily resolved.

Identification of the subject matter of movement education is broadly referred to as "games, sports, dance, aquatics, and equitation." The meaning of dance within these differentiating categories varies from one program to another. In general dance programs include the social, creative, and theatre forms of dance. Included in the social forms are traditional rhythmic games and folk dances at the elementary level, and folk, square, and social dance at the secondary level. The past fifteen years has seen a change in emphasis within the social forms to a much broader representation of international dances at all levels and an extension into advanced skills and exhibition dancing at secondary and college levels. There are fine student groups who make extensive tours each year. From this writer's observation, square dancing is not as widely employed in school programs, but is an activity which has experienced growing popularity among adults in civic recreation.

Less social dance is being taught in the schools. Several reasons may be cited: (1) most dance in secondary schools and colleges is taught by women and social dance is most successfully taught by men; (2) current fad dances are highly individualized and partnering (leading and following) is not as important; (3) with the exception of the Latin American style, most popular music does not encourage a motor response in specifically defined step patterns.

Changes in content and emphases in the category of theatre or spectacular dance reflects in part the opportunity for mass media viewing of dance from theatrical and commercial sources. Tap and clog dance are now rarely included in dance curricula. More and more secondary and college programs are now adding ballet and jazz for both professional and elective classes. In those instances where opportunity is provided for students to pursue the study of theatrical dance, the administrative direction is frequently in a special department of dance or is in affiliation with the theatre department. There are, of course, some exceptions, with excellent programs of theatre dance in physical education departments.

It is the creative dance form which has expanded the most in the past twenty years. The demand for creative dance in the educational program may stem from a number of social forces which have influenced the direction of educational programs. In the 1930s and 1940s public education was directed toward meeting the needs of the individual as he related to—and became a part of—the social group. Dance activity in this educational context was strongly oriented to the social forms of dance and geared to the kind of group interaction inherent in these forms. Even in the modern dance of this period, group effort was strongly encouraged in choreographic conception and thematic material.

The past decade has seen a shifting social emphasis to individualism, avoidance of conformity, and stress on the need for the creative approach in all educational endeavor. Paralleling this social movement was the rapid dissemination of scientific knowledge in psychology and the application of psychological principles to educational method. Self-realization and individuality became of singular importance. Psychiatry was quick to recognize the importance of creative movement as an implement of communication at the non-verbal level. The use of creative movement for both diagnosis and as an adjunct to therapy opened up a new area for professional careers in dance.

In short, creative dance was the one activity in all dance and physical education activities which had the best potential for fulfilling both social and psychological needs. Rapid implementation of programs occurred at all educational levels, but the most rapid development took place at the two extremes of the educational ladder—the elementary school at the one end and the college or university professional preparation program at the other.

Scrutiny of elementary school dance programs containing the word "creative" in their titles revealed that course content ranged from a mere motor response to an external beat—keeping time to music—to the exploration of the full range of the movement potential and to the development of sensitivity to the multifold rhythms in the environment. "Creative dance" might mean only a pantomimic posturing or it could be a means of communicating significant statements about natural and personal phenomena in the child's personal world.

Today most elementary students have some opportunity to move freely, creatively, and rhythmically because teachers have had pertinent professional training from the combined disciplines of education psychology and physical education. For the most part the elementary programs are handled by the elementary classroom teacher or the specialist in physical education. Much more needs to be done in stimulating the interest of dance educators to work at the elementary level. It is significant to note that some remarkably fine work with children is being done by professional dancers and in private schools or studios. Among these are Bruce King, Martha Nishitani, Ann Halprin, Virginia Tanner, Nadia Chilkovsky, and Bonnie Bird.

Some of the problems which have existed in the past concerning the inclusion of dance in the physical education curricula for secondary schools seem to persist today. In spite of the educational acceptance of dance as a major curricular offering for physical education, there are still some communities in the U.S. where the antagonism to dance is so real that it is not permitted to be taught in the schools. The antagonism extends to all forms of dance, but is strongest against social dance.

Where modern dance is offered in secondary physical education curricula, it is predominately administered through the departments for girls and taught by women. Boys are directly or indirectly discouraged from participation, except through the avenue of the theatre. The emphasis placed on physical fitness by our national government has added some impetus to dance as a physical conditioner, and many secondary school dance programs do not extend beyond this point. Where this condition exists, students are often further deprived of a good dance experience because only techniques are taught and there is little done in relating dance to the other artistic disciplines or to its understanding as an independent art.

In spite of the persistent problems for dance within the secondary school physical education curricula, many excellent programs exist. In some of the larger educational systems, dance specialists are hired for the secondary schools and students may earn credit in dance equal to that granted for other subjects. In these instances students are usually allowed to elect dance for a larger block of time than is possible under the activity unit plan. In other situations fine work is being done in extracurricular arrangements such as clubs or performing groups.

The problems which surround dance in the secondary school physical education programs exist as well on the college level. However, the tremendous growth of professional dance programs in the colleges and universities has far surpassed that of any other single division in the "games, sports, aquatics and equitation" complex of physical education. While dance educators are strongly in accord that dance should exist as an independent art, the administrative ties are today—as in the past—predominately with physical education. It is not the purpose here to define the advantages and disadvantages of the administrative placement of dance in either theatre, physical education, fine arts, or liberal arts; it suffices to state that dance programs in institutions of higher learning continue to expand under varying administrative alliances. This expansion occurs in numbers, quality, variety of program content, and in degrees granted.

In 1950 there were thirteen major dance curricula in colleges and universities in the U.S.; in 1956 there were twenty-five. Data obtained from the National Section on Dance publication, *The Dance Directory: Programs of Professional Preparation and General Education* (1963 rev.), reveals that there are sixty-five institutions offering major curricula in dance. Many of these offer both the performing arts major and the educational dance major. The main difference in the two curricula is that the educational dance curricula are directed toward preparation for teaching.

Eighty schools offer a concentration in dance equivalent to what is commonly referred to as a minor or a second area of specialization. In twenty-seven institutions, dance specialization is combined with the physical education major in which from six to twelve of the required term hours in professional physical education courses are in dance. Four institutions list programs leading to the doctor of philosophy degree.

The Dance Directory further reveals administrative affiliations for major dance curricula as follows: nine are in independent dance departments; eight in theatre departments; one in allied arts and architecture; five interdisciplinary. Of the remaining forty-one, all are under the administration of physical education schools, departments, or divisions. Dance majors, programs of dance concentration, and requirements for dance within the physical education major, make up a total of ninety-eight programs that are administered by physical education—and most of these are within the women's departments. However, the *Directory* reveals that there are ninety-one men on instructional staffs.

It seems appropriate to cite some trends which characterize dance programs in today's colleges and universities. Some of these are: (1) the establishment of increasing numbers of independent dance departments within the educational structure; (2) provisions for many opportunities for students to see professional performances and to work with professional dancers in special workshops, master lessons, and symposia; (3) extension of interdisciplinary courses with improved rapport with the other arts; (4) many more men students are participating in both major and general dance curricula; (5) a demand for men in teaching and administrative positions on an increase; (6) higher standards of performance and production in college and university dance programs.

It is encouraging to note the progress of dance in schools in the last two decades. It is to be hoped that in the next two decades those problems which seem to have been persistent for dance in education will have been solved by perception, keen insight and research.

Dance Archives Museum of Modern Art, N.Y., was founded in 1940 by Lincoln Kirstein, whose private collection of books, pictorial material, manuscripts, etc., formed the basis of the Archives. Paul Magriel was first curator of the Archives, serving in that capacity until he joined the U.S. Army at the beginning of World War II. In 1943 George H. Amberg became curator. Soon after his appointment the Archives were made part of the newly created Dept. of Dance and Theatre Design, of which Amberg became curator. In 1946 the name of that department was changed to Dept. of Theatre Arts and Amberg was placed at the head of it. The Archives arranged special exhibits, among which those dedicated to the works of Eugene Berman, Pavel Tchelitchev, and Joan Junyer were outstanding. In 1947 the part of the collection which dealt with pre-twentieth century material was transferred, conditionally, to the Harvard College Theatre Collection. The reason for the transfer was the Museum's desire to adhere to its policy of reflecting modern art and the lack of space in the Museum for housing that part of the collection. In 1948 the department became a division of the Music Library of the Museum, at which time Amberg resigned. The collection was given to the Dance Collection of the New York Public Library (1961). See also KIRSTEIN, LINCOLN, COLLECTION.

Dance Business Group. See FOUNDATIONS, PHILANTHROPIC.

Dance Collection, The New York Public Library.

BY GENEVIEVE OSWALD, Curator of the Dance Collection.

The Dance Collection of the New York Public Library is a reference collection devoted to the literature and iconography of the dance, stressing historical, theatrical, educational, therapeutic, and socio-economic aspects and covering every form of dance: ballet, modern, "expressionist," social, ethnic, primitive, folk, and national. Included in the Collection are over 13,800 books and 3,500 librettos, many of them rare; 4,600 prints, original drawings, costume and stage designs; 40,000 programs; 60,000 photographs; 350,000 newspaper and magazine clippings; 26,851 manuscripts and letters; dance notation scores; microfilms; motion picture films; and current and back issues of domestic and foreign periodicals. These groups of material form small collections in themselves in completeness and size.

Special attention was given to dance in the Music Division at the New York Public Library as early as 1944. In 1947 the Collection was re-organized and a curator was appointed to develop its resources. To acquaint the public with the small but good collection then available, a series of exhibitions and lectures—Dance and Its Allied Arts—was given by distinguished persons in the dance world. Since that time the Collection has attempted to contribute to the artistic life of the city and to illuminate the riches of its collections by having exhibitions, lectures, and other public events honoring organizations or individuals on special occasions. Among these have been the concert of French ballet music and the exhibition, "French Court and Opera Ballet," of books and prints from the collection of George Chaffee (1948); the exhibition, "British Ballet," and reception for the Sadler's Wells Ballet on the occasion of their first visit to the U.S. (1949); and the exhibitions "Ted Shawn, American Dancer" (1950); "Fanny Elssler, a 100th Anniversary of her Last Performance" (1951); "Dance Notation" (1952); "Enrico Cecchetti" (1954); "The Magic of Anna Pavlova" (1956); "The Royal Danish Ballet" (1956); "The Cia Fornaroli Collection" (1957); "Marius Petipa" (1958); "José Limón, Ambassador Extraordinary" (1958); "The New York City Ballet" (1959); "Laban Dance Notation, 1940–1960" (1960); "Stravinsky and the Dance" (1962); and "Galina Ulanova" (1962). The exhibitions honoring the Royal Danish Ballet's first visit to the U.S. and the New York City Ballet's anniversary were accompanied by other public events.

But the true history of any archive is found in the great collections it has acquired. The Dance Collection of the New York Public Library is in the possession of the following collections, listed here in alphabetical order: Gabriel Astruc–Diaghilev Archives, Louise Branch, Tatiana Chamié, Irving Deakin, Denishawn, Roger Pryor Dodge, Isadora Duncan, Cia Fornaroli, Hanya Holm, Humphrey-Weidman, Lincoln Kirstein, La Meri. Descriptions of these collections appear under their names, listed in alphabetical sequence in this volume. They afford an insight into the strength and riches of the archive.

Because of the enormous scope of theatrical dance activity and the need to document it, the Collection depends heavily on gifts from dancers and performing companies. Yearly deposits of clippings, programs, and photographs are made by major companies throughout the world as well as by the regional ballet companies in the U.S. A concentrated effort is made also to document the careers of individual dancers. Among those well represented through gifts of material are Nora Kaye (1956), Agnes De Mille (1956), Catherine Littlefield and the Philadelphia Ballet (1954). S. Hurok's collection (1959) of 150 press books compiled in his office during the past thirty years provide a detailed history of performance for the artists and companies under his management.

When the Museum of Modern Art's Library decided to curtail its coverage of the subject of dance (1956), it transferred to the Dance Collection 250 volumes and

30 boxes of clippings, photographs, and miscellaneous materials. This ephemera has special value since most of it was collected prior to 1940, is contemporary in nature, and strengthens the files for the two decades prior to the establishment of the Dance Collection. Important are the more than 2,000 clippings and programs documenting the performances and tours of the American Ballet and Ballet Caravan. Of great value also is the correspondence and manuscript material relevant to the W.P.A. which provides a history of its Dance Project.

The picture files must rely on gifts from photographers for their growth. Two large gifts of photographs representative of dance activity in N.Y. over a thirty-year period were received from Walter Owen and Carl Van Vechten. In 1955 Mr. Owen presented 5,000 photographs taken by him during his career here. Carl Van Vechten established the Fania Marinoff Collection in 1956, honoring his wife with a gift of 3,500 photographs, unusual art studies of the more celebrated artists who have performed here during the past three decades. More recently four fine archives of negatives have been received, those of George Platt Lynes (1958), Wilbur Hulin Stephan (1959), Frederick Melton (1961), and Constantine Hassalevris (known professionally as Constantine, 1964). More than 12,000 negatives, the work of the last four mentioned photographers, now enrich the documentation of contemporary American dance.

In 1962 Robert W. Dowling donated to the Collection 6,000 negatives of photographs taken by Albert Kahn of Galina Ulanova. This unique photographic study of one of the great ballerinas of our time presents a comprehensive account of her recent performances and her day-to-day activities as dancer and teacher and in private life.

The scope of the book collection is broad, with a fine group of 19th-century American ballroom dance handbooks and guides and a good collection of anti-dance tracts of the same period. Among rare books and librettos are many exceptional items: a "balletto à cavallo," *In Mondo Festeggiante,* beautifully illustrated and published in 1661; the *Medea Vendicativa,* 1662, a "drama di fuoco," the argument of which suggests spectacular employment of stage machinery; and the "ballet tragique" *Les Horaces,* choreographed by Noverre, dated 1777. Of particular interest is a manuscript volume prepared by the choreographer Henri Justament of drawings for costumes, notations for choreography, and numerous other details for the production of Offenbach's *Le Voyage dans la Lune,* Paris, 1879. In many ways the rarest item in the collection is the *Receuil des devises et des poésies,* 1689, by Claude François Abbé Ménéstrier, author of the famous *Des Ballets Anciens et Modernes* (which is also included in the collection). This fascinating and fragile volume is a collection of small publications on the fêtes, horse ballets, marriage processionals, and ceremonials of Ménéstrier's day, with descriptions of the decorations and edifices built for each. Interleaved and bound with it are handwritten notes, letters and pages in manuscript on which the author has added further observations and reminiscences.

The archive has also been enriched through the generosity of the Committee for the Dance Collection, a group organized to aid the Library in acquiring rare and unusual material. Because of their efforts, in addition to the Gabriel Astruc –Diaghilev Archives, a fine group of ballet stage designs including the work of such artists as Boris Anisfeldt, Alexandre Bénois, Eugene Berman, Léon Bakst, Nathalie Gontcharova, Michel Larionov, Mstislav Doboujinsky, and Isamu Noguchi are now available to the public. The Doris Humphrey Committee has raised funds and made available films and notated scores of Miss Humphrey's works.

Although mentioned by collections here, all the special archives are integrated with the main body of dance literature. In reference to the Dance Collection as a whole, it can be said that the archive has the most comprehensive collection of books on dance available in a single location; it has a superb collection of manuscripts; a strong print collection; the most complete documentation available on the dance of the 20th century; and a rare book collection that includes most of the incunabula recorded in the various dance bibliographies.

The material is arranged in a workable, serviceable manner and is well-indexed and catalogued. Although there is still much to be added, a three-year Rockefeller Foundation grant in 1956 greatly facilitated this aspect of the work. In addition to the card index or catalogue of books, there are several expansive supplementary files; a Dance Subject File, which is an index of articles in publications filed under artists, company name, or subjects, such as ballet, décor, technique, etc.; a Concert Dance Title File, which is an index of premières of concert dance (modern dance) works giving pertinent data; a Dance Title File, giving references on the history, directions, and/or descriptions of individual dances such as tango, hornpipe, etc.; an Iconography File, an index of references to pictures and print material found in the print and photograph collections and in published sources as well; a Dance Index File (made by the W.P.A.), an annotated index of dance references in various works on anthropology, ethnology, comparative religion, etc., in institutional libraries of greater N.Y. With the aid of these files the Dance Collection serves an estimated 6,000 readers a year and answers inquiries by mail from such widely separated places as Brazil, Burma, Ceylon, Czechoslovakia, Iceland, India, Japan, Korea, and the U.S.S.R.

In an effort to stimulate serious research on the dance, the Collection, in cooperation with the Library's editor of publications, has published a series of studies on dance. Included are: *When All the World Was Dancing, Rare and Curious Books from the Cia Fornaroli Collection,* by Marian Eames (1957); *Isadora Duncan, Pioneer in the Art of Dance,* by Irma Duncan (1958); *Famed for Dance, Essays on the Theory and Practice of Theatrical Dancing in England, 1660–1740* by Ifan Kyrle Fletcher, Selma Jeanne Cohen, and Roger Lonsdale (1960); *New York's First Ballet Season, 1792,* by Lillian Moore (1961); *Stravinsky and the Dance,* by Selma Jeanne Cohen (1962), and the companion volume, *Stravinsky and the Theatre,* a catalogue of décor and costume designs for his stage works (1963); *The Professional Appearances of Ruth St. Denis and Ted Shawn, a Chronology and an Index of Dances, 1906–1932,* by Christena Schlundt (1962).

In the spring of 1964 the Dance Collection, hitherto a part of the Music Division, was made a regular division, but the staff preferred to retain the former designation. In July, 1965, the Dance Collection became part of the Library-Museum of the Performing Arts at Lincoln Center, where its facilities and services are being greatly expanded.

The Dance Collection at the New York Public Library, Fifth Avenue and 42nd Street, closed on Feb. 1, 1965 to prepare for the transfer of its material to the Library and Museum of the Performing Arts at Lincoln Center, which was just being completed at the time. In the new building it became part of the Research Library of the Performing Arts, with the Theatre and Music Libraries forming the other parts. The Collection began limited operations July 19, 1965. On November 30 dedication ceremonies were held. The Collection opened full operations immediately following the ceremonies. At the opening the Collection included 26,000 volumes plus archival material. For the opening the Library published a pamphlet entitled *The Dance Collection,* written by Marian Eames, outlining the character and importance of some of the material in the Collection.

Soon after the opening of the Dance Collection the Library published three books on dance topics: *The Library and Museum of the Performing Arts,* by Rosine Raoul, with drawings by Susanne Suba (Dec. 15, 1965); *Images of the Dance: Historical Treasures of the Dance Collection, 1581–1861,* by Lillian Moore (Dec. 15, 1965); and, also by Lillian Moore, *Bournonville's London Spring* (Jan. 1, 1966).

Dance Director, person in charge of staging dances for musical comedies, revues, and motion pictures. See CHOREOGRAPHER.

Dance Films, Inc., a non-profit tax-exempt educational organization devoted to the promotion of the use of audio-visual material, such as 16 mm. non-theatrical motion pictures, projection slides, and film strips to record dance and performances of dancers for posterity and as aids in teaching dance and dance appreciation on professional, student, and layman levels. Located in N.Y., its services are available throughout the U.S. to members and non-members alike. They include information on motion pictures and correlative audio-visual material, production and circulation of such material and housing it in its archives. Susan Braun is director.

Dance for Percussion. Modern dance work; chor.: Joyce Trisler; music: Malloy Miller and Carlos Chavez. First prod.: Joyce Trisler and Company, YM–YWHA, N.Y., Jan. 21, 1961, with Joyce Trisler, James Truitte and group. Although this is a themeless work, the great central pas de deux is a passionate dance of love.

Dance, History of.

BY WALTER TERRY.

If we are to be certain when and how primitive man began to dance, we must, paradoxically, turn to the present for much of our information. Archaeologists can find bones, rough tools, and weapons, and perhaps even cave paintings which tell us something of our early forebears, but dance, which existed in time and space and then only in terms of living bodies, died with them, leaving no physical remains.

We can surmise that primitive man danced simply because the dance impulse has been evident throughout recorded history. We can be reasonably certain of the types of dances familiar to early man by studying the dances of contemporary tribal or primitive peoples.

Havelock Ellis and Curt Sachs point out that dancing probably preceded man himself, that dance in recognizable forms is to be found in the movement patterns of animals and birds. Thus, we might say that dance begins with life itself.

It is safe to assume that early man danced first out of sheer physical exuberance, perhaps next in connection with courtship, and lastly in terms of ritual. A fourth dance purpose might be found in the need of or desire for communication, a communication based upon gesture and mimesis.

Through tribal dances existing to this day, we can guess that when man emerged from the Stone Age era and arrived at a neolithic culture, he had ritual dances for every important occasion: marriage, birth, circumcision, propitiation of the gods, illness, war, and, in fact, any occasion requiring the aid of magic, of increased powers, of dedication.

With the consolidation of Egyptian cultures and the founding of the Egyptian nation, tribal dance patterns were forged into permanent and generally accepted rituals and ultimately developed into the foundations of a dance art. Written and pictorial records attest to the importance of dance in Egypt. In its ritual forms, it not only provided discernible manifestations of mythology, but it offered a means of contacting deity, and by incorporating local beliefs into a master dance ritual, the Egyptian ruler and his priesthood were able to bring the peoples of the land from tribal to national loyalty.

On the other side of the world, the Incas of Peru were destined to follow a similar course of incorporating the customs of those they vanquished into the national culture, thus assuring to a reasonable degree the ultimate loyalty of the conquered.

As the rituals of Egypt increased in scope and complexity, it was inevitable that on certain occasions only the initiated would participate while the general public, the tribal dancers of an earlier day, watched.

When this occurred, dance spectacle, albeit religious in purpose, was born and theater dance heralded. There were, of course, people's dances and professional dances of non-religious purpose in addition to the major ritual dances. Egyptian wall paintings depict musicians and dancers assembled for the entertainment of royalty and a letter written by an Egyptian monarch speaks of his majesty's desire to see a dancing dwarf.

In Greece, as in Egypt, dancing was to be found as ritual, as entertainment, and as a form of popular expression. Here, however, it seemed to be on a broader scale than in Egypt, for not only were there dances for almost every religious occasion, there were Pyrrhic dances for the training of soldiers; gymnopedia, basically religious, but manifestly spectacular and appropriate to the theater; dances of a dramatic nature concerned with the enactment of legends. From this Greek dance, from the dithyramb in honor of Dionysos, was born the drama.

Roman dance, like the Roman theater, was similar to that of the Greeks but far less imaginative. Ritual dances in the temples survived, but dancing within the framework of the drama played a lesser role than it did in Greece. Ritual and mimetic dances of the people were probably to be found in rural sections, and the circus, of course, found its dance importations among captives brought to Rome from Africa, Iberia, Britain, and Germany. In the pantomime shows of Rome one might discern the beginning of what we today call ballet.

While the Western dance was progressing to its theatrical fulfillment, the Oriental dance was pursuing a similar but culturally distinct course. In India, particularly, dance evolved styles, techniques, and codifications long before a permanent form of Western dance emerged. As far back as the fifth century A.D. the rules of Indian dance had been set down in the *Natya Sastra* of Bharata and the *Abhinaya Darpana* of Nandikesvara, rules which have governed the classic dance of India ever since.

One could trace the foundation, the progress, and the ultimate forms of dance in China, Japan, Mexico, in places great and small, remembered and forgotten, and find that man in all those places danced for similar reasons. Theater dances might be absent in some, but their potential would be present in mimetic dances, in ritual dances, and in the customary combinations of both. In the West, theater dance died—or at least slept—with the fall of Rome and the dominance of the Christian Church. Although the church may be blamed for a centuries-long hiatus in theatrical dance, it also must be credited with keeping the theater alive and of giving it a new birth. As the church damned pagan Rome and the cruel spectacles which mirrored its decadence, it maintained within its own sphere of action those aspects of art adaptable to its religious plan and desired by the common man.

Dance and drama continued to exist in the ritual of the mass, in the pageant which permitted enactments of Bible scenes; ultimately and inevitably, secular material crept in and the religious drama crept out of the church to the church steps, to the church grounds, to the village green, and, finally, to the theater again. Dance, of course, crept right along and was joined eventually by the folk dances of the people which no church could ever completely abolish. Many of these folk dances, by the way, had their roots in the tribal dances of antiquity, the maypole dance, for example, being a descendant of an ancient fertility dance.

From the festival dances which survived the disapproval of the church, from the religious ceremonies and from the pagan-Christian mythology which the folk had evolved in order to maintain a desirable activity in a new era, dance headed for the theater.

In 1489 in Milan a banquet-ball was given which has been termed the first ballet. Songs, pantomimes, declamations, etiquette activities, and dances were woven into a spectacle for the entertainment of a Duke, his bride, and their party.

In 1581 Catherine de Medici, the Queen of France, provided a noble audience of approximately ten thousand people with *Le Ballet Comique de la Reine,* a spectacle with verse and dance which cost the nation several million francs. A few years later Thoinot Arbeau published his *Orchesographie,* a treatise on the dances and dancing of his day, illustrated by sketches of dance positions and movements.

During the seventeenth and eighteenth centuries, the art of dancing developed quickly. Louis XIV founded the Royal Academy of Music and the Dance; Jean-Baptiste Lully created his opera-ballets; through the Academy the technical foundation of the ballet d'école was laid; Pierre Beauchamp and Louis Pécourt and, later, Pierre Rameau (through *The Dancing Master*) helped to codify the terminology of the growing ballet.

Great dance figures appeared during the eighteenth century in the persons of Marie Camargo, a dancer whose costume innovations and dance skill soon eclipsed the names of Marie Sallé and Françoise Prévost, her immediate predecessors and rivals; Jean-Georges Noverre, a distinguished choreographer and dance leader; Vestris, Auguste and Salvatore, father and son, and other lesser figures who carried the avant-garde ideas of French ballet to Italy, Central Europe, Scandinavia, England, and Russia.

With the nineteenth century, ballet deserted France as a headquarters and shifted to Italy. With Salvatore Vigano, the art of dancing gave added accent to the dramatic element through the weaving of pantomime with the action of dance. This policy was in line with the tenets of Noverre which had called upon the dance to be expressive, tenets passed on to Vigano by Jean Dauberval whose ballet, *La Fille Mal Gardée,* is still performed.

Later Italy produced Carlo Blasis, whose book, *The Code of Terpsichore,* became standard reading for ballet students throughout Europe. It was during this century that the great ballerinas—Maria Taglioni, Fanny Elssler, Carlotta Grisi, Lucile Grahn, and Fanny Cerito added their immortal names to ballet and ushered in the Romantic period regarded as classic by audiences today.

The ballerina rose upon points, she rose into the air higher than ever before, the vocabulary of movement grew to enable her to say more through her art, and the world, for a time, was at her feet. Taglioni danced *La Sylphide* to the plaudits of adoring followers, while the more earthy Elssler aroused her admirers with her "Cachucha." *Giselle,* destined for repeated performances during the ensuing century, was created in 1841 by Jules Perrot with his wife, Carlotta Grisi in the title role.

Slowly the focus of ballet activity shifted, and by the latter part of the nineteenth century Russian ballet became preeminent. It would require a book to tell the story of Russian ballet. Suffice it to say that the Russian Imperial Ballet gave us Marius Petipa and his great ballets, *The Sleeping Beauty* and *Swan Lake,* to name but two, the latter in collaboration with Lev Ivanov, who also staged *The Nutcracker*.

Later Michel Fokine emerged as the leading choreographic figure in the so-called Golden Age of Russian ballet and such great dancers as Vaslav Nijinsky, Tamara Karsavina, and Anna Pavlova appeared. Through the impresario, Serge Diaghilev, Russian ballet advanced tremendously not only in art production but in world-wide prestige.

Under his direction, much of the best in Russian ballet left Russia for France and, later, for other parts of the world where such Fokine ballets as *Les Sylphides, Petrouchka,* and *Schéhérazade* became almost synonymous with the word ballet itself.

In America, theatrical dance had existed from colonial times. Early performers were primarily of French training. The second major influx in the mid-eighteenth century was led by Italian artists of the ballet, and the third balletic invasion, during the second decade of this century, was concluded by the Russians. Following a brief hiatus, Russian ballet returned to America in 1933 and remained permanently. Slowly and inevitably it absorbed American dancers and choreographers. The names of the companies were still Russian but only a few stellar performers were of Russian origin.

America had produced dance artists of distinction, among them Augusta Maywood and Mary Ann Lee, who represented the traditional ballet. It was not until the turn of the century that America began to produce dance artists who were willing and able to break away from the traditions of Europe. The first of these were Isadora Duncan and Ruth St. Denis.

Duncan, completely rejecting the technique of the ballet and deriving her artistic inspiration from ancient Greece, stated the principle of freedom of movement, of the freedom of the dancer to dance how and what he pleased. St. Denis, with a similar precept, but concerned with the spiritual manifestations of dance, turned to the Orient for thematic and stylistic guidance, and later, with Ted Shawn and their Denishawn dancers, was able, over a period of sixteen years, to bring her version of dance to almost every city and town in America and to many capitals of the world. On his own, Shawn began to exploit the possibilities of American dance through music, décor, movement, concepts, and themes. He pioneered in the field of dance for men.

From Denishawn emerged a new generation with new dance ideas. Calling themselves modern dancers, for want of a better name, Martha Graham, Charles Weidman, and Doris Humphrey evolved techniques of their own and established a way of dance, expressional rather than spectacular or pictorial dance it might be called, and established themselves as leaders of American dance not only in the theatre but in education.

In Europe a similar revolution against ballet had occurred. Instigated perhaps by the appearances of Duncan, it culminated in the schools and techniques of Rudolf von Laban and Mary Wigman. Now, neither in Europe nor in America is the modern dance regarded as revolutionary, although recurring avant-garde experiments keep the field of modern dance from becoming static. So it is that the once artistically heretical Martha Graham has built a repertory, performed by brilliant dancers in lavish productions, which became enormously successful both in America and abroad, leaving the controversial side of modern dance to such experimenters as Merce Cunningham, Paul Taylor, or Alwin Nikolais. As for the initial rift between ballet and modern dance, it slowly faded away as both schools borrowed from each other and, in many instances, achieved a genuine fusion of techniques. In the musical comedy theatre, choreography almost demanded that the dancer be competent in ballet, modern, tap, and even ethnic dance forms.

In fact, interest in and use of ethnic dance developed at high speed following World War II. Not only were there visiting artists and troupes from Spain and India, with whom Americans had become familiar, but also companies from Bali, Japan, China, the Soviet Union, Poland, Hungary, Mexico, Ceylon, and the newly independent countries of Africa. These views of national dance not only broadened the horizons of American dance followers but also influenced the popular theater, both with respect to musicals and revues and also to movies and television.

The great international cultural exchanges which were instituted after World War II greatly affected the history of dance around the world. American dance companies—ballet, modern, variety, or ethnic (Negro, American Indian, etc.)—have traveled around the world under the auspices of the U.S. State Dept. and have strongly influenced the dance in lands visited. The New York City Ballet had a tremendous impact on ballet circles in the Soviet Union, just as the visits to America of the Bolshoi and Kirov Ballets swiftly injected new colors and aspects of style into American ballet or as Graham influenced dance education in, say, Indonesia. Never, therefore, in the history of dance has dance been exploited so thoroughly on the international level nor has dance ever experienced a more successful period of achievement and popular respect in the world. In America alone, in the two decades following the U.S. entry into World War II, interest in dance (aided by mass exposure via TV) has reached the point where it is now considered a major box office attraction. Esthetically it has reached a peak where it could be said that in range of techniques, styles, forms, and source materials, American dance has no rival anywhere in the world. See also History of Ballet, Music for Dance, etc.

Dance Index (publication). See Periodicals, Dance (U.S.).

Dance International, the name given to a dance festival held at Rockefeller Center, N.Y., Nov. 29, 1937, to Jan. 2, 1938, organized by a committee which included Louise Branch (chairman), C. M. Girard, R. H. Mansfield. The program included an exhibition of paintings, sculptures, costumes, and motion pictures related to the dance; daily programs of dance films and lectures by Lincoln Kirstein, Rolf de Maré, John Martin, Curt Sachs; small stage and folk dance performances at the Center Theatre by the American Ballet, Ballet Caravan, Mordkin Ballet, Ruth Page Ballet, Philadelphia Ballet and the Martha Graham, Hanya Holm, Humphrey-Weidman, Helen Tamiris groups. In one way or another the following countries were represented at Dance International: Austria, Brazil, Chile, China, Cuba, Czechoslovakia, Denmark, England and British colonies, Estonia, Finland, France, Germany, Holland and colonies, Hungary, Italy, Japan, Mexico, Norway, Peru, Poland, Sweden, United States of America, Yugoslavia. Original plans called for the festival to be held every four years, but unsettled European conditions, followed by World War II, forced the abandonment of the project.

Dance Masters of America. See Teachers' Organizations (U.S.).

Dance Museum (Dansmuseet), a museum devoted to the dance of Asiatic people, opened in 1953 and located in the Royal Theatre of Stockholm. Contains a unique collection of costumes, masks, instruments, attributes from India, China, Japan, Ceylon, Indonesia, Siam, and Tibet, gathered by Rolf de Maré during his travels before World War I and in the 1930's and 1960's and contributed to the Museum. A large part of the collection had originally been housed in Les Archives Internationales in Paris, established by de Maré, but was transferred to Stockholm. The Museum is also a repository for some 15,000 meters of motion picture films and about 10,000 still photographs of dance taken in these countries. The Curator of the Museum, Bengt Haeger, collected additional material in 1959 and 1960 in China, Ceylon, and India, and in South America in 1961. Material relating to Les Ballets Suédois (1920–25) is also kept in the Dance Museum.

Dance News (publication). See PERIODICALS, DANCE (U.S.).

Dance Notation, History of.

BY ANN HUTCHINSON.

Through the centuries attempts have been made to devise a satisfactory system of dance notation, that is, the recording of movement. Some scholars believe that the ancient Egyptians made use of hieroglyphs to notate dances, and that the Romans employed a method of notation for salutatory gestures.

However, the first attempt of which we have a record are two Spanish manuscripts of the middle fifteenth century, preserved at the Municipal Archives at Cervera, Spain. The dance steps are recorded by means of vertical and horizontal strokes, and one of the manuscripts has also the abbreviations of the names of the dance steps: R—reverencia; P—paso; DE—doble; RE—represa. This method of using letter names is also found in the Burgundy manuscripts, in *The Dance Book of Margaret of Austria,* and in *L'art et instruction de bien danser* of the late fifteenth century.

It was Thoinot Arbeau in his *Orchésographie,* published in 1588, who explained dance terms and steps in detail and through whom the method had widespread use. Many books using the system were printed at that time in England, France, and Italy. While the system was simple and obviously limited, it was sufficient to record the dances of the period, known as basse danse (low or ground dance), so called because the feet never left the floor. When the haute danse became popular, it soon became clear that the notation was inadequate to record jumps, kicks, and the wider variety of steps being used. Words and pictures were added to describe the new steps, and eventually the notations became too complicated to be of practical use.

In the time of Louis XIV when professional dancing first became distinguished from social dancing, the method of notation that served the period was that originated by Raoul Feuillet. His method, first published in 1700 as *Chorégraphie, ou l'Art de Décrire la Danse* is based on "track drawings"; the dancer's relation to the room is given and the floor pattern is shown by a line, along which the steps and a few arm movements are written.

Feuillet also published a *Recueil des Danses* which he composed, as did his contemporary Louis Pécourt. Many others used this notation to publish dances, notably John Weaver in England in 1706, Kellom Tomlinson in 1736, and others in Germany, Spain, and Italy who adapted it to their own needs.

Pierre Rameau, ballet master at the court of Spain adapted the system and brought out his *Abbrege de la Nouvelle Methode dans l'Art d'Ecrire ou de Tracer Toutes Sortes de Danses de Ville* in 1752. It is Favier's version of the Feuillet notation which is explained in detail in the *Encyclopédie* of Diderot and d'Alembert (1751–1772). By the end of the eighteenth century the notation had become too complex and too inflexible to be adapted to the changing dance.

As the classic ballet technique became established, dance writers began to introduce stick figures to show the leg and also the body and arm positions. A transition system, using both Feuillet and pictorial figures, was that of E. A. Theleur who explained his "Chirography" in his *Letters on Dancing* (1832).

The system of Arthur Saint-Léon, *Stenochorégraphie,* was published in 1852. It used only stick figures, placing them on a musical staff for clarification; steps done on the ground were placed on the five lines, and those which rose from the floor were drawn in the spaces. The skeleton drawings were written from the point of view of the audience, so that right and left were reversed.

An "amplification and perfection" of this system was published as the *Grammar of the Art of Dancing* by Albert Zorn (1887). The work attained comparative success and was used as a textbook in dancing academies in Europe and by the American National Association of Masters of Dancing. The method was not only too complicated to be of lasting use, but also required a certain ability to draw, and did not accurately represent the third dimension.

Subsequent methods adapted music notation to show dance steps. While the duration of the movements was clear, they failed to cover the more complicated steps and body movements. The German Bernard Klemm, after studying previous methods of notation, based his own on music notation, but it never became successful due to the complicated variety of signs and symbols he included.

It was Vladimir Stepanoff, dancer and teacher at the Imperial Maryinsky Theatre in St. Petersburg, who devised the most practical music-note dance notation. It was published in his book, *Alphabet des Mouvements du Corps Humain* (1891), and was taught as part of the curriculum in the Ballet School. Stepanoff is credited with having recorded the most important ballets by Marius Petipa; however, the notation was not complete enough, and today the ballets can only be reconstructed approximately.

The most recent notation of this type is that of Antonio Chiesa, an officer in the Italian air force whose *Motographie* was published in 1934.

The important systems developed in the twentieth century have been based on abstract symbols, though there have been recurrences of the use of adaptations of stick figure, notably in *Dance Writing,* published in a pamphlet by Sol Babitz (1939), and of adapted music notes used with other signs by Jap Kool (1927) and Pierre Conte (1931). The Babitz system appears simple and logical at first but investigation reveals that it contains the usual pitfalls.

Of the invention of Vaslav Nijinsky little is known, since it has never been published or taught.

The three most highly developed and widely used notation systems developed recently are those of Margaret Morris, Rudolf von Laban, and the Benesh method. Margaret Morris published her *Notation of Movement* in book form in England (1928). Her system is written with abstract symbols on two three-line staves, positions for the arms and head are written on the upper staff, the legs and feet on the lower; the body is written in between. It is based on the fact that all human movements take place around an imaginary central axis. The Morris notation avoids entirely the use of words or letters, with the result that the notation can be international. The symbols are not pictorial and so have to be learned by heart. They do not include the rhythmic content of the movement, which has to be written above with music notes. While every type of movement can be written, the Morris system is complex to learn and slow to read.

In 1928 Rudolf von Laban published his *Schrifttanz,* or *Kinetographie Laban,* as he later called it. His system is the most complete and has several advantages over the Morris notation. For a description of the Laban system see LABAN DANCE NOTATION SYSTEM.

The Benesh Dance Notation System was developed by Rudoph and Joan Benesh and copyrighted in 1955. Since 1956 this system has been included in the syllabus of the Royal Academy of Dancing Teachers' Training Course. *An Introduction to Benesh Dance Notation System* was published by A. and C. Black, London, 1956. The system is now being taught in the

Royal Ballet School and Ballet Rambert, both in London.

Almost every choreographer and many teachers have made use of their own systems of arbitrary symbols as an aid in memorizing dances. These systems are only intelligible to their originators, and often are confusing even to them. The advantages of a universal and scientific system of notation are plain. See also DANCE NOTATION BUREAU.

For a bibliography of dance notation systems consult *A Bibliography of Dancing* by Paul David Magriel, published by The H. W. Wilson Company, N.Y., 1936.

Dance Notation Bureau, was formed in N.Y. in 1940 by Henrietta Greenhood (Eve Gentry) and Janey Price, who had studied the Laban Notation System with Irma Otte-Betz in N.Y.; Ann Hutchinson, who had been a student at the Jooss-Leeder School in England; and Helen Priest (Rogers), who had studied with Albrecht Knust in Germany. Hanya Holm and John Martin were the original advisers to the Bureau.

When the founders first met, they found many discrepancies in the notation as they had learned it. This was inevitable, since the system was still quite new and was being improved and perfected by all who were using and teaching it. There was an obvious need for a central clearing house to which a student or teacher could write for information and clarification. For this purpose the Bureau was formed.

The Bureau's first efforts were directed toward standardizing the system through consultations with Rudolf von Laban. Though it now investigates all systems of dance notation, the Bureau is primarily concerned with the Laban system, which it now calls Labanotation. It has also functioned as a center for the discussion and exchange of ideas and material, as a school providing qualified teachers of Labanotation, as a recorder of dances in Labanotation, and as a reference library of notated dance works.

Since its formation, the Bureau has done much to promote the use of Labanotation in the U.S. In large part its success has been due to the perseverance of Miss Hutchinson, who was for many years its president. Bureau members have taught Labanotation, have written textbooks on the method, have given lecture-demonstrations, and have notated dances in many idioms—ballet, modern dance, musical comedy, etc. As a result of their endeavors, many works, notably by George Balanchine, Hanya Holm, and Doris Humphrey, have been preserved by and re-staged from Labanotation scores. Among the individuals who have made distinct contributions to the work of the Bureau are Irma Bartenieff and Els Grelinger in N.Y., Nadia Chilkovsky in Philadelphia, and Katrine Hooper in Boston. Martha Hill has introduced Labanotation into the modern dance curriculum of the several schools she has directed, while Josephina Garcia, Virginia Moomaw, Helen Priest Rogers, and Carol Scothorn have promoted the notation in various liberal arts colleges. The Dance Notation Bureau has also been instrumental in arranging for the copyrighting of dances through registration of the notated score with the Copyright Office, Library of Congress, Washington.

In 1967 the officers of the Bureau were: Ann Hutchinson, Honorary President. Lucy Venable, President; Mireille Backer, Irmgard Bartenieff, Martha Davis, Betsy Martin, Anna Wilson, Vice Presidents; Yvonne Parker, Secretary; Nona Schurman, Assistant Secretary; Billie Mahoney, Treasurer. Bureau marked its 25th anniversary in 1965.

Dance Observer (**publication**). See PERIODICALS, DANCE (U.S.).

Dance of Death. See DANSE MACABRE.

Dance Perspectives (**publication**). See PERIODICALS, DANCE (U.S.).

Dance Players, ballet company organized by Eugene Loring, sponsored by

Dance Players, Inc. (Mrs. Winthrop Palmer, Pres.), Nov., 1941, with a group of dancers headed by Janet Reed, Joan McCracken, Lew Christensen, Eugene Loring, Michael Kidd. The group made a short tour in the spring of 1942, then opened at the National Theatre, N.Y., Apr. 21, 1942, for a two-week season. Following that they took up summer residence at a specially rented farm in New Hope, Penn., where they rehearsed and gave occasional performances. After a short fall tour the company gave its last performance in Trenton, N.J., Nov. 12, 1942. In the repertoire were *Billy the Kid, City Portrait, The Duke of Sacramento, Harlequin for President, The Man from Midian, Prairie* (all by Loring), and *Jinx* (Lew Christensen).

Dance Project, a branch of the Federal Theatre Project, organized in the U.S. in 1935 to help solve unemployment in the dance field, was subsidized by the Works Progress Administration (W.P.A.). Under the general direction of Mrs. Hallie V. Flanagan, head of the Theatre Project, the Dance Project was administered by supervisors in various cities, among which New York and Chicago were the most active.

The New York Dance Project was organized late in 1935 with some one hundred dancers. Don Oscar Becque was its first supervisor; choreographers included Doris Humphrey, Charles Weidman, Helen Tamiris, Gluck-Sandor, Arthur Mahoney and Don Oscar Becque. The project's first production, Gluck-Sandor's *The Eternal Prodigal,* to Herbert Kingsley's music, opened Nov. 30, 1936, at the Ritz Theatre, after eight months of preparation. The cast included the following soloists: Felicia Sorel, Lisa Parnova, Valya Valentinoff, Kohana, Roger Pryor Dodge, Gluck-Sandor. The ballet was very successful and played twenty-eight performances.

On Jan. 2, 1937, Lincoln Kirstein replaced Don Oscar Becque as supervisor of the Project, but resigned after one day in office because he was unwilling to cope with the Project's politics and resented the attitude of most of the choreographers toward his plan of presenting an elaborate pageant, "The History of American Dancing." Opposition to Kirstein grew out of the fact that five of the six choreographers on the Project were modern dancers, while Kirstein, as ever, was a supporter of ballet. After Kirstein's resignation no new supervisor was appointed. Stephen Karnot, administrative assistant to Kirstein, was left in charge of the Project. In January of that year the Project's Young Choreographers Laboratory gave its first performance, presenting works by Lillian Mehlman, Saida Gerrard, Mura Dehn, Roger Pryor Dodge, Bill Matons, Nadia Chilkovsky, and Susanne Remos. Lazar Halpern succeeded Arthur Mahoney, who had resigned as ballet choreographer.

On May 6, the Project opened a season of forty-one performances of Tamiris's *How Long Brethren?* and Weidman's *Candide,* at the Nora Bayes Theatre, with the choreographers taking the principal roles in their respective productions. On June 15th of that year Congress cut the appropriation for the Federal Theatre Project by fifteen percent, and the activities of the New York Project diminished in scope. Administrator Karnot was subsequently transferred to Los Angeles and Evelyn David was appointed Co-ordinator of Dance Activities in New York.

In April, 1938, the Project presented a Children's Festival, "Folk Dances of All Nations," choreographed by Lillian Mehlman, at the Hippodrome. During the same month Tamiris and Harold Bolton presented the dance-drama, *Trojan Incident,* at the St. James Theatre. This was actually the last major activity of the New York Dance Project. The Federal Theatre came to an official end on July 31, 1939, but the dance activities of the New York Project petered out long before then, due chiefly to improved theatre business in the country.

In Chicago the Federal Dance Project was first directed by Grace and Kurt Graff and Berta Ochsner. Its first production was in the revue *O Say, Can You See,* which opened Dec. 11, 1936, at the Great Northern Theatre. Ballets were choreographed by the Graffs and Ochsner, tap and chorus routines were by Sammy Dyer and Hazel Davis. The program included *Renaissance, Gambolero* and *Night After Night* by the Graffs, and *The People's Choice* and *Fugitive From Rhythm* by Ochsner.

A new edition of the revue opened at the same theatre on June 17, 1937. Later that year Louise Dale Spoor became supervisor of the Dance Unit. On Jan. 27, 1938, an all-dance program opened at the Great Northern Theatre under the title "Ballet Fedré." The Graffs, Ochsner, and Katherine Dunham were the choreographers, the orchestra was under the direction of Edward Wurtzebach, settings were by Clive Rickebaugh. The program opened with *Midsummer Triptych* and *Two Cautionary Tales* by Berta Ochsner. The Graffs repeated their *Renaissance* and did a new ballet, *Viennese Trilogy*. In the company were Richard Reed, Kenneth MacKenzie, and David Ahdar. The program closed with Dunham's *L'Ag'ya.*

On June 19, 1938, the Project presented three ballets: *Frankie and Johnny,* and *American Pattern,* both with choreography by Ruth Page and Bentley Stone and music by Jerome Moross, with Page, Stone, Bettina Rosay, Betsy Ross, Ann Devine, Richard Reed, Sean Marino, David Ahdar, and Edwin Gibson in the cast; and *Behind This Mask,* with choreography by the Graffs and music by David Scheinfeld.

With Ruth Page and Bentley Stone as directors of the Project, another long-run program opened in Mar., 1939, at the Blackstone Theatre. The program consisted of *Love Song* (Page), *Guns and Castanets,* and *Scrapbook* (Stone and Page). Daniel Saidenberg conducted the orchestra. The company, in addition to Page and Stone, included Bettina Rosay, Pearl Lang, Betsy Ross, Ethel Sarasohn, Dorothy Davies, Leila Volkoff, Walter Camryn, David Nillo, John Kriza, and Kenneth MacKenzie.

Later that year Walter Camryn was named director of the Project. He began work on a Stephen Foster ballet, *Thunder in the Hills,* but the project was terminated before the ballet could be presented.

Dance Script. See DANCE NOTATION and LABANOTATION.

Dance Sonata. Modern dance work; chor.: May O'Donnell; commissioned music: Charles Jones. First prod.: May O'Donnell Dance Company, YM–YWHA, N.Y., Apr. 6, 1952. A group work, led by Nancy Lang and Robert Joffrey, which was a perfect introduction to May O'Donnell's particular style of movement and choreography. It was later reset to a score by Ray Green and given in this form Apr. 14, 1953, in a two week season of American Dance presented by the B. de Rothschild Foundation at the Alvin Theatre, N.Y.

Dancing Doll, The. See PUPPENFEE, DIE.

Dancing Master, The. See RAMEAU, PIERRE.

Dancing Times, The (London), monthly illustrated magazine devoted to all forms of theatrical dancing. First published in 1894 by Edward Humphrey as a small non-illustrated house organ of the Cavendish Rooms, London, where he taught dancing. Purchased 1910 by Philip J. S. Richardson and T. M. Middleton, Richardson assuming editorship and Middleton controlling advertising and business. A. H. Franks joined the magazine in 1946 and became editor in 1958, and Mary Clarke joined in 1954 as assistant editor, becoming editor upon Franks's death in 1963. In 1956 the magazine, which until then had covered all forms of dance, including social dancing, was divided into two magazines thus enabling *The Dancing Times* itself to concentrate entirely on the theatrical forms while the new magazine, *The Ballroom Dancing Times,* specialized in all the social forms. The policy of *The Dancing Times* is to maintain the highest possible standards of ballet criticism, to give a voice to leading authorities on all forms of theatrical dancing, and to encourage the highest teaching standards.

Dancing Tragedy. Ballet in 1 act, chor.: Dennis Gray; music: Richard Strauss (ballet music from the opera *Salomé*) ; book: Tiago de Melo; décor: Mario Conde. First prod.: Ballet da Cultura Artística, S. Paulo, Brazil, 1957, with a cast headed by Veronika Mlakar, Raul Severo, Ismael Guiser, Roberto Barrientos. The same year presented at Teatro Municipal, Rio de Janeiro, with Berta Rozanova (Salomé) , Decio Otero, Sebastian Araujo, Antonio Barros, Ricardo Abelan, Aldo Lotufo, Edmund Carijó, Arthur Ferreira (The Seven Men) . A unique approach to the story of Salomé: Salomé searches for her ideal on the roads of the world but none of the six men she meets fulfills her dreams, they only bring her a fleeting illusion of happiness. However, one day, trying to escape the gloom which dominates her, she meets a strange man who, she feels, is going to bring her the dream of happiness. She conquers him only to feel in his love the taste of death.

Dandré, Victor E. (1870–1944), husband of Anna Pavlova and manager of her company. Wealthy landowner and outstanding balletomane of old Russia, he married the great Russian dancer in 1914 and soon afterwards became her lifelong manager. It was due to his managerial talent that Anna Pavlova became known to the world at large. Pavlova's unmatched genius won her world-wide fame, but it was Dandré who made it possible. A few years after the death of Pavlova (1931), Dandré organized a company of his own which toured Europe, South America, India and Australia. In 1938 he (with German Sevastianov) took over Col. de Basil's Ballet Russe de Monte Carlo, renamed it Royal Covent Garden Russian Ballet and later, Original Ballet Russe, and presented it in London and Australia. Dandré last visited the U.S. (1937) for the purpose of presenting in this country the film *The Immortal Swan,* assembled from a multitude of shots made of Pavlova during her travels. The film has never been released in the U.S.

Danieli, Fred (Alfredo Carlo Danieli), American dancer, teacher and choreographer, b. N.Y. City, 1917. Studied with Mikhail Mordkin and at School of American Ballet, N.Y. His professional debut was in the musical *On Your Toes* (1938), followed by a tour of the Eastern U.S. with the Mordkin Ballet. Soloist with Ballet Caravan for two years, touring U.S., Canada, and Cuba. Leading dancer in the Ford Ballet's *A Thousand Times Neigh* (chor. William Dollar) at New York World's Fair 1940. After a season as soloist with Ballet Theatre in conjunction with the Chicago Civic Opera Company, which gave him the opportunity to work and study with Michel Fokine, he toured South America as leading dancer and lecturer with Ballet Caravan (1940). In the same year he organized his own company, El Ballet de las Americas, for which he staged three original ballets. From 1941–46 was with Army Ground Forces, touring all overseas Theaters of Operations. After his Army discharge, joined the cast of *Call Me Mister,* also appearing in ballets on C.B.S. television. Choreographed *Punch and the Child* for Ballet Society (1946); staged a ballet for the Ford Motor Show at the Waldorf Astoria Hotel (1948). Staged dances and musical numbers for Ray Bolger's musical, *Where's Charley?* Since 1950 has been chairman of the faculty of the Newark Ballet Academy. He is also artistic director of the Garden State Ballet, a New Jersey civic ballet company which is a member of the Northeast Regional Ballet Festival Association. See REGIONAL BALLET.

Danielian, Leon, American dancer, choreographer, teacher, b. New York City, 1920. Studied with Mikhail Mordkin, Michel Fokine, Anton Dolin, Antony Tudor, Igor Schwezoff, School of American Ballet. Made his debut with the Mordkin Ballet (1937); danced in the Rogers and Hart musical *I Married an Angel* (1938); soloist, Ballet (now American Ballet) Theatre (1939–41), his ballets including *Swan Lake* (pas de trois), *Lady into Fox, Goyescas, Carnaval, Les Sylphides,* and others; Col. de Basil's Original Ballet Russe (1942), dancing *Carnaval, Cimarosiana, Coq d'Or, Francesca da Rimini, Blue Bird* pas de deux, and others. From 1943 to 1961 (as guest artist during the last few seasons), premier danseur with Ballet Russe de Monte Carlo, dancing Harlequin (*Carnaval*), *Blue Bird, Black Swan* and *Don Quixote* pas de deux, and *Les Sylphides,* Franz (*Coppélia*), Sugar Plum Fairy's Cavalier (*The Nutcracker*), Hussar and King of the Dandies (*Le Beau Danube*), title role (*Le Spectre de la Rose*), Faun (*Afternoon of a Faun*), Poet (*Night Shadow*), Peruvian (*Gaîté Parisienne*), and others. During this period he made many guest artist appearances, including a season with Ballets des Champs-Elysées, Paris, (1951) dancing *Don Quixote* and *Black Swan* pas de deux and *Impromptu au Bois.* During the same year partnered Yvette Chauviré in *Coppélia, Giselle,* and *The Nutcracker* on a tour of North Africa and the south of France. Choreographed *Sombreros* for Ballet Russe de Monte Carlo (1956); as guest artist with *San Francisco Ballet* (1957) toured Far East, and South and Central America, (1958), dancing *Con Amore, Black Swan, Nutcracker* and *Don Quixote* pas de deux. Choreographed *Mazurka* for Ballet Russe de Monte Carlo (1958); again guest artist with San Francisco Ballet (1959) touring

Leon Danielian, American dancer, choreographer.

Middle East, Far East and North Africa. Choreographed *España* (1962) for Ballet Russe de Monte Carlo. Currently teaching.

Daniels, Danny (Daniel Giagni), American dancer and choreographer, b. Albany, N.Y., 1924. Studied dance with Thomas Sternfield (Albany), Edith Jane (Hollywood, Calif.), Jack Potteiger, Vincenzo Celli, Elisabeth Anderson-Ivantzova, Anatole Vilzak (N.Y.). Made his debut in the chorus of *Best Foot Forward* (1941) and *Count Me In* (1942), graduating to juvenile lead of *Billion Dollar Baby* (1945), and dancing leads in *Street Scene* (1947), *Make Mine Manhattan* (1948), *Kiss Me, Kate* (1951). Created *Tap Dance Concerto* in collaboration with Morton Gould which had its first performance in Rochester, N.Y. (1952). Has since performed it with the N.Y. Philharmonic, L.A. Philharmonic (in Hollywood Bowl), and with other leading U.S. orchestras. Presented it in Berlin and in London (Albert Hall, 1957). Soloist with Agnes de Mille Dance Theatre (1953). Has choreographed for many television series (Martha Raye, Ray Bolger, Patrice Munsel, "Firestone Hour," "Revlon Revue"); also many television specials, starring Milton Berle, Bing Crosby, and Danny Kaye, as well as "Fabulous 'Fifties" (for which he received the "Emmy" Award, 1960).

Choreographed Broadway musicals *All American* (1962), *High Spirits* (1964); off-Broadway revival of *Best Foot Forward* (1963), also directing the last-named.

Danilova, Alexandra, contemporary ballerina, b. Peterhof, Russia, now an American citizen. Educated at Imperial (later State) Ballet School, Petrograd, from which she was graduated into the corps de ballet of the Soviet State Ballet at the Maryinsky (now Kirov) Theatre and later advanced to soloist (1922–23). She left Russia with a small group including George Balanchine, Tamara Geva, and others to tour Western Europe (1924). Was engaged by Serge Diaghilev for the winter season of his Ballets Russes (1924–25), promoted to ballerina in 1927, and remained with his company until his death in 1929. Her roles included *Firebird,* Can-Can Dancer (*La Boutique Fantasque*), Terpsichore (*Apollon Musagète*); creations included Fairy Queen (*The Triumph of Neptune*), Serving Maid (*The Gods Go a'Begging*), Masked Lady (*Le Bal*), among others. Soloist Monte Carlo Opera Ballet (1929–30); danced in operetta *Waltzes from Vienna,* Alhambra Theatre, London (1931); ballerina, Col. de Basil's Ballets Russes (1933–38, except for the fall season, 1934, when she appeared as ballerina in the operetta *The Great Waltz,* Center Theatre, N.Y.); prima ballerina Ballet Russe de Monte Carlo (1938–52). Her great range of roles from the classic tragedy of her Odette (*Swan Lake,* Act 2), to the soubrette charm of her Street Dancer (*Le Beau Danube*) included Swanilda (*Coppélia*), Glove-Seller (*Gaité Parisienne*), Mazurka and pas de deux (*Les Sylphides*), and, during the American period of Ballet Russe de Monte Carlo, such creations as Sleepwalker (*Night Shadow*), ballerina (*Danses Concertantes*), and the title role in the revival of *Raymonda.* She danced a season with Sadler's Wells (now Royal) Ballet at Royal Opera House, Covent Garden, London (1949) appearing in *Coppélia, Giselle, La Boutique Fantasque;* guest artist with London's Festival Ballet at Stoll Theatre (1951); guest ballerina with Slavenska-Franklin Ballet (1952–53); formed own group, Great Moments of Ballet (1954–56), touring U.S., Canada, Japan, Philippines, South Africa. Made her farewell N.Y. appearance as guest ballerina of Ballet Russe de Monte Carlo at Metropolitan Opera House (1957), following this with a second Far Eastern tour. Danced and acted in the musical *Oh Captain!* (1958); Capezio Award Winner (1958). Staged ballets for the Metropolitan Opera House in *La Giaconda* (1959), *Gypsy Baron* (1960), *Boris Goudonov* (1961). Staged *Coppélia* for La Scala, Milan, and the full *Nutcracker* for Washington (D.C.) Ballet (both 1961). Currently lecturing and teaching.

Alexandra Danilova, prima ballerina and subsequently teacher, in Swan Lake.

Danilova, Maria (1793–1810), the greatest Russian dancer of the 19th century, entered the St. Petersburg Imperial School of Ballet at the age of eight. The choreographer Charles Didelot recognized the exceptional talent of the young pupil, and she began to get roles of Cupid in various ballets a year after she had entered the school. Within a few years, while still a student, she began to dance ballerina roles, competing successfully with the foreign ballerinas visiting Russia. Beautiful, graceful, light, technically very strong, Danilova was considered a phenomenon on the Russian stage. She was graduated from the school in Nov. 1809, ahead of her class, but never reached the "official" status of dancer. Her delicate health was undermined by constant rehearsals and the hard tasks demanded by Didelot. Despite excellent care given her by the director of the theatre and many balletomanes, despite the careful medical attention of the court physicians sent to her bedside by the Czar, Danilova died on January 8, 1810, at the age of seventeen. Lincoln Kirstein in his authoritative *Dance* (N.Y., 1935) says that the French dancer Duport who went to St. Petersburg as a guest artist accompanied by his mistress, a famous actress, "managed to seduce her (Danilova), being skilled in ways the natives did not know, and abandoned the Frenchwoman. But not for long. His engagement over, he made peace with her and quit Russia without so much as a word to poor Danilova who adored him. She fell ill, crushed, and quite as in a romance by Pushkin, died, at the age of seventeen, of a broken heart." Russian sources, however, fail to substantiate Mr. Kirstein's story. They state, in fact, that many romantic rumors had been circulated about Danilova's death but none of them withstood careful research. No other Russian dancer, before or after Danilova, had so much poetry written about her. The Russian poets of that period—Karamzin, Ismailov, Gniedich, and Milanov—have all contributed to immortalize the memory of the great artist who was actually never a full-fledged dancer.

Danish Ballet and Music Festival, first held in 1950 and repeated every year since, is the only international festival in which greater prominence is given to ballet than to any other event. The Festival takes place during the final two weeks in May and includes performances in the Royal Theatre, the New Stage, and at Tivoli Pantomime Theatre. The August Bournonville ballets are a feature of the Festival which attracts visitors from all over the world. Retiring dancers usually choose to give their farewell performance during a Festival, when they take a solo call (never allowed at any other time) and receive flowers and gifts while the orchestra plays a fanfare. The King of Denmark, sometimes accompanied by members of his family and sometimes alone except for an equerry, attends performances frequently, the company giving its first bow to the royal box before acknowledging the applause from the rest of the audience. During the Festival, one (occasionally two) curtain calls are taken, a custom which is not allowed at any other time. The Festival is always held May 15–31.

Danse d'Ecole, classic dance, the technical system formulated by Pierre Beauchamp (ca. 1700), a break from the ballet de cour in which the dancers were restricted by heavy court costumes. The five absolute positions and the turn-out (en dehors) are basic. Gaetan Vestris added a great deal to this foundation. Carlo Blasis's *Code of Terpsichore* (1830) became the standard book of instruction in his time and is still a valid textbook of the classic dance. He prepared the way for the greatest possible extension of the legs and arms, which hastened the development of the danse d'élevation. Even today the language of the classic ballet is French, though the influence is international—the collective expression of the dance in Europe, Russia, England, and America during the past 300 years.

Danse Macabre (Dance of Death, Danse des Morts, Totentanz), a standard part of 14th century German morality plays, but the concept existed also in France, England, and Spain. Actually Danse Macabre existed more in painting and literature than in movement. There are Danse Macabre frescoes in churchyards in Lubeck, Dresden, Lucerne, London (Old St. Paul's). The idea of the usual Danse Macabre is that all men are equal before death. The text is usually satiric. Original Danses Macabres showed only men. One of the earliest is a wall painting made in 1312 in Klingenthal, Switzerland. In 1424 one was painted on the walls of the cloister in the Church of the Holy Innocents, Paris. During the bubonic plague the Danse Macabre became a social dance.

Danseomanie, dancing mania, legend that young people cursed by priest got danseomania. Dr. Paracelsus (d. Salzburg, 1541) tried to cure it scientifically.

Danses Concertantes. Ballet in 6 movements; chor.: George Balanchine; music: Igor Stravinsky; décor: Eugene Berman. First prod.: Ballet Russe de Monte Carlo, N.Y. City Center, Sept 10, 1944, with Alexandra Danilova and Leon Danielian (later Frederic Franklin) in main roles. A ballet to this score with choreography by Kenneth MacMillan, in décor by Nicholas Georgiadis, was presented by Sadler's Wells Theatre Ballet at Sadler's Wells Theatre, London, Jan. 18, 1955, with Maryon Lane, Donald Britton, David Poole in leading roles. MacMillan staged this version for Royal Danish Ballet. It is a plotless work.

Dante Sonata. Ballet in 1 act; chor.: Frederick Ashton; music: Franz Liszt's *Dante Sonata* (d'après une lecture de Dante), orch. by Constant Lambert; décor: Sophie Fedorovitch, after illustrations for Dante's *Divine Comedy* by John Flaxman, English illustrator (1755–1826). First prod.: Sadler's Wells (now Royal) Ballet, Sadler's Wells Theatre, London, Jan. 23, 1940, with a cast headed by Margot Fonteyn, Pamela May, Robert Helpmann, Michael Somes. The struggle between the forces of good and evil, the ballet's theme, had at the period of its creation a very special emotional significance for its audiences in wartime London.

Danton, Henry, English dancer, ballet master, teacher, b. Bedford, 1919. Educated Wellington College and Royal Military Academy, Woolwich (King's Honour Cadet), and Regular Army commission in the Royal Artillery. Studied dance with Vera Volkova and Stanislas Idzikowski (London), Olga Preobrajenska, Victor Gzovsky (Paris), Pierre Vladimiroff (N.Y.). After a season with Allied Ballet, London (1943), joined International Ballet, dancing male lead in *Les Sylphides* and *Swan Lake* (1943–44); leading soloist with Sadler's Wells (now Royal) Ballet, his ballets including *Les Sylphides, Sleeping Beauty, Swan Lake, Symphonic Variations* (in which he created one of the three male roles), and others; season with Metropolitan Ballet (1947) and was the first English dancer to dance *Flower Festival at Genzano* pas de deux (with Elsa-Marianne von Rosen); danced *Nutcracker* and *Black Swan* pas de deux during Ballets des Champs-Elysées Paris season (1947–48), also touring Europe as partner to Lycette Darsonval, dancing *Les Sylphides, Giselle, Coppélia, Sylvia, Nutcracker* pas de deux; Ballets de Paris de Roland Petit U.S. tour (1949–50), dancing *Le Combat, Le Rendez-vous, Pas d'Action;* toured South America and U.S. with Mia Slavenska (1950–51) dancing classic pas de deux; guest artist, Australian National Ballet (1951–52), dancing classic repertoire, *Protée, Graduation Ball,* and staging *Pas de Quatre, The Nut-*

cracker, Don Quixote, and re-staging full-length *Swan Lake* and *Aurora's Wedding.* First dancer, artistic director, and ballet master of Venezuelan National Ballet (1953–58), for which he staged *Swan Lake* (Acts 2 and 3), *Giselle* (for Alicia Alonso and Igor Youskevitch, guest artists), *Aurora's Wedding, Coppélia, Le Spectre de la Rose,* and others. Staged *Giselle* (Act 2), and *Peasant* pas de deux, and *Swan Lake* pas de trois for Washington Ballet. Currently teaching in N.Y.

D'Antuono, Eleanor, American dancer, b. Boston, Mass., 1939. Studied dance with Maria Papporello and E. Virginia Williams in Boston, and danced with the latter's New England Civic Ballet before joining corps de ballet of Ballet Russe de Monte Carlo (1954). She danced her first solo roles, Prayer (*Coppélia*), Seamstress (*Le Beau Danube*) in 1956. Other leading roles as she was promoted to leading soloist included Daughter (*Le Beau Danube*) (1957), leading girl (*Sombreros*) (1959), *Blue Bird* pas de deux, *Minkus* pas de trois (from *Paquita*), Mazurka and Prelude (*Les Sylphides*), First and Second leads (*Variations Classiques*), second ballerina (*Ballet Imperial*—all 1959), *Don Quixote* pas de deux, Glove Seller (*Gaîté Parisienne*), Waltz and Pas de deux (*Les Sylphides*—all 1960). Danced a season with Robert Joffrey Ballet (1960–61). Joined American Ballet Theatre in fall of 1961, as soloist, dancing a leading Swan (*Swan Lake,* Act 2) Girl in Yellow (*Les Patineurs*); promoted to ballerina in 1963, dancing ballerina (*Theme and Variations*), Woman in His Past (*Lilac Garden*), and others.

Eleanor d'Antuono, ballerina of the American Ballet Theatre.

Danza. Six Variations on a Caribbean theme; chor.: Heinz Rosen; music: Werner Egk: décor: Helmut Jürgens; costumes: Charlotte Flemming. First prod.: Feb. 16, 1960, at Staatsoper, Munich, with Natasha Trofimova, Dulce Anaya, Margot Werner, Heino Hallhuber, Rainer Köchermann. This is a folklore ballet staged on a classic foundation after a Haitian folk song. The following season (Dec., 1960) a version was staged by Heino Heiden for Mannheim National Theatre.

Daphnis and Chloë. Ballet in 3 scenes; chor. and book: Michel Fokine; commissioned music: Maurice Ravel; décor: Léon Bakst. First prod.: Diaghilev Ballets Russes, Théâtre du Châtelet, Paris, June 8, 1912, with Tamara Karsavina and Vaslav Nijinsky in the title roles, Adolph Bolm as Dorkon. Fokine revived it at Theatre Royal, Drury Lane, London in 1914 with himself and Vera Fokina in the title roles. His original (1904) scenario called for two acts, but the second was never completed. Fokine again revived it for the Paris Opéra, June 20, 1921. Catherine Littlefield also staged the ballet for her company. The story and the score has a great allure for choreographers and among other versions are those by George Skibine and John Cranko. However, the most successful of all the versions is that of Frederick Ashton, in décor by John Craxton, premièred by Sadler's Wells (now Royal) Ballet at Royal Opera House, Covent Garden, London, Apr. 5, 1951, with Margot Fonteyn (Chloë), Michael Somes (Daphnis), John Field (Dorkon in this production), Alexander Grant (Pirate Chief). The subject is a simplified version of the tale (possibly the first novel ever written) by the Roman author Longus, who tells this story of ancient Greece. Chloë the shepherdess and Daphnis the goatherd love each other with a complete innocence. When Chloë is carried off by a band of pirates, Daphnis invokes the aid of Pan who disperses the pirates in terror, and the lovers are united in a triumphal dance of celebration.

Dark Elegies. Ballet in 1 act; chor. and book: Antony Tudor; music: Gustav Mahler's *Kindertotenlieder;* décor: Nadia Benois. First prod.: Ballet Rambert, Duchess Theatre, London, Feb. 19, 1937, with Peggy van Praagh, Agnes de Mille, Maude Lloyd, Antony Tudor, Hugh Laing. Staged by Tudor for Ballet (now American Ballet) Theatre, Jan. 24, 1940, with Lucia Chase, Miriam Golden, Nina Stroganova, Laing, Tudor, and Dimitri Romanoff in the principal parts. Later Nora Kaye danced Stroganova's role. The ballet is accompanied by a vocal rendering of Mahler's song cycle. The set of dances reflects the atmosphere of these songs on the death of children, the anguish of bereavement, the ultimate acceptance of loss in the knowledge that life will go on. Tudor used a very free ballet style for his choreography, with very little pointe work. The two back cloths and the simple costumes suggest a fishing village. Tudor staged the ballet for the Royal Swedish Ballet in Stockholm (1963). It is also in the repertoire of National Ballet of Canada. The ballet was revived for the American Ballet Theatre's twenty-fifth anniversary season, March 16 to April 11, 1965.

Dark Meadow. Group dance by Martha Graham; commissioned music: Carlos Chavez; décor: Isamu Noguchi; costumes: Edythe Gilfond. First prod.: Plymouth Theatre, N.Y., Jan. 23, 1946, with Martha Graham (She Who Seeks), May O'Donnell (She of the Ground), Erick Hawkins (He Who Summons). Commissioned by the Elizabeth Sprague Coolidge Foundation, Library of Congress, Washington, D.C. The work is in four sections: Remembrance of Ancestral Footsteps (*Ancestral Footsteps* was the working title of *Dark Meadow*), Terror of Loss, Ceaselessness of Love, Recurring Ecstasy of the Flowering Branch. A ritual celebrating the mysteries of birth, life, death and rebirth.

Darkling, The. Ballet in 1 act, chor.: Brian Macdonald; music: Benjamin Britten's *Variations on a Theme by Frank Bridge;* décor: Peter Symcox. First prod.: Royal Winnipeg Ballet, Playhouse Theatre, Winnipeg, Oct. 17, 1958, with Marilyn Young (The Darkling), Michael Hrushowy (Her Lover). The ballet shows the metamorphosis through love of the girl, called here the Darkling. At the end the metamorphosis is complete and she has moved from shadow into light.

Darrell, Peter, English dancer, choreographer, director, b. Richmond, Surrey, 1929. Studied at Sadler's Wells (now Royal) Ballet School and was one of the original members of Sadler's Wells Theatre Ballet. Later joined London's Festival Ballet. Choreographed *Harlequinade* for Festival Ballet; *Les Chimères, Tell-Tale Heart* for Ballet Workshop; *The Gift* for Ballet der Laage Landen. Cofounder and artistic director with Elizabeth West of Western Theatre Ballet (1957–59), subsequently principal choreographer, then re-assumed directorial responsibilities after the death of Elizabeth West. His ballets for this company include *Prisoners, Non-Stop, Impasse, Chiaroscuro, Ode, Bal de la Victoire, Mods and*

Lycette Darsonval, première danseuse étoile of the Paris Opéra Ballet (1940–57), currently teaching.

Rockers (to music by England's singing group, The Beatles).

Darsonval, Lycette, French ballerina, b. Coutances, Brittany, 1912. Studied under Carlotta Zambelli at the Paris Opéra. Created leading roles in, among others, *Elvire* (1937), *David Triomphant* (1937), *Oriane et le Prince de l'Amour* (1938) and, after her promotion to première danseuse étoile in 1940, *La Princesse au Jardin* (1941), *Joan von Zarissa* (1942), *L'Amour Sorcier* and *Suite en Blanc* (1943), *Phèdre* and *La Grande Jatte* (1950), *Salomé* (1955), *Variations* (1957). Darsonval was one of the most popular French ballerinas, not only at the Opéra but all over France, where she appeared in provincial towns with her own group. In addition to the ballets of Lifar and other contemporary choreographers, she danced *Giselle* for many years with Lifar as partner and was very successful in *Sylvia* and *Coppélia*. Darsonval had also toured in U.S., Germany, etc., with her own group. She was director of the Paris Opéra Ballet School (1957–60). Now has her own studio in Paris, teaching and directing a ballet group. Is a Chevalier de la Légion d'Honneur, Chevalier des Arts et Lettres, Medaille de la Ville de Paris. Her brother, Serge Perrault, is also a dancer; he created the Toreador in Roland Petit's *Carmen*.

Dauberval, Jean (or d'Auberval, stage name of Jean Bercher, 1742–1806), French dancer and choreographer, who did much to further the theories of Jean Georges Noverre, his teacher. Dauberval's best known ballet, *La Fille Mal Gardée,* first produced in 1789, is one of the oldest ballets still being performed, although probably in an entirely different form, his original choreography having long disappeared. He was married to the famous ballerina Mlle. Théodore.

Davis, Mike. See PHOTOGRAPHERS, DANCE (ENGLAND).

Day, Mary, teacher, choreographer, b. Washington, D. C. A pupil of Lisa Gardiner, the two of them established the Washington (D.C.) School of the Ballet in 1944. Their productions of ballets for children such as *Hansel and Gretel, Cinderella,* and *Adventures of Oz,* for which the National Symphony Orchestra played, became a feature of Washington's Christmas season. Out of these performances grew the Washington Ballet, one of the best of the regional groups, for which Mary Day choreographed a number of works, among them *Hi Spri, Modern Madrigal, Schubertiana,* and *Ondine* (to music by Sibelius). The company danced at Jacob's Pillow Dance Festival in 1960. Mary Day visited the Soviet Union (May, 1961) as a guest of the U.S.S.R. under the sponsorship of the U.S. State Dept.

to study the schools of the Bolshoi and Kirov Ballets. On returning, the Washington National Ballet Foundation was set up to establish the Washington School of the Ballet as a resident academic and professional school, the first of its kind in the U.S. This program began with the Sept., 1962, term.

Day on Earth. Modern dance work; chor.: Doris Humphrey; music: Aaron Copland's Piano Sonata; costumes: Pauline Lawrence. First prod.: José Limón Dance Company, City Center, N.Y., Dec. 21, 1947, with José Limón (Man), Letitia Ide (Woman), Miriam Pandor (Young Girl), Melisa Nicolaides (Child). Day on Earth is man's cycle of life and all that goes into the making of it, conceived within the framework of his daily work in which is contained his love, his anguish, and the processes of birth and death.

Daydé, Bernard, French theatrical and ballet designer, b. Paris, 1921. Earliest works were *Romeo and Juliet* and *Les Sylphides* for Metropolitan Ballet (London, 1947). His striking décors include *La Nuit est une Sorcière* (chor. Pierre Lacotte, 1955), Harald Lander's *Etudes* (London's Festival Ballet, 1956), *Promethée* (Maurice Béjart for Miskovitch Ballet, 1956), *Les Liens* (Janine Charrat, 1957), *Pulcinella* (Béjart, 1957), *Señor de Mañara* (Miskovitch Ballet, 1959), *Qarrtsiluni* (Harald Lander, Paris Opéra, 1960), *Jugando el Toro* (Antonio, 1961); *The Lesson* (Flemming Flindt, Opéra Comique, 1964); also the settings and costumes for African Ballet of Keita Fodeba. In 1962 designed the new production of *Etudes* and *Le Triomphe de l'Amour* with which Lander returned as guest choreographer to Royal Danish Ballet. Daydé is an extremely original designer, modern in spirit and style.

Daydé, Liane, French ballerina, b. Paris, 1934. Studied at Paris Opéra with Albert Aveline, Leo Staats, Carlotta Zambelli, Blanche d'Allesandri, Serge Lifar, and with Alexandre Volinine. Entered Paris Opéra company in 1948 and was promoted to première danseuse étoile in 1951, creating title role in *Blanche Neige* (Serge Lifar) the same year. Other roles include *Giselle, Swan Lake, Romeo and Juliet* (Lifar, 1955). Since leaving the Opéra (1959) has toured all over the world partnered by Michel Renault, appearing five times in Soviet Russia where she was the first European dancer to dance *Giselle* at the Bolshoi Theatre. Has been guest artist at Colón, Buenos Aires; La Scala, Milan; with London's Festival Ballet. Guest ballerina, with Ballet International du Marquis de Cuevas (1961–62), dancing Aurora in *The Sleeping Beauty,* partnered by Serge Golovine, Rudolf Nureyev. Appeared at Jacob's Pillow in the summer of 1962 partnered by Golovine. Toured the U.S. as prima ballerina of Grand Ballet Classique de France (fall-winter, 1965). Married to impresario Claude Giraud (1961).

Liane Daydé, prima ballerina of Grand Ballet Classique de France.

Deakin, Irving, English-born writer, lecturer, b. at sea, 1901, d. New Milford, Conn., 1958. Educated at Eastbourne College, and at Royal College of Music with Aubrey Brain, Ralph Vaughan Williams, Sir Henry Wood. Editor and music critic, *British-American,* London (1925–27); European music and theatre correspondent, International Feature Syndicate (1926–30). Wrote and lectured on dance; originated and conducted first ballet radio program in U.S. on music and ballet over WQXR (1937–43), N.Y. General manager, San Francisco Civic Ballet Association (1947–48). Worked for several years in the press department of Hurok Attractions, Inc. His books include *To the Ballet* (1935), *Ballet Profile* (1936), *At the Ballet* (1956).

Deakin, Irving, Collection, an integral part of the Dance Collection of the New York Public Library, consists of 2,700 photographs, the manuscripts of Irving Deakin's books, typescripts and records of the author's interview programs on radio station WQXR, N.Y. (1937–43), and a collection of letters from prominent dancers of the period. Especially interesting is the correspondence concerning the organization of Ballet Theatre (1939–40).

Dean, Beth, American dancer, b. Denver, Colo., m. Victor Carell. Studied dance as a child with Leo Staats in Paris and Nicholas Legat in London. Has lived in Australia since 1947, making a study of aboriginal dancers and developing a program with her musician husband with which they have toured in Australia, New Zealand, and all over the world. Has also choreographed ballets on Australian themes, including a version of John Antill's *Corroboree,* and for musicals, opera, etc. In addition to her research in Australia she and her husband undertook a world tour in 1962 for studying and filming dance in the Far East, Spain, Ireland, Mexico, Tahiti, etc., and dances of the American Indian. Co-author (with Victor Carell) of *Dust for the Dancers,* a travel book about Central and Northern Australia, and *Softly Wild Drums,* on New Guinea.

Death and the Maiden. Ballet in 1 act; chor. and costumes: Andrée Howard; music: the Andante con moto from Franz Schubert's String Quartet in D minor—the movement which is known as "Death and the Maiden," developed from the Schubert song. First prod.: Ballet Rambert, Duchess Theatre, London, Feb. 23, 1937, with Andrée Howard as the Maiden. It was later danced with great success by a long line of Rambert dancers, some of them being Elisabeth Schooling, Sally Gilmour, Joan McClelland, Brenda Hamlyn, June Sandbrook. The choreographer staged it for Ballet (now American Ballet) Theatre at Center Theatre, N.Y., for its initial 1940 season, with herself and Annabelle Lyon alternating as the Maiden. The ballet shows the young girl in all her innocent happiness overtaken by the shadow of Death but finding, at the very end, that Death is gentle. A ballet of the same name using the Schubert quartet in full was choreographed by Erick Walter for the Wuppertal State Opera Ballet (Jan. 30, 1964), with Denise Laumer and Joachim Koenig in the principal roles.

Death of a Bird. Ballet in 1 act; chor.: Ismael Guiser; music: Heitor Villa-Lobos (*Bachiana No. 8*); book: Vinicius de Morais; décor: Emiliano Di Cavalcanti. First prod.: Ballet Rio de Janeiro, Teatro Municipal, 1960, with Yolanda Verdier, Nelly Laport, Raul Severo, Arthur Ferreira, Aloisa Menezes, Decio Otero. In a clearing in the jungle the tropical birds are occupied with their daily tasks. At the approach of evening the birds join one another in love. The gavião, a tropical bird of prey, appears and kills the male sabiá and tries to abduct the female sabiá. All the little birds attack the dreadful gavião and kill him in revenge.

Deaths and Entrances. Modern dance work; chor.: Martha Graham; music: Hunter Johnson; décor: Arch Lauterer; costumes: Edythe Gilfond. First prod.: Bennington College, Vt., July 18, 1943, with Martha Graham, Jane Dudley, and Sophie Maslow as the Three Sisters, Merce Cunningham as the Poetic Beloved, Erick Hawkins as the Dark Beloved. The title comes from a Dylan Thomas poem, the subject is a searching of the inner mind of the Brontë sisters. With this work Graham made her first use of symbols—here a vase, a shell, a goblet, the sight or touch of which evokes memories which temporarily become more powerful than the present. *Deaths and Entrances* had its N.Y. première Dec. 26, 1943, at the Forty-Sixth St. Theatre, and was revived in 1947 with Graham, May O'Donnell, and Pearl Lang as the Sisters, and John Butler as the Poetic Beloved.

De Basil, Col. W. (Vassili Grigorievitch Voskresensky, 1888–1951), m. Olga Morosova. A former officer of the Russian army, he began his theatrical career in 1925 as assistant to Prince Zeretelli, director of an itinerant Russian opera company. In 1932 was accepted by René Blum as co-director of the Ballets Russes de Monte Carlo. Eventually Blum retired, leaving de Basil in full charge. In 1938 Leonide Massine left de Basil's organization. With Massine, de Basil lost a number of other dancers and the title of the company which reverted to Blum. In 1939 de Basil obtained control of the Original Ballet Russe, which he managed until it disbanded in 1948.

Déboulé, in ballet, a quick turn from one foot to the other with a rolling movement, usually in a series, in a straight line (chaîné) or in a circle (en manège).

Debut, first appearance of a dancer on the stage, in general, or first appearance in a given city, in a new part, or in a new ballet.

Marquis George de Cuevas, American patron of the arts and ballet impresario.

De Cuevas, Marquis George (eighth Marquis de Piedrablanca de Guana de Cuevas), American patron of the arts, b. 1886, Chile, of a Spanish father and Danish mother (American citizen since 1940), d. Feb. 22, 1961, Cannes, France; m. Margaret Strong, granddaughter of the late John D. Rockefeller; Sponsor of the Masterpieces of Art exhibition at the N.Y. World's Fair (1939–40); founder and director of Ballet Institute (1943) and Ballet International which made its N.Y. debut in 1944. Although the season was a disastrous financial failure, the Marquis did not lose interest in ballet. He took over the company of Nouveau Ballet de Monte Carlo (summer, 1947), changed its name to Grand Ballet de Monte Carlo, and brought to Europe such American dancers as Rosella Hightower, Marjorie Tallchief, William Dollar, and others, and engaged Bronislava Nijinska as ballet mistress. Some French elements remained for a short time but after the first season at the Vichy Opéra (summer, 1947), the company lost both Serge Lifar and the principal French dancers. The big Paris season in the Alhambra Theatre, Nov. 1947, included ballets by American choreographers: *Constantia* (Dollar), *Sebastian* (Edward Caton), and American ballerinas Hightower and Tallchief. The new style was extremely significant for the future of the French school. From 1947 to 1960 the Marquis toured the company all over the world, thanks to the financial support offered by the Rockefeller fortune of his wife. In 1950 the company became Le Grand Ballet du Marquis de Cuevas and, in its final years International Ballet of the Marquis de Cuevas. The Marquis became one of the most popular figures in the European ballet world and his personality was especially loved by his public. He combined the elegance of a "grand seigneur" with a real simplicity of heart. One of the most talked of episodes of his career was the costume ball he gave in 1953 in Biarritz on Lake Chiberta—a scene of incomparable magnificence. His apartment in Paris at 7, quai Voltaire, was known to all ballet lovers. He usually received his visitors lying in his bed surrounded by his favorite Pekingese dogs. He devoted much passion and energy to his company; most of the big stars of the day appeared as guest artist during one or another of his annual Paris seasons: Alicia Markova, Tamara Toumanova, Leonide Massine, David Lichine, Erik Bruhn, and others. Among his ballet masters at various times were Bronislava Nijinska, William Dollar, Nicholas Beriosoff and, for a larger period than anyone else, John Taras. The Marquis's company produced such young dancers as Serge Golovine, gave George Skibine his start as a choreographer, and played a big part in developing the public taste for the classic ballet, especially in France. The Marquis loved the classic repertoire. Few of the new works in the company's repertoire will be remembered. The most successful were *Le Prisonnier du Caucase* (Skibine-Aram Khachaturian, 1951)., *Piège de Lumière* (Taras-Jean-Michel Damase, 1952), *Idylle* (Skibine-François Serrette, 1954). The final production (1960), when the Marquis was already dangerously ill, was the full-length *The Sleeping Beauty* in new, magnificent sets by Raymundo de Larrain, young designer and a Chilean relative of the Marquis. The Marquis was present at the sumptuous première at the Théâtre des Champs Elysées, Oct. 27, 1960, attended by nurses. It was his final "folie," for he was desperately ill. He died in his villa, "Les Delices," in Cannes, Feb. 22, 1961. The company continued its engagements directed by young Larrain and, at the end of 1961, became International Ballet of the Marquese de Cuevas. By then its principal stars had left the troupe—Hightower, Tallchief, Skibine, and many others. The company lost the personality which the Marquis had given to his beloved ballet, and gave its final performances in 1962.

Deege, Gisela, German dancer, b. Berlin, 1928. Pupil of Tatiana Gsovska. Made her debut at fifteen as Juliet in *Romeo and Juliet,* Leipzig, Germany. From 1947 to 1950 at the State Opera, Berlin; also appeared in Hamburg and other big German cities, and with the Berliner Ballett of Tatiana Gsovska (1955). Since 1952, prima ballerina of the Berlin Municipal (now German) Opera. Among her roles are Desdemona (*The Moor of Venice*), Medusa (title role), Isabeau (*Joan von Zarissa*), Electra (*Black Sun*), and others. Often dances on German and British television.

De Face, in ballet, facing the audience. The position of a dancer's body when presented squarely to the audience.

De Falla, Manuel (1877–1946), Spanish composer. Wrote scores for *El Amor Brujo* and of *The Three-Cornered Hat* (chor. Leonide Massine, 1919).

Defense of Paradise. Ballet presented by Catherine de Medici on Aug. 18, 1572. The theme was Catholicism versus Protestantism with the Catholics defending

Heaven and the Protestants defending Hell. Characters included the Zodiac, Cupid, Mercury, and nymphs.

Defilé, or to give the full title, Defilé du Corps de Ballet, is a spectacular, on-stage parade of the entire ballet company of the Paris Opéra, for which the full depth of the stage is opened, including the backstage Foyer de la Danse. The company, beginning with the pupils (petits rats) and finishing with the étoiles, in proper succession, enter in groups, by pairs and, finally as singles, depending on their position in the company, and assume carefully planned places on the stage, to music from Hector Berlioz' *Les Troyens à Carthage*. Defilés are staged a few times a year on very special occasions, such as state visits, certain national holidays, in honor of some great artists, etc. It is a most effective spectacle. The Royal Ballet (British) staged a defilé in honor of Dame Ninette de Valois at the Royal Opera House, Covent Garden, on May 7, 1964. Whether the defilé will become a feature at the Royal Ballet has not been announced.

De Gaetani, Thomas, contemporary American stage director, designer, b. New York City. Graduate of Brander Matthews School of Dramatic Arts, Columbia Univ. Director, U.S. Center of International Association of Theatre Technicians; President, U.S. Institute for Theatre Technology (since 1960); Director, Stage Dept. and Lecturer in Theatre Arts for Dance Dept., Juilliard School of Music (1953–63). Appointed Managing Director, Theatres and Concert Halls of Lincoln Center for the Performing Arts (1963). Currently (1967) consultant on construction of theatres and art centers.

Dégagé, literally, disengaged; in ballet, to free the foot in preparation for the execution of a step; to transfer weight.

De Galantha, Yekaterina, Russian dancer, ballet mistress and teacher, b. St. Petersburg (now Leningrad), Russia, 1898. Studied dance with Nicholas Legat, Samuel Andrianov, Alfred Bekefi, Enrico Cecchetti, and Claudia Kulichevskaya. In Western Europe she studied with Anna Pavlova, Vaslav Nijinsky, and once again with Cecchetti. She was a member of Diaghilev Ballets Russes (1915–16), dancing in the corps and as soloist. Remaining in the U.S. after the company's visit here, she appeared as ballerina in operettas and films (1917–18). Left the U.S. to join the Anna Pavlova Company as character ballerina and danced in Uruguay and Argentina. In 1921 Joined Teatro Colón in Buenos Aires as character ballerina. Helped form many of the present Argentine dancers who studied in the school which she opened in Buenos Aires in 1933.

Degas, Edgar Hilaire Germain (1834–1917), French painter. A member of the impressionist school who painted many pictures of ballet dancers, among them "The Star Dancer," "Dancers Practicing at the Bar," "The Rehearsal," "Dancer Fastening Her Sandal," etc. He also executed a series of bronzes of dancers of varying sizes, casts of which, like his pictures, are in many art galleries. The Metropolitan Museum, N.Y. and the Sterling and Francine Clark Art Institute, Williamstown, Mass. have particularly good representative collections. Degas was not interested in the dancer as an artist, but in the play of light and shade on working muscles.

De La Bye, Willy, Dutch dancer, b. Leiden, Holland, 1934. Soloist of Ballet Recital, Nederlands Ballet, both under Sonia Gaskell; since 1959 soloist of Nederlands Dans Theater. Her repertoire includes *Designs for Six* (John Taras), *Firebird* (Fokine), both 1954; *Giselle* (the first Dutch dancer to dance the title role), *Night Shadow* (Balanchine) both 1956; the Siren in *The Prodigal Son* (Lichine), the Ballerina in *Petrouchka* (Fokine), both 1958; *Sleeping Beauty,* Act 3 (Petipa), 1960; Clorinda in *The Duel* (William Dollar), 1961; and *Les Sylphides, Pas de Quatre* (Dolin); as well as leading roles in the following ballets by Dutch choreographers: *Feestgericht* (Hans van Manen), *Beauty and the Beast* (Aart Verstegen), *The Trial* (Jaap Flier), *Euridyce* (v. Manen), *Giovenezza* (Rudi van Dantzig).

De Lappe, Gemze, American dancer, b. Portsmouth, Va., 1921. Her career has been mainly in musicals, among them *Miss Liberty* (Jerome Robbins), *Oklahoma!, Paint Your Wagon, Juno,* and the New York City Center revival of *Brigadoon* (1962), all with choreography by Agnes de Mille. Frequently acts as assistant to Miss de Mille in the theatre and on television programs. A leading dancer with Rod Alexander's Dance Jubilee touring U.S. (1958–59) and the Middle and Far East (1959–60). Danced a leading role in Agnes de Mille's *The Harvest According* for Ballet (now American Ballet) Theatre.

Delarue, Allison, contemporary American writer, b. N. J. Studied at the Peddie School (1924), Princeton Univ. (A.B. 1928, M.A. 1929), graduate studies Oxford Univ. (1931). Has contributed many articles on ballet to *Dance Index, Dance News, Art News, N.Y. Times, American Collector,* etc. Balletomane and collector of Romantic Ballet memorabilia and stage designs of Eugene Berman, and others. On staff The Cooper Union Museum for the Arts and Decoration, N.Y. (1938–47). Currently House Photographer, Princeton Univ.'s McCarter Theatre.

De Lauze, F., French author. He wrote *Apologie de la Danse* (1623) which was translated into English by Joan Wildeblood under the title *A Treatise of Instruction in Dancing and Deportment* (London, 1952). F. Lauze may or may not have been a dance teacher; there is no definite information about it. His book bridges the gap between the well-known treatise of Thoinot Arbeau, *Orchésographie,* (1588) and Pierre Rameau's *Le Maître à Danser* (1725).

De Lavallade, Carmen, contemporary American dancer, b. New Orleans, La.; m. Geoffrey Holder (1955). Studied with Lester Horton in Los Angeles, becoming leading soloist of his company. Made her N.Y. debut with that group on Mar. 28, 1953. Soon after the death of Horton in Nov. of that year, she moved permanently to N.Y., where her first important engagement was in the musical *House of Flowers* (1954–55). Was first dancer of the Metropolitan Opera Ballet (season 1955–56), where her greatest role was in *Aida.* She also has danced in modern dance companies, among them Geoffrey Holder's and John Butler's; also on television and with the New York City Opera Ballet, creating one of the few leading roles in Butler's *Carmina Burana.* In 1962 she joined the Alvin Ailey Co. as featured dancer and made a 15-week tour of Asian countries with that company on behalf of the President's International Cultural Exchange Program. At present dancing in concerts, recitals, and television; also teaching at the New Dance Group Studio. Is a frequent guest artist with various companies, including the Donald McKayle Dance Co. (creating the Girl in *Reflections in the Park,* 1964). Danced with Holder in the Josephine Baker season at Henry Miller Theatre (1964). Guest artist with American Ballet Theatre for the 25th anniversary season at N.Y. State Theater (Mar.–Apr., 1965), creating the principal role in *The Four Marys* and the Wife in the revival of *Tally-Ho* (under the title *The Frail Quarry*).

Carmen de Lavallade, American modern dancer

Delavalle, Hugo (Hugo Ramón Amado Delavalle), Argentine dancer, b. Rosario, Argentina, 1935. Studied dance with Michel Borovski, Amalia Lozano, and Roberto Giachero. Premier danseur, Teatro Argentino de La Plata (1954). In 1956 joined Grand Ballet du Marquis de Cuevas as soloist. At present premier danseur of the Opera Ballet, Stuttgart, Germany.

Deldevez, Edward Ernest (1817–1897), French dramatic writer and composer, assistant conductor of the Grand Opéra and Paris Conservatory. He composed the score for Joseph Mazilier's *Paquita* (1846) and, with J. B. J. Tolbecque composed the score for Mazilier's *Vert-Vert* (1851). He was a prolific composer for the now-forgotten French ballets of his time.

Delibes, Clément Philibert Léo (1836–1891), French composer. Wrote scores for the ballets *La Source* (chor. Arthur Saint-Léon, 1866), *Coppélia* (Saint-Léon, 1870), *Sylvia* (Louis Mérante, 1876). Also composed the opera *Lakmé* (1883).

Delius, Frederick (1863–1934), English composer whose nocturne *Paris* Frederick Ashton used for his ballet *Nocturne* (1936). Antony Tudor used Delius's music for his ballet *Romeo and Juliet* (1943). The music (arr. by Antal Dorati) included excerpts from *A Village Romeo and Juliet* (*"Walk to the Paradise Garden"*), *Brigg Fair, Eventyr, Over the Hills and Far Away.*

Dellanoy, Marcel, French composer, b. La Ferté, 1898. His principal scores for ballet are *Le Fou de la Danse* (Opéra Comique, 1929), *La Pantoufle de Vair* (Ruth Page, Chicago Opera, 1931), *Les Noces Fantastiques* (Serge Lifar, Paris Opéra, 1955). Is Chevalier de la Légion d'Honneur; awarded Grand Prix of the Blumenthal Foundation in U.S.

Dell'Ara, Ugo, Italian dancer, b. 1921. Studied at the School of Teatro dell' Opera, Rome. Made his debut in 1939; became principal dancer of ballet company in 1945. Transferred to Teatro alla Scala, Milan, in 1946 and continues there as principal dancer. Appointed ballet master, he created *Conte d'Hiver* (1955), *Lumawig et la Flèche* (1956), and others.

Dell'Era (also Dellera), **Antonietta,** Italian dancer, b. 1865. Came to St. Petersburg in 1886 and at first appeared in a privately-owned summer theatre, where she danced between the acts of an operetta. Her success was so great that the Imperial Maryinsky Theatre was forced to engage her as ballerina, where her success continued. She earned her place in the history of ballet by creating the role of the Sugar Plum Fairy in the original production of *The Nutcracker,* choreographed by Lev Ivanov to Peter Tchaikovsky's score (1892). Paul Gerdt was her partner. Dell'Era, with Virginia Zucchi and Maria Giuri, began a long succession of Italian ballerinas who dominated the Russian Imperial Ballet for some sixteen years. The "Italian Invasion," as it was called, led to the improvement of the technique of Russian dancers. The year of Dell'Era's death has not been established.

Dello Joio, Norman, composer, b. New York City, 1913. Educated at All Hallows Institute, City College, and at Juilliard School of Music. Has composed a number of scores for dance works, including *Prairie* (chor. Eugene Loring, Dance Players, 1942), *Diversion of Angels* and *Seraphic Dialogue* (Martha Graham), *On Stage!* (Michael Kidd for Ballet Theatre) and *There Is A Time* (José Limón). His orchestral compositions include works for orchestra, chamber music, choral music, piano, voice and piano, and incidental music for television. Teaches composition at Sarah Lawrence College and Mannes College of Music, N.Y. Won the Pulitzer Prize for Music (1957); N.Y. Music Critics Award (1948; 1958). Is an Hon. Doc. of Music of Colby College and Lawrence College.

Delsarte, François (1811–1871), French teacher whose studies of classic rhetoricians as well as of anatomy led to the accumulation of considerable information which forms the foundation of expression and the use of gesture. He started his career as a successful singer at the Opéra Comique, but because of poor training at the Conservatory his voice failed four years later (1834). This induced him to devote himself to a more intelligent method of instructing students. The combination of an artist's enthusiasm and a surgeon's science made Delsarte a remarkable teacher, numbering Jenny Lind and Rachel among his pupils, though he was comparatively unknown during his lifetime. Through his disciples, notably Steele Mackaye whose plans to bring him to America were prevented by the latter's death, Delsarte's philosophy gained renown. His system of gesture is a complex one, based on a triune division of the human being (intellectual, emotional, physical) restricted by the triune conditioning of natural law (time, motion, space); and the predominance of one of these natures causes differences in personality. The three main divisions of the body are head (intellectual), trunk (emotional), limbs (physical), and for each major division there are triple subdivisions which in turn are divided. The Delsartean system has nine laws of gesture on which are based exercises for freedom and relaxation of every part of the body with the object of educating each part to express an intelligible idea or emotion. Delsarte's theories are probably the best available source for learning gesture and pantomime, and the record of these we owe to his pupil Genevieve Stebbins. He has had great influence on the modern dance. Ruth St. Denis was early influenced by American teachers of his principles; Irene Lewisohn, a pupil of Stebbins, was influential in developing a type of dance that was definitely theatrical, basing her dances on symbols derived from folk cultures. Ted Shawn's book *Every Little Movement* (1954), is both a biography and a statement of Delsarte's aims and theories.

De Lutry, Michel, dancer, b. France, 1924; m. Domini Callaghan. Studied with Lubov Egorova in Paris. Principal dancer, Châtelet Theatre, Paris. To England in 1946 (subsequently becoming a British subject) and joined International Ballet, making his debut in *Comus,* and later dancing virtuoso demi-caractère roles, such as *Blue Bird* pas de deux (*The Sleeping Beauty*), pas de trois (*Swan Lake*), and others. Danced for Ballet Workshop, Walter Gore Ballet, in television, and films. Ballet master Theater am Gärtnerplatz, Munich (1958–60). Currently director, Zurich Stadttheater company and ballet school.

Delza, Sophia, contemporary dancer and teacher, b. New York City. Graduate of Hunter College, N.Y., danced from early childhood. An American modern dancer who has made an intensive study of Chinese theatre dance; lived in Shanghai (1948–51) and was the first American dancer to teach modern dance in Chinese theatre and dance schools. Studied Chinese action dance roles of the classic Chinese Theatre with Wang-Fu-Ying and Cheng Ch'uan-Chien. Has given many recitals throughout the U.S., also appeared on television. Demonstrates and lectures on T'ai Chi Ch'uan, the ancient Chinese exercise art, and has written the first book in English on the subject. Lectures and teaches, and is the official teacher of T'ai Chi Ch'uan at the United Nations (since 1958).

De Maré, Rolf, Swedish patron of the arts and collector, b. Stockholm, 1886, d. Barcelona, 1964. He formed Les Ballets Suédois (1920), with himself as director and Jean Börlin as choreographer and principal dancer. Leading composers, painters and librettists of the time participated in the production of some

Rolf de Maré, Swedish patron of the arts and ballet impresario.

twenty-five ballets in Paris, where the company made its home. The company was disbanded in 1925. Later de Maré became director of the Théâtre des Champs-Elysées. He has presided over or acted as committee member on all international congresses of dance in Europe of the period. After Jean Börlin died in 1931 de Maré, with Dr. Pierre Tugal, founded in his memory Les Archives Internationales de la Danse in Paris, which for a number of years was the center of dance activity in western Europe. In 1932 Rolf de Maré, with the Archives, organized an International Choreographic Competition in Paris, at which Kurt Jooss's ballet *The Green Table* won first prize, Trudi Schoop's *Fridolin,* second. Only a few days before his sudden death, he had been planning another such competition to be held in Stockholm in 1965. De Maré visited the United States in connection with the Dance International in N.Y. (1937–38). In 1950 the Archives Internationales de la Danse was dissolved. The greater part of the material was transferred to the Musée de l'Opéra, Paris, and the remainder to the Dance Museum, directed by Bengt Haeger, at the Royal Swedish Opera House, Stockholm.

Demi (lit. half), in ballet, a movement, position, or pose executed in less than full measure or strength, as demi-plié.

Demi-Caractère (dancer), in ballet, a dancer who takes character and mime roles; not a strictly classic dancer. All non-classic roles and dances in ballet are called demi-caractère in French. The English terms are character dancers, character dance.

Demi-Contretemps, step in ballet. Technique: start 4th pos., L toe pointed back; demi-plié and jump upward off R ft., bringing L ft. sur le cou-de-pied back; land in 5th pos. L ft. front and immediately slide L ft. forward to 4th pos., R toe pointed back.

De Mille, Agnes George (Mrs. Walter Prude), American choreographer, dancer, author, b. New York City, 1909. Graduate, Univ. of California (A.B., cum laude). Studied dance with Theodore Koslov, Marie Rambert, Lydia Sokolova, Antony Tudor, Carmalita Maracci, Edward Caton, Nina Stroganova. Gave dance concerts U.S., Europe, Denmark, France (1929–40). Choreographed: *Black Ritual* (1940); *Three Virgins and a Devil* (1941); Drums Sound in Hackensack (for Jooss Ballet, 1941); *Rodeo* (1942); *Tally-Ho* (1944); *Fall River Legend* (1948); *The Harvest According* (1952); *Rib of Eve* (1956); *The Wind in the Mountains* and *The Four Marys* (1965). All but *Black Ritual, Drums Sound in Hackensack,* and *Rodeo* were created for Ballet Theatre. *Rodeo* (first staged for the Ballet Russe de Monte Carlo) has been in the Ballet Theatre repertoire since the mid-1940's. She also choreographed a program toured by her group, the Agnes de Mille Dance Theatre (1953–54). Created *The Bitter Weird* (using music from *Brigadoon*) for the Royal Winnipeg Ballet and for the same company staged and appeared in *The Rehearsal* (Oct. 29, 1965), Hunter College

Agnes de Mille, American choreographer

Playhouse, N.Y. Choreographed the musicals *The Black Crook* (1929); *Nymph Errant* (1933); *Oklahoma!* (1943); *One Touch of Venus* (1943); *Bloomer Girl* (1944); *Carousel* (1945); *Brigadoon* (1947); *Gentlemen Prefer Blondes* (1949); *Paint Your Wagon* (1951); *The Girl in Pink Tights* (1954); *Goldilocks* (1958); *Juno* (1959); *Kwamina* (1961); *110 in the Shade* (1963). Choreography for films includes *Romeo and Juliet* (1936); *Oklahoma!* (1955). For television choreographed the following "Omnibus" programs: "The Art of Ballet" (1956); "The Art of Choreography" (1956); "Lizzie Borden" (1957). Other television choreography includes *Bloomer Girl* (1956); "Gold Rush" (1958). Directed the plays *Allegro* (1947); *The Rape of Lucrecia* (1948); *Out of This World* (1950). Has received the following academic honors: Hon. Litt. D. (Mills College, 1952); Alumni Medal (Univ. of Calif., 1953); Hon. Litt. D. (Russell Sage College, 1953); Dr. of Human Letters (Smith College, 1954); Spirit of Achievement Award (Albert Einstein College of Medicine, Yeshiva Univ., 1958); Dr. of Humane Letters (Hood College, 1959); Dr. of Fine Arts (Northwestern Univ., 1960). Other awards include: Donaldson Award (1943, 1944, 1945, 1947); Antoinette Perry Award (1947); Lord and Taylor Award (1947); named Woman of the Year by American Newspaper Woman's Guild (1946); Capezio Dance Award (1966). Author of *Dance to the Piper* (Boston, 1952); *And Promenade Home* (Boston, 1956); *To a Young Dancer* (Boston, 1962); *The Book of the Dance* (N.Y., 1963); also of numerous articles in periodicals. She was an original member of the National Council on the Arts and first chairman of its Dance Panel (1965); first president of the Society of Stage Directors and Choreographers, Inc., formed in the fall of 1965.

Demi-Plié, in ballet, a half-plié; pose with knees half bent and heels on the floor in any of the five positions.

Demi-Pointe, in ballet, on the half-toes, reached by rising on the balls of the feet.

Demoiselles de la Nuit, Les. Ballet in 1 act, 3 scenes; chor.: Roland Petit; music: Jean Françaix; book: Jean Anouilh; décor: Léonor Fini. First prod.: Ballets de Paris de Roland Petit, Théâtre Marigny, Paris, May 22, 1948, with guest artist Margot Fonteyn (Agathe, the White Cat), Roland Petit (Young Man), Gordon Hamilton (Cat Baron de Grotius). Among the cat people who assume human characteristics at their private revels is the beautiful Agathe with whom a young man, happening upon such a revel, falls in love. He takes her to his home, but, though she loves him, her natural instincts are too much for her and she flees over the rooftops. In following her, both fall to their deaths, but are united at the last. Colette Marchand assumed the role of Agathe after Fonteyn had given her special guest performances and created it in the Ballet (now American Ballet) Theatre version, with John Kriza as the young man and Eric Braun as the Cat Baron, Metropolitan Opera House, N.Y., Apr. 13,

1951. Later Agathe was one of Mary Ellen Moylan's most successful roles.

De Molas, Nicolas (1900–1944), Russian-American painter. Came to U.S. in early 1920's and became a citizen a few years before he died. The work for which he is best known in this country was a series of paintings under the general title, "Conversation Pieces." Also designed décor and costumes for various ballets, including Ballet Theatre's *Black Ritual* (Agnes de Mille), *Capriccioso, Gala Performance, Goyescas, The Beloved.*

De Moroda, Derra, dancer, teacher, b. Hungary, 1897. Studied under Enrico Cecchetti and is co-founder of the Cecchetti Society, London. Has written numerous articles on dance and is author of *The Csardas and Sor Tanc* (Line Dance) (1929), and co-author with Margaret Craske of *The Theory and Practice of Advanced Allegro* (1956). Currently teaching in Salzburg, Austria. Is often seen at ballet performances at Festivals and in the opera houses of London, Paris, Vienna, Munich, and others.

Denby, Edwin, American writer and critic, b. Tientsin, China, 1903. Studied Harvard Univ.; Univ. of Vienna; Hellerau-Laxenburg Schule (ballet, 1925–28). Dancer-choreographer in Europe and the U.S. (1929–35). Dance critic *Modern Music* (1936–42), *N.Y. Herald Tribune* (1942–45); contributor to *Dance Encyclopedia* and numerous periodicals in the U.S. and Germany. Awarded Guggenheim Fellowship (1948) for comparative study of ballet in the U.S. and Europe. Author of *Looking at the Dance* (N.Y., 1949), *Dancers, Buildings and People in the Streets* (N.Y., 1965), and two books of poems.

Edwin Denby, American writer, poet and critic

Denham, Sergei I., b. Moscow, Russia, of a rich merchant family. Director of Ballet Russe de Monte Carlo from 1938. When the company temporarily discontinued its annual U.S. tours at the end of the 1951–52 season he organized a small Ballet Russe de Monte Carlo Concert Group which toured for two seasons until the large company was reorganized for the 1954–55 season with Maria Tallchief as guest ballerina for that season. The company then continued its annual tours until 1962. Denham organized the Ballet Russe de Monte Carlo School in Mar., 1954, taking over the Swoboda-Yurieva School and retaining Madame Maria Swoboda as head of the faculty. Organized Ballets de Monte Carlo (1966) under the patronage of Prince Rainier III of Monaco, with the Monte Carlo Opera House as its home.

Denishawn.

BY WALTER TERRY.

Denishawn, the Ruth St. Denis and Ted Shawn School of Dancing and Related Arts, first opened its doors to dance students in Los Angeles in 1915. Prior to that time, both artists had established themselves separately as dancers of distinction. St. Denis had made her New York debut as a dancer in 1906 in her own ballet, *Radha,* and had achieved international fame long before she met the younger Ted Shawn. He, on the other hand, had given up studying for the ministry in order to become a dancer and had taught, choreographed, and performed for several years before his meeting and marriage with St. Denis (Aug. 13, 1914).

The Denishawn school was predicated upon the principle that all techniques and styles were the rightful heritage of the dance student. The leaders and their staff offered classes in ballet, Oriental dance, movement techniques devised for their own specific needs, primitive dance, and later the German modern dance. From a single Los Angeles studio, where pupils dropped their fees into a cigar box as they entered the classroom, Denishawn grew into a major educational institution with branches in several cities and, towards the end of the Denishawn era, with Denishawn House in New York.

The story of the Denishawn dancers runs parallel to that of the school. For sixteen years, until St. Denis and Shawn separated in 1931, the Denishawn dancers toured the United States and much of the world, including the Orient (1925–26), bringing to audiences full-scale ballets, opulently produced and concerned with a myriad of themes. Among their most notable productions—some choreographed by St. Denis, others by Shawn, and a few jointly—were *A Dance Pageant of Egypt, Greece and India, The Garden of Kama, Xochitl, The Spirit of the Sea, The Vision of the Assouia, Ishtar, The Feather of the Dawn, The Lamp, Jurgen,* and *Job*. In addition, there were literally hundreds of ballets, ensemble dances, pas de deux, and solos in the Denishawn repertory, ranging from simple pieces performed against a neutral backdrop to Shawn's *The Feather of the Dawn,* which had a pueblo upon the stage, and St. Denis's *Ishtar* which originally (for one presentation only) required eight hundred tons of scenery. Although Miss St. Denis continued to run Denishawn for a brief period following her separation from her husband, the last Denishawn performance by the company and its two founders occurred in 1931 at the Lewisohn Stadium, New York City. The pair did not dance together again until the summer of 1942 at Jacob's Pillow, near Lee, Mass., and then without a company.

The name "Denishawn" originated in connection with a contest conducted by a theater manager in Portland, Oregon, the object of which was to find a name for an untitled dance performed by St. Denis and Shawn. Miss Margaret Ayer suggested *The Denishawn Rose Mazurka;* shortly thereafter the name was given to both the school and the company.

Among Denishawn students to become prominent in the dance field were Martha Graham, Doris Humphrey, Charles Weidman, Jack Cole, Pauline Lawrence, Gertrude Shurr, Margaret Severn, Ada Forman, Florence O'Denishawn, Margaret Loomis, Harry Losee, Klarna Pinska, and numerous others. Louis Horst, composer-conductor, was for many years musical director for Denishawn.

Available for study by historians, students and dancers is the Denishawn collection of thousands of items—programs, press clippings, photographs and other memorabilia—housed in the Dance Collection of the New York Public Library, a presentation to the Library by St. Denis and Shawn. The Library has published (1962) a valuable illustrated book for dance researchers: *The Professional Appearances of Ruth St. Denis and Ted Shawn; A Chronology and an Index of Dances, 1906–1932,* prepared by Christena L. Schlundt.

Denishawn Collection, an integral part of the Dance Collection of the New York Public Library, was a gift of Ted Shawn and Ruth St. Denis in 1951. It consists of 8,000 photographs, 25,000 clippings and programs, and more than 600 letters and manuscript items documenting the careers of these artists beginning with the first performances of Miss St. Denis (ca. 1902). Covered also are the early careers of Martha Graham, Doris Humphrey, and Charles Weidman, the men's group formed by Ted Shawn which toured from 1933 to 1940, and the organization and development of Jacob's Pillow. These records constitute the documentation of American growing awareness of dance as an art form. The collection also represents the work of some of the fine photographers of the period, among them Arnold Genthe and Arthur Kales.

Denmark, Ballet in.

BY SVEND KRAGH-JACOBSEN, M.A.

The origins of Danish ballet are traceable, as in other European countries, to the court ballets which in Denmark flourished under Frederick II (1559–1588), Christian IV (1588–1648), and Frederick III (1648–1670). Ballet became associated with the theatre as a stage art form with the opening of the first theatre in which Danish was spoken from the stage, the Lille Grönegade-Theatre (1722). There, as at the Royal Theatre which was opened on Kongens Nytorv in 1748, the ballet was dominated at the beginning by foreign ballet masters, choreographers, and ballerinas who were invited by the changing managements to build up and popularize the repertoire. First to arrive were representatives of the Italian school, among them Gaetano Orlando, Angelo Pompeati, Antonio Como, Antonio Sacco, Innocente Gambuzzi, Vincenzo Piattoli, and Domenico Andreani. Then came a few Frenchmen, among them Des Larches, who led the way and Pierre Laurent. In time dancers began to be recruited among Danish aspirants and to attract attention. By the 1750's there was an almost regular teaching schedule established at the Royal Theatre, although the actual school was not founded until 1771 by Laurent. Considered the most important contributor to the early development of Danish ballet, Laurent came to the Royal Theatre from the Paris Opéra and remained in Denmark until his death (1807). A number of Danes whom he trained contributed to the first flowering of the Danish ballet.

In 1775 the Florentine Vincenzo Galeotti (1733–1816) came to Copenhagen and remained the Royal Theatre's ballet master for more than a generation, becoming a naturalized Danish citizen in 1781. He continued to dance until 1811 when he appeared, at the age of 78, as Lorenze in his own ballet *Romeo and Juliet.* He retired only because he had received the Knight's Cross of Dannebrog (the first Danish ballet artist to be so honored), a distinction which prevented him from dancing on the stage. A man wearing the Knight's Cross did not dare at that time to expose himself to public criticism (some one hundred and forty-five years later Ted Shawn became the first American dancer to be awarded this order).

Galeotti was a talented man with a fertile imagination and a knowledge of the international repertoire and its great masters, from Jean-Georges Noverre to Casparo Angiolini. He established in Denmark a large international repertoire and presented it in a style which won praise not only from the Danes but also from distinguished foreigners who were acquainted with the international standard of ballet of the period. His productions ranged from dramatic ballets based on literature, such as Voltaire's *Orphelin de la Chine* and Shakespeare's *Romeo and Juliet* and *Macbeth,* to ballets on subjects taken from Scandinavian history. These included numerous divertissements and entrées, many of them comedies. His only extant work, *Amors og Balletmastererns Luner* (*Les Caprices du Cupidon et le Maître de Ballet*), first produced in 1786, is the oldest ballet to remain in the world repertoire with choreography of the original production. Its longevity can be explained in that the ballet has never been out of the repertoire long enough to be forgotten. It is still being performed in Denmark in the version staged by Harald Lander with music by Jens Lolle. The ballerina in Galeotti's ballets was Anna Margrethe Schall (1775–1852).

In 1792 the French dancer Antoine

Bournonville (1760–1843), who was at the time a star in the Gustav III Theatre in Stockholm, came to Copenhagen as a guest artist, and remained a permanent member of the company at the Royal Theatre. From 1816 to 1823 he was the leader of the Danish ballet. Although a man of culture, he was uninventive as a choreographer and a poor administrator. The Copenhagen ballet, therefore, began to decline and reached a very low state before his son August replaced him in 1829. August Bournonville (1805–1879) administered the Danish ballet for nearly a half century with a firm hand. He was responsible for its second flowering and gave it the distinctive character which it still possesses. Despite his French blood and education he succeeded in giving Danish ballet a coloring intimately associated with the cultural life of Denmark of the period, especially its literature and music.

August Bournonville was born in Copenhagen and received his first training under his father. He made his first appearance at the Royal Theatre in 1813. His style and artistic development were strongly influenced by his periods of study—especially with Auguste Vestris—in Paris between 1820 and 1828. During his last four years there he danced at the Opéra and was on the verge of making an international career. However, he was drawn back to Denmark by his desire to become a leading figure in Danish theatrical life and to raise the Danish ballet to a level where it would be respected by the Danish citizenry. Another reason for his desire to return to Denmark was his dislike of the social status to which dancers were relegated abroad from which he had suffered during a short stay in London. His choreographic training was international; he was hard working, impulsive, gifted, and ambitious. He became the intimate friend of such artists as Hans Christian Andersen and the sculptor Bertel Thorvaldsen and felt himself an honored member of Danish cultural life.

Bournonville's works bear definite marks of the golden period of Danish Romanticism in literature and painting. He established a performing company of his own pupils, a repertoire of his own ballets and a ballet organization so firmly based that his spirit dominated the Danish ballet theatre for a half century after his death. A brilliant dancer, he created many parts for himself in his early repertoire, a fact that has given Danish male dancing an outstanding position. The ballerinas whom he trained included Lucile Grahn (1819–1907), the most famous of Danish ballerinas. She was one of the few to rebel against her mentor and left Denmark to become an international star, the first Dane in the European ballet firmament. Other prominent ballerinas were Augusta Nielsen (1822–1902), followed by Juliette Price (1893–1906)—Bournonville's own ideal as a dancer—and Betty Schnell (1850–1939). Miss Schnell left the ballet when still very young to become the world's greatest Ibsen actress. She created Nora (*The Doll's House*) and Hedvig (*The Wild Duck*), among other famous roles.

Of Bournonville's fifty or so ballets and many more arrangements, about ten are still being danced and are considered to be the greatest treasure of the Danish ballet repertoire. His compositions range from spirited ballets based on colorful folklore, such as *Napoli* (1841), to historical pantomimes, which are no longer performed. He also composed works, a few of which still charm, in the form of divertissements, such as *Danseskolan af Konservatoriet* (The Conservatory's Dance School) (see KONSERVATORIET) which displays the classic French (Vestris) style in a well-preserved purity. Danish Romanticism found expression in his medieval ballet *Et Folkesagn* (A Folk Tale), created in 1854. Throughout his long career he inspired the finest Danish musicians, including Niels William Gade, Johan Peter Emilius Hartmann, and one of the great names in Danish music, Hans

Christian Lumbye, to compose original ballet music.

August Bournonville left the theatre in 1877 and almost immediately the Danish ballet began to decline. His last pupil, Hans Beck (1861–1952), ballet master of the Royal Theatre from 1894–1915, succeeded with Valborg Borchsenius (1872–1948) in keeping alive much of Bournonville's repertoire. But the Danish ballet was suffering more and more from the absence of an original choreographer and the lack of contact with the new currents which—chiefly emanating from the Diaghilev period—produced a fantastic upsurge of the international ballet just outside Danish frontiers. Although Michel Fokine lived for a long time in Copenhagen and worked fruitfully in Sweden, he was asked only to recreate three of his most famous ballets, *Les Sylphides,* (known in Denmark as *Chopiniana*), *Petrouchka* and *Prince Igor* (1925). In these works the best Danish dancers of the period at long last received some inspiration for their careers, among them the romantic Ulla Poulsen (b. 1905) and the greatest of all Danish dancers of this century, Elna Lassen (1901–1930) who unfortunately died just when she found in George Balanchine the inspiration her great talent deserved.

It was under Harald Lander, a pupil of Hans Beck, that new life was infused into the Danish ballet. These new trends produced the Danish ballet's third flowering in the 1930's and 1940's, before the Danes became "international" in the 1950's. The effects of the Lander period were clearly perceptible up to 1960. Trained in the Danish-French Bournonville style, Harald Lander went abroad in the 1930's and returned after fruitful years of study in Russia and the U.S. He was ballet master of the Royal Theatre in the 1940's and 1950's during which time he revived the repertoire (including the Bournonville works) and kept a firm hold on the organization. As a choreographer he proved less original and imaginative than Bournonville, but among his more than twenty-five ballets were several of great artistic quality which have been admired even when given by other companies than the Danish. The best are *Qarrtsiluni* (1942) and *Etudes* (1948), both choreographed in collaboration with the composer Knudaage Riisager, who has also worked successfully with Birgit Cullberg. Also of great importance were Lander's adaptations of a number of works from the international repertory in the 1930's and 1940's which brought Danish ballet closer to the main streams of contemporary ballet. Among these were his *Bolero, La Valse, The Sorcerer's Apprentice,* and classics like *Coppélia* (of which he created a definitive "Danish version"), and *Swan Lake.*

During his tenure as ballet master Lander taught many of the soloists who have since contributed much towards establishing Danish ballet on a high international level. After Lander left Denmark in 1951 he was engaged by the Paris Opéra. In Jan.–Feb., 1962, he re-created his *Etudes* for a new cast at the Royal Danish Ballet and created—again with Riisager—the Jean Baptiste Lully court-ballet *Le Triomphe de l'Amour,* under the title, *Les Victoires de l'Amour.*

Throughout the 1930's and 1940's the outstanding dancers of the Royal Danish Ballet were Margot Lander and Børge Ralov, both of whom measured up to international standards but who preferred to remain in their own country. Both danced an enormous repertoire which included the Bournonville ballets and the standard classic ballets: *Swan Lake, Giselle, Chopiniana.* Ralov was also a great Petrouchka. The team of Margot Lander and Børge Ralov was followed by a host of young dancers whose talents Lander had moulded by his teaching and his repertoire. First among them were the three ballerinas Mona Vangsaa, Kirsten Ralov, and Margrethe Schanne. The last named has shown herself to be the most original as a representative of the Romantic repertoire and the best Danish *Sylfiden* (*La Sylphide*) in the generation of 1930–60. After these come Inge Sand and Toni Lander (the former wife of Harald Lander). Toni Lander gained international fame after she left Denmark with her husband, particularly with the American Ballet Theatre. Among the male dancers who were trained by Lander much talent has emerged, outstanding examples being Frank Schaufuss, Stanley Williams, Poul Gnatt, Erik Bruhn, and Fredbjørn Bjørnsson; also Henning Kronstam and Flemming Flindt who were only boys when Lander left. Flindt studied with Lander in Paris and is now famous as a guest artist of some prominence in international ballet. He and Toni Lander returned to Copenhagen to be guest artists in *Etudes* when Harald Lander recreated the work in 1962. A special and very rare artist—also trained by Lander—is Niels Bjørn Larsen, artistic director of the Royal Danish Ballet since 1961 and one of the great names in the world of ballet.

Just before he left Denmark in 1951, Harald Lander engaged the internationally renowned ballet pedagogue Vera Volkova for the Royal Ballet, where she has since been the principal teacher of the neo-Russian style. Through her best pupils she has influenced the creation of a repertoire in a neo-Russian style, not quite without threat to the pure-Bournonville dance. Her most promising pupils are Kirsten Simone, Kirsten Petersen, and Solveig Østergaard, who have been elevated to solo dancer status. The greatest contemporary Danish ballet artist, Erik Bruhn, received his first training and achieved his first success at the Royal Theatre where he displayed extraordinary gifts even before the departure of Lander. He has achieved his high stature through years of training and performing outside Denmark, although officially he is still with the Royal Ballet. As often as possible he is guest artist in Copenhagen. His exceptional range of artistic imagination, and brilliant technique make it possible for him to dance classical virtuoso roles as well as modern character parts such as Don José in Roland Petit's *Carmen* and Jean in Birgit Cullberg's *Miss Julie* with equal impact. The youngest of the Danish male dancers include a growing number of new talents, including Niels Kehlet, Jørn Madsen, Ole Fatum, and Eske Holm.

Danish ballet, however, is stronger in boys than in girls, though Anna Laerkesen (trained outside the company's school until she was 17) has recently shown herself of international caliber. Danish choreography has been much weaker since Lander's departure. Birger Bartholin, who with Nini Theilade and Børge Ralov, was the best in Lander's time, is now creating choreography on only a small scale. A whole regiment of the younger artists have tried but no one has thus far created a work which has had more than passing interest and warranted being kept in the repertoire beyond one or two seasons. The newest Danish choreographers are Niels Bjørn Larsen, Frank Schaufuss, Erik Bruhn, Fredbjørn Bjørnsson, Ole Palle Hansen, Kirsten Ralov, and Lizzie Rode.

The Danish ballet has fortunately had the opportunity to work with the great international choreographers. The succession began in 1925 with Michael Fokine and continued with George Balanchine, directly or indirectly represented in Denmark. Leonide Massine was in Copenhagen during Lander's term. Balanchine himself staged his *Serenade* and *Apollo,* while Vida Brown staged his *Symphony in C,* and John Taras represented him in *Concerto Barocco* and *Night Shadow.* Taras also staged his own *Designs with Strings.* Frederick Ashton created his *Romeo and Juliet* for the Royal Danish Ballet to Prokofiev's score and staged his *La Fille Mal Gardée,* while Anton Dolin staged his *Pas de Quatre,* David Lichine his *Graduation Ball,* and Jerome Robbins his *Fanfare.* Birgit Cullberg created her *Moon Reindeer* for the Royal Theatre and revived her *Miss Julie* and *Medea.* Roland Petit revived his *Carmen* and

Cyrano de Bergerac and created *La Chaloupée* (1961). Alfred Rodrigues staged *Vivaldi Concerto* and *Blood Wedding;* Kenneth MacMillan *Danses Concertantes, The Burrow,* and *Solitaire.* Elsa-Marianne von Rosen staged *Irene Holm,* created for the Royal Swedish Ballet, and created *The Virgin Spring,* both in 1964.

In Sept., 1965, it was announced that Flemming Flindt would become director of the Royal Danish Ballet Jan. 1, 1966. He had previously staged with success his first ballet for the company, *The Private Lesson,* based on Ionesco's famous one-act play *The Lesson,* which he had first created for television. His first ballet after his assumption of the position of director was the full-length *Three Musketeers* based on the Alexandre Dumas novel, with a score by the French composer Claude Delerue and scenery and costumes by the French designer Bernard Daydé. This was premièred on May 11, 1966, with Henning Kronstam as d'Artagnan and Kirsten Simone as Milady. One of Flindt's foremost concerns is to restore the Bournonville repertoire to mint condition, with new productions in new décors but with the original choreography preserved in its purest form. *Kermesse in Bruges* was the first on the list for restoration.

After the 1966 Royal Danish Ballet and Music Festival Margrethe Schanne retired as ballerina.

Danish ballet enjoys a reputation which its best dancers are upholding with élan, but it is based on foreign choreography and the Danish classics—especially August Bournonville's works—as far as they can be preserved and given in proper form. The Danes have gained their present reputation through a series of tours of Europe and America and the very popular Ballet Festivals held in Copenhagen annually in May, during which the best ballets of the repertoire are displayed for an international audience.

Nomenclature of dancers in the Royal Danish Ballet differs from that in any other company. When a student graduates into the company from the school after examination, he or she is an "aspirant" for the first year. After one final examination the aspirant, if taken permanently into the company, becomes a ballet dancer. There is only one other rank, that of solo dancer. A solo dancer at the top level is the equivalent of a ballerina (première danseuse) or premier danseur. The exceptions were Margot Lander and Børge Ralov who were designated prima ballerina and premier danseur, the only dancers in the history of the Royal Danish Ballet to receive this distinction.

De Quesada, Alfonso, Argentine impresario, b. Madrid, Spain, 1918. Head of the Buenos Aires branch of Conciertos Daniel, the Artists' Management Bureau, since 1941. The Bureau, the biggest and most important in South America, was founded in Spain by his father, Ernesto de Quesada. It has world-wide connections and its clients include ballet and modern dance companies, individual dancers, choreographers, as well as the usual complement of singers, instrumentalists, conductors, and others. The Buenos Aires branch, which is also known as Sociedad Musical Daniel, was founded in 1917 by Ernesto de Quesada and Cirilo Grassi Diaz. Sr. Grassi Diaz resigned in 1924 to occupy an important post at the Teatro Colón. Two brothers of Alfonso are heading the Mexican and Venezuelan offices. Since the recent retirement of Ernesto de Quesada, Alfonso de Quesada is in charge of the entire Conciertos Daniel organization.

Derain, André, French painter and designer, b. Chatou, 1880, d. Chambourcy, 1954. A member of "Les Fauves" group of painters in the early years of the century, he designed his first ballet, *La Boutique Fantasque* for the Diaghilev Ballets Russes (1919). His other outstanding works for ballet were *Jack in the Box* (Diaghilev Ballets Russes, 1926), *La Concurrence* (Ballet Russe de Monte Carlo,

1932), *Songes* (Les Ballets 1933), *Salade* (Paris Opéra, 1935), *L'Epreuve d'Amour* (Ballet de Monte Carlo, 1936), *Mam'zelle Angot* (Sadler's Wells Ballet, 1947), *Que le Diable l'Emporte* (Ballets de Paris de Roland Petit, 1948), Ravel's *La Valse* (Opéra Comique, 1951).

Descombey, Michel, French premier danseur, ballet master, b. Bois Colombes (Seine), 1930. General education at Lycée Condorcet; ballet with Lubov Egorova and at Paris Opéra ballet school, entering corps de ballet 1947. First important role: Jester in Serge Lifar's *Blanche Neige,* followed by Sorcerer in Harald Lander's *Qarrtsiluni.* Also danced Eros in Gene Kelly's *Pas de Dieux* and others. As choreographer worked with small, private groups, his ballets including *Les Frères Humains* (1951), etc. For the Opéra Comique staged *Fièvres, Les Baladins, Clairère,* and also choreographed for stage shows, among them *Plumes Rouges* (Alhambra, 1962). Succeeded George Skibine as ballet master at Paris Opéra (1962), since when he has choreographed *Symphonie Concertante,* and the ballet in the opera *Tannhäuser.* Choreographed many ballets for French television, one of the most notable being *Pour Piccolo et Mandolines* to music by Vivaldi.

Deshayes, a family name of several French authors, dancers, choreographers, and composers of the 18th and 19th centuries, among them: Jacques, a dancer of the Théâtre de l'Académie Royale de Musique (now Paris Opéra), 1680–1722; Jean-François (1705–1779), choreographer and author; Prosper-Didier (d. 1815), choreographer, dancer and composer, father of André Jean-Jacques Deshayes.

Deshayes, André Jean-Jacques (1777–1846), son of Prosper-Didier Deshayes. Entered the ballet school of the Paris Théâtre de l'Académie Royale de Musique (now Paris Opéra) in 1788. Was accepted into the company in 1794, eventually becoming premier danseur demi-caractère. Pierre Gardel choreographed for him *Le Retour de Zéphire.* His talent as a mime brought him great success in Gardel's *Déserteur.* Appeared in Gardel's *Judgment of Paris.* Danced in Madrid in 1799 and the same year was engaged as first dancer at Teatro alla Scala, Milan. Danced Jean Dauberval's *Les Jeux d'Eglé* at the King's Theatre (later Her Majesty's) London in 1800 and remained as dancer and, later choreographer, until 1842. His *Pastoral Symphony* to Beethoven's music (1829) is probably the earliest example of "symphonic ballet," more than a hundred years before Leonide Massine's *Les Présages* inaugurated a new form. Among his other ballets were *Masaniello* (1829), *Kenilworth* (1831), *Faust* (1833), *Beniowsky* (1836) and *Le Brigand de Terracina* (1837), in which Pauline Duvernay's mirror dance was also a very early, perhaps the earliest, example of its kind. He actively assisted Jules Perrot with the first London production of *Giselle,* Mar. 12, 1842, and again collaborated with Perrot and wrote the book for *Alma,* premièred June 23, 1842, which was one of Fanny Cerito's greatest triumphs. His wife was also one of the best known dancers of the period, dancing under his name as Mme. Deshayes.

Design for Theatrical Dance.

BY GEORGE AMBERG.

Stage design for the dance theatre may be defined as the artistic creation of a realistic, illusionistic, or decorative environment by means of architecture, construction, painting, and lighting. For practical purposes the history of dance décor may be identified with the evolution of the ballet. The contributions of other forms of theatrical dancing to the art of stage design today are as yet negligible.

Ballet is essentially theatrical. From its beginning in the 16th century it was conceived as an elaborate spectacle which required and stimulated visual elaboration, attracting and inspiring many artists of fame and stature throughout its long and brilliant history. Ballet design as an art and craft originated at the Renaissance courts of Italy where dancing was essentially a spectacular display of human skill and beauty.

In the middle of the sixteenth century, Sebastiano Serlio's interpretation of Vitruvius's work on the Hellenistic theatre, although inaccurate, had an incalculable influence on scene design. It resulted eventually in the monumental painted architectures which dominated the stages of the world until today. The effectiveness of painted scenery increased with the designers' mastery in accurately drawing architectural perspective, thus creating the illusion of space and distance. Simultaneously, stage machinery was technically perfected in order to permit transformation scenes—the change of settings in view of the audience—and other surprising and magical effects. At the same time Italian (or Italian-trained) artists introduced their scenic arts and crafts in France, England and Austria. In England, the most outstanding scenic artist was Inigo Jones (1575–1652). After traveling extensively abroad, he returned with an accumulation of knowledge and experience in Renaissance art and architecture to the court of James I, where he created superb and highly original scenes for the court masque.

The eight members of the prodigious Bibiena family—painters, architects, and stage designers—reigned for three consecutive generations in many European court theatres (mainly in Italy and Austria), carrying the essence of Baroque feeling into their magnificent stage architectures. But long before, the main theatrical interest in Italy had turned from ballet to opera.

The ballet flourished in France, beginning with the lavish staging of the *Ballet Comique de la Reine* (1581). Following this immensely successful production, the talents of the designers working at the French court were primarily applied to the creation of sumptuous costumes. Of the notable scene designers at the Royal court, Torelli (1608–1678), Vigarani (1586–1663), and Servandoni (1695–1766) should be mentioned. Subsequently stage design in France is of only moderate artistic interest; the Romantic period, glorious in the art of dancing, produced no scenic work of consequence.

Modern ballet design originated almost spontaneously; at least there is no traceable connection with the historical past, nor with the major changes and advances in the concept of modern theatrical design. However, just as the ballet itself, even in its most progressive acceptance, has to respect tradition, the design which serves it is determined by specific traditional principles and requirements. Since the scene is often destined for the fast and sweeping movements of large groups of performers, it is essential that the widest possible floor area be free and on an even level. Consequently the settings—with the exception of a few experimental endeavors—use the theatrically obsolete system of flat painted canvas wings and backdrops. It is obvious that this spatially limited arrangement suggests a pictorial rather than a functional treatment. This two-dimensional character is further stressed by the lyrical quality and the frequently naïve and simple subject matter of the average ballet. The remarkable success of contemporary ballet design is mainly due to the contributions of easel painters of distinction. For all the wealth of magic, vision, and imagination contributed by great artists to the present ballet theatre, there are few indications as yet of the emergence of essentially new scenic concepts and solutions. As a category, ballet design still lives on borrowed art, rather than on its own theatrical resources.

Modern ballet design started with the organization of Serge de Diaghilev's Ballets Russes in Paris (1909). This was not the actual beginning of our century's most consequential ballet reform; actually it had been conceived, formulated, and promoted, in its essence, by a group of Russian avant-garde artists some years before. But Paris was the center and model of Western culture and art. The distinction between scene design and costume, choreography, and music is somewhat arbitrary; particularly in view of the fact that the new, signal principle which Diaghilev advocated was the complete integration of all these elements into one unified work of art. Once this idea had been categorically stated and successfully demonstrated, it was followed fairly consistently; at least the designers conceived the costumes in relation to and as a part of the setting. Until the beginning of World War I the Ballet Russe was an exclusively Russian company with Russian designers. After 1917, under the influence of Boris Kochno and Jean Cocteau, Diaghilev became fascinated by the work of modern easel painters and avant-garde artists, many of whom he employed. The success of these artists was great, for the results were magnificent. However, while the performances gained immensely in pictorial interest and visual appeal, they lost proportionately in the essential justification of their existence, i.e. ballet dancing of impeccable style and technique. This was, and still is, the danger of fashionable trends in modern design. There are, however, many fine examples demonstrating that great easel painters and sculptors are capable of adjusting their self-sufficient creations to an objective purpose and the exigencies of the ballet theatre. Those who have been particularly successful include Pablo Picasso, Georges Rouault, Marc Chagall, Isamu Noguchi, and Ben Shahn. Others, such as Jean Cocteau, Pavel Tchelitchev, Christian Bérard, Henri Matisse, Alexander Benois, Nathalie Gontcharova, Michael Larionov, Maurice Utrillo, and Raoul Dufy played a decisive role in elevating the style and technique of ballet décor to the level of the ballet. Recent developments in many lands indicate a clearer awareness of the essential functional principles which alone warrant a sound and lasting future for the ballet as an art.

Designs with Strings. Ballet in 1 act; chor.: John Taras; music: Tchaikovsky's Trio in A minor; décor: George Kirsta. First prod.: Metropolitan Ballet, Edinburgh, Scot. Feb. 6, 1948, with Svetlana Beriosova, Sonia Arova, Celia Franca, Delysia Blake, Erik Bruhn, David Adams; staged for Ballet (now American Ballet) Theatre, Center Theatre, N.Y., Apr. 25, 1950, in costumes by Irene Sharaff, with Diana Adams, Norma Vance, Lillian Lanese, Dorothy Scott, Erik Bruhn, Michael Lland (then Holland Stoudenmire). Although a themeless ballet reflecting the music, there is a hint of first love offered and gently refused. This ballet is in the repertoire of several companies, among them the Royal Danish Ballet.

Despréaux, Jean Étienne (1748–1820), dancer at Paris Opéra. Son of a musician at the Opéra, he made his debut there in 1764 as a supernumerary. An injury to a foot ended his career as a dancer but he became a violinist and maître de ballet. In 1789 he married Madeleine Guimard and they retired to a house in Montmartre where he wrote poems and parodies on dance. The title of his book published in 1806 was *Mes Passe-Temps: Chansons, suivies de l'Art de la Danse, poème en quatre chants, calqué sur l'art Poetique de Boileau Despréaux*. Despréaux was a gentle, wise and humorous man. The most notable part of his career was during his happy married life with Guimard.

Desrat, G., French writer on dance of the 19th century. Among his works are *Nouveau Traité de Danse Historique et Pratique* (1883) and *Le Petit Traité de Danse* (a condensation of the above, 1890). His most important, although not very accurate, work is *Dictionnaire de la Danse, Pratique et Bibliographique depuis l'origine de la danse jusqu'a nos jours*

(1895). It has a preface by Charles Nuitter, the famous Librarian of the Paris Opéra.

Dessous (lit. under), in ballet, designates the direction in a movement when the working leg passes behind the supporting leg.

Dessus (lit. over), in ballet, designates the direction in a movement when the working leg passes in front of the supporting leg.

Destiné, Jean-Léon, dancer, b. St. Marc, Haiti, 1925. Graduate of the Ethnological Institute, Port-au-Prince. In 1944 received a two-year scholarship from the Rockefeller Foundation for study of journalism and typographic arts in the U.S. Made his N.Y. debut as soloist and choreographer in the opera *Troubled Island,* N.Y. City Center (1949). Between 1949 and 1961 appeared six times at Jacob's Pillow Dance Festival. Has toured with his group in U.S., Canada, Mexico, and in Europe. His motion picture *Witch Doctor,* was a prize winner at Venice and Edinburgh Film Festivals (1952). Appointed Cultural Attaché for the Republic of Haiti in U.S. (1960), having previously been decorated by his Government: Chevalier Honneur et Mérite (1951) and Officer de l'Ordre National Honneur et Mérite (1958). Teaches at New Dance Group Studio, N.Y.

Detcher, Abi (Abraham Deutscher, 1932–57), Ballet and art critic, b. Antwerp. One of the great ballet lovers and balletomanes in Rio de Janeiro's dance world, an avid supporter of all dancers and ballet activities, notable for his knowledge of ballet. Considered the best of the new generation of art critics, especially ballet. Travelled to Europe and Israel in 1953, watching ballet in Paris, London, and Rome. Ballet and drama critic of *Aonde Vamos?,* an Israelite weekly. Was also founder of Amigos do Ballet, a ballet club in Rio de Janeiro. His early death in a street accident was a great loss to Brazil's dance world.

Détourné, in ballet, turning on both feet in the direction of the foot that is in back.

Deuil en 24 Heures (Mourning Clothes in 24 Hours). Ballet in 1 act, 5 scenes; chor.: Roland Petit; music: Maurice Thiriet; décor: Antoni Clavé. First prod.: Ballets de Paris de Roland Petit, at Théâtre de l'Empire, Paris, Mar. 17, 1953, with Colette Marchand (Widow), Serge Perrault, George Reich. A burlesque of Paris in the 1900's done somewhat in the manner of a two-reel silent comedy. A beautiful lady who fancies herself in black is quite reconciled to the duel between her husband and her latest admirer since it gives her the opportunity to dress up in a coveted black dress and make merry at Maxim's. Leslie Caron made her debut as a dancer in the U.S. in the role of the Widow when the company appeared at the Broadway Theatre, N.Y., Jan. 19, 1954. The ballet was called *The Beautiful Widow* (in translation) and was filmed as *A Merry Mourning,* when it formed part of the quartet of Petit ballets made into film under the title *Black Tights.* Cyd Charisse danced the Widow.

Deux Pigeons, Les. See TWO PIGEONS, THE.

De Valois, Ninette, Dame (Edris Stannus, Mrs. Arthur Connell), dancer, teacher, choreographer, director, b. Ireland, 1898. Studied dancing with various teachers including Edouard Espinosa and Enrico Cecchetti. Made her debut as principal dancer in a pantomime at the Lyceum Theatre, London (1914); was so successful that she danced there every year until 1919; also danced in revues (1918) and was première danseuse of the Royal Opera, Covent Garden (1919). Joined the Diaghilev Ballets Russes

Dame Ninette de Valois, founder of the Sadler's Wells Ballet (now Royal Ballet) of London and its director until her retirement in 1964.

(1923) and soon became a soloist. She left the company in 1925 but appeared with it occasionally the following year, Diaghilev sending for her to dance the "finger" variation whenever he wished to present *Aurora's Wedding*. In May, 1926, de Valois opened a ballet school in London which she called the Academy of Choreographic Art. Later the same year her pupils danced in some of the Shakespeare productions at the Old Vic, the theatre at that time being under the direction of Lilian Baylis. De Valois also produced dances for the Abbey Theatre, Dublin, and the Festival Theatre, Cambridge. In 1928 she staged her first ballet at the Old Vic, *Les Petits Riens* to the Mozart music, presented as a curtain-raiser to the Christmas production of Humperdinck's *Hansel and Gretel.* After that she presented ballets there each year. In 1931 Miss de Valois closed her first school and opened a second school at the newly rebuilt Sadler's Wells Theatre, also under Lilian Baylis' direction. The first, small company appearing on alternate weeks at the Old Vic and Sadler's Wells became known as the Vic-Wells Ballet and was the beginning of the company that in later years became first, the Sadler's Wells and ultimately, the Royal Ballet. Among the ballets she choreographed are *Le Création du Monde* and *Job* (originally staged by the Camargo Society), *Douanes, The Haunted Ballroom, The Rake's Progress, The Gods Go a'Begging, Orpheus and Eurydice, Checkmate, The Prospect Before Us, Promenade,* and, after the company moved to the Royal Opera House, Covent Garden, *Don Quixote* (1950). For Ballet Rambert she created *Bar aux Folies-Bergère* (1934). During the early years of the Sadler's Wells company she frequently appeared as a dancer: Swanilda (*Coppélia*), Tightrope Walker in her own *Douanes,* creating Pas de Trois (*Les Rendez-vous*) and Webster (*A Wedding Bouquet*) making her last appearance as a dancer in that ballet (1937), though she gave a single performance (off point and forgetting most of it to the delight of the audience) at the twenty-first anniversary performance of the company (1950). In Jan., 1947, Miss de Valois was awarded the C.B.E. (Commander of the Order of the British Empire) by King George VI in recognition of her work at the Sadler's Wells School and for the part she played in the development of British ballet; in 1951 Queen Elizabeth II created her a Dame of the British Empire (D.B.E.). Her long list of honors include Hon. Mus.D. London Univ., 1947; Hon. D.Litt.Mus., Reading Univ., 1951; Hon. D.Litt., Oxford Univ., 1955; Hon. D.Litt., Sheffield Univ., 1955; Hon. Mus.D. Trinity Coll. Dublin, 1957; Doctor of Fine Arts, Smith Coll., U.S.A., 1957; Hon. LL.D. Aberdeen Univ., 1958. Also Chevalier of Legion of Honor, 1950. She is the author of *Invitation to the Ballet* (1937), *Come Dance With Me* (1957). In 1947 she went to Turkey to advise on the formation of the first national school of ballet and has returned several times to see and report on progress. On Mar. 15, 1963, she announced her retirement as Director of the Royal Ballet which she watched grow from the first half dozen dancers in the Shakespeare plays at the Old Vic to a great, internationally renowned and respected company. She continues to take a guiding interest in the Royal Ballet School of which she has been appointed a Life Governor.

Devant, in ballet, forward, or in front of.

Développé, in ballet, unfolding of the working leg into any desired pose such as à la seconde, arabesque, and other poses. When the extended leg is bent in and closed down, it is called développé fermé. In *Swan Lake* (Act 2), Odette performs a développé supported by the Prince before falling sideways at the end of the adagio. She starts her variation in the same act by performing a series of développés fermés.

Devi, Ragini, American dancer and teacher specializing in Hindu dance; mother of Indrani. For many years had her own group and gave solo and group performances. Established a school of Hindu dance in N.Y.

Devil's Holiday. Ballet in prologue, 3 scenes, 2 entr'actes; chor.: Frederick Ashton; music (arr. from themes of Paganini) and book: Vincenzo Tommasini; décor: Eugene Berman. First prod.: Ballet Russe de Monte Carlo, Metropolitan Opera House, N.Y. Oct. 26, 1939, with Simon Semenoff (Old Lord), Alexandra Danilova (His Daughter), Frederic Franklin (Young Lover), George Zoritch (Fiancé), Marc Platoff (The Devil). The Devil takes a hand in straightening out the love affair between the daughter of an impoverished lord and a poor young man when she is about to be contracted in marriage to a fiancé who will save the family fortunes. At a carnival the presence of the Devil spoils the gaiety until, on the stroke of midnight, he vanishes and all ends happily. This was Ashton's only ballet for Ballet Russe de Monte Carlo. The outbreak of World War II in Europe in 1939 prevented him from polishing it at final rehearsals and he always felt it was never seen to proper advantage.

Devil's Violin, The. See VIOLON DU DIABLE, LE.

De Zoete, Beryl, writer and authority on the dances of Southeast Asia, d. London, 1962. She was a student of the Dalcroze system of eurythmics. She travelled widely, and her books *Dances of Bali, The Other Mind: A Study of Dancing in South India,* and *Dance and Magic Drama in Ceylon* are standard works on their subjects. During its existence she was a frequent contributor to Richard Buckle's magazine, *Ballet.* See PERIODICALS, DANCE (ENGLAND).

Diable Boiteux, Le. Ballet in 3 acts, 5 scenes; chor.: Jean Coralli; music: Casimir Gide; book: Burat de Gurgy and Jean Coralli; décor: Feuchères, Séchan, Diéterle, Philastre, Cambon. First prod.: Théâtre de l'Académie Royale de Musique, Paris, June 1, 1836, with Barrez (the Devil), Joseph Mazilier (Cléophas), Fanny Elssler (Florinda); London première: King's Theatre, the same year under the title *The Devil on Two Sticks,* with Pauline Duvernay as Florinda; St. Petersburg première: Oct. 23, 1839. The "Cachucha" in this ballet was sensational and became so popular that it was included in many later ballets. The ballet has an unimaginably complicated scenario. In outline it deals with an impecunious student, Cleophas, setting free Asmodeus (the Devil on Two Sticks) from a carboy where he had been imprisoned by an alchemist. In return for his freedom Asmodeus attends to Cleophas's amatory pursuits.

Diaghilev, Serge, and His Ballets Russes. Serge Diaghilev (1872–1929) was born in Perm, Russia, a member of the Russian nobility. After graduating from the Perm Gymnasia (High School) in 1890, he went to St. Petersburg to study law. His university studies interested him much less than the artistic life of the capital. His ambition was to become a composer, but Nicholas Rimsky-Korsakov, for whom the young Diaghilev played a composition he had written, persuaded him to abandon his intention of devoting himself to music.

He joined a circle of young painters and musicians of which Alexandre Benois was the moving spirit and which included Dmitri Filosofov (a cousin of Diaghilev), Léon Bakst, and Walter Nouvel. With his friends he founded (1899) the magazine *Mir Isskoustva* (The World of Art), which exercised a strong influence on the development of the arts in Russia. Diaghilev's interest in ballet can be traced back to his first year in St. Petersburg, when he saw the famous Italian ballerina Virginia Zucchi on the stage of the Imperial Theatre.

In the fall of 1899 Prince Serge Volkonsky, then director of the Imperial Theatres, appointed Diaghilev to the post of "Official for Special Missions" at the Theatres and gave him the task of editing the 1899–1900 edition of the *Annual of the Imperial Theatres.* Subsequently he was entrusted with the supervision of the production of the opera *Sadko* at the Maryinsky Theatre. The production was very successful and led to the commission of supervising the revival of the ballet *Sylvia.*

Diaghilev's independent manner made it very difficult for him to work under the strict regime of the Imperial Theatres. He made a number of influential enemies at the Theatre and was forced to resign in 1901, a little more than a year after his appointment.

In 1904 *Mir Isskoustva* discontinued publication. Between the years 1904 and 1908 Diaghilev staged a number of art exhibitions in St. Petersburg and Paris.

In 1908 Diaghilev made his debut as a theatrical impresario with the presentation of the opera *Boris Godounoff* at the Paris Opéra with the famous Russian basso Feodor Chaliapine in the title role. While in Paris Diaghilev signed a contract with the Théâtre Châtelet to present a season of Russian ballet in 1909.

Back in Russia after the opera season, Diaghilev assembled a group of dancers of the Imperial Theatres headed by Michel Fokine and including, among others, Anna Pavlova, Tamara Karsavina, Vera Karalli, Ida Rubinstein, Vaslav Nijinsky, Adolph Bolm, Mikhail Mordkin, and Theodore Kosloff. The repertoire selected for the season consisted of *Les Sylphides, Cléopâtre, Le Pavillon d'Armide, Prince Igor, Le Festin* (all except the last by Michel Fokine), and the opera *Ivan the Terrible.* After innumerable difficulties the Paris season opened in May, 1909, and was a triumph for the company and Diaghilev.

This season may be considered the beginning of a new era in ballet: the modern ballet. If Michel Fokine is rightly called the father of the modern ballet, Diaghilev was the man who made possible the emergence of the modern ballet as a concrete organization.

The success of the season determined the future career of Diaghilev. He became attached to the ballet in preference to all other art forms in which he had been interested. This season also marked the beginning of the strong attachment Diaghilev developed for Vaslav Nijinsky, an attachment which some historians of ballet feel was one of the strongest stimuli in Diaghilev's desire to make his ballet a permanent institution rather than a more or less loose series of ballet seasons, similar to his series of art exhibitions.

The next season (1910) saw the Diaghilev company at the Paris Opéra. *Schéhérazade* (with Ida Rubinstein and Nijinsky), *The Firebird* (with Karsavina and Bolm) and *Giselle* (with Karsavina and Nijinsky) were added to the repertoire and the Moscow ballerina Catherine Geltzer appeared as guest artist.

In 1911 Nijinsky resigned from the Maryinsky Theatre and Diaghilev decided to establish his company as a permanent organization. Up to then the Diaghilev company had been composed of artists of the Russian Imperial Theatres on leave of absence. It could perform only when the artists were free and thus depended on the good will of the Imperial Theatres for its existence. Its seasons were limited to the summer months. In 1911 the Diaghilev

Serge Diaghilev, ballet impresario

company opened the season in Rome, played in Monte Carlo and Paris, and gave two seasons in London, one in June during the festivities for the coronation of George V, and the other from Oct. to Dec.

During the long 1911 season the following ballets were added to the repertoire: *Petrouchka* (Karsavina, Nijinsky, Bolm), *Le Spectre de la Rose* (Karsavina, Nijinsky), *Le Dieu Bleu* (Karsavina, Bronislava Nijinska, Nijinsky), *Narcisse* (Karsavina, Nijinsky), all by Fokine; and *Swan Lake,* in two acts and three scenes (Karsavina, Nijinsky), *Aurora and the Prince,* a pas de deux from *The Sleeping Beauty* (Mathilde Kchessinska and Nijinsky), and the under-water ballet from the opera *Sadko.*

The following season the Diaghilev ballet appeared in Paris, London, Berlin, Vienna, and Budapest. Additions to the repertoire included Nijinsky's first choreographic attempt, *The Afternoon of a Faun* with Marie Piltz and Nijinsky, and two ballets by Fokine, *Daphnis and Chloë* (Karsavina, Nijinsky) and *Thamar* (Karsavina, Bolm).

The 1913 season was a crucial one in the life of Diaghilev and the history of his organization. Fokine had left the company at the end of the season to return to Russia and for the first time since its inception the company did not present any new ballets by Fokine. New in the repertoire that season were two ballets by Nijinsky, *Le Sacre du Printemps* with Marie Piltz as the Chosen Virgin and *Jeux,* with Karsavina, Ludmila Shollar and Nijinsky; *The Tragedy of Salome* by Boris Romanov; and Stravinsky's opera *Le Rossignol* with choreography by Romanov. During this season the company appeared in Monte Carlo, Paris (where it opened the new Théâtre des Champs-Elysées) and London (Covent Garden and Drury Lane).

After the London season the company, headed by Baron Dmitri Ginzbourg, one of Diaghilev's chief lieutenants, left for a South American engagement. Diaghilev, who had an inexplicable fear of the ocean, stayed behind. While the company was playing in Buenos Aires, Nijinsky married a dancer in the corps de ballet, Romola de Pulszky, whom he had met the year before during the Budapest season. Soon after Diaghilev was notified of the marriage he cabled Nijinsky that he was dismissed. As it later developed, Nijinsky's marriage meant the end of his close friendship with Diaghilev.

Fokine returned to the company after a year's absence and Diaghilev went to Russia to look for a dancer and choreographer who could replace Nijinsky. After a long search he chose Leonide Massine, a pupil of the Moscow Imperial School.

The 1914 season was the first to be given without Nijinsky. To the repertoire were added *Le Coq d'Or,* a three-act opera which was given with singers in the pit and dancers upon the stage, the cast of which included Fokine and Karsavina (Queen of Shemakhan); *The Legend of Joseph,* in which Massine made his debut; *Papillons* (Karsavina, Yelisaveta Vill, Shollar, Lubov Tchernicheva); *Midas* (Karsavina, Bolm, Froman), all choreographed by Fokine.

At the beginning of World War I Diaghilev was resting in Venice. He remained there until 1915 and then moved to Switzerland. It was here that he received an invitation from Otto Kahn, Chairman of the Board of the Metropolitan Opera House in N.Y., to bring his company to the U.S.

Karsavina was unavailable for the American tour and Fokine had returned to Russia after the outbreak of the war. But Diaghilev, aided by Bolm who was living in Geneva, succeeded in assembling a company for the American tour. It included, among others, Vera Nemtchinova, Stanislas Idzidowski, and Leon Woicikowski. After many efforts Diaghilev also succeeded in obtaining the release of Nijinsky, who had been a civilian prisoner of war in Austria-Hungary, his wife's country. The release came too late for Nijinsky to participate in the first N.Y. season, but he joined the company in N.Y. when it returned there for its second U.S. tour.

Diaghilev surmounted his fear of the sea sufficiently to join the company on its voyage to the U.S. Here he met Nijinsky after a long interval. The company brought a repertoire of some twenty ballets, among them Massine's first ballet, *The Midnight Sun.*

Diaghilev returned to Europe after the first American season and did not accompany the ballet on its subsequent tours to the U.S. and South America.

The highlights of the Diaghilev company from 1916 to 1929 included:

1916: Production of Nijinsky's *Til Eulenspiegel.* Olga Spessivtzeva joined the company.

1917: Production of Massine's *Good-Humored Ladies, Contes Russes,* and *Parade;* seasons in Italy, Spain, France, and South America.

1919: Production of Massine's *La Boutique Fantasque* (Lopoukhova and Massine) and *The Three-Cornered Hat* (Karsavina and Massine); three seasons in London, one in Paris.

1920: Production of Massine's *Chant du Rossignol, Le Sacre du Printemps* (new choreography), and the opera-ballets *Pulcinella* and *Le Astuzzie Femminili;* seasons in London and Paris.

1921: Production of the full-length version of *The Sleeping Beauty* with Vera Trefilova, Lubov Egorova, Olga Spessivtzeva, Lydia Lopoukhova, Pierre Vladimiroff; season in London.

1922: Production of *Aurora's Wedding,* Nijinska's *Le Renard;* seasons in France and Belgium. Boris Kochno joined the company.

1923: Company signed a contract with the Principality of Monaco to become the official ballet of the Monte Carlo Opera and changed its name to Les Ballets Russes de Monte Carlo, direction Serge de Diaghilev. Production of Nijinska's *Les Noces* (Felia Doubrovska as the Bride); season in Paris.

1924: Production of Nijinska's *Les Biches, Les Facheux, Les Tentations de la Bergère, Le Train Bleu,* and Massine's *Mercure.* Ninette de Valois, Anton Dolin, and Serge Lifar joined the company; seasons in Paris and London.

1925: Production of Massine's *Les Matelots* and *Zephyr and Flora,* Balanchine's *Barabau* and *La Pastorale.* Alexandra Danilova, Alicia Markova, Tamara Gevergeva, and George Balanchine joined the company; seasons in Paris and London.

1926: Production of Balanchine's *Jack-in-the-Box* (Danilova and Idzikowski), *The Triumph of Neptune* (Danilova, Sokolova, Lifar, Idzikowski, Balanchine), and *Le Rossignol* (new choreography, Markova in title role); seasons in London, Paris, Berlin, Turin, Milan.

1927: Production of Balanchine's *La Chatte* (Spessivtzeva and Lifar) and Massine's *Pas d'Acier;* performances in London, Paris, Germany, Austria, Budapest, Prague, Geneva.

1928: Production of Massine's *Ode* and *Les Facheux,* Balanchine's *Apollon Musagète* and *Les Dieux Mendiants;* seasons in London, Paris, and Brussels (opening of the Palais des Beaux Arts).

1929: Production of Balanchine's *Le Fils Prodigue* and *Le Bal,* Lifar's *Le Renard* (new choreography); seasons in Paris, Berlin, Cologne, London.

The last performance of the Diaghilev ballet was given at Covent Garden in London, July 26, 1929. The bill included Balanchine's *Le Bal* and *Le Fils Prodigue,* and *Aurora's Wedding.* The printed program of this performance lists the following artists: *Le Bal:*—Danilova and Dolin; *Le Fils Prodigue:*—Lifar and Doubrovska; *Aurora's Wedding:*—Danilova (Aurora), Lifar (Prince), Markova and Dolin (the Blue Birds).

Following the London season Diaghilev, who had long suffered from diabetes, went to take a rest in Venice, Italy. His condition grew worse and he died on August 19. He was buried on the Venetian island of San Michel.

Diaghilev's artistic and managerial activities, as well as his private life, have undergone minute examination and interpretation by his friends and enemies. Because of what has been written about him rather than because of what he did, Diaghilev's name has become a symbol and a legend. This tends to obscure the significant ends which he achieved and to lend unwarranted importance to his methods. However, the perspective of time has made his achievements very clear.

Diaghilev was the greatest impresario ballet has ever known. A man of high culture and exquisite taste, he gave Western Europe and the U.S. Russian ballet. In doing so, he made the Russian ballet, reared and cultivated within its national borders, a cosmopolitan art form, an art form which Western Europe and America had thought dead for more than half a century. He was possessed of the intelligence, artistic ability, personal magnetism, and will power to attract to the ballet the major talents of his time. He also had the taste and the knowledge necessary to weld individual talents into a concerted effort. Choreography, music and painting had always served the ballet, but Diaghilev made possible the true fusion of these elements, achieving by his efforts the most important characteristic of modern ballet. This was his greatest feat and his particular genius.

During the twenty-one years of the existence of the Diaghilev Ballets Russes he drew into close collaboration almost all the outstanding choreographers, dancers, composers, and painters of his period, including the following: *Choreographers:* Michel Fokine, Vaslav Nijinsky, Leonide Massine, Bronislava Nijinska, George Balanchine; *Dancers:* Anna Pavlova, Vaslav Nijinsky, Tamara Karsavina, Vera Karalli, Mikhail Mordkin, Adolph Bolm, Serge Grigorieff, Enrico Cecchetti, Mathilde Kchessinska, Bronislava Nijinska, Ludmila Shollar, Marguerite Froman, Seraphima Astafieva, Alexander Kochetovsky, Pierre Vladimiroff, Leonide Massine, Lydia Lopoukhova, Lubov Tchernicheva, Vera Nemtchinova, Anatole Bourman, Leon Woicikowski, Stanislas Idzikowski, Leokadia Klementovitch, Felia Doubrovska, Alicia Markova, Anton Dolin, Alexandra Danilova, Alice Nikitina, Serge Lifar, Anatole Vilzak, George Balanchine, Olga Spessivtzeva, and Vera Trefilova; *Composers:* Stravinsky, Ravel, Tcherepnine, Glazounov, Prokofieff, Debussy, Auric, Satie, Milhaud, and Nabokov; *Painters:* Bakst, Benois, Korovin, Derain, Picasso, Gontcharova, Larionov, Sert, Tchelitchew, Rouault, de Chirico, and Cocteau.

Diaz, Cirilo Grassi, Argentine impresario and theatre director, b. 1883, Uruguay. Former president of Mozarteum Argentino, co-founder of Associación Wagneriana Argentina (1912) and, with Ernesto de Quesada, of Conciertos Daniel (1917), from which he resigned in 1924. In 1922 he organized the Buenos Aires Teatro Colón resident ballet company which became official in 1925. That year he was made Technical Director of the Ballet company, orchestra and chorus, and established the Teatro Colón ballet school after visits to the Paris Opéra, Vienna Staatsoper, and Teatro alla Scala, Milan, where he studied teaching methods. In 1956 he resigned from Teatro Colón. In 1961 the Italian Embassy offered him the directorship of Teatro Coliseo in Buenos Aires (owned by the Italian government), of which he had been artistic advisor as far back as 1921. 1962 marked Grassi Diaz's 50th anniversary with Argentina's cultural and artistic life.

Dickson, Charles, dancer and ballet master, b. Bellwood, Pa., 1921. Studied classic ballet with several teachers; modern dance with Charles Weidman. Member of Ballet Russe de Monte Carlo (1938–40), American Ballet Caravan (South American tour), 1941, Ballet Theatre (1940–42). After service in U.S. Army (1942–45) appeared in Broadway musicals *Annie Get Your Gun; Look, Ma, I'm Dancin'; Music in My Heart.* Soloist and ballet master for Alicia Alonso's Ballet de Cuba, and Borovansky's Australian Ballet (for which he staged the full-length *Swan Lake*). Ballet master, London's Festival Ballet (1961–62). Since 1963 ballet master in Lima, Peru.

Didelot, Charles Louis (1767–1836), outstanding French dancer, choreographer and teacher, b. Stockholm, Sweden, d. Kiev, Russia. The son of the choreographer and first dancer of the Swedish Royal Theatre, he studied first with his father and later at the school of the Paris Opéra. He made his debut at the age of twelve in Paris; studied subsequently with Auguste

Charles Didelot, French dancer, choreographer, teacher. (Charcoal drawing by A. O. Orlovsky, ca. 1810. Original in Pushkin Museum, Moscow.)

Vestris and danced at the Opéra with the great 18th century ballerina Madeleine Guimard, making his debut in 1790. Staged first ballet, *La Métamorphose,* in Lyons, then appeared in London, where he also staged one of his most famous ballets, *Zephyr and Flora* (1796). Didelot is credited with introducing considerable changes in stage costume and originating flesh colored tights for women. He also invented "flights" on the ballet stage. From 1801 to 1811 Didelot was choreographer of the St. Petersburg Imperial Ballet. In 1811 he left St. Petersburg to work in London and Paris, but returned to St. Petersburg in 1816 and remained there to the end of his days. Didelot produced some fifty ballets, most of them in the romantic vein characteristic of his generation. His ballets were notable for their interesting plots, clear and expressive pantomime, and vividness of situation. The famous Russian poet Alexander Pushkin said that there was more poetry in Didelot's ballets than in the entire French literature of that period. Among Didelot's ballets are *Apollo and Daphne, Rolland and Morgana, Apollo and Perseus, Don Quixote, Paul and Virginia.* Didelot's work as head of the St. Petersburg ballet school was remarkable. He revolutionized the entire system of teaching and his is considered a vital epoch in the history of the school on a par with that of Cecchetti, Fokine, and Vaganova.

Dieken, Sandra, contemporary Brazilian dancer, b. Rio de Janeiro. Began to study 1944 with Yuco Lindberg, Teatro Municipal; later with Igor Schwezoff, Suiza Carbonell, Nina Verchinina. Made her debut in 1945 in Schwezoff's *Bacchanale,* while still a student. Joined Original Ballet Russe, 1948. Toured Spain and Portugal with Ballet Nina Verchinina as first dancer. Back in Brazil, entered Rio's Teatro Municipal Ballet (1950) as soloist; promoted to first dancer (1958). Dances most ballets of the repertoire and frequently appears on television. Ballerina of Ballet do Rio de Janeiro IV Centenário.

Dieux Mendiants, Les. See THE GODS GO A'BEGGING.

Dim Lustre. Ballet in 1 act; chor. and book: Antony Tudor; music: Richard Strauss's *Burleske for Piano and Orchestra;* décor: Motley. First prod.: Ballet (now American Ballet) Theatre, Metropolitan Opera House, N.Y., Oct. 20, 1943, with Nora Kaye, Hugh Laing, Rosella Hightower, Janet Reed, John Kriza, Antony Tudor. Two who meet at a ball might have become lovers had they not constantly found themselves carried back to the past on a tide of memories by a dropped handkerchief, a touch, a kiss. *Dim Lustre* was revived at the same theatre, Apr. 26, 1956, with Nora Kaye and Hugh Laing re-creating their original roles, and Ruth Ann Koesun, Sonia Arova, Ivan Allen, Darrell Notara. Tudor staged it for New York City Ballet at N.Y. State Theater, May 6, 1964, with Patricia McBride, Edward Villella, and Patricia Neary.

Dirtl, Willy, Austrian dancer, b. Vienna, 1931. Studied at the ballet school of the Vienna State Opera under Adele Krausenecker, Willy Fränzl, Erika Hanka, Gordon Hamilton. Premier danseur of the Vienna State Opera Ballet since 1951. His roles include Albrecht (*Giselle*), Othello (*The Moor of Venice*), Joan (*Joan von Zarissa*), Prince (*Swan Lake*), Mandarin (*The Miraculous Mandarin*), Zedelmeier (*Hotel Sacher*), various pas de deux, and others. Visited New York in Feb., 1962, to dance the *Blue Danube Waltz* with Viennese prima ballerina Edeltraud Brexner at the (charity-sponsored) Vienna Opera Ball; returned in Feb., 1963, with Edeltraud Brexner to dance the *Voices of Spring Waltz* at the Ball of that year.

Discovery of Brazil, The. Ballet in 4 scenes; chor.: Tatiana Leskova (scenes 1 and 3) and Eugenia Feodorova (scenes 2 and 4); music: Heitor Villa-Lobos, originally composed for an historical Brazilian motion picture of the same title; book: Circe Amado; décor and staging: Gianni Ratto; costumes: Bela Pais Leme. First prod.: Teatro Municipal, Rio de Janeiro, 1960, with Berta Rozanova, Johnny Franklin, Ruth Lima, Aldo Lotufo, David Dupré, Eleonora Oliosi. An historical work which is danced theatre rather than pure ballet. The scenes are entitled "Departure from Portugal," "Voyage," "Myths of Brazilian Jungle," and "Landing," but director Gianni Ratto united the parts and presented them without intermissions, leading up to a strong climax in the last scene: "The First Mass."

District Storyville. Modern dance work; chor.: Donald McKayle; music: Dorothea Freitag; décor: Normand Maxon. First prod.: Donald McKayle Company, YM–YWHA, N.Y. Apr. 22, 1962, with Thelma Oliver, Jacqueline Walcott, Pearl Reynolds, Herman Howell, Gus Solomons, Jr., William Louther, Kenneth Scott, Alfred De Sio, Eliot Feld, and others. New Orleans in the great days of jazz when a night on the town culminated in the crowning of the king of the horns.

Diversion of Angels. Modern dance work; chor.: Martha Graham; music: Norman Dello Joio; décor: Isamu Noguchi. First prod.: Martha Graham Dance Company, 1st American Dance Festival, Conn. College, New London (under the title *Wilderness Stair*), Aug. 13, 1948, with May O'Donnell, Pearl Lang, Helen McGehee, Dorothea Douglas, Joan Skinner, Dorothy Berea, Natanya Neumann, Erick Hawkins, Mark Ryder, Robert Cohan, Stuart Hodes, Dale Sehnert. Under its present title it was given at Eighth St. Theater, Chicago, Mar. 20, 1949, and had its N.Y. première at 46th Street Theater, Jan. 22, 1950, with Yuriko instead of May O'Donnell. The décor was subsequently discarded and Edythe Gilfond designed new costumes. The title comes from a poem by Ben Bellitt, and the program note calls it "a lyric ballet about the loveliness of youth, the pleasure and playfulness, quick joy and quick sadness of being in love for the first time."

Diversions. Ballet in 1 act; chor.: Kenneth MacMillan; music: Arthur Bliss's *Music for Strings;* décor: Nicholas Georgiadis; costumes: Philip Prowse. First prod.: Royal Ballet, Royal Opera House, Covent Garden, London, Sept. 16, 1961, with Svetlana Beriosova, Donald Macleary, Maryon Lane, Graham Usher, and four other couples. A themeless ballet.

Divertimento. Ballet in 1 act; chor.: George Balanchine; music: Alexei Haieff's score of the same name. First prod.: Ballet Society, Hunter College Playhouse, N.Y., Jan. 13, 1947, with Mary Ellen Moylan, Elise Reiman, Gisella Caccialanza, Beatrice Tompkins, Tanaquil LeClercq, Francisco Moncion, Lew Christensen, Todd Bolender, Fred Danieli, John Taras. First perf. by New York City Ballet (the name given by Ballet Society to its performing company the following year): Nov. 2, 1948, with Maria Tallchief, Tanaquil LeClercq, Elise Reiman, Jocelyn Vollmar, Beatrice Tompkins, Francisco Moncion, Dick Beard, Roy Tobias, Nicholas Magallanes, Herbert Bliss. The five brief musical sections are Prelude, Aria, Scherzo, Lullaby, Finale. Although the ballet is themeless, there are hints of romance between the five pairs of dancers. Lullaby, for the leading girl, is the one solo passage.

Divertimento No. 15 (original title *Caracole*). Ballet in 5 movements; chor.: George Balanchine; music: Mozart's Divertimento in B flat major, K. 287; costumes: Christian Bérard (for Les Songes [Dreams]). First prod.: New York City Ballet, City Center, N.Y., Feb. 19, 1952, with Maria Tallchief, Melissa Hayden, Patricia Wilde, Diana Adams, Tanaquil LeClercq, André Eglevsky, Nicholas Magallanes, Jerome Robbins. A considerably revised version under its present title, was presented May 31, 1956, during the Mozart Festival at Stratford, Conn., organized by Ballet Society and the American Shakespeare Theatre and Academy, this version having its N.Y. première at City Center, N.Y., Dec. 19, 1956, with new costumes by Barbara Karinska, and the James Stewart Morcom backcloth originally designed for *Symphonie Concertante.* The reason for the revisions was that in the time that elapsed between the last performance of *Caracole* and its revival as *Divertimento No. 15,* the choreographer and the dancers had forgotten most of the choreography. The N.Y. première was danced by Melissa Hayden, Patricia Wilde, Yvonne Mounsey, Diana Adams, Barbara Milberg (substituting for Allegra Kent who was absent through illness but subsequently danced the role), Jonathan Watts, Nicholas

Magallanes, Roy Tobias. A superb series of variations, pas de deux and ensembles, one of the most dazzling of Balanchine's abstract ballets, though many feel that the original *Caracole* was even finer than its second version.

Divertissement. A series of dances, called entrées, inserted into a classic ballet; or a group of dances put together for the purpose of presenting several individual dancers in a series of separate numbers. The separate dances in a divertissement are often erroneously called divertissements by spectators. In the classic ballet a divertissement was generally inserted toward the end of the last act, as in *The Sleeping Beauty,* from which *Aurora's Wedding* and *Princess Aurora* were taken, or into the next to last act, as in *Swan Lake,* from which the *Magic Swan* was taken. A typical divertissement is to be found in Act 3 of *Coppélia.* It is interesting to note that although this divertissement has no connection with the ballet proper, it was originally planned with a definite continuity which, however, has been lost in the current revivals of *Coppélia.* This divertissement carries the title *The Fête of the Bell,* and the original score of the ballet outlines the following scenario:

1. Waltz of the Hours. The Toller of the Bell, with an hourglass in his hand, calls the hours. The morning hours, led by Dawn, answer his call.
2. Dawn. Dawn appears surrounded by field flowers. The morning hours dance around her.
3. Prayer. This is the hour of prayer. Prayer blesses the beginning of the day, and rises to heaven.
4. Work. The time for work arrives. Dawn and her morning hours depart, and their places are taken by the hours of the midday. The spinners and field workers begin their tasks.
5. Hymen. The god of marriage arrives at the head of a procession, accompanied by Cupid. A village wedding takes place.
6. War. The gay scene is succeeded by a scene of discord. Mournful sounds fill the air. Arms are raised. Flames light up the darkened sky.
7. Peace. Peace appears with an olive branch in her hand. Everything calms down; the discord ends.

Finale. The hours of the evening and of the night appear and introduce a procession of pleasures and games.

Parts of this divertissement exist in most productions of *Coppélia,* but it is at present never given in its entirety.

Dixon, Norman, contemporary English dancer and choreographer, b. Northampton. Studied at Ballet Rambert School; joined the company (1949); principal dancer (1953). Choreographed ballets for the Sunday Ballet Club; also staged a two-week season of his ballets at Pembroke Theatre-in-the-Round, Croydon (Mar., 1960). Working in Portugal since 1960. His ballets include *Voice in the Wilderness* (1958), *The Cord* (1959), *Violent Rhythm* (1959), *Preciosa* (1960).

Doboujinsky, Mstislav, Russian painter and stage designer, b. Novgorod, 1875, d. N.Y., 1957. A graduate of the Russian Imperial Academy of Art, he contributed to Serge Diaghilev's magazine *The World of Art* (Mir Iskoustva) (1899–1904). For the Diaghilev Ballet Russes he designed décor for *Papillons* (1912) and *Midas* (1914). His other work included *The Fairy Doll* (Anna Pavlova company 1915); *Coppélia* (Ballets de Monte Carlo, 1935); *The Nutcracker* (Sadler's Wells Ballet, 1937); *Ballet Imperial* (American Ballet, 1941); *Russian Soldier* (1942), *Mademoiselle Angot* (1943), *Graduation Ball* (revival, 1944), all for Ballet Theatre; *The Gentleman Chooses a Bride* (1946), for Boris Romanov; *The Prisoner of the Caucasus* (1951), for the Grand Ballet du Marquis de Cuevas; this décor was originally designed for Boris Romanov's ballet *Prince Goudal,* produced by de Cuevas' Ballet International in N.Y., 1944; *Coppélia* (for Ballet Rambert, 1956).

Dodge, Roger Pryor, Collection, an integral part of the Dance Collection of the New York Public Library, was given to the Library by Mr. Dodge in 1937 and contains more than 500 photographs of Vaslav Nijinsky, many of them rare. This record of Nijinsky's career covers most of his roles, among them *L'Après-Midi d'un Faune, Carnaval, Le Festin, Giselle, Petrouchka, Jeux, Les Orientales, Le Spectre de la Rose, Pavillon d'Armide, Schéhérazade,* as well as informal off-stage photos. Among the dancers who performed with Nijinsky represented are Tamara Karsavina and Anna Pavlova.

Dokoudovsky, Vladimir, dancer, choreographer, teacher, b. Monte Carlo, 1922; m. Nina Stroganova. Began his dance studies with Olga Preobrajenska in Paris at age twelve. Won the first prize at the International Competition organized by the Archives Internationales de la Danse, Paris. Made his professional debut at thirteen as soloist during the season of opera organized by Col. de Basil in Monte Carlo; soloist, at the Opéra Comique, Paris; first dancer, Polish Ballet, directed by Bronislava Nijinska (1937); soloist, Ballet Russe de Monte Carlo (1938); Mordkin Ballet and Ballet Theatre (1938–1940). Premier danseur, Original Ballet Russe (1942–1952), with a season as guest artist with Ballet Russe de Monte Carlo (1951). His repertoire included a wide range of classic, demi-caractère, and caractère leads in *Swan Lake, Schéhérazade, Le Coq d'Or, Graduation Ball, Paganini, Giselle, Les Présages, Gaité Parisienne, Le Spectre de la Rose, Bluebird* pas de deux, etc. Restaged *Graduation Ball* for Ballet Russe de Monte Carlo (1949); was ballet master and regisseur for the same company (1953). Has choreographed several ballets for his own ballet group (with Stroganova) for educational television and for regional companies. Currently teaches in N.Y.

Dolin, Anton (Sydney Francis Patrick Chippendall Healey-Kay), English premier danseur, choreographer, director, b. Sinfold, Sussex, 1904. Studied dance with Lily and Grace Cone in Brighton as a child; later with Seraphima Astafieva in London, and with Bronislava Nijinska. Was a child actor, playing Michael in *Peter Pan,* among other roles. Appeared in corps de ballet of the Diaghilev Ballets Russes revival of *The Sleeping Beauty* (Alhambra Theatre, London, 1921–22); engaged as soloist (debut in Monte Carlo, Jan. 1, 1924). Was with the company until 1925, and again 1928–29. *Le Train Bleu* was created for him (1924). He and Leon Woicikowski created the Evil Companions (in George Balanchine's *Prodigal Son*); also created the leading male role (*Le Bal*), and others. Danced Blue Bird (*Aurora's Wedding*), male role (*Les Sylphides*), pas de trois—with Felia Doubrovska and Alexandra Danilova—(*Swan Lake,* Act 2), Moor (*Petrouchka*), Harlequin and Eusebius (*Carnaval*), and others, including the Fop (Les Facheux), in which he danced a solo on point. Partnered Tamara Karsavina in *Le Spectre de la Rose* (1927); with Vera Nemtchinova founded ballet group (1927–28) for which he choreographed George Gershwin's *Rhapsody in Blue* and Chopin's *Revolutionary Etude.* After the death of Diaghilev, Dolin came to N.Y. with the *International Revue.* Upon his return to London he helped found the Camargo Society (1930), for which he created the role of Satan in *Job* (1931). He also danced in early performances of the Vic-Wells (later Sadler's Wells, now Royal) Ballet. Danced Albrecht to Olga Spessivtzeva's *Giselle* in the Camargo Society's summer season (1932). Principal dancer and later guest artist with Vic-Wells (1931–35), creating title role in Frederick Ashton's *The Lord*

Anton Dolin as the Prince in Princess Aurora, *produced by Ballet (now American Ballet) Theatre.*

of Burleigh and partnering Alicia Markova when she danced her first *Giselle* (1934). With Markova (financially sponsored by Mrs. Laura Henderson), he founded, was director, and principal dancer of the Markova-Dolin Ballet (1935–38). Toured with Original Ballet Russe in Australia (1939). Joined Ballet Theatre as premier danseur or guest artist from its inception until 1946, restaging *Swan Lake, Giselle,* and *Princess Aurora,* and choreographing *Quintet, Pas de Quatre, Capriccioso, Romantic Age.* Created title role in *Bluebeard,* Red Coat (*Fair at Sorochinsk*), etc. Premier danseur and choreographer of the ballet in the revue *Seven Lively Arts* (N.Y., 1944–45). Organized new Markova-Dolin group which toured in U.S., Central America, and Mexico between 1945 and 1948. Guest artist, Original Ballet Russe (season 1946–47); with Sadler's Wells Ballet, Royal Opera House, Covent Garden, London (June, 1948); Ballet Russe de Monte Carlo (fall-winter, 1948). In 1949, again with Markova, he formed a group in England which became London's Festival Ballet (1950) and of which he was artistic director and principal dancer until 1961. Formed and toured with group, Stars of the Ballet (1961). Director and choreographer, Rome Opera Ballet (1962). Author of *Divertissement* (1930), *Ballet Go Round* (1938), *Pas de Deux: the Art of Partnering* (1949), *Alicia Markova* (1953), *Autobiography* (1960). Awards include Order of the Sun, Lima, Peru (1960); Queen Elizabeth II Coronation Award of Royal Academy of Dancing (1957). Dolin will always be remembered as one of the outstanding partners in classic ballet. He was also the first English male dancer to earn international fame.

Dollar, William, dancer, choreographer, teacher, b. St. Louis, Mo., 1907. Studied dance with Michel Fokine, Mikhail Mordkin, George Balanchine, Pierre Vladimirov, N.Y.; Alexandre Volinine, Paris. Leading dancer, Philadelphia

Opera; American Ballet (1936–37); Ballet Caravan (1936–38); Ballet Theatre (1940); American Ballet Caravan (1941); New Opera Co., N.Y. (1942); Ballet International (1944). Also danced in musicals and was Vera Zorina's partner in the dance sequences of the film *Goldwyn Follies* (1938). He was one of the first male dancers to make a name in contemporary American ballet. Ballet master, American Concert Ballet (1943); Ballet Society (1946). Choreographed and was dance director of Ford Ballet, N.Y. World's Fair (1940), and various musicals and television programs. Ballet master, Grand Ballet de Monte Carlo—later Grand Ballet du Marquis de Cuevas (1948). Created Herr Drosselmeyer in George Balanchine's *The Nutcracker* (1954). In 1956 he helped establish a state ballet school in Teheran, Iran. Has also worked extensively as choreographer and teacher in South America. His ballets include *Five Gifts; Constantia,* first staged for Ballet International and later taken into the repertoires of Original Ballet Russe and American Ballet Theatre; *Mendelssohn Concerto,* also for American Ballet Theatre. His best known ballet is *Le Combat* (The Duel) originally commissioned by Roland Petit for his Ballets de Paris, and also in the repertoires of New York City Ballet and American Ballet Theatre. Has staged several ballets for Detroit City Ballet, a regional company. For Le Théâtre d'Art du Ballet he has choreographed Francesca da Rimini, *Fountain of the Blind* (based on the story of Pelléas and Mélisande), and *Simple Symphony.* Dollar has been a member of the faculty of the Ballet Theatre School for several years. In the spring of 1965 he took a leave of absence to become ballet master and guest choreographer of the Teatro Municipal in Rio de Janeiro, Brazil. The same year he staged *Marguerite Gautier* for Théâtre d'Art du Ballet company.

Domenico of Ferrara, c. 1400, dancing master at the court of the Marquis Leonello d'Esté of Ferrara. He was the first to codify a theory of dance teaching. His students passed on his ideas orally at first and then in writing, the most important manuscripts being those of William the Jew (Guglielmo Ebreo). He made many innovations in court dance, particularly in the Basse Danse and created new forms known as Balli and Balletti. He came from Piacenza (hence is sometimes known as Domenico of Piacenza).

Dominic, Zoe. See PHOTOGRAPHERS, DANCE (ENGLAND).

Don Juan. Ballet in 3 scenes; chor.: Michel Fokine; music: from the ballet by Christoph Wilibald Gluck, based on the Molière play; book: Eric Allatini and Michel Fokine; curtain and décor: Mariano Andreù. First prod.: René Blum's Ballet Russe, Alhambra Theatre, London, June 25, 1936, with Anatole Vilzak (Don Juan), Jeannette Lauret (Donna Elvira), and André Eglevsky (Jester) in the leading roles. Allatini spent considerable time locating the complete score of *Don Juan,* composed to fit specific situations in Molière's play, and originally choreographed by Angiolini in Vienna (1761). The première of the Fokine ballet had been scheduled for June 19, 1939, but all costumes were destroyed by a fire on June 16, and the première had to be postponed until June 25.

Fire also caused trouble to the Vienna production of *Don Juan* in 1761. The première went on as scheduled but at a subsequent performance the Kärntnertortheater, where the ballet was being given, burned down as a result of the overheating of Hell. Based on Molière's drama, the ballet tells the story of Don Juan's duel with the Commander, who was killed protecting the honor of his daughter, Elvira. At a feast given by Don Juan, the ghost of the Commander makes an appearance, but refuses the invitation of Don Juan to drink a glass of wine with him. After a while the ghost re-appears and invites

Don Juan to visit him at the cemetery. Don Juan accepts the invitation and at the cemetery is caught by the stone arm of the Commander's statue. The loosed furies almost tear him to pieces and he dies. Fokine's *Don Juan* had its N.Y. première Oct. 22, 1938, when Michel Panaieff assumed the title role.

Don Juan. Ballet in 1 act; chor.: Frederick Ashton; music: Richard Strauss's tone poem of the same title; décor: Edward Burra. First prod.: Sadler's Wells (now Royal) Ballet, Royal Opera House, Covent Garden, Nov. 25, 1948, with Margot Fonteyn (La Morte Amoureuse), Moira Shearer (The Young Wife), Robert Helpmann (Don Juan). The theme is taken from Théophile Gautier's poem "La Morte Amoureuse," ["The love that caught strange light from Death's own eyes"] Ashton's *Don Juan,* though he pursues many women, is in love with death.

Don Juan de Zarissa. See JOAN VON ZARISSA.

Don Quichotte chez la Duchesse. Ballet-comique by Favart produced at the Académie Royale, Paris, 1743, with music by Boismortier and costumes by Louis Boquet. Marie Allard danced the leading role.

Don Quixote. Ballet in prologue, 4 acts, 8 scenes; chor. and book: Marius Petipa; music: Leon Minkus. First prod.: Bolshoi Theatre, Moscow, Dec. 26, 1869. Based on Cervantes' novel of the same name, the ballet was produced chiefly to introduce Spanish dances. Other ballets inspired by the same novel were Jean Georges Noverre's production in Vienna (1750's); *Les Noces de Gamache* by Louis Milon, Opéra, Paris, Jan. 18, 1801; Paul Taglioni's ballet in Berlin (1850). Petipa's ballet was produced in 5 acts, 11 scenes, at the Maryinsky, Nov. 21, 1871; a revised version by Alexander Gorsky was produced at the Moscow Bolshoi Theatre (1900). Anna Pavlova had a ballet, *Don Quixote* (by Laurent Novikov), in her repertoire.

Don Quixote. Ballet in 3 acts, 7 scenes; chor.: Alexander Gorsky, revived by Rostislav Zakharov, with new mis-en-scène and dances; music: Leon Minkus; décor: Vadim Ryndin. First prod.: Bolshoi Theatre, Moscow, Feb. 10, 1940. This version is still in the repertoire of the Bolshoi. The interpolated gypsy dance in Act 2 was choreographed by Kasian Goleizovsky to music by Konstantin Korchmaryev. Like the Petipa-Gorsky version on which this production is based, it has only a very vague connection with Cervantes's novel, but it has been an important part of the Bolshoi repertoire ever since the Gorsky production in 1900 was staged under the influence of the Moscow Art Theatre. Its virtuoso pas de deux in the last act of both the Petipa and Gorsky versions, is known the world over, and is one of the reasons the ballet survives. This version, staged by Witold Berkowski of the Warsaw State Opera, is in the repertoire of Ballet Rambert (première: July 26, 1962, Sadler's Wells Theatre, London), with Lucette Aldous and Kenneth Bannerman as the lovers Kitri and Basilio, and John Chesworth in the title role.

Don Quixote. Ballet in 5 scenes; chor.: Ninette de Valois; commissioned music: Roberto Gerhard; décor: Edward Burra. First prod.: Sadler's Wells (now Royal) Ballet, Royal Opera House, Covent Garden, London, Feb. 20, 1950, with Robert Helpmann (Don Quixote), Margot Fonteyn (Dulcinea), Alexander Grant (Sancho Panza). The ballet shows episodes from the Cervantes' novel, including the tilt with the windmills, the meeting with Dulcinea at the inn, the Don's illusions, madness, and death.

Don Quixote. Ballet in 3 acts, 5 scenes; chor.: George Balanchine; commissioned score: Nicolas Nabokov; décor: Esteban Francés; costumes executed by Karinska. First prod.: New York City Ballet, N.Y. State Theater, May 28, 1965, with Richard Rapp (Don Quixote) Suzanne Farrell (Dulcinea), Deni Lamont (Sancho Panza). At a Ballet Society benefit preview (May 27), Balanchine appeared in the title role. The first evening-length American ballet staged to a commissioned score, *Don Quixote* is based on a number of episodes from the Cervantes masterpiece.

Dona Ines de Castro. Ballet in 1 act, 5 scenes; chor. and book: Ana Ricarda; commissioned music: Juaquin Serra; décor; Celia Hubbard. First prod.: Grand Ballet du Marquis de Cuevas, Casino Municipal, Cannes, Mar. 1, 1952, with Rosella Hightower (Dona Ines), George Skibine (Don Pedro), John Taras (King of Portugal), Wladimir Skouratoff (King's Counsellor), Ana Ricarda (Infanta of Navarre). Based on a Portuguese legend of the early Middle Ages in which Ines is beloved by Don Pedro, heir to the throne of Portugal, who must marry the Infanta of Spain. The King's Counsellor persuades the King of Portugal to order the murder of Ines. He does, but dies in horror at his own act. Don Pedro, now the King, carries the dead body of Ines to the Throne Room, where he goes through the macabre act of having her crowned and seated on the throne. Out of his mind with grief, he dances with the body of Ines until he himself falls dead.

Donald of the Burthens. Ballet in 1 act, 2 scenes; chor.: Leonide Massine; commissioned music: Ian Whyte; décor: Robert MacBryde and Robert Colquhoun. First prod.: Sadler's Wells (now Royal) Ballet, Royal Opera House, Covent Garden, London, Dec. 12, 1951, with Beryl Grey (Death), Alexander Grant (Donald), Leslie Edwards (King). Closely allied to the Faust theme, the story tells how a poor woodcutter (Donald) makes a pact with Death promising that, in return for his becoming a great doctor, he will never offer a prayer. He tricks Death in saving the life of a king but himself dies when he returns to prayer. The ballet did not stay long in the repertoire, possibly because the death of King George VI shortly after the ballet's première made the theme of the ballet painful to British audiences.

Donizetti Variations (original title, *Variations from Don Sebastian*). Ballet in 1 act; chor.: George Balanchine; music: from Gaetano Donizetti's opera *Don Sebastian;* décor: David Hays; costumes: women's designed and executed by Barbara Karinska; men's designed by Esteban Francés, executed by Karinska. First prod.: New York City Ballet, City Center, N.Y., Nov. 16, 1960, with Melissa Hayden, Jonathan Watts, and Carole Fields, Hester Fitzgerald, Leda Roffi, Suki Schorer, Victoria Simon, Carol Sumner, Michael Lland, Richard Rapp, William Weslow. The variations for the ensemble and for the two soloists in various entrées, singly and together, are brilliant and frequently satirical. Violette Verdy, Jacques d'Amboise, and Edward Villella have also danced the leads. This ballet was premièred, with *Monumentum Pro Gesualdo* on "Salute to Italy" night, in honor of the centennial celebration of the unification of Italy.

Dorati, Antal, conductor, b. Budapest, Hungary, 1906; American citizen since 1942. Former conductor of Royal Opera, Budapest; State Operas of Dresden, Muenster, Frankfurt, etc.; also conducted orchestras in opera houses in various European cities; toured Mexico, Cuba, Australia. Was second conductor, Ballet Russe de Monte Carlo (1935–37); conductor, Original Ballet Russe (1938–41); musical director, Ballet (now American Ballet) Theatre (1941–45; except for one season with New Opera Company, N.Y., 1942). Musical director, Dallas (Tex.) Symphony Orchestra (1945–49); Minneapolis Symphony Orchestra (1949–60). Conductor, British Broadcasting Corporation (B.B.C.) Symphony Orchestra (since 1962); also conducts operas and concerts in various European cities. Arranged and orchestrated the music for *Graduation Ball, Bluebeard, Helen of Troy, Romantic Age, Harvest Time, Fair at Sorochinsk, Giselle* (for Ballet Theatre, 1946), and various pas de deux. His recordings with the Minneapolis Symphony Orchestra of the full-length *Swan Lake, The Sleeping Beauty,* and *The Nutcracker* (for Mercury Records) are considered the definitive versions.

Douairiere de Billebahaut, La, a grotesque and fantastic ballet given in the time of Louis XIII (1626). It burlesqued deformity, misfortune, and crime.

Doubler, Margaret N. See H'DOUBLER, MARGARET N.

Doubrovska, Felia (Felizata Dlužhnevska), ballerina and teacher, b. 1896; m. Pierre Vladimiroff. Graduated from the St. Petersburg Imperial School of Ballet (1913). Although she made rapid progress at the Maryinsky Theatre, she resigned and left Russia to join the Diaghilev Ballets Russes (1920), making her debut with the company as the Blue Bird and Fairy of the Pine Woods in *The Sleeping Beauty* (London, 1921), and creating The Bride (*Les Noces,* 1923), Film Star (George Balanchine's *Pastorale,* 1925), Calliope (Apollon Musagète, 1928), and her most important role, the Siren (*The Prodigal Son,* 1929), among others. In 1938–39 she was première danseuse of the Metropolitan Opera Ballet, under Boris Romanoff. Currently teaches at School of American Ballet, N.Y.

Felia Doubrovska, Russian-born ballerina, at present teaching in New York.

Douglas, Scott, dancer, b. El Paso Tex. 1927. Began dance training at age of six. Toured the Orpheum Circuit as a tap dancer at age nine. After service in the Navy, began studies with Ruth St. Denis and Lester Horton in Los Angeles; after two years began ballet training in San Francisco with Willam Christensen. Joined San Francisco Ballet (1948) and became leading male dancer. Joined Ballet (now American Ballet) Theatre (1950) for its European tour. Remained with the company until 1962, rising to premier danseur, with time out for appearances with the Metropolitan Opera Ballet (1958–59) and as partner to Nora Kaye at 1959 Festival of Two Worlds, Spoleto, and later in Moscow. Also that year danced in John Butler's production of *Carmina Burana* by N.Y. City Opera. Toured Europe with Jerome Robbins's Ballets: U.S.A. (1961). His roles with Ballet Theatre included Prince (*Swan Lake,* Act 2), male dancer (*Les Sylphides*), Third Sailor (*Fancy Free*), Billy and Pat Garrett (*Billy the Kid*), Boy in Green (*Les Patineurs*), Jean (*Miss Julie*), Friend (*Pillar of Fire*), Pastor (*Fall River Legend*), Paris (*Helen of Troy*), Tancredi (*The Combat*), male lead (*Theme and Variations*), Head Wrangler and Champion Roper (*Rodeo*), etc. Joined Nederlands National Ballet as premier danseur (1963); returned to American Ballet Theatre (1964).

Scott Douglas, principal dancer of the American Ballet Theatre.

Douvillier, Suzanne Theodore, née Vaillande (1788–1826). Known throughout much of her career as "Madame Placide," Suzanne Douvillier was the first ballerina to attain fame in the U.S. as both a dancer and choreographer. Born in Dole, France, she was educated in Paris (probably at the Opéra). With Alexandre Placide, her partner and companion, she made her debut at the John St. Theatre, N.Y. Jan. 25, 1792, in the ballet *The Bird Catcher.* After appearances in Philadelphia, Boston, and Newport, she and Placide settled in Charleston, where she danced in such important ballets as Gardel's *La Chercheuse d'Esprit* and Jean Georges Noverre's *The Whims of Galathea.* In 1796 she staged her first original work, *Echo and Narcissus.* Following a duel between Placide and the singer, Louis Douvillier, Suzanne (who had never been Placide's legal wife) married Douvillier and went with him to New Orleans. Noted for her beauty and versatility, she was not only ballerina of the New Orleans theatre, but staged many ballets (some of them original) and designed and painted the scenery for her productions. She died in New Orleans on Aug. 30, 1826.

Dowell, Anthony, British dancer, b. London, 1943. Began dance training with Mrs. June Hampshire; later entered the Royal Ballet School. While a senior student at the School, joined the Covent Garden Opera Ballet. Transferred to the Royal Ballet in 1962 and the same year danced his first solo role: in the *Napoli* divertissement, staged for the company by Erik Bruhn. His first created role was Oberon in Frederick Ashton's *The Dream.* Among his other roles are Romeo in MacMillan's *Romeo and Juliet,* Country Boy in Andrée Howard's *La Fête Etrange,* soloist in *Diversions* and Boy in *The Invitation* (both by MacMillan), pas de trois in Ashton's *Monotones,* as well as Florestan pas de trois in *The Sleeping Beauty* (Act 3), and pas de quatre in *Swan Lake* (Act 1).

Doyle, Desmond, South African dancer, b. Cape Town, 1932; m. Brenda Taylor. Dance training University of Cape Town Ballet. Joined Sadler's Wells (now Royal) Ballet (1951); promoted to soloist (1953); currently principal dancer. His repertoire includes Siegfried (*Swan Lake*), Prince (*Cinderella*), Franz (*Coppélia*), Red Knight (*Checkmate*), etc. Created The Husband (*The Invitation*), Mark (*Sweeney Todd*), two episodes in *Images of Love,* and others. Created Tybalt in Kenneth MacMillan's *Romeo and Juliet* (1965).

Draper, Paul, American dancer, b. Florence, Italy, 1909, of American parents; m. Heidi Vosseler. His father Paul Draper, Sr. was a talented lieder singer; his mother Muriel later became a noted author and lecturer; his aunt Ruth was the famous monologist. He is a famous American tap dancer who is credited with elevating this dance form to concert proportions and creating a new style in tap dance, popularly known as ballet-tap. His formal training in tap lasted no more than a few weeks in beginners' class for which he was persuaded to withdraw as being without talent. Every element in his tap dancing has been worked out by himself. His training in ballet was mainly with Anatole Vilzak, and with Anatole Oboukhoff at School of American Ballet, N.Y. he borrowed from ballet technique to bring to tap the elegance of manner, precision of execution, arm movements, turns, and jumps associated with ballet. Made his first professional appearance at a vaudeville theatre in London (1932) and between 1940 and 1949 toured with Larry Adler, the harmonica virtuoso. Lived abroad between 1951 and 1954, touring in Israel in 1951. Since his return to the U.S., has continued to give solo performances of his dances to classic (Bach, Couperin, etc.) and modern dance music to piano accompaniment. These include his satirical sketches such as *A Sharp Character, Dance Hall* and others,

Paul Draper, American tap dancer, choreographer and teacher.

some of them danced without music. His *Sonata for Tap Dancer* is a major contribution to tap dance without music.

Dream, The. Ballet in 1 act; chor.: Frederick Ashton; music: Felix Mendelssohn. Overture and incidental music for *A Midsummer Night's Dream* arr. by John Lanchbery; scenery: Henry Bardon; costumes: David Walker. First prod.: Royal Ballet, Royal Opera House, Covent Garden, London, Apr. 2, 1964, with Antoinette Sibley (Titania), Anthony Dowell (Oberon), Alexander Grant (Bottom), Carole Needham (Helena), Vergie Derman (Hermia), David Drew (Demetrius), Derek Rencher (Lysander). *The Dream* was Ashton's contribution toward the quadricentennial celebrations in England of Shakespeare's birth. He tells the story only as it is concerned with the magical happenings in the forest. Oberon was Anthony Dowell's first created leading role. Alexander Grant danced on point (in black shoes and high stockings) as Bottom in his metamorphosis into an ass.

Drehtanz, 16th century German turning dance. Dancers placed hands firmly on back of partner and turned. The Ländler, and later the waltz, descended from it.

Drew, Roderick, American dancer, b. San Francisco, 1940. Studied ballet with Lew and Harold Christensen at San Francisco Ballet School. Made his debut with San Francisco Opera Co.; member of San Francisco Ballet (1954–62), being promoted to soloist in 1957. His roles included Sugar Plum Fairy Cavalier (Lew Christensen's *The Nutcracker*), title role (*Jinx*), last movement (*Serenade*), 1st movement (*Symphony in C*), Thief (*Con Amore*), Station Attendant (*Filling Station*), Beast (*Beauty and the Beast*); created Adam (*Original Sin*) and others. Leading dancer with National Ballet (Washington, D.C.) from its inception, repeating his role in *Con Amore* and dancing 2d movement (*Serenade*), Prince Siegfried (*Swan Lake,* Act 2), Franz (*Coppélia*); leading male roles in *Hommage au Ballet* and *Tribute,* both choreographed by Frederic Franklin. In 1963 danced Carnival Boy in *Carousel* in summer stock. Danced with Sonia Arova at Jacob's Pillow Dance Festival (1964). In 1965 joined Harkness Ballet.

Drigo, Riccardo (1846–1930), Italian musician and composer. For many years conductor of the Maryinsky Imperial Theatre in St. Petersburg. Composed the music to several ballets in the repertoire of Russian ballet companies, among them *The Talisman* (Petipa, 1889), *The Magic Flute* (Ivanov, 1893), *Harlequinade* (also known as *Les Millions d'Arlequin;* Petipa, 1900). The last named is also in the repertoire of Ballet Russe de Monte Carlo, staged by Boris Romanov.

Du Boulay, Christine, English dancer and teacher, b. Ealing, Middlesex, 1923; m. Richard Ellis. Studied dance with various English teachers, at Sadler's Wells School, and with Stanislas Idzikowski, Judith Espinosa, Vera Volkova, Molly Lake, Anna Northcote. Made her professional debut as a Page in the Sadler's Wells (now Royal) Ballet production of *The Sleeping Beauty* (1939). Member of the Sara Payne Ballet, Gate Theatre, Dublin (1941–1942); soloist with International Ballet (1943–1945) and with Sadler's Wells Ballet (1946–1952). Her repertoire included Lead Mazurka (*Coppélia*), Girl with Stockings (*The Rake's Progress*), Mother (*Miracle in the Gorbals*); also danced in *Les Patineurs, Hamlet, Daphnis and Chloë,* and others. Emigrated to U.S. (1952) and with Richard Ellis teaches in Chicago; also with him is co-founder and director of Illinois Ballet (1959) and co-author of *Partnering, the Fundamentals of Pas de Deux* (Chicago, 1954).

Dudinskaya, Natalia, Peoples' Artist of the USSR, Soviet prima ballerina, b. 1912; m. Konstantin Sergeyev. Daughter of a dancer and musician who, under the theatrical name of Taglioni headed a ballet studio in Kharkov in the 1920's. She watched classes in her mother's studio and at the age of eight took part in them. In 1923 she was entered into the second year class of the then Petrograd Ballet School, graduating in 1931 after studying for the final three years under Agrippina Vaganova, who considered her (with Marina Semyonova) to have assimilated her teaching to perfection. Six months before graduation, Dudinskaya made her debut as Princess Florine in the *Blue Bird* pas de deux of *The Sleeping Beauty*. Six months after joining the Kirov ballet company she danced Odette-Odile in the original St. Petersburg version of *Swan Lake*. She has also danced the same role in three other versions, those of Vaganova (1932), Fedor Lopukhov (1945), and Konstantin Sergeyev (1950). Her other ballets in the classic repertoire included *Raymonda, Giselle, Don Quixote, La Bayadère, Esmeralda, Le Corsaire*. She also danced important roles in many of the new ballets created at the Kirov Theatre after 1931: Mireille de Poitiers (*Flames of Paris*), Corali, alternating with Galina Ulanova (*Lost Illusions*), Pannochka (*Taras Bulba*), title role (*Gayané*), title role (*Cinderella*), Parasha (*Bronze Horseman*), Girl-Bird (*Shurale*), Sarie (*Path of Thunder*), many of which she created. Her greatest role in modern ballet was Laurencia in the Vakhtang Chabukiani ballet of that name. She currently dances less frequently than before but remains the Kirov's prima ballerina. During the past few years she has taught

Natalia Dudinskaya, ballerina of the Kirov Ballet as Kitri in Don Quixote.

the classe de perfection for the company's ballerinas, thus replacing her teacher, Agrippina Vaganova, of whose method she is an esteemed specialist. In 1961 she visited London as ballet mistress with the Kirov Ballet. In 1964 on the second U.S. visit of the company she bore the title Principal Ballet Mistress.

Dudley, Jane, American dancer, choreographer, teacher, b. New York City, 1912. Studied dance with Hanya Holm, Martha Graham, and Louis Horst. A leading dancer, and later guest artist, of the Martha Graham Dance Company (1937–1944), creating the Ancestress (*Letter to the World*) and one of the three sisters (*Deaths and Entrances*). Between 1942 and 1954 she was also a member of the Dance Trio with Sophie Maslow and William Bales, giving many performances in works choreographed by herself and the other two members of the Trio. Some of her choreographic works created between 1938 and 1948 were *Four Middle-Class Portraits, The Ballad of Molly Pitcher, Adolescence, Harmonica Breakdown, New World a'Comin', Swing Your Lady, Cante Flamenco* (all solos), *Short Story* (trio danced by Jane Dudley, Pearl Lang, and Marjorie Mazia); and *Caprichos* and *Furlough,* danced with Sophie Maslow and William Bales, respectively. Later works (1949–1953) included *The Lonely Ones,* based on the William Steig cartoons with sound effects score by Zoe Williams, danced by the Dance Trio; *Reel* (Woody Guthrie) also by the Trio; a number of solos: *Lullaby for a Child, Faces of Woman, Vagary;* and *Passional,* a group work performed by the Dance Trio with the New Dance Group performing company and presented at the 3rd American Dance Festival, Conn. College, New London (1950). Her final large scale work was *Family Portrait,* danced by Maslow and Bales and the New Dance Group at the 1953 American Dance Festival. She retired from the stage in 1954, but continues to teach. Is President and instructor at New Dance Group Studio, N.Y.

Duel, The. See COMBAT, LE.

Dukas, Paul (1865–1935), distinguished French composer. Though he occupies an important position in French music, he contributed only two works to ballet: *The Sorcerer's Apprentice,* which was written as a symphonic poem in 1897 (one of his earliest compositions), and *La Péri,* written as a dance-poem in 1911, one of his last. *The Sorcerer's Apprentice* was first staged as a ballet by Michel Fokine in St. Petersburg (1916). There are many balletic and even pantomimic versions of *The Sorcerer's Apprentice,* but few of them of any artistic merit. *La Péri* was first performed by the Russian dancer Natasha Truhanova, for whom Dukas wrote the score, with choreography by Ivan Clustine at the Châtelet Théâtre, Paris, 1912, and after that by many ballerinas, among them Anna Pavlova, Olga Spessivtzeva, Yvette Chauviré, Alicia Markova, Margot Fonteyn, and others. Recent versions are by Frederick Ashton and George Skibine.

Duke, Vernon (Vladimir Dukelsky), composer, b. Pskoff, Russia, 1903, m. Kay McCracken. Studied music at Kiev Conservatory: composition under Reinhold Glière; piano under M. Dombrovsky and B. Yavorsky. Has written score for the ballets *Zéphire et Flore* (Diaghilev Ballets Russes, Leonide Massine, 1924); *Jardin Public* (Col. de Basil's Ballets Russes de Monte Carlo, Massine, 1934), *Le Bal des Blanchisseuses* (Ballets des Champs-Elysées, Roland Petit, 1946), *Emperor Norton* (San Francisco Ballet, Lew Christensen, 1957). Also composed the music for the ballets in the films *Ziegfeld Follies* (1935), *Goldwyn Follies* (1938), *Cabin in the Sky* (1940), *Lady Comes Across* (1941), all with choreography by George Balanchine. Has written many articles for music and theatre magazines, the autobiographical *Passport to Paris* (Boston, 1955), *Epistles* (Munich, 1962) and *Listen Here: A Study in Music Depreciation* (N.Y., 1963).

Duncan, Irma, dancer, b. nr. Hamburg, Germany, 1897. A pupil of Isadora Duncan at her school founded in Grünewald, Berlin, 1904, she made her debut as a child with Isadora Duncan at the Royal Opera House (Krolls) in 1905, and toured Europe, including two weeks at the Maryinsky Theatre, St. Petersburg (1908). Began teaching junior classes at the age of 14 at the Elizabeth Duncan School in Darmstadt and at the Isadora Duncan School in Bellevue-sur-Seine, nr. Paris (1914) where she continued her dance studies with Isadora. Made her American debut at Metropolitan Opera House with the Duncan group (1914). One of the six Isadora Duncan Dancers who toured U.S. (1918–1920) and again danced with Isadora in Paris (1920–1921). Helped found the Isadora Duncan School in Moscow (1921) and, after the dancer's death in 1927, was head of the school. Headed a group of twelve pupils from the Moscow school in a performance of songs and dances to music by Russian composers (including Tchaikovsky's Symphony No. 6) at Manhattan Opera House, N.Y. (Dec., 1928), presented by S. Hurok, and then on tour in U.S. and China. This was the first time a group of dancers from the Soviet Union toured in U.S. They returned in 1930, Irma Duncan remaining in U.S., becoming an American citizen in 1935. Taught and performed (1930–1934) making her farewell as a dancer Jan. 25, 1934, in a concert-pageant staged by Walter Damrosch to the Beethoven Ninth Symphony at Madison Square Garden, for which she choreographed the *Ode to Peace,* danced by herself and a group of dancers she had trained. Continued to teach and paint, her work having appeared in many exhibitions since 1952. Author of *Isadora Duncan's Russian Days* (with Allan Ross Macdougall, N.Y., 1929); *The Technique of Isadora Duncan* (N.Y., 1937); *Duncan Dancer* (autobiography, Middletown, Conn., 1966).

Duncan, Isadora (1878–1927), was born in San Francisco, California, of Irish parents. Her mother was a music teacher, and from her Isadora absorbed an understanding of the relation between music and movement. She studied ballet as a child, but soon broke away from the conventional classic form to express herself in her own way. Her debut in Chicago (1899) was not successful, so she went with her family to Europe where she danced for the first time in Paris in 1900 and was appreciated much more than in the U.S.

Her vaguely expressed theory of dance was that movement, or dance, basically was the expression of an inner urge or impulse. She tried to locate the source of this impulse, which she considered fundamental and universal, physically, in the solar plexus. Though she had little formal education, she was self-educated to a remarkable degree. She was much influenced by Greece and Greek art. Her usual costume was a flowing tunic, and she was the first Western dancer to dance barefooted and to appear on the stage without tights.

Duncan's Paris success led to engagements in Budapest, Berlin, Florence, and other European cities. In 1904 she founded her own school in Berlin and two years later appeared with a group composed of her pupils. By then she had established a firm attitude toward her dance form, which she called the "free dance" as opposed to the formal dance form of ballet.

In 1905 Duncan made her first appearance in Russia where she created a heated and lasting controversy between the old-school balletomanes and critics on one side and advocates of the reform of the ballet on the other. It is an established fact that she had a strong influence on

Michel Fokine, who was then formulating his ideas about the "new" ballet. His ballet *Eunice,* in which the dancers appeared barefoot and in Greek tunics, was a manifestation of this influence.

The art of Isadora Duncan was closer to pantomime than to actual stage dance. It avoided definitely set movements and steps and transformed the dance into seldom, if ever, repeated improvisations which were never solidified into an unchangeable formal system. For this reason the strength and charm of Duncan's art was destined to disappear with the retirement of the dancer. Sympathetic critics always considered Duncan a personal phenomenon in the art of dance. Her influence on modern dance is felt now more than it was during her lifetime.

Duncan revisited Russia in 1907 and 1912. She established schools in France, Germany, and the U.S., but these were only schools, not a new system of training. Attracted by the Russian revolution, Duncan returned to Russia in 1921 and established there a school which existed through 1924. Though the U.S. at first received her coldly, she returned to her mother country at various times (1909, 1911, 1917, and 1922—the last time under the aegis of impresario S. Hurok).

Isadora Duncan died tragically near Nice, France, on Sept. 14, 1927, as a result of a weird accident. The end of a long scarf which she was wearing around her neck while taking a trip in an open automobile became caught in the rear wheel of the car and strangled her.

During her lifetime, Duncan had been unique in that she seemed to belong not so much to the dance world alone as to the world of art. She dared to use the music of master composers for her dances and although she was criticized for this, her superb musical taste was soon recognized. Cosima Wagner presided herself over Duncan's dancing to music of Wagner at the near-sacred Bayreuth Festival; the pianist Harold Bauer worked with her and felt that he learned of undiscov-

Isadora Duncan. (An enlargement of a postal card which had a wide distribution in Europe ca. *1919. Part of the Duncan Collection of the New York Public Library.)*

ered musical details through watching her dance. Sculptors, painters, poets, essayists and, indeed, many artists of the century (Rodin, Clara, Craig, Bourdelle, Walkowitz, Grandj'ouan, Van Vechten, among them) found in her an inspiration. And after her death, artists of all kinds—not dancers alone—found in her a continuing source of inspiration.

Many books and chapters within books have been written about her but the most famous is her own (*My Life*), in which she touched upon her art concepts but dwelt more with her tempestuous personal life, her flaunting of conventions (she bore three children out of wedlock; two were drowned in a tragic accident, the third died soon after birth); her much publicized marriage to the hard-drinking, mentally unbalanced Soviet poet (Yessenin) who ultimately committed suicide; and other aspects, both tragic and ecstatic, of a remarkable life.

Duncan (Isadora) Collection, an integral part of the Dance Collection of the New York Public Library, given to the Library by Irma Duncan in 1956. It contains material belonging and pertaining to Isadora Duncan. More than 750 items: photographs, manuscripts of her writings, letters, posters, playbills, programs, clippings, books, original drawings, and other memorabilia, most of them rare, some unique, document this American dancer's personal life and career. Choice items are Isadora Duncan's early journals written in Paris in 1901; an album of photographs taken by E. Gordon Craig in 1905; an album of clippings, which are reviews of her early performances in Russia in 1907 and 1913, letters written during her post-revolutionary tours through Russia; photographs by the distinguished photographer Arnold Genthe, who understood Duncan's work so well; drawings by Auguste Rodin, José Clara, Antoine Bourdelle, Jules Grandj'ouan, and E. Gordon Craig. Photographs and press books documenting the growth and activity of the Schools of Duncan Dancing both in Western Europe and Russia, and the tours of the Duncan Dancers, under the direction of Irma Duncan, are also part of this collection. The collection continues to grow as new material is being added. Recent additions are one hundred programs covering Duncan's performances (1900–1913) and 300 drawings made during rehearsals and performances of Isadora Duncan's most celebrated works by Jules Grandj'ouan.

Duncan, Jeff, American modern dancer, b. Cisco, Tex., 1930. Studied music at North Texas State College, being trained as a pianist. Began dance training with Martha Wilcox at Denver Univ. (1950), also studying drama and acting in plays presented by the Univ.'s Dept. of Drama and Dance. Also studied with Hanya Holm; Alwin Nikolais at Henry Street Settlement Playhouse (joining the dance company late in 1951); José Limón and Doris Humphrey on a Connecticut College scholarship. Was chosen by Doris Humphrey to dance the Young Lover in her revival of *With My Red Fires* at the 1953 American Dance Festival. Joined New Dance Group for its Mar., 1954, Festival at the YM–YWHA, and danced the duet in Anna Sokolow's *Lyric Suite.* Made his debut as a choreographer with a program at N.Y.'s Educational Alliance the same year, and has since given many programs of solo and group works, including *Antique Epigrams, Four Preludes, Frames, Terrestrial Figure* (solos), *Three Fictitious Games, Winesburg Portraits, Outdoors Suite* (group works). Has danced in Broadway musicals and choreographed for summer theatres; also teaches. In 1964 received a $1500 award from the Ella Lyman Cabot Trust Fund to help in creating a performance and lecture-demonstration program for presentation in schools and colleges.

Dunham, Katherine, dancer, choreographer, director, ethnologist, b. Chicago, Ill.

Katherine Dunham leading her company in "Congo Pailette," a section of Bal Nègre, *a great work.*

1914; m. designer John Pratt. Ph.B. (Anthropology) and M.A., Univ. of Chicago; recipient of two Rosenwald Travel Fellowships and a Rockefeller Fellowship. Eminent exponent of the Negro dance. Established first school in Chicago (1931), where she was director of ballet for the Federal Theatre (1938). Dance director, choreographer and dancer for many motion pictures, revues, and musicals, of which the best known are *Cabin in the Sky* (musical, 1940), and *Stormy Weather* (motion picture, 1943). Organized her own company which for several years performed all over U.S. and Europe. At the end of a triumphal season in London, England, the British ballet critic Richard Buckle collaborated with photographer Roger Wood on a book of text and pictures of Dunham and her group. Returned for a N.Y. season (1950) after two years in Europe. Lived for several years in Haiti. Presented a new dance revue, *Bamboche* (1962), which included dancers from Africa, among them the Royal Dancers of the Court of the King of Morocco. She has contributed articles to many magazines, written an account of her experiences in Jamaica while on an anthropological field trip, *Journey to Accompong* (N.Y., 1946), and a third person autobiography of her childhood and youth, *A Touch of Innocence* (N.Y., 1959), as well as several short stories. Choreographer for the Metropolitan Opera production of *Aïda* (season 1963–64). Re-opened her school in N.Y. (1964). Chevalier–Legion d'Honneur & Merit, Haiti (1949); Commander (1959). Member, Women's Hon. Scientific Fraternity, Univ. of Chicago; Member, Royal Society of Anthropologists, London.

Duport, Louis (1781–1853), French dancer and principal rival of Auguste Vestris. Danced in Russia between 1808 and 1812 and was a sensational success in the ballets of Charles Didelot. Made his London debut in 1819. Retired with a great fortune and died in Paris. (See "The Duport Mystery," by Lillian Moore, *Dance Perspectives* No. 7.)

Dupré, David (David José), Brazilian dancer, b. São Paulo, 1930. Began studies in 1946 at the Ballet School of the Teatro Municipal, Rio de Janeiro, with Marilia Franco. Danced in Ballet Society with Tatiana Leskova (1948); Conjunto Coreografico Brasiliero (1950), with Vaslav Veltchek. Joined Teatro Municipal (1951), dancing first roles. In 1955 danced with Ballet do IV Centenário of São Paulo. Went to Paris to study with Nora Kiss and Serge Peretti (1955–56). Upon his return to Rio de Janeiro resumed his roles at Teatro Municipal, which include most classic and romantic ballets. Presented his first ballet at the Workshop of Teatro Municipal, Dec., 1961: *Scènes de Ballet* to Igor Stravinsky's score. Won the Nijinsky Contest as the Best Brazilian Dancer (1961).

Dupré, Louis (1697–1774), French dancer noted for his grace and style, the prototype of the danseur noble. He was known as "Le Grand Dupré." At the age of sixty he danced in *Les Fêtes Venitiennes* and still displayed great finish and fine style. He was the teacher of Jean Georges Noverre.

Durang, John (1768–1822), American dancer, b. York, Pa. Appeared with the Old American Company of Lewis Hallam in Phila. and N.Y. (1784–96), dancing hornpipes and in harlequinades and also appearing in full ballet productions. Married Mary McEwen, a dancer and actress. Engaged in 1796 to direct pantomimes for circus troupe at Ricketts' Amphitheatre, Phila. In 1800 joined stock company of the Chestnut Street Theatre, remaining there till he retired in 1819. His children were all trained as dancers. His son Charles was also an actor and teacher and was the author of *The Ball-room Bijou,* and *Art of Dancing* (ca. 1855). Charles Durang died in 1870.

Dust Bowl Ballads. Two solos by Sophie Maslow; music: Woody Guthrie ("I Ain't Got No Home in This World Any More"; "Dusty Old Dust"); costume: Edythe Gilfond. First prod.: May, 1941.

Dying Swan, The. Solo dance created by Michel Fokine for Anna Pavlova; music: Camille Saint-Saëns "Le Cygne," from his *Le Carnaval des Animaux*. First danced by Pavlova at a special performance in the Hall of Noblemen, St. Petersburg, 1905, given by the artists of the Maryinsky Theatre for a charitable cause. The costume was designed by Léon Bakst. This is the dance for which Pavlova was best known, and it belongs to her alone. However, other great ballerinas, among them Alicia Markova, Galina Ulanova, and Maya Plisetskaya, have given their own notable interpretations.

Dynamism, according to John Martin, one of the four basic principles of the modern dance, the other three being substance, Metakinesis and form.

E Minor. Ballet in 1 act; chor.: Arnold Spohr; music: Frédéric Chopin's Piano Concerto in E minor; décor: John Hirsch; costumes: Grant Marshall. First prod.: Royal Winnipeg Ballet at Playhouse Theatre, Winnipeg, Jan. 15, 1959, with Marilyn Young, Fredric Strobel and supporting dancers. An interpretation of the music in a free classical style.

Eames, Marian, contemporary writer and editor, b. Buffalo, N.Y. Educated in private schools. Studied acting at Clare Tree Major Dramatic School, American Laboratory Theatre. Danced as a child with Isadora Duncan and the Denishawn School; studied with Mikhail Mordkin and Serge Nadejdin. Associate, Museum of Modern Art, N.Y. (1944–46); editor, *Dance Index* (1946–49), director *Life Magazine* Filmstrips (1949–53). Currently freelancing; has done a number of small publications for the Dance Collection of the N.Y. Public Library, Library and Museum of the Performing Arts in Lincoln Center.

Eaters of Darkness. Ballet in 1 act. Chor. and book: Walter Gore; music: Benjamin Britten's *Variations on a Theme of Frank Bridge;* décor: Hein Heckroth. First prod.: Frankfurt State Opera Ballet, Jan. 29, 1958 (as *Die Im Schatten Leben*), with Paula Hinton (The Bride), Paul Herbinger and Wolff Winter. Revived by Walter Gore for his London Ballet at Edinburgh Festival, Aug. 14, 1961; décor: James Deakin. A young bride is wrongfully committed to an asylum by her husband and becomes insane as a result. The ballet is also in the repertoire of American Festival Ballet with Christine Hennessy dancing the role of The Bride.

Ebony Concerto. See JAZZ CONCERT.

Ecart, Grand, balletic version of the acrobatic split. Stand in 5th position, R. ft. in front. Slide R. ft. forward diagonally and L. ft. backward diagonally until both legs are stretched flat on the floor. The concluding step of the Can-Can, the term came into being in 1861. A good example of grand écart is in the finale of the Can-Can for the ballerina and corps de ballet in Leonide Massine's *Gaîté Parisienne.*

Ecarté, in ballet, pose in which one leg is raised at an oblique angle to the body and the body is at an oblique angle to the spectators. It is one of the expressions used to define the position of the dancer's body in relation to the audience, the others being en face, de face, croisé, and effacé.

Echappé (lit. escaped), in ballet, a movement from a closed to an open position. Technique: Échappé sauté—start 5th pos., R ft. front; demi-plié and jump off both feet, opening into 2nd pos. in the air;

land in 2nd pos.; with another jump return to 5th pos., demi-plié. Échappé sur les pointes—Start 5th pos., R ft. front; demi-plié and slide and open both feet sidewards to 2nd pos. on pointes; return to 5th pos. à terre, demi-plié. Échappé may be done en face, croisé, effacé, battu, et al. In the coda of the famous pas de deux of Odile and the Prince in the ballroom scene of *Swan Lake* (in the Royal Ballet version), Odile performs a series of échappés traveling backwards.

Echoes of Trumpets. Ballet in 1 act; chor. and book: Antony Tudor; music: Bohuslav Martinu's *Fantaisies Symphoniques;* décor: Birger Bergling. First prod.: Royal Swedish Ballet, Royal Theatre, Stockholm, Sept. 20, 1963, with Gerd Andersson, Svante Lindberg, Annette Wiedersheim-Paul, Kari Sylwan, Mario Mengarelli. The total destruction of the village of Lidice, Czechoslovakia, during World War II, following the slaying of the Nazi governor, Heydrich, is the dramatic source of this ballet, the first original work staged by Tudor for the Royal Swedish Ballet. A man returns to the ruined village to seek his beloved. He is captured and executed. The girl dances a lament with his dead body. Although there is this thread of story, *Echoes of Trumpets* is basically a group work.

Revived by the Metropolitan Opera Ballet, N.Y. in 1966 under the title *The Echoing of Trumpets.*

Ecossais, Ecossaise (Fr., lit. Scotch). 1. A sedate dance in 3/2 or 3/4 time. 2. A quick country-dance in 2/4 time.

Edinburgh International Ballet. A company under the direction of Peggy van Praagh and sponsored by the directors of the Edinburgh Festival for its twelfth anniversary (1958). Five different programs were presented between Aug. 25 and Sept. 1, the works being: *Circle of Love* (Birgit Cullberg), *Secrets* (John Cranko), *Night and Silence* (Walter Gore), *Concerto for Dancers* (Wendy Toye), *Les Fâcheuses Rencontres* (George Skibine), *Octet* (John Taras), *Dreams* (Dmitri Parlic), *Midsummer's Vigil* (Björn Holmgren), *The Seventh Sacrament* (Deryk Mendel), *La Belle Dame Sans Merci* (Andrée Howard), *Changements de Pieds* (Alan Carter), *The Great Peacock* (Peter Wright). It had been hoped to follow the Festival appearances with a London season but this was dropped and the company, recruited for the occasion with guest artists brought by the respective choreographers, did not outlive the Festival. However, *La Belle Dame Sans Merci* was briefly added to the repertoire of the Royal Ballet and *Night and Silence* became one of the most successful ballets in the reportoire of Gore's London Ballet.

Eduardova, Eugenia, 1882–1960, Russian ballerina and teacher. Was graduated from the Russian Imperial Ballet School in St. Petersburg in 1901; danced with the ballet company of the Maryinsky (now Kirov) Theatre until 1917, when she resigned and left Russia. Her greatest successes were in demi-caractère roles in which she had no peer. Outside Russia she danced with the Anna Pavlova company in London, Berlin, and on tour. In 1920 she settled in Berlin where she opened a ballet school and married Joseph Lewitan, the Russian-born editor of the German magazine *Der Tanz.* During the fifteen years Mme. Eduardova taught in her school she molded most of the principal German ballet dancers now active, as well as a number of outstanding teachers. She also contributed substantially to the professional education of several German choreographers. In 1935 Mme. Eduardova and her husband left Germany and settled in Paris, where she continued to teach. In 1947 they moved to N.Y., where she taught for a short while.

Edwards, Leslie, English dancer, ballet master and teacher, b. Teddington, 1916. Studied ballet with Marie Rambert, Margaret Craske, Stanislas Idzikowski, Alexandre Volinine, Vera Volkova, et al. Member of Ballet Rambert (1935–37). Joined Vic-Wells Ballet in its early days and has remained with the organization ever since, being currently a principal character dancer and mime with the Royal Ballet. His very large repertoire over the years includes the King (*Donald of the Burthens*), Magician (*Noctambules*), King (*Prince of the Pagodas*), Thomas (*La Fille Mal Gardée*), (all creations); The Charlatan (*Petrouchka*), Red King (*Checkmate*) and, in the classic repertoire, von Rothbart (*Swan Lake*), Catalbutte (*The Sleeping Beauty*), Hilarion (*Giselle*). He teaches mime at the Royal Ballet School and company classes for the Royal Ballet and is also one of the company's rehearsers, becoming a member of the staff in 1958. Guest teacher, Wilderness Camp, Canada (1954–61); guest director and teacher of the Washington Ballet (1962). Has danced in and choreographed for British television and appeared on American television.

Effacé, in ballet, pose of the body when it is at an angle to the audience and working leg is extended away from the body, not crossing it in the spectators' line of vision. Effacé may be en avant, en arrière, à terre, or en l'air.

Egk, Werner, German composer; b. Auchsesheim, Bavaria, 1901. Studied music in Augsburg and Frankfurt. Conductor of the Berlin Staatsoper (1936–41); director of the Berlin College of Music (Hochschule fur Musik, 1950–53). His compositions for ballet include *Joan von Zarissa* (1940), *Abraxas* (1948), *A Summer Day* (1950), *The Chinese Nightingale* (1953), *Danza* (1960).

Eglevsky, André, premier danseur and teacher; b. Moscow, 1917; American citizen since 1939; m. Leda Anchutina. Began to study ballet for health reasons when a small boy, first with Maria Nevelska in

André Eglevsky in the coda of the pas de deux of The Nutcracker.

Nice, later with Lubov Egorova, Mathilde Kchessinska, Alexandre Volinine (Paris), Nicholas Legat (London), and still later at School of American Ballet (New York). Joined Col. de Basil's Ballet Russe de Monte Carlo when only fourteen, and six months later was dancing leading roles in *Swan Lake,* Act 2, *Les Sylphides, Les Présages,* et al. His dozen or so perfectly controlled slow pirouettes in the last named always caused a sensation. After a season with Leon Woicikowski's company (1935), he joined the René Blum Ballets de Monte Carlo (1936), creating the Young Lover (*L'Epreuve d'Amour*), and Leader of the Jesters, and Leader of the Demons (Michel Fokine's *Don Juan*). Came to U.S. as a permanent resident (1937). Premier danseur American Ballet

(1937–38); Ballet Russe de Monte Carlo (1939–42), Ballet (now American Ballet) Theatre (1942–43 and 1945); he also danced a season with Ballet International (1944) for which he created the title role in Massine's *Mad Tristan,* and choreographed *Sentimental Colloquy;* danced with Leonide Massine's Ballet Russe Highlights (summer, 1945). For Ballet Theatre he created Paris (*Helen of Troy*) and danced Albrecht (*Giselle*), Prince (*Swan Lake,* Act 2), title role *Apollo, Blue Bird* pas de deux, *Black Swan, Nutcracker, Don Quixote* pas de deux, et al. With Original Ballet Russe (1946–47), *Grand Ballet du Marquis de Cuevas* (1947–50) repeating the title role in Leonide Massine's *Mad Tristan* (now called *Tristan Fou*) and dancing the classic repertoire. Joined New York City Ballet early in 1951, remaining until 1958. During that period George Balanchine staged many works which displayed Eglevsky's great virtuosity, among them *Pas de Trois* (Minkus), in which he performed the famous single cabriole during which he appeared to be hanging for seconds in the air; the revival of *Apollo, Swan Lake* (Act 2; the Balanchine version with a variation taken from a piece of music in Act 3, never actually used in the Russian versions), *Caracole, Scotch Symphony, Roma, Pas de Trois* (Glinka), *Pas de Dix.* He also danced brilliantly in the *Sylvia* pas de deux and in Balanchine's *The Nutcracker.* The Sugar Plum Fairy Cavalier was intended for him but an injury prevented his appearing during the first season. He left New York City Ballet after its Oriental and Australian tour in 1958. Opened his own school in that year in Massapequa, L.I. He has a small group which gives performances, sometimes with special guest artists. He appeared with it in its early days but he now confines himself to directing it and to teaching in his own school and at School of American Ballet, N.Y. Danced with Melissa Hayden in Charles Chaplin's film *Limelight* (1952).

Egorova, Lubov (Princess Nikita Troubetzkoy), Russian ballerina, b. St. Petersburg, 1880. Pupil of the Imperial Ballet School of the Maryinsky Theatre, St. Petersburg, graduated into the company, was promoted to coryphée in 1898 and to ballerina in 1912. Her ballets included *Giselle, Raymonda, Sleeping Beauty, Swan Lake.* Left Russia in 1917. Was one of the Auroras of the 1921 Diaghilev Ballets Russes production of *The Sleeping Beauty* at the Alhambra Theatre, London, alternating this role with that of the Lilac Fairy. Opened her Paris ballet studio in 1923. Formed a company, Ballets de la Jeunesse in 1937 in which her young pupils, who included Tatiana Leskova, Genevieve Moulin, Vassili and Oleg Tupine and George Skibine made their debuts. She revived *Aurora's Wedding* for the Royal Danish Ballet and taught briefly in London but otherwise never left her Paris studio. Among her pupils are Solange Schwarz, Janine Charrat, Ethery Pagava, and many other famous French dancers. Prince Troubetzkoy died Aug. 31, 1963. On Dec. 19, 1964, Mme. Egorova was awarded the rank Chevalier de l'Ordre des Arts et Lettres by the French Government.

8 Clear Places. Modern dance work; chor.: Erick Hawkins; commissioned music: Lucia Dlugoszewski; designs: Ralph Dorazio. First prod.: Hunter College Playhouse, N.Y., Oct. 8, 1960, with Erick Hawkins and Barbara Tucker. The composer, Lucia Dlugoszewski, kneels downstage surrounded by her hand-made instruments: boxes with pebbles, handbells, tissue paper to be torn or crushed, Japanese wind glasses, and so on. The dances (with lower case titles) are: north star, inner feet of the summer fly, they snowing, etc.

Electronics. Ballet in 3 movements; chor.: George Balanchine; music: an electronic tape score by Remi Gassmann in collaboration with Oskar Sala; décor: David Hays. First prod.: New York City Ballet, City Center, N.Y., Mar. 22, 1961, with Diana Adams, Jacques d'Amboise, Violette Verdy, Edward Villella and corps. The first electronic score for ballet in this country was also the first for which all of the sounds were artificially created, i.e., without the use of any kind of musical instruments, natural sources or sine-tone generators. The music and the sparkling, stalactite-like scenery, also from synthetic materials, dominated the choreography and dwarfed the dancers who, although the ballet was themeless, appeared to be engaged in some kind of struggle which is never actually resolved.

Elektra. Ballet in 1 act; chor.: Robert Helpmann; music: Malcolm Arnold; décor: Arthur Boyd. First prod.: Royal Ballet, at Royal Opera House, Covent Garden, London, Mar. 26, 1963, with Nadia Nerina (Elektra), David Blair (Orestes). A violently theatrical re-telling of the famous Greek myth.

Elevation, the capacity of a dancer to jump, leap and perform movements in the air. Elevation consists of two equally important component parts: (a) elevation proper, which is the ability to jump, to tear oneself away from the ground; and (b) ballon, which is the ability to remain in the air for a length of time. A well developed elevation makes for high jumps, a good ballon lets a dancer perform movements in the air, makes him appear to soar.

Elfes, Les. Ballet in 1 act; chor.: Michel Fokine; music: Felix Mendelssohn's overture to *A Midsummer Night's Dream* and Violin Concerto. First prod.: Fokine Ballet, Metropolitan Opera House, N.Y., Feb. 26, 1924. Revived with costumes by Christian Bérard for René Blum's Ballet Russe de Monte Carlo at Monte Carlo (1937). Revived by Ballet Russe de Monte Carlo for the 1942–43 season with Mia Slavenska and Igor Youskevitch in leading roles. Themeless but depicting the half-human, half-insect creatures of the forest disporting in the moonlight.

Ellis, Angela (previously Anne Ashley, Angela Dukes), English dancer and teacher, daughter of Dame Marie Rambert and the late Ashley Dukes; b. London; m. David Ellis. Educated privately. Studied dance with her mother and Vera Volkova, Victor Gsovsky, Margaret Craske. Dancer, Ballet Rambert (1943–47). Co-founder Ballet Workshop, London (1951). Associate director and principal teacher, Ballet Rambert School.

Ellis, David, English dancer, choreographer, teacher, b. London, 1921; m. Angela Dukes. Educated at Westminster School and University College, Oxford (with a degree in medicine). Studied ballet with Vera Volkova, Marie Rambert, Victor Gsovsky. Member Ballet Rambert since 1946, currently associate director of that company. Choreographed *Le Diable s'Amuse,* for Ballet Guild (1945–46); *Last Train,* for Anglo-Russian Ballet (1945). Co-founder Ballet Workshop (1951); director, Mercury Theatre Trust (1951). Choreographer, Glyndebourne Opera (1957–58).

Ellis, Richard, dancer and teacher, b. London, 1918, m. Christine Du Boulay. Studied dance with Grace and Lillie Cone, Ninette de Valois, Margaret Craske, Stanislas Idzikowski, Anna Pruzina, Anton Dolin and, later, Vera Volkova. Made his debut as a child actor in repertory (1932), and after appearances in cabaret with Anton Dolin's small company and with Camargo Society joined Sadler's Wells (now Royal) Ballet (1933) rising to soloist rank and dancing a large repertoire of classic and modern roles including Mercury (*The Gods Go A'Begging*), Black Knight (*Checkmate*), Gemini Twin (*Horoscope*), Lawyer (*Prospect Before Us*) (all creations). Volunteered for the Royal Navy (1940), was commissioned a Lieutenant (1942) and demobilized (1945), having been mentioned in dispatches for services on D Day. Returned to Sadler's Wells, creating Officer (*Mam'zelle Angot*), Husband (*Don Juan*), and dancing Summer Fairy Cavalier and Hairdresser (*Cinderella*), Catalbutte, Russian Prince (*The Sleeping Beauty*) among many other roles. Emigrated to U.S. (1952) and taught in Chicago, opening own school in 1954. Co-director, with his wife of the school and of the Illinois Ballet (founded 1959) which gives performances in the Chicago area.

Elssler, Fanny (1810–1884). Fanny Elssler, one of the most glorious names in ballet, was born in Vienna, the daughter of Karl Ludwig Ferdinand Elssler, a valet and copyist for the composer Franz Joseph Haydn. Apparently Haydn was not too generous with Elssler, because Fanny's mother had to take in washing to help support their six children.

However, Haydn did show some interest in his valet's family: he sent the two youngest daughters, Theresa and Fanny, to study ballet. Fanny took lessons from Herschelt and later from Aumer, the ballet master of the Kaernthertor Theatre in Vienna. At the age of nine, after three years of study, she was taken into the corps de ballet of the Vienna Hoftheater.

The ballet master of the Hoftheater was Filippo Taglioni, the father and teacher of Maria Taglioni. Fanny, whose lifelong rival she was later to become, made her debut in 1822 in *La Reception d'une Jeune Nymphe à la Cour de Terpsichore,* a ballet specially staged for the occasion by Filippo Taglioni. Fanny left the Hoftheater a short while later to appear in Naples; her next meeting with Maria Taglioni did not take place until 1833, when both dancers were engaged to appear at the King's Theatre in London.

During the intervening eleven years Fanny Elssler had become famous and had grown used to being the first dancer wherever she appeared. When she saw Taglioni dance, however, she realized that she was not the only great dancer, that here was a rival with whom it would not be easy to compete. Elssler's success at the King's Theatre was great, but she could not break through or even approach the popularity of the older dancer.

With the two dancers appearing simultaneously, the basic difference between them came to the fore. Taglioni was light, ethereal, sylphlike; Elssler was human, close to earth, voluptuous. Taglioni was a vision of a demi-goddess, cool and detached; Elssler a beautiful woman who made use of every charm she possessed to attract the audience. The conservative London public was not used to Elssler's fire and abandon; it seemed to prefer Taglioni's abstract style.

However, Dr. Véron, the director of the Paris Opéra, who visited London and saw Elssler on the stage, thought differently. He was certain that Paris would love Elssler for the very reason that she was so different from Taglioni. Her dancing would suit the French temperament much better than the crystalline aloofness of Taglioni. Besides, he had an axe to grind.

Conscious of the power she wielded over the audience and certain of lavish support from the Paris press, Taglioni's demands on the management grew more unreason-

Fanny Elssler (from a lithograph by Henri Grevedon, Paris, 1835.)

able every season, her whims created situations difficult to cope with. Dr. Véron had been looking for someone whose presence in the Paris ballet would help deflate Taglioni. After watching Elssler for several weeks, he decided that she was just the dancer he was looking for and lost no time in offering her a contract. Elssler accepted Dr. Véron's offer, but her first action upon her arrival in Paris was to begin a three-month period of intensive study with the celebrated Auguste Vestris.

Her debut at the Opéra took place in Sept., 1834. She danced the title role of Alcine in Jean Coralli's ballet *La Tempête,* which was based on Shakespeare's

The Tempest. She was an immediate success and at her very first appearance divided Paris into two camps: the Elsslerites and the Taglionists. The poet Théophile Gautier, an ardent balletomane and until then a staunch supporter of Taglioni, came out with his famous article in which he compared the two dancers. He said:

"Fanny Elssler's dancing is quite different from the academic idea, it has a particular character which sets her apart from all other dancers. It is not the aerial and virginal grace of Taglioni, it is something more human, more appealing to the senses. Mlle. Taglioni is a Christian dancer . . . she flies like a spirit in the midst of transparent clouds of white muslin . . . she resembles a happy angel. Fanny is quite a pagan dancer; she reminds one of the muse Terpsichore, tambourine in hand, her tunic exposing her thigh, caught up with a golden clasp . . . After all, dancing consists of nothing more than the art of displaying beautiful shapes in graceful positions and the development from them of lines agreeable to the eye; it expresses the passions. Mlle. Fanny Elssler has fully realized this truth . . ."

Fanny Elssler brought to the ballet what we now call the character dance: the fiery Hungarian, Polish, Spanish, and Russian dances; and in her dancing made use, for the first time, of the entire body. She realized very clearly that her success lay mainly in the character dance, and she selected for her repertoire ballets in which the character dance played an important part. Coralli's *Le Diable Boiteux,* produced in 1836, contained the "Cachucha"; Mazilier's *La Gypsy,* produced in 1839, was made famous by "La Cracovienne."

In 1838 Taglioni accepted an invitation to dance with the St. Petersburg Imperial Ballet, and Elssler remained the sole star of the Paris Opéra. Her popularity was greater than ever, but she resented the fact that people considered her the greatest character dancer and reserved for Taglioni the title of the greatest classic ballerina. She wished to prove to Paris and the world that she could be the greatest classic dancer, too. Thus, she decided to appear in *La Sylphide,* the ballet created for Taglioni by her father, and so closely identified with Taglioni that the dancer was often referred to as La Sylphide.

Contrary to all advice, Elssler appeared in *La Sylphide* in Sept. 1838, and failed. Gautier was the only critic who found it possible to say a kind word about the performance, everybody else openly and frankly declared it a fiasco.

About a year and a half after her debut in *La Sylphide,* Fanny Elssler left for America where she danced with great success through July, 1842. For an account of Elssler's success in America see ELSSLER IN AMERICA.

Fanny Elssler continued to dance until she was forty-one. She appeared with undiminished success in London, Vienna, Berlin, Brussels, Budapest, St. Petersburg, Moscow, and Naples. She was welcomed everywhere except at the Paris Opéra, where the management could not forget nor forgive her breach of contract in connection with the American tour. Her official leave of absence from the Opéra had expired when she was offered an extension of the tour. She was having too good a time in America to return to Paris and so told the management of the Opéra.

Her last performance took place on June 21, 1851, in Jules Perrot's ballet *Faust,* in Vienna.

She retired, as she had planned, while still young, graceful, and beautiful. During her career she had accumulated a fortune reported to have been in excess of one million dollars.

Fanny Elssler died in her native Vienna on Nov. 27, 1884, at the age of seventy-four.

Elssler in America.

In 1840, Fanny Elssler came to America for a three-month visit and stayed two years. The eighth President of the U.S., Martin Van Buren, and his cabinet received her in an official audience; Congress adjourned every evening she danced in Washington because most members attended her performances and no quorum could be made; at a formal banquet in the Capitol her health was drunk from a dance slipper; a carpet was stretched in front of the Park Theatre in New York for her to walk on.

In *The Letters and Journal of Fanny Elssler,* published in America in 1845, the dancer wrote under a Nov., 1839, dateline:

"I am about to cross the Atlantic and proceed to America! . . . I cannot look upon this strange intention as other than a mad freak that has seized my fancy in a thoughtless moment . . . My sober judgement could never have brought me to such a resolution . . . My professional career has reached its zenith; here I am, sitting securely on an operatic throne, that has dazzled my eyes and fired my ambition since my girlhood . . . Never was an artiste more completely seated in public sympathy, undisturbed by rivalry, unassailed by critics . . ."

This was not, however, the full truth. Elssler's position in the Opéra had been seriously shaken because of the failure of *La Sylphide* (see ELSSLER, FANNY). At the end of the same letter she writes:

". . . I do taste of sours as well as of sweets, for these messieurs of the press often write rudely in order to dispel one's fanciful dreams, and so melt down to the chilling reality of a helpless subjection to their invincible domination."

On Apr. 15, 1840, Fanny Elssler boarded the Great Western at Bristol, England, and sailed for America. She was accompanied by her manager Henry Wickoff, her cousin Katy Prinster, and two dancers —James Sylvain, whose real name was Sullivan, and a young lady whose name is variously reported as Mlle. Arraline, Jardaines, and Jardienne.

The crossing was rough but uneventful except for one incident. Fanny Elssler had taken with her all her jewelry, and one evening she wore most of it for a gala dinner given in her honor by the captain of the ship. A sailor decided to rob her and a few nights later crept into her cabin, knife in hand. Fanny had not yet retired. Taken by surprise, she stepped back and not knowing how else to defend herself, she took a preparation and did a turn during which she hit him with her extended leg with such force that he fell to the floor. It was later discovered that he was seriously injured; a few days later he died.

Fanny Elssler landed in New York on May 3rd, and took up residence at the American Hotel, close to the Park Theatre, where she was to dance. The Park Theatre was located in Park Row, near what is now the southern approach to the Brooklyn Bridge.

The newspapers gave Elssler a hearty welcome. Everyone who had ever seen her dance in Europe thought it necessary to write to the papers about his impressions. Music and drama critics tried to evaluate Elssler's talent, basing their opinions on European clippings and information cheerfully supplied by her manager, Henry Wickoff.

Letters of introduction from Parisian acquaintances opened the doors of society for her. Invitations to dinners, parties, teas followed one another in a steady stream. President Van Buren's son John established himself as a more or less permanent escort, and the brilliant financier August Belmont offered to act as her financial adviser, an offer which Elssler gratefully accepted. Reporters followed her every step and described everything they saw in the florid style of the 'Forties.

In spite of the whirl of social activities Elssler devoted most of her time to the selection of a corps de ballet and practice. Today one can come to New York and assemble a fine corps de ballet within a few weeks. In 1840 it was more difficult, and Elssler had to be content with what she could find. However, James Sylvain did the best he could under the circumstances, and Fanny Elssler's American debut took place on May 14th. She danced the pas seul "La Cracovienne" and Coralli's ballet *La Tarentule*.

The next day newspapers could not find enough adjectives to describe Elssler, her dancing, the reception and reactions of the audience. The spectators went wild, and the Park Theatre was sold out during the entire two-week engagement. It is reported that the box office receipts reached the unheard-of sum of twenty thousand dollars, of which Elssler received seven thousand. No matter what Elssler danced and how she danced it, the ovations were always the same. *La Sylphide* was as successful as *Tarentule,* and flowers filled the stage every night.

It was during these two weeks at the Park Theatre that Elsslermania, which was later to sweep the country and last for two solid years, received its impetus. The first manifestation of it was given by a few young men who unharnessed Elssler's horses and pulled her carriage from the theatre to the hotel. The crowd which collected nightly at the stage door joined in the fun, and a tradition was established.

A week in Philadelphia followed the New York engagement. When she appeared at the old Chestnut Street Theatre (between 6th and 7th Streets) for the first time, the Philadelphians knew exactly what to do.

Ellsler opened with *Tarentule* and later in the week gave *La Gypsy, Natalie, La Sylphide,* and *Le Dieu et la Bayadère,* changing the bill apparently every day. The Philadelphia success was in no way less clamorous than that of N.Y.

As the tour continued, music publishers decided that it would be a good idea to print up a few thousand copies of the music to which Elssler had danced. Within ten days of publication they sold out all the sheet music they had printed, and had to begin publishing on a larger scale. "Cachucha," "La Cracovienne," "La Mazurka," "La Smolenska," and many other numbers flooded the country.

Photography was just about a year old at that time so there wasn't much it could do for Elssler, or Elssler for it. But pen and ink artists produced many Elssler portraits, and very soon thousands of lithographs were snatched up by the public. The whiskey industry paid its tribute to Elssler by including her in the series of portrait-bottles which were in great vogue in the 'Forties. One side of these bottles contained a more or less accurate representation of a notable person, produced in relief. Elssler was pictured in a full length dance pose. Shirt studs bearing the likeness of Elssler were brought out by an enterprising jeweler. They were made in the form of a pillbox about an inch in diameter and a quarter of an inch thick, backed by metal and covered with glass. The little box contained a figure of a dancer, supposedly Elssler.

In Baltimore, which she visited next, the demand for tickets was so great that the smart theatre owner placed them on auction and sold them to the highest bidders. After the performance, Baltimorians not only unharnessed her horses and pulled her carriage to her hotel, but went N.Y. one better by lifting Elssler on their shoulders and carrying her into the lobby. Not to be outdone by other cities, stately Richmond, Va., greeted Elssler with tolling bells and salutes from cannons.

At West Point, which Elssler visited without her company, appearing only in a divertissement, the Academy staged a full dress parade in her honor.

Fanny Elssler's first American tour ended in August with a repeat engagement in N.Y. By that time her official leave of absence from the Paris Opéra had expired, but she was having much too good a time in America to think of going back to Paris. Her second American tour lasted more than eight months, covered practically every principal city in the U.S. and took her to Havana, Cuba.

During her two-years' stay in America Essler appeared, in addition to the already mentioned ballets and solo numbers, in *La Somnambule, La Rose Animée* and *La Fée et le Chevalier*. While in Cuba she composed a very successful number, "El Zapateado de Cadiz," which fitted well her "El Jales de Jerez" which she brought from Spain.

Cheered and waved, Fanny Elssler left the U.S. on Aug. 16, 1842, in the Caledonia, which sailed from Boston.

It is surprising to note that her unprecedented and unrepeated success notwithstanding, Fanny Elssler had practically no influence on the dance in this country. Ballet in America after Elssler's tours remained exactly in the same state of artistic poverty as it had been before her arrival. As before, it continued to be considered something between tightrope walking and fancy dancing. It is true that for a year or so provincial dancing masters continued to teach the Cachucha, Mazurka, Cracovienne, "as danced by Fanny Elssler," but this was the only manifestation of Elssler's influence, and it was soon forgotten.

Elssler, Theresa (1808–1878), dancer, sister of Fanny Elssler. She was an excellent dancer, but very tall and strong. She often danced with her sister and frequently appeared *en travesti,* partnering and supporting Fanny. She staged several numbers and short ballets for her sister. She became the morganatic wife of Prince Adalbert of Prussia. The Prince's cousin, King Wilhelm I of Prussia, subsequently conferred upon Theresa the title Baroness von Barnim.

Elvin, Violetta (Prokhorova), ballerina, b. Moscow, 1924. Studied at Bolshoi Ballet School with Agrippina Vaganova, graduating in 1942. Ballerina, Tashkent State Theatre (1943) rejoining Bolshoi Ballet in Kuibyshev to which it was evacuated during World War II (1944), and was promoted to soloist on the company's return to Moscow. Emigrated to England with her first husband, Harold Elvin (later adopting his name professionally), in 1945, and made her debut with Sadler's

Violetta Elvin, Russian-born former ballerina of the Sadler's Wells (now Royal) Ballet, 1946–56.

Wells (now Royal) Ballet in *Blue Bird* pas de deux (with Alexis Rassine), Feb. 21, 1946, the second night after the re-opening of Royal Opera House, Covent Garden with the full-length *Sleeping Beauty*. Subsequently danced Aurora in that ballet, Odette-Odile (*Swan Lake*), *Giselle,* created Summer in Frederick Ashton's *Cinderella,* Lykanion (*Daphnis and Chloe*), Water (*Homage to the Queen*), La Favorita (*Veneziana*), danced the Miller's Wife (revival of *The Three-Cornered Hat*), and a large repertoire. Guest artist at Teatro alla Scala, Milan (1952). Gave her farewell performance in *The Sleeping Beauty* June 23, 1956. Married Fernando Saveressi and now lives in Italy.

Embattled Garden. Modern dance work; chor.: Martha Graham; music: Carlos Surinach; scenery: Isamu Noguchi. First prod.: Martha Graham and Dance Company, at Adelphi Theatre, N.Y., Apr. 3, 1958, presented by B. de Rothschild Foundation, with Matt Turney (Lilith), Yuriko (Eve), Bertram Ross

(Adam), Glen Tetley (Stranger). A satirical glimpse of the Garden of Eden. In subsequent seasons, Paul Taylor took over the role of the Stranger.

Emblen, Ronald, English dancer, b. Port Said, Egypt, 1933. Studied at Sadler's Wells School and with Anna Severskaya. Began his professional career with International Ballet (1951–54) and has been with Walter Gore Ballet (1954), London's Festival Ballet (1955), Western Theatre Ballet (1958). Went to Australia with Margot Fonteyn's Concert Ballet (1962). Returned as leading dancer with London's Festival Ballet, dancing Jester (*The Snow Maiden*), title role (*Witch Boy*), Dr. Coppelius (*Coppélia*), Sailor (*London Morning*), leading male role (*Symphony for Fun*). Joined Royal Ballet in 1963 dancing Mother Simone (*La Fille Mal Gardée*) and creating the Great Deity (Kenneth MacMillan's *La Création du Monde*), among other roles.

Emboîté, Pas, in ballet, a boxed-in step, usually performed in a series, in which the feet are held as close together as possible. Technique—Start 5th pos. R ft. in front; demi-plié and jump upward off both feet, bringing L leg front, knee slightly bent; land on R ft., keeping L leg bent at knee. Emboîté on pointes—Stand on pointes in 5th pos. and pass R ft. in front of L in 5th pos., then L ft. in front of R in 5th pos. and proceed. Emboîté en tournant—same as simple emboîté except one complete turn is done with two emboîtés; working ft. is brought sur le cou-de-pied. A series of emboîté en tournant is usually performed on the diagonal.

Emery, Fernando, Argentine journalist, dance critic and lecturer, b. 1904. He studied both law and for a diplomatic career, but chose journalism instead. Took ballet lessons from Boris Romanov and Yelena Smirnova to get first hand knowledge of technique. His articles have appeared in *El Hogar, Mundo Argentino* and *Sinfonia* in Buenos Aires, *Ballet* (Líma, Peru) and *Toute la Danse* (Paris). Has lectured on classic ballet and modern dance throughout Argentina; has had radio and television programs devoted to dance. At present dance critic of the newspaper, *Correo de la Tarde,* and the magazines *Lyra* and *El Mundo de la Danza,* all in Buenos Aires. Teaches History of Dance at the Institute Superior de Arte de Teatro Colón and at the Escuela Nacional de Danza de Buenos Aires.

Emperor Jones. Modern dance work; chor.: José Limón; music: Heitor Villa Lobos; décor: Kim Swados; costumes: Pauline Lawrence. First prod.: José Limón Dance Company at Empire State Music Festival, Ellenville, N.Y., July 12, 1956, with José Limón (Emperor Jones), Lucas Hoving (White Man) and company. The Eugene O'Neill play told in dance terms which show us the Emperor Jones at the moment of his downfall, remembering his days of slavery and triumph and now undergoing the degradation of pursuit and capture. Commissioned by Empire State Music Festival.

Empire Ballets, a name coined by the English writer and publisher Cyril W. Beaumont for the series of ballet performances given at the Empire Theatre, London, during the years 1887 to 1914 which, with the Alhambra Ballets, were the only ballet performances in England of the period. The Austrian ballerina and choreographer Katti Lanner was the first ballet mistress of the theatre. Among the premiers danseurs during the first ten years of the Empire Ballets was Enrico Cecchetti. In 1897 Adeline Genée made her London debut at the Empire Theatre and remained its ballerina for ten years. In 1907 Lydia Kyasht and Adolph Bolm made their London debuts there. As a footnote to ballet at the Empire Theatre, a ballet company was formed in 1951 (with Alan Carter as ballet master) and presented short programs of ballet between feature films to which the theatre had long since been given over. See THE EMPIRE BALLET by Ivor Guest, publ. by The Society for Theatre Research, London, 1962.

En Arrière, in ballet, backward, or in back of.

En Avant, in ballet, forward, or in front of.

Enchaînement, in ballet, a chain of movements; a complete dance phrase, corresponding to a sentence in speech. As a sentence consists of words, so an enchaînement consists of pas, temps and poses.

Encore (Fr.), again. In the theatre a call for a repetition of the performance of a short number, used in U.S. and England; the French usually shout *Bis!*

En Dedans, in ballet, a term used to describe inward circular movements of legs or arms, such as fouetté en dedans, pirouette en dedans, etc. Compare with en dehors.

En Dehors, in ballet, term used to describe outward circular movement of legs or arms, such as fouetté en dehors, pirouette en dehors, etc. Compare with en dedans.

En Face, in ballet, facing spectators, body squarely forward.

Engel, Lehman, composer, b. Jackson, Miss., 1910. Attended College of Music and Conservatory, Cincinnati, awarded fellowship in composition, Juilliard Graduate School, three times winner of Antoinette Perry Award. Composed music for many of Martha Graham's early works (*Ceremonials, Ekstasis, Transitions, Marching Song, Imperial Gesture*), and for Charles Weidman, Doris Humphrey, Erick Hawkins, and others. Also composed incidental music for many plays, and is well known as a musical director and conductor on Broadway.

English Style, a phrase used to imply the style of ballroom dancing developed in England which has since found favor in many other countries of the Eastern Hemisphere. It has also been cultivated in several parts of the United States where, as a rule, it is known as International Style. It pays great attention to carriage and deportment and favors smooth gliding movements with appropriate rise and fall and contrary body movement. Its basic technique was developed shortly after World War I and is based on natural movement, the feet going forward in alignment and not turned out as in the old style. The style is seen at its best in the English slow foxtrot. Only this style is seen in competitive dancing. A full description of this style of dancing is given in textbooks by A. H. Franks, Victor Silvester, Alex Moore, Eve Tynegate Smith and Henry Jacques.

En Haut, in ballet, a high position of arms; identical to en couronne.

Enkelmann, Siegfried, German ballet photographer, b. 1905 in Russia. Has lived in Germany since 1921 and is a self-taught photographer in Berlin since 1931. Published the following collections of dance photographs in book form: *Tanzer Unserer Zeit* (*Dancers of Our Time*), 1936; *Schönheit im Tanz* (*Beauty in the Dance*), 1939; *Ballett in Deutschland* (*Ballet in Germany*), 1956; second edition, 1958; *Ballett in Deutschland II* (*Ballet in Germany II*), 1957; *Gisela Deege,* 1957; *Gert Reinholm,* 1957. Has also had a studio in Munich since 1960.

En l'Air. See AIR, EN L'.

E.N.S.A., Entertainment National Service Association, English equivalent of the American U.S.O. during World War II.

Sir Basil Dean, the English stage director and producer, was head of the organization.

Ensemble, in ballet, a group; dancers who appear in a group and, generally, not soloists. See CORPS DE BALLET.

Enters, Angna, dancer-mime, choreographer, painter, writer, b. New York City, 1907. Originator of her own distinctive form of dance and pantomime with which she has created nearly 300 characters, performing in U.S. and all over the world as The Theatre of Angna Enters since 1928. Performed an original pantomime, *Pagan Greece,* playing 13 different characters, at Metropolitan Museum, N.Y. (1938), the first theatre performance ever held in that museum. Has since performed in many other museums. She designs and executes all her own costumes. Has held exhibitions of her own paintings and sculpture in U.S., Canada and London since 1933, and has lectured on mime and working in the arts at many universities. Received a Guggenheim Fellowship for study in Greece (1934) and Egypt (1935). Has written many articles on mime for various magazines, also motion picture scripts for M.G.M. and Samuel Goldwyn, and is the author of *First Person Plural* (Stackpole, 1937), *Silly Girl* (Houghton Mifflin, 1944), *Among the Daughters* (Coward McCann N.Y., 1954, W. H. Allen, London, 1955), *Artist's Life* (Coward McCann, 1958, W. H. Allen, 1959). Artist in residence, Dallas Theatre Center and Baylor University (1961–62), Fellow at Center for Advanced Studies, Wesleyan University, Middletown (1962–63).

Angna Enters, American mime and dancer-choreographer.

Entrechat, in ballet, a movement in which the dancer crosses his legs repeatedly while in the air. There exist entrechat-trois, entrechat-quatre, entrechat-cinq, entrechat-six, entrechat-sept, entrechat-huit. The number following the word entrechat indicates the movements of each leg; thus, in entrechat-six, for instance, there are actually only three crossings, but six movements of the legs, hence the designation. Even-numbered entrechats are finished with both feet on the ground; in the odd-numbered entrechats, one foot remains in the air at the end of the movement. Entrechat-six is quite common in contemporary ballet; entrechat-sept is done more seldom. There is a series of entrechat-sept in the male *Blue Bird* variation in *Princess Aurora.* Entrechat-huit is done very rarely. One example of it is in Albrecht's variation in *Giselle* (Act 2) when this role is danced by Igor Youskevitch, Erik Bruhn and a few others. To count the actual crossings of the dancer's legs on the stage is impossible. There is, however, a way of knowing how many entrechats a dancer does: an entrechat-quatre and an entrechat-huit end with the same foot front with which it begins; and an entrechat-six ends with left foot front if it begins with right foot front, and vice versa. The difference between entrechat-quatre and entrechat-huit is noticeable without any special attention. The word entrechat is supposed to be derived from the Italian capra intercciata (lit. a bound or braided goat). The step does remind one of the jumps of a goat whose hind legs have been tied so that it cannot run away. Technique: Entrechat-quatre—start 5th pos. R ft. front; demi-plié and jump upward off both feet, opening feet slightly to 2nd pos. en l'air; beat calves together, R ft. back; land in 5th pos., demi-plié, R ft. front. Entrechat-six—same as entrechat-quatre except that calves beat together once more with R ft. in front, and land in 5th pos., L ft. front. Entrechat-huit—add one beat to entrechat-six. Entrechat-trois—same as royal, but land on one ft., other ft. sur le cou-de-pied, front or back. Entrechat-cinq—entrechat-quatre, landing on one ft. Entrechat-sept —entrechat-six, landing on one ft. There also exists, more or less theoretically, an entrechat-dix, i.e. five crossings of each leg. Ballet tradition has it that Nijinsky could do an entrechat-dix, not only in rehearsal or during a lesson, but on stage as well. But more insistent questioning reveals that not one of his colleagues interviewed had actually seen him do it. Vecheslav Svoboda, a graduate of the Moscow Ballet School and a soloist of the Bolshoi Ballet, told this writer that a classmate of his, Domashov, could do an entrechat-dix at almost any time, but had never dared to try it on stage. Domashov also used to do an entrechat-six on the way up and come down in fifth.

Entrée, in ballet, a dancer or group of dancers executing a number in a divertissement, or, more rarely, in a ballet.

Eoline, ou la Dryade. Ballet in 6 scenes; chor.: Jules Perrot; music: Cesare Pugni. First prod.: Her Majesty's Theatre, London, Mar. 8, 1845, with Lucile Grahn and Perrot in the leading roles. Given in St. Petersburg with new settings by Roller, Shishkov, Tchushkine, Wagner, Nov. 16, 1858 with Amalia Ferraris in the title role. A typical Romantic ballet, it is based on a Bohemian legend. The story tells of the dryad Eoline whose life as a mortal woman depends on the continued life of a great oak tree, of which she is the dryad. She is about to marry Edgar, whom she loves, when Rübezahl, whom she does not love, sets fire to the oak, and Eoline dies.

Épaulé (Fr., shouldered), in ballet, pose of body when one shoulder is turned forward, one shoulder back; head is turned with chin over forward shoulder. The changing from one shoulder to the other during the progression of steps (for example in a series of jetés) is typical of the beautiful Russian style which very rarely presents a dancer absolutely en face. American dancers and some Europeans pay much less attention to this aspect of technique.

Epaulement (Fr., lit. shouldering), in ballet the use of the shoulders in presenting a step to the audience. See ÉPAULÉ.

Episodes. Ballet in 2 unrelated parts; chor.: Martha Graham and George Balanchine; music: Anton Webern (for Graham: Passacaglia, Op. 1, and Six Pieces, Op. 6; for Balanchine: Symphony, Op. 21; Five Pieces, Op. 10; Concerto, Op. 24; Variations, Op. 30; Ricercata in 6 voices from Bach's *Musical Offering*); décor: David Hays. First prod.: New York City Ballet and Martha Graham and Dance Company, City Center, N.Y., May 14, 1959. The first part of *Episodes,* choreographed by Martha Graham, showed Mary, Queen of Scots, on her way to the scaffold, reliving her lifelong struggle with Queen Elizabeth of England. Martha Graham was Mary, and members of her company appearing with her were Bertram Ross (Bothwell), Helen McGehee, Ethel Winter, Linda Hodes, Akiko Kanda (The Four Marys), Gene McDonald, Richard Kuch, Dan Wagoner (Darnley, Rizzio, Chastelard), while Sallie Wilson of New York City Ballet, was Elizabeth. The second part was a series of dances, some the merest wisps, like the music, and all of them choreographic realization of the score, danced by Violette Verdy and Jonathan Watts, Diana Adams, and Jacques d'Amboise, Allegra Kent and Nicholas

Magallanes, Melissa Hayden and Francisco Moncion. The modern dancer, Paul Taylor, was introduced to dance one section which Balanchine choreographed very much in Taylor's personal style. Only the second part is now given, and the Taylor episode has been dropped. Although the collaboration of a master modern dance and a master classic ballet choreographer was greatly talked of beforehand as making dance history, the actual collaboration was no more than the two choreographers using music performed in succession instead of on different occasions as they might equally well have been.

Epreuve d'Amour, L'. Ballet in 1 act; chor.: Michel Fokine; music: attributed to Wolfgang Amadeus Mozart; book: Fokine and André Derain; décor: André Derain. First prod.: René Blum's Ballet Russe, Théâtre de Monte Carlo, Apr. 4, 1936 with Vera Nemtchinova (Chung-Yang), André Eglevsky (Her Lover), Jean Yazvinsky (Mandarin), Anatole Oboukhov (The Ambassador), Hélène Kirsova (Butterfly). The Mandarin designs a marriage between his daughter Chung-Yang and the pompous Ambassador. But her poor young Lover disguises himself as a dragon and his friends as brigands, steals the Ambassador's treasure, whereupon the Mandarin withdraws his consent to the marriage. When the deception is revealed and the treasure is restored, the Ambassador retires in dudgeon, realizing that his money was his only attraction, and the path is clear for the young couple to marry. Alicia Markova and Nathalie Krassovska later danced the role of Chung-Yang. Krassovska danced it for the U.S. première Oct. 14, 1938 at Metropolitan Opera House, N.Y. The music, composed for a carnaval in 1791, does not appear in the Köchel or any other listing of Mozart's works and, in fact, was not discovered until 1928 in Graz, Austria.

Equity (Actors Equity Association). See TRADE UNIONS, THEATRICAL.

Jean Erdman, American dancer, choreographer, teacher.

Erdman, Jean, contemporary American dancer, choreographer, teacher, b. Honolulu, Hawaii; m. Joseph Campbell. Graduate of Sarah Lawrence College (1938). Studied dance with Martha Graham, Bennington Summer School of Dance, School of American Ballet, N.Y., José Fernandez (Spanish), Hisamatsu (Japanese), Kawena Pukui and Huapala (Hawaiian). Member, Martha Graham company (1938–43); guest artist with Graham (1945–46). Organized her own group (1944) and has since given many solo and group performances all over the U.S. Among her most important solos are *The Transformations of Medusa* (1942), *Creature on a Journey* (1943), *Ophelia* (1946), *Hamadryad* (1948), *Changing-woman* (1951), *Duet for Flute and Dancer* (1956), *Fearful Symmetry* (1957), *Four Portraits from Duke Ellington's Shakespeare Album* (1958); and group works: *The Perilous Chapel* (1949), *Solstice* (1950), *Song of the Turning World* (1953), *Strange Hunt* (1954), *20 Poems—from e. e. cummings* (1960). Arranged the choreography for Jean Paul Sartre's *Les Mouches* (The Flies), Vassar Experimental Theatre (1947); for Jean Giraud's *The Enchanted* on Broadway (1950), and a ballet-play *Otherman—Or the Beginning of a New Nation,* text by William Saroyan, music by Alan Hovhaness which she also directed for Bard Theatre (1954). Adapted, directed, choreographed, and staged *The Coach With the Six Insides* from James Joyce's *Finnegans Wake* which won 1963 Vernon Rice and Obie awards for the best off-Broadway production and subsequently was presented at Festival of Two Worlds, Spoleto; Théâtre des Nations Festival, Paris; Dublin Theatre Festival; also toured the U.S. and concluded world appearances in Tokyo (1964).

Erlanger, Frederic d', Baron (1868–1943), Paris-born English banker who composed several operas and the scores for the ballets *The Hundred Kisses* and Michel Fokine's *Cinderella.*

Errand into the Maze. Duet by Martha Graham; music: Gian-Carlo Menotti; costumes: Edythe Gilford; décor: Isamu Noguchi. First perf.: Ziegfeld Theatre, N.Y., Feb. 28, 1947 with Martha Graham and Mark Ryder. The myth of Theseus and his journey into the labyrinth translated into a psychological exploration of a woman journeying "into the maze of the heart's darkness, where she encounters and conquers the Creature of Fear."

Errante. Ballet in 1 act; chor. and book: George Balanchine; music: "Der Wanderer," Schubert-Liszt; décor: Pavel Tchelitchev. First prod.: Les Ballets 1933 in London and Paris with Tilly Losch in leading role; revived for American Ballet in New York 1935, with Tamara Geva; revived for Ballet Theatre, Metropolitan Opera House, N.Y., May 21, 1943 with Vera Zorina. The ballet had no clear plot. Its production and choreographic contents were motivated by the moods which Schubert's "Wanderer" Fantasy for piano inspired in Balanchine.

Escudero, Vicente, Spanish dancer, b. Valladolid, ca. 1882. Danced as a child in cabarets in Spain. Made his Paris debut in 1920 with Carmita Garcia, his partner for many years. Danced with Anna Pavlova in 1931 and with La Argentina in 1934. Then toured in Europe and U.S., both as a soloist and with his own company, making his last American appearance as a dancer in 1961. Recently active as a lecturer on flamenco dancing, devoting himself to preserving what he considers its characteristic principles: purity, sobriety and style.

Esmeralda, La. Ballet in 3 acts, 5 scenes; chor. and book: Jules Perrot; music: Cesare Pugni; décor: W. Grieve; machinery: D. Sloman; costumes: Mme. Copere. First prod.: Her Majesty's Theatre, London, March 9, 1844 with Carlotta Grisi (Esmeralda), Jules Perrot (Gringoire), Antoine Louis Coulon (Quasimodo). First perf. in St. Petersburg, Jan. 2, 1849 with Fanny Elssler (Esmeralda), Perrot (Gringoire), Peter Didier (Quasimodo). Elssler danced this ballet at her farewell performance at the Bolshoi Theatre, Moscow, March 14, 1851. Esmeralda was the favorite role of the great Maryinsky ballerina, Mathilde Kchessinska. A version of this ballet had its first performance in the U.S. by the Monplaisir Ballet Company, New York, Sept. 18, 1848. It had long been unknown outside Russia when Nicholas Beriosov staged his own version of it (in décor by Nicola Benois) and with the Pugni music arranged by Geoffrey Corbett, for London's Festival Ballet, tried out at the Liceo Theatre, Barcelona, Spain in May 1954 and with its actual première at Royal Festival Hall, London, July 14, 1954, with Nathalie Krassovska (Esmeralda), John Gilpin (Gringoire), Keith Beckett (Quasimodo), Belinda Wright (Fleur de Lys), Oleg Briansky (Phoebus), Anton Dolin (Frollo). The plot is based on Victor Hugo's famous novel *The Hunchback of Notre Dame* and tells the complicated story of Quasimodo's hopeless love for the Gypsy girl, Esmeralda, the machinations of an evil priest, Frollo, about how Quasimodo sacrifices his life to save that of his beloved. Tamara Toumanova and Violette Verdy also danced the roles of Esmeralda and Fleur de Lys. Subsequently the ballet as a whole was dropped and only the divertissement retained. The first ballet based on this story was Antonio Monticoni's *Esmeralda,* Teatro alla Scala, Milan, 1839.

Espinosa. Famous family of dancers of Spanish extraction who settled in London and became famous as teachers, among them: Leon (1825–1904); his son Edouard (1817–1950) founder of British Ballet Organisation; and daughters Judith (1876–1949), Lea (b. 1883) and Ray (b. 1885). See also KELLAND-ESPINOSA.

Estancia. Ballet in 1 act, 5 scenes: Dawn, Morning, Afternoon, Night and Dawn; chor.: Michel Borovski; music: Alberto Ginastera; décor: Dante Ortolani. First prod.: Aug. 19, 1952, Teatro Colón, Buenos Aires, Argentina, with Esmeralda Agoglia (Young Farm Girl), Enrique Lommi (Young Townsman) and corps de ballet. It is inspired by rural life in Argentina and is very popular for the Malambo scene which closes the ballet.

Etchévery, Jean-Jacques (Marie Ernest Jean-Jacques de Peyret-Chappuis), French dancer and choreographer, b. Paris, 1916. Awarded Bachelor's degree; studied dance with Lydia Karpova, Gustave Ricaus, Nicholas Zverev. Premier danseur, Nouveau Ballet de Monte Carlo from May, 1941 until Nov., 1944, when he formed his own company, Ballets de l'Oiseau Bleu. Ballet master, Opéra Comique, Paris (beg. Oct. 1, 1946). Choreographed *Le Cerf* (Debussy, 1944), *Printemps* (Debussy), *Chanson Sentimentale* (Leo Unger, 1945), *La Bourrée Fantasque* (E. Chabrier), *La Précaution Inutile* (*Barber of Seville,* Rossini, 1946); also restaged *La Péri, Sylvia,* and others.

Eternal Struggle, The. Ballet in 1 act; chor. and book: Igor Schwezoff; music: Robert Schumann's *Etudes Symphoniques;* décor: Kathleen and Florence Martin. First prod.: Original Ballet Russe, Sydney, Australia, 1939, with a cast headed by Tamara Toumanova, Schwezoff,, and Borislav Runanin. Schwezoff also staged this ballet in Rio de Janeiro.

Eternal Triangle. Ballet in 1 act; chor. and book: Dennis Gray, inspired by the Ninth Commandment; music: George Ribalowsky; décor: Fernando Pamplona; costumes: Tomás Santa Rosa. First prod.: 1955 by Teatro Municipal, Rio de Janeiro, with Tatiana Leskova (the Wife), Dennis Gray (the Husband), Johnny Franklin (the Other Man).

Ethnic Dance.

BY LA MERI.

The term "ethnic dance" designates all those indigenous dance arts which have grown from popular or typical dance expressions of a particular race. Properly speaking the term excludes folk-dances which, however typical racially, are still communal dances executed for the pleasure of the executant, as distinguished from art-dances executed for the edification of the spectator. The ethnic dance includes those created for worship, such as Hindu Natya or the ancient Hawaiian Meles; highly stylized theatre dances, such as the Javanese Wayang-Wang and Japanese Noh; dances used as social entertainment, such as the Moslem forms; and communal dances introduced to theatre relatively recently, such as the Spanish.

The Orient is the richest field for the ethnic dancer, where every race and nation has its dance-art which is widely supported and understood by the aristocracy and population alike. It is the fruit of their culture and of interest to all classes. In the larger sense the term "ethnic" is so all-embracing that it is easier to define it by saying what it isn't than what it is.

The ballet is not an ethnic dance because it is the product of the social customs and artistic reflections of several widely-differing national cultures. It has been built for the edification of the aristocratic, international minority and is not, therefore, a communal expression. The dance-arts which have grown up in Europe and North America in the last century are not ethnic because each is the product of one genius and not of a communal cultural expression. Most of the folk dances of South America and Europe must also be excluded, for they have not yet passed into the realm of art; that is, they do not possess a technical terminology, a traditional style, or a clearly-defined school of instruction. Strictly speaking, neither are the folk-dances of the Orient ethnic, for anyone from any country might dance them for pleasure and entirely correctly, since they have no traditional style. Yet these dances, like the South American and European, will be a part of the repertoire of the ethnic theatre dancer because in transplanting them to the stage the artist must not only re-choreograph them into theatre pieces, but must project them with the physical style and spiritual approach which mark them when they are danced by natives on their native soil.

The dances of the natives of South and Central Africa and of the Indians of North and South America are difficult to define in this respect. Among both these races there exist "theatre" dances. Although they are a part of communal worship, they are executed by selected dancers who perform traditional movements in stylized costumes for the edification of the spectator.

Ethnic dance includes all forms of exotic dance created by all classes. It is the most democratic, for it is the product of both the folk of the soil and the aristocracy of the palace and common to all classes of the blood which engendered it. Ethnic dance must be born of a people to whom dancing is an integral part of the worship, education, and everyday life of all classes.

Etoile, a star; in ballet, the French designation of a prima ballerina or premier danseur, such as première danseuse étoile or premier danseur étoile.

Etude. Ballet in 1 act; chor.: Ludmilla Chiriaeff; music: Robert Schumann's *Scenes of Childhood.* First prod.: Les Grands Ballets Canadiens, Comédie Canadienne Théâtre, Montreal, Apr. 12, 1956, with Milenka Niderlova and Eric Hyrst and ensemble of five girls and three men. In practice tights and leotards a ballerina and her premier danseur, with dancers from the corps de ballet, go through the basic classic exercises, developed into dances. A long pole, representing the practice bar, manipulated by the dancers themselves as they begin the exercises, forms part of the choreographic pattern.

Etudes. Ballet in 1 act; chor.: Harald Lander; music: Karl Czerny arranged by Knudage Riisager; décor: Nordgren. First prod.: (as *Etude*) Royal Danish Ballet, Copenhagen, Jan. 15, 1948, with Margot Lander, Hans Brenaa, Svend Erik Jensen. Lander staged it for the Paris Opéra, Nov. 19, 1952, with Micheline Bardin, Michel Renault, Alexander Kalioujny, when it was titled *Etudes,* by which name it is now generally known. Lander staged it for American Ballet Theatre, 54th St. Theatre, N.Y., Oct. 5, 1961, in décor by Rolf Gerard (costumes executed by Barbara Karinska), with Toni Lander (Lupe Serrano later danced the role), Royes Fernandez and Bruce Marks. After a lapse since 1951, *Etudes* returned to the Royal Danish Ballet repertoire Mar. 4, 1962 with Toni Lander, Flemming Flindt, Frank Schaufuss, Eske Holm. London's Festival Ballet produced a version Aug. 8, 1955 with Toni Lander, John Gilpin, Anton Dolin. A themeless ballet, *Etudes* is an exposition of the entire technique of classic ballet from the first pliés at the bar to the brilliance of batterie and allegro.

Eukinetics.

BY ANGIOLA SARTORIO.

Eukinetics is a system developed by Kurt Jooss of controlling the dynamics and expression of the dancer's body.

Absolute control of the body does not mean only the ability to perform all technically difficult steps; it means the ability to control the body like an impersonal instrument, the ability to tense consciously any part of the body and to know what that tension will mean to the audience.

According to Delsarte the body is divided into three parts or centers. The upper chest is the spiritual or intellectual center, the middle body is the emotional center, the lower body (abdomen and hips) is the animal force or physical center.

Any movement can be given a variety of expressions by tensing different centers of our body. Let us take, for example, the jeté en tournant. If we tense the chest, our jeté will be light, our movement detached from the earth. If we tense the region of the waist, we shall have a soft, flowing jeté en tournant, because this is the middle of the body, the balance point. If we tense the hips, a strong forceful jeté results, full of vitality and animal force.

All dancers can more or less be divided into three categories. Basing himself on the Delsarte principle, Rudolf von Laban classified dancers as high, middle, and low. Ballet divides its dancers into classic, demi-caractère, and character, very much on the same basis without perhaps realizing it. We find an analogous division in singing: soprano, mezzo-soprano and contralto, or tenor, baritone, and bass. These are types of people and not just chance styles of dancing or singing.

In spite of this division into categories, there is no reason why a dancer in complete control of his body should not be able to do any type of dance. Unlike the singer, who is limited in style by the range of his voice, the dancer can control his instrument of expression in all ways not limited by the laws of nature. Each movement can be performed in many different styles. It is like taking a drawing and coloring it differently—each new combination of colors will produce a different impression.

With the help of Eukinetics the dancer is able to execute the typical movements of the personality he is portraying, project the special style the choreographer desires, and bring out the characteristic style of the dances of different nations. The dancer can be classic, demi-caractère or character, as may be required; moreover, he can create the impression of being tall, short, thin, fat, heavy, light, strong, weak, etc.

According to Eukinetics, all movement can be divided into two great categories: out-going and in-coming. All else is a variation of these two. These two divisions are called central (i.e. movements originating in a center and radiating or spreading out to the periphery, the outer regions) and peripheral (i.e. originating in the outer, peripheral regions and moving to a center).

If we tense the back, the outside of the arms or hands, we create a peripheral movement. If we tense the abdomen, the inside of the arms or hands, we create a central movement. The same applies to the legs. In general, movements with tension in hands and feet are peripheral; movements emanating from the center of the body are central.

Within each of these great divisions—central and peripheral—we can further divide movements as to intensity (i.e. strong and weak) and as to speed (i.e. slow and fast). For example, if you hit the table with the palm of your hand peripherally, that is, putting the tension in your fingers, you can do it in four different ways: strong and fast, strong and slow, weak and fast, or weak and slow. As an example of a central movement, let us take a step to the right and push out the right hip. This movement can also be done in four ways: strong and slow, strong and fast, weak and slow, or weak and fast.

For the sake of simplicity these eight possibilities of movements can be classified thus: *Peripheral:* draw (slow-strong), float (slow-weak), strike (fast-strong), flutter (fast-weak); *Central:* press (slow-strong), slide (slow-weak), thrust (fast-strong), shake (fast-weak).

To illustrate, if you were dancing the Wilis in *Giselle,* you would do floating movements, while the sailors in Jerome Robbins's *Fancy Free* would use mainly slides, shakes, and thrusts; Hagar in Antony Tudor's *Pillar of Fire* would require presses, draws, and thrusts. Any dance, whether it is ballet or modern, folk, tap, or ballroom, can be analyzed in this manner.

An interesting individual experiment in Eukinetics is to take a simple definite movement and change it by gradually changing its characteristics. You might begin with our first example—hitting the table with the palm of the hand peripherally. Your first movement will be: *Peripheral:* strong-fast (i.e. obviously a strike).

Having changed one by one the origin of the movement, its intensity and speed, you will find your final movement to be: *Central:* weak-slow (i.e. a slide, a kind of caress). If you substitute a cheek for the table, it immediately becomes apparent that the difference between a slap and a caress is not only in the emotion which motivates the movement.

The value of Eukinetics for the dancer, however, is not in the fact that it supplies a ready label for any movement, but that mastery of the system enables the dancer to express himself in any dance media in which he may be called upon to work. See also CHOREUTICS.

Eurhythmics, a system of education in the arts, originated by Emile Jaques Dalcroze, based on a thorough study of musical rhythm through bodily movement. Intended for the teaching of music, it proved effective also as a general mental and physical education using rhythm as a coordinating factor in all the arts. In practically all schools in U.S. and abroad music, physical education, dramatic and art departments show the influence of the principles expounded by Dalcroze since his system was officially recognized in 1905. In the dance field, it is of particular value in training children and beginners to understand rhythm; progressive dance educators consider it a prerequisite for proper dance training.

Evan, Blanche, contemporary dancer and teacher; b. New York City. Studied with Bird Larson, Hanya Holm, Martha Graham, Ella Daganova, Harald Kreutzberg, Doris Humphrey, Emile Jaques Dalcroze, Vilzak-Shollar, La Meri, Veola. Has appeared in solo and joint recitals in various N.Y. theatres; in Norwalk, Conn.; Newark, N.J.; Boston, Mass.; Moscow, U.S.S.R. (1935–37). Choreographs own dances. Has taught, lectured and given demonstrations in various schools and colleges since 1933; contributed to *Theatre Arts, Dance Magazine, Parents Magazine, Jewish Survey,* etc. Has had own studio in N.Y. since 1935.

Evans, Edwin (1874–1945), English music and ballet critic, *Daily Mail* (1933–45). Musical adviser to Serge Diaghilev; chairman of the Camargo Society. A true friend of British ballet in its early, struggling days, he wrote the scenario and arranged the Mendelssohn music for Frederick Ashton's *The Lord of Burleigh* (1931), and selected the Haydn music for Ninette de Valois' *Promenade* (1943). Author of *Music and the Dance;* also wrote a monthly article on music and the ballet for *The Dancing Times,* London.

Evans, Meriel, English dancer and choreographer, b. Ceylon, 1934. Dance training, University of Cape Town Ballet, and at Elmhurst Ballet School, Royal Ballet School in England. Joined Sadler's Wells (now Royal) Ballet (1949), promoted to soloist shortly after. Choreographed her first ballets when only 14 (for Royal Academy of Dancing Production Club and later on television), and appointed resident choreographer, Covent Garden Opera, 1957, leaving in 1960. Guest artist with Royal Ballet (1961). Artistic director, National Ballet, Dublin since 1961 for which she choreographed *Musicale* the same year. Also teaches as guest at R.A.D., Royal Ballet School and Elmhurst Ballet School, and occasionally acts as examiner for R.A.D.

Every Soul Is a Circus. Modern dance work; chor.: Martha Graham; music: Paul Nordoff; décor: Philip Stapp; costumes: Edythe Gilfond. First prod.: St. James Theatre, N.Y., Dec. 27, 1939 with Martha Graham (Empress of the Arena), Erick Hawkins (Ringmaster), Merce Cunningham (Acrobat). The title, and the motto of the piece, is from Vachel Lindsay's lines: 'Every soul is a circus/ Every mind is a tent/ Every heart is a sawdust ring/ Where the circling race is spent.' Martha Graham presented a parade of the characteristics which have distinguished women from Eve, or Lilith, throughout time. This work marked the beginning of what has become generally known as The Theatre of Martha Graham. It was also Merce Cunningham's first appearance with Graham.

Excelsior. Monumental spectacular ballet, or set of related episodes in 12 scenes; chor.: Luigi Manzotti; music: Romualdo Marenco; décor: Alfredo Edel. First perf.: Jan. 11, 1881 at Teatro alla Scala, Milan with Bice Vergani and Carlo Montanara in the principal parts. It was presented at Her Majesty's Theatre, London, in 1885, with Giovanni Limido and Enrico Cecchetti. According to C. W. Beaumont, Manzotti was the inventor of the propaganda ballet and *Excelsior* was propaganda for science and the arts. As a ballet being produced forty years after the première of *Giselle, Excelsior* was, of course, retardative in its artistic, musical and choreographic aspects. It may have had a retardative influence on ballet in Italy that is still being felt.

Expressional Dance, a term coined by John Martin, author and at the time critic of the *N.Y. Times,* to include the modern dance, which in his opinion is "art and not entertainment." Says he in his *Introduction to the Dance* (New York, 1939): ". . . it has built a structure of its own that is broader, simpler and closer to the nature of human experience than anything the arts have contrived."

Extension, in ballet, stretching of the leg at any angle from the body.

Fabbri, Flora, Italian ballerina of the 19th century, b. Florence (date unknown). She was one of the six pupils of Carlo Blasis who were called the "Pleiades of Blasis." She made her debut in the Fenice Theatre, Venice; also danced in Rome (1838) and Bologna (1841). Married the French choreographer Louis Bretin (1842). Was a leading dancer at the Paris Opéra (1845–51). Her repertoire included *La Sylphide, Paquita,* Arthur Saint-Léon's *Les Nations, Idalia, ou La Fleur Inconnue* (which Bretin, with Cazzoletti, choreographed for her in 1855), and others.

Fables for Our Time. Modern dance work; chor.: Charles Weidman; music: Freda Miller (for 2 pianos). First prod.: Charles Weidman Dance Theatre Company, Jacob's Pillow Dance Festival, July, 1947; N.Y. première: Mansfield Theatre, Apr. 18, 1948. Weidman received a Guggenheim Fellowship (1947) to stage this work, which in its Jacob's Pillow performance was still only roughly sketched. It was completed for its N.Y. première. Weidman chose four of the famous James Thurber fables for his dance pantomimes: "The Unicorn in the Garden," "The Shrike and the Chipmunk," "The Owl Who Was God," "The Courtship of Al and Arthur" (another—"The Little Girl and the Wolf"—was dropped before the N.Y. première). Weidman and Betty Osgood led the company. Jack Ferris, the dry and droll narrator, has always been a highly successful element in what has proved to be Weidman's most successful work. A set of five *Further Fables for Our Time,* premièred Feb. 12, 1960, Henry St. Playhouse, N.Y. were of no more than passing interest. These Fables were: "The Clothes Moth and the Lunar Moth," "The Tigress and Her Mate," "The Rose, the Fountain and the Dove," "Oliver and the Other Ostriches," "What Happened to Charles?"

Façade. Ballet in 1 act; chor.: Frederick Ashton; music: William Walton (originally written as an accompaniment to poems by Edith Sitwell); book: adapted from the Sitwell poems; décor: John Armstrong. First prod.: Camargo Society, Cambridge Theatre, Apr. 26, 1931, with Lydia Lopoukhova, Pearl Argyle, Alicia Markova, Frederick Ashton in leading parts. Ballet Rambert immediately took it into its repertoire and it was presented at the Mercury Theatre, May 4, 1931, with Andrée Howard as the Milkmaid and Tango dancer in place of Lopoukhova. Ashton staged it for Vic-Wells (later Sadler's Wells, now Royal) Ballet Oct. 8, 1935, when a Country Dance was added for Pearl Argyle and Robert Helpmann. After the costumes and scenery were lost in Holland early in 1940, the ballet was presented (July, 1940) with new décor by John Armstrong and two more numbers added—one which preceded the previous opening Scottish dance, the other a Foxtrot satire (later dropped). Ballet Rambert continued to perform *Façade* in its original décor (which is superior to the later version) and with the basic six dances and finale: Scottish Rhapsody, Yodelling Song, Polka, Waltz, Popular Song, Tango. Alicia Markova created the Polka (which ends with a double tour en l'air), and danced it with both Ballet Rambert and Vic-Wells. Ashton's seedy Tango dancer was one of his most successful creations and Moira Shearer later had a big comic success in the Tango. This work, slight as it is, might fairly be said to mark the true beginning of British ballet, for it established Ashton as a genuine creative talent.

Facsimile. Choreographic observation; chor. and book: Jerome Robbins; music: Leonard Bernstein; décor: Oliver Smith; costumes: Irene Sharaff. First prod.: Ballet Theatre, Broadway Theatre, N.Y., Oct. 24, 1946, with Nora Kaye, Jerome Robbins, John Kriza. A psychological treatment of the eternal triangle situation, which in this case is motivated by sex, not love. Not a very pleasant ballet to watch, *Facsimile* never enjoyed audience acceptance, but it was nevertheless a very well-conceived composition.

Fadetta. Ballet in 3 acts and 4 scenes; chor.: Leonid Lavrovsky; music Léo Delibes (from his ballet *Sylvia*). First prod.: Leningrad, 1934. The plot of the ballet is based on a chapter of George Sand's novel *La Petite Fadette,* and deals with the love of a rich peasant's son for Fadette, the grand-daughter of a poor old woman with whom she lives in a broken-down hut on the edge of a forest. The old woman is rumored to be a witch and Fadette is an outcast who but seldom dares to come down to the village. The rich peasants side with the boy's father in trying to prevent the marriage, but do not succeed in the end. *Fadetta* is intended as a quasi-propaganda work in that the well-to-do peasants are represented as villains, the poor as heroes.

Fadeyechev, Nicolai, Honored Artist of the RSFSR, Soviet premier danseur, b. 1933. Entered the Bolshoi School in 1943; graduated 1952 (class of Nicolai Rudenko). While still at school, Fadeyechev was considered an excellent prospect to grow into a leading soloist. However, while possessing both an excellent physique and good line, he was not very strong and had to work hard to gain the stamina to dance leading roles in evening-length ballets. Within two years of graduating into the company he was given the roles of Siegfried (*Swan Lake*), and Prince Desiré (*The Sleeping Beauty*); then followed Albrecht (*Giselle*), which remains his best role as he has a great feeling for the Romantic style. He is a fine actor and partner in addition to his strong, unobtrusive technique. Danced with the Bolshoi Ballet in London (1956), and on tour; also danced on television in London (1958) with Nadia Nerina in *Giselle.* Danced with the Bolshoi Ballet in N.Y. and on tour in the U.S. and Canada (1966). He is Maya Plisetskaya's principal partner and danced *Swan Lake* with her as guest artists of the Paris Opéra (1961). Also partnered Nerina in *Swan Lake* when she was guest artist at the Bolshoi Theatre (1961). Other roles include Frondozo (*Laurencia*), Harmodius (*Spartacus*), Danila (*The Stone Flower*). Was awarded the title People's Artist of the RSFSR in 1964.

Faier, Yuri, Peoples' Artist of the USSR, leading ballet conductor of the Bolshoi Theatre and of Soviet Ballet, b. 1890. Conductor of the Bolshoi Ballet since 1923, beginning in its orchestra as a violinist. Faier's knowledge of the technique of the classical dance is unsurpassed by any other conductor. He has an extraordinary ability of identifying himself with the dancer and his tempo and interpretation invariably assist the artist in the execution of the role. Author of a book of memoirs, *Notes of a Ballet Conductor* (1960). Retired in 1963.

Failli, a movement in ballet. Technique: start 5th pos., R ft. front facing R corner; demi-plié and bound forward off both feet, raising L leg to grande quatrième en effacé derrière; land on R ft. and slide L ft. through 1st pos. to 4th pos. croisé, R toe pointed back. This movement is done on one count.

Fairy Doll, The. See PUPPENFEE, DIE.

Falk, Per, Swedish painter and stage designer, b. Göteborg, 1924. Studied at the Academy of Art, Stockholm. Designed décor for several Swedish theatres, among them the Malmö City Theatre (1951–58). Created the décor for Birgit Cullberg's ballets *The Moon Reindeer* (1957) and *Eden* (1961) used in all productions of these ballets.

Fall-Recovery, in modern dance the expression of the dynamic principle upon which the modern dance is based. This term was used especially by Doris Humphrey to describe a synthesis resulting from the interaction of two opposites: a period of unbalance and a period of balance. All movement from the simple change of weight onward is an alternation of these two periods. (Paul Love.)

The principle was originally formulated by the German dancers of the first and second decade of this century, stemming probably from the great theoretician of movement, Rudolf von Laban, and the equally great practicing dancer Mary Wigman. Its original designation was Anspannung-Abspannung. Compare with CONTRACTION-RELEASE.

Fall River Legend. Ballet in 1 act; chor. and book: Agnes de Mille; commissioned music: Morton Gould; décor: Oliver Smith; costumes: Miles White. First prod.: Ballet Theatre, Metropolitan Opera House, N.Y., April 22, 1948, with a cast headed by Alicia Alonso (subsequently Nora Kaye) as The Accused, Diana Adams (Mother), Peter Gladke (Father), Muriel Bentley (Stepmother), Ruth Ann Koesun (The Accused as a Child), John Kriza (Pastor). The book of the ballet is based on the story of Lizzie Borden. When Lizzie's mother dies, the father marries another woman who is a cruel stepmother to her. She interferes with Lizzie's life and when Lizzie does not obey her she spreads rumors that she is mentally deranged, thus destroying Lizzie's only chance of romance. Unable to bear her persecution any longer, Lizzie takes an ax and kills both her stepmother and her father.

Fallis, Barbara, dancer, teacher, b. Denver, Colo., 1924; m. Richard Thomas. Moved with her family to London in 1929. Studied dance at Mona Clague Ballet School; also with Joan Lawson and at Vic-Wells (now Royal Ballet) School (1937–40), appearing with Vic-Wells Ballet (1938–40). Returned to U.S. (1940). Joined corps de ballet of Ballet (now American Ballet) Theatre (1941), rising to soloist. Danced Waltz (*Les Sylphides*), Lamb (*Helen of Troy*), Calliope (*Apollo*), Impromptu Dance (*Graduation Ball*); created Grahn (*Pas de Quatre*), and others. Joined Ballet Alicia Alonso as ballerina (1948–52), dancing Ballerina (*Petrouchka*), Young Girl (*Le Spectre de la Rose*), Aurora (*Aurora's Wedding*), Queen of the Willis (*Giselle*), and others. Soloist, New York City Ballet (1953–58), dancing Pony and Hortense, Queen of the Swamp Lilies (*Cakewalk*), 2nd and 3rd movements (*Western Symphony*), Marzipan (*The Nutcracker*), Pas de Neuf (*Swan Lake,* Act 2); also created role in *Pas de Dix,* and others.

Toured with Nora Kovach and Istvan Rabovsky (1958), partnered by Royes Fernandez. Also had leading dancing and acting roles in seasons at St. Louis Municipal Opera, Palm Beach Playhouse, Pocono Playhouse, Gateway Playhouse. Assistant to choreographer Ray Harrison for the musical *The Student Gypsy* (1963). Currently teaching in N.Y.

Falls the Shadow Between. See PERSEPHONE (chor. Pearl Lang).

Fanciulla delle Rose. Ballet in 1 act; chor.: Frank Staff; music: Anton Arensky's *Variations on a Theme of Tchaikovsky;* décor: Guy Sheppard. First prod.: Metropolitan Ballet, Scala Theatre, London, June 10, 1948, with Svetlana Beriosova as the Young Girl, her first created leading role. The Young Girl, on her way to lay a wreath of roses on the statue of the Madonna, is beset by a vision of the seven deadly sins to which she succumbs. The roses fade and wither, but she ventures to lay them at the foot of the Madonna who accepts them with her repentance.

Fancy Free. Ballet in 1 act; chor. and book: Jerome Robbins; music: Leonard Bernstein; décor: Oliver Smith; costumes: Kermit Love. First prod.: Ballet Theatre, Metropolitan Opera House, N.Y., Apr. 18, 1944, with Harold Lang, John Kriza, Jerome Robbins as the three sailors, Janet Reed, Muriel Bentley, Shirley Eckl, the three girls, and Rex Cooper as the Bartender. Three sailors on shore leave enjoy their free time having a few drinks, dancing, and flirting with girls. This was Robbins' first ballet and has been a permanent and beloved part of the Ballet (now American Ballet) Theatre repertoire since its première.

Fandango (Sp.), a lively Spanish dance in triple time danced to the accompaniment of castanets or tambourine.

Fanfare. Ballet in 1 act; chor.: Jerome Robbins; music: Benjamin Britten's *Young Person's Guide to the Orchestra;* décor: Irene Sharaff. First prod.: New York City Ballet, City Center, N.Y., June 2, 1953, with Yvonne Mounsey, Irene Larsson, Jillana, Jacques d'Amboise, Brooks Jackson, Edward Bigelow, Todd Bolender, Herbert Bliss, Frank Hobi. Britten took a theme from Henry Purcell's *Abdelazor,* writing a series of variations on it for the various sections of the orchestra, bringing in the entire orchestra for a final fugue. Robbins's dancers represent the instruments, dancing short, illustrative variations, the whole company coming together for the final mighty fugue. The ballet's première was to celebrate the Coronation of Queen Elizabeth II. Jerome Robbins has also staged *Fanfare* for the Royal Danish Ballet (première: Apr. 29, 1956). Allegra Kent attracted attention for the first time when she danced the Viola pas de deux (with d'Amboise) on Jan. 12, 1954.

Fantasy. Ballet in 1 act; chor.: John Taras; music: Franz Schubert's Fantasy for piano duet, op. 103, orch. by Felix Mottl. First prod.: New York City Ballet, City Center, N.Y., Sept. 24, 1963, with Patricia McBride, Edward Villella (First Couple), Carol Sumner, Robert Rodham (Second Couple), Marlene Mesavage, Earle Sieveling (Third Couple). Young Lovers are keeping trysts in a wood. As the night deepens and mysterious Watchers of the Night invade the open glade, one of the girls turns into a creature of fury who hounds her lover to death. The other couples are untouched by the magic and unaware that anything has happened. Dressed and set from existing costumes and décor, the program did not list any designers, but imagination and magnificent lighting made *Fantasy* a beautiful presentation.

Far from Denmark, or a Costume Ball on Board Ship (Fjernt Fra Danmark eller Et Costumebal Onbord). Vaudeville-ballet in two acts; chor.: August Bournonville; music: Hans Christian Lumbye and Joseph Glaeser. First perf.: Royal Danish Ballet, Copenhagen, 1860. A Danish frigate anchored in an Argentinian port is the locale of a complicated musical comedy-like romance involving a lieutenant in the Danish navy, the daughter of a consul, and her sweetheart Alva. A masked ball aboard ship offers an occasion for a number of character dances. Only these dances have ever been seen outside Denmark, although the ballet in its entirety remains in the Danish repertoire.

Farandole, an old dance in 6/8 time originating in Provence, France, and Catalonia, consisting mainly of a galop step danced in a chain. The dancers, led by a conductor, hold hands and wind in and out very much like follow-the-leader. It is also known in France as *L'Escargot* because of the snail-like formation. An example of the farandole adapted to ballet can be found in the Hunt Scene of *The Sleeping Beauty*.

Farewell, The. Modern dance work; chor.: Pauline Koner; music: final section of Gustav Mahler's *Das Lied von der Erde;* costumes: Pauline Koner, executed by Nellie Hatfield. First prod.: Virginia Museum Theatre, Richmond, Va., Feb. 9, 1962, sponsored by the Virginia Dance Society (a preview performance). Its official première was Feb. 28 on the concert series of the Hartford (Conn.) Symphony; N.Y. première: YM–YWHA, Apr. 30, 1962. This long solo, lasting nearly a half hour, is Pauline Koner's tribute to the memory of Doris Humphrey, her friend, teacher, and adviser.

Farjeon, Annabel, English dancer and writer on ballet, b. Buckleberry, Berks, 1919. Her father, Herbert Farjeon, was a noted writer (particularly famed for his intimate revues) and dramatic critic. Studied with Phyllis Bedells and at Sadler's Wells School, becoming a member of the company (1935–40). Began reviewing ballet books for *Time and Tide* when assistant literary editor (1946–48); ballet critic, *New Statesman and Nation* since 1949, *Evening Standard* since 1959. Has contributed to other newspapers and ballet periodicals, and lectured on ballet. Member of the Critics' Circle, London.

Farmaniantz, Georgi, Honored Artist of the RSFSR, Soviet dancer, b. Bezhetsk, 1921; m. Bolshoi soloist Elmira Kosterina. Entered the Bolshoi school in 1929, following in the steps of his sister and partner, Yevgenia Farmaniantz. In his first year he played Cio-Cio San's baby in the Puccini opera *Madama Butterfly*. His proper debut came in 1930 when he took the part of a Russian doll in Igor Moiseyev's *Football Player*. He showed an early aptitude for character dance and was the best pupil in Anatole Kusnetsov's character class. Was accepted into the Bolshoi Ballet in 1940. His first role, that of Ataman Shilo in *Taras Bulba,* showed him as an outstanding demi-caractère dancer. His large repertoire of roles which require both outstanding virtuosity and characterization include: Basil (*Don Quixote*), Franz (*Coppélia*), Colin (*La Fille Mal Gardée*), Blue Bird (*The Sleeping Beauty*), Nur-Ali (*The Fountain of Bakhchisarai*), Jester (*Swan Lake*), Warrior Chieftain (*Polovetzian Dances from Prince Igor*), Devil (*Mirandolina*), Karen (*Gayané*), Letika (*Crimson Sails*), Satyr (*Walpurgis Night*). He has danced all over the U.S.S.R. and in 25 foreign countries. Retired as a dancer in 1963; currently teaching.

Farrally, Betty (Betty Hey), Canadian teacher, b. Bradford, England, 1915. Studied at Toren School of Dance, Leeds, England. In 1938 went to Winnipeg, Canada, with Gweneth Lloyd as co-founder-director of Canadian School of Ballet. Co-founder-director also of the Winnipeg (now Royal Winnipeg) Ballet Company the same year. Was with the company as ballet mistress or artistic director until 1957. Currently teaching.

Suzanne Farrell, ballerina of the N.Y. City Ballet, as one of the aspects of Dulcinea, in Balanchine's Don Quixote.

Farrell, Suzanne (Roberta Sue Ficker), dancer, b. Cincinnati, 1945. Studied ballet with Marian LaCour at College Conservatory of Music, Cincinnati. Won a Ford Foundation Scholarship to School of American Ballet, N.Y., and a year's tuition at Professional Children's School, N.Y. (1960). Joined New York City Ballet (1961), her first solo—one of the three female leads in *Serenade*—coming ten months later while the company was on tour. Danced the second lead in *Concerto Barocco* for the first time on tour with the company in Cologne, Germany (1962). Danced the first lead in this ballet during the 1963 fall season at City Center, N.Y. Her first important creation was the female lead in *Arcade,* Mar. 28, 1963, followed Apr. 9 with the lead in *Movements for Piano and Orchestra* when she took over the role originally created for Diana Adams who was ill; officially promoted to soloist prior to the fall season of 1963, when she added Titania (*A Midsummer Night's Dream*) to her repertoire. Since that time she has created lead roles in George Balanchine's *Meditation* (pas de deux with Jacques d'Amboise), *Clarinade* and the revival by New York City Ballet of *Ballet Imperial.* Her first great role came on May 28, 1965, when she danced Dulcinea in George Balanchine's full-length *Don Quixote.* The role brought her the title principal dancer, which is more or less the equivalent of ballerina in more traditional companies.

Farren, Fred (1874–1956), English dancer, choreographer and maître de ballet, b. and d. London. Made his debut in pantomime (1885) and was for many years principal dancer at Empire Theatre, London, partnering Lydia Kyasht in many ballets, some of which he also choreographed. Was Dr. Coppelius, to Adeline Genée's Swanilda in the Empire production of *Coppélia* (1906).

Farriss, Audrey, contemporary English dancer, b. Croydon; m. William Wilson. Studied locally with Joan Beste, with Stanislas Idzikowski and at Royal Ballet School. Member, International Ballet (1953); Ballet de l'Europe (1954). Joined Sadler's Wells Theatre Ballet (1956); soloist, Royal Ballet, since 1957. Her roles include Fairy Autumn (*Cinderella*), Songbird Fairy (*The Sleeping Beauty*), title role (*Pineapple Poll*), and others.

Farron, Julia (Farron-Smith), English dancer, b. London, 1929; m. Alfred Rodrigues. Studied at Sadler's Wells (now Royal) Ballet School from age twelve and attracted attention when, as a very little girl she created Pepe, the Dog in *A Wedding Bouquet* (1937). Her first leading creation was Psyche in Frederick Ashton's *Cupid and Psyche* (1939) and from then until she retired in 1961 she had a distinguished career as a leading soloist, particularly striking in character and demi-caractère roles. Her creations included Hannah (*A Mirror for Witches*), Diana (*Sylvia*), Tarantella—with Alexander Grant (*Swan Lake,* Act 3—Ashton arrangement), Berthe (*Ondine*), Jocasta (*Antigone*). She danced a wide variety of other roles including Black Queen (*Checkmate*), Young Girl (*The Rake's Progress*), Prostitute (*Miracle in the Gorbals*), Fairy Godmother (*Cinderella*), Lykanion (*Daphnis and Chloe*). She retired in 1961. Came out of retirement to create Lady Capulet in Kenneth MacMillan's *Romeo and Juliet* (1965). The same year played the Princess Mother in *Swan Lake* on the Royal Ballet's U.S. tour.

Farruca, a Spanish Flamenco dance often called the most "gypsy" of all Spanish dances (see SPANISH DANCE). Leonide Massine very effectively used the farruca for the Miller's solo in his ballet *The Three-Cornered Hat.*

Fascilla, Roberto, Italian dancer, b. 1937. Entered the ballet school of Teatro alla Scala, Milan, in 1948, graduated in 1956; appeared in his Passo d'Addio in 1957; promoted to soloist in 1958. He is tall and strong and is considered an excellent partner. His most notable ballet is probably *La Giara.*

Faust. Ballet in 3 acts, 7 scenes; chor. and book: Jules Perrot; music: Panizza, Costa, Bajetti; décor: Carlo Fontana; machinery: Giuseppe Ronchi. First prod.: Teatro alla Scala, Milan, Feb. 12, 1848, with Fanny Elssler (Marguerite), Effisio Catte (Faust), Jules Perrot (Mephistopheles); Russian première: Nov. 16, 1854, with Mme. Yella (Marguerite), Marius Petipa (Faust), Perrot (Mephistopheles). *Faust,* one of Perrot's greatest successes, was in the Russian repertoire for a long time. Fanny Elssler danced it for her farewell performance in Vienna, June 21, 1851. The choreographer used Goethe's tragedy as a thread for a ballet about the principal characters of the tragedy with the addition of many others of his own invention. The ballet ends with Faust escaping from Mephistopheles and joining Marguerite in heaven.

Feast of Ashes. Ballet in 1 act; chor.: Alvin Ailey; music: Carlos Surinach (*Doppio Concertino,* a section of *Ritmo Jondo* not used in Doris Humphrey's work of that name, and a short musical bridge specially composed by Surinach to link the two scores); décor: Jack Venza. First prod.: Robert Joffrey Ballet, in a Workshop performance at Fashion Institute of Technology, N.Y., Sept. 30, 1962, with Françoise Martinet, Lisa Bradley, Paul Sutherland, in leading roles. *Feast of Ashes* is based on Federico García Lorca's *House of Bernarda Alba.* Two great Spanish houses are united in the marriage of a son to the elder of two daughters, but he loves the younger daughter and they flee together. The haughty matriarch orders their recapture and death, for nothing less can obliterate the shame. This ballet was given during the Robert Joffrey Ballet's tour of the Near and Far East (1962–63), and was one of the works presented on the company's opening night at the Kirov Theatre, Leningrad, Oct. 15, 1963.

Federal Dance Theatre. See DANCE PROJECT.

Fedorova, Alexandra, Russian ballerina and teacher, b. 1884; graduated from the

St. Petersburg Imperial School (1902) and was accepted into the ballet company of the Maryinsky Theatre; m. Alexander Fokine, brother of Michel Fokine. In 1906 became first soloist of the Maryinsky Theatre, dancing important roles; also appeared as prima-ballerina of the Troitzky Theatre owned by her husband. Left Petrograd in 1922 and moved to Riga, Latvia, where she became ballet mistress of the Latvian State Theatre of Opera and Ballet and contributed much to the development of the company. Came to N.Y. in 1937, eventually becoming an American citizen. Her son Leon Fokine a dancer and teacher, works in N.Y. Mme. Fedorova conducted her own ballet school until 1965 when she retired.

Fedorova, Sophia (called Fedorova II in the official register of the Moscow Bolshoi Theatre, 1879–1963), one of the great character ballerinas, she graduated from the Moscow Bolshoi School in 1899 and was accepted into the company. Among her ballets were *La Fille Mal Gardée, Don Quixote, The Daughter of Pharaoh, The Humpbacked Horse, Esmeralda, Le Corsaire, Bayaderka,* and others. In 1909 Serge Diaghilev invited Fedorova to dance in the first Paris season of his company and she created a sensation opening night as the Polovetzian Girl in *Prince Igor.* She remained in the company until the summer of 1913, continuing to dance in *Prince Igor* and adding to her repertoire roles in *Cléopâtre, Schéhérazade,* and several others. She returned to Moscow in 1913 but left again in 1922, ostensibly for a cure abroad. In 1928 Diaghilev invited her to re-join his company for the Paris season. Again, after nineteen years, she danced the Polovetzian Girl and again she delighted the Paris audience. She did not have an easy time in Paris after the season and eventually suffered a complete nervous breakdown in 1930, as a result of which she was placed in a hospital for mental cases. When her condition improved, a balletomane friend, Grigory Stolpovsky, arranged for her discharge from the hospital and looked after her to the end of her days. Very little was heard of Sophia Fedorova between 1928 and the time of her death: Jan. 3, 1963.

Fedorovitch, Sophie, one of England's most noted theatrical designers, b. Minsk, Russia, 1893, d. London, 1953. She had lived in London since 1920 and was a British subject. She was closely associated with British ballet from its beginnings, having designed the costumes and décor for Frederick Ashton's first ballet, *A Tragedy of Fashion* (1926). This was followed by *Les Masques, Mephisto Valse, Valentine's Eve, Valse Finale, La Fête Etrange* (for Ballet Rambert); *The Scorpions of Ysit,* Ashton's *Le Baiser de la Fée, Nocturne, Horoscope, Dante Sonata, Symphonic Variations,* Ninette de Valois' *Orpheus and Eurydice;* Andrée Howard's *Veneziana* (all for Sadler's Wells (now Royal) Ballet; also for Sadler's Wells Theatre Ballet: *Summer Interlude* (Michael Somes) and Valses Nobles et Sentimentales, the latter an enlarged and re-designed version of the original *Valentine's Eve.* Sophie Fedorovitch had not entirely completed her designs for *Veneziana* (and was also engaged on designing a production of Gluck's *Orfeo ed Euridice*) when she died in a tragic domestic accident—overcome by the fumes from a faulty gas pipe while sleeping.

Felicitas (Felicitas Bauer Barreto), Brazilian dancer, choreographer, painter, writer, and lecturer on dance, b. Niteroi. As a child learned native dances at a neighboring "macumba." Began to study classic dance at Teatro Municipal ballet school under Maria Olenewa, later Ricardo Nemanoff and Yuco Lindberg. Danced in Teatro Municipal Ballet and in her own recitals until 1943, when she began to study Brazilian Indian and other folklore dances, living for many years in Brazil's jungle and hinterland. Returned several times to civilization: in 1948 to form her Ballet Folklorico Felicitas, the first Brazilian Negro dance company; in 1957 to present some Brazilian dances in Paris; in 1959 to publish her first book, *Dances of Brazil.* From 1959 to 1962 travelled through Latin America to study the dances of lost Indian civilizations. Author of *Dances of Brazilian Indians* (Mexico City, 1961) and *One Continent, One People* (Rio, 1962). Sponsored by the National Cultural Council, she is currently lecturing and demonstrating aboriginal dances.

Femmes de Bonne Humeur, Les. See GOOD-HUMORED LADIES, THE.

Fenonjois, Roger, dancer and choreographer, b. Paris, 1920. Studied at Paris Opéra under Gustav Ricaux from 1931. Became premier danseur étoile in 1944, and was one of the most popular male dancers of the Opéra, possessing exceptional ballon. Danced principal roles in *Les Deux Pigeons, Chevalier et la Demoiselle,* and others. Choreographer of *Chansons de France, Jeu de Cartes, La Calle, Pagliacci, Hermaphrodite, Le Faune, Quadrille* (Georges Auric-Jean Hugo, 1943). Appeared in concert performances with Renée Jeanmaire (1943–44); South American concert tours (1946–48); ballet master in Montevideo, Uruguay (1949–55), combining this with seasons as ballet master of Bordeaux Opera (1952–53). Teacher and choreographer in Lima, Peru, since 1958. Established Lundis de la Danse (Dance Thursdays) there (1961).

Fenster, Boris (1916–1960), Peoples' Artist of the RSFSR, Soviet choreographer. Graduated from the Leningrad Ballet School (1936); was accepted into the ballet company of the Maly (Little) Opera Theatre, Leningrad, dancing Harlequin in Fedor Lopukhov's version of *Les Millions d'Arlequin* (Riccardo Drigo), and other ballets. His dance career served merely as an introduction to his real calling. He choreographed his first ballet, *Ashik-Kerib,* to music by Boris Asafiev (1940), and thus started a long and productive career as a choreographer that ended at the Kirov Theatre with his final production *Masquerade* (K. Laputin) on Dec. 29, 1960. Was chief choreographer of the Maly Opera Ballet (1936–56); chief choreographer of the Kirov Ballet (1956–60). Among his other ballets are: *False Bridegroom* (music: Mikhail Chulaki, 1946), *Tale of the Dead Tzarevna and the Seven Giants* (Anatole Liadov and V. Deshevov, 1949), *Youth* (Chulaki, 1949), *The Merry Prankster* (K. Korchmaryov, 1951), *Mistress into Maid* (Asafiev, 1951), *Twelve Months* (K. Bitov, 1954), and, at the Kirov Theatre *Taras Bulba* (Vasily Solovyov-Sedoy, 1955). Fenster was married to Svetlana Sheina, ballerina of the Maly Opera Theatre.

Feodorova, Eugenia, dancer, teacher, choreographer, ballet mistress, b. Kiev, Russia. Studied ballet in the school of the Kiev State Ballet and later at the Kirov in Leningrad. Left Russia in 1947 as a member of a folkloric group appearing in the western zone of Germany. Remained in Europe and danced in Berlin, Milan, and Bilbair; taught in Madrid and Paris. Went to Brazil in 1954 as teacher and ballet mistress for the Ballet do Rio de Janeiro; founded her own school in 1956. Guest choreographer at Teatro Municipal (1958–61), staging *Walpurgis Night, Serenade for Strings, The Discovery of Brazil,* and the full-length *Swan Lake.* Currently ballet mistress and choreographer for the new Brazil Ballet Foundation.

Fermé, in ballet, a closed position or pose. 1st, 3rd, and 5th positions are closed positions.

Fernandez, Royes, dancer, b. New Orleans, La. 1929. Began dance studies with Lelia Haller, a pupil of Laurent Novi-

koff. In summer of 1945 took classes with Alexandra Danilova in N.Y. Later that year auditioned for Alicia Markova and Anton Dolin who encouraged him to make dancing his career. The following summer began to work with Vincenzo Celli and continues to study with him when in N.Y. Made his professional debut with Col. W. de Basil's Original Ballet Russe (1946–47); soloist Markova-Dolin company tour of U.S., Canada, and Mexico (1947–48), dancing *Swan Lake* pas de trois, *Les Sylphides;* soloist Ballet Alicia Alonso (now Ballet de Cuba) (1948–50); principal male dancer and partner of Mia Slavenska in Mia Slavenska Ballet Variante (1951); again Ballet Alicia Alonso (1952–54) as soloist, then premier danseur and partner to Alonso, touring Central and South America, with seasons in Havana, Cuba. Danced Siegfried in the full-length *Swan Lake* staged by Mary Skeaping in Havana, *Le Spectre de la Rose, Apollo,* Albrecht in *Giselle, Black Swan, Nutcracker,* and *Bluebird* pas de deux, Colin in *La Fille Mal Gardée,* and others. Premier danseur with Borovansky Ballet in Australia (1954–56), dancing the Sugar Plum Fairy Cavalier in David Lichine's version of *The Nutcracker,* in his revival of *Francesca da Rimini,* and other leading roles; with Nora Kovach-Istvan Rabovsky Concert Group (fall, 1957); premier danseur, American Ballet Theatre since 1957, having had earlier seasons with this company as soloist between 1950 and 1953. His repertoire includes Albrecht (*Giselle*), Prince (*Swan Lake,* Act 2), male leads (*Theme and Variations, Grand-Pas Glazounov*), the classic pas de deux. Creations include Sailor (*Lady from the Sea*), Nilas (*Moon Reindeer*), one of the two male leads (*Etudes*), James in the American Ballet Theater production of *La Sylphide* (1964), and others. Toured Near East as guest artist with San Francisco Ballet (1959). Has made many television appearances. His pure, virtuoso classic style made a deep impression when American Ballet Theatre toured in the Soviet Union (1960). Appeared as guest artist with London's Festival Ballet for its London summer season (1962) and with Australian Ballet (spring, 1964), always returning as premier danseur of the American Ballet Theatre. Danced James to Toni Lander's *La Sylphide,* choreographed by Harald Lander, in the San Antonio, Tex., première of the ballet (Nov. 11, 1964).

Royes Fernandez, premier danseur of American Ballet Theatre.

Ferrari, Beatriz, Argentine dancer and choreographer, b. Buenos Aires, 1922. Studied dance at the Conservatorio Nacional de Música y Declamación and later at Teatro Colón School with Michel Borovski and Esmée Bulnes, as well as with Margaret Wallman, Vania Psota, and Tatjana Gsovska. Entered Teatro Colón as corps de ballet dancer but soon advanced to solo roles in *Protée, Offenbachiana, The Three-Cornered Hat, La Boutique Fantasque, Joan von Zarissa, The Legend of Joseph, Swan Lake, Schéhérazade, Apollon Musagète, Gli Ucelli,* and others. She left Teatro Colón in 1951 to open a dance school for children. For the past few years she has been specializing in creating ballets for television, presenting some twenty-six programs a year. In 1954 she received the award of the Asociación Periodista Argentina. She is the sister of dancer Victor Ferrari.

Ferrari, Victor, Argentine dancer, b. Buenos Aires, 1923. Studied dance with Dora del Grande, Mercedes Quintana, Esmée Bulnes, and Michel Borovski. Joined Teatro Colón in 1940 and became premier danseur in 1947, the first Argentine to reach this rank at Teatro Colón. In 1952 he was guest artist at the Maggio Musicale Fiorentino. In 1953 went to Paris and danced *Coppélia* with Argentine ballerina Adela Adamova. While in Europe he danced with Tamara Toumanova at Teatro alla Scala, Milan, and with Vera Zorina at the Salzburg Festival. At Colón his repertoire included *Hamlet, Joan von Zarissa, Bolero, Evolución de Movimiento, Apollon Musagète, Coppélia, Les Sylphides, Swan Lake, Protée, Capriccio Espagnol, The Three-Cornered Hat,* and others.

Ferraris, Amalia (1830–1904), Italian-born ballerina of the Paris Opéra during the latter years of the Romantic period, pupil of Carlo Blasis. Appeared as guest ballerina at the St. Petersburg Imperial Theatre. Was particularly noted for her dancing in *Giselle, Les Elfes* (1856), *Marco Spada* (1857) *Sacountala,* and *Faust* (1858).

Ferreira, Arthur (Arthur dos Santos), Brazilian dancer and teacher, b. S. Paulo, 1922. Began dance studies under Maria Olenewa, (1943); later studied under Igor Schwezoff, Vaslav Veltchek, Tatiana Leskova. Made his debut with Ballet da Juventude, Rio de Janeiro (1947); danced in Ballet Society (1948–49); joined Teatro Municipal as first dancer, (1950); leave of absence (1959); danced Stadtheater, Lucerne, Switzerland, (1959–60), under Fred Stebler. Returned to Rio as first dancer and teacher, Ballet Rio de Janeiro (1960–61). Currently at Teatro Municipal. Created roles in *Zuimaaluti, The Scarecrow, Hymn to Beauty, Salamanca do Jarau, The Seven Sins, Bachianas No. 1, Rondo Capriccioso, A Dancing Tragedy, The Sorcerer's Apprentice.*

Ferri, Olga (Olga Ethel Ferri de Lommi), Argentine ballerina, b. Buenos Aires, 1931; m. Enrique Lommi. Graduate of Teatro Colón ballet school where she studied with Esmée Bulnes. While still at school she danced in the Teatro Colón corps de ballet. In 1947 she joined the company as soloist and was made ballerina in 1949. Her repertoire includes: *Giselle, Les Sylphides, Swan Lake, Coppélia, The Nutcracker, Hamlet, Romeo and Juliet, Bourrée Fantasque, The Lady and the Unicorn.* Went to Europe to dance with Milorad Miskovitch in Jack Carter's *El Señor de Mañara* (1959), especially created for them. She was guest artist with the ballet of the State Opera in Munich in the role of the Unicorn which she had danced at the première at the Teatro Colón. Later she was guest artist with Tatjana Gzovska's Berliner Ballett. Danced for nine months with London's Festival Ballet (1960); appeared in the main role of *The Life and Loves of Fanny Elssler,* a film made for European television with choreography by Jack Carter (1961). At present she continues as ballerina of Teatro Colón. She was guest ballerina with London's Festival Ballet and Royal Swedish Ballet (1963).

Festin de l'Araignée, Le. Ballet-pantomime by Gilbert de Voisins; chor.: Leo Staats; music: Albert Roussel; décor: Maxime Dethomas. First prod.: Théâtre des Arts, Paris, Apr. 3, 1913, with Sara-Djeli as the Spider; revived at Opéra-Comique, Paris, Dec. 5, 1922, with an acrobat, Mado Minty. New version (chor.: Albert Aveline; décor: Leyritz); first prod.: Paris Opéra Ballet, May 1, 1940, with Suzanne Lorcia. A Spider waits in her web for her prey: ants, a pair of praying mantis, and a mayfly. See also SPIDER'S BANQUET, THE.

Festival Ballet, London's. This English company owes its origin to a touring company led by Alicia Markova and Anton Dolin in 1949. In 1950 it became the Festival Ballet with Dr. Julian Braunsweg as manager. Its first London season was at the Stoll Theatre (Oct. 24, 1950–Jan. 1, 1951) over which period a number of guest stars appeared, among them Leonide Massine, David Lichine, Tatiana Riabouchinska. The company at that time was headed by Markova and Dolin, with John Gilpin, Nathalie Krassovska, Anna Cheselka, Anita Landa, Noel Rossana, Daphne Dale, and Louis Godfrey, among others. Since that time, while based at the Royal Festival Hall, London, the company has toured widely in Europe, was the first English company to dance in Monte Carlo (1951), toured Canada and the U.S. (1954–55), South America (1960, 1965), and the Near East. The company has always made a feature of guest artists which have included Alexandra Danilova, Tamara Toumanova, Sonia Arova, Beryl Grey, Royes Fernandez, Bruce Marks, Niels Kehlet, Karl Musil, and (for the 1966 London season) Madalena Popa (Romania) and Olga Ferri (Buenos Aires). David Adams and Galina Samtsova who joined the company as guest artists remained as permanent members. Other principal dancers have included Belinda Wright, Violette Verdy, Toni Lander, Marilyn Burr, Dianne Richards, Jeanette Minty, Lucette Aldous, Oleg Briansky, Vassili Trunoff, André Prokovsky, Ben Stevenson, and many others. Markova left in 1952 and Dolin, though dancing less and less, remained as artistic director until 1961 when he was succeeded in that position by John Gilpin who continued also as leading male dancer. In Sept., 1962, London's Festival Ballet Ltd., (the holding company) was liquidated and in its place London's Festival Ballet Trust Ltd. was organized as a non-profit organization, to enable the company to make applications to the Arts Council, local authorities, cultural foundations, etc. for grants. It had been for many years the only major British company receiving no official financial assistance of any kind. Discussions with Ballet Rambert regarding a possible merger in the spring of 1964 came to nothing. In 1965 after consultations with the Greater London Council and the Arts Council regarding continued financial difficulties a new holding company was formed, London Festival Ballet Enterprises Ltd. Donald Albery, an experienced impresario and theatre manager, was appointed chairman and company administrator with Dr. Braunsweg remaining in a purely consultant capacity. A small experimental group, London Dance Theatre, formed by Norman McDowell, was reported to be merging with Festival Ballet. This did not occur, but McDowell was appointed artistic director of the company. The repertoire is composed largely of the standard classics, several Michel Fokine ballets, Harald Lander's *Etudes* and his staging of a one-act version of *Napoli* and the Royal Danish's Ballet's *Coppélia;* also newer works such as *Symphony for Fun* (1952), Nicholas Beriosoff's *Esmeralda* (1954), *The Witch Boy* (1957) Soviet choreographer Vladimir Bourmeister's *The Snow Maiden* (1961), and Vaslav Orlikovsky's *Peer Gynt* (1963). Orlikovsky also staged a full-length *Swan Lake* (1964) but this was replaced by Jack Carter's version which uses the Tchaikovsky score as it was originally written for the 1877 Moscow production (prem.: Mar. 8, 1966, New Theatre, Oxford). Another full-length Carter ballet, *Beatrix* (based on the 1842 François Albert ballet *La Jolie Fille de Gand* and using the same Adolphe Adam music) had its première Aug. 31, 1966 at Royal Festival Hall, London. The company has a two month summer season and a four week Christmas season annually in London.

Festival of Two Worlds, a month-long summer festival of music and dance organized by Gian-Carlo Menotti which, since 1958, has taken place annually in the small Italian hill town of Spoleto, within easy driving distance of Rome. Performances are given either in the Teatro Nuovo or the Teatro Caio Meliso. Jerome Robbins's Ballets: U.S.A. made its first public appearances (June 8, 1958) in the Teatro Nuovo, with a program which included *The Concert, Afternoon of a Faun* and the première of *N.Y. Export:*

Opus Jazz, together with Todd Bolender's *Games* to the Pergolesi-Stravinsky *Pulcinella* Suite. John Butler's Chamber Ballets appeared at the Teatro Caio Meliso but did not give any new works. Both companies returned in 1959, at which time Robbins's *Moves* (performed without sound) was premièred and John Butler premièred *The Sybil* to a score by Carlos Surinach. That year *Album Leaves,* a kind of revue mixing sketches, folk songs, dance and pantomime, was inaugurated. Herbert Ross also presented several new works with a company called the American Ballet, headed by Nora Kaye with Scott Douglas, Glen Tetley, Carmen de Lavallade, Sondra Lee, Bambi Linn. A group under the title New American Ballets and including Mary Hinkson, Akiko Kanda, Arthur Mitchell, Paul Taylor, and others, presented works by Karel Shook, Herbert Ross, Donald McKayle, and Paul Taylor (1960); Taylor's group also appeared in the new edition of *Album Leaves.* American Ballet Theatre performed in its regular repertoire. Robbins's Ballet: U.S.A. returned (1961), and premièred *Events* to a score by Robert Prince in décor by Ben Shahn; Maurice Béjart appeared for the first time, showing his *Symphonie pour un Homme Seul* and his version of Stravinsky's *Le Sacre de Printemps.* In 1962 a group under the title of Ballet of the Festival of Two Worlds was organized by Milan stage director Beppe Menegatti at the request of Menotti. It was headed by Carla Fracci and Milorad Miskovitch, with Janine Monin, André Prokovsky, Antonio Gades, Anna Razzi, and Alfredo Koellner in a repertoire specially choreographed for the Festival. Talley Beatty's company and that of Alwin Nikolais appeared at that Festival, also for the first time. Ballet Rambert appeared at the 1963 Festival and premièred Norman Morrice's *The Travellers.* Dance events at the 1964 Festival included the touring company of the Royal Ballet in Rudolf Nureyev's restaging of *Raymonda,* with Margot Fonteyn and Nureyev in the principal roles; Paul Taylor dance company offering the première of *The Red Room,* choreographed by Taylor to Gunther Schuller's composition *Seven Studies on Themes of Paul Klee,* and two other works from the company's repertoire. In 1965 the ballet companies participating in the Festival were the New York City Ballet and the Württemberg State Opera Ballet of Stuttgart, Germany, with the Nederlands Dans Theater as guests in 1966.

Festivals, Ballet Summer. All over Europe summer festivals of music, dance, and drama, are placing an increasing emphasis on dance. Most important is the Royal Danish Ballet and Music Festival, given annually since 1950, with ballet getting priority both in title and fact. This is unique in presenting productions of the Royal Danish Ballet with no guest artists or guest companies. The Royal Swedish Festival of Opera, Drama, Music and Ballet which takes place early in June makes ballet only a minor part of its schedule, but of historical importance are the recreations of 18th century ballets presented in the little Court Theatre at Drottningholm just outside Stockholm, an exquisite example of the late baroque style in architecture. All the 18th century stage machinery enabling scenery to be changed in ten seconds is still in use, and there are three gloires and other special effects still in perfect order.

Widest in artistic scope of the European Festivals are the Holland Festival and the International Festival of Music and Drama in Edinburgh, Scotland. Neither makes a great feature of dance events though both invite visiting companies. In Edinburgh in particular, the facilities for presenting dance are very inadequate and, unless the event is of exceptional significance, e.g. the appearance in 1963 of Martha Graham and her company, local patrons rather than Festival visitors make up the bulk of the audience.

The famed Salzburg Festival naturally

concerns itself mainly with opera and orchestral concerts but usually offers a few ballet performances, the 1964 visitors being the Yugoslav National Opera Ballet from Zagreb.

There are a number of major Festivals in Italy every year. The Venice Biennale (held every other year) always offers performances by invited companies. One of the oldest European festivals, the Maggio Musicale Fiorentino, held in Florence in May and June, invites companies and sometimes commissions works specially for the occasion, as in 1964 (the 27th Festival) when Aurel Milloss staged a new version of *The Miraculous Mandarin.*

A festival devoted exclusively to dance is the International Ballet Festival held in the beautiful park at Nervi, outside Genoa. The 7th Festival in 1964 featured a group of dancers from the Bolshoi Theatre as well as Kurt Jooss's revival of his master work *The Green Table,* and a number of internationally famous artists, among them Yvette Chauviré dancing the title role in *Giselle.*

Gian-Carlo Menotti directs the annual Festival of Two Worlds in Spoleto, of which dance is always an important part. Jerome Robbins's Ballets: U.S.A. made its debut at the 1958 Festival. In 1964 Rudolf Nureyev staged his version of Marius Petipa's *Raymonda* for England's Royal Ballet as the major dance contribution of that year.

The state opera houses of Germany have in recent years begun to present important ballet festivals, usually with guest artists. Typical was the 1964 season in Munich, May 27 to June 1, when in addition to the Bavarian State Opera Ballet, guest artists from the New York City Ballet, American Ballet Theatre, Paris Opéra, Royal Ballet, Bolshoi Ballet and Sofia (Bulgaria) Opera were presented.

Todd Bolender celebrated the end of his first season as ballet director in Cologne with a special ballet week in July, 1964, which will probably grow into an annual festival. In addition to the resident company Merce Cunningham and his company and Yuriko appeared.

Since John Cranko became ballet director of the State Opera Ballet of Württemberg, Stuttgart has become the most important ballet center in Germany. The annual Ballet Festival Cranko established is becoming one of the major summer events in Europe. His version of the Prokofiev *Romeo and Juliet* in 1963 definitely put Stuttgart on the international ballet map.

Many European cities make dance a feature permanent or occasional, of their annual Art Festivals, among them the great International Festival in Berlin, the Bath (England) Festival and the music festivals in such resort towns as Aix-en-Provence (France) and Wiesbaden (Germany). Dubrovnik (Yugoslavia) always presents ballet during its Summer Festival, and Bregenz (Austria) stages a ballet against the background of Lake Constance.

Fête Etrange, La. Ballet in 2 scenes; chor.: Andrée Howard; music: Gabriel Fauré (six piano pieces and two songs: "Mandoline" and "Soir"; book: Ronald Crichton; décor: Sophie Federovitch. First prod.: London Ballet, Arts Theatre, London, May 23, 1940, with Frank Staff (Julien—the Boy), Maude Lloyd (The Young Chatelaine), David Paltenghi (The Young Nobleman). A month later, June 20, Ballet Rambert gave its first performance with the same cast. It was taken into the repertoire of Sadler's Wells Theatre Ballet (with orchestration by Lennox Berkeley) Mar. 25, 1947, with Donald Britton, June Brae and Anthony Burke in the principal roles; Leo Kersley and David Poole later danced the two male roles with particular success. This production (the music re-orchestrated by Guy Warrack) was taken into the repertoire of Royal Ballet late in 1957 when the two companies were combined under one name. Pirmin Trecu, who had possibly his greatest personal success as the Boy, gave his farewell performance in this ballet. Basil Crichton, who also selected the music, was inspired by an episode from Alain Fournier's novel *Le Grand Meaulnes.* In his own words (to quote Cyril W. Beaumont), the ballet is concerned with "the tragedy of sensitive adolescence, symbolized not only by the sequence of events, but by the gradual though pronounced change of mood; anticipation leading through increasing happiness to ecstasy, which in its turn falls into sadness and disillusion."

Fêtes Chinoises. First ballet by Jean Georges Noverre presented in 1749 at the Foire St. Laurent, Paris. The décor was by François Boucher and the costumes by Louis Boquet.

Feuillet, Raoul Ager, inventor of a dance notation system published in 1701 under the title *Chorégraphie ou l'Art d'Écrire la Danse.* It was published in England in 1728 as *Choreography or the Art of Writing Dancing.* Feuillet was a maître de ballet and composer of ballets in Paris. He also published a *Recueil de Danses* which described a number of the dances performed at the Opéra. His collaborator was André Lorin, conductor of the Académie Royale and officer in charge of the dancing masters of the court. P. Siris, an English dancing master, published in 1706 *The Art of Dancing,* a translation of Feuillet's *Chorégraphie.*

Fibers. Modern dance work; chor.: Paul Taylor; music: Arnold Schoenberg's Five Pieces for Orchestra, op. 16; décor: Rouben ter-Arutunian. First prod.: Paul Taylor and Dance Company, Hunter College Playhouse, N.Y., Jan. 14, 1961, with Maggie Newman, Akiko Kanda, Paul Taylor, Dan Wagoner. An evocation of some unknown rite, perhaps involving tree worship, since the stage is dominated by the mystery of the strange fibrous growth which appears to regulate the actions of the dancers.

Field, John (John Greenfield), English dancer, ballet master, director, b. Doncaster, 1921; m. Anne Heaton. Studied with Shelagh Elliott Clarke and Edna Slocombe in Liverpool and made his debut with Liverpool Ballet Club (1938). Entered Sadler's Wells (now Royal) Ballet (1939), becoming principal dancer. Was with the company, except for service in World War II, until he retired from dancing in 1956 upon his appointment as director of Sadler's Wells Theatre Ballet, retaining this position until the company was merged with the Royal Ballet. He then assumed the title Assistant Director, Royal Ballet, and remains in charge of the touring portion. He was noted for the clean elegance of his style in the great classic roles, dancing Siegfried (*Swan Lake*), Albrecht (*Giselle*), Florimund (*The Sleeping Beauty*), male dancer (*Les Sylphides*), also dancing Caricaturist (*Mam'zelle Angot*), Red Knight (*Checkmate*), and others.

Fifield, Elaine, dancer, b. Sydney, Australia, 1931. Studied dance with Elizabeth Scully; won Overseas Scholarship of Royal Academy of Dancing (1945). Went to London (1946) to study at Sadler's Wells (now Royal) Ballet School from which she was taken into the Sadler's Wells Theatre Ballet (1947), becoming principal dancer. Created title role (*Selina*), and her most important creation—Poll in *Pineapple Poll;* also danced leads in *Les Rendez-vous, The Nutcracker, Swan Lake* (Act 2), and others. Transferred to Sadler's Wells (now Royal) Ballet (1954); as ballerina (1956) she danced Odette-Odile (*Swan Lake*), created title role (*Madame Chrysanthème*). Returned to Australia (1954) and, after a few performances with Borovansky Ballet, retired upon her marriage to a non-professional.

Figure in the Carpet, The. Ballet in 5 scenes; chor.: George Balanchine; music: George Frederick Handel's *Royal Fireworks Music* and *Water Music;* décor: Esteban Francés (costumes executed by Barbara Karinska). First prod.: New York City Ballet, City Center, N.Y., Apr. 13, 1960. Scene 1 (The Sands of the Desert) is a big, typical Balanchine ensemble headed by Violette Verdy, the only connection with sands of the desert being the color of the costumes. Scene 2 (The Weaving of the Carpet) is more of the same with men added to the previously all-girl ensemble. Scene 3 (The Building of the Palace) is a pastiche of an 18th century court ballet, in keeping with the period of the music, with entrées for representatives of various nationalities, culminating in a pas de deux for the Prince and Princess of Persia (Melissa Hayden and Jacques d'Amboise), after which Scenes 4 and 5 (The Gardens of Paradise and Apotheosis—The Fountain of Paradise) show the completed carpet hanging as the back cloth. The ballet was presented in honor of the Fourth International Congress of Iranian Art and Archeology which opened in N.Y., Apr. 27, 1960. The underlying ideas in the organization of the sequences of scenes were suggested by Dr. Arthur Upham Pope, Director of the Congress.

Fille de Marbre, La. Ballet in 2 acts, 3 scenes; chor. and book: Arthur Saint-Léon; music: Cesare Pugni; décor: Cambon and Thierry. First prod.: Théâtre de l'Académie Royale de Musique, Paris, Oct. 20, 1847, with Fanny Cerito (title role), Arthur Saint-Léon (Sculptor), H. Desplaces (Prince); St. Petersburg première: Dec. 1, 1856, with Cerito in title role. Possibly this ballet was a revival of *Alma* (chor.: Jules Perrot, 1842) in which Cerito was so successful. *The Marble Maiden* by Vernoy de Saint-Georges and Albert, music by Adolphe Adam, produced at Theatre Royal, Drury Lane, London, in 1845, with Adèle Dumilâtre in title role, Albert (Sculptor), Lucien Petipa (Prince), had a theme similar to the first scene of this ballet. As the title implies, the ballet has a Pygmalion-like story in which the sculptor of a statue of a beautiful woman begs the Devil to bring the girl to life. The Devil agrees on the condition that if the girl ever falls in love with a mortal she will be turned back into a marble statue. After numerous adventures the girl falls in love with a Moorish Prince and is changed back into a statue.

Fille du Danube, La. Ballet in 2 acts, 4 scenes; chor. and book: Filippe Taglioni; music: Adolphe Adam; décor: Pierre Ciceri, Despléchin, Diéterle, Feuchère, Séchan; costumes: Henri d'Orchevillers. First prod.: Théâtre de l'Académie Royale de Musique, Paris, Sept. 21, 1836, with Maria Taglioni and Joseph Mazilier in principal parts; London première: Theatre Royal, Drury Lane, Nov. 21, 1837; St. Petersburg première: 1837, with Taglioni and her father in the principal roles. A girl called the Daughter of the Danube because she was found on the shore of the Danube river as an infant, and Rudolph, a young squire of the local baron, are very much in love. But the baron decides to marry and orders all nubile village girls to come to the castle to a ball during which he will choose a bride. At the ball his choice falls on the Daughter of the Danube; but she, remaining faithful to Rudolph, jumps from the castle balcony into the Danube. In his grief Rudolph follows her into her watery grave. There the Nymph of the Danube unites the two lovers and restores them to the outer world.

Fille du Pharaon, La. Ballet in 3 acts, 7 scenes with prologue and epilogue; chor.: Marius Petipa; music: Cesare Pugni; book: Vernoy de Saint-Georges and Marius Petipa. First prod.: Maryinsky Theatre, St. Petersburg, Jan. 30, 1862, with Carolina Rosati in the title role and Nicholas Goltz, Marius Petipa, Lev Ivanov in the cast. *Le Roman de la Momie* by Théophile Gautier was the inspiration for this ballet, which Petipa produced for Rosati's final appearance in St.

Petersburg. It was so successful that Petipa was appointed second ballet master of the Imperial Theatre. The ballet deals with an Englishman, Lord Wilson, and his servant, John Bull, who are touring Egypt. In the desert they join a merchant's caravan. A simoom arises and the company seeks shelter in a nearby pyramid, which contains the mummy of the beautiful Princess Aspicia, the daughter Pharaoh. Waiting for the sand storm to subside, the bored men begin to smoke opium. Soon they fall into a dream during which Aspicia comes to life and the pyramid is transformed into Pharaoh's palace. Lord Wilson becomes Taor, a young Egyptian in love with Aspicia, and John Bull assumes the image of his slave, Passifont. Then begins Act 1 and the long story of Taor's love for Aspicia and the adventures of the two lovers pursued by the King of Nubia, who is also attracted by Aspicia. The performance of the original version lasted some four hours and required the participation of nearly four hundred dancers and supernumeraries.

Fille Mal Gardée, La. Ballet in 2 acts, 3 scenes; chor. and book: Jean Dauberval; music: various composers—later Peter Ludwig Hertel. First prod.: Bordeaux, France, 1789, with Mlle. Theodore as Lise. Jean Aumer staged it at the Paris Opéra (1828) to music by François Joseph Hérold (to which Frederick Ashton reverted for his version). *La Fille Mal Gardée* was first presented in the U.S. at the Lafayette Theatre, N.Y., July 31, 1828, and Fanny Elssler gave her farewell performance in America as Lise (July 1, 1842). In 1864 new music by Peter Ludwig Hertel was used and when the ballet was re-staged (under the title of *Useless Precautions*) in St. Petersburg by Marius Petipa and Lev Ivanov (1882), this was the score used (with additions by Delibes, Minkus, Pugni, Drigo, and Anton Rubinstein). It is the St. Petersburg version on which all others are based, with the exception of Ashton's for the Royal Ballet. Lise was a favorite role of Anna Pavlova, whose company had the ballet in its repertoire for many years. Enrico Cecchetti often played the part of Mother Simone, traditionally played by a man. *La Fille Mal Gardée* was revived by Mikhail Mordkin (largely with his own choreography) in décor by Serge Soudeikine for the Mordkin Ballet, Alvin Theatre, N.Y., Nov. 12, 1938, with Lucia Chase (Lise), Dimitri Romanoff (Colin), Mordkin (Mother Simone). It was re-staged by Ballet (now American Ballet) Theatre, with choreographic revisions by Bronislava Nijinska, Jan. 19, 1940, at Center Theatre, N.Y., with Patricia Bowman (Lise), Yurek Shabelevsky (Colin), Edward Caton (Mother Simone); in the repertoire of Ballet Theatre as *The Wayward Daughter* (1941) and *Naughty Lisette* (1942) with Irina Baronova (Lise), Romanoff (Colin), Simon Semenoff (Mother Simone). Reverting to its original title, Romanoff staged a revival Apr. 17, 1949, with Nana Gollner, Igor Youskevitch, and Caton. Since then Janet Reed, Alicia Alonso, and Lupe Serrano have all enjoyed a great success in this most delightful soubrette role. Fernand Nault staged a version of *La Fille Mal Gardée* for the Robert Joffrey Ballet, as did Ludmilla Chiriaeff for Les Grands Ballets Canadiens. *La Fille Mal Gardée* shares with the Royal Danish Ballet's *The Whims of Cupid and the Ballet Master* the distinction of being one of the only two 18th century ballets still extant although, obviously, in a very different form from that in which it was originally seen in 1789. It was one of the first ballets to be based on people who might have a real life existence instead of on traditional mythological beings of the ballets before this time. It was also one of the earliest comic ballets. The story tells how Lise and her lover Colin foil the attempts of her mother and a neighboring rich farmer to marry her off to the farmer's son (who is himself quite happy to escape matrimony).

Fille Mal Gardée, La. Ballet in 2 acts, 3 scenes; chor.: Frederick Ashton; music: François Joseph Hérold, arr. re-orch. and augmented by John Lanchbery; décor: Osbert Lancaster. First prod.: Royal Ballet, Royal Opera House, Covent Garden, London, Jan. 28, 1960, with Nadia Nerina (Lise), David Blair (Colas), Stanley Holden (Mother Simone), Alexander Grant (Alain). This is a completely new version of the old ballet, only the story remaining and, to some extent, the Hérold music. The score for the 1828 Paris Opéra production, which Ivor Guest arranged to have sent to Ashton, proved to be almost entirely in 6/8 time and was, in general, a disappointment. Ashton went over it with Lanchbery and the Royal Ballet conductor began a new orchestration and composed little additions. Then Guest discovered a violin score (dated 1837) which included a pas de deux that had been added for Fanny Elssler and which contained many quotations from the Donizetti opera *L'Elisir d'Amore*. Finally Ivor Guest unearthed the original Bordeaux score from which Hérold had composed his version. None of these various scores contained any indication of how the score fit the action of the ballet, so Ashton and Lanchbery pieced it together to make music and action match. The ballet follows exactly the original story line and contains virtuoso dance passages for Lise and Colas (as Colin is called here) and a wonderful character study of humor and pathos in the farmer's simple-minded son, Alain, a part which is one of Alexander Grant's great triumphs. Ashton's *La Fille Mal Gardée* is also the first British ballet which uses English folk dance as source material (maypole, Morris, sword dance, and Lancashire clog, this last being adapted for the dance of Mother Simone). Merle Park, Antoinette Sibley, Doreen Wells, Maryon Lane have also danced Lise, and Donald Macleary, Christopher Gable, and Graham Usher, Colas. The roles, however, remain closely identified with their creators: Nerina and Blair.

Filling Station. Ballet in 1 act; chor.: Lew Christensen; music: Virgil Thomson; book: Lincoln Kirstein; costumes: Paul Cadmus. First prod.: Ballet Caravan, Avery Memorial Theatre, Hartford, Conn., Jan. 6, 1938, with Jane Deering, Marie Jeanne, Todd Bolender, Harold Christensen, Lew Christensen, Marjorie Moore, Douglas Coudy, Fred Danieli, Erick Hawkins, Eugene Loring. A ballet in the tradition of the comic strip set in the period of bootleggers, speakeasies and Chicago gangsters, in which the noble filling station attendant Mac, is shown as the Great American Hero. It was revived by New York City Ballet, City Center, N.Y., May 12, 1953, with Jacques d'Amboise (Mac), Janet Reed (Rich Girl), Michael Maule (Rich Boy), Robert Barnett and Edward Bigelow (Truck Drivers), Stanley Zompakos (Motorist), Shaun O'Brien (His Wife, in travesty), Edith Brozak (Child). The original version had a tragic ending as the Rich Girl (who is also very drunk) is killed by a gangster's bullet. In the revival, she fools all by gaily waving just as her funeral procession carries her out of sight.

Fine Arts, The, the arts that create things of beauty or of the imagination for their own sake and not for utility. The major fine arts include architecture, drawing, music, painting, poetry, and sculpture; the minor arts are dance and drama.

Fini, Leonor, Italian born painter and designer, working in Paris. Extremely original style of a troubled romanticism. Her ballets include *Le Palais de Cristal* (George Balanchine, Paris Opéra, 1947), *Les Demoiselles de la Nuit* (Roland Petit, Ballets de Paris de Roland Petit, 1948), *Le Rêve de Leonor* (Frederick Ashton, Ballets de Paris de Roland Petit, 1949), *Orféo* (Janine Charrat, Fenice Theatre, Venice, 1952), *Le Spectre de la Rose* (Teatro alla Scala, Milan).

Finishing School. Ballet in 1 act; chor.:

Gweneth Lloyd; music: an album of rediscovered music by Johann Strauss, including *"Explosions Polka," "Serail Tanze," "Paroxysm Waltz,"* and *"Festival Quadrille"*; décor: John Russell; costumes: Dorothy Phillips. First prod.: Winnipeg (now Royal Winnipeg) Ballet, Walker Theatre, Winnipeg, Nov. 6, 1942, with Betty Farrally and Paddy Stone heading the cast. The ballet takes place in a fashionable girls' school in the Paris of the 1870's. A rebellious new girl is admitted and upsets the entire school with her mischievous pranks.

Finland, Ballet in. Finland has had a state-supported ballet company since 1879 when the Russian government built an opera house in Helsingfors (now Helsinki), the seat of the Russian Governor-General of the Grand Duchy of Finland, a part of the Russian empire since 1809. It declared its independence in 1917 following the Russian revolution; two years later it officially became a republic, with Helsinki as its capital.

When the theatre opened to the public it was called the Alexander Theatre in honor of Czar Alexander II, then emperor of Russia. The theatre is now called Suomen Kansallisooppera (The National Opera House). A ballet school was established at the theatre almost from the very beginning and within a few years Finnish dancers replaced the Russian in the operettas and occasional operas which were being given in the theatre. The theatre is small but stately; it seats seven hundred and is decorated in white and gold.

During the first decade of this century the Russian impresario Edward Fazer became director of the theatre. He introduced opera and also arranged frequent visits of Russian ballerinas and premiers danseurs and small ballet groups from the Maryinsky Theatre in St. Petersburg.

First to be mentioned as resident ballet master and choreographer of the theatre was George Gué (d. 1962), a Russian of Finnish extraction who had worked in St. Petersburg. He is credited with raising the ballet school to a professional level and contributing much to the development of the Finnish ballet. Among the instructors in the school were the Russian dancer and ballet master Alexander Saxelin (d. 1959), a pupil of Paul Gerdt; also Nicholas Legat and Michel Fokine, as well as the ballerina Senta Will (of Finnish extraction), who after her marriage was known as Senta Will von Knorring.

In 1922 Gué produced the first full-length ballet ever to be staged in Finland, *Swan Lake,* with Marie Paischeff as Odette-Odile. A year later came a program of shorter works, including *Chopiniana* (*Les Sylphides*) and *Schéhérazade,* with von Knorring as première danseuse. In 1932 Saxelin replaced Gué as ballet master. The first Finnish choreographer was Irja Koskinen, who staged a ballet to Jan Sibelius's *Scaramouche* (1935). She revived this ballet in 1965 and still continues teaching and coaching in the school. She stopped dancing in 1959, having been prima ballerina since 1935. Another Finnish dancer to become a choreographer is Elsa Silvesterson who staged *Festivo* to music by Sibelius (1966).

Guest choreographers over the years included Birger Bartholin, Mary Skeaping (*Swan Lake* and *The Sleeping Beauty*), Rostislav Zakharov (*The Fountain of Bakhchisarai*), Birgit Cullberg (*Miss Julie* and *Odysseus*), Serge Lifar (*Firebird, Suite en Blanc, Romeo and Juliet*), Harald Lander (*Etudes, Aubade, Qarrtsiluni*). Nicholas Beriosoff also served as ballet master (1963–64).

The Finnish National Ballet lists a roster of fifty-three dancers; it can also call on the services of fifteen trained mimes and supernumeraries. The principal dancers at this writing are Margaretha von Bahr, Doris Laine, Maj-Lis Rajala, Virpi Laristo, Liisa Taxell, Seija Silverberg, Arija Nieminen; also Heikki Värtsi, Matti Tikkanen, Uuno Onkinen, Leo Ahonen, Klaus Salin, Fred Negendank, Helmer Salmi (mime). The ballet company gives

Uuno Onkinen (center) in Harald Lander's Qarrtsiluni, *staged for the Finnish National Ballet.*

frequent performances throughout Europe. Its most recent tour was in the fall of 1966 when it danced in Lausanne, Bern, and Stockholm with success. A group of dancers from the company made a tour of the U.S. (fall–winter, 1959). A group of four dancers (Virpi Laristo, Seija Silverberg, Helmer Salmi, and Heikki Värtsi) danced in the Finnish Pavilion at the N.Y. World's Fair (1964).

Among Finnish dancers well known outside Finland are the famous Soviet-born dancer and choreographer Vasily Vainonen (d. 1964); ballerina and motion picture star Taina Elg; Kari Karnakoski, soloist of Ballet Theatre, now teaching in Helsinki; Lucia Nifontova and Arvo Martikainen, soloists with the Ballet Russe de Monte Carlo in the mid-1930's. Of Finnish extraction are the Tyven sisters, Gertrude (d. 1966) and Sonia, the latter using a stage name of Taanila. Both were soloists with the Ballet Russe de Monte Carlo. Sonia married Robert Lindgren, dean of the Dance Dept. of the North Carolina State School of the Arts, where she is a member of the ballet faculty.

Fiorato, Hugo, conductor, violinist, b. New York City, 1914. Associate conductor of New York City Ballet since 1955, he also was a member of the WQXR String Quartet (radio station of the *N.Y. Times*). His musical training was at the Frankfurt (Germany) Conservatory, with Arnold Volpé, and at the Damrosch School (violin). A musical prodigy who made his debut as a violinist at the age of five, he became a child actor with the Clare Tree Major Children's Theatre until, at eighteen, he formed the Gotham Trio. Entered National Orchestral Association (1932), becoming concert master in the 1940's, and conductor and supervisor of training of orchestra (1956–57 season). Became concert master of WQXR String Orchestra (1943); organized the string quartet (1947). Concert master and personnel director of Ballet Society orchestra (1946), remaining with the organization when the performing company became New York City Ballet. Has conducted at many music Festivals in U.S. and abroad.

Firebird. Ballet in 1 act, 3 scenes; chor. and book: Michel Fokine; music: Igor Stravinsky—his first score for ballet; décor: Alexander Golovine. First prod.: Diaghilev Ballets Russes, Paris Opéra, June 25, 1910, with Tamara Karsavina (Firebird), Michel Fokine (Ivan Tsarevich), Enrico Cecchetti (Kostchei), Vera Fokina (Tsarevna). *Firebird* was revived in 1926 with new décor by Nathalie Gontcharova (the original having been damaged), Felia Doubrovska assuming the title role. George Balanchine was the Kostchei of this production. It was one of the Diaghilev ballets revived by Col. de Basil's Ballets Russes de Monte Carlo and provided Alexandra Danilova with one of her greatest roles. Irina Baronova and Tamara Toumanova also danced *Firebird* for the de Basil company. In 1954 Serge Grigoriev and Lubov Tchernicheva staged a careful revival for Sadler's Wells (now Royal) Ballet as part of the commemoration of the twenty-fifth anniversary of the death of Serge Diaghilev; it was premièred at the Edinburgh Festival, Aug. 23, 1954, with Margot Fonteyn (Firebird), Michael Somes (Ivan Tsarevich), Frederick Ashton (Kostchei), Svetlana Beriosova (Tsarevna). Nadia Nerina and Annette Page have also danced the title role in this production. Another version, with choreography by Adolph Bolm, in décor by Marc Chagall, was staged for Ballet (now American Ballet) Theatre, Metropolitan Opera House, New York, Oct. 24, 1945, with Alicia Markova and Anton Dolin in the principal roles. New York City Ballet acquired this décor and George Balanchine choreographed his own version,

Final scene of Fokine's Firebird *in décor by Nathalie Gontcharova for Col. de Basil's Ballets Russes.*

using the score shortened by Stravinsky himself in 1945 expressly for a smaller ballet orchestra. The Balanchine *Firebird* was premièred at City Center, N.Y., Nov. 27, 1949, with Maria Tallchief and Francisco Moncion as the Firebird and Ivan Tsarevich. Melissa Hayden and Patricia Wilde have also danced the title role. Yet another version is that of Serge Lifar (Paris Opéra, July 4, 1954, with Nina Vyroubova and Youly Algaroff). Aurel Milloss is only one of many other choreographers who have been attracted by the story, which is taken from Russian fairy tales. Hunting in the forest, Ivan captures the Firebird who wins her freedom by giving him one of her magic feathers with which the young prince may summon her in time of danger. Into the forest comes a troupe of young girls—princesses under the spell of the evil and immortal Kostchei. He and his creatures come upon the scene before Ivan and the princess, with whom he has fallen in love, can make their escape. But Ivan summons the Firebird, who shows him where to find the egg which holds the Kostchei's life. Ivan breaks the egg, the Kostchei dies, and the spell is broken. In the final scene Ivan Tsarevich is crowned, his beautiful bride beside him and all the princesses united with the princes to whom they were formerly betrothed.

Firebird. Ballet in 3 scenes; chor.: Adolph Bolm; music: Igor Stravinsky; décor: Marc Chagall. First prod.: Ballet Theatre, Metropolitan Opera House, N.Y., Oct. 24, 1945, with Alicia Markova (Firebird), Anton Dolin (Ivan Tzarevich), John Taras (Kostchei), Diana Adams (Tsarevna). Serge Lifar and Aurel Milloss have also staged their own versions of this ballet.

Firebird. Ballet in 3 scenes; chor.: George Balanchine; music: Igor Stravinsky; décor: Marc Chagall (from the Adolph Bolm production for Ballet Theatre, purchased by New York City Ballet from S. Hurok). First prod.: New York City Ballet, City Center, N.Y., Nov. 27, 1949, with Maria Tallchief (Firebird), Francisco Moncion (Ivan Tsarevich), Pat McBride (Tsarevna). This follows the general story line of the Fokine work except that the Firebird, when summoned by Ivan, brings him a magic sword with which to overcome the Kostchei and his evil entourage. The score is the shortened version arranged by Stravinsky, more in the nature of a suite.

First Chamber Dance Quartet, The, group of four dancers, Lois Bewley, Nadine Revene (later Janice Groman), Charles Bennett, Bill Carter, which made its debut Nov. 12, 1961, at the YM–YWHA, N.Y. The dancers choreograph all their own works and Lois Bewley's *Pi–r²* which she dances with Bennett and Carter is one of the most completely successful pieces of choreographic satirical comment ever invented, the object of the satire being the Balanchine themeless and costumeless ballets to very advanced music. The group (with Janice Groman taking Nadine Revene's place after the first season) has travelled all over the U.S. and was invited to stage and choreograph a new chamber opera *Masque of Angels* (libretto by John Olon; music by Dominick Argento), and John Blow's 17th century chamber opera *Venus and Adonis,* at the Tyrone Guthrie Theatre, Minneapolis, Minn. (Jan. 9 and 11, 1964). The troupe were Artists-in-Residence at the Fort Wayne (Ind.) Cultural Center, sponsored by the Fine Arts Foundation (May, 1965).

Fisherman and His Soul, The. Ballet in 1 act; chor.: Grant Strate; music: Harry Somers; décor: Kay Ambrose. First prod.: National Ballet of Canada, Palace Theatre, Hamilton, Nov. 5, 1956, with Earl Kraul (Fisherman), Harold da Silva (His Soul), Lilian Jarvis (Mermaid), Angela Leigh (Leading Witch). Based on a fairy tale by Oscar Wilde, the ballet shows the attempts of the Fisherman to rid himself of his Soul so that he may consummate his love for the Mermaid. The Witch provides the solution which is also the final tragedy.

Flamenco, a Sevillian gypsy; also dances of the Sevillian gypsy and, loosely, all non-formal Spanish dances. The rhythm-forms of flamenco dances are: Alegrias, Soleares, Bulerias, Farruca, Zapateado, Tango, and Zambra. See also SPANISH DANCE, THE.

Flames of Paris, The. Ballet in 4 acts and 6 scenes; chor.: Vasily Vainonen; music: Boris Asafiev; book: Nicolai Volkov and Vladimir Dmitriev; décor: Vladimir Dmitriev. First prod.: Kirov Theatre, Leningrad, Nov. 7, 1932, with Vakhtang Chabukiani (Jerome), Olga Jordan (Jeanne), Nina Anisimova (Thérèse), Galina Ulanova (Mireille de Poitiers). Asafiev's music uses melodies typical of the period, including the "Ça Ira" and "Carmagnole," sung by a chorus. The ballet deals with episodes in the French Revolution of 1789, including the march of the Marseillais on Paris and the storming of the Tuileries. Jerome leads the Marseillais battalion and Jeanne, Thérèse, and Mireille de Poitiers join the Revolution. The ballet ends with a grand divertissement modelled after the open-air celebrations in the style of Louis David, the French painter who was dictator over the arts during the Revolution.

Fleming, Robert, Canadian composer, b. Prince Albert, Saskatchewan, 1921. Studied music in Saskatoon and at Royal College of Music, London, and Royal Conservatory of Music, Toronto. Is a Licentiate of the Royal Schools of Music (LRSM). Composed scores for the ballets *Chapter 13* (1947) and *Shadow of the Prairie,* both commissioned by the Winnipeg (now Royal Winnipeg) Ballet; and *Ballet Introduction* (1960) for Les Grands Ballets Canadiens, choreography by Eric Hyrst. Currently music director of National Film Board of Canada, Montreal.

Flic-Flac, in ballet, a brushed or flicked step used as a connecting step. Technique: start 2nd pos. L toe pointed; brush or flick L toe on floor in front of R ft., finishing sur le cou-de-pied in front; rise on R half-toe, executing one turn to R at same time flicking L toe back of R ft.; finish facing front, L ft. sur le cou-de-pied in back. This is flic-flac en tournant. It can also be done without the turn.

Flickers. Modern dance work; chor.: Charles Weidman; music: Lionel Nowak. First perf.: Dec. 27, 1941, N.Y. with Weidman, Doris Humphrey, Beatrice Seckler and company. Four satires on silent film plots: "Hearts Aflame"—the old mortgage theme; "Hearts Courageous"—the traditional Western; "Flowers of the Desert"—Weidman as a Valentino-type Sheik; "Wages of Sin"—Doris Humphrey as an old-style movie vamp, à la Theda Bara.

Flier, Jaap, Dutch dancer, b. The Hague, 1934. Studied with Sonia Gaskell and Benjamin Harkarvy. Has danced with both the Nederlands Ballet and Nederlands Dans Theater (see HOLLAND, DANCE IN) and is currently with the latter as soloist. His roles include *Les Sylphides,* Albrecht (*Giselle*), Siegfried (*Swan Lake,* Act 2), Tancred (*The Duel*), Poet (*Night Shadow*), title role in *The Prodigal Son,* and others.

Flindt, Flemming, Danish dancer, b. Copenhagen, 1936. Entered Royal Danish Ballet school (1946); accepted into the company (1955); promoted to soloist (1957). Soon after gaining the title of soloist he obtained a leave of absence to be guest artist with other companies, among them London's Festival Ballet, Paris Opéra Ballet, Ruth Page's Chicago Opera Ballet. Returned to Copenhagen as guest artist with his old company (1962), his repertoire including the leading male roles in *Carmen, Moon Reindeer, Etudes* (which he also danced with Festival Ballet), *Graduation Ball* (Drummer), and

Flemming Flindt as guest choreographer for the Metropolitan's production of Faust *(1965)*.

others. Guest artist with England's Royal Ballet (May–June, 1963), dancing *Flower Festival at Genzano* pas de deux, *Les Sylphides, Don Quixote* pas de deux, *La Fille Mal Gardée, Sylvia* (the last three with Melissa Hayden). Dances as guest artist in many European opera houses but retains his title as premier danseur étoile of the Paris Opéra where, on Dec. 18, 1963, he created the leading male role in George Balanchine's *Scotch Symphony* for that company. Choreographed Ionesco's short play *The Lesson* for Danish television (Sept. 20, 1963); later staged for the Opéra Comique, Paris, Apr. 6, 1964, and in 1965 for the Royal Danish Ballet (U.S. prem.: Dec. 7, 1965, under the title *The Private Lesson*). On Sept. 27 of that year the Metropolitan Opera Ballet presented a new production of *Faust* with choreography by Flindt. In Jan. 1966, Flindt was appointed director of the Royal Danish Ballet. His first new ballet for this company (prem.: May 11, 1966) was the full-evening work *The Three Musketeers,* based on the Dumas novel.

Floor-Work, in modern dance the general term used to describe the sequence of technical exercises done on the floor at the beginning of each technique class, before a rehearsal and before a performance.

Flore. Ballet produced in Paris in 1669 which bears the distinction of being the last ballet in which Louis XIV appeared.

Flower Festival at Genzano. Ballet in 1 act; chor.: August Bournonville; music: Edward Helsted and Holger Simon Paulli. First perf.: Royal Danish Ballet, Copenhagen, 1858. The action is based on a real event which occurred at the beginning of the 19th century: it recounts the romance and trial of the lovely Rosa and her sweetheart, the sharpshooter Paolo. Outside Denmark only the typically Bournonville pas de deux is known. It is in the repertoire of Ruth Page's Chicago Opera Ballet, England's Royal Ballet, Robert Joffrey Ballet and others. The Festival itself is still an annual event at Genzano, taking place in June.

Fokina, Vera (Antonova) (1886–1958), Russian dancer and widow of Michel Fokine. Graduated from the St. Petersburg Imperial Ballet School (1904); married Fokine (1905) and became his most faithful disciple. Very successful in the Fokine repertoire in Russia, she achieved her greatest fame in Western Europe where she made her debut in 1909 in the Diaghilev Ballets Russes. In 1916 she was promoted to first soloist of the Maryinsky Ballet, but resigned in 1918. Among her outstanding ballets were *Carnaval, Cléopâtre, Schéhérazade,* and *Le Spectre de la Rose,* all choreographed by her husband. She died in N.Y., July 29, 1958. Their son Vitale survives her.

Fokine, Michel (1880–1942), great choreographer and reformer of ballet, was born in St. Petersburg, Apr. 26, 1880. He entered the Imperial School of Ballet in 1889 and was graduated from it nine years later. Upon his graduation he was accepted into the company of the Maryinsky

Michel Fokine

Theatre with the official rank of soloist. This was contrary to general practice, which required that every graduate begin his career on the Imperial Stage as a member of the corps de ballet.

His debut took place on his eighteenth birthday, Apr. 26, 1898, in a pas de quatre in *Paquita,* a ballet by Joseph Mazilier, restaged for the Imperial Theatre by Marius Petipa.

Michel Fokine was regarded in his time an excellent dancer; he was strong, graceful, expressive and he possessed a considerable technique. But he earned his place in the history of ballet not as a dancer, but as a choreographer and teacher. His teaching career began in 1902 when he was appointed to take charge of an intermediate class at the Imperial School. Three years later he was given the advanced class.

Fokine's first choreographic effort was a short ballet, *Acis et Galathée,* staged in 1905 for a pupils' performance at the Imperial School. The same year he produced one of his most popular compositions, *The Dying Swan,* a solo dance for Anna Pavlova to Saint-Saëns' music, performed by the great dancer at a charitable function.

It was not until late in 1907 that the management of the Imperial Theatre permitted Fokine to stage a ballet for the theatre proper. This was *Le Pavillon d'Armide,* a ballet in three scenes to music by Nicholas Tcherepnine and décor and costumes by Alexandre Benois. Anna Pavlova, Vaslav Nijinsky, and the choreographer himself danced the main roles.

Long before this event took place, Fokine began to think about the necessity for reform in ballet. In 1904 he submitted to the Imperial Theatre a scenario for a ballet based on Longus' *Daphnis and Chloë* and appended to it notes outlining his plan for a reform of ballet.

He demanded in this plan inspired music, unity of construction, unity of expression; he elaborated on the necessity of an organic fusion of the three elements of ballet: dance, music and painting.

The management did not accept Fokine's scenario and ignored his suggestions.

A year after the production of *Le Pavillon d'Armide* Serge Diaghilev invited Fokine to stage several ballets for the proposed season of the Russian Ballet in Paris in 1909. Fokine accepted. This was the real beginning of Fokine's career as a choreographer and the beginning of a new era in ballet.

It would not be amiss to note here that Fokine staged some sixty-odd ballets, but only a few of them were choreographed for the Imperial Theatre and one for the present Russian State Theatre. Among them were: *Acis et Galathée* (1905), *A Midsummer Night's Dream* (1906), *Le Pavillon d'Armide* (1907), *Eunice* (1908), *Chopiniana* (1908), the *Polovetzian Dances* in the opera *Prince Igor* (1909), *Egyptian Nights* (1909), *Orpheus and Euridice* (1911), *Judith* (1912), *Eros* (1915); the dances in the opera *Russlan and Ludmila* (1917); and, for the post-revolutionary State Theatre, *Stenka Razin* (1917).

Beginning in 1909 Fokine spent most of his time in France returning to Russia only to fulfill his contractual obligations to the Imperial Theatre. From 1911 to 1914 he actually lived in France. He returned to Russia at the outbreak of World War I, but left it again in 1918, never to return. In 1923 he settled in N.Y., but made several trips to Europe, South America and Australia, answering invitations from ballet companies to stage new ballets or revive old ones.

According to Soviet sources, Fokine made an attempt in 1923 to return to the Russian State Theatre. His letter outlining the conditions of his return, addressed to the then director of the State Academic Theatres, I. Exkouzovitch, was found in the archives of the Leningrad Theatre. In Aug., 1925, Exkouzovitch made a trip to Paris to negotiate with several Russian dancers (among them Fokine) and musicians about their return to the Soviet Union. Reporting about this trip Exkouzovitch said that Fokine would be willing to return but that his fee was too high for the State Theatre. The impression which the Soviet document creates is that Exkouzovitch had personal reasons to hinder the return of Fokine to the Soviet Union and that the question of the choreographer's fee was a convenient excuse to prevent Fokine's return.

Contemporary ballet companies retain in their repertoire the following ballets created by Fokine: *Prince Igor* (1909), *Les Sylphides* (1909), *Carnaval* (1910), *Schéhérazade* (1910), *Firebird* (1910), *Le Spectre de la Rose* (1911), *Petrouchka* (1911), *Paganini* (1939), *Bluebeard* (1941).

As mentioned before, Fokine as far back as 1904 saw the necessity of freeing the ballet from arbitrary academic limitations which hampered its development and kept it in a magnificent state of splendid decay. He realized that the fault of the academic ballet lay in the approach of choreographers to their task of creating ballets, and he began his reform from that approach.

He subjected the choreography of his ballets to the music to which they were planned, to the locale and period in which they were laid. The style of the dances, the manner of their execution, was adapted to the character of the ballet.

While the classic tradition was apparent in everything he created, he knew how to separate the true tradition from the conventional barnacles of usage, of pseudo-tradition.

Fokine formulated the fundamental ideas of his reform in the now historic letter to the London *Times* on July 6, 1914. These are his famous Five Principles:

"1. To create in each case a new form of movement corresponding to the subject matter, period and character of the music, instead of merely giving combinations of ready-made and established steps.

"2. Dancing and mimetic gesture have no meaning in ballet unless they serve as an expression of dramatic action.

"3. To admit the use of conventional gesture only when it is required by the style of the ballet, and in all other cases to replace the gestures of the hands by movements of the whole body. Man can and should be expressive from head to foot.

"4. The group is not only an ornament. The new ballet advances from the expressiveness of the face and the hands to that of the whole body, and from that of the individual body to groups of bodies and the expressiveness of the combined dancing of a crowd.

"5. The alliance of dancing with other arts. The new ballet, refusing to be the slave either of music or of scenic decoration, and recognizing the alliance of arts only on the condition of complete equality, allows perfect freedom both to the scenic artist and to the musician."

These Five Principles were a great reform in ballet. They have revitalized the classic ballet, given it a new foothold, a new impetus that will let itself be felt for generations to come.

The influence of Fokine on the modern

ballet is tremendous not only because he was a great reformer, but also because he was a choreographer of genius, active to the very last weeks of his life.

Dancers the world over considered it a rare privilege to work under Fokine, and the experience of artistic association with him is something no dancer will ever forget.

Fokine died in N.Y. on Aug. 22, 1942. Ten days before his death he returned from Mexico City where he had revived his *Petrouchka* for Ballet Theatre. Double pneumonia complicated by pleurisy was the cause of his death.

Folía, Portuguese carnival dance. It was originally based on fertility rites but developed into a noisy romp that included castanets and masked figures, executed at a very fast tempo. It was copied in Spain and eventually became a theatre dance.

Folk Dance, dance created by a people without the influence of any one choreographer but built up to express the characteristic feelings of a people, according to the peculiarities of a racial temperament. Folk dances include the square dance in U.S., the polka and czardas in Central Europe, the rumba in Cuba, etc. Folk dances have been incorporated into ballets. In a modified form, some folk dances have become popular as ballroom dances. See also ETHNIC DANCE.

Folk Dance and Song Society, English, founded in 1911 by Cecil Sharpe and others to preserve and make known English folk dances, folk music, and singing games, and also to encourage research in those subjects. The society has many branches in England and a very large membership. The only forms of dancing dealt with are Country Dancing, Morris Dancing, and Sword Dancing. It possesses very fine premises and a valuable library in London. The current administrator is Stephen Pratt. The Country Dance Society of America fulfills the same function of preserving English folk dance and music in the U.S., with May Gadd as National Director.

Folk Dancing in America.

BY WALTER TERRY.

In spite of skyscrapers, humming factories and the rush and competition of daily living, Americans have not forgotten the joys of folk dancing. With more leisure than ever before Americans are probably dancing more than at any time in their history. It cannot be said, of course, that everyone in America knows how to tread the measures of a Hoe-Down, or an Alabama Tatervine, or even a Virginia Reel, for most Americans have never experienced the pleasures of folk dancing. But it would be equally wrong to say that folk dancing in America is dying out.

The folk dance has been and is being used on the stages of our theatres with outstanding artistic success. The late Catherine Littlefield's *Barn Dance* (1937), Eugene Loring's *Billy the Kid* (1938), Agnes de Mille's *Rodeo* (1942) are perhaps prime examples of the use of folk dance in modern ballet. Miss de Mille's choreography for *Oklahoma!* (1943) was an outstanding first in the application of folk dance to modern musical comedy. Television programs use folk dances from time to time, although rarely with distinction.

But the interest in folk dance is limited neither to the country barn, the theatre or television. Even city dwellers are joining in. In N.Y. alone there are enough folk dance sessions to offer anyone an opportunity to join in folk dancing almost every day of the week. Perhaps there are few barns in which to hold these sessions, but with the help of a fiddler, a caller and a group of enthusiasts, studios in the Young Men's and Young Women's Christian Associations or Young Men's and Young Women's Hebrew Associations, or the meeting rooms of other organizations, or even city parks are occasionally transformed into temporary folk dance floors.

For N.Y. and other big cities, folk dancing is something of a tonic, because it leads the city inhabitant away from his traditional self-sufficiency and his pattern of rarely knowing his neighbor, into a social activity where he meets others in a spirit of social harmony.

Strictly speaking, our native dances are limited to dances of the American Indians, to the tap and juba dances of the Negro American. The beautiful dances of American Indians and the superb dance forms of the Negro American, which have contributed so richly to our theatre do not represent the true dance heritage of the majority of Americans. We may share in these heritages and cherish them, borrow from them and contribute to them, but in the realm of the pure folk dance the real heritage leads back to the folk dances of Europe. We can trace our folk or country dances by following the travels of our forebears.

In the American folk dance one finds patterns, rhythms, and steps which stem from England, Scotland, Ireland, France, Italy, Germany, Russia, Greece, and all those nations whose sons and daughters contributed to the development of a new world and a new nation. With these pioneers came the dances of their native lands. In time mother tongues were forgotten, old loyalties faded as a new loyalty to the adopted country grew, but the dances lived, sometimes under their old names but more often under new, American titles. Perhaps, too, the movements changed slightly, not so much in actual steps as in manner. But that was inevitable for the dancers were also changing and inevitably reflected in their movements the space, speed, vigor, and rough lustiness of a new land.

If the older importations in folk dance have been absorbed by American culture right along with those early settlers who built the new culture, European folk dances continue to exist in purer form through the dance activities of the subsequent immigrants. In N.Y. alone there are French, English, Russian, Polish, Ukrainian, Greek, Israeli, and other national folk dance groups. Through these groups the newcomers maintain contact with the pleasantest aspects of their heritage and their sons and daughters learn to share in that heritage. The most important phase of this folk dance activity is that it does not tend to isolate various heritages, for at these folk dance sessions and many of the larger gatherings, all types of folk dances are demonstrated and taught. It is possible, then, for those of Scotch and Italian heritage to learn and participate in the dances of the Ukraine or Lithuania; in turn, those who, or whose forebears came from the Ukraine or Lithuania, can take part in the dances of Scotland and Italy.

There is yet another quality inherent in folk dancing which is of importance not only to America but to the world, and that is its universality. Each nation brings its own characteristics to bear upon its folk dances, yet all have much in common, for these dances are usually simple to do, communal in spirit, and demand that participants move together in harmony. It is not suggested here that folk dancing could be a solution for the world's problems, or American "melting pot" problems, or that a global folk dance session would resolve all difficulties. It is, however, unsophisticated to ignore the magic qualities of folk dancing. If folk dancing in a New England barn can bring fun and friendship to individuals with varying interests and different social backgrounds, folk dancing may bring fun and friendship to American citizens of various national strains. Most people desire joy and friendship rather than sorrow and fear. They find the symbol of that desire in the folk dance, for it is difficult to clasp the hand of another and not experience the pull of friendship; it is difficult to participate in a folk dance and not experience the tug of communal joy. Thus, the renascence, or at least the continuing growth, of folk dance in America can be considered a healthy sign.

Most, if not all states in the Union, have folk dance groups of various nationalities and instruction groups for people who prefer some rudimentary or advanced instruction before joining an active dance group. Nation-wide organizations which furnish detailed information about dance groups in the U.S. include: Folk Arts Center, Inc., 271 Hicks Street, Brooklyn, N.Y. 11202 (the American Folk Dance Society is the Center's Division of Folk Dance and Music); Country Dance Society of America, 55 Christopher Street, N.Y., N.Y. 10014 (this organization publishes semi-annually *The Country Dance*); International Folk Dance Foundation, Inc., 300 West End Avenue, N.Y., N.Y. 10023 (a non-profit educational foundation devoted to the promotion and stimulation of folk dancing throughout the world).

Folk dance festivals in the U.S. are local or at best regional in character, despite the occasional "national" in their titles. Among the festivals are Southern Arizona Square Dance Festival, Tucson, Ariz. (Jan.); Annual National Folk Festival, Nashville, Tenn. (May); Annual Folk Festival of the College of the Pacific, Stockton, Calif. (July–Aug.); Northwest Folk Dance Festival, Enumclaw, Wash. (Aug.). There are also several Conferences, the most comprehensive of which is sponsored by the Dept. of Arts and Humanities, University Extension, Univ. of California, Los Angeles, Calif., 90024. The Conference is usually held in Aug. at the Santa Barbara Campus, Goleta, Calif.

A useful little book containing much information about folk dance groups, etc., is the *Annual Folk Dance Guide,* published by Paul Schwartz ($1.00), P.O. Box 342, Cooper Station, N.Y., N.Y. 10003.

Folk Legend (Folkesagn). Ballet in 3 acts; chor.: August Bournonville; music: Niels W. Gade and Johan Peder Emilius Hartman. First performed by the Royal Danish Ballet, Copenhagen, 1854, and still occasionally revived. The action takes place in Jutland in the beginning of the 16th century. It recounts the story of the beautiful Hilda who in her childhood was stolen by the trolls and substituted by the sorceress's daughter, the capricious Birthe. This romantic ballet is based on a legend in which the natural world and the Christian faith triumph over the world of trolldom and superstition. The wedding dance in the last act is played at Danish weddings to this day.

Folksay. Modern dance work, chor.: Sophie Maslow; music: folk songs arr. by Woody Guthrie; costumes: Edythe Gilfond. First prod.: New Dance Group, Studio Theatre, N.Y., Mar. 10, 1942, with William Bales, Sophie Maslow, Mark Ryder and company. Based on a text taken from Carl Sandburg's "The People, Yes," this suite of dances recreates a small town atmosphere at the turn of the century. At its première Guthrie and Earl Robinson played their guitars, sang and told the old, old jokes which are part of the charm of one of the true modern dance classics.

Folkwangballett. See Jooss Ballet.

Fonaroff, Nina, dancer, choreographer, teacher, b. New York City, 1914. Studied dance with Welland Lathrop, Cornish School, Seattle; Martha Graham, School of American Ballet, N.Y.; costume and stage design in Zurich, Switzerland; drawing and painting with George Grosz, N.Y. Soloist, Martha Graham company (1937–46). Taught at Teachers College (Columbia Univ.), YM–YWHA, N.Y., Bennington College, Martha Graham School, Neighborhood Playhouse School of the Theatre, N.Y. Assistant to Louis Horst (1937–52). Early dance compositions included *Yankee Doodle, American Prodigy, Café Chantant, 5 A.M., Yankee Doodle Greets Columbus, Little Theodolina* (1942); and, after she formed her own company, *The Feast* (1945), *Of Tragic Gesture, Of Sondry Wimmen, Born to Weep* (1946), *Mr. Puppet, Aria and Recitative* (1947), *Masque* (1949),

Lazarus (1952), *Requiem* (1953). Since 1955 she has conducted special movement classes for actors.

Fondu, in ballet, a lowering of the body made by bending the knee (demi-plié) of supporting leg, such as battement fondu, arabesque fondue, etc. The arabesque fondue is typical of the current Soviet style.

Fontán, Rodolfo (Rodolfo José Fontanetto), Argentine dancer, b. Santa Fe City, Argentina, 1932. Studied with Vassili Lambrinos, Amalia Lozano, Michel Borovski, Aída Mastrazi, Mme. Poliakova, Tamara Grigorieva, Gloria Kazda, Nicholas Zverev. Joined Teatro de La Plata, Buenos Aires, as soloist, later becoming premier danseur. In 1957 was invited to dance at the Teatro Municipal, Santiago de Chile. In 1958 was selected among other dancers to join Teatro Colón. Made his debut in *The Nutcracker* (1959), at performances organized by the Dirección General de Cultura under the direction of Vassili Lambrinos which led to a contract with Teatro S.O.D.R.E. of Montevideo, Uruguay. On return to Buenos Aires renewed performances of *The Nutcracker* and danced as soloist at Teatro Colón under the direction of Antony Tudor, John Taras, and Vassili Lambrinos. His repertoire included *Les Sylphides, Swan Lake, Giselle, Don Quixote, Pillar of Fire, Interplay* (Lambrinos), *Aurora's Wedding,* Bizet's *Symphony in C, Paganini, Metamorphosis* (replacing Skibine), *Concierto Coreográfico.* In 1962 he won the scholarship given by the Federal Republic of Germany to study under Tatiana Gsovska (Berlin) and Kurt Jooss (Essen).

Fontenla, Norma (Norma Beatriz Fontenla de Moneo), Argentine ballerina, b. Buenos Aires, 1933. Graduate of Conservatorio Nacional de Música y Arte Escénico and of Escuela de Baile del Teatro Colón, Buenos Aires; she also has a Dance Teacher's Diploma. Joined Teatro Colón at a very early age, becoming soloist (1953) and ballerina (1961). As guest ballerina of the Ballet do Rio de Janeiro she danced in Europe (1960) under the direction of William Dollar. Her repertoire in Teatro Colón includes *Coppélia, Choreartium* (1st and 4th movements), *Swan Lake, Paganini* (Florentine Beauty), *Giselle* (Myrtha), *Pas de Quatre, Les Sylphides, Don Quixote, Apollon Musagète, Daphnis and Chloë, Interplay* (Lambrinos), *Aurora's Wedding, Firebird.* On Feb. 16, 1963, she made her successful debut in the title role of *Giselle;* also danced Odette in the full-length *Swan Lake* staged by Jack Carter, May 28, 1963.

Fonteyn, Dame Margot (Hookham), English ballerina, b. Reigate, 1919; m. Dr. Roberto Arias (1955), former Panamanian Ambassador to the Court of St. James. Studied as a child in Shanghai with George Goncharov; later with Vera Volkova and at the Sadler's Wells Ballet School in England. Began her professional career as a Snowflake in the Vic-Wells (later Sadler's Wells, now Royal) Ballet Christmas production of *The Nutcracker* (1934); first important role was lead in revival of Frederick Ashton's *Rio Grande* (1935). After Alicia Markova left the company, Fonteyn took over many of her roles. Her first major creation was the Bride in Ashton's *Le Baiser de la Fée* (1935) and from that time on she created a long line of roles in Ashton ballets: Woman in ball-dress (*Apparitions*), Flower Girl (*Nocturne*), White pas de deux (*Les Patineurs*), Julia (*A Wedding Bouquet*), Girl (*Horoscope*), Bride (*The Wise Virgins*), Leader, Children of Light (*Dante Sonata*), Una (*The Quest*), ballerina (*The Wanderer*); and after the company moved to the Royal Opera House, Covent Garden in 1946; leading ballerina (*Symphonic Variations*), La Bolero (*Les Sirènes*), La Morte Amoureuse (Ashton's *Don Juan*), ballerina (*Scènes de Ballet*), Chloë (*Daphnis and Chloë*),

title role (*Sylvia*), female Tiresias (*Tiresias*), title role (*La Péri*), title role (*Ondine,* probably her greatest creation), *Raymonda* pas de deux, Spirit of the Air (*Homage to the Queen*), first ballerina (*Birthday Offering*), Marguerite (*Marguerite and Armand*). The title role of Ashton's *Cinderella* was also intended for Fonteyn but an accident prevented her from dancing the première. In Robert Helpmann ballets she created the Lady (*Comus*) and Ophelia (*Hamlet*); in Ninette de Valois ballets, Love (*Orpheus and Eurydice*) and Dulcinea (*Don Quixote*). As guest artist with Les Ballets de Paris de Roland Petit she created Agathe (*Les Demoiselles de la Nuit,* 1948). She has danced many other roles including the title role in *Firebird* and the Ballerina in *Petrouchka* in the revivals of these ballets for The Royal Ballet; the Miller's Wife (*The Three-Cornered Hat*) and the title role in *Mam'zelle Angot,* staged by Leonide Massine; also first ballerina in George Balanchine's *Ballet Imperial,* all of these being creations in the Royal Ballet's repertoire. She dances the great classic repertoire, *Giselle,* full-length *Swan Lake, The Sleeping Beauty,* her Aurora in the latter being generally considered the definitive interpretation of our time. Her importance in the history of British ballet can hardly be exaggerated. She was the first ballerina of international status developed by a British school and company. Since the (then) Sadler's Wells Ballet first danced in the U.S. (1949–50) she has been a great favorite in America as well as in her own country. Since 1959 she has been guest artist with the Royal Ballet, though she appears with it so frequently that she is still considered its prima ballerina. Since that time, however, she has been able to make more guest appearances all over the world. She took a group of dancers for an Australasian tour (1962), and to Europe (1963). She has been President of the Royal Academy of Dancing since 1954 and annually organizes and presents a Gala Matinee in which she is able to persuade to appear famous dancers from all the major companies. She was created C.B.E. (Commander of the Order of the British Empire) in 1951, and D.B.E. (Dame of the Order of the British Empire) in 1956. Other honors include: Hon. Litt.D., Leeds Univ., 1952; Hon. Mus.D., London Univ., 1954; Hon.D.Mus., Oxford Univ., 1959; Order of the Finnish Lion, 1960.

Dame Margot Fonteyn, as Chloë in Daphnis and *Chloë.*

Forains, Les. Ballet; chor.: Roland Petit; music: Henri Sauguet; book: Boris Kochno; décor: Christian Bérard. First prod.: Ballets des Champs-Elysées, Théâtre des Champs-Elysées, Paris, Mar., 1945 with Janine Charrat, Ethery Pagava, and Roland Petit in principal roles. This, Petit's first ballet, is a sentimental work about a troupe of strolling entertainers—a magician, acrobats, clowns, Siamese twins, etc.—who give a performance in a public square. The passer-by spectators applaud the several acts but at the end of the show when the magician passes the hat they disappear. The performers, hungry and cold, move on dejectedly. In its original production *Les Forains* was a true work of art, sincere and perfect in its every facet.

Ford Ballet, a company sponsored by Ford Motor Company during the summer of 1940 at the N.Y. World's Fair. It appeared in a specially built theatre in the Ford Pavilion. Two units, each composed of twenty-four dancers of the Ballet Caravan, gave twelve shows a day (each unit six shows) of the ballet *A Thousand Times Neigh,* choreographed by William Dollar and supervised by Lincoln Kirstein. The music was by Tom Bennett. Marie Jeanne, Leda Anchutina, Nicholas

Magallanes, Fred Danieli, Newcomb Rice, Sergei Temoff, Vladimir Dokoudovsky were among the soloists. The Ford Ballet was the first attempt by an industrial concern to utilize ballet as a publicity medium. The theme of the ballet was the replacement of the horse by the automobile treated in a humorous way.

Ford Foundation. See FOUNDATIONS, PHILANTHROPIC.

Fornaroli, Cia (1888–1954), Italian ballerina and teacher. Studied at the ballet school of Teatro alla Scala, Milan, where she became the favorite pupil of Enrico Cecchetti. Was engaged as ballerina of the Metropolitan Opera Ballet, N.Y., where she remained from 1910 to 1913. On her return to Milan she became prima ballerina of Teatro alla Scala until 1934. In 1928 she was appointed director of the ballet school of La Scala, but Mussolini discharged her from this post in 1933 after she married Dr. Walter Toscanini, who was under the attack of the Fascists. She left the theatre and both of them moved to N.Y. where she subsequently had her own school for a few years. She was considered one of the great Italian ballerinas of her generation. Gualtiero Martini wrote a book about the dancer entitled *Cia Fornaroli e l'Arte della Danza* (Milan, 1923). In 1957 Dr. Toscanini contributed a large collection of memorabilia to the Dance Collection of the N.Y. Public Library, designated the Cia Fornaroli Collection in her honor.

Fornaroli, Cia, Collection, an integral part of the Dance Collection of the N.Y. Public Library, was formerly one of the great private dance libraries. It was given to the Dance Collection by Dr. Walter Toscanini as a memorial to his wife, the famous Italian ballerina Cia Fornaroli, in 1955. The gift consists of more than 2,000 prints, 3,300 books, 3,500 librettos, 850 pieces of music, 23,000 letters and manuscripts and 15,000 clippings, photographs, and playbills. This historic collection is especially strong in Italian materials of the 19th century. Superb documentation and special attention in collecting have been given by Dr. Toscanini to the choreographers Gasparo Angiolini, Salvatore Vigano, and to the teacher and theoretician Carlo Blasis. Although the print collection included many of French and of English origin, the representation of rare and unique Italian items makes it particularly valuable in this country.

The earliest and most significant item in the manuscript collection is one, hitherto unknown, written by Guglielmo Ebreo (called in English-language dance literature William the Jew of Pesaro), probably in Tuscany, ca. 1460 and intended for use as a teaching tool by the master himself. Another item from this period is a manuscript of directions, written down about 1500 by Cosimo Ticcio, for a group of ballets created at the time by the ballet masters Giovannino, De Lanzino, and Il Papa. A more recent manuscript of great interest is the manual of exercises and technique studies written in Enrico Cecchetti's hand in 1894 in St. Petersburg.

Another fascinating item is the manuscript, a two volume compilation made by the choreographer Salvatore Taglioni (1789–1868), brother of Filippo and uncle of Maria, of librettos, production notes and drawings, cast lists, costume and prop designs, and other bits of evidence relating to his career as choreographer. The material provides insight into the theatre of Taglioni's time and detailed information not only of his career but of other dancers who worked with him, among them Fanny Elssler.

The book collection contains rare editions, or in some instances, unique copies of works of Noverre, Caroso, Blasis, Pemberton, Rickham, Angiolini, Negri, Nivelon, and Taubert. The subject of ballet technique is also well covered, as Mr. Toscanini was particularly interested in searching for little known or unknown items on this practical aspect of dance.

In the libretto collection, ranging from 1700 to 1900, both French and Italian productions are well represented. The collection of 15,000 clippings, predominantly from European newspapers, is especially valuable because it adds another dimension to the Library's files which consists mainly of clippings from contemporary American newspapers.

The collection has many other facets: a body of original material on Italian folk and national dance, arranged by province, the result of field research done by Cia Fornaroli and Walter Toscanini; ballet scores and piano music for dance, including variations and classroom music written by Cecchetti; many excellent 18th and 19th century theatrical almanacs and a fine collection of manuscripts and letters. The collection continues to grow as new material is added to it yearly.

Fortner, Wolfgang, German composer, b. Leipzig, 1907. Wrote the score for the ballet *The White Rose,* based on Oscar Wilde's *The Birthday of the Infanta.*

Fossé, Bob, dancer and choreographer, b. Chicago, 1927; m. Gwen Verdon. Outstanding choreographer of musicals, he has received three "Tony" Awards and one Donaldson Award. Choreographed *Pajama Game, Damn Yankees, New Girl in Town, Bells Are Ringing, Little Me* (for which he received the 1963 "Tony" Award); choreographed and directed *Redhead;* staged the musical numbers for *How to Succeed in Business Without Really Trying;* also choreographed and danced in *My Sister Eileen* and choreographed *Pajama Game* and *Damn Yankees* for motion pictures. Performed title role in the New York City Center revival of *Pal Joey* (1963), which he also choreographed. Director and choreographer of musical *Sweet Charity,* which opened on Broadway Jan., 1966.

Fouetté, in ballet, a "whipped" step. Technique: Fouetté relevé—start facing L, R toe pointed front; step on R ft., relevé onto R demi-pointe (or pointe), bringing L leg to grande quatrième devant; half turn on R ft. to the R (finish facing R wall), L leg remaining extended but turning on hip socket so it is now in arabesque ouverte; sink onto R heel. Fouetté sauté—same as fouetté relevé, substituting a jump on the R foot for the relevé. Fouetté may be done back or front as well as side, and with a complete turn (when it is called fouetté en tournant) as as well as with various arm and body positions. The Lilac Fairy in *The Sleeping Beauty* concludes her variation with a series of this type of fouetté. The coda to the *Swan Lake* pas de trois begins with the female dancer performing fouettés sautés with a beat (fouettés battus).

Fouetté en Tournant, one of the most spectacular movements in ballet, in which the dancer, standing on one foot, makes a rapid circular movement with the other leg, thus propelling herself around the supporting leg as an axis, without moving from the spot. Fouettés en tournant, done separately from other movements, are performed in series. A well-executed series of fouettés should be divisible by four. Thus, eight fouettés, for example, are considered a finished enchaînement, while ten are considered an unfinished series of twelve. For a long time thirty-two fouettés were considered the acme of achievement of any dancer. Now, however, there are many dancers who do thirty-two fouettés on the stage and twice that number in class. The term fouetté is taken from the French verb fouetter, meaning to whip, and the working leg of a dancer doing fouettés does remind one of the movement of a lashing whip. Technique: after executing a pirouette en dehors (or other turn) as preparation, whip R leg to grande seconde, L leg fondu; R leg executes a rond de jambe en l'air en dehors, at the same time relevé on L pointe and turn to R on L ft.; finish facing front, fondu on L, R leg whipping out again in grande seconde, and continue doing turns in a series on one spot. Fouetté turns are also done bringing the working leg to demi-quatrième devant after each turn and whipping it to 2nd pos. before turning.

Foundations, Philanthropic. Although the U.S. did not have a program of direct subvention of the arts prior to Sept., 1965 (when the National Foundation on the Arts and Humanities was established by Congress), the Federal Government has been the largest source of financial support of the arts and humanities for a long time. This seemingly paradoxical situation is the result of two provisions of the Federal Tax Code. One allows a deduction of twenty percent (and in some cases thirty) of an individual's personal income tax liability for his contributions to educational, scientific, or charitable purposes. Another provision exempts from inheritance taxes bequests for similar philanthropic purposes. Due to these provisions the individual—personal or corporate—becomes a direct contributor to the support of the arts in the U.S. It should be noted, however, that the arts as a beneficiary of these contributions can claim only a small share of the total, ranking far behind education, religion, health, and social welfare in the amount of private or individual gifts.

There is also a new factor in the picture of grants to the arts in the U.S.: the philanthropic foundation. In the period 1956–60 four such foundations contributed roughly $20,000,000 to the support of the arts, excluding gifts to the Lincoln Center for the Performing Arts in N.Y.

$20,000,000 is a large sum, but it is very small in comparison with the total budgets of the foundations. While the foundations' activity in the arts is an emergent trend of quite recent years it has yet to prove of significance to the pent-up demands in the arts, but it could foreseeably do so quickly under proper conditions. The foundations, big and small, between them should be able to meet most (if not all) of the many intellectual and artistic needs of this country.

THE ROCKEFELLER FOUNDATION was established in 1913 but the program in arts did not begin until 1953 (although the program in humanities, of which the arts are a part, is much older). For the humanities the Foundation has available only a fraction of its income. The budget in recent years has allotted $3,000,000 a year for use in all fields of the humanities all over the world. Only part of this can be devoted to the arts and from that only a part to dance.

As for grants in the arts, the Foundation is interested in cases where temporary and limited support might enable one or another organization in the arts to develop to a new level of competence, a level which might find its own support from the public or from other sources in society, so that the level could be maintained after the Foundation support had ceased, as the Foundation must anticipate it would.

In general, the Foundation does not wish to become involved in long-term support of any organization. When the Foundation makes a grant the grant is, so to say, self-contained. The assumption is that the grant carries with it no obligation of future support for the same venture. This is one of the reasons why any of the organizations in the arts finds it difficult to depend on the Foundation's help for maintaining its regular budget.

From 1953 to 1960 the Rockefeller Foundation made grants to dance organizations and individuals totaling $417,150. The Foundation hoped that the program could continue in the future on the same basis, but felt that it would be unrealistic to expect that it would expand because it is difficult for a foundation such as the Rockefeller (which operates not only nationally but internationally) to deal with projects that are primarily local in character or which are of a type in which the need is almost universal.

Between 1960 and 1965 the Rockefeller Foundation did not make any grants to the dance. In 1965 Norman Lloyd, a composer with leanings toward the modern dance, was appointed Director for Arts. Since his appointment the Foundation has given two rather small grants to Connecticut College in the springs of 1965 and 1966, both for the production of new works during the annual American Dance Festival which the College presents every Aug. In Apr., 1966, the Rockefeller Foundation awarded a grant of $370,000 to the Univ. of Utah, Salt Lake City, to be used in establishing a modern dance repertory company.

THE FORD FOUNDATION began its program in the arts in 1957 and, as W. McNeil Lowry, Director of the Program in Humanities and the Arts of the Ford Foundation (until June, 1964, when he was elected Vice President for Policy and Planning), once said: "For the Ford Foundation, the decision in 1957 to spend two to three million dollars a year on creative artists and artistic experiments was less significant than its decision to permit a full-scale national inquiry of the economic and social positions of the arts at this point of American history, and to do so with the artists and artistic directors as full participants.

"Nothing finally will be done for the arts in enlightened patronage until it is done for the art itself and not simply that it is icing on the cake. If art is left to be icing on the cake, it will be treated by people in power and people with influence and people with money as icing on the cake."

In addition to the national inquiry of the economic and social positions of the arts in the U.S. in which dance was included along with the other art forms, the Ford Foundation, between 1957 and 1963, made only one grant to dance: $150,000 (1959).

Describing the reason for the grant in its 1959 Annual Report, the Foundation wrote:

"Since many communities with ballet schools lack continuing performing outlets for the dancer, a program for talented young dancers will provide them with advanced training at the School of American Ballet in New York or at the School of the San Francisco Ballet and, afterwards, opportunities to perform with the corps de ballet of the New York City Ballet or the San Francisco Ballet. Selections to be made over a three-year period during which dancers will be observed in their local ballet schools."

Much as the Rockefeller Foundation's in the arts, the budget of the Ford Foundation for the arts is only two and one-half percent of the Foundation's total budget. Another limitation was also in line with that of the Rockefeller Foundation. For the duration of the exploratory program (at least) with which the program in arts of the Ford Foundation began, the board of trustees issued a flat prohibition against any direct financing of any institution, organization, or association in the arts, or the humanities for that matter.

Mr. Lowry was of the opinion that, should the program in the arts be substantially increased in years to come, it would still be mostly on a matching basis with institutions or communities; but none of it would take care of deficit financing per se.

The exploratory program mentioned by Mr. Lowry having been completed, the Ford Foundation announced on Dec. 16, 1963, a $7,756,000 program "to strengthen professional ballet in the United States." This was the largest contribution to ballet in the U.S. (and probably anywhere else) from any source private, institutional, or governmental. The awards were allocated as follows: $1,500,000 to the School of American Ballet to improve instruction and performance in local communities; $2,425,000 to the School of

American Ballet over the next ten years to strengthen it as a national ballet-training institution; $2,000,000 to the New York City Ballet over a ten-year period; $644,000 to the San Francisco Ballet over ten years, to be matched by $250,000 in new funds; $400,000 to the National Ballet, Washington, D.C., to be matched by $550,000 of other contributions over a five-year period; $295,000 to the Pennsylvania Ballet, Philadelphia, of which $45,000 was in assistance to the 1963–64 training and performance activities, and $250,000 to be matched by $500,000 over a ten-year period; $175,000 to the Utah Ballet, Salt Lake City, to be matched by $100,000 over a five-year period; $173,750 to the Houston Ballet to be matched equally over a five-year period; $144,000 to the Boston Ballet to assist in the development of a permanent company with four new productions in each of the next three seasons.

The Ford Foundation continues its generous support of the dance. In Nov., 1964, it announced an award to the Robert Joffrey Ballet (now the City Center Joffrey Ballet) of $155,000 of which $35,000 was a direct contribution; the balance of $120,000 was a matching grant. In Dec. the Foundation awarded $72,000 to the Dance Collection (now part of the Library and Museum of the Performing Arts at Lincoln Center) to develop techniques in connection with the creation of a computerized catalogue.

In Aug., 1966, the Foundation announced grants totaling $1,250,000 to three ballet companies which, in the Foundation's opinion, were to become major new forces on the American dance scene. The recipients were the City Center Joffrey Ballet, $500,000; the Pennsylvania Ballet Company, $450,000; the Boston Ballet, $300,000. The grants involved matching and supplementary funds to be raised by the recipients in some measure for a total of $1,425,000. Each of the companies had received previous Ford Foundation grants for their initial periods. W. McNeil Lowry said that the new grants were intended to insure the companies' continuing momentum.

The Rockefeller and the Ford Foundations are institutional giants and have no equals among foundations which include humanities and/or art divisions. But there are a number of smaller foundations which occupy a very important place on the periphery of the performing arts. As mentioned above, the big foundations can rarely pay attention to the problems of the individual—company or single person—creator-performer, or engage in the distribution of small contributions. Yet the need for small contributions is always there and always acute.

A very active foundation in this category is the BETHSABEE DE ROTHSCHILD FOUNDATION FOR THE ARTS AND SCIENCES. Its founder-president is Baroness Bethsabee de Rothschild, daughter of Baron Edouard de Rothschild, head of the French branch of the famous family. The first dance activity of the Foundation was the sponsorship in 1953 of a two-week engagement of "The American Dance" on Broadway, in which six modern dance companies participated. In the spring and summer of 1954 the Foundation underwrote a European tour of Martha Graham and company. In the winter of 1954–55 the Foundation contributed toward the establishment of the Juilliard Dance Theatre, directed by the late Doris Humphrey. In the spring of 1955 the Foundation sponsored another Broadway engagement of "The American Dance," this time for three weeks. Six American modern dance companies and six solo dancers participated in the greatest assemblage of choreographers and dancers in the modern dance field ever seen in N.Y.

Since that year the Foundation has contributed to the support of the Martha Graham company's performances in N.Y. and sponsored some of its foreign tours, furthered the production of new works, and helped to sustain the Martha Graham School of Contemporary Dance. According to Miss Rothschild, the objective of her Foundation in the dance is to help the dancer reach a wider audience than he could on his own. "Success in art is often accompanied by financial loss, and it is the function of the Foundation to make it possible for the dancer to fail financially."

The newest foundation active in dance is THE REBEKAH HARKNESS FOUNDATION, presided over by Mrs. Rebekah Harkness. The Foundation was established to promote American cultural achievement and to foster recognition of such achievement throughout the world. Its first activity in dance was the sponsorship of a three-month European tour of major cities and festivals of the Jerome Robbins' Ballets: U.S.A. beginning in June, 1961. Upon the return of the company from Europe the Foundation underwrote a three-week engagement of the company on Broadway (Oct., 1961). In 1962 the Foundation sponsored the African tour of the Pearl Primus Dance Troupe and, in the summer of that year, a twelve-week rehearsal and workshop period of the Robert Joffrey Ballet at Mrs. Harkness' estate, Watch Hill, R.I. In Sept. a contribution from the Foundation made possible a six-day Dance Festival at the open-air Delacorte Theatre in Central Park, N.Y. The performances were free to the public. They have been repeated with the participation of various performing groups every summer through 1966.

In 1962 and 1963 the Rebekah Harkness Foundation sponsored two foreign tours of the Robert Joffrey Ballet in the Middle and Far East and in the Soviet Union, in co-operation with the Cultural Exchange Program of the U.S. Dept. of State. In the spring of 1964 the Rebekah Harkness Foundation, in association with the William Hale Harkness Foundation (named after Rebekah Harkness' late husband) announced the formation of a ballet company, the Harkness Ballet. The company spent the summer of 1964 rehearsing at Watch Hill and began its performing career with a European tour in the spring of 1965.

Although Jerome Robbins' Ballets: U.S.A. has been a beneficiary of the Rebekah Harkness Foundation, Jerome Robbins himself is heading a foundation which he established in 1958, THE LENA ROBBINS FOUNDATION, so named in memory of his mother. The major function of this Foundation is to assist young choreographers in bringing their work to the attention of the public. Among American choreographers who have benefited from the Foundation's grants during the past few years are Talley Beatty, Pearl Lang, Katherine Litz, Anna Sokolow, Paul Taylor, Yuriko. On occasion the Foundation has been known to contribute to worthy causes in the dance not necessarily connected with choreographers.

A foundation which is very active in many other fields of the arts but less so in dance is THE GUGGENHEIM FOUNDATION. Its contributions to dance-oriented activities are smaller than the dance field would hope. Among recent beneficiaries were Merce Cunningham, grants for choreography (1954, 1959); Pearl Lang, grant for choreography (1960); Paul Taylor, grant for choreography (1961–62). The late Doris Humphrey received a grant to write a book on choreography (*The Art of Making Dances*, N.Y., 1959), published posthumously.

There also exist foundations whose support goes to specific organizations. Best known among these are BALLET FOUNDATION, a non-profit organization founded in 1939 for the stated purpose of promoting ballet as a nation-wide cultural movement, and sponsoring Ballet Russe de Monte Carlo; and the BALLET THEATRE FOUNDATION, established in 1947 as a non-profit corporation for the purpose of supporting Ballet (now American Ballet) Theatre as a performing unit.

Fountain of Bakhchisarai, The. Ballet in 4 acts; chor.: Rostislav Zakharov; music: Boris Asafiev; book: Nicolai Volkov after Alexander Pushkin's poem of the same title; décor: Valentina Khodasevich. First prod.: Kirov Theatre, Leningrad, Sept. 28, 1934, with Galina Ulanova (Maria), Tatiana Vecheslova (Zarema), M. Dudko (Khan Guirei). Khan Guirei of Bakhchisarai falls in love with Maria, a captive Polish princess. Zarema, his favorite wife, kills Maria in a paroxysm of jealousy. Guirei, ever mourning for Maria, erects a Fountain of Tears in her memory. The role of Zarema in the Bolshoi Ballet production is one of Maya Plisetskaya's most spectacular parts.

Four Marys, The. Ballet in 1 act; chor.: Agnes de Mille; music: Scots ballad ("Ballad of Mary Hamilton," also called "The Ballad of the Four Marys"), adapted and scored by Trude Rittmann; orch. by Rittmann and Mordechai Sheinkman; décor: Oliver Smith; costumes: Stanley Simmons; lighting: Jean Rosenthal. First prod.: American Ballet Theatre, N.Y. State Theater, Mar. 23, 1965, with Carmen de Lavallade (Mary Hamilton), Judith Lerner (The Mistress), Paul Sutherland (Her Suitor). The ballad, based on a true episode at the court of Mary, Queen of Scots, was brought to America by Scottish immigrants. Agnes de Mille adapts the story which becomes an episode in the ante-bellum South. The suitor to the mistress of a great house seduces one of her maids. The girl drowns the child and is hanged; but the suitor, whose guilt is known to all, remains silent.

Four Temperaments, The. Ballet in 1 act; chor.: George Balanchine; music: Paul Hindemith score of that name; décor: Kurt Seligmann. First prod.: Ballet Society, Central High School of Needle Trades, N.Y., Nov. 20, 1946, with Gisella Caccialanza, Georgia Hiden, Rita Karlin, Tanaquil LeClercq, Mary Ellen Moylan, Elise Reiman, Beatrice Tompkins, Todd Bolender, Lew Christensen, Fred Danieli, William Dollar, José Martinez, Francisco Moncion. A somewhat revised version was presented by Ballet Society at City Center Feb. 9, 1948; its first performance by the newly-styled New York City Ballet in its initial season came Oct. 25, 1948, with Beatrice Tompkins, Elise Reiman, Jocelyn Vollmar, Brooks Jackson, Dick Beard, and Francisco Moncion setting the opening theme of the music, and with Maria Tallchief and Nicholas Magallanes (Sanguinic Variation), Francisco Moncion (Melancholic), Todd Bolender (Phlegmatic), and Tanaquil LeClercq (Choleric). The ballet was originally commissioned with décor and costumes by Pavel Tchelitchev for The American Ballet's South American tour (1941). However, Hindemith and Tchelitchev did not seem to agree on the visual presentation of the ballet, so it was not given at that time. On Nov. 29, 1951, the ballet was given without décor and in practice costumes for the first time and has been performed in this way, with far greater success, ever since. It is one of the greatest of all Balanchine's translations of music into pure dance. Also in the repertoire of the (Nederlands) Nationaal Ballet and Royal Swedish Ballet; premièred by Paris Opéra Ballet Dec. 18, 1963.

Foxtrot, a ballroom dance of American origin in 4/4 time, based on the two-step, but with a broken instead of an even rhythm. The basic rhythm of the foxtrot is *slow,* slow, *quick*-quick. There are many variations of foxtrot.

Foyer de Danse. Ballet in 1 act; chor., and book: Frederick Ashton; music: Lord Berners; costumes: after Degas. First prod.: Ballet Rambert, Mercury Theatre, London, Oct. 9, 1932, with a cast headed by Alicia Markova (L'Etoile) and Ashton (Maître de Ballet). The occurrences of fact and fancy at a ballet rehearsal.

Foyer de la Danse. Ballet in 1 act; chor. and book: Adolph Bolm; music: Emmanuel Chabrier; décor Nicholas Remisoff. First prod.: Chicago Allied Arts,

Eighth Street Theatre, Chicago, Nov. 27, 1927, with Ruth Page and Adolph Bolm in principal roles. The ballet was inspired by Degas' painting of the same title. The plot is a ballet rehearsal during which all the things happen that usually do or do not happen during an actual rehearsal.

Fracci, Carla, Italian ballerina, b. Milan, 1936. Entered the ballet school of Teatro alla Scala, Milan (1946); was graduated (1954), and appeared in her Passo d'Addio (1955); promoted to soloist (1956); prima ballerina (1958). Was guest ballerina with London's Festival Ballet (1959); Ballet Festivals, Nervi (1960, 1962); Festival of Two Worlds, Spoleto (1962). Her first role as a ballerina was in Alfred Rodrigues' *Cinderella* (Prokofiev), which Violette Verdy had premièred in 1955. This was Fracci's first full-length ballet, but she performed it as if she had been doing three-act ballets for years. A romantic ballerina par excellence, her ballets include *Giselle, La Sylphide* (which she premièred in 1962), *The Nutcracker, Les Sylphides, Pas de Quatre,* and others. She appeared in the U.S. on television in 1961 and 1962. Was guest artist with Royal Ballet (May-June, 1963), dancing in *Les Sylphides, Le Bal des Voleurs,* and *Flower Festival at Genzano* pas de deux. Guest artist with American Ballet Theatre April-May, 1967, dancing *La Sylphide* and *Giselle* in New York.

Franca, Celia (Celia Franks), English dancer, choreographer, artistic director National Ballet of Canada, director, National Ballet School of Canada, b. London, England, 1921. Studied at Guildhall School of Music in London, received a scholarship at the Royal Academy of Dancing; also studied with Stanislas Idzikowski and other teachers in London. Her first stage experience was in the chorus of a revue, *Spread it Abroad,* London (1935). Was a member of Ballet Rambert

Carla Fracci, Italian ballerina, in La Sylphide.

(1936–39); her roles included Woman in his Past (*Lilac Garden*), Mazurka (*Les Sylphides*), *Blue Bird* pas de deux, among others. She was one of the original cast of Antony Tudor's *Dark Elegies.* With a short-lived company known as Three Arts Ballet she danced a season at the Lyric Theatre, Hammersmith, when she choreographed her first ballet, *Midas,* to music by Elizabeth Lutyens. She danced with the Arts Theatre Ballet (1940) which amalgamated with Ballet Rambert, and after a season with International Ballet joined Sadler's Wells Ballet (1941). Her large repertoire included Queen of the Wilis (*Giselle*), Dawn (*Coppélia*), Prelude (*Les Sylphides*), a Leading Swan, Spanish Dance, and Mazurka (*Swan Lake*), Danse Arabe (*The Nutcracker*), and others; creations included the Queen (*Hamlet*), Spider (*The Spider's Banquet*), Prostitute (*Miracle in the Gorbals*), as well as roles in many other works of the modern repertoire. When Sadler's Wells Theatre Ballet was organized in 1946 she choreographed for it *Khadra* and *Bailemos* (1947). In 1948–49 she was commissioned by British Broadcasting Corporation to create two dance dramas, *Dance of Salome* and *Eve of St. Agnes.* During this period she also spent some time teaching classic ballet to the Ballets Jooss in exchange for training in modern dance, and she danced in many Jooss ballets. When Metropolitan Ballet was formed (1948), she joined as leading dancer and ballet mistress, but returned to Ballet Rambert as guest artist (1950). In 1951 was invited to organize the new National Ballet of Canada and National Ballet Summer School and has been with both organizations ever since. The summer school was expanded to the National Ballet School (1959) which is a full time residential and day school offering both academic and dance subjects with Betty Oliphant as principal. For the National Ballet of Canada Celia Franca has choreographed *Dance of Salome* and new version of L'Après-midi d'un Faune, among others, and staged *Les Sylphides, Giselle, Swan Lake, The Nutcracker, Polovetsian Dances from Prince Igor, Coppélia, Princess Aurora.* In addition to being artistic director of National Ballet of Canada from the beginning, she also danced during the early years, creating the ballerina role in the Canadian production of Antony Tudor's *Offenbach in the Underworld.* After retiring as a performer for several years, she returned in the spring of 1964 to dance Lady Capulet in John Cranko's *Romeo and Juliet* in the National Ballet of Canada production.

Françaix, Jean, French composer, b. Mans, 1912. Composer of *Scuola di Ballo* (Boccherini-Françaix, Ballet Russe de Monte Carlo, 1933), *Beach* (Ballet Russe de Monte Carlo, 1933), *Le Roi Nu* (Serge Lifar, Paris Opéra, 1936), *Les Malheurs de Sophie* (Robert Quinault, Paris Opéra, 1948), *Les Demoiselles de la Nuit* (Ballets de Paris de Roland Petit, 1948), *Le Jeu Sentimental, Le Roi Midas* (Strasbourg Opera, 1957). George Balanchine choreographed *A La Françaix* to the composer's *Serenade for Small Orchestra* (1951).

Francés, Esteban, Spanish artist and designer, b. 1915. His first theatre work was *Le Renard* for Ballet Society (1947). For New York City Ballet he has designed décor and costumes for *Tyl Eulenspiegel, Con Amore, Jeux d'Enfants* (1955), *Figure in the Carpet;* also décor for *La Sonnàmbula,* costumes for *Pas de Dix,* and men's costumes for *Donizetti Variations* (girls' were by Barbara Karinska). Also designed décor and costumes for Eugene Loring's *The Capital of the World* (Ballet Theatre, 1954) and Zachary Solov's Vittorio (Metropolitan Opera Ballet, 1954). Designed décor and costumes for George Balanchine's production of *Don Quixote,* N.Y. State Theater, Lincoln Center, premièred May 28, 1965.

Francesca da Rimini. Ballet in 1 act, 2 scenes; chor.: David Lichine; music: Peter Tchaikovsky's *Fantasy Overture* of the same name; book: Lichine and Henry Clifford; décor: Oliver Messel. First prod.: Col. de Basil's Ballet Russe, Royal Opera House, Covent Garden, London, July 15, 1937, with Lubov Tchernicheva (Francesca), Paul Petroff (Paolo), Marc Platoff (Malatesta), Alexandra Danilova and Roman Jasinski (Vision of Guinevere and Lancelot); N.Y. première: Metropolitan Opera House, Oct. 24, 1937. The famous love story of Paolo and Francesca: Francesca is betrothed to the brutal and ugly Malatesta, but loves his younger brother Paolo. Seeking a moment together, the two young lovers read of two other ill-fated lovers and the vision of Guinevere and Lancelot appears to them. They are discovered by Malatesta who murders Paolo. Francesca dies with him. Michel Fokine choreographed an earlier version to the same music at the Maryinsky Theatre, St. Petersburg (1915); another version of the same story, choreographed by Nicolai Kholfin to music by Boris Asafiev, was staged for the Stanislavsky company in Moscow (1947). William Dollar staged yet another version to the Tchaikovsky music for Le Théâtre d'Art du Ballet (1961).

Franco, Marilia (Marilia Franco Ferraz), Brazilian dancer, teacher, choreographer, b. Araraquara, ca. 1924. Studied in Brazil with Chinita Ullman, Vaslav Veltchek, Maria Olenewa, and several teachers in U.S. and Europe. Made her professional debut as first dancer of S. Paulo's Teatro Municipal (1942); became ballerina of Teatro Municipal, Rio de Janeiro (1943). Danced with Original Ballet Russe (1944–47). In 1947 became choreographer and teacher at S. Paulo's Teatro Municipal, a post she still occupies. She also directs the Municipal Dance School with some one thousand pupils and eleven teachers. Has choreographed dances in all operas as well as a number of ballets.

Franco, Rodolfo (1890–1954), Argentine painter and stage designer. Studied in Buenos Aires and Paris. Was professor at the Escuela Superior de Bellas Artes, Academia de Bellas Artes of the University La Plata, Argentina; member also of the Comisión de Bellas Artes. From 1925 to 1930 was Stage Director of Teatro Colón, Buenos Aires. He designed décor for *Petrouchka, Les Noces* (Nijinska), *La Flor del Irupe, Le Coq d'Or, The Afternoon of a Faun, Les Sylphides, Le Spectre de la Rose, Pulcinella, Schéhérazade, El Amor Brujo, Giselle, Daphnis and Chloë,* and others.

Frankie and Johnny. Ballet in 1 act; chor.: Ruth Page and Bentley Stone; music: Jerome Moross; book: Michael Blandford and Jerome Moross; décor: Paul Dupont. First prod.: WPA Theatre Project; Page-Stone Ballet, Great Northern Theatre, Chicago, June 19, 1938, with Ruth Page and Bentley Stone in title roles. It was based on the well-known song of the same name. Revived for Ballet Russe dé Monte Carlo with décor by Clive Rickabaugh, N.Y. City Center, Feb. 28, 1945, with Page and Stone in the roles of Frankie and Johnny, subsequently danced by Ruthanna Boris and Frederic Franklin.

Franklin, Frederic, dancer, teacher, choreographer, b. Liverpool, England, 1914. Began dance training with Shelagh Elliott-Clarke in Liverpool; then studied in London with Lydia Kyasht and Nicholas Legat, and in Paris with Lubov Egorova. Made his professional debut at the Casino de Paris (1931), partnering Mistinguette, singing and dancing. Returned to London, danced with Wendy Toye in cabaret and West End musical shows. Joined the Markova-Dolin company as soloist (1935–37); signed by Leonide Massine as premier danseur of the then newly-formed Ballet Russe de Monte Carlo (1938), creating during the first two seasons the Baron (*Gaîté Parisienne*), Spirit of Creation (*Seventh Symphony*), Young Lover (*The Devil's Holiday*), Second Movement (*Rouge et Noir*). Came to America with the company (1938) and in 1944, after a season with *Song of Norway* in which Ballet Russe de Monte Carlo performed the ballets, was made ballet master. His repertoire of classic, demi-caractère and character roles included Albrecht (*Giselle*), Prince (*Swan Lake,* Act 2), Favorite Slave (*Schéhérazade*), Franz (*Coppélia*), Gypsy Youth (*Capriccio Espagnol*), Poet (*Night Shadow*), and many others; also such creations as Champion Roper (*Rodeo*), title role (*Billy Sunday*), male lead (*Danses Concertantes*), and others. He was renowned, not only for the charm and brio of his dancing but for his partnering of such great ballerinas as Alexandra Danilova, Alicia Markova, Mia Slavenska, Tamara Toumanova, Irina Baronova, Yvette Chauviré, and others. Danced a summer season as guest star with Danilova at Royal Opera House, Covent Garden,

Frederic Franklin, director and choreographer of National Ballet of Washington, D.C.

London, with Sadler's Wells (now Royal) Ballet (1949). With Mia Slavenska formed Slavenska-Franklin Ballet (1951), touring U.S. and Far East and created the role of Stanley in Valerie Bettis' ballet version of *A Streetcar Named Desire* (1952). Rejoined Ballet Russe de Monte Carlo as premier danseur and maître de ballet (1954–56), again leaving to tour South Africa with Alexandra Danilova. Became director of Washington Ballet performing group of Washington School of Ballet (1956–60), choreographing *Etalage* and *Homage au Ballet* to music by Liszt and Gounod respectively. Early in 1961 rehearsed and staged ballets at Teatro alla Scala, Milan; appointed artistic adviser to American Ballet Theatre later that year and (with Danilova) mounted Grand-Pas Glazounov. Choreographed *Tribute* (to César Franck's *Symphonic Variations*) for the 1961–62 season of Ballet Russe de Monte Carlo. Director of National Ballet and of its school since its formation in 1962. In addition to mounting their versions of *Swan Lake* (Act 2), *Les Sylphides, Coppélia* (in which he returned to the stage to play Dr. Coppelius), he set his *Tribute* and *Homage au Ballet* for the company. Rehearsed New York City Ballet in the revival of George Balanchine's *Ballet Imperial* (1967).

Franklin, Johnny (João Franco Oliveira), contemporary Brazilian dancer, teacher, choreographer, b. São Paulo, 1930. Educated at Mackenzie College, São Paulo. Began to study dance under Maria Olenewa (1944), and later with Igor Schwezoff, Nina Verchinina, Vaslav Veltchek, Tatiana Leskova. Made his professional debut in the corps de ballet of Teatro Municipal, Rio de Janeiro (1945); promoted to first dancer 1951. Dances a full repertoire of classic and modern ballets. Has also toured all over Brazil in concert performances, was ballet master and choreographer for Ballet da Juventude (1952–55); has also danced and choreographed for local television since 1953. Choreographer of *Maracatu,* first prize winner in the New Choreographers' Workshop (1961). Since 1955 has also taught in his own ballet school.

Franks, Arthur H., English editor and writer on ballet, b. Blackheath, 1907, d. London, Sept. 25, 1963. Director and editor, *The Dancing Times,* and *The Ballroom Dancing Times,* London. Associated from 1946 with P. J. S. Richardson, founder-editor of *The Dancing Times,* he assumed full editorship in 1958. Franks founded *The Ballroom Dancing Times* in 1956 realizing that the two reading publics are almost entirely separate, and also changed the fifty-year-old format in 1962. Author of *Approach to the Ballet* (1948), *Ballet for Film and T.V.* (1950), *Twentieth Century Ballet* (1954), *Svetlana Beriosova* (1958); editor: *Girl's Book of Ballet* (1953), *Ballet: A Decade of Endeavour* (1955), *Pavlova* (which was translated into Russian, 1956), *A History of Social Dancing,* and *Dancing as a*

Career (1963). Was a member of the Critics' Circle, London.

Frappé, in ballet, beating of the toe of working ft. against the ankle of supporting leg. See BATTEMENT FRAPPÉ.

Fraser, Moyra, dancer, b. Sydney, Australia, 1923. Studied at Sadler's Wells School; entered Sadler's Wells (now Royal) Ballet (1938), becoming soloist. She was particularly effective in roles where her height could be used to advantage—as Queen of the Wilis (*Giselle*), and in two creations, Sabrina (*Comus*), Hen (Robert Helpmann's *The Birds*), among others. Played Venus in the opera *The Olympians,* Royal Opera House, Covent Garden (1949). Left Sadler's Wells Ballet in 1946; now dances and acts in intimate revues, films.

French, Ruth, English dancer and teacher, b. London, 1906. Studied with Sasha Goudin and Serge Morosoff. Principal dancer with the Anna Pavlova company (*Blue Bird* pas de deux, and other roles); danced in many London Hippodrome revues; principal dancer in the early days of Vic-Wells Ballet before it became Sadler's Wells (now Royal) Ballet. Her roles included Sugar Plum Fairy (*The Nutcracker*), Swanilda (*Coppélia*), and others. Has her own school of ballet in London and is a Member of the Grand Council and Examiner, Royal Academy of Dancing.

Fricassée (Fr.), an 18th century dance, with pantomime.

Fris, Maria, ballerina, b. Berlin, 1932, d. Hamburg, 1961. A prima ballerina of the Hamburg State Opera and leading classic ballerina of Germany, she was a pupil of Tatiana Gsovska (Berlin) and Serge Peretti (Paris). She danced her first principal role in the Berlin State Opera (Dulcinea in *Don Quixote,* 1949), and was subsequently engaged by Wiesbaden State Opera (1951–52), Ballets de France de Janine Charrat (1952–54), Municipal Opera, Frankfurt (1958–59), and lastly the Hamburg State Opera. Maria Fris committed suicide by throwing herself from the catwalk on the empty stage of the Hamburg Opera House on May 27, 1961, a few hours before she was to rehearse the role of Juliet. She had suffered from a nervous breakdown earlier that year but appeared to have recovered completely. She was depressed by fears that a chronic ankle weakness would make it necessary for her to give up dancing. She had attempted suicide (1960) by taking an overdose of sleeping pills while in Spain with the Maurice Béjart company.

Friska, the fast movement of the czardas.

Froman, Margarita, Russian ballerina, ballet mistress, and choreographer. Studied at the school of the Moscow Bolshoi Ballet, was graduated into the company in 1915. Toured with the Diaghilev Ballets Russes in Europe and the U.S. (1916). Returned to Moscow (1917) and was promoted to ballerina of the Bolshoi. Left Moscow (1921) and settled in Yugoslavia to become the head of the Zagreb National Ballet as ballerina and choreographer. Her brother, Maximilian Froman, went with her as premier danseur. She had a decisive influence on the establishment and development of ballet in Yugoslavia. In the course of her years in Yugoslavia she, first in Zagreb and then in Belgrade, succeeded in transplanting the tradition and the art of Russian ballet to the Yugoslav stage. She founded a ballet school at Zagreb and with the abundant talent and enthusiasm she found there she enlarged the Zagreb troupe and proceeded to choreograph a vast number of ballets for Zagreb and Belgrade. Among her pupils were Mia Corak, better known to ballet goers in the U.S. and Europe as Mia Slavenska, and Ana Roje, who subsequently headed her own company in Split, and is now teaching in the U.S. Among the ballets choreographed by Margarita Froman are *Swan Lake,* Act 2 (1921), *The Polovetzian Dances from Prince Igor, Schéhérazade, Les Papillons* (Schumann), *The Jilted Pierrot* (Carl Maria von Weber), all in 1922; *Thamar* (Balakirev), *Coppélia, Petrouchka,* and excerpts from *The Nutcracker* with her own choreography were presented in 1923. In 1924 the first ballet based on Yugoslav theme, *The Gingerbread Heart,* in two acts by the Croatian composer Kresimir Baranovic and choreography by Froman, was presented to an enthusiastic public. The music as well as the plot were based on Croatian folk songs and the choreographer made use of Croatian folk dances. Also in 1924 Froman produced Schumann's *Carnaval* and Rimsky-Korsakov's *Capriccio Espagnol.* Between 1927 and the second world war she staged in Zagreb Debussy's *Box of Toys* (1927), *The Firebird* (1928), *The Three-Cornered Hat* (1930), Stravinsky's *Les Noces,* and the full *Nutcracker* (both in 1932), *Swan Lake* and *The Afternoon of a Faun* (both in 1940). For three years after 1926–27 Froman divided her choreographic activities between Zagreb and Belgrade, reviving for Belgrade several ballets she had staged in Zagreb and choreographing for the first time *Raymonda* (1927) and *The Humpbacked Horse.* In 1937 she revived the full *Nutcracker* and staged *Imbrek-with-the-Nose,* a comic ballet based on a folktale, to music by Baranovic, the composer of *The Gingerbread Heart; Harnasie,* a ballet on a Polish folk theme to music by Karol Szymanowski; and a ballet with a Caucasian motif to the popular music *Caucasian Sketches* by Mikhail Ippolitov-Ivanov. During the German occupation of Yugoslavia the ballet did not perform. It was not until 1947 that she staged another ballet for the Belgrade National Ballet: the four-act *The Legend of Ohrid,* to a score by Stevan Hristic. Produced by Yugoslav Radiotelevision, *The Legend of Ohrid* was telecast for American viewers in the summer of 1962. This ballet, with *The Gingerbread Heart* and *The Devil in the Village,* choreographed by Pia and Pino Mlakar to a score by Fran Lhotka (1935 and 1937), are considered the national ballets of Yugoslavia. In 1949 she staged Prokofiev's *Romeo and Juliet* with Nenad Lhotka as Romeo and Sonia Kastl as Juliet. Margarita Froman emigrated to the U.S. in the early 1950's and now devotes herself to teaching in Connecticut.

Frontier. An American Perspective of the Plains: Solo by Martha Graham; music by Louis Horst; décor: Isamu Noguchi. First prod.: Guild Theatre, N.Y., Apr. 28, 1935. One of Graham's great early solos, notable for its being her first use of décor and the beginning of her collaboration with Noguchi. The setting was a section of rail fence with two lines of white rope extending upward to the right and left. It was a dance of the American pioneer woman and possibly foreshadowed her later group work, *Appalachian Spring.*

Fuller, Loie (1862–1928), American performer who began her career as a child temperance lecturer. At an early age she took a few dance lessons but gave them up on account of difficulty. After some singing lessons she obtained a speaking and singing part in a show. While in this show she received a present of a long scarf of very light silk. Playing with the scarf and admiring its lightness and floating power she conceived the idea of creating a spectacular stage number consisting of manipulation of a length of light silk illuminated by variegated lights. She named the number *The Serpentine Dance,* although the dance itself contained only a few movements, the main attraction being the floating silk. Troy and Margaret West Kinney (in their admirable book *The Dance*) say the following about Miss Fuller and her *Serpentine Dance:* "The success of the Serpentine was not one of those victories gained after long experimenting for a perfect expression . . . It was instantaneous and complete; a few weeks sufficed to make Loie Fuller a national figure. A period of tremendous popularity followed, popularity amounting to a fashion . . . In Paris Miss Fuller had a sketch in which she, a solitary figure, stood on a height at dawn, silhouetted against the sky . . . The figure, on being touched by the rays (of the rising sun), represented its awakening by the fluttering . . . of its hundred yards or so of drapery . . . An audience mistook the intent of the effect, and greeted it as a dance of fire. The upward rush of the cloth, obviously, had suggested flame. "La Loie" lost not a moment in seeing the possibilities, nor an hour in setting to work on their development. Stage electric lighting was new . . . Electricians were enthusiastic over new problems . . . the colours and movement of flame were almost counterfeited . . ." *La Danse de Feu* became as strong a hit as *The Serpentine Dance.* Subsequently Miss Fuller developed a long list of similar numbers, which were all startling and agreeable to the eye. She danced at the Paris Universal Exposition (1900) and with her company toured in Europe and America, appearing at the Metropolitan Opera House (1910). Her machinery and effects were a closely guarded secret. She had many imitators, but not one of them ever approached the smooth performance of her act. Her autobiography, *Quinze Ans de ma Vie,* was published in France (1908), with a preface by Anatole France. An English language edition of the book was published in London (1915). For a detailed biography and appreciation of Loie Fuller see *Dance Index,* Mar., 1942.

Fuoco, Sofia (Maria Brambilla, 1830–1916) Italian ballerina. Began to study ballet at the school of Carlo Blasis at the age of seven. She was one of his "Pleiades." Made her debut at Teatro alla Scala, Milan (1839), becoming ballerina (1843). In this position she danced the première of the ballet *Gisella, ossia la Willi,* choreographed by Antonio Cortesi to music by Giovanni Bjetti (1811–76). In 1846 she was acclaimed with Maria Taglioni, Carolina Rosati, and Carolina Vente in Jules Perrot's *Pas de Quatre.* She made her Paris debut at the Théâtre de l'Académie Royale de Musique (now Paris Opéra) July 10, 1846, in *Betty, ou la Jeunesse de Henry V* (choreographed by Joseph Mazilier) to music by Ambroise Thomas, inspired by the play *La Jeunesse de Henry V* by Alexandre Duval). Théophile Gautier, having praised in his day Maria Taglioni, Fanny Elssler, and Carlotta Grisi, had this to say about Sofia Fuoco: "From her appearance Mademoiselle Sofia Fuoco made a distinct impression. She has the merit of originality so rare in the dance, a limited art if there ever was one: she does not remind one of Taglioni, Ellsler, [Carlotta] Grisi, or [Fanny] Cerito . . . Hers is one of the most brilliant debuts in dancing that we have had to notice for a long time." Fuoco enjoyed a similar success in London, Madrid, and other European cities. Her repertoire included, in addition to the works mentioned, *Il Prestigiatori* (Blasis, 1852), *Zuleika* (A. Coppini, 1852), the revival of Perrot's *Catarina, ou La Fille du Bandit* (1853), *La Nozze di Ninetta e Nane* (by Dario Fissi, choreographer, dancer, and inseparable partner of Fuoco, 1854). Very little is known of the career of Sofia Fuoco after 1858. She died a rich and well-loved old lady in Carate Lario in her villa on Lake Como. She was one of the strongest dancers on pointe of her time and, during her four years at the Paris Opéra, earned the nickname "La Pointue" because of this.

Fuzelier, Louis (1677–1752), choreographer at the Académie Royale. Best-known of his ballets are *Les Indes Galantes* (Rameau, 1735), *Les Amours des Dieux* (1727), and *Les Amours Désguisés.* Also choreographed *Arion* (1714), *Les Fêtes Grecques et Romaines* (1723), *La Reine de Féris* (1725), *Les Amours des Déesses, Le Carnaval du Parnasse* (1749).

G

Gable, Christopher, English ballet dancer, b. London, 1940; m. Carole Needham. Studied at Royal Ballet School; danced with Covent Garden Opera Ballet (1956) and then entered Royal Ballet, of which company he is now a premier danseur. Made a great impression with his creations of The Cousin (*The Invitation*) and The Young Man (*The Two Pigeons*). Also dances Siegfried (*Swan Lake*), Colas (*La Fille Mal Gardée*), Solor (*La Bayadère—Kingdom of Shades*), Franz (*Coppélia*) and others. Created two roles in *Images of Love*. He rose to his present position through the touring section of the Royal Ballet but since 1963 has been with the resident group at Covent Garden. Kenneth MacMillan created the role of Romeo (*Romeo and Juliet*) on Christopher Gable, although Rudolf Nureyev danced the première (Feb. 9, 1965).

Gabovich, Mikhail (1905–1965), Peoples' Artist of the RSFSR, Soviet premier danseur. Gabovich belongs to the first group of dancers developed by Soviet ballet who contributed much to the development of its present style. After attending one of the numerous ballet studios popular in Moscow in the 1920's, he was accepted into the Bolshoi school when in his mid-teens, and was graduated in 1924 after three years of study under Alexander Gorsky. Soon after entering the Bolshoi company he danced his first important part, the Genie of the Ocean in Gorsky's production of *The Humpbacked Horse*. Within a few years he was one of the leading Bolshoi dancers, with great dramatic gifts in addition to his strong technique. His roles included the Prince in *The Sleeping Beauty,* Solor in *La Bayadère,* and all the classic repertoire. As a young dancer Gabovich appeared in the first Soviet ballet *The Red Poppy* (1927) as a foreign sailor and one of the phoenix-birds who partnered Yekaterina Geltzer in a dream scene. He was the first Vaclav in the Bolshoi's production of *The Fountain of Bakhchisarai* (1936), created Vladimir in Rostislav Zakharov's *Prisoner of the Caucasus* (1938), and Andrei in the same choreographer's *Taras Bulba* (1941). Other Soviet ballets in his repertoire included *Romeo and Juliet* (Bolshoi production, 1946), *Bronze Horseman* (Bolshoi production, 1949), *Cinderella* (1945), *The Red Flower* (1950). He retired in 1951 following a leg injury. Was artistic director of the Moscow ballet school (1954–58) and taught there until his death, July 15, 1965. Author of a paper on his teacher Gorsky and numerous articles on ballet in leading Soviet newspapers.

Antonio Gades, Spanish concert dancer

Gades, Antonio, Spanish dancer, b. Madrid, 1936. Began studying dance at age thirteen and three months later made his debut at the Circo Price. Pilar Lopez took him into her company a year later where he remained for nine years, performing and studying. He then went to the Rome Opera House where he collaborated with Anton Dolin on a version of Ravel's *Bolero.* Appeared at Festival of Two Worlds, Spoleto (1962), dancing with Carla Fracci in Beppe Menegatti's *Pavane for a Dead Infanta* (Ravel) and *Teatrino di Cristobal,* for both of which works he was also co-choreographer. Guest dancer for nine months at Teatro alla Scala, Milan where he was also choreographer and teacher of Spanish dance. In 1963 returned to Spain to play a leading role in the film *Los Tarantos,* in which Carmen Amaya made her final appearance. Formed his own company, appearing in the Spanish Pavilion at the N.Y. World's Fair (1964).

Gagaku, is a Japanese word meaning noble and elegant music. It is the name of the all-male Japanese Imperial Household Musicians and Dancers and also designates the style of their music. Gagaku was introduced into Japan in the 8th century from China. It reached its greatest popularity in the Heian period (9th–11th centuries). Since its introduction into Japan it has been associated with the life of the Imperial Court. Membership in Gagaku is hereditary and the musicians and dancers are interchangeable. A dance performance of Gagaku is called Bugaku, meaning dance and music. An instrumental performance of Gagaku is called Kangen, meaning pipes and strings.

The Bugaku style is quite different from other types of Japanese dance in that the dramatic elements are of far less importance than the pure dance form. Also, in contrast to other styles of Japanese dance, Bugaku emphasizes symmetry, not only in the frequent use of paired dancers but also in the basic movement patterns of the solo dancers.

Until Lincoln Kirstein, general director of the New York City Ballet, succeeded in arranging a guest season of the Gagaku in the U.S. (May–June, 1959), few people outside the Imperial Music Pavilion in Tokyo or one of the great shrines at Ise or Nara had ever seen Gagaku. Performances outside Japan were unprecedented. The U.S. performances were undertaken in some measure as a celebration of the marriage of Crown Prince Akahito with Michiko Shoda in mid-April of that year and as a reciprocity for the performances of the New York City Ballet in Japan in Mar.–Apr., 1958. The Gagaku dancers appeared in the U.S. on an exact replica of the platforms on which they dance in Japan. It is quite possible that more people have seen Gagaku in the U.S. than have ever beheld it in Japan.

Those who saw Gagaku in the U.S. participated in the rare experience of seeing the oldest institution performing dance and music in the world. Gagaku was founded in 703 A.D. and has existed and been performed without interruption ever since. Gagaku is actually not a theatrical performance, but a ritual or entertainment designed for the palace. Slow moving by Western measurements of time, refined into a near abstraction when the dance has a definite plot, Gagaku is probably the ultimate in artistic formalism or formal art achieved through the talents of generations of dancers and musicians, who not only follow one another in time, but are descended, one from another, in a very definite family succession. By its performances, American audiences were brought a little closer to understanding the human element of a people so different from and yet essentially so like Americans. The performances also offered the opportunity to observe a civilization a millennium older than the American.

Gaîté Parisienne. Ballet in 1 act; chor.: Leonide Massine; music: Jacques Offenbach; book and décor: Comte Étienne de Beaumont. First prod.: Ballet Russe de Monte Carlo, Théâtre de Monte Carlo, Apr. 5, 1938, with Nina Tarakanova (Glove-Seller), Eugenia Delarova (Flower-Girl), Jeannette Lauret (La Lionne), Lubov Roudenko (Can-Can Dancer), Leonide Massine (Peruvian), Frederic Franklin (Baron), Igor Youskevitch (Officer). The role of Glove-Seller was later danced by Alexandra Danilova, with whose name the role is associated. This ballet, in the current repertoire of the same company, was filmed in technicolor by Warner Brothers (1941) under the title *The Gay Parisian.* The story deals with the exploits of a rich Peruvian in a Paris nightclub towards the end of the last century.

Gala Performance. Ballet in 1 act, 2 scenes; chor. and book: Antony Tudor; music: Serge Prokofiev's *Classical Symphony,* preceded by the 1st movement of his Piano Concerto No. 3; décor: Hugh Stevenson. First prod.: London Ballet, Toynbee Hall Theatre, London, Dec. 5, 1938, with Peggy van Praagh (La Reine de la Danse, from Moscow), Maude Lloyd (La Déesse de la Danse, from Milan), Gerd Larsen (La Fille de Terpsichore, from Paris), with Antony Tudor and Hugh Laing as cavaliers. It was taken into the repertoire of Ballet Rambert at Arts Theatre, London, June 28, 1940, and is still being performed by that company. Sally Gilmour and Lucette Aldous have been enchanting as the ballerina from Paris, Joan McClelland and Gillian Martlew have been particularly outstanding as the ballerina from Milan. Produced by Tudor for Ballet (now American Ballet) Theatre, Majestic Theatre, N.Y., Feb. 11, 1941, in new décor by Nicolas de Molas, with a cast headed by Nora Kaye (Ballerina from Moscow), Nana Gollner (Ballerina from Milan), Karen Conrad (Ballerina from Paris). Irina Baronova and Alicia Alonso are only two of the many who subsequently danced the Ballerina from Milan. Tudor also staged *Gala Performance* for the Royal Swedish Ballet and Mariane Orlando made something quite outstanding of this role, while Bjorn Holmgren presented a dazzlingly comic vignette as the apologetic partner to the Ballerina from Paris. The scene is backstage before a gala performance, then the performance itself with all three ballerinas vying for attention and growing more and more outrageous as the ballet proceeds.

Galaxy. Dance theatre piece; chor., sound score, costumes, lighting: Alwin Nikolais. First prod.: Henry Street Settlement Playhouse, N.Y., Mar. 19, 1965, by the combined Alwin Nikolais Dance Co. and Henry St. Playhouse Dance Co., headed by Gladys Bailin, Bill Frank, Phyllis Lamhut, Murray Louis. This experiment in movement, pattern, light, shape, and sound, included the use of fluorescent lighting. The four solos by the artists mentioned above were performed to recorded accompaniment of brief lectures on armadillos, bacteria, astronomy, and aviaries.

Galeotti, Vincenzo (Tomaselli), (1733–1816), Italian dancer, choreographer, teacher. He devoted most of his activities to the Royal Danish Ballet, which he headed and reformed. Among his pupils was August Bournonville. In his ballets he strove toward dramatic and pantomimic expressiveness. Among his works were several on themes from Shakespeare, such as *Romeo and Juliet, Macbeth,* etc. He also staged *Nina, or Insane from Love, Inez de Castro, Bluebeard,* and others. He is still represented in the repertoire of the Royal Danish Ballet today by *The Whims of Cupid and the Ballet Master* (Les Caprices du Cupidon et le Maître de Ballet), first staged in 1786.

Galina, Anna, French dancer, b. New York City, 1936. Pupil of Tatiana Piankova, with whom she founded Le Théâtre d'Art du Ballet (1957) and of which she is ballerina. Her ballets include *Les Sylphides, Carnaval,* and others. She created the Goddess in *Ballade* (Leonide Massine) and the title role in *Francesca da Rimini* (William Dollar), among other roles.

Galli, Rosina (1896–1940), première danseuse and ballet mistress of the Metropolitan Opera Ballet. Her husband was Giulio Gatti-Casazza, director of the Metropolitan Opera (1908–35). He first saw his future wife when she was a six-year-old girl taking an entrance audition at the ballet school of the Teatro alla Scala, Milan, of which he was then director. Rosina Galli came to the U.S. as a soloist of the Chicago Opera Ballet (1912). She joined the Metropolitan as ballerina (1914), becoming its ballet mistress (1919). She was an excellent dancer and a strict ballet mistress. A devoted follower of the classic tradition, she insisted on hard work. Her greatest success as a dancer was Rimsky-Korsakov's opera-ballet *Le Coq d'Or* staged by Adolph Bolm at the Metropolitan (1916), with singers in the pit and dancers on stage. Other triumps were the Polovetzian dances in *Prince Igor* (Bolm), with Giuseppe Bonfiglio as her partner (1916); *Petrouchka,* staged by Bolm with the choreographer in the title role, Galli as the ballerina, Bonfiglio (Moor), and Ottokar Bartin (Charlatan) (1919); *La Giara* (1927). In 1930 Galli married Gatti-Casazza, and retired as ballerina, but continued as ballet mistress. After the 1934–35 season Gatti-Casazza retired from the Metropolitan and the husband and wife moved to Milan where Rosina Galli died five years later of pneumonia.

Galliard (or Gaillard), a court dance, sprightly and in triple time. At one time it had five steps and was known as "cinq-pas"; in Italy it is known as saltarelli. The galliard which was full of tricks and turns was usually followed by the statelier pavan. One form of galliard included exchange of kisses. The origin is said to be Roman and it is similar to the tordion.

Gallini, Giovanni Andrea, a director of opera in London (1784). Published a *Treatise on the Art of Dancing* (London, 1762; re-published 1772). It contained chapters on the history of dance, descriptions of dancing in various parts of the world, and a section on mime. There were also "critical observations on the art of dancing," rules on theatrical dancing, and a collection of "cotillons or French dances."

Galop, a late 18th century dance used as a finale to voltas and contredanses. It was in 2/4 time and consisted of a glissade with one foot and a chassé, then alternate. It is often used in classic ballet.

Gambarelli, Maria, contemporary American dancer, b. Italy of Italian-American parentage. Studied as a child at Metropolitan Opera Ballet School, N.Y. Member of the original Roxy Gang, one of the first groups to do nationwide radio broadcasts, where she was affectionately known as "Gamby." Première danseuse, Capitol Theatre, N.Y. for a number of years; première danseuse, Metropolitan Opera Ballet (1939–41). Has also danced in films, revues, and on television.

Maria Gambarelli, American ballerina

Gamelan, a native musical instrument of the Siamese, Javanese, and Balinese. It is actually a collection of a variety of percussion instruments. All forms of gamelan can be traced to ancient China, but the Balinese gamelan owes its more direct origin to the similarly composed but quite different sounding gamelan of Java. The Balinese gamelan includes metallophones, bronze gongs, gong chimes, cymbals, drums, and reeds. Most of the rhythms and melodies have been handed down through generations. The diapason of the gamelan ranges from the deepest gong to the highest metallophone—over seven octaves. The word gamelan also defines the orchestra playing on the various instruments forming the gamelan.

Gamelan. Ballet in 1 act; chor.: Robert Joffrey; music: Lou Harrison's of the same title; décor: Villa Kim. First prod.: Robert Joffrey Ballet, Kirov Theatre, Leningrad, Oct. 15, 1963, with Lisa Bradley, Brunhilda Ruiz, Gerald Arpino, Lawrence Rhodes and company. A series of impressions, echoing the oriental style of the music. Two sections of Gamelan were given, in practice costume, at a workshop performance at N.Y.'s Fashion Institute of Technology, Sept. 30, 1962.

Games. Modern dance work; chor.: Donald McKayle; music: traditional songs, sung by June Lewis and Donald McKayle; décor: Paul Bertelsen; costumes: Remy Charlip. First prod.: Hunter College Playhouse, N.Y., May 25, 1951, with Donald McKayle, Esta (Beck) McKayle, Eve Beck, Louanna Gardner, Remy Charlip, John Fealy, George Liker, John Nola. Children of a city's slums play their games, traditional and improvised to street songs, while behind their absorption lies always the terror of their natural enemy, "the cops." At subsequent performances Shawneequa Baker sang with Donald McKayle.

Garatuja, O. Ballet in 1 act; chor.: Dennis Gray; music: Alberto Nepomuceno (an arrangement of several short pieces); story from a novel by José de Alencar; décor: Nilson Penna. First prod.: Ballet de Rio de Janeiro, Teatro Municipal, 1960, with a cast headed by Alice Calino, Dennis Gray, Nelly Laport. It is a gay episode of the colonial days of Rio de Janeiro. O Garatuja, a young imaginative boy, who delights in using his talent for drawing whatever he sees in the streets (mainly to play practical jokes), falls in love with a nice girl and has to reform to please her parents.

Gard, Alex (Alexis Kremkoff-Gard) (1900–1948), American theatrical caricaturist, born in Kazan, Russia. Studied at Imperial Russian Naval Academy, left Russia after revolution. Studied art in Paris, worked there on publications *Le Matin, Sourire, Rire*. Came to U.S. in 1925. Published *Ballet Laughs* (1941), *More Ballet Laughs* (1946), *Stars Off-Gard* (1947). Served in U.S. Navy 1942–45, during which time he published books of Navy caricatures: *Sailors in Boots, Getting Salty, Sick Bay*. Was on staff of *N.Y. Herald Tribune*. His book on Reno divorcées was in preparation when he died suddenly June 1, 1948.

Gardel, Maximilien (1741–1787), son of a court ballet master to Stanislas, King of Poland, prominent French dancer connected with the Académie Royale de Musique. With Auguste Vestris he is credited with having invented the rond de jambe. He was the first dancer to dance without the heavy mask, then part of stage equipment. He removed it in 1722 to let the audience know that it was he rather than Vestris (who had been scheduled to dance a role). Gardel was ballet master at the Paris Opéra and composed many ballets including *Ninette à la Cour* (1778), *Mirza* (1779), *La Chercheuse d'Esprit* (1777), *Le Déserteur* (1784), *La Rosière* (1784), *Le Premier Navigateur* (1785), *Le Coq du Village* (1787). Madeleine Guimard danced the leading role in *La Chercheuse d'Esprit* and *Le Premier Navigateur*.

Gardel, Pierre (1758–1840), dancer in the Paris Opéra, brother of Maximilien Gardel. He married the danseuse Mlle. Miller. In 1787 he became maître de ballet at the Opéra, a post he retained for forty years. He produced *Télémaque dans l'Ile de Calypso* and *Psyche*, among other ballets.

Gardiner, Lisa (1894–1956), American dancer, choreographer, ballet teacher, b. Washington, D.C. Educated at Friends School and Univ. of Wisconsin. Studied dance with Protopovitch, Adolph Bolm, Vera Trefilova. Member of Adolph Bolm's Ballet Intime (1917), Anna Pavlova company (1918–21), Michel Fokine's Ballet (1922). Began teaching in Washington, D.C. (1922), first at the Tchernikoff-Gardiner School of Ballet, later the Lisa Gardiner School. In 1945 became co-director (with Mary Day) of Washington School of Ballet. In 1956 the two directors founded the Washington Ballet, a regional company with standards close to professional. She died suddenly in her sleep on Nov. 4, 1956.

Gargouillade, lit. "paddling" step; in ballet, step consisting of a pas de chat with a rond de jambe en l'air en dehors with the leg that starts the movement, and a rond de jambe en l'air en dedans with the leg that completes the step done simultaneously. The Sugar Plum Fairy (*The Nutcracker*—Ivanov version) has a series of gargouillades in her variations, but today most dancers content themselves with pas de chat. Patricia Wilde performed a brilliant series in *Caracole,* but the step disappeared when the ballet was revived as Divertimento No. 15.

Garth, Midi, contemporary American modern dancer, b. New York City, of Czechoslovakian and Austrian parentage. Studied dance with Francesca de Cotelet,

Sybil Shearer (with whom she also danced at Goodman Theater, Chicago), at New Dance Group Studio; composition with Louis Horst; acting, music and dance at Roosevelt College, Chicago. An Audition Winner at the YMHA (1949), she has since presented solo programs at the YMHA, Henry Street Playhouse, Hunter College, and at various universities where she has also taught and conducted workshops. Received an Ingram Merrill Award for Choreography (1961) and a Yaddo Fellowship (1962). Some of her best known solo pieces are *Prelude to Flight, No Refuge—Waking and Dreaming, Predatory Figure, Time and Memory, Juke Box Pieces,* and, perhaps her best known work, *Anonymous,* danced to the beat of a metronome. Has also composed group works. Currently teaching in N.Y.

Gaskell, Sonia, b. Kiev, the Ukraine, 1904. Artistic Director of Netherland's state-supported national ballet company, Het Nationaal Ballet, Amsterdam. She began working as teacher and ballet mistress in Paris in 1936 and in 1939 moved to Holland where she taught ballet, mostly to children. A good administrator, after the war she formed her own group, Ballet Recital, with which she created some interesting experimental productions. She became director of Het Nederlands Ballet (1958), a new company organized in The Hague. Also in The Hague she founded the first Netherland Academy of Ballet. In 1959 two of Holland's ballet troupes, the Opera Ballet of Amsterdam and the Ballet der Lage Landen were combined into one company under the name Amsterdams Ballet. After many vicissitudes the Amsterdams Ballet and the Nederlands Ballet were amalgamated into Het Nationaal Ballet with Sonia Gaskell as artistic director. See also HOLLAND, DANCE IN.

Gassmann, Remi, composer, educator, critic, pianist, b. St. Mary's, Kan., 1908. An A.B. (Mus.M.) Univ. of the Eastman School of Music, he also studied at the Hochschule fuer Musik, Berlin (1931–36), class of Paul Hindemith, and studied privately with Guy Maier, Roger Sessions, Eugene Goossens, Isidor Phillip, Frederick Stock. His compositions for ballet include *Billy Sunday* (Ruth Page, Ballet Russe de Monte Carlo, 1948), *Paean* (Tatiana Gsovska, Berlin Opera Company Ballet, 1960), *Electronics* (George Balanchine, New York City Ballet, 1961). Has composed many other scores performed by leading orchestras, companies and soloists, in U.S. and abroad; has written and lectured extensively; for many years engaged in research in electronic sound. The music for *Electronics,* created in collaboration with Oskar Sala in West Berlin, was the first major work of symphonic proportions achieved entirely by electronic means.

Gautier, Théophile (1811–1872), famous French poet and writer, leader in the Romantic movement, one of the greatest critics of all time. He took an active part in the development of the ballet of his time, the golden era of the French ballet. He wrote the libretto for *Giselle* and actively participated in its production. Although he did a great deal in sponsoring the careers of Fanny Elssler and Maria Taglioni, his name is most closely linked with Carlotta Grisi, for whom *Giselle* was staged. The ballerina is supposed to have left her husband, Jules Perrot, for Gautier, but this is not so; she much preferred her partner, Lucien Petipa, for whom she did leave her husband. Gautier found solace with Carlotta's sister Ernesta who bore him two daughters. Gautier's philosophy or art can be summed up in two of his favorite formulas: "Art for art's sake," and "Everything proceeds from form." Among his principal works concerning ballet are: *L'Art Dramatique, Les Beautés de l'Opéra, Souvenir du Théâtre, Portraits Contemporains,* and *Ballet Romantique,* the latter translated into English by Cyril W. Beaumont (1932) under the title *The Romantic Ballet as seen by Théophile Gautier.*

Gautier's poem, *La Mort Amoureuse* was the inspiration for Frederick Ashton's ballet, *Don Juan*. See also ROMANTIC BALLET; GISELLE.

Gavotte, in the 14th century was a peasant dance; later popularized by Marie Antoinette it became a fashionable court dance. Gluck composed music for it and when revived by Maximilien Gardel at the Paris Opéra to music by Grétry it became basis for brilliant solos. It included pas de basque, jetés, bourrées, and pas de zéphires.

Gavrilov, Alexander (1892–1959), dancer of the St. Petersburg Maryinsky Theatre. Was graduated from the Maryinsky School in 1911; left the Imperial Ballet the same year to join the Diaghilev Ballets Russes, where he often understudied Nijinsky and alternated with him in several roles. Came to the U.S. in the early 1930's and did some dancing and teaching, becoming ballet master of the then being formed Ballet Theatre (1939). Later toured with a small ballet troupe, and from the middle 1940's devoted himself entirely to teaching, first in N.Y. and later in Miami, Fla.

Gay Swindles of Courasche, The (Die Gaunerstreiche der Courasche). Ballet in 5 scenes; chor.: Rudolf Kölling; music: Richard Mohaupt; décor: Paul Haferung; book after the novel *Simplicius Simplicissimus*. First prod.: Deutsches Opernhaus, Berlin, 1936, in connection with the XI Olympiad. In the confusion of the Thirty-Years War, Courasche and her Friend Springinsfeld carry out daring thievery and liberation scenes. Army officers and guards, a village magistrate, a merry widow, and shopkeepers are fooled and swindled. The rogues succeed even in freeing themselves from the gallows and triumphing over the people. The ballet has been danced on many German stages.

Gayané. Ballet in 4 acts, 6 scenes; chor.: Nina Anisimova; music: Aram Khachaturian; book: Konstantin Derzhavin; décor: Natan Altman. First prod.: Kirov Ballet in evacuation at the Perm Opera, Dec. 9, 1942; revived in a new version also with choreography by Nina Anisimova in settings by Valery Dorrer, Kirov Theatre, Leningrad, Feb. 20, 1945, with Natalia Dudinskaya, Feya Balabina, Nina Anisimova, Nikolai Zubkovsky, Konstantin Sergeyev. The fourth act from the ballet was revived by Nina Anisimova for the Bolshoi Ballet, Nov. 19, 1961. Gayané, an Armenian mountain girl, loves Armen, but Giko is jealous and attacks Armen. After many tribulations, Giko catches one of the enemy who has crossed the frontier. Gayané and Armen are reunited after the enemy has attempted to kill her, and all become friends again. The ballet ends in a celebration at which guests from other republics perform their dances. The famous "Sabre Dance" is among the dances performed in this divertissement.

Geitel, Klaus, German writer and ballet critic, b. Berlin, 1924. Studied at the Universities of Halle, Berlin, and Paris. Contributor to various German and foreign publications and German television companies; ballet critic of the newspaper *Die Welt*. Author of *Ballet Center Paris* (1960), *Ballet Before the Première* (1961), both in German; wrote television film script *Mary Wigman and Her Studio* (1960).

Geltzer, Yekaterina (1876–1962), People's Artist of the RSFSR, outstanding ballerina of Russian and Soviet ballet. Prima ballerina from 1901. Daughter of Vassily Geltzer, brilliant mime of the Bolshoi Theatre, Moscow and regisseur of its ballet company in the 1890's. Entered Bolshoi school at the age of eight; graduated into the company in 1894. Her first roles were one of the four animated frescoes in *The Humpbacked Horse* and a Greek goddess in the "Walpurgis Night" from *Faust*. In 1896, after seeing Pierina Legnani dance in Moscow, Geltzer asked

Yekaterina Geltzer (1876–1962), ballerina of the Moscow Bolshoi Ballet, in the Directoire Polka.

her father to send her to St. Petersburg to study under Christian Johansson and Marius Petipa. While she had received a strong pointe and pirouette technique from her Moscow teacher Joseph Mendes, a pupil of Carlo Blasis, she felt a want of harmonious coordination, poise, and grace in her dancing. Two years of work under Johansson provided the young dancer with an excellently balanced school that allowed her to become an indisputable "queen of adagio." Her great power of projection was connected with a pronounced dramatic talent inherited from her father. All these gifts came to full blossoming after the revolution with her unforgettable renderings of the roles of *Esmeralda* and Tao-Hoa (*The Red Poppy*). She not only created the latter role but actively participated in the creation of this important landmark in Soviet choreography. In 1925 Geltzer became one of the first artists to be awarded the (at that time highest) title of Peoples' Artist of the Republic, equal in importance to the present Peoples' Artist of the U.S.S.R. Her large and varied repertoire included *Swan Lake, The Sleeping Beauty, Raymonda, Coppélia,* as well as a great number of solo dances. Her 85th birthday was celebrated in Moscow by the Theatre Society in Nov., 1961. She was married to Vassily Tikhomirov, her partner and teacher for many years. In 1910 she danced with Alexandre Volinine in the second Paris season of the Diaghilev Ballets Russes (*Les Sylphides* and in the divertissement). Geltzer died in Moscow, Dec. 12, 1962.

Genée, Dame Adeline (Anina Jensen), ballerina, b. Aarhus, Jutland, Denmark, 1878. Studied with her aunt and uncle, M. and Mme. Alexandre Genée. Made debut age ten in Christiania (now Oslo), Norway, dancing a polka. When her uncle took over the management of the Centralhallen Theater in Stettin, Germany, she was engaged as dancer, often being given principal roles. In 1895 danced the leading role (created for Maria Taglioni) in *Robert the Devil* at Stadttheater, Stettin. The following year made her debut at the Berlin Opera, also dancing the same year in Munich where she danced her first Swanilda in *Coppélia* (Nov. 21, 1896), the role with which she was ever after identified. Made her debut at the Empire Theatre, London, Nov. 22, 1897, and from then on became to all intents and purposes a British ballerina for, though engaged for only a few weeks, Genée remained for ten years and later made return appearances. During this period she appeared with the Royal Danish Ballet (1902), dancing *Coppélia* and Flower Festival at Genzano with Hans Beck. Her repertoire at the Empire included *The Press, Les Papillons, High Jinks, The Dancing Doll, Cinderella, Fête Galante, The Dryad,* and others, and, above all, *Coppélia,* revived especially for her (1906). Made her U.S. debut in *The Soul Kiss,* New York Theatre, 1907. After five seasons in U.S. with her own company, producing *La Danse* and dancing *Coppélia* at the Metropolitan Opera House, she returned to England (1910) and married Frank Isitt. Appeared at the Coliseum in *Butterflies and Roses* (1911), *Camargo* (1912), *Robert the Devil* (1914), *La Danse* (1915), *The Pretty Prentice* (1916), and at the Alhambra (1916). She also visited Australia and New Zealand (1913). Genée made her farewell appearance in 1917 at the Coliseum. She was persuaded out of her retirement to appear in a suite of old dances (called *The Love Song*) for a charity matinee, June 7, 1932; repeated it in Copenhagen went she went there with a troupe of English dancers Sept. 24–28, dancing it at the final performance in the presence of the King and Queen of Denmark and the Prince of Wales (now the Duke of Windsor), and finally dancing it for a season at the Coliseum in Feb., 1933. Anton Dolin was her partner. In 1920 Adeline Genée was elected Founder President of the Association of Operatic Dancing in London, and in 1935 the Association was granted a Royal Charter and became the Royal Academy of Dancing. She retired from the presidency in 1954. She was also a founder member of the Camargo Society (1930–33). In 1935 she received the Order of Ingenii et Arti (M.I. et A.) from the King of Denmark; shortly after World War II King Christian X awarded her the Medal of Liberty in acknowledgment of her efforts to restore Anglo-Danish relations; and in 1953 King Frederik IX created her a Commander of the Order of Dannebrog. In 1950 she was created Dame of the Order of the British Empire (D.B.E.) for her services to dancing in England.

Gennaro, Peter, dancer and choreographer, b. New Orleans, La., 1924; m. Jean Kinsella. With very little formal dance training except for eighteen months with Katherine Dunham (1947–48), he developed a strongly individual style combining elements of ballet and jazz. His choreography for the "Perry Como Show" on television was considered tops in its field and his own appearances from time to time became real dance events. His first professional engagement was with the San Carlo Opera Company which toured the U.S. Danced in the musical *Guys and Dolls,* and came to the fore dancing "Steam Heat" with Carol Haney in *Pajama Game.* He worked as assistant to Jerome Robbins in *West Side Story,* and Robbins has been quick to say that the famous musical owes a great deal to Gennaro; had the dance lead in *Bells Are Ringing;* choreographed the musicals *The Unsinkable Molly Brown* (also the film version), *Mr. President,* and in the fall of 1964, *Bajour.* What is particularly remarkable about his choreography and dancing is that he has overcome the handicap of having less than 50 per cent normal hearing.

Gentry, Eve (Henrietta Greenhood), modern American dancer, b. Los Angeles, Calif.; studied with Ann Mundstock (San Francisco), Hanya Holm, Harald Kreutzberg, Michio Ito, Benjamin Zemach, Martha Graham, Doris Humphrey, Charles Weidman, Helen Tamiris; also studied ballet, mainly with Julia Barashkova and Lisan Kay. Leading group member and soloist with Hanya Holm group (1936–41); choreographer and soloist Doris Humphrey Workshop; co-founder Dance Notation Bureau (1940). Until 1945 danced under own name of Henrietta Greenhood, since then as Eve Gentry, taking her husband's surname. Has presented many solo programs in N.Y. and throughout the country, forming the Eve Gentry Dance Company (1948–49). Solo performer in training film of *Joseph H. Pilate's Technique of Body Control, Conditioning and Rehabilitation* (1957); has also appeared in many television programs. She designs her own costumes and those of her company for all performances. Has her own school since 1954, specializing in technique and improvisation for teenage student dancers and professionals.

Eve Gentry, American modern dancer, choreographer in her Antenna Bird.

Georgi, Yvonne, dancer, choreographer, ballet mistress, b. Leipzig, Germany, 1903. Studied dance with Dalcroze-Hellerau, Mary Wigman, Victor Gsovsky. Made her debut as a soloist in 1923, appearing in Germany, Austria, Holland, U.S., and Poland between that year and 1939. Between 1926 and 1932 she was also partner of Harald Kreutzberg, touring with him in Germany, Austria, Switzerland, Holland, Sweden, Italy, France, Czechoslovakia, U.S., and Canada. Her last appearance in the U.S. was in 1939 with her Dutch ensemble. She has also had an extended career as ballet mistress and choreographer, begining with the Gera (Germany) Opera (1925–26), Hannover Opera (1926–31), Amsterdam Opera (and private company, 1932–34), Düsseldorf Opera (1951–54), and again Hannover Opera since 1954. She has also been guest choreographer at Berlin State Opera (1932), Vienna State Opera (1959), Salzburg Festival (1959). Her choreographic works include *Orpheus and Eurydice, Electronic Ballet, Evolutions, Woman of Andros* to music by Henk Badings (all except the first to electronic scores); *Prometheus* (Beethoven), *Symphonie Fantastique* (Hector Berlioz), *Moor of Venice* (Boris Blacher), *Glück, Tod und Traum, Ballade, Pas de Coeur* (all to music by Gottfried von Einem); *Bolero* (Maurice Ravel); *Legend of Joseph* (Richard Strauss); *Pulcinella, Petrouchka, Sacre du Printemps, Orpheus, Apollon Musagète, Agon, Firebird* (all to the Igor Stravinsky scores); *Goyescas* (Enrique Granados); *Straw Hat* (Jacques Ibert's Divertissement); *Bacchus and Ariadne* (Albert Roussel); *Prisma—Opus 16* (Arnold Schönberg); *Goldfish Bowl* (Jurriaan Andriessen); *Carmina Burana* (Carl Orff), and many others, as well as staging most of the classic and romantic works of the international repertoire. Also choreographed for German and Austrian television and for the French film *Ballerina.*

Georgiadis, Nicholas, Greek painter

and designer, b. 1925. Studied in Athens, N.Y. and London. Ballets include *Danses Concertantes* (1955), and *House of Birds* (1955) for Sadler's Wells Theatre Ballet; *Noctambules* (1956), *The Burrow* (1958), *Agon* (1958), *The Invitation* (1960), and *Diversions* (1961) for Royal Ballet. For American Baliet Theatre designed *Winter's Eve* (1957). All are Kenneth MacMillan ballets. Designed décor and costumes for the Kenneth Macmillan *Romeo and Juliet* at the Royal Ballet (1965).

Gerdt, Paul (1844–1917), probably the greatest classic dancer and partner of all time on the Russian Imperial Stage. Began his career in 1860 and six years later became premier danseur; continued to dance until the end of 1916. Gifted, tall, strong and handsome, he was the perfect partner, and during his fifty years as premier danseur he danced with all the great ballerinas. He was also an excellent teacher, specializing in supported adagio and mime, of which he was a past master.

Gerdt, Yelizaveta, Honored Art Worker of the RSFSR, leading Soviet teacher and former ballerina of the Maryinsky Theatre, b. 1891. Through her principal teacher, Anna Johansson, she assimilated the style of the latter's great father, Christian Johansson. Entered the Maryinsky school 1899, graduating 1908 under Michel Fokine, dancing the Waltz and Mazurka in the graduation performance of *Chopiniana* which he choreographed for the occasion. The year previously, Fokine gave her the role of Armide in *The Animated Gobelin* (*Le Pavillon d'Armide*) which he staged for Vaslav Nijinsky's graduation. Yelizaveta Gerdt inherited the beauty, grace and exceptional line of her celebrated father, Paul Gerdt. She was strictly a classical dancer, lovely, technically impeccable but slightly cold. She began dancing ballerina roles in 1910 and by 1913 was officially made ballerina. Her ballets included *The Sleeping Beauty, Swan Lake, La Fille du Pharaon, La Bayadère, Raymonda,* and others. For some ten years after the revolution she continued as leading ballerina of the former Maryinsky (now Kirov), dancing during the first period under very difficult conditions. In 1918 she began teaching at the Kirov school and giving company classes. In 1934 she was invited to work at the Bolshoi Theatre and school where she has formed many outstanding ballerinas, among them Maya Plisetskaya, Raisa Struchkova, Yekaterina Maximova, and the young Yelena Ryabinkina, whom she has coached in all her roles at the Bolshoi. She continues to coach young dancers but has retired from teaching.

Gesture, strictly speaking, is all movement of the human body (and by no means of arms alone), the aim of which is to express or signify something. Dance is generally silent, and it uses gestures to express that which cannot be expressed in dance alone. Carlo Blasis in his *Code of Terpsichore* said that gesture is primitive speech taught to humans by nature itself. According to Blasis, there exist two kinds of gestures: natural and artificial, or conventional. The first is inherent in us, and is the outward expression of what goes on within us, the physical expression of our feelings. These gestures depict emotions. The second kind of gestures is created by art, through imitation. These gestures depict objects and conceptions independent of us. They are emblems of that which is outside our moral world. They are adopted by usage to indicate that which cannot be described by natural gestures. See also PANTOMIME.

Geva, Tamara, (Tamara Gevergeyeva), choreographer, dancer, actress, b. St. Petersburg, 1908, of Russian, Swedish, and Italian descent. Studied at State Ballet School of Maryinsky Theatre. During the revolution left Russia at sixteen with a small group including George Balanchine and Alexandra Danilova which performed in Germany and England until it was seen by Serge Diaghilev and invited to join his company. Geva remained two years, then came to U.S. with Nikita Balieff's *Chauve Souris* show and was shortly thereafter signed by Florenz Ziegfeld for the musical *Whoopee*. Apart from a guest artist appearance with American Ballet in Balanchine's *Errante* (1935), her career has since been in musicals (notably *On Your Toes,* 1936), plays, and films.

Giachero, Roberto, Argentine dancer, choreographer and teacher, b. Mercedes (San Luis), Argentina, 1925. Studied dance with Maria Ruanova, Esmée Bulnes and Boris Kniaseff. Joined the ballet of Teatro Argentino de La Plata, Argentina (1946) as soloist for the performances organized by the Comisión Nacional de Cultura. He founded the Compañía Argentina de Ballet (1948) and worked with it seven seasons during which he choreographed *Romeo and Juliet* (Tchaikovsky), *Kingdom of Ys* (Poulenc), *Psyché* (Debussy), *Promenade à Vienne* (Johann Strauss). In 1954–57 he was choreographer for the Teatro Argentino where he revived standard ballets and staged *La Boutique Fantasque* (Rossini-Respighi), among other new works. In 1958 he choreographed *Apollo and Daphne* to music by Handel and *L'Ivrogne Corrige* to Gluck. These two works were later presented at the Théâtre des Nations, Paris, and at the Brussels Exposition (1958). He returned to Teatro Argentino de La Plata as guest choreographer (1959) and staged *David and Bathsheba,* a danced oratorio to music by Presbítero Angel Colabella. He choreographed *The Portrait of Marguerite Gautier,* to music by Carrera Urquiza, for the Ballet del Sur at Bahia Blanca, Argentina (1961).

Giara, La. Ballet in 1 act; chor.: Jean Börlin; music: Alfredo Casella. First prod.: *Les Ballets Suédois,* Théâtre des Champs-Elysées, Paris, 1924 (as *La Jarre*). Comic ballet, based on a short story by Luigi Pirandello, about eloping lovers, an indignant father, and the precious jar which an old itinerant mender of pots and pans is brought in to mend. He does so, but leaves himself inside it, so that the only way to extricate him is to break the jar again. Ninette de Valois choreographed a version for the Sadler's Wells (now Royal) Ballet (1934) with Walter Gore as the jar mender. There are several Italian and Central European versions, including Luciana Novaro's at Teatro alla Scala, Milan.

Gift of the Magi. Ballet in 6 scenes; chor. and book: Simon Semenoff; music: Lukas Foss; décor: Raoul Pène du Bois. First prod.: Ballet (now American Ballet) Theatre, Metropolitan Opera House, N.Y., Oct. 15, 1945, with Nora Kaye and John Kriza as Della and Jim. Based on the O. Henry story of the poor young married couple who each sells the most precious possession so that the other may have a Christmas present. The wife cuts off and sells her hair to buy her husband a chain for his valuable watch, while he sells his watch to buy her a tortoise shell comb for her hair. The ballet was later briefly revived for London's Festival Ballet with John Gilpin and the young American dancer Melinda Plank.

Gigue, a lively dance generally in 6/8, 12/8, 4/4, but also in 6/4 and 2/4 time, popular in France ca. 1700. In music it is often used as a movement in a suite. See also MUSIC FOR DANCE.

Gill, Laurel. See MARTYN, LAUREL.

Gillies, Don, Canadian dancer and choreographer, b. Toronto, 1926. Studied dance with Boris Volkoff, Toronto and at Sadler's Wells Ballet School in London. Danced in English musicals, including the London productions of *High Button Shoes* and *Carousel;* joined Sadler's Wells Theatre Ballet (1951), touring U.S.A. and Canada. Was in Gene Kelly's *Invitation to the Dance* film (1951). Returned to

Canada in 1952, joining Canadian Broadcasting Corporation as dancer-choreographer.

Gillot, Claude (ca. 1720), designer of ballet costumes at the Paris Opéra. He followed Jean Bérain II. Watteau and Lancret worked in Gillot's studio. One of his best known works was *Les Éléments.* He replaced the stiff brocades of his time with softer materials. The simplicity of his costumes was charming but he lacked the nobility of his predecessor Bérain.

Gilmour, Sally, English dancer, b. Malaya, 1921. Was sent to London in 1930 and studied there with Tamara Karsavina and Marie Rambert. Became famous overnight when she created the title role in *Lady into Fox* (Andrée Howard, 1939) with Ballet Rambert. As ballerina of the Ballet Rambert her range extended from strong tragedy to delicate comedy. She danced *Giselle, Swan Lake* (Act 2), Caroline in *Jardin aux Lilas,* and *Dark Elegies;* her creations included the Duck in *Peter and the Wolf* (Frank Staff, 1940), *Confessional* (Walter Gore, 1941), Younger Sister in *The Fugitive* (Howard, 1944), Tulip in *Sailor's Return* (Howard, 1947), *Winter Night* (Gore, 1948). Just before she retired, she danced the young girl in the Agnes de Mille ballet in the London production of *Carousel* (1951). Now lives (since 1953) with her doctor husband in Australia.

Gilpin, John, English dancer, director, b. Southsea, 1930; m. Sally Judd. Studied at June Ripman School and Ballet Rambert School. Well known as a child actor in straight plays. Joined Ballet Rambert (1945), becoming principal dancer, and creating Rabbit-Catcher (*The Sailor's Return*), dancing *Blue Bird* pas de deux, *Peasant* pas de deux (*Giselle*), *Swan Lake* pas de trois, *Le Spectre de la Rose,* and others. London season of Ballets de Paris de Roland Petit creating leading male role in Frederick Ashton's *Le Rêve de Leonor* (1949). With London's Festival Ballet since 1950, becoming principal dancer; assistant artistic director (Apr. 1959); artistic director and principal dancer (1962). A virtuoso whose range encompasses demi-caractère as well as danseur noble roles, his large repertoire includes Sugar Plum Fairy's Cavalier (*The Nutcracker*), Albrecht (Giselle), Franz (*Coppélia*), and such creations as title role (*The Witch Boy*), male lead (*Symphony for Fun*), one of the two male leads (Festival Ballet's *Etudes*), second movement (Festival Ballet's *Bourrée Fantasque*), title role (*Peer Gynt*), and others. Guest artist, Royal Ballet, making his debut as the Blue Skater (*Les Patineurs*) in Apr. 1961, A back injury prevented him carrying out his full schedule of performances. He again danced as guest artist with the Royal Ballet's touring section in its June, 1963, season at Covent Garden. Was guest artist with the American Ballet Theatre during its 25th Anniversary Season in New York (March 16–April 11, 1965), dancing Albrecht in *Giselle, La Esmeralda* pas de deux with Lupe Serrano, and principal male role in Harald Lander's *Etudes.* In September, 1965, resigned as artistic director of London's Festival Ballet but continues as premier danseur.

Giselle.

Giselle, a romantic ballet in two acts by Vernoy de Saint-Georges, Théophile Gautier, and Jean Coralli, with music by Adolphe Adam, scenery and costumes by Pierre Ciceri and choreography by Jean Coralli and Jules Perrot, was first produced at the Théâtre de l'Académie Royale de Musique, Paris, June 28, 1841, with Carlotta Grisi in the title role and Lucien Petipa as Albrecht.

The composer, Adolphe Adam, was a prolific craftsman who had composed some fifty theatrical scores, among them a dozen or so for ballets. Vernoy de Saint-Georges was a professional, not to say hack, ballet librettist who worked with Jean Coralli,

Lucien Petipa, Arthur Saint-Léon, Jules Perrot, Marius Petipa, and others, but never created anything outstanding before or after *Giselle*. Pierre Ciceri, who designed the scenery and costumes, was a popular landscape painter with some theatrical experience. The choreographer, Jean Coralli, was a ballet master of note who always worked in very definite and closely circumscribed outlines.

Jules Perrot, probably the greatest of all choreographers of the Romantic period, staged the solo dances for Carlotta Grisi, to whom he was then married, but due to backstage intrigues he was not given credit for his work on the program. Théophile Gautier, the poet, writer and leader of the Romantic movement, officially did not get credit for more than writing the story of the ballet, which later had to be adapted to the requirements of the stage by Saint-Georges. What is more, the story was not even original; Gautier found it recorded as a popular legend by the German poet Heinrich Heine in his *De l'Allemagne*.

The story is of the peasant girl Giselle, who falls in love with Count Albrecht who is living in her village disguised as a peasant. Though warned by the gamekeeper Hilarion, who loves her, Giselle refuses to believe any ill of her lover until his uncle, the Duke of Courland and his daughter, Bathilde, who is Albrecht's fiancée, discover him when they seek refreshment while out hunting. Hilarion denounces Albrecht by showing his sword with the crest on it to the company. The shock is too much for the fragile Giselle; she loses her mind and then falls dead in her mother's arms. In the second act, the repentant Albrecht goes to pray at her tomb. Hilarion has preceded him; has been captured by the Wilis (the spirits of maidens who loved to dance and who died before their wedding day), and has been thrown into the lake. The Queen of the Wilis decrees a similar fate for Albrecht, but the gentle spirit of Giselle appears to save him. Albrecht is condemned to dance himself to death, but Giselle, dancing with him, is able to save him, for when dawn comes, the Wilis must return to their graves. Giselle, too, must return, and Albrecht gently carries her back to her tomb.

There are innumerable slight variations from the basic story. Hilarion, once generally considered a villain, is now usually depicted as an honest man, genuinely in love with Giselle, who wishes only to save her from what he knows can only be the bitter disillusionment of discovering Albrecht's duplicity. In this particular interpretation Alexander Lapuri and Vladimir Levashev in Russia and Leslie Edwards in England are outstanding. Albrecht is similarly open to various interpretations. He is sometimes portrayed as a youthful philanderer, shocked into seriousness only when he sees the tragedy he has brought about. Other Albrechts take the decisive line of a young man genuinely in love with Giselle from the beginning, but momentarily struck dumb by the sudden appearance of the Duke and Bathilde. The original St. Georges-Gautier-Coralli scenario makes it clear that Giselle was intended to kill herself with Albrecht's sword. Nowadays most Giselles have it snatched away from them and it is established that they die from a combination of shock and "a broken heart." Some Giselles indicate in pantomime while dancing with the villagers that they have a weak heart, which makes their death rather more convincing if they do not intend to stab themselves. All these variations are part of the endless fascination of Giselle for its interpreters and public alike.

Gautier thought the story would make a good ballet. More than that, touched by Gautier's talent, ignited by his inspiration, the mechanical collaboration of the people who were working on the production of Giselle was transformed into a fusion of their creative efforts which resulted in a composition of artistic strength and validity. In this respect, Gautier bears a distinct resemblance to Serge Diaghilev, who also succeeded in bringing out the finest in his collaborators.

Gautier's long-standing interest in ballet continued for years after *Giselle* was first produced. His passionate attitude toward the ballet had a romantic as well as an artistic aspect.

A great friend of the dancers Maria Taglioni and Fanny Elssler at the height of their careers, Gautier fell in love with the twenty-year-old Carlotta Grisi when she arrived in Paris from Italy. He saw in her a synthesis of everything he had admired in Taglioni and Elssler. Grisi, in Gautier's opinion, possessed both the lyric quality of the "Christian" Taglioni and the fire and enchantment of the "pagan" Elssler. She alone could do justice to the inherent quality of the subject matter of a romantic composition, to the opposition of earthly suffering and spiritual happiness.

Whether or not Carlotta Grisi actually was the great dancer Gautier imagined her to be is open to question. Since most of the information we have about her personality and talent is contained in the writings of Gautier himself, his evaluations on this subject require a very careful approach and a stricter-than-usual critical attitude. One thing is clear: Grisi never reached the lofty heights inhabited by her predecessors Taglioni and Elssler. These two brought something new to the theatrical dance, made possible new approaches to choreographic composition, which formed the basis for future creations. Their art touched wide groups of people not necessarily connected with theatre arts. Grisi continued on the road opened by Taglioni and Elssler. Through her efforts these roads were widened and lengthened. But it was not she who cut the first direct footpath through the clichés and antiquated pseudo-traditions of the pre-Romantic ballet. Consequently, the appearance of Grisi was a great event only in theatrical circles. [No one could take the places of Taglioni and Elssler in ballets, such as *La Sylphide* or *Le Diable Boiteux*. Consequently these ballets did not survive the retirement of the dancers.] Grisi, on the other hand, was by no means the only interpreter of the role of Giselle, nor even the finest. The apparent timelessness of *Giselle* is due to the fact that a hundred years ago, as now, *Giselle* was the ideal romantic ballet.

Giselle is a remarkable ballet chiefly because all its component parts—story, choreography, music, décor—blend into a homogeneous artistic unit. From the choreographic aspect alone, *Giselle* has not been surpassed in a hundred years. For the first time in ballet a choreographic composition was based and carried out on the development of dance themes. The dances are saturated with systematically developed ideas through the introduction of leitmotifs, passages associated with or expressive of a certain person, mood, sentiment or situation.

Adolphe Adam's music for *Giselle* may sound antiquated to the modern listener. Like the story of the ballet, it is simple and naïve, but it is moving and sincere. The structure of the score contains the same unaffected simplicity and economy which characteristize the choreographic structure. And this in spite of the fact that *Giselle* had been composed on order in some three weeks. It is perhaps for this reason that Adam used in *Giselle* rhythms and melodies borrowed from some of his other compositions. Many melodies were taken from his ballet *The Pirate,* which he had composed in 1840 for Filippo Taglioni, who planned to produce it in St. Petersburg.

The score of *Giselle* created a trend toward more serious ballet music. Léo Delibes in his *La Source* and *Coppélia* and Tchaikowsky in *Swan Lake, Sleeping Beauty,* and *The Nutcracker* made use of the experience and technique of the rhythmic phrasing in *Giselle*.

Giselle has undergone many changes, but has never been off the boards since its première.

In 1842 it was produced for the first time in St. Petersburg. The choreographer of the first Russian version was Antoine

Titus, who had been sent to Paris by the management of the Imperial Theatres to look for novelties. The production was a great success and featured Elena Andreyanova in the title role. In 1848 Fanny Elssler danced *Giselle* for her Russian debut, and two years later Carlotta Grisi appeared in it in St. Petersburg. By that time Titus' choreography was somewhat rearranged by Jules Perrot and Marius Petipa. Later on Arthur Saint-Léon made some additional changes in the choreography, and that version prevailed until 1887 when Petipa reconstructed the ballet for the debut of the French ballerina Emma Bessonet.

Ever since *Giselle* was first presented, every ballerina in the world has coveted the title role and every premier danseur has aspired to dance Albrecht. More tears have been shed and contracts broken over *Giselle* than over any other ballet. The names of dancers who have appeared in these roles read like a roster of the greatest men and women in ballet. They include: Carlotta Grisi, Maria Taglioni, Fanny Elssler, Lucile Grahn, Fanny Cerito, Tamara Karsavina, Anna Pavlova, Olga Spessivtzeva, Vera Nemtchinova, Alexandra Danilova, Alicia Markova, Mia Slavenska, Tamara Toumanova, Nana Gollner, Annabelle Lyon, Patricia Bowman, Alicia Alonso, Margot Fonteyn, Lycette Darsonval, Yvette Chauviré, Galina Ulanova, Marina Semenova, Raissa Struchkova, Marina Kondratieva, Irina Kolpakova, Alla Shelest, Yekaterina Maximova, Natalia Makarova, Nina Vyroubova, Rosella Hightower, Nora Kaye, Lupe Serrano, Liane Daydé, Violetta Elvin, Beryl Grey, Moira Shearer, Nadia Nerina, Anya Linden, Lynn Seymour, Carla Fracci, Sally Gilmour; and Vaslav Nijinsky, Mikhail Mordkin, Laurent Novikoff, Pierre Vladimiroff, Anatole Vilzak, Anatole Oboukhoff, Anton Dolin, Igor Youskevitch, André Eglevsky, Serge Lifar, Robert Helpmann, Frederic Franklin, Royes Fernandez, George Zoritch, Michael Somes, Walter Gore, David Blair, Youly Algaroff, George Skibine, Konstantin Sergeyev, Yuri Zhdanov, Nicolai Fadeyechev, Maris Liepa, Rudolf Nureyev.

In Paris the Diaghilev Ballets Russes presented *Giselle* in its 1910 season with Tamara Karsavina and Vaslav Nijinsky. It was revived again in 1924 for the debut of Olga Spessivtzeva in Paris. Spessivtzeva and Serge Lifar later danced the ballet in the Opéra in 1932. It was revived again in 1938 in Lifar's version, which the Opéra still uses. Lycette Darsonval, Yvette Chauviré, and Liane Daydé are three notable French Giselles.

In London Carlotta Grisi danced *Giselle* for the first time in 1842. The ballet was revived on Oct. 9, 1843, at the Princess Theatre with an English ballerina, Miss Ballin, in the title role. Another English dancer, Alice Holt, danced it at the Empire Theatre, December 26, 1844. The Diaghilev company had presented it with Karsavina and Nijinsky at the Royal Opera House, Covent Garden, London, on October 16, 1911; and the Anna Pavlova Company had produced it in 1913 with Pavlova as Giselle.

Among English productions of note is that of the Camargo Society during its Savoy Theatre, London, season in 1932, when Spessivtzeva danced the title role with a company of English dancers. Anton Dolin was Albrecht, Frederick Ashton Hilarion and Ninette de Valois was Berthe, Giselle's mother. Victor Dandré's gift of the Pavlova costumes and scenery made this production possible.

The first all-English production was given by the Vic–Wells (later Sadler's Wells, now Royal) Ballet at the Old Vic Theatre, Jan. 1, 1934, with Alicia Markova in the title role and Dolin as Albrecht. The following year (May 27, 1935) when Markova and Dolin formed their own company, they presented the ballet with themselves in the principal roles. Margot Fonteyn succeeded Markova in the Vic-Wells version which had been staged by Nicholas Sergeyev, former regisseur of the Maryinsky Theatre, St. Petersburg. This version included the "Peasant" pas de deux, to music by Norbert Bergmüller, which is often dropped from American productions. When the Royal Ballet production was revised by Frederick Ashton under the supervision of Karsavina in 1960, he choreographed an entirely new dance for the girl in this pas de deux, using the music which was originally used for Giselle's own variation in Act. 1. Karsavina staged the pantomime scene, dropped elsewhere, in which Giselle's mother foretells Giselle's doom.

Sergeyev also revived the ballet for International Ballet in 1942. Other English productions are those of Ballet Rambert (with Sally Gilmour and Walter Gore as the first Giselle and Albrecht), and London's Festival Ballet.

In the United States the first *Giselle* was given Jan. 2, 1846, in Boston with Mary Ann Lee, the American ballerina who had studied under Jean Coralli. The first New York performance was at the Park Theatre, Feb. 2, 1846, with the French dancer Mme. Augusta in the title role. Katti Lanner (daughter of the famous Viennese composer), who was later the choreographer of London's Empire Theatre, danced *Giselle* in N.Y. in 1870, and Anna Pavlova and Mikhail Mordkin danced it at the Metropolitan Opera House in 1910. The latter's own company, the Mordkin Ballet presented *Giselle* at the Majestic Theatre, N.Y., in 1937 with Lucia Chase in the title role. This production became part of the original repertoire of Ballet Theatre (now American Ballet Theatre); Alicia Alonso and Igor Youskevitch were renowned for their interpretations of the leading roles in this company's version. The Leonide Massine-René Blum Ballet Russe de Monte Carlo made its debut in New York in 1938 with *Giselle.* Due to an injury, Alicia Markova was able to dance only the first act (this was her U.S. debut); Mia Slavenska substituted for her in the second act.

Mary Skeaping staged an exceptionally fine production for the Royal Swedish Ballet in 1953, restoring many musical cuts, among them a long fugue in the second act during which the Wilis were seen as spirits destroying any man who crossed their path, thus preparing the way for the later entries of Hilarion and Albrecht.

Giselle's Revenge. Modern dance satire; chor. and costumes: Myra Kinch; music: Manuel Galea. First prod.: Myra Kinch and Company at Jacob's Pillow Dance Festival, Lee, Mass. (1953), with Myra Kinch (Giselle), and William Milié (Albrecht); N.Y. première: Henry Street Playhouse, Nov. 22, 1953. A satire on the famous romantic ballet in which a Charles Addams–like (not an Adolphe Adam–like) Giselle lures the unsuspecting Albrecht into her coffin and nails him down with blood-curdling glee.

Gissey, Henri (d. 1673), designer of costumes for many ballets in which Louis XIV danced. His masterpiece, *Carrousel de Louis XIV,* was given in front of the Louvre in 1662.

Gitana, La. Ballet in prologue and 3 acts, 5 scenes; chor. and book: Filippo Taglioni. First prod.: Bolshoi Theatre, St. Petersburg, Dec. 5, 1838, with Maria Taglioni (Lauretta) and Nicholas Goltz (Ivan); London première: Her Majesty's Theatre, June 6, 1839, with Taglioni in the title role. The incredibly complicated plot is basically the story of a girl stolen by Gypsies who falls in love with the son of a nobleman and is spurned until her true identity is revealed.

Gittana (It.), a Spanish dance.

Giuliano, Juan, dancer, b. Montevideo, Uruguay, of Argentinian parentage; m. Hélène Trailine. Studied dance in the school of the Colón Theatre, Buenos Aires. Left Argentina in 1950 to make his debut in the S.O.D.R.E. Theatre, Montevideo. Was engaged in 1953 by the Ballet do IV Centenário, São Paulo, then directed by Aurel Milloss; danced *Petrouchka, Bolero,* and others, and continued his dance studies with Milloss. Principal dancer for a season at Teatro Municipal, Rio de Janeiro (1956). Later that year joined Grand Ballet du Marquis de Cuevas in Europe, dancing *Prisoner of the Caucasus, La Somnambule, Prince Igor,* and *Swan Lake* and partnering all the ballerinas of the company, including Rosella Hightower with whom he danced the pas de deux *Soirée Musicale* (Rossini-Britten), choreographed by John Taras. Between 1957 and 1959 was premier danseur in Janine Charrat's company, dancing in Europe, U.S., Central and South America, his biggest success being in *Grieg Concerto,* partnering Charrat in this long pas de deux. He also danced at various European festivals, and was Nora Kaye's partner in the European season of Ballet of Two Worlds (1960), organized by Herbert Ross and Nora Kaye, dancing *The Dybbuk, Within the Grove* (based on the Japanese play *Rashomon*), and *Persephone.* Again partnered Janine Charrat, when her company and the company of the Théâtre Royal de la Monnaie, Brussels, directed by Maurice Béjart, played a joint season at Sadler's Wells Theatre, London, Apr., 1960. Premier danseur with Ballet Russe de Monte Carlo for its 1961–62 U.S. tour, his outstanding partnering and brilliant *batterie* being particularly notable in the classic pas de deux: *The Black Swan, The Nutcracker, Don Quixote.* Appeared with a group of French dancers at Jacob's Pillow Dance Festival (1963). Currently premier danseur at Opéra Comique, Paris.

Glazounov, Alexander (1865–1936), Russian composer. He did much to raise the quality of ballet music. He wrote three ballets for the Maryinsky Theatre, St. Petersburg, which were choreographed by Marius Petipa: *Raymonda* (1898), *Ruses d'Amour* (1900) and *The Seasons* (1900). The bacchanale from *The Seasons* (Autumn), danced by Anna Pavlova and Mikhail Mordkin, was an outstanding number in the ballerina's company. Parts of the music from *The Seasons* were used by Bronislava Nijinska for her Snow Maiden (1942). George Balanchine and Alexandra Danilova staged *Raymonda* for Ballet Russe de Monte Carlo in N.Y. (1946). Balanchine staged the pas de dix from *Raymonda* for the New York City Ballet, where it is known as *Pas de Dix.* Danilova and Frederic Franklin staged a version known as Grand Pas Glazounov for American Ballet Theatre. Frederick Ashton's *Birthday Offering* uses music of Glazounov taken from his concert works and ballets arranged by Robert Irving.

Glebov, Igor. See Asafiev, Boris.

Glière, Reinhold (1875–1956), Russian composer. Provided the music for the ballets *Chrysis* (1912), *Egyptian Nights* (based on a narrative poem by Alexander Pushkin, 1925), *The Red Poppy* (now called *The Red Flower,* 1927), *The Comedians* (1930), *The Bronze Horseman* (based on a narrative poem by Pushkin, 1949).

Glissade, in ballet, a gliding step; a preparatory movement for leaps; a running start, as it were. Technique: Start in 5th pos. R ft. front; demi-plié and slide R ft. to 2nd pos., toe pointed; change weight to R ft. and slide L ft. to 5th pos. back, demi-plié. Glissade may be done back or front, changing ft. to 5th pos. back or front, etc.

Glissé, in ballet, a gliding movement.

Gloire, machine for stage effects, introduced into France in the early 17th century by Francini, an engineer, and causing as much of a sensation as the singers and dancers whom it carried on stage. These contrivances were more elaborate than the Italian nuvola, credited to the 15th century architect Filippo Brunelleschi, let down from the ceiling to represent heaven. About the same time in England Inigo Jones accomplished Paradises of scenic wonders. Jerome Servandi, machinist and designer of Jean Georges Noverre's ballets (1727–1809) made even more wonderful gloires and other mechanical inventions for unusual stage settings. The court theatre at Drottningholm, just outside Stockholm, Sweden, still uses gloires among its stage effects and is one of the few remaining theatres where such machinery is in use today.

Gloire, La. Ballet in 1 act, 3 scenes; chor.: Antony Tudor; music: Ludwig von Beethoven (overtures *Egmont, Coriolanus, Leonore* No. 3); costumes: Robert Fletcher. First prod.: New York City Ballet at City Center, N.Y., Feb. 26, 1952, with Nora Kaye (the actress La Gloire as Lucretia, Phaedra, Hamlet), Hugh Laing (Hippolytus, Laertes), Francisco Moncion (Sextus Tarquinius, Claudius), Diana Adams (Aspirant). A great, but fading, star, La Gloire, seen in three of her famous roles, while offstage she watches the inexorable passage of time which will elevate a young aspirant to the position she clings to so desperately. Although this ballet lasted only a short time in the repertoire, it is notable as being one of the two ballets (*Lady of the Camellias* is the other) which Tudor created for N.Y. City Ballet. Since that time his only other works created for a major company have been *Offenbach in the Underworld* for National Ballet of Canada and American Ballet Theatre and *Echoes of Trumpets* for Royal Swedish Ballet.

Gluck, Christoph Wilibald (1714–1787), German composer. Michel Fokine used his *Don Juan* for his ballet of the same title (1936). His opera *Orfeo ed Euridice* was staged as an opera-ballet by George Balanchine (1936) under the title *Orpheus,* in which the singers were seated in the orchestra pit and the dancers were on the stage, a style of production which the Metropolitan Opera audience could not accept with favor. Ninette de Valois used most of the music from the opera for her ballet *Orpheus and Eurydice* (1941) in which the dancers were on stage and two singers sat in the orchestra pit and sang certain parts of the opera. Agnes de Mille used some of Gluck's music for her ballet *Tally-Ho!* (1944).

Gnatt, Poul, Danish dancer, choreographer, director, b. Baden bei Wien, Austria, 1923, of Danish parents; brother of Kirsten Ralov. Studied at Royal Danish Ballet School, graduating into the company and being appointed solo dancer (1952) where he was an outstanding James in *La Sylphide.* Guest artist, Les Ballets des Champs-Élysées (1945–46), Metropolitan Ballet (1946–47, 1950), Royal Swedish Ballet (1949), Original Ballet Russe (1950–51), Borovansky's Australian Ballet (1951–52). Founded New Zealand Ballet (1953) and is currently artistic and touring director. Still dances occasionally. His ballets for New Zealand Ballet include *Valse Triste, Waltz in Vienna, Sonata, Satan's Wedding, Prismatic Variations* (in collaboration with Russell Kerr). Guest artist, Borovansky Ballet, Melbourne (1960). In 1962 invited his sister and her husband, Fredbjørn Bjørnsson, to dance in New Zealand. They staged *Napoli* for the company.

Godfrey, Louis, South African dancer, b. Johannesburg, 1930; m. Marilynn Burr. Studied with Ivy Conmee and Marjorie Sturman, then in London with Vera Volkova, Stanislas Idzikowski, at Sadler's Wells Ballet School, etc. Leading dancer, Johannesburg Festival Ballet Society (1946–48). With Alicia Markova and Anton Dolin on concert tour (1949–50); appeared with Sadler's Wells Ballet, Jan.–Mar., 1950; joined Dolin and Markova Apr., 1950 for gala performance and remained when the company expanded to become London's Festival Ballet (1951). Currently a principal dancer at the last named company; his roles include: Sugar Plum Fairy's Cavalier (*The Nutcracker*), Franz (*Coppélia*), Golden Slave (*Schéhérazade*), Dandy (*Le Beau Danube*), Moor and Petrouchka (*Petrouchka*), Leil (*The Snow Maiden*), and others.

Gods Go a'Begging, The. Ballet in 1 act; chor.: George Balanchine; music: George Frederick Handel, selected and arr. by: Sir Thomas Beecham from various operas, principally *Alcina* but also *Admeto, Teseo, Il Pastor Fido,* etc., and a Hornpipe transcription from Handel's Concerto Grosso Op. 6 No. 7; book: Sobeka (Boris Kochno); décor: Léon Bakst (the opening scene of Fokine's *Daphnis and Chloë*); costumes: Juan Gris (only the gods' costumes were new; the others were the costumes for Bronislava Nijinska's *Les Tentations de la Bergère*). First prod.: *Diaghilev's Ballets Russes,* His Majesty's Theatre, London, July 16, 1928 with Alexandra Danilova (Serving-Maid), Leon Woicikowski (Shepherd), Felia Doubrovska, Lubov Tchernicheva, Constantin Tcherkas. David Lichine staged a version of this ballet, in décor by Juan Gris after the original Bakst setting, for Col. de Basil's Ballets Russes de Monte Carlo (1937). An entirely new version by Ninette de Valois in décor by Hugh Stevenson was premièred by Vic-Wells (later Sadler's Wells, now Royal) Ballet at Sadler's Wells Theatre, London, Feb. 21, 1936, with Elizabeth Miller and William Chappell as the Serving-Maid and the Shepherd, respectively. Pearl Argyle and Richard Ellis later danced these roles. A young shepherd intrudes upon a fête champêtre of youthful nobles. He is attracted by the beautiful young serving-maid, their attendant. Laughed at by the nobles when they are discovered, the young pair strike awe into the group when a metamorphosis reveals them as two gods.

Golden Age, The. Ballet in 3 acts, 5 scenes; chor.: E. I. Kaplan and Vassily Vainonen (special numbers by V. P. Tchesnokoff and Leonid Yacobson); music: Dimitri Shostakovitch; book: A. V. Ivanovsky; décor: V. M. Khodasevich. First prod.: Moscow, 1930. The book was the prize winner in a contest for ballets with Soviet themes; the score was the first Shostakovitch wrote for a ballet. It has been out of the repertoire since the middle 1930's.

Goldwyn, Beryl, English dancer, b. Pinner, Middlesex, 1930. Studied at Sadler's Wells School and Ballet Rambert School. Joined Ballet Rambert (1949), becoming principal dancer (1953). Her repertoire included *Giselle,* Swan Queen (*Swan Lake,* Act 2), and others. Retired on her marriage to a non-professional (1955), returning briefly when the Ballet Rambert danced at Jacob's Pillow Dance Festival (1959). Beginning 1962, artistic director, Masque Ballet.

Goleizovsky, Kasian, Honored Art Worker of the Lithuanian SSR, Soviet choreographer, b. 1892. Began ballet training in Moscow but in 1907 moved to St. Petersburg where he studied for another three years in the ballet division of the Theatre School, graduating into the Maryinsky company in 1909, but being transferred to the Moscow Bolshoi Theatre Ballet in 1910. While in St. Petersburg the young dancer closely observed Michel Fokine's work and in Moscow was attracted by Alexander Gorsky's progressive artistic outlook—a search for new forms of the theatrical dance and dislike of conventional classical ballet. Nevertheless he was bent on developing a style of his own. In that period he met the founder and director of the *Chauve Souris,* Nikita Balieff, for whom he produced several one act plays, operettas and many dance numbers. This work gave Goleizovsky the opportunity to develop his talent for the miniature and grotesque styles which later interested him as a choreographer. His real opportunity came after the revolution when, for at least a decade, he exerted a strong influence, not only on the Moscow ballet but also on young choreographers in Leningrad, including George Balanchine. While remaining with the Bolshoi company as choreographer, he maintained a private ballet studio which was a testing center of the latest ideas in choreography. Much of his choreography of the 1920's was very beautiful though at times acrobatic and devoid of action—the dancers were required to take intricate poses rather than to dance. His most important work of that period was *Joseph the Beautiful* (1925) to music by Sergei Vasilenko, given at the Experimental Theatre-Filial of Bolshoi. Serge Diaghilev sent him repeated offers to join his Ballets Russes as dancer and choreographer but he did not wish to leave his country. In 1927 he staged *The Red Whirlwind* at the Bolshoi to music by Boris Ber, and resigned in protest when the revolutionary spectacle aroused violent resentment on the part of the supporters of the classical ballet at the Bolshoi. However, he returned at different times for single productions. In the late 1920's and early 1930's his "Goleizovsky Thirty Girls" at the Moscow Music Hall were famous. His staging of the Polovetsian dances for *Prince Igor* at the Bolshoi (1933) is still in use, after revisions during the past few years. He is an expert on national dances, particularly those of Gypsy, Spain, Hungary, and Old Russia. In 1960 he presented an evening of short dance numbers choreographed by talented young Bolshoi dancers at the Tchaikovsky Concert Hall, Moscow. In 1961 he choreographed a concert program to music by Scriabine and young Soviet composers, including Rodion Shchedrin, for the Kirov Ballet, and a suite of dances to music by Sergei Prokofiev at the Maly Opera Theatre, Leningrad. Seventy-five at this writing, he has many plans including a production of *Le Sacre du Printemps*. He is married to Vera Vasilieva, formerly a soloist in the Bolshoi Ballet and currently teaching in the Bolshoi school.

Gollner, Nana, ballerina, teacher, b. El Paso, Texas, 1920; m. Paul Petroff. After recovering from infantile paralysis in early childhood studied dance to strengthen her muscles, first with Theodore Kosloff in California, later in N.Y. and London. First professional engagement in Max Reinhardt's *A Midsummer Night's Dream*. Soloist, American Ballet (1935), Col. de Basil's Ballet Russe (1935–36); ballerina, René Blum's Ballets Russes de Monte Carlo (1936–37); Ballet (now American Ballet) Theatre (1936–37); prima ballerina Original Ballet Russe (1941–43), again with Ballet Theatre (1943–45). Guest ballerina with International Ballet in London and on tour in England (1947) and with Ballet Theatre (spring, 1948). Her repertoire included *Swan Lake, Giselle, Helen of Troy, Undertow* (created Medusa), *Aurora's Wedding* and *Princess Aurora, Gala Performance* (Italian Ballerina), *Pas de Quatre* (Taglioni), and others. Since 1948 has undertaken occasional tours with Petroff and a small group, or performances in Los Angeles, but mainly teaches in California.

Nana Gollner, American ballerina in Swan Lake.

Golovine, Alexander (1864–1930), Russian painter for many years attached to the Russian Imperial Theatre and later active in the early period of the Diaghilev Ballets Russes for which company he designed the décor for the operas *Boris Godounov* (1908) and *Ivan the Terrible* (the Russian title: *Pskovitianka*) (1909), the original décor for the ballet *The Firebird* (1910), and collaborated with Constantine Korovine on the designs for *Swan Lake* (Act 2, 1911).

Golovine, Serge, French dancer, b. Monaco, 1924, of French mother and Russian father; m. dancer Lilian van de Valde. First training with Julia Sedova in Nice. During World War II became soloist of Monte Carlo Opera Ballet, dancing *Le Spectre de la Rose, Les Sylphides,* and others. Became a member of Paris Opéra ballet after examination (1947). Soloist, then premier danseur, of Grand Ballet du Marquis de Cuevas which he joined in 1950, becoming one of the darlings of the Parisian and European publics in such ballets as *Spectre de la Rose, Black Swan* pas de deux, *Piège de Lumière, Le Moulin Enchanté, Blue Bird* pas de deux, *Tarasiana;* also dancing James in August Bournonville's *La Sylphide* with Alicia Markova, Albrecht in *Giselle,* partnering Nina Vyroubova, Margrethe Schanne. Danced one of the Princes in the 1960 production of *The Sleeping Beauty,* partnering Liane Daydé as Aurora. One of the most popular dancers in France, he is light, elegant, with beautiful leaps and batterie. Choreographed *Feu Rouge Feu Vert* (Pierre Petit), *Narcisse* (Y. Brothier). After the dissolving of the Marquis de Cuevas' company, formed his own group touring Europe. Partnered Liane Daydé at Jacob's Pillow Dance Festival (1962).

Golovkina, Sophia, Peoples' Artist of the RSFSR, Soviet ballerina and, since 1961, principal of the Bolshoi Theatre School, b. 1915. Graduated from the Bolshoi school (1933), pupil of Victor Semyonov, Alexander Chekrygin, Fedor Lopukhov, and of Agrippina Vaganova when that great teacher spent one year in Moscow (1944). Golovkina possessed a very strong technique, particularly par terre. Her best roles were Tsar-Maiden (*The Humpbacked Horse*), the title role in *Raymonda,* Mireille de Poitiers (*Flames of Paris*), Tao-Hoa (*The Red Poppy*), Swanilda (*Coppélia*). Besides being principal of the Bolshoi school, Golovkina also teaches there. In 1961 she visited Washington, D.C., as guest of the Washington Ballet School and danced, as guest artist, with the Washington Ballet.

Gonta, Leonid, b. Kharkov, Ukraine, 1918. Studied at the Kharkov ballet school and later with ballet master Vladimir Ponomariov in Leningrad. Danced as soloist in Kiev and Odessa, and with the Vienna State Opera (1944). In 1947–48 toured with Yugoslav ballerina Natalia Boskovic through Germany. Ballet master of the Munich (Germany) Volksoper and later of the Bremen Opera. Currently company instructor at the Munich State Opera Ballet.

Gontcharova, Nathalie (1881–1962), Russian painter and stage designer, b. Moscow, d. Paris; m. Michel Larionov. One of the "Moscow futurists" of the early 20th century, she became a close collaborator with Serge Diaghilev in his ballet company. Among her outstanding works were the décor for *Le Coq d'Or* (1914), *Igrouchki* (1921), *Le Renard* (1922), *Les Noces* (1923), and costumes for the revival of *Firebird* (1926). Later she designed Michel Fokine's *Cinderella* (1938), and Leonide Massine's *Bogatyri* (1938). The décor and costumes for the latter were used in 1943 for Bronislava Nijinska's *Ancient Russia.* She often worked with her husband Larionov. She came out of retirement to recreate her costumes and décor for the Royal Ballet revival of *Firebird* (1954). Died in Paris where she had lived for many years.

Good-Humored Ladies, The. Ballet in 1 act; chor.: Leonide Massine; music: 22 sonatas of Domenico Scarlatti, arr. and orchestrated by Vincenzo Tommasini; décor: Léon Bakst. First prod.: Diaghilev Ballets Russes, Teatro Constanza, Rome, Apr. 12, 1917, with Guiseppina Cecchetti (Marquise Silvestra), Lydia Lopoukhova (Mariuccia), Lubov Tchernicheva (Constanza), Enrico Cecchetti (Marquis di Luca), Stanislas Idzikowski (Battista), Leonide Massine (Leonardo), Sigmund Novak (Count Rinaldo), Leon Woicikowski (Niccolo); revived for Col. de Basil's Ballets Russes de Monte Carlo with Alexandra Danilova as Mariuccia. Grand Ballet du Marquis de Cuevas staged it with Rosella Hightower as Mariuccia. Revived by Massine for the Royal Ballet at Royal Opera House, Covent Garden, London, July 11, 1962, with Antoinette Sibley (Mariuccia), Lydia Sokolova (Silvestra), Ronald Hynd (Leonardo), Brian Shaw (Battista), Alexander Grant (Niccolo), Stanley Holden (Marquis di Luca). This ballet is based on *Le Donne di Buon Umore,* a comedy by Goldoni, and has an extremely complicated plot of chaperones and young lovers, disguises and mistaken identities ending with the triumph of the lovers and the discomfiture of the old people in their attempts to thwart them. 22 sonatas of Scarlatti are used in all, the seven principal ones (and those used most often for recording suites from the ballet) being Longo Nos. 388 (Entrance of Constanza and Mariuccia); 361 (Entrance of Battista); 33 (Constanza's dance of sorrow); 209 (Disguising of Niccolo); 499 (Ladies mock Silvestra); 463 (Supper dance of Leonardo and Mariuccia); 385 (Finale).

Gopak. See HOPAK.

Gopal, Ram, Hindu dancer, choreographer, teacher, b. Bangalore, India, 1920. Studied under Kunju Kurup (Kathakali), Sundaram (Bharata Natya), Misra (Kathak), Nabakumar (Manipuri). Opened first school of Indian classical dancing in Bangalore (1935). Made his debut with La Meri in India (1937). First came to U.S. from India (1938) by way of China, Japan, and Hawaii. Following his American appearances he danced in Warsaw, Paris, and London. At the beginning of World War II, Gopal returned to India where he continued dancing and studying. Early in 1947 won the competition at the All-India Festival in Delhi. In July, 1947, returned to London with his own company, and then toured Europe. India's prime minister, Pandit Nehru selected Ram Gopal to represent India at the Greater N.Y. Golden Anniversary International Dance Festival at City Center, Sept. 30–Oct. 3, 1948. Since then, Gopal and his group have toured extensively and done much to enlighten Western audiences about Indian dancing. He taught and danced at Jacob's Pillow in 1958. Author of *Rhythm in the Heavens* (autobiography). Opened Academy of Indian Dance and Music, London (1962). He devotes most of his time to teaching in the Academy.

Gore, Walter, English dancer and choreographer, b. Waterside, Scotland, 1910; m. Paula Hinton. Studied dance and acting at Italia Conti School, and danced with Leonide Massine in London. Joined Ballet Rambert (then known as the Rambert Dancers) for its first season at Lyric Theatre, Hammersmith, 1930, and was with the company until 1935 when he danced a season with Vic-Wells (later Sadler's Wells, now Royal) Ballet, creating the role of the Rake in *The Rake's Progress.* Choreographed for musicals and then returned to Ballet Rambert as leading dancer and choreographer, his first ballet being *Paris Soir* (1939) and his first important work *Confessional* (1941). After war service in the British navy, he again returned to Ballet Rambert, his ballets including *Simple Symphony* (1944), *Mr. Punch* (1946),

Plaisance and *Winter Night* (1948), *Antonia* (1948), dancing the leading male roles in all except *Plaisance.* During the same period danced many leading roles in the repertoire, including an exceptionally sensitive and dramatic Albrecht in *Giselle.* In 1952 returned with his wife, Paula Hinton, to Australia where he had toured with Ballet Rambert (1947–48), but was back the same year to stage some ballets for Ballet Workshop. Choreographed *Carte Blanche* for Sadler's Wells Theatre Ballet (1953); organized his own group (1954) and again toured in Australia heading company called Australian Theatre Ballet (1955–56). Guest choreographer for Ballet Der Lage Landen (see HOLLAND, BALLET IN) 1956 and for the Paris season of Milorad Miskovitch's Ballet the same year. From 1957 to 1959 was ballet master and chief choreographer of Frankfurt (Germany) State Opera Ballet, for which company he staged one of his most important works, *Eaters of Darkness* (1958). Choreographed *Night and Silence* for Edinburgh International Ballet, a company specially organized for the Edinburgh Festival of 1958. Formed London Ballet (1961), with a repertoire of classic and new works including his *Eaters of Darkness* and *Night and Silence.* His version of *The Nutcracker* originally staged by him in Holland, had its British première Oct. 11, 1962, at the Brighton Hippodrome. In the summer of 1964 choreographed *Sweet Dancer* for Ballet Rambert, premièred July 20 at the Sadler's Wells Theatre, London, with Paula Hinton and John Chesworth in the leading roles. Since 1965 ballet master of a private ballet company in Lisbon. On leave from that post he staged his *Street Games* for the Harkness Ballet (summer, 1966).

Gorham, Kathleen, contemporary dancer, b. Sydney, Australia, m. Robert Pomie. Studied ballet with Lorraine Norton and Leon Kellaway and joined the Borovansky Ballet in Australia when only 15. When Ballet Rambert toured Australia in 1948 she joined that company and returned with it to England to study at Sadler's Wells School (1949). Danced with Sadler's Wells Theatre Ballet as soloist (1951–52); soloist with Grand Ballet du Marquis de Cuevas in Europe (1953). Rejoined Borovansky company as leading dancer (1954) and after his death in 1959 returned to Europe to dance with various companies. First dancer of the Australian Ballet (under the direction of Peggy van Praagh) since 1962, her repertoire including Odette-Odile (*Swan Lake*), Swanilda (*Coppélia*), and others.

Gorsky, Alexander (1871–1924), Russian dancer and choreographer, b. St. Petersburg suburb. Was accepted into the St. Petersburg Imperial School of Ballet in 1880 and began his training under Platon Karsavin, father of ballerina Tamara Karsavina; was graduated in 1889 and six years later promoted to soloist. Always interested in the arts, Gorsky had attended evening courses at the Academy of Arts while a student at the ballet school, and after graduation from the ballet school he continued to paint. He also studied languages. In 1896 he was appointed assistant instructor of the Ballet School under Paul Gerdt. In the theatre Gorsky was a close friend of Vladimir Stepanov, a dancer and teacher who had invented a system of dance notation. Gorsky was instrumental in placing Stepanov's dance notation system on the curriculum of the Ballet School. In 1898, in a desire to raise the standing of the Moscow Ballet, the director of the Imperial Theatres decided to stage there *The Sleeping Beauty,* which Moscow audiences had not yet seen. Gorsky was selected for the job and left for Moscow early in Dec., 1898. The première of the ballet took place Jan. 17, 1899, and the program noted that the ballet was staged "according to dance notations based on the system of V. I. Stepanov." Gorsky was satisfied that a ballet could be reproduced from dance notations, but wanted to prove that a new ballet could also be staged in this manner. Accordingly, on his return to St. Petersburg, he decided to choreograph "on paper" a one-act ballet, *Chlorinda, the Queen of the Mountain Fairies.* On Apr. 11 of that year the ballet was given at a ballet school performance and the program note said that it was "the first attempt at composing a ballet . . . on paper by the use of the alphabet of movement invented by V. I. Stepanov. The roles were rehearsed from written-out parts, similar to those used in opera, during the current school year." On Sept. 1, 1900 Gorsky was promoted to premier danseur and at the same time transferred to the Moscow Bolshoi Theatre as regisseur. The Moscow Ballet, stepchild of the Imperial Theatres, was in a catastrophic condition. The company listed only about seventy dancers, the repertoire was poor, attendance at performances was often not more than one-third of capacity. Only the School was in a fair state owing to the pedagogical talents of I. D. Nikitin and Vassily Tikhomirov. The instructors as well as the dancers and students lacked leadership. Gorsky's arrival in Moscow supplied this leadership. His debut as independent choreographer took place Dec. 6 with *Don Quixote,* which he staged entirely differently from the St. Petersburg version of Petipa, retaining, however, certain parts. The young painters Constantine Korovine and Alexander Golovine, who did the décor and costumes, closely collaborated with Gorsky. The ballet provoked a lively controversy in the press, most critics considering Gorsky's work decadent, incompatible with the conception of great art, unworthy of "the model ballet stage." The spectators, however, immediately accepted Gorsky's production, and the attendance at *Don Quixote* began to grow quickly. The choreographer himself considered the production of *Don Quixote,* only as a first step in his chosen direction. Said he: "The distinction of my production is that there is a continuous movement of groups on the stage; the scenes are based on a plan new and original with me; I do not recognize any rules of symmetry." In January, 1911, Gorsky restaged *Swan Lake,* which had not been given in Moscow since the original and unsuccessful production staged in 1877 by Julius Reisinger. As in *Don Quixote,* Gorsky kept all that was valuable from the Petipa-Ivanov St. Petersburg production of *Swan Lake,* but changed the first and third acts considerably, abolished the symmetry of the dance groups, introduced a number of strong character dances which created a contrast with the lyric scenes, established a definite direction in the development of the story, increased the expressiveness of the classic dances. During the same year Gorsky also staged *The Humpbacked Horse* and two other ballets. The following year (1912) Gorsky was appointed ballet master of the Moscow Theatre. In Nov. of that year he presented a new ballet at the Bolshoi Theatre, *Nôtre Dame de Paris,* which again created a lively controversy. Sophie Fedorova, famous Moscow character dancer, made her debut in this ballet in the role of Esmeralda. Among the other ballets staged by Gorsky at the Bolshoi Theatre were: *The Magic Mirror, La Fille du Pharaon* (both in 1905), *Raymonda* (1908), *Salambo* (1910), *Giselle* (1911), *Le Corsaire* (1912), *Eunice and Petronius* (1915), *La Bayadère* (1916), *Stenka Razin* (1918), *The Nutcracker* (1919). In 1911 Gorsky was invited by the London Alhambra Theatre to stage a ballet for the festivities in connection with the coronation of King George V. He staged *The Dance Dream,* to a collection of musical pieces by Brahms, Glazounov, Tchaikovsky, Luigini and Rubinstein. The Moscow ballerina Yekaterina Geltzer and premier danseur Vassily Tikhomirov were guest artists. Gorsky's last ballet was presented in the 1923–24 season. It was *The Grotto of Venus,* staged to the ballet music from Wagner's *Tannhäuser.*

Goslar, Lotte, contemporary dancer, pantomimist, b. Dresden, Germany, now an American citizen. Apart from a short period at the Mary Wigman School and with Gret Palucca's Dance Co. is self-taught. Left Germany (1933) and toured very successfully through Czechoslovakia, Holland, Belgium, and Switzerland as a dance mime and as a member of Erika Mann's (daughter of Thomas Mann) anti-Hitler show, *The Peppermill,* which came to the U.S. in 1937. After three trans-continental solo tours, starred (with Imogene Coca) in *Who's Who in New York,* also *Reunion in New York* and at the Rainbow Room, then a nightclub. Went to Hollywood in 1943 for a four-week engagement at the Turnabout Theatre (alternating with Elsa Lanchester) and remained ten years. Founded her first pantomime company at that time and toured widely on the West Coast. In 1954 this developed into her pantomime show, *For Humans Only,* which has since gone into a number of editions and toured all over the U.S. and in Europe. A fourth U.S. and European tour of a new edition, *All in Fun,* began in Oct., 1963. Lotte Goslar is on the staff of the Pasadena Playhouse, has taught master classes in pantomime at UCLA, and staged dances for films and stage shows, among them the late Charles Laughton's production of Berthold Brecht's *Galileo,* and special material for the late Marilyn Monroe in *River of No Return.* In Sept., 1966, appeared with her company in *Clowns and Other Fools* as part of the Dance Festival sponsored by the Rebekah Harkness Foundation, at the open-air Delacorte Theatre in Central Park, N.Y. Continues to tour with her company in the U.S. and abroad.

Gosling, Nigel. See BLAND, ALEXANDER.

Goth, Trudy, dancer, dance director, writer, b. Berlin, Germany, 1913, of Hungarian parentage. Educated in Florence, Italy; studied dance with Harald Kreutzberg. Studied photography in Vienna, Budapest, and Berlin; continued dancing with Angiola Sartorio in Florence and with members of Ballet Jooss. Assistant to Angiola Sartorio, director of school and company of Corpo di Ballet della Città di Firenze, with appearances with same company and in operas during May Festivals in Florence (1936–39). To U.S. in 1940, studying with Agnes de Mille, José Limón, Cia Fornaroli, Vincenzo Celli. Appeared with Henry Schwarze (formerly of Ballet Jooss), at Jacob's Pillow Dance Festival, summer camps, and others. Founded Choreographers' Workshop (1946). Currently writes on dance and music events, mainly European.

Gould, Diana, English dancer, b. London, 1913. Studied with Marie Rambert in London and Lubov Egorova in Paris. Principal dancer in the early Rambert seasons, creating a number of roles in the early ballets of Frederick Ashton and Antony Tudor, e.g. Pavane (*Capriole Suite*), Mars (*The Planets*), and Grille d'Egout in Ninette de Valois' *Bar aux Folies-Bergère.* Danced briefly with Col. de Basil's Ballet Russe de Monte Carlo; soloist with Markova-Dolin Ballet (1935–37). Retired upon her marriage to violinist Yehudi Menuhin.

Gould, Morton, American composer and conductor, b. 1913. Jerome Robbins used his *American Concertette* for *Interplay* (1945). He composed the score for Agnes de Mille's ballet *Fall River Legend,* staged by Ballet Theatre (1948). George Balanchine's *Clarinade* (1964) is set to Gould's *Derivations for Clarinet and Jazz Band.*

Gounod Symphony. Ballet in 4 movements; chor.: George Balanchine; music: Charles Gounod's Symphony No. 1 in D major; décor: Horace Armistead (his set for *Lilac Garden*); costumes: Barbara Karinska. First prod.: New York City Ballet, City Center, N.Y., Jan. 8, 1958, with Maria Tallchief, Jacques d'Amboise and ensemble. Considerable revisions were made after the first season, the dancing for the two soloists being considerably extended, Partricia Wilde and Jonathan Watts most often dancing this version. It is a very elegant ballet in abstract style, following the movements of the score: Allegro Molto, Allegretto (pas de deux and variations), Minuetto, and Adagio and Allegro Vivace.

Goviloff, George, French dancer, b. Monaco, 1932 of French mother and Russian father; brother of Serge Golovine. Pupil of Marika Besobrasova in Monte Carlo, Olga Preobrajenska, Nora Kiss, and Serge Peretti in Paris. Started dancing professionally in 1949. Joined Grand Ballet du Marquis de Cuevas (1951); promoted to premier danseur (1956). Ballets include *Prisonnier du Caucase, Moulin Enchanté, Piège de Lumière, Prince Igor,* and almost the entire Cuevas repertoire. Danced Blue Bird in that company's final full-length production of *The Sleeping Beauty* (1960). Joined London's Festival Ballet (1963).

Govrin, Gloria, dancer, b. Newark, N.J., 1942. Studied at Tarassoff School, American Ballet Academy (Fred Danieli) Newark, N.J.; won scholarship at age ten to School of American Ballet, N.Y. Apprentice, New York City Ballet at age fifteen; full company member two years later, dancing first solo, Scotch Girl (*The Figure in the Carpet*), when the company was touring Calif. Promoted to soloist at age nineteen. Her roles include 4th move-

Gloria Govrin, soloist of the N.Y. City Ballet, in the Arabian Dance in Balanchine's Nutcracker.

ment (*Western Symphony*), 4th movement (*Symphony in C*), Harp (*Fanfare*), Captain of the Amazons (*Con Amore*), Queen (*The Cage*), Siren (*The Prodigal Son*), Bach section (*Episodes*), 2nd Regiment (*Stars and Stripes*), and others. Her first important creation was Hippolyta (*A Midsummer Night's Dream,* 1962). Also created one of the leading roles in George Balanchine's *Clarinade* (1964); the new "Danse Arabe" in *The Nutcracker* (1965); La Bonne Fée (*Harlequinade*) (1965); "Rigaudon Flamenco" (with Arthur Mitchell) in the Act 2 divertissement in George Balanchine's *Don Quixote;* also the Night Spirit in the same ballet.

Goya, Carola (Carola Goya Weller), contemporary Spanish and ethnic dancer, b. New York City. Studied dance at Metropolitan Opera Ballet School, with Michel Fokine and with Manuel del Castillo Otero, LaQuica and Maria Esparsa in Spain. After dancing with Metropolitan Opera Ballet for two years, made N.Y. solo debut as Spanish dancer (1927). Since then has presented innumerable recitals in N.Y., all over the U.S. and Canada, in London, Rio de Janeiro, Buenos Aires. Inaugurated Community Concerts in the Union of South Africa (1939), followed by appearances in Hong Kong. Danced at the White House for President and Mrs. Roosevelt at the Ambassadors' Banquet (1936). Joined José Greco's company as leading dancer when it was formed in Madrid (1947), touring Europe and South America; returned to U.S. with the company (1951). Formed partnership with Matteo in 1954. Was the first person to play the castanets as a solo instrument with symphony orchestras (Detroit, Kansas City symphonies; Symphony of the Air, Carnegie Hall). Has written articles, primarily on Spanish dance, for many periodicals; contributor of articles on Spanish dance to the *Enciclopedia dello Spettacolo.* Conducted a study and performance tour with Matteo.

Carola Goya and Matteo in their "Horseback" dance.

Goya (Carola) and Matteo, Spanish and ethnic dance team. Partnership was formed in 1954, since when they have presented their program A World of Dancing on extensive tours in U.S. and abroad. Also appear as solo artists with symphony orchestras and have appeared on "Firestone Hour," "Omnibus," and "Camera Three" television presentations. Have appeared annually since 1953 at Jacob's Pillow Dance Festival and headed the ethnic dance department at the Jacob's Pillow University of the Dance since 1955. They jointly choreographed and danced in the New York City Opera production of Manuel de Falla's *La Vida Breve.* In 1964 toured India, performing and studying.

Goyescas. Ballet in 1 act; chor.: José Fernandez; music: piano pieces by Enrique Granados of that name, orchestrated by Harold Byrns; book: Alder Jenkins; décor: Nicolas de Molas. First prod.: Ballet Theatre, Center Theatre, N.Y., Jan., 1940. Completely revised with new chor. by Antony Tudor, book by Nicolas de Molas for Ballet Theatre, Majestic Theatre, N.Y., Feb., 1941, after a single performance at Lewisohn Stadium, N.Y., Aug. 1, 1940, with Nora Kaye, Alicia Alonso, Hugh Laing, Jerome Robbins, Eugene Loring, Antony Tudor and Tilly Losch. A series of sketches based on Goya's drawings, again restaged by Argentinita for Ballet Theatre.

Graduation Ball. Ballet in 1 act; chor., and book: David Lichine; music: innumerable pieces by Johann Strauss, principally "Perpetuum Mobile," "Acceleration Waltz," "Tritsch-Tratsch Polka," et al. (inset classic pas de deux to music from the operetta *A Night in Venice*), arr. and orch. by Antal Dorati; décor: Alexandre Benois. First prod.: Original Ballet Russe, Theatre Royal, Sydney, Australia, Feb. 28, 1940, with Tatiana Riabouchinska and David Lichine in the leading roles, Borislav Runanine (Head Mistress), Igor Schwezoff (General), Nicholas Orlov (Drummer), Tatiana Leskova (Impromptu), Alexandra Denisova and Geneviève Moulin (Dance Competition), Natasha Sobinova and Paul Petroff (La Sylphide and the Scotsman); opened in New York at the Fifty-First St. Theatre Nov. 6, 1940, with the same cast except for Tatiana Stepanova and Michel Panaieff (La Sylphide and the Scotsman); revived for impresario S. Hurok by the choreographer with new décor by Mstislav Doboujinsky and first presented by Ballet (now American Ballet) Theatre, Metropolitan Opera House, N.Y., Oct. 8, 1944, with Riabouchinska and Lichine in their original roles, Alpheus Koon (Head Mistress), John Taras (General), John Kriza (Drummer), Rosella Hightower (Impromptu), Margaret Banks and Marjorie Tallchief (Dance Competition). In place of La Sylphide and the Scotsman a new pas de deux was added for Alicia Alonso and Richard Reed and a new number (subsequently dropped), the Tyrolean Boy (Harold Lang). After the guest appearances of Riabouchinska and Lichine their roles were taken by Janet Reed and Lang, and the Tyrolean Boy by André Eglevsky or Tommy Rall. Lichine staged *Graduation Ball* (reproducing the Benois décor) for Royal Danish Ballet in 1952 with Inge Sand and Fredbjørn Bjørnsson in the leading roles, Mette Mollerup and Henning Kronstam having their first big successes in the Impromptu dance and as the Drummer, respectively. He again staged it for London's Festival Ballet, July 9, 1957, in the Benois décor.

Graeme, Joyce (Platts), English dancer, teacher, b. Thorner, Yorkshire, 1918. Student member of Vic-Wells (later Sadler's Wells, now Royal) Ballet (1936–38). Dancer, Open Air Theatre, Regent's Park (1939–40); soloist, International Ballet (1941–43). Leading soloist, Ballet Rambert (1945–48) where her large repertoire included a remarkable Queen of the Wilis (*Giselle*) and the creation of Mrs. Punch (*Mr. Punch*). Director, choreographer and ballerina, Australian National Ballet (1948–51); took this company on Commonwealth Centenary Celebration tour of Australia, New Zealand and Tasmania (1951). Guest artist, London's Festival Ballet (1952). Assistant director and ballet mistress, Ballet Rambert for three months in 1952–53. Also danced in musicals, revues. Taught mime and character, make-up and repertoire, pas de deux, history of dance and pointe work at ballet school of Teatro alla Scala, Milan (1955–62), and danced Madge, the Witch (*La Sylphide*), The Head Mistress (*Graduation Ball*), Stepmother in Raymundo de Larrain's *Cinderella,* première Dec. 4, 1963, International Dance Festival, Paris. Ballet mistress, Scapino Ballet, Holland (1963–64).

Graham, Margaret (Margaret Graham de Barbon), ballerina of Teatro S.O.D.R.E., Montevideo, Uruguay, b. Buenos Aires, Argentina, 1937; m. dancer-choreographer Tito Barbon. Studied with Esmée Bulnes,

Yekaterina de Galantha, and Roberto Giachero. After a brief connection with Teatro Argentino de La Plata, she joined Ballet Alicia Alonso of Cuba but returned to the Teatro Argentino (1951) and was made ballerina, remaining until 1957. Her repertoire included *Giselle, Firebird, Les Sylphides, Romeo and Juliet, Paganini, Sinfonia Clasica* (Tamara Grigorieva). Left Teatro Argentino to join Teatro S.O.D.R.E., Montevideo, as danseuse étoile (1957). Was guest artist at Teatro Argentino (1958) for the premières of *Giselle* and *Firebird.* Both Miss Graham and Tito Barbon visisted the U.S. Dec., 1963–Apr., 1964 as Foreign Specialists on a grant from the Bureau of Education, U.S. Dept. of State. While in the U.S., Sr. Barbon choreographed his ballet *Opus 2* to music by Gian-Carlo Menotti for the Pacific Ballet in San Francisco, and *La Péri.* (Paul Dukas) for the Washington (D.C.) Ballet.

Graham, Martha. (1893–).

BY WALTER TERRY.

The senior star and greatest exponent of the American modern dance is no longer a controversial figure in the theatre as she was in the 1920's and 1930's. Her artistry both as a dancer and choreographer has been recognized not only in her homeland, but in Europe, the Middle East, and Asia, as well. Still, she remains an experimenter, a searcher, a nonconformist.

Martha Graham was born at the turn of the century in a suburb of Pittsburgh, Pa., to a New England family of Scottish and Irish extraction. She is a tenth-generation American and a direct descendant of Miles Standish. She was brought up in Santa Barbara, Calif., and while still in high school she determined to become a

Martha Graham (on elevation left) and company in the great dancer's work, Alcestis, *in which she dances the title role.*

dancer. Upon graduation in 1916 she prevailed upon her physician father and her mother to permit her to study at the Denishawn School in Los Angeles. Three years after her first lessons she was given the leading feminine role in Ted Shawn's Aztec ballet, *Xochitl,* playing first opposite Robert Gorham and later Shawn himself. During her seven years at Denishawn, she studied with both Ruth St. Denis and Ted Shawn, primarily with the latter, and appeared with the Denishawn company and with the vaudeville units which were sent out over the country.

Discontented with Denishawn, Miss Graham severed her connection with the company in 1923 and obtained an engagement with the *Greenwich Village Follies* as solo dancer. But she was not satisfied with revue dancing and in 1925 left the *Follies* for a position on the teaching staff of the Eastman School of Music in Rochester, N.Y. Here she found the opportunity to explore new dance paths, to study and experiment. Her New York debut in 1926 disclosed many changes, but reflections of Denishawn heritage were still apparent in such dances as *A Study in Lacquer, Three Gopi Maidens, Maid with the Flaxen Hair,* and others. In succeeding seasons, however, the new Graham, the revolutionary (in the artistic sense), began to emerge in such works as *Immigrant, Revolt, Four Insincerities,* and *Heretic.* In the 1930's she rooted her work in American Indian material and American behavior patterns. To the works created during this period *Two Primitive Canticles, Primitive Mysteries, Ceremonials,* and, in later seasons, *El Penitente,* belong to the former group, while to the latter belong *American Provincials, Frontier, American Document,* and many other works; timeless human experiences found form and substance in such creations as *Lamentation, Imperial Gesture, Frontier,* and many of her subsequent works.

In later years, assisted by a handsome and magnificently trained company of men and women, she turned more and more to theatre works, striking in both theme and production. The first of what might be described as modern dance ballets included *Letter to the World,* suggested by the life and the inner nature of the New England poet Emily Dickinson; *Deaths and Entrances,* based upon the violent sentiments and memories of the Brontë sisters (described as "doom eager"); two fine comedies, *Every Soul Is a Circus* and *Punch and the Judy;* the lovely, stern yet sweet testament to America's pioneer spirit, *Appalachian Spring,* and a stunning repertory of contemporary dance-dramas deriving from classical Greek sources: *Cave of the Heart* (Medea), *Errand Into the Maze* (the transforming of the Minotaur legend of the labyrinth into a psychological exploration of deep-rooted human fears), *Night Journey* (Oedipus and Jocasta), *Clytemnestra, Alcestis,* and *Phaedra.* Miss Graham has also been praised and honored for the musical scores she has commissioned (some through the Elizabeth Sprague Coolidge Foundation in the Library of Congress, the Alice M. Ditson Fund of Columbia University, the B. de Rothschild Foundation for the Arts and Sciences). Her composer-collaborators have included Samuel Barber, Paul Hindemith, Gian Carlo Menotti, Aaron Copland, Carlos Surinach, Carlos Chavez, William Schuman, Robert Starer, Halim El-Dabh, and Norman Dello Joio.

Like all modern dancers, she has avoided the crystallizing of a set technique. Indeed, even in her teaching, she explores with her pupils new areas of action. In her own personal performing, however, there are recurrent movements and gestures which have become characteristic of her special style. The movement vocabulary of her youthful company is, of course, larger and more varied, but a general Graham theatrical style colors all. She believes that new dance movements must be born in order to serve choreographic ideas of all kinds, emotional manifestations, character-comment, and all the other elements involved, with continually fresh creative effort.

Martha Graham's dance purpose is to give physical substance to things felt—to lamentation, to celebration, to hate, to passion, to the experience of the personal frontier, to bigotry, to the underlying passions, dreams, fears, and tragedies which made possible the work of a poet such as Dickinson. When in her dances she is concerned with a specific character, situation, or plot, she is actually using it as a starting point or, perhaps, a frame for the revelation of human behavior. Thus, when as the irked wife in *Punch and the Judy* she turns away from her husband and jumps upon the back of Pegasus, she is making manifest the escape urge, not in the specific and homely terms of going home to mother, visiting a psychiatrist, taking to drink or cards, but in an imaginative and dream-like way which may apply to any woman's experience. This pattern she follows in almost all her works in order that "Frontier" may be not just one frontier but all frontiers—physical, mental, emotional, and in order that *Errand Into the Maze* may not deal with the conquest of a specific fear but with the individual's battle against the chemistry of fear itself. Far from being a cultist or an obscurantist, she endeavors to remove the cloak of obscurity from the purposes and aspects of human behavior and to reveal in dance architecture the architecture of the inner man.

Since 1926, she has created well over one hundred dances, ranging from solos through ensemble compositions to full-scale modern dance theatre pieces. In addition to the works already mentioned, other important early compositions include *Tanagra, Danza, Ekstasis, Frenetic Rhythms, Integrales, Course, Horizons, Chronicle, Immediate Tragedy,* and *Deep Song*. More recent works include *Legend of Judith, A Look at Lightning, Secular Games, Acrobats of God,* and *The Witch of Endor*. While she has continued to choreograph new works, she has been, until recently, reluctant to revive past successes in which she herself figured largely as a performer. However, for the memorial program honoring her long-time musical director, Louis Horst, presented at the American Dance Festival, Connecticut College, in August, 1964, she revived three works for which Mr. Horst had composed the scores: *Frontier* (with Ethel Winter), *El Penitente* (with Marni Thomas in the choreographer's role, David Wood, and Gene McDonald), and *Primitive Mysteries* (with Yuriko). The latter work was also included in her 1965 N.Y. season, as well as *Cave of the Heart* (with Helen McGehee) and *Appalachian Spring* (with Ethel Winter).

Miss Graham and her company have toured Europe and the Middle East, sponsored by the Cultural Exchange Program of the U.S. State Department and by the Bethsabee de Rothschild Foundation. In 1964 they appeared with great success in England and set in motion there an immense interest in the American modern dance. In addition to her tours she has created a number of dance motion pictures, among them *A Dancer's World, Appalachian Spring,* and *Night Journey*.

Born in 1893, Martha Graham was having her greatest success as choreographer and performer in the 1960's. Winner of the Capezio Award (1960), she received the Aspen Award in the Humanities (May, 1965) given to honor "the individual anywhere in the world judged to have made the greatest contribution to the advancement of the humanities." The National Council on the Arts awarded her a matching grant of $141,000 (Feb., 1966) to take her company on an eight-week tour of the U.S. and a grant-in-aid to create two new works. Harvard Univ. also invested her with an honorary degree of Doctor of Arts (June, 1966). In Oct. *Martha Graham: Portrait of the Lady as an Artist* (N.Y., 1966), with text by LeRoy Leatherman and photographs by Martha Swope was published.

Grahame, Shirley, English dancer, b. Teddington, 1936. Studied at Sadler's Wells Ballet School from 1948; entered the company (now Royal Ballet) (1954); soloist (1958). One of the principal dancers of the touring section, she dances Odette-Odile (*Swan Lake*), Aurora (*The Sleeping Beauty*), Queen of the Wilis (*Giselle*), Black Queen (*Checkmate*), and others.

Lucile Grahn, Danish-born Romantic ballerina, youngest member of the Pas de Quatre.

Grahn, Lucile (1819–1907), famous Danish ballerina of the Romantic period, b. Copenhagen. A pupil of the Royal Danish Ballet School and protégée of August Bournonville, she danced her first role (Sabi in *Jocko, the Brazilian Ape,* 1829) when not quite ten years old. Bournonville created *Waldemar* (1835) and his version of *La Sylphide* (1836) for her. But her ambition for international acclaim after successful appearances in Paris (1838) and Hamburg (1839) caused her to rebel against Bournonville's despotism and after bitter quarrels she left the Royal Theatre in 1839 and never danced in Denmark again. She became a guest artist at the Paris Opéra and an internationally famous star, dancing in St. Petersburg (1843) and being one of the four ballerinas in the famous Jules Perrot *Pas de Quatre* in London with Maria Taglioni, Carlotta Grisi and Fanny Cerito (1845). She was a particular favorite in Germany and Austria and the Danes never forgave her for the pro-German sympathy she displayed during the brief war of 1848–49 when the Danish provinces of Schleswig-Holstein revolted and demanded independence under the protection of Prussia. Her best known creations were *Eoline* (1845) and *Catarina* (1846) and she also danced *Giselle, Esmeralda* and, of course, *La Sylphide,* with great success. She retired as a dancer on her marriage to opera singer Friedrich Young (1856), but continued as ballet mistress at the Leipzig State Theatre (1858–61) and at the Munich Hofoper (1869–75) where she choreographed many of the opera ballets, including one of the earliest versions of the "Bacchanale" in Wagner's *Tannhäuser.* When she died she left nearly a million marks to the City of Munich, which named a street for her close to the opera house, Lucile Grahn Strasse.

Grand, in ballet, a qualifying adjective added to the name of a step which is performed so that the leg forms an angle with the body of approximately 90 degrees, such as grand battement, grand jeté, grand pirouette, etc.

Grand Ballet du Marquis de Cuevas, the company directed by Marquis George de Cuevas, growing out of his Ballet International, Nouveau Ballet de Monte Carlo, and Grand Ballet de Monte Carlo. The last assumed the name of Grand Ballet du Marquis de Cuevas in 1950. Its repertoire in its early years was largely that of the

Ballet International and Grand Ballet de Monte Carlo to which, with the passing years were added works by George Skibine, John Taras (ballet master during most of the period of the company's existence), Ana Ricarda, and others. Best known were Skibine's *Le Prisonnier du Caucase* and *Idylle,* Taras's *Piège de Lumière,* and Ricarda's *Ines de Castro.* Leading dancers included Rosella Hightower (from the beginning until her retirement in 1961), Marjorie Tallchief (1947–56), George Skibine (1947–56), Jacqueline Moreau (1951–59), Vladimir Skouratoff (1952–57), Nina Vyroubova (1957–61), Serge Golovine, Genia Melikova, Nicholas Polajenko and others; in addition most of the leading French and European dancers of the day appeared as guest artists, among them Alicia Markova, Tamara Toumanova, Leonid Massine, David Lichine, Erik Bruhn, Margrethe Schanne. For its Paris season in Mar., 1958, the company reverted to its original name and, for the last years of the Marquis' life was known as Ballet International du Marquis de Cuevas. His final great production was the full-length *Sleeping Beauty* staged by Bronislava Nijinska and Robert Helpmann from the Petipa version, premièred Oct. 27, 1960, at the Théâtre des Champs-Élysées, Paris, in décor and costumes by his nephew Raymundo de Larrain. After the death of the Marquis early in 1961, his widow, with Larrain as artistic director, carried on the company which at the end of 1961 became Ballet International de la Marquese de Cuevas. The Marquese de Cuevas disbanded the company on June 30, 1962.

Grand Ecart. See ECART, GRAND.

Grand Jeté. See JETÉ.

Grand Pas de Deux, this designation of a set dance in ballet very often used by press agents and managers of ballet companies does not really exist in classic ballet. A pas de deux is always a pas de deux. What does exist is a Grand Pas, which is a set dance for a group of soloists with an ensemble or corps de ballet. Typical Grands Pas known to contemporary audiences are the Grand Pas d'Action in Act 1 of *The Sleeping Beauty,* usually called the Rose Adagio; the Grand Pas des Sylphides in Act 2 of *La Sylphide.* The *Pas de Dix,* which Balanchine staged for the New York City Ballet to some of Glazounov's music from *Raymonda,* is an excellent example of a classic Grand Pas staged by a contemporary choreography.

Grand Pas–Glazounov. Ballet in 1 act; chor.: after Marius Petipa re-created by George Balanchine and Alexandra Danilova, revived by Frederic Franklin. First prod.: American Ballet Theatre, Broadway Theatre, N.Y., Apr. 25, 1961, with Toni Lander and Royes Fernandez, and Susan Borree, Sallie Wilson, Janice Groman, Patricia Carleton, Martin Scheepers, Ivan Allen, Felix Smith, Gayle Young. Maria Tallchief and Erik Bruhn shared the leading roles. The pas de dix is from the last act of *Raymonda,* originally staged by Balanchine and Danilova in the 1940's for Ballet Russe de Monte Carlo. As *Pas de Dix,* a somewhat different version not attributed to any choreographer other than Balanchine, it is in the repertoire of New York City Ballet. *Grand Pas–Glazounov* has a variation for each of the four supporting female dancers but there are many resemblances between the two versions.

Grands Ballets Canadiens, Les, founded in 1952 for performances on Canadian television out of Montreal and at that time and for its first short tours was known as Ballets Chiriaeff after its director and choreographer Ludmilla Chiriaeff. The reputation it gained because of its television appearances led to an increase in the number of dancers, though it remains a group of about twenty dancers, and a change of name to its present title. Eric Hyrst joined the company in 1953 as leading male dancer, choreographer and artistic adviser. Les Grands Ballets Canadiens made its U.S. debut at Jacob's Pillow Dance Festival in 1959, returned in 1960, and now tours both in its own country and the U.S. Its repertoire contains such standard works as *Swan Lake, Coppélia, Petrouchka, Les Sylphides,* but its reputation rests on the original works by Ludmilla Chiriaeff (*Night on the Bare Mountain, Jeu de Cartes, Kaleidoscope, Les Noces, Etude, Nonagone, Jeux d'Arlequins, 4e Concert Royal,* and many others) and Eric Hyrst (*Drawn Blinds, Psyché, Variations on a Theme of Haydn, Première Classique, Sea Gallows,* and many others). On Jan. 18, 1962, Les Grands Ballets Canadiens became the first Canadian ballet company to present *La Fille Mal Gardée.* This version, to the J. W. Hertel score, was set for the company by Edward Caton and staged with certain adaptations by Ludmilla Chiriaeff and Eric Hyrst. Members of the company include, among others: Milenka Niderlova, Véronique Landory, Andrée Millaire, Brydon Paige, and the American dancer Vincent Warren. Anna-Marie and David Holmes, formerly of Royal Winnipeg Ballet, who spent several months in 1963 dancing and studying at the Kirov Theatre, Leningrad, joined the company as leading dancers at the beginning of the 1964–65 season, when Roger Rochon, formerly a leading dancer, was appointed company manager.

Grant, Alexander, British dancer, b. Wellington, New Zealand, 1925. Awarded a Royal Academy of Dancing Scholarship (1944), entered Sadler's Wells Ballet School (1946) and danced with the company the same year, with a brief period as a member of Sadler's Wells Theatre Ballet. Currently principal dancer with Royal Ballet. Since he created the role of the Barber in Leonide Massine's *Mam'zelle Angot* (1947) for this company when it was still known as Sadler's Wells Ballet, his reputation as a great character dancer has grown steadily until he is today internationally known as one who ranks with the greatest in that area. Other creations are Sancho Panza (Ninette de Valois' *Don Quixote*), Jester (Frederick Ashton's *Cinderella*), Cannibal King (*Bonne-Bouche*), Pierre (*Madame Chrysanthème*), Eros (Ashton's *Sylvia*), Tirrenio (Ashton's *Ondine*), Alain—possibly his greatest creation (Ashton's *La Fille Mal Gardée*), Mercury (*Persephone*), Niccolo (Massine's revival of *The Good-Humored Ladies*), Bottom (*The Dream*). The little Neapolitan dance Ashton created for him (with Julia Farron) in *Swan Lake* (Act 3) is always a show stopper. He also dances The Miller (*The Three-Cornered Hat*), title role (*Petrouchka*) in the Royal Ballet productions, Fire (*Homage to the Queen*), one of the three male dancers (*Symphonic Variations*), and others. In 1964 created Bottom in Sir Frederick Ashton's *A Midsummer Night's Dream* and the Bridegroom in the revival of the same choreographer's *A Wedding Bouquet.* In the Birthday Honors of 1965 he was named by Queen Elizabeth II a Commander of the Order of the British Empire (C.B.E.)

Grant, Pauline, English dancer and choreographer, b. Birmingham, 1915. Studied at Ginner-Mawer School and with Antony Tudor and Vera Volkova. Had her own Ballet Group (1944–45). Has choreographed for Sadler's Wells Opera, Glyndebourne Opera where she was also principal dancer (1951–56), and Royal Opera House, Covent Garden (*The Olympians,* 1950; *The Bohemian Girl,* 1952). Choreographer Royal Shakespeare Theatre, Stratford-on-Avon since 1949. Also choreographer of musicals and ice shows.

Grantzeva, Tatiana, Russian-born American ballet dancer who made her debut as soloist with Ballet Russe de Monte Carlo (1938) and continued with that company until 1944. Première danseuse in the musical *A Lady Says Yes* (1945); co-founder and ballerina of Ballet for America (1946); ballerina of the Metropolitan Opera production of *Die Fledermaus* with which she toured an entire season. Appeared with Ballet Russe de Monte Carlo frequently as ballerina and ballet mistress until 1962. In Jan., 1962, married architect Count Robert de Veyrac, opening a ballet school soon after. In the summers of 1963 and 1964 she was choreographer, ballet mistress, and ballerina of the Cincinnati Summer Opera Festival. In 1965 moved with her husband to Paris where she began to teach. After watching several of her classes, Maurice Béjart, choreographer and director of Les Ballets du XXme Siècle at the Brussels Théâtre Royal de la Monnaie, invited her to join his company as instructor (1966).

Grantzova, Adele (1843–1877), German ballerina who was considered a perfect technician with a clean, soft style and excellent elevation. She created the ballets *Trilby* and *Camargo* and danced in *Meteor, Fiammetta, Esmeralda, Le Corsaire, Giselle, Faust, La Source, The Humpbacked Horse,* and others. She appeared in Paris, Berlin, Vienna, St. Petersburg and Moscow. She died following an operation on her foot.

Grasslands. Ballet in 1 act; chor. and décor: Robert Moulton; music: Virgil Thomson (music from the film, *Louisiana Story*). First prod.: Royal Winnipeg Ballet at Playhouse Theatre, Winnipeg, Oct. 18, 1958, with Marilyn Young (Floozie) and company. The joys and hardships of farm life on the Great Plain.

Gray, Dennis (Nelson Rodrigues), Brazilian dancer and choreographer, b. Aracatuba, Brazil. Began his performing career in a circus. Studied ballet with Maria Olenewa and Igor Schwezoff. After his debut with the Original Ballet Russe (1944) and performing with Ballet da Juventude (1947), was engaged as first character dancer of the Teatro Municipal. Choreographed *Eternal Triangle* (1955), *The Swan of Tuonela* (1956), *Dancing Tragedy* (1957), and others. Currently choreographing chiefly for television and revues.

Gray, Felicity (also known as Felicity Andreae), English dancer and choreographer, b. Southampton, 1914. Studied with Phyllis Bedells. Danced in Camargo Society seasons, with Vic-Wells Ballet and Leon Woicikowski Ballet; also in vaudeville, choreographer for Carl Rosa Opera, numerous musicals, and revues. Associated with a very successful television program "Ballet for Beginners." Author of *Ballet for Beginners* (1952).

Graziana. Ballet in 3 movements; chor.: John Taras; music: Wolfgang Amadeus Mozart's Violin Concerto No. 3, K. 216; costumes: Alvin Colt. First prod.: Ballet (now American Ballet) Theatre, Metropolitan Opera House, N.Y., Oct. 25, 1945, with Alicia Alonso, Nora Kaye, André Eglevsky in the leading parts. Themeless ballet following the musical line. Although it did not last long in the repertoire it has an importance as Taras's first choreography.

Greanin, Leon (1895–1948) impresario, b. Russia, d. Israel. Among dancers and dance groups that he managed were Argentinita (1926), Nemtchinova-Oboukhov Ballet (1928–29), La Argentina (1933–35), Markova-Dolin Ballet (1937–38), as well as groups of Margaret Froman, Boris Romanov, the Sakharovs, Mikhail Mordkin, and others. Was representative of Ida Rubinstein (Paris, 1935–36), Ballet Theatre (Mexico, 1941, 1942), Carmen Amaya (Mexico, 1944). Was impresario of Jooss Ballet, following the company's winning the first prize at the choreographic competition organized by Archives Internationales de la Danse (Paris, 1932) and remained general manager of the company through 1941. After acquiring U.S. citizenship went to Israel (then Palestine), where he organized dance and music seasons until his death.

Great American Goof, The. Ballet-play by William Saroyan; chor.: Eugene Loring; music: Henry Brant; décor and costumes: Boris Aronson. First prod.: Ballet Theatre, Center Theatre, N.Y., Jan. 11, 1940, with a cast headed by Eugene Loring (title role), Miriam Golden (the Woman), Antony Tudor (the Dummy), Lucia Chase (a Little Girl). The rather disjointed plot of this ballet dealt with the trials and tribulations of a young innocent (the Goof) amid the city slickers of both sexes. The main interest was supposed to be in the story and spoken text written by William Saroyan, who stated in the program that he had never seen a ballet before he wrote this one. The production was a pseudo-Diaghilev stunt, which might have come off twenty-five years earlier in Monte Carlo or Paris, but not in 1940 in N.Y. The ballet died a well deserved early death during the first season of Ballet Theatre and was never revived.

Greco, José (Costanzo José Greco), director, dancer, b. Montorio-Nei-Frentani, Italy, 1919, of Spanish-Italian parentage. Began his dance career as partner of Argentinita (1944–45); partnered Pilar Lopez in Europe (1947–48). Since 1949 has headed his own Spanish Ballet Company, touring annually in America and Europe. Has appeared in several motion pictures—*Manolete* (Spain, 1949), *Som-*

Don José Greco in Farruca.

brero, Around the World in 80 Days, Holiday for Lovers, Ship of Fools (all in U.S.). Has appeared many times on such television shows as those of Ed Sullivan, Perry Como, Dinah Shore, Gary Moore, and Bob Hope. In 1962 was decorated with the Cross of the Knight of Civil Merit from the Spanish Government which bestows the title of "Don."

Greek Dance Association (England), an association of teachers founded by Miss Ruby Ginner at Stratford-on-Avon in 1923 to standardize the teaching of the Revived Greek Dance with the object of promoting mental and physical development by the use of that method in schools. Entrance is by examination. The Association is incorporated in the Imperial Society of Teachers of Dancing and conducts children's examinations.

Green Table, The. Dance of Death in 8 scenes; chor. and book: Kurt Jooss; music: Dr. Frederick (Fritz) Cohen; costumes: Hein Heckroth. First produced Jooss Ballet, Théâtre des Champs-Elysées, Paris, July 3, 1932, with the choreographer as Death. Inspired by World War I and its aftermath, it won first prize in a competition organized by Rolf de Maré, founder-director of Les Archives Internationales de la Danse, Paris, and has since been given in all parts of the world. It depicts the various facets of a war, beginning with a conference at a long table covered with regulation green cloth (hence the title) and going through mobilization, combat, war profiteering, refugees, etc., and ending with the conference with which the work began. And all the time Death is in the foreground dancing out the rhythm of the ballet. *The Green Table* is Kurt Jooss' greatest work. It has never been equalled by any other choreographer nor by Jooss himself. Jooss staged *The Green Table* for the Chilean National Ballet in 1948. It was revived in N.Y. by the Joffrey Ballet in Sept. 1967.

Gregory, Jill, English dancer and ballet mistress, b. Bristol, 1918. Studied at Abbey Theatre School, Dublin under Ninette de Valois. An early member of Vic-Wells Ballet, joining in 1933 and making her debut in *Création du Monde.* Remained to become soloist of Sadler's Wells Ballet, creating one of the giggling bridesmaids in *A Wedding Bouquet* and the Gold Fairy in its 1939 production of *The Sleeping Beauty,* and many other roles. After a short break during World War II, she rejoined the company when it was performing at the New Theatre, and became ballet mistress (1952) a position she still holds now that it is the Royal Ballet.

Gregory, John, English dancer and teacher, b. Norwich, 1914, m. Barbara Vernon. Studied with Igor Schwezoff, Mme. Nadine Legat, Stanislas Idzikowski, etc. in London. Principal dancer with Anglo-Polish Ballet in the early days of World War II; then, after service with an entertainment unit, with Jay Pomeroy's Russian Ballet, operettas, and musicals; with Ballet Jooss and Col. de Basil's Original Ballet Russe (1947). Started school with his wife (1949) and founded Federation of Russian Classical Ballet (1950). From this he launched Harlequin Ballet (1959). He has written numerous articles and pamphlets on the ballet.

Gremo, Maryla, Polish dancer and choreographer born in Lvov. Studied with Eugenia Edouardova (Berlin), Enrico Cecchetti, and Nadine Nicolaeva-Legat (London) and Olga Preobrajenska (Paris). Went to Brazil in 1932 to dance at the Polish Embassy for a national fête and settled in Rio de Janeiro. Danced at Teatro Municipal beginning 1934 and was ballet mistress of Ballet da Juventude; resident choreographer of Teatro Municipal. Her ballets include *Mephisto Valse, Rondo Capriccioso* and *Bachianas No. 1, The Sorcerer's Apprentice, Concerto Brasileiro, Romeo and Juliet.* Received award as Best Choreographer of 1959.

British ballerina Beryl Grey as Odile, in Swan Lake, *Act 3, produced by the Sadler's Wells (now Royal) Ballet.*

Grey, Beryl (Groom), English ballerina, b. Highgate, London, 1927; m. Dr. Sven Svenson. Studied with Madeline Sharp in Bromley, and at Sadler's Wells Ballet School from age nine (with Nicholas Sergeyev, Ninette de Valois, Vera Volkova), later with Anna Severskaya and Audrey de Vos. Entered Sadler's Wells (now Royal) Ballet (1941). Her first important roles came in the spring of 1942 when, due to illnesses in the company on tour, she danced leading roles in *Les Sylphides, Comus, The Gods Go a'Begging,* and *Swan Lake* (Act 2). A few months later, on her fifteenth birthday, she danced Odette-Odile in the full-length *Swan Lake* at Sadler's Wells Theatre, adding *Giselle* (1944) and *The Sleeping Beauty* (1946). She created the Duessa (*The Quest*), Rendez-vous (*Promenade*), Second Ballerina (*Ballet Imperial* in Sadler's Wells production), Countess Kitty (*Les Sirènes*), Fairy Winter (Frederick Ashton's *Cinderella*), Death (*Donald of the Burthens*), and others. Her large repertoire also included Queen of the Wilis (*Giselle*), Prayer (*Coppélia*), Lilac Fairy (*The Sleeping Beauty*), Black Queen (*Checkmate*), ballerina (*Scènes de Ballet*), and many others. She left the Royal Ballet in 1957 but has since returned frequently as guest artist, most recently in 1963. Since 1953 she has regularly made guest appearances with the Royal Swedish Ballet and is a great favorite in Sweden, having married a Swedish doctor and taken the trouble to learn the language. She has made innumerable other guest appearances with companies all over the world, including the Soviet Union where she danced with the Bolshoi, Kirov, Kiev State, and Tiflis State companies (1957). She wrote *Red Curtain Up* (1958), an account of her experiences in Russia and *Through the Bamboo Curtain* (1966), concerning her guest appearances in China. Appointed head of Arts Educational School, London (1966).

Griffith, Dennis, English dancer, b. India, 1938. Studied ballet with Kathleen Crofton and at Royal Ballet School. Danced in revue, International Ballet, at Edinburgh Festival (1958); joined Western Theatre Ballet later that year, dancing leads in *Love Duet, One in Five, Bal de la Victoire* (Hero), and others.

Grigoriev, Serge, former dancer of the St. Petersburg Maryinsky Theatre, b. 1883; m. dancer Lubov Tchernicheva (1909). Joined the Diaghilev Ballets Russes at its inception (1909), participated in its organization and became dancer and regisseur. In 1912 left the Imperial Theatre to devote all his time to the Diaghilev company. His administrative and rehearsal duties took up so much time that he had few opportunities to dance. However, his Shah Shariar in *Schéhérazade* and the Russian Merchant in *Boutique Fantasque* remain memorable creations. After the death of Diaghilev and the disbandment of the company, she joined Col. de Basil's Ballet Russe de Monte Carlo as regisseur-general and remained with the company until it was dissolved (1951–52). In 1953 Grigoriev wrote a very factual and well documented book, *The Diaghilev Ballet 1909–1929,* published by Constable, London. It has since become a standard reference volume on the subject. In 1954, Grigoriev and Tchernicheva staged a very careful revival of Fokine's *The Firebird* for Sadler's Wells (now Royal) Ballet as part of the commemoration of the 25th anniversary of the death of Serge Diaghilev. In 1957 they staged *Petrouchka* for the same company, and have restaged its production of *Les Sylphides.* The Grigorievs have been living in London in semi-retirement, occasionally sharing their vast knowledge of the classic ballet, and the Diaghilev repertoire in an advisory capacity with choreographers and directors of ballet companies.

Grigorieva, Tamara, director, ballet mistress and choreographer of the Ballet of Teatro Colón, Buenos Aires, Argentina, b. 1918, Petrograd (now Leningrad), Russia. Argentine citizen. First ballet teacher Olga Preobrajenska and later George Balanchine, Anatole Vilzak, Lubov Tchernicheva, Anatole Oboukhov, Pierre Vladimirov, Stanislas Idzikowski, Igor Schwezoff, Boris Kniaseff, Alexandre Sakharov. Began in George Balanchine's Les Ballets 1933, later same year joined Col. de Basil's Ballets Russes de Monte Carlo and stayed with Col. de Basil's company, renamed Original Ballet Russe, until 1944. Rose rapidly from corps de ballet to soloist and became ballerina in 1938. Her repertoire there included *L'Après-midi d'un Faune* (Nymph), *Prince Igor* (Polovetsian Woman), *Carnaval* (Chiarina), *Firebird* (Princess), *Symphonie Fantastique, Les Présages, Choreartium, Schéhérazade, Paganini, Cotillon, Prodigal Son, Coq d'Or, Francesca da Rimini.* In 1944 left the company to settle in Rio de Janeiro and work with Ballet da Juventude and Teatro Municipal. Guest ballerina Teatro Colón, Buenos Aires (1947–48); guest artist at Teatro S.O.D.R.E. in Montevideo, Uruguay (1949). Danced and acted in Buenos Aires in musical comedy *Así Se Ama en Sud America* (1950). Ballet mistress, choreographer and director of the ballet at Teatro S.O.D.R.E. in Montevideo (1951–54), where she revived many standard ballets and choreographed her first work, *Concierto Coreográfico,* to Tchaikovsky's First Piano Concerto in B flat minor, and in which she danced the principal part. Was engaged as ballet mistress and director of the Ballet at Teatro Colón (1956); ballet mistress, choreographer and director of the ballet at Teatro Argentino de La Plata (Buenos Aires) (1957–59), where she revived a number of ballets and choreographed two new ones: *Sinfonia Clásica,* to Serge Prokofiev's *Classic Symphony* (1957); and Symphonic Variations, to Brahms' *Variations on a Theme by Haydn* (1959). In 1961 she returned to Teatro Colón as ballet mistress, choreographer, and director of the ballet company, a post which she continues to occupy.

Grigorovich, Yuri, Honored Artist of the RSFSR, Soviet dancer and choreographer, b. 1927. Graduated from Leningrad Ballet School in 1946 to become one of the leading demi-caractère soloists of the Kirov company. He dances in the same kind of roles as his famous uncle, George Rosai of the first Diaghilev Ballets Russes season in Paris. Grigorovich is the son of Rosai's sister. At an early age he showed a predilection for choreography and, while still at school, began choreographing short numbers. In 1956 he choreographed Glinka's *Valse Fantaisie* for the school graduation performance. In 1957, with a group of young enthusiasts at the Kirov, he started working on a new version of *The Stone Flower,* returning the Sergei Prokofiev score to its original state and creating inventive new choreography. The entire production was conceived as a succession of dance suites. His artistic credo is the creation of characterization through dance, integrally blended with mime. His production of *The Stone Flower* was re-created at the Bolshoi Theatre in Moscow (1959) and was also performed in the Novosibirsk opera house. His second ballet *Legend of Love* (1961) carried further his artistic principles of modern dance idiom grounded in the classical technique with themes of profound dramatic content. In Sept., 1964, he was appointed chief choreographer of the Moscow Bolshoi; beginning work there during the 1963–64 season, when he produced a new *Sleeping Beauty*. On Apr. 15, 1965, revived his *Legend of Love* for the Bolshoi. Choreographed a new version of *The Nutcracker* which was acclaimed in N.Y. during the Bolshoi Ballet's 1966 American tour.

Grimaldi, Joseph (1779–1837), English actor of Italian parents, famous for his pantomime. At the age of two he danced at Sadler's Wells and Drury Lane Theatres and in 1806 appeared in *Mother Goose* at Covent Garden. He was a clown without equal in his day. His *Memoirs* were edited by Charles Dickens (1838).

Grinwis, Paul, contemporary Dutch dancer and choreographer, b. Holland. Studied at Théâtre Royal de la Monnaie, Brussels. Member, Col. de Basil's Ballet Russe de Monte Carlo (1946); Borovansky Ballet (1951); Original Ballet Russe (1952). Principal dancer and choreographer, Borovansky Ballet (1954–61). Roles included Can-Can Dancer (*La Boutique Fantasque*), Headmistress (*Graduation Ball*). His ballets include *Les Amants Eternels* (1951), *Los Tres Diabolos* (1954).

Grisi, Carlotta (1819–1899), Italian ballerina of the Romantic period, creator of the role of *Giselle.* Born in Milan, she studied ballet at the Conservatory of Music there and began to dance at the age of eight. When she was fourteen she went to Naples where she met Jules Perrot who took her with him to Paris and subsequently married her. She made her debut at the Paris Opéra in the dances in Donizetti's opera *La Favorita.* Her real success came with the title role in *Giselle* (1841). Another great role of Grisi was *La Péri* (1843). She also created *La Esmeralda* (1844) and *Paquita* (1846). The famous writer and critic Théophile Gautier, hitherto a staunch supporter of Taglioni and Elssler in turn, took a great liking to Grisi, but the ballerina preferred her partner Lucien Petipa, for whom she left her husband. Gautier found solace with Carlotta's sister Ernesta, who bore him two daughters. In 1845 Grisi appeared in the famous *Pas de Quatre,* staged by Perrot in London with her, Taglioni, Grahn and Cerito. In 1849 she danced in the St. Petersburg Imperial Theatre.

Grossvater, an old social dance of German origin. A theatrical version of this dance is incorporated in the first act of *The Nutcracker.*

Gsovska (also called Gsovsky), **Tatiana,** German teacher, ballet mistress and choreographer, b. Moscow, 1902, m. Victor Gsovsky. Studied in Moscow and St. Petersburg, was ballet mistress of the Moscow Experimental Theatre. Went to Berlin (1925) and opened her ballet school (1929), out of which emerged a number of outstanding German dancers, among them Natasha Trofimova, Gisela Deege,

Maria Fris, Helga Sommerkamp, Peter van Dijk, Gert Reinholm, Rainer Köcherman, Erwin Bredow. Ballet mistress of the Berlin (Eastern Zone) State Opera, (1945–52) and of the Teatro Colón, Buenos Aires (1952–53). Returned to Germany and settled in the Western Zone of Berlin (1953), resumed her teaching activities and founded her Berliner Ballett (1953) which frequently tours Europe and has also visited North and South America. Ballet mistress of the Municipal Opera, Berlin (Western Zone) and since 1959 also of the Frankfurt Opera. She has revived some thirty ballets of the standard repertoire and many of the modern middle-European repertoire. Her own choreographic works include *Medusa, Agon, Othello (Moor of Venice), Undine, The Black Sun, Lady of the Camellias, The Deed* (based on Dostoyevsky's *Crime and Punishment*).

Gsovsky, Victor, Russian dancer, teacher and choreographer, b. St. Petersburg, 1902; m. Tatiana Gsovska. Studied in St. Petersburg. Went to Berlin in 1925 and became ballet master of the Berlin State Opera with which he remained until 1928. During that period opened his ballet school. Joined the Markova-Dolin ballet troupe in London (1937). Later taught in Paris, and became ballet master of the Paris Opéra (1945). In 1946–47 held the same position with Ballets des Champs-Élysées, for which company he staged *La Sylphide* (1946). Later he was ballet master of the Metropolitan Ballet (London) for whom he staged *Dances of Galatea and Pygmalion.* His other works include *Hamlet* (Munich, 1950), *Road to Light* (Munich, 1952), *The Pearl* (Paris, 1953). From his Paris school came a number of outstanding dancers, among them Colette Marchand, Irène Skorik, Violette Verdy, Heino Hallhuber, Serge Perrault.

Gué, George (Grönfeld) (1893–1962), Finnish ballet master and choreographer, b. St. Petersburg, Russia. Studied ballet with Nicholas Legat and music with Alexander Glazounov. Organized the National Ballet of Finland and was its ballet master (1921–35). Produced the first ballet ever to be staged in Finland: *Swan Lake* (1922). In 1936 went to France, where he worked with several ballet companies, among them Monte Carlo Opera Ballet. Was a choreographer for the theatres Châtelet, Mogador, and Folies-Bergère, all in Paris. Was ballet master of the Royal Swedish Ballet (1939–48). Returned as ballet director of the Finnish Ballet (1955), where he died after a recurring illness.

Guérard, Roland, dancer, b. Flat Rock, N.C., 1905. Studied Cooper Union Technical School, Pace Institute of Accounting; dance with Chester Hale, Fokine, Celli, Vilzak, Vladimiroff (N.Y.), Egorova, Volinine (Paris). Member, Ballets Franco-Russe (1930–31); Folies-Bergère, Paris (1931–32); Ballet Russe de Monte Carlo (de Basil) (1933–38); René Blum Ballet (1937), Ballet Russe de Monte Carlo (1938–42). As soloist he danced in *Les Sylphides, Swan Lake* (Friend), *Blue Bird, Carnaval,* and others, as well as demi-caractère roles. Danced in musicals *Merry Widow* (1943–44), *Song of Norway* (1944–46), *Brigadoon* (1947). Currently teaching ballet in U.S.

Guerra, Antonio, dancer, choreographer, maître de ballet, b. Naples, 1810, d. Vienna, 1846. Studied with Pietro Hus in Naples and made his debut at San Carlo Theatre (1826). Danced in Milan, Turin, Florence, and at Paris Opéra. Was one of Maria Taglioni's partners. Principal dancer and maître de ballet, Her Majesty's Theatre, London (1838), partnering Fanny Elssler in his own version of *La Gitana* (1839). Choreographed a number of ballets in London, including *Le Lac des Fées* for Fanny Cerito (1840). Choreographer, Imperial Theatre, Vienna (1842), his ballets including *Nankin, Angelica, Manfred, Fortuna.*

Guerra, Nicola (1862–1942), dancer, choreographer, teacher, b. Naples, d. Italy. At age seventeen had already attained position of premier danseur at Teatro alla Scala, Milan; later danced in London, St. Petersburg, Paris and N.Y. and was principal dancer and maître de ballet at Vienna State Opera for ten years. Staged the revival of Jean Philippe Rameau's opera, *Castor and Pollux* for Paris Opéra (1918). Choreographed *La Tragédie de Salome* for Ida Rubinstein (1919) and *Artemis Troublée* (1922), both presented at the Paris Opéra. He directed the Paris Opéra Ballet School (1927–29) during which period he created a number of ballets, among them *Cyrca* (1927), *Turandot* (1928), and *Salamine* (1929).

Guest, Ivor, English writer on ballet, mainly its history, b. Chislehurst, Kent, 1920; m. Ann Hutchinson (1962). Educated at Lancing College, and Trinity College, Cambridge, he is a lawyer by profession and a writer by avocation, specializing in ballet of the 19th century. His books include *The Ballet of the Second Empire 1858–1870* (1953), *The Romantic Ballet in England* (1954), *The Ballet of the Second Empire 1847–1858* (1955), *Fanny Cerrito* (1956), *Victorian Ballet Girl* (1957), *Adeline Genée* (1958), *The Dancer's Heritage* (1960), *The Empire Ballet* (1962), and "The Alhambra Ballet" (*Dance Perspectives,* 1959). Edited *La Fille Mal Gardée* (1960), the history of the ballet and of its Royal Ballet version, and wrote *The Romantic Ballet in Paris* (Middletown, Conn., 1966). The last named was honored with a special exhibition arranged by the Harvard Theatre Collection at the Houghton Library (summer, 1966). He was an associate editor of the *Ballet Annual* in London until its final issue (1964); is also adviser on ballet to the Italian *Enciclopedia dello Spettacolo,* and, since 1964, editorial adviser to the *London Dancing Times.* Organized National Book League Exhibition of books on ballet (1957–58). Wrote the text for the catalogue of the collection of dance prints at the Mercury Theatre, London, entitled *A Gallery of Romantic Ballet* (London, 1966).

Guest Artist, an outstanding dancer engaged for a limited time to appear with a company with which he or she is not regularly associated. Guest artists are frequently invited by company directors to stimulate the sale of tickets. The appearance of a dancer as a guest artist is called a guest performance.

Guests, The. Ballet in 1 act; chor.: Jerome Robbins; music: Marc Blitzstein. First prod.: New York City Ballet at City Center, N.Y., Jan. 20, 1949, with Maria Tallchief, Francisco Moncion, Nicholas Magallanes. Jerome Robbins' first ballet for this company. Although danced in practice costume and without any definite plot, there is an unmistakable theme of discrimination of class or race, or both, implicit in the action.

Guggenheim Foundation. See FOUNDATIONS, PHILANTHROPIC.

Guglielmo Ebreo. See WILLIAM, THE JEW OF PESARO.

Guiablesse, La. Ballet in 1 act; chor. and book: Ruth Page; music: William Grant Still; décor: Nicholas Remisoff. First produced: Century of Progress Exhibition, Chicago, June 16, 1933; Chicago Opera House, Chicago, June 23, 1933, with an all-Negro cast. *La Guiablesse* is a she-devil found in the folklore of Martinique and Guadeloupe, the French islands in the West Indies. She is a temptress who entices men into her arms only to cast them down the mountain where she lives.

Guimard, Madeleine (1743–1816), illegitimate daughter of an inspector of a Paris cloth factory. At the age of fifteen she became a member of the corps de ballet at the Comédie Française. From there she went to the Académie Royale where in 1761 she understudied Allard. In 1762 she made her debut at the Opéra in Fuzelier's *Les Fêtes Grecques et Romaines*. In the following year she was designated as première danseuse noble. In 1764 Guimard appeared in Rameau's *Castor and Pollux*. She danced many demi-caractère roles and was in many ballets including Maximilien Gardel's *La Chercheuse d'Esprit, Le Premier Navigateur, Ninette à la Cour, La Fête de Mirza,* and *Le Déserteur*. Her best role in Noverre's works was in *Les Caprices de Galatée*. Guimard was very slight of build, in fact disparaging remarks arout her thinness were often made. When she was in her prime she had smallpox and was left with a scarred face, but this did not seem to affect her attraction for men. Her dancing was more graceful than virtuoso. She was definitely a terre à terre dancer, lively and vivacious and an excellent mime. Her taste in dress was excellent. She preferred simple rather than the ornate costumes which were the vogue. She excelled in naive shepherd girl roles which in view of her famous love affairs always delighted her audiences. Her lovers included Jean Benjamin de la Borde, valet de chambre to Louis XV, and the Prince de Soubise. The latter endowed her with a pension which she gave up voluntarily when the house of Soubise came upon lean days. Guimard had a sumptuous house in a suburb of Paris, decorated by Fragonard, and a town house with a private theatre called Temple of Terpsichore wherein many ballets, some of reportedly scandalous nature, were given. *Les Fêtes d'Adam* was supposed to have been such a spectacle. In 1789 Guimard married choreographer and poet Despréaux and retired to a house high above Montmartre and had a long and happy marital life. She did return to dance and sing in a revival of Rameau's *Talents Lyriques* in which she was one of the Three Graces.

Guns and Castanets. Ballet in 1 act; chor.: Ruth Page and Bentley Stone; music: Georges Bizet, selected and adapted by Jerome Moross; songs: poems of Federico Garcia Lorca, trans. by A. L. Lloyd; book: Ruth Page; décor: Clive Rickabaugh; costumes: John Pratt. First prod.: Page-Stone Ballet, Great Northern Theatre, Chicago, Ill. Mar. 1, 1939 (as a WPA Theatre Project), with Ruth Page (Carmen), Bentley Stone (Escamillo), Walter Camryn (José), Bettina Rosay (Micaela). Adapted from the story of Carmen by Prosper Mérimée, but set in the period of the Spanish Civil War.

Gusev, Pyotr, Honored Artist of the RSFSR, Soviet dancer, choreographer and teacher, b. 1905. Gusev graduated from the former Maryinsky school in 1922 after only four years of training. He remained at the Kirov Theatre until 1935, but in 1934–35 worked also at the Maly Opera Theatre as one of its leading male dancers. With his partner Olga Mungalova he became the pioneer of the semi-acrobatic, semi-classical pas de deux very popular on the concert stage at that time. He began teaching at the Bolshoi school in 1935. From 1937 to 1940 and again in 1950 he headed the school. Between 1945 and 1951 he headed the Kirov Ballet company and, in 1956, the Bolshoi ballet company. At various periods (1935–41, 1943–46, 1951–57) he was ballet master at the Stanislavsky and Nemirovich-Danchenko Lyric Theatre, in 1953 staging the second act (after Lev Ivanov) of the Vladimir Bourmeister *Swan Lake*. He worked at the Peking Dance School as senior teacher and choreographer (1957–60), and also as director and teacher of courses for the training of choreographers. From Oct., 1960 to Dec., 1961, he headed the ballet company of the Maly Opera Theatre, Leningrad. In the summer of 1961 he visited New Zealand and Australia. Since his retirement (1961), the Maly Opera Theatre company is headed by Konstantin Boyarsky. Gusev was for many years Olga Lepeshinskaya's partner on the concert stage. As a teacher he was renowned for his instruction of supported adagio.

Gypsy, La. Ballet in 3 acts, 5 scenes; chor.: Joseph Mazilier; music: François Benoist and Ambroise Thomas, two talented composers of the period, and Marliani, a hack tunesmith; book: H. Vernoy de Saint Georges and Mazilier; décor: Philastre and Cambon; costumes: Paul Lormier. First prod.: Théâtre de l'Académie Royale de Musique, Paris, Jan. 28, 1839, with Fanny Elssler in the title role; London première: Her Majesty's Theatre, June 24, 1839, also with Elssler. The ballet has an unimaginably complicated scenario which deals mainly with the story of a daughter of a lord being abducted by a band of Gypsies. This was the ballet in which Fanny Elssler established her reputation as a dancer of genius.

Haakon, Paul, dancer, b. Denmark, 1914. Brought to N.Y. as a child, he had already begun his ballet studies at the school of the Royal Danish Ballet. In the U.S. he studied with Michel Fokine, Mikhail Mordkin, and at the School of American Ballet, N.Y. Made his debut with the Fokine Ballet in *Harlequinade* (1927) at age thirteen. After solo performances here, he went to Europe (1930) where he studied in France, Spain, and England; later danced in the Anna Pavlova company. After his return to the U.S., was premier danseur of the American Ballet (1935), starred in several musicals, and in Radio City Music Hall; appeared in hotels and the better nightclubs. Since 1963 ballet master and instructor of the José Greco Spanish Ballet.

Habanera, a Cuban dance of African origin. The name is derived from Habana (Havana), the capital of Cuba. Known at one time as Creole Country Dance, it was taken to Spain and later France. Bizet used the habanera in his opera *Carmen*. Among other composers Ravel and Chabrier composed musical pieces which were named "Habanera."

Hadassah (Hadassah Spira), contemporary dancer, b. Jerusalem, Israel; m. Milton Epstein. Descended from a long line of prominent Rabbinical and Hassidic families, she became interested in Hindu dance and music at an early age after witnessing a Hindu cremation in Sarafend, Palestine. Studied dance in U.S. and abroad with Devi Ritha and Pryagopal (Manipuri), Damayanti Joshi (Kathak), Raghavan Nair and Ram Gopal (Bharata Natya), Radem Mas Kodrat and R. M. Wiradat (Javanese court-dances), and

Hadassah in Shuvi Nafshi *(Return, Oh My Soul), based on Psalm 116.*

Kenfi Hinoki (Japanese dance); modern dance with Jack Cole. Has appeared in recital and dance groups presenting Indian, Javanese, Balinese, and Israeli suites since 1938, making her N.Y. debut in Times Hall, 1945. Appeared at Jacob's Pillow Dance Festival, Lee, Mass. (1951, 1954, 1961). Toured India and Israel 1959–60. Was commissioned by the Tagore Centenary Committee to create a Tagore Suite, premièred at the YM–YWHA, with the Indian actor Saaed Jeffrey as narrator (1961). On the faculty, member of the board of directors, and chairman of the ethnic division, New Dance Group Studio, N.Y., teaching Hindu dance.

Haeger, Bengt, Swedish writer, ballet critic, curator of the dance museum in the Royal Theatre, Stockholm, b. 1916; m. Indian dancer Lilavati. Author of *Ballet Classic and Modern* (1945), *Ballets from the Whole World* (1947); also edited Rolf de Maré's book *Les Ballets Suédois* (1947). He is president of Dansfrämjandet, an organization founded to stimulate interest in dance.

Haieff, Alexei, American composer of Russian origin, b. 1914. Came to the U.S. (1932) and won a scholarship to the Juilliard School of Music. Was granted the Lili Boulanger Memorial Award (1942) and a medal from the American Academy in Rome. Won a Guggenheim Fellowship (1946) and the grant of $1,000 from the National Academy of Arts and Letters (1947); also awarded the American Prix de Rome (1947, 1948). Among his compositions used for dance is *Zanilda and Her Entourage* which he composed for Merce Cunningham (1946). George Balanchine used his *Divertimento for Small Orchestra* for the ballet *Divertimento,* choreographed in 1947 for Ballet Society and later in the repertoire of New York City Ballet. On Feb. 9, 1948, Ballet Society announced that it would present a two-act ballet, *Beauty and the Beast,* on Mar. 22, to be choreographed by Balanchine to a score by Haieff. The ballet has not yet been produced.

Hale, Chester, dancer and teacher, b. Jersey City, N.J., 1897. Educated at Univ. of Chicago. Former member, Diaghilev Ballets Russes in U.S.; Anna Pavlova company. Ballet master, Capitol Theatre, N.Y. (1925–34). Staged dance numbers in films (*The Painted Veil, Anna Karenina, Rose Marie, A Night at the Opera*). Teaches ballet in N.Y.

Halévy, Jacques (1799–1862), French composer. Noted chiefly for his operas (*La Juive, L'Eclair, La Reine de Cypre,* and others), he wrote the score for one ballet, *Manon Lescaut* (1830).

Half-Toe. See DEMI-POINTE.

Hall, Fernau, contemporary writer on ballet, b. Victoria, B.C., Canada. Studied dance with Nesta Brooking, Margaret Craske (at Vic-Wells School); Ernest Berk (modern) and Rosandro (Spanish). Danced with Sakuntala Company (a Hindu group); Ballets Nègres; Dance Theatre; corps de ballet of Col. de Basil's Original Ballet Russe; also in the film *The Little Ballerina.* Stage director for several dance companies, including the Imperial Ballet of Japan and the Azuma Kabuki European tours. Contributor to *The Dancing Times* (since 1957), *Dance Magazine, Saturday Review, N.Y. Times* (magazine); ballet critic, *Ballet Today* (since 1958). Author of *Ballet* (1948), *Modern English Ballet* (1950), *An Anatomy of Ballet* (1953; U.S. title: *World Dance*).

Hallhuber, Heino, German dancer, b. Munich, 1927. Studied under Erna Grebl, Pino Mlakar, Rudolf Kölling, Victor Gsovsky. Made his debut at the Munich State Opera in *Don Juan* (1949). Dances principal roles in all classic, romantic, and modern ballets in the repertoire; also appears often on television.

Halte de Cavalerie. Ballet in 1 act; chor. and book: Marius Petipa; music: Ivan Armsheimer; décor: Levogt; costumes: Ponomarev. First prod.: Maryinsky Theatre, St. Petersburg, Feb. 2, 1896, with Pierina Legnani and Paul Gerdt in the principal roles. A most popular ballet up to the revolution of 1917, it is a gay little comedy dealing with a pretty country girl being paid court by officers of a cavalry regiment which has halted in the village for a rest. The point of the story is that in this pursuit each officer is being displaced by one of a higher rank, from the youngest subaltern to the colonel, while the girl is actually in love with a boy in the village. Mikhail Mordkin in staging his *Voices of Spring* for the Mordkin Ballet (later Ballet Theatre) incorporated his version of a scene from *Halte de Cavalerie.*

Hambo, Swedish folk dance in 3/4 time which dates back to the 16th century and is still danced everywhere in Sweden. Ivó Cramér has used this dance in his ballet *The Prodigal Son.*

Hamilton, Gordon (1918–1959), dancer, ballet master and teacher, b. Sydney, Australia. Studied to be a concert pianist, but changed to dancing after seeing the Col. de Basil's Ballet Russe de Monte Carlo in Australia (1934). Studied with Olga Preobrajenska in Paris and Marie Rambert in London. After brief periods with Ballet Rambert and Anglo-Polish Ballet, joined Sadler's Wells Ballet (1940–46) as soloist. Danced many character roles including Dr. Coppelius (*Coppélia*), Carabosse (*The Sleeping Beauty*), Mr. Taylor (Ninette de Valois' *The Prospect Before Us*), and others; created Lepidopterist (de Valois' *Promenade*), Polonius (Robert Helpmann's *Hamlet*), and others. Joined Ballets des Champs-Elysées (1946) as ballet master and principal character dancer in *La Sylphide, Les Forains, Los Caprichos,* etc. Returned to Sadler's Wells Ballet briefly (1947); rejoined Petit in his Ballets de Paris (1949), creating roles in *Carmen, La Croqueuse de Diamants.* Stayed in America after the tour of that company and appeared in musicals. Appointed ballet master and teacher of Vienna State Opera (1954), staging *Swan Lake* (Act 2) and *Giselle.* Died in Paris while on leave of absence.

Hamlet. Ballet in 1 scene; chor.: Robert Helpmann; music: Peter Tchaikovsky's "Fantasy Overture," *Hamlet;* décor: Leslie Hurry. First prod.: Sadler's Wells (now Royal) Ballet, New Theatre, London, May 19, 1942, with Robert Helpmann (title role), Margot Fonteyn (Ophelia), Celia Franca (Queen), David Paltenghi (King), Gordon Hamilton (Polonius), John Hart (Laertes), Leo Kersley (Gravedigger), Margaret Dale (Messenger). The ballet begins and ends with the bearing away of the dead Hamlet. In that last moment of time before death, he relives the events that have brought him to this end. Paltenghi and Michael Somes also danced the role of Hamlet, and, after a lapse of several years, it was revived Apr. 2, 1964, for Rudolf Nureyev and given, together with Frederick Ashton's *The Dream* and Kenneth MacMillan's *Images of Love,* on a special program as part of England's Shakespeare Quatercentenary Celebrations.

Hamlet. Ballet in prologue and 3 scenes; chor.: Victor Gsovsky; music: Boris Blacher; book: Tatiana Gsovska; décor: Helmut Jürgens. First prod.: Bayerische Staatsoper, Munich, Nov. 19, 1950, with Franz Baur (Hamlet), Irène Skorik (Ophelia), Heino Hallhuber (Laertes), Walter Matthes (Polonius). The ballet follows the spirit of the Shakespeare play in its principal scenes rather than the simplified libretto by Tatiana Gsovska. Mme. Gsovska staged her version of the ballet for the Berlin Städtische Oper; it was later taken over by the Berliner Ballett, which toured the U.S. in 1955 and presented with Gert Heinholm in the title role. An enlarged version by Tatiana Gsovska in décor and costumes by Ludvig Zuckermandel was premièred Aug. 30, 1951, at Teatro Colón, Buenos Aires, Argentina, with Victor Ferrari (Hamlet), Adela Adamova (Ophelia), Maria Ruanova (Queen), Enrique Lommi (King), José Neglia (Laertes).

Handel, George Frederic (1685–1759), German-born composer. He made England his home and his artistic inspiration. Some of his music has been used for ballet, including *The Gods Go a'Begging* (George Balanchine, 1928; Ninette de Valois, 1936); *Origin of Design* (de Valois, 1932), both scores arranged as suites from various pieces by Sir Thomas Beecham. In 1960 Balanchine staged *The Figure in the Carpet* to the *Water Music* and the *Fireworks Music*. Modern dancer Paul Taylor used Handel's music for his *Aureole*.

Haney, Carol (1925–1964), American dancer and choreographer, b. New Bedford, Mass. After studying dance from childhood, she had her own school in New Bedford at age fifteen. Three years later went to Hollywood; studied with Ernest Belcher, worked in nightclubs and was assistant to Jack Cole and Gene Kelly in musicals, including *American in Paris, Singin' in the Rain,* and *Brigadoon*. Was also Cole's partner in nightclubs. Danced with Bob Fosse in the movie version of *Kiss Me, Kate*. Had her first Broadway success in *Pajama Game* (1954), especially the number "Steam Heat." Had a straight role in the play *A Loss of Roses*. Choreographed the annual Oldsmobile industrial shows; also the musicals *Bravo Giovanni* (1962), *She Loves Me* (1963), *Jennie* (1963), *Funny Girl* (1964). Choreographer for television's "Garry Moore Show" (1963). She had just returned from staging her dances for the London production of *She Loves Me* when she was taken ill and died a few days later in N.Y., Mar. 10, 1964.

Hanka, Erika (1905–1958), Director of the Ballet of the Vienna Staatsoper, came from an old Austrian military family. She was born in Bozen and received her dance education in Vienna and Germany. Her first job was as soloist at the Düsseldorf Opera, where she soon became acting ballet mistress. Later she joined the Jooss Ballet with which she toured Europe and the U.S. After several seasons of touring she became ballet mistress at the Cologne Opera and later in Essen and Hamburg. From Hamburg she was invited to Vienna as guest choreographer (1941). Here she staged the ballet *Joan von Zarissa* to Werner Egk's music. The ballet had a great success and she became permanent ballet mistress. In her sixteen years in Vienna she staged some fifty ballets, among them many world premières. Perhaps her greatest work was *The Moor of Venice,* to Boris Blacher's score, in décor and costumes by Georges Wakhevitch (premièred Nov. 29, 1955, on the occasion of the opening of the re-built Vienna Staatsoper). She worked mainly in a modern ballet style. It was due to Erika Hanka's talent, initiative, perseverance, and indefatigable effort that the ballet began to play a proper part in the artistic plan of the Vienna Opera. She died May 15, 1958, of a heart attack, which followed an appendectomy performed two days before.

Hansen, Émile (1843–1927), Danish dancer and choreographer of the Royal Danish Ballet. A pupil of August Bournonville, he numbered among his works the two-act ballet *Aditi,* to music by Frederik Rung; the ballet-divertissement *The Gypsy Camp* to music by the same composer (both in 1880); dances to Weber's opera *Oberon* (1886–87); dances in the fairy-comedy *Once Upon a Time* to music by Peter Erasmus Lange Müller (1887); one-act ballet *A Carnival Joke in Venice* to music by Rung (1890). He was ballet master of the Moscow Bolshoi Theatre (1879–89), where he revived the original Reisinger version of *Swan Lake* (1880 and

1882). He was apparently permitted frequent leaves of absence during which he worked in Copenhagen, and also staged ballets at the Alhambra Theatre, London (1884–87). He was ballet master of Paris Opéra (1890–94), during which period Russian ballerina Olga Preobrajenska studied with him.

Harding, Kathleen (Mrs. Joseph J. Snyder, 1885–1958), English-born secretary of the Metropolitan Opera Ballet School since its establishment in 1909 until 1950, and of the Opera Ballet Company from 1914 to her death. Came to the United States as secretary of Malvina Cavallazzi, founder of the school. She was an accomplished pianist and for a time played for the ballet classes. Miss Harding's modest title does not convey the skill, extent, and importance of her administrative work in the School and Company. Her vast experience and knowledge of the ways of the Metropolitan Opera complex was of great help to a succession of ballet school directors, ballet masters, and choreographers in the discharge of their administrative duties.

Hari, Eugene (Otto Ulbricht). See MATA AND HARI.

Harkarvy, Benjamin, teacher, choreographer, director, b. New York City, 1930. Studied ballet with George Chaffee, Elizabeth Anderson-Ivantzova, Edward Caton, School of American Ballet, N.Y., and Olga Preobrajenska, Paris. After four years of training, made his debut at eighteen with Brooklyn Lyric Opera, for which he also choreographed the dances in *La Traviata.* After dancing and choreographing in summer stock, began teaching and opened own school in N.Y. (1955), also forming concert group which danced at Jacob's Pillow Dance Festival (1957). Director, choreographer, ballet master of Royal Winnipeg Ballet (1957–58), during which time he conducted a weekly television series on ballet for three months. Ballet master, Nederlands Ballet for a year from Sept., 1958. Formed his own company, The Nederlands Danse Theater, with headquarters at The Hague. This has received a government subsidy since 1962. This group has toured extensively in Europe and in Israel, making its U.S. debut at the Jacob's Pillow Dance Festival (1965). In addition to works choreographed by himself and by young Dutch choreographers, he has invited Anna Sokolow, Ivó Cramér, Glen Tetley, John Butler to stage works. Glen Tetley also danced with the company. See also HOLLAND, DANCE IN.

Harkness Ballet, the newest U.S. ballet company, founded in N.Y. in the spring of 1964, sponsored by Mrs. Rebekah Harkness, president of the Rebekah Harkness Foundation (see FOUNDATIONS, PHILANTHROPIC). The activities of the Harkness Ballet began with a summer study and rehearsal session at Watch Hill, R.I. Vera Volkova, famous instructor of the Royal Danish Ballet School; Erik Bruhn, a premier danseur of the same company who was a guest artist with the Harkness Ballet, and Leon Fokine, scion of the famous ballet family and a well-known N.Y. teacher taught the classes. George Skibine was engaged as artistic director and choreographer. His wife, Marjorie Tallchief, a former première danseuse étoile of the Paris Opéra, was named prima ballerina and Nicholas Polajenko, until recently premier danseur of Marquis de Cuevas' International Ballet, became premier danseur. Donald Saddler, a choreographer in his own right, was appointed assistant artistic director. Choreographers working with the company were Alexandra Danilova, Mme. Volkova, Skibine, Saddler, Brian Macdonald, Alvin Ailey, Richard Wagner, Michael Smuin, and Thomas Andrew. To take care of the financial needs of the company the Rebekah Harkness Foundation, together with the William Hale Harkness Foundation (named after the late Mr. Harkness), provided a grant of $2,000,000. The company made its debut with a European tour beginning Feb. 19, 1965, with a three-week season at the Municipal Casino, Cannes, France. Five performances at the Opéra Comique, Paris, from Mar. 12 followed, with appearances also in Copenhagen, Malmo (Sweden), Berlin, several Italian cities, Bucharest (Romania), and in Lisbon and Oporto, Portugal. The most successful ballets appeared to be Ailey's *Feast of Ashes,* Macdonald's *Time Out of Mind,* Skibine's *Daphnis and Chloë,* Stuart Hodes' *The Abyss.* Its first U.S. tour was in the fall of 1965. On Nov. 18, Harkness House for the Ballet Arts was opened in N.Y. as the official school and headquarters for the company, with a gallery for the display of special exhibitions in connection with ballet. A second tour of Europe to which Greece and North Africa and Egypt were added began again in Cannes where John Butler's version of Gian-Carlo Menotti's *Sebastian* had its première (Mar. 4, 1966) at the Casino Theatre. During this tour the company appeared at the open-air Festival de Marais, Paris (June 16–18). A second U.S. tour (including Hawaii) began Sept. 12 in Los Angeles where *The Abyss* had its U.S. première. Principal dancers of this season were Brunilda Ruiz, Lone Isaksen, Elisabeth Carroll, Margaret Mercier, Lawrence Rhodes, Helgi Tomasson, and Panchita DePeri, Finis Jhung, Ali Pourfarrokh, Richard Wagner, Roderick Drew. The repertoire included the following: *The Abyss* (Hodes-Marga Richter), *After Eden* (Butler-Lee Hoiby), *Ariadne* (Ailey-André Jolivet), *Canto Indio* (Macdonald-Carlos Chavez, *Capers* (Macdonald-Vittorio Rieti), *Cindy* (Saddlers-R. Harkness), *Daphnis and Chloë* (Skibine-Maurice Ravel), *Daughters of the Garden* (Donald McKayle-Ernest Bloch), *Feast of Ashes* (Ailey-Carlos Surinach), *Hearts, Meadows and Flags* (Wagner-Hoiby), *Highland Fair* (Smuin-Malcolm Arnold), *Idylle* (Skibine-François Serrette), *Koshare* (Saddler-Louis Ballard), *La Venta* (Skibine-Surinach), *Macumba* (Ailey-Harkness), *Sarabande* (Skibine-François Couperin), *Sebastian* (Butler-Menotti), *Time Out of Mind* (Macdonald-Paul Creston), *Youth* (Wagner-Samuel Barber).

Harkness, Mrs. Rebekah (Rebekah Semple West Pierce Harkness), American composer and sponsor of dance, b. St. Louis, Mo.; children: Allen Pierce, Terry Pierce, Edith Harkness. Advanced studies in harmonic structure and composition at the Dalcroze School; with Nadia Boulanger at Fontainebleau, France; with Frederick Werle at the Mannes College of Music, N.Y.; and with Lee Hoiby. President of the Harkness Foundation (see FOUNDATIONS, PHILANTHROPIC), promoting American dance and American dance companies, among them Jerome Robbins' Ballets: U.S.A. (European tour, 1961, in cooperation with the U.S. Dept. of State); ethnological dance tour of Africa by Pearl Primus (1962); Robert Joffrey Ballet (U.S. and overseas tours 1962, 1963, the latter in cooperation with the Dept. of State); Harkness Foundation Ballet Workshop at Watch Hill, R.I. (1963); Harkness Ballet, established 1964; annual open-air Dance Festival, free to the public, as part of N.Y. Shakespeare Festival in Central Park's Delacorte Theatre, beginning 1962. Established Harkness House for Ballet Arts, N.Y. (1965) which includes the Harkness Ballet School, rehearsal studios and a gallery, as well as offices. Among Mrs. Harkness' compositions are *Journey to Love* (a ballet), *Barcelona* (a dance piece for José Greco), *Safari in Africa, Letters from Japan, Macumba* (suite for New Orleans Philharmonic and ballet for Alvin Ailey), *The Gift of the Magi, Dreams of Glory* (ballet), *The Palace* (ballet).

Harkness, Rebekah, Foundation. See FOUNDATIONS, PHILANTHROPIC.

Harlequin, one of the characters in

commedia dell'arte whose masks as well as costumes and movements peculiar to each became very familiar and popular in Paris, Vienna, London. Harlequin, mocking and grotesque in his diamond patch costume, had great influence on stage dancing in England, and was often introduced in a danced scene following ordinary plays. John Rich and Henry Woodward were famous Harlequins in England in the early 18th century. The character is used in *Carnaval* (Michel Fokine, 1910), and in George Balanchine's ballets *Le Bourgeois Gentilhomme* (1944), *Night Shadow* (1946) and *Harlequinade* (1965).

Harlequin Ballet Company, a small English company formed in Sept., 1959 by John Gregory and Barbara Vernon to take ballet to smaller provincial towns, schools, and colleges. The company receives an Arts Council grant and makes regular tours.

Harlequin in April. Ballet in prologue, 2 acts and epilogue; chor. and book: John Cranko; commissioned music: Richard Arnell; décor: John Piper. First prod.: Sadler's Wells Theatre Ballet at Sadler's Wells Theatre, London, May 8, 1951, with Patricia Miller (Columbine), David Blair (Harlequin), Stanley Holden (Pierrot). The ballet was suggested by the lines from T. S. Eliot's *The Waste Land,* beginning: "April is the cruellest month, breeding/Lilacs out of the dead land . . ." There is no straightforward story, but Man is born from the barren earth, struggles to maturity, loves, triumphs, fails, grows old, and returns to the earth. The fumbling, bumbling Pierrot looks on and comments without in any way being able to help.

Harlequinade. Ballet in 2 acts; chor.: George Balanchine; music: Riccardo Drigo (*Les Millions d'Arlequin*); décor: Rouben Ter-Arutunian. First prod.: New York City Ballet, N.Y. State Theater, Feb. 4, 1965, with Patricia McBride (Colombine), Edward Villella (Harlequin), Suki Schorer (Pierrette), Deni Lamont (Pierrot), Gloria Govrin (La Bonne Fée), Michael Arshansky (Cassandre), Shaun O'Brien (Leandre). George Balanchine's completely new version of the old Maryinsky ballet, *Les Millions d'Arlequin,* by Petipa. Harlequin foils Leandre, Colombine's elderly suitor, and La Bonne Fée (The Good Fairy) bestows upon him the "millions" which make him acceptable to Cassandre (Colombine's father) as a suitable husband. The scenery was adapted by Ter-Arutunian from that originally designed by him for the New York City Opera production of Rossini's opera *La Cenerentola.*

Harlequinade, pantomime, an English descendant of commedia dell'arte, extravaganzas with dance and songs which became popular in America in the late 18th century. Here for the first time American national themes and heroes were represented: Indian chiefs, Pocahontas, the spirit of Benjamin Franklin, etc. Some of these companies performed in England and continental Europe, where they introduced real Indians in their own war dances.

Harmonica Breakdown. Modern dance solo, choreographed and danced by Jane Dudley; music: Sonny Terry's *Harmonica and Washboard Breakdown;* created in 1940 and given on a special program in N.Y., May, 1941 called America Dances. A solo of syncopated body rhythms, shuffles, bends, slides and swings, which for many years remained one of the great successes in the Dudley-Maslow-Bales repertoire.

Harris, Joan, dancer, ballet mistress, director, b. London, 1920. Studied with Stanislas Idzikowski, Vera Volkova, and at Sadler's Wells School. Member of Anglo-Polish Ballet (1941); soloist, International Ballet (1941–45); leading dancer, Sadler's Wells Theatre Ballet

(1945–47). Also danced in musicals, revues, pantomimes, and was ballet mistress for the films *The Red Shoes* and *Steps of the Ballet;* assistant choreographer for the film *The Tales of Hoffmann* (between 1947 and 1949). Ballet mistress, Bavarian State Opera, Munich (1954–61); choreographed *Purcell Suite* for Bayreuth Festival (1957). Ballet director, Opera House, Oslo, 1961–66, when she was succeeded by Sonia Arova.

Harrold, Robert, English dancer and teacher, b. Wolverhampton, 1923. Studied at Rambert School, and with Olga Preobrajenska, Lubov Egorova, Alexandre Volinine (Paris); with Pericet (Seville and Madrid). Made his debut with Anglo-Polish Ballet (1940). Danced with Ballet Rambert (1941–44), dancing Lover (*Lilac Garden*). Dances 2 and 5 (*Dark Elegies*), male dancer (*Les Sylphides*), and others; created Personage with Long Ears (Andrée Howard's *Carnival of Animals,* 1943). Served with British Army (1944–47). Has appeared in films, television, toured schools and ballets clubs as lecture-recitalist. Choreographer, Turkish State Opera, Ankara (1959–60); Glyndebourne Opera from 1959. His ballets include *El Amor Brujo* (1960), *St. George in Provence* (Western Theatre Ballet, 1960).

Hart, John, English dancer, ballet master, b. London, 1921; m. Ann Howard. Studied with Judith Espinosa. Won Adeline Genée Gold Medal of the Royal Academy of Dancing (1939). Joined Sadler's Wells (now Royal) Ballet (1938) and, except for service in the Royal Air Force in World War II (1942–47), has remained ever since, first as principal dancer, then as ballet master from 1955 and principal of ballet staff. He is currently assistant director of the company. Has the distinction of having danced Siegfried (full-length *Swan Lake*), Prince Florimund (*The Sleeping Beauty*), Albrecht (*Giselle*), and Franz (*Coppélia*) before he was twenty, this being an essential forcing because of the loss of male dancers to war service at that time. His creations included the Governor (*The Three-Cornered Hat,* staged for Sadler's Wells Ballet), Laertes (*Hamlet*), a Brother (*Comus*), Orion (*Sylvia*); also danced leads in *Symphonic Variations* and *Scènes de Ballet,* White Skater (*Les Patineurs*), the Official (*Miracle in the Gorbals*), and many others. Published a book of photographs, *Ballet and Camera* (1956). His position as assistant director assumed greater importance on the retirement of Dame Ninette de Valois, Dec. 1963.

Hartong, Corrie, Dutch dancer, teacher and choreographer, b. Rotterdam, 1906. Studied dance at the Mary Wigman School in Dresden, Germany. Began teaching in Chemnitz (1927), then headed the Wigman school in Magdeburg. Returned to Holland (1931) and founded the Rotterdamse Dansschool in association with Gertrud Leistikow. The school under her direction became part of the Conservatory of Music (1935). At the same time she continued dancing, staging, and lecturing. In 1954 she established the Rotterdamse Dansacademie. She is taking part in activities for furthering the dance in Holland as a member of several committees and of the Arts Council of the Dutch Government. Her books include *Danskunst* (Introduction to the theory and practice of the dance) and *Mijn Balletboek* (for children). Her major choreographic works include *Aubade* (Poulenc), *Ballade* (Oscar van Hemel), *Danse sacrée et danse profane* (Debussy), *Valses Nobles et Sentimentales* (Ravel), *The Concert* (Jurriaan Andriessen).

Harvard Theatre Collection, housed in the Houghton Library, Harvard Univ., Cambridge, Mass., possesses a great number of pictorial material, scores, books, manuscripts, and letters pertaining to the dance. The collection is especially strong in 18th and 19th century material. The curator of the collection (1940–60) was Dr. William Bird Van Lennep, who was largely responsible for the growth and quality of the collection. The present curator is Helen Willard.

Haskell, Arnold Lionel, English writer, critic, educator, b. London, 1903. Educated at Westminster School and Cambridge Univ. (M.A.). Co-founder of Camargo Society 1930; a director of Ballet Club; founder of plan for Vic-Wells (later Sadler's Wells, now Royal) Ballet School (1936); dance critic for *Daily Telegraph* (1935–38) and other publications; director of Sadler's Wells (now Royal) Ballet School since 1947 when full academic training was added to its dance curriculum. Retired Jan. 1, 1965, and left London to settle in Bath. On his retirement was named Honorary Director of the Royal Ballet School. Among his many books about the dance are: *Some Studies in Ballet* (1928), *Balletomania* (1934), *Diaghilev* (1935), *Prelude to Ballet* (1936), *Balletomane's Scrapbook* (1936), *Dancing Round the World* (1937), *Ballet Panorama* (1938), *Ballet, a Complete Guide to Appreciation* (1938), *Balletomane's Album* (1939), *Waltzing Matilda; A Background to Australia* (1940), *The National Ballet* (1943), *The Making of a Dancer* (1946), *In His True Centre* (his autobiography; 1951), *The Russian Genius in Ballet* (1963). Editor of *Ballet Annual* since 1947. Received the Legion of Honor (1951); C.B.E. (Commander of the Order of the British Empire, 1954). Member of Critics' Circle, London.

Arnold L. Haskell, as director of the Royal Ballet School (ca. *1961*).

Haunted Ballroom, The. Ballet in 2 scenes; chor.: Ninette de Valois; commissioned music and book: Geoffrey Toye; décor: Motley. First prod.: Vic-Wells (later Sadler's Wells, now Royal) Ballet, Apr. 3, 1934, with Alicia Markova (Alicia), Ursula Moreton (Ursula), Beatrice Appleyard (Beatrice), Robert Helpmann (Master of Tregennis), Freda Bamford (The Young Master), William Chappell (The Stranger Player). This was Helpmann's first leading role and established him as England's first native premier danseur. The Young Master of Tregennis was also Margot Fonteyn's first important (though non-dancing) role which she took over from Freda Bamford after the first season. Although it has not been performed for many years it was an important ballet in the early development of the company which was destined to become the Royal Ballet. The story tells of the mysterious ballroom in which all the Masters of Tregennis are destined to dance themselves to death when their hour comes. The young girls of the prologue become the ghostly dancers who compel the Master to his doom. The Young Master, coming in search of his father, finds him lying dead and foresees his own inevitable end.

Hawaiian (Hula) Dance.

BY LA MERI.

Like many ancient dances, the hula can be traced only through Hawaiian legend. One legend says that a male and a female god arrived in the islands from the South Seas. The gods danced and, when the male of the pair vanished, the female (Lakawahine) remained to dance alone. Her worshippers adopted her dance, the hula. Another legend has it that two male gods were the sole inventors and practitioners of the hula. When Hiaka, sister of the volcano goddess Pele, learned the hula from Laka, the dance became open to women and was expressive of religious devotion.

Thus Hawaiian dance was born as a form of worship, a sacred thing. The morai or place of worship was built in the form of a square enclosed by the small temples (halua). The open space in the center, called the wailua, was the place where the hulas were performed. During the maka hiki or festival time, leaving the morai was *kapu* (taboo). At the first kuaha (altar) of Laka, the protector of the hula art, special prayers were offered up for inspiration and proficiency in rhythmic movement. The first mele (chant) was an invocation chanted during the donning of the hula costume.

Until fairly recently the major part of the education of the young Hawaiian was the mastery of the mele and hula. Their cultural importance cannot be overestimated, for since there is no Hawaiian written language, the songs and dances are regarded as a valuable repository of history and customs. Being respected as a worship and an art, not regarded as an entertainment for performer or beholder, they were preserved until the fall of the monarchy in Jan., 1893, by the court, and the performers selected from the loveliest of the native youths and maidens. Today there is a Conservatory of Hawaiian Music and Dancing in Honolulu established to preserve this folk expression.

The word "hula" simply means dance and is applicable to all Hawaiian forms of that art. Since priest and warrior dance no more, we have come to associate hula exclusively with the lyric dances of the olapa (dancer). In ancient times the women performed the hula sitting on their heels. (Samoans sit cross-legged; Tahitians on the heels with the opposite knee up.) In this sitting position the olapa mimed, with sinuous gestures, the meaning of the accompanying mele. It was not until the end of the nineteenth century that the missionary ship The Morning Star arrived in Hawaii with grass skirts from Tahiti. With the donning of this new garment, the olapa created the first standing hula, moving softly eight steps forward and eight steps backward with a gentle flow in the hips. Today the hip movements are more accentuated and the footsteps more varied, but the main interest and beauty of the hula is still in the undulating gestures of the hands and arms.

The hip movements which, until recently, have been so misrepresented and misunderstood by the foreigner, are merely a natural, rhythmic accompaniment to the gestures. The hip movements are: (1) hooleilei, the up-beat swing from side to side; (2) ami, the circular swing; and (3) ami-poipoi, the figure eight movement. It is said that all the hip movements were imported from Tahiti with the first grass skirts, but the Hawaiian performs them in a slower tempo and with a sinuous grace which is lacking in the staccato speed of the Tahitian. Of the noho hulas (sitting-down dances) still extant, the most notable are those performed with the ipu (large gourd), the puili (bamboo wands), the ili-ili (pebbles), and the uli-uli (small, feathered gourds which are also used in standing hulas). Eulogy hulas (kui) were among the first of the standing dances. It is believed that *Liliu E,* dedicated to Queen Lilioukalani, was the first of these, and we know there was a whole drama dedicated to Pele, fire goddess of Mauna Loa. There were also animal dances, therapy dances, great warrior dances and game hulas.

In the beginning the dance was an accompaniment to the music, the chant being rendered by voices in homophonic chorus, polyphony later being adopted from Christian hymns. Ancient instruments which accompanied the voices were the noseflute, the conch-shell trumpet, gourds, rattles, bamboo sticks, pebbles and drums. The ukelele and the guitar are imported instruments, the former Portuguese in origin. The guitar was brought in from Spain, but is strung, tuned and played in a manner entirely local. The rhythm of Hawaiian music is regular, unbroken by accelerando or diminuendo. The tempo, usually in a 4/4 beat, may be very fast or quite slow; the musicians are generally dancers grown too old to be agile. The true hula is naive, bucolic, and of unparalleled grace. It is a dance of great innocence and joy for, whatever else may have been forgotten, it has kept intact the motivation of its being, the idyllic religion of children of Nature.

Hawkins, Erick, contemporary American modern dancer, b. Trinidad, Colo. Began his career as a ballet dancer, having studied at the School of American Ballet. Member of the American Ballet (1935–37) and Ballet Caravan (1936–39). In 1938 he joined the Martha Graham company as guest artist, but remained to become leading dancer and danced with the company until 1951. Soon after he organized his own small group to pursue an avant-garde policy, working in close association with composer-pianist Lucia Dlugoszewski. Nearly all of his ballets are abstract compositions, despite elaborate costuming, and for the spectator bear little relation to their rather esoteric titles. His better-known works are entitled *Sudden Snake-Bird, inner feet of a summer fly, 8 Clear Places, Early Floating, Here and Now with Watchers.* In 1963 his group, consisting of himself, Miss Dlugoszewski and three girl dancers, appeared in Paris as part of the annual Théâtre des Nations Festival.

Haydée, Marcia (Marcia Pereira da Silva), contemporary Brazilian dancer, b. Niteroi, Brazil. Studied dance under Yvonne Gama e Silva, Yuco Lindberg,

Erick Hawkins, American dancer-choreographer, in his work Early Floating.

Vaslav Veltchek. Made her professional debut with Ballet Madeleine Rosay, in Quitandinha, Petropolis (1953). Joined Teatro Municipal, Rio de Janeiro, the same year. Received a scholarship to Sadler's Wells Ballet School, London (1954–55). Joined Grand Ballet du Marquis de Cuevas (1957), rising to rank of soloist. Left in 1961 to become ballerina of Stuttgart Opera Ballet, where she created the role of Juliet in John Cranko's *Romeo and Juliet* (1963), also dancing the role as guest artist when Cranko staged it for National Ballet of Canada (1964). She also dances Odette-Odile in Cranko's version of the full-length *Swan Lake.*

Hayden, Melissa (Mildred Herman), American ballerina, b. Toronto, Canada, 1923. Began her dance studies with Boris Volkov in Toronto at age twelve. At seven-

Melissa Hayden, ballerina of the N.Y. City Ballet as Titania, partnered by Edward Villella as Oberon, in Balanchine's ballet A Midsummer Night's Dream.

teen went to N.Y. to continue her studies with Anatole Vilzak and Ludmila Shollar, almost simultaneously finding her first job as a member of Radio City Music Hall corps de ballet. Joined Ballet (now American Ballet) Theatre (1945), dancing Bird (*Peter and the Wolf*), pas de deux (*Interplay*), Chrisothemis (*Helen of Troy*), Page (*Bluebeard*), and others; then danced a season with Ballet Alicia Alonso. Joined New York City Ballet (1950) and, apart from a return to American Ballet Theatre (1953–55) and various guest appearances with Ruth Page's Chicago Opera Ballet, has been with that company ever since. She has a dazzling, virtuoso technique and great dramatic ability which gives her an enormous range of roles. Some of her most important creations are Profane Love (*Illuminations*), Clorinda (*The Duel*), Young Girl (*The Still Point*), title role (*Medea*), pas de trois and variation (*Agon*), one of the five ballerinas (*Caracole*—later known as *Divertimento No. 15*), pas de deux (*Stars and Stripes*), Titania (*A Midsummer Night's Dream*), and others, in addition to many other ballets including *Age of Anxiety, Allegro Brillante, Sylvia Pas de Deux, Pas de Trois* (*Minkus*), 1st movement (*Symphony in C*), 2nd movement (*Western Symphony*). She has made many television appearances, dancing with André Eglevsky on the "Kate Smith Show" as early as 1952, when ballet was little known in that medium. Again with Eglevsky danced in Charles Chaplin film *Limelight* (1952). Awarded the Albert Einstein Award for Woman of Achievement of the Year (1962). She is on the committee of the Ford Foundation to choose dance scholarship students. Guest artist with Royal Ballet (May–June, 1963), dancing *Flower Festival at Genzano* pas de deux, *La Fille Mal Gardée, Sylvia, Don Quixote* pas de deux, in all partnered by Flemming Flindt. Guest artist with Cullberg Ballet, Stockholm, March 1967.

Hays, David, American stage designer, b. New York City, 1930. Graduated from Harvard Univ. (1952); to London on a Fulbright scholarship (1952–53); Yale Drama School (1953–54); M.F.A., Boston Univ. (1954–55). Has designed décor for many New York City Ballet productions, including *Pastorale, Stars and Stripes, Episodes, Native Dancers, Liebeslieder Walzer, Monumentum pro Gesualdo, Electronics, A Midsummer Night's Dream, Bugaku, Arcade,* and others. Designed operas for the Metropolitan Opera, New York City Opera, etc., and *A Midsummer Night's Dream* and *A Winter's Tale* for Shakespeare Festival, Stratford, Conn. His designs for plays include *Long Day's Journey Into Night, Tenth Man, All the Way Home, No Strings* (for which he won the New York Drama Critics' Award for Best Designer, 1961–62); also off-Broadway productions of *The Iceman Cometh, The Quare Fellow* and *The Balcony,* his work winning two OBIE (Off-Broadway) awards.

Haythorne, Harry, Australian dancer and ballet master, b. Adelaide, 1926. Member, England's Metropolitan Ballet (1949); International Ballet (1950–51). Ballet master, London Coliseum (1955); Drury Lane Theatre (1956); Leonide Massine's Ballets Européens (1960); Walter Gore's London Ballets (1962–63). Created an Ugly Sister in the Vaslav Orlikovsky-Raymundo de Larrain *Cinderella* (International Dance Festival, Théâtre des Champs-Elysées, Paris, Dec. 4, 1963). Has notated in Labanotation George Balanchine's ballets in Europe; also been chairman of British Dance Notation Society.

Hazana (Achievement). Ballet in 1 act; chor. and libretto: Norman Morrice; music: Carlos Surinach (from *Tientos* and *Doppio Concertino*); décor: Ralph Koltai. First prod.: Ballet Rambert, Sadler's Wells Theatre, London, May 25, 1959, with John Chesworth (The Husband), June Sandbrook (His Daughter), Gillian Martlew (His Wife). Overcoming terrible obstacles, a cross is raised for a religious festival in a South American village.

H'Doubler, Margaret N., outstanding American dance educator, b. Beloit, Kan., 1889; m. Prof. Wayne L. Claxton, Director of Arts Dept., Wayne State Univ., Detroit, 1934. Educated in Warren, Ill.; began graduate work in teaching at Univ. of Wisconsin, Madison, Wis. Given Assistant Professorship in Physical Education at Univ. of Wisconsin and later promoted to Associate Professor. In 1916 came to N.Y. to work at Teachers College at Columbia Univ. Dr. Blanche Trilling, at the time Director of the Dept. of Physical Education at the College, suggested that Miss H'Doubler study dance. Following the suggestion she began to work with Gertrude Colby and Bird Larson and continued to study with Porter Beegle, Alys Bentley, and at the Isadora Duncan School in N.Y. Fourteen months later she returned to the Univ. of Wisconsin, where she began to teach dance as part of the physical education program. Her new method of teaching was well received by teachers and students alike. As a result of her work dance became an integral part of the physical education curriculum. In her teaching dance she advocated creativity rather than strict discipline of technique. Her work in initiating and developing the idea of college dance clubs, which she named Orchesis in 1918, led to further substantially the interest in dance in universities and colleges throughout the U.S. Miss H'Doubler expressed her philosophy of dance and dance education in her book, *Dance, a Creative Expression* (N.Y., 1940; Madison, Wis., 1957). Through her work with teachers and, over the years, with thousands of students, she exerted a great influence on dance in education. She retired from active teaching in 1959.

Hear Ye! Hear Ye! Ballet in 1 act; chor.: Ruth Page; music: Aaron Copland; book: Ruth Page and Nicholas Remisoff; décor: Nicholas Remisoff. First prod.: Ruth Page Ballet Co., Chicago Opera House, Chicago, Nov. 30, 1934 with Ruth Page and Bentley Stone in leading parts. A murder is committed in a night club in the presence of several guests. Some of the guests dance out their versions for the judge, the versions little agreeing among themselves.

Heart of the Hills, The. Ballet in 5 scenes; chor.: Vakhtang Chabukiani; music: André Balanchivadze; book: G. Leonidze and Nicholas Volkov; décor: S. Virsaladze. First prod.: Kirov Theatre, Leningrad, 1938, with Tatiana Vecheslova and Vakhtang Chabukiani in leading parts. Based on an episode in Georgian history (a revolt because of high taxes in the feudal realm of Eristav), the ballet contains many authentic folk dances of Georgia and neighboring states.

Heaton, Anne, English dancer, b. Rawalpindi, India, 1930; m. John Field. Studied with Janet Cranmore, Birmingham (1937–43), then at Sadler's Wells (now Royal) Ballet School. Soloist with Sadler's Wells Theatre Ballet from its inception (1945), creating Girl (*Mardi Gras*), Lover (*Khadra*), Yellow Girl (*Assembly Ball*), and dancing many other roles; transferred to Sadler's Wells Ballet (1948) becoming soloist, and creating Doll (*A Mirror for Witches*), The Woman (*The Burrow*), the Wife (*The Invitation*), and others; also danced in *Les Sylphides, Giselle* (title role). Resigned from the Royal Ballet (1959), due to arthritis in the foot, but danced occasionally as guest artist until end of 1962. Also principal dancer in the pantomime *Aladdin,* London Coliseum (1959).

Heckroth, Hein, German stage designer. Studied in Düsseldorf, Munich, and Paris. A collaborator of Kurt Jooss for whose company he designed the décor, costumes, and masks for *The Big City* (1926) and *The Green Table* (1932), as well as for *The Prodigal Son, The Seven Heroes,* and others. Also designed the décor for the films *The Red Shoes* (1948) and *The Tales of Hoffmann* (1952). Currently staff designer for the municipal theatres of Frankfurt where he has designed several ballets for Walter Gore and Tatiana Gsovska, most notably *Eaters of Darkness.*

Hedeby, Kerstin, Swedish painter and stage designer, b. Linköping, 1926. Entered Swedish Academy of Arts in 1948. Designed décor for ballet, opera and drama in the Malmö City Theatre and Royal Theatre, Stockholm, working mainly for Ingmar Bergman. Her most recent work was for the Birgit Cullberg ballets *The Lady from the Sea* and *Odysseus.*

Heinel, Anne (1753–1808), ballerina of the Stuttgart Theatre and the Paris Opéra; m. Gaetan Vestris. She was a great virtuoso and is credited with introducing the multiple pirouette.

Heinrich, Annemarie (Ana Maria Erna Erica Heinrich de Sol), Latin American dance photographer, b. Darmstadt, Germany, 1912. No North American or European dancer ever returns from Argentina without a portfolio of photographs signed "Annemarie Heinrich." In addition to photographing dancers living in or visiting Buenos Aires, she has exhibited in photographic salons in Argentina, Brazil, Milan (Italy), and other countries. In 1960 she was named Argentine photographer to have had the greatest number of photographs accepted at foreign exhibitions. She is Permanent Member of the Jury of Federacion Argentina de Fotografia. In 1962 began working on a definitive book of ballet photographs, *Ballet En La Argentina.*

Heinrich, Helga, German dancer, b. Munich, 1933. Studied with Pino Mlakar, Marcel Luipart, Victor Gsovsky, Vaslav Orlikovsky. Ballerina of the Classic Russian Ballet of Orlikovsky, dancing all classic ballets.

Held, Helga, German dancer, b. Berlin, 1935. Studied with Lotte Sevelin, Gustav Blank, Tatiana Gsovska, Erich Walter. Soloist of the Wuppertal Opera Ballet (1953–60); at Cologne since 1960. Classic ballerina dancing principal roles of the classic and modern repertoire.

Helen of Troy. Ballet in prologue and 3 scenes; chor.: David Lichine; music: Jacques Offenbach (*La Belle Hélène*); arr. by Antal Dorati; book: David Lichine and Antal Dorati; décor: Marcel Vertès. The ballet was begun by Michel Fokine in Mexico and was close to being completed, when Fokine was taken ill and had to return to N.Y. Lichine was then commissioned to restage the ballet. According to Fokine, all that was necessary to complete the ballet were some rehearsals during which a few changes could be made. To the deep regret of everyone concerned Fokine died Aug. 22, 1942, without a chance to complete his work. The ballet was first produced by Ballet Theatre, Nov. 29, 1942, Detroit, Mich., with the following dancers in the leading parts: Irina Baronova (Helen), André Eglevsky (Paris), Simon Semenov (Menelaus), Jerome Robbins (Hermes), Jean Hunt (Lamb), Nicolas Orloff (Faun), Sono Osato (Aphrodite), Rosella Hightower (Hera), Lucia Chase (Pallas Athena). First presented in New York Apr. 3, 1943 at the Metropolitan Opera House with Vera Zorina in the title role. George Balanchine restaged a few of her dances. Subsequently Maria Karnilova, Nana Gollner, Diana Adams, Mary Ellen Moylan, Sonia Arova have all danced the title role. The plot of the ballet follows the general line of the Offenbach operetta, omitting some of the details, but preserving the important highlights: the Judgment of Paris, the beautiful Helen, the henpecked Menelaus, etc. It was a delightful ballet-bouffe, which regrettably has not been performed for a long time and would need to be re-choreographed.

Robert Helpmann in the principal role of the Stranger in his ballet Miracle in the Gorbals.

Helena, Vera (Vera Helen Favilla), Brazilian dance critic, b. Rio de Janeiro. Began ballet studies under Yuco Lindberg at Teatro Municipal ballet school; later studied with Carlos Leite at Ballet da Juventude, Vaslav Veltchek, Madeleine Rosay, Maryla Gremo, Juliana Yenakieva. Began as ballet critic in 1950 in Government Broadcasting (Radio Roquete Pinto); later became writer on ballet in several local magazines, such as *Queria* and *Aonde Vamos?* Currently has her own ballet program on Radio Roquete Pinto with international dance news, interviews, criticism, and comments.

Hellerau and Hellerau-Laxenburg. See DALCROZE.

Helpmann, Robert, premier danseur, choreographer, actor and director, b. Mount Gambier, South Australia, 1909. Began his dance training with Anna Pavlova company when it was in Australia; danced in Australia under management of J. C. Williamson (1926–30). Went to England (1933) and became member of Vic-Wells (later Sadler's Wells, now Royal) Ballet corps de ballet while continuing his studies in the company's school. Premier danseur, Sadler's Wells Ballet from 1934 until his resignation in 1950. His personality and sense of the stage attracted attention from the beginning and as early as 1933 he danced Satan in *Job*. His first important creation was the Master of Tregennis (*The*

Haunted Ballroom) (1934), followed by Red King (*Checkmate*), Mr. O'Reilly (*The Prospect Before Us*), Orpheus (Ninette de Valois' *Orpheus and Eurydice*), Poet (*Apparitions*), Young Man (*Nocturne*), Bridegroom (*A Wedding Bouquet*), White Skater (*Les Patineurs*), Leader, Children of Darkness (*Dante Sonata*), title role (*The Wanderer*), St. George (*The Quest*), The Tenor (*Les Sirènes*); title roles, *Don Juan* and *Don Quixote* (Ninette de Valois' version) and others. Choreographed and danced the title roles in *Comus, Hamlet,* and *Adam Zero;* danced The Stranger in his ballet *Miracle in the Gorbals,* and choreographed *The Birds* (1942). He also danced Siegfried (*Swan Lake*), Albrecht (*Giselle*), Sugar Plum Fairy's Cavalier (*The Nutcracker*), Franz and a hugely comical Dr. Coppelius (*Coppélia*), *Les Sylphides, Façade* and others. He created Prince Florimund in the first Sadler's Wells production of *The Sleeping Beauty* (1939) and was both its Florimund and Carabosse when this ballet re-opened the Royal Opera House, Covent Garden (1946). During his years with the Sadler's Wells Ballet he took occasional leaves of absence to appear in the theatre as an actor and revue artist. He played Oberon opposite Vivien Leigh in *A Midsummer Night's Dream* at the Old Vic Theatre, and repeated this role opposite Moira Shearer (when he was also choreographer) for the production which S. Hurok brought to the Metropolitan Opera House and a coast-to-coast tour of the U.S. (1954). He also played *Hamlet* (alternating with Paul Scofield) at the Shakespeare Memorial Theatre, Stratford-on-Avon, and then at the New Theatre, London. Also appeared in a number of films, notably *The Red Shoes* (1948) and *The Tales of Hoffmann* (1950). Since leaving Sadler's Wells Ballet he has returned from time to time as guest artist, both with Sadler's Wells Theatre Ballet (revival of *The Prospect Before Us,* 1951) and the Royal Ballet, touring his native Australia with the company (1958–59). Director and choreographer of the opera *Le Coq d'Or,* Royal Opera House, Covent Garden (1954, 1956, 1958–59). Completed the staging of the Ballet International du Marquis de Cuevas' production of *The Sleeping Beauty* when Bronislava Nijinska left after setting the choreography (1960). Returned to Royal Ballet to choreograph *Electra* (premièred Mar. 26, 1963) and (with Frederick Ashton) staged the new production of *Swan Lake* (Dec. 12, 1963). Choreographed in 1964–65 two ballets for the Australian Ballet: *The Display,* based on a legend about the Australian native lyrebird (a symbol of eroticism) to a score by Malcolm Williamson; and *Yugen,* based on a Japanese legend, to a score by Yuzo Toyama. As guest artist of the Royal Ballet served as Narrator for the revival of *A Wedding Bouquet* (1965). In the revival of Ashton's *Cinderella* for the same company (1965) he appeared as one of the stepsisters, with the choreographer appearing as the other (as they had done in the original production of the ballet in 1948). Helpmann has directed and acted in many plays for the Old Vic and other managements. Received the Order of the Star of the North (Sweden, 1954), Order of the Cedar of Lebanon (1957), and Queen Elizabeth II Coronation Award of the Royal Academy of Dancing (1961); was made a Commander of the Order of the British Empire (C.B.E.) by Queen Elizabeth II (1964). His name will always be associated with the early history of the Sadler's Wells Ballet, and especially with the war years when, with the burden of almost the entire male repertoire upon him, he brought an unflagging zest to every performance.

Hennessy, Christine, American dancer, b. Providence, R.I., 1936. Studied with Maria Swoboda at Ballet Russe de Monte Carlo School of Ballet, N.Y. Danced with that company for two years, then became ballerina at Bremen State Opera House, Germany (1956). The following year toured Germany and Austria with American Concert Ballet; became second ballerina of American Festival Ballet (1958); made a four-ballet television series for German, Swiss, and Austrian television (1959). The same year was promoted to first ballerina of American Festival Ballet, a position she continues to hold. Her repertoire includes *Swan Lake* (Act 2), *Don Quixote* and *Black Swan* pas de deux, Walter Gore's *Eaters of Darkness,* Job Sanders' *Bachianas Brasileiras,* and others.

Henry Street Settlement Playhouse, built in 1915 by the Lewisohn sisters as the original Neighborhood Playhouse and School of the Theatre. Among the famous artists of the day who appeared there were Isadora Duncan, Sarah Bernhardt, Eleonora Duse. When the Neighborhood Playhouse moved to East 54th Street (1927), Herman Gettner and Louis Abrams took the theatre over and donated the building to the Henry Street Settlement. Helen Hall, director of the Settlement, invited Alwin Nikolais to become director of the theatre and head of the dance school (1948) with Betty Young as co-director on the administrative side. Henry Street Settlement maintains the theatre building and underwrites the school which offers many scholarships to talented students who cannot afford even the modest fees. Nikolais has built up the performing side so that the theatre, while continuing to present many performances for children, has become famous as the home of the Nikolais company and of the experimental works they perform.

Henze, Hans Werner, German composer, b. 1926. Studied at the Musikhochschule (Musical College), Braunschweig; was a pupil of Fortner and Leibowitz. His dance compositions include *Variations* (1948), *Jack Pudding* (1949), *Rosa Silber* and *Labyrinth* (1950), *The Sleeping Princess* (after Tchaikovsky) (1951), *Pas d'Action* and *The Idiot* (the latter a ballet pantomime for Tatiana Gsovska) (1952), *Dance Marathon* (1957), *Ondine* (for the Royal Ballet, London, 1959). Was artistic director of the ballet at the Hessisches Staatstheater, Wiesbaden (1949–52).

Herbertt, Stanley, dancer, choreographer, teacher, b. Chicago, Ill., 1919. Bachelor of Education, Chicago Teachers College (1942). Studied dance with Edna McRae, Nathan Vizonsky in Chicago; Antony Tudor, Edward Caton, Elizabeth Anderson-Ivantzova, N.Y. Directed Maltz Marionette Troupe, Chicago (1935–36); member, Polish Ballet (1940–41); also with Ruth Page's Chicago Opera Ballet, Littlefield Ballet, San Carlo Opera Ballet before joining Ballet (now American Ballet) Theatre (1943–47), dancing the following character roles: Hilarion (*Giselle*), von Rothbart (*Swan Lake*), Popolini, King Bobiche (*Bluebeard*), Charlatan (*Petrouchka*), Silenus (*Undertow*), and others. In *Carousel* touring company (1947–48), *Inside U.S.A.* (1948). Teaching in St. Louis, Mo. since 1951, establishing his own company incorporated in 1958 as St. Louis Civic Ballet. Has created many ballets for this group and for television and commercial shows. Also teaches for various teachers' organizations.

Here and Now with Watchers. Modern dance work; chor.: Erick Hawkins; music: Lucia Dlugoszewski; décor: Ralph Dorazio. First prod.: Hunter College Playhouse, N.Y., Nov. 24, 1957, with Erick Hawkins and Nancy Lang. A sequence of dances for either or both dancers with titles such as i. now: THE, iii. (vulnerable male is), or iv. now HERE MADE OF FALLING (and my body).

Hering, Doris, writer, critic, lecturer, b. New York City. B.A. (cum laude, Phi Beta Kappa) Hunter College; scholarship for M.A. in Romance Languages, Fordham Univ. Associate editor, critic, Regional Ballet editor, *Dance Magazine* (See PERIODICALS, DANCE, U.S.). Author *Dance* *in America* (for U.S. Dept. of State, 1950). Editor of *25 Years of American Dance* (1950). Contributes to periodicals, encyclopedias, and annuals.

Hernandez, Amalia, contemporary Mexican dancer, teacher, choreographer, company director, b. Mexico City. Studied ballet and modern dance and was trained in Spanish dance by Argentinita, but has specialized in the study of the dances and folklore of Mexico. In the mid-1940's began teaching modern dance at the Instituto Nacional de Bellas Artes (National Institute of Fine Arts), and in 1952 formed a small group to present Mexican folklore programs on television. This original group has grown through the years into Mexico's national company, Ballet Folklorico of Mexico. Amalia Hernandez choreographs the entire repertoire which is based on authentic source material.

Herodiade. Modern dance work; chor.: Martha Graham; music: Paul Hindemith; décor and artistic collaboration: Isamu Noguchi; costumes: Edythe Gilfond. Both music and choreography were commissioned by the Elizabeth Sprague Coolidge Foundation and the first performances (under the title *Mirror Before Me*) were given Oct. 28 and 30, 1944 in the Library of Congress, Washington, D.C., as part of the Coolidge Chamber Music Festival, with Martha Graham (Herodiade), May O'Donnell (Attendant); N.Y. première: National Theatre, May 15, 1945. Very typical of the great symbolical works of Graham at that period, Herodiade is perhaps Everywoman gazing into a mirror which pitilessly reveals to her both her present and her future. She takes up the burden of what must come. On Mar. 15 and 16, 1963, Ethel Winter and Linda Hodes, under the direction of Martha Graham, re-created the two roles for performances at Juilliard Concert Hall, N.Y., conducted by Paul Hindemith.

Hertel, Peter Ludwig (1817–1899). One of a family of musicians of the same surname. He composed the ballet score for *La Fille Mal Gardée* in current use, except by the Royal Ballet in its Frederick Ashton production.

Herzberg, Tana, contemporary German dancer, b. Berlin. Studied under Gustav Blank, Tatiana Gsovska. Since 1951 ballerina of the Berlin Municipal (now German) Opera. Among her roles are Bellastriga (*Abraxas*), Bianca (*The Moor of Venice*), Clytemnestra (*Black Sun*), and *Improvisations to Mallarmé* (music: Pierre Boulez).

Hesitation, in ballroom dancing the holding of a position for one or two counts of music; used most often in waltzes; said to have been introduced by Vernon and Irene Castle.

High Dancer. See EUKINETICS.

Highland Fling, dance of the Scottish Highlands, in 4/4 time, highly formalized, symbolizing victory. This and the Sword Dance are probably the most representative of the dances of Scotland.

Hightower, Rosella, American ballerina, b. Ardmore, Okla., 1920. First studied dance under Dorothy Perkins, Kansas City, Mo. Member, Ballet Russe de Monte Carlo (1938–41); soloist and later ballerina, Ballet Theatre (1941–45), Ballet Russe Highlights of Leonide Massine (1945–46), Original Ballet Russe (1945–46), dancing *Giselle* (title role), *Sebastian, Constantia, Black Swan* pas de deux. Joined Nouveau Ballet de Monte Carlo (1947) when it was being taken over by the Marquis de Cuevas and became first Grand Ballet de Monte Carlo and then Grand Ballet du Marquis de Cuevas. Except for short guest seasons with American Ballet Theatre in U.S. and Europe, she remained first ballerina of the Marquis' company until his death (1961).

Rosella Hightower in the variation from the Don Quixote *pas de deux.*

Her enormous repertoire included the great classic roles and *Piège de Lumière, Ines de Castro, Rondo Capriccioso, La Sylphide* (Bournonville version staged by Harald Lander for the Grand Ballet). She created Aurora in the Grand Ballet's full-length version of *The Sleeping Beauty* (1960). For almost fifteen years, she toured all over the world with the Marquis' company. She was his favorite dancer and also one of the most popular ballerinas in continental Europe, her brilliant virtuosity and striking musicality bringing her triumphs on Parisian and most European stages. After the death of the Marquis, she retired from the company, making only guest appearances from time to time. The success of the three performances she gave in Paris in Jan., 1962 with Sonia Arova, Erik Bruhn, and Rudolf Nureyev attested to her immense popularity. She now has a ballet studio in Cannes, but still dances occasionally, including a guest appearance with Les Grands Ballets Canadiens (Oct. 14–16, 1963) in Toronto, and a tour with a group of French dancers in North Africa and South America (1964). She also choreographed a few ballets: *Henry VIII* for the Markova-Dolin company (1949), *Pleasuredrome* (Metropolitan Ballet, England, 1949), *Salomé* (1950), *Scaramouche* (1951) for Grand Ballet du Marquis de Cuevas. She married French designer Jean Robier and has a daughter, born in the U.S. (1955).

Hilarides, Marianna (née Boedijn), Dutch dancer, b. 1933. Danced with Nederlands Ballet and Nederlands Dans Theater and has been a soloist with Het Nationaal Ballet since 1962, dancing leading parts in the divertissement from *The Sleeping Beauty,* Pas des Fiancées in *Swan Lake, Firebird, Giselle, Night Shadow, Francesca da Rimini, Rencontre, Les Mirages, Shirah* (Pearl Lang). Won third prize in the competition for ballet dancers, Rio de Janeiro (1961).

Hill, Margaret, English dancer, b. Ilford, Essex, 1924, m. Michael Boulton. Studied at Ballet Rambert School, entering the company 1944 and becoming soloist, then principal dancer, dancing most of the company's repertoire and being an outstanding Queen of the Wilis (*Giselle*). Soloist, Sadler's Wells Theatre Ballet (1952), creating the Girl (*Solitaire*). Transferred to Royal Ballet as soloist, but resigned in 1959 and has now retired.

Hill, Martha, contemporary modern dance teacher and educator, b. East Palestine, Ohio. Studied music, Dalcroze eurythmics, ballet and modern dance. B.S. Teachers' College, Columbia Univ.; M.A. New York Univ. Member, Martha Graham company (1929–31). On the faculty of Kansas State Teachers' College, Univ. of Chicago; director of dance, Univ. of Oregon; faculty, Lincoln School of Teachers' College. Director, Bennington School of the Dance (1934–39), which became Bennington School of the Arts, where she continued until 1942. Director of Dance, New York Univ. (1930–51); chairman of dance and choreographer, Bennington College (1932–51). Founder, Connecticut College School of the Dance and American Dance Festival (1948). Has been director of the Dance Dept. of Juilliard School of Music since it was founded (1951). Member, Advisory Commission of School of Performing Arts, N.Y.; member, Dance Advisory panel of Cultural Exchange Program. Received the American Academy of Physical Education Award for services in dance education. At the 1965 commencement of Adelphi Univ., she was awarded an Honorary Doctorate of Humane Letters.

Hilverding, van Wewen, Franz (1710–1768), Austrian ballet master of Dutch extraction who worked in Vienna and in Stuttgart, Germany. Jean Georges Noverre followed him in his Stuttgart post and was influenced by him in the development of the ballet d'action. In 1758 Hilverding, as he was generally called, went to St. Petersburg, where he contributed to raising the standard of ballet. As a child, Emperor Paul I of Russia took dance lessons from Hilverding. In 1765 Hilverding returned to Vienna, exchanging places as it were with Gasparo Angiolini, who was leaving Vienna for St. Petersburg.

Hindemith, Paul (1895–1963), composer, b. Hanau, Germany; studied composition with Arnold Mendelssohn and Sekles; played viola in Frankfurt Opera orchestra (1915–23), after which period was active mainly as a composer of orchestral and chamber music, operas, oratorios and songs. Composer of music for *St. Francis* (Leonide Massine, 1938), *Herodiade* (Martha Graham, 1944), *Four Temperaments* (George Balanchine, 1946). Balanchine also used his *Symphonic Metamorphosis on Themes of Carl Maria von Weber* for the ballet *Metamorphoses* (1952). This music was originally written (but not used) for Massine's *Vienna—1814,* the choreographer deciding to use "straight" Weber. His dance-pantomime, *The Demon,* had its first U.S. performances Mar. 13 and 14, 1963, in Juilliard Concert Hall, choreographed by José Limón, and danced by the Limón company, with the composer conducting, only a few weeks before his death.

Hindu Dance.

BY LA MERI.

Hindu dance is more properly called Hindu Natya since the term Natya means both dance and drama and in the Eastern view the two arts are inseparable. Natya is something more than an art; it is a science. It is based on a profound knowledge of human anatomy, and its study follows natural lines so easily that the hard-working Westerner is often fooled into believing the art itself is an easy one.

As in all oriental dance forms, the upper body is considered far more important in dance expression than the lower body, but it is not to be supposed that technique of the legs is lacking. There are definite positions of the feet on the ground (boumya mandala pada) and in the air (akasa pada); movements of the legs on the ground (boumya cari) and in the air (akasa cari); gaits (gati), spiral movements (bhramari), and leaps (utplavana). Within these categories are embraced every possible movement of the legs and feet.

Technique of the upper body includes movements of the waist (kati), shoulders (kaksa), neck (griva), and arms (vartanam), in addition to the beautiful and complete gesture language of the hands (hasta-mudras). The facial expression (mukhaja) includes movements, with their meanings, of brows (bhru), eyes (dristi), nose (nasa), cheeks (ganda), mouth (asya), and chin (cibuka). Ground contacts, or movements of the feet on the ground (thattadavu), are greatly prized by the Hindu, the mastery of contra-tempo, or syncopating effect in beatings, being considered a feat of great virtuosity.

The science of Natya was born in the temple as a means of worship. It is believed that the hasta-mudras were first used to illustrate the chanting of the Rig-Vedic hymns, the oldest scripture of Hinduism. Legendary lore claims that Natya itself is the fifth Veda, having been formed by Brahma from parts of the four original Vedas. "Thus, recalling all the Vedas, the Blessed Brahma framed the Natya-Veda from the several parts of the four Vedas as desired. From the Rig-Veda he drew forth the words, from the Sana-Veda, which was a re-arrangement of the hymns from the Rig-Veda, the singing, from the Yajur-Veda, gesture, and from the Atharva-Veda the flavour." (First chapter of the *Natya Sastra of Bharata;* translated by Ananda Kentish Coomaraswamy.)

There is a sharp difference in style between the northern and southern dance. In the south, the dance is highly stylized. It is believed that Bharatra Natya dates back to 1500 B.C., although Bharata Muni, the compiler (author) of his scriptures of the dance did not write them until about 1000 A.D. Essentially the style has changed very little in the last 300 years. There are several outstanding schools or styles in south India; foremost among these being Bharata Natya and Kathakali.

BHARATA NATYA is the style practiced by the devadasis (temple dancers) since the beginning; it is found in and around Madras—the old Vigayanager Empire where once it flourished under royal protection. It is the dance represented in the bas-relief of the Natya Sabha (Hall of the Dance) in the Chidambaram Temple. The floor design, like the air design, is built along architectonic lines, and the whole has great strength and austerity, even in the lighter passages. The repertoire of the Bharata Natya dancer includes nrtta, nrtya, and nautch. Nrtta is an abstract dance of pure lyricism; nrtya is an expressive dance, pantomimic in content; nautch is a combination of song and dance. The song, in nautch, whether sung by the devadasi or a member of the orchestra, is illustrated with pantomimic gestures and laced with steps of pure dance. The typical Bharata Natya program continues without interval for some three hours. Dancers and musicians never leave the platform, which is primitively lit and without curtains.

Orissa is another secular dance form, similar to Bharata Natya, but more legato in movement. It is believed to be closer to the original style of the ancient Vigayanager Empire temple dancers.

KATHAKALI (literally, story-play) is the Passion play of Hinduism. Although its roots lie in the uncharted past, the present form dates from the close of the 16th century. Practiced in Malabar, it represents the whole gamut of great Hindu literature in its repertoire: the *Ramayana* (the story of Rama, the great epic of India), the *Mahabharata* (including the *Bhagavad Gita*), the *Gita of Jayadeva,* and many other plays. The actor-dancers are generally boys and young men. The costumes and make-up are highly stylized and include the characteristic great circular wooden headdresses, gaudily painted. The lower body is covered by wide crinoline-like white skirts. Make-up is applied in colors and designs to represent masks. Pantomimic gestures (hasta-mudras) are used lavishly, and are as highly stylized as the facial expressions (mukhaja). Body movements are descriptive; and traditional dances appear in every play. The plays are presented at night on an outdoor platform without scenic effects. The orchestra, consisting mostly of ear-splitting percussives, sits across the back of the stage, sometimes behind a small curtain. The traditional lighting is a pot of burning butter.

Female dancers in the Kathakali play perform in a style called Mohini Attam, which is as expressive, but far less violent than the male technique. The name derives from Vishnu's incarnation as the dancer Mohini.

In the north the outstanding schools are the Kathak, Manipuri, and the popular dances of the Nautch-Wali.

The KATHAK dance was originally practiced by a group of Brahmin priests called Kathaks. These dancers told stories of their faith and illustrated them with pantomime and dances. The Kathak dance technique is divided into gaths and torahs. The torahs are passages of thattadavu—complicated, lively, and strong—set to bolos, or sentences of rhythm which the dancer gives by means of spoken syllables to the tabla-wallah (drummer). The gaths are pantomimic passages employed by the dancer as periods of rest from the torahs. The gaths depict with a few simple mudras such everyday actions as kite-flying or anecdotes about the gods—such as Krishna's dalliance with the gopis, the milk-maids who always accompany him. Kathak dance, traditionally executed, is spontaneously created. A complete artistic understanding between dancer and drummer makes this possible. Rhythmic passages of hands, brow, and neck are often used by women protagonists of the art. Women generally wear saris; men, wide-skirted coats (achkans) and round caps, a costume presumably of Persian origin. The dance itself, intended as entertainment, is designed to be performed with the spectators seated on all sides—a floor-show dance—as compared to the South Indian forms, which are essentially stage dances, choreographed for spectators on one or three sides and at a lower level.

As performed today, the feminine protagonist of Kathak uses much nritya. In the 19th century the priest Prakash Kathak annotated some three hundred and sixty gats. Of these an estimated twenty-odd are presently in use. There are eleven types of music fit for nritya.

Male dancers of Kathak lay emphasis on nrrta (the bolas, or rhythmic passages). There are twelve types of bolas which are capable of infinite variation.

The NAUTCH-WALI (nautch girls) dates from the time of the Moguls (1526–1707). These dancers were originally imported from Persia for the entertainment of the rulers. The dancers borrowed from Kathak and created a form of dance which has long been popular at home and abroad. Unfortunately the morals of the Nautch-Wali were somewhat loose, and so they were responsible for the belief, widespread in the 19th century, of the immorality of all Indian dancers.

The MANIPURI dance originated in the territory of Manipur in northeast India. The Lai Haroba of Manipur is a religious, dramatic dance which has grown out of the local folklore and Hindu mythology. The style is indigenous and the entire community takes part in the performance. In the 18th century, when Manipur turned to Hinduism, the Ras Lila was adopted. This was a devotional re-creation of Lord Krishna and the Brindaban gopis.

The Manipuri dance uses only a few of the traditional Hindu mudras. The soft, flowing, restful quality of its style, its body carriage and projection savor of the Far East.

The great Indian poet Rabindranath Tagore (1861–1941), who founded the Santiniketan School in Bengal in 1901, devoted much thought to the pronounced decline of Indian dance and other arts, particularly evident during the second decade of this century. On a visit to distant Manipuri in 1917 he was happy to realize that there the arts were flourishing. He watched the Manipuri dance, liked its style, and decided to bring it to Bengal and the rest of India, hoping that it would play a salutary role in his planned revival of the Indian dance. To achieve this he engaged several teachers of the Manipuri dance for the Santiniketan School, and the School led the renaissance movement of Indian dance.

To Tagore and Uday Shankar belong the greatest credit for this. Shankar combined the outstanding classical schools into a theatre art which is compatible with our times. This is in keeping with tradition, for the sage Muni Bharata, who wrote the rules of Natya, said in the 9th chapter of his treaties (Slokas 151–2) that the teacher (guru) must devise new forms to move with the changing times.

Other dance-dramas recently revived include Bhagawata Mela Nataka of Tanjore, a religious drama-dance in Bharata Natya style, performed by men of the Brahmin caste; and Yaksha Gana of Karnataka, a rural dance in early Kathakali style.

Hinkson, Mary, contemporary American modern dancer, b. Philadelphia; m. Julian Johnson. Graduate Univ. of Wisconsin. Studied dance mainly with Martha Graham and Louis Horst. Member, Martha Graham Dance Company since 1951, dancing many featured roles including creations in *Canticle for Innocent Comedians, Seraphic Dialogue, Acrobats of God,* and others, and taking over Martha Graham's role as The Awakener in *Samson Agonistes.* Created the title role in *Circe* for its London and N.Y. premières (1963). Soloist, New York City Opera Ballet (1952, 1955). Created the only woman's role in Donald McKayle's *Rainbow 'Round My Shoulder* (1959). Featured dancer in *Figure in the Carpet* (New York City Ballet, 1960). Danced in television programs *"Omnibus," "Camera 3,"* et al. On faculty of Martha Graham School since 1951; Juilliard School of Music Dance Department since 1952; School of Performing Arts since 1955. Frequent guest artist with New York City Ballet, American Ballet Theatre and other companies.

Mary Hinkson, as Earth in Martha Graham's Canticle for Innocent Comedians.

Hinton, Paula, English dancer, b. Ilford, Essex, 1924; m. Walter Gore. Studied dance with H. Delamere-Wright (Liverpool). Professional debut in Old Vic Co.'s production of *Tragedy of Dr. Faustus* (Liverpool, 1944). Joined Ballet Rambert (1944), becoming principal dancer and creating leading roles in *Winter Night, Antonia* (title role), and others. Danced in Australia with Walter Gore (1952, 1955). Has been guest artist with Ballets des Champs-Elysées, Original Ballet Russe, London's Festival Ballet; appeared also with Pilar Lopez (1958). Ballerina, Frankfurt State Opera Ballet (1956–58); International Ballet of Edinburgh Festival (1958); guest artist, Ballet Rambert (1961). Ballerina, London Ballet, organized by Walter Gore, since 1961 where her creations include *Night and Silence, Eaters of Darkness,* and others. She also dances *Giselle,* Sugar Plum Fairy in Gore's version of *The Nutcracker,* and others. She is one of the finest actresses in ballet.

Hirsch, Georges, Director of the French National Lyric Theatres, Paris Opéra and Opéra Comique, from 1946 to 1951 and again from 1956 to 1959. During the first period he devoted most of his time to reconstruction of both companies after the disruption during World War II. Early in 1947 he invited George Balanchine to stage four works for the Opéra Ballet. Balanchine revived his *Serenade, Baiser de la Fée* and *Apollon Musagète,* and choreographed a new work, *Le Palais de Cristal,* to Bizet's Symphony in C major. In Sept. of that year Hirsch reinstated Serge Lifar in his post of maître de ballet of the Opéra, which he had lost following the liberation of Paris in Aug., 1944. It was during Hirsch's administration that the ballet company of the Opéra visited the U.S. and Canada in 1948.

History of Ballet (From Ballet Comique de la Reine to Petipa).

It is to the court festivities of Renaissance Italy that the roots of ballet can be traced. During the 15th century it became customary for wealthy nobles to amuse and impress their guests with splendid banquets and balls. The stimulation and gratification of the senses, expressed in the appetite of the age for spectacle, encouraged the presentation of ever more lavish entertainments. Thus, Lorenzo de Medici (1449–92) in quest of diversion during a Florentine carnival season, invented the "triumph," so named after a kind of chariot upon which the masked spectacle was mounted. Classical antiquity provided the "triumph's" theme and Lorenzo himself often wrote the accompanying verses. The "triumph" was hospitable not only to poetry, but also made use of interludes of music, dance, and pantomime, basic elements in ballet.

While the "triumphs" were chiefly for outdoor entertainment, the banquets were the scenes of lavish indoor amusements. A spectacular example of the Renaissance banquet was that given in honor of Gian Galeazzo, Duke of Milan, and his wife by Bergonzio di Botta in 1489. In the banquet hall a splendid parade of figures prominent in classical mythology—Jason and the Argonauts, Diana and her nymphs, Orpheus and his lyre, and so on—paid tribute in music, verse, pantomime, and dance to the ducal couple. The various entries were interspersed with eating and drinking. Artists such as Botticelli and Leonardo da Vinci provided decorations for such fêtes. Leonardo was responsible for the intricate representation of *Il Paradiso* which honored the entry of the same Gian Galeazzo into Milan.

Coming from this background of prodigal display, it is not surprising that Catherine de Medici, as wife of Henry II and Queen of France, was responsible for the continuation and development of the Italian type of entertainment at the French court.

Catherine had witnessed dance entertainments in Italy and had brought a group of strolling players to the court of France. She had also imported a well-known violinist, Balthasar de Beaujoyeux, and appointed him Valet de Chambre and organizer of court entertainments. His great achievement under her patronage was the Ballet Comique de la Reine (1581).

The Ballet Comique de la Reine made lavish use of verse, instrumental and vocal music, dance, and scenic machinery which provided some spectacular effects (including Jupiter posed upon a cloud). Its importance to the development of ballet lay chiefly in the coordination of these elements into something approaching dramatic unity.

The principles embodied in this production also influenced the development of England's sole contribution to spectacular theater during this period—the masque. Introduced by Henry VIII into the English court in 1512, the masque reached its height in the early 16th century in the collaboration of Ben Jonson (author) and Inigo Jones (designer). The coordination of verse and action with dance interludes and scenic effects made the masque the English equivalent of the French court ballet.

With the accession of Louis XIV (1643) ballet took another step forward and gained great popularity due chiefly to the fact that the king himself was an enthusiastic dancer and took part in the court performances. Ballet was at the time being cultivated only by the ladies and gentlemen of the court. The steps scarcely differed from those of the ballroom dances, and the performers were encumbered by heavy costumes, wigs, and masks. The king and his nobles invariably appeared as heroic characters.

Feeling that from a technical standpoint the court ballets left much to be desired, Louis XIV founded a school for the training of the dancers; the ballets soon began to acquire a professional quality that permitted their performance in public. In spite of the fact that in the court ballets women appeared together with the men, no women took part in the professional performances on the stage. Female parts in the theatre were taken by boys. The invariable masks and wigs helped to sustain the illusion.

The first public appearance of women in the professional ballet dates back to 1681, when the composer Jean Baptiste Lully, then director of the Académie, presented a ballet in which four female dancers took part.

The ballets were still composed of a mixture of music, singing, and dancing. Owing to the heavy costumes, the dancers could not accomplish much beyond the stately steps of the minuet, gavotte, etc., all strictly à terre.

Marie Camargo, a famous dancer of this period, is credited with having made an attempt to increase the range of steps in the ballet. Camargo was an exponent of the more lusty and vigorous style of dancing which originated in Italy. She was a virtuoso dancer with a brilliant technique for that period. To give her legs greater freedom she wore a much shorter skirt than was the custom. From the famous painting of her by Nicholas Lancret we see that it was well above the ankle. She also wore soft slippers instead of high-heeled shoes and an undergarment which was the forerunner of tights, now an accepted part of the regulation costume for the classic ballet.

Marie Sallé, another famous dancer of that period, went even further in freeing the costume and anticipated the flowing draperies of Isadora Duncan.

It is to one of the principal figures in the history of ballet—Jean-Georges Noverre—that we are directly indebted for many of the principles which govern ballet down to the present day. Noverre was born in Paris in 1727, studied under Louis Dupres, a celebrated dancer of that period, and at the age of sixteen made his debut at the Opéra Comique, where four years later he was appointed ballet master. Noverre was one of the first to realize the possibilities of ballet as an artistic medium and set forth his ideas and ideals in his famous *Lettres sur la Danse et sur les Ballets,* published in 1760. He made an effort to do away with the formal, conventionalized movements which had hitherto comprised most of the ballets, and was one of the first to advocate reform in the matter of costume. He was particularly opposed to the wearing of masks, a convention finally discontinued in 1773, when the famous dancer Maximilien Gardel discarded his mask in a performance at the Opéra.

Noverre's theories were considered too advanced for Paris and he was unsuccessful in obtaining the much coveted post of ballet master at the Opéra. He was forced to go abroad for an opportunity to develop his theories, eventually making a visit to England. France and England were at this time on the verge of war and Noverre met with a hostile reception. However, he profited much by his association with the famous English actor David Garrick, from whom he gained valuable instruction in the art of mime and who dubbed Noverre "the Shakespeare of the dance."

As a result of this Noverre is credited with becoming the creator of the ballet d'action, in which the story was expressed entirely in dumb show, without the help of spoken interludes. The composer Christoph Gluck, a close friend of Noverre, was at this time experimenting with opera, much as Noverre was with ballet, and the two collaborated on a production of *Iphigenie en Tauris* (1774).

At the court of the Duke of Wuerttemberg in Stuttgart Noverre at last found an outlet for his ideas. He was appointed ballet master of the Wuerttemberg Ducal Theatre, was given a company of twenty principal dancers and a corps de ballet of one hundred; the most famous designers of scenery and costumes were put at his disposal. Under Noverre's direction Stuttgart soon became the center of the dance world.

It was not until 1775 that Noverre was finally appointed ballet master of the Paris Opéra, due to the influence of Queen Marie Antionette, whose teacher he had been in Vienna. He succeeded Gaetano Vestris in this post. A few years later Noverre retired on a pension. After the outbreak of the French Revolution Noverre was forced to flee to England, together with many other artists. This time he was received more kindly. Later he was able to return to France, where he died in 1809.

The best known male dancers of this period were Gaetano Vestris and his son Auguste. Vestris was excessively vain, a characteristic in which he was equalled if not surpassed by his son. Both men were fine dancers, Auguste being particularly famous for his high leaps and ability to remain as if suspended in the air; among the women, in addition to Camargo and Sallé, were Anna Heinel, who married Gaetano Vestris, and Madeleine Guimard.

Ballet costume underwent a further change at the time of the French Revolution. It became customary for the dancers to wear tunics of light transparent material, modelled on the dress of ancient Rome and Greece, through which the entire length of the dancer's leg was visible. To retain the illusion of flesh, and at the same time satisfy the demands of modesty, there was a further evolution of the undergarment introduced by Camargo, which resulted in the wearing of skin-colored tights, known as maillots, after the costumer of the Paris Opéra at that time. When the costume barriers were broken down, the technical expansion of the ballet went ahead at much greater speed than before.

To Carlo Blasis (1803–1878), for many years ballet master of Teatro alla Scala in Milan, we are indebted for the establishment of a system of training which has been adopted by all important schools. Blasis is also credited with the invention of the ballet position known as attitude, which was suggested to him by the statue of Mercury by Giovanni di Bologna. His *Code of Terpsichore,* published in 1830, was the first comprehensive textbook designed for dancers and teachers.

The thirties of the 19th century ushered in one of the most glorious periods in ballet, the Romantic period. Three great dancers made distinct contributions to the glory of the Romantic period and possibly made the period a reality. They were Maria Taglioni, Fanny Elssler and Carlotta Grisi.

Maria Taglioni (1803–1884) was the daughter of a famous dancer, teacher and ballet master, Filippo Taglioni. She was an almost legendary figure, whose dancing had a rare spiritual quality, and whose lightness produced the effect of floating over the stage rather than dancing on it. Although it has never been definitely established, Taglioni is often credited with being the first dancer to raise herself on her toes, thus enlarging the vocabulary of ballet and creating a wider field of artistic expression within the ballet. Her most famous ballet was *La Sylphide* staged for her by her father in 1832.

Fanny Elssler (1810–1884) was born in Vienna, the daughter of Karl Ludwig Ferdinand Elssler, valet and copyist for the composer Franz Joseph Haydn. At the age of nine she was taken into the corps de ballet of the Vienna Hoftheater, and fifteen years later she made her debut at the Paris Grand Opéra in Jean Coralli's ballet *La Tempête,* based on Shakespeare's *The Tempest.*

Paris, which up to then had been devoted to Taglioni, divided itself into two camps: the Elsslerites and the Taglionists. Théophile Gautier, poet, balletomane, and leader in the Romantic movement, had been a staunch supporter of Taglioni. When he first saw Elssler dance he wrote his famous article in which he compared the two dancers. He said among other things:

"Fanny Elssler's dancing is quite different from the academic idea, it has a particular character which sets her apart from all other dancers. It is not the aerial and virginal grace of Taglioni, it is something more human, more appealing to the senses. Mlle. Taglioni is a Christian dancer . . . She flies like a spirit in the midst of transparent clouds of white muslin . . . she resembles a happy angel . . . Fanny is quite a pagan dancer; she reminds one of the muse Terpsichore, tambourine in hand, her tunic, exposing her thigh, caught up with a golden clasp. . . . After all, dancing consists of nothing more than the art of displaying beautiful shapes in graceful positions and the development from them of lines agreeable to the eye; it is mute rhythm, music that is seen. Dancing is little adapted to render metaphysical ideas; it only expresses the passions. Mlle. Fanny Elssler has fully realized this truth . . ."

Fanny Elssler brought into the ballet what we now call the character dance: the fiery Hungarian, Polish, Spanish, Russian dances; and in her dancing made use of the entire body, instead of dancing only with her feet, as dancers did before her.

Carlotta Grisi (1821–1899), the youngest of the three, was of Italian origin. She came to the ballet with an artistic background: most of her family were singers. At the age of seven she was entered in the ballet school of Teatro alla Scala in Milan and later studied with the great ballet master and teacher Jules Perrot, whom she subsequently married.

While Fanny Elssler, Maria Taglioni and Carlotta Grisi were great dancers in their own right, their importance to ballet would have been limited to their time only, had they not been a part of the Romantic period.

The essential characteristic of the art of the Romantic period was the exposition of events, the treatment of subject matter, on two planes: reality, or as it was often referred to, the bitter reality, and the fantastic, or, the beautiful dream. From this premise originated the basic theme of the romanticists: the never-ending struggle between the actual and the ideal, between the flesh and the spirit; the never-ending struggle, in which bitter reality triumphs tragically over the beautiful dream.

In literature, painting, and music the romantic period was a great progressive development; in ballet it was little short of a revolution.

Everything underwent a change. The subject matter of the pre-Romantic ballet —its mythological, heroic, and pastoral themes—gave way to dramatic love themes, fairy tales, folk legends. The dance itself was all but transformed. For the first time in the history of the ballet the ballerina raised herself on her toes, manifesting outwardly the yearning of her time for greater heights, for closer proximity to the ideal, for less contact with the earth—the symbol of bitter reality. Along with it there appeared a change in the general pattern of the ballet dance: the technique was enriched with new steps and greater deftness in their execution. Ballet moved further in its defiance of the laws of gravity and balance, laws which were holding the human body so realistically close to earth, so far away from the ideal, the dream world. Woman began to reign supreme in ballet; she became both the principal subject and object of the new romantic lyricism. In costuming the theatricalized court costume was abandoned in favor of a more or less standardized dress for the dancer—the tarlatan tunic, or tutu as it is often called, flesh-colored tights, and specially designed soft, heelless shoes. Renewed attention was paid to the artistic value of the music and décor used for ballet.

These changes were deep-rooted and artistically significant. The Romantic dance brought forth new choreographic designs not known to the pre-Romantic ballet. In the simplicity of lines, poses and movements there began to be noticed the expressive force possible in the choreographic arrangement of lyric movements.

It is doubtful whether the Romantic ballet could have achieved its significance if Théophile Gautier, one of the leaders of the Romantic movement, had not taken such an active part in it. Filippo Taglioni, who staged the ballets for his great daughter, Maria Taglioni, was a skillful choreographer. However, his education and cultural background were not sufficient to make him realize the significance of this period, much less prepare him for leadership in it. He sensed, rather than understood, the Romantic movement. He was an apt craftsman, and little more. Gautier, though an outsider to ballet, was a writer and poet of great talent, a true representative of the movement which embraced all that was outstanding in European art. Gautier, more than any person in the Romantic period, was the logical man to create the masterpiece which would serve as an example of the Romantic ballet, even for us, more than a century after its creation.

This masterpiece was *Giselle,* a Romantic ballet in two acts by Vernoy de Saint-Georges, Théophile Gautier, and Jean Coralli, with music by Adolphe Adam, scenery by Pierre Ciceri, and choreography by Jean Coralli. It was first produced at the *Théâtre de l'Académie Royale de Musique,* Paris, on June 28, 1841.

The Romantic period had begun some ten years before the first performance of *Giselle,* and *Giselle* was not the first ballet to reflect the characteristics of the Romantic period. This honor belongs to the ballet *La Sylphide,* produced in 1832 for Maria Taglioni by her father. A few years later Taglioni danced in another Romantic ballet, *La Fille du Danube.* These compositions were in the nature of preliminary experiments, stepping stones leading to the creation of *Giselle.*

The importance of Théophile Gautier in the creation of *Giselle* was not so much in what he actually did himself, as in the inspiration and influence he wielded on the people who created the ballet. The coauthors of *Giselle* had had a great deal of experience in their respective fields, both before *Giselle* and after it; yet in no instance had they achieved a composition as harmonious and vital. (For further details consult the entry.)

Toward the middle of the 19th century ballet began to lose favor in Western Europe, and the center of interest in ballet shifted to Russia.

Practically unknown to the outside world, Russia had had an Imperial School of Ballet since 1738. Empress Anna had engaged a Frenchman, Jean Baptiste Landet, to teach manners and dancing to the cadets of the Military School for Nobles in 1734. So successful was he in his teaching that four years later he was commanded to organize a separate School of Ballet. The succeeding monarchs, Empress Elizabeth, Catherine the Great, and Paul I, continued to take an active interest in ballet. As a boy Paul I took ballet lessons from Franz von Hilverding, who was ballet master in St. Petersburg in the 1750's and '60s. Paul later danced in ballets in the Court Theatre. In 1786 the Alsatian Charles Felix Reinhardt August Le Picq came to St. Petersburg as first dancer, and ten years later became chief ballet master and choreographer. He was a pupil of Noverre and a talented dancer. During his stay, in 1794, the first Russian-born ballet master gained recognition in the Imperial Theatre. His name had been Ivan Lesogoroff, but since Russian names at that time were not considered to carry enough prestige and glamour on the ballet stage, his name was promptly changed to Jean Waldberg (a literal translation into the German of his family name).

In 1801 Charles Louis Didelot, a Swede by origin and a pupil of Auguste Vestris, became teacher and ballet master of the Imperial Theatre. By that time Russian dancers were making definite progress toward stardom. Years later one of them, Elena Andreyanova, a pupil of Didelot, was considered equal to Taglioni in talent and technique. She danced most of the roles of the famous Italian and there was a certain amount of rivalry between the two dancers.

Didelot produced more than forty ballets on the Imperial stage. Most of his ballets were in the romantic vein; they all had interesting stories, clearly and expressively unfolded in dance and pantomime. He was an untiring worker and a revolutionist in his methods of teaching. He died in 1837 while on his way to a vacation in the South of Russia. The great Russian poet Alexander Pushkin is quoted as stating that there was more poetry in Didelot's ballets than in the entire French literature of that time.

Didelot was followed by Jules Perrot and Arthur Saint-Leon, who left their imprints on the ballet in Russia, but not nearly as powerfully as those of Marius Petipa, another Frenchman, who followed them.

Petipa arrived in Russia as a dancer in 1847. A few years later he became ballet master and in 1862, with his production of a ballet called *La Fille du Pharaon* to music by Cesare Pugni, despotic ruler over everything balletic. He ruled over the St. Petersburg Imperial Theatre for almost half a century, retired in 1903, and died seven years later at the age of ninety-one.

It was Petipa who gave the world classic ballets which are still considered among the greatest of all time, and it is Petipa who should be credited with the development of what we now call the classic ballet.

The term classic as applied to ballet is arbitrary. It denotes a style in the dance rather than a period. The term academic would be more accurate, but it has never gained general acceptance. In a broad sense, a classic ballet is one that is based on the classic tradition developed through the centuries of the existence of ballet. It was Petipa who by strict adherence to and constant repetition of the same principle in the composition of ballet developed the rules, or rather the tradition, of the classic ballet. It must be reiterated that classicism in ballet is in no sense a category that can be compared with or opposed to romanticism. Classicism applies to style and structure only, romanticism to period and content; hence a classic ballet can be and often is Romantic (*Swan Lake,* for instance), and a Romantic ballet can be and often is classic (*Giselle,* for instance).

By the time Petipa took over the St. Petersburg Imperial Theatre, ballet in Russia was just about one hundred years old, a youngster as art forms go, and it was Petipa's task to nurture the Russian ballet to maturity. He did this with notable success though not without pitfalls. Petipa's achievements were great and many, but from the point of view of our time Petipa's period possessed quite a number of defects. These shortcomings are just as important to us as his achievements, for it is on these shortcomings that the modern ballet learned to develop and to progress.

The defects of the classic ballet were not so much in its traditional framework or in its choreography, as in the general manner in which ballets were created.

Petipa was a great believer in the priority of choreography over everything else that went into the composition of a ballet. Music to him was merely an accompaniment, serving the needs of choreography, furnishing the dancers the necessary tempi and rhythms, without which it would have been difficult for them to dance. There was nothing new in this point of view. Petipa's predecessors, Didelot, Perrot, Saint-Leon, were of the same opinion. Everybody else in the Imperial Theatre, including the audience, fully concurred with it.

Because of this attitude, the composition of ballet music had become a routine job relegated to staff composers in the Theatre. During Petipa's reign the Italian Cesare Pugni and the Austrian Leon Minkus and later the Italian Riccardo Drigo were the most famous.

Pugni, whose first ballet on the Russian stage, *The Artist's Dream,* was produced by Perrot in 1848, is credited with nearly three hundred ballets, large and small. He was a facile composer. Minkus, who was not so prolific, nor so able as Pugni, used to compose in advance, filing away separate pieces for future use. He had constructed an ingenious pigeonhole file with labels: Waltzes, Marches, Polkas, Galops, Variations, Adagios, etc. As soon as he received an order for a ballet—and Petipa's orders were very explicit—Minkus would lay out an outline, assemble the most suitable melodies from his pigeonholes, write in the necessary modulations to connect the separate pieces, and the ballet was ready.

For one thing, however, these composers must be given credit: their music was easy to dance to. No more than craftsmen at best, their product was generally artistically poor and often meaningless, but from a functional point of view it served its purpose. More than that, these composers seemed to have had an understanding of the nature of the ballet dance and a knowledge of the principles of choreography as practiced by their contemporary ballet masters.

Quite often it would happen that the choreographer or the ballerina would not like some of the melodies. In such cases it was the task of the composer to substitute another number, of his own composition or some other composer's; they were not fussy about it. An example of this practice is *Le Corsaire,* which was kept in the repertoire of the Imperial Theatre for more than fifty years and sections of which are still being performed in the U.S.S.R. It was first staged in Paris in 1856 by Joseph Mazilier to music composed by Adolphe Adam, the composer of *Giselle.* Two years later Jules Perrot restaged it in Russia, still with the original music. As it continued to be given, however, the music of it began to undergo changes dictated by this or that ballerina, choreographer, director of the theatre. At the time the last generation of the great ballerinas of the Imperial Theater danced the main role of Medora (i.e. about 1915–1916), the music of *Le Corsaire* was officially credited on the program to Adam, Pugni, Delibes, Drigo, Tchekrygin, Prince Oldenburg, and others. These anonymous "others" appeared frequently on ballet programs of the Imperial Theatre and who they were will probably remain a mystery forever.

In 1905 Michel Fokine staged his first ballet, and a new era in ballet was begun. See FOKINE, DIAGHILEV, etc.

Hitchins, Aubrey, contemporary dancer and teacher, b. Cheltenham, England, now living in the U.S. Educated at Cheltenham College; dance studies with Enrico Cecchetti, Nicholas Legat, Lubov Egorova. Had his early experience under Michel Fokine; partnered Anna Pavlova on world tours (1925–30); first dancer, Royal Albert Hall, London, in *Hiawatha* (three seasons). Lecturer on "Anna Pavlova, Her Life and Art." Assistant in construction of film *The Immortal Swan,* a biographical film of Pavlova. Toured with *Le Chauve-Souris;* toured Holland with Vera Nemtchinova and Anatole Oboukhov; organized own company (1943). Since 1947 has been teaching in N.Y. with one or two interruptions for guest teaching.

Hobi, Frank, dancer and teacher, b. Aberdeen, Wash., 1923. Studied dance with Mary Ann Wells (Seattle), Anatole Vilzak, Anton Dolin, Antony Tudor, Anatole Oboukhoff, Pierre Vladimiroff, Muriel Stuart, Felia Doubrovska, Leon

Fokine, Vera Nemtchinova, George Balanchine. Joined Ballet (now American Ballet) Theatre (1941–42), then enlisted in U.S. Army Air Force, serving as a photo lab technician and photographer until discharged (1945). Soloist, Ballet Russe de Monte Carlo (1945–49), his repertoire including *Swan Lake, Les Sylphides, The Nutcracker, Coppélia,* and the Balanchine ballets (*Serenade, Ballet Imperial, Danses Concertantes, Le Baiser de la Fée, Concerto Barocco*), and one of the four male dancers in *Raymonda* (Act 3), staged by Balanchine. Leading male dancer with New York City Ballet (1949–54), dancing in most of the Balanchine repertoire and creating Mr. Interlocutor in Ruthanna Boris' *Cakewalk;* also dancing in *Age of Anxiety, Pied Piper,* and *Interplay.* Toured two seasons with Ruthanna Boris and Stanley Zompakos in a concert group (1954–56). Premier danseur, co-director, and teacher *Royal Winnipeg Ballet* (1956–57); stage manager New York City Ballet (1958–60). Currently teaching.

Hoctor, Harriet, contemporary American dancer and teacher, b. Hoosick Falls, N.Y. Studied dance with Ivan Tarasov, Louis H. Chalif, Anton Dolin (N.Y.), Merriel Abbott (Chicago), Nicholas Legat (London). A brilliant dancer, Harriet Hoctor began her professional career just a few years before ballet gained a place among the performing arts in the U.S. Consequently she danced in vaudeville, musical comedies, revues in theatres and large restaurants, the so-called presentation houses such as the Roxy, the Palace and the Paramount (N.Y.) and the Hippodrome (London). From 1934 to 1937 she danced in films. She opened her ballet school in Boston (1941), but still managed to dance in the Diamond Horseshoe (1942–43) and stage its revues (1943–45). Currently teaching in Boston.

Hodes, Linda (Linda Margolies), contemporary American modern dancer, b. New York City; m. Stuart Hodes. Began dance training in Martha Graham School's children's classes at age nine and entered the company in 1953. Created many roles including Joan (*Seraphic Dialogue*—in which she has also performed the role of Joan the Martyr), Cassandra (*Clytemnestra*), Young Judith (*Judith*), Pasiphae (*Phaedra*), one of the girls in *Acrobats of God* etc. Also danced important roles in *Deaths and Entrances, Ardent Song, Diversion of Angels,* and others. Has been guest artist with Paul Taylor, Yuriko, Glen Tetley; also has appeared in works by Nina Fonaroff, Stuart Hodes, Robert Cohan, Normand Maxon, Norman Walker. Created a number of solo and group works, among them *Demonium* (1952), *World on a String* (1953), *Curley's Wife* (1953), *Reap the Whirlwind* (1955), *Annabel Lee* (1961). Has also appeared on television. She is a member of the faculty of the Martha Graham School.

Hodes, Stuart, American modern dancer, choreographer, teacher, b. 1924; m. Linda (Margolies) Hodes. Studied at Martha Graham School (Martha Graham, Erick Hawkins); ballet at School of American Ballet, N.Y. (Muriel Stuart), and with Lew Christensen, Ella Daganova, and others. A B-17 Pilot in the U.S. Army Air Corps (1943–45), he holds the Air Medal. A leading member of Martha Graham's company (1947–58), he danced with her in *Every Soul Is a Circus, Appalachian Spring, Deaths and Entrances, Errand Into the Maze,* was the Seer in *Night Journey,* created Fire (*Canticle for Innocent Comedians*), and appeared in most of the Graham works during that period. Leading dancer on Broadway in *Paint Your Wagon* (1950), *Kismet* (1955), revival *Annie Get Your Gun* (1957), and others. Gave performances of his own works at the YM–YWHA (N.Y.), 1950, 1952, 1953, including *Lyric-Percussive, Surrounding Unknown, Drive, Flak* (all 1950), *I Am Nothing, No Heaven in Earth, Musette for Four, Murmur of Wings* (all 1952). On the faculty of

Stuart Hodes, American modern dancer, choreographer and teacher.

Martha Graham School, Juilliard School of Music Dance Department, School of Performing Arts, for which last-named he has created a number of works for student dancers; guest choreographer at Utah State Univ. Summer Workshop in the Performing Arts (1959, 1960); choreographer for concerts and musical shows. Assistant choreographer to Jonathan Lucas for the Broadway musical *First Impressions* (1959) and to Donald Saddler in *Milk and Honey* (1961), *We Take The Town* (1962), *Sophie* (1963), and in Saddler's N.Y. World's Fair Show, *To Broadway With Love* (1964). His own later choreographic works include: *Suite for Young Dancers, Folk Dances of Three Mythical Lands, The Waters of Meribah,* (all 1959), *Offering and Dedication, Simon Says, Balaam* (all 1960), *La Lupa* (1961). Choreographer for Santa Fe (New Mexico) Opera Company operas and evening of new ballets (summer 1963). Choreographed *The Abyss* for the Harkness Ballet (1965). Currently choreographer and instructor with Harkness Ballet, which presented the première of his first ballet *The Abyss,* to a score by Marga Richter, during its European tour (spring, 1966).

Höfgen, Lothar, German dancer, b. Wiesbaden, 1936. Studied with Peter Roleff, Hedy Dähler, Peter van Dijk. Danced in Nuremberg, Mannheim, Lubeck, and Mainz. Principal character dancer, Cologne Opera (1959–64); left company to go to Maurice Béjart's Ballet du XXme Siècle, Théâtre Royal de la Monnaie, Brussels, (spring, 1964).

Hogan, Michael, English dancer, b. Leicester, 1929; m. *Anita Landa.* Studied at Sadler's Wells Ballet School, making his debut with Sadler's Wells Opera in the ballet *The Bartered Bride* (Belfast). One of the Three Ivans in *The Sleeping Beauty* when Sadler's Wells (now Royal) Ballet re-opened Royal Opera House, Covent Garden (1946). Soloist, Sadler's Wells Theatre Ballet from its inception (Dec. 1945), dancing Peasant Boy (*Promenade*), Lover (*Khadra*), Tango Dancer (*Façade*), and others, until he joined London's Festival Ballet as a soloist (1952).

Holden, Stanley (Stanley Waller), English dancer, b. London, 1928; m. Stella Farrance. Studied at Bush-Davies School, London. Joined Sadler's Wells (now Royal) Ballet (1944), transferring to Sadler's Wells Theatre Ballet (1948) where he became a leading character dancer, creating Agnes, a Witch (*Selina*), Pierrot (*Harlequin in April*), and others, and dancing Mr. O'Reilly in the revival of *The Prospect Before Us*. Went to South Africa to teach (1954), returning to Royal Ballet as soloist (1957). His greatest creation to date with this company is Mother Simone in Frederick Ashton's *La Fille Mal Gardée;* also created the Marquis di Luca in Leonide Massine's revival of *The Good-Humored Ladies* (July 11, 1962). Alternated with Alexander Grant as the Bridegroom in the 1965 revival of *A Wedding Bouquet*.

Holder, Geoffrey, dancer, b. Port-of-Spain, Trinidad, 1930; m. Carmen de Lavallade. Studied native dances in the West Indies, taught at Katherine Dunham School, N.Y. Danced in Broadway musicals, first attracting attention with portrayal and dance as Baron Samedi in *House of Flowers*. Appeared with the Metropolitan Opera Ballet (1955). Formed own company, choreographing works based on ethnic sources for concert performances and on television. Received a Guggenheim Fellowship in painting (1957).

Holland, Dance in.

BY PAULA BALMA AND NEL ROOS.

Until 1934 no dance tradition such as was known in France, Italy, Russia, Denmark, and other European countries existed in Holland. This was due to the lack of a permanent national opera. It was Gertrud Leistikow, a well known European modern dancer, who first brought dance to Holland. She toured the country during 1914–16, returned in 1922, and remained to found schools in Amsterdam, Rotterdam, The Hague, and Utrecht. The first Dutch professional dancers of note included Jacoba van der Pas, Else Dankmeyer, and Angele Sydow. The more important dancers, alone or with their pupils, gave occasional recitals in Amsterdam, The Hague, or Rotterdam, but only a small part of the public was interested in dance. From time to time international ballet companies and dancers visited Holland, among them the Diaghilev Ballets Russes, Anna Pavlova, Argentina, Ballet Russe de Monte Carlo, Argentinita, Jooss Ballet, Trudi Schoop, and Harald Kreutzberg.

In the 1930's the classic dance was introduced to Dutch pupils by two members of the Pavlova company, Alperova and Helden; later Igor Schwezoff and others taught classic ballet technique and Dutch dancers went abroad to study with well known ballerinas.

The Dutch public, however, was by nature more interested in the more modern forms of dance, of which the Jooss and Schoop companies were representative. Gradually the interest in dance grew and more Dutch dancers began to appear before the public. No ballet group of importance developed, however, until Yvonne Georgi came to Holland in 1934 and laid the foundation for a national ballet. At first Miss Georgi visited Holland with dancers of the Hanover (Germany) Opera, where she was first dancer. Later she gave performances with a few Dutch dancers who formed the first important Dutch ballet group (1936). The group was founded under the patronage of the Wagner Association in Amsterdam. The Georgi group became independent after a few years under the name Georgi Ballet and in 1939 made a short American tour.

Due to the efforts of the Wagner Association a Dutch opera was founded. In 1941 the opera company became the Amsterdam Municipal Opera and the Georgi Ballet was engaged as the Opera Ballet. Among the ballets performed by the Georgi company and later by the Opera Ballet were *Coppélia, Diana* (Voormolen), *Pulcinella, Shadows* (Wydeveld), *The Nutcracker, Bolero,* and *Prometheus.* Leading dancers included Mascha Ter Weeme, Rita Nauta, Rini Hopman, Marie-Jeanne van der Veen, Nora de Wal, Greet Lintsz, Maud Kool, Nel Roos, Antony Raedt, Karel Poons, Kyril Alban,

Jan Beuchli, Cor van Muyden, Lucas Hoving, Johan Mittertreiner, and Bob Nyhuis. A few foreign dancers were engaged for leading parts, among them Victor Gsovsky, Nicolas Orloff, Constant Yolas, and Herbert Freund.

Apart from the Georgi Ballet, a smaller group was directed by Florrie Rodrigo, a modern dancer. Other dancers and teachers in Rotterdam and The Hague were Corrie Hartong, Nettie van der Valk, Puck Santhagens, Else van Egmond, and Iril Gadescov.

During the German occupation several independent dancers stopped dancing for reasons of principle and dancers belonging to the Hebrew faith were not allowed to appear on stage; but the majority continued their activities. Ballet performances were meeting with increased success and the public gave greater support. Apart from the full-evening ballet performances, so-called "Ballet Parades" were given. These consisted of solo dances and pas de deux, created and performed by the soloists of the Opera Ballet. The "Ballet Parades" gave the younger dancers an opportunity to present themselves to the public and were highly appreciated.

Over the years the classic ballet technique came more and more into vogue and from 1941 Yvonne Georgi began to use the classic technique in combination with modern expression for the choreography of her ballets. On several occasions she even used pointes, but the choreographing of classic works was not her strongest talent.

After the liberation of Holland (1945), the opera and the ballet were discontinued for some time by the authorities. Some dancers who were barred from the so-called art-dance were permitted to appear in musical shows, cabarets, etc. As they had to earn their living, most of them were compelled to choose this field of activity. As a result the Opera Ballet was depleted.

In 1945 Hans (Johanna) Snoek organized the Scapino Ballet, a company designed to give performances for young people. The company is still in existence and under her direction is doing excellent work in furnishing civilized entertainment for young audiences and acquainting them with ballet. During the 1963 Christmas season the company appeared at Philharmonic Hall at Lincoln Center, N.Y.

In July, 1946, the Amsterdam Opera was re-organized. Only a small ballet group was kept for the purposes of the opera. Two members of the Georgi Ballet, Nel Roos and Max Dooyes, were in this group and did much to keep it going. Darja Collin, a Dutch dancer and choreographer who for many years worked abroad, including the U.S.A., was invited to organize and direct a new troupe, the Opera Ballet Company, to provide ballets for the Opera and to give separate performances. She worked with the company for several years and many Dutch dancers benefitted from her serious classic training. When she left Holland to open a school in Florence, Françoise Adret became ballet mistress and choreographer of the company.

In 1948 Nettie van der Valk, a talented teacher and choreographer, founded a semi-professional ballet group, Ballet Ensemble, with which she worked until 1951, when it was dissolved. The group showed great promise, but Miss van der Valk's death in 1958 prevented the reactivation of the group as had been planned.

Mascha Ter Weeme, former soloist in Yvonne Georgi's company, became artistic director of a new company, Ballet Der Lage Landen, founded in 1947. The company did excellent educational work in making the Dutch public ballet minded, especially outside the larger cities.

Sonia Gaskell, a gifted administrator, worked with a small group called Ballet Recital and did quite a lot of experimentation. In the spring of 1958 she became director of the newly established Het Nederlands Ballet in The Hague. During a visit to New York that summer, she engaged as ballet masters Benjamin Harkarvy and Karel Shook. After her return to Holland she succeeded in engaging a Russian ballet master from Leningrad, Abdurahman Kumysnikov. Mr. Harkarvy resigned from the company in 1959 and in April of that year organized his own troupe, Het Nederlands Dans Theater, with some dancers from Het Nederlands Ballet. The new company had a difficult struggle to survive as it received no government subsidy, but in 1961 the troupe moved its headquarters to the Hague and is now receiving financial assistance from that city. Hans van Manen and Benjamin Harkarvy are artistic directors.

In 1959 the Opera Ballet Company and the Ballet der Lage Landen were combined into one company under the name Amsterdams Ballet, with Mascha Ter Weeme as artistic director. In the autumn of 1961 the Amsterdams Ballet and the Nederlands Ballet were amalgamated to form a national company under the name Het Nationaal Ballet, with Sonia Gaskell as artistic director and Mascha Ter Weeme as head of the Opera Ballet department.

Academies of dance exist in The Hague, Amsterdam, and Rotterdam, and there are good private schools in the smaller towns for the training of both professional and amateur dancers. Since 1959 state examinations for dancers and teachers have been held annually to determine their qualifications to join professional dance companies or to teach dance in schools.

Holm, Eske, soloist of the *Royal Danish Ballet,* b. Copenhagen, 1940. Entered the Royal Danish School of Ballet (1952); accepted into the company (1958). His roles include *Peter and the Wolf, Cyrano de Bergerac, Danses Concertantes, Etudes,* and a very successful Romeo in the revival of Frederick Ashton's *Romeo and Juliet* (Feb. 2, 1963). His first choreographic work, *Tropisms,* was premièred May 29, 1964, during the Danish Ballet and Music Festival.

Hanya Holm, modern dancer, choreographer and teacher.

Holm, Hanya, contemporary choreographer, teacher and dancer, b. Worms-am-Rhein, Germany; U.S. citizen. After convent school in Germany, studied at Hoch Conservatory and Dalcroze Institute, Frankfurt-am-Main; graduate Dalcroze Institute, Hellerau and Mary Wigman Central Institute, Dresden. Appeared in one of the first productions of Max Reinhardt's *The Miracle;* toured throughout Europe as member of original Wigman Group. Chief instructor and co-director, Mary Wigman Central Institute (10 years); Dance Director, Ommen, Holland (2 summers); Assistant director and dancer with Wigman in *Totenmal* (Munich, 1930). Founded N.Y. Mary Wigman School (1931), called Hanya Holm Studio since 1936. Organized own company, debut in Denver, Colo. (1936); N.Y. debut (Dec. 1937). Appeared with group in N.Y., Bennington College and on tour throughout U.S. Among her many dance compositions are *Trend* (1937), which won N.Y. Times award for best dance composition of year; *Metropolitan Daily*

(1938), first modern dance to be televised; *Tragic Exodus* (1939). Established Center of the Dance in the West, Colorado Springs (1941), and continues this summer course annually at Colorado College. Has choreographed, staged musical numbers and/or directed many of the outstanding Broadway musicals: "The Eccentricities of Davy Crockett' (*Ballet Ballads*) and *Kiss Me, Kate* (1948), *The Liar* and *Out of This World* (1950), *My Darlin' Aida* (1952), *The Golden Apple* (1954), *Reuben, Reuben* (1955), *My Fair Lady* (1956), *Christine* and *Camelot* (1960); choreographed and staged musical numbers for *Kiss Me, Kate, Where's Charley?* and *My Fair Lady* in the London productions; went to Israel to do the same for a production of *My Fair Lady* in Tel Aviv (1964). Directed and choreographed the opera *The Ballad of Baby Doe,* Central City, Colo. (1956), and Gluck's *Orfeo ed Euridice* for the Second Annual Vancouver International Festival (1959). Choreographed for the 1955 film version of *The Vagabond King* for Paramount and has also worked for television. Has written numerous articles in periodicals, books, and *World Book Encyclopedia* including *Dance, a Basic Educational Technique,* edited by Frederick Rand Rogers (N.Y., 1941), "The Dance," for *World Book Encyclopedia,* and others. Her Labanotated choreography for *Kiss Me, Kate* was the first choreographic composition accepted for copyright by the Library of Congress, Washington, D.C., thereby establishing an important precedent for future choreographers. Her dances for *Kiss Me, Kate* won the N.Y. Drama Critics Award for choreography (1948–49); won an award from the Federation of Jewish Philanthropies for outstanding contribution to the modern dance movement in America (1958) and received an Honorary Degree of Doctor of Fine Arts from Colorado College (1960). In addition to her N.Y. school and summer school in Colorado Springs, she has taught in numerous colleges and universities across the U.S. In the summer of 1965, the choreographer-teacher celebrated her 25th anniversary as Director of the Summer Dance Session of Colorado College, Colorado Springs. To honor the occasion the College organized a dance festival in addition to its regular events. Since 1961 she has been head of the dance department of The Musical Theatre Academy of N.Y.

Holm, Hanya, Collection, an integral part of the Dance Collection of the New York Public Library, a gift of the dancer in 1952, reflects a facet in the development of the modern dance which stems from Mary Wigman. More than 500 photographs, 10 scrapbooks and 200 programs trace the growth of Hanya Holm as a force in American dance. Her major works are fully represented. Valerie Bettis and Eve Gentry are among the dancers whose careers are documented. Also included are many rare photographs of Mary Wigman. This collection, like the Denishawn and Humphrey-Weidman Collections, continues to grow as more recent material is being added to it. In the case of Hanya Holm the documentation also covers her career as a choreographer for musical comedy.

Holmes, Berenice, contemporary American dancer, choreographer, teacher, b. Chicago, Ill. Studied ballet with Adolph Bolm (1922), Alexandra Maximova, Marcel Berger, Harald Kreutzberg, School of American Ballet, Bronislava Nijinska. With Chicago Civic Opera (1923); Allied Arts (1925–26); created role of Polyhymnia in Bolm's production of *Apollo,* at Library of Congress (1928). Performed with Vincenzo Celli and with Arthur Corey, touring in *The Thursday Musical* (1932–33). Established her own group in Chicago (1935) for which she choreographed many dance numbers. Currently teaching in Chicago.

Holmgren, Bjørn, Swedish dancer and

choreographer, b. Stockholm, 1920. Graduate of the Royal Swedish Ballet school; studied later with Mme. Rousanne, Boris Kniaseff and Mary Skeaping. Was accepted into the Royal Swedish Ballet in 1939; became premier danseur in 1946. Was guest artist with International Ballet (London) in 1949 and 1950 and with several other companies in Scandinavia and on the continent. Danced all principal roles in the classic as well as Swedish repertoires. His choreographic work includes *Suite Classic* to music by Lalo (1952); *Swedish Rhapsody* to music by Alfvén (1958); *Pastoral* to music by Larsson (1961). Birgit Aakesson created the title roles of *The Minotaur* and *Icaros* (a ballet for a solo dancer) for him (1963). He is one of the teachers at the Choreographic Institute connected with the Music Academy, Stockholm, founded in the fall of 1963. Retired as dancer from the Royal Swedish Ballet (1965), but continues to choreograph and teach.

Holz, Rudolf, German dancer, b. Berlin, 1938. Studied with Ines Mesina and Gustav Blank. Made his debut (1952) at the Berlin Municipal (now German) Opera. He is a classic dramatic dancer who dances *The Moor Of Venice, Joan von Zarissa, Agon, Ondine* (Tatiana Gsovska version), *Romeo and Juliet* (Prokofiev), and others.

Homage to the Queen. Ballet in 1 act; chor.: Frederick Ashton; commissioned music: Malcolm Arnold; décor: Oliver Messel. First prod.: Sadler's Wells (now Royal) Ballet, at Royal Opera House, Covent Garden, London, June 2, 1953, with Margot Fonteyn and Michael Somes (Air), Nadia Nerina and Alexis Rassine (Earth), Violetta Elvin and John Hart (Water), Beryl Grey and John Field (Fire). This was an "occasion" ballet, the occasion being the Coronation of H. M. Queen Elizabeth II. The elements pay homage to the queen. Unlike many such pieces, this had a long life in the repertoire, being full of typical Ashton inventions, particularly the Air pas de deux, and the slow undulations of Elvin's arms as Water.

Honegger, Arthur (1892–1955), composer, b. Le Havre, France of German-Swiss parentage. Member of the group called Les Six. One of the composers of *Les Mariés de la Tour Eiffel* (Les Ballets Suédois, 1921) and, for the same company, *Skating Rink* (1922); for *Ida Rubinstein, Les Noces de Psyché et de l'Amour* (Bach-Honegger, 1931), *Amphion* (1931), *Semiramis* (1934); for Serge Lifar, at the Paris Opéra: *Cantiques des Cantiques* (1938); for Nouveau Ballet de Monte Carlo, one part of *Chota Rustaveli* (1946); for Paris Opéra, *L'Appel de la Montagne* (1945), *Naissances des Couleurs* (1949). Andrée Howard used a selection of his piano pieces for *Lady Into Fox* (1939).

Honer, Mary, English dancer, actress, teacher, b. London, 1914, m. actor Peter Bell. Studied with Judith Espinosa, Margaret Craske, Nicholas Legat, Olga Preobrajenska, Mathilde Kchessinska. Started her career in musical comedy and had her first ballet experience when she joined the Vic-Wells (later Sadler's Wells, now Royal) Ballet, becoming a ballerina in 1936. Created Bride (*A Wedding Bouquet*), Blue (fouettés) Girl (*Les Patineurs*), Leader of the Furies (Ninette de Valois' *Orpheus and Eurydice*), and others, and danced a sparkling Swanilda (*Coppélia*); also danced Sugar Plum Fairy (*The Nutcracker*), Blue Bird pas de deux (*The Sleeping Beauty*), Girl (*The Rake's Progress*), Waltz (*Les Sylphides*), and others. After leaving the ballet (1942) she played juvenile leads and was choreographer for the Shakespeare company at Stratford-on-Avon for two years and at Open Air Theatre, Regent's Park for three. Had her own ballet school in London and was a member of the Royal Academy of Dancing major committee. She died in London on May 6, 1965.

Hoofer, a rapidly disappearing name for a dancer on the vaudeville stage or in night clubs; now used only as a derisive term to denote an inartistic male tap dancer.

Hootchy-Kootchy, a pseudo-Turkish, sensual dance executed by women in short skirts and tight breastbands, which originated at the Philadelphia Centennial Fair (1876). The term has been carried over to mean any so-called "sexy" dance at fairs, carnivals, etc.

Hopak (also spelled gopak), a Ukrainian folk dance performed by men; has often been used in ballets as a solo or ensemble dance.

Horoscope. Ballet in 1 act; chor.: Frederick Ashton; music and book: Constant Lambert; décor: Sophie Fedorovitch. First prod.: Vic-Wells (later Sadler's Wells, now Royal) Ballet, Sadler's Wells Theatre, London, Jan. 27, 1938, with Michael Somes (Young Man born under Leo), Margot Fonteyn (Young Woman born under Virgo), Pamela May (Moon), Richard Ellis and Alan Carter (The Gemini). Young lovers born under conflicting signs of the zodiac are united by the Moon under their common sign, the Gemini. This was the first creation of a leading role by Michael Somes. The score and the décor were lost in Holland when the Sadler's Wells Ballet had to evacuate at a few hours' notice in 1940, and *Horoscope* has never been performed since.

Horst, Louis, (1884–1964), pianist, composer, writer, teacher, b. Kansas City, Mo. and d. New York City. Studied piano and violin in San Francisco, music composition in Vienna (1925). Musical director for Ruth St. Denis (1915–25), Martha Graham (1926–48). Composed scores for Graham's Primitive Mysteries (1931), *Frontier* (1935), *El Penitente* (1940) and others, and *Born to Weep, Little Theodolina* (Nina Fonaroff), and

Louis Horst, American composer, pianist, dance theoretician, writer, editor, teacher of dance composition.

Transformation of the Medusa (Jean Erdman). Taught dance composition at Neighborhood Playhouse School of Theatre, N.Y. (1928–64); Bennington College Summer Sessions (1934–45); Connecticut College Summer School (1948–63); Juilliard School of Music Dance Dept. (1951–64). Founded *Dance Observer* (see PERIODICALS, DANCE, U.S.) in 1934 and edited it up to the final Jan. 1964 issue. His books include *Pre-Classic Dance Forms* (*Dance Observer,* 1937) and *Modern Dance Forms* (Impulse Publications, 1960); also wrote sixteen short articles on Renaissance dance forms for *Encyclopedia Britannica* during the 1950's.

Horton, Lester (1906–1953), American dancer, choreographer, teacher, b. Indianapolis, Ind. Studied dance in Indianapolis and later with Adolph Bolm and Andreas Pavley in Chicago. Began his professional career as designer and stage manager for the Indianapolis Civic Theatre. He was interested in the dances of the American Indian on which he became an authority; also worked for two years with Michio Ito. His work in the

Japanese theatre developed his approach to theatre-dance in its usage of props in conjunction with the dance. Moved to California in 1928 where he directed dance festivals, largely based on his knowledge of American Indian dance, and also appeared in solo performances. In 1934 he organized his own group, known as the Lester Horton Dancers, which gave regular performances in Hollywood and toured on the West Coast. From 1948 his dance seasons were given in his own theatre, most of the works being both choreographed and designed by him. His company made only two appearances in N.Y., one in 1943 and the other in the spring of 1953, also appearing at Jacob's Pillow Dance Festival in the summer of 1953. These appearances, however, were instrumental in creating great interest in his particular approach to modern dance technique, and Horton stands with Martha Graham and Doris Humphrey as the American teachers whose methods have established a school. Some of his pupils are Janet Collins, Carmen de Lavallade, Joyce Trisler, James Mitchell, Alvin Ailey, James Truitte. After his death (Nov. 2, 1953), his school and theatre were continued for several years but closed at the end of 1960.

Lester Horton, American dancer, choreographer, teacher.

House of Birds, The. Ballet in 1 act; chor.: Kenneth MacMillan; music: Federico Mompou (*Chants Magics, Préludes, Fêtes Lointaines, Trois Variations, Charmes, Suburbis, Impressions Intimes, Scenes d'Enfants*), piano solos orch. and arr. by John Lanchbery; décor: Nicholas Georgiadis. First prod.: Sadler's Wells Theatre Ballet, Sadler's Wells Theatre, London, May 26, 1955, with Doreen Tempest (Bird Woman), Maryon Lane and David Poole (Lovers). The libretto was devised by MacMillan and Lanchbery from "Jorinda and Joringel" by the Brothers Grimm. A Catalonian village is dominated by a Bird Woman whose magic has transformed the women of the village into birds. The witch is worshipped by the men. When a young couple from another region arrive the girl is claimed by the Bird Woman, but the girl's lover rouses the other men, enters the witch's house and frees the women from the spell. The ballet was revised and enlarged for production at the Royal Opera House, Covent Garden (1963) with a major dance sequence added when Christopher Gable danced the Lover.

House Party, The. See Les Biches.

Hovhaness, Alan, American composer, of Armenian extraction, b. Somerville, Mass., 1911. Studied piano with Heinrich Gebhard, composition with Frederick Converse; also had lessons with Bohuslav Martinu. Has made intensive study of Indian and oriental systems and his works frequently show this influence combined with the use of typical Armenian traditional musical patterns. A prolific composer, both modern dance and classic ballet choreographers frequently use his music. He composed *Ardent Song* (1954), and *Circe* (1963) for Martha Graham; *Black Marigolds* (1959) and *Shirah* (1960) for Pearl Lang; *Upon Enchanted Ground* (1951) and *Dawn Song* (1952) for Jean Erdman.

Hoving, Lucas (Lucas Hovinga), modern dancer, teacher, choreographer, b. Groningen, Holland; now U.S. citizen; m. Lavina Nielsen. Studied dance with Florrie Rodrigo and Yvonne Georgi in Holland; at the Kurt Jooss School, Dartington Hall, S. Devon, England. Danced with the Jooss Ballet (*Green Table, Big City,* and others), with Martha Graham (*Letter to the World*), Valerie Bettis (*As I Lay Dying, Yerma*); joined José Limón group, creating many important roles beginning 1949 with El Conquistador in *La Malinche,* and including the Friend (*The Moor's Pavane*), Leader (*The Traitor*), White Man (*Emperor Jones*), all choreographed by Limón, and in many Doris Humphrey works including *Night Spell, Ruins and Visions.* Is on the faculty of Juilliard School of Music Dance Dept., Connecticut College Summer School of the Dance, is vice-president of Contemporary Dance, Inc., artistic director of The Merry-Go-Rounders. For his own dance group has choreographed *Wall of Silence, Aubade, Strange, To Wish Wishes No Longer, Has the Last Train Left?, Incidental Passage, Icarus* and others. Danced and taught in Holland and in English universities (1964).

How Long Brethren. Modern dance group work; chor.: Helen Tamiris; music: Negro songs, collected and recorded by Lawrence Gellert, arr. by Genevieve Pitôt;

Lucas Hoving, modern dancer and choreographer in his work Icarus.

costumes: James Cochrane. First prod.: Nora Bayes Theatre, N.Y., May 6, 1937. This was a Dance Project production and Tamiris's second work for the Federal Theatre. It ran for ten weeks (together with Charles Weidman's *Candide*), and had a further two-week run at the end of 1937 at the Forty-Ninth Street Theater. These were songs of protest, and the choreography of the dances (performed by Tamiris with an ensemble) underscored the titles: "Pickin' off de Cotton," "Upon de Mountain," "Railroad," "Scottsboro," "Sistern and Brethren," and "Let's go to de Buryin'." This work established Helen Tamiris as a leader in her field.

Howard, Alan, dancer, teacher, choreographer, b. Chicago, Ill. Studied dance in Chicago with Edna McRae. Joined Ballet Russe de Monte Carlo (1949), rising to premier danseur and remaining (except for one season with New York City Ballet, 1953) until 1960. Over that period he danced most of the leading male roles in both the classic and modern repertoire, his style easily encompassing classic and demi-caractère roles. Now teaching in San Francisco where he has his own group, Pacific Ballet, giving fall and spring performances, and for which he has choreographed a number of works.

Howard, Andrée, English choreographer, dancer and designer, b. 1910. Studied dance with Marie Rambert, Lubov Egorova, Mathilde Kchessinska, Olga Preobrajenska, Vera Trefilova. Was an original member of the Ballet Club (later Ballet Rambert) and was one of its principal choreographers, her ballets including *Our Lady's Juggler* (1933), *The Mermaid* (1934), both in collaboration with Susan Salaman; *Cinderella, Rape of the Lock* (1935), *Alcina Suite* (1934), *La Muse s'Amuse* (1936), *Death and the Maiden* (1937), *Croquis de Mercure* (1938), *Lady into Fox* (1939), *La Fête Etrange* (1940—first for London Ballet which a month later joined with Ballet Rambert), *Carnival of Animals* (1943), *The Fugitive* (1944), *Sailor's Return* (1947). She frequently danced in her own ballets and also in the general repertoire, including *Dark Elegies, Bar aux Folies-Bergère, Façade, Les Sylphides,* and others. Guest artist with Ballet (now American Ballet) Theatre (1940) staging and dancing in *Death and the Maiden* and *Lady into Fox.* For International Ballet she choreographed a ballet version of Shakespeare's *Twelfth Night* (1942), and for Sadler's Wells Ballet, *The Spider's Banquet* (1944). Choreographed *Mardi Gras, Assembly Ball* and *Selina* for Sadler's Wells Theatre; *A Mirror for Witches, Veneziana* and *La Belle Dame Sans Merci* (1959) for the Royal Ballet. She choreographed Edward German's operetta, *Merrie England* for Sadler's Wells Opera (1960), and the same year was guest artist with Royal Ballet dancing one of the Stepsisters in Frederick Ashton's *Cinderella.* Andrée Howard often designs both décor and costumes for her ballets and occasionally for other choreographers. She designed the décor for an early production of *Les Sylphides* by Ballet Rambert, for Walter Gore's *Confessional,* and for *The Sleeping Beauty* staged by Anna Ivanova for the Turkish National Ballet (1964).

Howes, Dulcie (Cronwright), South African dancer and teacher, b. Mossel Bay, Cape Province, 1910. Studied with Helen Webb, Margaret Craske, Tamara Karsavina, and Elsa Brunelleschi. Founded Univ. of Cape Town Ballet School (1934) and Company (1937), which has produced a number of well known dancers including Alfred Rodrigues, Meriel Evans, Desmond Doyle, Johaar Mosaval. Currently Head of Dept. of Ballet and Director of Univ. of Cape Town Ballet Company. Given the Cape Tercentenary Award of Merit for services to ballet (1950–55).

Hoyer, Doré, German modern dancer. Pupil of Mary Wigman and member of her company. From 1949 to 1951 she was ballet mistress of Hamburg State Opera, during which time she created a number of works, among them *Vision* (Stravinsky's Concerto in D), *Revolving Dance* (Maurice Ravel's Bolero), *Gypsy* (Bartók's *Divertimento in 3 Movements*), *The Wooden Prince* (Bartók, Sonata for Two Pianos and Percussion), *The Stranger* (Dimitri Wiatowitsch). By 1951 she felt that she did not want to be further tied down to one place and returned to independent work. She toured through Europe and visited South America twice. In 1957 she made her U.S. debut at the American Dance Festival at Connecticut College, where she appeared Aug. 18 in *The Great Song,* to the music of Dimitri Wiatowitsch, her composer-pianist. On Aug. 26 Miss Hoyer appeared at an invitational recital at McMillin Academic Theatre of Columbia Univ., N.Y. She is a major artist of an impressive individuality and consummate technique, the last of a line of Central European dancers which began with Mary Wigman.

Hughes, Allen, dance and music critic, b. Brownsburg, Ind., 1921. Studied at George Washington Univ., Washington, D.C. (1940–42); Univ. of Michigan (1942–43), and again (1946–47), after service in the U.S. Navy as Ensign and Lieut. (j.g.); music lecturer and organist, Toledo (Ohio) Museum of Art (1947–48); N.Y.U. (1948–50). Assistant editor and critic, *Musical America* (1950–53). Lived in Paris until 1955 when he became a music critic on the N.Y. *Herald Tribune,* at the same time being an instructor in music at Brooklyn College (1958–60). Joined *The N.Y. Times* as music critic (1960); became assistant to John Martin in the dance dept. (1961) and succeeded him as dance critic and editor (July 1, 1962). In Sept., 1965, he returned to the music department, succeeded by Clive Barnes as dance critic and editor of the dance department. In 1957 he went on a seven-week lecture tour of Europe for the U.S. Dept. of State Leaders and Specialists Program; has also lectured widely in the U.S. and contributed articles and reviews to many publications.

Huis Clos. See SONATE À TROIS.

Humpbacked Horse, The. Ballet in 5 acts, 10 scenes; chor. and book: Arthur Saint-Léon; music: Césare Pugni. First prod.: Dec. 15, 1864 at the Bolshoi Theatre, St. Petersburg, with Martha Muravieva in the principal role. Based on a Russian fairy tale by P. Yershov, this was the first ballet on a Russian theme ever staged by the Imperial Theatres. Its production evoked a strong protest among the St. Petersburg balletomanes who felt that the administration of the Imperial Theatres should have selected a Russian composer and a Russian choreographer for the first ballet on a Russian theme. This protest notwithstanding, *The Humpbacked Horse* became one of the most popular ballets on the Russian stage and was kept in the repertoire for some ninety-six years.

Humpbacked Horse, The. Ballet in 3 acts; chor.: Alexander Radunsky; music: Rodion Shchedrin; book: Vasily Vainonen and Pavel Maliarevsky, based on a fairy-tale by P. Yershov; décor: Boris Volkov. First prod.: Bolshoi Theatre, Moscow, Mar. 4, 1960. This is a new version of *The Humpbacked Horse,* with new choreography and a modern score. The part of the half-witted old Czar was created by Radunsky, a brilliant mime. Rimma Karelskaya was the Czar-Maiden, Vladimir Vasiliev, Ivanushka. The Humpbacked Horse helps Ivanushka win the love of the beautiful Czar-Maiden, fool the old Czar and become a handsome young prince. In Oct., 1962, a Soviet-produced film of the ballet had its première in N.Y. Maya Plisetskaya acted and danced the Czar-Maiden and Vladimir Vasiliev repeated his role of Ivanushka.

Humphrey, Doris (1895–1958).

BY WALTER TERRY.

One of the leading dancers and choreographers of modern dance and a featured soloist with the Denishawn company, Doris Humphrey received her first dance training in her home state of Illinois. Of New England ancestry and Middle West upbringing, she began dancing at the age of eight at the Parker School in Chicago. Her dance teacher, Mary Wood Hinman, trained her in ballroom, clog, folk, and "esthetic" dancing, and was so impressed with her native facility that she urged her to continue her studies under other teachers. She studied ballet under the Viennese ballet mistress, Josephine Hatlanek, and under Andreas Pavley and Serge Oukrainsky, "interpretive" dance under F. E. Balph, and ultimately other forms of dance under Ruth St. Denis and Ted Shawn. While still in Chicago she danced at garden parties, in charity performances, and whenever opportunity presented itself. Following her high school graduation, she taught dancing in her home town of Oak Park, and finally, in 1917, set out for California and Denishawn.

As a member of the Denishawn company, she learned to dance featured roles in Hindu, Japanese, Siamese, and other Oriental ballets in the repertory and in the music visualization works. One of her most popular solos during this period was her *Hoop Dance*. She was encouraged to test out her choreographic ideas and was helped, particularly by Miss St. Denis, to produce *Tragica,* the first contemporary dance to be performed without musical accompaniment. She remained with the Denishawn company through that organization's two-year tour of the Orient. Following the tour, she and Charles Weidman headed the faculty at Denishawn House in New York City while the principals were appearing in the *Ziegfeld Follies*.

Doris Humphrey, pioneer of the American modern dance; dancer, choreographer, teacher, author.

In 1928 Miss Humphrey left Denishawn and joined forces with Charles Weidman, who had severed connections with Denishawn at the same time, to found a school and a company. In order to base her dance activity upon new principles in keeping with her new dance goals, she spent considerable time working before a mirror and investigating the motor possibilities and limitations of her body, kinetic rhythms, and the laws which governed action. She arrived at the theory that the movement of dance, with all its inherent dramatic properties, existed upon that arc which ranged from balance to unbalance, fall to recovery, that between the motionlessness of perfect balance and the destruction implicit in completely yielding to the pull of gravity lay the "arc between two deaths," the area of movement. With this discovery she came upon the rhythm which exists in human action, the dynamics which give shading and color to dance, and structure evolving from the sway which leads a body away from its balance and the compensatory movements which restore its equilibrium. By forsaking set dance vocabularies and forms and rediscovering fundamental laws of movement, Miss Humphrey felt that she had found a basic dance which would not only be universal in appeal—since its principles applied to every moving being—but would enable her to create fresh works dependent not upon musical forms, traditional steps, and accepted styles, but upon the laws of movement alone.

Working from the principle of balance and unbalance, fall and recovery and, later, upon the application of gestural material, she created many works of immediate significance and enduring value. Her early efforts included *Color Harmony, Water Study, Drama of Motion, Life of the Bee, Circular Descent, Pointed Ascent,* and others in which the titles reflected her immediate concern with the application of her discovery. That the application of her "arc between two deaths" was not esoteric was borne out in her many Broadway assignments, which included the musical revue *Americana,* Molière's *School for Husbands,* and other stage productions.

In 1936, Miss Humphrey completed her great dance trilogy, *Theatre Piece, With My Red Fires,* and *New Dance,* the first dealing with man's rivalries, competitions and efforts wasted in oppositions; the second with the tragedy of possessive love; and the third with the advancement to the ideal human relationship—group harmony co-existing with cherished individuality.

In her trilogy, in some of her earlier dances, and particularly in *Passacaglia,* Miss Humphrey made it clear that she had few if any rivals in the field of large-scale choreography for mass groups. With her growing interest in the field of gesture—universal gesture as opposed to balletic or codified pantomime—she began to create highly dramatic theatre pieces such as *Inquest, Lament for Ignacio Sanchez Mejias,* and *The Story of Mankind,* the latter two composed for José Limón and his company. Even in this later aspect of her work, however, she did not forsake her concern with the problems which beset mankind, nor her realization that behind specific incidents and characters lay dramatic problems and behavior which pertained to any man—rich or poor, educated or uneducated.

With her retirement as a performer in 1945, she turned all her energies to choreography. She became artistic director of the Limón troupe (with which Pauline Koner performed for fifteen years) and for the remaining years of her life devoted herself to the building of a remarkable repertory for that company while also guiding Limón in his choreographic ventures. Among her outstanding works of this period were *Day on Earth, Ritmo Jondo, Night Spell, Ruins and Visions, Invention, Theater Piece No. 2,* and *Brandenburg Concerto No. 4,* the latter completed by Ruth Currier following Miss Humphrey's death.

In addition to her work as a choreographer and artistic director, she found the time and strength, despite years of constant pain and lameness from arthritis, to teach technique, choreography, and repertory. In 1955, with the assistance of Martha Hill, director of dance at the Juilliard School of Music, she founded the Juilliard Dance Theater, for which she created new works, revived some of her major works from the past, and enlisted the services of guest choreographers. Her final contribution to choreography was her book, *The Art of Making Dances* (N.Y., 1959), a definitive work on the subject, published posthumously.

The dance world held Doris Humphrey's compositions in high esteem. Shortly after her death a committee was formed to raise funds to preserve her works in motion pictures (as danced by the Limón and Juilliard Workshop companies) and in Labanotation. Still photographs and musical scores were also secured by the Doris Humphrey Fund, administered by the New York Public Library which also provided a permanent repository for the Humphrey choreographic material in its Dance Collection. Contributions to the Fund, which ranged from a dollar to hundreds of dollars, came from individuals and organizations.

In addition to the compositions listed above, her other major works included *The Shakers* (which though originally staged for a Broadway musical, has subsequently become something of a classic through repeated performances over the years in various Humphrey-directed companies), *Air on a Ground Bass, Dionysiaques, Song of the West, Decade,* and many pieces created in collaboration with Charles Weidman.

Humphrey-Weidman Collection, an integral part of the Dance Collection of the New York Public Library, containing more than 800 photographs, 30 volumes of press clippings, 200 programs, set designs, playbills and miscellaneous items documenting the careers of Doris Humphrey and Charles Weidman. It was presented to the Library by Mr. Weidman in 1951. The material dates from 1928 when both dancers left Denishawn. Miss Humphrey's growth as a choreographer is evident from a succession of photographs, reviews, and interviews; Mr. Weidman's works are also fully represented. Outlined also are the early careers of members of their company who were to become well known in their own right, among them Sybil Shearer, Katherine Litz, and José Limón. This collection is valuable also because it mirrors so well the great excitement attending the development and fruition of the modern dance of the 1930's. Additions to this collection have been made with funds raised by the Doris Humphrey Committee which was organized after the dancer's death to preserve her works in dance notation and on film. Sound tapes of Miss Humphrey's lectures, as well as additional personal photographs and manuscript material (gifts of Charles F. Woodford, the late dancer's husband), have further enriched this collection.

Hundred Kisses, The. Ballet in 1 act; chor.: Bronislava Nijinska; music: Frederic d'Erlanger; book: Boris Kochno; décor: Jean Hugo. First prod.: Col. de Basil's Ballet Russe, Royal Opera, Covent Garden, London, July 18, 1935, with Irina Baronova (Princess), David Lichine (Prince); Metropolitan Opera House, N.Y., Oct. 18, 1935, also with Baronova and Lichine. The ballet is based on a fairy-tale by Hans Christian Andersen. The proud princess scorns the prince when he comes to her in disguise, offering only a rose. But when he returns, again disguised, but with the magic bowl and spoon which causes everyone to dance, she pleads with him and offers him her hand in return for the bowl. He throws away his disguise, stands revealed as the prince and scorns her for her pride. Her father banishes her from his kingdom and she is left with nothing.

Hurde, Patrick (David Higgins), English dancer, b. Bristol, England, 1936. Studied dance at Royal Ballet School, London, and from 1954 to 1958 was a soloist with that part of the company which was originally Sadler's Wells Theatre Ballet. His roles included Bootface (*The Lady and the Fool*), Jasper (*Pineapple Poll*), Scotch and Popular Song (*Façade*), among others. Danced in Sweden and Germany as guest artist with many companies (1958–59). Since 1959 has been a soloist of National Ballet of Canada, some of his roles being Toby (*Antic Spring*), The Soul (*Fisherman and His Soul*), Jasper (*Pineapple Poll*), Pas de Trois (*Les Rendez-vous*), Chinese and Trepak (*The Nutcracker*). Has danced all over Europe, in North and South Rhodesia, and South Africa.

Hurok, Solomon, contemporary American impresario, born in Russia. Arriving in the United States in 1906, he began his managerial activities in 1910 organizing concerts in a Brooklyn community center. His first commercial venture was characteristically a big one: he hired the New York Hippodrome (since demolished) for a series of Sunday night concerts, presenting the greatest instrumental and vocal talent available. The venture proved a success, and Hurok gave up the miscellaneous jobs he had held prior to that venture to try to make a living in the concert and dance field. With his share of financial setbacks as well as successes, Hurok managed through the years a brilliant array of dance attractions, among them Anna Pavlova, Isadora Duncan, Loie Fuller, Mary Wigman, Trudi Schoop, Uday Shan-Kar, Vincente Escudero, Argentinita, Martha Graham Company, Ballet Russe de Monte Carlo, Original Ballet Russe, Ballet (now American Ballet) Theatre, the Markova-Dolin Company, the Sadler's Wells (now Royal) Ballet, the Sadler's Wells Theatre Ballet, the Moscow Bolshoi Ballet, the Leningrad Kirov Ballet, the Moiseyev Dance Company, the Beryozka Dance Troupe, the Azuma Kabuki Dancers and Musicians from Toyko, the Śląsk and Mazowsze State Dance Companies from Poland, Roland Petit Ballets de Paris, the Agnes de Mille Dance Theatre, Antonio and His Spanish Ballet, The Spanish Ballet of Roberto Iglesias, the Georgian State Dance Company, the Ukrainian Dance Company, the Yugoslav State Company, the Kolo from Belgrade, the Inbal from Israel, Bayanihan Philippine Dance Company, Ballet Folklorico of Mexico, Alexandra Danilova and Her Ensemble, the Katherine Dunham Dancers, and others. Hurok has an equally imposing list of vocal and instrumental concert artists. In other fields of the concert business Hurok was responsible for the record-making telecasts of *The Sleeping Beauty* (1955) and *Cinderella* (1957), both danced by the Sadler's Wells Ballet. Two volumes of the impresario's memoirs have been published: *Impresario,* written in collaboration with Ruth Goode (N.Y., 1946), and *S. Hurok Presents* (N.Y., 1953). A colorful figure in the dance and concert field Hurok has been called America's Impresario No. 1, and the legend "S. Hurok Presents," which appears in all his advertisements, posters, etc. has long been accepted as a symbol of the quality of the attraction being presented. Hurok contributed a great deal of time and effort to the preliminary discussions in Washington and Moscow of the conditions of an agreement between the U.S.A. and the U.S.S.R. about cultural exchanges between the two countries. When the agreement was signed Jan. 27, 1958, Hurok's organization, Hurok Attractions, Inc., was mentioned by name in the official document, an event without precedent. Hurok honors include an honorary Commandership of the Order of the British Empire (C.B.E.), an Officership of the French Legion of Honor, honorary doctorates from Boston and Wayne Universities, and several honors from American cities, educational institutions and organizations.

Hurry, Leslie, English painter and designer, b. London, 1909. Studied at St. John's Wood Art School and Royal Academy. His décor for Robert Helpmann's *Hamlet* (1942) was a sensation and brought him into prominence as a designer for the theatre. He designed the production of the full-length *Swan Lake* for Sadler's Wells (now Royal) Ballet (1943) and re-designed it in 1952. Designed *Scherzi Delle Sorte* (also called *The House of Cards*) for Ballet Rambert (1951). In recent years Hurry has done many designs for the legitimate theatre and for opera.

Hutchinson, Ann, dancer and notation specialist, b. New York City; m. Ivor Guest. Went to live in Europe at age eight and attended schools in England and on the continent. Studied modern dance at Jooss-Leeder Dance School, Dartington Hall, Devon, England (which included courses in music appreciation, costume design, and Laban dance notation), and in N.Y. with Hanya Holm, Martha Graham, José Limón, and others; studied ballet with Laura Wilson in London, Vincenzo Celli, Antony Tudor, Margaret

Ann Hutchinson, dancer, dance notation specialist.

Craske, Edward Caton, Vera Nemtchinova, Muriel Stuart, Anatole Oboukhoff, in N.Y., and at various times studied ballroom, folk, tap, Spanish, Hindu. As a performer she appeared in modern dance concerts in N.Y., and for eight years in Broadway musicals such as *One Touch of Venus, Billion Dollar Baby, Great to be Alive, Finian's Rainbow, Kiss Me, Kate.* Her principal work in the dance field has been as a notator and teacher of the Laban notation system. After three years' study at the Jooss-Leeder Dance School she stayed on for a further year to notate four Jooss ballets. Worked personally with Rudolf von Laban on movement analysis problems, effort observation, etc. and also has done intensive work with other leaders in the field, notably Albrecht Knust of Germany (author of *Handbook of Kinetography Laban*). Has studied twenty-two different systems of notation for comparison and evaluation. In addition to the Jooss works, *The Green Table* and *Big City,* she has notated a number of Balanchine ballets: *Symphony in C, Orpheus, Bourrée Fantasque, Theme and Variations,* and others, as well as works by Doris Humphrey, and various musicals. Was one of the founders (1940) of the Dance Notation Bureau, retiring as president in 1961. Has written many textbooks on Labanotation, and for her work in this area has been the recipient of three Rockefeller Foundation grants (see FOUNDATIONS, PHILANTHROPIC). Was one of the three teachers to establish the Dance Dept. of the School of Performing Arts, N.Y., where over two separate periods she taught ballet and Labanotation, a term she originated for this particular system. Headed the notation department of the Juilliard School of Music Dance Dept. (1951–61), and has taught and lectured at many schools and universities in the U.S. and Europe. Contributor to *Encyclopedia Britannica, Dance Encyclopedia,* and other publications. Founding member the International Council of Kinetography Laban (1961). Now living in London, but still teaches at Jacob's Pillow, for the Cecchetti Council of America, and special sessions of the Dance Notation Bureau, N.Y.

Hymn. See PROTHALAMION.

Hymn to Beauty. Ballet in 1 act; chor.: Leonide Massine; music: Francisco Mignone's *Fantasia Brasileira;* book: inspired by the Baudelaire poem of the same title; décor: Georges Wakhevitch. First prod.: Teatro Municipal, Rio de Janeiro, 1955, with Lupe Serrano, Ricardo Abellan, Michael Lland, Helga Loreida, Arthur Ferreira, Jaques Chaurand, Yara von Lindenau, Zeni Lacerda and Mercedes Batista and her Folkloric Ballet. Reminiscent of Massine's symphonic and surrealist ballets, suggesting rather than stating, the dancers being symbols.

Hynd, Ronald, English dancer, b. London, 1931; m. Annette Page. Studied at Rambert School; joined Ballet Rambert (1946), becoming soloist. Joined Sadler's Wells (now Royal) Ballet (1951), becoming soloist (1960); currently principal dancer. Roles include all the leading male parts in the classic ballets, also Bridegroom (*La Fête Etrange*), Moondog (*The Lady and the Fool*), Leonardo (Leonide Massine's revival of *The Good-Humored*

Ladies), a creation. Guest artist, National Ballet of Ireland (1960).

Hyrst, Eric (Hertzell), English dancer and choreographer, b. London, 1927. Studied at Italia Conti Stage School; later at Sadler's Wells Ballet School and with Vera Volkova. Graduated into Sadler's Wells Ballet at the age of sixteen, and two years later became soloist with the newly-formed Sadler's Wells Theatre Ballet. Joined Metropolitan Ballet as leading dancer (1947), dancing all the classic repertoire, and one of the two male roles in *Designs With Strings.* Formed his own company for a London season (1949), joined New York City Ballet (1950), leaving in 1952 to dance in South America with Ballet Alicia Alonso. Following a season with Royal Winnipeg Ballet, he joined Les Grands Ballets Canadiens (Oct., 1953), as premier danseur, choreographer, and artistic adviser. He has choreographed many ballets for this company, among them *Première Classique, Sea Gallows,* and *Hommage* (to miscellaneous selections from music of Peter Tchaikovsky).

I, Odysseus. Modern dance work in 12 episodes; chor.: José Limón; music: Hugh Aitken; properties: Thomas Watson and William McIver; lighting: Thomas Skelton. First prod.: José Limón Dance Company, 15th American Dance Festival, New London, Conn., Aug. 18, 1962, with José Limón (Odysseus), Simon Sadoff (Zeus), Betty Jones (Athena), Ruth Currier (Circe), Harlan McCallum (Poseidon), Lola Huth (Calypso), Louis Falco (Hermes), Lucy Venable (Penelope). Episodes from the *Iliad* developed in a mainly satirical manner, with Circe and Calypso as vamps impelled by jazz rhythms. Simon Sadoff is a Zeus who controls mortals and immortals from his piano, which is set to one side of the stage.

Ibert, Jacques (1890–1962), French composer. After winning the Prix de Rome (1919), he composed many scores for ballets, including *Rencontres* (1925), *Gold Standard* (Ruth Page, 1934), *Diane de Poitiers* (Serge Lifar at Paris Opéra, 1934), *Les Amours de Jupiter* (Roland Petit, Ballets des Champs-Élysées, 1946), *Ballad of Reading Goal* (Jean-Jacques Etchévery, Opéra Comique, 1947), *Escales* (Lifar, Opéra, 1949; composed in 1924), *Le Chevalier Errant* (Lifar, Opéra, 1950). He also wrote the music for the motion picture *Invitation to the Dance,* staged and choreographed by Gene Kelly (1958). His *Divertissement* has been used by many choreographers, among them Aurel Milloss (*Indiscretions*), and most recently Joseph Lazzini for Milorad Miskovitch's company (1964). Taught at the Berkshire Music Center, Tanglewood, Mass. (1950). Appointed director of the French National Lyric Theatre, i.e. the Paris Opéra and Opéra Comique (1955), but resigned after one year. He was a Commander of the Légion d'Honneur.

Icare. Ballet in 1 act; chor. and book: Serge Lifar; rhythms: Serge Lifar, orch. by J. E. Szyfer; décor: P. R. Larthe. First prod.: Paris Opéra Ballet, Théâtre de l'Opéra, Paris, July 9, 1935, with Serge Lifar in title role. The ballet is based on the Greek myth of Daedalus and Icarus. Basically a long solo with the group taking a very minor part, it was a novelty at the time because of its use of rhythmic drum beats of varying tempi instead of the conventional orchestral score.

Iconography of Dance.

BY GEORGE CHAFFEE.

The iconography of dance is both the art of representing dance by pictures or images and the study of whatever pictorial sources may be contributory to recording the history and art of dance. The latter is a much broader yet often much more specific field than the former, as, for instance, civilian portraits of dancers or scenographic designs for ballets. Compared with all the other theatrical arts, this representational record is of exceptional importance in the field of dance.

Théophile Gautier once described dance as "music seen" ("une musique qu'on voit"). The iconography of folk and social dance is valuable; however, these forms are primarily dances to be danced. Theatrical dance is that conceived and executed for the benefit of an audience. It is this that is in the last analysis a purely visual art. Here the iconography is of great importance. For all that may be written about it and whatever its musical accompaniment, both words and musice are secondary to the dance itself and are rarely able to give more than a vague, suggestive account in an inadequate medium. The one medium of direct record for theatrical dance (no abstract notation of the flexibility and universality of musical notation ever having been invented) that speaks its own language is the image as rendered by the pictorial arts: painting, drawing, sculpture, engraving, and photography. For dance, this is universal and timeless. The iconography of dance (especially of theatrical dance) is not merely an aid to literature on the subject but is itself a true "literature," of equal and sometimes of greater importance than the written word. The subject has special pertinence in relation to ballet, because ballet is a fixed academic theory and system of dance technique and of dance as theatre which has developed by enrichment rather than by any basic change and now has behind it almost five centuries of unbroken historical continuity in our European culture. Thus, present practice and past performance remain directly connected and intelligibly explicable. The history (and so, the iconography) of ballet is dominant in dance in our modern European culture, i.e., from the Renaissance on, particularly as concerns the stage, but also in social dancing down far into the 19th century, and reflexively in traditional folk-dance.

The iconography of dance in general is world-wide and of immemorial antiquity, long preceding any written accounts. In time it may be said to go back to the prehistoric cave paintings of Europe and to the sculptural monuments of the ancient peoples of the New World. The history becomes definitive and begins the great stream of dance in our European realm with the picture writings and other remains of ancient Egyptian civilization and the earliest Aegean relics of Greece and its islands. With the rise of the ancient Greek civilization of the Eastern Mediterranean, the iconography takes a form, variety, and distinction (especially in theatre dance) that has persisted in European cultures for more than 2000 years, through the age of the Roman Empire and medieval times, with the Renaissance drawing its inspiration and models directly from Greco-Roman antiquity.

This vast gallery of art works on dance falls inevitably into the great compartments of dance itself: folk, social, religious, and theatrical; West and East; ancient, medieval, and modern (i.e. from 15th–16th centuries on), etc. As art it ranges from original paintings, drawings, and sculptures (whether isolated or engaged and ornamental, in whatever application), to prints (including book illustrations) of all sorts—woodcuts, linecuts, etchings, mezzotints, aquatints, lithographs, etc., and finally, to photography and its process prints. These works can be subdivided further into full-length "action" studies (of dancers in their costumes or roles, dancing) and, historically, into portrait studies of known dancers, scenographic and costume designs, technical plates and the like, even including a sizable category of fantasy and caricature.

In such material a vast amount of widely scattered fine art is found, usually in great art galleries, known only to the public through reproductions. Students and researchers wishing to consult source material directly will do best to confine themselves historically to old prints, of which there are many collections. (In this connection, the collection of photographs of old paintings, designs, and prints of the theatre, made under the direction of Dr. Allardyce Nicoll through a Rockefeller grant, at Yale College, will be found to contain much rare dance material.)

Theatrical dance is universal and constant—and so is its art record. In Europe in the course of the Renaissance theatrical revival, the academic system of dance and the dance spectacle known as ballet emerged by degrees, to become definitively and permanently established in the second half of the 16th century. It is at this time that its iconography also begins, and we find that the most important and extensive body of dance prints are ballet items.

Apparently the earliest of all ballet prints are two plates found in Jean Dorat's brochure, *Magnificentissime Spettacoli* (Paris, 1573), and some Ecole de Fontainebleau engravings of masks and headdresses for ballets of about the same decade. There followed the famous *Balet Comique de la Royne* (Paris, 1581/82) by Balthazar de Beaujoyeux, and the earliest illustrated ballet program-libretto manuals: Fabritio Caroso's *Il Ballarino* (Venice, 1581) and the *Orchesographie* of Thoinot Arbeau (Jehan Tabourot) (Langres, 1588), the former with quite static technical plates, the latter with more animated ones.

The earliest identified print of a professional dancer (a dancing master) is the bust portrait frontispiece of himself in Caroso's volume.

The earliest identified full-length studies of professional dancers "in action" are some French linecuts of 1675–1700 (Mlles. Subligny, Desmatins, Dufort; MM. Balon, Dumoulin, Lestang, etc.). Earlier engravings by Daniel Rabel for *La Delivrance de Renault* ("Discours au vraj . . ," Paris, 1617) and the *Balli di Sfessania* etchings by Jacques Callot (Nancy, 1662) record identifiable figures; Callot's are even named, but only by their roles, on the plates.

By the end of the 16th century ballet prints were being issued in many European capitals, and they continued to appear from then on. The French sequence is the richest and most sustained. Italian works of the 16th–17th centuries are numerous and splendid, but after 1650 little seems to have been produced until the beginning 19th century. Central Europe (the Germanies, Poland, Moravia, etc.) offers an interesting and fairly consecutive series of works; Scandinavian countries and Russia published little before 1800. The publication of ballet prints in England may be said to have begun timidly in Restoration times (1660–1700) and to have been fitful during the 18th century, reaching its productive peak in the "action" studies of the 19th century. Probably the earliest American dance (ballet) print is one dated 1827 ("Mr. and Mrs. Conway and Miss Deblin of the Park Theatre, N.Y."), a New York work. Between 1827 and 1860 literally hundreds of different ballet prints (lithographs) came from American presses, a fever then common to all Europe, from whence the contagion had spread. Little of note was done anywhere other than in France between 1870 and 1900, but the genius of Serge Diaghilev and the stimulus of his Ballets Russes in Paris revived the fashion in 1909–10. Art prints as well as art photographs have been numerous ever since.

Material concerned specifically with dance iconography is sparse and fragmentary, apart from what dance literature and theatre works in general contribute in passing. Unfortunately, most writers (or their publishers) title or edit their dance illustrations in a careless, incomplete and frequently erroneous fashion.

On the iconography of ballet a number of essays written and published by Cyril W. Beaumont are important, particularly his *Five Centuries of Ballet Design* (London, 1947) and *The Romantic Ballet in Lithographs of the Time* (London, 1939). Also this writer's series of methodical catalogues of French, English, and American prints, with introductory essays and critical remarks, published in the periodical *Dance Index* (New York) under the title "The Souvenir Lithographs of the Romantic Ballet."

In addition, such works as Mrs. Lillian Arvilla Hall's *Catalogue of Engraved Dramatic Portraits in the Theatre Collection of the Harvard College Library* (Cambridge), and the Arrigoni-Bertarelli catalogue, *Ritratti di Musicisti* (Milan), on the Castello Sforzesca collection, and a hundred like volumes may be fruitfully culled for dance items buried among an endless amount of other theatre prints. As a valuable forerunner on dance iconography, G. Bapst's *Essai sur l'Histoire du Théâtre* (Paris, 1893) should also be consulted.

Icosahedron, a geometric figure having twenty sides, nearest in form to the sphere. Rudolf von Laban used the icosahedron in the development of his theories of movement. See CHOREUTICS.

Idiot, The. Ballet pantomime; chor.: Tatiana Gsovska; music: Hans Werner Henze; book: Tatiana Gsovska and Ingeborg Nachmann, based on Dostoevsky's novel of the same name; décor: Jean-Pierre Ponelle. First prod.: Hebel Theatre, Berlin, during the 1952 Berlin Festival with Wiet Palar (Nastasia), Natasha Trofimova (Aglaia), Harald Horn (Rogozhin), Wolfgang Leistner (Gania). The work is a combined form of dance, pantomime, and dialogue and follows the action of the novel in its main features and characters.

Idylle. Ballet in 1 act; chor.: George Skibine; music: François Serette; book and décor: Alwyn Camble. First prod.: Grand Ballet du Marquis de Cuevas, Théâtre de l'Empire, Paris, Jan. 2, 1954, with Marjorie Tallchief, George Skibine, and Vladimir Skouratoff. A little parable of human frailty in which the beautiful white filly, quite happy with her simple black horse lover, is momentarily overcome by the splendor of a gray circus horse, magnificent in his trappings. But once she has torn away the plumes and epaulettes in the ecstasy of her infatuation, she sees he is just a poor little horse after all, and she returns to her faithful, though countrified, lover. This ballet is also in the repertoire of Ruth Page's Chicago Opera Ballet.

Idzikowski, Stanislas, contemporary dancer and teacher, b. Poland. Studied dance with Enrico Cecchetti. Made his professional debut in Empire Theatre ballets; danced with Anna Pavlova, Lydia Lopoukhova, and the Diaghilev Ballets Russes. For the last named he created Battista (*The Good-Humored Ladies*), Cat (*Contes Russes*), Snob (*La Boutique Fantasque*), Dandy (*The Three-Cornered Hat*), Caviello (*Pulcinella*), and was a notable Bluebird (*The Sleeping Beauty*), Harlequin (*Carnaval*), and *Petrouchka.* Guest artist, Vic-Wells (later Sadler's Wells, now Royal) Ballet, dancing *Carnaval, Le Spectre de la Rose,* and creating the leading male role in *Les Rendez-vous.* Co-author with C. W. Beaumont of *A Manual of Classical Theatrical Dancing.* Currently teaching in London.

Iglesias, Roberto, contemporary Spanish dancer, b. Guatemala. Studied dance at the Bellas Artes School, Mexico City; also with Elisa Cansino, San Francisco. With the company of Rosario and Antonio (1947) and Ballet Español Ana Maria (1948). On Feb. 26, 1951, appeared with his own group, Ballets de España, in a performance at the YMHA, N.Y. Joined Rosario as her leading dancer (1953), then formed his own company (1955). This group had its first N.Y. season at the Broadway Theatre, opening Oct. 7, 1958.

Illuminations. Ballet in 1 act; chor.: Frederick Ashton; music: Benjamin Britten's *Illuminations,* a setting of Arthur Rimbaud's series of poems of that name, for tenor and strings; décor: Cecil Beaton. First prod.: New York City Ballet, City Center, N.Y., Mar. 2, 1950, with Nicholas Magallanes (Poet), Melissa Hayden (Profane Love), Tanaquil LeClercq (Sacred Love), Robert Barnett (Dandy and Drummer). This was the first ballet by a foreign choreographer to be commissioned by New York City Ballet. The action is in part a realization in dance of the poems and a choreographic comment on the life of the young poet. Revived April 7, 1967, by Nicholas Magallanes with John Prinz (Poet), Mimi Paul (Sacred Love), Sara Leland (Profane Love).

Images of Love. Ballet in 1 act; chor.: Kenneth MacMillan; commissioned music: Peter Tranchell; décor: Barry Kay; lighting: William Bundy. First prod.: Royal Ballet, Royal Opera House, Covent Garden, London, Apr. 2, 1964. The nine episodes derive from Shakespeare quotations, as follows: "She never told her love" (*Twelfth Night;* Svetlana Beriosova and Donald Macleary); ". . . the remembrance of my former love/ Is by a newer object quite forgotten" (*Two Gentlemen of Verona;* Nadia Nerina, Desmond Doyle, Keith Rosson, Derek Rencher); ". . . while idly I stood looking on/ I found the effect of love in idleness" (*Taming of the Shrew;* Georgina Parkinson, Desmond Doyle, with ten dancers); ". . . love is blind" (*Two Gentlemen of Verona;* Lynn Seymour, Christopher Gable); "Love, lend me wings to make my purpose swift" (*Two Gentlemen of Verona;* Nadia Nerina, Alexander Grant); "When love begins to sicken and decay/ It useth an enforced ceremony" (*Julius Caesar;* Beriosova and Macleary); "Two loves I have of comfort and despair" (Sonnet CXLIV; Rudolf Nureyev, Lynn Seymour, Christopher Gable); "I break my fast, dine, sup and sleep,/ Upon the very naked name of love" (*Two Gentlemen of Verona;* Alexander Grant, Georgina Parkinson and five dancers); "If music be the food of love, play on" (*Twelfth Night;* full company). This ballet, with Frederick Ashton's *The Dream,* was created for a special Shakespeare Quatercentenary program, the evening being completed by Robert Helpmann's *Hamlet.*

Imago. Modern dance work; chor., sound score, costumes, lights: Alwin Nikolais; color consultant, George Constant. First prod.: Nikolais Dance Company, Hartford, Conn., Feb. 24, 1963; N.Y. première: Henry Street Settlement Playhouse, Feb. 28 (by invitation), Mar. 1 (public performance), with Murray Louis, Gladys Bailin, Phyllis Lamhut, Bill Frank, Peggy Barclay, Albert Reid, Roger Rowell, Ray Broussard. The most extended and complete of all the Nikolais experiments up to that time in which the dancers are as important, but no more so, than the other components that make up the work. Forms, color, shapes, costumes which are extensions of the dancer, all make up an endlessly fascinating kaleidoscope of movement.

Imperial Society of Teachers of Dancing, Inc. (England), founded in 1904, by far the largest body of teachers in the British Commonwealth, with headquarters in London. The Society was remodeled in 1924 and now each form of dancing has its own branch in the Society. The ballroom and stage branches are the largest; there are two classical ballet branches, one known as the Imperial Ballet Branch and the other as the Cecchetti Society Branch. The Cecchetti Society (which follows the methods of that maestro) was an independent organization until incorporated into the Imperial Society (1924). Entrance is by examination and further examinations have to be passed before a member becomes a Fellow. From time to time examiners are sent abroad. At home the ballroom branch makes a feature of what is known as Medal Tests for amateurs. Current president is Victor Silvester; chairman, C. W. Beaumont.

Impresario, a person who engages a ballet company or other dance organization and presents it in performances. The basic difference between an impresario and a manager is that an impresario pays the company a stipulated sum for each week of the season, guarantees the number of weeks the company will perform during the season, pays for its transportation, hires an orchestra, and assumes the financial risk. A manager works for the company generally on a percentage basis, assumes no financial risk, and does not share in the expenses. See also BOOKING AGENT.

Inbal (Dance Theatre of Israel). The Hebrew word "Inbal" means the tongue of the bell, the clapper which transforms the bell from a piece of dead cup-shaped metal into a source of living sound. It was aptly chosen as the name of the dance troupe, for one of the intentions of Inbal is to give sound to an aspect of Jewish art which has been practically unknown outside Israel. Director Sara Levi-Tanai and the dancers who constitute Inbal are with one or two exceptions Yemenite Jews (or as the Bible calls them, Temanites)—those Jews who have lived since antiquity in the little country of Yemen, situated in the south-western part of the Arabian peninsula on the Red Sea. Soon after Israel became an independent state in May, 1948, virtually all the Jews of Yemen left the country to join their brethren in Israel. Inbal was founded in 1950.

The founder-director-choreographer of Inbal is Sara Levi-Tanai, a small frail-looking, shy, retiring woman in her forties. Although she has had no formal dance education, she possesses an enormous talent for choreography which makes it possible for her to stage intricate dance compositions which have all the earmarks of great craftsmanship as well. She has had no formal musical training, yet she is able to reconstruct the melodies of her people from simple chants and give them form, body, and color, and compose an occasional tune that has the style, cadence, and melodic line of a true folk song. Mrs. Tanai had a two-fold aim in assembling her troupe: she wanted to preserve the basic cultural elements of her people in their new surroundings and at the same time try to integrate the art of her people into the art expression of Israel as a whole. These aims may seem contradictory, but they are not in reality. It must be realized that Israel is not homogeneous country; some ninety percent of its nearly two million population are Jews, but they are Jews who came to Israel from three continents—Europe, Asia, and Africa. Each group brought with it cultural influences from the countries where they had lived. In Israel they found cultural influences from other countries and it became obvious that eventually the various cultures would become integrated into a new culture likely to produce new art forms and its own traditions. Some groups would continue to preserve their cultural heritage and add to the new culture, others would be absorbed by the new culture. It was Sara Levi-Tanai's feeling that the Yemenite community of Israel could and should not only make its definite contribution to the culture of Israel through its dances and songs, but could also lend color to the very basis upon which the culture of Israel was to develop.

Most of the work of the Inbal troupe is based on Yemenite tradition and folklore. Influences of many nations are reflected in the Yemenite dance; there is first the influence of the traditional dance of the time of the Jewish prophets and kings as described in the Bible, an influence that is also apparent in the use of percussion instruments—the drum, tambourine, finger-cymbals, anklebells—all mentioned in the Bible, as well as the Biblical flute

Queen of Sheba, a ballet in the repertoire of Inbal. Margalith Oved in the title role (center), Meir Ovadia as King Solomon (on the throne).

(halil). There is also the influence of the long forgotten (by the Western Jew) liturgical dance, only the faintest traces of which are left in contemporary Jewish public worship. The influence of the Arabic dance is obvious, but there is also the influence of the African Negro dance. Yemenite music is often syncopated and the syncopation is reflected in the dance which here and there approaches what is now called modern jazz. Other clear influences include head and shoulder movements from India; the use of the kerchief by the girls and the barely accented shuffling steps from the Caucasus; the languid movements of the Turkish odalisque; and many others.

Most of the girls in the Inbal troupe are dark-complexioned and beautiful. Nearly all have straight backs and small heads proudly sitting on a long neck set on square shoulders. The heads and backs reflect the pride of a small nation but there is also a physical explanation: for untold generations Yemenite women have been used to carrying loads on their heads. Most of the men in the troupe are also dark, a little above average height, square shouldered, and handsome. They are strong and their dance technique is more elaborate than that of the girls. When dancing as a group by themselves, they vie with one another in the execution of intricate steps, despite the definite choreography set for them.

The repertoire of Inbal consists of Yemenite folk themes, religious themes which are closely interwoven with the Yemenite way of living (such as *Sabbath Eve,* a tender piece of spiritual love and beauty), stories from the Bible (such as the heroic *Deborah the Prophetess,* or the somewhat humorous episode of King Solomon and the Queen of Sheba), dances on the eternal theme of love between man and woman (such as the romantic *Longing*), and works based on Yemenite customs (the elaborate and absorbing *Wedding*).

Inbal has visited the United States twice (1958, 1959), touring the country under the management of Hurok Attractions. In 1963 they appeared in the film *The Greatest Story Ever Told.*

Indes Galantes, Les, ballet by Fuzelier, given at the Académie Royale (1735). The music was by Jean Philippe Rameau, the costumes by Jean Baptiste Martin. An entirely new version was staged at the Paris Opéra June 18, 1952, and has remained in the repertoire. Choreography was by Albert Aveline (prologue and 1st entrée), Serge Lifar (2nd and 4th entrée) and Harald Lander (3rd entrée). Seven prominent designers were responsible for the various scenes: Arbus and Jacques Dupont (prologue, "The Palace of Hebe"); George Wakhevitch (1st entrée, "The Generous Turk"); Jean Carzou (2nd entrée, "The Incas"); Fost and Moulène (3rd entrée, "The Flowers"); Roger Chapelain-Midy (4th entrée, "The Savages"). It is one of the greatest successes of recent years at the Opéra, due to the richness and fantasy of the productions, the harmony of the elements of singing, dance, lighting, settings, and the excellence of the interpreters.

Indiscretions. Ballet in 1 act; chor.: Aurel Milloss; music: Jacques Ibert's *Divertissement;* idea: Eduardo Anahory and Milloss; décor: Eduardo Anahory. First prod.: Ballet do IV Centenario, Teatro Municipal, Rio de Janeiro, 1954, with Ady Addor, Lia Marques, Raul Severo, Cristian Uboldi, Ismael Guiser, Norberto Neri. A very elegant, stylized, satire leaning toward the grotesque.

Indo-Chinese Dance. See ORIENTAL DANCE.

Indrani, Indian dancer specializing in the more recondite styles of the classic Indian dance.

Indrani, contemporary Hindu dancer, b. Madras, India. The daughter of Ragini Devi, she studied Bharata Natya with Pandanallur Chokkalingam Pillai and Sikkil Ramaswami Pillai. Later became interested in the lesser known styles of the classic Indian dance, studying Orissi with Devas Prasad Das, Mohini Attam with Kerala Kalamandalam, and Kuchipudi with Narasimha Rao. She was the first dancer to present the Orissi classic dance (of Orissa state) and the Kuchipudi dance-dramas outside India. She has toured extensively in Europe, the U.S., and Canada.

Inglesby, Mona (Kimberley), English dancer, company director, b. London, 1918. Studied at Rambert School and danced with Ballet Rambert, creating La Môme Fromage, and Can-Can dancer in Bar aux Folies-Bergère (1934), and later dancing La Goulue in the same ballet; Papillon (*Carnaval*), and others. Founder of International Ballet (1940), of which company she was director, choreographer, and ballerina, dancing *Coppélia, Swan Lake, The Sleeping Beauty,* and others. Choreographed *Endymion, Everyman,*

Masque of Comus, Amoras, Panetomania, etc. Retired in 1953.

Inquest. Modern dance work; chor.: Doris Humphrey; music: Norman Lloyd; costumes: Pauline Lawrence. First prod.: Humphrey-Weidman Studio Theater, Mar. 5, 1944, with Doris Humphrey (Mother), Charles Weidman (Father), Peter Hamilton (Son). *Inquest* was based on a famous chapter, "Of King's Treasuries," in John Ruskin's *Sesame and Lilies.* A narrator read extracts from a coronor's report on a death from starvation of a poor cobbler in the England of 1865. This work also marked Doris Humphrey's last appearances as a dancer.

Insects and Heroes. Modern dance work; chor.: Paul Taylor; music: John Herbert McDowell; décor: Rouben Ter-Arutunian; costumes: George Tacet. First prod.: Paul Taylor and Dance Company, 14th American Dance Festival, Connecticut College, New London, Aug. 18, 1961, with Maggie Newman, Linda Hodes, Elizabeth Walton, Elizabeth Keen, Paul Taylor, Dan Wagoner; N.Y. première: Hunter College Playhouse, Nov. 24, 1961. Like most of Taylor's titles, whether this one has anything to do with the action remains in doubt. His strange creatures move with a kind of aimless compulsion in and out of little lighted booths or indulge in mimic battles which resolve nothing and end as inconclusively as they begin.

International Ballet, company founded in London, England, in Feb., 1940, by Mona Inglesby. Gave its initial performance at Alhambra Theatre, Glasgow, May 19, 1941, followed by a tour of the provinces and a season at the Lyric Theatre, London. From then until 1953 when it was disbanded, it toured all over Great Britain and Northern Ireland (its season at the Grand Opera House, Belfast, in July, 1947, was the first visit of a major ballet company since 1912, when Anna Pavlova danced in Belfast with her group), in Italy, Spain, Sicily and Switzerland, and gave annual seasons in London. The repertoire included the full-length classic ballets, *Coppélia, Swan Lake, The Sleeping Beauty,* all staged by Nicholas Sergeyev, the company's ballet master; Michel Fokine's *Les Sylphides* and *Carnaval;* the Lev Ivanov *Polovetsian Dances from Prince Igor,* also staged by Sergeyev; Andrée Howard's *Twelfth Night;* Harold Turner's *Fête en Bohème;* Mona Inglesby's *Endymion, Everyman, The Masque of Comus, Planetomania,* and others. Celia Franca, Moira Shearer, Sonia Arova danced with International Ballet early in their careers. In the season of 1947 Nana Gollner and Paul Petroff appeared as guest artists.

Interplay. Ballet in 4 movements; chor.: Jerome Robbins; music: Morton Gould's *American Concertette;* décor: Carl Kent. First prod. (as part of Billy Rose's *Concert Varieties*): Ziegfeld Theatre, N.Y., June 1, 1945, with Janet Reed, Muriel Bentley, Bettina Rosay, Roszika Sabo, John Kriza, Jerome Robbins, Michael Kidd, Erik Kristen. Produced by Ballet (now American Ballet) Theatre, with décor by Oliver Smith and costumes by Irene Sharaff, Metropolitan Opera House, N.Y., Oct. 17, 1945, with Janet Reed, Muriel Bentley, Melissa Hayden (then Mildred Herman), Roszika Sabo, John Kriza, Fernando Alonso, Harold Lang, Tommy Rall. Produced by New York City Ballet, with new costumes by Irene Sharaff, at City Center, N.Y., Dec. 23, 1952, with Janet Reed, Todd Bolender, Michael Maule, Jacques d'Amboise. Vassily Lambrinos has staged his own version for Teatro Colón, Buenos Aires. It is a themeless ballet, although these dancers and this choreography could only be American.

Invitation, The. Ballet in 1 act; chor.: Kenneth MacMillan; commissioned music: Matyas Seiber; décor: Nicholas

Georgiadis. First prod.: Royal Ballet, New Theatre, Oxford, Nov. 10, 1960, with Lynn Seymour (The Girl), Christopher Gable (Her Cousin), Anne Heaton (The Wife), Desmond Doyle (The Husband). The libretto was based on two novels—*The Ripening Seed* by Colette and *House of the Angel* by Beatriz Guido. It tells of a double seduction and the loss of innocence. This ballet confirmed Lynn Seymour as a great, new dramatic dancer and also focussed attention on Gable as one of the most promising of a rising generation of English male dancers. Donald Macleary, Anya Linden and Monica Mason have danced the roles of the Cousin and the Wife.

Irman, Vladimir (Vladimir Georges Irman Sknaksareff), Argentine dancer and choreographer, b. Anapa, Kuban (Russia), 1919; now a citizen of Argentina. Studied ballet with Olga Preobrajenska in Paris. Soloist of the Original Ballet Russe, 1939–44. In 1944 he was engaged as choreographer and dancer by Casino de Urca, Rio de Janeiro, of which he later became artistic director. While at the Casino he appeared as guest artist at Teatro Municipal, where he danced the Russian Sailor in Igor Schwezoff's production of *The Red Poppy*. In 1947 he was invited as guest artist by Teatro Colón, Buenos Aires. In 1950 he toured Uruguay as guest artist of the ballet company of Teatro SODRE. Subsequently danced with Adela Adamova, première danseuse of the Colón in operettas for which he choreographed the dances, in Argentina, Brazil and Uruguay. In 1961 he was choreographer-dancer-actor of Harold Hecht's film production of *Taras Bulba,* Buenos Aires. Currently guest choreographer and dancer with the Argentine and Brazil ballet companies.

Irving, Robert A., musical director and conductor, b. Winchester, England, 1913; educated Winchester College; New College, Oxford; Royal College of Music. After serving during World War II with the Royal Air Force Coastal Command (being decorated with the Distinguished Flying Cross and bar), became associate conductor of the B.B.C. (British Broadcasting Corporation) Scottish Orchestra, Glasgow (1946–48); musical director and adviser to Sadler's Wells (now Royal) Ballet (1949–58); musical director and principal conductor, New York City Ballet since 1958. Has also conducted for New York City Opera and for Martha Graham. He has made many recordings with Philharmonia, Royal Philharmonic, Royal Opera House orchestras, and Sinfonia of London; between 1952 and 1958 conducted many symphony concerts with Philharmonia, Royal Philharmonic, and London Philharmonic orchestras. Composed the music for the N.Y. Theatre Guild production of Shakespeare's *As You Like It* (1949), and for British documentary films, *Floodtide* (1948) and *British Travel Association* (1958). Also serves as one of the two on-stage pianists in *Liebeslieder Walzer* for the New York City Ballet.

Isaac d'Orleans, Sieur, Jewish dancing master at the French court, ca. 1700. English poet Jenyns wrote of him:
"And Isaac's Rigadoon shall live as long
As Raphael's painting or as Virgil's song."

Isaksen, Lone, Danish dancer, b. Copenhagen, 1941. Made her debut as a teen-ager with Elsa-Marianne von Rosen's Scandinavian Ballet, dancing the title role in *La Sylphide* and solo roles in ballets by von Rosen, Ivó Cramer, and others. Came to N.Y. in 1962 to study at American Ballet Center on an American-Scandinavian Foundation scholarship; shortly thereafter joined the Robert Joffrey Ballet. Created the leading role in Gerald Arpino's *Incubus* (1962); also had a leading role in his *Palace,* and others. After the dissolution of the Joffrey company following its U.S. tour (spring, 1964) she joined the Harkness Ballet (June, 1964) as ballerina. Her repertoire includes *The Abyss, After Eden, Highland Fair, Daphnis and Chloë, Sebastian.* Appeared as guest artist with Niels Kehlet of the Royal Danish Ballet at the Jacob's Pillow Dance Festival, dancing *Le Spectre de la Rose* (summer, 1966).

Ismailov, Serge, dancer, teacher, b. Moscow, 1912; m. Anna Istomina. Educated in Russia and Belgium. Studied dance with Olga Preobrajenska, Lubov Egorova, Bronislava Nijinska, Nicholas Legat, Pierre Vladimirov, Anatole Oboukhoff. Member, Nijinska's company (1932), Les Ballets 1933, Col. de Basil's Ballet Russe (1933–40), Ballet Russe de Monte Carlo (1943–44), Ballet International (1944). Also danced in television, musicals. Among his roles were Swineherd (*The Hundred Kisses*), Chief Cossack (*La Boutique Fantasque*), Favorite Slave (*Schéhérazade*). Currently teaching in N.Y.

Israel, Dance Theatre of. See INBAL.

Istomina, Anna (Audrée Ruth Thomas), dancer, teacher, b. Vancouver, B.C., Canada, 1925; m. Sergei Ismailov. Studied dance with June Roper. Member, Ballet Russe de Monte Carlo (1940–44), becoming soloist. Danced pas de trois (*Swan Lake*), *Blue Bird* pas de deux, leading roles in *Rouge et Noir, Snow Maiden, Les Sylphides,* and others. Danced in *Song of Norway* (1944); soloist in operetta *La Vie Parisienne* (1944–45); ballerina of Leonide Massine's Ballet Russe Highlights (1945–46), Teatro Colón, Buenos Aires, Argentina (1947). Has appeared on television. Currently teaching.

Istomina, Avdotia (1799–1848), Russian ballerina of the St. Petersburg Ballet who was graduated from the Imperial School of Ballet in 1815. While still in school she danced solo parts in many ballets. According to contemporary writers, Istomina was of medium height, dark, very beautiful, had an excellent figure and fiery black eyes veiled by long eyelashes. She was very strong, had excellent aplomb and, at the same time, was very graceful and light. Her pirouettes and elevation were extraordinary. Istomina was very successful on the stage and had a most romantic life. At least two duels were fought over her during one of which an officer of the Imperial Guard, Count V. V. Sheremetieff, was killed and the famous Russian playwright Alexander Griboyedoff was wounded. The great Russian poet Alexander Pushkin dedicated some verses to Istomina in his *Eugene Onegin.* Istomina left the stage in 1836 and died twelve years later of cholera.

Itelman, Ana, Argentine dancer and choreographer, b. Santiago de Chile, 1932. Studied dance in Buenos Aires, Argentina, with Miriam Winslow and became a member of her company. In U.S. studied with Martha Graham, Hanya Holm, José Limón, Louis Horst; in Montevideo, Uruguay, with Nina Fonaroff. In 1954 she formed a company and presented her ballet *"Esta Ciudad de Buenos Aires . . ."* In 1956 she choreographed the dances in the musical comedy *Plain and Fancy* in Buenos Aires. Her other works include *Gymnopedies* (Satie), *Yorubas* (popular music), *Choros* (Villa-Lobos), *Sarcasmo* (Prokofiev), *Ebony Concerto* (Stravinsky), and Gian-Carlo Menotti's *The Unicorn, the Gorgon and the Manticore.* At present Ana Itelman teaches dance at Bard College, Annandale-on-Hudson, N.Y.

Ito, Michio (1894–1961), Japanese dancer and dance director; m. Hazel Wright, American dancer, marriage ending in divorce in 1936. Studied dance in Germany. Came to U.S. during World War I and appeared in the Theatre Guild production of the Japanese play *Bushido.* In 1920 (and later) worked in John Murray Anderson's productions of the *Greenwich Village Follies,* remaining to teach and do concert work in the U.S. In 1930 he presented a series of popular Japanese plays at the Booth Theatre. He returned to Japan in 1948 and produced in Tokyo the Gilbert and Sullivan *Mikado*. He operated a television studio in Japan and arranged for the appearance of Oriental dancers in the U.S. He last visited the U.S. in 1959.

Iuqui, Leda (Leda Rivas), contemporary Brazilian dancer and teacher, b. Pelotas. Began studies at the School of the Teatro Municipal in 1936 with Maria Olenewa; later worked with Yuco Lindberg and Vaslav Veltchek. Became soloist of the Teatro Municipal in 1943; left to dance with the Original Ballet Russe (1944); returned as guest ballerina for the 1946–47 season. Danced subsequently in the Copacabana Casino. Since 1958 has directed her own school in Copacabana.

Ivanov, Lev (1834–1901), Russian dancer, teacher, choreographer of the St. Petersburg Russian Imperial Ballet. Graduated from the St. Petersburg School in 1852. A talented dancer and one of the greatest choreographers of the 19th century, Ivanov was kept in the background during his entire career, dominated first by Jules Perrot, who did not like him, and later by Marius Petipa, who considered him a dangerous rival. Contemporary Russian sources agree that had Ivanov not been a Russian, his fame would have at least equalled that of Petipa. From his early years at school he displayed a phenomenal musical aptitude. The director of the Imperial School of Music made several unsuccessful attempts to have Ivanov transferred from the ballet school to the music school. The authorities of the ballet school did not appreciate his musical genius and he was often reprimanded and punished for his great interest in music. Felix Kchessinski, father of Mathilda Kchessinska, tells in his memoirs: "Our rehearsals were usually conducted to the accompaniment of two violins rather than

Lev Ivanov, great Russian choreographer, best known for The Nutcracker *and Acts 2 and 4 of* Swan Lake.

a piano. Once one of the violinists did not show up for rehearsal. Ivanov calmly sat down at the piano and played the whole ballet from the beginning to the end, as if he had the music before him." In 1882 Ivanov was appointed regisseur-in-chief of the ballet company. In 1885 he was promoted to the post of second ballet master under Petipa. Ivanov staged nearly a score of ballets for the Imperial Theatre, new ones and revivals, most of them "in collaboration" with other choreographers, especially Petipa. This collaboration was due not to Ivanov's need of help but to the ruling of the director of the theatre. His most important works are *The Nutcracker* and *Swan Lake*. He staged all of *The Nutcracker* since Petipa was ill at that time, and Acts 2 and 4 of *Swan Lake*. The other ballets staged or revived by Ivanov are *La Fille Mal Gardée* (with Petipa), *The Enchanted Forest, The Haarlem Tulip, Cupid's Pranks, The Magic Flute, Cinderella* (Act 2), *The Awakening of Flora* (with Petipa), *Acis et Galatée, Mikado's Daughter, Sylvia* (unfinished due to Ivanov's death). Most of Ivanov's works were attributed to Petipa even during the former's lifetime because Petipa's name, as ballet-master-in-chief, had to be placed on the program. In addition, Petipa often interfered with Ivanov's work just so he would have a "moral" right to have his name on the program.

Ivanovsky, Nicolai (1893–1961), professor, Honored Art Worker of the RSFSR. From the end of World War II until his death, Ivanovsky was artistic director of the Vaganova Choreographic School (Ballet School) of the Kirov Theatre, Leningrad. He was graduated from the same school (then called Theatre School) under Michel Fokine, who mentions him in his memoirs as an outstanding dancer and a member of the great choreographer's brilliant class of 1911 (which also included Pierre Vladimirov and Alexander Gavrilov). Danced character roles with the Diaghilev Ballets Russes (1912–15). In 1915 worked in the Troitzky Theatre Miniature founded by Fokine's brother, Alexander. Returned to the Maryinsky (now Kirov) Theatre, Leningrad, as soloist end of 1915 and remained until the late 1930's. His importance, however, is as a pedagogue, his activities placing him among the outstanding figures of the Soviet Ballet. He was a leading authority on historical dance, teaching it to the day of his death at the Leningrad ballet school and in the teachers' training department. He was the author of *Ballroom Dance of the 16th and 19th Centuries,* published in Leningrad in 1948.

Ivesiana. Ballet in 6 episodes; chor.: George Balanchine; music: Charles Ives' "Central Park in the Dark," "Hallowe'en," "The Unanswered Question," "Over the Pavements," "In the Inn," "In the Night." First prod.: New York City Ballet, City Center, N.Y., Sept. 14, 1954, with Janet Reed and Francisco Moncion (1st episode), Patricia Wilde and Jacques d'Amboise (2nd episode), Allegra Kent and Todd Bolender (3rd episode), Diana Adams and Herbert Bliss (4th episode), Tanaquil LeClercq and Bolender (5th episode). The 2nd episode ("Hallowe'en") was revised and became "Arguments," and then revised again and called "Barn Dance." The six unrelated scenes created an atmosphere of foreboding, despair, mystery, joyless frenzy and final hopelessness (in the last episode the dancers simply move about the stage on their knees, passing and re-passing as they shuffle from one side to the other) that welds the work into a coherent whole. A shortened and somewhat revised version was premièred Mar. 16, 1961, the 1st, 3rd, 5th (almost completely new), and 6th remaining. Now becoming 1st, 2nd, 3rd, and 4th, they were danced by Patricia McBride and Francisco Moncion, Allegra Kent and Deni Lamont, Diana Adams and Arthur Mitchell. The final episode remained unchanged.

Izmailova, Galia, Peoples' Artist of the U.S.S.R., Soviet ballerina, b. 1923. Izmailova is the first Uzbek classical ballerina (in contrast to the numerous folk dancers headed by Tamara Hanum). She studied ballet in Tashkent under the Maryinsky-trained teacher Yevgenia Oboukhova, and is leading ballerina of the Uzbek State Theatre of Opera and Ballet. She also excels in Uzbek national dances and in 1946 received a prize for performing the national dance, Zang. In 1952 the Uzbek ballet, *Ballerina,* was created in Tashkent, using the story of her life; a simple girl from a Uzbek village becomes a ballerina. In 1953 she danced with great success in London.

Jackson, Rowena, New Zealand dancer, b. Invercargill, 1926; m. Philip Chatfield. Studied with the Misses Powell and Lawson in New Zealand. She was the first New Zealand recipient of a Royal Academy of Dancing Scholarship. Entered Sadler's Wells School (1946); won the Adeline Genée Gold Medal (1947). Became a member of the Sadler's Wells (now Royal) Ballet; promoted to ballerina (1954). She danced all the leading classic roles and was especially dazzling in the third act of *Swan Lake* where she performed the thirty-two fouettés, alternating singles with doubles, perfectly sur place. She first attracted public attention, in fact, when she stepped at a moment's notice into an injured dancer's place during a performance of *Les Patineurs* and performed the almost equally famous fouettés that occur towards the end of that ballet. Other roles included *Blue Bird* pas de deux, Fire (*Homage to the Queen*), and the creation of one of the seven ballerina roles in *Birthday Offering*. She returned to New Zealand shortly after her marriage to Philip Chatfield (1958). Dances as ballerina with United Ballet Company of New Zealand since 1959. Awarded M.B.E. (Member of the Order of the British Empirc), 1961.

Jacob, Kurt, German choreographer and ballet master in the modern dance style, b. Berlin, 1922. Student of Max Terpis and Sabine Ress. Soloist of the Theater am Nollendorfplatz, Berlin (1939–43); then of the Opera House, Düsseldorf, and later of the City Theatre in Malmö, Sweden. Returned to the Berlin Theatre where he staged the dances for *Lady in the Dark* by Kurt Weill. Since 1953 has choreographed for motion pictures and television in Berlin, Stuttgart, and Munich. His television ballets include *Frankie and Johnny, Leather and Lavender, The Matchmaker, Parallels, Terminus: Longing*. Guest choreographer for *Kiss Me, Kate* (Munich), *Mirror of Memory* (television station Granada, London), *La Paloma* (Hamburg), and others.

Jacob's Pillow, an 18th century farm near Lee, Mass. which was purchased in 1930 by Ted Shawn. The name comes from an old wagon road which zig-zagged over this particular Berkshire hill and was named Jacob's Ladder by New England settlers. The farm was called Jacob's Pillow because of one huge boulder on the side lawn of the "salt-box" style farm house. Ted Shawn used the house and the two adjacent barns as a summer dance theatre and residence for his group of men dancers between 1933 and 1939. After the group was disbanded in the spring of 1940, Mary Washington Ball, professor of physical education at the State Normal

School in Cortland, N.Y., leased the farm for the summer to conduct the Jacob's Pillow School of Dance and Festival. The following summer Alicia Markova and Anton Dolin leased Jacob's Pillow to run an International Dance Festival and School. Most of the Ballet Theatre company lived and rehearsed at Jacob's Pillow that summer and many of its artists took part in the performances which were given in a converted barn which was also used as a studio. In Oct. of that year a group of people bought the farm from Ted Shawn and incorporated Jacob's Pillow Dance Festival as an educational, artistic, non-profit organization, appointing Mr. Shawn managing director of the enterprise. The first move of the new organization was to build a separate dance theatre with a seating capacity of some five hundred. In 1959 a major job of reconstruction enlarged the entrance and increased the seating capacity by seventy-one by means of a small balcony. Now called the Ted Shawn Theatre, it was especially designed by architect Joseph Franz who designed the Music Shed at Tanglewood, Mass., for the Berkshire Music Festival. Construction began in the spring of 1942 and was finished in July. During the summers of 1942–46 Jacob's Pillow continued under the directorship of Ted Shawn, assisted by Fern Helsher. Early in 1947 Shawn decided to take a vacation from Jacob's Pillow and the directors of the corporation appointed Arthur Mahoney and Thalia Mara as managing directors of the School and Festival for the summer of 1947. Shawn returned as director in 1948 and has continued in that capacity ever since, with John Christian as his associate director. He has maintained a consistent policy of presenting modern, ethnic dance, and ballet on his programs, but he has departed from this practice on special occasions, such as when he has imported such important foreign visitors as National Ballet of Canada (1953), ten dancers from the Royal Danish Ballet (1955), and Ballet Rambert (1959), all of them making their U.S. debuts and all of them presenting the entire program. Jacob's Pillow has also given the opportunity to regional ballet groups to be seen outside their areas: Miami Ballet (1957), Atlanta Civic Ballet (1958), Washington Ballet (1960), Boston Ballet (1962). The Jacob's Pillow Dance Festival remains unique as the only festival extending over a period of ten weeks (65 performances), which is entirely devoted to dance. Europe has many festivals devoted to music and dance, but all except that in Copenhagen place the emphasis on music. Connecticut College annually presents its American Dance Festival of modern dance (the longest to date in 1962—11 performances) in connection with and at the culmination of its summer school session. Smaller festivals of two or three performances take place in the U.S., such as the Perry-Mansfield Theatre Festival at Steamboat Springs, Colo., and a few others. In dance, however, there is nothing anywhere on the scale of the Jacob's Pillow Dance Festival.

Japanese Dance. See ORIENTAL DANCE.

Jaques-Dalcroze, Émile. See DALCROZE, ÉMILE JAQUES.

Jardin aux Lilas. See LILAC GARDEN.

Jarre, La. See GIARA, LA.

Jarvis, Lilian, Canadian dancer, b. Toronto, 1931. Studied dance with Mildred Wickson and Boris Volkov in Toronto. Went to London, England (1950) to study dance and appear in *Carousel* at Drury Lane Theatre. On returning to Canada (1951) joined the newly-formed National Ballet of Canada of which she is one of the principals. Her roles include Swanilda (*Coppélia*), Sugar Plum Fairy and Snow Queen (*The Nutcracker*), *Giselle,* Odette (*Swan Lake,* Act 2). She also dances leads in many ballets of the contemporary repertoire including *Lilac Gar-*

den, Pineapple Poll, Winter Night, and Grant Strate's ballets for the National Ballet of Canada.

Jasinski (Czeslaw), Roman, dancer and teacher, b. Warsaw, Poland, 1912; m. Moscelyne Larkin (Moussia Larkina). After seven years of study at Warsaw Opera Ballet School (from which he was graduated as the honor student of his class and winner of three prizes), he was engaged by Bronislava Nijinska for the Paris season of the Ida Rubinstein company (1928), which gave him the opportunity for further studies with Nijinska and Lubov Egorova in Paris. Gave concert performances with Serge Lifar in France (1931); danced with Leonide Massine at Teatro alla Scala, Milan (1932); was one of the original members of Col. de Basil's Ballets Russes (1932). Left that company to join George Balanchine's Les Ballets 1933 as premier danseur, creating roles in *Les Songes, Errante, Mozartiana,* and *Seven Deadly Sins.* Made his U.S. debut later that year with a group of dancers led by Serge Lifar. Rejoined Ballets Russes de Monte Carlo (1933) and remained as premier danseur until 1947 (by which time the company was known as Original Ballet Russe). Joined Sergei Denham's Ballet Russe de Monte Carlo (1948–50). One of the outstanding interpreters of the male role in *Les Sylphides,* his large repertoire also including Prince (*Swan Lake*), Albrecht (*Giselle*), Blue Bird (*Aurora's Wedding*), Hussar (*Le Beau Danube*), Baron (*Gaîté Parisienne*), Poet (*Night Shadow*), title roles in *Le Spectre de la Rose, Protée, Icare, Afternoon of a Faun, Prodigal Son* (Lichine version). He travelled all over the world with these companies; also toured in South America with Alicia Markova (1950) and Tamara Toumanova (1953). Ballet master and premier danseur, Ballet Russe de Monte Carlo Concert Company (1951 and 1952); with Alexandra Danilova's Great Moments of Ballet group (1954–55). Now teaches in Tulsa, Okla., where he and his wife also direct the Tulsa Civic Ballet (see REGIONAL BALLET), for which he stages works from the standard repertoire and choreographs original ballets.

Jason and the Argonauts. Ballet by Bergonzio di Botta of Tortona, presented at the banquet-ball given in 1489 for the Duke of Milan. It is this spectacle that set the pattern for later ballets.

Jazz Concert. A four-part entertainment as follows: *Creation of the World,* Darius Milhaud's 1923 score choreographed by Todd Bolender; Igor Stravinsky's 1918 *Ragtime,* choreographed by George Balanchine; Francis Poulenc's 1923 *Les Biches* (The House Party), choreographed by Francisco Moncion; Igor Stravinsky's 1946 *Ebony Concerto,* choreographed by John Taras. First prod.: New York City Ballet, City Center, N.Y., Dec. 7, 1960. This was the first of two "Jazz Evenings" (see MODERN JAZZ: VARIANTS). The first and the last ballets survived the occasion and have been given occasional performances since. *Creation of the World,* in décor by David Hays, begins with Adam and Eve, rushes swiftly down the centuries and arrives at the 1920's with a gold digger and a poor but faithful lover who remains true after the Wall Street crash erases everything and everybody else. The gold digger, Peaches, was Janet Reed's last creation before she retired entirely as a dancer. *Ebony Concerto,* danced in practice costume, with décor by David Hays, was in three movements, Allegro Moderato, Andante, and Vivo. Patricia McBride and Arthur Mitchell led a small corps de ballet in choreography which reflected the music and had an effective opening with all the dancers in silhouette.

Jeanmaire, Renée (Zizi), French ballerina and motion picture star, b. Paris, 1925; m. Roland Petit. A "petit rat" of the Paris Opéra, trained by Alexandre

Renée Jeanmaire, in rehearsal for her most famous role in the ballet Carmen, *choreographed by Roland Petit.*

Volinine and Boris Kniaseff, she joined the company in 1939. Gave some Paris performances partnered by Roger Fenonjois and (in 1945) Wladimir Skouratoff. Appeared with Roland Petit at the Soirées de la Danse at Sarah Bernhardt Theatre organized by Irène Lidova and Claude Giraud (1944); created leading role in *Quadrille* (choreographed by Fenonjois, 1945). Ballerina with Nouveau Ballet de Monte Carlo (directed by Eugene Grunberg and Serge Lifar 1946), creating *Aubade* (Lifar–Francis Poulenc). Ballerina with Col. de Basil's Original Ballet Russe for its final London and Paris seasons (1947) dancing *Graduation Ball, Prodigal Son* (Lichine version), and others. Joined Les Ballets de Paris de Roland Petit for its initial season at the Marigny Theatre, Paris (1948), dancing leading roles in *Que le Diable l'Emporte, Études Symphoniques.* Her career reached its climax with Petit's *Carmen,* premièred in London (1949). When this was followed by a N.Y. season, she became internationally famous. Sang for the first time in *La Croqueuse de Diamants* (1950). Went to Hollywood (1951) to make the motion picture *Hans Christian Andersen* with Danny Kaye. Starred on Broadway in *The Girl in Pink Tights* (1953). Married Roland Petit (1954) and is now mother of a daughter, Valentine. Now combines singing and acting with her dancing. Her stage shows include *Revue des Ballets de Paris* (1956), *Le Patron* (1959), and an especially designed show called *An Evening with Zizi* with which she appeared in U.S. (1964). Star of the film *Black Tights* (released in U.S., 1962), consisting of four Petit ballets, Jeanmaire appearing in the first and last–*La Croqueuse de Diamants* and *Carmen.*

Jeanne d'Arc. Ballet in 3 acts, 7 scenes; chor.: Vladimir Bourmeister; music: Nicolai Peico; book: Vladimir Pletnev; décor: Vadim Ryndin. First prod.: Stanislavsky and Nemirovich-Danchenko Lyric Theatre, Dec. 29, 1957, with Violetta Bovt as Jeanne. The ballet follows the story of Jeanne d'Arc (Joan of Arc). The action takes place in France in the 15th century. In the third act Jeanne is offered freedom by the English officer Lionel, whom she loves, in exchange for the betrayal of her people. In her indignation, Jeanne kills Lionel. The ballet ends with the scene of Jeanne being burned at the stake.

Jensen, Svend Erik, solo dancer and teacher, Royal Danish Ballet, b. Copenhagen, 1913. Entered the Royal Danish Ballet School in 1923; accepted into the company in 1933; made solo dancer in 1942. Dances important character roles in *Coppélia, The Sorcerer's Apprentice, Qarrtsiluni, Graduation Ball, Kermessen i Brügge, Petrouchka, Romeo and Juliet, Fanfare, La Sylphide, Peter and the Wolf,*

Night Shadow. Has taught ballet at the Royal Danish Conservatory of Music since 1958. His Old General in *Graduation Ball* is one of the great comic portraits in ballet. Is a Knight of the Order of Dannebrog.

Jesuit Ballet. The Jesuit priests have made great use of the stage for didactic purposes, educational and theological, and in the 17th century began presenting ballets at openings of sessions or at prize-givings. These ballets formed an important part of Jesuit drama, especially in France, and the scenery and stage effects of the College of Louis-le-Grand in Paris were said to be more varied and numerous than those of the Théâtre Français, but not quite so good as those of the Académie Nationale de Musique. Students of the College gave ballet performances at the French court. Elaborate programs were prepared and the ballets were on pious or sacred themes. Much criticism was levelled against the Jesuits for their use of ballet, which they attempted unsuccessfully to answer in a ballet by P. C. Porée, *L'homme instruit par les spectacles* (Paris, 1726). The Jesuit priests Claude François Ménéstrier (1682) and P. Le Jay (1725) wrote important treatises on ballet. (*G.B.L.W.*)

Jeté (more correctly, pas jeté), in ballet, a thrown step, a jump to any side. The following are some of the forms of jeté: 1. Jeté derrière—start 5th pos. R ft. front; slide L ft. to demi-seconde and demi-plié on R leg; jump upward off R ft.; land on L ft. in demi-plié, R ft. sur le cou-de-pied back. Jeté may also be done devant, starting with front ft. and bringing supporting ft. sur le cou-de-pied front. 2. Grand jeté, a large leap forward. It can be done in open position or in croisé. It can also be done going back. This leap is a true test of a dancer's elevation and ballon, for it requires both a high jump and a soar, altitude and distance. Almost every ballet contains a number of grands jetés. It is also used very often as an exit step in a man's variation. Good examples of grands jetés are the beginning of the ballerina's mazurka in *Les Sylphides* and Myrtha's variation in *Giselle* (Act 2). 3. Jeté en tournant (often incorrectly called tour jeté), usually preceded by a glissade dessus—start in 4th pos., R toe pointed back; glissade dessus to R; facing R side, step on R ft. throwing L leg up to grande quatrième devant; jeté onto L ft. while turning to R and finish facing L wall, bringing R leg up to grande quatrième derrière. Jeté en tournant may also be done with a beat, when it becomes jeté en tournant battu.

Jeu de Cartes. Ballet in 1 act and 3 hands; chor.: Janine Charrat; music: Igor Stravinsky; book: Stravinsky and M. Malaieff; décor: Pierre Roy. First prod.: Ballets des Champs-Elysées, Théâtre des Champs-Elysées, Paris, Oct. 12, 1945, with Jean Babilée as the Joker. Babilée made his first sensational success in this ballet, which also established Charrat as an important choreographer. Ludmilla Chiriaeff has also choreographed a version for Les Grands Ballets Canadiens. See also CARD GAME.

Jeune Homme et la Mort, Le. Ballet in 1 act; chor.: Roland Petit; book, dance, décor and costumes suggested by Jean Cocteau; music: J. S. Bach (Passacaglia and Fugue in C minor); décor: Georges Wakhevitch. First prod.: Ballets des Champs-Elysées, Théâtre des Champs-Elysées June 25, 1946, with Jean Babilée and Nathalie Philippart. One of the most striking ballets in the post-war French (or any other) repertoire and Babilée's greatest triumph. The same dancers recreated their roles for the American Ballet Theatre, Metropolitan Opera House, N.Y., Apr. 9, 1951. A young artist, waiting with desperate impatience for the arrival of his mistress, is brutally rejected by her and hangs himself in his attic. The girl returns masked as a figure of death, hands him a similar mask and leads him over the rooftops of Paris. The dancers were rehearsed by counts to jazz music and only at the dress rehearsal heard the actual music of Bach.

Jeux d'Enfants. Ballet in 1 act; chor.: Leonide Massine; music: Georges Bizet's suite of the same name; book: Boris Kochno; curtain and décor: Joan Miró. First prod.: Col. de Basil's Ballet Russe, Théâtre de Monte Carlo, Apr. 14, 1933, with Tatiana Riabouchinska (Child), Tamara Toumanova (Top), David Lichine (Traveller). The Child dreams that her nursery toys come to life and play with her. She falls a little bit in love with the Traveller. Albert Aveline staged a version at the Paris Opéra (July 16, 1941). Another version with choreography by George Balanchine, Barbara Milberg, and Francisco Moncion was premièred by New York City Ballet, City Center, N.Y., Nov. 22, 1955, with Melissa Hayden (The Doll) and Roy Tobias (Toy Soldier), and with décor by Esteban Francés. It was briefly revived (attributed only to Balanchine) Sept. 8, 1959.

Jew of Pesaro, William. See WILLIAM THE JEW OF PESARO.

Jig, a gay spirited dance in 6/8 or 12/8 time. In music often used as a movement in a suite. See also GIGUE; MUSIC FOR DANCE.

Jillana (Zimmermann), American dancer, b. Hackensack, N.J., 1936. Began her dance studies with Emily Hadley (mother of Diana Adams) and then went on scholarship to School of American Ballet, N.Y. Made her debut with Ballet Society (1948) and remained until 1957 with the company which became New York City Ballet, being promoted to soloist in 1955. Was with American Ballet Theatre (1957–58), danced in the musical *Destry Rides Again* (1959). Rejoined New York City Ballet in the fall of that year as leading soloist. Retired end of 1966. Her roles included the Lady (*Con Amore*), leader of the pas de neuf (Balanchine's *Swan Lake,* Act 2), Coquette (creation in the N.Y. City Ballet's production of *Night Shadow*), Helena (creation) and Titania (*A Midsummer Night's Dream*), one of the four girls in *Liebeslieder Walzer* (creation), and many others.

Jinx. Ballet in 1 act; chor.: Lew Christensen; music: Benjamin Britten's *Variations on a Theme of Frank Bridge;* décor: James Stewart Morcom; costumes: Felipe Fiocca. First prod.: Dance Players, National Theatre, Apr. 24, 1942, with Janet Reed (Girl), Conrad Linden (Boy), Lew Christensen (Jinx). This production was taken into the repertoire of San Francisco Ballet. Lew Christensen restaged it for New York City Ballet, premièred Nov. 24, 1949, N.Y. City Center, with Janet Reed (Girl), Herbert Bliss (Boy), Francisco Moncion (Jinx). A story of circus superstition and the tragedy that ensues when a clown is believed to be the jinx that causes a series of accidents.

Jitterbug, a generic term now almost obsolete for unconventional, often formless and violent, social dances to syncopated music, generally in 4/4 time. The best known forms of jitterbug were the Charleston, Black Bottom, Shag and Lindy Hop, dances of the 1920's and 1930's.

Joan von Zarissa. Ballet in prologue, 4 scenes and epilogue; chor.: Lizzie Maudrik; music and book: Werner Egk; décor: Josef Fenneker. First prod.: Staatsoper, Berlin, Jan. 20, 1940. The ballet, with a singing chorus, treats the Don Juan theme according to medieval French sources, among them the poet Charles d'Orléans (1391–1465), father of King Louis XII of France. Choreographed for many German stages, the latest Feb. 16, 1960, by Heinz Rosen for the Staatsoper, Munich, with Heino Hallhuber, Natasha Trofimova, Dulce Anaya. Serge Lifar choreographed the ballet for the Paris Opéra (1942). On Sept. 17, 1949, the ballet was premièred at the Volksoper by the Vienna Staatsoper Ballet choreographed by Erika Hanka, in décor and costumes by Georges Wakhevitch, with Willy Dirtl in the title role and Edeltraud Brexner (Isabeau). A version by Tatiana Gsovska (called *Juan de Zarissa*), with décor by Hector Basaldúa, was premièred Oct. 31, 1950, at Teatro Colón, Buenos Aires, Argentina, with Victor Ferrari in the title role, Maria Ruanova (Isabeau), Olga Ferri (La Belle Florence), Victor Moreno (Jester).

Job. Masque for dancing in 8 scenes; chor.: Ninette de Valois; music: Ralph Vaughan Williams; book: Geoffrey Keynes; décor: Gwendolen Raverat; wigs and masques: Hedley Briggs. First prod.: Camargo Society, Cambridge Theatre, London, with John McNair in title role, Anton Dolin as Satan. First performance by Vic-Wells (later Sadler's Wells, now Royal) Ballet, Old Vic Theatre, London, Sept. 22, 1931; revived by Sadler's Wells Ballet, Royal Opera House, Covent Garden, May 21, 1948, with Robert Helpmann as Satan, a role he danced frequently after Dolin left the Vic-Wells company. The Covent Garden production had décor by John Piper. The ballet is adapted from William Blake's illustrations from the Book of Job. The scenario (by probably the world's greatest expert on Blake) and the score had been offered to and declined by Serge Diaghilev. At the composer's request *Job* has always been called "A Masque for Dancing," not a ballet. The story of *Job,* as seen through the eyes of the poet-mystic, is unfolded in a formal stylization in which the dances and poses are a constant reminder of the original pictures.

Joel, Lydia, editor-in-chief *Dance Magazine,* dancer, teacher, b. New York City; m. Edwin Miller. Received her general education at New York Univ. (B.A.); additional study Cornell Univ. Studied dance with Harald Kreutzberg, Hanya Holm School, School of American Ballet, Bennington (Vt.) College Summer School of Dance. Member, Advisory Commission on Dance, N.Y. School of Performing Arts; Doris Humphrey Memorial Committee; Advisory Committee, National Regional Ballet Association; Dance Magazine Annual Award Panel. Danced with Hanya Holm company in Max Reinhardt's production of *The Eternal Road.* Taught dance Texas Christian Univ. (1938); Southern Methodist Univ. (1938–44). On staff of *Dance Magazine* since 1947; appointed editor, 1952; editor-in-chief from 1954. Contributes as writer and photographer to various publications.

Joffrey Ballet, Robert. This company made its first appearance as the Robert Joffrey Ballet Concert May 29, 1954, at the YM–YWHA, N.Y. at which Joffrey's *Pas de Déesses* was premièred. From the very beginning the troupe was attached to the American Ballet Center, its official school. In the fall of 1956, now called Robert Joffrey's Theatre Dancers, the group began its first tour with a repertoire of four Joffrey ballets and six dancers. By 1958 the company had become the Robert Joffrey Theatre Ballet and enlarged to eight dancers. In 1960 the company, much enlarged and travelling with an orchestra, became the Robert Joffrey Ballet. An engagement to appear at the 1962 Festival of Two Worlds, Spoleto, was offered to Joffrey. The engagement did not include transport expenses and Mrs. Rebekah Harkness, hearing that the engagement would have to be turned down, offered to cover the expenses through the Rebekah Harkness Foundation. Instead, Robert Joffrey asked if the money could be used to pay his dancers for a rehearsal period prior to their annual tour—a luxury the group had never been able to afford. The Rebekah Harkness Foundation not only decided to do this but undertook the sponsorship of a summer workshop at Watch Hill, R. I., for which a number of choreographers were invited to create new works. These were seen at two performances before an invited audience (Sept. 28 and 30, 1962) at the N.Y. Fashion Institute of Technology. Robert Joffrey Ballet toured the Near and Middle East, India, and Pakistan (winter, 1962–63) under the Cultural Presentations Program of the U.S. Dept. of State, sponsored by the Harkness Foundation. The company again spent the summer of 1963 in Watch Hill. During this summer the company was invited by the Soviet Government to tour in the U.S.S.R. in the winter of 1963. The company danced contemporary works only, its repertoire including ballets by Joffrey, Gerald Arpino, Brian Macdonald, Alvin Ailey, and others. After the Soviet tour and the U.S. tour which followed it (ending Mar. 14, 1964, in Bridgeport, Conn.) the association between the company and the Rebekah Harkness Foundation came to an end and the Robert Joffrey Ballet was disbanded. However, with Alexander Ewing as aide on the business administration and fund-raising side, Joffrey set to work to develop another company from a few of the dancers who remained with him, students from his school, and by open auditions. On Nov. 24, 1964, the Ford Foundation awarded a grant of $155,000 to enable the company to resume active production and inaugurate a training program for dancers. $35,000 was an outright grant for the necessary preliminary activities in building a repertoire and $120,000 (on a matching basis) became available Jan. 1, 1965. The newly-constituted company made its debut at Jacob's Pillow Dance Festival (Aug. 10–14, 1965), its N.Y. debut at the open-air Delacorte Theater, Central Park (Sept. 8–12), and danced at the first Harper Theatre Dance Festival, Chicago (Nov., 1965). A seven-performance season at New York City Center (Mar. 30 to Apr. 3, 1966) was such a success that Morton Baum, chairman of the board of directors of City Center, invited the company to become the official resident company of that theatre. The company name was changed to City Center Joffrey Ballet (which see) at that time. Robert Joffrey is artistic director, with Gerald Arpino as principal choreographer and assistant director. Alexander Ewing is general director and heads the Foundation for American Dance formed for fund-raising purposes. Also in 1966 an arrangement was made whereby the company would spend a period of each year in Seattle-Tacoma for performances and rehearsals of new works and perform in the Northwestern U.S.

Joffrey, Robert (Abdullah Jaffa Anver Bey Khan), dancer, choreographer, teacher, director; b. Seattle, Wash., 1930, of an Afghan father and Italian mother. Began his dance training with Mary Ann Wells in Seattle and later studied in N.Y. at School of American Ballet, and with Alexandra Fedorova; modern dance with

Robert Joffrey, American dancer, choreographer, teacher, director of the City Center Joffrey Ballet.

May O'Donnell and Gertrude Shurr. Made his professional debut with Roland Petit's Ballets de Paris (1949–50). Between 1950 and 1953 danced many times in performances of May O'Donnell's company. Faculty member of N.Y. High School of Performing Arts (1950–1955); his earliest ballets were staged largely with students of the school. His first ballet, *Persephone,* was staged for a Choreographers' Workshop program (1952); *Scaramouche* and *Umpateedle* were given at Jacob's Pillow Dance Festival (1953). Formed his first company, Robert Joffrey Ballet Concert, for a performance at the YM–YWHA (1954), when his *Pas des Déesses* and *Le Bal Masqué* (to Francis Poulenc's score of that name) were premièred, with a second performance the following year when *Harpsichord Concerto* (Manuel de Falla) and Arnold Schoenberg's *Pierrot Lunaire* were the premières. Invited to choreograph for Ballet Rambert (1955), for which he staged *Pas des Déesses* and *Persephone* (using for the latter music by Vivaldi—*The Seasons*—instead of the original score by Robert Silverman). His own company, Robert Joffrey Theatre Ballet, now known as the Robert Joffrey Ballet, toured the U.S. every season from 1956 to 1964. In addition to his own works it had a repertoire which included works by George Balanchine (*Pas de Dix*), Francisco Moncion (*Pastorale*), Antony Tudor (*Soirée Musicale*), Gerald Arpino (the company's leading male dancer), and others. Toward the end of 1962 the company was sent by the State Dept. on a tour of the Near East as part of the Cultural Presentations Program. This tour was co-sponsored by the Rebekah Harkness Foundation, which had previously assumed financial responsibility for a three-month rehearsal and study period at Watch Hill, R.I., when six choreographers (Joffrey, Arpino, Brian Macdonald, Fernand Nault, Alvin Ailey, Donald Saddler) created new works later seen on two Workshop programs in N.Y. The Rebekah Harkness Foundation continued to sponsor the company, which again was sent by the State Dept. for another official tour, this time to the Soviet Union, at the end of 1963 and beginning of 1964. After the U.S. tour which followed, the association between the Robert Joffrey Ballet and the Foundation was dissolved. Joffrey found himself temporarily without a company. With Alexander Ewing and Gerald Arpino, he set to work to rebuild and with the aid of a Ford Foundation grant had a new company prepared for performance in 1965. This company, as City Center Joffrey Ballet, is now the official resident ballet company of the New York City Center. A feature of this company is its apprentice program with special classes and rehearsals designed to prepare selected dancers for entry into the company. Joffrey founded his own school in 1953, has taught at many teachers' conventions, and has staged for television. Was choreographer for New York City Opera Company (1957–62), his work including choreography for new operas such as Douglas Moore's *Wings of the Dove* and *The Devil and Daniel Webster,* Carlisle Floyd's *Wuthering Heights* and *Susannah,* Robert Kurka's *The Good Soldier Schweik,* Marc Blitzstein's *Regina,* as well as operas from the standard repertoire, and Monteverdi's *Orfeo.* He also staged the dances (in which his company appeared) in the Dallas Civic Opera production of Handel's *Alcina* in which Joan Sutherland made her American debut (1960). During the ballet company's inactivity, Joffrey devoted his time to teaching at the American Ballet Center, the official school of the company. As soon as the company was reactivated in Mar., 1965, he resumed his post of director.

Johansson, Anna (1860–1917), Russian ballerina and teacher. The daughter of the famous dancer and teacher Christian Johansson, she graduated from the St. Petersburg Imperial School in 1878, making her debut in *Esmeralda.* She was one of the greatest dancers of her generation.

Retired in 1900 to devote herself to teaching at the St. Petersburg School. From 1911 until her death she headed the classe de perfection.

Johansson, Christian (1817–1903), dancer and teacher, b. Stockholm, Sweden. Trained under August Bournonville, Copenhagen. Made his debut with the St. Petersburg Imperial Ballet (1841), as a result of which he became premier danseur. The greatest dancer of his time, he also became (in 1860) one of the greatest teachers the St. Petersburg School ever had. He stopped dancing in 1869, devoting himself entirely to the School. Since then and up to his death he trained all the great dancers of the Russian ballet including his daughter, Anna Johansson.

Johansson, Ronny, Swedish dancer and teacher, b. Riga, Latvia, 1891. Went to Stockholm in 1913; studied modern dance there and in Germany. Toured Europe (1918–25), then went to the U.S. where she was assistant teacher at the Denishawn school and gave a series of recitals and demonstrations in colleges and universities. Opened her own school in Stockholm (1932); became teacher at the Royal Dramatic Theatre (1942). Founded the Swedish Dance Teachers Organization (1939) and was its secretary for many years.

Johnson, Hunter, contemporary American composer, b. 1906. Wrote the music for Martha Graham's *Letter to the World* (1940), and *Deaths and Entrances* (1943); Erick Hawkins' *Yankee Bluebritches* (1940), and *In Time of Armament* (1941).

Johnson, Louis, contemporary American dancer and choreographer, b. Statesville, N.C., moving to Washington, D.C. as a boy, where he began working at acrobatics at the local YMCA. Began dance studies with Doris Jones and Clara Haywood. After a year, he and a fellow student, Chita Rivera, were taken by their teachers to audition under George Balanchine for School of American Ballet and both received scholarships. Johnson deferred entrance for a year in order to graduate from high school, majoring in commercial art. Made his debut with New York City Ballet as a soloist in Jerome Robbins' *Ballade* (Feb. 14, 1952); then appeared in several Broadway musicals including the leading male dancer in *Damn Yankees,* a role he repeated in the film. He first attracted attention as a choreographer with *Lament,* performed on the N.Y. Ballet Club's Choreographers' Night program (1953); since then has continued to present himself and his group in performances of original solos and group works which include a beautiful suite of *Negro Spirituals.* He staged and choreographed for the Modern Jazz Quartet's 1961 European tour, and has also performed with them in the U.S. Choreographed summer stock musicals for several years; was assistant choreographer for the Broadway show *Jamaica.* He is working in Harlem Youth Activities (HAR–YOU ACT) teaching youngsters. In June, 1965 he presented a program of Har–You Dancers at the YM and YWHA, 92nd St., N.Y.

Johnson, Nancy, dancer and teacher, b. San Francisco, Calif. 1934; m. Richard Carter. Studied at San Francisco Ballet School with the Christensen brothers and Gisella Caccialanza. Principal dancer with San Francisco Ballet (1950–59), creating leading roles in *Dryad, The Masque of Beauty and the Shepherd, Beauty and the Beast, Con Amore* (which she also danced during its first season in the repertoire of New York City Ballet), *Emperor Norton,* and others. During the same period she was principal dancer for San Francisco Opera seasons, and was a frequent guest artist in performances of the Univ. of Utah Theatre Ballet directed by Willam Christensen. Now teaches with her husband (also a former leading dancer with San Francisco Ballet), heading the Dept. of Dance, California Western Univ.,

Nancy Johnson, ballerina, choreographer and co-director of San Diego Ballet, shown here in Lew Christensen's ballet Beauty and the Shepherd.

which they founded in 1960. Also organized the San Diego Ballet Company (1961), which made a very successful appearance at the Jacob's Pillow Dance Festival in 1966.

Joko (or to give it its full title, *Danina, or Joko the Brazilian Ape*), one of the strangest ballets with a complicated plot to be produced in a period when strange ballets with complicated plots were the rule rather than the exception. *Joko* began its theatrical life as French melodrama in Paris (1825), with the famous character dancer Charles Mazurier in the title role. In Nov. of that year *Joko* was brought over to the Royal Opera House, Covent Garden, London, with Mazurier as the Ape (whose name was now spelled Jocko) and the style of the production was labeled "Melo-Drama." According to the printed program, it had ballet music by Signor V. Castelli, and the overture and incidental music were arranged from the works of Bishop and Piccini. On Dec. 26 of the same year, another company of *Joko* opened in N.Y. in the form of a pantomime. *Joko* was apparently liked by American audiences because there are mentions of the pantomime in 1833–34–35. The first ballet production of clear record took place in Stuttgart, Germany, where Filippo Taglioni, father of the great Maria Taglioni, staged *Joko* as a "Grand Pantomimic Ballet" in 4 acts, to music by Peter Joseph von Lindpaintner (1791–1856), one of the most popular works of this prolific German composer and conductor. Its première was given Mar. 12, 1826. Maria Taglioni danced Danina, Anton Stuhlmüller (later partner of Fanny Elssler) was Alvar, and Jean Briol had the title role. Unconcerned with melodrama, Melo-Drama or straight pantomime, the choreographer with the assistance of the composer was able to simplify somewhat the unwieldy scenario. According to this scenario, Danina, a Brazilian native girl, slave of a rich Portuguese landowner Don Alonzo, is secretly married to Alvar, commander of the Portuguese fleet. They have a five-year-old son, Sabi. Danina makes friends with the ape Joko, after saving him from a venomous snake. Alvar returns from a voyage, and after a general celebration comes to join his wife and son in the forest. Jeafre, the overseer of the plantation, who is also in love with Danina, spies on the affectionate reunion of the little family. When Danina and Alvar leave Sabi asleep in a grotto, Jeafre tries to kidnap him. Joko rescues the child and restores him to Danina. Don Alonzo blesses the union of Danina and Alvar, which is now announced to all, and the ballet ends with a general celebration and divertissement. The Taglioni-Lindpaintner ballet version of *Joko* had an even greater popular success than the melodramatic and straight pantomime versions. No attempt is made here to list the scores of productions of *Joko* which mushroomed over Europe, but a few of these are worth mentioning. Thus, J. L. Lewis, a director-producer of English pantomime, presented the ballet with great success in the Königstädtisches Theater in Berlin on July 15, 1826 and later on tour, just four months after the Stuttgart première (a case of very fast piracy). The Imperial Bolshoi Theatre, St. Petersburg, presented *Joko* (called *Zhako*) as a comedy with dances, premièred Oct. 24, 1827. No names of choreographer, composer or dancers appear in any available source. On May 5, 1829, the prolific Danish choreographer, P. J. Larcher, staged *Joko,* "after" Taglioni, to the Lindpaintner music, for the Royal Danish Ballet in Copenhagen. Lucile Grahn, then a ten-year-old pupil of the company's ballet school, made her stage debut in the role of the boy Sabi. The attraction of *Joko* faded on the European continent by the begining of the 1830's, and the ballet was not being seen nor written about. The production of *La Sylphide,* a ballet-pantomime in 2 acts with music by Jean Schneitzhöffer, choreographed by Filippo Taglioni, with Maria Taglioni in the title role, was premièred Mar. 12, 1832, at the Académie Royale de Musique (now Paris Opéra). It ushered in a new epoch in ballet, the Romantic Ballet, and *Joko* was firmly forgotten. But in 1940, one hundred and fourteen years after *Joko's* première, choreographers Pino and Pia Mlakar, revived it in Munich. Their daughter, Veronika, age five, made her stage debut in the role of Sabi.

Jones, Betty, American modern dancer and teacher, b. Meadville, Pa., 1926. Studied dance with José Limón, Ted Shawn, Alicia Markova, La Meri, spending five summers as a scholarship student at Jacob's Pillow. Made her debut with the USO unit of *Oklahoma!,* touring the Philippines (1945). Toured with the musical *Bloomer Girl* (1946). Joined José Limón Dance Company in 1947 and has been a leading member ever since, dancing a large repertoire of Limón and Doris Humphrey works and being especially noted for her creation of the Moor's Wife in *The Moor's Pavane.* She has also created roles in works choreographed by Ruth Currier, the most famous being the Victim in *The Antagonists.* Her beautiful singing voice has often been used in works requiring an off-stage voice. Has taught master classes in the U.S. and at Academia de Bellas Artes, Mexico City. Is on the faculty of José Limón dance studio, Connecticut College Summer School of the Dance, Juilliard School of Music Dance Dept.

Jones, Inigo (1575–1652), architect and designer of masques, active in the theatre from 1605 to 1640. He travelled in Italy and his work shows some of the influence of the Italian masquerie. He designed the costumes as well as the settings and paid great attention to the lighting of the spectacle, achieving special effects by placing glass vessels of colored water in front of lights. Some of his masques include *Hue and Cry after Cupid* (with Ben Jonson, 1608), *Oberon* (1611), *The Twelve Goddesses* (with *Samuel Daniel,* 1604), *Masque of Flowers at Gray's Inn* (1614), *Masque of Blackness* (with Jonson), *Tethy's Festival* (with Daniel), and *Salmacida Spolia* (1640), his last masque.

Jones, Marilyn, contemporary Australian dancer. Won a scholarship to the Royal Ballet School at age sixteen; joined the Royal Ballet a year later. Returned to Australia (1958) as a leading member of the Borovansky Ballet. When the company disbanded she returned to London, again on a scholarship. Joined Ballet International du Marquis de Cuevas as leading soloist and subsequently ballerina. Joined Australian Ballet for its 1962–63 season, her roles including Odette-Odile in the full-length *Swan Lake,* among others. Guest artist, London's Festival Ballet (summer 1963), dancing Ingrid in *Peer Gynt,* and other roles.

Jones, Robert Edmond (1887–1954), American designer and the only American artist chosen by Serge Diaghilev to design a work for his Ballets Russes. This was Vaslav Nijinsky's *Til Eulenspiegel* (1916). Also designed *The Birthday of the Infanta* (Adolph Bolm, 1919) and *Skyscrapers* (1920), for which he and its composer, John Alden Carpenter, also collaborated on the choreography, assisted by Sammy Lee. He was especially well known for his designs for the theatre.

Jonson, Ben (1573?–1637), writer of masques popular in England in early 17th century. These had literary as well as spectacular elements. The nobility took part, including Queen Anne and the Countess of Bedford. The dramatic interlude with song, music and dance was an element that gave rise to opera ballet. Jonson's most famous masques were *Masque of Blackness* (1605), *Masque of Beauty* (1608), and *Hue and Cry after Cupid* (1608). Inigo Jones usually designed the costumes and sets for Jonson's masques.

Jooss Ballet, company organized in 1932 by Kurt Jooss as director and principal choreographer, Dr. Fritz (Frederick) Cohen, as composer and musical director and Sigurd Leeder, as dancer, teacher and choreographer. The company was originally (1930) called the Dance Group of the Essen (Germany) Opera House and, subsequently, the Folkwangballet of Essen. The troupe became self-sustaining when Jooss's *The Green Table* won first prize at the Choreographic Competition held in Paris by the Archives Internationales de la Danse, headed by Rolf de Maré (1932). It was after the competition that the company took on the name Jooss Ballet. Under the management of Leon Greanin the company made its first world tour (1933–34), after which its headquarters and school were established at Dartington Hall, Devon, England. The beginning of World War II found the company in the U.S. It returned to England in a U.S. ship convoy escorted by destroyers. There, Jooss moved his headquarters to Cambridge and became part of E.N.S.A. Most of the ballets in the repertoire were by Jooss, with music by Dr. Cohen. These included *The Green Table, The Big City, Prodigal Son, A Ball in Old Vienna, The Seven Heroes, Chronica, A Spring Tale,* and others. Additional ballets were *Drums Sound in Hackensack* (Agnes de Mille), *Sailor's Fancy* (Sigurd Leeder) and *Le Bosquet* (Hans Zullig). In 1947 the company was disbanded. When Jooss re-organized the Folkwang school in Essen (1949), he also revived the performing group. Several members of the previous company rejoined the new troupe, among them Zullig, Noelle de Mosa, Ulla Soederbaum, and Rolf Alexander. New works were choreographed by Jooss and Zullig for a tour of Western Europe and a London season (1953). After the tour the company was disbanded once more. It remained inactive for some nine years. In 1964 a new company under a former name, Folkwangballet of Essen, appeared with enormous success in the XXV Maggio Musicale Fiorentino (Florence May Music Festival) dancing *The Green Table* on May 20. On May 29 the company danced *The Green Table* at the Munich Ballet Festival Week and in July the company appeared at VII International Festival of Dance at Nervi (Genoa), repeating the Florence success on both occasions.

Jooss, Kurt, choreographer, dancer and director of dance company, b. Wasseralfingen, Württemberg, Germany, 1901. Educated at Realgymnasium, Aalen; College for Music, Stuttgart; dramatic school. First met Rudolf von Laban in 1920 and began to study with him at the National Theater, Mannheim, the following year, later becoming his assistant and principal dancer. Subsequently became producer for the Dance Group at the State Theatre, Münster, which gave separate performances and appeared in dramatic productions and operas. Here he met Dr. Fritz

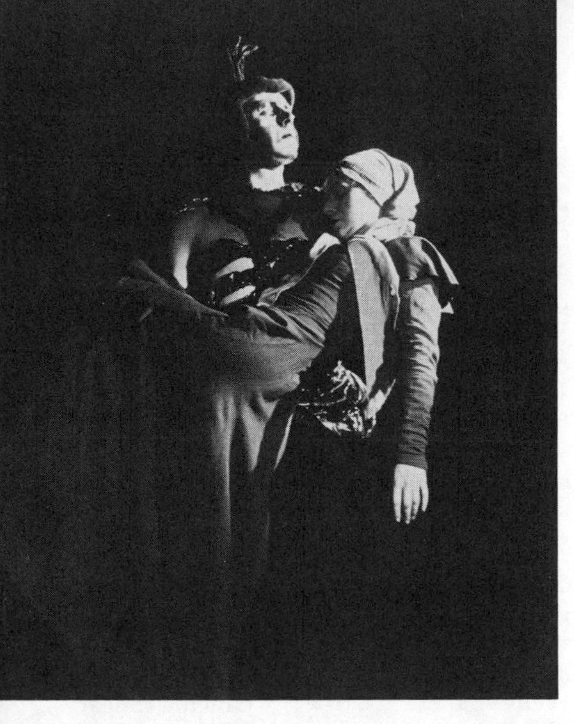

Kurt Jooss, founder of the Jooss Ballet, choreographer and dancer, in the role of Death in his ballet The Green Table.

(now Frederick) Cohen, Sigurd Leeder, and Aino Siimola. This dance group, known as the Neue Tanzbühne (New Dance Stage), had a repertoire by Jooss and toured Germany (1924–26). In Oct., 1926, Jooss went to study in Paris and Vienna. He returned to Germany (1927) and founded the Folkwangschule fur Musik, Tanz, und Sprechen, with Leeder as head instructor. He founded the Folkwangbuhne and Dance Theatre Studio (1928), with Dr. Cohen, Leeder, Siimola, and Elsa Kahl as original members. He married Aino Siimola (1929). He was supervisor of the Dance Group of the Essen Opera House (1929), and ballet master (1930), at which time the group became the official ballet of the Opera House. In 1932 Jooss decided to enter the Choreographic Competition organized by the Archives Internationales de la Danse, Paris, and his ballet *The Green Table,* to music by Dr. Cohen, won first prize. Just prior to the competition the Jooss group had left the Essen Opera House to become a self-sustaining organization under the name of Folkwangballet of Essen. After winning the competition the company assumed the name Jooss Ballet (or Ballets Jooss). From that time Jooss headed the company and choreographed most of the ballets in its repertoire with Dr. Cohen as musical director. In 1947 he disbanded the company. When he re-organized his school in Essen (1949) he also revived the performing company. The company made a tour of Europe and danced in London in 1953. After 1953 it remained inactive but Kurt Jooss continued with his very successful school in Essen. In 1963–64 Jooss organized a new company which danced with great success at several of the annual ballet festivals in Western Europe.

Joseph the Beautiful. Ballet in 1 act; chor.: Kasian Goleizovsky; music: Sergei Vassilenko. First produced.: Leningrad, 1924. Based on the Bible story of Joseph and Potiphar's wife.

Jota, a quick Spanish folk dance in 3/8 time often used by Spanish theatre dance troupes and in ballets on Spanish themes. Michel Fokine staged a ballet in one scene to Mikhail Glinka's "Jota Aragonesa," Maryinsky Theatre, St. Petersburg (1916).

Journal. Modern dance work; chor. and costumes: Murray Louis; music: Ottorino Respighi's Notturno, George Antheil's *Serenade for Strings,* Charles Ives' *The Unanswered Question,* Ferdinando Sor's *Etude,* and from Jacques Ibert's *Impressions of Paris.* First prod.: Henry Street Playhouse, N.Y., Nov. 8, 1957, with Louis, Peggy Barclay, Clare Lorenzi, Laura de Freitas, and Anne Sherman. A series of recollections ranging from the hopes of youth to the acceptance of age.

Juana (Johanna Jurgens), ethnic dancer, b. Englefield Green, Surrey, England, 1926. Studied music at Guildhall School of Music, London; voice in Salzburg and London; dance at Ethnologic Dance Center with La Meri (1940–48); special studies with Sophia Delza (Taichi Chüan), Nala Najan, Nataraj Vashi, Sita Poovia (Indian), Argentinita, Antonio de Cordoba (Spanish), Miyoko Watanabe (Japanese), Kim Sun Young and Taikwon Cho (Korean), Tai Ai-lien (Tibetan), and others. Was a member of La Meri's company (1940–48), making her own debut as a concert soloist at the Barbizon-Plaza Theatre (1947). Was first Western dancer to set ancient classical dance of India to music of Bach (*Bach Karanas,* 1944); first to interpret a contemporary social theme by means of traditional Bharata Natya (India Today, 1946). Between 1946 and 1954 toured extensively in U.S., Europe, Africa, with solo programs showing a wide range of authentic dances of many countries, and with a variety of lectures. Special research projects have included study of Ouled Nail tribes of the Sahara and Berber dances in Morocco (1951), Polynesian dances in Hawaii (1952), Yugoslav and Northern Turkey folk, religious, classical, and popular (1951–52). Taught and performed several times at Jacob's Pillow. Has been televised in U.S., Europe, and Near East. Filmed *Three Ethnic Dances* (Dynamic Films, 1946), *One Pair of Hands* (Henri Storek for Belgian Ministry of Education and Culture, 1962).

Judgment of Paris. Ballet in 1 act; chor.: Antony Tudor; music: Kurt Weill (from *Dreigroschenoper*—The Threepenny Opera); book and costumes: Hugh Laing. First prod.: Westminster Theatre, London, June 15, 1938, with Agnes de Mille (Venus), Thérèse Langfield (Juno), Charlotte Bidmead (Minerva), Antony Tudor (Client), Hugh Laing (Waiter). It was first given by London Ballet at Toynbee Hall, London, Dec. 5, 1938, and by Ballet Rambert (which still has it in its repertoire), at Arts Theatre, London, Oct. 1, 1940. Sally Gilmour and Marguerite Stewart as Juno, Gerd Larsen, Elisabeth Schooling and Peggy van Praagh as Venus, Margaret Scott and Joan McClelland as Minerva, were all outstanding later interpreters. Staged for Ballet (now American Ballet) Theatre with décor by Lucinda Ballard, Center Theatre, N.Y., Jan. 23, 1940, with Viola Essen (Juno), Agnes de Mille (Venus), Lucia Chase (Minerva), Tudor, Laing. The Greek legend transferred to a French café, late at night, where a drunken boulevardier makes his choice from three sad and aging ladies of pleasure.

Judson, Stanley, contemporary English dancer and choreographer. Danced with Pavlova Ballet (1927). Was one of the stalwarts of the early days of British ballet, and a principal dancer with the Vic-Wells Ballet (1931–34), dancing Sugar Plum Fairy Cavalier (*The Nutcracker*), Franz (*Coppélia*) and many other roles in the repertoire of that period. When Anton Dolin was taken ill a few hours before the second performance of *Giselle* (Jan. 1934), he stepped in and danced a fine Albrecht to Alicia Markova's Giselle. Soloist with Markova-Dolin Ballet (1935–36), and with René Blum Ballet de Monte Carlo (1936). Was for many years a successful choreographer of ice shows in the U.S. Associate director, Cork Ballet, Eire, since 1960, where his works include a version of *La Fille Mal Gardée.*

Juilliard Dance Theatre, was organized in 1955, under the direction of Doris Humphrey to offer training and performance experience to young professional dancers. Its members were chosen through competitive auditions and included a number of graduate students of the Juilliard Dance Dept. From that year it gave brief seasons annually in the Juilliard Concert Hall and made occasional appearances elsewhere. Its repertoire included revivals of several early Humphrey works, such as the 1929 *Life of the Bee,* the 1934 *Race of Life,* and 1940 *Bach Partita No. 5 in G Major.* Its most substantial new work was Doris Humphrey's *Dawn in New York* to Hunter Johnson's Concerto for Piano and Chamber Orchestra, commissioned by the Juilliard School of Music and performed Apr. 27–29, 1956, as part of the school's 50th anniversary Festival of American Music. In Mar. 1957, the company danced the action (arranged by Doris Humphrey) in Frederic Cohen's production of Maurice Ravel's *L'Enfant et les Sortileges,* staged for Juilliard Opera Theater. It joined the José Limón Dance Company for the première of Limón's *Missa Brevis* (1958). The company was dissolved in 1959, a few months after Doris Humphrey's death.

Juilliard School of Music, Dance Department. The Dance Department was added to the Juilliard School in 1952, under the direction of Martha Hill. The curriculum, as announced by Juilliard president Dr. William Schuman, was designed to give dance students of college age a comprehensive program in the study of the techniques and repertoire of modern dance and ballet, with the possibility of matriculating as candidates for Bachelor and Master of Science Degrees, Diploma, Post-Graduate Diploma, or as Special Student. The original faculty included Agnes de Mille, Martha Graham, Martha Hill, Doris Humphrey, José Limón, Jerome Robbins and Antony Tudor. Louis Horst was engaged to teach dance composition and Ann Hutchinson dance notation. During Doris Humphrey's lifetime, Juilliard Dance Theatre, composed mainly of advanced students and former students, gave performances. The Dance Department presents annual performances as part of the graduating exercises.

Junk Dances, modern dance work; chor.: Murray Louis; music: a medley of practically everything; décor: Robert Wilson. First perf.: Murray Louis & Company, Henry Street Settlement Playhouse, N.Y., Nov. 27, 1964. A funny piece of "pop" art which omits nothing except possibly the kitchen stove. The music ranges from the Galli-Curci rendition of Lo, Hear the Gentle Lark," to Brahms' *Variations on a Theme of Haydn,* via "Bye, Bye, Blackbird," and "Nola." Murray Louis and Phyllis Lamhut are the principal culprits.

Junk, Victor (pronounced Yoonk), Viennese professor and composer, b. 1875. Wrote numerous musical compositions for dance. Author of *Handbuch des Tanzes* (1930), a German language biographical dictionary of dance and related material.

Jurgens, Hellmut, German stage designer, b. Westfalen, 1902. Studied at the Academy of Arts, Düsseldorf. Worked at Bühnen Düsseldorf (1930–38); Municipal Stages of Frankfurt a/M (1938–45); State Opera, Munich, since 1947. Professor at the Academy of Arts, Munich, since 1953. Among the ballets he designed are *Swan Lake, The Legend of Joseph, Joan von Zarissa, The Chinese Nightingale, The Tragedy of Salome, Princess Turandot, Bolero, Carmina Burana, Catulli Carmina, Danza, La Buffonata, La Tragedia di Orfeo.*

Kabuki, a Japanese theatre-dance form. The indigenous Japanese theatrical dance has never been a separate art form. There are hints of theatre in the first form of Japanese dance—Princess Ame-No-Uzume attempting to entice the brooding Sun Goddess from her cave. There are hints of theatre in the archaic prayer dances—the Kagura, performed by the Miko (or Shrine Virgins), on the open lawn before the shrine and in an encirclement of pines, which later developed into the actual setting of the stage of the Noh Theatre. These seeds, intermixed with importations from the Asia mainland, specifically China and Korea, and from the South Pacific islands, bore fruit in the form of the three classic theatre arts of Japan: Noh (religious drama), Bunraku (marionettes), and Kabuki (dance-drama). Kabuki is said to have originated with a certain O-Kuni of Izuma, a Miko (or Shrine Virgin), from the Shrine of Izumo on the main island of Honshu, some time between 1586 and 1603. As a Shrine dancer, she carried the tradition of prayer dances into her style and added to it comic interludes, peasant dances and mimes, and erotic innovations of her own. As the popularity of O-Kuni's dances increased, she began to do dance-playlets, augmented her rather primitive musical accompaniment, and finally added a larger stage.

Kabuki as a word and a style of dance-theatre art was first applied to O-Kuni's dancing, and the term O-Kuni Kabuki is still being used. At the beginning men danced together with women, but after O-Kuni's death women gradually took over the identity of Kabuki until it became known as Women's Kabuki (Onna Kabuki). These all-women Kabuki led to corrupt and immoral practices and were eventually banned by law. The same immorality and the same ban were the fate of the next manifestation, that of Young Men's Kabuki (Wakashu Kabuki). The final development of Kabuki resulted in the all-male, mature, Men's Kabuki, which became fixed as the tradition for Kabuki theatre. It is often called the Grand Kabuki. This tradition holds true to this day and the Kabuki Theatre (drama) is denied to women. The Kabuki dance, however, is open to women as a means of learning and performing the Japanese classical dance. If a woman becomes a great enough dancer she may inherit the leadership of a Kabuki Dance School from her natural or adopted father. A contemporary example is Tokuho Azuma Kabuki, head of the Azuma School of Kabuki Dance.

With the creation of these dynasties—the bequeathers and beneficiaries of the Kabuki tradition—Kabuki as an inte-

Tsuchigumo *by Masaya Fujima.*

Kabuki Odori: *Tokuho Azuma and Kikonojo Onoe (center, holding spears).*

grated art form of dance began to assume perfection. The Kabuki dance is a stylized choreographic movement almost always telling a story which is chanted by narrators or the dancers themselves to the accompaniment of an orchestra. Kabuki dance troupes employ both female and male dancers, most of them belonging to one dynasty or another.

In watching the Kabuki dance (and, in fact, most of Japanese dancing) one must bear in mind that while in the Western dance lines of the body dominate the costume, the costume is an integral part of the expression in Japanese dancing. The costume is part of the body and the use of sleeves, the slight twitch of the hem or the skirt, is as much of a vital part of the choreography and feeling as are the more external balances and spectacular steps of the ballet dancer. The artist is molded into the costume and such properties as fans, scarves, and spears are considered as extensions of the dancer's body.

The American public had the opportunity of seeing Kabuki dancers in the winter-spring season of 1954 and again in the winter of 1955–56, when impresario S. Hurok brought the Azuma Kabuki Dancers and Musicians to the U.S. The troupe also danced in Paris and at the Edinburgh Music Festival (1955).

Kaesen, Robert, Dutch dancer and choreographer, b. Wilrijk, Belgium, 1931. Among his ballets are *Walking in Circles* (Kringloop), for Ballet de Lage Landen; *The Chameleons,* for the Amsterdams Ballet; *Contrasten* (Contrasts), for National Ballet. See HOLLAND, DANCE IN.

Kahl, Elsa, contemporary dancer and teacher, b. Hamburg, Germany; m. Frederic Cohen. Educated at Firgau Lyceum, Hamburg, and Westphalian School for Dance, Drama and Music, Muenster; also Folkwang School for Dance, Drama and Music, Essen, under Kurt Jooss (1924–30). Solo dancer, Handel Festival, Goettingen; Heidelberg Festival; Jooss Group, Essen; director, Bewegungschor Wuerzburg (1927–30); solo dancer, Bayreuth Festival (1930, 1931). Soloist, Jooss Ballet (1932–42), creating Woman in Red (*The Green Table*), Mother (*Prodigal Son*), Devil's Grandmother (*Johann Strauss Tonight*), Worker's Wife (*Mirror*). In 1936 received Medaille des Archives Internationales de la Danse. Instructor in dance and consultant in dramatics, Black Mountain College, N.C. (1942–44). Conducted courses in N.Y. (1945–46), including one in operatic acting at the Juilliard Opera Theatre, N.Y. Retired in 1963.

Kaleidoscope. Ballet in 1 act; chor.: Walter Gore; music: Johannes Brahms' *Variations on a Theme of Paganini;* décor: Ronald Wilson. First prod.: Ballet at Eight, Mercury Theatre, London, May 30, 1949, with Paula Hinton, Margaret Hill, Barbara Grimes, Walter Gore. Though themeless, the costumes suggested glittering insects whose constant, restless movements brought about kaleidoscopic shifts of pattern. The ballet was taken into the repertoire of Ballet Rambert following its première.

Kaleidoscope. Modern dance work; chor.: Alwin Nikolais; music: excerpts from George Antheil, Edgard Varèse, Alan Hovhaness, Heitor Villa-Lobos, John Cage, Henry Brandt, and ethnic; color design: George Constant; lighting: Tharon Musser. First prod.: Henry Street Playhouse Dance Company, May 25, 1956, and at 9th American Dance Festival, Connecticut College, New London, Aug. 17, 1956, with Gladys Bailin, Beverly Schmidt, Phyllis Lamhut, Dorothy Vislocky, Coral Martindale, Murray Louis, Bill Frank. A further excursion (begun with *Masks—Props—Mobiles*) into the world of props, colors, and lighting effects in which the dancers are of no greater importance than the other elements.

Kaleidoscope. Ballet by Ruthanna Boris. See COMEDIANS, THE.

Kalioujny, Alexandre, Russian-born French dancer, b. ca. 1926. Early dance training was with Olga Preobrajenska. Won first prize at the International Dance Competition for children in Brussels (1939). A leading dancer with Nouveau Ballet de Monte Carlo (1946), gaining wide recognition for his performance as a warrior chief in Chota Rustaveli. Appointed premier danseur étoile of the

Paris Opéra (1947), one of the few dancers trained outside the Opéra school to achieve this position. Created 1st movement of *Palais de Cristal* and the Fiancé in *Le Baiser de la Fée* (both George Balanchine, 1947). Partner of Tamara Toumanova in her guest seasons at Opéra. One of his great roles was the Polovetsian Chief in the *Dances from Prince Igor.* Appeared on Broadway with Renée Jeanmaire in *The Girl in Pink Tights* (1953). After several seasons as guest artist rather than as permanent member of the Paris Opéra, he retired definitely to open a ballet studio in Nice (1961).

Kamadjojo, Indra, Indonesian dancer, b. Banjoemas (Java), Indonesia, 1906. Educated at Royal School of Dancing, Djokjakarta. Has given solo dance recitals on tours through Holland (where he lives when not touring), Belgium, and Switzerland.

Karalli, Vera, Russian ballerina, b. 1888. Studied under Alexander Gorsky at the ballet school of the Bolshoi Theatre, Moscow. Was graduated in 1906; became ballerina in 1909. Danced two seasons with the Diaghilev Ballets Russes, appearing in *Le Pavillon d'Armide* (1909), the title role in *Thamar* (1919). Currently living in Vienna, where she is also known as Coralli.

Karina, Lilian (married name Vasarhelyi), dance teacher, b. St. Petersburg, Russia, 1910. Studied with Eugenia Edouardova and Victor Gsovsky in Berlin; with Olga Preobrajenska, Lubov Egorova, and Bronislava Nijinska in Paris. Opened a ballet school in Budapest with her partner Aurel Milloss (1937). Went to Sweden (1939) and eventually opened a school in Stockholm (1943). Birgit Cullberg and most of the leading Swedish dancers have worked in her studio.

Karina, Tania, dancer, b. Cannes, France, 1930; m. Oleg Sabline. Began dance studies at age six with Ivan Clustine and then Julia Sedova; later studied in Paris with Lubov Egorova and Olga Preobrajenska. Joined Grand Ballet de Monte Carlo (which became Grand Ballet du Marquis de Cuevas) in 1944; promoted to soloist in 1947; danced her first leading part in William Dollar's *Five Gifts* (1948); became leading soloist (1954), dancing Sleepwalker (*Night Shadow*), *Paquita* pas de trois, Anton Dolin's *Pas de Quatre,* Myrtha (*Giselle*), Prelude (*Les Sylphides*), and others. Guest artist at European opera houses and in concert tours with Jeunesses Musicales de France (1957–58). Emigrated to U.S. (Apr. 1958); danced at Jacob's Pillow (1958, 1960); toured with André Eglevsky's group (1958–59); with Nora Kovach and Istvan Rabovsky (1959–60). Joined Ballet Russe de Monte Carlo as ballerina for the 1960–61 season under her family name of Chevtchenko, dancing *Swan Lake, Schéhérazade, Le Beau Danube, Gaîté Parisienne,* and the classic pas de deux. Guest ballerina, Ballet National de Venezuela (Feb., 1962). Frequent guest artist with U.S. and South American ballet companies; also teaches in U.S.

Karinska, Barbara, contemporary costume maker and designer, b. Russia. Left Russia after the Revolution to live in Paris where she made her first ballet costumes, those designed by Christian Bérard for George Balanchine's *Cotillon* (1933). From then on she made costumes from the designs of some of the most famous designers of the day, among them André Derain, Salvador Dali, and Cecil Beaton. Has been living and working in N.Y. since 1938, and from the early days of New York City Ballet she has been responsible for almost all their costumes, at first making and later also frequently designing them. *Bourrée Fantasque* was the first ballet for which she designed the costumes, followed by *La Valse.* Her most elaborate work for N.Y.C. Ballet was *The Nutcracker.* Won the Capezio Award in 1962.

Karnilova, Maria, American dancer, musical comedy actress, b. Hartford, Conn., 1920. Studied dance at Metropolitan Opera Ballet School, and with Alexandra Fedorova, Michel Fokine, Antony Tudor, Edward Caton, Anton Dolin, Hanya Holm. First professional appearance was as member of Children's Ballet under Rosina Galli at the Metropolitan Opera House. Toured South America with Victor Dandré's Opera Company (1935); appeared at Lewisohn Stadium with Michel Fokine and Mikhail Mordkin companies (1936); with Salmaggi Opera Co. at Hippodrome (1937). Also danced in the Broadway musical *Stars in Your Eyes* (1938). Original member of Ballet (now American Ballet) Theatre (1939–46), rising from corps de ballet to soloist, dancing in *Helen of Troy, Bluebeard* (Boulotte), *Three Virgins and a Devil, Lilac Garden* (An Episode in His Past), *Judgment of Paris,* and others. Ballerina of Metropolitan Opera Ballet (1951–52). Except for this engagement and for guest appearances with American Ballet Theatre, at Jacob's Pillow, and with Jerome Robbins' Ballets: U.S.A. in N.Y. (1958–59, dancing in *The Concert*), she has been engaged mainly in Broadway musicals, making an entirely new career as a dancer-comedienne, most particularly as the stripper Tessie Tura in *Gypsy* (1959–61), also in *Bravo, Giovanni* (1962). In 1964 she created the role of the Wife in the musical *Fiddler on the Roof,* directed and choreographed by Jerome Robbins, for which she was awarded a "Tony" by the American Theatre Wing.

Tamara Karsavina and Vaslav Nijinsky in Fokine's ballet Le Spectre de la Rose.

Karsavina, Tamara, former ballerina of the Maryinsky Theatre and the Diaghilev Ballets Russes, b. St. Petersburg, Russia, 1885, daughter of famous Russian dancer Platon Karsavin; m. Vasily Moukhin, later divorced; m. Henry J. Bruce (1917). Made her debut with the Imperial Ballet in Javotte (1902). Among her other ballets were *The Awakening of Flora, The Humpbacked Horse, Swan Lake, Le Corsaire, The Sleeping Beauty, Giselle, The Nutcracker, Raymonda, La Bayadère, Harlequinade,* and others. With Michel Fokine and Anna Pavlova she was active in the organization of the Diaghilev Ballets Russes which she joined at its inception (1909), dividing her time between it and the Maryinsky Theatre. The most outstanding ballerina of the Diaghilev company, she created for it the principal roles in *Les Sylphides* (Waltz), *Carnaval*

(Columbine), *Petrouchka* (Ballerina), *Le Spectre de la Rose* (Girl), *Firebird* (title role), *Thamar* (title role), *Daphnis and Chloë* (Chloë), *Le Coq d'Or* (Queen of Shemakhan), *The Three-Cornered Hat* (Miller's Wife), *Pulcinella* (Pimpinella). A follower and exponent of Fokine's theories, she was considered a great classic ballerina, free of the acrobatic exhibitionism of her predecessors at the Maryinsky. Although she had virtually retired, except for a few guest appearances with the Diaghilev company in its final years, she came out of retirement to dance as guest artist with Ballet Rambert in its earliest days, appearing in *Les Sylphides, Le Spectre de la Rose, Carnaval,* in Frederick Ashton's *Mercury* (Venus), Susan Salaman's *Waterloo* and *The Crime* (Jenny), and her own solo *Mademoiselle de Maupin* (1931). These were her final creations before she retired permanently. Her book *Theatre Street* (1931) remains one of the great books on ballet of all time and an intimate picture of the Maryinsky Theatre and its school. Her second husband's two books, *Silken Dalliance* and *Thirty Dozen Moons,* give an intimate glimpse of the great dancer as a wonderful human being. She has also written the textbook *Classical Ballet: The Flow of Movement.* She staged *Le Spectre de la Rose* for Sadler's Wells (now Royal) Ballet (1943), coached Margot Fonteyn in *The Firebird* and *Le Spectre de la Rose,* assisted in the production of mime scenes in Frederick Ashton's *La Fille Mal Gardée* (1960), re-creating the pantomime of Lise's imagining herself as bride and mother from her memories of the Maryinsky version; also staged Carnaval for Western Theatre Ballet (1961).

Kastl, Sonia, Yugoslav ballerina, b. Zagreb, 1929. A pupil of Margarita Froman and Ana Roje, she joined the Zagreb National Ballet in 1945; was promoted to ballerina in 1950. She is considered the prima ballerina of Yugoslavia. Her ballets include *Romeo and Juliet* (Prokofiev-Froman), *The Devil in the Village* (Fran Lhotka-Pia and Pino Mlakar), *Classical Symphony* (Prokofiev-Parlic), and *Ballet Concerto* (Vivaldi), *Les Forains* and *Candelaria* (Carlo Riesco), all choreographed by O. Cintolesi, as well as all the standard ballets in the company's repertoire.

Katcharov, Michel, dancer, ballet master, b. Iran, 1913. Began studying ballet in U.S.S.R. at age thirteen. Moved to Paris (1930) and studied with Olga Preobrajenska and Bronislava Nijinska. Danced in Russian Opera Season, Paris (1930); member, Ida Rubinstein's company (1931); Col. de Basil's Ballet Russe (1932–37); Ballet Russe de Monte Carlo from 1938, becoming ballet master and remaining, except for brief intervals, until 1959. Ballet master, Geneva (Switzerland) Opera Ballet, (1961–62, 1962–63). Taught in Europe until spring, 1966; in fall of that year joined the newly formed Ballets de Monte Carlo as ballet master.

Kathak. See HINDU DANCE.

Kathakali. See HINDU DANCE.

Kay, Hershy, composer, orchestrator, arranger, b. Philadelphia, Pa., 1919. Won scholarship at age sixteen to study the 'cello at the Curtis Institute of Music, Phila., but taught himself orchestration by taking short piano pieces and working them out in each composer's style. Began his professional career by playing the 'cello in Broadway theatre orchestras and did his first professional arranging for Brazilian soprano Elsie Houston with a group of Brazilian songs for a Rainbow Room presentation. Night club assignments followed until his classmate at the Curtis Institute, Leonard Bernstein, engaged him to orchestrate the musical *On the Town* (1944). Innumerable musicals have succeeded this one: *Peter Pan, Candide, Once Upon a Mattress, Milk and Honey,* etc. He made his first arrangements in the dance field for Martha Graham (1947); wrote his first ballet score (based on music by Carl Maria von Weber) for Herbert Ross's *The Thief Who Loved a Ghost* (Ballet Theatre, 1950). The following year he arranged and orchestrated piano music by Louis Moreau Gottschalk for the New York City Ballet's *Cakewalk.* In 1954 he was commissioned to write the score for George Balanchine's *Western Symphony,* this four-movement work based on folk songs of the American West. He arranged (and orchestrated certain of the pieces) a selection of waltzes, preludes and mazurkas of Frédéric Chopin for Jerome Robbins' *The Concert* (1956) and, again for Balanchine, made a score for Stars and Stripes from the marches of John Philip Sousa (1958). Has also done extensive work for radio, television, and motion pictures.

Kay, Lisan (Elizabeth Hathaway), contemporary American dancer, teacher, b. Conneaut, O. Studied dance with Andreas Pavley, Serge Oukrainsky, Ruth Austin; later with Yeichi Nimura and Vera Trefilova. Made her professional debut with Chicago Civic Opera Co. (1926–27); toured U.S. and Canada with Pavley-Oukrainsky Ballet. Won American scholarship for the First International Dance Congress held in Buxton, England, when Ruth St. Denis was dean of judges (1932). Chosen as partner by Yeichi Nimura and, after a successful debut at Theatre Vieux-Colombier, Paris (1932), toured Europe, Palestine, and Egypt for five years; then returned in 1937, touring U.S., Canada, Cuba, Hawaii. Gave solo recitals in N.Y. (1943). Was dance lead in *Lute Song* (1945–46), later remounting Nimura's choreography and style for the London production (1948). Dance lead in *Desert Song,* St. Louis, Memphis, Toronto, (summers 1946–47). Also composed dance sequences for Republic Pictures and *N.Y. Times* Style Show (1944). Currently partner and teacher at Ballet Arts, N.Y.

Kaye, Nora (Nora Koreff), ballerina, b. New York City, 1920, of Russian parentage; m. Herbert Ross. Studied at Metropolitan Opera Ballet School, with Michel Fokine, Anatole Vilzak, Ludmila Shollar; also at School of American Ballet, N.Y. Appeared in children's ballets at Metropolitan Opera House from age of nine to fifteen. When the American Ballet became the official ballet company of the Metropolitan Opera, she joined the company. Later was a member of Radio City Music Hall ballet and appeared in musicals. Joined Ballet (now American Ballet) Theatre at its inception (1939), first doing corps de ballet and small soloist roles. With her performance of Hagar in *Pillar of Fire* (Apr. 8, 1942) she was raised to the rank of ballerina, dancing classic as well as dramatic roles. Among her other creations were Russian ballerina (*Gala Performance*—Ballet Theatre production), Princess (*On Stage!*), and others. *Fall River Legend* was intended for her, but she missed the première due to illness. Among her other roles were Caroline (*Lilac Garden*), Queen of the Wilis and the title role (*Giselle*), Juliet (*Romeo and Juliet*), Swan Queen (*Swan Lake,* Act 2), Polyhymnia (*Apollo*), and many others. It was during her period with Ballet

Nora Kaye, American dramatic ballerina.

Theatre that her performances brought about a new title, that of dramatic ballerina. Between the spring of 1951 and the fall of 1954 she was with New York City Ballet, where she repeated her Caroline for this company's production of *Lilac Garden* and had another major creation as the Novice in *The Cage*. She also created the title role in *La Gloire*. On the whole, however, the company's style was not the one best suited to display her own very special talents. Her first creation after her return to Ballet Theatre (1954) was the role of Blanche in Valerie Bettis' *A Streetcar Named Desire,* following this with the Operetta Star in *Offenbach in the Underworld* and the Wife in Agnes de Mille's *Rib of Eve* (both in 1956) as well as principal roles in Kenneth MacMillan's *Winter's Eve* and *Journey,* and Herbert Ross's *Paean* (all 1957—*Journey* and *Paean* were premièred at Ballet Theatre Workshop performances and later went into the repertoire); *Tristan,* a pas de deux for herself and Erik Bruhn, also by Ross (1958). In 1953, 1955, and 1956 she toured with Paul Szilard in Japan. In the summer of 1959 she and her husband organized a group which appeared at the Spoleto Festival of Two Worlds. She also danced with Scott Douglas in Moscow in connection with the U.S. Exposition at the Sokolniki Park (Aug., 1959). Her final creation with American Ballet Theatre was in Ross's *Dialogues* to Leonard Bernstein's *Serenade for Violin Solo, Strings and Percussion.* Unfortunately, none of the ballets in which she created roles after her return to the company where she had so glorious a career, have survived in the repertoire. She and her husband again appeared at the Spoleto Festival (1960) and then toured with their Ballet of Two Worlds for a season in Europe, the company's most important work being *Within the Grove,* based on the Japanese play *Rashomon* and danced to music composed by Laurence Rosenthal for the Broadway production. She retired as a dancer following this season. Currently assistant to Herbert Ross on the musicals which he choreographs both in America and Europe.

Kchessinska, Mathilda (Mathilda-Maria Kchessinska-Nechui, Princess Krassinska-Romanovska), former prima ballerina of the Maryinsky Theatre; b. 1872. The daughter of Felix Kchessinsky, famous Polish character dancer at the Maryinsky Theatre and the morganatic wife of Grand Duke André of Russia (d. Paris, 1956), she graduated in 1890 from the St. Petersburg Imperial Ballet School, and became ballerina in 1895. Owing to her proximity to Czar Nicholas II, she wielded extraordinary influence and power in the Imperial Ballet. It was due to her, for instance, that Prince Serge Volkonsky, director of the St. Petersburg Imperial Theatres, was dismissed from his post. It is incorrect to assume that her success and fame were due only to her connection with the Court. She was a light, precise, clean dancer who made the best of every role entrusted to her. She was one of the strongest technicians of her period; her dancing, according to a contemporary critic, reminded one of the most beautiful and precious filigree work in gold. It is a

Mathilda Kchessinska, great Russian ballerina of an older generation, teaching in her Paris studio, ca. 1947.

matter of record that the advent of Kchessinska put Russian dancers on an equal artistic footing with their foreign colleagues. Among her ballets were: *Le Roi Candaule, Cinderella, La Sylphide, The Nutcracker, The Sleeping Beauty, Paquita, The Awakening of Flora, La Fille Mal Gardée, The Daughter of Pharaoh, Esmeralda, The Humpbacked Horse,* etc. She also appeared in the season of the Diaghilev Ballets Russes company in London (1911), dancing *Swan Lake.* Since 1917 she has resided in Paris where she conducts a ballet school. Her last appearance on the stage was in 1936 when she danced a Russian dance at a charity performance given by the Ballet Russe de Monte Carlo at Covent Garden, London. In 1960 Kchessinska wrote a book *Dancing in St. Petersburg; The Memoirs of Kchessinska,* which was published in Paris, London, and N.Y.

Niels Kehlet, outstanding soloist of the Royal Danish Ballet.

Kehlet, Niels, Danish dancer, b. Hobro, 1938. Entered Royal Danish Ballet School in 1948; graduated into the company (1957); solo dancer since May, 1961. Dances *Blue Bird* pas de deux (*The Sleeping Beauty*), *Don Quixote* pas de deux, Peter (*Peter and the Wolf*), Gennaro (*Napoli*), Magician (*Moon Reindeer*), Drunken Peasant (*Miss Julie*), one of the two leading male parts (*Etudes*), 3rd movement (*Symphony in C*). Guest artist with International Ballet of Marquis de Cuevas (June–July, 1961). Had his greatest success to date creating Colas in Frederick Ashton's *La Fille Mal Gardée,* staged for the Royal Danish Ballet (1964). Guest artist with Lone Isaksen at Jacob's Pillow Dance Festival, dancing *Le Spectre de la Rose* with great success (summer, 1966).

Kelland-Espinosa, Edward, English dancer, teacher, stage producer, b. London, 1906. Studied with his father, Edouard Espinosa (see ESPINOSA). First connection with the stage was at Tivoli, Cape Town, South Africa, as call-boy at age eleven. First English engagement as Bobby in the musical *The Arcadians on Tour.* Principal dancer in London for many musical shows; has staged innumerable dances and ballets for pantomimes and summer shows. On the death of his father (1950) became Chairman of the British Ballet Organization on behalf of which he periodically undertakes world tours. He is also principal of the Espinosa School of Dancing.

Kellaway, Leon (Jan Kowsky), contemporary dancer and teacher, b. London, England. Studied ballet with Seraphima Astafieva and Nicholas Legat. His dance career included two years with Anna Pavlova's company, partnering Lydia Kyasht, and dancing with Olga Spessivtzeva in Australia. He stayed there to produce ballet for operettas until the formation of the Borovansky Ballet, of which he was ballet master and character dancer for fifteen years. Many of Australia's well-known dancers studied at his school in Sydney where he is currently teaching. Is also associate ballet master of the Australian Ballet.

Kelly, Gene, stage, motion picture, television actor, dancer, choreographer, director, b. Pittsburgh, Pa., 1912. Attended Penn. State Univ. and Univ. of Pittsburgh (B.A., 1933), and while in college directed the annual Cap and Gown shows. His dance studies began in his mother's school and he continued teaching in Pittsburgh until 1938; staged dances for Diamond Horseshoe, N.Y. (1940); also appeared in several musicals, playing the title role in *Pal Joey* (1941). Danced and acted in a number of highly successful film musicals, among them *For Me and My Gal, Cover Girl, Les Girls;* choreographed and danced in *Anchors Aweigh, Take Me Out to the Ball Game, The Pirate, An American in Paris* (which won a special Academy Award in 1952), *Brigadoon,* and others; directed, choreographed, and danced in *On the Town, Singin' in the Rain, Invitation to the Dance* (an all-dance full-length film which won the Golden Bear Award—first prize, best picture at the Berlin Film Festival, 1956), *It's Always Fair Weather,* and others. His television show on Omnibus, "Dancing is a Man's Game" (1958), was a major contribution to the very small number of important dance features in that medium. Directed the Rodgers and Hammerstein musical *Flower Drum Song* on Broadway (1958). Created and choreographed *Pas de Dieux* for the Paris Opéra Ballet (1960), and in that year was nominated a Chevalier of the Legion of Honor by the French Government; also received a citation from the Paris American Legion for "meritorious services and outstanding contribution toward Franco-American relations." He is the first American-born choreographer ever to create a ballet for the Paris Opéra. His alma mater, the Univ. of Pittsburgh, awarded him an honorary Doctorate of Fine Arts (1961). In

Gene Kelly, American dancer, choreographer, actor; star of stage, screen and television.

addition to his many dance achievements, he has also played many "straight" roles in motion pictures: *Christmas Holiday, The Happy Road* (which he also directed and which won the Foreign Press Association Award as the best international picture of the year, 1956), *Marjorie Morningstar, Inherit the Wind,* and others. He also directed *Tunnel of Love* and *Gigot.* He has frequently lectured on dance. The Museum of Modern Art, N.Y., honored him with the presentation of "The Art of Gene Kelly," a retrospective film series running in the Museum's cinema (Sept. 2–Oct. 6, 1962), at the same time publishing an illustrated brochure covering his entire career. Returned to a dancing-acting role in films with *What a Way to Go* (1964). In 1963 the U.S. State Dept. sent him on a 3-week good-will tour of African nations. At present choreographing and directing films in Hollywood and appearing occasionally on television.

Kelly, Jennifer, dancer, b. Tanganyika, East Africa, 1936. Studied dance in England at Arts Educational School and School of Ballet Rambert. Soloist with Ballet Rambert, dancing Lucile Grahn (Robert Joffrey's *Pas de Déesses*), Presque

Classique and Nuages, (*Czernyana*), Girl Blackamoor (*Night Shadow*), and others; created Friend (*Two Brothers*), Girl Monkey (*The Wise Monkeys,* chor. Norman Morrice, 1960), Child (*A Place in the Desert*), and others.

Kemp, William, a professional dancer and comedian whose most noteworthy achievement was dancing all the way from London to Norwich in 1599. He did Morris dances and was attended by Thomas Slye. A record of this was published in 1600 as *Kemp's nine daies wonder.* Kemp was a comedian in Shakespeare's company where he was listed as "head master of Morrice dancers."

Kennedy, Elisabeth, English dancer and teacher, b. London, 1918. Studied with Mme. Sismondi, Tamara Karsavina, Phyllis Bedells, Lydia Kyasht, Anne Northcote (Anna Severskaya). Joined Vic-Wells (later Sadler's Wells, now Royal) Ballet (1936); assistant ballet mistress, Sadler's Wells Ballet (1946–56); joined teaching staff (1955). Currently teaching at Royal Ballet School.

Allegra Kent, ballerina of the N.Y. City Ballet.

Kent, Allegra, American dancer, b. Los Angeles, 1938; m. Bert Stern. Began dance training in California, then entered School of American Ballet, N.Y. Joined New York City Ballet (1953) and first attracted public notice when she danced the Viola pas de deux in *Fanfare* (Jan. 12, 1954). Later the same year she danced her first creation, "The Unanswered Question" episode in *Ivesiana.* A ballerina since 1957, she dances a large repertoire including Swan Queen (*Swan Lake,* Act 2), 2nd movement (*Symphony in C*), one of the five ballerinas (*Divertimento No. 15*), The Novice (*The Cage*), the Girl (Jerome Robbins' *Afternoon of a Faun*), Leader of the Bacchantes (*Orpheus*), Terpsichore (*Apollo*), pas de deux (*Agòn*), and others. Her many creations include the Girl (*Pastorale*), the dancing Annie (*Seven Deadly Sins*), one of the lead roles (*Episodes*), Sleep Walker (*La Sonnàmbula*), and others. Has appeared many times on television and very successfully as lead dancer in the otherwise unsuccessful Broadway musical *Shinbone Alley.*

Kermis in Bruges, The, or The Three Gifts (Kermesse i Brugge Eller de Tre Gaver). Romantic ballet in 3 acts; chor.: August Bournonville; music; Holger Simon Paulli. First prod.: Royal Danish Ballet, Copenhagen, 1851. The action takes place in Bruges, Flanders, towards the end of the 17th century. On the evening of a folk festival three brothers save the beautiful Eleonore, daughter of the alchemist Mirewelt, from being kidnapped. As a reward, Mirewelt presents each with a gift: Geert with a ring which attracts all hearts, Adrian with a sword that brings victory, and Carelis with a fiddle which forces all who hear it to dance. After many adventures Geert, Adrian, and Mirewelt are accused of sorcery and are to be burnt. They are saved by Carelis who forces the judges and the population to grant a pardon after making everybody dance to his viola de gamba. Geert and Adrian return to their sweethearts, Carelis wins Eleonore. The fiddle is stored in the city hall only to be taken out once a year at Kermis time to bring joy and merriment in the old capital of Flanders. In the contemporary production, Svend Erik Jensen, Poul Wessel, and Fredbjorn Bjornsson have given memorable performances as the three brothers.

Kerr, Russell, New Zealand dancer, teacher, company director, b. Auckland, 1930. Studied with Kathleen Whitford, Elsa Brunelleschi, Stanislas Idzikowski, and at Royal Ballet School. Danced with José Greco's Spanish Company (1951), Ballet Rambert (1953); soloist, London's Festival Ballet (1954). Currently teaching in Auckland, N.Z.; is also artistic director of New Zealand Ballet and director of Repertory Ballet Company. Has choreographed a number of ballets, including several in collaboration with Poul Gnatt.

Kersley, Leo, English dancer, teacher, b. Watford, 1920; m. Janet Sinclair. Studied with Stanislas Idzikowski and Marie Rambert. Soloist with Ballet Rambert (1936–41), Sadler's Wells Ballet (1941–42), Anglo-Polish Ballet (1942–43). Leading male dancer with Sadler's Wells Theatre Ballet from its inception (1946) to 1951, creating roles in *Assembly Ball, Khadra,* and others. After several years of teaching in the U.S. and Holland, he returned to England (1959) and now has his own school in Harlow, Essex. With his wife, he wrote *A Dictionary of Ballet Terms* (1953); has also written many articles for English dance publications. Has staged several ballets for Sunday Ballet Club.

Keynes, Lord (John Maynard) (1882–1946), British economist, parliamentarian, patron of the arts; m. Lydia Lopoukhova (1925). Lord Keynes gained world fame as an economist, but his services to the theatre, especially the ballet, will always be remembered. He was co-founder and moving spirit of the Camargo Society (1930), the source of contemporary English ballet. While teaching at Cambridge Univ., he founded the Cambridge Arts Theatre which was the home of the Jooss Ballet during World War II. Was co-founder of C.E.M.A. (Council for the Encouragement of Music and the Arts), out of which developed the Arts Council of Great Britain which made possible the existence of ballet (together with the theatre, music, and the visual arts) in Great Britain during World War II by subsidizing it. Remained president of the Council until his death.

Khachaturian, Aram, Soviet composer, b. Tbilisi (then called Tiflis), 1903. He wrote the scores for the ballets *Gayané,* first produced in 1942 in Perm (then called Molotov), whereto the Leningrad Kirov Ballet company was evacuated, and *Spartacus,* produced by the same company in Leningrad (1951). A symphonic composer of great importance in U.S.S.R., he is often considered an elder statesman of music in his country.

Khokhlov, Boris, Soviet dancer, b. Moscow, 1932. Entered Bolshoi Ballet School in 1942, graduating with the 1951 class of Asaf Messerer. In his first season with the Bolshoi Ballet he danced the pas de trois in *Swan Lake* (1951–52). Was promoted to first soloist after dancing Prince Desiré (*The Sleeping Beauty*) in 1955; has since danced all the danseur noble parts in the repertoire: Siegfried (*Swan Lake*), the Princes in *The Nutcracker* and *Cinderella,* Vaslav (*The Fountain of Bakhchisarai*), Basil (*Don Quixote*) and Albrecht (*Giselle*), the last named for the first time on June 11, 1962. He has danced with all the leading ballerinas of the Bolshoi including Galina Ulanova, whom he partnered on her last appearance at the Bolshoi in *Chopiniana* (*Les Sylphides*).

Kidd, Michael, dancer, choreographer, director, b. Brooklyn, N.Y., 1919; m. Mary Heater. Studied for three years at the School of Engineering, City College, N.Y.; studied ballet with Anatole Vilzak, Ludmila Shollar, Muriel Stuart. Made his debut in the musical *The Eternal Road* (1937); member, American Ballet (Metropolitan Opera, 1937); Ballet Caravan (1937–40), his roles including title role in *Billy the Kid,* among others. Danced at N.Y. World's Fair (1939, 1940) and at Radio City Music Hall (1941). Soloist and assistant director, Dance Players (1941–42). Soloist, Ballet Theatre (1942–47), dancing title role in *Billy the Kid,* First Sailor (*Fancy Free*), Devil (*Three Virgins and a Devil*), etc., and creating one of the four male roles (*Interplay*). Choreographed his only ballet *On Stage!* (1945), in which he created the role of the Handyman. Staged dances and musical numbers for musical *Finian's Rainbow* (1947) for which he won the Antoinette Perry (Tony) Award, since when he has had a long string of musical successes, also winning Tony's for *Guys and Dolls* (1951) and *Can-Can* (1953). Both directed and choreographed the musicals *Li'l Abner, Destry Rides Again, Wild Cat, Subways Are For Sleeping*. Staged dances and musical numbers for *Here's Love* (1963), *Ben Franklin in Paris* (1964). Staged the dances for the 1964 N.Y. World's Fair spectacular *Wonder World.* Has also choreographed for many films beginning with *Seven Brides for Seven Brothers* (1954); also *Knock on Wood* and *Merry Andrew* for Danny Kaye, and the film version of *Guys and Dolls.*

Kinch, Myra, contemporary modern dancer, choreographer, teacher, b. Los Angeles, Calif.; m. Manuel Galea. B.S. Univ. of California at Los Angeles. Studied dance with Dorothy Lyndall,

Myra Kinch, American modern dancer, choreographer and teacher.

Bertha Wardell, Doris Carl, Mary Clare Sale, Vincenzo Celli, Muriel Stuart, La Meri, and Eugenia Eduardova. Made her debut in a solo performance at the Rheinhardt Theatre, Berlin, and later was dance soloist at the Politeama Theatre, Mexico City. She was director and choreographer of the West Coast Dance Project of the Federal Theatre Project and choreographer for the opera department of the Federal Music Project. Has toured U.S. and Canada for many years, as a solo performer and with her group which includes her pianist-composer husband Manuel Galea, who has composed much of the music for her many works. She is known particularly for her dance satires: *Giselle's Revenge, Tomb for Two* (based on *Aïda*), *A Waltz is a Waltz is a Waltz, To Unfurl the Fan,* and others, but has also a considerable body of serious works to her credit including *Sundered Majesty, Veni Creator,* and others. Has headed the modern dance department at Jacob's Pillow since 1948, and has appeared many times on its Dance Festival programs. Choreographs for many music festivals, outdoor dramas, etc., and has appeared on "Frontiers of Faith" and "Camera Three" television programs.

King, Eleanor, modern dancer, lecturer, teacher, b. Middletown, Pa., 1906. Studied dance at Clare Tree Major's School of the Theatre (1925–26); Theatre Guild School (1926); seven years with Doris Humphrey and Charles Weidman; also mime with Etienne Decroux. Was a member of the original Humphrey-Weidman group (1927–35), appearing with it in U.S. and Canada. Danced in Leonide Massine's *Le Sacre du Printemps,* Philadelphia and Metropolitan Opera Houses (Apr., 1930). Developed own repertory group in Seattle, Wash., touring U.S. and Canada. Her first large work with poetry (Lauro de Bosis) and music (David Diamond and Franczeska Boas) was *Icare,* premièred at Brooklyn Museum Dance Center (1937). She has subsequently choreographed works based on the writings of James Joyce, Walt Whitman, Petrarch. Since 1955 has been associate professor, Dept. of Speech and Dramatic Arts, Univ. of Arkansas, teaching Dance in Fine Arts, and Mime, and also choreographing for Theatre of the Imagination. Took a sabbatical (1960–61) to study dance in Japan, where she also lectured.

Kinney, Troy (1872–1938), American etcher, painter, writer on dance. His major contribution to dance literature was the comprehensive and definitive volume *The Dance, Its Place in Art and Life,* written in collaboration with his wife, Margaret West Kinney (N.Y., 1924). This was one of the first important books on dance published in the U.S. He also wrote a number of essays and articles on various personalities and subjects. His many etchings and dry-points are considered among the finest graphic representations of dance.

Kirov Ballet, the company domiciled in the Kirov (formerly Maryinsky) Theatre, Leningrad. The Kirov Ballet still retains much of the style of the old Imperial Russian Ballet of the Maryinsky days, as opposed to the more florid Soviet style exemplified in its finest flowering by the Bolshoi Ballet of Moscow.

With the exception of the official Soviet ballet hierarchy, the Kirov Ballet is recognized as the leading ballet organization of continental Europe by what is generally referred to as the ballet world. At this writing (summer, 1967) the performing personnel is composed of 182 artists divided into: Highest Group (ballerinas and premiers danseurs: 15); First Group (first soloists: 27), First Group non-soloists (coryphés and coryphées: 25), Second Group (corps de ballet: 95), Third Group (older members of the company: mimes, walk-ons, etc.: 20). Artistic Direction: Konstantin Sergeyev, artistic director: 1; Ballet Masters and Associates: 7; Rehearsal and Coaching Personnel (usually former dancers): 6; Company Teachers (not to be confused with teachers in the company's school) 4. The current active repertoire, i.e., ballets which can be given with one rehearsal or without any rehearsal if the cast is available: 34 ballets, mostly full-evening in length. New ballets in rehearsal at this time: 6. Toured the U.S. and Canada for the second time, (Sept. 6–Dec. 14, 1964). Ballets new to this country were Prokofiev's *Cinderella,* Glazounov's *Raymonda* and B. S. Maizel's *A Distant Planet,* all choreographed by Konstantin Sergeyev; and the *Polovetzian Dances from Prince Igor,* with choreography after Michel Fokine.

Kirov Theatre of Opera and Ballet, Leningrad, the name of the Maryinsky Theatre since 1935. The Maryinsky Theatre was renamed The State Academic Theatre of Opera and Ballet at the beginning of the Revolution (1917) and was known under its Russian initials (GATOB) until 1935. It was then given its present name in honor of the Soviet hero Sergei Kirov. Its present correct name in full is State Academic Theatre of Opera and Ballet, named after Kirov.

Kirsova, Hélène (Ellen Wittrup), Danish dancer, teacher, choreographer, d. Feb. 22, 1962, in London. Danced with Santiago Ballet, Col. de Basil's Ballet Russe de Monte Carlo, René Blum Ballets de Monte Carlo. She was particularly noted for her Valse in *Les Sylphides* and the role of the Butterfly which she created in *L'Epreuve d'Amour.* Toured Australia with the de Basil company (1936–37) and settled in Sydney, founding a school and later an Australian National Ballet company (1941) which was very successful for several years. Her ballets for that company included *A Dream and a Fairy Tale, Faust* (using Heinrich Heine's scenario), *Waltzing Matilda,* using Australian themes. After she retired, she visited Russia and under her married name of Bellew wrote *Ballet in Moscow Today* (1956).

Lincoln Kirstein, writer, producer, director-general of the New York City Ballet.

Kirstein, Lincoln Edward, b. Rochester, N.Y., 1907. An outstanding American authority on dance, especially ballet, he has contributed more than any other contemporary American toward the development of the theatrical dance in the U.S. He is co-founder and director, the School of American Ballet, N.Y. (1934); co-founder and director, the American Ballet (1935); founder and director, Ballet Caravan (1936); founder, Dance Archives of the Museum of Modern Art, N.Y. (1940), closed a few years later by the Museum for lack of space; founder and editor, *Dance Index* (1942–49, except during his service in the U.S. Army during World War II); co-founder and secretary, Ballet Society (1946); general director, the New York City Ballet since its establishment (1948). Kirstein was graduated from Harvard Univ. (A.B., 1929; A.M., 1930). While there he was founder and editor of the literary magazine *Hound and Horn* (discontinued in 1935) and founder of the Harvard Society for Contemporary Art. His books include *Fokine* (London, 1934), a biography of the great choreographer; *Dance* (N.Y., 1935), a monumental volume on the history of the art form); *Blast at Ballet, a Corrective for the American Audience* (N.Y., 1938), an analysis of what was wrong with ballet in the U.S.; *Ballet Alphabet, a Primer for Beginners* (N.Y., 1939); with Muriel Stuart, *The Classic Ballet, Basic Technique and Terminology* (N.Y., 1952). Lincoln Kirstein served with distinction in the U.S. Army from Feb., 1943, to Oct., 1945. Shipped out as a Private in the Corps of Engineers, he served subsequently as a dispatch rider and after the invasion was attached to the Monuments, Fine Arts and Archives office, under the direction of the American Commission for the Protection and Salvage of Artistic and Historic Monuments in War Areas. His activities in recovering works of art stolen by the Nazi leaders earned him the Commission's citation and a medal from the Netherlands Government. Since the middle 'fifties Kirstein's interests have also included theatrical expressions not closely connected with ballet. Among them are The Shakespeare Memorial Theatre, Stradford, Conn., in which he continues to be active; *The Play of Daniel,* the 12th century musical drama which he produced in 1959 and has revived annually at Christmas in N.Y. and at other times on tour; Gagaku, the Dancers and Musicians of the Japanese Imperial Household, which he presented in the U.S. in 1959; the Japanese Classic Dramatic Theatre, The Grand Kabuki, which he imported from Japan in 1960. The Japanese Government took cognizance of his sponsorship of Japanese theatre in the U.S. by awarding him (Sept. 27, 1960) the Order of the Sacred Treasure, Fourth Class, for his "outstanding contribution to the cultural exchange between the two nations."

Kirstein, Lincoln, Collection, an integral part of the Dance Collection of the New York Public Library, was given by Mr. Kirstein to the Library in 1961. This historical collection includes books, prints, rare clipping material, and motion picture films, more than 3,000 items in all. Among the iconographic material are original designs by Cecil Beaton, Eugene Berman, Alvin Colt, James Stewart Morcom, and Rouben Ter-Arutunian; engravings of Shaker rituals; a selection of early caricatures; nearly 100 playbills, mainly relevant to 19th century English ballet; prints of the 19th century French opera ballet, Floradora girls, masked balls, and 18th century social dance.

Kiss, Nora, outstanding Paris teacher of ballet, b. Piatigorsk, Russia, 1908. Studied with Vera Alexandrova, Carlotta Brianza, Alexandre Volinine, Rousanne Sarkissian. Danced in French and Russian ballet companies (1929–1935) under Boris Romanov and George Balanchine. Began teaching in Paris in 1938. During World War II taught in Rome. Has had a studio in Paris since 1946. Guest teacher for summer courses in Helsinki, Krefeld, Cologne, etc.

Kitchell, Iva (Mrs. Stokely Webster), dancer and dance satirist, b. Junction City, Kan., 1912. Studied ballet with Edward Caton, Vincenzo Celli, Konstantin Kobeleff, Vera Nemtchinova; modern and oriental, with Yeichi Nimura, all in N.Y.; ballet with Lubov Egorova, Leo Staats, Alexandre Volinine, Paris; acting with Percival Vivian. Made her professional debut with the Chicago Opera Ballet; later became soloist, Radio City Music Hall; toured Germany with her satiric dances (1938), including two months at the Scala, Berlin. First solo program in N.Y. was at Barbizon Plaza Theatre (1940); first Carnegie Hall recital (1946). Has given hundreds of concert performances in U.S. and Canada, appearing many times at the Jacob's Pillow Dance Festival; toured South America (1951, 1958); two-week one-woman show at Bijou Theatre on Broadway (1956). In 1958–59 toured assisted by her daughter Stephanie Kitchell (Webster). Her best known dances were probably *Ze Balley, Soul in Search, Non Objective, Carmen Kitchell from Kansas, Bacchanale (as seen in the Opera)*. Wrote chapter on satiric dance for Walter Sorell's *The Dance Has Many Faces.* Retired as a performer in 1961 and now teaches in Huntington, L.I., N.Y.

Klavsen, Verner, Danish dancer in the Royal Swedish Ballet, b. 1931. Studied with Harald Lander and Vera Volkova; went to Stockholm (1952) and was accepted into the Royal Swedish Ballet. Has danced nearly all the principal classic roles and most of the modern Swedish repertoire; awarded the first Carina Ari Foundation fellowship (4,000 Sw. kr.) for his creation of the role of the Sailor in Birgit Cullberg's *Lady from the Sea* (1961); created role of Danila, the young stone cutter, in the Royal Swedish Ballet's production of *The Stone Flower* (Feb. 27, 1962); created the Friend in Antony Tudor's *Pillar of Fire* and Tybalt in his *Romeo and Juliet,* staged for Royal Swedish Ballet (Dec. 30, 1962). Invited by Soviet Union to dance in Moscow, Kiev, Tallin, as partner to Finnish ballerina Doris Laine (fall, 1963).

Klebe, Giselher, German composer, b. Mannheim, 1925. Studied music with Kurt von Wolfurt, Rufer, Boris Blacher, and others. In addition to his operatic and orchestral works he has composed for ballet *Pas de Trois, Signale* (1955, in the repertoire of Berliner Ballet), *Fleurenville* (1956), *Menagerie* (1958), and others.

Klemisch, Dietlinde, Austrian dancer, b. Vienna, 1938. Studied under Ewald Vondrak and at the ballet school of the Vienna State Opera. Accepted into the company in 1952; promoted to soloist in 1957. Dances both classic and demi-caractère roles. Among her roles are the interpolated *Peasant* pas de deux (*Giselle,* Act 1), the Girl (*The Miraculous Mandarin*), Perette (*Joan von Zarissa*), the *Paquita* pas de trois, and principal roles in *Swan Lake, Hotel Sacher, The Fairy Doll,* and others.

Kniaseff, Boris, French teacher and former dancer, b. St. Petersburg, 1905. Studied dance with Kassian Goleizovsky, St. Petersburg. Danced in Paris and elsewhere (1921–32), often as partner of Olga Spessivtzeva. Ballet master of Opéra Comique (1932–34); opened his own studio 1937 where such dancers as Yvette Chauviré, Renée Jeanmaire studied with him. Choreographer with Col. de Basil's Original Ballet Russe (1947), *Ballets de Paris de Roland Petit* (1948). Opened a school in Lausanne, Switzerland (1953), and later in Geneva and Rome. He developed a system of exercises to be performed while lying on the floor, substituting for the barre. His best known ballet is *Legend of the Birchtree* (Beryozka, 1930). Engaged as ballet master by the Colón Theatre, Buenos Aires for one year beginning Jan., 1967.

Kobeleff, Konstantin, Russian dancer and teacher, b. 1885. Was graduated from the St. Petersburg Imperial School of Ballet (1903) and accepted into the ballet company of the Maryinsky Theatre. Danced with the Diaghilev Ballets Russes in Western Europe on leave of absence from the Maryinsky (1909–11). Resigned from the Theatre (1912) to return to Diaghilev. Came to the U.S. with the Diaghilev company (1916) and remained here to become an American citizen. Was dancing in U.S. in big vaudeville touring acts until the advent of talking films which spelled the end of vaudeville. He began teaching in N.Y. in the late 1920's and continued until 1960, when he retired. He died Aug. 7, 1966, after a fall in which he suffered a broken pelvis.

Köchermann, Rainer, German dancer, b. Chemnitz, 1930. Pupil of Tatiana Gsovska. Has danced at the State Opera Berlin (1949–51); Berlin Municipal (now German) Opera (1951–55); first soloist, Frankfurt (1955–59); Hamburg (since 1960). Dances all classic and modern ballet principal roles; appears often in television also.

Kochno, Boris, b. Russia, 1903, the son of an officer in the Russian Imperial Army. Co-founder and artistic director of Ballets des Champs-Elysées. Interested in literature and the arts from his early youth, he wrote poetry, painted a little, and had an excellent ear for and a fine understanding of music. He went to Paris in 1922 and soon afterwards became the secretary and later close friend of Serge Diaghilev. By 1925 his friendship with Diaghilev had matured to a point where he became an advisor and spokesman for the impresario and exercised a strong influence on him. In the course of his association with the Diaghilev Ballets Russes he wrote the books for a number of ballets, among them *Les Facheux, Zephyr and Flora, Les Matelots, La Chatte, The Gods Go a'Begging, Ode, Le Pastorale, Le Fils Prodigue, Le Bal.* After Diaghilev died, Kochno joined the Ballets Russes de Monte Carlo as artistic collaborator (1932) and wrote the books for *Cotillon* and *Jeux d'Enfants.* The following year he left the company and joined George Balanchine in the founding of Les Ballets 1933. He subsequently re-joined the Ballets Russes and stayed with the organization through 1937. In Mar., 1945, together with Christian Bérard, he was responsible for the production of Roland Petit's *Les Forains* at a private performance at the Théâtre des Champs-Elysées. This led to the founding of Les Ballets des Champs-Elysées, of which he became artistic director in Oct. of that year. Wrote the books for *Les Forains, La Fiancée du Diable, Les Amours de Jupiter,* and others. He was with the company until it was disbanded in 1949 and, with Petit gone, tried to revive it in 1951 with the collaboration of Jean Robin and Ruth Page. Wrote and edited, in collaboration with Maria Luz, *Le Ballet* (Paris, 1954).

Koegler, Horst, German writer and ballet critic, b. Neuruppin, 1927. Studied at the Universities of Kiel and Halle/Saale. Playwright and opera regisseur in Görlitz (1949–51); free lance journalist (1951–59) in Berlin, and since 1959 in Cologne. Ballet critic of the newspapers *Die Welt* and *Stuttgarter Zeitung,* contributor to the Cologne magazine *Das Tanzarchiv.* Among his books are *Ballett in Deutschland II* (with Siegfried Enkelmann, 1957), *Bolshoi Ballett* (1959), *Modernes Ballett in Amerika* (1959), *Ballett International* (1960).

Koellner, Alfredo, Italian dancer, b. Genoa, 1933; m. Vera Markovic. Studied under Ettori Caorsi and the sisters Placida and Teresa Bataggi. Accepted into the ballet company of Teatro dell'Opera, Rome (1950); promoted to premier danseur (1955). Soloist, Ballet Européen of Nervi (1960). Since that autumn premier danseur of the Stuttgart Opera Ballet.

Koesun, Ruth Ann, American dancer, b. Chicago, Ill., 1928. Studied dance with Edna Lucile Baum, Bentley Stone and Walter Camryn in Chicago; with Vecheslav Swoboda in N.Y. Joined Ballet (now American Ballet) Theatre (1946) and has remained ever since, dancing leading roles which include Prelude (*Les Sylphides*), Mother and Sweetheart (*Billy the Kid*), Impromptu Dance (*Graduation Ball*), Dead Girl (creation–*Los Caprichos*), Lise (*La Fille Mal Gardée*), Fanny Cerito (*Pas de Quatre*), and others. Has also done night club work with John Kriza, summer stock musicals, various guest artist appearances, and appeared at the Jacob's Pillow Dance Festival.

Kolpakova, Irina, Peoples' Artist of the RSFSR, Soviet ballerina, b. 1933; m. Vladilen Semyonov. She was the last ballerina trained by Agrippina Vaganova, having graduated from the Leningrad school in 1951 only a few months before her great teacher's death. A lyrical, classic ballerina, her excellent line and cleancut, exact technique enable her to shine particularly in such roles as Aurora or the Princess Florine in the *Blue Bird* pas de deux in *The Sleeping Beauty.* She also has a feeling for contemporary roles, and had a marked success as the Beloved in Igor Belsky's first ballet, *Coast of Hope,* sharing its creation with Alla Osipenko. Her reper-

toire includes the title role in *Giselle,* Maria (*Fountain of Bakhchisarai*), Desdemona (Vakhtang Chabukiani's *Othello*), Katerina (*The Stone Flower,* Yuri Grigorovich version), Shiriene (*Legend of Love*). Has danced in Paris, London, and N.Y. with the Kirov Ballet.

Kondratov, Yuri, Peoples' Artist of the RSFSR, Soviet dancer and teacher, b. 1921. Entered Bolshoi School in 1930 as a pupil of Pyotr Gusev; graduated in 1940. One year before graduation he created the leading role of Ilko in *Svetlana* in which Olga Lepeshinskaya created the name role. Shortly after danced another important role, the athlete Tybul in *Three Fat Men.* When the Bolshoi Ballet was evacuated to Kuibyshev at the beginning of World War II, Kondratov danced Siegfried in *Swan Lake* for the first time and subsequently danced it with all the leading ballerinas of the period. He was Galina Ulanova's partner for many years, dancing with her on her first appearance outside the Soviet Union at the Maggio Musicale in Florence (1951). He partnered Marina Semyonova (1945–49) and Olga Lepeshinskaya (1949–50). His most famous creation was Fabricio in Vassily Vainonen's *Mirandolina* (1949). His other great role was Basil in *Don Quixote,* a role which showed the robust manliness, brio and virtuosity of his dancing. His other roles included Colin (*La Fille Mal Gardée*), Vaslav (*The Fountain of Bakhchisarai*), Grey (Crimson Sails), Prince Desiré (*The Sleeping Beauty*), Albrecht (*Giselle*), Jean de Brienne (*Raymonda*), Franz (*Coppélia*), Ma Lie-chen (*The Red Flower*). He retired from the stage in 1959 and in Jan., 1960, was appointed Artistic Director of the Bolshoi Ballet School where he had for many years been teaching the art of supported adagio, on which subject he is an authority. Currently conducts one of the boys' classes at the school.

Irina Kolpakova, ballerina of the Leningrad Kirov Ballet and outstanding example of the St. Petersburg style of dancer; shown here in Raymonda, *Act 1.*

Kondratyeva, Marina, honored Artist of the RSFSR, Soviet ballerina, b. 1933. Daughter of a well-known scientist, she entered the Bolshoi School in 1943 and was graduated in 1952 (class of Galina Petrova). She danced her first ballerina role, *Cinderella,* during the 1953–54 season. The lyrical and gentle image of this role suits her fragile type to perfection, though she possesses a strong, virtuoso technique in contrast to her lightness and seeming fragility. It was considered that she had passed her ballerina test when she danced Aurora in *The Sleeping Beauty* (1956). Her performance as Maria in *The Fountain of Bakhchisarai* is considered closest to that of its creator, Galina Ulanova. When the Leningrad production of *Shurale* was transferred to Moscow she alternated with Maya Plisetskaya in the leading role of the Bird-girl. She also dances Juliet in *Romeo and Juliet,* the Muse (creation) in Leonid Lavrovsky's *Paganini,* and her most important role to date, *Giselle.* She has toured abroad many times.

Koner, Pauline, modern dancer and choreographer, b. New York City, 1912. Attended Columbia Univ.; studied dance with Michel Fokine, Michio Ito, Angel Cansino. Made her debut in the children's corps of Fokine Ballet (1926); toured U.S. as soloist with Michio Ito (1928–29). Made her debut as a solo dancer in her own works in a recital at Guild Theatre, N.Y., 1930, and from then until 1946 appeared in N.Y. and on tour in U.S. in solo performances. Joined José Limón Dance Company (1946) and remained on a "permanent guest artist" basis until 1960. She created a great number of roles in the Limón and Doris Humphrey repertoire of the company, including title role (*La Malinche*), Friend's Wife (*The Moor's Pavane*), Mary (Limón's *The Visitation*), Mother (*Ruins and Visions*), and many others. She also continued creating solo and group works, including *Cassandra* (solo), *Concertino, The Shining Dark* (inspired by the story of Helen Keller and premièred, to a score by Leon Kirchner, at the 1956 American Dance Festival, Connecticut College, New London), all staged for her own company which she founded in 1949. Her long solo, *The Farewell,* premièred in 1962, is a major contribution to the modern dance repertoire. She has appeared on many television programs, taught and staged works in Rome, Amsterdam, The Hague, Santiago de Chile, Buenos Aires. Has also lectured and taught in many universities in the U.S. and contributed articles to many dance publications. In Jan. 1965, Miss Koner left for Japan for a six-month performing and teaching engagement in Tokyo. She also danced and lectured in Kyoto, Osaka, and other cities. On her return she joined the dance faculty of the North Carolina School of the Arts, Winston Salem, and performed at the Jacob's Pillow Dance Festival (summer, 1966).

Pauline Koner with Lucas Hoving in José Limón's Moor's Pavane.

Köning, Joachim, German dancer, b. Kassel, 1939. Studied with Marianne Vogelsang, Michael Piel. His major engagements include the German Opera, Berlin, as corps de ballet dancer; Municipal Stages Wuppertal as soloist. Has danced principal roles in *Concerto for Orchestra* (Béla Bártok), *Construction Humaine* (Spitzmüller), the role of Triptolemos in *Persephone* (Igor Stravinsky), and others.

Koren, Sergei, Honored Artist of the RSFSR, Soviet character dancer and ballet master, b. 1907. Koren belongs to the outstanding group of Leningrad dancers who, during the 1930's played a most important role in the creation of the style of Soviet ballet of that period. He also has the distinction of belonging to that small number of male dancers who gained the highest possible position in spite of not starting ballet training in early childhood. Koren became interested in ballet in his 'teens. He joined the evening courses of the Leningrad ballet school organized in the 1920's for the benefit of talented young people who had missed the proper entrance age to the former Maryinsky school. After a year he was transferred to the regular school where he continued to develop as a character dancer of great promise. He was graduated in 1927 into the Kirov company and soon achieved a leading position as character soloist. Outstanding creations of that period include Karim (*Partisans' Days*—Vasily Vainonen–Boris Asafiev), Ostap (*Taras Bulba*), Zaal (*Heart of the Hills*—Vakhtang Chabukiani–Andrey Balanchivadze), Nurali (*The Fountain of Bakhchisarai*), and others. In 1942 he joined the Bolshoi Ballet, making his debut as Espada, the matador, in *Don Quixote,* offering a fine study of true Spanish dance in contrast to the ballet-Spanish character dancing of traditional ballet repertoire. His greatest characterization at the Bolshoi was Mercutio in *Romeo and Juliet*. His other important creation is Lie Shang-foo in *The Red Flower*. He retired from active dancing in Jan. 1961, appearing only occasionally in mime roles. As ballet master at the Bolshoi he is passing on his vast experience in characterization to young dancers. He has also choreographed dances in operas and dance ensembles.

Korovine, Constantine, Russian painter, b. Moscow, 1861, d. Paris, 1939. Korovine, with his friend and colleague Alexander Golovine, was responsible for much that was new, original, and colorful in the Russian Imperial and private theatres at the end of the 19th and the first decade of the 20th centuries. His style of painting and stage design did much to change the taste of the European, especially the French, public in the years just before World War I. His designs for the Diaghilev Ballets Russes included *Le Festin* (1909), the opera *Russland and Ludmilla* (Paris Opéra), *Prince Igor* (1927); for the Anna Pavlova company *Don Quixote;* for Col. de Basil's Ballet Russe de Monte Carlo *Danses Slaves et Tziganes* (Bronislava Nijinska, 1935).

Koslov, Alexis, Russian dancer of the Moscow Imperial Theatre, b. 1887; brother of Theodore Koslov. Graduated from the Moscow school in 1905; danced in *Daughter of Pharaoh, Humpbacked Horse, The Sleeping Beauty, Giselle, Fairy Doll.* Resigned from the Imperial Theatre (1910) and appeared with various companies in Western Europe. Currently residing in U.S.

Koslov, Theodore (1881–1956), Russian dancer, teacher; m. Alexandra Baldina; brother of Alexis Koslov. Graduated from the Moscow Imperial Theatre School into the company (1901); joined the Diaghilev Ballets Russes (1909), resigning from the Imperial Theatre a year later. Organized a small group, among them Tamara Karsavina, for a season at the London Coliseum, and in 1911 joined Gertrude Hoffman's company for a N.Y. season and U.S. tour for which he restaged *Les Sylphides, Cléopâtre* and *Schéhérazade.* Opened a school in N.Y., but in 1917 assembled a troupe of six dancers which played the Keith Vaudeville Circuit. When the troupe reached Hollywood, Koslov met Cecil B. de Mille and subsequently appeared in many of his and other films of the old silent days. Opened a school in Hollywood in 1922 (continuing to appear for some time in films) and taught until the day of his death.

Kotchetovsky, Alexander (1889–1952), Russian dancer of the Moscow Imperial Ballet. Graduated from the Moscow School in 1907. Left early in his career to join the Diaghilev Ballets Russes, remaining until 1914 as a leading character dancer and mime. Returned to Russia at outbreak of World War I and became ballet master for the Petrograd and later Kiev state opera theatres. Joined the Chauve-Souris company (1919) with which he came to the U.S., remaining to become ballet master for Shubert, Paramount and Fox Theatres and opening a school in N.Y. Moved to Houston, Tex. (1930) where he opened a school and taught until his death.

Kovach, Nora. See KOVACH AND RABOVSKY.

Kovach and Rabovsky (Nora Kovach, b. 1932; Istvan Rabovsky, b. 1930), Hungarian-born prima ballerina and premier danseur of the Budapest State Opera Ballet. Were graduated from the State Opera Ballet school and also studied at the Leningrad Kirov Ballet School for six months (1949–50). In May, 1953, when the Hungarian Government sent the dancers to East Berlin to appear at an important function at the Berlin Opera House, they defected to the West by taking a subway train to the Western Zone of Berlin and reporting to the British Military Police. They eventually arrived in London as guest artists with London's Festival Ballet at Festival Hall, and subsequently came to the U.S. where they made their debut on the Ed Sullivan television show, "Toast of the Town," on Nov. 22. They later appeared as guest artists with Roland Petit's Ballets de Paris which was then playing an engagement in the U.S. In the little more than fourteen years since their arrival here, the dancers (they are married) have toured the U.S., Latin American countries, Japan with a concert group; danced in night clubs and hotels. In the summer of 1963 they organized a small Hungarian group, called Bihari, which made its debut in Aug. at Lewisohn Stadium, N.Y. Kovach and Rabovsky are now U.S. citizens.

Kozhukhova, Maria (1897–1959), Honored Art Worker of the RSFSR, and of the Uzbek SSR, prominent Soviet ballet teacher. Kozhukhova entered the St. Petersburg Theatre School (of the Maryinsky Theatre) in 1907. She was fortunate to have been a pupil of Michel Fokine and he mentions her favorably in his memoirs. She was graduated from the school in 1915 and was soon promoted from corps de ballet to solo parts. She possessed great personal charm and her dancing was full of life and temperament. When many of the Maryinsky ballerinas left after 1917, she became one of the leading ballerinas of the Kirov Ballet. She retired in 1933 to devote herself to teaching, which she had begun as early as 1919. In 1933 she was invited to teach at the Bolshoi School and soon became its leading teacher for girls, some of her pupils being Violetta Prokhorova (Elvin), Violetta Bovt, Ludmilla Bogomolova. From 1947 she taught classes for the artists of the Bolshoi theatre.

Kozlovsky, Albert, teacher and choreographer, b. Liepaja (Latvia), 1902. Studied ballet at the Moscow Bolshoi Ballet School. Went abroad in 1925 and danced in several French, Russian, Spanish, and Italian companies. Returned to Latvia in 1931 and became ballet master and choreographer of the Liepaja Opera House and the Dramatic Theatre. He established the official ballet company in Liepaja and staged several ballets for it, among them *Swan Lake.* Left for Sweden in 1944 with his wife, Nina Dombrovska. He founded a private school in Stockholm in 1945. In 1947 he was engaged as teacher by the Oscarsteatern and in 1949 was chosen instructor of the Royal Swedish Ballet school. He staged for this company the *Grand Pas de Dix Hongrois* (from *Raymonda*) and *Don Quixote.* He is a naturalized Swedish subject.

Kozlovsky, Nina, née Dombrovska, b. Liepaja (Latvia), 1908; m. Albert Kozlovsky. Studied ballet at the Riga, Latvia, Opera Ballet school with Alexandra Fedorova and later with Olga Preobrajenska in Paris. Engaged by the Liepaja Opera Ballet as dancer; became première danseuse in 1931. Left for Sweden in 1944 with her husband and since 1949 has been teaching at the Royal Swedish Ballet school. She is a naturalized Swedish subject.

Kragh-Jacobsen, Svend, Danish author, critic and lecturer, b. Copenhagen, 1909. M.A. in Literature, Univ. of Copenhagen (1931); studied in Bureau d'Etudes Internationales, Geneva (1934, 1935). Began his career in journalism with *Nationaltidende,* a small Copenhagen newspaper (1936–37); since Feb. 1938 has been with the Copenhagen *Berlingske Tidende,* the oldest European daily (founded in 1749) and the biggest in Denmark; since 1951 principal critic of drama, dance, and film there with an international reputation. Also broadcasts on television and radio on theatre subjects. His books include *Ballettens Blomstring* (1945), *Margot Lander* (1947), with Torben Krogh the monumental volume *Den Kongelige Danske*

Ballet (1952), *The Royal Danish Ballet* (in English, 1955). Since 1955, also editor and publisher of *Danish Theatre Annual* (in Danish); contributor to *Dance Encyclopedia.*

Krakoviak, Cracovienne (Fr.), a Polish dance with syncopation in 2/4 time, made famous in ballet by Fanny Elssler.

Kramer, Leonie (Leonie M. H. Kruisdijk), Dutch dancer, b. The Hague, 1941. After four years in Nederlands Ballet is now (1967) a member of Het Nationaal Ballet (see HOLLAND, DANCE IN). She danced solo parts in *Night Shadow, Concerto Barocco, Etudes, Suite en Blanc, Graduation Ball, The Prisoner of the Caucasus, Pas de Quatre,* and others.

Krassovska, Nathalie (Natasha Leslie), ballerina, b. Petrograd, U.S.S.R., 1921. She began her dance studies with her grandmother, who had been a member of the Bolshoi Ballet; but her principal studies were with Olga Preobrajenska in Paris, and Nicholas Legat in London. Her first professional appearance was in Bronislava Nijinska's Ballet (1932). Member, George Balanchine's Les Ballets 1933; toured South America with Serge Lifar (1934); with Ballet Russe de Paris (1935). Joined Ballet Russe de Monte Carlo (1936), rising to ballerina rank and dancing a large repertoire including *Giselle, Les Sylphides, Swan Lake, The Nutcracker, Coppélia, Ballet Imperial, Serenade, Firebird, Paganini, Francesca da Rimini,* and others. She left the company in 1950, though she returned many times for guest artist seasons. With London's Festival Ballet (1950–55), dancing *Esmeralda, Napoli, Romeo and Juliet* (Oleg Briansky), all classic pas de deux, etc. She has also returned to this company as guest artist, has made guest appearances with Ballet Rambert, Grand Ballet du Marquis de Cuevas, and has toured in South America with Igor Youskevitch (1961). Guest ballerina with Thomas Andrew's Santa Fe Opera Ballet at Jacob's Pillow Dance Festival (1962). Has appeared on television and in films for television in Europe and South America. Currently living in Dallas, Tex., where she teaches. She continues to make occasional guest appearances, frequently for Igor Youskevitch's Ballet Romantique (1964).

Nathalie Krassovska, Russian-born American ballerina and teacher, in her costume for Raymonda.

Krassovskaya, Vera, Soviet historian and critic of ballet, Dr. of Arts, b. Leningrad, 1915. Graduated from the Leningrad Choreographic School, danced with the Kirov Ballet (1933–41). Her books include *Vakhtang Chabukiani* (1956), *Russian Ballet Theatre from the Beginning to the Middle of the 19th Century* (1958), *Leningrad Ballet* (1961), *Russian Ballet Theatre of the Second Half of the 19th Century* (1963) (for which she received her doctorate), *Anna Pavlova* (1964). She has also written a number of articles about Soviet and foreign ballets which have appeared in the Soviet Union. At present is working on a book, *Russian Ballet from the Beginning of the 20th Century to 1917.*

Kraul, Earl, Canadian dancer, b. London, Ont., 1929. Studied dance with Bernice Harper and Stanislas Idzikowski in London; in Canada with Betty Oliphant and Celia Franca. Joined National Ballet of Canada for its first season (1951) and has remained ever since. His first leading role was the male dancer in *Les Sylphides* (1953), and since then he has added Siegfried (*Swan Lake*), Franz (*Coppélia*), Albrecht (*Giselle*), Sugar Plum Fairy's Cavalier (*The Nutcracker*), *Blue Bird* pas de deux, Harlequin (*Carnaval*), Prince Florimund (*Princess Aurora*); in the modern repertoire, Lover (*Lilac Garden*), 3rd and 5th Songs (*Dark Elegies*), Painter (*Offenbach in the Underworld*), Ben (*Ballad*), male dancer in *Concerto Barocco, Le Corsaire* pas de deux (with Galina Samtsova), and one of the Clowns in Ray Powell's *One in Five.* Romeo in John Cranko's *Romeo and Juliet* (1964) is his most important role to date.

Harald Kreutzberg, modern German dancer in his solo dance With a Book.

Kreutzberg, Harald, German dancer, b. Czechoslovakia, 1902. Studied with Rudolf von Laban and Mary Wigman. Appeared in solo concerts of his own works and with Yvonne Georgi and Ruth Page. Danced in U.S. in the early 1930's and again in 1937, 1947, 1948, and 1953. Made his farewell appearance as a dancer in Frankfurt (1959), but continued to choreograph for other performers, notably Dore Hoyer, and to teach at his school in Berne, Switzerland.

Krieger, Victorina, Honored Art Worker of the RSFSR. Soviet ballerina, b. 1896. Daughter of well-known actor Vladimir Krieger and actress and playwright Nadezhda Krieger-Bogdanovskaya, Victorina Krieger was born in St. Petersburg. When her father was invited as leading actor of the well-known Korsh Theatre, the family moved to Moscow where she entered the Bolshoi Ballet School in 1903, graduating in 1910 (Vassily Tikhomirov's class). At an unprecedentedly early age for those days, she received her first ballerina part in 1915—the Tzar-Maiden in *The Humpbacked Horse.* In 1916 she danced Kitri in *Don Quixote* which became her best role, though her Lise in *La Fille Mal Gardée* and Swanilda in *Coppélia* were also memorable. She had steel points and was unsurpassed for her thirty-two fouettés which she was able to perform alternately en dedans and en dehors. In Sept., 1921, Krieger received an invitation to dance as alternate ballerina with Anna Pavlova's company. She danced *Coppélia* with great success in Ottawa, Quebec, and Montreal, and then left, as Pavlova considered there was a place for only one prima ballerina in her company. Krieger signed some independent American contracts and danced *The Fairy Doll* (billed as *The Toyshop*) and a recital program that included the "Bacchanal" from Camille Saint-Saëns' opera *Samson et Dalila* in N.Y. After dancing in Europe, she returned to the U.S.S.R. in 1923, touring with Mikhail Mordkin

(1923–24). In 1925 she rejoined the Bolshoi company and also danced periodically at the Kirov Theatre, Leningrad. She organized the Moscow Art Theatre of Ballet (1929), aiming at introducing content and dramatic depth into choreography. The company toured all over the country. Krieger created Lise in *The Rivals* (new version of *La Fille Mal Gardée*), The Miller's Wife in *Le Tricorne* and Zarema in *The Fountain of Bakhchisarai*. Among the company's young soloists was Vladimir Bourmeister, whose artistic education began there. The company's artistic credo was close to that of the famous Moscow Art Theatre, which is why Vladimir Nemirovich-Danchenko, co-director with Konstantin Stanislavsky of the Moscow Art Theatre, invited Krieger and her group to form the nucleus of the ballet of his Lyric Theatre. Krieger continued working at the Bolshoi where she created the Stepmother in *Cinderella* in 1945. Since 1958 she has been director of the Bolshoi Theatre Museum. She is author of a book, *My Notes* (Moii Zapiski, 1930), and writes articles about ballet performances in leading Moscow newspapers. She is a member of the Union of Soviet Journalists.

Kriner, Dora (Mrs. Roberto García Morillo), Argentine dancer, choreographer, writer, lecturer, b. Buenos Aires, Argentina, 1920. Studied ballet at Conservatorio Nacional de Música y Arte Escénico with Yelena Smirnova, Dora del Grande, and Mercedes Quintana; modern dance with Inés Pizarro and Otto Werberg; choreography with Clothilde Sakharov; Japanese dance with Sestko Nakandakaré. In 1940 she joined the corps de ballet of Teatro Colón, Buenos Aires. In 1952 she received a grant from the Dante Alighieri Association to study dance in Italy. Has published articles on dance in many Argentine and Uruguayan publications, and in collaboration with Roberto García Morillo has written *Estudios Sobre Danza*. Has lectured in Argentina, France, and Italy, as well as for the Cultural Dept. of the U.S. Embassy, in the interior of Argentina. Has choreographed for Saski-Naski, a group of Basque folklore dancers. In 1960 she organized the First Festival of Songs, Dances, and Poems of Japan, Thailand, India, China, and Indonesia at the request of the Comité Oriente-Occidente attached to UNESCO. The Festival took place in Aug., 1960, at Teatro Nacional Cervantes. At present she is writing a book, *Otros Estudios Sobre Danza.*

Krisch, Winfried, German dancer, b. Hamburg, 1936. Studied with Anneliese Sauer, Kurt Peters (Hamburg), Nora Kiss, Olga Preobrajenska (Paris), Victor Gsovsky (Berlin). His principal engagements include those with the Malmö Municipal Opera, Maurice Béjart company, Municipal Theatre (Bonn), Municipal Theatre (Essen), Cologne Opera. Dances principal roles in *Apollon Musagète, Orpheus, Firebird, Les Sylphides, Pulcinella,* and the classic pas de deux.

Kriza, John, American dancer, b. Berwyn, Ill., 1919, of Czechoslovakian parentage. Studied dance for two years at Morton Junior College; then with Mildred Perchal (Berwyn); principal instruction with Bentley Stone, Walter Camryn, Anton Dolin, Pierre Vladimirov, Valentina Pereyaslavec. Made his debut in W.P.A. Federal Project and Chicago City Opera Ballet (then under Ruth Page, 1939). A charter member of Ballet (now American Ballet) Theatre, which he joined in 1940, he rose from corps de ballet to leading dancer, becoming a national favorite from the time he created the role of the sentimental Second Sailor in *Fancy Free* (1944). Since then he has created many roles including Blues pas de deux (*Interplay*), Hero (*On Stage!*), Pastor (*Fall River Legend*), pas de deux with the dead girl (*Caprichos*), Tancredi (Ballet Theatre version of *Le Combat*). He also dances a large repertoire ranging from the solo male dancer (*Les Sylphides*) to the title roles in *Bluebeard* and *Billy the Kid,* Colin (*La Fille Mal Gardée*), Hermes (*Helen of Troy*), Champion Roper (*Rodeo*), Jean (*Miss Julie*), and many others. He has been guest artist with Ruth Page's Chicago Opera Ballet, has appeared on television, in night clubs and in summer stock, but his entire career is closely identified with the history of American Ballet Theatre.

Kröller, Heinrich (1880–1930), German dancer, ballet master, choreographer. A one-time premier danseur of the Dresden Opera, he subsequently became ballet master at the Munich, Vienna, and Berlin state opera houses. Among his many ballets are Richard Strauss' *Schlagobers* (1924) and John Alden Carpenter's *Skyscrapers* (1929).

Kronstam, Henning, solo dancer of Royal Danish Ballet, b. Copenhagen, 1934. Entered the Royal Danish Ballet school (1941); accepted into the company (1952); promoted to solo dancer (1956). Toured Europe and U.S. with Inge Sand's group (1955, 1957). Guest artist, Oslo (1957); also in England and Scotland (1959, 1960). Appeared in films with Roland Petit in Paris (1960). Guest artist, International Ballet of the Marquis de Cuevas (1961). Has also been guest artist, with Kirsten Simone, with Ruth Page's Chicago Opera Ballet for several seasons. Among his roles are Romeo (*Romeo and Juliet*—Frederick Ashton version), Poet (*Night Shadow*), Drummer (*Graduation Ball*), title role (*Apollo*), Prince Florimund (*The Sleeping Beauty*)—all creations for Royal Danish Ballet; also Albrecht (*Giselle*), Jean (*Miss Julie*), Don José (*Carmen*), Prince Siegfried (*Swan Lake,* Act 2), and many others. He is a Knight of the Order of Dannebrog since Dec., 1964.

Krupska, Dania, American dancer and choreographer, b. Fall River, Mass., 1923, of Polish parentage. Studied ballet with Ethel Philips, Catherine Littlefield, Mikhail Mordkin, Aubrey Hitchins, Sevilla Forte in U.S., and with Lubov Egorova in Paris. Toured (as Dania Darling) in Poland, Roumania, Hungary, and the Balkan countries, Palestine, Vienna; joined Catherine Littlefield's Philadelphia Ballet for European tour (1937) and its season with Chicago Opera (1938). Member of American Ballet until it disbanded; also danced in Broadway musicals and at Radio City Music Hall. Assistant to Agnes de Mille in a number of productions, including *Girl in Pink Tights* (appearing for Renée Jeanmaire several times). Choreographed *Seventeen* as her first Broadway musical, followed by the first *Shoestring Revue, The Most Happy Fella,* Gypsy scene in the Metropolitan Opera production of *The Gypsy Baron;* nominated for Tony Award for choreography in *The Happiest Girl in the World,* etc. Choreographed prize-winning Italian musical show *Rugantino* (1962), staged in N.Y. (1964). Choreographed New York City Center revivals of *The Most Happy Fella* (1959), *Show Boat* (1961), *Fiorello* (1962). Has staged dances in many television shows. Has choreographed ballets *Outlook for Three* (Jacob's Pillow Dance Festival) and *Pointes on Jazz* (Dave Brubeck, American Ballet Theatre, 1961).

Kurgapkina, Ninel, Honored Artist of the RSFSR, Soviet ballerina, b. Leningrad, 1929. Entered the Kirov Ballet School in 1938; graduated with honors (class of Agrippina Vaganova) in 1947 and was taken into the corps de ballet of the Kirov Opera and Ballet Theatre. Kurgapkina had shown exceptional talent as a child and was taken into the School of Artistic Education for Children (now

Henning Kronstam, premier danseur of the Royal Danish Ballet; due to his frequent television appearances almost as well known in the U.S. as in Europe.

named for Vaganova) where she was prepared for entrance into the theatre school proper. She is an impeccable virtuoso dancer and conducts the daily company class whenever the ballet mistress is absent. She dances all the classic ballerina roles: Aurora (*The Sleeping Beauty*), Odette-Odile (*Swan Lake*), Kitri (*Don Quixote*), and Myrtha (*Giselle*), but her warmth and power of projection also enables her to dance such roles as Galia (*Home Fields*), Parasha (*The Bronze Horseman*) and, especially, the Beloved (*Coast of Hope*).

Kurtz, Efrem, Russian-American conductor, b. 1900. He directed the orchestra in a recital given by Isadora Duncan (1921) and was subsequently musical director of the Anna Pavlova Ballet, the Ballet Russe de Monte Carlo (1938–42), and conductor of the Kansas City Symphony Orchestra. He arranged the music for the Ballet Theatre production of *Mam'zelle Angot* (1943).

Kyasht, Lydia (properly Kyaksht), former first soloist of the Russian Imperial Theatres, b. St. Petersburg, 1885, d. London, 1959. Studied at School of the Maryinsky Theatre, St. Petersburg, under Paul Gerdt. Made her debut with the company in 1902; became first soloist 1908. Due to intrigues, left the Imperial Theatre and Russia the same year, never to return. Married M. Ragozin and settled in London where she appeared with great success in the Empire Ballets. During the 1940's she had her own company, Ballet de la Jeunesse, developed mainly from her school. Author of *Romantic Recollections* (1929).

La Meri (Russell Meriwether Hughes), ethnic dancer, teacher, lecturer, writer, b. Louisville, Ky., 1898. Educated in Texas Woman's Univ., Denton and Columbia Univ., N.Y. Studied ballet, Spanish, and Mexican dance with local teachers in San Antonio (1913–20); Hawaiian dance in Hawaii (1917); Spanish dance in Barcelona (1922); ballet with Aaron Tomaroff and Ivan Tarasoff; and modern dance with Michio Ito, N.Y. (1925). Between 1926 and 1939 studied dance in Mexico, South America, Spain, Africa, India, Ceylon, the Philippines, Japan. She made her professional debut with a tour down the Rio Grande Valley and in San Antonio and Dallas (1923); also danced in various motion picture houses in N.Y. (1925). Until the outbreak of World War II in Europe (1939), she toured all over the world, performing and studying. Returned to N.Y. and with Ruth St. Denis founded the School of Natya (May, 1940), which was absorbed into the Ethnologic Dance Center which La Meri founded in Oct., 1942. The school continued until 1956, offering a complete training in many forms of national dance to countless students, among whom were Juana and Matteo. During this period La Meri continued her own tours of performances and lectures, and created many ethnic dances (Hindu, Chinese, Burmese, Polynesian, Indian, Moroccan, Spanish, Latin American, and others), including *El Amor Brujo* (Manuel de Falla), a Bharata

La Meri, ethnic dancer, writer, choreographer, teacher, lecturer.

Natyam interpretation of *Swan Lake* (Act 2) and *Schéhérazade.* She has appeared many times at the Jacob's Pillow and Connecticut College Dance Festivals, taught and presented works for Juilliard School of Music Dance Dept., and in universities all over the U.S. Currently teaching and giving lecture-demonstrations in colleges and dance schools. She has written articles for many periodicals and encyclopedias (including *Dance Encyclopedia, Encyclopedia Britannica, Enciclopedia dello Spettacolo*). Her books include *Principles of the Dance Art* (London, 1933), *Dance as an Art Form* (N.Y., 1933), *Gesture Language of the Hindu Dance* (N.Y., 1941), *Spanish Dancing* (N.Y., 1948), together with six volumes of *Collected Poems* (between 1917 and 1938). Teaches at the Jacob's Pillow summer dance school, occasionally lectures and choreographs for dance groups and individual dancers. In 1965, Jacob's Pillow Dance Festival, Inc., published her book *The Basic Elements of Dance Composition.*

La Meri Collection, an integral part of the Dance Collection of the New York Public Library, was presented by the dancer to the Library in 1948. It includes more than 1,000 photographs, 3,000 clippings, programs, and memorabilia documenting her career and her experiences as an ethnic dancer. In 1962 she further enriched the collection with her library of material gathered during a lifetime of research and study. Included are clippings and photographs of American-Indian, European, Far Eastern, and Asian forms of dance, customs, and costumes indigenous to these areas.

La Scala, Milan. See TEATRO ALLA SCALA, MILAN.

Laban Dance Notation System.

BY ANN HUTCHINSON.

Rudolf von Laban published his method of dance notation, called "Schrifttanz" in 1928. Two years later other editions appeared, written in English, French, and German. This work was the result of years of study and research to find a notation which would be suitable to all kinds of movement. In the past the drawback of the notation systems invented was that each served only one form of dance and was not adaptable to others. The Laban notation, or "Kinetographie" as he called it, is based on the body and its possibilities for movement. While it is the most logical of all notations, and for the most part pictorial, it is not a shorthand; it reflects in detail the intricacies of the body in motion.

The principal use for notation is for recording dances, ballets and movement patterns. Today the film is becoming an easy though expensive way to record large ballets. Although it serves as an excellent reminder, a film is, at best, a more or less imperfect performance and may not show the exact intentions of the choreographer. Reconstructing through films ballets that have been forgotten is tedious, slow, and usually inaccurate rhythmically. With the Laban script of a ballet to study, any step at any place in the ballet can be analyzed and its relation to other steps, or other performers, can easily be seen. There have been many instances when the notated works of the Jooss ballets have simplified their reconstruction and rehearsing. Notation is also a valuable aid in training dancers; by analyzing movements the student gains a clearer perception of space and rhythm, and of the physiological source of movements.

The Laban notation is written from the point of view of the dancer and all directions are taken from the body, with the exception of up and down which are constant due to gravity. The staff used in the notation consists of a vertical center line with vertical columns on either side. The staff represents the body; all columns on the right of the center line are for the right side of the body, and those on the left are for the left side of the body. Each part of the body has its column and the symbols are placed in the appropriate columns. The basic symbol is a rectangle which is altered in shape to show direction, in color to show level, and in length to indicate rhythm. Thus one symbol gives the part of the body which moves, and the direction and speed of the movement. The notation alphabet includes signs for the joints (shoulders, knees, fingers, etc.); for various surfaces of the body (palm, face, chest, etc.); signs for turning, touching, sliding, stamping, clapping, dynamics, etc. While floor plans are used to clarify group dances, they are not necessary for a solo dance since the size and direction of the steps and jumps will show how the dancer travels across the floor.

During the 1940's Laban adapted his notation for industrial purposes, concentrating on work movements and effort control. In his booklet, *Laban Lawrence Industrial Rhythm* (1945), he shows the same operation being done by three different people, and by means of the notation shows just how and where one loses and the other gains. Several plants and factories in England use the system to speed production and make industrial work safer. The notation has also been used by doctors for physiotherapy. See also DANCE NOTATION.

Laban, Rudolf, von. See VON LABAN, RUDOLF.

Labanotation, a term coined by the Dance Notation Bureau, N.Y. to refer to the Laban system of dance notation, also the title of book on the system, by Ann Hutchinson.

Labis, Attilio, French dancer; m. Christianne Vlassi. Trained in the Paris Opéra school; promoted to premier danseur étoile (1961). His repertoire includes Gene Kelly's *Pas de Dieux, Marines* (George Skibine–André Jolivet), *Le Combat* (William Dollar), *Etudes* (Harald Lander), *Swan Lake* (the full-length version staged by Vladimir Bourmeister, 1961). Toured with Claude Bessy in the U.S.S.R. (fall, 1961), appearing in concert programs and with the Bolshoi Theatre Ballet. Made his U.S. debut at the Jacob's Pillow Dance Festival with a group of French stars (1963). Guest artist with Royal Ballet during summer season, 1965, at Covent Garden, London.

Labyrinth. Ballet in 4 scenes; chor.: Leonide Massine; music: Franz Schubert; book: Salvador Dali; décor and costumes: Salvador Dali. First prod.: Ballet Russe de Monte Carlo, Metropolitan Opera House, N.Y., Oct. 8, 1941, with André Eglevsky (Igor Youskevitch alternating) as Theseus, Tamara Toumanova (Ariadne), Frederic Franklin (Minotaur), George Zoritch (Castor), Chris Volkoff (Pollux). This, the sixth of Massine's symphonic ballets, was adapted from Greek mythology, and set to Schubert's Seventh Symphony.

Lac des Cygnes, Le. See SWAN LAKE.

Lacotte, Pierre, French dancer and choreographer, b. Chatou, France, 1932. Studied at Paris Opéra school with Gustave Ricaux, and with Lubov Egorova, Boris Kniaseff, Rousanne Sarkissian. Promoted to premier danseur of Opéra (1953), dancing principal roles in *Etudes, Le Palais de Cristal, Septuor, Les Santons, Les Caprices de Cupidon et le Maître de Ballet,* and others. Left the Opéra (1955) to organize his own company, Les Ballets de la Tour Eiffel, with a season at Théâtre des Champs-Elysées. Guest artist, Metropolitan Opera Ballet, N.Y. (1956), partnering Melissa Hayden and Mary Ellen Moylan. Partnered Violette Verdy during the London season of *The Princess* (1960). Choreographer of *La Nuit est une Sorcière* (music: Sydney Bechet; décor: Bernard Daydé), *Gosse de Paris* (music: Charles Aznavour), *Such Sweet Thunder* (music: Duke Ellington) for Berlin Festival (1958), and many others.

Ladré, Marian, contemporary dancer, b. Czestochowa, Poland; m. Lara Obidenna. Studied at Ballet School of Theater Wielki, Warsaw for seven years. Left Warsaw in 1924. Member, Comte Etienne de Beaumont's Soirées de Paris and Boris Romanoff's Romantic Theatre until 1927 when he joined the Diaghilev Ballets Russes. Soloist, Col. de Basil & René Blum Ballets Russes from its inception (1932) until 1947; also regisseur for his last two years with company (later Original Ballet Russe). Created role of Nicoletto (*Scuola di Ballo*), pas de trois (*Jeux d'Enfants*), Artist (*Le Beau Danube*), Sister (*Cinderella*); also danced Eunuch (*Schéhérazade*), Marquis di Luca (*Good-Humored Ladies*), Athlete (*Le Beau Danube*), Polkan (*Coq d'Or*), The Three Ivans (*Aurora's Wedding*), Fate (*Les Présages*), Tarantella (*Cimarosiana*), Professor (*Scuola di Ballo*), Charlatan (*Petrouchka*), Pantalon (*Carnaval*), and others. Currently teaching in Seattle, Wash.

Lady and the Fool, The. Ballet in 1 act, 3 scenes; chor.: John Cranko; music: selections from the following operas by Giuseppe Verdi (in the order in which they are first played)—*Alzira, Jerusalem, Sicilian Vespers, Il Finto Stanislau, Joan of Arc, Arnoldo, I Due Foscari, Ernani, I Masnidieri, Macbeth, Attila, I Lombardi, Don Carlos, Oberto, Luisa Miller,* arr. by Charles Mackerras; décor: Richard Beer. First prod.: Sadler's Wells Theatre Ballet, New Theatre, Oxford, Feb. 25, 1954, with Patricia Miller (La Capricciosa), Kenneth MacMillan (Moondog), Johaar Mosaval (Bootface); revived and revised for Sadler's Wells (now Royal) Ballet, Royal Opera House, Covent Garden, London, June 9, 1955, with Beryl Grey, Philip Chatfield, and Ray Powell. On a whim the spoiled beauty, La Capricciosa, takes two poor clowns with her to an extravagant ball. But in the course of the evening she has a change of heart and falls in love with Moondog. They leave together, though not forgetful of Bootface in their new happiness.

Lady and the Unicorn, The. Ballet in 1 act, chor.: Heinz Rosen; music: Jacques Chailley; book, décor, and costumes: Jean Cocteau. First prod.: Gärtnerplatztheater, Munich, May 9, 1953, with Geneviève Espagnol (Lady), Boris Trailine (Knight), Veronika Mlakar (Unicorn). According to legend, the Unicorn accepts nourishment only from the hands of a virgin. When he sees that the Lady has a lover in the person of a Knight, he dies, mourned by the Lady who now does not want to see the Knight. The ballet was inspired by the unicorn tapestry in the Cluny Museum, Paris. Rosen staged the ballet in several other countries, among them the U.S., where it was produced by Ballet Russe de Monte Carlo, with Irina Borowska, Igor Youskevitch, Nina Novak (première Royal Alexandra Theatre, Toronto, Canada, Oct. 14, 1955).

Lady from the Sea. Ballet in 1 act, based on the play by Henrik Ibsen; chor. and book: Elizabeth Leese; music: Saul Honigman; décor: Jean de Belleval; costumes: Kay Ambrose. First prod.: National Ballet of Canada, Carter Barron Amphitheatre, Washington, D.C., June 13, 1955, with Celia Franca (The Lady), Yves Cousineau (Stranger), Ray Moller (Husband). The Canadian première took place in Montreal in Nov. of the same year with the same cast. An earlier version, created by Elizabeth Leese for her own semi-professional group, was first staged in May, 1952. A young girl, born and bred by the sea, plights her troth with a Stranger and promises to await his return. After years of waiting, she marries a widower but finds it hard to adjust herself to life with him and his three children. When the Stranger finally returns and she must choose between the romantic ideal and warm reality, she chooses reality.

Lady from the Sea. Ballet in 1 act, 5 scenes; chor. and book: Birgit Cullberg; music: Knudage Riisager; décor: Kerstin Hedeby. First prod.: American Ballet Theatre, Metropolitan Opera House,

N.Y., Apr. 20, 1960, with Lupe Serrano (the Girl), Royes Fernandez (the Sailor), Glen Tetley (the Husband). The ballet was inspired by the Henrik Ibsen play of the same name. The main theme is the magic attraction of the sea. A young girl is torn between the kind but stolid husband (a widower with two children) whom she marries and her romantic attachment to a sailor who left her years before. She finally realizes that the sailor has really been the symbol of her love for the sea, and only then is she able to accept fully the happiness offered by her husband and the children. Cullberg mounted this ballet for the Royal Swedish Ballet in Stockholm, Mar. 1, 1961, with Kari Sylwan (the Lady) and Verner Klavsen (the Sailor). Kari Sylwan assumed the role (her first important creation) when Mariane Orlando was taken ill only five days before the première.

Lady into Fox, ballet in 3 scenes; chor.: Andrée Howard; music: Arthur Honegger—Toccata and other piano pieces, arr. by Charles Lynch; book: based on the novel by David Garnett; décor: Nadia Benois. First prod.: Ballet Rambert, Mercury Theatre, London, May 15, 1939, with Sally Gilmour and Charles Boyd as Mrs. Tebrick (the Lady of the title) and Mr. Tebrick. Staged for Ballet (now American Ballet) Theatre, Center Theatre, N.Y., Jan. 26, 1940, with Andrée Howard and William Dollar. Mrs. Tebrick turns into a fox shortly after members of a local hunt have visited her house. At first she still responds to her husband's love but finally she loses all memories of her human past, and he sadly lets her go to make her own life in the forest. The title role made Sally Gilmour famous overnight and will always be associated with her.

Lady of the Camellias. Ballet in 4 acts, based on the novel by Alexandre Dumas; chor.: Tatiana Gsovska; music: Henri Sauguet; décor: Jean Ponelle. First prod.: Berliner Ballett (during the Berlin Festival), Sept. 29, 1957, with Yvette Chauviré and Gert Reinholm; revived for the Paris Opéra (1960) with Yvette Chauviré and George Skibine.

Laerkesen, Anna, dancer of the Royal Danish Ballet, b. Copenhagen, 1942. Accepted as a second-year student at the company's school in 1959, after having been trained by Edith Feifere Frandsen, former prima ballerina of the Riga, Latvia, Opera (now teaching in Copenhagen). Made her debut in August Bournonville's *La Sylphide* while still a student (1959); promoted to dancer (1960). Toured in U.S. as soloist with the Inge Sand group (1961). Dances principal roles in *Graduation Ball, Solitaire, Lady from the Sea* and others. Had a sensational success as Juliet in the revival of

Danish ballerina Anna Laerkesen as Queen in Flemming Flindt's The Three Musketeers *(1967)*.

Romeo and Juliet (Frederick Ashton version), Feb. 2, 1963. Promoted to soloist (1964). Dances principal female role in Birgit Cullberg's *Moon Reindeer* since promotion.

Lafon, Madeleine, French dancer, b. Paris, 1924. Studied at the Paris Opéra school and with Alexandre Volinine. Promoted to première danseuse étoile (1952). Except for a few guest appearances, her entire career has been with the Paris Opéra. Her principal ballets were *Les Mirages, Le Palais de Cristal, Soir de Fête, Coppélia.* She was a precise and strong technician. Died April 6, 1967.

Lafontaine, Mlle. (1665–1738), first woman dancer in the Académie Royale and the first French première danseuse. Her first public appearance was in *Le Triomphe de l'Amour* (1681).

Lagerborg, Anne-Marie, Swedish dancer, b. 1919. Entered the Royal Swedish School of Ballet (1926); accepted into the company (1937); became soloist (1947), and Associate Ballet Director of the Royal Swedish Ballet (1957). Her roles include the Lilac Fairy in *The Sleeping Beauty, Medea,* and Kristin in *Miss Julie* (both by Birgit Cullberg). Has been Cullberg's choreographic assistant on many occasions. Spent two weeks in N.Y. in Jan. 1966, rehearsing Antony Tudor's ballet *Echoing of Trumpets* for the Metropolitan Opera Ballet. In Sept. 1966, went to Göteborg to stage Cullberg's *Adam and Eve, Medea,* and *Miss Julie* for the Göteborg Ballet.

Laiderette. Ballet in 1 act; chor.: Kenneth MacMillan; music: Frank Martin's *Petite Symphonie Concertante;* décor: Kenneth Rowell. First prod.: Sadler's Wells Choreographers' Group, Sadler's Wells Theatre, London, Jan. 24, 1954, with Maryon Lane and David Poole. Staged for Ballet Rambert; first London performance July 4, 1955, with Patricia Ashworth and Ronald Yerrell. Lucette Aldous has also had a big success in the title role. The "Little Ugly One" is a wretched youngster from the streets, whose ugliness carries her into a masked ball where she momentarily attracts a rich young man. The revelation that her pitiable appearance is not assumed causes her to be rejected once again.

Laine, Doris, prima ballerina of the Finnish National Ballet, b. Helsinki, 1931. Studied in Helsinki, Moscow, and with Anna Severskaya in London. Joined National Ballet of Finland (1947); became soloist (1952); ballerina (1956). Created title role in *Esmeralda* (1963). Dances *Swan Lake* (Odette-Odile), *Giselle, Fountain of Bakhchisarai* (Maria), *Cinderella, Coppélia* (Swanilda), *Miss Julie, Stone Flower* (Mistress of the Copper Mountain), *The Sleeping Beauty* (Aurora), *Etudes, Firebird, Don Quixote* (Kitri), and others. Guest artist with Bolshoi Ballet, Moscow (1960); also with Bolshoi, Kirov (Leningrad), and Tallin (Estonia), partnered by Verner Klavsen, premier danseur of the Royal Swedish Ballet (1963). Visited the U.S. (winter, 1965) under a Leaders and Specialists Grant of the Dept. of State. Holder of Pro Finlandia Award, King's Medal (Sweden), Order of Arts and Letters (France).

Laing, Hugh, dancer, b. Barbados, British West Indies, 1911, of English and Irish parents. Studied with Margaret Craske, Marie Rambert in London; Olga Preobrajenska in Paris. Soloist, Ballet Club (which became Ballet Rambert), and then with London Ballet. He created leading roles in the early ballets of Antony Tudor, among them Mortal under Mars (*The Planets*), Mercury (*The Descent of Hebe*), Lover (*Jardin aux Lilas*), Waiter (*Judgment of Paris*), and others. Joined Ballet (now American Ballet) Theatre for its first season and, except for a season (1945–46) in the musical *The Day Before Spring,* remained until

Doris Laine, prima ballerina of the Finnish National Ballet with premier danseur Matti Tikkanen in Romeo and Juliet.

1950. During this period, he re-created his roles in *Jardin aux Lilas* (now called *Lilac Garden*) and *Judgment of Paris,* and created Young Man from the House Opposite (*Pillar of Fire*), Romeo (Tudor's *Romeo and Juliet*), Young Gypsy (*Aleko*), Transgressor (*Undertow*), and others. Joined New York City Ballet (1950), again dancing the Lover in *Lilac Garden,* creating Hippolytus and Laertes in *La Gloire,* and giving an outstanding performance in the title role of *The Prodigal Son.* Danced Harry Beaton in the Gene Kelly film version of *Brigadoon.* Though never a great technician, his intense, dark good looks and wonderful artistry made him an outstanding performer. It is unlikely that he will ever be equalled in the Tudor creations. Is now a successful commercial photographer.

Lake, Molly, English dancer, teacher and choreographer, b. Cornwall, 1909; m. Travis Kemp. Studied with Seraphima Astafieva. Made her debut with Anna Pavlova company. Soloist, Markova-Dolin Ballet (1935–36). Director, Ballet Guild Company from 1942 (in which year she staged a centenary performance of *Giselle,* dancing the title role); later of Embassy Ballet and Continental Ballet. Teaching in Turkey since 1954.

Lambert, Constant (1905–1951). English composer, conductor, author. Educated at Christ's Hospital and Royal College of Music. He was the only English composer to be commissioned to write a score for the Diaghilev Ballets Russes (Bronislava Nijinska's *Romeo and Juliet,* 1926). He was musical director of Sadler's Wells Ballet from its earliest days and his influence in shaping the style and development of the company was only slightly less than that of Ninette de Valois and Frederick Ashton. He composed the music for *Pomona,* presented by the Camargo Society (1930) and subsequently taken into the repertoire of Sadler's Wells Ballet. His choral work *Rio Grande* was also performed by the Camargo Society (1932) and then taken over by Sadler's Wells. He was the composer of *Horoscope* (1938) and *Tiresias* (1951), for both of which he wrote the book. His wife, Isabel Lambert, designed the décor for the latter. He arranged some of Henry Purcell's *Fairy Queen* music for *The Birthday of Oberon* (1933), a mixture of song and ballet; also the Meyerbeer music for *Les Patineurs.* Selected and arranged the William Boyce music for *The Prospect Before Us,* the music of Henry Purcell for *Comus,* Emanuel Chabrier's music for Ballabile, among others. He would undoubtedly have been a more prolific composer in other fields had not his devotion to the ballet taken up so much of his life. During World War II when the company could not travel with an orchestra, he played one of the two pianos. His witty, beautifully spoken and timed commentary for *A Wedding Bouquet* (words by Gertrude Stein) was one of the major pleasures of that ballet. His *Music Ho!* (1933) is one of the best books on music written in this century, and during the 1930's his music column in the now defunct *Sunday Referee* revealed him as one of the most perspicacious of ballet critics.

Lambert, Isabel. Contemporary English artist and designer; m. Constant Lambert. Designs for ballets include *Tiresias, Madame Chrysanthème,* Alfred Rodrigues' *Jabez and the Devil,* all for the Royal Ballet; *Blood Wedding* for Sadler's Wells Theatre Ballet.

Lambeth Walk, an English social dance in vogue in the late 1930's. It was created by Lupino Lane (member of England's famous theatrical family, the Lupinos) for a musical comedy about London's Cockneys, *Me and My Girl* (1937), and unexpectedly caught the public fancy.

Lambranzi, Gregorio, Venetian ballet master who invented a system for setting down or recording dances. His book, *Nuova e curiosa scuola de'balli teatrali,* was published in Nürenberg (1716). It is an illustrated textbook for dancing masters with an ingenious manner of presenting each dance. The author gives the theme and air of music and suggests steps and also includes a picture which gives the costume and style of the dance. From this the professional dancer could be stimulated to improvise or arrange a dance. The dances presented include many comedy dances based on commedia dell'arte characters. There are also dances of various trades and professions, such as grenadier, blacksmith, cobbler, and dances of sports and other activities. An English translation of the work by Derra de Moroda was published by Cyril W. Beaumont (London, 1927).

Lambrinos, Vassili, dancer, teacher, choreographer, b. Greece, ca. 1927. Began his ballet training in Athens, later moved to Paris, where he studied with the great Russian ballerinas of the former Imperial theatres and outstanding French teachers. He danced in several continental ballet companies. His first important choreographic works were for London's Festival Ballet, among them the *Grieg Piano Concerto in A minor,* with Nathalie Krassovska and John Gilpin, and *The Laurel Crown,* to a score by the late Michael Hobson (both 1953). In 1957 he staged *Contrepointe d'Amour* for the Grand Ballet du Marquis de Cuevas, with Maria Ruanova, Daphne Dale, and Nicholas Polajenko. He accepted an invitation from Teatro Colón, Buenos Aires, to become dancer, ballet master, and choreographer. In the season 1958–59 he choreographed *Daphnis and Chloë* to the Maurice Ravel score, with José Neglia and Esmeralda Agoglia in the title roles, and Morton Gould's *Concertette* (the music used by Jerome Robbins for *Interplay*). In addition he staged the full-length *Nutcracker* in a specially built tent-theatre in a square in Buenos Aires, with Amalia Lozano as the Sugar Plum Fairy and Rodolfo Fontan as her Cavalier. The ballet ran 120 performances. Lambrinos came to New York in Oct., 1959, to stage the dances in the revue *New Faces.* While waiting for rehearsals to begin he taught at the International Dance School, N.Y. At present (fall, 1966) he lives in Los Angeles and is acting and occasionally choreographing films.

Lament. Modern dance work; chor.: Louis Johnson; music: Heitor Villa-Lobos' *Bachianas Brasileiros No. 5.* First prod.: Central High School of Needle Trades, N.Y., New York Ballet Club's Third Choreographers' Night, Apr. 12, 1953, with Louis Johnson, Margaret Newman, Tania Makaroff, David Vaughan, Arthur Mitchell. A haunting evocation of the aching loneliness of lost souls in limbo. A then-unknown Gloria Davey (later of the Metropolitan Opera) was the singer.

Lament for Ignacio Sanchez Mejias. Modern dance work; chor.: Doris Humphrey; music: Norman Lloyd; décor: Michael Czaja; costumes: Pauline Lawrence. First prod.: José Limón Dance Company, Belasco Theatre, N.Y., Jan. 5, 1947, with José Limón, Letitia Ide, and Meg Mundy (narrator). The famous poem by Federico Garcia Lorca is spoken as two dancers act out the tragedy of the bullfighter who finds death in the afternoon. Louis Falco danced the role of Mejias for the first time at the American Dance Festival, Conn. College (Aug. 15, 1964).

Lamentation. Solo modern dance; chor.: Martha Graham; music: from Zoltan Kodaly's Suite of 9 pieces for piano; costumes: Martha Graham. First prod.: Maxine Elliot Theatre, N.Y., Jan. 8, 1930. The first and one of the greatest of Graham's solo works in which she created a universal figure of grief. The dance was performed in its entirety by the dancer seated upon a bench.

Lamont, Denis, ballet soloist, b. St. Louis, Mo. 1932. Educated in his home town. First professional performances in summer musicals and an occasional television appearance. Joined Ballet Russe de Monte Carlo in 1951, remaining with the company until 1953, when he joined Ballet Theatre. Returned to Ballet Russe de Monte Carlo in 1954 and stayed with the company through 1958. His repertoire included Leonide Massine's *Harold in Italy,* in which he danced a pas de deux with the ballerina Nina Novak, as well as *Gaîté Parisienne, Sombreros, Cirque de Deux,* the *Blue Bird* pas de deux from the *Sleeping Beauty,* et al. Joined the New York City Ballet in 1954, where he continues to be one of the principal dancers. His ballets include *La Sonnàmbula, The Nutcracker, Ivesiana* and *The Prodigal Son,* all choreographed by George Balanchine, and *Fanfare* by Jerome Robbins. His most recent creations are Pierrot in Balanchine's *Harlequinade* and Sancho Panza in *Don Quixote,* both in 1965.

Lancaster, Osbert, English author and artist, b. 1908. Educated at Charterhouse School and Lincoln College, Oxford; art studies at Slade School. Cartoonist, *Daily Express* (since 1939). His designs for ballet, which reflect his delight in architectural quirks include *Pineapple Poll* (Sadler's Wells Theatre Ballet), *Bonne-Bouche, Coppélia, La Fille Mal Gardée* (all for the Royal Ballet), *Napoli* (London's Festival Ballet, 1954). He is an Hon. Associate of the Royal Institute of British Architects (A.R.I.B.A.) and was created a Commander of the Order of the British Empire (1953).

Lanchbery, John, English musician and conductor, b. London, 1923. Musical director, Metropolitan Ballet (1947–49); musical director and principal conductor, Royal Ballet. His connection with the latter company began in 1951 as conductor of Sadler's Wells Theatre Ballet. His compositions include ballet scores for

Rosella Hightower, John Cranko, Celia Franca; arrangements and adaptations include *House of Birds* (1955), and *La Fille Mal Gardée* (Frederick Ashton version, 1960). Has written various articles, including a series for International Federation for Theatre Research. Made an Associate of the Royal Academy of Music for Services to Theatre Music (1953); awarded the Bolshoi Theatre Medal, Moscow (1961).

Landa, Anita, English dancer, b. Las Arenas, Vizcaya (Basque Province, N. Spain), 1929, of half-Spanish parentage; m. Michael Hogan. Studied with Elsa Brunelleschi and at Cone-Ripman School. Made her debut with Esmeralda's Spanish Company, (1948). Joined the Markova-Dolin Ballet (1949), remaining when it became London's Festival Ballet, becoming leading dancer. She dances the Doll (*Petrouchka*), the Girl (*Le Spectre de la Rose*), Chief Polovetsian Girl (*Prince Igor*), and others; creations include the leading girl (*Symphony for Fun*).

Lander, Harald, dancer, choreographer, director, ballet master, teacher, b. Copenhagen, Denmark, 1905; m. (1) Margot Lander, (2) Toni Lander. Education and dance training in the Royal Danish Ballet School, Copenhagen (from 1913); graduated into the company (1923); first solo role was as the Spanish dancer in *Far from Denmark* (1925). Studied in U.S. with Michel Fokine, Ivan Tarasoff (1926–27), and with Juan de Baucaire (1927). Starred in many Paramount-Publix Circuit shows including *Vienna Life* all over U.S. Studied dance in Mexico (1929) returning to Royal Danish Ballet later that year as leading dancer; ballet master (1932–51). As a dancer his leading roles (up to 1945 when he retired as a performer) included Gennaro (*Napoli*), Don Alvarez (*Far from Denmark*), Toreador (*The Toreadors*), Man (*Bolero*), Officer (*La Valse*), and others. He choreographed many ballets between 1931 and 1951, some of the best known being *Bolero* (1934), *Seven Deadly Sins* (1936), *Thorvaldsen* (1938), *La Valse* (1940), *L'Apprenti Sorcier* (1940), *Qarrtsiluni* (1942), *Spring* (1942), *Slaraffenland* (1942), *La Vida Espagnola* (1945), *Phoenix Bird* (1946), *Aubade* (1951). His most famous ballet *Etudes* was created in 1948 and has been staged for many other companies, always with great success. His careful staging and preservation of the Bournonville repertoire (*Napoli, La Sylphide, Conservatoriet, Far From Denmark, La Ventana, Folk Tale, Kermesse in Bruges, Hunters from Amager,* remain the foundation upon which the Royal Danish Ballet rests. He also revised the Hans Beck production of *Coppélia* (1934) which continues to be one of the most successful ballets in the Danish repertoire. In 1952 he choreographed an act (*Les Fleurs*) of the famous Paris Opéra production of *Les Indes Galantes.* He was appointed ballet master of the Paris Opéra (1953) and director of the Paris Opéra Ballet School (1959), which post he held until the end of the 1962–63 season. His works for the Paris Opéra Ballet included *The Whims of Cupid and the Ballet Master* (1952), based on his own version of

Harald Lander, international choreographer, director, ballet master.

the ancient Vincenzo Galeotti ballet which he had originally presented in Copenhagen in 1933, *Hop-Frog* (1953), *Printemps à Vienne* (Franz Schubert, 1956), *Rendez-vous* (Mozart, 1961), and others; also restaged *Etudes* (1952), *La Valse* (1958), and *Qarrtsiluni* (1960); arranged dances for a number of the operas including *Oberon, Don Giovanni, Salomé, Ballo in Maschera, Les Troyens.* As guest choreographer he has staged *Etudes, Coppélia, Napoli,* and a new ballet, *Vita Eterna,* for London's Festival Ballet; *La Sylphide* for International Ballet of the Marquis de Cuevas and Teatro alla Scala, Milan; *Etudes* and *La Sylphide* for American Ballet Theatre, Nederlands Nationaal Ballet; *Etudes* for Teatro Municipal of Rio de Janeiro; *The Whims of Cupid and the Ballet Master* for Nederlands Nationaal Ballet. He staged a special program comprising *Etudes, Qarrtsiluni* and *Napoli,* Act 3, for the Finnish National Ballet (prem.: Jan. 14, 1965). Early in 1962 he returned as guest choreographer to Copenhagen to re-stage *Etudes* (not performed there since his departure in 1951) and a new ballet, *The Triumph of Love,* based on the old French ballet by Jean Baptiste Lully. Opened his own studio in Paris early in 1964. His decorations include Dannebrogsman and Ridder (Knight) of Dannebrog (Denmark), Chevalier of Vasaorder (Sweden), Chevalier of Belgian Royal Order (Belgium), Medal of Honor of the City of Paris (France).

Lander, Margot (Margot Florentz-Gerhardt), Danish ballerina, b. 1910, d. Copenhagen, July 19, 1961. Studied in the Royal Danish Ballet School, mainly with choreographer and teacher Harald Lander, whom she married in 1931. Made her debut with the company in the Eskimo dance in *Far from Denmark;* became solo dancer (1931); was named prima ballerina (1942), the only Danish dancer ever to have this title (see DENMARK, BALLET IN). Her large repertoire included Lander's ballets, a wide range of August Bournonville's, and the standard classic ballets. She was especially outstanding in *Napoli, Swan Lake, Giselle, Coppélia,* and as the Broom in *The Sorcerer's Apprentice.* She retired in 1948, dancing for her final performance *Giselle* and the last act of *Napoli,* on which occasion the King of Denmark decorated her with the Fortjensmedalle (she had previously received the Ingenio et Arti decoration). Married Erik Nyholm (1950) after her divorce from Lander. She was the unique star of the Royal Danish Ballet of her time with an international style of rare brilliance and poetry.

The late Margot Lander, prima ballerina of the Royal Danish Ballet.

Lander, Toni (Toni Pihl Petersen), ballerina, b. Copenhagen, 1931; m. Harald Lander, divorced 1965; m. Bruce Marks, 1966. Received her dance training and general education in the school of the Royal Danish Ballet, Copenhagen. In

American Ballet Theatre's ballerina Toni Lander in "Black Swan" variation.

1947, while still a student, she danced her first solo role in the pas de trois in *The Life-Guard Corps on Amager.* Was graduated into the company in 1948; became a solo dancer (the Danish equivalent of ballerina) in 1950. She created her first major role in *Etudes* soon after her promotion. Guest ballerina in London (1951–52) during the final season of Original Ballet Russe; ballerina with London's Festival Ballet (1954–59), with a leave of absence to dance a leading role in the Françoise Sagan ballet *Le Rendez-vous Manqué* (Broken Date) in 1958. Ballerina with American Ballet Theatre (1960–61, and again beginning 1963), dancing Odette (*Swan Lake,* Act 2), title role (*Miss Julie*), Italian Ballerina (*Gala Performance*), Bulotte (*Bluebeard*), ballerina in *Theme and Variations, Etudes,* and *Grand Pas–Glazounov,* and others. She returned to Denmark for the first time to re-create her role in Etudes (1962), which she has also danced with London's Festival Ballet. Was guest ballerina with that company (summer 1962) at Royal Festival Hall. She is a Ridder (Knight) of Dannebrog. Danced the title role in *La Sylphide,* choreographed by Harald Lander for American Ballet Theatre, at the American premiere of the ballet in San Antonio, Tex., partnered by Royes Fernandez (Nov. 11, 1964). Continues to dance the ballet with great success.

Ländler, Austrian dance, a gliding and turning one which included a love pantomime and kissing one's partner; the forerunner of the waltz. See also DREHTANZ.

Landory, Veronique (Edith Landori), Hungarian dancer, b. Budapest, 1940. Received academic and dance training at Budapest State Opera and Sadler's Wells (now Royal) Ballet School. In 1953 joined Les Ballets Chiriaeff as soloist for television and stage presentations and continued with the company when it became Les Grands Ballets Canadiens, dancing in all television and stage performances. Her repertoire includes *Le Spectre de la Rose, Swan Lake* pas de trois, *Les Sylphides,* and many of the ballets choreographed by Ludmilla Chiriaeff and Eric Hyrst for the company.

Lane, Maryon, South African dancer, b. Zululand, 1931; m. David Blair. Studied at Sadler's Wells School (1946), joining Sadler's Wells Theatre Ballet the following year and becoming principal soloist. Her creations for that company included the leading roles in *House of Birds* and *Laiderette,* among others. She was transferred to Sadler's Wells (now Royal) Ballet in 1955 and is currently a leading soloist. She is a favorite dancer of Kenneth MacMillan, and he has continued to create roles for her: *Danses Concertantes, Diversions,* and possibly most outstanding, the terrified little hypnotist's assistant in *Noctambules.* She is an outstanding Swanilda in *Coppélia.* Other roles include Fairy of the Golden Vine (the "Finger" variation) (*The Sleeping Beauty*), *Swan Lake* pas de trois, title role (*Madame Chrysanthème*), and others.

Lang, Harold, American dancer, b. San Francisco, Calif. Studied ballet with Theodore Kosloff, Hollywood, and Willam Christensen, San Francisco; tap with Carlos, N.Y. Made his debut with San Francisco Opera Ballet, then joined Ballet Russe de Monte Carlo (1941–43) where his roles included Melon Seller and Snob in *La Boutique Fantasque,* King of the Dandies (*Le Beau Danube*), and others. Joined Ballet (now American Ballet) Theatre (1943–45) dancing Bluebird and Pas de Trois (*Aurora's Wedding*), First Cadet (*Graduation Ball*), Faun (*Helen of Troy*), Gypsy (*Aleko*), and others, and creating First Sailor (*Fancy Free*) and variation (*Interplay*). Since 1946 has been featured dancer and/or male lead in a long line of Broadway musicals including *Mr. Strauss Goes to Boston, Three to Make Ready, Look, Ma, I'm Dancin', Kiss Me, Kate, Make a Wish, Pal Joey* (title role in revival), and others, together with many leads in musicals and straight comedies in summer stock. Has made guest appearances with New York City Ballet and American Ballet Theatre since the beginning of his Broadway career, and has appeared on all the important television shows featuring dance. Has received three Donaldson Awards for "best dancer on Broadway," for *Look Ma, I'm Dancin'* (1947), *Make a Wish* (1950–51), and *Pal Joey* (1951–52).

Lang, Pearl, American modern dancer, b. Chicago, 1922. Received her general education at Chicago City Junior College of Univ. of Chicago (1938–41); dance studies at Frances Allis Studio, and with Martha Graham, Louis Horst, Muriel Stuart, Nenette Charisse, and others. Soloist with Martha Graham company (1942–52), dancing many important roles in *Cave of the Heart, Deaths and Entrances, Punch and the Judy, Night Journey, Letter to the World, Diversion of Angels, Canticle for Innocent Comedians, Ardent Song,* and others, many of them creations. She was the first dancer ever to take over a Graham role when she danced the Three Marys in *El Penitente* at the Ziegfeld Theatre, N.Y. in 1947, and the Wife in *Appalachian Spring* at the Alvin Theatre, 1953. Formed her own dance company in 1952, for which she has choreographed many works, among them *Legend, Rites, And Joy Is My Witness, Song of Deborah, Juvenescence, Nightflight, Falls The Shadow Between, Shirah, Apasionada.* She has also choreographed many solo dances for herself, the best known being *Windsung* and *Moonsung*. Was guest artist with the Martha Graham company during its European tour in 1954; featured dancer in a number of Broadway productions including *One Touch of Venus, Carousel, Finian's Rainbow, Touch and Go;* was Solveig opposite John Garfield in *Peer Gynt*. Has choreographed and danced in many musicals in summer stock and frequently appeared on television; has danced at Connecticut College American Dance Festivals and at Jacob's Pillow where she has also been guest teacher; has taught and danced in many universities in U.S. Has been guest teacher at Kurt Jooss's Folkwangschule, Essen, Germany; Schweizer Berufsverband für Tanz, Zürich, Switzerland; and Svenska Danspedagog Forb., Stockholm, Sweden. In 1960 received a Fellowship from the Guggenheim Foundation and a grant from the Lena Robbins Foundation. Currently on faculties of Yale Univ. School of Drama, Juilliard School of Music Dance Department, Neighborhood Playhouse.

Pearl Lang, American modern dancer in Persephone.

Lanner, Katti (1831–1908), Austrian ballerina, choreographer, teacher. Made her debut in 1845 at the Hoftheater, Vienna. She danced *Giselle* in N.Y. in 1870. In the early 1880's she moved to England and established a ballet school in London. In 1887 she was engaged as choreographer and ballet mistress of the Empire Ballets. During her ten years at that theatre she staged some fifteen successful ballets and also trained the dancers. Her father, Joseph Lanner (1801–1843), was a famous Viennese composer of waltzes and rival of Johann Strauss, Jr.

Lany, Jean (1718–1786), dancer at the Paris Opéra. Was an important soloist and later became maître de ballet. Thérèse Vestris, sister of Gaetan, was his mistress. He was challenged to a duel by Gaetan who was jailed for a short time after Lany withdrew.

Lany, Louise, danseuse at the Paris Opéra, ca. 1770. She is credited with the invention of the entrechat-six.

Lapauri, Alexander, Honored Artist of the RSFSR, Soviet dancer, b. 1926; m. Raisa Struchkova. Entered the Bolshoi School in 1935, graduating in 1944 (class of Nicolai Tarasov). His first important role with the Bolshoi company was Maners, Sr. in *Crimson Sails,* which demonstrated his great dramatic gifts. He went on to become one of the leading dancer-actors in the Bolshoi, high marks in his career in this field being Hilarion in *Giselle* and Khan Guirei in *The Fountain of Bakhchisarai.* He is also an unsurpassed partner. With his wife, ballerina Raisa Struchkova, he began appearing in recitals with difficult, semi-acrobatic duets soon after graduation of which *Moszkovsky Waltz,* choreographed by Vasily Vainonen, is an outstanding example. He and Struchkova have performed it all over the world. His other most outstanding role as a partner is Bacchus in *Walpurgis Night,* from the opera *Faust.* Tall, masculine, strong, he represents to perfection the type of male dancer for which the Bolshoi company was famous for many generations, particularly in the days of Alexander Gorsky. While still dancing in the Bolshoi company, Lapauri was graduated from the Choreographers' Dept. of the State Theatre Institute. With his classmate, Olga Tarasova, he choreographed for the Bolshoi the ballet *Song of the Woods* (to music by G. Zhukovsky) in 1960, and *Lieutenant Kije* to music by Sergei Prokofiev (1963). He has also choreographed several of his own concert numbers, such as *Claire de Lune* (Debussy) and *Reverie* (Glinka). He teaches supported adagio classes at the Bolshoi School. With Struchkova he has danced in more than fifteen countries outside the Soviet Union.

Laport, Nelly (Kyra Nelidova), contemporary dancer and designer, b. Buenos Aires, Argentina, of American parents. Began studying dance in 1942 under Roman Jasinski; later with Lubov Tchernicheva, Olga Kirowa, Tatiana Leskova. Joined Original Ballet Russe (1944), touring South America and rising from corps de ballet to soloist. Her ballets included *Carnaval* (pas de trois), *Symphonie Fantastique* (3rd movement), among others. Danced with Ballet Society, 1949. Has lived in Rio de Janeiro since 1948 and is a Brazilian citizen by marriage. Dancer and artistic director of Ballet do Rio de Janeiro (1958–60). Currently teaching at the Ballet Academy of Tatiana Leskova.

Lapson, Dvora, dancer, teacher, writer, b. New York City, 1907. B.A., Hunter College; studied dance with Michel Fokine, Irma Duncan, Evelyn Gates, Doris Humphrey. A leading exponent of the Jewish folklore dance which she helped to develop to stage proportions; authority on history and theory of the Biblical and Palestine dance; creator of a repertoire of over 100 original dance compositions. Leading dancer and choreographer for *The Pioneers,* the first Hebrew opera (1936). Between 1929 and 1954 toured in

U.S., Canada, Mexico, and Europe, performing and gathering research material, especially in Palestine (1929) and Poland (1937), where she visited Chassidic communities. She was the first American dancer to be invited to dance in the new state of Israel (1949). Is director of the Dance Education of the Jewish Education Committee of N.Y. (formerly Bureau of Jewish Education) since 1932; instructor in Dance Education of the Hebrew Union College–Jewish Institute of Religion, N.Y., since 1952. Dance critic of Yiddish newspaper *The Day* (1934–36). Her books include *New Palestine Dances* (1948), *Dances of the Jewish People* (1954), *Folk Dances for Jewish Festivals* (1961), all published by the Jewish Education Press. Has also written many articles on Jewish dance for magazines and periodicals; contributor to *Encyclopedia Judaica.*

Larionov, Michel, painter and stage designer, b. Odessa, Russia, 1881, d. Paris, 1964. Lived in Paris since 1914 when he went there at the suggestion of Serge Diaghilev and became closely associated with the Diaghilev Ballets Russes. Among his outstanding works for the stage were the décor for Leonide Massine's first ballet, *The Midnight Sun* (1915), *Contes Russes* (1918), *Chout* (1921), and (stage set only) for *Renard* (1922). He often worked as a team with his wife, Nathalie Gontcharova (d. 1962), though he seldom took official credit for such work. Before leaving for Paris Larionov headed a Moscow group of futurists. Eventually he came under the influence of cubism. A frequent exhibitor in Paris, his works were shown in N.Y. in 1922 at the Kingore Galleries, and in 1952 and 1954 at the Solomon R. Guggenheim Museum.

Larkin, Moscelyne, American dancer, b. Miami, Okla., 1925; m. Roman Jasinski. Had her early dance training with her mother, Eva Matlagova (Tulsa), and in 1938 she began to study in N.Y. with Vincenzo Celli, and later with Mikhail Mordkin, Anatole Vilzak, and Ludmilla Shollar. Member of Original Ballet Russe (1941–47), when she danced under the name of Moussia Larkina, rising from corps de ballet to soloist and later ballerina, dancing Guile (*Paganini*), Waltz and Mazurka (*Les Sylphides*), Frivolity (*Les Présages*), Love (*Eternal Struggle*), Papillon (*Carnaval*), Daughter (*Le Beau Danube*), and others; joined Ballet Russe de Monte Carlo (1948), dancing Zobeide (*Schéhérazade*), Harlequin (*Night Shadow*), Cowgirl (*Rodeo*), *Blue Bird* pas de deux, *Paquita* pas de trois, Glove Seller (*Gaîté Parisienne*), Odile (*Swan Lake,* Act 2), and others. Headed this company's Concert Company (1952–53). With Alexandra Danilova's Great Moments of Ballet (1954–55). Has danced with St. Louis and Pittsburgh Municipal Operas as guest ballerina. Appeared at Jacob's Pillow and in 1961 was guest ballerina with the Ballet Russe de Monte Carlo on summer dates. Since 1954 has taught with her husband in Tulsa and with him is co-founder and director of Tulsa Civic Ballet (see REGIONAL BALLET). She received a special Citation from the Governor of Oklahoma for her part in organizing the Oklahoma Indian Ballerina Festival (1957), which brought together Maria Tallchief, Rosella Hightower, Yvonne Chouteau, and Moscelyne Larkin herself in two special performances at the Municipal Auditorium, Tulsa, as part of the Semi-Centennial Celebrations of Oklahoma's entry into the Union.

Larkina, Moussia. See LARKIN, MOSCELYNE.

Larsen, Gerd, Norwegian dancer, b. Oslo, 1921; m. Harold Turner. Studied with Antony Tudor; was soloist of the then newly formed London Ballet, creating French Ballerina (*Gala Performance*). Also danced with Ballet Rambert, International Ballet, and Sadler's Wells (now Royal) Ballet (soloist since 1954).

Since 1956 has been teaching company classes and plays important mime roles such as Berthé (*Giselle*), Demeter (*Persephone*—creation), Queen (*The Sleeping Beauty*), Princess Mother (*Swan Lake*). Created the Nurse in Kenneth MacMillan's *Romeo and Juliet* (1965).

Larsen, Niels Bjorn, Danish dancer, ballet master and choreographer, b. Copenhagen, 1913; m. Elvi Henricksen. Artistic director of the Royal Danish Ballet, since 1961. Studied at the Royal Ballet School, graduating in 1929. On leave of absence (1935–37) to dance with the Trudi Schoop company; returned to the Royal Danish Ballet (1937); became soloist (1942). In 1946 formed own company and toured Scandinavia and the Netherlands. Became teacher at the Royal Danish Ballet School and (in 1947) instructor to the artists of the ballet. Ballet master of the company (1951–56), taking the place of Harald Lander. Appointed director of the Tivoli Pantomime Theatre (1955). Guest artist with British (1957, 1958) and U.S. (1957, 1959) companies. Leading roles in *Gaucho* (Lander), *A Folk Tale* (Bournonville), *Qarrtsiluni* (Lander), *Coppélia* (Børge Ralov), *Episode* (Massine), *La Sylphide* (Bournonville), *Night Shadow,* (Balanchine), and others. Devised choreography for *The Dethroned Lion Tamer* (1943), *Desire* (1951), *Till Eulenspiegel* (Tivoli), *Capricious Lucinda* (1954), *Flitter* (Tivoli), *Vision* (in collaboration with Elvi Henricksen), *Peter and the Wolf* (1960), *Wild West* (Tivoli, 1961). Is a Knight of the Order of Dannebrog. Resigned as director of the Royal Danish Ballet at the end of its U.S. tour in Dec., 1965 (succeeded by Flemming Flindt), but continues as mime and actor of the Royal Theatre and director of Copenhagen's Tivoli Pantomime Theatre.

Larson, Bird (d. 1927), American teacher of physical education at Barnard College, N.Y. Her researches into orthopedics led to her "Natural Rhythmic Expressions," and affected not only her pupils but subsequently the whole system of physical education in U.S. schools. She turned from the strictly educational field to the professional dancer. Her system stressed first the necessity of learning the possibilities of natural body movements, then the assimilation of movements of gymnastic origin, and finally combining controlled movements with musical form to express an idea.

Lassu, the slow movement in a czardas.

Last, Brenda, English dancer, b. London, 1938. Studied ballet with Biddy Pinchard, Vera Volkova, and at Royal Ballet School. Won Adeline Genée Gold Medal of Royal Academy of Dancing (1955). Danced with West Country Ballet at Edinburgh Festival (1955). Joined Western Theatre Ballet (1957), and is currently a leading dancer. Her repertoire includes *Peasant* pas de deux (*Giselle*), Bird (*Peter and the Wolf*), Girl (*Sonate à Trois*), leading girl (Chiaroscuro), Papillon (*Le Carnaval*), Bride (*A Wedding Present*), and others. Joined Royal Ballet (1963), where her first important part was one of the soloists in the *Napoli* divertissement.

Laubin, Reginald and Gladys, contemporary dance team, exponents of American Indian Dance (Reginald Karl Laubin, b. Detroit, Mich.; Gladys W., his wife, b. Paterson, N.J.). Both studied at Art School and among the Sioux, Crow, Cheyenne, and other Plains Indians. Adopted by Sioux Indians and given names Tatanka Wanjila (One Bull) and Wiyaka Wastewin (Good Feather Woman). Have given demonstration lectures featuring dance, arts, and lore of American Indians at many leading art and historical museums, colleges, universities; recommended by anthropologists and staff members, U.S. Office of Indian Affairs; contributors to *Dance Encyclopedia.*

Laumer, Denise, German ballerina, b. Berlin, 1930. Studied under Gustav Blank, Tatiana Gsovska. Made her debut in 1947 at State Opera House, Berlin; later danced at the opera houses of Wiesbaden, Munich, Wuppertal. Her roles include Eurydice, Chloë, Terpsichore, title role in *Firebird, Juliet,* and others. Awarded Preis Land Nordrhein, Westfallen (1958).

Laurencia, ballet in 3 acts, 5 scenes; chor.: Vakhtang Chabukiani; music: Alexander Krein; book: Yevgeny Mandelberg, after Lope de Vega's drama Fuente Ovejuna; décor: Simon Virsaladze. First prod.: Kirov Theatre, Leningrad, Mar. 22, 1939, with Natalia Dudinskaya (Laurencia), and Vakhtang Chabukiani (Frondozo). Laurencia, a girl from a Castilian village, raises her fellow-villagers against the tyrannical Commendatore and the entire village follows her to storm the castle. Frondozo, betrothed to her, kills the Commendatore in battle. Rudolf Nureyev staged the pas de six from this ballet for the Royal Ballet, premièred Mar. 24, 1965, at the annual Royal Ballet Benevolent Fund Gala, dancing the leading male part with Christopher Gable, Graham Usher, Nadia Nerina, Antoinette Sibley, Merle Park. The British company spells the title *Laurentia.*

Laurençin, Marie (1885–1956), French painter and stage designer. Her work for ballet includes *Les Biches* (Diaghilev Ballets Russes, 1924), *Les Roses* (Count Etienne de Beaumont's Soirées de Paris, 1924), *Un Jour d'Eté* (Opéra Comique, Paris, 1940), *Le Déjeuner sur l'Herbe* (Ballets des Champs-Elysées, Paris, 1945).

Laurentia. See LAURENCIA.

Lauterer, Arch (1905–1957), American stage designer. His work includes sets for Martha Graham's *El Penitente, Letter to the World, Deaths and Entrances;* Hanya Holm's *Trend;* Doris Humphrey's *Decade,* and others.

Lavrovsky, Leonid, Peoples' Artist of the RSFSR, professor, Soviet choreographer, b. 1905. Entered the Theatre School (Ballet Department) in Petrograd in 1916, graduating in 1922, a pupil of Samuel Andrianov and Vladimir Ponomaryov. Leading roles in the Kirov Ballet included Siegfried (*Swan Lake*), Jean de Brienne (*Raymonda*), Amoun (*Cléopatre*), the male role in *Les Sylphides,* and others. While a member of the company he joined the group of young dancers and choreographers known as The Young Ballet (Molodoi Balet), founded in 1921 by George Balanchine and Vladimir Dmitriev. Performances included extracts from classic works and new compositions, mostly staged by Balanchine, in which Lavrovsky appeared. Later, Lavrovsky parted from the group to devote his entire energy to dancing in the Kirov Ballet maintaining, however, his interest in modern choreography. In 1930 he participated in one of the first attempts at creating a ballet on a contemporary theme at the Kirov Theatre, and danced the role of the Fascist in *The Golden Age,* with choreography by Vasily Vainonen, Leonid Yacobson, and others, and music by Dmitri Shostakovich. His own first venture in choreography also came in 1930, when he staged a suite of dances to Robert Schumann's *Symphonic Etudes* for the graduation performance of the Leningrad Ballet School. It was acclaimed by the press as a sign of new trends in choreography. His next work, also for the school was to Peter Tchaikovsky's *The Seasons* (1931), followed by his first full-length ballet, *Fadette* (1934), basing the story on part of George Sand's novel *La Petite Fadette,* but using the music of Léo Delibes' *Sylvia.* At that time Lavrovsky was studying drama and theatrical production and was considerably influenced in his work by the stage director V.N. Solovyov who collaborated with him on the scenario of *Fadette.* In this work, Lavrovsky for the first time used classic dance as a means of enhancing the characterization of each character in the ballet. The behavior of each dancer was psychologically motivated and all dances were given a definite meaning. This principle became his artistic credo. In 1935 in the ballet *Katerina,* to music by K. Korchmaryov, also done for the Leningrad school, he used Russian folk dance steps to express the despair of the peasants. In 1936 Lavrovsky re-created *Fadette* on a larger scale for the Maly (Little) Opera Theatre of Leningrad and became artistic director of the ballet department (until 1937), staging new versions of *La Fille Mal Gardée* (1937) and *The Prisoner of the Caucasus* (1938). In 1937 he was invited to the post of artistic director of the Kirov Ballet, creating his most important work, *Romeo and Juliet* (1940). The outbreak of World War II interrupted his activity with the Leningrad ballet. He spent the first part of the war as artistic director of the Armenian ballet in Erevan. In 1944 he was appointed artistic director of the Bolshoi Ballet, remaining until 1956 and resuming the post again in 1960. To mark the centenary of *Giselle* in Russia, Lavrovsky revived the ballet at the Bolshoi, (1944). This production was hailed as the definitive *Giselle* when it was shown in London in 1956 by the Bolshoi Ballet on tour. In 1946 he staged his *Romeo and Juliet* at the Bolshoi, creating many new mise-en-scènes. In 1952 came his (first) version of *The Stone Flower.* He choreographed a new version of *The Red Poppy* under the title of *The Red Flower* (1957), and in 1960 devised an original version of Sergei Rachmaninov's *Paganini* to his own scenario (which has nothing in common with that used by Michel Fokine). In 1961 he created a new ballet, *Night City* to Béla Bartók's *The Miraculous Mandarin,* and a one-act ballet, *Pages of Life,* to music by Andrei Balanchivadze. He is chief choreographer and artistic director of the Soviet Ice Ballet, and Professor of the Theatre Institute of Moscow where he heads a course in choreography in the Choreographers Dept. Lavrovsky is married to Natalia Chidson, retired Bolshoi dancer. His son Mikhail (by his first marriage to ballerina Yelena Chikvaidze) is a member of the Bolshoi company, and promises to develop into an outstanding dancer. In 1964 Leonid Lavrovsky was appointed Director of the Moscow Academic Choreographic School (the new name of the Moscow Bolshoi School of Ballet). He was succeeded in his post as chief choreographer of the Bolshoi by Yury Grigorovich. In May, 1965, Mr. Lavrovsky was awarded the title of Peoples' Artist of the USSR on the occasion of his 60th birthday and the 25th anniversary of his creation of *Romeo and Juliet.*

Lawrence, Bryan (Palethorpe), British dancer, b. Birmingham, 1936. Studied at Sadler's Wells (now Royal) Ballet School from 1949. Entered Sadler's Wells Theatre Ballet (1954); soloist (1956); transferred to Royal Ballet (1959). Roles include The Lover (*House of Birds*), *Blue Bird* pas de deux and *Florestan* pas de trois (*The Sleeping Beauty*), *Peasant* pas de deux (*Giselle*), Siegfried (*Swan Lake*), and others. Joined Australian Ballet as premier danseur (1964).

Lawrence, Pauline, b. Los Angeles, 1900; m. José Limón. Pianist and accompanist at Hollywood High School while a student there; joined Denishawn Company (1917) as pianist, also dancing minor roles. Pianist for Martha Graham. Joined Humphrey-Weidman company when its leaders broke away from Denishawn. With José Limón company from its inception, designing costumes for many of her husband's dance works. Now acts as his personal representative.

Lawson, Joan, English writer, dancer, teacher, b. London, 1908. Studied with Margaret Morris and Serafima Astafieva; later in Moscow and Leningrad. Soloist, Nemtchinova-Dolin Ballet (1933–35). Lecturer to Central Advisory Council for Education among H.M. Forces (1939–48).

Critic, *The Dancing Times* (1940–54). Has lectured for Arts Council and many educational bodies; Royal Ballet School Courses for Teachers (1947–59). Teacher of classic ballet and national dance. Fellow, Imperial Society of Teachers of Dancing; member, Critics' Circle, London. Author of *European Folk Dance* (London, 1953), *Mime* (London, 1957), *Dressing for the Ballet* (with Peter Revitt, London, 1958), *Classical Ballet, Its Style and Technique* (London, 1960); in preparation: *A History of Ballet and Its Makers.*

Layton, Joe, American dancer, choreographer, stage director. Studied dance with Joseph Levinoff, N.Y. After nearly ten years as a dancer in the choruses of Broadway musicals, he was engaged to choreograph summer shows at Camp Tamiment (where Jerome Robbins also received his early professional experience). This led to his engagement for the off-Broadway revival of the Jerome Robbins-Leonard Bernstein musical *On the Town.* His choreography was a success and this production was followed in quick succession by choreographic assignments in *Once Upon a Mattress, The Sound of Music, Greenwillow, Tenderloin,* and *Sail Away* (which he also re-created in London). In 1962 he both staged and directed the musicals *No Strings* and *Cock of the Walk.* Staged and choreographed London production of *On the Town* (1963); the same year choreographed *The Girl Who Came to Supper.*

Lazowski, Yurek, American dancer and teacher, b. Warsaw, Poland, 1917, American citizen since 1944; m. Galina Razoumova. Received his dance training and general education in the school of the Warsaw Opera Ballet, in which company he made his debut aged thirteen. While still only seventeen he danced with the Ida Rubinstein company in Paris (1934), then became first dancer of the Flemish Opera, Belgium. Joined Col. de Basil's Ballets Russes de Monte Carlo (1935), remaining until 1941 (by which time it was known as Original Ballet Russe). As leading character dancer, his roles included Prince Guidon (*Le Coq d'Or*), Dandy (*Le Beau Danube*), Bird-Catcher (*The Hundred Kisses*), Scandal (*Paganini*), Domenico (*Francesca da Rimini*), and others, all except the Dandy being creations. First character dancer and regisseur, Ballet (now American Ballet) Theatre (1941–43), dancing Orestes (*Helen of Troy*), staging and dancing the title role in the revival of *Petrouchka,* and creating the title role in *Russian Soldier,* among other roles. Returned to Ballet Russe de Monte Carlo (1944–46); soloist, Leonide Massine's Ballet Russe Highlights (1946). Has staged dances for television; choreographed the dance scene in *Boris Godounov* for Metropolitan Opera (season 1961–62). Teaches in N.Y. at School of Performing Arts, and in private schools in and around N.Y.

Lazzini, Joseph, French choreographer, ballet master, b. Marseille, France, 1927, of Italian parents; m. Alberte Clauzier. His career as a dancer was mainly at the San Carlo Opera House, Naples. Ballet director, Liège, Belgium (1955–57); Toulouse (1958), where he staged a sensational ballet to Ravel's *La Valse.* Director, ballet master, and choreographer, Marseille Opera Ballet since 1959 for which company his work has made him one of the most talked-about choreographers in European state theatres. Won the medal for best choreographer at the 1964 International Ballet Festival in Paris for his program: presentation of Stravinsky's *Orpheus, La Valse,* Benjamin Britten's *Les Illuminations* and *Le Voyage* (to percussion). Staged *The Miraculous Mandarin* (1963) and recreated it for the Metropolitan Opera Ballet Evening (Apr. 11, 1965). Was invited to be choreorapher and coordinator of movement with director Jean-Louis Barrault for the Met's production of *Faust* (1965–66 season), but could not fulfill the engagement due to an

Yurek Lazowski, leading American character dancer and teacher.

automobile accident in which he was seriously injured. Flemming Flindt was subsequently given the commission.

LeClercq, Tanaquil, American dancer, b. Paris, 1929, of French-American parentage; m. George Balanchine. Studied at School of American Ballet, N.Y., where she won the scholarship competition (1941) and Ballet Society Fellowship (1946). She was a leading dancer with Ballet Society from its inception and continued as a ballerina of New York City Ballet creating many roles, among them Choleric variation (*Four Temperaments*), 2nd movement (*Symphony in C*),

American ballerina Tanaquil LeClercq in Balanchine's Symphony in C.

1st movement (*Bourrée Fantasque*), Young Girl (*La Valse*), Girl (Jerome Robbins' *Afternoon of a Faun*), 4th movement (*Western Symphony*); also dancing *Concerto Barocco,* George Balanchine's *Swan Lake* (Act 2), and others. While in Copenhagen, during the company's 1956 European tour, she was stricken with poliomyelitis which terminated her career. She was a dancer of unique personality and style, with very long, slender arms and legs which gave a strange, angular grace to all she did. In summer, 1964, she wrote a book, *Mourka: The Autobiography of a Cat,* illustrated with photographs by Martha Swope. Her second book, *Ballet Cookbook,* was published in 1967.

Lecocq, Alexandre Charles (1832–1918), French composer. Music from his musical comedies *La Fille de Mme. Angot* and *Giroflé-Girofla* was used by Leonide Massine for his ballet *Mam'zelle Angot* (1943).

Lederman, Minna, writer and critic, b. New York City. Studied at Academy of Dramatic Arts, and Vassar College, Barnard College, and Columbia Univ. Studied ballet with Mikhail Mordkin. After two years on N.Y. newspapers reporting news and writing reviews on music and dance, became editor and dance critic of *Modern Music,* a quarterly review, a position she held until the magazine discontinued publication in 1946. Contributor on dance, criticism, and general artistic matters to leading American periodicals; editor *Stravinsky in the Theatre* (N.Y., 1949).

Lediakh, Gennady, Soviet dancer, b. 1928 into a peasant family in the Altai region. He began his theatrical studies as a member of an amateur dramatic group at the Novosibirsk Pioneers' Palace while attending a regular high school. When the Novosibirsk Opera House was completed in 1945 it recruited gifted amateurs for its ballet school. Lediakh, who was also a fine athlete, attracted attention and by the end of 1945 was already a member of the Novosibirsk ballet company. In 1948 he was sent to study at the Bolshoi School, graduating with the class of Asaf Messerer (1951). He is one of the small group of Bolshoi dancers who did not begin studies in the school at an early age. He made extraordinary progress, partly due to his tremendous endurance. His first roles with the Bolshoi were usually grotesques, jesters, etc., but he also proved an excellent cavalier in supported adagio. His first important role was Philippe (*Flames of Paris*) in 1953, and this has been followed by Frondozo (*Laurencia*), Basil (*Don Quixote*), which shows his virtuoso technique to particular advantage, Prince (*Cinderella*), Franz (*Coppélia*), and others.

Lee, Kathryn (Catherine Lee Scales), dancer, b. Denison, Tex., 1926. Studied dance with Maria Domina, Ernest Belcher, San Francisco Ballet School, School of American Ballet, N.Y., Ludmila Shollar, Anatole Vilzak. Made her debut in Opera Under the Stars, Dallas, Tex. (1941.). Appeared in musicals, operettas, and revues (1942–45); Leonide Massine's Ballet Russe Highlights (1945–46); and on television. Currently teaching in N.Y.

Lee, Mary Ann (1823–1899) American ballerina, b. Philadelphia, Pa. She began her ballet training in Philadelphia and in 1837 made her debut as Fatima in *The Maid of Cashmere,* an English version of François Auber's opera-ballet *Le Dieu et la Bayadère.* Two years later she appeared for the first time in N.Y. in the same work. When Fanny Elssler came to the U.S. in 1840, Mary Ann Lee began to take lessons from James Sylvain, Elssler's partner. He taught her also most of Elssler's spectacular character solo numbers, such as the *Cracovienne, Cachucha, Bolero, El Jaleo de Jerés,* and others. She made many successful U.S. tours and in 1844 left for Paris, where she studied with Jean Coralli at the Opéra ballet school. She returned to the U.S. in 1845 and brought with her authentic versions of *Giselle, La Fille de Danube,* and *Jolie Fille de Gand* with which she toured the U.S. On Jan. 1, 1846, she became the first American to dance *Giselle* at the Howard Atheneum, Boston, partnered by George Washington Smith. Mary Ann Lee's health began to fail toward the end of 1846, but she continued to appear intermittently until 1854. According to available records, she was the best American ballerina of the period, with the exception of Augusta Maywood, but she was not in the class of Fanny Elssler, the Taglionis, or even the European stars of lesser magnitude who visited the U.S. For details on Mary Ann Lee see Lillian Moore's monograph, "First American Giselle," *Dance Index,* May, 1943. (L.M.)

Leeder, Sigurd, dancer, ballet master, teacher, b. Hamburg, 1902. For many years a close associate of Kurt Jooss. He met Jooss in Münster, where he joined the newly organized Neue Tanzbühne (New Dance Stage) and toured Germany (1925–26). In 1928 he became one of the original members and head instructor of the Folkwangschule für Musik, Tanz and Sprechen, which Jooss founded. Participated in the performance of *The Green Table* at the Choreographic Competition in Paris (1932), when the ballet won the first prize; toured the U.S. with the company (1933–34). Was co-director with Jooss of the Jooss-Leeder School, Dartington Hall, Devon, and later in Cambridge, both in England (1934–41). Was ballet master of the Jooss Ballet (1942–47); choreographed *Sailors' Fancy* (1943). Left the organization when Jooss disbanded the company (1947). Taught in London until 1960, when he went to Chile as Director of Studies and Teacher in the University School of Dance.

Leese, Elizabeth, German-born Canadian dancer, choreographer, teacher. Studied modern dance at the Jooss-Leeder School; ballet with Lubov Egorova in Paris. First came to the U.S. with the Trudi Schoop Company (1937). Settled in Canada, where she married journalist and writer Kenneth Johnstone. Was soloist with Boris Volkov's Canadian Ballet in Toronto (1939–42); director of Canadian Government Recreational Dance Project (1942–45). Opened her own school in Montreal (1945) and formed a company (with herself as choreographer and soloist) which gave performances between 1945 and 1958. Choreographed *Lady from the Sea* for her own company; later the ballet was taken into the repertoire of National Ballet of Canada. Introduced the Cecchetti method of teaching to Montreal (1955), with Margaret Saul as guest teacher. In addition to her stage and television appearances as dancer, she also played leading parts in *I Remember Mama* and *Anna Christie* for the Montreal Repertory Theatre and frequently broadcast in French for the French radio network from Montreal. She died in 1962 at the height of her career.

Legat, Nadine Nicolaeva (née de Briger), Russian dancer and teacher, b. St. Petersburg, Russia, 1895. Studied at Bolshoi Ballet School. Married Nicholas Legat and continued his school in England after his death (1937), creating a boarding school at Tunbridge Wells (now at Goudhurst, Kent). Has lectured on ballet to schools and clubs. Author of *Ballet Education* (London, 1947), *Preparation for Ballet* (London, 1953).

Legat, Nicholas (1869–1937), Russian dancer and teacher, son of dancer Gustaf Legat, of Swedish extraction. Graduated from the St. Petersburg Imperial School in 1888. An outstanding dancer of his time and an excellent partner, he was best known as a great teacher, both at the Imperial School and later in Western Europe. He left Russia in 1914 and subsequently opened a school in London with his wife, Nadine Nicolaeva-Legat, who continues the school to this time. He was a talented caricaturist, as attested by his volume *Russky Balet* (The Russian Ballet), published in St. Petersburg. He also wrote *The Story of the Russian School* (British-Continental Press, London, 1932). Among the famous contemporary dancers trained by Legat are Ana Roje, Alan Carter, André Eglevsky. Legat died in London.

Legat, Serge (1875–1905), Russian dancer and teacher, son of dancer Gustaf Legat, of Swedish extraction, younger brother of Nicholas Legat. Graduated from the St. Petersburg Imperial School in 1894. An outstanding dancer of his generation and later an excellent teacher, Legat was well on the way to becoming a major influence in Russian ballet when he committed suicide. According to Russian prerevolutionary sources, his suicide was the result of a series of quarrels with his common-law wife, Maria Petipa, daughter of Marius Petipa. Soviet sources imply that his suicide was due to political oppression from the management of the Imperial Theatres. He was considered the finest classic partner of his time.

Legend. Modern dance work; chor.: Pearl Lang; music: Morton Feldman; costumes: Eleanor de Vito. First prod.: Brooklyn High School of Homemaking, Brooklyn, N.Y., Nov. 14, 1951, with Pearl Lang, Bertram Ross, Irving Burton, Sheldon Ossossky. The theme is taken from S. A. Ansky's famous play, *The Dybbuk,* and is concerned with the scene in which the soul of the dead lover, imprisoned in the body of his beloved, is exorcised and floats away. This was Pearl Lang's first important group work.

Legend of Impossible Love, The. Ballet in one act; chor.: Aurel Milloss; idea, plot, and décor: Emiliano Di Cavalcanti. First prod.: Ballet do IV Centenário, Teatro Municipal, Rio de Janeiro, Brazil, 1954, with Edith Pudelko, Raul Severo, Vera Maia, Yoko Okada, Lucia Villar, Miriam Hirsch, Rachel Wainer, and Ruth Rachou. This is the most Brazilian of all Brazilian ballets created by a foreign choreographer. Milloss used no music, only recorded sounds of Brazilian-Indian folklore and noises of the forest. From the bottom of the waters Yara entices everything and everyone. The despair of the Lonely Man who waits for her forces to emerge from the lake. Stronger than the power of her eyes is the love inspired by him who desires her. All except the Lonely Man die in the forest around them. This impossible love takes Yara back to the bottom of her kingdom. It is love, not Yara, that makes the Lonely Man die on the shore of the lake.

Legend of Joseph, The. Ballet in 1 act; chor.: Michel Fokine; music: Richard Strauss; book: Hugo von Hofmannsthal and Count Harry Kessler; décor: José

Maria Sert; costumes: Léon Bakst. First prod.: Diaghilev Ballets Russes, Théatre National de l'Opéra, Paris, May 14, 1914, with Leonide Massine as Joseph; Maria Kusnetzova, Vera Fokine, Alexis Bulgakov. This was Massine's first important role in a ballet. The ballet was a choreographic re-telling of the Biblical story of Joseph and Potiphar's wife. Margaret Wallman staged her version for Teatro alla Scala, Milan (1952). Erika Hanka and Yvonne Georgi have also staged versions.

Legend of Judith. Modern dance work in 1 act; chor.: Martha Graham; commissioned score by Mordecai Seter; décor: Dani Karavan. First prod.: Martha Graham Dance Company, Habima Theatre, Tel-Aviv, Israel, Oct. 25, 1962, with Martha Graham (Judith), Linda Hodes (the Young Judith), Bertram Ross (Holofernes and Manasse), David Wood (Tyrant), Yuriko (His Courtesan), Helen McGehee (Teller of the Tale), Robert Powell (Listener); N.Y. première: Lunt-Fontanne Theatre, Oct. 13, 1963, with the same cast. The legend of the slaying of Holofernes by the young widow Judith, who thereby saves the besieged town of Bethulia, retold as a ritual. Martha Graham's program note states that the action "takes place entirely within the unknown landscape of the mind of a woman, a kind of Judith."

Legend of Love. Ballet in 3 acts; chor.: Yuri Grigorovich; music: Arif Melikov; book: Nazym Hikmet; décor: Simon Virsaladze. First prod.: Kirov Theatre, Leningrad, Mar. 23, 1961. The Turkish writer Nazym Hikmet used for the plot of his play and subsequent ballet an old legend about Queen Mehmene-Banu who sacrificed her beauty and personal happiness to save her sister Shiriene, while the youth Ferhad, who loved Shiriene, renounced his love to sacrifice himself for his people. Principal roles were created by Irina Kolpakova (Shiriene), Inna Zubkovskaya (Mehmene-Banu), Alexander Gribov (Ferhad), Anatole Gridin (Stranger). On Apr. 15, 1965, the ballet was premièred at the Moscow Bolshoi, with Maya Plisetskaya in the principal role of Mehmene-Banu.

Legerton, Henry, Australian dancer and ballet master, b. Melbourne, 1917. Studied with Stanislas Idzikowski, Hélène Kirsova, Vera Volkova. With London Ballet at Arts Theatre (1940); Kirsova Ballet (Australia, 1940–41). Served with Australian Army (1941–46) in Australia, New Guinea, Morotai, and Amboina. Danced in the musical *Bullet in the Ballet* (1946). Joined Sadler's Wells (now Royal) Ballet (1947), remaining to present time. Currently ballet master of the touring section. He was a dancer-actor of great intelligence and style in a wide range of parts, among them The Rake (*The Rake's Progress*), Dr. Coppelius (*Coppélia*), Carabosse (*The Sleeping Beauty*).

Legnani, Pierina (1863–1923), Italian ballerina assoluta. She made her debut at La Scala, Milan, and danced with great success in Paris, Madrid, and London. She was skyrocketed into fame, however, when she made her debut at the Maryinsky Theatre, St. Petersburg (1893), in the ballet *Cinderella* and performed for the first time in the history of the Imperial Ballet thirty-two consecutive fouettés. Her success was so great that evening that she had to repeat her variation. More than any other event this feat made the Russian dancers technique-conscious and they began to strive for technical brilliance. Although engaged as a guest artist for one season, the ballerina remained with the Imperial Theatre until Jan., 1901. She created the role of Odette in the St. Petersburg version of *Swan Lake* (1895). She also danced *Caterina, Coppélia, The Talisman, The Halt of Cavalry, Bluebeard, Camargo, Raymonda,* and other ballets. After leaving Russia she danced in Italy and France and appeared in some of the Alhambra ballets (London) during the first decade of this century.

Lehmann, Maurice, French theatrical impresario, b. 1895. He was twice director of the National Lyric Theatres of France (Opéra and Opéra Comique, 1945–46 and 1951–56). Among his innovations was the introduction of the defilé of the ballet of the Opéra on special occasions.

Leistner, Wolfgang, German dancer, b. Zwickau (Saxony), 1933. Studied with Herbert Freund in Leipzig, Sabine Ress in Berlin, Peter van Dijk in Wiesbaden, Harold Turner and Cleo Nordi in London; attended the Sadler's Wells (now Royal) Ballet School. Made his debut in Leipzig (1949). Other engagements include those at Comic Opera, Berlin; State Theatre, Wiesbaden; State Opera, Munich; Municipal (now German) Opera, Berlin, appearing in principal roles in classic and modern ballets.

Leite, Carlos, Brazilian dancer, choreographer and ballet master, b. Porto Alegre, 1914. Made his debut as a singer in an opera company (1932), then went to Rio de Janeiro (1934) to study drama. Began his dance studies at the ballet school of the Teatro Municipal under Maria Olenewa; later with Yuco Lindberg, Vaslav Veltchek, Yurek Shabelevsky, and Igor Schwezoff. Made his debut as a dancer in the opera-ballet in *Romeo and Juliet* (1935); soloist (1940); first dancer (1943). Appeared with Original Ballet Russe for the two seasons (1942, 1944). Founder of Ballet da Juventude (1945); dancer and stage director of Ballet da Juventude (1947), as well as assistant to choreographer Schwezoff. Went to Belo Horizonte (1948), doing pioneer work by establishing its first ballet school from which emerged the Ballet de Minas Gerais, an important civic ballet in Brazil. Currently choreographer and director for Ballet de Minas Gerais and for local operas and television; also teaches in his own school and at Universidade Mineira de Artes. Danced principal roles in most of the repertoire of Ballet de Minas Gerais. Choreographed *Salomé* (Richard Strauss), *Comedia Balletica* (Jerkinson), *Dance of Yaras* (João Sepe), *Cuadro Flamenco* (Albeniz-Falla), *Batuque* (Alberto Nepomuceno), *Mozartiana* and *Les Petits Riens* (Mozart), *Galatea* (von Suppé), *Uirapurú* (Heitor Villa-Lobos), and revived several ballets of the standard repertoire.

Leland, Sara, American dancer, b. Melrose, Mass., 1941. Studied with E. Virginia Williams in Boston and danced with her regional group, the Boston Ballet. Joined the Robert Joffrey Ballet for the season 1959–60. Joined New York City Ballet (summer 1960); promoted to soloist (1963). Her first created leading role was in Francisco Moncion's version of *Les Biches* (fall, 1960). Dances solo roles in *Symphony in C, Agon, Scotch Symphony, A Midsummer Night's Dream, La Valse, Creation of the World, Raymonda Variations.* Has often returned to Boston to appear as guest artist with the Boston Ballet.

Lemanis, Osvald (Janis Osvalds Lemanis), dancer, choreographer, teacher, b. Riga, Latvia, 1903; d. Flint, Michigan, Sept. 9, 1965. Studied ballet at the Latvian National Ballet School under Nicholas Sergeyev and Alexandra Fedorova. In 1922 was given a scholarship by the Latvian Government for further study with Michel Fokine and Lubov Egorova. In 1926 was accepted into the corps de ballet of the Latvian National Ballet company; the following year promoted to soloist and in 1928 to premier danseur. In 1931 he danced in Max Reinhardt's Berlin production of *La Belle Hélène* and, under Boris Romanoff's direction, the *Polovetsian Dances* in the film *Congress Dances.* In 1933 he partnered Olga Spessivtzeva in her gala performance in Riga. In 1934 choreographed dances for Reinhardt's production of *The Merchant of Venice,* at Venice, in which dancers from the Milan's La Scala and the Latvian Ballet appeared. The same year was appointed artistic director and chief choreographer of the Latvian Ballet, a position he held until 1944. During that time he staged original choreography for the full-length *Swan Lake, Le Triomphe d'Amour, Don Quixote, Ilga, Esmeralda, The Fountain of Bakhchisarai,* and *Raymonda,* as well as a number of shorter works and opera ballets. In 1935 the Latvian National Ballet under his direction, gave three guest performances at the Stockholm Royal Theatre. The following year he partnered Olga Spessivtzeva in a gala performance at the Opéra Comique, Paris. In 1945–48 he was artistic director, choreographer and dancer of the newly organized Latvian Ballet, for which company he created a number of ballets. In 1948–50 he was choreographer and premier danseur of the Stuttgart Opera House, where he choreographed several works, among them *In Scripto Satanis* (Otto-Erich Schilling), 1949. After 1950 he, together with his wife Mirdza Tillak, ballerina of the Latvian Ballet, headed the Dance Dept. of the Institute of Musical Arts, Detroit, Mich. In 1954 they began to teach at Michigan Mercy College and created choreography for the College's Artists Series musical shows. In 1959 he staged the full-length *Cinderella* (Prokofiev) for the Detroit City Ballet. He received the Three-Star Decoration from the Latvian Government; the Vasa Order, First Class, from the King of Sweden; and a medal from the Royal Theatre, Stockholm.

Leningrad, since 1924 the name of the Russian city formerly called St. Petersburg and Petrograd.

Lensky, Fedor (Schlicker), dancer and ballet master, b. Arnsberg, Germany, 1913. Studied modern dance in Folkwangs-Jooss-School, Essen; classic dance in Gsovsky School, Berlin. First dancer of Opera, Essen (from 1934), and of first dance group for German State Theatres and Tatiana Gsovsky's Ballet. Ballet master, premier danseur, Nouveau Ballet de Monte Carlo (from 1941), dancing in *Coppélia, La Grisi, Soir de Bal Masqué, Le Poéte et ses Rêves,* etc. His choreographed works include *Farandole, Rhapsodie Slave,* and *Snow White.* Staged Czech folk dances for Czechoslovakian children's chorus; gave solo recitals of his own creations. Currently heads the International Dance School, N.Y.

Leonard, Claudie. See ALGERANOVA, CLAUDIE.

Leotard, a practice and stage costume for dancers, in its simplest form resembling a sleeveless one-piece bathing suit. A variation of it has long sleeves. It is worn with tights by ballet dancers, sometimes without tights by modern dancers. Because the strenuous physical demands of the classic technique make it vitally important for the leg muscles to be kept warm and soft during practice, dancers usually wear leotards with ankle-length tights. The leotard has been used as a basis of theatrical costumes by ballet and modern dancers. The name stems from Jules Leotard, a famous French acrobat who wore it in his trapeze act and who was seen in the U.S. in 1868.

Lepeshinskaya, Olga, Peoples' Artist of the U.S.S.R. Soviet ballerina, b. 1916. Entered Bolshoi Ballet School in 1925 and one year later danced as a Cupid in *Don Quixote.* A year before graduation she danced the principal part of Masha in *The Nutcracker.* She was graduated in 1933. In 1935 created the role of Suok, the Circus Dancer, in *Three Fat Men.* Her exuberant buoyancy and strong technique, coupled with a winning personality and considerable power of projection, made her ideal for interpreting contemporary roles, one of them being the title role in *Svetlana* (1939). Among her many important roles are Aurora (*The Sleeping Beauty*), Lise (*La Fille Mal Gardée*), Jeanne (*Flames of Paris*), Kitri (*Don Quixote*), Tao-Hoa (*The Red Poppy*), and others. She also has a varied concert repertoire. Has danced in Paris, Japan, China, Hungary, Czechoslovakia, and Mexico.

Le Picq, Charles (1749–1806), French dancer and ballet master. A favorite pupil of Jean Georges Noverre, he was known as the "Apollo" of the dance. He made his debut at the Paris Opéra (1783) in *Apollon et les Muses* and danced the same ballet at the King's Theatre, London (1785). He often partnered Madeleine Guimard in *Les Caprices de Galatée*. In 1786 he went to St. Petersburg and for the next twelve years was choreographer and ballet master of the Imperial Ballet there. It was at his appeal that Emperor Alexander I of Russia ordered the publication of a definitive edition of Noverre's *Lettres sur la danse, sur les ballets et les arts* (1803–04) in French.

Leskova, Tatiana (Tatiana Hélène Leskova), dancer, ballet mistress, choreographer, b. Paris, 1922, Brazilian citizen since 1953. Attended Sion and Ecole des Arts. Studied ballet with Lubov Egorova; later with Boris Kniaseff and Anatole Oboukhov. Made her debut at Opéra Comique de Paris (1937). Danced in Ballet de la Jeunesse (1938) and at the Comédie Française. Joined Original Ballet Russe (1939) and rose from corps de ballet to first dancer, dancing entire repertoire. Left in 1945 to settle in Rio de Janeiro, Brazil. Danced in the Copacabana Casino shows. Guest artist, Teatro Municipal (1946–47). Presented her own company, Ballet Society (1948–49). Dancer, ballet mistress, choreographer of Teatro Municipal (1950–60). Choreographed *Symphonic Variations* (1948), *Mascarade* (1949), *Prometheus Chained* and *Walpurgis Night* (1950), *Star of the Circus* (1951), *Salamanca do Jarau* (1952), *Peter and the Wolf* (1953), *The Scarecrow* (1954), *The Seven Sins* (1954), *Foyer de la Danse* (1955), *The Kid's Parrot* (1957), *The Discovery of Brazil* (1960). Restaged *Giselle, Coppélia, Aurora's Wedding, Les Sylphides, Swan Lake, Pas de Quatre, Protée, L'Après-midi d'un Faune, Prince Igor. Schéhérazade.* Danced virtually all ballets of the repertoire. Recipient of Leaders and Specialists Grant, U.S. Dept. of State (1959). Ballet mistress, Leonide Massine's Ballets Européens de Nervi (1960). Received Municipal (Rio de Janeiro) Award as Best Dancer of the Year (1960). Director of Ballet and ballerina of Teatro Municipal (since 1961); also teaches in her own school in Copacabana. Married Antonio de Bouza, director of the SODRE of Uruguay (Dec., 1965). Continues to work at the Teatro Municipal, Rio de Janeiro, as guest choreographer.

Lesson, in ballet, the arrangement of exercises into daily periods to instruct a dancer in technique and to maintain technical proficiency during an active stage career. The lesson consists of approximately the same movements from a pupil's first introduction to the barre down to the last year of his professional appearance. There is a natural difference bred by the ease of familiarity, but even the youngest student immediately tries to execute steps which will later be part of his accustomed vocabulary.

The class starts easily while progress is at first, by necessity, slow. Children without previous training, as well as accomplished dancers, commence with bar and follow by work in the center of the floor, in a dry and rather invariable sequence. Soon, combinations of more complex movements are permitted at the bar, and then without its aid, in the center. The five fundamental positions, their variants in arms and legs, as well as principles of opposition and plasticity, are mastered.

An easy adagio combination is ventured to prepare for instruction in balance. The adagio becomes increasingly complex and difficult to sustain. Later on, new combinations are continually substituted for others. The student cannot afford to make any short-cut. Everything follows inexorably from the simple sources: self-control, aplomb, balance, stamina, and limberness become the normal properties of a body which will finally be prepared to begin the more difficult group exercises, allegro. The slower exercises (adagio), coming first, warm up the muscular mechanism for its peak load of exertion.

Allegro cannot be undertaken until the feet are so correctly trained that their behavior is almost instinctive. The turn-out of the legs must be broad and effortless. The instep must be firm and well-muscled. The exercises begin with simple jumps in which both feet are used to spring: temps levé and changement de pieds. These are first practiced with the hands on the bar, the dancer facing the wall. Then comes the more complicated assemblé. The assemblé correctly performed is a base for the rest of the division of allegro. The legs must co-ordinate into the rise and fall, and yet be turned out in landing. There is no possibility of muscular laxity. Afterwards follow the glissade, jeté, échappé, pas de basque, and balancé. Having mastered the primary jetés, the lesson passes to jumps in which only one foot is used for a spring (the other resting sur le cou-de-pied, after the jump) and to sissonne ouverte in various directions. More difficult jumps, as the saut de basque, come later, with cabrioles and the rest of batterie. Allegro is the basis of the rapid enchaînements which constitute most of classic stage dancing. In advanced classes every one of these steps is varied in execution by being practiced en tournant.

This is a rough outline for most of our standard "Russian" ballet classes, and does not apply to character dance, which has its own bar system, or to supported adagio, or to lessons for pointes. Agrippina Vaganova, the author of the best modern work on the subject (*Fundamentals of the Classic Dance,* translated by Anatole Chujoy, publ. by Kamin, N.Y., 1946 and A. & C. Black, London, 1948) and academician of the Soviet Technicum for ballet in Leningrad, gives almost the same order. She wisely insists on no absolutely rigid rule for planning her class, recognizing that dancers are artists, not soldiers, and that theatrical life is variable. Fatigue must be taken into consideration as well as the individual progress of pupils. (From Lincoln Kirstein's *Ballet Alphabet*).

Lester, Keith, dancer, choreographer, ballet master, b. Guildford, Surrey, England, 1904. Studied dance with Serafima Astafieva and Nicholas Legat. Made his debut in dances choreographed by Michel Fokine for *Hassan* (1923). Partnered Lydia Kyasht and Tamara Karsavina in London, Olga Spessivtzeva at Colón Theatre, Buenos Aires (under Fokine); danced in Max Reinhardt's *The Miracle* (London, 1932); with Ida Rubinstein company in Paris (1934); toured U.S. in ballet revue. Joined Markova-Dolin company as dancer and choreographer (1935), choreographed *David* (1935), for which Jacob Epstein designed the curtain, *Death in Adagio,* and *Pas de Quatre,* which Anton Dolin later revised and restaged in the version now in the repertoire of American Ballet Theatre and other companies; *Bach Suite No. 2 in B Minor* (all 1936). Director and choreographer of Arts Theatre Ballet (1939–40) and Ballet Guild (1941), for both of which he staged a number of ballets. Since 1945 has been ballet master and choreographer of the Windmill Theatre (London's famous non-stop revue whose wartime story was told in the motion picture *Tonight and Every Night*). He has staged well over 200 ballets for the Windmill, and is reputed to arrange the most outstanding fan dances. He also belongs to the Westminster Morris, a well known team performing traditional English Morris dances.

Let the Heavens Open, that the Earth May Shine. Modern solo; chor.: Sybil Shearer; music: Vivaldi-Bach; costume: Sybil Shearer. First prod.: N.Y. Times Hall, May 3, 1946.

Letter to the World. Modern dance work; chor.: Martha Graham; music: Hunter Johnson; spoken text from lines of poems by Emily Dickinson, selected by Martha Graham; décor: Arch Lauterer; costumes: Edythe Gilfond; first prod.: Bennington College, Vt., Aug. 11, 1940, with Martha Graham (The One Who Dances), Margaret Meredith (an Actress, The One Who Speaks), Jane Dudley (The Ancestress), Erick Hawkins (The Lover), Merce Cunningham (March); revised and presented at Mansfield Theatre, N.Y., Jan. 20, 1941, with Jean Erdman as The One Who Speaks. One of the greatest of the early group works of Martha Graham.

Lettres sur la Danse, et sur les Ballets, a collection of letters by Jean Georges Noverre (1727–1809), an excellent introduction to the criticism of theatrical dance. Noverre's inability to get into the Paris Opéra led to the writing of these epistles, an angry testament of his ideas on the art of dancing and rules governing the dance. He realized the importance of having music adapted to dance instead of simply setting steps to music already composed. He wished to discard needlessly cumbersome costumes and over-complicated steps and grimaces, to allow the body freedom to make full use of the vocabulary of classic dance and of natural expressions and gestures. Though Noverre failed in his lifelong struggle to attain his goal, his influence was felt through his letters in Italy and Russia; even today they stand as a monument to his greatness and brilliance as a dance critic.

Levashev, Vladimir, Honored Artist of the RSFSR, Soviet character dancer, b. Moscow, 1923. Entered the Bolshoi School in 1932, graduating in 1941. Accepted into the Bolshoi Ballet where, due to wartime conditions, he began dancing responsible roles while technically still at school. Levashev is not merely a character dancer in the accepted sense, rather is he a dancing actor of the type produced by Soviet ballet in the 1930's. He has danced all the mazurkas and Spanish dances in the classic repertoire, but it was his acting in the role of Nur-Ali in *The Fountain of Bakhchisarai* that gave Leonid Lavrovsky the idea of entrusting the tall, handsome youth with the role of Mercutio in *Romeo and Juliet.* He is also an outstanding Hilarion (*Giselle*), and an extraordinary Severian, the wicked bailiff (*The Stone Flower*).

Levinson, André, Russian writer and ballet critic, b. St. Petersburg, 1887, d. Paris, 1933. Levinson moved to Paris after the Russian revolution and soon began to write about ballet in the Paris press. French ballet and literary circles considered him the first dance critic in France because before him dance criticism was written by music and drama critics and consequently did not offer a proper reflection of the art form and its practitioners. He was not a follower of Serge Diaghilev and considered that Diaghilev committed a serious aesthetic error in subjecting the dancer "to the arrogant dictatorship of the painter of the décor," and in having given "the musical elements precedence over the choreographic inspiration,"—in short, in having lowered the dance to an imitation of fashions of pictorial figurations or the conventions of plastic art. He believed that the art of dance should be self-sufficient, an end in itself. Levinson wrote for Parisian dailies and several magazines in French and in English. Among his books are *La Danse au Théâtre* (1924), *La Vie de Noverre* (1925), *Anna Pavlova* (1928), *La Argen-*

tina (1928), *Marie Taglioni* (1929 in French, 1930 in English), *La Danse d'Aujourd'hui* (1929), *Les Visages de la Danse* (1933).

Levi-Tanai, Sara. See INBAL.

Levitov, Alexander, European and Australian impresario, b. Russia, 1892, d. Paris, 1958. Among the companies and individual dancers managed by Levitov were Yekaterina Geltzer, great ballerina of the Moscow Bolshoi Ballet; the Anna Pavlova Ballet and, after her death, the ballet company organized by her husband, Victor Dandré, with Olga Spessivtzeva as ballerina; the Original Ballet Russe on its Australian tour; Les Ballets de l'Amerique Latine. Levitov, who had his business in Paris, moved to Australia in the 1930's and remained there until the early 1950's when he returned to Paris to continue his business.

Ley, Olga, dancer, teacher, writer, b. St. Petersburg, Russia, 1912. Studied dance with Mikhail Mordkin, Vecheslav Swoboda, Ludmila Shollar, Anatole Vilzak, Marion Venable. Danced with Gavrilov Ballet, Philadelphia Opera Ballet; soloist, Mordkin Ballet (1936–38), and other companies. Director and originator of Helena Rubinstein's exercise salon (1934–40); dance editor and columnist for newspaper *PM* (1940–45). Author of *It's Fun to be Fit* (N.Y., 1942). Dance consultant for Capezio, Inc.; teacher of dance exercises, free-lance writer, illustrator, photographer, designer.

Lhotka, Nenad, Yugoslav dancer and choreographer, b. Zagreb, 1922. Studied with Ana Roje and Lubov Egorova. Joined Zagreb National Ballet as principal dancer (1942). After dancing with the Janine Charrat company (1950–52), returned to Zagreb. In 1949 and 1950 was awarded the Yugoslav State Prize for his dancing Romeo in Margarita Froman's *Romeo and Juliet* (Prokofiev), a role which he created. Choreographed *Tragedy of Salomé* (Florent Schmitt, 1953), and *Classical Symphony* (Prokofiev, 1954), both in Zagreb. Was ballet master of the Royal Winnipeg Ballet (1955–56).

Liberty Tree. Modern solo; chor.: Erick Hawkins; music: Ralph Gilbert; costumes: Edythe Gilfond; décor: Carlos Dyer. First prod.: Bennington College, Vt., July 13, 1940.

Libidins, David, concert manager and impresario, b. Constantinople (now Istanbul), Turkey, of Russian parentage, d. N.Y.: 1958. Studied voice in Moscow and spent several years as a singer with opera companies and in shows. S. Hurok engaged him in the early 1930's to handle the U.S. tours of Col. de Basil's Ballets Russes. Became administrative director of the Léon Blum–Leonide Massine Ballet Russe de Monte Carlo (1938). Resigned in 1943 and opened his own managerial office and from then, until his death, was the booking manager for Ballet Russe de Monte Carlo, except for two brief periods, during one of which he was administrative director of Ballet (now American Ballet) Theatre. Among the individual artists he handled, outside his ballet activities, were musicians Wanda Landowska and Vladimir Horowitz.

Lichine, David (David Lichtenstein), dancer and choreographer, b. Rostov-on-Don, Russia, 1910; m. Tatiana Riabouchinska. Studied dance with Lubov Egorova and Bronislava Nijinska in Paris. Made his debut with Ida Rubinstein's company in Paris; joined Col. de Basil's Ballets Russes de Monte Carlo (1932) and remained with the company (Original Ballet Russe) until 1941, creating many roles including the Hero (*Les Présages*), King of the Dandies (*Le Beau Danube*), one of the two leading male dancers (*Cotillon*), title role (*Protée*), title role in his own version of *The Prodigal Son,* Junior Cadet (*Graduation Ball*),

David Lichine, dancer, choreographer, teacher.

and others. He choreographed *Nocturne* (1933, based on the fairy characters of *A Midsummer Night's Dream*), *Les Imaginaires* (1934), *Le Pavillon* (1936), *Francesca da Rimini* (1937), *The Gods Go a'Begging* (1938), *Protée* (1938), *Prodigal Son* (1939), *Graduation Ball* (1940). His later works include *La Création* (a ballet without music) and *La Rencontre* for Les Ballets des Champs-Elysées (1948), and the London's Festival Ballet production of *The Nutcracker* (1957). He has also staged *Graduation Ball* for American Ballet Theatre, Royal Danish Ballet, and London's Festival Ballet, which work has been filmed (Mexico, 1961). He has been guest choreographer at La Scala, Milan, and the Royal Opera House, Amsterdam. Teaches in California and directs his own group, Los Angeles Ballet Theatre.

Lidholm, Ingvar, Swedish composer, b. 1921. Created the score for Birgit Aakesson's ballet *Rites* (1960).

Lido, Serge, French ballet photographer, b. Moscow, of Russian parentage, was granted diploma from Ecole des Sciences Politiques. Served in French Army (1939–40). Started as reporter for magazines *Vu* and *France,* inaugurating a new style of ballet reportage. In 1947 opened his studio on the Ile Saint-Louis, Paris, and published the first of his series of books of dance photographs, *Dance No. 1.* These books were published annually from 1950 to 1960 under the title *Ballet.* Began a new series, *Ballet Panorama* (1961).

Lidova, Irène, French ballet critic, writer, producer, b. Moscow. Studied in Paris; granted diploma from Licence de Lettres de la Faculté de Paris. Began writing dance criticism in *Marianne,* a weekly (1939). Organized the first concert performances of Janine Charrat and Roland Petit (1943–44). Founder of Soirées de la Danse (1944) to discover new talents, which then included Renée Jeanmaire, Jean Babilée, and others. One of the founders and general secretary of Les Ballets des Champs-Elysées (1945–46). In 1956 founded a ballet group with Milorad Miskovitch which gives opportunities to new choreographers and artists of the younger generation. Author of *17 Visages de la Danse Française, Roland Petit,* and several studies. Collaborates with her husband, Serge Lido, on his photographic publications. General Secretary of French Association of Ballet Critics and Writers; Paris correspondent for *Dance News.*

Liebeslieder Walzer. Ballet in 1 act, 2 scenes; chor.: George Balanchine; music: Johannes Brahms' *Liebeslieder Walzer,* Op. 52 and Op. 55, for four hands, songs for soprano, contralto, tenor, and baritone; décor: David Hays; costumes: Barbara Karinska. First prod.: New York City Ballet, City Center, N.Y., Nov. 22, 1960, with Diana Adams and Bill Carter, Melissa Hayden and Jonathan Watts, Violette Verdy and Nicholas Magallanes, Jillana and Conrad Ludlow; Louise Sherman and Robert Irving, pianists. The ballet, which is danced with a short interval between the two sets of waltzes, takes place in an elegant Victorian drawing room. The couples dance with a certain reserve, for all their pleasure in the compelling rhythm. In the second half (with the girls now on point and in filmy dresses instead of their former stately satins), the dancers seem to have been transported out of place and time, only to return, once more composed and quiet, to applaud politely as the music ends.

Liepa, Maris, Soviet dancer, b. Riga, Latvia, 1930. Enrolled in the Riga Choreographic School (1945). In 1950 was sent to Moscow to participate in a program of pupils of provincial ballet schools and attracted the attention of teachers of the ballet school of the Moscow Bolshoi Theatre. In 1953 he was accepted into the Moscow School where he studied for two years under Nicolai Tarasov. He returned to Riga for the season 1955–56, but then became a soloist of the Ballet of the Stanislavsky and Nemirovich–Danchenko Theatre in Moscow, where he worked under ballet master Vladimir Bourmeister. In 1957 he received a gold medal at the International Contest of Classic Dancing in Moscow for his variations in *Le Corsaire.* After four years at the Stanislavsky, Liepa made his debut with the Bolshoi Ballet in the ballet *The Path of Thunder* (1961). His other roles include the classics and Bacchus in *Walpurgis Night,* the title role in *Spartacus,* and others. He made a very strong impression during the Bolshoi's U.S. tour (1962). He is considered one of the bright lights of the young generation of Soviet male dancers.

Lieutenant Kije. Ballet in one act, based on the story by Yury Tynianov; music: Sergei Prokofiev's symphonic suite of the same title; chor.: Alexander Lapauri and Olga Tarasova; décor: B. A. Messerer. First prod.: Bolshoi Theatre, Moscow, Feb. 2, 1963, with G. T. Bovt (Paul I), Raisa Struchkova (Lady-in-Waiting), Liudmila Bogomolova (The Feather). An army clerk copying an Order of the Day to be signed by Emperor Paul of Russia, enters by mistake the name of a non-existing Lieutenant Kije among officers assigned to guard duty. The signature of the Czar brings Lieutenant Kije to life, so far as the senior officers are concerned. For fear of the Czar's wrath they continue the fiction of Kije's service and private life. As time goes on he is promoted from rank to rank, and finally dies of wounds received during a battle. Paul orders a funeral with full military honors for the hero who is now a general. The night before the funeral Paul visits the church where Kije lies in state. He looks into the coffin, finds it empty, and has a terrible hallucination. Michel Fokine used the same music for his ballet *Russian Soldier,* staged in N.Y. for Ballet Theatre (1942).

Lifar, Serge, choreographer and dancer, b. Kiev, Russia, 1905. Received a high school education; studied piano and violin at Kiev Conservatory of Music; dance at the State School. Bronislava Nijinska brought him to Paris to join the Diaghilev Ballets Russes (1923). He became premier danseur (1925), his greatest triumph being the creation of the title role in George Balanchine's *The Prodigal Son* (1929). His first choreography was for *Le Renard* for the final Diaghilev season the same year. Premier danseur and

Serge Lifar, French dancer, choreographer, director, shown here as the original Apollo in Balanchine's Apollon Musagète, *in the Diaghilev company (1928).*

maître de ballet of the Paris Opéra (1930–44), being given the title Professor (1932). His ballets at the Opéra include *Promethée* (1929), *Icare* (1935), *David Triomphant, Le Roi Nu* (1936), *Alexandre le Grand* (1937), *Oriane et le Prince d'Amour, Aeneas, Le Cantique des Cantiques* (1938), *Joan de Zarissa* (1942), and others. Left the Opéra to become artistic director and choreographer of Nouveau Ballet de Monte Carlo (1944–46), choreographing *Dramma per Musica, Chota Rustavelli,* and others, remaining with the company for a season after the Marquis de Cuevas took it over and renamed it Grand Ballet de Monte Carlo (summer, 1947). Returned as choreographer, ballet master, and dancer to Paris Opéra, Oct., 1947, creating many other ballets including, among others, *Zadig, Escales, Lucifer* (1948), *Endymion, La Naissance des Couleurs* (1949), *Septuor, L'Inconnue, Le Chevalier Errant, Phèdre* (1950), *Astrologue, Blanche-Neige* (1951), *Les Fourberies* (1952), *Cinéma, Variations, Grand Pas* (1953), *Nauteos* (1954), *Les Noces Fantastiques,* Prokofiev's *Romeo and Juliet* (1955), *Le Chemin de Lumière* (1957), *Le Bel Indifférent* (for Opéra Comique), and *Daphnis et Chloë* (1958). The last named was his final creation for the Opéra. He had retired as a dancer with a performance as Albrecht in *Giselle,* partnering Yvette Chauviré, Dec. 5, 1956. Since leaving the Opéra (1959), he has created ballets for other companies, including *The Moor of Venice* (Netherlands Ballet, 1960), *Bonaparte at Nice* (London's Festival Ballet, Nice Festival, 1960), *Pique Dame* (Monte Carlo Opera, 1960), *On ne badine pas avec l'Amour* (Nice Opera, 1961). In 1962 he staged ballets at the Colón in Buenos Aires, Argentina (including *Phèdre* with Tamara Toumanova as guest artist), and in Chile. In the summer of 1962 Georges Auric, newly-appointed General Administrator of the National Lyric Theatres of France, invited Lifar to return to the Opéra as choreographer. Lifar is the author of many books, articles, etc., among them *Le Destin d'un Danseur* (1934), *Le Manifeste du Chorégraphe* (1935), *Diaghilev* (in Russian 1939, in French 1954), *L'Histoire du Ballet Russe* (in Russian 1939, in French 1950), *Pensées sur la Danse* (1946), *A L'Aube de mon Destin* (1948), *Traité de Danse Académique* (1949), *Vestris, Dieu de la Danse* (1950), *Traité de Chorégraphie* (1952), *Meditations sur la Danse* (1952), *Dix Ans à l'Opéra* (1953), *Les Trois Graces du XXe Siècle* (1957), *Au Service de la Danse* (1958).

Light Opera. See MUSICAL COMEDY.

Lilac Garden (Jardin aux Lilas). Ballet in 1 act; chor.: Antony Tudor; music: Ernest Chausson's *Poème;* book: Hugh Stevenson and Antony Tudor; décor: Hugh Stevenson. First prod.: Ballet Rambert, Mercury Theatre, London, Jan. 26, 1936, with Maude Lloyd (Caroline, the Bride-to-Be), Hugh Laing (Her Lover), Antony Tudor (The Man She Must Marry), Peggy van Praagh (An Episode in His Past). At a party on the eve of an arranged and loveless marriage, Caroline tries to say a last good-bye to her lover. But there are interruptions—from her husband-to-be, from his former mistress and from the other guests—and when she leaves, the farewell is still unsaid. Tudor has marvellously given us the emotions held in restraint by the rigid conventions of Edwardian etiquette, and Chausson's *Poème* is probably the finest score ever to accompany a ballet for which it was not composed. Tudor staged *Lilac Garden* (still at that time called *Jardin aux Lilas*), for Ballet Theatre, Center Theatre, N.Y., Jan. 15, 1940 in décor after Stevenson, with Viola Essen (Caroline), Karen Conrad (An Episode in His Past), and Tudor and Laing in their original roles. Caroline later became one of Nora Kaye's greatest parts. Tudor staged it with himself, Kaye, Laing, and Tanaquil LeClercq for New York City Ballet, in décor by Horace Armistead and costumes by Barbara Karinska, at City Center, N.Y.,

Nov. 27, 1951. It is also in the repertoire of National Ballet of Canada (since 1954).

Lilavati, Devi (Bose), contemporary Indian dancer, b. Calcutta. Studied under Krishna Rao and joined the Ram Gopal company (1947). After touring with the company she settled in Sweden and married Bengt Haeger, writer and curator of the Swedish Dance Museum, Stockholm. She has given dance recitals in Scandinavia, Germany, China, and Paris. Was guest artist with the Royal Swedish Ballet in 1961.

Lima, Ruth, Brazilian dancer, b. Rio de Janeiro. Began dance study in the ballet school of Teatro Municipal (1947), under Yuco Lindberg, later studied with Luiza Carbonell. Joined corps de ballet of Teatro Municipal (1954). Currently first dancer of Teatro Municipal; dances roles in *Narcisse, The Seven Sins, Concerto Dançante, Les Présages, The Scarecrow, Serenade for Strings, Giselle, Masquerade, Constantia.* Also dances on television and her own recitals.

Limón, José, dancer, choreographer, teacher, company director, b. Culiacan, Sinaloa, Mexico, 1908; m. Pauline Lawrence. Brought to U.S. by his parents at the age of seven, he majored in painting at school. After a year at Univ. of California, he went to N.Y. and enrolled in an art school, but after attending a single dance performance joined the school of Doris Humphrey and Charles Weidman. Also studied ballet with Nenette Charisse and Ella Daganova. A member of the Humphrey-Weidman company (1930–40), during the same period and until 1942 he danced in many Broadway musicals. His first notable choreographic works (both solos for himself) were *Danzas Mexicanas* (Mills College, summer, 1939) and Bach's *Chaconne in D Minor* (1942). After service with the U.S. Army during World War II, he formed his own group for which he and Doris Humphrey, his artistic director for many years, choreographed many works, including the early *Lament for Ignacio Sanchez Mejias* and *Day on Earth* (both Humphrey, 1947), his own *La Malinche,* and his first major work, *The Moor's Pavane* (1949). For many years his group consisted of himself, Betty Jones, Ruth Currier, and Lucas Hoving, with Pauline Koner as a permanent guest artist. In the mid-1950's this nucleus was considerably expanded and the repertoire began to include works necessitating an ensemble, such as *Ritmo Jondo, There Is a Time, The Traitor, Missa Brevis,* and others. His was the first company to be sent abroad (South America, 1954) under the International Cultural Exchange Program of the U.S. State Dept. He went under the same auspices to Europe (including Poland and Yugoslavia, 1957), and again to South and Central America (1960 and 1963). He has for many years been on the faculties of the Juilliard School of Music Dance Dept. and Connecticut College School of Dance, and has presented many dance performances at the Juilliard Concert Hall and during the Connecticut College American Dance Festivals. He frequently uses the students at these schools to augment his own company, as for *Missa Brevis,* and for *Performance,* a work commissioned by the Juilliard School, danced by its students (Apr. 14, 1961), and restaged for the students of Connecticut College for the American Dance Festival the same year. He has on numerous occasions been invited to perform and choreograph for the Academy of Dance of the National Institute of Fine Arts, Mexico, and staged *Missa Brevis* (and performed in it) for the Academy (1962). Since 1946 he has toured annually in U.S. Received an honorary doctorate from Wesleyan University (1960). He received the Capezio Dance Award for 1965. In Oct., 1964, the New York State Council on the Arts named José Limón artistic director of a modern dance group named The American Dance Theatre. The company, which was considered to be the first step

in the endeavors of the Council to establish a permanent repertory company, gave two performances (Nov. 18 and 19) at the New York State Theater, Lincoln Center.

The two performances were very successful artistically and financially; this success raised hopes of the possibility of forming a large modern dance company, able to appear in a repertoire created by several choreographers. On March 2 to 7, 1965 the American Dance Theatre presented a week's performances, again under the artistic direction of José Limón. Discussions still continue about the creation of a modern dance company, but progress is very slow.

On Jan. 22, José Limón and his company opened the inaugural performance of the Hunter College Dance Series, presented in cooperation with the New York State Council on the Arts.

On August 19, Limón presented a new work, *My Son, My Enemy,* at the 18th American Dance Festival at Connecticut College, New London, Conn. The work was inspired by a letter Peter the Great, first Emperor of Russia, wrote to his weakling son, Alexis, the heir-apparent to the throne. The score was by Vivian Faine. Limón's *Choreographic Offering* and *Missa Brevis* completed the program.

During the rest of the year José Limón and company gave performances on tour and in New York.

On Jan. 21, 1966 the dancer-choreographer was accorded a signal honor by National Educational Television Network: an hour's telecast of three of his outstanding creations, *Lament for Ignacio Sanchez Mejias* (with choreography by the late Doris Humphrey), *The Moor's Pavane,* and *Missa Brevis.* Limón choreographed the last two works and danced the principal roles in all three.

José Limón with Betty Jones in his Moor's Pavane.

Lindberg, Yuco (Johannes Lindberg) (1906–1948), dancer, teacher, and choreographer, b. Estonia. Began dance studies in Tallinn. Emigrated to Brazil (1925), and became Brazilian citizen, continuing dance with Ricardo Nemanoff and Maria Olenewa at Teatro Municipal, Rio de Janeiro. Became first dancer of this theatre (from 1934). When Olenewa resigned (1942), he assumed direction of ballet school which he held until his death. A fighter for the cause of ballet in Brazil, his dedication was responsible for the school of Teatro Municipal's survival through difficult years. Such talented Brazilian dancers as Maria Angélica, Marcia Haydée, and Yvonne Meyer began studies under his tutelage. He was a versatile choreographer, staging for ballet, operas, movies, revues, shows, and social parties. Directed the ballet performance in honor of the visiting President Truman, Sept., 1947. His most important work was *Happiness* (1943), in prologue and three acts, to music by Alberto Lazzoli. Others include *Batuque* (Alberto Nepomuceno), *Muiraquitã* (Batista Siqueira), *Congada* (Mignone), *Senzala* (José Siqueira), *Uirapurú* (Villa-Lobos), *Garimpeiro's Dream* (Eleazar de Carvalho), and many others.

Linden, Anya (Elinton), English dancer, b. Manchester, 1933, of English-Russian parentage. Studied in the U.S. under Theodore Koslov. Entered Sadler's Wells School (1947), joining Sadler's Wells (now Royal) Ballet (1951); soloist (1954); ballerina (1958). Dances all the leading classic ballerina roles, also *Blue Bird* pas de deux (*The Sleeping Beauty*), Queen of the Wilis (*Giselle*), Bride (*La Fête Etrange*), The Wife (*The Invitation*), Ophelia (*Hamlet*); created Poor Girl (*Noctambules*), lead (Kenneth MacMillan's *Agon*), title role (*Antigone*), and others.

Lindgren, Robert, dancer and teacher, b. Vancouver, Canada, 1923, now an

American citizen; m. Sonya Taanila (Tyven). Began his dance studies with Dorothy Wilson and June Roper, Vancouver. Later studied in N.Y. with Anatole Vilzak, Maria Yurieva-Swoboda, Igor Schwezoff, and others; also with Olga Preobrajenska in Paris. Joined Ballet Russe de Monte Carlo (1942) and returned to this company after service in the Royal Canadian Air Force during World War II. Danced leading roles in *The Red Poppy, Rodeo, Schéhérazade, Graduation Ball, Polovetsian Dances from Prince Igor, Night Shadow, Raymonda, Gaîté Parisienne,* and others. Left in 1951 and appeared regularly on C.B.S. and N.B.C. network television shows and in several Broadway musicals. Toured South Africa and the Orient with Alexandra Danilova (1956–57). Soloist, New York City Ballet (1957–59), dancing in *Interplay, Western Symphony, Night Shadow, Fanfare, Square Dance,* and others. Taught with his wife in Phoenix, Ariz. until Mar., 1965, when he was appointed Dean of the School of Dance of the North Carolina School of the Arts, Winston-Salem, and his wife joined the ballet faculty.

Lindsay, Rosemary (Scott Giles), English dancer, b. London, 1927. Entered Sadler's Wells School (1941); became member of Sadler's Wells (now Royal) Ballet (1943); promoted to soloist (1943). Her repertoire included Aurora and Lilac Fairy (*The Sleeping Beauty*), Queen of the Wilis (*Giselle*), The Aristocrat (Leonide Massine's staging of *Mam'zelle Angot* for Royal Ballet), Swanilda (*Coppélia*), Red Queen (*Checkmate*), Young Girl—creation (*The Shadow*), and others. Retired in 1961.

Lindy. See JITTERBUG.

Line of Dance, in ballroom dance, direction followed in moving around a ballroom, i.e. counterclockwise.

Linn, Bambi (Linnemeier), American dancer, b. Brooklyn, N.Y., 1926. Studied at the Professional Children's School, N.Y., and had her dance training with Mikhail Mordkin, Ballet Arts School, Elisabeth Anderson-Ivantzova, Helena Platova, Hanya Holm. The original Aggie in *Oklahoma!* (1943–45), she also created the role of Louise in *Carousel* (1945–46) for which she received the Donaldson Award; played it again in the N.Y. City Center revival (1956). With her first husband, Rod Alexander, she was a featured dancer in many television series, including "Your Show of Shows" (1952–54), "Max Liebman Specials" (1954–56), and others. Toured abroad with Rod Alexander in *Dance Jubilee* (1958–59), and appeared as guest soloist with American Ballet Theatre at Spoleto Festival of Two Worlds (1959). Had a featured dancing and acting role in the Broadway musical *I Can Get It For You Wholesale* (1962).

Lippincott, Gertrude, modern dance choreographer, dancer and teacher, b. St. Paul, Minn., 1913. Studied Univ. of Chicago (1931–32), Univ. of Minnesota (1932–35), B.S., Phi Beta Kappa, magna cum laude; studied dance with Jan Veen, Leslie Burrowes (Wigman technique), London (1936); Bennington School of the Dance, Vt. (1937–38); and with Martha Graham, Doris Humphrey, Charles Weidman, Hanya Holm, Louis Horst, and Ella Daganova (ballet); also at N.Y.U. (Master's Degree in Dance, 1943). Her career in dance began when she was asked to join the Univ. of Minnesota Dance Group in the early 1930's (she was originally asked because she was the only dancer to own a car, but she quickly established herself as its outstanding member). Since then she has given solo recitals, group performances, demonstrations all over the country, and has taught at Mt. Holyoke College, Hamline Univ., Minneapolis YWCA, Colorado College of Education, Louisiana State Univ., Mills College, Univ. of Oregon, and other institutions. She was a co-editor of *Dance Ob-*

server (1945–57); author of many articles in *Journal of Health and Physical Education,* and others; contributing editor as well as writer for *Impulse* since 1952. In recent years her dance programs have experimented in the field of speech and dance movement. Established her own Modern Dance Center in Minneapolis (1937) which is still the headquarters of her teaching and performing activities.

Liszt, Franz (1811–1886), Hungarian composer who originated the symphonic poem. A well-known example of this musical form is *Les Préludes,* used by Michel Fokine for a ballet (1913). He composed a number of *Hungarian Rhapsodies,* the second of which is much used by dancers. His music is used in part (the other composer is Franz Schubert) for *The Beloved* (Bronislava Nijinska, 1928). George Antheil orchestrated his *Etudes d'éxécution transcendante* for *Transcendence* (George Balanchine, 1934). Constant Lambert selected and Gordon Jacob orchestrated a number of his piano pieces for *Apparitions* (Frederick Ashton, 1936) and also orchestrated his *Dante Sonata* (subtitled: "D'après une lecture de Dante") for Ashton's ballet of the same name (1940). Liszt's *Mephisto Waltz: At the Inn* was the score for Ashton's *Mephisto Waltz* for Ballet Club (afterwards Ballet Rambert) in 1934 and for his re-working of this ballet as *Vision of Marguerite* for London's Festival Ballet (1952). Ashton again used Liszt music—the *Piano Sonata* in *B minor* and *La Gondole Lugubre,* orchestrated by Humphrey Searle—for *Marguerite and Armand* (1963).

Littlefield Ballet, The (1935–42), founded by Catherine Littlefield, Philadelphia, Pa. First ballet company entirely staffed and directed by Americans; later known as Philadelphia Ballet. Appeared in Philadelphia, N.Y., other U.S. cities. First season presented complete *Daphnis and Chloë, Bolero, The Fairy Doll, Fête Champêtre,* and others. The following season, besides first American presentation of complete version of *The Sleeping Beauty,* ballets with American themes (*Barn Dance, Terminal*) were produced. Company appeared in Paris, Brussels, London (summer, 1937); was official ballet of the Chicago Civic Opera Company (1938–40; 1941–42). Had planned tour (1942), but was forced to disband, due to World War II and the dearth of male dancers.

Littlefield, Catherine, choreographer, ballerina, teacher, b. Philadelphia, Pa., 1908, d. N.Y. 1951. Received her early training in her mother's school (Mrs. Caroline Littlefield, d. May 7, 1957); later with Luigi Albertieri, N.Y.; Leo Staats, Lubov Egorova, Paris. Made her professional debut in the musical *Sally* (1923); danced at Roxy's Theatre, N.Y., for some months; then returned to help at her mother's school. Première danseuse for several years of Philadelphia Grand Opera Co.; choreographer and dancer (season 1934–35). Founder, choreographer, première danseuse, The Littlefield Ballet (1935–42). Director of American Jubilee, N.Y. World's Fair (1940). Choreographed *Barn Dance, Terminal, Fête Champêtre, Café Society;* restaged *The Fairy Doll, Daphnis and Chloë,* the complete *Sleeping Beauty,* etc., for her company. Choreographed the musicals *Hold Your Hats, Crazy with the Heat, A Kiss for Cinderella, Follow the Girls,* etc. Choreographer and director of *It Happens on Ice, Stars on Ice, Hats Off to Ice, Icetime* (Center Theatre, N.Y.). Choreographed Sonja Henie's *Ice Revues* (on tour, 1942–48). Catherine Littlefield was one of the most important pioneers of American ballet. She was the first American to take a full company to Europe (London and Paris, 1937), and the first to stage a full-length version of *The Sleeping Beauty.* She was an outstanding teacher, numbering among her many pupils who made names for themselves Karen Conrad, Dania Krupska, Zachary Solov and Edward Caton.

Littlefield, Dorothie (1916–1952), American dancer, sister of Catherine Littlefield, b. Philadelphia, Pa. Studied at her mother's school; later at her sister's school and the School of American Ballet, N.Y. Member, Bronislava Nijinska company; American Ballet (1935). Ballerina and ballet mistress, Philadelphia Ballet, in Europe (summer, 1937) and U.S.; Chicago Civic Opera Company (1939); American Jubilee company, N.Y. World's Fair (1940). Guest artist, Ballet (now American Ballet) Theatre in her original role in *Barn Dance* (1944); featured dancer in musical *Song of Norway* (1946–47), staged and choreographed by George Balanchine. Assistant to and later associate with Catherine Littlefield in staging Broadway musicals and ice shows.

Litz, Katherine, modern dancer and choreographer, b. Denver, Colo., 1918. Studied dance with Doris Humphrey and Charles Weidman; composition with Youri Bilstin and Louis Horst; ballet with Helena Platova and Richard Thomas; also studied acting and voice. Made her debut with the Humphrey-Weidman company (1936–42), and was also a soloist and group member of Agnes de Mille's concert company (1940–42). Danced in Broadway musicals *Oklahoma!* and *Carousel;* choreographed and danced leading role in *Susanna and the Elders (Ballet Ballads,* 1948). Made her debut as performer-choreographer at the YMHA in Apr., 1948. Since then she has continued to give programs of her own works, both solos and for groups, at the YMHA, Juilliard Concert Hall, Hunter College Playhouse; also at Jacob's Pillow and American Dance Festivals, Connecticut College, New London, and others. Has danced, lectured, and taught at colleges throughout the U.S. Has also appeared on television programs and had an acting-dancing role in the off-Broadway musical *The Crystal Heart* (1960). Her dances are frequently satirical comments on human foibles. Some of the best known are *The Glyph, Story of Love from Fear to Flight, Twilight of a Flower, Fall of a Leaf.* Was a recipient of a grant from the Lena Robbins Foundation (see FOUNDATIONS, PHILANTHROPIC) for choreography (1960).

Livry, Emma (1842–1862), French ballerina of the Paris Opéra. She was a pupil and protégée of Maria Taglioni, who watched over her development like a second mother, hoping to see her art flower again in Livry. Taglioni staged the ballet *Le Papillon* (1860) as a vehicle to display Livry's talent, providing the young dancer with her first great triumph. During a rehearsal of the ballet *La Muette de Portici,* Livry's ballet skirt caught fire from a gas jet which was hanging from a piece of scenery; she died eight months later.

Ljung, Viveka, Swedish dancer, b. 1935. Entered Royal Swedish Ballet School (1942); was accepted into the company (1952); danced solo parts, among them Miss Julie in Birgit Cullberg's ballet of the same name. Left the Royal Swedish Ballet to join the American Ballet Theatre (1961). Joined the Nederlands Nationaal Ballet (1962).

Llanto. Modern trio dance; chor.: Sophie Maslow; music: traditional (recordings); costumes: Edythe Gilfond.

Lloyd, Gweneth, English teacher, choreographer, b. Eccles, Lancs., 1901. Studied dance at Liverpool Physical Training College and the Ginner-Mawer School of Dance and Drama in London. In 1938 she and Betty Farrally founded the Canadian School of Ballet in Winnipeg, which later opened other branches, and the same year founded the Winnipeg (later Royal Winnipeg) Ballet, Canada's first professional company. Between 1939 and 1958, Gweneth Lloyd choreographed thirty-five ballets for her company, the best known being *The Wise Virgins* (1942), *Finishing School* (1942), *Chapter 13* (1947), *Visages* (1949), *The Shooting of Dan Mc-*

Grew (1950), *Shadow on the Prairie* (1952). The last named was filmed by the National Film Board of Canada. In 1961 she won a Senior Fellowship Award for study from the Canada Council. Currently teaching.

Lloyd, Margaret (1887–1960), American writer and dance critic, b. South Braintree, Mass., d. Brookline, Mass. Dance critic of *Christian Science Monitor* from 1936 until her death. She was the wife of Leslie A. Sloper, music and drama editor of *Christian Science Monitor* (d. 1949). Previous to Margaret Lloyd's appointment as dance critic she had been feature writer and film critic for the paper for many years. She wrote for many periodicals and encyclopedias and was the author of the *Borzoi Book of Modern Dance* (1949), the best informed book on the subject of the period.

Lloyd, Maude, dancer and critic. b. Cape Town, South Africa. She was a pupil of Marie Rambert and a member of her company from its earliest days; première danseuse (1936–40). Also was member of Markova-Dolin Ballet and London Ballet (1938–41). She created roles in many Antony Tudor and Andrée Howard ballets, the best known being Caroline (*Lilac Garden*), solo (*Dark Elegies*), Italian Ballerina (*Gala Performance*), Chatelaine (*La Fête Etrange*). Now writes on ballet in the London *Observer* with her husband Nigel Gosling, under the pseudonym Alexander Bland.

Lloyd, Norman, composer, b. **Pottsville,** Pa., 1909. B.A. and M.A., N.Y. Univ. He studied piano with Robert Braun and Abbey Whiteside; composition with Vincent Jones and Aaron Copland. His long-time association with the dance includes playing and conducting for Elna Lillbach, Martha Graham, Doris Humphrey, Charles Weidman, Hanya Holm, Martha Hill, Bessie Schonberg. He has composed a number of dance works, including *Panorama* (Martha Graham), *Dances of Work and Play* (Hanya Holm), *Quest* (Charles Weidman), *To the Dance, Inquest, Lament for Ignacio Sanchez Mejias, Invention* (Doris Humphrey), *La Malinche, Dialogues, Interlude for the Indecent* (José Limón), *Restless Land* (a choral ballet for Martha Hill). With his wife, Ruth Lloyd, has developed a course in Rhythmic Training for Dancers which they have taught at N.Y. Univ., Barnard College, Sarah Lawrence College, Bennington School of the Dance, Connecticut College School of the Dance. His dance music, published by Orchesis Publications, includes *Accompaniments for Modern Dance, Restless Land* (for chorus and piano), *Five Dance Pieces* (piano solo). Has written articles on music and dance for *Journal of Health and Physical Education, Juilliard Review,* and *Dance Observer.* In addition to his work in the dance field he has written musical scores for documentary and experimental films, has published various compositions, and taught on the music faculties of N.Y. Univ. and Sarah Lawrence College. Since 1946 has served on the music faculty of Juilliard School of Music, of which he was also director of education (1946–49). Director for Arts, Rockefeller Foundation, since Feb. 1, 1965.

Lommi, Enrique, Argentine dancer, b. Buenos Aires; m. Olga Ferri. Graduate of Teatro Colón Ballet School. Joined corps de ballet of Teatro Colón (1945); two years later was promoted to soloist; became premier danseur (1949). Repertoire includes *The Prodigal Son, Rouge et Noir, Jeux des Cartes, Orpheus, The Three-Cornered Hat, Swan Lake, Giselle, Joan von Zarissa, Capriccio Espagnol,* and others. Created the leading role in the Argentine ballet *Estancia* (1952); was invited to dance with the Berliner Ballett in Europe under the direction of Tatiana Gsovska (1959). Has staged dances for several Argentine films. Danced Siegfried in Jack Carter's *Swan Lake* (1963).

London Ballet, The, company founded in 1938 by Antony Tudor with dancers Hugh Laing, Peggy van Praagh, Maude Lloyd, Gerd Larsen, Charlotte Bidmead, Pauline Clayden, Sylvia Hayden, David Paltenghi, Guy Massey. The company first gave joint performances with Agnes de Mille (June, 1938). In Dec. it began to give regular performances in Toynbee Hall. In the repertoire of the London Ballet were *Judgment of Paris, Gallant Assembly, Soirée Musicale,* and *Gala Performance,* created for the company by Tudor; some Tudor ballets already produced by Ballet Rambert; Keith Lester's *Pas des Déesses,* Frank Staff's *The Seasons,* Andrée Howard's *Fête Étrange,* and others. The outbreak of World War II and subsequent shortage of male dancers led to the combining of London Ballet with Ballet Rambert into the Rambert-London Ballet (June, 1940). This arrangement continued until Sept., 1941, when the group was disbanded.

London Ballet (Walter Gore's), English ballet company launched in Edinburgh, Aug. 1961, directed by Walter Gore. Since its formation has toured in England and abroad with Michael Pilkington as musical director. The company's repertoire includes *Les Sylphides, Swan Lake* (Act 2), *Giselle,* Walter Gore's version of *The Nutcracker,* and the following modern works (mostly Gore's choreography): *Eaters of Darkness, Night and Silence, The Fair Maid, Light Fantastic, Les Joyeux, Peepshow, Shindig, Rencontre.* The company is led by Paula Hinton, Walter Gore, Alexis Rassine, Jane Evans, Robin Haig, Vicky Carriss, Barry Wilkinson, Harry Haythorne.

London Morning. Ballet in 1 act; chor.: Jack Carter; libretto and commissioned music: Noel Coward, orch. by Gordon Jacob; décor: William Constable; costumes: Norman MacDowell. First prod.: London's Festival Ballet, Festival Hall, London, July 14, 1959, with Jeanette Minty (American Girl), John Gilpin (The Sailor), Anton Dolin (The Gentleman in the Bath Chair), tourists, and others sightseeing in London. The ballet is conceived as a humorous work about summertime tourists in London.

London's Festival Ballet. See FESTIVAL BALLET, LONDON'S.

Longway Set, type of American square dance in which the dancers form into two lines with partners facing each other (ladies in one line, men in the other). An example of this is the Virginia Reel. See SQUARE DANCE.

Look at Lightning, A, modern dance work; chor.: Martha Graham; music: Halim El-Dabh; décor: Ming Cho Lee; costumes: Martha Graham. First prod.: Martha Graham Dance Company, Broadway Theatre, N.Y., Mar 5, 1962, with Matt Turney, Bertram Ross, Richard Kuch, Robert Powell. Inspiration in the shape of a beautiful young woman strikes suddenly, unexpectedly, and fleetingly—as does lightning—in adolescence, youth, and maturity, and each responds in its own way.

Lopez, Pilar, contemporary Spanish dancer. Sister of Argentinita with whom she danced in Europe, South America and U.S. until Argentinita's death (1945). Formed her own company (1946) with José Greco and Manolo Vargas, both formerly with Argentinita, and made a fresh start in Madrid. Continues to tour although Greco, Vargas, and Roberto Ximenez, who joined the company in 1950 when Greco left, have long since formed their own companies.

Lopokova, Lydia. See LOPOUKHOVA, LYDIA.

Lopoukhova, Lydia (also spelled Lopokova) (Lady Keynes), dancer of the Russian Imperial Ballet, b. 1891. Was graduated from the School in 1909; left the

Lydia Lopoukhova (Columbine) with Stanislas Idzikowski (Harlequin) in Fokine's Carnaval.

Imperial Theatre the following year to join the Diaghilev Ballets Russes, and never returned to Russia. Among her roles in the Diaghilev company were *Carnaval* (Columbine), *Petrouchka* (Ballerina), *The Sleeping Beauty* (Aurora, Lilac Fairy, Blue Bird); also created *The Good-Humored Ladies* (Mariuccia), *Parade* (Acrobat), *La Boutique Fantasque* (Can-Can Dancer). She also appeared in Frederick Ashton's *Façade* (Camargo Society, London, 1931); as the Street Dancer in Massine's *Le Beau Danube* (Soirées de Paris, 1924); as Swanilda in the Vic-Wells production of *Coppélia* (London, 1933). In 1925 she married the famous English economist, John Maynard Lord Keynes (d. 1946).

Lopukhov, Andrei (1898–1947), Honored Artist of the RSFSR. Leading Soviet character dancer and teacher. Entered St. Petersburg Imperial School in 1908, graduating in 1916. Was a pupil of Michel Fokine, Mikhail Oboukhov, Paul Gerdt; classmate of Anatole Vilzak, was accepted into the school in spite of extreme myopia, only because his brother Fedor and sisters Yevgenia and Lydia were already well-known dancers. He developed into a brilliant character dancer of a virtuosity and ease that enabled him to concentrate on characterization. Besides numerous national dances in old and new ballets he created many important parts, such as Espada (*Don Quixote*), Nur-Ali (*Fountain of Bakhchisarai*), and, in particular, Mercutio (*Romeo and Juliet*), in which role he remained an unsurpassed performer. He began teaching early and became a leading character teacher, training many outstanding Soviet character dancers. He was co-author of the book *Fundamentals of Character Dancing* (Leningrad, 1939) and lectured at the Leningrad ballet school on the methodology of teaching.

Lopukhov, Fedor, Peoples' Artist of the RSFSR, Soviet choreographer, b. 1886. Entered the St. Petersburg Imperial School in 1896, graduating in 1905. Was a pupil of Nicholas Legat. Soon transferred to Moscow (1907–09). He became interested in choreography very early and was staging individual dances by 1910. Has choreographed for various ballet groups since 1917. Headed ballet of the Kirov Theatre (1922–30; 1944–47; 1955–58); founder and artistic director of the ballet of the Maly (Little) Opera Theatre, Leningrad (1930–35). He choreographed *Ballad of Love* (to Tchaikovsky's *The Seasons*) for that company (1960), retiring shortly afterwards following fifty years service in the theatre. However, he continued choreographing and in 1962 was contemplating several works, among them *The Gypsy* to music selected from Mikhail Glinka, a new version of Stravinsky's *Sacre du Printemps,* a ballet to Modest Mussorgky's *Pictures from an Exhibition, Organ-Grinders* (Scenes of Old St. Petersburg), and a revival of his 1921 version of *The Firebird.* Lopukhov's role in the development of Soviet ballet is all-important. Immediately following the revolution, he was instrumental in preserving and reviving the classic ballets and is still considered one of the greatest experts on the classical heritage. He was also the leader of the modern Leningrad choreographers of the early 1920's. It was Lopukhov who introduced elements of the acrobatic into ballet and who began breaking many conventions, combining classic dance with new movements either borrowed from sports and acrobatics or newly invented. He had great influence on the Young Ballet group, among whom George Balanchine was the most active innovator and follower. In his *Ice Maiden* (1927) he introduced beautiful high lifts for Pyotr Gusev and Olga Mungalova which became a model for many Soviet choreographers. Choreographed the first version of *Taras Bulba* (1940). He was the first to use the 1877 score for his revival of *Swan Lake* (1945) and to make von Rothbart's role one for a dancer rather than a mime. In his last period as director of the Kirov Ballet he encouraged young choreographers which led directly to the production of *The Stone Flower* by Yuri Grigorovich and the birth of a new choreographer. He is the only artist to receive from the Soviet government the title of Honored Ballet Master. All leading Soviet choreographers have been his pupils or come under his influence. He is the brother of Andrei Lopukhov, Yevgenia Lopukhova (1884–1941) and Lydia Lopukhova. Author of the book *Paths of a Ballet Master* (Berlin, 1925), in which he summed up his views on the art of choreography. His autobiography *Sixty Years in Ballet* was published in 1966.

Lorin, André, conductor of the Académie Royale in Paris and officer in charge of the dancing masters to the court (ca. 1700). Collaborating with Feuillet, he invented a system of dance notation.

Loring, Eugene (LeRoy Kerpestein), choreographer and dancer, b. Milwaukee, Wis., 1914. Studied at School of American Ballet, N.Y. Appeared with Michel Fokine's ballet at Lewisohn Stadium, N.Y. (1934, 1935). Member, American Ballet from the time of its organization, including its appearances as official ballet of Metropolitan Opera. Soloist and choreographer, Ballet Caravan, choreographing *Harlequin for President, Yankee Clipper, Billy the Kid, City Portrait.* Soloist, Ballet Theatre (1940–41), for which he revived *Billy the Kid* and choreographed *The Great American Goof.* Organizer, choreographer, and dancer, Dance Players (1941–42), creating the ballets *The Man from Midian, Prairie, The Duke of Sacramento,* as well as reviving some of his old works. Appeared in the play *Madame Sans-Gêne;* had leading role in play *The Beautiful People* by William Saroyan. Currently in Hollywood staging dance numbers for motion pictures and teaching in his American School of Dance. In 1966 staged his ballet *The Sisters* for the San Diego Ballet.

Lorrayne, Vyvyan (Mackay), South African dancer, b. Johannesburg, 1939. Winner of South African Classical Ballet Championships. Member, Durban Centenary Ballet Company (1953). Entered Royal Ballet School (1956). Joined Covent Garden Opera Ballet (1956); transferred to Royal Ballet; soloist since 1957. Dances Lilac Fairy (*The Sleeping Beauty*), White pas de deux (*Les Patineurs*), Prelude (*Les Sylphides*), Fairy Summer (Frederick Ashton's *Cinderella*), and others.

Losch, Tilly (Ottilia Ethel Leopoldine; form. Countess of Caernarvon); dancer, actress, choreographer, b. Vienna, 1907. Studied in Vienna Opera Ballet School from age of six; graduated into the ballet and had her first solo when she created Princess Teaflower in *Schlagobers* (1924), with Richard Strauss conducting. Her first dramatic part was in *Leonce and Lena* at Vienna Burgtheater. Was First

Fairy in Max Reinhardt's *A Midsummer Night's Dream,* for which she created the choreography (Salzburg, 1927); gave recitals with Harald Kreutzberg the same summer. Came to America with Reinhardt, choreographing and dancing for him; also gave recital with Kreutzberg (1928). Ballerina, Les Ballets 1933, which her first husband (Edward James) financed for seasons in Paris and London and for which she created the leading role in *Errante* and the dancing Anna in George Balanchine's original version of Kurt Weill's *Seven Deadly Sins.* Appeared in many musicals in London and N.Y., being noted particularly for her "hand dances." Mimed and danced the role of the Nun in Reinhardt's *The Miracle* (1932). Appeared in the film *The Good Earth;* choreographed the dances (and danced) for the films *Duel in the Sun* (1945) and *Song of Schéhérazade* (1946). Is now a successful painter.

Lost Illusions. A Soviet ballet; music: Boris Asafiev; chor.: Rostislav Zakharov. First prod.: Kirov Theatre, Leningrad, 1936, with Galina Ulanova, Tatiana Vecheslova, and Vakhtang Chabukiani. This work is based on Honoré de Balzac's novel of the same name.

Lotufo, Aldo, Brazilian dancer, b. Cuiabá, 1926. Educated at high school and Escola Nacional de Arquitetura (National School of Architecture). Began his dance studies (1947) under Carlos Leite; later studied with Maryla Gremo, Vaslav Veltchek, Tatiana Leskova, Eugenia Feodorova. Made his professional debut with Ballet da Juventude (1948). Joined Teatro Municipal of Rio de Janeiro (1950); promoted to soloist (1953); first dancer (1956). Dances both classics and modern repertoire. Won critics' award as best dancer of the year (1959).

Louis, Murray (Murray Louis Fuchs), American modern dancer and choreographer, b. New York City, 1926. After one year at San Francisco State College, went to N.Y. and received his Bachelor of Science degree at N.Y. Univ. (1951). His dance studies began with Ann Halprin on the West Coast (1947), continued with Colorado College summer course (1948) and at Henry Street Playhouse (from 1949). Has appeared in all Alwin Nikolais' productions since 1951, including seven television performances on the "Steve Allen Show" and three Montreal programs. His own choreographic works include (solos for himself), *Little Men* and *Antechamber* (1953), *Man in Chair* and *Figure in Grey* (1956), *Rialto* (1960), and others; group works include *Bach Suite* (1956) (televised by Canadian Broadcasting Company, Montreal, 1959), *Incredible Garden* (1956), *Journal* and *Entre-Acte* (1958), *An Odyssey* (1960), *Signal* (1961), *Facets,* and *Caligraph for Martyrs,* a revised version of *Signal*

American modern dancer Murray Louis in his Landscapes.

(1962), and others. He is a staff member of Henry St. Playhouse (since 1951), assistant to Nikolais, and director of Young Peoples' Division. He has taught special courses at a number of colleges.

Louis XIV (1638–1715), King of France (1643–1715), known as the "Sun King." During his reign the arts were greatly advanced. Interested in the dance, he himself often danced in the ballets produced for court fêtes. In 1661 he granted permission to a group of ballet masters to establish an Academy of Dancing which led to the establishment of the Royal Academy of Music and Dance (now the Paris Opéra).

Loup, Le (The Wolf). Ballet in 1 act; chor.: Roland Petit; music: Henri Dutilleux; book: Jean Anouilh and Georges Neveux; décor: Jean Carzou. First prod.: Ballets de Paris de Roland Petit, Théâtre de l'Empire, Paris, Mar. 17, 1953, with Violette Verdy (Bride), Roland Petit (The Wolf), Claire Sombert (Gypsy), George Reich (Husband). This fantastic story has the cruelty and gentleness found in many fairy tales. A young husband, running off with a gypsy girl, persuades his bride that he has actually been transformed into a wolf. At first afraid, she is won over by the kindness of the wild animal the husband has tricked into taking his place, and learns to love him for his sweetness and courage. But the villagers, discovering they are living with a wolf in their midst, decide to kill him.

Love Duet. Ballet in 1 act; chor.: Meriel Evans; music: Hector Berlioz (from *Les Troyens à Carthage*); costumes: Alix Stone. First prod.: Sunday Ballet Club, Dec. 13, 1959, with Vyvyan Lorrayne and Derek Rencher; revived by Western Theatre Ballet, with Hazel Merry and Dennis Griffith.

Love, the Sorcerer. See AMOR BRUJO, EL.

Low Dancer. See EUKINETICS.

Lozano, Amalia, Argentine dancer, choreographer, teacher, b. Buenos Aires, 1926. Graduate of Conservatorio de Música y Danza; studied dance with Dora del Grande, Esmée Bulnes, Nina Verchinina, Igor Schwezoff, Vaslav Veltchek, Yekaterina de Galantha, Otto Werberg, Vassili Lambrinos. Joined the corps de ballet of Teatro Colón (1941); the following year George Balanchine gave her the role of Polyhymnia in *Apollon Musagète*. In 1943 she danced with the Original Ballet Russe. Was first dancer of Teatro Municipal, Rio de Janeiro, under the direction of Igor Schwezoff (1944–49); then followed engagements with Vassili Lambrinos company (1950), appearance in the Argentine film *Pájaros de Cristal* (1955), Lambrinos' ballet *Contrepoint d'Amour* (1957), and *The Nutcracker* (1958). In 1959 she and Nestor Perez Fernandez founded their own company, Ballet de Camara Argentino, with which she performs. She does choreography for television shows, for Ballet del Sur, and for her own company. Since 1953 she also teaches professional dancers.

Ludlow, Conrad, dancer, b. Hamilton, Mont., 1935; m. Joyce Feldman. Studied dance in San Francisco with Willam, Harold, and Lew Christensen at San Francisco School of Ballet, graduating into the San Francisco Ballet, his first creation being the Student in *Con Amore* (1953); promoted to principal dancer in 1955. Creations included Paris (*Masque of Beauty and the Shepherd,* 1955), Death (*Tarot,* 1955), Hunter (*The Dryad,* 1956), all choreographed by Lew Christensen. Principal dancer, San Francisco Opera Ballet (1956). Joined New York City Ballet (1957) and after a few months began his Army service, rejoining the company end of 1959. Promoted to soloist (fall, 1960); leading soloist (summer, 1961). Created one of the four male roles in *Liebeslieder Walzer* (1960), Titania's Cavalier and leading male dancer in Act 2 pas de deux (*A Midsummer Night's Dream,* 1961), and others. Also dances a large repertoire of solo roles.

Luipart, Marcel (Fenchel Luipart), German dancer, b. 1915 in Mülhausen, Alsace. Studied with Nicholas Legat, Eugenia Edouardova, Laurent Novikov, Victor Gsovsky, Major engagements include assignments in Düsseldorf, Hamburg, Berlin, Munich (1935–36); Ballets de Monte Carlo (1936); Milan and Rome (1940); Derra de Moroda Ballet, Frankfurt a/M. Ballet master in Munich, Bonn, Essen, Cologne, until 1961. Has choreographed *Abraxas* (Egk), *Orpheus* (Stravinsky), *Don Juan* (Richard Strauss), and others.

Luisillo (Luis Pérez Davila), dancer, b. Mexico City, 1928. Studied both classic and Spanish dance in Mexico City and was discovered by Carmen Amaya who took him with her to Spain (1948). Had his first big successes in her company in Paris and London that year, with his partner Teresa. He and Teresa then formed their own company with which they toured. It was disbanded following its tour of the U.S. (1954). Luisillo then formed his own group, Luisillo and his Theatre of the Spanish Dance which, since 1956, has toured almost all over the world. In addition to the classic Spanish and Flamenco dances in which he excels, he has introduced a new style to Spanish dance with his own choreography, based on the traditional dance vocabulary and using Spanish music and sounds. This style has been employed in a series of dramatic works, among the best being *The Prisoner and the Rose, The Blind Man, Luna de Sangro, The Awaiting, Sanlucar de Barrameda.*

Lukom, Yelena, Honored Art Worker of the RSFSR, Soviet ballerina, b. 1891. A pupil of Michel Fokine, she was graduated from the St. Petersburg School in 1909. Danced with Diaghilev Ballets Russes; promoted to soloist (1912). Although she was trained before the revolution, Lukom actually became the first ballerina of Soviet ballet, being promoted to that rank in 1918 and being principal ballerina of the Kirov company for many years after. Her importance was connected with the new elements introduced by her and her partner, Boris Shavrov, into Soviet ballet. They were the first to use daring high lifts of a semi-acrobatic nature, especially in their concert repertoire. At the same time Lukom was a perfect classic ballerina, and her *Giselle* was unforgettable. She was also an excellent actress, creating Tao-Hoa in the first Leningrad version of *The Red Poppy* (1929). She retired in 1941, having been partnered during her career by Vakhtang Chabukiani and Konstantin Sergeyev. Since her retirement as a dancer she has worked as rehearsal ballet mistress of the Kirov ballet and has influenced a whole generation of dancers, particularly Inna Zubkovskaya.

Lully, Jean Baptiste (1632–1687), musician, composer and dancer, b. Florence, Italy. The son of a wealthy miller, he was christened Giovanni Batista Lulli. He was taken to the court of Louis XIV of France as a dancer and violinist and there changed his name to the French form. At first he served as garçon de chambre to Louise d'Orleans; later danced in *Ballet de la Nuit* (1653). He appeared in a number of ballets with Louis XIV with whom he was on friendly terms. He was instrumental in creating and developing the Académie Royale de la Musique, of which he became director, stage manager, and conductor (1672). Lully composed the music for many ballets, conducted the orchestra at the Académie and composed popular songs. He believed a ballet should be an integrated whole, a unit rather than a string of disconnected dances. Among his collaborators were the designer Bérain, the dancer Charles Beauchamp, and the poets Benserade, Racine, and Molière.

Lully composed the entrées for many of Molière's plays, starting in 1664 with *Le Mariage Forcé,* in which he and Beauchamp danced. Lully's ballets included *Cadmus et Hermione, Proserpine, Isis,* and others.

Lumley, Benjamin (1811–1874), English author and lawyer. In charge of finances at Her Majesty's Theatre, London (1836–41), and its manager from 1842 until it closed in 1858. He produced the *Pas de Quatre* at the theatre in 1845. Author of a volume of memoirs, *Reminiscences* (1864).

Lunnon, Robert, contemporary dancer, teacher, choreographer, b. Bristol, England; m. Doreen Tempest. Trained at Sadler's Wells School of Ballet (1944–47). Danced with Sadler's Wells (now Royal) Ballet (1947–49), rejoining after service in the Royal Air Force. Because of his height, he was transferred to Sadler's Wells Theatre Ballet to partner Svetlana Beriosova in *Swan Lake* and *The Nutcracker* (1951). Headed the faculty of the Turkish State Ballet School, Ankara (1952–55), which had been founded by Dame Ninette de Valois; ballet master of Norwegian Ballet, Oslo (1955–57). Has taught in Chicago since 1957 and was artistic director of Regional Ballet Ensemble of Chicago and of the Allegro American Ballet Company (see REGIONAL BALLET), for which he has choreographed several works and staged productions of the standard classic repertoire. Returned to England in 1966.

Lynch Town. Modern group dance; chor. and costumes: Charles Weidman (from his suite *Atavisms*); music: Lehman Engel. First prod.: Guild Theatre, N.Y., Jan. 26, 1936.

Lynham, Deryck (1913–51), English writer on ballet. Educated in France. One of the founders of the Ballet Guild (1942) and a Trustee of the London Archives of the Dance. Author of *Ballet Then and Now* (1947), and *The Chevalier Noverre* (1950).

Lynne, Gillian (Pyrke), English dancer, teacher, choreographer, b. Bromley, 1926. Studied with Madeleine Sharp, Royal Academy of Dancing, and at Cone-Ripman School. With Arts Theatre Ballet (1940); Ballet Guild (1942); Sadler's Wells (now Royal) Ballet (1943–51), becoming soloist. From 1951 principal dancer in many musicals and revues, most notably taking the Gwen Verdon role in *Can-Can.* She is leading exponent of modern stage dancing and contributor of articles on the subject to the *Dancing Times.* Choreographed *The Owl and the Pussycat* for Western Theatre Ballet (1962). Spent a month in N.Y. (May, 1963), observing the American modern dance in the classroom and on stage.

Lyon, Annabelle (Mrs. Julius Borah), dancer and teacher, b. New York City, of Russian parentage. Studied dance with Michel Fokine, Leon Fokine, George Balanchine, Anatole Vilzak, Alexandra Fedorova, Pierre Vladimirov. Member, American Ballet (from 1935) and Ballet Caravan. Danced in the film *Goldwyn Follies* (1937); musical *Great Lady* (1938). Ballerina, Ballet (now American Ballet) Theatre from its inception to 1943, creating Youngest Sister (*Pillar of Fire*), Page (*Bluebeard*), The Lustful One (*Three Virgins and a Devil*), Butterfly (*Aleko*). She also danced in *Giselle, Les Sylphides, Le Spectre de la Rose,* Fanny Cerito (*Pas de Quatre*), Caroline (*Lilac Garden*), French Ballerina (*Gala Performance*), and others. Principal dancer in musical *Carousel* (1945–47). Now teaching in N.Y.

Lyonnois, Marie, danseuse at the Paris Opéra. Made her debut in 1746. She was known for ability to do pirouettes and is credited with the invention of the gargouillade.

Lyric Suite. Modern dance work; chor.: Anna Sokolow; music: Alban Berg's quartet of the same name. First prod.: YM–YWHA, N.Y., on the second annual concert series presented by the New Dance Group, Mar. 30–Apr. 4, 1954, with Donald McKayle (Allegretto), Beatrice Seckler (Allegro), Eve Beck, Jeff Duncan (Largo), Mary Anthony (Andante). An abstract work in the modern idiom which explores the emotions in terms of dance. It was originally staged for Ballet de Bellas Artes, Mexico City (1953).

Lysistrata. Ballet in 3 acts; chor.: Gustav Blank; music and book: Boris Blacher; décor: Ita Maximova. First prod.: Berlin Festival, Sept. 30, 1951, with Ingeborg Höhnisch (Lysistrata), Friedl Herfurth (Myrrha), Jockel Stahl (Lysistratos), Rainer Köchermann (Kinesias). In accordance with the comedy of Aristophanes on which the ballet is based, the married women of Athens refuse their attention to their husbands, despite some temptations, thus forcing their husbands to make peace with Sparta. A ballet based on the Aristophanes comedy has also been staged by Antony Tudor (London), Rezsö Brada (Budapest), Lilo Gruber (to music by Richard Mohaupt, Berlin).

M

Mabry, Iris, contemporary modern dancer, choreographer, teacher, b. Clarksville, Tenn.; B.A. Smith College. Studied dance at Neighborhood Playhouse, N.Y., Bennington College School of the Dance, Vt. Audition winner YMHA dance series (Feb., 1943); solo debut, Times Hall, May, 1946; appeared on Ballet Society programs (Jan. 13, 14, 1947). Presented many solo performances of works choreographed by herself, usually to the music of her composer-pianist husband, Ralph Gilbert, who is also her accompanist. Among her best known solos are *Sarabanade, Dilemma, Rally, Litany, Cycle, Witch, Dreams, Rhapsody, Doomsday.* Now appears but rarely in N.Y., but danced *Doomsday* at the annual Freda Miller benefit performance, YMHA, May 4, 1963.

Macdonald, Brian, Canadian dancer, choreographer and teacher, b. Montreal, 1928. B.A., McGill Univ., Montreal, and for two years after graduation was a music critic. His dance training was with Gerald Crevier and Elizabeth Leese. When National Ballet of Canada was formed, he became a charter member, leaving after two years because of a serious arm injury. Has choreographed for variety shows in Montreal, Winnipeg, and Quebec; created six major works for CBS television between 1954 and 1958 and two series of children's television shows with the Royal Winnipeg Ballet. Four of his ballets, *The Darkling, Les Whoops-de-Doo, A Court Occasion,* and *Prothalamion* are in the repertoire of the Royal Winnipeg Ballet. Has also directed and choreographed both for stage and television many Canadian productions of famous musicals, including *Guys and Dolls, Pajama Game, Damn Yankees, Carousel, Oklahoma!* and others; also *My Fur Lady,* the McGill Univ. skit on *My Fair Lady* that played in Canada for eighteen months. Was on the staff of the Banff School of the Fine Arts and is dance teacher and director at the National Theatre School. In Mar. 1962, received a Canada Council grant for study in N.Y., Europe, and the Soviet Union. While in the U.S. he staged *Time Out of Mind,* a ballet to music by Paul Creston for the Robert Joffrey Ballet (premièred at the company's Workshop performance Sept. 28 at Fashion Institute of Technology, N.Y.). In the spring of 1963 he staged *Prothalamion* (under the title *Hymn*) for the Norwegian Ballet, Oslo (with Hanne Thorstenson and Palle Damm). Appointed Director of Swedish Royal Ballet, Stockholm, for season 1964–65. He was married to Olivia Wyatt, a soloist of Royal Winnipeg Ballet (d. 1959). Married Annette Weidersheim-Paul, a soloist of the Royal Swedish Ballet (Dec. 20, 1965). On April 16, 1966, the Royal Winnipeg Ballet presented *Rose Latulippe,* choreographed by Macdonald, at the Shakespeare Festival Theatre, Stratford, Ont., the first evening-length Canadian ballet with Miss Wiedersheim-Paul in the title role. Since June, 1967, director of Harkness Ballet, N.Y.

Mackerras, Alan Charles, composer, b. Schenectady, N.Y., 1925. Educated Sydney (Australia) Grammar School, King's School, Conservatory of Music, all in Sydney; Academy of Music, Prague, Czechoslovakia. Conductor and arranger of music, lecturer. Conductor, Sadler's Wells Theatre (1948–54); British Broadcasting Corporation Concert Orchestra (1954–56). Now freelance and guest conductor. Arranged the Arthur Sullivan music for *Pineapple Poll* and the Giuseppe Verdi music for *The Lady and the Fool.* He is a specialist in the interpretation of baroque and contemporary music.

Mackinnon, Kaye, contemporary dancer, choreographer, company director, b. Boston, Mass. A Phi Beta Kappa of Tufts Univ., she studied ballet with Olga Preobrajenska, Mathilde Kchessinska, Vera Trefilova, and others in Paris; modern dance at the Mary Wigman School and with Harald Kreutzberg; Spanish with Maria del Villar and others in Spain. Made her professional debut with Bronislava Nijinska's Russian Ballet company at Théâtre du Châtelet, Paris (1934), then travelled in Europe for several years with French musical comedies, acting and dancing. Married Luis Pacheco (N.Y., 1939), a leading symphonic conductor and composer of Peru, and went to live in Lima, Peru in 1940, giving recitals and directing the school of ballet of the Association of Amateur Artists. Presented the first evening of ballets ever inspired by Peruvian themes, *Selva, Sierra y Costa* (Jungle, Mountain and Coast), in 1942, for which her husband composed the music; the libretto was by Elvira Miró Quesada and designs and production were by members of the Association of Amateur Artists. Founded her own school, Escuela del Ballet Peruano, in 1946 from which, in 1948, the professional company Ballet Peruano of which she is director, choreographer, and dancer was formed. She has received silver medals and diplomas from Municipality of Callao (1957), Municipality of Lima (1959), Municipality of Trujillo, and Institute of Hispanic Culture, Madrid (1961).

Kaye Mackinnon with partner in La Moza Mala, *a Peruvian ballet.*

Macleary, Donald, Scottish dancer, b. Glasgow, 1937. Studied with Sheila Ross (1950–51), Sadler's Wells School (1951). Joined Sadler's Wells Theatre Ballet (1954); promoted to soloist (1955), before transferring to Sadler's Wells (now Royal) Ballet of which he is currently a principal dancer. His repertoire includes the leading male roles in the classic ballets, Colas (*La Fille Mal Gardée*), Cousin (*The Invitation*), and the following creations: Young Lover (*The Burrow*), Bridegroom (*Le Baiser de la Fée*—Kenneth MacMillan version), Haemon (*Antigone*), Jabez (Alfred Rodriguez' *Jabez and the Devil*), male lead (*Diversions*), Knight (Andrée Howard's *La Belle Dame Sans Merci*), and others. He has also appeared as Romeo (Kenneth MacMillan's *Romeo and Juliet*), and in the pas de deux with Svetlana Beriosova in the Royal Ballet's *La Bayadère*.

MacLeish, Archibald, American poet and dramatist, b. 1892. He wrote the book for the ballet *Union Pacific,* staged by Leonide Massine to music by Nicholas Nabokov, (1934).

MacMillan, Kenneth, Scottish dancer and choreographer, b. Dunfermline, 1930. Studied at Sadler's Wells School; entered Sadler's Wells Theatre Ballet (1946), Sadler's Wells (now Royal) Ballet (1948) where he danced *Florestan and His Sisters* pas de trois (*The Sleeping Beauty*), pas de trois, with Beryl Grey and John Field (*Ballet Imperial*), one of the Prince's four attendants (Frederick Ashton's *Cinderella*), and others. Returned to Sadler's Wells Theatre Ballet (1952), making debut as choreographer with *Somnambulism* (1953) with Sadler's Wells Choreographers' Group. The following year another ballet for this group, *Laiderette,* was staged and later taken into the Ballet Rambert repertoire. For Sadler's Wells Theatre Ballet he created *Danses Concertantes* and *The House of Birds* (1955), *Solitaire* (1956). For the Royal Ballet he staged the following works: *Noctambules* (1956), *The Burrow* and *Agon* (1958), *Le Baiser de la Fée* (1960), *The Invitation* and *Diversions* (1961), *The Rite of Spring* (1962), *Symphony* (1963), *Song of the Earth* (1966). Created his first full-evening ballet, *Romeo and Juliet* (1965). For American Ballet Theatre he created *Journey* (to Béla Bartók's *Music for Strings, Percussion and Celeste*), and *Winter's Eve* (to Benjamin Britten's *Variations on a Theme of Frank Bridge*), both in 1957. *The Burrow, Danses Concertantes,* and *Solitaire* were staged in 1961 for the Royal Danish Ballet. Guest choreographer, Stuttgart State Opera Ballet (spring, 1965). MacMillan was resident choreographer of the Royal Ballet through the 1965–66 season; currently resident choreographer of the German Opera Ballet, West Berlin.

Mad Tristan. Surrealist ballet in 2 scenes; chor.: Leonide Massine; music: Richard Wagner (excerpts from *Tristan and Isolde,* orch. by Ivan Boutnikov); book, décor, and costumes: Salvador Dali. First prod.: Ballet International, International Theatre, N.Y., Dec. 15, 1944, with a cast including Francisco Moncion (Tristan), Toni Worth (Isolde), Lisa Maslova (Chimera of Isolde). This surrealist version of the drama of Tristan and Isolde made little sense as a whole but had some exciting moments. Dali's décor was considered the most interesting part of the ballet and dominated both the choreography and the plot. The work did not survive its first season.

Madame Chrysanthème. Ballet in 1 act and 5 scenes; chor.: Frederick Ashton; commissioned music: Alan Rawsthorne; décor: Isabel Lambert. First prod.: Sadler's Wells (now Royal) Ballet, Royal Opera House, Covent Garden, London, Apr. 1, 1955, with Elaine Fifield (Chrysanthème), Alexander Grant (Pierre), Ray Powell (Marriage Broker). The story is based on the novel by Pierre Loti and tells of a sailor who, while on shore leave in Japan, contracts a for-the-duration-of-the-leave marriage with a Japanese girl. Returning for a last glimpse of her after he has said good-bye, he is disillusioned to find her chinking his money and testing it to make sure it is genuine.

Mademoiselle Angot. See MAM'ZELLE ANGOT.

Madsen, Jørn, soloist of the Royal Danish Ballet, b. Copenhagen, 1939. Entered Royal Danish Ballet School (1949); accepted into the company (1958); made soloist (1961). While still in school danced in *Lunefulde Lucinda* (Capricious Lucinda, 1954) and in *Romeo and Juliet* (1955). Dances leading roles in *Peter and the Wolf, Romeo and Juliet, Festa, La Chalupée, Cyrano de Bergerac, Graduation Ball, Ballet in D, Etudes.*

Magallanes, Nicholas, contemporary American dancer, b. Camargo, Chihuahua, Mexico. Educated in U.S. and studied dance at School of American Ballet, N.Y. Made his professional debut in the Ford Pavilion ballet *A Thousand Times Neigh* at the N.Y. World's Fair (1940); soloist, Ballet Caravan (South American tour, 1941); Littlefield Ballet (1942). With Ballet Russe de Monte Carlo (1943–46), working up from corps de ballet to leading roles, creating Poet (*Night Shadow*), Cléonte (*Le Bourgeois Gentilhomme*), Jean de Brienne (*Raymonda*), and others, and dancing the leading classic male roles. Joined Ballet Society at its inception (1946) and has danced continuously as a premier danseur with that organization which became New York City Ballet. His enormous repertoire includes such important creations as the title role in *Orpheus,* the Poet (*Illuminations*), 2nd movement (*Western Symphony*), Second Intruder (*The Cage*), one of the four male dancers in *Liebeslieder Walzer*), and others; leading roles in *Concerto Barocco, Serenade, Four Temperaments, Symphony in C, Bourée Fantasque,* etc.

Nicholas Magallanes, premier danseur of the N.Y.C. Ballet, in Western Symphony.

Magic Flute, The. Ballet in 1 act; chor. and book: Lev Ivanov; music: Riccardo Drigo. After being presented at the Imperial Ballet School (Mar. 22, 1893), it was produced at the Maryinsky Theatre, St. Petersburg (Apr. 23, 1893) with Michel Fokine in the role of Luke and with Agrippina Vaganova and Serge Legat in the cast. This ballet was in the repertoire of Anna Pavlova's company with Pavlova (Lise), Alexander Volinine (Luke), Enrico Cecchetti (the Marquis). Luke, a country youth, is in love with Lise, a country girl. But the Marquis, a rich landowner, selects Lise as his fiancée and Lise's mother chases Luke away. While the Marquis and everyone else are in Lise's hut, Oberon, disguised as a beggar, gives Luke a magic flute which makes everyone dance when it is played. At the end Oberon reveals himself to the people and forces Lise's mother to agree to the marriage of Lise and Luke. The village celebrates the reunion of the lovers while the Marquis and his retinue leave.

Magriel, Paul, American writer, b. Riga, Latvia, 1906. Educated at Columbia Univ., N.Y. Compiler of *Bibliography of Dancing* (N.Y., 1936) and subsequent Cumulated Supplements through 1940. Author of *Ballet—An Illustrated Outline* (N.Y., 1938); editor of *Nijinsky* (N.Y., 1946); *Pavlova* (N.Y., 1947); *Isadora Duncan* (N.Y., 1947); *Chronicles of the American Dance* (N.Y., 1948). In addition, he is the author of many articles on dance. He was one of the original editors of *Dance Index* and first curator of the Dance Archives of the Museum of Modern Art, N.Y. (1939–42).

Mahler, Gustav (1860–1911), Austrian composer. Composed the song cycle *Kindertotenlieder,* music used by Antony Tudor for his ballet *Dark Elegies* (1937), and *Das Lied von der Erde,* which Tudor used for *Shadow of the Wind* (1948). Pauline Koner also used the final section of *Das Lied von der Erde* for her great solo *The Farewell,* composed in memory of Doris Humphrey.

Mahler, Roni, American dancer, b. New York City, 1942. Studied ballet with Maria Swoboda in her own school and at Ballet Russe de Monte Carlo School of Ballet (1954–60). Joined Ballet Russe de Monte Carlo (1960), rising to soloist rank before joining National Ballet, Washington, D.C. at its inception (1962) as soloist; promoted to leading soloist (Sept., 1963). For this company she created one of the leading roles in Frederic Franklin's *Hommage au Ballet,* Captain of the Amazons (*Con Amore*), Dawn (*Coppélia*), Choleric variation (*Four Temperaments*), Tomboy (Valerie Bettis's *Early Voyagers*), and others; dances Waltz (*Les Sylphides*), *Swan Lake,* etc. Guest soloist, Philadelphia Arts Festival (1962). Has appeared on several "Sing Along With Mitch" television programs (1963–64) in dances arranged by James Starbuck.

Left the company in 1967.

Mahoney, Arthur, contemporary dancer, teacher, choreographer, b. Boston, Mass.; m. Thalia Mara. Studied voice, violin, piano; ballet with Luigi Albertieri, Michel Fokine, Nicholas Legat, Bronislava Nijinska; Spanish dance with Helene Veola and Escudero. Made his debut with Metropolitan Opera Ballet and was a member of the Ida Rubinstein company in Paris (1928). Appeared in vaudeville and musicals in N.Y., and toured with Thalia Mara in the U.S. Was one of the choreographers for the Dance Project of the W.P.A.; also directed the Jacob's Pillow season (1947). Has specialized in the French and English court dance of the 16th, 17th, and 18th centuries. Founded with his wife the School of Ballet Repertory, N.Y. (1948) and, also with her, is co-founder of the National Academy of Ballet, a nonprofit educational institution chartered by the Univ. of the State of N.Y., dedicated to setting high professional standards for ballet teaching in the U.S. Has choreographed several works, among them several for the Ballet Repertory Dancers. Separated from his wife in 1964 and moved to California where he is teaching.

Maillot. French name for tights, said to be derived from the name of their inventor, M. Maillot (d. ca. 1838), who manufactured hosiery for the Paris Opéra in the 19th century.

Maiocchi, Gilda, Italian ballerina, b. Milan, 1925. Graduated from the ballet school of Teatro alla Scala, Milan; appeared in her Passo d'Addio in 1947; promoted to ballerina in 1953. Left the theatre soon after to do freelance work; returned to become assistant ballet mistress.

Maître de Ballet. See BALLET MASTER.

Makarov, Askold, Peoples' Artist of the RSFSR, Soviet dancer, b. 1925. Was graduated from the Leningrad school in 1943; began dancing in the company in Dec., 1942. Created the role of Ostap in the Boris Fenster version of *Taras Bulba*

(1955), the title role in *Spartacus* (1956), and the Soviet Fisherman in *Coast of Hope* (1959). His repertoire also includes Danila (*The Stone Flower*), both Vaslav and Guirei (*The Fountain of Bakhchisarai*), Va Lie-chen (*The Red Flower*), Philippe (*Flames of Paris*), Prince Charming (*Cinderella*), Frondozo (*Laurencia*). He excels in roles of an heroic nature, is a fine dramatic actor and an excellent partner, both in the modern and classic ballets. He is married to Kirov ballet soloist Ninel Petrova.

Makarova, Maria, Russian ballet teacher, b. St. Petersburg, 1885. Graduated from the Russian Imperial Ballet School in 1903 (class of Paul Gerdt). Artist of the Maryinsky Theatre until 1936. Honored Artist of the Republic (1934). Appointed teacher of the State Theatre in Kiev (1936). After World War II, went to Paris and then to Brazil (1955). Currently teacher and ballet mistress of Ballet Rio de Janeiro.

Makarova, Natalia, ballerina of the Leningrad Kirov Ballet; b. Leningrad, 1940; graduated from the Leningrad Choreographic School (1959). Received Gold Medal at the Second International Ballet Competition at Varna, Bulgaria (1965). Danced her first *Giselle* at the Royal Opera House, Covent Garden, London (summer, 1961), during the first appearance there of the Kirov Ballet. Other ballets include *Swan Lake, Chopiniana* (*Les Sylphides*), *The Sleeping Beauty, Cinderella, Raymonda,* and others.

Make-Up. The art of applying cosmetics to produce the proper appearance of a character as he is seen by the spectators. The essentials of good make-up include the base, such as cold cream, which is applied to protect the skin and must be smooth; the foundation, colored grease paint or liquid powder applied evenly over all the exposed area of skin; lines, used to accentuate eyebrows, to make wrinkles, etc.; highlights, made with light grease paint to give an appearance of fullness where necessary; shadows, made with dark grease paint or eye-shadow to complement highlights; blending or smoothing out the whole effect, usually with theatrical face powder. Other indispensable items in addition to those mentioned are rouge, eyebrow pencils, mascara, lip rouge or lipsticks, cotton, cleansing tissue, orangesticks, powder puffs, etc. In recent years pancake make-up is often used instead of grease paint because it can be applied quickly and easily; false eyelashes are also used instead of mascara. The term make-up is also applied to the cosmetics used.

Malaguena (Sp.). A variety of fandango.

Maletic, Vera, Yugoslav dancer, choreographer, and artistic director of the Studio for Contemporary Dance, Zagreb (her native city). She is the daughter of choreographer Ana Maletic, former head of the State Dance Ensemble Lado and author of books on dance. Her initial dance training was at her mother's school and she studied subsequently at the Art of Movement School, London; received her master's degree from the Univ. of Zagreb. Like her mother she is a pioneer and a leader in the modern dance in Yugoslavia. Since 1958 she has been on the faculty of the State School of Rhythm and Modern Dance, Zagreb, teaching modern dance, choreography, and dance notation and lecturing on history of dance. In addition, she has instituted at the School a dance workshop and a performing group. In 1964 and 1965 she led a modern dance workshop at the International Youth Festival, Bayreuth, West Germany. She is a member of the International Council of Kinetography Laban (I.C.K.L.). In 1966 she spent six months in the U.S. (Feb.–July) during which time she gave a workshop in choreography at the Dance Notation Bureau, attended a course in American Modern Dance at the Extension Division of the Juilliard School of Music's Dance Dept., and visited dance performances and modern dance schools. Her choreographic work is mostly abstract. Among her productions are *Formations* (Ruben Radica), *Equilibres* (Milko Kelemen), *Dessins Commentés* (Kelemen). Her predominant field is telegenic choreography, i.e., most of her productions are first staged for the theatre and later re-worked for television where she finds her largest public. Some of her works are produced by Yugoslav TV (such as *Dessins Commentés*), while *Formations* was the first co-production of TV Zagreb and TV Vienna. Her *Equilibres* was screened at the International Congress on Dance, Ballet, and Pantomime in Television and Films, organized by UNESCO in Aug., 1965 at Salzburg, Austria. It was favorably received by the participants and guests and laudably commented upon by Arne Arnbom, famous producer and director of TV Stockholm who presented the work. From N.Y. Maletic went to England to teach at the Art of Movement Studio, Addlestone, Surrey.

Malinche, La. Modern dance work in 1 scene; chor.: José Limón; music: Norman Lloyd; costumes: Pauline Lawrence. First prod.: José Limón Dance Company, Ziegfeld Theatre, N.Y., Mar. 31, Apr. 1 and 2, 1949, with Limón (El Indio), Pauline Koner (La Malinche), Lucas Hoving (El Conquistador). Malinche, a young and beautiful Mexican Indian, became the companion and interpreter of the conqueror Cortez. Her people looked upon her as a traitor and in their legends punished her until, during the last great revolution, she returned to aid them in their struggle for liberty. Limón tells the story as though it were being performed by the simple people of a Mexican village during a fiesta.

Maly (Little) Opera Theatre of Leningrad, The, established in 1918 in the former Imperial Mikhailovsky Theatre which used to present French drama and comedy and German, French, and Italian opera. Fedor Lopukhov was head of the ballet company assembled (1932–33 season) mainly from dancers graduating from the Evening Course of the Leningrad Ballet School. Within a short time the group had become a strong, professional company famous for its experimental ballets, particularly during the period (1932–35) when Lopukhov was artistic director. He choreographed new versions of *Les Millions d'Arlequin* (*Harlequinade,* 1933) and *Coppélia* (1934). When Leonid Lavrovsky took over from Lopukhov he created *Fadette* (1936), a new version of *La Fille Mal Gardée* (1937), and his version of *The Prisoner of the Caucasus* to music by Boris Asafiev (1938). Boris Fenster was principal choreographer (1935–56), staging *The False Bridegroom* to music by Mikhail Chulaki (1946); *Youth,* considered his most important ballet (1949); *Blue Danube* to music by Johann Strauss (1956), and others. Galina Isayeva, still one of the company's leading dancers, headed the company (1956–60). Pyotr Gusev was leading male dancer from Oct., 1960 to Dec., 1961, earlier having choreographed for the company *Seven Beauties* (to music by Kara Karayev, 1953) and a new version of *Le Corsaire* (1955). The present chief choreographer is Konstantin Boyarsky, a graduate of the Kirov ballet school (1935). Although a young man, he is interested primarily in revivals of old works and has carried out, under the supervision of Fedor Lopukhov, a reconstruction of the authentic 1895 St. Petersburg production of *Swan Lake* (1958), and revivals of *Petrouchka* and *The Firebird.* His original works include *On the Eve* (3 act ballet to part of Turgenev's novel of the same name), Prokofiev's *Classical Symphony* (1961), and Stravinsky's *Orpheus* (1962).

Mam'zelle Angot. Ballet in 3 scenes; chor. and book: Leonide Massine; music: Charles Lecocq, from his comic opera *La*

Fille de Madame Angot; décor: Mstislav Doboujinsky. First prod.: under the title *Mademoiselle Angot* by Ballet (now American Ballet) Theatre, Metropolitan Opera House, N.Y., Oct. 10, 1943, with Leonide Massine (Barber), Nora Kaye (Mam'zelle Angot, later danced by Janet Reed), André Eglevsky (Artist), Rosella Hightower (Aristocrat), Simon Semenoff (Official); restaged by Massine for Sadler's Wells (now Royal) Ballet in décor by André Derain, Royal Opera House, Covent Garden, London, Nov. 26, 1947, with Margot Fonteyn in title role (later danced by Nadia Nerina, among others), Alexander Grant (Barber), Michael Somes (Artist), Moira Shearer (Aristocrat), Franklin White (Official). The Barber in the English production was Alexander Grant's first major creation. A typically complicated comic opera plot in which Mam'zelle Angot falls in love with the Artist, who falls in love with the Aristocrat (mistress of the Official). All ends happily as Mam'zelle Angot discovers that she really loves her faithful Barber after all.

Man from Midian, The. Ballet, chor.: Eugene Loring; music: Stephan Wolpe; book: based on a poem by Winthrop Palmer; décor: James Stewart Morcom; costumes: Felipe Fiocca. First prod.: Dance Players, spring, 1942. The plot of the ballet is a free treatment of the Biblical account of the emergence of Moses as a leader of the Israelites.

Manager. There are various types of managers connected with the business aspect of dance; among them, the manager is a person engaged by a dance company to take care of the business dealings of the organization, i.e. secure bookings, arrange for advertising and publicity, furnish transportation, hire the necessary help such as musicians, stagehands, etc., supervise the box office, etc. A manager should be distinguished from an impresario. A booking manager is a booking agent; a personal manager is a dancer's personal representative or agent (both these agents usually working on a percentage basis); a company manager is a person who handles the business end of the company within the company itself, pays salaries, etc.; a stage manager is a person who runs the show, supervises stagehands, is in charge of light and music cues, occasionally assigns parts, etc. The duties and responsibilities of a manager and a booking agent are often vested in one person, while a company manager occasionally performs some of the duties of a manager. A company manager and a stage manager are salaried employees.

Mancenilha. Ballet in 1 act; book and chor.: Madeleine Rosay; music: Heitor Villa-Lobos (Bachianas Nos. 2 & 4); décor and costumes: Tomás Santa Rosa. First prod.: Teatro Municipal, Rio de Janeiro, Brazil, 1953, with Berta Rozanova (Mancenilha), Johnny Franklin (Caboclo), and Rosemary Brantes, Sebastião Araujo, Dennis Gray, Edmundo Carijo, Mercedes Batista, Ezy Garro, Joan Santos. Maria Angélica and Edgard Deporte danced later the principal roles. The ballet deals with a tale of the Brazilian hinterland. The "cangaceiros" (northern bandits) are returning to the village. Their chief, the Caboclo, is loved by the most beautiful girl of the region. However, at night he meets Mancenilha, according to the legend the intoxicating flower that changes into a woman. Mancenilha seduces the Caboclo and leaves him after a dance during which she toys with his feelings. In despair the Caboclo goes to the local Witch who by sorcery brings back the Mancenilha. Seeing the Caboclo enthralled by this strange passion and thus lost to the gang, the cangaceiros call a "capoeira" (a danced duel) to choose a new leader. After a war dance the bandits seize the Caboclo. He dies poisoned at the feet of the Mancenilha.

Manchester, P. W. (Miss), contemporary editor and critic, b. London. Educated at private schools; studied dance. Interest in ballet began with the Diaghilev Ballets Russes in the late 1920's. Ballet critic for *Theatre World* (1941–43); secretary to Marie Rambert (1944–46). Assumed editorship of a new magazine, *Ballet Today,* published in London (first issue: Mar., 1946). Invited to U.S. as guest editor of *Dance News* (1951); remained as managing editor. N.Y. dance critic, *Christian Science Monitor* (since 1960). Author of *Vic-Wells: A Ballet Progress* (London, 1942); co-author with Iris Morley of *The Rose and the Star* (1948). Contributor to *Ballet Annual* and other dance publications; co-editor, *Dance Encyclopedia.*

Manège. In ballet, an imaginary circle around the outer edge of the visible stage; also a circle described by a dancer moving in fast, short turns around the stage, such as petits tours en manège, déboulés, jetés en tourant, etc.

Manipuri. See HINDU DANCE.

Manon Lescaut. Ballet-pantomime in 3 acts, 5 scenes; chor.: Jean Aumer; book: Eugene Scribe; music: Jacques Halévy; décor: Ciceri; costumes: Lecomte, Lami, Duponchel. Principal dancers were Maria Taglioni, Pauline Montessu, Mademoiselle Ferdinand. Taglioni's pas was choreographed by Filippo Taglioni. The plot is much the same as the opera of the same name.

Mansfield, Portia, dancer and teacher, b. Chicago, Ill., 1887. B.A., Smith College; M.A., 1933; D. Ed., 1955, N.Y.U. Studied dance with Louis Chalif and at Cambridge Normal School of Dance with Luigi Albertieri and Michel Fokine; also with Mme. Theodore, Paris; character dance in Milan; modern dance with Doris Humphrey, Charles Weidman; two seasons of Dalcroze studies; anatomy and research in corrective exercises; one year's study of sculpture at Art Students League, N.Y.; two years' study of 'cello. A member of the Pavley-Oukrainsky Ballet, she has been since 1914 co-director and co-owner (with Charlotte Perry) of the Perry-Mansfield School of the Theatre and Dance, and Camps for girls; also choreographer and director of Portia Mansfield Dancers and later Perry-Mansfield Dancers (four companies which toured for nine seasons in U.S. and Canada). Author of six volumes, *Rhythmic Movement,* a set of books of exercises with music for the exercises by Louis Horst; producer, photographer, distributor of 12 sound-color films on dance and horsemanship.

Mara, Thalia, contemporary dancer, teacher, choreographer, author, b. Chicago, Ill.; m. Arthur Mahoney. Studied music; ballet with Alexandra Maximova, Adolph Bolm, Olga Preobrajenska, Nicholas Legat, Michel Fokine, Ella Daganova; Spanish dance with Veola and Calvol. Made her debut with Ravinia Park Opera Ballets, Chicago (1926–27); soloist, Carina Ari Ballet, Paris and Switzerland (1928). Made concert tours of U.S. and Canada and appeared as featured dancer with St. Louis and Detroit operetta companies. Co-director of Jacob's Pillow (1947). With her husband founded School of Ballet Repertory, N.Y. (1948) and, with him, is co-founder of the National Academy of Ballet. Author of *First Steps in Ballet, Second Steps in Ballet, Third Steps in Ballet, On Your Toes, So You Want to Be a Ballet Dancer.* Separated from husband in 1964.

Maracatú. Ballet in 1 act; chor.: Johnny Franklin; décor: Sorensen. First prod.: Teatro Municipal, Rio de Janeiro, 1961, with a cast headed by Aldo Lotufo, Sandra Dieken, Julia Rodrigues, Johnny Franklin. A colorful stage version of the old and popular Brazilian folklore dance, Maracatú. The ballet is accompanied by percussion.

Maracci, Carmalita, American dancer, choreographer, teacher, b. Montevideo, Uruguay, 1911, of Italian and Spanish extraction. She was brought to the U.S. as a child; studied ballet and the Spanish dance in Calif. She succeeded in working her balletic and Spanish techniques into a personal vocabulary of movement and style of dance. Made her professional debut in Los Angeles, Calif. (1930). Has appeared with own group throughout the U.S. Among her dance compositions are solos *Viva Tu Madre, Nightingale and the Maiden, Etude, Cantine, Fandanguillo, Gavotta Vivace;* trios *Another Fire Dance, Sonate, Portrait in the Raw España, ¿Por Qué? Flamenco;* group dances *Narrative of the Bull Ring, Suite;* the ballet *Circo de España,* choreographed for Ballet Theatre (1951). Currently teaching in Los Angeles.

Marchand, Colette, French dancer, b. Paris, 1925. Pupil of Paris Opéra School, graduating into the company and remaining until 1946. Also studied with Victor Gsovsky, Alexandre Volinine. Ballerina, Metropolitan Ballet (England, 1947). Leading dancer, Ballets de Paris de Roland Petit (1948), creating *L'Oeuf à la Coque* and *Le Combat* (1949), and dancing *Les Demoiselles de la Nuit* after Margot Fonteyn's first few guest performances at the company's opening Paris season. She was hailed as "Les Legs" during the company's first successful N.Y. season. With the same company created leading roles in *Deuil en 24 Heures, Ciné-Bijou, Lady in the Ice* (1953). The same year starred in a stage show *Plein Feu* with Maurice Chevalier. Was a big success in a purely acting role in the motion picture *Moulin Rouge* (1953), directed by John Huston in which José Ferrer played Henri de Toulouse-Lautrec. Toured Japan with Milorad Miskovitch (1955) and joined his company for its South American tour (1959). Danced Roxane in Roland Petit's *Cyrano de Bergerac* (London, 1960). Is often seen on television in Paris and makes guest appearances in opera houses in France and Italy. Starred in the musical *Eugène le Mystérieux,* Châtelet Theatre, Paris (1964). Married to conductor Jacques Bazire.

French ballerina Colette Marchand in Roland Petit's L'Oeuf à la Coque.

Marchowsky, Marie, contemporary American modern dancer and teacher, b. New York City. Studied ballet with Ella Daganova; modern dance at the Martha Graham School, becoming a member and soloist of the Martha Graham Company (1934–40), and dancing in *Primitive Mysteries, American Document,* and others. During same period was soloist with the Anna Sokolow group. Between 1940 and 1945 presented her own works on group programs sponsored by the New Dance League and The American Dance Association. Has presented her own solo programs since 1946, mostly at the YM-YWHA and Henry Street Playhouse. Taught and gave lecture-demonstrations in Paris (1950–51). Has made several television appearances. Some of her best known solos are *Ebb Tide* (original score by Isaac Nemiroff); *Two Portraits: After Toulouse-Lautrec* and *Odalisque; Age of Unreason,* based on the Goya *"Los Caprichos"; Three Amiable Foibles,* and others. Teaches in her own studio in N.Y.

Mardi Gras. Ballet in 1 act; chor.: Andrée Howard; commissioned music: Leonard Salzedo; décor: Hugh Stevenson. First prod.: Sadler's Wells Theatre Ballet, Sadler's Wells Theatre, London, Nov. 26, 1947, with Anne Heaton (The Girl), Donald Britton (The Boy), Nadia Nerina (Circus Dancer), John Cranko (The Pugilist). A young girl caught up in the feverish gaiety of a carnival realizes that her experiences then are the foreshadows of what her future life is to be.

Margolies, Linda. See HODES, LINDA.

Marguerite and Armand. Ballet in 1 act; chor.: Frederick Ashton; music: Franz Liszt's Piano Sonata in B minor and "La Lugubre Gondole," orch. by Humphrey Searle; décor: Cecil Beaton. First prod.: Royal Ballet at Royal Opera House, Covent Garden, London, Mar. 12, 1963, with Margot Fonteyn (Marguerite), Rudolf Nureyev (Armand), Michael Somes (Armand's Father). The famous novel by Alexandre Dumas fils, made into a ballet which tells its story in flashbacks as Marguerite lies dying. The role of Armand was Nureyev's first creation in a ballet produced outside the Soviet Union.

Marie Jeanne (Marie-Jeanne Pelus), dancer and teacher, b. New York City, 1920, of French parents; m. Dwight Godwin. Started her dance studies with School of American Ballet, N.Y. (1934) and joined Ballet Caravan (1937–40), creating the role of Mother and Sweetheart (*Billy the Kid*), Debutante (*Filling Station*), and others. Guest artist with Ballet Russe de Monte Carlo (1940), when she danced the leading role in George Balanchine's restaged version of *Serenade;* with American Ballet on its South American tour (1941), creating leading roles in *Concerto Barocco* and *Ballet Imperial* and dancing in *Apollon Musagète, Serenade,* and many others; Original Ballet Russe (1942), dancing leading roles in *Paganini, Choreartium,* and others, in South America; Marquis de Cuevas' Ballet International (1944), creating leading roles in William Dollar's *Constantia,* André Eglevsky's *Colloque Sentimental,* and dancing many other roles. Ballerina, Ballet Russe de Monte Carlo (1945–47), dancing in *Concerto Barocco, Ballet Imperial, Le Baiser de la Fée, Les Sylphides, Night Shadow,* and others. Danced with Ballet Society (1948), creating role of Nymph in *Triumph of Bacchus and Ariadne* and dancing many other Balanchine ballets. Joined the Grand Ballet du Marquis de Cuevas, returning briefly to New York City Ballet for its 1953 European tour. Retired as a dancer in 1954 and now teaches. Author of *Yankee Ballerina* and *Opera Ballerina.*

Mariemma, contemporary Spanish dancer, b. Valladolid. Studied Spanish dance with Estampio; also studied ballet as a child in Paris, becoming principal dancer of the children's ballet at the Théâtre du Châtelet at age eleven. Noted for the purity of her classic Spanish style, she has toured widely in Europe, the U.S., and South America, as well as in her own country.

Markert, Russell Eldridge, dance director, b. Jersey City, N.J., 1899. Producer of the stage shows at Radio City Music Hall, N.Y., and director of the Rockettes since 1932. Started professional career dancing in Earl Carroll's *Vanities* (1923) and subsequently staged dances for many revues, including *Greenwich Village Follies, Rain or Shine,* the Marx Brothers'

Animal Crackers, George White's *Scandals,* and others, and for road companies. Organized the Roxyettes, Roxy Theatre, N.Y. (1928) and staged all their routines until, with Roxy, he joined the staff of the then newly-founded Radio City Music Hall. In the early days of talking pictures he staged dances for Paul Whiteman's film *The King of Jazz* and for *Moulin Rouge,* starring Constance Bennett.

Markova, Dame Alicia (Lilian Alicia Marks), prima ballerina, b. London, 1910. Studied with Seraphima Astafieva, Nicholas Legat, Enrico Cecchetti, Vincenzo Celli. Accepted in the Diaghilev Ballets Russes at age fourteen and remained with the company until Diaghilev's death (1929). She created the title role in George Balanchine's *Le Rossignol* (1926), danced Papillon (*Carnaval*), *Blue Bird* pas de deux (*Aurora's Wedding*), and others. Danced with Ballet Rambert, creating leading roles in Frederick Ashton's *La Péri, Foyer de Danse, Les Masques, Mephisto Valse;* Antony Tudor's *Lysistrata;* Ninette de Valois' *Bar aux Folies-Bergère.* Also danced in Camargo Society performances, creating the Polka in *Façade,* among other roles; danced in the early performances of the Vic-Wells (later Sadler's Wells, now Royal) Ballet (1931–33) and became its first prima ballerina (1933–35), creating *Les Rendez-vous* (1933), *The Haunted Ballroom* (1934), *The Rake's Progress* (1935). During this period became the first English dancer to dance the title role in *Giselle* and Odette-Odile in the full-length *Swan Lake.* With Anton Dolin she organized the Markova-Dolin Company of which she was prima ballerina (1935–38). Joined the René Blum–Leonide Massine Ballet Russe de Monte Carlo as ballerina (1938–41), her performance of *Giselle* during its first N.Y. season establishing her immediately as an idol with the American public. Her creations for this company included *Seventh Symphony* (3rd movement–Sky) and *Rouge et Noir* (The Woman), among others. Ballerina of Ballet (now American Ballet) Theatre (1941–44; 1945–46), creating Zemphira (*Aleko*), Juliet (Antony Tudor's *Romeo and Juliet*), title role (Adolph Bolm's *Firebird*), Princess Hermilia (*Bluebeard*); also dancing *Swan Lake* (Act 2), *Les Sylphides, Giselle,* and others. Ballerina in the revue *Seven Lively Arts* (1944–45). Formed new Markova-Dolin company which toured U.S. (season 1945–46). Guest artist Original Ballet Russe (1946–47) for which she created title role in John Taras' *Camille.* The Markova-Dolin group toured Central America (spring, 1947) and were guest artists with the Mexican Ballet, Mexico City (summer, 1947); toured U.S. (1947–48); toured the Philippines with Anton Dolin (1948). Returned to England as guest artist with Sadler's Wells Ballet at Royal Opera House, Covent Garden, London, June, 1948, dancing *Giselle,* the full-length *Swan Lake,* and her first Aurora in *The Sleeping Beauty.* Guest artist, Ballet Russe de Monte Carlo (fall–winter, 1948); toured South Africa with Anton Dolin (1949). Co-founder with Dolin and prima ballerina of London's Festival Ballet (1950–51). Since leaving that company she has been guest artist with companies all over the world—many times with American Ballet Theatre; with Grand Ballet du Marquis de Cuevas, dancing title role in August Bournonville's *La Sylphide* (1955); with Royal Winnipeg Ballet, Royal Danish Ballet, ballets of Teatro alla Scala, Milan, and of Teatro Municipal, Rio de Janeiro; with Ruth Page's Chicago Opera Ballet, dancing *The Merry Widow* (1955–56). Danced in the ballet of *Die Fledermaus* and in Gluck's opera *Orfeo ed Euridice* at Metropolitan Opera House, N.Y. during two separate seasons. Has returned as guest ballerina with London's Festival Ballet on various occasions; danced a season with Italian Opera Co., Theatre Royal, Drury Lane, London, choreographing and dancing in *William Tell* and *The*

Pearl Fishers. Has danced in Israel, and been guest artist with Ram Gopal and his company of Indian dancers and musicians in London. Made her final appearances as a dancer with London's Festival Ballet in 1962. She announced her retirement Jan. 1, 1963, and three months later was appointed director of the Metropolitan Opera Ballet in which capacity she also directed the group of dancers from the company known as Metropolitan Opera Ballet Studio which gave performances for school children. She has appeared frequently on television in U.S. and Britain from 1950 on; gave a series of twelve radio talks, "Markova's Ballet Call" for the British Broadcasting Corporation (summer, 1960). Author of *Giselle and I* (1960). For her services to British ballet she was created C.B.E. (Commander of the Order of the British Empire, 1960) and Dame of the Order of the British Empire (1963). Her dancing was noted for its delicacy and its incredible lightness. These very special qualities made her *Giselle,* her Taglioni in the Dolin *Pas de Quatre,* her Prelude and pas de deux in *Les Sylphides* famous everywhere. Crispness, added to these qualities made her Sugar Plum Fairy (*The Nutcracker*) the outstanding interpretation of her time. She also danced the famous Anna Pavlova solo, *The Dying Swan,* and a delightful piece of Spanish pastiche, *Bolero 1830,* arranged for her by Ana Ricarda. Markova belongs to that select list of dancers who have influenced ballet in their own time. On Nov. 15, 1964, Dame Alicia presented the Metropolitan Opera Ballet in a performance of *Les Sylphides* at the Metropolitan. On Nov. 30, at a champagne party in her honor, Rudolf Bing, general manager of the Metropolitan, announced that a separate ballet evening would be presented—for the second time in the 80-year existence of the Opera House. The evening took place Apr. 11, 1965. The program included *Les Sylphides; The Miraculous Mandarin,* staged by Joseph Lazzini, in décor by Bernard Dayde; *Pas de Quatre,* with choreography by Anton Dolin, staged by Dame Alicia; and the Bacchanale from *Samson et Dalila,* with revised choreography by Zachary Solov, in décor by Robert O'Hearn.

Dame Alicia Markova as Taglioni in Pas de Quatre.

Markova-Dolin Ballet. A company organized by Anton Dolin and Alicia Markova in London under the sponsorship of Mrs. Laura Henderson (owner of the famous non-stop variety theatre The Windmill). The company gave its first London season at the Duke of York's Theatre (1935) and toured England and Europe until 1938 when Markova joined Ballet Russe de Monte Carlo. In the winter of 1945 Markova and Dolin formed a new group in the U.S. of the same name which toured (1945–46), danced in Central America (spring, 1947), appeared with the Mexican Ballet in Mexico City (summer, 1947), and toured again in U.S. (1947–48).

Markovic, Vera, Yugoslav dancer, b. Zagreb, 1931. Studied with Margarita Froman, Ana Roje, and Nadine Nicolaieva-Legat. Joined the Zagreb National Ballet (1945); becoming principal soloist (1949). Her repertoire includes *Romeo and Juliet* (Froman), *The Legend of Ohrid* (Froman), *Bolero* (Boris Romanov), *The Devil in the Village* (the Mlakars), *Classical Symphony* (Parlic), and the classics.

Marks, Bruce, dancer, b. New York City, 1937; graduate of N.Y. School of Performing Arts and Juilliard School of Music Dance Department, he received his higher education at Brandeis Univ. While still at school he began performing at age fourteen, creating the role of the young boy in Pearl Lang's *Rites,* and later created a leading male role in *And Joy Is My Witness, Nightflight,* and Mercury in *Falls the Shadow Between* (Persephone). Was Pearl Lang's partner in *Black Mari-*

golds (1958) and later in *Shirah* and *Apasionada*. He is the rare example of a dancer who is equally prominent in both the ballet and modern dance fields. He began ballet training with Margaret Craske and Antony Tudor at the Metropolitan Opera Ballet School and joined the corps de ballet (1956), subsequently being promoted to premier danseur (1958). Appeared at the Spoleto Festival of Two Worlds (1959) in the company organized by Herbert Ross and Nora Kaye. Joined American Ballet Theatre as leading dancer in Sept., 1961, and created one of the two leading male roles in Harald Lander's *Etudes*. Guest artist with Royal Swedish Ballet (1963–64 season), dancing leading male role in Birgit Cullberg's *Seven Deadly Sins* (Aug., 1963) in twelve open-air Stockholm theatres. Also danced Adam in her *Eden* pas de deux as part of the ballet film Cullberg made in 1963. Returned to the American Ballet Theatre in 1964. Guest artist with London's Festival Ballet (summer 1965). Dances a wide repertoire including a number of classic pas de deux as well as the standard and modern works. Married Toni Lander, ballerina of American Ballet Theatre, in 1966.

Marsicano, Merle, (Merle Petersen), contemporary American modern dancer, b. Philadelphia, Pa.; m. painter, Nicholas Marsicano. Studied ballet with Ethel Phillips and, when she became ballet mistress of the Pennsylvania Opera Co., danced in the opera ballets. Also studied with Mikhail Mordkin; modern dance with Ruth St. Denis and, later, with Erna Wassell, a pupil of Mary Wigman; two years with Martha Graham at Neighborhood Playhouse; dance composition with Louis Horst. Began to give dance performances in Philadelphia, then moved to N.Y. after her marriage and continued to dance at first under the auspices of Theatre Dance. Since 1952 she has presented her own programs of solos for which she frequently uses music specially composed for her by John Cage, Morton Feldman, Stefan

Merle Marsicano

Wolpe, Jerry Petersen. Some of her best known dances are *Figure of Memory* (Feldman), *Fragment for a Greek Tragedy* (Cage), *Time Out of Season* (Wolpe), *Maenad* (Petersen), *Way Out* (Albert Ammons), *Gone!* (Miles Davis). She is one of the true individualists of modern dance with a style completely underivative of her former teachers.

Martin, John, outstanding American dance critic and writer on dance, b. Louisville, 1893; m. Hettie Louise Mick, 1918. Began brief acting career in 1912 and was with the Chicago Little Theatre (1915–17). After holding down jobs as press agent for Stuart Walker (1922) and drama director Swarthmore Chautauqua (1923), became executive secretary of Richard Boleslavsky's Laboratory Theatre (1924–26). In 1927 became dance editor and critic of *The New York Times,* remaining with the newspaper until his retirement (June, 1962). Director of summer theatre productions in Johnstown, Pa.

(1929), Locust Valley, N.Y. (1933), New Rochelle, N.Y. (1934). Member of the faculty of the New School for Social Research, N.Y. (1930–34); Bennington College School of Dance (1934–38), and lecturer on dance history and criticism (1930–45). Served in the United States Army Air Force, Signal Corps, World War I. Author of *The Modern Dance* (1933); *Introduction to the Dance* (1939); *The Dance* (1945); *World Book of Modern Ballet* (1952), and a number of plays produced by various companies. Editor of *Dramatic Mirror,* N.Y. (1919–22). Contributor to various periodicals and encyclopedias, including *Dance Encyclopedia.* John Martin is a key figure in the dance in America, one who played a decisive role in the development of the modern dance. When the history of modern dance in the U.S. is written it will be realized that it was due to his support and criticism in innumerable articles in *The New York Times* and elsewhere that the modern dance assumed the image it had and took the line of growth and development it did. He fought its battles against an apathetic public and almost singlehandedly succeeded in establishing it as a recognized art form. At present he is free-lancing, writing articles, working on books, and lecturing. Since summer, 1965, is lecturer on dance at the University of California at Los Angeles, to which city he moved in the summer of 1966.

John Martin

Martinez, Enrique, American dancer, b. Havana, Cuba, 1926. Studied ballet in Cuba with Alicia Alonso and in N.Y. with Igor Schwezoff. Joined Ballet (now American Ballet) Theatre (1947) and after a season with the Ballet Alicia Alonso (1950), returned to Ballet Theatre for its European tour. Promoted to soloist (1954) in that company, he danced Mercutio (Antony Tudor's *Romeo and Juliet*), Third Sailor (*Fancy Free*), Boy in Green (*Les Patineurs*), Devil (*Three Virgins and a Devil*), Drummer (*Graduation Ball*). Has been assistant ballet master since 1960. Has choreographed pas de deux and ballets for Ballet Alicia Alonso, Grand Ballet du Marquis de Cuevas, and others as well as for the Denver Civic Ballet and Detroit City Ballet, both regional groups (see REGIONAL BALLET).

Martlew, Gillian, English dancer, b. Ashbourne, Derbyshire, 1934. Studied dance at King Slocombe School of Dance, Cambridge, and Ballet Rambert School, London. Joined the latter's company (1950), of which she is currently a ballerina. Her creations include Girl (*Two Brothers*), Wife (*Hazana*), Daughter (*A Place in the Desert*), and others, while her wide repertoire includes Swan Queen (*Swan Lake,* Act 2), Queen of the Wilis and Bathilde (*Giselle*), Tango (*Façade*), Episode in His Past (*Lilac Garden*), Italian Ballerina (*Gala Performance*), Venus (*Judgment of Paris*), 1st and 2nd Dances (*Dark Elegies*), and many others.

Martyn, Laurel, Australian dancer and choreographer, b. Brisbane, Queensland, 1916. Studied with Phyllis Bedells; awarded the Adeline Genée Gold Medal of the Royal Academy of Dancing and a choreographic scholarship from the same organization. Danced with Sadler's Wells Ballet (as Laurel Gill, 1935–38), being one of the first Australian dancers to make a name outside that country. Ballerina, Borovansky Ballet (1947). Since 1948, director, choreographer, and teacher of Victorian Ballet Guild, Melbourne.

Marwari. A form of Hindu dance practiced in North India. Other forms in this region are Kathak and Manipuri. See HINDU DANCE.

Maryinsky Theatre. Imperial Russian theatre in St. Petersburg, home of the Russian ballet since 1889. This, the greatest of Russian Imperial theatres, was built on the spot formerly occupied by a theatre-circus which burned down in 1859. The Maryinsky Theatre was opened Oct. 2, 1860, but ballet was not presented there until 1880. Prior to that time ballet was given at the Bolshoi Theatre (which see). Beginning Apr. 12, 1889, all official ballet performances were given at Maryinsky Theatre, with occasional ballets performed at the small theatres attached to the various Imperial palaces, such as the Hermitage Theatre, Theatre of Krasnoye Selo, and others. In 1935 the name Maryinsky Theatre was changed to Kirov State Academic Theatre of Opera and Ballet.

Masks—Props—Mobiles. Modern dance work; chor.: Alwin Nikolais, Murray Louis, and Dorothy Vislocky; music: sound score devised by Alwin Nikolais and Alan Hovhaness, with an excerpt from the Sibelius incidental music for *Pelléas and Mélisande*. First prod.: Playhouse Dance Company, Henry Street Playhouse, Jan. 26, 1953; revised version: Dec. 10, 1955. This work was the first which focused public attention on the new experiments in movement, sound, light, and décor which were to develop into a new modern dance form in which dancers lost their own individuality in the experimentation with shapes, forms, lights, and the development to the ultimate of the possibilities in the handling of props.

Maslow, Sophie, contemporary American modern dancer, choreographer, teacher, b. New York City, of Russian-American parentage. Studied dance at Neighborhood Playhouse School of the Theater (now Henry Street Playhouse) with Blanche Talmud and appeared in

American modern dancer and choreographer, Sophie Maslow.

the children's Christmas productions. From the Playhouse School joined Martha Graham's concert group, becoming a soloist. Her first choreographic work was a solo, *Themes From a Slavic People,* to music by Béla Bartók, performed in a New Dance Group performance at Civic Repertory Theatre, N.Y. (1934). In 1941 came *Dust Bowl Ballads* to Woody Guthrie's songs, "Dusty Old Dust," and "I Ain't Got No Home in This World Any More." *Folksay* (1942) brought her general recognition as being in the forefront of modern dance choreographers. In May, 1948, she premièred *Champion,* based on the Ring Lardner short story with music composed for it by Samuel Matlowsky. The same year she was a founding member of the American Dance Festival, Connecticut College, New London, where she both taught and performed on the first Festival program. From this period she also teamed with Jane Dudley and William Bales, the three dancers performing as the Dudley-Maslow-Bales Trio and also as members of the New Dance Group company. She again taught and performed at the 2nd American Dance Festival when *Festival* (one section of the work which a year later became her great *The Village I Knew*) was premièred at New London. Appeared in many dance performances and staged a number of other works, best known being *Manhattan Transfer* (American Dance Festival, 1953), *Celebration,* a suite of dances based on Israeli songs and authentic source material (YM–YWHA, 1954), *Prologue* (1959). She has also choreographed for New York City Opera (dances and movement in *The Dybbuk,* 1951, were the outstanding feature of the opera), for plays on and off-Broadway, for the Hanukah Festivals for Israel held annually at Madison Square Garden, and frequently repeated in Philadelphia and Boston (1952, 1955, 1956, 1960–62), for television, summer theatres, etc. Is on the board of directors and teaching staff of the New Dance Group Studio with which she has been associated since its inception, and is also head of the dance department of Hebrew Arts School for Music and Dance, N.Y. Choreographed *The Dybbuk* (m.: Robert Starer), based on the Solomon An-sky play, as part of the annual Hanukah Festival, Madison Square Garden, N.Y. (Nov. 30, 1964), with Ethel Winter as Leah, Bertram Ross as Hanon, Dick Gain as the Messenger. Later in the year the Harkness Ballet invited her to stage *The Dybbuk* for its company. Rehearsals began July 6, 1965, at Watch Hill, R.I., but at this writing (spring, 1967) the ballet has not yet been produced.

Mason, Monica, South African dancer, b. Johannesburg, 1941. Studied with Nesta Brooking and at Royal Ballet School, entering the company (1958); currently soloist. Her roles include Gypsy (Kenneth MacMillan's *Le Baiser de la Fée*), Woodland Glades Fairy and Florestan's Sister (*The Sleeping Beauty*), Mazurka (*Les Sylphides*), one of the principals (*Diversions*), Gypsy (*The Two Pigeons*), two episodes in *Images of Love*. Her most important role to date is her creation of the Chosen Virgin in MacMillan's *The Rite of Spring.*

Masque of Beauty. Sequel to *Masque of Blackness* by Ben Jonson and Inigo Jones, produced in 1608. The Queen Consort and ladies of the court took part in its presentation.

Masque of Blackness. First masque produced by Ben Jonson and Inigo Jones. It was given on Twelfth Night (1605) at Whitehall, London.

Masquerade. Ballet in 1 act; chor.: Tatiana Leskova; music: Aram Khachaturian; book: Edla Ipanema Moreira; décor: Mario Conde. First prod.: Rio de Janeiro Ballet Society, Teatro Fenix, 1949; in 1951 presented by Teatro Municipal, Rio de Janeiro, with Beatriz Consuelo, Johnny Franklin, Berta Rozanova, Aldo Lotufo. Bitter-sweet flirtations during a masquerade.

Masquerade. Ballet after the Mikhail Lermontov drama of the same name in 4 acts and 9 scenes; chor. and book: Boris Fenster; music: Lev Laputin; décor: Tatiana Bruni. First prod.: Kirov Theatre, Leningrad, Dec. 29, 1960. An earlier version with book and choreography by Oleg Dadishkiliani was premièred at the Novosibirsk Theatre of Opera and Ballet, Mar. 23, 1956. The Stanislavsky and Nemirovich-Danchenko Lyric Theatre produced this ballet with choreography by Igor Smirnov in décor by Valery Dorrer. The Kirov Theatre version is with Irina Kolpakova (Nina), Konstantin Sergeyev (Arbenin), Natalia Dudinskaya (Baroness Strahl). In the Stanislavsky and Nemirovich-Danchenko production Ella Vlasova is Nina and Alexei Chichinadze is Arbenin. At a grand masquerade ball Nina, wife of Arbenin, drops her bracelet. It falls into the hands of Prince Zvezdich who mistakenly thinks it belongs to Baroness Strahl because the Baroness had exchanged costumes with Nina. Arbenin, a Byronic character, suspects his wife of unfaithfulness and, disillusioned with life, poisons her. Baroness Strahl tells him the true story and he loses his mind.

Masques, or masks. Allegorical or mythological presentations given in England in the first half of the 17th century. It was the English equivalent to the

French ballet de cour and was related to the Italian masquerie. A masque consisted of verse, comedy with plot, and included entrances for dancers. They were particularly notable for their décor. Ben Jonson was the most famous writer of masques, although John Milton (1608–1674) also wrote some. The names of Samuel Daniel (*The Twelve Goddesses,* 1604) and Campion are also noteworthy. The best designer for masques was Inigo Jones (an architect who had travelled in Italy), with whom Jonson often collaborated. Their two most famous productions were the *Masque of Blackness* (1605) and the *Masque of Beauty* (1608). Alfonso Ferabosco composed music for masques and Thomas Giles and Hieronimius Herne were known as maîtres de ballet. The big feature of every masque was the "grand masque dance," which occurred in about the middle of the performance and in which all the noblemen took part. The masque was followed by social dancing. The dances in the production were usually moriscos. This type of entertainment had a definite influence on Shakespeare and the development of the English theatre. The masque gradually placed more emphasis upon singing than upon dancing, but the anti-masque, first presented by Jonson (1609) as a dance or show to precede and act as a foil to the masque, was the greatest contribution England made to theatrical dancing. Anti-masques were presented by professional actors, not members of the aristocracy, and were healthier in humor than the masque.

Masques, Les. Ballet in 1 act; chor. and book: Frederick Ashton; music: Francis Poulenc's Trio for Piano, Oboe and Bassoon; décor: Sophie Fedorovitch. First prod.: Ballet Rambert, Mercury Theatre, London, Mar. 5, 1933, with Frederick Ashton (A Personage), Alicia Markova (His Lady Friend), Pearl Argyle (His Wife), Walter Gore (Her Lover). A Personage, who takes his lady friend to a masked ball, finds himself very attracted to another lovely lady. He discovers that she is his wife, who has also gone accompanied by her lover. The couples re-pair and leave happily. Sophie Fedorovitch's beautiful black and white scenery and costumes added to the chic and sophistication of this early Ashton work.

Massine, Leonide (Leonid Fedorovitch Miassine), choreographer, b. Moscow, 1896; m. Tatiana Milisnikova (Orlova). Educated Imperial Ballet School, Moscow; pupil of Domashov, Enrico Cecchetti, Nicholas Legat. Choreographer and principal dancer, Diaghilev Ballets Russes (1914–20); choreographer, dancer, artistic director, Ballet Russe de Monte Carlo (1932–41); Ballet Theatre, N.Y., (1941–44); organized Ballet Russe Highlights (1945–46); guest choreographer, Ballet International (U.S.); Sadler's Wells Ballet, Royal Danish Ballet, Teatro alla Scala, Opéra Comique (1947–51); Ballets Européens (1960); Royal (British) Ballet (1962). Among his ballets are *The Midnight Sun* (1915); *Good-Humored Ladies, Contes Russes, Parade* (1917); *La Boutique Fantasque, The Three-Cornered Hat* (1919); *Le Sacre du Printemps, L'Astuzzie Feminili, Pulcinella, Le Rossignol* (1920); *Salade, Le Beau Danube, Les Facheux* (1924); *Les Matelots, Zéphire et Flore* (1925); *Cimarosiana* (1926); *Le Pas d'Acier, Ode, Mercure* (1927); *Les Enchantement d'Alcine, Le Roi David, Amphion* (1929–30); *Belkis, La Belle Hélène* (1932); *Les Présages, Les Jeux d'Enfants, The Miracle* (1933); *Choreartium, Scuola di Ballo* (1933–34); *Le Bal, Union Pacific, Jardin Public* (1935); *Symphonie Fantastique* (1936); *Gaîté Parisienne, Seventh Symphony, St. Francis* (Nobilissima Visione) (1938); *Capriccio Espagnol, Rouge et Noir, Boga-*

Leonide Massine in final scene of Firebird *(1916).*

White
N.Y.

tyri, Bacchanal (1939); *Vienna 1814, The New Yorker* (1940); *Saratoga* (1941); *Aleko* (1942); *Mlle. Angot* (1943); *Antar, Daphnis and Chloë, Mad Tristan* (1944); *Capriccio* (Stravinsky), *Symphonie Fantastique* (Berlioz), *Clock Symphony* (Haydn), *Sacre du Printemps* (rev., 1948); *Quattro Stagioni, Suite Bergamasque, Le Peintre et son Modèle* (1949); *La Valse* (Ravel) (1950); *Donald of the Burthons* (1951); *Laudes Evangelii* (1952; television production, 1962); *The Fall of the House of Usher* (1955). Films in which Massine staged dances and appeared include *Carnaval in Costa Rica* (1945), *Red Shoes* (1948), *Tales of Hoffmann* (1951), *Neapolitan Carousel* (1953). Film versions of Massine's ballets *Capriccio Espagnol* and *Gaîté Parisienne* were produced by Warner Brothers (1941) under the titles *Spanish Fiesta* and *The Gay Parisian,* respectively. Joined the newly organized Ballets de Monte Carlo (summer, 1966) as choreographer and artistic supervisor.

Mata and Hari

Mata, Ruth (Meta Krahn). See MATA AND HARI.

Mata and Hari, contemporary dance team; American citizens since 1945. Ruth Mata studied music and Isadora Duncan style dance; Eugene Hari studied athletics and acrobatics. Both had the same professional training: ballet with Volkart, Zürich; modern dance with Mary Wigman and Rudolf von Laban, Berlin; acrobatics and tap in Zürich, London, N.Y.; pantomime with Trudi Schoop, Zürich, whose dance company they joined for its 1937–39 U.S. tours. They remained in N.Y. where they married, and ever since have toured as a team, sometimes with a small supporting company, sometimes as a duo. In this country they studied ballet with Edna McRae (Chicago), Alexandra Fedorova, Elisabeth Anderson-Ivantzova (N.Y.), and others. Their first N.Y. appearance as a team was on a program with Agnes de Mille, Jack Cole, and Jerome Robbins, followed by a recital at the National Theatre. Since then they have toured all over the U.S., Canada, South Africa, South America, and in Europe, appearing in theatres and night clubs. They played in the motion picture *Meet the People* (1944) and the musical *Laffing Room Only* (1944–46). They have danced many times on television in "The Show of Shows," "Ed Sullivan Show," "Dinah Shore Show," and others. All their repertoire is their own choreography and includes *Carnegie Hall* (their "signature number"), *Circus Acrobats, Apache Dance, Woman on the Couch, Kiss Me My Love, Have Gun, Get Gold,* and others; *The Lady Unobserved, A Lady Takes a Shower, Hollywood "Pop" Singer,* all Ruth Mata solos; *Physical Culture, The Angler,* Eugene Hari solos; *The Yellow Envelope, The Fight, Fight for a Woman's Love,* and others, all group works. Opened their Pantomime Studio in N.Y. in Feb., 1962; also continue to perform.

Matelots, Les. Ballet in 5 scenes; chor.: Leonide Massine; music: Georges Auric; book: Boris Kochno; curtains, décor, and costumes: Pedro Pruna. First prod.: Diaghilev Ballets Russes, Théâtre Gaité-Lyrique, Paris, June 17, 1925, with Vera Nemtchinova, Lydia Sokolova, Leon Woizikowski, Tadeo Slavinsky, Serge Lifar (debut); Coliseum Theatre, London, June 29, 1925; revived by Massine for Ballet for America with décor by Eugene Dunkel, with Tatiana Grantzeva, Galina Razoumova, Yurek Lazowski, Yurek Shabelevski, Paul Petroff Sept. 14, 1946. The plot of the ballet deals with a young girl who becomes engaged to a sailor just before he leaves on a voyage. When the sailor and his friends return they put on false beards to test the fidelity of the girl by making love to her, but she remains true to her fiancé. The sailors remove their disguises and the lovers embrace.

Matisse, Henri (1869–1954), great French painter and sculptor. Designed *Le Chant du Rossignol* (1920) for the Diaghilev Ballets Russes and *Rouge et Noir* (1939) for René Blum's Ballet Russe de Monte Carlo. He actually painted the designs directly on the dancers' costumes in the latter.

Matizes (Nuances). Ballet in 2 movements with an all-female cast; chor.: Nina Verchinina; music: Johann Sebastian Bach (a collection including a saraband, intrata, prelude, chorale, menuet, gigue, and bourrée); décor: Fernando Pamplona. First prod.: Ballet Universidade de Cuyo, Argentina, 1953. In 1955 presented by Teatro Municipal, Rio de Janeiro, Brazil. One of the best works of Verchinina in her typical style, influenced by both classic and modern dance. The first movement, called the "Sacred," suggests the sentiment of Bach's music and is choreographed in the modern dance style; the second, the "Profane," presents ancient dances stylized in the classical idiom.

Mattachins (Matassins). 16th century sword dance used in court ballets.

Matteo (Matteo Vittucci), contemporary Spanish and ethnic dancer, b. Utica, N.Y. B.S., Cornell Univ., M.S. in Dance Education, Springfield College. Studied dance at Metropolitan Opera Ballet School, La Meri's Ethnologic Dance Center (Artist's Diploma), Jacob's Pillow, etc.; with LaQuica and Maria Esparsa (Spain); Mme. Azuma (Japan); Guneya (Ceylon); Balasaraswati (India). Member, Metropolitan Opera Ballet (1947–51). Made his N.Y. solo debut as ethnic dancer (1953). Formed partnership with Carola Goya (1954) (see GOYA AND MATTEO). Teaches ethnic dance forms (which he introduced to the curriculum) at High School of Performing Arts; instructor of dance, American Theater Wing (1959–61); has lectured extensively. Author of the definitive works *The History of Castanets* and *Castanets and How to Play Them.* Contributor of articles on ethnic dance to *Enciclopedia dello Spettacolo;* ethnic dance consultant for the MGM doc-

Matteo, ethnic dancer, choreographer and teacher.

umentary film *Dance Beat*. Made a study and performance tour (with Carola Goya) in India (1964).

Mattox, Matt, American modern dancer, choreographer, teacher, b. Tulsa, Okla., 1921. Studied dance with Ernest Belcher, Nico Charisse, Eugene Loring, and Jack Cole in Los Angeles. Has danced in films (*Seven Brides for Seven Brothers, Pepe*), Broadway musicals, (*Carnival in Flanders, Once Upon a Mattress, Jenny*), etc. Has choreographed for television, for the Broadway musical *Say, Darling,* for the Dunes Hotel (Las Vegas) *Revue La Parisienne,* and others. Taught modern jazz at the second International Ballet Seminar (May 25–June 7, 1964) Copenhagen, Denmark. Also teaches in N.Y.

Maule, Michael, dancer, b. Durban, South Africa, 1926; American citizen since 1956; m. Joan Watson (1965). Educated in South Africa, where he also began his dance studies. Served as Lieut. in the South African Naval Forces during World War II. After emigrating to U.S. studied dance with Vincenzo Celli and made debut in the musical *Annie Get Your Gun* (1946). Danced briefly with Ballet (now American Ballet) Theatre, and then partnered Alicia Alonso in the classic repertoire with Ballet Alicia Alonso (1949–50). Joined New York City Ballet as soloist (1950–53); toured as Alexandra Danilova's partner (1954–56); partnered Alicia Markova in Gluck's opera *Orfeo ed Euridice,* Metropolitan Opera House, N.Y. (1958); acted, sang, and danced the juvenile lead in a summer stock production of the musical *Happy Hunting,* the same year. With Jerome Robbins' Ballets: U.S.A. for European tour (1959); two seasons as leading dancer with Zachary Solov's Ballet Ensemble (1960–61). Makes frequent guest appearances. In 1964 organized a touring ensemble booked by Columbia Artists Mgt.

Mauri, Rosita, (1849–1923), leading dancer Teatro Principal, Barcelona. She made her debut at the Paris Opéra in 1878, dancing in the Charles Gounod opera *Polyeucte.* She was such a success that Louis Mérante choreographed *La Korrigane* for her (1880). Her greatest success was as Gourouli in *Les Deux Pigeons* (1886). In this original version of the ballet, Gourouli, the young girl, masquerades as the Gypsy who entices her lover Pepio. This duality was a tour de force for the dancer. She was one of the great étoiles of her time and continued to dance at the Opéra as late as 1907.

Maximova, Yekaterina, Soviet ballerina, b. 1939. Entered the Bolshoi Theatre School in 1949, graduating in 1958 (class of Yelizeveta Gerdt). She immediately attracted attention at the graduation performance when she danced the adagio from *The Sleeping Beauty* and the second pas de deux in *Giselle.* In her first season at the Bolshoi Theatre (1958–59), she created the role of Katerina in *The Stone Flower,* newly produced by Yuri Grigorovich, and danced it in the U.S. and Canada (1959). She was coached for *Giselle* by Galina Ulanova (1960). Among her other ballets are *Chopiniana* (Waltz and Prelude), *Song of the Woods* (Mavka), *Flames of Paris* (Jeanne), *The Nutcracker.* In the 1966 American visit of the Bolshoi Ballet she made a great impression as a classic-romantic ballerina as well as a technician without peer in the company. Her greatest success was in the full-length *Don Quixote* as Kitri, the principal ballerina role. She is married to her classmate and partner, Vladimir Vasiliev.

May, Pamela, English ballerina, teacher, b. Trinidad, 1917. Entered Sadler's Wells (now Royal) Ballet School at fifteen and graduated into the (then) Vic-Wells Ballet. First danced under the name of Doris May. Danced pas de trois in the full-length version of *Swan Lake* (1934) and, except for a leave of absence (1941–43), remained until 1952, becoming ballerina.

Ballerina of the Moscow Bolshoi Yekaterina Maximova as Giselle.

She created many roles, among them Red Queen (*Checkmate*), Moon (*Horoscope*), Girl in Brown (*Les Patineurs*), Lover—with Michael Somes (*The Wanderer*), Mlle. Theodore (*The Prospect Before Us*), one of the Children of Light (*Dante Sonata*), Fairy Godmother (Frederick Ashton's *Cinderella*), and others; also danced Odette-Odile (*Swan Lake*), Aurora, Lilac Fairy, *Blue Bird* pas de deux (*The Sleeping Beauty*), Prelude (*Les Sylphides*), Rich Girl (*Nocturne*), Queen of the Wilis (*Giselle*), and many others. Guest artist with Royal Ballet since 1952, currently appearing in mime roles such as Princess Mother (*Swan Lake*), Bathilde (*Giselle*), Queen (*The Sleeping Beauty*). Has appeared as guest artist at Teatro alla Scala, Milan. Currently teacher, Royal Ballet School.

Maywood, Augusta (1825–1876?), American ballerina. When Mrs. H. A. Williams divorced her husband in 1828 and later married Robert Campbell Maywood, an actor-manager, Augusta's family name was changed to Maywood. She began her ballet study with M. and Mme. Paul Hazard, the French-Belgian dancers, who had established a school in Philadelphia. She made her debut in Philadelphia at the age of twelve (1837) in *The Maid of Cashmere,* an English version of the opera-ballet *Le Dieu et la Bayadère* by François Auber. She had a great success which she repeated a year later in N.Y. in the same work. In 1838 she went to Paris to study at the Paris Opéra ballet school and made her debut at the Opéra in Nov. of that year in Jean Coralli's *Le Diable Boiteux* (known in England as *The Devil on Two Sticks*). Théophile Gautier, among other French critics, admired her dancing and wrote laudatory reviews of her performances. She remained at the Opéra almost exactly one year and disappeared from it and Paris with the dancer Charles Mabille after a performance of Joseph Mazilier's *Le Diable Amoureux* in which they both danced. She later married M. Mabille. In 1843–44, and again in 1845–46, she was a ballerina in Lisbon, dancing *Giselle,* among other ballets. Also in 1845, she was guest ballerina of the Vienna Opera Ballet, at the time a stronghold of Italian ballerinas. In 1848 she became ballerina of Teatro alla Scala, Milan. She retired from the stage about 1863. She was the first American ballerina to gain an international reputation. The year of her death was never properly established, but is accepted by some historians as 1876. For detailed information on Augusta Maywood see Marian Hannah Winter's monograph in *Dance Index,* Jan.–Feb., 1943.

Augusta Maywood, first American ballerina to gain international recognition.

Mazilier, Joseph (Giulio Mazarini) (1797–1868), French dancer and choreographer, b. Bordeaux, of Sicilian parentage. Made his debut in Paris at the Théâtre de la Porte Saint-Martin (1822); later danced at the Opéra where he became first character dancer (1833) and ballet master and choreographer (1839). His best known ballets include *La Gypsy* (1839), *Paquita* (1846), *Le Corsaire* (1856); others are *Le Diable Amoureux* (1840), *Le Diable à Quatre* (1845), *Betty* (1846), *Vert-Vert* (1851), *Jovita, ou Les Boucaniers* (1853), *Les Elfes* (1856), *Marco Polo, ou la Fille du Bandit* (1857). Mazilier was not appreciated sufficiently by his contemporaries and still less by later generations. It was true that he was not successful in handling masses, but his choreography for smaller groups, pas de deux, and individual dancers displayed a vivid imagination, a developed sense of invention, and fine musicality. His was a choreographic talent akin to that of Jean Coralli and Jules Perrot. At least two of his ballets survive, restaged and changed by other choreographers and probably bearing little resemblance to the original versions. They are *Paquita* and *Le Corsaire,* originally danced by Carlotta Grisi and Carolina Rosati, respectively.

Mazowsze. Polish song and dance company. Founded in 1948 by the late Tadeusz Sygietynski and his wife, Mira Ziminska. The selected boys and girls are chosen by audition and trained and housed in a great country estate called Karolin, some miles outside Warsaw. They receive a complete general education as well as dance training. The purpose of the group is to create for the stage the traditional songs and dances of Poland. The costumes are either originals or very carefully reproduced copies of originals. Mira Ziminska carries on as director since her husband's death and is also the company's designer. The company has toured widely all over Europe, and was awarded the Gold Medal at the Brussels World's Fair (1958). It made its U.S. debut in 1961, appearing at City Center, N.Y., Nov. 15–Dec. 3.

Mazurka. A Polish folk dance in 3/4 time; a ballroom dance in Eastern and Central Europe based on the folk dance; a character dance in ballet.

McBride, Patricia, American ballerina, b. Teaneck, N.J. Attended Professional Children's School, N.Y. Studied dance with Ruth A. Vernon, Teaneck, N.J.; Dance Circle, N.Y.; School of American Ballet, N.Y., where she was awarded a scholarship. Began her dance career with André Eglevsky Ballet Company (1958); joined New York City Ballet (1959); promoted to junior soloist (1960); ballerina (1961). Her roles include Girl (Jerome Robbins' *Afternoon of a Faun*), Sugar Plum Fairy and Dewdrop (George Balanchine's *The Nutcracker*), Central Park in the Dark movement (*Ivesiana*), Sleepwalker (*La Sonnàmbula*), 3rd Movement (*Symphony in C*), 1st Movement (*Stars and Stripes*), 2nd Movement (*Western*

Patricia McBride (Columbine) and Edward Villella (Harlequin) in Balanchine's Harlequinade.

Symphony), and others. Her creations include Chinese Entry (*Figure in the Carpet*), leading girl (*Ebony Concerto*—see JAZZ CONCERT), Hermia (*A Midsummer Night's Dream*), Columbine (Balanchine's *Harlequinade*). Dances a number of pas de deux in the company's repertoire, usually partnered by Edward Villella with whom she also often appears on television. Danced in *Concerto Barocco* as guest with Washington (D.C.) Ballet (1960).

McBride, Robert, contemporary American composer. He wrote the scores for *Punch and the Judy* (Martha Graham), *Show Piece* (Erick Hawkins), and *Furlough* (William Bales).

McCracken, Joan (1923–1961), American dancer, b. Philadelphia, Pa. Studied dance with Catherine Littlefield, Eugene Loring, Elizabeth Anderson-Ivantzova. Was one of the original members of American Ballet; member of Catherine Littlefield's Philadelphia Ballet; joined Ballet Caravan for its 1941 South American tour. The same year danced at Radio City Music Hall. Was with Dance Players throughout its existence and then created The Girl Who Falls Down in the musical *Oklahoma!* (1944) which launched her on a successful career on Broadway in such musicals as *Bloomer Girl, Billion Dollar Baby, Dance Me a Song, Me and Juliet*. Also appeared in the film musicals *Hollywood Canteen* and *Good News*. Won Donaldson Award twice: best supporting role (*Bloomer Girl*), best dancer (*Billion Dollar Baby*). She gave up dancing early because of heart trouble but appeared in several straight plays, her last performance being in a revival of Jean Cocteau's *The Infernal Machine* at the Phoenix Theatre.

McGehee, Helen, contemporary American modern dancer, choreographer, teacher, b. Lynchburg, Va. Graduated Phi Beta Kappa from Randolph-Macon Woman's Univ. Studied modern dance there and later with Martha Graham. She has been a member of the Graham company since the late 'forties. An early leading role was one of the Three Remembered Children in *Deaths and Entrances* (1947), since when she has danced in most of the Graham repertoire, some of her later creations being *Acrobats of God, Clytemnestra* (Electra), *Phaedra* (Artemis). She has presented programs of her own works from time to time, and Apr. 11, 1965, staged probably her most important work to date—*After Possession*. Devised for herself and Clover Roope, it is based on the legend of the nun who became mother of the magician Merlin. The Greek government invited her to teach and to act in Greece during the summer of 1965.

Helen McGehee as "Water" in Martha Graham's Canticle for Innocent Comedians.

McGrath, Bill, Canadian dancer, b.

Cumberland, British Columbia. Studied dance with Wynne Shaw. Danced four seasons with Theatre Under the Stars, Vancouver. Was leading dancer with Royal Winnipeg Ballet (1952–54, 1955–56). From 1957 danced with his wife, Carlu Carter, in many television programs. Currently in Australia appearing on television.

McKayle, Donald, modern dancer, choreographer, teacher, b. New York City, 1930; m. Esta Beck, subsequently divorced; m. Lea Levin (1965). Attended New York City College. Studied dance at New Dance Group, also with Martha Graham, Merce Cunningham, Nenette Charisse, Karel Shook, Hadassah. Has danced as guest artist for many of the leading modern dance choreographers, including Anna Sokolow, Merce Cunningham, Jean Erdman, and Martha Graham on her company's tour of the Orient (1955–56). For his own dance company he has choreographed (and usually performed in) *Games* (1951), *Nocturne* (1953), *Her Name Was Harriet* (1952), *Rainbow 'Round My Shoulder* (1959), *District Storyville* (1962), *Blood of the Lamb* (1963), and others. Has appeared in a number of Broadway musicals, among them *House of Flowers* and *West Side Story;* was assistant choreographer for *Copper and Brass* and *Redhead.* His works have been given on several C.B.S. television shows and he has performed at the Spoleto Festival of Two Worlds. Staged the off-Broadway *Trumpets of the Lord* (1964). Teaches at New Dance Group Studio, Martha Graham School, Juilliard School of Music Dance Department, Bennington College, Sarah Lawrence College, Neighborhood Playhouse. Won the 1963 Capezio Dance Award. Choreographer of the musical version of *Golden Boy* (1965). Was invited (Oct., 1966) by director Michael Benthall of *Two Cities* (based on Dickens' *A Tale of Two Cities*) to choreograph the musical.

Donald McKayle in his Rainbow 'Round My Shoulder.

McKenzie, Jean, Canadian ballerina, b. Regina, Saskatchewan. A pupil of June Roper in Vancouver and Gweneth Lloyd in Winnipeg, she joined the Winnipeg (now Royal Winnipeg) Ballet in 1939, a year after its beginning, and danced in most of its early repertoire, creating the leading role in *Ballet Premier.* Also choreographed and danced for two seasons in Vancouver's Theatre Under the Stars. Now teaching ballet in Winnipeg.

McRae, Edna L., contemporary teacher, b. Chicago, Ill. Graduate of Chicago Normal School of Physical Education, Harvard Summer School of Physical Education. Studied ballet with Madeline B. Hazlitt, Pavley-Oukrainsky, Adolph Bolm, Vecheslav Swoboda, Chester Hale, Nicholas Legat, Lubov Egorova, Mathilda Kchessinska, Olga Preobrajenska, Vera Trefilova, Tamara Karsavina, Phyllis Bedells; Spanish dance with Angel and Elisa Cansino; tap with James Hess, John Bubbles, Charles Shelton, Sammy Dyer. Danced with Adolph Bolm's Ballet Intime, Allied Arts, Pavley-Oukrainsky Ballet (all in Chicago). Taught at Francis Parker School, Chicago (1920–24), Pavley-Oukrainsky Ballet School (1920–23), Perry-Mansfield Camp (1920–33). Director of the Edna L. McRae School of the Dance which she established in 1923. Accepted Keith Allison as co-director, 1962. Retired from teaching in 1964.

Mead, Robert, English dancer, b. Bristol, 1940. Studied with Lilian Houleden and at Royal Ballet School. Recipient of a Leverhulme Scholarship administered by the Royal Academy of Dancing. Entered Royal Ballet (1958). Roles include the Gypsy Lover (*Les Deux Pigeons*), pas de trois (*Swan Lake*), *Blue Bird* pas de deux (*The Sleeping Beauty*), Moon (*Blood Wedding*), Mark (*Sweeney Todd*), male role (*Les Sylphides*), pas de trois (*Les Rendez-vous*).

Measure. A stately dance, popular in England at the time of Queen Elizabeth I. The term is still used in English and American square dances.

Medal Tests (England). A series of examinations in modern ballroom dancing arranged for amateurs and conducted by the Imperial Society of Teachers of Dancing and all other associations of teachers. They are of several grades, the lowest gaining a Bronze Medal, the next a Silver Medal, and the higher ones a Gold Medal or Gold Star. They serve the purpose of letting the amateur know what progress he or she is making. Many thousands of dancers take them each year. They were instituted in 1934 by Mr. Newton of the National Association of Teachers of Dancing.

Medea. Ballet in 1 act and 5 scenes; chor.: Birgit Cullberg; music: Béla Bartók's piano pieces (including *Microcosmos*), arr. by Herbert Sandberg; décor: Alvar Grandstrom. First prod.: Riksteatern, Gaevle, Sweden, Oct. 31, 1950, with Anne-Marie Lagerborg (Medea), Maurice Béjart (Jason), Inga Noring (Creusa). The following year Elsa-Marianne von Rosen brought a company called the Swedish Ballet to London and *Medea* was premièred Feb. 12, 1951, at the Princess Theatre, with Elsa-Marianne von Rosen (Medea), Julius Mengarelli (Jason), and Inga Noring (Creusa). A somewhat revised version was taken into the repertoire of the Royal Swedish Ballet, Apr. 11, 1953, again with Elsa-Marianne von Rosen, but with Willy Sandberg (Jason) and Gerd Andersson (Creusa). Mariane Orlando has also had one of her biggest successes in the title role. The ballet is based on the Greek tragedy of Euripides and tells how Medea, rejected by her husband Jason, revenges herself on his new love, Creusa, by offering her a poisoned robe. In the final madness of her rage, Medea kills her own two children. Birgit Cullberg staged this ballet for New York City Ballet, Nov. 26, 1958, in costumes by Lewis Brown, with Melissa Hayden (Medea), Jacques d'Amboise (Jason), Violette Verdy (Creusa). The Royal Danish Ballet added *Medea* to its repertoire, Apr. 24, 1959, with Margrethe Schanne (Medea), Henning Kronstam (Jason), Kirsten Simone (Creusa).

Medici, Catherine de (1519–1589); m. Henri, Duc d'Orleans, later King of France. As Queen of France she introduced the type of entertainments that her father Lorenzo, Duke of Urbino, produced in Italy. The first and greatest of these spectacles, *Ballet Comique de la Reine* (1581), influenced the direction of the history of ballet.

Meister, Hans, Swiss dancer, b. Schaffhausen, Switzerland, 1937. Studied dance in Opera Ballet School, Zurich, and at Sadler's Wells (later Royal Ballet) School, London. Joined National Ballet of Canada (1957); became a soloist (1959); principal dancer (1961). He dances Siegfried and the Pas de Trois in *Swan Lake,* Sugar Plum Fairy Cavalier (*The Nutcracker*), Franz (*Coppélia*), male dancer in *Les Sylphides, Blue Bird* pas de deux, male lead (*Les Rendez-vous*), French Cavalier (*Gala Performance*), title role in *The Remarkable Rocket,* the single male dancer in *Concerto Barocco,* among others. In Aug., 1961, he danced *Blue Bird* and *Black Swan* pas de deux at Jacob's Pillow Dance Festival, partnering Galina Samtsova. Joined Metropolitan Opera Ballet in 1962; resigned at the end of the 1965–66 season and returned to Switzerland.

Melikova, Genia (Eugenie Melnichenko), ballerina, b. France, of Russian parents. Emigrated with her parents to the U.S.; eventually became U.S. citizen. She studied with Julia Sedova in Nice and with Anatole Vilzak and Igor Schwezoff in N.Y. Danced in Radio City Music Hall, as well as in musical comedies and revues in N.Y.; soloist, Ballet Theatre (1949–50). Left for Europe to join the Marquis de Cuevas company where she subsequently became a ballerina (1954). She remained with that company until its dissolution in 1962. Joined London's Festival Ballet (spring, 1963). In 1964 she was invited by the Grand Ballet Classique de France which she joined at expiration of her contract. Toured the U.S. with this company in Oct.–Dec., 1965.

Melville, Kenneth (Griffiths), English dancer, b. Birkenhead, Cheshire, 1932. Won a scholarship to Sadler's Wells (now Royal Ballet) School, entering the corps de ballet of the company and rising to leading soloist rank. Among his roles were Albrecht (*Giselle*) opposite Violetta Elvin, title role (*Don Juan*), leading male dancer (*Ballet Imperial*), Poet (*Apparitions*), Caricaturist (*Mam'zelle Angot*). Left Sadler's Wells Ballet in 1954; danced in film *Oh, Rosalinda!,* which starred Ludmilla Tcherina. Joined London's Festival Ballet as leading dancer (1955), his repertoire including Albrecht (*Giselle*), Gennaro (*Napoli,* Act 3), Phoebus (*Esmeralda*), Mephisto (*Vision of Marguerite*), Sugar Plum Fairy Cavalier (*The Nutcracker*), Siegfried (*Swan Lake,* Act 2), one of the male leads (*Etudes*). Joined the Borovansky Ballet (1957, 1958) touring Australia and New Zealand, partnering Elaine Fifield. Returned to Festival Ballet (1958) as guest artist; danced concert tours in England and U.S. with Marina Svetlova (1959). Joined National Ballet of Canada as principal dancer (1960). In addition to the classic

Franco-American ballerina Genia Melikova as Odile, Swan Lake, *Act 3.*

repertoire he dances Captain Belaye (*Pineapple Poll*), Officer (*Offenbach in the Underworld*), Faune (*L'Après-midi d'un Faune,* Celia Franca version), leading male dancer (*Les Rendez-vous*), Preacher (*Barbara Allen*), and leading roles in David Adams' *Pas de Chance* and Ray Powell's *One in Five.*

Ménéstrier, Claude François (Père Ménéstrier) (1631–1705), French Jesuit priest who wrote several books on ballet. Among his works are *Ballets Anciens et Modernes selon les Régles du Théâtre,* the first printed history of the dance (Paris, 1681); and *Traité des Ballets* (1682). Ménéstrier was an advocate of dancing and demonstrated that it was connected with the ritual of the church. See also JESUIT BALLET.

Mengarelli, Julius (1920–61), Swedish dancer. Studied at the Royal Swedish Ballet School, becoming premier danseur (1945). He created the role of Jean in Birgit Cullberg's ballet *Miss Julie.* During his last years with the Royal Swedish Ballet he developed into an excellent mime.

Mengarelli, Mario, b. 1925, Swedish dancer, brother of Julius Mengarelli. Studied at the Royal Swedish Ballet School, becoming premier danseur (1960). His best roles are in the modern ballets of Birgit Aakesson. Created the leading Nazi soldier in Antony Tudor's *Echoes of Trumpets* (1963).

Menotti, Gian-Carlo, composer, b. Cadegliano, Italy, 1911. His mother was his first music instructor; later studied at Milan Conservatory of Music (1923–28), then completed his formal training at Curtis Institute of Music, Philadelphia, majoring in composition under Rosario Scalero. Has lived in the U.S. ever since, but keeps his Italian nationality. His first ballet was *Sebastian* commissioned by the Marquis de Cuevas Ballet International (1944). He wrote the score for Martha Graham's *Errand Into the Maze* (1947). A prolific composer of operas, musical dramas, orchestral, and chamber works, he has used dance as an important part of many of his compositions for the theatre. One of the four roles in his famous chamber-opera, *The Medium* (1946), is for a dancer-mime playing a deaf mute. The little dance interlude in *Amahl and the Night Visitors,* the first opera ever composed for television (1949), is one of the key episodes. His madrigal fable, *The Unicorn, the Gorgon and the Manticore,* originally commissioned by the Elizabeth Sprague Coolidge Foundation, was premièred in the Library of Congress, Washington, D.C. (1956) and was given the following year by New York City Ballet with choreography by John Butler. He founded the Festival of Two Worlds, Spoleto, Italy (1958), where dance has always been an important feature of the programs.

Menuet (Minuet). Dance of French origin introduced at time of Louis XIV, but achieving its greatest popularity much later. Name comes from "menu," or small steps. It was a dignified dance in 3/4 time with many deep bows and curtsies. There were many kinds of menuet, the best known being "Le Menuet de Dauphin," "Le Menuet de la Reine," "Le Menuet de la Cour," and "Le Menuet d'Exaudet."

Mephisto Valse. Ballet in 1 act; chor.: Frederick Ashton; music: Franz Liszt's *Mephisto Valse;* décor: Sophie Fedorovitch. First prod.: Ballet Club (afterwards Ballet Rambert), Mercury Theatre, London, June 13, 1934, with Alicia Markova, Walter Gore, and Frederick Ashton. Ashton used the episode in the inn of the Faust legend in which Faust is drawn to the innocent Marguerite but is forced by Mephistopheles, playing his violin, to draw her into wilder and wilder dancing, eventually to seduce and then abandon her. Using the same music and theme, Ashton staged an entirely re-choreographed version for London's Festival Ballet as *Vision of Marguerite* (which see).

Mephisto Valse. Ballet in 1 act; chor.: Maryla Gremo; music: Franz Liszt; décor and costumes: Fernando Pamplona. First prod.: Teatro Municipal, Rio de Janeiro, 1952, with Maryla Gremo (Marguerite), Aldo Lotufo (Faust), Richard Adama (Mephisto). Tatiana Leskova and Lupe Serrano danced Marguerite and Arthur Ferreira was Mephisto in later performances. Revived in 1955 for Ballet Museu de Arte of S. Paulo, with Juan Giuliano and Neyde Rossi.

Mérante, Louis (1828–1887), French dancer and choreographer. Made his debut when only six at the Théâtre Royal, Liège, Belgium, in the ballet in Auber's opera *Gustave III*. Premier danseur, Marseille (1846); appointed premier danseur of the Paris Opéra (1848). Created leading roles in many of the ballets of the period, among them *L'Etoile de Messine, Néméa, La Source,* and, only five years before his death, *Namouna*. As a choreographer, his most famous works were *Sylvia* and *Les Deux Pigeons,* others being *Gretna Green* (1873), *Yedda* (1879), and *La Korrigane* (1880), in which he also danced leading roles. He married a Russian dancer, Zina Richard, who subsequently danced under the name of Mérante.

Mercier, Margaret, Canadian dancer, b. Montreal. She began studying ballet in Montreal and then received four years advanced training at the Sadler's Wells (now Royal Ballet) School, graduating into the company as its youngest member (1954). Danced in the corps de ballet and later as soloist during its London seasons and its European, U.S., and Canadian tours (1954–58). Her first small individual roles were as the Peasant Girl in *Swan Lake* (Act 1), one of the Four Little Swans and one of the three girls in the Pas de Six in Act 1 (also in *Swan Lake*). Later danced in the Pas de Trois (*Swan Lake,* Act 1) and the Florestan and His Sisters divertissement (*The Sleeping Beauty,* Act 3). Joined Les Grands Ballets Canadiens (1958), making her debut creating the Young Girl in Ludmilla Chiriaeff's *Horoscope* for Canadian television. Her theatre debut with the company was in May, 1959, when she created the leading role in *Labyrinthe,* choreographed by Eric Hyrst, and also danced the Rose Adagio from *The Sleeping Beauty*. She dances a large repertoire which includes *Black Swan* pas de deux (Eric Hyrst choreography), *Don Quixote* pas de deux, *Raymonda* pas de deux, *The Nutcracker* pas de deux, Swanilda (*Coppélia*), ballerina (*Première Classique*), Lise (*La Fille Mal Gardée,* version by Edward Caton, re-staged by Ludmilla Chiriaeff and Eric Hyrst), and others. She had a great success when the company appeared at Jacob's Pillow Dance Festival (1959, 1960). Joined Robert Joffrey Ballet (summer, 1963); joined the Harkness Ballet (spring, 1964). Married Richard Wolf, a member of the Harkness Ballet, in Lisbon (May 1, 1965) while on tour with the company.

Margaret Mercier, Canadian-born ballerina of the Harkness Ballet.

Mercury Theatre. See BALLET RAMBERT.

Meridian. Modern dance work; chor.: Paul Taylor; music: Pierre Boulez's *Le Marteau Sans Maître;* costumes: Louise Thompson. First prod.: Paul Taylor and Dance Company, Hunter College Playhouse, Feb. 13, 1960, with Akiko Kanda, Paul Taylor, and Dan Wagoner. A gentle, almost lyric trio, though the manipulation of the girl by her two partners comes close to acrobatics at times.

Merlin, Olivier, French dance, music, and drama critic. Perceptive, with an independent mind and cultivated taste, he is on the staff of the daily newspaper *Le Monde* and the magazine *Paris-Match.*

Merry, Hazel, English dancer, b. London, 1938; m. Oliver Symons. Studied at Royal Ballet School; joined Western Theatre Ballet upon its formation (1957). Created leading roles in *Non Stop, The Prisoners, Chiaroscuro, Bal de la Victoire, Street Games, One in Five, Love Duet,* Maurice Béjart's *Sacre du Printemps, Sonate à Trois,* and others; also dances *Nutcracker* pas de deux, *Swan Lake* pas de trois, *Peasant* pas de deux (*Giselle*), Chiarina (*Carnaval*), and others. Has danced frequently on television and in pantomime, revues, and musicals.

Merry-Go-Rounders. A professional repertory performing group giving performances for children, mainly in high schools in the N.Y. area, and at the 92nd St. YM–YWHA, N.Y., where the idea originated in the dance department (1952). The company serves the dual purpose of giving entertainment to children and offering performing experience to young dancers. Doris Humphrey was the first artistic director. Lucas Hoving is currently director of the group with Bonnie Bird, one of the original members of the advisory board, as artistic director and Paul Spong as musical director.

Merry Widow, The. See VILIA.

Message, The. See BIBLISKA BILDER.

Messel, Oliver, English painter and designer, b. 1905. Educated at Eton College. One of the most famous stage designers of the day, his décors for ballets include *Francesca da Rimini* (Col. de Basil's Ballet Russe de Monte Carlo, 1937), *Comus* (1942), *The Sleeping Beauty* (1946), *Homage to the Queen* (1953), all for Sadler's Wells (now Royal) Ballet. Created Commander of the Order of the British Empire (C.B.E.) by Queen Elizabeth II (Jan., 1958).

Messerer, Asaf, Peoples' Artist of the RSFSR, Soviet premier danseur and teacher, b. 1903. Messerer belongs to the small number of Soviet dancers of the 1920's who started ballet training when well into their 'teens. In spite of this he quickly attained the position of leading male dancer at the Bolshoi Theatre. After taking private lessons in Mikhail Mordkin's school and dancing in the ballet company of the Theatre of Working Youth, Moscow, he entered the Bolshoi school (1920), going straight into the senior class, and was graduated in 1921 under Alexander Gorsky and Vassily Tikhomirov. His first important role was Siegfried in *Swan Lake* (1922). He caused a turmoil in the theatre by boldly replacing conventional mime with expressive acting, and by performing steps of unprecedented virtuosity. He greatly enriched the vocabulary of the male classic dance by per-

Asaf Messerer with applicants for children's parts in Bolshoi Ballet's Ballet School *during the N.Y. season in 1962.*

forming multiple tours en l'air and other virtuoso steps. While remaining the undisputed premier danseur noble of the Bolshoi for many years, he was equally at home in demi-caractère roles and danced all the principal male roles in the Bolshoi repertoire. He was one of the first Soviet dancers to tour outside the Soviet Union, with his sister and constant partner, Sulamith Messerer, and later with his wife, ballerina Irina Tikhomirnova. He began teaching at the Bolshoi school in 1923 and since 1942 has conducted a classe de perfection for artists for the Bolshoi Ballet. He learned much from his teacher Tikhomirov who, in turn, was a pupil of Christian Johansson, but everything he learned he developed and expanded according to his own experience. He retired from the stage in 1954 and is now considered the most important teacher at the Bolshoi. He has choreographed several ballets, among them a divertissement, *The Battle of Toys,* and *Schumanniana* (both in 1924) for the Victorina Krieger Art Ballet. The fourth act of *Swan Lake* currently in the Bolshoi repertoire is his choreography. In 1952 he choreographed this ballet for the Budapest Opera. In 1960–61 he was invited to instruct the company classes and help launch the ballet school at the Théâtre Royal de la Monnaie, Brussels (Brussels Opera), where he worked with Tikhomirnova as his assistant. He was ballet master of the foreign tours of the Bolshoi Ballet (1956, 1958 and 1962). For the 1962 tour he created *Ballet School,* the most successful work of the entire tour. In a very clever and elegant manner it depicts the development of a ballet dancer, beginning with exercises at the bar for the youngest pupils and culminating in breathtaking solo and group exhibitions of technique by the company's featured dancers. Asaf Messerer is an uncle of prima ballerina Maya Plisetskaya.

Messerer, Sulamith, Peoples' Artist of the RSFSR, Soviet ballerina and teacher, b. 1908. Entered Bolshoi School in 1920 and was graduated into the company (class of Vassily Tikhomirov) in 1926, quickly rising to ballerina status. Her best roles were Lise in *La Fille Mal Gardée,* Swanilda in *Coppélia* and, particularly, Kitri in *Don Quixote*. She began teaching at the Bolshoi school in 1938 and for the Bolshoi company in 1948 and has devoted herself entirely to teaching since she retired from the stage in 1950. Alone, and with her brother, Asaf Messerer, she has toured many foreign countries. In 1958 she went to Ceylon to help form a national theatre there. In 1960–61 she was invited to teach at the ballet school in Tokyo. She was once prominent in the world of sport and between 1927 and 1931 was the USSR swimming champion. She is an aunt of prima ballerina Maya Plisetskaya.

Metakinesis. The psychical, as opposed to physical, overtones accompanying movement; according to John Martin it is one of the four basic principles of the modern dance, the other three being substance, dynamism, and form. In the opinion of the writer all movement is done with a purpose and is in some degree functional. The conscious recognition of this fact distinguishes the modern dance from other forms.

Metamorphoses. Ballet in 1 act; chor.: George Balanchine; music: Paul Hindemith's *Symphonic Metamorphoses on Themes of Carl Maria von Weber;* costumes: Barbara Karinska. First prod.: New York City Ballet at City Center, N.Y., Nov. 25, 1952, with Tanaquil LeClercq, Todd Bolender, Nicholas Magallanes. The metamorphoses of the ugly creatures of the insect world into flashing dragonflies and other winged beauties.

Metropolitan Ballet. A company formed in London in 1947 by Leon Hepner, with Victor Gsovsky as ballet master and choreographer. After its initial season it was re-organized with Cecilia Blatch as director and backer, Nicholas Beriosoff as regisseur, and Celia Franca as ballet mistress. Financial difficulties caused its dissolution in 1949, but during its three years' existence it introduced a fifteen-year-old Svetlana Beriosova, Colette Marchand, Erik Bruhn, Serge Perrault, and others to English audiences. Other outstanding dancers who appeared at various times were Celia Franca, Sonia Arova, David Adams, Henry Danton, Poul Gnatt. John Taras created *Designs with Strings* for the Metropolitan Ballet (1948).

Metropolitan Daily. Modern group work; chor.: Hanya Holm; music: Gregory Tucker. First prod.: Feb. 19, 1939. The first dance production ever to be shown on television, it was an amusing group work depicting the various parts of a newspaper: politics, crime, theatre, sports, comic strips, etc.

Metropolitan Opera Ballet Studio. A group of dancers of the Metropolitan Opera Ballet organized by John Gutman, Assistant General Manager, Metropolitan Opera, at the end of 1962 for the dual purpose of presenting ballet programs in N.Y. schools, sponsored by the Board of Education and of giving opportunities to young choreographers. Ron Sequoio, Thomas Andrew, and Mattlyn Gavers staged ballets during the 1962–63 season. Antony Tudor choreographed *Fandango* to music by Antonio Soler; Hans Meister staged Ray Powell's *One in Five;* Dame Alicia Markova, who assumed artistic direction of the group when she became director of the Metropolitan Opera Ballet in the spring of 1963, staged a special shortened version of *Les Sylphides* and the Rose Adagio from *The Sleeping Beauty.*

Metropolitan Opera House. The original theatre, located on Broadway between 39th and 40th Streets, N.Y. was opened Oct. 22, 1883, and from then until the end of the 1965–66 season housed the Metropolitan Opera Company and its resident opera ballet. From 1935, before the opera season opened each fall and after it closed in the spring, the Metropolitan Opera House was used for seasons (usually presented by S. Hurok) of most of the foremost dance companies of the world, among them Russia's Bolshoi and Kirov Ballets, England's Royal Ballet, Royal Danish Ballet, the Moiseyev and Ukrainian folk ensembles, and many others. Native companies such as Ballet Russe de Monte Carlo and American Ballet Theatre also gave seasons there, although not on a regular basis. The Bolshoi Ballet gave the last performance in the old house (May 8, 1966), the final day of its third American season. For the occasion Hurok invited every available leading dancer who had appeared there in the past to return for one final appearance in a polonaise with artists of the Bolshoi company. The new Metropolitan Opera House at Lincoln Center for the Performing Arts opened Sept. 16, 1966.

Mexico, Ballet Folklorico of. Company founded in 1952 by Amalia Hernandez. It began as a group of eight of her pupils from the modern dance department of the Instituto Nacional de Bellas Artes (National Institute of Fine Arts), Mexico City, presenting dances on folklore themes for television. The series of programs was sponsored by Emilio Ascarraga, director of Mexico's television syndicate Televicentro. Two years later, by which time the group had grown to twenty members, the Mexican government undertook the television sponsorship. Later the Department of Tourism became interested and sent the Hernandez Company, as it was still called, on tours in Mexico, Canada, Cuba, Festival of the Pacific (1958), and Los Angeles Fiestas Patrias in the same year. In 1959 the company, which had grown to fifty dancers and musicians, appeared in Chicago during the Pan-American games. So successful was this appearance that the President of Mexico, Senor Lopez Mateos, requested Celestino Gorostiza, Director General of the Instituto Nacional de

Bellas Artes to organize the troupe into an official national company. As Ballet Folklorico of Mexico it is now Mexico's national company. Its repertoire reflects in dance the history, customs, legends, and personality of Mexico, with its strains of Indian, Spanish, and Eurasian heritage. The company won first prize at the 1961 Théâtre des Nations Festival, Paris. It has toured in Germany, Belgium, Italy, and in South America, and danced at a command performance for President and Mrs. Kennedy (June 29, 1962) during their state visit to Mexico. It made its N.Y. debut, Sept. 11, 1962, at City Center while on its first U.S. tour.

Meyer, Laverne, Canadian dancer, b. Guelph, Ontario, 1935. Trained as tap and musical comedy dancer; studied ballet with Boris Volkov, dancing with his Canadian Ballet. Joined Sadler's Wells Opera Ballet, then became an original member of Western Theatre Ballet; appointed ballet master Feb., 1963. Created Bridegroom (*A Wedding Present*), Strong Man (Kenneth MacMillan's *Valse Excentrique*), the Man (*Sonate à Trois*); also choreographed *The Web*.

Meyer, Yvonne, Brazilian dancer, b. Rio de Janeiro. Studied under Yuco Lindberg, Maryla Gremo, Tatiana Leskova, Vaslav Veltchek. Made her debut with the Ballet da Juventude (1948). Soloist, Teatro Municipal (1953); joined Grand Ballet du Marquis de Cuevas (1954), becoming soloist (1955). Created role in *Romeo and Juliet;* danced in *The Mad Tristan, The Enchanted Mill, Designs for Strings, Fiesta, Aurora's Wedding, Chopin Concerto.* Left in 1957 to join Ballet Miskovitch and danced there for several seasons, creating title role in *La Belle Dame Sans Merci* (1958); danced at the Edinburgh Festival. Soloist of Massine's Ballets Européens, Nervi, Italy (1960). Created roles in *Human Comedy, Le Bal des Voleurs, Barber of Seville,* dancing also in *Choreartium* and *Le Beau Danube*. Created title role in Serge Lifar's *Pique Dame* (1960). Guest artist, Ruth Page's Chicago Opera Ballet (1961), dancing in *Die Fledermaus.* Joined Ballet Janine Charrat de France (1962) for the American tour, dancing *L'Amazone, Suite en Blanc, Forbidden Zone.* Joined Walter Gore's London Ballet for a short time, then returned to Brazil (summer, 1963).

Michaut, Pierre, (1895–1956), French writer and critic of ballet. Contributed to many French magazines and conducted weekly radio programs dedicated to dance and theatre. Author of *L'Histoire du Ballet* (1945) and *Le Ballet Contemporain* (1950). From 1945 to his death he was president of L'Association des Ecrivains et Critiques de la Danse. The Association organizes gala performances for young dancers and annually awards the René Blum Prize.

Middle Dancer. See EUKINETICS.

Midsummer Night's Dream, A. Ballet in 2 acts; chor.: George Balanchine; music: Felix Mendelssohn (Overture and Incidental music for *A Midsummer Night's Dream;* overtures to *Son and Stranger, Athalie, Fair Melusine,* Symphony for Strings No. 9, and the first *Walpurgis Night*); décor: David Hays; costumes: Barbara Karinska. First prod.: New York City Ballet, City Center, N.Y., Jan. 17, 1962, with Melissa Hayden (Titania), Gloria Govrin (Hippolyta), Patricia McBride (Hermia), Jillana (Helena), Edward Villella (Oberon), Arthur Mitchell (Puck), Nicholas Magallanes (Lysander), Bill Carter (Demetrius), Roland Vazquez (Bottom), Francisco Moncion (Theseus), Conrad Ludlow (Titania's Cavalier), with Violette Verdy and Conrad Ludlow heading the 2nd act divertissement. The story of Shakespeare's play developed in dance and pantomime, with a second act divertissement in symphonic ballet form as a substitute for the court entertainment offered by Bottom and the other "rude

Finale of Act 2 of A Midsummer Night's Dream; *front row (l. to r.) : Patricia McBride, Nicholas Magallanes; Gloria Govrin, Francisco Moncion; Jillana, Bill Carter.*

mechanicals" for the wedding celebrations of the various mortal couples involved. Conrad Ludlow danced the first few performances in this second act ballet, substituting for Jacques d'Amboise who had sustained an injury at the dress rehearsal.

In the summer of 1966 a motion picture of the ballet was filmed in New York, directed by Balanchine with Suzanne Farrell (Titania), Edward Villella (Oberon), Arthur Mitchell (Puck), Francisco Moncion (Theseus). It was premièred April 17, 1967 as a benefit for the New York City Ballet Scholarship Fund and shown to invited audiences later in the month.

Milhaud, Darius, French composer, b. Aix-en-Provence, 1892. One of "Les Six" and composer of several ballets by Jean Börlin for Les Ballets Suédois: *L'Homme et son Désir* (1921), *Les Mariés de la Tour Eiffel* (with other members of "Les Six," 1921), *La Création du Monde* (1923); also for *Le Train Bleu* (Bronislava Nijinska, 1924), *Imagined Wing* (Martha Graham, 1944), *The Bells* (Ruth Page, 1946), Adame Miroir (Janine Charrat, 1948), *La Rose des Vents* (Roland Petit, 1958). The music for *La Création du Monde* has frequently been used by other choreographers: Ninette de Valois (1931), Agnes de Mille for *Black Ritual* (1940), Todd Bolender (1960). Modern dancer-choreographer Alvin Ailey also used this for a work for two dancers which he subsequently revised and expanded into a group work. Milhaud's *Saudades do Brasil* provided the score for Peter Darrell's *Chiaroscuro* (Western Theatre Ballet, 1959).

Millaire, Andrée, Canadian dancer, b. Montreal. Studied ballet with Tatiana Lipkovska in Montreal; Lubov Egorova and Olga Preobrajenska in Paris; Kathleen Crofton in London. A member of London's Festival Ballet (1953–56), rising from corps de ballet to soloist. Joined Les Grands Ballets Canadiens (1958) and dances leading roles in *Première Classique, Etude, Labyrinthe* (Eric Hyrst), *Nonagone* (Ludmilla Chiriaeff), among other roles.

Miller, Mademoiselle (Marie Elisabeth Anne Houbert) (1770–1833), danseuse at the Paris Opéra, ca. 1790; m. Pierre Gardel. Jean-Georges Noverre called her the "Venus de Medici de la danse." She was a remarkable mime as well as an excellent dancer. Her greatest role was in the ballet *Psyche.*

Miller, Patricia, former ballerina of Sadler's Wells Theatre; b. Pretoria, South Africa, 1927; m. Dudley Davies. Studied dance in Cape Town with Cecily Robinson; danced with South African Ballet (1941) and Cape Town Ballet Club before going to London (1947) to study at Sadler's Wells Ballet School; joined the Sadler's Wells Theatre Ballet the same year, becoming a principal dancer. Her creations included Beauty (*Beauty and the Beast*), Columbine (*Harlequin in April*), La Capricciosa (*Lady and the Fool*), Love (*Pastorale*), all by John Cranko; one of the two leading female roles in Michael Somes' ballet *Summer Interlude* (1950), and others. Returned to South Africa to dance with Sadler's Wells (now Royal) Ballet at the Cecil Rhodes Centenary Exhibition (1953) and toured there with the company (1954), returning in 1956 to establish a school in Cape Town with her husband. Also dances from time to time in such productions as *The Nutcracker, Firebird, Pineapple Poll, Sylvia,* staged by David Poole, and the full-length *Swan Lake,* staged by Dudley Davies.

Milloss, Aurel (Aurel Milloss de Miholy; also, Aurel von Milloss), Hungarian-born, naturalized Italian dancer, choreographer, director, b. Ozora, Hungary (now Uzdin, Yugoslavia), 1906. Studied dance at the Ecole Blasis, Belgrade, and with Rudolf von Laban, Mary Wigman; ballet with Victor Gsovsky. First important professional engagement was as premier danseur of the Berlin Opera where he succeeded Harald Kreutzberg. His staging of a ballet on a theme of anti-tyranny, *Gaukelei* (Imposture), to music by Zillig, made him the target of Hitler and he left Germany in the early 1930's, touring Europe with a small group. After further dance study in Paris and Milan, he went to the Budapest Opera as guest premier danseur and choreographer (1933–35), and then to the National Hungarian Theatre in the same city (1936–38) as choreographer and maître de ballet. In 1936 he was invited as guest premier danseur and choreographer for a few months at the San Carlo Opera, Naples, where he staged *Aeneas* (Albert Roussel) and other works; then succeeded Boris Romanov as choreographer and ballet master of the Rome Opera (1938). Between 1939 and 1941 he also staged works at the Maggio Musicale Fiorentino (Florence May Festival of Music); since then he has frequently staged works for this Festival and for Venice Biennale and other European festivals. In 1942–43 worked at Teatro alla Scala, Milan, staging his version of Béla Bártók's *The Miraculous Mandarin.* In 1946 he was invited at the direct request of Arturo Toscanini to undertake the complete reform of the ballet company of La Scala where, with a leave of absence in 1947 to stage *Portrait de Don Quichotte* for the Ballets des Champs-Elysées in Paris, he stayed until 1950, at which time he returned to the Rome Opera for two seasons. Spent most of 1953 and 1954 in Brazil, reorganizing the ballet companies in Saõ Paulo and Rio de Janeiro. Returned to Europe in 1955, since when he has staged works in Rome, Germany, Belgium, Holland, Switzerland, Austria, and again in South America (1958). In 1959 was appointed ballet director of the Cologne (Germany) Opera, and in Sept. 1962, achieved full emancipation of the ballet from the opera. The ballet is now administered separately from the opera, while sharing the same theatre, a new situation for state theatres in Germany. In early 1963 he was appointed Director of Ballet at the State Opera, Vienna, beginning with the season 1963–64. Resigned his position at the State Opera, Vienna, at the end of the 1965–66 season to become choreographer of Teatro dell' Opera, Rome. With him as ballet mistress went the Franco-Russian dancer and teacher Marika Besobrasova, who had had her own company in Cannes, France. He is a prolific composer both of original works, including *La Follia di Orlando, Coup de Feu* (for Grand Ballet du Marquis de Cuevas), *Marsia, Anguish Sonata* (Bartók), and innumerable others; and rechoreographed versions of ballets, such as *Pulcinella, Petrouchka, Coppélia, The Prodigal Son, Firebird, Legend of Joseph, Le Sacre du Printemps,* and others.

Minkus, Leon (Aloysius Ludwig Minkus) (1827–1890), composer of ballet music and violinist, b. Vienna. Went to Russia as conductor of the orchestra of Prince Yusoupoff (1853); became staff ballet composer at the Bolshoi Theatre, Moscow (1864). Was transferred to St. Petersburg (1871) where he worked until 1886. In that year he was retired on a small pension because the position of staff composer had been eliminated. Dissatisfied with his miserly pension (570 roubles, i.e. about $285 a year), he left Russia for Austria, where he died four years later. A facile composer and excellent craftsman, he knew the demands of the choreographers and public of his period and composed more than twenty ballets, several of which were very successful. Among the ballets for which he composed scores were *Fiammetta, The Gold Fish, Don Quixote, Camargo, Papillons, The Bandits, The Adventures of Peleas, La Bayadère, Roxana, The Daughter of the Snows, Mlada, Day and Night, Paquita* (w. Deldevez), *La Source* (w. Delibes).

Minotaur, The. Ballet in 2 parts; chor.: John Taras; music: Elliott Carter; décor: Joan Junyer. First prod.: Ballet Society, Central H.S. of Needle Trades, N.Y., Mar. 26, 1947, with a cast headed by Elise Reiman (Pasiphae), Tanaquil LeClercq (Ariadne), John Taras (Theseus). The popular legend about the Minotaur, Ariadne, Theseus, and the Labyrinth told by the choreographer with more regard for the story than for the dance. Tanaquil LeClercq had the first principal role of her career in this ballet while still technically a student at the School of American Ballet, N.Y.

Minotaur, The. Ballet in 1 act, 3 scenes; chor.: Birgit Aakesson; music: Karl-Birger Blomdahl; book: Erik Lindegren; décor: Tor Hörlin. First prod.: Royal Swedish Ballet, Royal Opera Theatre, Stockholm, Apr. 5, 1958, with Bjorn Holmgren (Minotaur), Mario Mengarelli (Theseus), Mariane Orlando (Ariadne), Yvonne Brosset (Snake Priestess), Teddy Rhodin (Dionysus). The Greek legend of the fight to liberate the young men and maidens sacrificed to the monster. The fight between the Minotaur and Theseus was stylized in the manner of a bullfight.

Minty, Jeanette, English dancer, b. London, 1931; m. Peter White. Studied at Sadler's Wells (now Royal) Ballet School. Soloist, International Ballet; joined London's Festival Ballet (1953) and is currently a ballerina of that company. Dances

Sugar Plum Fairy (*The Nutcracker*), Juliet (Oleg Briansky's *Romeo and Juliet*), Swanilda (*Coppélia*), and others.

Minuet. See MENUET.

Mir Isskoustva (World of Art). The Russian art magazine established by Serge Diaghilev, Alexandre Benois, and Léon Bakst in 1899 in St. Petersburg, which exercised a strong influence on the development of the arts in Russia. It was published through 1904. Nearly all members of the group which later were to found the Diaghilev Ballet belonged to the circle which sponsored the publication of *Mir Isskoustva*.

Miracle in the Gorbals. Ballet in 1 act; chor.: Robert Helpmann; commissioned music: Arthur Bliss; book: Michael Benthall; décor: Edward Burra. First prod.: Sadler's Wells (now Royal) Ballet, Prince's Theatre, London, Oct. 26, 1944, with Pauline Clayden (Suicide), Moira Shearer and Alexis Rassine (Lovers), Leslie Edwards (Beggar), Gordon Hamilton (Street Boy), David Paltenghi (Official), Celia Franca (Prostitute), Robert Helpmann (Stranger). A dance-drama which presents the thesis that if Christ were to return, it would be necessary for people to destroy him again. The Stranger restores a Suicide to life, but when the formerly powerful Official sees his influence over the poor people jeopardized, he starts the lie that sends the Stranger to his death.

Miraculous Mandarin, The. Dance pantomime in 1 act; chor.: Hans Strobach; music: Béla Bartók; book: Bartók, after Melchior Lengyel. First prod.: Municipal Stage, Cologne, Germany, Nov. 28, 1926. It was banned on the grounds of immorality as was the Prague production (1927). The plot of the ballet concerns a prostitute who acts as a decoy for three gangsters who rob and murder their victims, but who is absolved by the omnipotence of the love between her and the Mandarin which conquers violence and death. No other ballet in modern times and no classic ballet over the same time period (thirty-five years) has had so many different productions as *The Miraculous Mandarin*. The reason for its popularity is most probably the strong dramatic plot, something uncommon in modern ballet. Of the productions which followed the two banned in Cologne and Prague mentioned above, the following are noteworthy: 1942–43, Teatro alla Scala, Milan (Aurel v. Milloss); 1945, Budapest (Gyula Garangozô; banned on grounds of immorality, but the revised version staged in 1956 is still to be seen); 1950, Teatro alla Scala, Milan (Milloss; new production); 1951, New York City Ballet (Todd Bolender); 1955, Frankfurt a/M (Herbert Freund); 1955, Venice (J. J. Etchevery); 1956, Sadler's Wells Ballet, Edinburgh Festival (Alfred Rodrigues); 1957, Vienna State Opera Ballet (Erika Hanka); 1957, Belgrade National Theatre (Dmitri Parlic); 1957, Munich State Opera House (Alan Carter); 1957, Zürich (Hans Macke); 1958, Ballet de France de Janine Charrat, Paris (Arno Vashegi); 1959, Nederlands Ballet, Amsterdam (Arno Vashegi and Vera Pasztor); 1961, Brussels, Théâtre Royal de la Monnai (Parlic); 1961, Moscow Bolshoi Ballet (Leonid Lavrovsky, entitled *The Night City*).

Mirages, Les. Ballet in 1 act, 2 scenes; chor.: Serge Lifar; music: Henri Sauguet; décor: A. M. Cassandre; book: Lifar and Cassandre. First prod.: Paris Opéra, Dec. 15, 1947, with Yvette Chauviré, Michel Renault, Micheline Bardin, Madeleine Lafon in the leading roles. A neoromantic ballet, it deals in its essence with a Young Man who reaches out for love, riches, and dreams, only to find that they are only mirages and cannot be possessed. At the ballet's end, he is alone with his shadow as before. Revived Sept. 26, 1962, with Josette Amiel, Claire Motte, and Flemming Flindt.

Miranda, Nicanor, Brazilian critic, b. S. Paulo. A Professor of the Faculty of Philosophy at S. Paulo's Univ., he has been writing about dance since 1937; has been dance critic for *Diario de S. Paulo* since 1949. He was organizer and director of the ballet activities during the celebrations for the Fourth Century of S. Paulo. Teaches History and Aesthetics of Dance in the Music Academy; is director of the ballet school of S. Paulo's municipality. Translated Curt Sachs' *Eine Weltgeschichte des Tanzes* from the German and contributed the chapter, "Ballet in Brazil," to the *Enciclopedia dello Spettacolo* (Rome, 1960).

Miró, Joan, Spanish artist, b. Catalonia, 1893. With Max Ernst he designed the drop curtains, accessories, and costumes for Bronislava Nijinska's *Romeo and Juliet* for the Diaghilev Ballets Russes (1926). His surrealist designs and costumes were the outstanding features of Leonide Massine's *Jeux d'Enfants* for Col. de Basil's Ballets Russes de Monte Carlo (1933).

Mirror Before Me. See HERODIADE.

Mirror for Witches, A. Ballet in prologue and 5 scenes; chor.: Andrée Howard; commissioned music: Dennis ApIvor; décor: Norman Adams; costumes: Andrée Howard and Norman Adams. First prod.: Sadler's Wells (now Royal) Ballet, Royal Opera House, Covent Garden, London, Mar. 4, 1952, with Anne Heaton (Doll), Julia Farron (Hannah), Leslie Edwards (Bilby), Philip Chatfield (Titus), John Hart (The Stranger). The libretto was based on a novel by Esther Forbes about 17th century New England. Hannah is bitterly jealous of the affection her husband Bilby shows for a young girl he has adopted and whose mother was burnt as a witch. When her husband dies, she finds a way to have Doll denounced as a witch, although Doll's lover, Titus, tries to protect her.

Milorad Miskovitch as Prométhée.

Miskovitch, Milorad, dancer, b. Yugoslavia, 1928. Studied dance with Nina Kirsanova in Belgrade; and Olga Preobrajenska, Boris Kniaseff in Paris. Soloist, Ballets des Champs-Elysées (1946); Mona Inglesby's International Ballet; Col. de Basil's Original Ballet Russe (1947); Grand Ballet de Monte Carlo (1948), making his debut with last named as Albrecht to Rosella Hightower's *Giselle.* Leading dancer, Ballets de Paris de Roland Petit (1949), creating *Le Combat* (William Dollar), *Adame Miroir* (Janine Charrat), and dancing the Hussar in *Le Beau Danube,* among other roles. Concert tours with *Lycette Darsonval, Yvette Chauviré* (1950–51); leading dancer, Ballets Janine Charrat (1952); guest star, London's Festival Ballet, the same year. Concert performances with Alicia Markova in England, U.S. and Paris (1954); with Colette Marchand in Japan (1955). Formed his own company (1956) and has since appeared with it all over Europe and South America. Guest artist, Ruth Page's Chicago Opera Ballet (1961). As ballet master and director he has produced such talents as Veronika Mlakar, Duska Sifnios, Yvonne Meyer, and others, as well as young choreographers such as Milko Sparemblek, Dirk Sanders, Vassili Sulich.

Apart from the roles which he dances in classic repertoire, he has created roles in his company's productions of *Prométhée* (Maurice Béjart; Maurice Chana), *Señor de Mañara* (Jack Carter; Tchaikovsky), *Echelle* (Dirk Sanders; Turjac), *Heros et son Miroir* (Sparemblek; Kelemen).

Miss Julie. Ballet in 1 act, 4 scenes; chor.: Birgit Cullberg; music: Ture Rangstrom; décor and book: Allan Fridericia, based on August Strindberg's play of the same title. First prod.: Swedish Ballet (a company organized by Elsa-Marianne von Rosen and her husband, Allan Fridericia), Riksteatern, Vasteros, Sweden, May 1, 1950, with Elsa-Marianne von Rosen, Julius Mengarelli; first performance by Royal Swedish Ballet, Stockholm (with the same principals); Sept. 7, 1950, with décor by Sven Erixon. After a London season (1951) the ballet was revised, very much to its advantage, and it is today one of the most successful story ballets in the contemporary repertoire. It follows closely the Strindberg story of Miss Julie, a young noblewoman brought up to hate and fear the idea of love between man and woman, who cannot live with her shame after she has allowed herself to be seduced by her father's valet. Birgit Cullberg staged *Miss Julie* for American Ballet Theatre, Metropolitan Opera House, N.Y., Sept. 18, 1958, with Violette Verdy and Erik Bruhn, both of whom scored triumphs as Miss Julie and the valet, Jean. Other Julies for American Ballet Theatre have been Maria Tallchief and Toni Lander. It is also in the repertoire of the Royal Danish Ballet.

Missa Brevis. Modern dance work, commissioned by the Juilliard School of Music; chor.: José Limón; music: Zoltan Kodaly's *Missa Brevis in Tempore Belli;* back projection and costumes: Ming Cho Lee; lighting: Thomas de Gaetani. First prod.: José Limón and Dance Company with Juilliard Dance Theatre, Juilliard Concert Hall, N.Y., Apr. 11, 1958, with José Limón, Ruth Currier, Betty Jones, and group. Before the back-projection of a ruined cathedral, the dance matches the noble music in its affirmation of the unquenchable spirit of man in the face of direst peril.

Mr. Puppet. Modern dance work; chor. and costumes: Nina Fonaroff. First prod.: YM–YWHA, N.Y., Nov. 7, 1948, with Nina Fonaroff and Ray Malon. Mr. Puppet speaks a long soliloquy which expresses his search for a soul and his own destruction when he tries to find it in the little female doll who stands silently beside him. Anton Dolin and Alicia Markova gave several performances of this work in England the year after its N.Y. première.

Mitchell, Arthur, dancer, b. New York City, 1934. Educated and studied dance at School of Performing Arts, N.Y., winning the dance award in his graduating year; also a scholarship student at School of American Ballet, N.Y. After appearing in several musicals and with the modern dance companies of Donald McKayle,

Arthur Mitchell as Puck in Balanchine's Midsummer Night's Dream.

John Butler (in Europe), and others, joined New York City Ballet (1956); promoted to soloist (1959). His repertoire includes Fourth Movement (*Western Symphony*), male solo (*Interplay*), Jason (*Medea*), and others; creations include Unicorn (*The Unicorn, the Gorgon and the Manticore*), pas de deux, with Diana Adams (*Agon*), male lead (*Ebony Concerto*—see JAZZ CONCERT). His most important role to date is that of Puck in George Balanchine's *A Midsummer Night's Dream*. Has frequently appeared on television and danced at Spoleto's Festival of Two Worlds (1960, 1961). As guest artist with Stuttgart State Opera Ballet, he danced Mercutio in John Cranko's *Romeo and Juliet* (1963).

Mitchell, James, contemporary American dancer, b. Hollywood, Calif. Majored in dramatics at Los Angeles City College; studied dance with Lester Horton and appeared with his group on West Coast. Danced in musicals *Bloomer Girl, Billion Dollar Baby, Brigadoon*. His success in the last named in 1947 took him to Hollywood and straight acting in films for several years. Returned to Broadway for *Paint Your Wagon* (1951); played MacHeath in the revival of *The Three-Penny Opera* (1954); had a big success acting and dancing in *Carnival* (1961).

Mlakar, Pia, Yugoslav dancer and choreographer, b. Hamburg, Germany, 1908. Wife of choreographer Pino Mlakar and mother of dancer Veronika Mlakar. Studied in Berlin with Rudolf von Laban and in Belgrade with Yelena Poliakova, a former soloist of the Imperial Maryinsky Theatre, St. Petersburg. She made her debut in Darmstadt (1929), and was principal dancer in Dessau (1930–33), Zurich (1935–38), Munich (1939–43). Retired as dancer (1947) to devote herself to choreography in collaboration with her husband.

Mlakar, Pino, Yugoslav dancer and choreographer, b. Novo Mesto, 1907. Husband of Pia Mlakar and father of Veronika Mlakar. Pupil of Rudolf von Laban in Berlin; Yelena Poliakova in Belgrade. After seasons in Darmstadt and Dessau, won Bronze Medal in the competition organized by Les Archives Internationales de la Danse in Paris (1932) for his ballet *Un Amour du Moyen Age* (Handel-Vivaldi), a ballet which he re-choreographed, with his wife, to commissioned music by Fran Lhotka and premièred Feb. 6, 1937 at Stadttheater, Zurich, under the title *The Ballad of a Medieval Love*. Other ballets choreographed by this gifted couple include *The Legend of Joseph* (Richard Strauss), Belgrade, 1934; *The Devil in the Village* (Fran Lhotka), Zurich, 1935 and 1937; *Prometheus* (Beethoven), Zurich, 1935; *The Little Ballerina* (Prek), Liubliana (Yugoslavia) company, 1947, in which their daughter made her debut; other original works and revivals in Yugoslavia, France, and Germany.

Mlakar, Veronika, soloist American Ballet Theatre, b. Zurich, Switzerland, 1935. The daughter of the Yugoslav dancers and choreographers Pia and Pino Mlakar, she began her dance training with her mother and later studied at the Sadler's Wells (now Royal) Ballet School, London (1952–54); also with Mme. Rausanne in Paris; at the Ballet Arts School (with Vladimir Dokoudovsky), the School of American Ballet, and the Ballet Theatre School, all in N.Y. She made her debut in Ljubljana, Yugoslavia (1947) and danced her first leading role (Swanilda in *Coppélia*) with the Munich State Opera Ballet (1951). She created the role of the Unicorn in the Jean Cocteau–Heinz Rosen *La Dame à la Licorne* (1953) and in the following year the roles of Florence in *Joan von Zarissa* and the Queen of Hearts in Janine Charrat's *Jeu de Cartes*. Joined Roland Petit's Ballets de Paris and created *La Chambre* (1955). After a season with Milorad Miskovitch's Ballet

Veronika Mlakar as Hagar in Tudor's Pillar of Fire.

de l'Etoile, she returned to the Petit company and created *La Dame dans la Lune* (1957). Later that year she came to the U.S. with the Petit company and subsequently joined Ruth Page's Chicago Opera Ballet. In 1961 she joined Jerome Robbins' Ballets: U.S.A. for its European tour and N.Y. season. Her repertoire included *The Cage* (the Novice), *The Concert* (the "Mad" Ballerina), and perhaps the finest role in the repertoire: the Girl in *Afternoon of a Faun*. She remained in N.Y. after the season and married the psychiatrist Dr. Arthur Brandt. Veronika Mlakar joined the American Ballet Theatre for its 25th Anniversary Season (1964) having taken time to rest after the European tour and to have a child. Her roles in the company included corps de ballet, a variety of small roles, and later more important ones such as the Mother of the Groom in Robbins' staging of *Les Noces,* Myrtha in *Giselle,* and Antony Tudor's *Dark Elegies*. She danced Hagar in Tudor's *Pillar of Fire* for the first time on Feb. 2, 1966. She danced the title role in Birgit Cullberg's *Moon Reindeer* (Oct., 1966) and in 1967 she danced *Miss Julie* with Eric Bruhn.

Modern Dance (definition). According to Paul Love, modern dance is a form of dance based on dynamism, on the collision of two opposites, such as contraction and release, fall and recovery, etc., which were formulated from natural rhythms, originally used literally. Technically, movement is regarded as the substance of the modern dance and the body is the instrument. All movement comes from a central source, the torso, which is the controlling force, and contains psychical (or mental) overtones of meaning (see METAKINESIS). According to John Martin, modern dance is based on four principles: substance (movement), dynamism, metakinesis, form (as a result of movement, not dependent on musical or other forms). See also AMERICAN MODERN DANCE.

Modern Galop. Ballet in 1 movement; chor.: Dennis Gray; music: George Ribalowsky; décor: Henrique Peyceré. First prod.: Teatro Municipal, Rio de Janeiro, 1954. An abstract ballet inspired by the fusion of several colors.

Modern Jazz: Variants. Ballet in 5 variants and finale; chor.: George Balanchine; music: Gunther Schuller, commissioned by New York City Ballet (1960). First prod.: New York City Ballet, City Center, N.Y., Jan. 4, 1961, with Diana Adams, Melissa Hayden, Arthur Mitchell, John Jones. The second of the "Jazz Evening" programs (see JAZZ CONCERT). Gunther Schuller conducted in the orchestra pit and the chief attraction was the presence on stage of the Modern Jazz Quartet (John Lewis, piano; Percy Heath, double bass; Connie Kay, drums; Milt Jackson, vibraharp). A companion piece, to music by Milton Babbitt, had been announced for this performance, but was cancelled at short notice on the plea that the orchestration was not ready.

Mohaupt, Richard (1904–1957), German composer. Resided in the U.S. (1939–

55). Composed the ballets *Gay Swindles of Courasche* (1936), *Max and Moritz* (1949), *Lysistrata* (1955).

Moiseyev, Igor, Peoples' Artist of the U.S.S.R., Soviet choreographer, artistic director of the State Folk Dance Ensemble of the U.S.S.R., b. Kiev, 1906. Moved with his parents to Moscow, where he saw his first ballet at the age of thirteen. He entered one of the private ballet studios functioning at that period and in 1921 was accepted into the fourth grade of the Bolshoi School, graduating from it in 1924. In the Bolshoi company he was a versatile dancer in classic, demi-caractère, and grotesque styles, some of his ballets being Sergei Vassilenko's *Joseph the Beautiful* (title role), *Theolinda* (Raoul), *La Bayadère* (Slave), *Le Corsaire* (Slave), *The Red Flower* (Phoenix Bird). His earliest choreography was *The Football Player* to music by Oransky (1930) with himself in the title role. Later the same year he established himself as a choreographer with his dances for Sergei Prokofiev's opera-ballet *Love for Three Oranges.* His first major ballet was *Salammbo* to music by Andrei Arends (1932), previously choreographed in 1910 by Alexander Gorsky. He himself played the principal male role of Mato. His next important creation was *Three Fat Men,* also with music by Oransky, with which he proved himself to be an inventive choreographer and a master of stagecraft.

In 1936 Moiseyev's interests became attracted to a new field of choreography. In that year a Theatre of Folk Art was established in Moscow with the idea of assembling amateur talent from all parts of the country. Moiseyev was asked to head the choreographic department of the theatre. He accepted and also became one of the organizers of a nation-wide Folk Dance Festival, for which he was asked to put together one big program of separate dance numbers brought to the Festival from all parts of the country. He realized it was time to assemble all these riches together, collecting the experience of the national dancers and improving upon it artistically by creating new choreography on the basis of the authentic folk dance idioms.

Igor Moiseyev, founder, choreographer, director of the State Folk Dance Ensemble of the U.S.S.R.

In 1937 the State Folk Dance Ensemble, headed by Igor Moiseyev, was officially founded (it celebrated its 25th Anniversary in Feb., 1962). It consisted of thirty-five dancers, many of them amateurs who had recently participated in the Folk Dance Festival. A group of "National Dancers," it could perform nothing but their own folk dances. Only about ten per cent of them were professionals—graduates of the Bolshoi or some other ballet school. All the dancers who formed the ensemble had to be taught how to perform all folk dances in a highly professional way without sacrificing the proper national style. On Oct. 7, 1937, the first program was shown at the Hall of Columns in Moscow. It included Russian, Ukrainian, Georgian, Byelorussian, Armenian, Kazakh, Azerbaijan, and Moldavian dances.

In the first year the ensemble was given the task of learning dances of the eleven republics then forming the Soviet Union.

In 1939 Latvian, Lithuanian and Estonian dances were added.

Moiseyev showed from the first his great gift for attaining magnificent theatrical effects with very simple means. He developed and literally re-created folk dances, patterns, often concealing the primitivism of the few basic steps which usually constitute a folk dance. He has also composed original dances which are completely true to the folk dance idiom. His Byelorussian *Bulba* is his own invention yet so completely true to the Byelorussian folklore, which had been lost before the revolution, that this dance has become the national dance of the Byelorussian people. *Bulba* is an object lesson of his artistic principles.

By 1941 the Ensemble was a large company of seventy professional dancers who had travelled widely all over the country. While it was and still is called an Ensemble, it is in reality a large and well-organized theatre of Folk Dance now numbering more than one hundred dancers. Every dancer has been trained in classic and character dance either at the Bolshoi Theatre School or its National Dance Department headed by Igor Moiseyev.

In his later programs Moiseyev has experimented with a more theatrical type of show based on a definite, but not too elaborate subject. Among these more recent numbers are *Red Navy Suite* (One Day in the Life of a Ship), *Football* (or Soccer), *May 1st* (celebrations in the streets of Moscow), *Ukrainian Suite* (betrothal of a young couple), *Pictures from the Past* (a whole series of brilliant characterizations), and *Partisans,* the famous choreographic scene in which the impression of men on horseback is conveyed in a unique way. In all Moiseyev has choreographed over 170 dances for the Ensemble.

The company has exerted a great influence, not only in the Soviet Union, where numerous ensembles built on the same lines have been founded, but in many other countries where folk dance has often been re-awakened following a visit from the Ensemble. In turn the Ensemble has studied and added to its repertoire dances of many of the countries it has visited, and taught other dances from its own repertoire to local dance groups. In many instances dances of other nations were commissioned from local choreographers, but in every case Moiseyev added to them his own inimitable style and knowledge of the theatre. In 1955 the Ensemble made a successful tour of France and England; in 1957 visited Egypt; in 1958, 1961 and 1965 the U.S.

In 1958 Moiseyev returned to the Bolshoi Theatre to create *Spartacus* for the Bolshoi Ballet, to music by Aram Khachaturian, in which he was particularly successful with the gladiators' scenes in the Roman circus.

In April, 1967 he announced plans for the formation of a company with "a new concert-stage repertoire of classic dance," which will specialize in one-act ballets and divertissements.

Moiseyev is married to Peoples' Artist of the RSFSR Tamara Zeifert, leading soloist of the Ensemble. His daughter, Olga, graduate of the Bolshoi school, is also a soloist with the Ensemble.

Moiseyeva, Olga, Honored Artist of the RSFSR, Soviet ballerina, b. 1928. Graduated from the Leningrad ballet school (class of Agrippina Vaganova, 1947), attracting attention in the ballerina part in the Shades scene from *La Bayadère.* Her first important role in the Kirov Ballet was that of Nikia, the leading part in the same ballet (1949). She was promoted to ballerina in 1953. Her repertoire includes *The Sleeping Beauty* (both Aurora and Princess Florine), *Swan Lake* (Odette-Odile), *Gayané* (title role), *Don Quixote* (Kitri), *Shurale* (Bird-Girl), and recently more dramatic roles such as *The Fountain of Bakhchisarai* (Zarema), *Spartacus* (Aegina), *Path of Thunder* (Sarie). Alternating with Inna Zubkovskaya, she

Olga N. Moiseyeva, ballerina of the Moscow Bolshoi, as Odette. (She is not related to Igor Moiseyev.)

created the role of Queen Mekhmene-Banu in *Legend of Love* (1961). She has danced in several foreign countries during Kirov Ballet tours, including France and England (1961) and the U.S. and Canada (1964).

Mollerup, Mette, soloist of the Royal Danish Ballet, b. Copenhagen, 1931. Entered the company's school (1947) after having been trained by her aunt, Asta Mollerup; accepted into the company (1950); made soloist (1956). Dances leading roles in *Graduation Ball, Symphony in C, Night Shadow, Pas de Quatre, Concertette, Far From Denmark, Don Quixote, Medea, Blood Wedding, Ballet in D, Apollon Musagète,* and others.

Monahan, James, English writer and critic, b. 1912. Controller, European Services of the British Broadcasting Corporation since Dec., 1952. Ballet critic, *The Guardian* (formerly *Manchester Guardian*), for over 25 years. Author of *Fonteyn: A Study of the Ballerina in Her Setting* (1958), and others. Member of Critics' Circle, London. Created Commander of the Order of the British Empire (C.B.E.), 1962.

Moncion, Francisco, contemporary American dancer, b. La Vega, Dominican Republic. Made his debut with New Opera Company (1942); danced in the operetta *The Merry Widow* (1943–44). Soloist, Ballet International (1944), creating title roles in *Sebastian* and *Mad Tristan.* Associated with New York City Ballet since its days as Ballet Society when he created leading roles in *Four Temperaments* (1946) and *Divertimento* (1947). Since then he has danced a large repertoire including important creations in *Age of Anxiety,* Jerome Robbins' *After-*

Francisco Moncion as King Midas in The Triumph of Bacchus and Ariadne.

noon of a Faun, in his own ballet, *Pastorale,* and giving a deeply impressive portrayal in the title role of *Prodigal Son.* He is also a fine painter and has given several exhibitions in N.Y. galleries.

Moncur, Pamela, English dancer, b. Manchester, 1938. Studied at Royal Ballet School, entering the company (1957) after dancing with Covent Garden Opera Ballet. Soloist, Royal Ballet, since 1959. Roles include Pas de Trois (*Swan Lake*), Golden Vine Fairy (*The Sleeping Beauty*), Pas de Trois (*Les Patineurs*), and others.

Monplaisir, Hippolyte (Hippolyte George Sornet), b. Bordeaux, France, 1821, d. Besana, Italy, 1877. Monplaisir studied under Guillemin in Brussels (where he made his debut in 1839), and with Carlo Blasis in Milan. He and his wife, Adele, were first dancers at Teatro alla Scala, Milan (1844–46). During this period Monplaisir partnered Fanny Elssler and worked with Maria Taglioni, Lucile Grahn, Carolina Rosati, and Jules Perrot. With his father-in-law, Victor Bartholomin, Monplaisir brought the first large-scale ballet company to the U.S. (1847). After 1848 Monplaisir alone directed this company, which produced here such ballets as Perrot's *L'Illusion d'un Peintre* and *Esmeralda,* Mazilier's *Le Diable à Quatre,* Monplaisir's *Azelia, Une Nuit à Venise,* and a version of *La Fille Mal Gardée.* They travelled as far as California. Due to a foot injury Monplaisir stopped dancing in 1856, while appearing at the Teatro de S. Carlos, Lisbon, where he succeeded Arthur St. Léon as choreographer. From 1861 until his death in 1877, Monplaisir produced a long series of successful ballets at La Scala, Milan. Outstanding were his *La Camargo* (1868, with Amalia Ferraris), *Brahma* (1869, also with Ferraris), and *La Semiramide del Nord* (1869, with Caterina Beretta). *Brahma,* in particular, was given all over the world, and remained in the repertoire as late as 1912. Virginia Zucchi danced it at the summer theatre "Abandon Sorrow" in St. Petersburg (1884), and Brianza (1896) —L.M.

Montez, Lola (Eliza Gilbert) (1818–1861), Irish dancer. She became the mistress of Ludwig I of Bavaria and held much political power until he abdicated. She is one of the characters in Leonide Massine's ballet *Bacchanale* (1939). Edward Caton staged *Lola Montez,* a ballet based upon her life, for Ballet for America (1946), and revived it for Ballet Russe de Monte Carlo (1947).

Monumentum Pro Gesualdo. Ballet in 3 movements; chor.: George Balanchine; music: three madrigals by Gesualdo di Venosa, re-composed for instruments by Igor Stravinsky (1960); costumes: Barbara Karinska. First prod.: New York City Ballet, City Center, N.Y., Nov. 16, 1960, with Diana Adams and Conrad Ludlow; Francia Russell and Roland Vazquez; Diane Consoer and Michael Lland; Janet Greschler and Shaun O'Brien; Hester FitzGerald and Deni Lamont; Marlene Mesavage and Bill Carter; Patricia Neary and Zbigniew Cichocki. The only importance of this tiny, eight minute work lies in its Stravinsky score. *Monumentum* and *Variations from Don Sebastian* (afterwards called *Donizetti Variations*) were premièred on "Salute to Italy" night, in honor of the centennial celebration of the unification of Italy.

Moon Reindeer, The. Ballet in 1 act; chor.: Birgit Cullberg; music: Knudage Riisager; décor: Per Falk. First prod.: Royal Danish Ballet, Royal Theatre, Copenhagen, Nov. 22, 1957, with Mona Vangsaa (Girl-Reindeer), Henning Kronstam (Nilas), Fredbjørn Bjørnsson (Sorcerer). It was staged by Royal Swedish Ballet, Stockholm, Jan. 31, 1959, with Mariane Orlando and Caj Selling in the two leading roles, and by American Ballet Theatre at 54th St. Theatre, N.Y., Oct. 2, 1961, with Lupe Serrano and Royes Fernandez. Later in the N.Y. season, Mariane Orlando and Caj Selling, guest artists with American Ballet Theatre at the time, repeated the roles they created for the Swedish production. The plot is based on a Lappland legend. The girl, spurned by the boy she loves, seeks help from a sorcerer. In return for winning the boy's love, she must turn into a white reindeer when the moon is full and, in this shape, lure hunters over the precipice to their deaths. Finally her lover must be the victim, but he kills her and in death she resumes her human form. Miss Cullberg revived the work for the American Ballet Theatre (Aug.–Sept., 1966) with Toni Lander and Bruce Marks, Sallie Wilson and Gayle Young alternating in the principal roles.

Moor of Venice, The. Ballet in 8 scenes, prologue and epilogue; chor.: Erika Hanka; music: Boris Blacher; décor: Georges Wakhevitch. First prod.: Vienna State Opera, Nov. 29, 1955, with Willy Dirtl (Othello), Christl Zimmerl (Desdemona), Richard Adama (Jago). The ballet is based on Shakespeare's *Othello* and follows the action fairly faithfully. In 1956 Yvonne Georgi staged this ballet in Hannover; also Tatiana Gsovska during the Berlin Festival (under the title *Othello*).

Moore, Jack, American modern dancer, b. Monticello, Ind., 1926. B.A., State Univ. of Iowa. Studied dance with Martha Graham and Merce Cunningham; ballet at School of American Ballet, N.Y. Was a Dance Audition Winner of the YW–YMHA, N.Y. (1951), and the recipient of the 1960 Doris Humphrey Fellowship at Connecticut College School of Dance. Performed with the Nina Fonaroff and Pearl Lang companies at American Dance season at the Alvin Theatre (1953), and appeared with the Martha Graham company for its season the same year at the Alvin. Has danced many times with Anna Solokow's company, his most important creation being one of the principal roles in *Rooms.* Has also danced with the José Limón and Merce Cunningham companies, among others. Has created many dance works, both solos and for groups, including *Somewhere to Nowhere, The Act* (1957), *The Cry of the Phoenix, The Greek* (1958), *Area Disabled* (1959), *Intaglios, Songs Remembered* (1960), *Target* (1961), *Excursions, Erasure, Chambers and Corridors* (1962). As a teacher he has been on the faculty of the Neighborhood Playhouse School of the Theatre, N.Y., as assistant to Louis Horst (1952–57), Juilliard School of Music Dance Department (1958–61); has taught at Connecticut College Summer School of Dance on various occasions, and is on the faculty of Bennington College Dance Dept. Has appeared in Broadway musicals and on television. Is on the board of directors of Contemporary Dance, Inc.

Moore, Lillian, dancer, writer, teacher, b. Chase City, Va., 1915; m. David C. Maclay. Studied ballet under George Balanchine, Pierre Vladimiroff, Margaret Curtis, and Rosina Galli (at Metropolitan Opera House), Alexandra Fedorova-Fokine, and others; modern dance with Charles Weidman. Joined Metropolitan Opera Ballet at sixteen, making her debut as soloist in *William Tell* (1931). Danced with American Ballet (1935–38); solo dancer, Metropolitan Opera Ballet under Boris Romanov (1938–42); guest artist, Fokine Ballet (1940), dancing Polovetsian Girl in *Prince Igor,* Prelude and Waltz in *Les Sylphides;* also appeared with various other groups. Toured Pacific as first dancer with the USO *Jerome Kern Show* (1945–46); toured Europe for Special Services, U.S. Army (1947–48); toured Austria, Italy, and Hungary (1948), and was the first American dancer to dance behind the Iron Curtain (Nov., 1948, Budapest). Between 1950 and 1953 she toured U.S. in a program of her own dances, mostly satirical and character, appearing at Jacob's Pillow Dance Festival for the first three years. Retired as a dancer in 1954 and then taught. Her many writings include the article, "Ballet," in the Encyclopedia Britannica, and others, as well as the "Dance-Ballet" section in the annual Encyclopedia Britannica *Book of the Year* (1950 to date); was American correspondent to the London *Dancing Times* (1943 to 1967); contributor to *Dance News, Dance Encyclopedia, Ballet Annual,* the Italian *Enciclopedia dello Spettacolo, Dance Index, Dance Perspectives, Chronicles of the American Dance* (ed. Paul Magriel), *N.Y. Times, N.Y. Herald Tribune.* Author of *Artists of the Dance;* monographs on Mary Ann Lee, John Durang, George Washington Smith, Moreau de St. Méry, Pierre Landrin Duport; co-author (with Erik Bruhn) of *Bournonville and Ballet Technique* (London and N.Y., 1962). In 1966 wrote *Images of the Dance: Historical Treasures of the Dance Collection, 1581–1861*), pub. by the N.Y. Public Library. That year was appointed director of the special apprentice program of City Center Joffrey Ballet. Died July 28, 1967.

Moor's Pavane, The. Modern dance work; chor.: José Limón; music: Henry Purcell, arr. by Simon Sadoff from *Abdelazer, The Gordian Knot Untied,* and the pavane from Pavane and Chaconne for Strings; costumes: Pauline Lawrence. First prod.: José Limón Dance Company, second American Dance Festival, Connecticut College, New London, August, 1949, with José Limón (The Moor), Betty Jones (His Wife), Lucas Hoving (His Friend), Pauline Koner (His Friend's Wife). The handkerchief episode from Shakespeare's *Othello* delineating the love, jealousy, passion, and tragedy of the play within the formal framework of a court dance.

Mordente, Tony (Anthony), American dancer, b. Brooklyn, N.Y., 1935; m. Chita Rivera. First studied ballet with Don Farnworth; graduated School of Performing Arts, N.Y., earning Dance Award. Several times premier danseur Radio City Music Hall, N.Y. A demi-caractère dancer rather than a straight classicist, he is shaping his career in Broadway musicals rather than in a ballet company. His first Broadway show was *Li'l Abner,* in which he created the role of Lonesome Polecat, choreographed by Michael Kidd. His reputation was established with his dancing of the role of A-rab in the original production of the Arthur Laurents–Leonard Bernstein–Jerome Robbins musical *West Side Story* (1957). In the original London company of the show he played the same role and in addition was assistant to Robbins and in charge of the company. In the original Broadway production of *Bye Bye, Birdie* he was assistant to director-choreographer Gower Champion; also choreographed the dances in the London production of the show. Played the part of Action in the film version of *West Side Story;* also appeared in the film *The Longest Day.* Played straight acting roles in television shows "Combat" and "Outer Limits." Appeared on the "Ed Sullivan Show," two "Sid Caesar Shows," assisting choreographer Lee Becker in one. Played Ensign Pulver in stock company of *Mr. Roberts.* Directed and choreographed *West Side Story* in St. Louis and *Bye Bye, Birdie* in Las Vegas. Assistant to Michael Kidd in the N.Y. World's Fair show *Wonder World* (1964); assistant to Michael Kidd for *Ben Franklin in Paris* (1964).

Mordkin Ballet. A ballet group organized by Mikhail Mordkin in N.Y. in 1937 as an outlet for the talents and ambitions of his pupils. The company subsequently formed the basis for Ballet Theatre.

Mordkin, Mikhail (1881–1944), Russian dancer, choreographer, and teacher, b. Moscow. He was a graduate of the Moscow Imperial School of Ballet and a

Mikhail Mordkin in his ballet studio (ca. *1938*).

premier danseur and ballet master of the Bolshoi Theatre, Moscow. In 1909 he joined the Diaghilev Ballets Russes for its initial season in Western Europe. Of an independent nature, characteristic of the dancer until his last days, Mordkin did not find it possible to stay with the company beyond the first season. He partnered with Anna Pavlova for appearances at the Paris Opéra. Their dancing at the Opéra impressed the late Otto Kahn, who invited the dancers to appear at the Metropolitan Opera House, N.Y., Jan., 1910. The first performance at the Metropolitan, which began after the regular opera performance and lasted into the morning, was nothing short of a sensation. The short N.Y. season was followed in 1910–11 by a coast to coast tour with a company especially engaged for it. In 1911 Mordkin returned to Russia where he organized for subsequent Western European and American tours a new company including, among others, Yekaterina Geltzer, Julia Sedova, Lydia Lopoukhova, Alexandre Volinine. Following the tours, Mordkin went back to Russia and was appointed ballet master of the Bolshoi Theatre. After the Oct., 1917, revolution he found it difficult to work under the new authorities. At the end of 1923 he left his native land to settle in U.S. In 1924 Mordkin and the company he had formed appeared in the Greenwich Village Follies, N.Y. During the next two years he toured America under the management of Morris Gest. His touring company included Vera Nemtchinova, Xenia Makletzova, and Hilda Butsova. After the tour Mordkin opened a ballet school in N.Y. and also taught in Philadelphia. In 1937 he organized the Mordkin Ballet Company as an outlet for the advanced students of his school. By 1938 the company had outgrown its original purpose and it became a professional organization. Among the ballets which Mordkin staged for his company were *Giselle, La Fille Mal Gardée, The Goldfish, Voices of Spring, Trepak,* and several others. In the fall of 1939 the Mordkin Ballet was reorganized into Ballet Theatre. Mordkin did not stay with Ballet Theatre, but returned to teaching. Mikhail Mordkin was married to Bronislava Pojitskaya, formerly a soloist of the Moscow Bolshoi Theatre. He died July 15, 1944, at his summer home in Millbrook, N.Y.

Moreau, Jacqueline, French dancer. Studied at Paris Opéra school and with Nora Kiss. Nominated première danseuse of Opéra (1948); leading dancer, Ballets des Champs Elysées (1951); ballerina, Grand Ballet du Marquis de Cuevas (1951–59). Her principal roles in the Marquis' company were in *Tertulia, Les Trois Soeurs, Du, Pas de Quatre, Les Sylphides, Swan Lake, Giselle,* and others.

Moreno, Blanca, soloist Teatro Colón, Buenos Aires, b. Traiguen, Chile, 1931; now an Argentine citizen. Graduate of Conservatorio Nacional de Música y Arte Escénico; dance teacher's diploma from Escuela Nacional de Danzas. Joined Teatro Colón as corps de ballet dancer (1947); promoted to soloist the following year. Her repertory includes *Bolero, Prometheus* (Milloss), *Suite des Danses,*

Aurora's Wedding, Les Sylphides, Paganini, Apollon Musagète, Interplay (Lambrinos), *Choreartium, Serenade, Ajedrez, La Flor de Irupé, Pas de Quatre, Mariposas Nocturnas, Pavana Real,* and others. In 1961 was invited by Teatro Argentino de La Plata, Buenos Aires, to dance in *Apollon Musagète.*

Moreno, Victor, Argentine dancer and teacher, b. Buenos Aires, 1928. Studied dance with Gemma Castillo, Michel Borovski, Francisco Gago, Yekaterina de Galantha, Vassili Lambrinos. Soloist, Teatro Colón (1947–52). His repertory includes *The Prodigal Son* (Lichine), *Capriccio Espagnol, Gaîté Parisienne, Schéhérazade, Swan Lake, Joan von Zarissa, Orpheo,* and others. Was premier danseur of Ballet Russe de Monte Carlo (1952–57). At present teaches dance in California and has his own regional ballet company.

Moreton, Ursula, English dancer, teacher, b. Southsea, 1903. Studied ballet with Enrico Cecchetti. Made her debut with Tamara Karsavina (1920). Member of the Diaghilev Ballets Russes (1920–22), dancing one of the two Porcelain Princesses in the famous revival of *The Sleeping Beauty* (1921). Joined Ninette de Valois as teacher (1926). Principal dancer, Vic-Wells (later Sadler's Wells, now Royal) Ballet, creating The Dancer (*The Rake's Progress*), President's Wife (*The Nutcracker*), Bathilde (*Giselle*), and others, and dancing many roles in the early repertoire. Assistant director, Sadler's Wells Theatre Ballet (1946–52); ballet principal of Royal Ballet School since 1952. Received the Royal Academy of Dancing's Queen Elizabeth II Coronation Award (1961).

Morillo, Roberto Garcia, Argentine composer, music professor and critic, b. Buenos Aires, 1911; m. Dora Kriner. Graduate of Conservatorio Nacional de Música y Arte Escénico. Music critic of the newspaper *La Nación* and author of many articles in a great many magazines. Among his many compositions are two ballets: *Harrild,* choreographed by Louis Bercher (1945), and *Usher,* choreographed by Leonide Massine (1955), both given by Teatro Colón, Buenos Aires. He is the author of a number of books and lectures in numerous universities, colleges, and to cultural organizations.

Morini, Elettra, Italian dancer, b. 1937. Entered the ballet school of Teatro alla Scala, Milan (1947); was graduated (1956); appeared in her Passo d'Addio (1957); promoted to soloist (1958). Dances mainly character roles in *Three-Cornered Hat, Capriccio Espagnol, La Giara,* and others.

Morlacchi, Giuseppina, b. Milan, Italy, 1843, d. Billerica, Mass., U.S., 1886. After studying with Carlo Blasis and Augusto Hus in Milan, Morlacchi made her debut in Genoa. Came to the U.S. as prima ballerina of *The Devil's Auction* (1867), a ballet spectacle similar to the famous *Black Crook.* Later she starred in the opera-ballet *La Bayadère,* as well as in *Esmeralda* and *L'Almée.* One of the finest exponents of the pure Italian school, she won the admiration of such critics as Brander Matthews and Philip Hale. While dancing in *The Scouts of the Prairie,* a spectacle based on the lives of famous Indian fighters, she married John Omahundro, an Indian scout known as "Texas Jack" who was a close friend and associate of "Buffalo Bill" Cody. After her husband's death in 1880, Morlacchi retired from the stage and lived quietly in East Billerica, Mass.–L.M.

Morosova, Olga, widow of Col. de Basil, a soloist in his Ballets Russes and ballerina of Original Ballet Russe in which she danced Street Dancer (*Le Beau Danube*), The Beloved (*Symphonie Fantastique*), and others. She is a sister of Nina Verchinina.

Moross, Jerome, contemporary American composer. Composed the music for *Frankie and Johnny* and *An American Pattern* (Ruth Page–Bentley Stone), *American Saga* (Charles Weidman). He also arranged and supplemented Georges Bizet's music for the Page-Stone ballet *Guns and Castanets.*

Morrice, Norman, British dancer and choreographer, b. Agua Dulca, Vera Cruz, Mexico, 1931. Studied dance at Royal Academy of Dancing, London, but mainly at the Rambert School of Ballet; entered Ballet Rambert (1953) and is currently choreographer and a principal dancer (mainly character roles). His roles include Dr. Coppelius (which he created for the Rambert production of *Coppélia*), Scottish Rhapsody and Popular Song (*Façade*), Hilarion (*Giselle*), Man She Must Marry (*Lilac Garden*), Third Dance (*Dark Elegies*), James (*La Sylphide*), Poet (*Night Shadow*), and others. His first ballet was *Two Brothers* (1958) in which he created the role of the younger brother, followed by *Hazana, The Wise Monkeys, A Place in the Desert,* and *Conflicts.* Visited U.S. (1961–62) for five months as recipient of a Fellowship in Choreography awarded by the Young Artists' Project of the Ford Foundation administered through the Institute of International Education. In the summer of 1964 choreographed *Cul de Sac* for Ballet Rambert to Christopher Whelan's commissioned score; London première: Sadler's Wells Theatre, July 19.

Morris, Margaret, English dancer and teacher, b. London, 1891. Studied with John d'Auban, ballet master, Drury Lane Theatre; also with Raymond Duncan (Greek dance). Evolved own technique of creative dance at the age of seventeen. Started own school in Bloomsbury, London, 1910. Choreography, on new technique, for production of Gluck's *Orfeo ed Euridice* at Savoy Theatre. Danced in various productions, then took own troupe to Paris (1913). Started small theatre in Chelsea (London) with a club for dancers, painters and musicians (1914). Adapted her technique for remedial purposes and created the Margaret Morris Movement, combining medical and aesthetic values (1925). Created a notation of human movement, Danscript (1928). Founded Celtic Ballet in Glasgow (1947), which appeared at Jacob's Pillow Dance Festival (1954). Founded Scottish National Ballet at Pitlochry (1960). Author of *Margaret Morris Dancing, Basic Physical Training* (textbook of Margaret Morris Movement).

Morris Dance (also Moresque, Morisque, Morisco, Morrisk, Morrice, or Moorish). Dance originating with the Moors in Spain ca. 1500. It had its most varied development in England where bells, kerchiefs, hobby-horses, and blackamoors were part of the dance. As a folk dance, a jog-trot was maintained as arms waved handkerchiefs. The steps were complicated. The Italian Morisco is done with bells tied on hands and feet. Frederick Ashton based the many ensemble dances in *La Fille Mal Gardée* for the Royal Ballet on traditional English Morris dances.

Mosaval, Johaar, South African dancer, b. Cape Town, 1934. Studied at Cape Town University Ballet (1947–50); Sadler's Wells School (1951). Entered Sadler's Wells Theatre Ballet (1952), becoming soloist (1953) where his principal creation was Bootface (*The Lady and the Fool*); also danced Jasper (*Pineapple Poll*), Harlequin (*Carnaval*), Tom (*Selinda*), and others. Currently soloist with Royal Ballet where his repertoire includes Blue Skater (*Les Patineurs*), *Blue Bird* pas de deux (*The Sleeping Beauty*), Punchinello (*Veneziana*), Dr. Coppelius (*Coppélia*), and others. Appears frequently on television and has also been guest soloist in a number of operas, notably in Benjamin Britten's *A Midsummer Night's Dream* (1961).

Mosolova, Vera (1876–1949), Honored Art Worker of the RSFSR, Soviet ballerina and teacher. Mistress of the classic ballet of the old tradition, Mosolova was one of the guardians of the heritage of the Russian school. She entered the Bolshoi School in 1886 and upon graduation in 1893 was accepted into the company. In 1896 she was transferred with Yekaterina Geltzer to St. Petersburg to dance in the Maryinsky company and to study in the classe de perfection of Christian Johansson. In 1911 Mosolova and Geltzer danced in the Alexander Gorsky production of *The Dance Dream* at the London Alhambra Theatre. In 1913 she danced and taught in the Anna Pavlova company at the Palace Theatre, London. She retired from the stage in 1918 after twenty-five years of service at the Bolshoi and devoted herself to teaching. Among her pupils were Asaf and Sulamith Messerer, Igor Moiseyev, Vera Vassilieva, and many others. She wrote a book of memoirs, the manuscript of which is preserved in the Bakhrushin Theatre Museum, Moscow.

Mossford, Lorna, contemporary English dancer and teacher, b. London. Studied with Violet Minifie and at Sadler's Wells (now Royal) Ballet School. Member of Sadler's Wells Ballet (1941–51), becoming soloist and dancing Crystal Fountain and Enchanted Garden Fairies (*The Sleeping Beauty*), Fairy Spring and Fairy Godmother (Frederick Ashton's *Cinderella*), among many other roles. Principal dancer, Opera House, Ankara, in first Turkish opera, *Kerem* (1953). Taught at Ankara Conservatoire. Ballet mistress, touring section Royal Ballet since 1957. Staged Kenneth MacMillan's *Solitaire* for Stuttgart Opera Ballet (1961).

Mother Goose Suite. Ballet in 1 act; chor.: Todd Bolender; music: Maurice Ravel's score of that name (*Ma Mère l'Oye*); décor: André Derain. Originally created for the short-lived American Concert Ballet (1943) with Mary Jane Shea and Francisco Moncion; New York City Ballet presented it for the first time at City Center, N.Y., Nov. 1, 1948, using the décor Derain had originally designed for *Les Songes* (Dreams) for Les Ballets 1933. The episodes of the music, based on the Mother Goose fairy tales, were "The Enchanted Garden," "Hop o'my Thumb," "Enchanted Princess," and "Beauty and the Beast." Bolender followed the mood of the music rather than the fact of the stories, using as his theme a Spectator who watches herself as a young girl imagining the various episodes. Marie Jeanne was the young girl, with Todd Bolender (Hop o'my Thumb), Dick Beard (Prince), Francisco Moncion (The Beast).

Motion. See Movement.

Motion Pictures, Ballet in.

by George Balanchine.

It is absurd to regard motion pictures as a mere relaxation or pastime. One should have the same attitude toward motion pictures as one has toward any other form of theatrical art. Films should be a product of greater imagination and fantasy than the theatre because of the larger scope which elements of space and time have in motion pictures. I also think that the responsibility of anyone working in motion pictures, whether he is a producer, director, or actor, is greater than he might have in the theatre because he is not addressing a selected group of people, a city public, but large masses of people all over the world. This is why I think a serious, creative, inventive, and imaginative approach to the films is an absolute necessity.

The importance of ballet for motion pictures lies in the element of pure fantasy. Although motion pictures have included quite a lot of fantasy, it has been mostly limited to the field of comedy as exemplified by the Chaplin and Marx Brothers films. The average picture seldom deals with free fantasy, but is tied up closely with real life. The fairy-tale type of unreality has up to now been employed in the field of animated cartoons. This field—the fairy-tale—through the medium of the technical tricks of the camera and the freedom it has over imaginative conceptions, is most suitable to the motion picture, but as yet remains practically unexplored.

People are in the habit of going to the movies to see their own lives or those of people they envy re-enacted, but the world of make-believe and pure fantasy is still only a by-product of present day production. Naturalistic theatre has always bored me. I think that essentially theatre art is based on the audience's desire to escape rather than to relive reality.

It is mainly because of its purely imaginative—I would even say artificial—quality that ballet is important for motion pictures. It introduces a completely imaginative world whose form is of a plastic nature—a visual perfection of an imaginary life. It has its own laws, its own meaning, and cannot be explained by the usual criteria of logic. This, for me, is the realm of complete fantasy.

On the other hand, the possibilities opened by motion pictures for the classic ballet are of an even greater importance and interest. The frame of the screen, for instance, is a far more mobile thing than the frame of the stage; it does not bind the ballet to the visual quadrangle of an x number of square feet. This also applies to the space and movability of the settings. It is far easier to create a complete space fantasy on the screen than on the stage. Natural elements like light and sound can be more freely employed on the screen than on the stage and thus become in the former medium far more important additions to ballet than is possible on the stage.

An additional point is that the spectator always sees a stage ballet from the same angle and from the same distance. On the screen, however, the spectator moves with the camera and thus can see the ballet not only from a wide range of angles but also from a wide range of distances. He may even feel himself to be amidst the ballet performance.

It is important to note that, visually, ballet in the film is equally complete, no matter from what seat in the auditorium one looks at it. The camera does the work. In the theatre a person sitting high in the balcony generally sees only wigs and heads and thus has an incomplete view of the ballet performance. This distorted view interferes with both his enjoyment and his appreciation. The movies correct this condition and make it possible for every member of the audience to enjoy ballet fully.

Creating dance for movies imposes completely new problems on the choreographer. It renders his task far more intricate and difficult, gives him new riddles to solve and opens a wide range of possibilities for the exercise of his invention.

Motta, Gilberto, Brazilian dancer and choreographer, b. Rio de Janeiro, ca. 1933. Began dance studies at Ballet da Juventude (1951) under Eduardo Sucena and Maryla Gremo; later with Maria Ruanova in Buenos Aires; Lubov Egorova in Paris; Aurel Milloss in S. Paulo. Danced in Ballets do IV Centenário in S. Paulo, Brazil. Became interested in modern dance after the first José Limón season in Rio (1954). Received a Dept. of State scholarship to study in N.Y. under Limón and Doris Humphrey (1955–57). Back in Rio (1958), presented his first choreography on television: *Hamlet* and *The Four Indefinitions.* Presented his group, Ballet Contemporàneo, for a short season at Teatro Copacabana (Aug., 1958). Received a scholarship to study mime with Marcel Marceau in Paris (1958–59). Choreographed for Ballet Contemporain and Théâtre d'Essai de la Danse (Paris, 1959–61) *Surrealisme, 2001, Antagonisme, Bachianas Brasileiras, Panneaurama,* and *Tryptique.* Currently in television.

Motte, Claire, French dancer. Pupil of the Paris Opéra school and Yves Brieux; promoted to première danseuse étoile in 1961. Her repertoire includes *Chemin de Lumière, Les Sylphides, Suite en Blanc, Giselle* (in which she has danced both the title role and Queen of the Wilis). A strong technician, she made a striking impression as Odette-Odile in the Vladimir Bourmeister version of the full-length *Swan Lake* staged at the Opéra (Dec., 1961). Danced Choleric variation in Balanchine's *Four Temperaments* and leading role in *Concerto Barocco,* both premièred at the Opéra, Dec. 18, 1963.

Mounsey, Yvonne, dancer, b. Pretoria, South Africa, 1921. Began her dance training at Poppins Salomon School in Pretoria; then studied with Igor Schwezoff in London; later with Olga Preobrajenska and Lubov Egorova, Paris; School of American Ballet, N.Y. Went to London in 1939 and in the same year joined the Massine-Blum Ballet Russe de Monte Carlo, dancing in Monte Carlo, Nice, Paris, and in Italy under the name of Irina Zarova. At the outbreak of World War II she returned to South Africa. Joined Col. de Basil's Original Ballet Russe in Sydney, Australia (1940), dancing leading roles in Serge Lifar's *Pavane* and Michel Fokine's *Le Coq d'Or.* Toured America with this company (1940–41) and was stranded with it in Cuba. Returned to South Africa (1948) and formed her own company. Joined New York City Ballet as a leading soloist (1949). She created many roles, including The Queen (*The Cage*), Harp (*Fanfare*), one of the five ballerinas (*Caracole,* later *Divertimento No. 15*), Venus (*Cakewalk*), Brangaene (*Picnic at Tintagel*), leader of the Pas de Neuf (*Swan Lake,* Act 2, Balanchine version), and others; also danced one of the ballerina roles in *Serenade,* 4th movement (*Symphony in C*), Woman in His Past (*Lilac Garden*), 1st movement (*Western Symphony*), and others. Probably her most outstanding role was that of the Siren in *The Prodigal Son.* Returned to South Africa in 1959 and helped found the Johannesburg City Ballet.

Moussorgsky, Modest Petrovitch (1835–1881), Russian composer. His opera *Fair at Sorochinsk* and the symphonic poem *A Night on Bald Mountain* were the sources of the music which David Lichine used for his ballet *Fair at Sorochinsk* (1943). Bronislava Nijinska also used his *Pictures at an Exhibition* for a ballet of the same title (1944).

Movement. The fundamental language of dance; a purposeful change of weight or position, as contrasted with motion, which in dance is considered as purely kinetic, i.e. physical, while movement is metakinetic. See METAKINESIS, MODERN DANCE.

Movements for Piano and Orchestra. Ballet in 1 act; chor.: George Balanchine; music: Igor Stravinsky's of the same name. First prod.: New York City Ballet, City Center, N.Y., Apr. 9, 1963, with Suzanne Farrell and Jacques d'Amboise, Elaine Comsudi, Gloria Govrin, Patricia Neary, Leslie Ruchala, Ellen Shire, Karin von Aroldingen. At the première the dancers wore white leotards and tights and the abstract choreography had an effect of living sculpture. At the second performance d'Amboise wore white shirt and black tights, the girls black practice costumes and this effect was lost, the choreography seeming a development of the *Agon* and *Episodes* experiments. Subsequently, the white leotards and tights were worn.

Moylan, Mary Ellen, ballerina, b. Cincinnati, Ohio, 1926. Studied ballet, tap, and acrobatics in St. Petersburg, Fla.; singing and dramatic training in N.Y.; was a scholarship student of School of American Ballet, N.Y. Made her debut as première danseuse in the musical *Rosalinda* (*Die Fledermaus*) (1942) and other ballerina roles in the New Opera Company season at Broadway Theatre, N.Y., beginning Nov., 1942, creating the first ballerina role in the revival of *Ballet Imperial.* Leading soloist with Ballet Russe de Monte Carlo (1943–44), her repertoire including *Etude* (Bronislava Nijinska), *Serenade, Les Sylphides, Snow Maiden* (Nijinska), *Ballet Imperial, Le Bourgeois Gentilhomme,* and others; also appeared with the company as soloist in the ballets in the musical *Song of Norway* (1944); ballerina of musical *Day Before Spring* (1945–46); ballerina with Ballet Society (1946), creating Sanguine (*Four Temperaments*) and ballerina (*Divertimento*); ballerina in the musical *The Chocolate Soldier* (1947); ballerina, Ballet Russe de Monte Carlo (1947–49), her new roles including Sugar Plum Fairy (*The Nutcracker*), Swan Queen (*Swan Lake,* Act 2), Myrtha (*Giselle*), Street Dancer (*Le Beau Danube*), Zobeide (*Schéhérazade*), the ballerina roles in *Paquita* and *Raymonda,* and others; ballerina of Ballet (now American Ballet) Theatre (1950–53), dancing Helen (*Helen of Troy*), Agathe (*Les Demoiselles de la Nuit*), Taglioni (*Pas de Quatre*), title role (*Princess Aurora*), *Black Swan,* and *Don Quixote* pas de deux, etc. Ballerina of Metropolitan Opera Ballet (1955–57), her principal creations being in the ballets for *Die Fledermaus, Aida, La Périchole,* and the ballerina in Zachary Solov's *Soirée.* Appeared on major television shows, lectured and taught. Retired in 1957 upon her marriage.

Mudras (more properly, Hasta-Mudras). The gesture language of the Hindu dance. See HINDU DANCE.

Mukhaja. In Hindu dance, facial expression. See HINDU DANCE.

Mulys, Gerard, French dancer and ballet master, b. Strasbourg, Alsace, 1915. Pupil of Gustave Ricaux, famous teacher at the Paris Opéra. Premier danseur, Nice Opéra (1932–38). Prisoner during World War II, escaping after seven months. Premier danseur and ballet master, Nouveau Ballet de Monte Carlo (1941), his repertoire including *Les Sylphides, Swan Lake,* The Blackamoor in *Petrouchka,* the Golden Slave in *Schéhérazade.* Stayed with the company under the direction of Eugene Gruenberg and Serge Lifar (1945–46), and until it became Grand Ballet de Monte Carlo under the direction of the Marquis de Cuevas. A knee injury ended his career as dancer and he became ballet master of Nice Opéra and director of its ballet school (1948–56), when he went to Paris Opéra Comique as teacher and ballet master. Became régisseur general, ballet master and teacher at Paris Opéra (1958). He is the owner of an important dance collection and author of *The Life of Monte Carlo Ballet, Michel Fokine, Ballets de Monte Carlo, 1914–1911.*

Mumaw, Barton, American modern dancer, b. Hazleton, Pa., 1912. Studied dance with Ted Shawn and first appeared with his company in *Job, A Masque for*

Barton Mumaw in The God of Lightning.

Dancing at the Lewisohn Stadium, N.Y. (1931); toured with Shawn's first company which included both men and women. Leading soloist with Shawn and His Men Dancers (1933–40). After the company was dissolved gave solo performances in N.Y. and on tour, interrupted by World War II during which he served in the U.S. Air Force (1942–46). On his return gave more solo performances, and toured briefly with Ted Shawn and La Meri giving benefit performances for Jacob's Pillow. Leading dancer in *The Promised Valley* (Helen Tamiris), Salt Lake City, an historical drama with music of the Mormon Trek. Has appeared in many musicals in N.Y., national companies, and summer stock, including *Annie Get Your Gun, Oklahoma!, Brigadoon, Chocolate Soldier, Song of Norway, Out of This World, The Golden Apple, My Fair Lady*. Choreographed the off-Broadway production of *Dark of the Moon*.

Musette. A pastoral air or symphonie de danse popular in opera ballets of the late 17th and 18th centuries and which was sometimes (but not necessarily) a dance.

Music for Dance (a brief history).

In the early stages of their development, the arts of music, dance, and drama were so closely connected that the history of one is at the same time the history of the others. The basic of the three arts was most probably dance. For the instrument of dance, the human body, did not have to wait to be invented; it was there from the very beginning.

In primitive times there was no separation of dance, music, and drama. They were all ritual acts performed by the whole community with no division between performers and audience. The first distinction between them appeared when the principle of the soloist, or leader of the dance, was introduced. After a period of time the soloist or leader became what we now call choreographer, and the chorus, or group, became the audience. Throughout these centuries dance, song, and music continued to be religious rituals rather than forms of entertainment or recreation.

The first forms of dance accompanied by music as an entertainment appears in Greek history. The highly developed Greek drama furnishes excellent proof of the variety of dance forms employed in the theatre. The leader and soloist of primitive times becomes now the "choregos," the conductor of the singing chorus and perhaps composer, as well as choreographer.

The Romans retained the entertainment features of the Greek comedy, but almost entirely discarded its moral and social significance and transformed tragedy into a circus-spectacle. Their contribution to the growth of the theatre was the development of dance. Dance, as a matter of fact, was given a secondary position. Dances were interpolated in pantomimes, much as dance divertissements are interpolated in operas in our times. It was in Rome that dancers, and with them singers and actors, became professional entertainers.

When the Christian Church triumphed over the Roman Empire, stage entertainment, especially dancing, was prohibited. But the Church realized the popular attraction of pageants and incorporated them into its rites. Within a few centuries the Mass, with all its ceremony and rituals, became a religious drama of the highest order. Dance was present in the early Mass only in the form of movement dictated by the words and music of the service. To a certain extent the Christian priest now became the "choregos."

Although the Church banished the professional stage as a form of entertainment, it did not, or could not, suppress folk customs which always included dancing. During the period of the early Renaissance, folk song-and-dance was highly popular and greatly developed in Central and Southern Europe. For the poor people of agricultural Europe the songs and dances of peasants celebrating the various events connected with the change of seasons was the only relief available from their none too happy daily life, and dancing, especially, gave them a certain illusion of freedom.

The release of Europe from church domination made possible the resurrection of drama, and with it dance and secular music, as forms of entertainment. People rediscovered the artistic principles of Greece and Rome. Composers began to develop a sustained melodic line with rhythmic accents adaptable to dancing. Heinrich Isaak (ca. 1450–ca. 1517), a composer of Dutch origin who worked in Italy, composed his "Carnival Songs" and the "Ballo," the latter a dance accompanied by vocal and instrumental music. In this dance the dancers were also singers. Our word "ballet" most probably stems from the diminutive of the term "ballo"—"balleti." About a century later Claudio Monteverdi (1567–1643) wrote his *Ballo delle Ingrate* (1608).

The court spectacles of France and Italy during the Renaissance period were complex and sophisticated theatrical performances, employing at first aristocratic amateurs as dancers, singers and actors, but later creating a demand for a theatrical profession. In 1489, at the court of Gian Galeazzo, at Milan, was held a famous spectacle based on a suite of dances which was the forerunner of ballet and opera.

In the 15th and 16th centuries social dancing was enormously popular. Throughout the Middle Ages there were fast, strong and lusty peasant dances which at times united with the slow, stately and elegant court dances. These dances required new music with a definite rhythm and cadence which would direct the rhythm of the movements. At the same time, the music would be directed in style and form by the dances themselves. Thus, for instance, the English folk-dance is responsible for the creation of the rondo, which was originally a round dance.

Italian dance teachers of that period collaborated with composers and gradually developed a definite sequence or order of formal ballroom dances which led to the creation of the musical form known as the suite. From the suite later evolved the sonata, the symphony and the tone poem.

In the sequence of ballroom dances the pavane was followed by a galliard. In Bach's time the allemande took the place of the pavane as the first dance in the suite. The basic dances in the suite were the allemande, courante, sarabande, and gigue. Later on one or two other dances began to be inserted between the third and fourth dances of the suite, among them the minuet, gavotte, rigaudon, or passepied. Forms of chaconne and passacaglia concluded the suite because they were the last dances to be danced at a ball.

Dance interludes at French court spectacles of the 16th and early 17th centuries, called entrées, demanded more elaborate music than that written for social dances. *Le Ballet Comique de la Reine,* given in 1581 and generally considered the first ballet to be performed in a form clear enough to create a succession of performances, demanded just such music.

A little less than a hundred years later (1669) the composer Jean Baptiste Lully received a charter from Louis XIV to create the French Academie Royale de Musique et de Dance, now the Paris Opéra. The Academie served as an example for similar institutions in other European capitals and metropolitan centers. The Russian academy was founded in 1738 in St. Petersburg. Vienna, Milan, Copenhagen, Berlin, and Warsaw soon imitated St. Petersburg. The theatre dance left the court ballroom and established itself on the stage for everybody to see.

Early in the 18th century the sonata, developed by Karl Philippe Emanuel Bach (son of Johann Sebastian), replaced the dance suite. Jean Philippe Rameau's opera ballets pushed into the background Lully's dance compositions. The opera-ballet continued as a standard tradition until the advent of the choreographer and reformer Jean Georges Noverre, who joined forces with the composer Christoph Willibald Gluck (1714–1787) in an effort to reform and advance the position and form of the theatrical dance.

The French Revolution marked the border line between two periods in dance music—the old and the new—the latter, dance music which is so close to our own period that it is hardly distinguishable from contemporary forms.

The innovations of the early 19th century lay in the more intense theatricalization of music for dance, in the development of the scope and instrumental effects of the orchestra. At the very beginning of the century the Italian choreographer Salvatore Vigano developed his "choreodrama" and can be considered the precursor of Leonide Massine, who originated the symphonic ballet in 1933. Vigano's *Creatures of Prometheus,* staged in 1801 to Beethoven's music, was revived as late as 1932 by Serge Lifar at the Paris Opéra.

In the 19th century the ballroom made greater use of folk music than ever before, and the simple tunes used in the ballroom were developed and theatricalized for the dance stage. Just as the earlier dance suites were built upon the patterns of the allemande, chaconne, etc., so ballet music of the 19th century consisted almost entirely of developed forms of the waltz, polka, polonaise, march, czardas, mazurka, etc.

Dance music in our century continues its development along with dance itself. New dance forms which demand new approaches to composition of dance music find willing innovators among modern composers, especially in America. The new works of Igor Stravinsky, Paul Hindemith, Aaron Copland, Gian-Carlo Menotti, Vittorio Rieti, Leonard Bernstein, Paul Bowles, Robert McBride, Elliot Carter, Jerome Moross, Walter Piston, William Schuman, Norman Dello Joio, Samuel Barber, Lukas Foss are a clear indication that dance music, perhaps more than any other part of dance as a theatrical art, has maintained a steady and a very healthy growth.

The main characteristic of our epoch in so far as ballet (not modern dance) is concerned is the use for dance of music which originally had not been composed as dance music. Examples of this characteristic date back to Michel Fokine's use of Chopin's piano music for his *Les Sylphides,* Rimsky-Korsakoff's symphonic poem for the *Schéhérazade* ballet. See also History of Dance; History of Ballet.

Musil, Karl, Austrian dancer, b. 1939. Studied with Willy Fränzl and the ballet school of the Vienna State Opera; accepted in the ballet company (1953); pro-

Karl Musil, premier danseur of the Vienna State Opera in rehearsal of his variation in Swan Lake.

moted to soloist (1958). Dances featured roles in *Giselle, Swan Lake, Symphony in C, Hotel Sacher,* and others, and the *Black Swan* and *Don Quixote* pas de deux, the *Paquita* pas de trois. Guest artist, London Festival Ballet (summer, 1963), sharing with John Gilpin title role in Vaslav Orlikovsky's *Peer Gynt.* Guest artist also in Monte Carlo, Hanover, and Stuttgart with the respective ballet companies. On Oct. 19, 1964, danced Prince Siegfried for the first time in Rudolf Nureyev's version of the full-length *Swan Lake,* staged for the Vienna State Opera (following the choreographer with great success in the role), to Christl Zimmerl's Odette-Odile. In Nov. of that year was guest artist with the Janine Charrat company appearing at the International Ballet Festival in her new ballet *Paris,* with French ballerina Tessa Beaumont as partner. Beginning Jan., 1965, he was guest artist for the season with the Ruth Page Chicago Opera Ballet, partnering Irina Borowska, whom he married in 1966.

Musitz, Suzanne, dancer, b. Hungary, 1937. Leading dancer Sydney (New South Wales) Ballet Group. Toured Europe with Grand Ballet du Marquis de Cuevas. An original member of Western Theatre Ballet, she left in 1961 but returned as guest artist for the company's appearance at the Edinburgh Festival the same year. She created the role of the wife in *The Prisoners* and has also danced the Woman in *Sonate à Trois,* among other roles.

Mute Wife, The. Ballet in 1 act; chor.: Antonia Cobos; music: Vittorio Rieti, ending with his orchestration of Niccolo Paganini's "Moto Perpetuo"; décor: Rico Lebrun. First prod.: Ballet International, International Theatre, N.Y., Nov. 22, 1944, with Antonio Cobos (Wife), Francisco Moncion (Husband), Sergei Ismailov (Doctor); revived in shorter version by Original Ballet Russe, Metropolitan Opera House, N.Y., October, 1946, with Cobos in title role, George Skibine (Husband), Moncion (Doctor). Based on Anatole France's *The Man Who Married a Dumb Wife,* the story tells how bitterly a loving husband regrets the operation which restores his wife's tongue. Her incessant chatter drives him to persuade the doctor to perform another operation to take away his hearing. The wife's playing of castanets to the *Moto Perpetuo* was a witty creation of ceaseless chatter. Ballet Russe de Monte Carlo re-staged the ballet (Metropolitan Opera House, N.Y., Sept. 16, 1949), to a new score of music by Scarlatti, orchestrated by Soulima Stravinsky, with Nina Novak (Wife), Leon Danielian (Husband), Robert Lindgren (Doctor). Cobos changed the choreography considerably for this version.

N

Nabokov, Nicolas, Russian-born American composer, b. 1903. Studied music in Russia and Germany (in Berlin with Ferruccio Busoni), specializing in piano and composition. His works for dance include two ballets: *Ode,* choreographed by Leonide Massine for the Diaghilev Ballets Russes (1928), and *Union Pacific,* also choreographed by Massine for Col. de Basil's Ballets Russes de Monte Carlo (1934). During World War II he worked for the U.S. State Dept.; for the U.S. Information Control Division in occupied Berlin (1945). Upon his return to the U.S. he taught music for several years. Was appointed (1950) Director of the Paris Exposition, "Masterpieces of the Twentieth Century," sponsored by the Congress for Cultural Freedom, (Apr. 20–June 6, 1951). Author of a book, *Old Friends and New Music* (Boston, 1951). He composed the score for George Balanchine's full-length ballet *Don Quixote,* premièred by the New York City Ballet, May 28, 1965, at the N.Y. State Theater.

Nadejdin, Serge (Osipov) (1880–1958), Russian dancer and teacher. Graduated from the St. Petersburg Imperial School of Ballet (1898); soon afterward enrolled in the School of Drama from which he graduated in 1901. Played on the stage of the Alexandrinsky (Dramatic) Theatre until 1905. Came to U.S. in the early 1920's and established his own ballet school in Cleveland, O. (1932). He was an accomplished pianist as well as dancer, actor, and excellent teacher.

Nadezhdina, Nadezhda, Peoples' Artist of the RSFSR, Soviet choreographer, b. St. Petersburg, 1908. Daughter of well-known Soviet writer Alexandra Brushtein and Professor of Surgery Sergei Brushtein. Began her dance education in Leningrad Choreographic Technicum. She was a character dancer with the Bolshoi Ballet but retired early due to illness and began choreographing for the variety stage. In the summer of 1948, after successfully choreographing Russian round dances for a group of amateur village dancers from the Kalinin region, she had the idea of founding the Beryozka dance company of which she has been the artistic director ever since. Her work, while true to Russian folk dance in every way, is firmly grounded in the best traditions and in the technique of Russian classic ballet. She has choreographed many dances in the company's repertoire, the most famous being *Beryozka* (Little Birch Tree) which gives the company its name, *Lebyodushka* (Little Swan), and *Northern Ring.* Men were accepted into the formerly all-girl company in 1961. "Beryozka" is also the title of a very popular Russian folk song, the melody of which Peter Tchaikovsky has used in his Symphony No. 4 in F minor.

Daniel Nagrin, modern dancer and choreographer.

Nagrin, Daniel, American modern dancer, b. New York City; m. Helen Tamiris, divorced 1964. B.S. in Education, City College, N.Y. Studied modern dance with Helen Tamiris, Martha Graham, Hanya Holm, Ray Moses, Anna Sokolow; ballet with Elizabeth Anderson-Ivantzova, Nenette Charisse, Edward Caton. After appearing as soloist in the dance companies and in the dance works of Helen Tamiris, Sophie Maslow, Charles Weidman, Anna Sokolow, he developed his own programs of solo works, many of which provide social commentary: *Strange Hero* (the glorification of the gangster type), *Man of Action* (the illusion of haste gets no one anywhere), *Indeterminate Figure* (the "little man" day-dreaming his reactions to the noises of the world about him); others being brilliant expositions of modern dance in all its styles: *Jazz, Three Ways; Spanish Dance; Dance in the Sun; A Dancer Prepares,* and others. Collections of these dances called *Dance Portraits* make up programs that he has shown all over the U.S. He has also choreographed a number of group works, several of them for the Tamiris-Nagrin Dance Company which was formed in 1960 and gave its first performance at the Phoenix Theatre, N.Y. He has been a featured dance soloist in the original Broadway productions of *Annie Get Your Gun, Lend An Ear, Touch and Go,* and *Plain and Fancy* (receiving the Donaldson Award for the Best Male Dancer of the 1954–55 season for the last named); has choreographed for the off-Broadway production of *Volpone* (1957) and for the film *His Majesty O'Keefe,* and has appeared as a dance soloist on television. Teaches extensively and in the summer of 1962 conducted with Helen Tamiris the first Summer Dance Workshop at C. W. Post College of Long Island Univ. In the summer of 1964 did choreography for *Emperor Jones* at Boston Arts Festival.

Napoli, or The Fisherman and His Bride. Romantic ballet in 3 acts; chor.: August Bournonville; music: Holger Simon Paulli, Edvard Helsted, and Niels W. Gade. First prod.: Royal Danish Ballet, Copenhagen, Mar. 29, 1842. The action takes place early in the nineteenth century in Naples and in the Blue Grotto on Capri. Rumors notwithstanding, the lovely Teresina is convinced that her fisherman-lover Gennaro has been faithful to her when he presents her with a ring. They sail away but a squall arises and Teresina is washed overboard. Gennarro seeks comfort at a priest's who gives him an amulet with a picture of the Madonna. Teresina, rescued by two naiads, is brought to the Blue Grotto to their King, Golfo, who falls in love with her and transforms her into a naiad. Gennaro arrives at the Grotto and finds Teresina, who does not remember her mortal lover. But Gennaro's prayers to the Madonna are heard, and Teresina's memory slowly returns to her and she once again takes her human shape. On their return to Naples Gennaro is accused of witchcraft for having brought back Teresina who was presumed dead. The priest explains that all was accomplished by Gennaro's faith. A joyous celebration including an exciting tarantella brings the ballet to a close. *Napoli* is the most popular of all Danish ballets. It contains every theatrical device as well as a great number of dances and action scenes. Bournonville composed the ballet after his return from a visit to Italy. On occasion the third act of *Napoli* is performed as a separate item on a program. It has been staged as a one act ballet by Harald Lander, adapted from Bournonville for London's Festival Ballet, Festival Hall, London, Aug. 30, 1954, in décor by Osbert Lancaster, with Toni Lander (The Bride) and Oleg Briansky (The Bridegroom). Erik Bruhn staged the last act divertissement for England's Royal Ballet, Royal Opera House, Covent Garden, London, May 3, 1962, with Antoinette Sibley, Merle Park, Lynn Seymour, Georgina Parkinson, Bryan Lawrence, Graham Usher, and Austin Bennett.

Narcissus (Narcisse). Ballet in 1 act; chor.: Nina Verchinina; music: Maurice Ravel's *Introduction and Allegro for Harp and Strings;* décor: Henrique Peyceré. First prod.: Ballet Vassili Lambrinos, Buenos Aires, 1950. Presented in 1954 by Teatro Muncipal, Rio de Janeiro, with Johnny Franklin in the title role (later danced by Aldo Lotufo). A choreographic version of the well-known myth about a handsome youth who saw his reflection in water, fell in love with it, and pined away. The gods changed him into the flower which bears his name.

Nathanson, Lucile Brahms, contemporary dance educator, dancer, b. Far Rockaway, N.Y. B.S., N.Y. Univ. (1942); M.A. in Dance Education (1947); matriculated for Ed. D. at same university. Also attended Univ. of Illinois and Adelphi College, and Bennington College Summer School of Dance (1943). Studied dance with Ruth St. Denis at Adelphi College (1938) and Jack Cole, Doris Humphrey, Charles Weidman, Martha Graham and others; ballet with Ella Daganova, Nenette Charisse, and others; in Europe studied with Mary Wigman, Harald Kreutzberg, Corrie Hartong, Rudolf von Laban, Lisa Ullmann; studied mime at Ecole de Jeu Dramatique, Paris. Has also studied ethnic dance, percussion for dance, Dalcroze eurythmics, body mechanics in relation to dance with Dr. Lulu Sweigard. Received a N.Y.U. teaching fellowship (1944–45); elected to Kappa Delta Pi, national educational honorary organization (1960). Performed with Ruth St. Denis' Rhythmic Choir, Adelphi College (1938), in student concerts, in own works on Program of Young Dancers at N.Y.U. (1945), and in various group performances at YM–YWHA. Co-producer, director, and choreographer of N.Y.U. Graduate Camp Show (1948–54). Has taught extensively in colleges, and since 1949 has been dance coordinator and instructor for Five Towns Music and Art Foundation. (The five towns, all on Long Island, N.Y., are Lawrence, Cedarhurst, Woodmere, Hewlett and Inwood.) Instructor in Children's Dance at YM–YWHA, N.Y., since 1953, organizing and directing the first program in U.S. of Teacher Training in Children's Dance (1954–61); originated and directed Annual Conference on Creative Teaching of Dance to Children at YM–YWHA (1954–60). Is associated with many other organizations connected with the teaching of modern dance, especially to children.

Natiez, Max, dancer, b. Leicester, England, 1938. Studied at school of Ballet Rambert from 1954, joining company (1957); joined Antonio's Spanish Ballet for three months later same year. Member, London's Festival Ballet (1958); promoted to soloist (1959), dancing Trepak and Harlequin dance (*The Nutcracker*),

Groom (*Petrouchka*), Blue Boy (*Symphony for Fun*), also creating leading role in Harald Lander's *Vita Eterna* (1960). Joined Western Theatre Ballet (1960), dancing *Giselle* peasant pas de deux, pas de trois (*Swan Lake*), one of the five (*One in Five*), Harlequin (*Carnaval*), and others.

National Ballet. A company sponsored in Washington, D.C. by the National Ballet Society, Inc. of which Mrs. Jean Riddell is president. Director of the company and of the school attached to it is Frederic Franklin. The school was opened June 1, 1962 and the company, for which auditions were held in Washington, New York and several other cities, gave its first performances Jan. 3, and 4, 1963, at Lisner Auditorium, Washington, D.C. Leading dancers were Andrea Vodehnal, Roni Mahler, Jacqueline Hepner, Lynne Kareken, Eugene Collins, Roderick Drew, James Capp, Franklin Yezer. National Ballet made its first metropolitan New York appearance with a single performance at Brooklyn College, Feb. 16, 1963. Repertoire included *Swan Lake* (Act 2), *Les Sylphides,* Franklin's *Hommage au Ballet, Tribute,* and *Rhythm in 3,* and Valerie Bettis's *Early Voyagers.*

The company made its New York (Manhattan) debut with eight performances March 27—April 2, 1967 at City Center with four new ballets *La Péri* (Skibine), *Night* (Anna Sokolow), *Idylle* (Skibine), *Through the Edge* (Michael Lopouszanski) and its regular repertoire. Marilyn Burr, Eugene Collins, Stevan Grebel, Ivan Nagy, Andrea Vodehnal were the principal dancers.

National Council on the Arts, The. Was established by the National Arts and Cultural Development Act of 1964. Its activity was limited, and when the National Foundation on the Arts and Humanities Act of 1965 was enacted by the Senate and House of Representatives and signed, on Sept. 29, 1965, by President Johnson, the National Council on the Arts was transferred from the National Development to the National Endowment for the Arts, an agency of the National Foundation. The National Council, through the National Endowment, could provide matching grants to nonprofit organizations, states and other public agencies, and to individuals engaged in the creative and performing arts for the whole range of artistic activity, including construction of necessary facilities. Under special circumstances matching would not be required.

Each of the two endowments—Arts and Humanities—would have $5 million to spend in fiscal 1966 and an additional $5 million in the form of matching funds to attract bequests from private sources. As used in the act, "the term 'the arts' includes, but is not limited to music (instrumental and vocal), dance, drama, folk art, creative writing, architecture and allied fields, painting, sculpture, photography, graphic and craft arts, industrial design, costume and fashion design, motion pictures, television, radio, tape and sound recording, and the arts related to the presentation, performance, execution, and exhibition of such major art forms."

Two significant paragraphs of Section 4 of the act state:

"The purpose of the Foundation shall be to develop and promote a broadly conceived national policy of support for the humanities and the arts in the United States pursuant to this Act."

"In the administration of this Act no department, agency, officer, or employee of the United States shall exercise any direction, supervision, or control over the policy determination, personnel, or curriculum, or the administration or operation of any school or other non-Federal agency, institution, organization, or association."

Theatrical producer Roger L. Stevens, who served as the White House cultural adviser, has been appointed the first

Chairman of the National Council on the Arts. Choreographer Agnes de Mille was chairman of the dance panel.

On Nov. 15, 1965, the National Council on the Arts announced the first grants totaling nearly $3 million for the support of the creative and performing arts in the United States. *The American Ballet Theatre* was the recipient of a grant of $100,000 toward the four-week January–February 1966 New York season and a second grant of $250,000 for a subsequent nationwide tour. Both grants were on a matching basis with private contribution. At the press reception during which Stanley Young, chairman of the Executive Committee of the National Council, acting in behalf of Mr. Stevens, presented the grant to Dr. Harold Taylor, president of Ballet Theatre Foundation, and made a brief speech, a sentence or two of which is worth preserving for posterity. He said: "This is the moment which we feel has come about 200 years late . . . It is the first time in American history that help to the arts has not been made part of a relief program—although some degree of relief must come into it."

National Endowment for the Arts, a part of the National Foundation on the Arts and Humanities (which see).

National Foundation on the Arts and Humanities came into existence on Sept. 29, 1965, when President Lyndon B. Johnson signed Public Law 89-209. This historically unprecedented law created an autonomous National Foundation "to develop and promote a broadly conceived national policy of support for the humanities and the arts in the United States." The structure of the National Foundation on the Arts and Humanities is somewhat complicated as government institutions are apt to be. It consists of the Federal Council on the Arts and the Humanities and the twin Endowments, a National Endowment for the Arts and a National Endowment for the Humanities, each of which has an advisory body (the National Council) respectively, on the Arts and on the Humanities. The new law amends the National Arts and Cultural Development Act of 1964 in transferring the National Council on the Arts from the Executive Office of the President to the National Endowment for the Arts. Authorized appropriation for each Endowment for each fiscal year 1966 through 1968 was $4,000,-000. Additional sums, up to $2,500,000 for the Endowment for the Arts were authorized to match total amounts donated to the Endowment in each fiscal year; $2,750,000 was authorized to assist individual states in supporting existing arts programs and in developing new arts projects and agencies. Amounts unspent in this manner may be used to match donations. The National Foundation of the Arts may use 20 per cent of its allotted funds for non-matching grants, but 80 per cent of the funds are for matching grants to non-profit organizations, state and other public institutions, and to individuals engaged in the arts.

The President appointed theatrical producer Roger L. Stevens as first Chairman of the National Council on the Arts. Serving with him were violinist Isaac Stern, conductor-composer Leonard Bernstein, choreographer Agnes de Mille, actor Gregory Peck, scenic designer and co-director of the American Ballet Theatre Oliver Smith, and others. The National Council on the Arts is assisted by an advisory panel on each of the art forms. The first Chairman of the Dance Panel was Agnes de Mille. The first grants were announced Nov. 15, 1965. They included two separate grants to the American Ballet Theatre: $100,000 to help it survive the 1965–66 season; and $250,000 to underwrite a nationwide tour. Both grants were on a matching basis. On Feb. 12, 1966, Martha Graham received a direct grant-in-aid of $40,000 to create two new works and a matching grant of $141,000 to enable her to take her company on an eight-week tour of the U.S. At the same time José Limón was granted $23,000 for the development of new works or the revival of old ones. Grants of $10,000 were awarded to Antony Tudor and Anna Sokolow; Alvin Ailey, Merce Cunningham, Alwin Nikolais, and Paul Taylor were granted $5,000 each. On May 16, 1966, the National Council allocated $300,000 for a project proposed by Jerome Robbins: the American Lyric Theatre Workshop, to be situated (most probably) in N.Y.

Natya. See HINDU DANCE.

Nault, Fernand, (Fernand Noel Boissonneault), French-Canadian dancer, choreographer, ballet master, teacher, b. Montreal, Canada, 1921. Studied ballet with Maurice Morenoff, modern dance with Elizabeth Leese in Canada; ballet in N.Y. with Anatole Vilzak, Margaret Craske, Vera Nemtchinova, Aubrey Hitchins, Valentina Pereyaslavec; also studied jazz. Made his debut in Montreal with Les Varietés Lyriques; joined Ballet (now American Ballet) Theatre (1944), as a member of the corps de ballet and rose to soloist and assistant regisseur. His roles included Wolf (*Peter and the Wolf*), principal Ivan (*Princess Aurora*), Hilarion (*Giselle*), Leading Gypsy (*La Fille Mal Gardée*), and later Mother Simone in the same ballet, Head Mistress (*Graduation Ball*), and others. Currently ballet master of American Ballet Theatre and co-director of Ballet Theatre School. He has taken considerable interest in the Regional Ballet movement, serving as artistic director of The Louisville Civic Ballet (1959 to date), and choreographing several ballets both for this group and for the Denver Civic Ballet Co. For the Robert Joffrey Ballet he staged a new version of *La Fille Mal Gardée*.

Navarre, Avril, English dancer, b. Wallasey, 1928. Studied at Sadler's Wells (now Royal) Ballet, entered company (1943) becoming soloist. Her roles included Swanilda (*Coppélia*), Golden Vine Fairy (*The Sleeping Beauty*), *Blue Bird* pas de deux in same ballet, title role (*Mam'zelle Angot*), The Blue Skater (fouetté girl) (*Les Patineurs*), and others. Retired in 1954.

Neary, Patricia, American dancer, b. Miami, Fla., 1942. Studied dance under Georges Milenoff and Thomas Armour in Miami; at National Ballet School, Toronto, Canada; School of American Ballet, N.Y. Danced in the Stravinsky Festival in Hamburg, Germany (1962), taking leading roles in *Apollo, Orpheus,* and *Agon*. Since 1962 has been a soloist with New York City Ballet, her roles including Polyhymnia (*Apollo*), Dewdrop (*The Nutcracker*), Choleric variation (*Four Temperaments*), Leader of Bacchantes (*Orpheus*), Ballerina in 1st and 4th movements (*Western Symphony*), 1st pas de trois (*Agon*), pas de neuf (*Swan Lake*), Hyppolita (*A Midsummer Night's Dream*), The Queen (*The Cage*), and variations in *Raymonda, Episodes, Scotch Symphony, La Valse,* and others.

Patricia Neary, a principal dancer of the New York City Ballet.

Nederlands Ballet. See HOLLAND, DANCE IN.

Nederlands Dans Theater. See HOLLAND, DANCE IN.

Nederlands Nationaal Ballet. See HOLLAND, DANCE IN.

Neglia, José, Argentine dancer, b. Buenos Aires, Argentina, 1935. Studied dance with Michel Borovski and Maria Ruanova. Joined Teatro Colón corps de ballet at an early age and received his first solo part in Aurel Milloss' ballet *Padmavati* (1947). In 1955 created the title role in *Usher* (chor. Massine), and the following year was promoted to premier danseur. His large repertoire includes *Les Sylphides, Swan Lake, Aurora's Wedding, Bolero, Hamlet, Three-Cornered Hat, Daphnis and Chloë, Capriccio Espagnol, Interplay* (Lambrinos), *El Amor Brujo, Rouge et Noir, Orpheus, Prometheus, Pillar of Fire, Gaîté Parisienne, Seventh Symphony, Petrouchka, Apollon Musagète, Joan von Zarissa, Estancia, Le Flor de Irupé, Supay, Pavana Real, Opus 34,* and others. Neglia is considered to be the most outstanding male dancer in Argentina.

Negri, Cesare, Italian author of the book *Nuove Inventioni di Balli,* published in Italy in 1604.

Neil, Sara, New Zealand dancer, b. Wellington, 1932; m. Walter Trevor. Entered Sadler's Wells Theatre Ballet (1951), soloist (1955). Her best role in the company was *Giselle.* Returned to New Zealand to become leading dancer of the United Ballet Company (1959).

Nemtchinova, Vera, ballerina, teacher, b. Moscow, Russia, 1903; m. Anatole Oboukhov. Her first dance teacher was Lydia Nelidova in Moscow; after three years began to study with Elisabeth Anderson; was with her for three months when Serge Grigoriev, regisseur-general of the Diaghilev Ballets Russes came to Moscow in search of dancers and engaged Nemtchinova. Starting in the corps de ballet she rose first to soloist, then to ballerina. Created the leading female roles in *Les Biches* (1924), *Les Tentations de la Bergère* (1924), *Les Matelots* (1925); also danced in *Swan Lake, The Sleeping Beauty, Pulcinella, La Boutique Fantasque* (creating the Queen of Hearts in 1919, later dancing the Can-Can Dancer), and others. With Anton Dolin formed the Nemtchinova-Dolin Ballet which gave a number of short seasons as part of the variety bill of the Stoll Theatre, London, and also toured, mainly in England (1927–28). Toured with her own company in Europe (1929) and in Argentina with Leo Staats Ballet Franco-Russe (1930). Later that year guest ballerina in Riga, dancing *The Sleeping Beauty, Swan Lake, Les Sylphides.* Prima ballerina, Lithuanian State Ballet (1931–35). Ballerina, René Blum's Ballet Russe de Monte Carlo, for which she created the leading role in *L'Epreuve d'Amour* (1936). Gave a few guest performances with Col. de Basil's company (called at that time Royal Covent Garden Ballet Russe due to litigation) at Royal Opera House, Covent Garden, London (1938), and stayed with this company as Original Ballet Russe for its Australian and U.S. tours (1939). Guest artist with Ballet (now American Ballet) Theatre, dancing title role in *Princess Aurora* (1943); danced full-length *Sleeping Beauty* (with Paul Petroff) with San Francisco Russian Opera and Ballet (1946). Currently teaching in N.Y.

Nemtchinova-Dolin Ballet. A small troupe organized in London in 1927 by Anton Dolin, Vera Nemtchinova, and Anatole Oboukhov which toured European countries until 1928 when Dolin rejoined the Diaghilev Ballets Russes.

Nerina, Nadia (Nadine Judd), South

Nadia Nerina with Nicolai Fadeyechev, in pas de deux, Giselle, *Act 2.*

African dancer, b. Cape Town, 1927, of British-Russian parentage. Studied with Eileen Keogan and Dorothea MacNair and from 1942 toured the Union of S. Africa. Went to England in 1945 where she studied with Marie Rambert, Elsa Brunelleschi and at Sadler's Wells School, joining the newly-formed Sadler's Wells Theatre Ballet (1946) where her first important role was the Circus Dancer in Andrée Howard's *Mardi Gras.* Transferred to Sadler's Wells (now Royal) Ballet (1947), becoming ballerina (1951). Small, fair, and piquante, she is noted for the lightness and aerial quality of her dancing and her great virtuosity. These qualities and her soubrette charm were exploited to the full by Frederick Ashton in *La Fille Mal Gardée,* her greatest role. Other creations include Earth (*Homage to the Queen*), Spring Fairy (Ashton's *Cinderella*), one of the seven ballerinas (*Birthday Offering*), title role (*Elektra*), and others. Also dances title roles in Royal Ballet's productions of Ashton's *Sylvia, Cinderella, Giselle, Firebird, The Sleeping Beauty,* and Odette-Odile (*Swan Lake*); ballerina roles in *Scènes de Ballet, Ballet Imperial,* and others. She has toured widely, notably appearing as guest artist with Bolshoi Ballet and Kirov Ballet in U.S.S.R. Has also appeared frequently on television. Created principal solo part in Royal Ballet's *Laurentia* pas de six. Guest ballerina with Western Theatre Ballet (1965), creating the leading role in *Home.*

New Dance. Modern group dance; chor.: Doris Humphrey (part of trilogy including *Theatre Piece* and *With My Red Fires*); music: Wallingford Riegger; costumes: Pauline Lawrence. First prod.: Guild Theatre, N.Y., Oct. 27, 1935.

New Dance Group. Organized during the Depression (1932) when many dance groups banded together as the Workers' Dance League. With nation's recovery all the groups gradually dispersed, only the New Dance Group remaining (though in a completely different form) to establish a school, offer classes in all forms of dance at modest fees, to hold studio lectures and demonstrations, and to present periodical dance performances. It was chartered by N.Y. State in 1944 as a non-profit institution. Outstanding modern dance works have been presented under the auspices of New Dance Group including *Harmonica Breakdown* (Jane Dudley) and *Dust Bowl Ballads* (Sophie Maslow, 1940), *Folksay* (Maslow, 1942), *Fable* (Hadassah, 1948), *Celebration* (Maslow), *Lyric Suite* (Anna Sokolow, 1954), and others. The performing company of New Dance Group appeared at the first American Dance Festival at Connecticut College, New London (1948) and in each subsequent Festival up to 1953, presenting works by Dudley, Maslow and William Bales. During the same period the company toured extensively.

In 1954, the building in which the school was situated was torn down, and it was decided to buy a building. The financial responsibilities involved caused a cessation of performance production for a number of years, but this was resumed with a performance of repertory works by Sophie Maslow, Anna Sokolow, and Donald McKayle at the YM–YWHA, Jan. 14, 1962. Among the dancers and dancer-choreographers who have presented works sponsored by New Dance Group are Pearl Primus, Jean Erdman, William Bales, Eve Gentry, Ronne Aul, Daniel Nagrin, Charles Weidman, and many others. The present (1966–67) officers are: Jane Dudley, president; Nona Schurman, vice-president; Judith Delman, secretary-treasurer. Directors: Charlotte Rahaim, executive director; William Bales, Judith Delman, Hadassah, Celene Keller, Billie Kirpich, Donald McKayle, Muriel Manings, Sophie Maslow, Betty Osgood, and Dorene Richardson.

New York City Ballet, The. When the American Ballet disbanded in 1941 it was not the end of the organization, for it must be understood that the American Ballet has always been and is still a movement in American ballet rather than just a ballet school and performing company. The future historian will refer to it as a school in ballet rather than just another company.

The years of World War II made it impossible to revive the company in any form. Those male dancers who were not drafted into the armed services and most of the female dancers had scattered among the performing companies and musical shows. It was felt that war time could not offer proper conditions in general to organize a new ballet company. In addition Lincoln Kirstein, who would be the moving spirit of the new troupe as he had been of the old, was drafted in Feb., 1943, and did not return until Oct., 1945.

Soon after his return, however, he and George Balanchine began to plan a new performing organization which they named Ballet Society. The stated purpose of the organization was the encouragement of the lyric theatre by the production of new works. The emphasis was to be on expert dance and musical direction "to insure essential elegance and freshness, rather than on famous stars or the residual prestige of the standard ballet repertoire." Performances were to be given four or five times a year. Between its first performance in Nov., 1946, and its last in Apr., 1948, Ballet Society produced a number of outstanding ballets by Balanchine, among them *Four Temperaments* (Hindemith), Divertimento (Alexei Haieff), *Symphonie Concertante* (Mozart), *The Triumph of Bacchus and Ariadne* (Vittorio Rieti), *Orpheus* (Stravinsky), *Symphony in C* (Bizet). Most of these are still in the repertoire of the New York City Ballet. Both Balanchine and Kirstein knew well that a professional ballet company could not exist on five performances a year, but they did not know how to achieve regular seasons for the company. The artistic success which the company achieved in Apr., 1948, with its performances at the New York City Center for

Music and Drama made a strong impression on Morton Baum, Chairman of the Executive Committee of the City Center, and he invited Ballet Society to join the complex of the New York City Center. Balanchine and Kirstein agreed and Ballet Society's performing company became the New York City Ballet.

It must be made clear that its title notwithstanding, the New York City Ballet is not an artistic or managerial function of the government of the City of New York, nor does New York City grant it financial support. The company bears its title by virtue of being part of the unique enterprise called the New York City Center.

The building which houses the City Center originally belonged to a fraternal order and was called Mecca Temple. During the depression of the 1930's the order could not keep up the payment of city taxes on the building. By 1941 the indebtedness of Mecca Temple reached such a sum that the City of New York could think of no alternative other than to foreclose on the organization for tax liens. Two years later, the late Newbold Morris, then president of the City Council, and Morton Baum, a member of the Council, persuaded the late Fiorello H. La Guardia, then Mayor of the City of New York, to permit them to form a non-profit membership corporation—The New York City Center of Music and Drama—to run the theatre (actually an auditorium with a stage) situated in the building on a non-profit basis, at low admission prices. The corporation would pay a rental fee to the City equivalent to the sum the City would have received from the owners of the building in taxes. The three basic organizations constituting the theatrical activities of the City Center—the New York City Ballet, the New York City Opera, and the New York City Light Opera—enjoy one important privilege: the City Center underwrites the seasons of the three companies.

However, if the New York City Ballet company's existence had depended solely on the City Center finances, it could not have long survived, because it was spending considerably more than the City Center budget permitted. The difference was made up from various sources: grants from foundations; contributions from individual patrons; profits from occasional television performances; an organization called Friends of the City Center.

Of great importance to the growth of the company were the foreign tours. The first of these took place in the summer of 1950, when David (now Sir David) Webster, General Administrator of the Royal Opera House, Covent Garden, London, invited the company to dance at Covent Garden for five weeks beginning July 10. The London season was very successful and did much for American art in Great Britain and, as it often happens, contributed to the prestige of the company at home. In 1952 the company toured Europe, dancing in Spain, France, Italy, Switzerland, The Netherlands, London, and at the Edinburgh and Berlin Festivals. In 1953 it danced at Teatro alla Scala, Milan, and in 1955 it again toured Europe, participating in a number of festivals, among them the Maggio Musicale Fiorentino, the Zurich and Holland festivals. In 1956 it made a ten-week European tour appearing (among other festivals) at the Biennale Music Festival of Venice. In 1958 it danced in Japan, Australia, and the Philippines under the management of Paul Szilard. In 1962 it toured overseas from Sept. 1 to Dec. 1, appearing in Germany, Switzerland, Austria, and the Soviet Union. In the Soviet Union it danced in Moscow, Leningrad, Kiev, Tbilisi, and Baku. The company made a strong impression on Soviet audiences, critics, and dancers alike. The visit of a ballet company, most of whose repertoire is in the abstract (or at least plotless) style, to a land whose official principle in art is "socialist realism" was bound to create at least a mild upheaval, and it did. The future influence of George Balanchine's choreography on the work of the young choreographers of the Soviet ballet cannot be doubted.

Since 1953 the President's Special International Program for Cultural Presentations (now called Cultural Presentations Program of the United States, but generally known as the Cultural Exchange Program) has been assisting foreign tours of American performing companies by furnishing funds for overseas transportation and by covering operational deficits under certain conditions. The great importance of these tours lies in the opportunity they create for American dance to be seen and evaluated by foreign countries and for American dancers to see and absorb some foreign cultural expressions, thus helping to bring about a closer international understanding. A residual benefit for the companies is the extension of the period performances.

Domestic seasons kept pace with foreign tours. In its first season as the New York City Ballet (1948–49), the company danced twenty-four performances between Oct. 11, 1948, and Jan. 23, 1949. Ten years later, during its anniversary season (1958–59), the company danced twenty-four weeks, a number which became the average for subsequent performance weeks. That season began with the thirteen-week European tour mentioned above. There was a six-week New York engagement in Mar.–Apr. 1963.

On Dec. 16, 1963, the Ford Foundation announced a $7,756,000 program "to strengthen professional ballet in the United States." This was the largest single contribution to ballet in the United States from any source. Among the awards were $2,000,000 to the New York City Ballet over a ten-year period; $2,425,000 to the School of American Ballet, the fountainhead of the New York City Ballet and the official school of the company, to strengthen it as a national ballet-training institution; and $1,500,000 to improve instruction and performance in local communities.

On Apr. 24, 1964, the New York City Ballet began its first season at the New York State Theater, the second building to be completed in the architectural complex called Lincoln Center for the Performing Arts.

The first season ran to May 17. The highlights of it were the Theater itself, the new costumes and scenery for several of the ballets, and one new (for this company) work, Antony Tudor's *Dim Lustre* to Richard Strauss' *Burleske*. It had its première on May 6. The ballet had originally been done for Ballet (now American Ballet) Theatre in 1943. The season opened with five performances of Balanchine's *A Midsummer Night's Dream*.

Everyone in the New York City Ballet from Balanchine and Kirstein down was proud and happy with the new theatre, probably one of the most beautiful and elegantly appointed playhouses anywhere. Philip Johnson, the architect of the theatre, has stated on many occasions that the theatre was being built for dance and more particularly for George Balanchine and the New York City Ballet.

During the summer the company rested and made a tour of the U.S. going as far as Los Angeles where it danced two weeks at the Greek Theatre. On its return to N.Y. the company rehearsed three new ballets: Balanchine's *Ballet Imperial,* Jacques d'Amboise's *Irish Fantasy,* and John Taras's *Piège de Lumière* (new for the company), as well as the regular repertoire. *Ballet Imperial* (new for the company) had been originally created for the South American tour of the American Ballet Caravan (1941) and was later in the repertoire of Ballet Russe de Monte Carlo (1945). Balanchine claimed that he had forgotten much of the choreography and asked Frederic Franklin to stage the revival. *Irish Fantasy* was staged to Camille Saint-Saëns' Ballet-Divertissement from the opera *Henry VIII* and was premièred Aug. 12, 1964, at the Greek Theatre. *Piège de Lumière* was originally staged for the Grand Ballet du Marquis de

Cuevas at Théâtre d'Empire, Paris, Dec. 23, 1952, to music by Jean-Michel Damase.

On Jan. 17, 1962, the New York City Ballet presented its second full-length ballet, *A Midsummer Night's Dream,* choregraphed by George Balanchine; the first was *The Nutcracker* in 1954, restaged in 1964, also by Balanchine. The third full-length ballet by Balanchine, his magnum opus, and the first to be staged for the stage of the New York State Theater, was *Don Quixote,* to commissioned music by Nicolas Nabokov, in décor and costumes by Esteban Francés. It was premièred on May 28, 1965, with Richard Rapp as the Don, Suzanne Farrell as Dulcinea, and Deni Lamont as Sancho Panza. At the gala preview which preceded the opening night Balanchine took the title role.

In Sept., 1964, the New York City Ballet became the first company to sign a Basic Agreement with the American Guild of Musical Artists (AGMA), the dancers' union, offering its dancers fifty-two weeks of employment during the year.

No list of ballets, however impressive, can make clear that George Balanchine and the New York City Ballet have established what may be considered the American style in ballet. This style is based on the Russian Imperial, and more specifically, the St. Petersburg style, which itself was a combination of the French and Italian schools with the addition of some Russian national characteristics. This was the style on which Balanchine and most of the teachers of the School of American Ballet, the official school of the New York City Ballet, were brought up.

This style has been further refined in the U.S. in conformance with the characteristics of American dancers: their better nourishment since infancy, their superior physical training since childhood, and, as a result of this, their stronger bodies and (in many cases) their greater height, especially their longer legs; their general alertness to their teachers' demands; their realization from the first years of their training that they are preparing to enter a company which is in the forefront of American ballet. Not unlike a person entering a monastic order, the corps de ballet dancers of the New York City Ballet are ready to accept a certain anonymity in order to help make the corps de ballet an artistic unit, rather than a collection of individuals each dancing for himself. The American style, further, demands a stronger than usual technique and a well developed musicality, an indispensable condition in a company headed by Balanchine.

Balanchine's aesthetic credo was expressed by him in an interview with a Moscow publication during the company's appearances there in the winter of 1962. Here is, in part, what he said:

"The contemporary public has grown up considerably and in the overwhelming majority has become intellectual and cultured. And by now no one will be satisfied with a sumptuous spectacle in which one hundred or two hundred supernumeraries will be walking around on stage. But stories, events, separate moments which are being reproduced on the stage by choreographic means should not be philosophically abstract.

"The ballet is such a rich art form that it should not be an illustrator even of the most meaningful literary primary source. The ballet will speak for itself. For fifteen years dancers develop every cell of their bodies, and all the cells must sing on the stage. And if the beauty of this completely trained body, its movements, its plastique, its expressiveness will bring aesthetic pleasure to the spectators in the auditorium, then ballet will have reached its goal.

"All my life I wanted—and I still want —to make it so that the beauty of the human body, the purity of lines, their plastic expressiveness should not be forgotten, that the ballet should not become a sauce, a seasoning for some other dish, because I am firmly convinced that ballet itself is one of the most beautiful art forms."

American dancers, and this is true of dancers in other American companies as well as in the New York City Ballet, generally dance with a great reserve of power and a still greater reserve of emotion, and for this they are often considered cold, dry, athletic by foreign audiences and critics. The writers and audiences do not realize that this reserve is a restraint designed by the choreographer as part of his aesthetics.

There exist, of course, other American ballet companies whose practices are at variance with the New York City Ballet in philosophy, style, and technique, but the fact that George Balanchine has produced such a large following of young choreographers in the U.S. and abroad, leads one to accept the New York City Ballet's style as the American style of ballet.

The 1966–67 season began for the company with a tour of the U.S. and Canada (Sept. 22–Oct. 30), prior to its twelve-week season at the New York State Theater. The company then danced its regular repertoire (Nov. 15–Dec. 4). This period was followed by a run of *The Nutcracker* (Dec. 8–Jan. 7, 1967), after which the company reverted to its regular repertoire. The season concluded with performances of *Don Quixote* (Jan. 26–Feb. 5).

For the 1966–67 season the company comprised the following artists (in alphabetical order): Principal dancers, Suzanne Farrell, Melissa Hayden, Jillana, Patricia McBride, Mimi Paul, Violette Verdy, Jacques d'Amboise, Anthony Blum, Conrad Ludlow, Nicholas Magallanes, Arthur Mitchell, Francisco Moncion, André Prokovsky, Edward Villella; and Gloria Govrin, Sara Leland, Kay Mazzo, Teena McConnell, Marnee Morris, Patricia Neary, Suki Schorer, Bettijane Sills, Carol Sumner, Deni Lamont, Frank Ohman, Richard Rapp, Earle Sieveling, Kent Stowell, Roland Vazquez, William Weslow. Ensemble: Karen Batizi, Diane Bradshaw, Marjorie Bresler, Elaine Comsudi, Gail Crisa, Rosemary Dunleavy, Suzanne Erlon, Deborah Flomine, Penelope Gates, Susan Hendl, Gail Kachadurian, Ruth Ann King, Johanna Kirkland, Linda MacArthur, Linda Merrill, Karen Morell, Jennifer Nairn-Smith, Delia Peters, Carolyn Peterson, Susan Pillersdorf, Nanette Reedy, Giselle Roberge, Donna Sackett, Lynne Stetson, Virginia Stuart, Karin von Aroldingen, Margaret Wood, Wilhelm Burmann, Alfonso Cata, Robert Maiorano, Paul Mejia, Larry O'Brien, Shaun O'Brien, Roger Peterson, John Prinz, Roger Pietrucha, David Richardson, Michael Steel, Robert Weiss.

Lincoln Kirstein is General Director; George Balanchine and John Taras, Ballet Masters; Una Kai, Associate Ballet Mistress; Francia Russell, Assistant Ballet Mistress; Robert Irving, Principal Conductor; Hugo Fiorato, Associate Conductor. Costumes by Karinska.

New York Export: Opus Jazz. Ballet in 3 movements; chor.: Jerome Robbins; music: Robert Prince; décor: Ben Shahn; costumes: Ben Shahn and Florence Klotz. First prod.: Jerome Robbins' Ballets: U.S.A., Festival of Two Worlds, Spoleto, Italy, June 8, 1958. N.Y. première, Alvin Theatre, Sept. 4, 1958, with Patricia Dunn, Jay Norman, Wilma Curley, John Jones. Progressive jazz choreography to progressive jazz music which created a furore all over Europe and was the ballet which introduced the style associated with the company.

New York Public Library Dance Collection. See DANCE COLLECTION, THE NEW YORK PUBLIC LIBRARY.

New York State Council on the Arts. Began its activities in an unofficial capacity in early 1960 with a survey of the state's cultural institutions. When the survey was completed, the Council submitted its findings to Governor Nelson A. Rockefeller and the Legislature together with a recommendation that the services of the cultural institutions of the state be extended to give people a greater opportunity to appreciate and to participate in the arts.

Formation of the Council was sponsored by the Governor, though not without opposition from the Legislature. However, the Legislature eventually passed the enabling legislation, establishing the Council and in April, 1961, approved a Budget Request for $450,000 to implement the recommendations of the Council. The Governor appointed Seymour H. Knox chairman of the Council. The first executive director was John H. MacFayden. He served until June 1, 1964 when he resigned to return to the practice of his profession, architecture. John B. Hightower, executive assistant to Mr. MacFayden during 1963–64, became executive director.

During its first season, which began in July, 1961, the Council presented performances of symphony orchestras, ballet companies, dramatic groups, and lectures and lecture-demonstrations, as well as art and photographic exhibitions in more than forty-five cities and towns. In October, 1961, the New York City Ballet gave six performances in as many cities under the auspices of the Council and groups from the company appeared in twelve lecture-demonstrations on the esthetics and technique of ballet, admission free. The second season began with a ten-city tour of the American Ballet Theatre in Oct., 1962.

Beginning in 1963 the Council has added a Professional Touring Arts Program involving support to performing groups, and a Technical Assistance Program providing professional guidance to organizations throughout the State who are interested in dance. It has also continued to sponsor lecture-demonstrations in N.Y. high schools.

In the fall of 1964 it sponsored the formation of a new modern dance group of 34 performers, The American Dance Theatre, under the artistic direction of José Limón, which gave two performances (Nov. 18 and 19) in the N.Y. State Theater at Lincoln Center. Lincoln Center for the Performing Arts presented a second series of performances (Mar. 2–7, 1965) in the same theatre, but the company itself has not survived as a performing unit. The idea behind the company's formation had been to create a group able to dance old and new works of a wide variety of modern dance choreographers in repertory.

Since early in 1965 the Countil has cooperated with the Hunter College Concert Bureau to present a modern dance subscription series in Hunter College Playhouse which has already established itself as a major annual event.

The broad objective of the Council is to bring art experience into the lives of as many of the State's citizens as possible. It seeks to develop programs based on community initiative, which will ultimately reach a point where the programs can exist and expand without further significant aid from the State. A pioneer in its particular area, the example of the N.Y. State Council on the Arts has been followed by almost every state of the Union.

New Yorker, The. Ballet in 3 scenes; chor.: Leonide Massine; music: George Gershwin; book: Rea Irwin and Leonide Massine; décor and costumes: Carl Kent, after Rea Irwin and Nathalie Crothers. First prod.: Ballet Russe de Monte Carlo, N.Y., Oct. 18, 1940, with a cast including Alexandra Danilova, Tatiana Chamié, Nathalie Krassovska, André Eglevsky, Frederic Franklin, Roland Guerard, Leonide Massine, Marc Platoff, Igor Youskevitch, George Zoritch. This ballet presents a view of characters out of *The New Yorker* magazine.

Newman, Claude, English dancer and teacher, b. Plymouth, 1903. Studied with Phyllis Bedells and Serafima Astafieva. Made his debut in Fokine Ballet, Drury Lane Theatre (1924), and between 1925 and 1931 appeared in many musicals. Joined Vic-Wells (later Sadler's Wells, now Royal) Ballet (1931), remaining until his service with the Royal Navy in World War II (1939–46). One of the real pioneers of English male dancing, he danced in almost all the early Sadler's Wells ballets, his creations including Tailor (*The Rake's Progress*), Mr. Taylor (*The Prospect Before Us*), Ernest (*A Wedding Bouquet*), and others. He was an outstanding Dr. Coppelius (*Coppélia*) and Drosselmayer (*The Nutcracker*), also dancing the Bouffon in the second act. Joined Sadler's Wells Theatre Ballet as ballet master and mime (1946), creating the Elderly Gentleman (*Assembly Ball*). Taught at Sadler's Wells School until 1952. Overseas Examiner for Royal Academy of Dancing and member of its Technical Committee. Currently teaching in England.

Newman, Ernest (1868–1959), English writer and music critic of various newspapers, including the Sunday *Times,* who wrote a series of articles in defense of Leonide Massine's symphonic ballets.

Newton, Joy, English dancer and teacher. Studied with Ninette de Valois at her Academy of Choreographic Art and was one of the original members of Vic-Wells (later Sadler's Wells, now Royal) Ballet, dancing in most of the early repertoire and always remembered for her Street Singer in *The Rake's Progress.* Ballet mistress Sadler's Wells Ballet (1942–46); principal of the National Turkish Ballet School founded by Ninette de Valois (1947–51).

Niblo's Garden. Famous amusement place opened by William Niblo in New York in 1828 under the name "Sans Souci." At first programs consisting of concerts, fireworks, etc., were held there in summer, but later it was given over to plays and almost every actor or performer of distinction appeared there. It burned down twice (1846, 1848), but each time was re-built and performances were given there until 1895. In 1866 its most famous production, *The Black Crook,* was presented there for the first time.

Nicholoff, Michael, contemporary dancer, teacher, b. Boston, Mass. Studied with Lilla Viles Wyman, Alexandre Volinine, Vera Trefilova. Member of Anna Pavlova company (1917–26); partnered Mistinguette (Paris, 1920). Has been teaching since 1926; in Baltimore since 1934.

Niderlova, Milenka, Canadian dancer, b. Czechoslovakia, now Canadian citizen. Began her dancing career at the Prague Opera House where she rose to the rank of soloist. Later became a leading dancer at the Théâtre Royal de la Monnaie, Brussels. After emigrating to Canada joined Les Grands Ballets Canadiens and has been one of its leading dancers from its early days. Created the Young Girl in *Sea Gallows* and the ballerina in *Etude,* among others, and dances a large classic and modern repertoire.

Niehaus, Max, German writer on ballet subjects, b. Wesel on the Rhine. Studied jurisprudence and history of arts at the Universities of Lausanne, Berlin, and Kiel. Privy Councillor in Düsseldorf and Wiesbaden. Author of *Ballett* (1954), *Junges Ballett* (1957), *Himmel, Hölle, and Trikot–Heinrich Heine und das Ballett* (1959), *Nijinsky* (1961). Publisher of annual "Balletkalender" since 1958; also writes articles for magazines and newspapers; contributor to *Dance Encyclopedia.*

Night and Silence. Ballet in 1 act; chor.: Walter Gore; music: Johann Sebastian Bach, keyboard music arr. for harpsichord and orchestra by Charles Mackerras: Prelude and Fugue in D (the fugue played as an overture), Adagio from Toccata, Adagio and Fugue in C, No. 1 of 12 Little Preludes for keyboard; Toccata in D minor, and Chromatic Fantasia; décor: Ronald Wilson. First prod.: Edinburgh International Ballet, Empire Theatre, Edinburgh, Aug. 25, 1958, with Paula Hinton and David Poole; revived for Ballet

Rambert, July 20, 1961, at Sadler's Wells Theatre, with Paula Hinton and Walter Gore, and now in the repertoire of Gore's London Ballet. A man awaiting the return of his mistress from a ball becomes insanely jealous as he sees the bouquet she carries. After a struggle in which he nearly strangles her, she is about to leave, but returns to forgive him when she sees his despair.

Night City, The. Ballet in 1 act; chor. and book: Leonid Lavrovsky; music: Béla Bartók's *Miraculous Mandarin;* décor: Vadim Ryndin. First prod.: Bolshoi Theatre, Moscow, May 21, 1961, with Nina Timofeyeva (Girl), Maris Liepa (Boy). This is a different version of Bartók's *The Miraculous Mandarin* libretto. A prostitute, used by three thugs to entice clients whom they rob and kill, accidentally meets a night repair hand. He is a kind and charming youth and she falls in love with him, but the thugs mortally wound him. She tries to save him so that they can flee together but he dies and she is alone again.

Night Journey. Modern group dance; chor.: Martha Graham, based on the Oedipus myth; music: William Schuman; décor and costumes: Isamu Noguchi. First prod.: Martha Graham group, Harvard Symposium on Music Criticism, Auditorium of the Cambridge High and Latin School, Cambridge, Mass., May 3, 1947, with a cast headed by Martha Graham (Jocasta), Erick Hawkins (Oedipus), Mark Ryder (Tiresias, the Seer); N.Y. première: Maxine Elliot Theatre, Feb. 17, 1948. The action takes place at the moment when Jocasta first realizes the fact of her incestuous relationship with Oedipus, and in her mind she recognizes the past up to the point of the intolerable present which only death can solve. Bertram Ross has subsequently danced the role of Oedipus and Stuart Hodes and Paul Taylor that of Tiresias.

Night Shadow. Ballet in 1 act; chor.: George Balanchine; music and book: Vittorio Rieti, orch. and arr. from operas by Vincenzo Bellini, principally *La Sonnàmbula* and *I Puritani,* and one aria from *I Capuletti ed i Montecchi;* décor: Dorothea Tanning. First prod.: Ballet Russe de Monte Carlo, City Center, N.Y., Feb. 27, 1946, with Alexandra Danilova (Sleepwalker), Nicholas Magallanes (Poet), Maria Tallchief (Coquette), Michel Katcharoff (Baron), with Ruthanna Boris, Leon Danielian, and Marie Jeanne in the divertissement. Balanchine staged it for Grand Ballet du Marquis de Cuevas, Cambridge Theatre, London, Aug. 26, 1948, in décor by Jean Robier (subsequently redesigned by André Delfau), with Ethéry Pagava (Sleepwalker), George Skibine (Poet), Marjorie Tallchief (Coquette). John Taras restaged this production, with the Delfau décor, for Royal Danish Ballet in Copenhagen, Jan. 9, 1955, with Margrethe Schanne (Sleepwalker), Henning Kronstam (Poet), Mona Vangsaa (Coquette), Borge Ralov (Baron). Balanchine staged it for New York City Ballet, assisted by Taras, City Center, N.Y., Jan. 6, 1960, in décor by Esteban Francés and costumes by André Levasseur, with Allegra Kent (Sleepwalker), Erik Bruhn, with Nicholas Magallanes in subsequent seasons (Poet), Jillana (Coquette), Taras (Baron), and Edward Villella in the Harlequin dance heading the divertissement. Ballet Rambert also has this ballet in its repertoire (July 18, 1961) in décor by Alix Stone. In 1961 Balanchine decided to rename the New York City Ballet production *La Sonnàmbula* from the title of the Bellini opera from which most of the music comes and from the French title *La Somnambule* by which the ballet was known when it was in the repertoire of the Grand Ballet. Except that sleepwalking is the basis of both the ballet and the opera, there is no connection between the two stories. In *Night Shadow* a Poet finds himself at an evening fête champêtre. He is first attracted by the mistress of the host (the Coquette), but when he is left alone as the other guests dance off to supper, the mysterious Sleepwalker (wife of the host), appears and they dance a strange pas de deux together in which she remains unaware of his presence. They are seen by the Coquette who in her jealousy betrays them to the Baron. Unable to control his rage, he enters the house and a moment later the Poet staggers out, stabbed to death. The Sleepwalker re-enters and, still without having wakened, bears him in her arms into the house and out of sight.

Night Spell (original title, *Quartet No. 1*). Modern dance work; chor.: Doris Humphrey; music: Priaulx Rainier's Quartet No. 1; costumes: Pauline Lawrence. First prod.: José Limón Dance Company, 4th American Dance Festival, Connecticut College, New London, Aug. 1951, with José Limón, Ruth Currier, Betty Jones, Lucas Hoving. José Limón as the sleeper is visited by three apparitions of his dreams.

Nijinska, Bronislava, dancer, choreographer, ballet mistress, teacher, b. Minsk, Russia, Jan. 8, 1891. Daughter of Thomas and Eleonora (Bereda) Nijinsky, dancers of the Government Ballet School and Theatre in Warsaw, Poland, and sister of Vaslav Nijinsky. She was graduated from the Imperial School of Ballet in St. Petersburg (1908) and very soon after entered the Maryinsky company, dancing one of the four Little Swans (*Swan Lake*), Dew (*Awakening of Flora*), one of the Precious Stones variations (*The Sleeping Beauty,* Act 3). She joined the Diaghilev Ballets Russes (1909) on leave of absence from the Maryinsky, her first outstanding role being Papillon in *Carnaval* (1910). In Feb. 1911, following the dismissal of her brother from the Imperial Theatres, she demanded to be permitted to resign from the organization. The management acceded to her demand but in retaliation stated in her certificate of resignation that she had no right to the title Artist of the

Bronislava Nijinska, dancer, choreographer, ballet mistress, teacher; sister of Vaslav Nijinsky.

Imperial Theatres. Following her resignation she joined the Diaghilev company as a permanent member, her roles including the Street Dancer in *Petrouchka* and the Bacchante in *Narcisse* (both 1911). She danced the Ballerina in *Petrouchka* the following year. For a short while she danced in her brother's short-lived company in London (1914); later returned to St. Petersburg where she was ballerina of the Opera of Prince Oldenbourg (1914–1915) and at the Kiev Opera (1915–18), establishing her own school in Kiev. In 1921 she left revolution-torn Russia and rejoined the Diaghilev company. Her first serious choreographic effort was her assistance in the revival of *The Sleeping Beauty* for the company in November of that year at the Alhambra Theatre, London. Her major contribution to this revival was a new number, "The Three Ivans," danced to the coda of the third act pas de deux. This number is still retained in the one-act divertissement from *The Sleeping Beauty* known either as *Aurora's Wedding* or *Princess Aurora,* while the form (though not the choreography) is followed in the Royal Ballet's production of the full-length ballet. She alternated with Lydia Lopoukhova in the role of the Lilac

Fairy. Following "The Three Ivans," she choreographed a number of ballets for the Diaghilev company, among them *Le Renard* (1922), *Les Noces* (1923), *Les Biches, Les Facheux* and *Le Train Bleu* (all 1924). In 1928 and 1929 she produced several ballets for the Ida Rubinstein company, among them *Nocturne, La Bien-Aimée, Bolero, Le Baiser de la Fée,* and *La Valse.* Between 1930 and 1934 she was ballet mistress of the Russian Opera season in Paris. She established her own Théâtre de Danse in Paris (1932) for which she revived some of her most successful ballets and staged some new ones, including her version of *Hamlet* (1934). (See SHAKESPEARE IN BALLET.) She had worked with Max Reinhardt for his *Tales of Hoffmann* production in Berlin (1931) and in 1934 was asked by him to choreograph the ballets for his film of *A Midsummer Night's Dream.* In 1935 she choreographed *Les Cent Baisers* for Col. de Basil's Ballet Russe de Monte Carlo and in 1936 *Danses Slaves et Tziganes* (to the ballet music from Dargomijsky's opera *Roussalka*) and revived *Les Noces* for the same company. In 1937 she revived *Les Biches* and *La Bien-Aimée* for the Markova-Dolin company. She settled permanently in California (1938) after directing seasons in Warsaw, Paris, London and N.Y. of the Polish National Ballet; established a school in Hollywood but has continued to stage works for various companies. These have included *Chopin Concerto* and *Snow Maiden* (1942) for Ballet Russe de Monte Carlo; *La Fille Mal Gardée* (1940), *The Beloved* (La Bien-Aimée, 1941), *Harvest Time* (1945) for Ballet (now American Ballet) Theatre; *Brahms Variations, Pictures at an Exhibition,* and *Bolero* for Ballet International (1944). After this company became Grand Ballet de Monte Carlo and then Grand Ballet du Marquis de Cuevas she spent many seasons from 1947 on as ballet mistress, re-staging a number of works. Her last work for this company under its final name of Ballet International du Marquis de Cuevas was the revival, with considerably revised choreography, of *The Sleeping Beauty,* Oct. 27, 1960, in Paris. She has also worked for several seasons at Teatro Colón, Buenos Aires.

Nijinsky, Vaslav (1890–1950).

To the vast majority of people, Anna Pavlova and Vaslav Nijinsky are still the personifications of the art of ballet. However, Pavlova toured throughout the world for many years, dancing before audiences numbering many hundreds of thousands. By contrast, so few people, comparatively speaking, ever saw Nijinsky dance, that if his fame were based on his actual appearances before the public, he would now have been completely forgotten. His entire ballet career lasted some nine years, including two war years (1914–1916) during which he did not dance.

Nijinsky's lasting fame is due mostly to the legend that has been created around him. This legend has been continually fed by the writings of people connected with (or disconnected from) the Diaghilev Ballets Russes, who considered it vital or profitable to delve into the most minute details of Nijinsky's dancing and, more often, Nijinsky's personal relations with Serge Diaghilev. Also, there is a group of people on the fringe of ballet which has made Nijinsky its demigod and continues to worship at his shrine.

Of Polish extraction, Nijinsky was born in 1890 in the Russian city of Kiev. He was the son of Thomas Nijinsky, in his day a well-known character dancer, and Eleonora Bereda, a pupil of the Warsaw State Ballet School. At the age of ten Nijinsky was accepted at the St. Petersburg Imperial School of Ballet, where he was considered a brilliant ballet student, but slow and not overly bright in his general studies. He failed twice in his examinations but was graduated from the School in 1908. His graduation role was in Michel Fokine's *Don Juan,* where he appeared as Ludmila Shollar's partner.

A few months after his debut on the

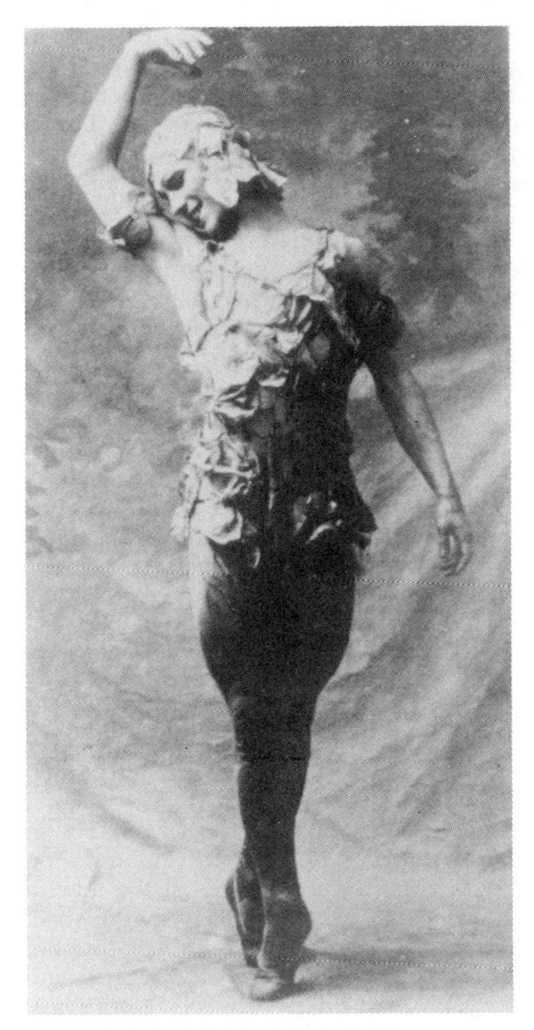

Vaslav Nijinsky in Le Spectre de la Rose.

Imperial stage Nijinsky met Serge Diaghilev. This meeting shaped the entire career of the dancer. It was during that winter that Diaghilev developed his plans for a ballet company, and Nijinsky figured in these plans as the premier danseur of the troupe.

In May, 1909, the Diaghilev Ballets Russes made its first appearance in Paris, and Nijinsky danced *Pavillon d'Armide, Les Sylphides, Prince Igor,* and *Cléopâtre,* all by Fokine. The success of the company was spectacular, but the personal success of Nijinsky was overwhelming. The following season Western Europe saw Nijinsky in *Schéhérazade* and *Carnaval,* also by Fokine. The artistic success of the second season surpassed that of the first.

The Diaghilev Ballets Russes was accepted as the finest organization of its kind Europe had ever seen, and Nijinsky acclaimed its greatest representative. At the end of the season Nijinsky returned once more to the Imperial Theatre from which he had been on leave of absence.

In 1911 while dancing the role of Albrecht in *Giselle* with Tamara Karsavina, Nijinsky neglected to wear a pair of shorts over his tights as was the custom at the Imperial Theatre. The stage manager told Nijinsky to correct this breach of custom. Nijinsky refused and Vladimir Teliakovsky, then director of the Imperial Theatres, suspended the dancer for insubordination and appearing in improper attire. Nijinsky, urged on by Diaghilev, Benois, and others sent in his resignation.

Up to that year the Diaghilev company had been organized on a temporary basis. Both in 1909 and in 1910 it was assembled for the European tour and disbanded after the tour was over. With Nijinsky free from the Maryinsky Theatre, Diaghilev decided to make his ballet a permanent organization based in Western Europe rather than in Russia.

During the 1911 season Nijinsky danced two of the finest roles in his repertoire, *Le Spectre de la Rose* and *Petrouchka.* His success was again phenomenal. The following season saw Nijinsky's first choreographic effort, *The Afternoon of a Faun,* to Debussy's prelude of the same title. With this ballet Nijinsky intended to create a new style of choreography, substituting angular and jerky movements for the curved and smooth movements of the traditional ballet.

The Faun enjoyed a measure of success, especially among sophisticated aesthetes and that part of the general audience which took its cues from them. This success was due not so much to the inventive

Vaslav Nijinsky, a year or so before his death.

genius of Nijinsky as a choreographer, as to the introduction of the sexual element to an extent hitherto unknown on the ballet stage.

In 1913 Nijinsky, continuing as premier danseur, staged two more ballets, *Le Sacre du Printemps* and *Jeux*. The first of these created a scandal at its opening. The audience's boos, stamping, and shouting made it necessary for Diaghilev to stand up in his box and shout at the crowd: "I beg you, permit us to finish the performance!" *Jeux* was accepted without protest, but also without interest. It was shelved after a few performances. *Sacre* was given only six times during the life of the company.

That same year (1913) the Diaghilev company left on a tour to South America. Diaghilev, who had an unreasoning fear of the ocean, stayed behind. While the company was playing in Buenos Aires Nijinsky married a dancer in the corps de ballet, Romola de Pulszky. As soon as Diaghilev heard about Nijinsky's marriage he cabled the dancer that he was dismissed. To all intents and purposes Nijinsky's marriage terminated not only his association with Diaghilev but also his career as a dancer.

In the spring of 1914 Nijinsky tried to organize his own company in London, but the plan collapsed when he became ill. There followed an enforced idleness during the first years of World War I when Nijinsky, as a Russian subject, was held as a civilian prisoner in Austria-Hungary, his wife's country.

In 1916 Nijinsky rejoined the Diaghilev company and came with it to the U.S. After this tour he organized a troupe of his own, composed of dancers from the Diaghilev company. Neither of the tours enjoyed any appreciable success. A new ballet, *Til Eulenspiegel,* which Nijinsky choreographed for his company, was given only a few times.

The two tours through the U.S. were followed by another season in South America, which turned out to be Nijinsky's final professional engagement. On his return to Europe he settled in Switzerland and soon began to display symptoms of the mental disease from which he never recovered. He died on April 8, 1950, in London. On June 5, 1953, his body was exhumed and on June 16 re-interred in the Montmartre cemetery, Paris. His grave is close to those of Gaetano Vestris, Théophile Gautier, and Emma Livry.

How great a dancer was Nijinsky? Undoubtedly, Nijinsky was a very talented dancer. He stemmed from a family of dancers; dancing was in his blood. At the time of his first appearance with the Diaghilev company ballet dancing in general was at a low ebb in Western Europe and outstanding male dancers had been unknown for generations. Fokine's *Polovetzian Dances from Prince Igor* came to Paris not only as a supreme example of the masculine dance but also as a complete surprise. Paris had forgotten that men existed who could actually dance with virility, power and technical polish. In these circumstances Nijinsky's extraordinary technique seemed a revelation.

From the material published about Nijinsky, and from people who saw him and dancers who danced with him, it appears very clearly that Nijinsky's elevation and ballon could not be matched by any other male dancer of his generation. His beats were clear and precise; he could do an entrechat-huit any time it was required, and occasionally would do an entrechat-dix.

Today there are several dancers whose technique, it is reasonable to assume, equals that of Nijinsky. A few years ago André Eglevsky and Igor Youskevitch could match most of the technical feats performed by Nijinsky. Of a younger generation, the Russians Yuri Soloviev of the Leningrad Kirov Theatre, Rudolf Nureyev, late of the same theatre, Vladimir Vasiliev of Moscow's Bolshoi, Erik Bruhn of the Royal Danish, our own Edward Villella and perhaps a few others match Nijinsky's virtuosity. It is doubtful, however, whether Nijinsky could have consistently given the number and quality of satisfying performances as the artists mentioned have given and are giving now. Whether they could match Nijinsky's personality must remain an unanswered question.

The artistic quality of Nijinsky's performances has become a matter of taste and memory. The further we are removed in time from Nijinsky, the more intense this artistic quality appears to those who saw Nijinsky dance. Our generation must take the statements of his contemporaries with some reservations. We can ask specific questions and receive more or less specific answers about his technique because ballet technique is clearly defined. There is no criterion, however, by which to measure the impressions of such a transcendental manifestation as artistic quality.

Nonetheless, Nijinsky was the greatest male dancer of his generation and would probably have achieved still greater heights had his career not been so tragically cut short by an incurable disease. But his role in the history of ballet and his influence on the art of ballet are extremely modest.

Nijinsky at the height of his career was a product of his friend and director, Diaghilev, and of Fokine, his choreographer. The moment the influence of Fokine's creative genius was removed, Nijinsky began to decline. When two years later Diaghilev, rightly or wrongly, disassociated himself from Nijinsky, the dancer's career came to an end.

Nikitina, Alice, Russian dancer, b. 1909. Studied with Olga Preobrajenska, Lubov Egorova, Nicholas Legat, and Enrico Cecchetti. A ballerina of the Diaghilev Ballets Russes, she made her debut at the Liubliana (Yugoslavia) Opera Ballet. She later danced with the Romantic Theatre of Boris Romanoff, and from 1923 to 1929 with the Diaghilev Ballets Russes. She created roles in *Zéphire et Flore* (1925), *La Chatte* (1927), in which she replaced Olga Spessivtzeva on 24-hour notice, *Ode* (1928). Her other ballets included *Pas d'Acier* (1927), *Apollon Musagète* (1928), and *Le Bal* (1929). Currently teaching in Paris.

Nikolais, Alwin, dancer, choreographer, director, teacher, composer, b. Southington, Conn., 1912. Attended Bennington College Dance Sessions (1937–39), Colorado College (1947). Between 1947 and 1950 studied in N.Y. principally with Hanya Holm but also with Martha Graham, Doris Humphrey, Charles Weidman, and Louis Horst. Had his own studio in Hartford, Conn. (1938–42). After his army service (1942–46) was assistant to Hanya Holm (1948–54). He began his professional career in the theatre as a musician, and in 1936 became a puppeteer, at which time he also began dance study in Hartford, Conn., with Truda Kaschmann from the Mary Wigman school. His

Alwin Nikolais, choreographer, composer, director of his own company.

first professional choreography was commissioned by Wadsworth Atheneum and Friends and Enemies of Modern Music, Hartford, when, with Truda Kaschmann and the composer Ernst Krenek, he staged a full evening production *Eight Column Line,* Avery Memorial Theatre, May 19 and 20, 1939. This was followed by numerous performances in Hartford and a transcontinental tour with Dancers en Route (1941). Appointed director of Henry Street Playhouse (1948), he built up a company of dancers for his very special form of dance-theatre in which lights, props, sounds (frequently electronic which he composes himself) are of equal importance with the dancers who are dehumanized to the degree that they become wonderfully accomplished instruments for the formation of ever-shifting patterns. His first work in this genre was *Masks, Props, and Mobiles* (1953), followed by *Forest of Three* (1953), *Village of Whispers* (1955), *Kaleidoscope* (1956), *Prism* (1956), *Bewitched* (music by Harry Partch, entire work commissioned for the 1957 Festival of Contemporary Arts at the Univ. of Illinois), *Runic Canto* (commissioned by American Dance Festival, Connecticut College, New London, 1957), *Cantos* (1957), *Mirrors* (1958), *Allegory* (1959), *Totem* (1960), *Stratus,* and *Nimbus* (1961), *Illusion* (commissioned by the Montreal, Canada, Festival, Aug. 9, 1961). Many of his individual dances (sometimes taken from the complete works) have been given on television, most notably a series given on the N.B.C. "Steve Allen Show" (1959). Canadian Broadcasting Company also presented a number of his works (1960, 1961). "Time to Dance" (1958) and "The Modern Arts" (1959) have been filmed. In addition to teaching at Henry Street Playhouse he has also taught at a number of colleges and various summer sessions. His book on dance theory, commissioned by Wesleyan Univ. Press, is due for publication and he has also written many articles for magazines, as well as "Sexual Dynamics in Contemporary Dance" for *Encyclopedia of Sexual Behavior* (Hawthorne Books, 1961). He was voted a member of ASCAP (American Society of Composers, Authors and Publishers) in 1959 and his scores have been played in concerts of contemporary music in the U.S., Canada, and elsewhere. They have also been heard in radio broadcasts and have been used on television broadcasts for theme and background music.

Nimura, Yeichi, choreographer and dancer, b. Suwa, Nagandken, Japan, 1908. Studied in Tokyo and N.Y.; professionally with his grandfather, a Shinto priest in Japan; also with Katherine Edson, Ivan Tarasoff, Konstantin Kobeleff, Alexander Kotchetovsky, Aurora Arriaza, Juan de Beaucaire. Made his debut as soloist in Ernest Bloch's *Israel,* Manhattan Opera House, N.Y. (1928); featured dancer in musicals and operettas; made concert debut and tour (1930); danced lead in *Pas d'Acier* (N.Y. and Phila., 1931); teacher, First International School of the Dance, England (1932), followed by tour through Europe, Near East, Africa. Returned to U.S. (1937); toured U.S., Canada, Cuba, Mexico, Hawaii (1937–38); helped found Ballet Arts School, N.Y. (1939) where he currently teaches. Choreographer of musical *Lute Song* (which he revised for the City Center revival in 1959) and various opera ballets for Metropolitan

Yeichi Nimura, choreographer, dancer, teacher, co-director Ballet Arts School, New York.

Opera Ballet. Is co-director of Ballet Arts Theatre, a performing group attached to the school, for which he created the ballets *Tropic Etude* (1960), and *Rashomon,* based on the Japanese legend (1962).

Nizzarda. An early 17th-century Italian couple dance in which the man lifts his lady high in the air.

Noack, Kjeld, dancer of the Royal Danish Ballet. Accepted into the company in 1942. Studied also in London and Paris. Guest artist, Marquis de Cuevas International Ballet, Ballets des Champs-Elysées, and others. Danced leading roles in *Romeo and Juliet, Night Shadow, Carmen, La Sylphide, Napoli,* and others. Appointed ballet consultant to Denmark's Radio and Television Company (1961).

Nobilissima Visione. See SAINT FRANCIS.

Noces, Les. Ballet in 4 scenes; chor.: Bronislava Nijinska; words and music: Igor Stravinsky; décor and costumes: Nathalie Gontcharova. First prod.: Diaghilev Ballets Russes, Théâtre Gaîté-Lyrique, Paris, June 14, 1923. The dancing was accompanied by a chanting, shouting, and wailing vocal chorus; revived by Nijinska for Col. de Basil's Ballet Russe for its 1936 American tour. The ballet is a stylization of ceremonies and rites connected with the marriage of peasants in Central Russia. The four scenes of the ballet tell the story: Benediction of the Bride; Benediction of the Bridegroom; Departure of the Bride from Her Parental Home; and the Wedding Feast. Nijinska used a very modern approach to the ballet (for 1923, actually a revolutionary one). Felia Doubrovska was the Bride at the première, Nicholas Semenov, the Bridegroom. Ludmilla Chiriaeff choreographed a version for Les Grands Ballets Canadiens. Nijinska revived *Les Noces* for the Royal Ballet, Royal Opera House, Covent Garden, London, Mar. 23, 1966, with Svetlana Beriosova as the Bride.

Noces, Les. Ballet in 1 act; chor.: Jerome Robbins; music: Igor Stravinsky; décor: Oliver Smith; costumes: Patricia Zipprodt. First perf.: American Ballet Theatre, N.Y. State Theater, Mar. 30, 1965, with Erin Martin (Bride), William Glassman (Bridegroom), Veronika Mlakar, Joseph Carow, Sallie Wilson and Bruce Marks (Parents), Ted Kivitt and Rosanna Seravalli (Matchmakers), Eliot Feld, Edward Verso (leaders of the friends). This work was the crowning achievement of American Ballet Theatre's 25th Anniversary Season. The American Concert Choir was the choral group for the N.Y. performances. At the première Leonard Bernstein conducted (on stage) the choir, percussionists, and the four pianists.

Noces Fantastiques, Les (The Fantastic Wedding). Ballet in 2 acts, 4 scenes; chor.: Serge Lifar; music: Marcel Delannoy; décor: Roger Chastel; costumes: André Levasseur. First prod.: Paris Opéra Ballet, Feb. 9, 1955, with Nina Vyroubova (Fiancée), Claude Bessy (Océanide, Queen of the Sea), Peter van Dijk (Captain). A ballet in neo-romantic style, and one of the best of Lifar's post-war works at the Opéra. A young sea captain leaves his betrothed to go to sea. He is shipwrecked and saved by the queen of a magic island, but when he spurns her love, remembering his fiancée, she has him thrown back into the sea to drown. His spectre, piloting a phantom ship and crew, returns to carry his bride to a ghostly wedding under the sea.

Noctambules. Ballet in 1 act, 2 scenes; chor. and book: Kenneth MacMillan; commissioned music: Humphrey Searle; décor: Nicholas Georgiadis. First prod.: Sadler's Wells (now Royal) Ballet, Royal Opera House, Covent Garden, London, Mar. 1, 1956, with Leslie Edwards (Hypnotist), Maryon Lane (Assistant), Nadia Nerina (Faded Beauty), Anya Linden (Poor Girl), Desmond Doyle (Rich Man), Brian Shaw (Soldier). The hypnotist's act does not please the audience, but when he begins to put them under a spell their suppressed longings cause strange happenings until the spell wears off. The little assistant, terrified by what has occurred, is left alone to express her terror by running in crazed circles, beating her little drum.

Nocturne. Ballet in 1 act; chor.: Frederick Ashton; music: Frederick Delius' *Paris;* book: Edward Sackville-West; décor: Sophie Fedorovitch. First prod.: Vic-Wells (later Sadler's Wells, now Royal) Ballet, Sadler's Wells Theatre, London, Nov. 10, 1936, with Margot Fonteyn (Poor Girl), June Brae (Rich Girl), Robert Helpmann (Young Man), Frederick Ashton (Spectator). A ballet of atmosphere with a slight theme. The Poor Girl—later called the Flower Girl—watches wistfully as the fashionable people arrive at a ball. The Young Man, bored with his surroundings, is momentarily attracted, but the Rich Girl lures him back and the Poor Girl is left to be consoled by the Spectator who then returns to his contemplation of Paris as the dawn comes up.

Nocturnes. Modern dance work; chor.: Merce Cunningham; music: *Five Nocturnes* of Erik Satie. First prod.: Merce Cunningham and Dance Company, Jacob's Pillow Dance Festival, Lee, Mass., 1956, with Merce Cunningham, Carolyn Brown, Viola Farber, Marianne Preger, Remy Charlip, Bruce King; N.Y. première: Brooklyn Academy of Music, Jan. 12, 1957. An exploration of the mood established by the music.

Noguchi, Isamu, Japanese-American sculptor, b. Los Angeles, Calif., 1904, of an American mother and a Japanese father (the poet Yone Noguchi). Educated in Yokohama, Japan, until age thirteen. Finished his high school education in Indiana and 2 years pre-medical training at Columbia Univ., N.Y. While still attending Columbia he was discovered by Onorio Ruotolo, director of the Leonardo da Vinci Art School, who recognized his potentialities as a sculptor and took him on as an apprentice. Within a short time he was elected a member of the National Sculpture Society of N.Y. Received a Guggenheim Foundation fellowship for study in the Orient in 1927 but got no further than Paris where he worked with Brancusi as an apprentice. Held his first exhibition of abstract carvings and sheet metal work at the Eugene Schoen Gallery in N.Y. (1928); since then he has held many exhibitions. Returned to the Orient in 1930. In 1935 went to Mexico where he carved a brick and colored cement wall sculpture called "History—Mexico." Won the competition for the Associated Press Plaque at Rockefeller Center (1938), the largest stainless steel sculpture ever cast. Received a Bollingen Fellowship (1950) for study and to write a book on sculpture and its relation to space and leisure. He spends part of every year in Japan where he has landscaped two gardens, one at Keyo Univ. as a memorial to his father. He also landscaped the gardens of the UNESCO Building in Paris, and has designed other gardens, including a proposed playground along Riverside Drive, N.Y. His main preoccupation continues to be sculpture for which he experiments with paper, wood, metals, bones, thread, stone, scrap, etc.

His works have been bought by art galleries in the U.S., Canada, England, and others. His sets for Martha Graham works have been making theatre history since 1934 and include those for *Night Journey, Seraphic Dialogue, Embattled Garden, Clytemnestra, Acrobats of God, Alcestis, Phaedra,* and others. He has also designed several ballets, of which the best-known is George Balanchine's *Orpheus* in the New York City Ballet repertoire.

Noir et Blanc. See SUITE EN BLANC.

Non Stop. Ballet in 1 act; chor.: Peter Darrell; jazz music by Williams and Palmer, played by Gillespie and Eldridge; décor: original by Barry Kay; later (which is current) by Ian Spurling. First prod.: Western Theatre Ballet, Theatre Royal, Bristol, England, June, 1958, with Hazel Merry, Jeffrey Taylor, Oliver Symons. A ten-minute piece of nonsense about the Twist.

Nonagone. Ballet in 1 act; chor.: Ludmilla Chiriaeff; music: several Preludes and Fugues from J. S. Bach's *The Well-Tempered Clavier,* orch. by Michel Perrault; costumes: Odette le Borgne. First prod.: Les Grands Ballet Canadiens, Comédie Canadienne Théâtre, Montreal, Apr. 16, 1959, with Véronique Landory, Margaret Mercier, Rona Nereida, Yvonne Laflamme, Andrée Millaire, Marianne Bigot, Jacques Claudel. An illustration in dance patterns of the contrapuntal designs of the music.

Nordi, Cleo, dancer and teacher, b. Kronstadt, Russia, 1899; m. Walford Hyden, for many years Anna Pavlova's conductor. Studied music and dancing in Russia (dancing with Nicholas Legat and Mme. Nicolaeva-Legat), later in Finland with George Gué. Studied in Paris with Olga Preobrajenska and Vera Trefilova. Entered Paris Opéra as danseuse rhythmique (1924); transferred to classic ballet (1925). Joined Pavlova Ballet (1926) and after her death (1931) appeared in musical productions in England. Has had her own school of ballet in London since the 1940's. Guest teacher, Royal Ballet (1952–55) and currently.

Nordoff, Paul, contemporary American composer of the music for Martha Graham's *Every Soul Is a Circus* (1939) and *Salem Shore* (1943). He also arranged Gluck's music for *Tally-Ho,* ballet by Agnes de Mille (1944).

North, Alex, composer, b. Chester, Pa., 1910. Studied music at Juilliard School of Music, N.Y., Moscow Conservatory, and with Aaron Copland and Ernst Toch. Composer of the music for Martha Graham's *American Lyric* (1937), Hanya Holm's *The Golden Fleece,* and a number of works by Anna Sokolow—*The Exile, Mama Beautiful, Ballad in Popular Style, Slaughter of the Innocents.* Composed ballet scores for *A Streetcar Named Desire* for the Slavenska-Franklin Ballet (1952) and *Mal de Siècle* for Grand Ballet du Marquis de Cuevas (1958), premièred at the Brussels World's Fair with the composer conducting. He has written incidental music for the theatre and for many films, the latest being *Cleopatra.* He received Academy Award nominations for his scores for *Spartacus, A Streetcar Named Desire* (which later became the score for the ballet), *Death of a Salesman, Viva Zapata, The Rainmaker, The Rose Tattoo, Unchained.* Has composed music for several television series. Received a Guggenheim Fellowship for musical studies in 1947.

Northcote, Anne. See SEVERSKAYA, ANNA.

Nouveau Ballet de Monte Carlo, ballet company formed in Monte Carlo during World War II (1942), under the sponsorship of Prince Louis II of Monaco and the direction of Marcel Sablon, director of the Monte Carlo Opéra. The company was composed of dancers who left Paris after the fall of France and young elements coming from local schools, mainly that of Julie Sedova. Between 1942 and 1944 leading dancers were Geneviève Kergrist, Marie-Louise Didion, Paul Goubé (all from the Paris Opéra), and also Marcelle Cassini, Lucienne Bergren, Ludmilla Tcherina, Edmond Audran, Gérard Mulys, Boris Trailine, Serge Golovine. Nicholas Zverev was one of the ballet masters, reviving works by Michel Fokine. Tony Gregory was another ballet master and choreographer (*L'Indiscret*). Jean Babilée appeared occasionally. After a lapse of two years the company was revived (1946) under the direction of the well-known Paris impresario Eugene Grünberg and the artistic direction of Serge Lifar, on leave from the Paris Opéra. Lifar created a number of ballets: *Dramma per Musica, Chota Rustaveli, Noir et Blanc, Salomé, Aubade,* and others. The company then included Yvette Chauviré, Janine Charrat, Renée Jeanmaire, Ludmilla Tcherina, Olga Adabache, Youly Algaroff, Alexander Kalioujny, Vladimir Skouratov, Boris Trailine. The company appeared in London in the summer of 1946. In the spring of 1947 Marquis George de Cuevas took over the company and became its director changing the name to Grand Ballet de Monte Carlo. Lifar remained for a few months as ballet master. Bronislava Nijinska was brought in by the Marquis to share this position, but after a season at the Vichy Opéra in July, 1947, the principal French artists and Lifar left. William Dollar became ballet master in 1948. From this time the company's story is that of the Grand Ballet du Marquis de Cuevas (which see).

Novak, Nina, ballerina, b. Warsaw, Poland, 1927. General education and ballet training in the school of the Warsaw Opera House; also studied with Bronislava Nijinska, Leon Woizikowski, and others. After suffering great privations during World War II she left Poland and joined Ballet Russe de Monte Carlo as soloist (1948), dancing Can-Can Girl (*Gaîté Parisienne*), First Hand (*Le Beau Danube*), Polovetsian Girl (*Dances from Prince Igor*), Lucile Grahn (*Pas de Quatre*), Mazurka lead (*Coppélia*). Danced more important roles in 1950–51 including title role (*The Mute Wife*), Queen of the Wilis (*Giselle*), *Blue Bird* pas de deux, and others. Promoted to ballerina (1952), dancing Swan Queen (*Swan Lake,* Act 2), Swanilda (*Coppélia*), Sugar Plum Fairy (*The Nutcracker*), *Black Swan* and *Don Quixote* pas de deux, and others. Headed the concert group of Ballet Russe de Monte Carlo for its 1952–53 and 1953–54 seasons for which she arranged six ballets for the sixteen dancers. When the company resumed at full strength (1954–55) she danced *Giselle* for the first time and during the 1955–56 season created the Unicorn in *La Dame à la Licorne* (The Lady and the Unicorn). For the 1957–58 season she choreographed *Variations Classiques* to Brahms' *Variations on a Theme of Haydn* and danced the ballerina role. Also danced first ballerina in the revival of Balanchine's *Ballet Imperial.* She has also staged the mazurka and czardas in the Ballet Russe de Monte Carlo's production of *Coppélia,* and with Anatole Vilzak restaged parts of the full-length *Swan Lake* (1960) in which she danced Odette-Odile. She returned to Poland for the first time in 1961 to dance with the State Ballet in Warsaw and with the Posnan company. She also danced several performances during the Festival of Dance in Warsaw, Lódz, Radom, and Gdansk. On Apr. 20, 1962, she married Roman Rojas Cabot, a Venezuelan diplomat. Soon afterwards she resigned from the company and settled in Caracas, Venezuela.

Novaro, Luciana, Italian dancer and choreographer, b. Genoa, 1923. Entered the ballet school of Teatro alla Scala, Milan (1933), where she studied with Paula Giussani, Ettorina Mazzucchelli,

Esmée Bulnes, Vera Volkova. Has been ballerina since 1946. Among her roles were *Legend of Joseph, Le Sacre du Printemps,* and others. She married an editor of the newspaper *La Notte,* has given up dancing and devotes her time to choreography. Among the ballets she has staged for La Scala are *Sebastian* (Gian-Carlo Menotti), *Jeu de Cartes* (Stravinsky), *La Giara* (new version), and others. She also does choreography for television.

Noverre, Jean Georges (1727–1810), famous French choreographer and reformer of ballet, born near Paris. His father, of Swiss extraction, was an adjutant of Charles XII of Sweden. Noverre was a pupil of Louis Dupré the famous dancer and ballet master of the Paris Opéra, and of the young dancer-choreographer Martel. He made his debut in a market theatre in Paris (1743). After a short time in Potsdam became dancer and ballet master at the Opéra Comique where he staged his first ballet *Les Fêtes Chinoises* (1749). Ballet is indebted to Noverre for many of the principles which govern this art form to the present day. He was one of the first to realize the possibilities of ballet as an artistic medium. He set forth his ideas and ideals in his famous *Lettres sur la Danse et sur les Ballets* published in 1760. He made an effort to eliminate the conventionalized movements and gestures which had hitherto comprised most of the ballets and he was one of the first to advocate reform in stage costumes. He was particularly opposed to the wearing of masks, which were eventually discontinued in 1773 when the famous dancer Maximilien Gardel discarded his mask in performances at the Paris Opéra. In the history of choreography Noverre is known as an excellent choreographer of more than 150 ballets and is credited with being the creator of the ballet d'action as well as a great theoretician and propagandizer of new ideas in theatrical dance. Noverre's reform of the ballet is often compared with Christoph Gluck's reform in music. Noverre's theories were considered too advanced for Paris and he was unsuccessful in obtaining the much coveted post of ballet master at the Opéra. He was forced to go abroad for an opportunity to develop his theories and made a visit to England. France and England were on the verge of war at that time (the Seven Years' War), and Noverre met with a hostile reception. However, he became acquainted with the famous English actor David Garrick, with whom he studied mime. Garrick called Noverre "the Shakespeare of the dance." Noverre traveled on to Stuttgart to find an outlet for his ideas. There at the court of the Duke of Württemberg, he was appointed ballet master of the Württemberg Ducal Theatre (1760). In Vienna (1767–74) he collaborated with Gluck, his close friend, who was experimenting with opera much as Noverre was with ballet. The two collaborated in the production of *Iphigenie en Tauris* (1774). In 1776 Noverre finally achieved his goal and was appointed ballet master of the Paris Opéra as successor to Gaetano Vestris. The appointment was made due to the influence of Marie Antoinette, whose teacher he had been in Vienna. After the French revolution Noverre was forced to flee to England. This time he received a more cordial welcome. While there he produced his last ballet, *The Loves of Tempe* (1793). He returned to France and just before his death edited a new edition of his *Lettres* and libretti. He died in his modest retreat at Saint-Germain.

Novikoff, Laurent (1888–1956), dancer and ballet master, b. Moscow. Graduated from the Moscow Imperial Ballet School (1906). Made his debut in *The Humpbacked Horse* (1908) with Vera Mosolova at the Bolshoi Theatre, Moscow. Joined Diaghilev Ballets Russes for first Paris season (1909). Premier danseur, Moscow Imperial Ballet (1910); same year danced *Don Quixote* with Yekaterina Geltzer in St. Petersburg. Joined Anna Pavlova as

Laurent Novikoff, dancer, ballet master, teacher.

her partner (1911). Michel Fokine choreographed *Les Preludes* (Liszt) and *Seven Daughters* (Spendiaroff) for them (1912). Novikoff returned to Russia (1914) and staged dances for the Moscow Opera: *Les Huguenots* (Meyerbeer), *Pan* (Koncarovitch), *Thamar* (Balakireff), *Narcisse* (Tcherepnine), and others. Following the revolution Novikoff left Russia (August, 1918); reached London (1919) and danced *Les Sylphides* and *Petrouchka* with the Diaghilev company; then danced as partner of Tamara Karsavina for two seasons. Rejoined Pavlova (1921), producing *Russian Folk Lore, Don Quixote,* and other ballets for the company; remained with her until 1928 when he established a school in London. Became ballet master, Chicago Civic Opera Company Ballet (1929), and remained for four seasons, producing *Swan Lake, El Amor Brujo, Chopiniana,* and others for this company. Ballet master, Metropolitan Opera Ballet (1941–45). Later taught in Chicago but lived in New Buffalo, Mich., until his death (1956).

Nowak, Lionel, composer, b. Cleveland, O., 1911. M. Mus., Cleveland Institute of Music. Musical director of the Humphrey-Weidman Dance Company (1938–42) for which he composed the music for Doris Humphrey's *Square Dances* (1939), *Green Land* (1941), and Charles Weidman's *On My Mother's Side* (1940), *Flickers* (1942), *House Divided* (1943). In addition composed *Danzas Mexicanas* for José Limón (1939), *Story of Mankind* (Humphrey, 1946), and has written scores occasionally for Jean Erdman, Harriette Ann Gray, and Gertrude Lippincott. Has also composed numerous chamber works. Is a member of American Composers' Alliance, a Visiting Artist for Association of American Colleges since 1946, and on the music faculty of Bennington College since 1948.

Nozze degli Dei. Spectacular ballet given in Florence (1637) in honor of the marriage of Duke Ferdinand II and Vittoria of Urbino. The settings were by A. Parigi.

Nuitter, Charles (Charles Louis Etienne Truinet) (1828–1899), French writer and practicing lawyer in the reign of Napoleon III. Director of the Archives of the Paris Opéra and author of several ballet libretti among them *La Source* (1866) and *Coppélia* (1870), both with Arthur Saint-Léon; and *Namouna* (1882) with Lucien Petipa.

Nureyev, Rudolf, Russian dancer, b. Ufa, capital of the Bashkir Republic, 1938. Studied with a private teacher and danced with amateur groups and later with the Ufa Opera Ballet. Entered the Leningrad Ballet School (1955) and studied there chiefly with Alexander Pushkin (no relation to the great Russian poet), an outstanding teacher. Three years later Nureyev was accepted into the Kirov Ballet Company as a soloist, dancing *La Bayadère, Le Corsaire, Don Quixote, Laurentia,* and *Taras Bulba.* Despite threats of punishment from the Ministry of Culture for his "insubordination," was occasionally permitted to dance with the Kirov Ballet outside the Soviet Union. In June, 1961, he was appearing with the company in Paris, the beginning of the Paris–London–New York–U.S. tour. The management of the company was apparently dissatisfied with his conduct during his free time outside the theatre. On the day of the company's departure for London when the dancers were boarding the London plane, Soviet officials attached to the company and members of the Soviet Embassy in Paris directed Nureyev to board the plane which was about to leave for Moscow. Nureyev did not obey the order and ran back into the airport building where he asked the protection of the French police. His escape from the ballet management and the Soviet authorities immediately brought him international attention. He remained in Paris, where he soon joined the Grand Ballet du Marquis de Cuevas, dancing the Prince and the Blue Bird in *The Sleeping Beauty.* Toured as partner to Rosella Hightower, also appearing with her at his London debut at the Royal Academy of Dancing Gala in Oct., 1961. In early 1962 he danced in U.S. on television and in a pas de deux with Sonia Arova as part of Ruth Page's Chicago Opera Ballet. That spring he was a guest artist with the Royal Ballet, London, returning to U.S. for further appearances with the Chicago Opera Ballet and with the American Ballet Theatre. Danced with the Royal Ballet in London and on its U.S. tour (1963) partnering Margot Fonteyn in *Giselle, Le Corsaire* pas de deux, *Les Sylphides, Swan Lake,* and in *Marguerite and Armand* in which he created the leading male role. He is more or less a "permanent" guest artist of the Royal Ballet as are Margot Fonteyn and Pamela May. He dances with the company during its London seasons and tours of the U.S., some of the summer festivals, etc., but finds many occasions to dance with little groups or as guest artist with various other companies. These peripatetic activities and his penchant for personal publicity have aroused criticism. Author of *Nureyev,* edited and with an introduction by Alexander Bland (London, 1962; N.Y., 1963). Staged the ballet *Raymonda,* and danced the role of Jean de Brienne for the Royal Ballet (touring section) at the 1964 Festival of Two Worlds, Spoleto. His partner was Doreen Wells, who replaced Dame Margot Fonteyn when the ballerina had to leave for Panama, where her husband had been seriously wounded by a political oppo-

Rudolf Nureyev in his variation of the pas de deux, Swan Lake, *Act 3, at the Vienna State Opera.*

nent. Dame Margot returned some ten days later to resume her role. Staged *Swan Lake* for the Vienna State Opera Ballet, dancing the première, Oct. 15, 1964, with Dame Margot. For the Royal Ballet he has staged *Le Corsaire* pas de deux, the Kingdom of Shades act of *La Bayadère,* dancing the male role in each; also the *Laurencia* pas de six, dancing the leading male part, and he choreographed a new Polonaise and Mazurka for *Swan Lake.* Created Romeo in Kenneth MacMillan's *Romeo and Juliet.* Created the Warrior Chief in the revival of the *Polovetzian Dances from Prince Igor* (1965). In Oct. 1966 he staged the full-length *Don Quixote* after Marius Petipa to the Ludwig Minkus music for the Vienna State Opera Ballet.

Nutcracker, The. Ballet in two acts, three scenes; chor. and book: Lev Ivanov; music: Peter Tchaikovsky; décor: M. I. Botcharov. First prod.: Maryinsky Theatre, St. Petersburg, Dec. 18, 1892, with Antonietta Dell-Era and Paul Gerdt as the Sugar Plum Fairy and her Cavalier. It is based on one of the famous *Tales* by E. T. A. Hoffmann. *The Nutcracker* under its French title of *Casse-Noisette* was revived by Nicholas Sergeyev for the Vic-Wells (later Sadler's Wells, now Royal) Ballet, Sadler's Wells Theatre, London, Jan. 30, 1934, with Alicia Markova and Harold Turner in the principal roles, and was later danced by Mary Honer, Margot Fonteyn, Nadia Nerina, and a long line of dancers, usually partnered by Robert Helpmann. *The Nutcracker* was in the repertoire of the Markova-Dolin Ballet, and other versions were or are danced by Ballet Russe de Monte Carlo, National Ballet of Canada, Ballet Rambert (in décor by Mstislav Doboujinsky), and others. It was revived by London's Festival Ballet with Alicia Markova and Anton Dolin (1950). A new version by David Lichine in décor and under the supervision of Alexandre Benois was presented at Festival Hall, London, Dec. 24, 1957, with Nathalie Krassovska and John Gilpin. The pas de deux of the Sugar Plum Fairy and her Cavalier from the Ivanov original is a popular number frequently given by companies and groups. The story tells of a Christmas party at which little Clara, daughter of the house, receives the gift of a Nutcracker from a strange old man Herr Drosselmeyer. She falls asleep and dreams that she watches a battle between the toy soldiers which were another gift, and some Mice. The Nutcracker fights the King of the Mice, and Clara saves the Nutcracker by throwing her shoe at the King. The Nutcracker is then transformed into a handsome young Prince who leads her through the Land of Snowflakes to Konfitürenburg, the home of the Sugar Plum Fairy, where everyone dances in her honor.

Nutcracker, The. Ballet in three acts and six scenes, with an epilogue; chor. and book: Vasily Vainonen; music: Peter Tchaikovsky; décor: Nicolai Seleznyov. First prod. (in this version): Kirov Theatre, Leningrad, Feb. 18, 1934, with Galina Ulanova (Masha) and Konstantin Sergeyev (Prince). First performed in the same version with décor by Vladimir Dimitriev at the Bolshoi Theatre, Moscow, Apr. 28, 1938. The ballet is currently in the repertoire of both theatres. In the Vainonen version, the name of the little heroine is Masha and it is she who dances the grand adagio and what is known as the Sugar Plum Fairy variation in the last act.

Nutcracker, The. Ballet in two acts, three scenes; chor.: George Balanchine; music: Peter Tchaikovsky; décor: Horace Armistead; costumes: Barbara Karinska. First prod.: New York City Ballet, City Center, N.Y., Feb., 1954, with Maria Tallchief and Nicholas Magallanes as the Sugar Plum Fairy and her Cavalier. Alberta Grant and Paul Nickel were the first Mary (in recent years she has become Clara as in the Russian version) and the Nutcracker Prince. This is a somewhat different version from the Ivanov original and has become a popular N.Y. Christmas event. Each year children and adults flock to see the Battle of the Mice and the Lead Soldiers, the Christmas tree that grows and the bed that travels right out into the forest where the Snowflakes dance. The Sugar Plum Fairy has been danced by almost all the leading dancers of the company: Diana Adams, Melissa Hayden, Patricia Wilde, Allegra Kent, Suzanne Farrell among them, while André Eglevsky, Jacques d'Amboise, Jonathan Watts, Conrad Ludlow have been among their cavaliers. An entirely new production with scenery and costumes by Rouben Ter-Arutunian was staged by Balanchine and premièred Dec. 11, 1964, at the N.Y. State Theater. The principal revision in the choreography was the Danse Arabe, which became a solo for Gloria Govrin.

It is usually danced for a month.

Obidenna, Lara (Illaria Obidennaya), contemporary dancer, b. Moscow; m. Marian Ladré. Studied ballet with Agrippina Vaganova at Maryinsky Theatre, Leningrad; with Lubov Egorova and Mathilde Kchessinska in Paris. Left Russia in 1924. Soloist, National Opera, Bucharest; Boris Romanoff's Romantic Theatre, Paris; Diaghilev Ballets Russes (1927–29); Col. de Basil & René Blum Ballets Russes from its inception (1932), remaining with the company (later Original Ballet Russe) as soloist and assistant to Serge Grigoriev until 1947. Among her roles were Chief Nursemaid (*Petrouchka*), Amazon (*Jeux d'Enfants*), Woman (*Eternal Struggle*), pas de trois (*Cimarosiana, The Gods Go a'Begging*), pas de sept (*Aurora's Wedding*), and others. Currently teaching in Seattle, Wash., with her husband in their own school.

Oboukhoff, Anatole (1895–1962), dancer, teacher, b. St. Petersburg, Russia; m. Vera Nemtchinova. Studied at the Ballet School of the Imperial Maryinsky Theatre, St. Petersburg (1907–13); graduated into the company and remained with it until 1920 (by which time it was known as the Russian State Theatre, Petrograd), rising to the position of premier danseur. His roles included Siegfried (*Swan Lake*), Prince Desiré (*The Sleeping Beauty*), Albrecht (*Giselle*), Gringoire (*Esmeralda*), and others. In 1914 he partnered Anna Pavlova in her final performances in Russia (Narodny Dom, St. Petersburg; Summer Auditorium, Pavlovsk; Aquarium Theatre, Moscow). Left Russia in 1920 and until 1922 was premier danseur of Opera Royal, Bucharest. Leading dancer, Boris Romanoff's Romantic Theatre, Berlin (1922–28); danced title role in *Petrouchka* as guest artist at Teatro alla Scala, Milan; danced with Vera Nemtchinova's company in Paris, Monte Carlo, and London (1929); guest artist with Riga State Ballet, Latvia (1930); director and leading dancer of Lithuanian State Ballet, Kaunas (1930–34); with Ballets Russes de Monte Carlo under René Blum's direction (1936–38), creating role of the Ambassador in *L'Epreuve d'Amour;* ballet master and instructor of Col. de Basil's Original Ballet Russe for its Australian tour (1939). Came with that company to U.S. (1940) when George Balanchine invited him to join the faculty of the School of American Ballet, N.Y., where he taught until his death. In 1944 he staged the *Don Quixote* pas de deux for Ballet (now American Ballet) Theatre, the first production of this virtuoso pas de deux to be seen in the U.S.

O'Brien, John, dancer, b. Melbourne, Australia, 1938. Studied dance in Melbourne, principally with Xenia Borovansky and Leon Kellaway; with Victor Gsovsky and others in Paris; with Marie Rambert, Angela Ellis, Kathleen Crofton, George Goncharov, and others in London.

Won scholarship to Royal Ballet School (1956) and appeared in the ensembles of the full-evening classic ballets. Danced with Covent Garden and Sadler's Wells Opera Ballets, then joined Ballet Rambert where he became a leading dancer. Roles include *Peasant* pas de deux (*Giselle*), Cavalier of Moscow Ballerina (*Gala Performance*), Blackamoor (*Night Shadow*), first Scottish solo (*La Sylphide*), Scottish Rhapsody (*Façade*), and others. Currently runs a bookstore in London.

O'Donnell, May, American modern dancer, choreographer, director, teacher, b. Sacramento, Calif., 1909; m. composer Ray Green. Studied dance with Estelle Reed in San Francisco (with whose concert group she made her debut), and with Martha Graham in N.Y. Was a soloist with the Martha Graham company (1932–38) and guest artist with the same company (1944–52), creating Pioneer Woman (*Appalachian Spring*), She of the Earth (*Dark Meadow*), The Attendant (*Herodiade*), Chorus (*Cave of the Heart*), and dancing principal roles in *Letter to the World, Deaths and Entrances, Punch and the Judy, Every Soul Is a Circus, Primitive Mysteries.* Gave a solo performance of original works in San Francisco (1939); organized San Francisco Dance Theatre with Gertrude Shurr and Ray Green (1939); toured with José Limón (1941–43); gave her first N.Y. program of original works at YMHA (1945). Since 1949 has directed, choreographed, and been soloist of her own May O'Donnell Dance Company, appearing in N.Y. and on tour in the U.S. Her works include *Cornerstone, Horizon Song, Our Rivers, Our Cradles, Suspension, Dance Sonata No. 1, Dance Sonata No. 2, Dance Concerto, Legendary Forest, Incredible Adventure, Drift, Dance Energies, Dance Theme and Variations, Dance Sonatinas, Illuminations, Sunday Sing Symphony, Contrasts for Three Dancers, The Queen's Obsession* (Lady Macbeth), *Spell of Silence,* and others. She has appeared with her company with many symphony orchestras throughout the U.S.; has given master classes all over the U.S. and has taught several special sessions at the Univ. of California Extension Division and Summer Session, Berkeley, conducting workshops at the university for three summers (1959–61). In N.Y. she teaches in her own school and at the School of Performing Arts and serves as National Adviser in Dance for the National Federation of Music Clubs, for which organization she prepared the Dance Section of the Junior Festivals Bulletin.

May O'Donnell, American modern dancer, choreographer, teacher.

Odyssey. Modern dance work; chor.: Murray Louis; music: Ivan Fiedel (percussion, brass and woodwind score). First prod.: Henry Street Playhouse, N.Y., Mar. 11, 1960, with Murray Louis, Beverly Schmidt, Gladys Bailin, and others. The wanderings of the Greek hero Odysseus seen as a twentieth century journey of the mind.

Offenbach, Jacques (1819–1880), French composer of music for *Le Papillon,* a ballet by Maria Taglioni (1860). Best known for his opera *The Tales of Hoffmann,* excerpts from his *La Vie Parisienne, Barbe-bleu,* and *La Belle Hélène* were produced as the ballets *Gaîté Parisienne* (Leonide Massine, 1938), *Bluebeard* (Michel Fokine, 1941), and *Helen of Troy* (David Lichine, 1942).

Offenbach in the Underworld. Ballet in 1 act; chor. and book: Antony Tudor; music: Jacques Offenbach (score for *Gaîté Parisienne* in a different orchestration); décor: Kay Ambrose. First prod.: National Ballet of Canada, Royal Alexandra Theatre, Toronto, Canada, Feb. 1, 1955, with Celia Franca (Operetta Star), Angela Leigh (Queen of the Carriage Trade), Lillian Jarvis (Debutante), David Adams (Artist), Earl Kraul (Officer). As Antony Tudor states, "There isn't an ending, only a closing time," so at the end of the evening in a fashionable café nothing has really been resolved but several people have had a wonderful time and only a few are sad. Tudor originally staged another version to different Offenbach music for the Philadelphia Ballet Guild, Convention Hall, Phila., May 5, 1954, with Viola Essen and Michael Lland as guest artists. The Canadian production with décor by René Bouché was taken into the Ballet (now American Ballet) Theatre repertoire and premièred at Metropolitan Opera House, N.Y., Apr. 18, 1956, with Nora Kaye (Operetta Queen), Lupe Serrano (Queen of the Carriage Trade), Ruth Ann Koesun (Debutante), Hugh Laing (Artist), Scott Douglas (Officer), John Kriza (Operetta Queen's Escort).

Oiseau de Feu, L'. See FIREBIRD.

Old-Time Dancing. A term given in England to the ballroom dances based on the old technique in which the turned-out five positions are used and which found favor prior to about 1914. The waltz of 1880, the polka, the barn dance, the schottische, the varsoviana (or varsovienne), and the lancers, are typical old time dances.

Olenewa, Maria, contemporary Russian choreographer, ballet mistress, teacher, b. Moscow. Began her dance studies in the private ballet school of Lydia Nelidova; made her professional debut at the Zimin Opera. Went to France after the revolution of 1917 and danced in the opera company of Maria Kouznetzov at the Théâtre des Champs-Elysées, Paris. Toured with the Anna Pavlova company in the U.S. Went to South America in 1921 to dance under the direction of Leonide Massine in opera ballets. Taught at Teatro Colón's ballet school in Buenos Aires, Argentina (1922–24). With critic Mario Nunes founded the dance school of the Teatro Municipal, Rio de Janeiro (1927), where she developed the first generation of Brazilian dancers and formed the first local corps de ballet which became official in 1936. Was also dancer and choreographer for Teatro Municipal. Resigned in 1942 and went to São Paulo, Brazil, to direct the ballet school of the Teatro Municipal; resigned in 1947. Formed the S. Paulo Ballet which toured from Santos to Amazonas (1948–49). The directors of the Teatro Municipal in Rio invited her back to participate in the festivities in connection with the 50th anniversary of the theatre. For the occasion she staged (1959) *Evocation of Two Periods* (Mozart-Kabalevsky, 1959). Still very active in her own ballet school in S. Paulo, she also maintains a dance group that tours the regions of Brazil. Olenewa formed almost all the present-day Brazilian dances and choreographed all operas during her years with Rio's Teatro Municipal. She was the first foreign choreographer to use Brazilian themes and the music of national composers. Her works include *Maracatu, Do Chico-Rei* and *Dionysian Feast* (Francisco Mignone), *Slaves* (Dinorá Carvalho), *The Herons* (José Siqueira), *Serenade* (Alberto Nepomuceno), *Negros Dance* (Frutuoso Viana), *The Neighbor's Apples* (Elpidio Pereira), *The Peace, Festa no Arraial* (Francisco Braga), *Batuque.*

Oliosi, Eleonora, Brazilian dancer, b. Pelotas, Brazil, 1939. Studied dance under Toni Seitz, Porto Alegre (from 1945); entered ballet school of Teatro Municipal, Rio de Janeiro (1952). Danced in Ballet da Juventude (1952–53). Joined ballet of Teatro Municipal (1955); appointed soloist (1957), then first dancer (1959). Won first prize in National Ballet Contest and second prize in International Ballet Contest (1961). Dances principal roles in most ballets of the repertoire and all classic pas de deux; also appears in a weekly television program.

Ombre, L'. Ballet in 3 acts; chor. and book: Filippo Taglioni; music: L. Wilhelm Maurer; décor: Fedorov, Serkov, Shenian, Roller; costumes: Mathieu. First prod.: Bolshoi Theatre, St. Petersburg, Dec. 10, 1839, with Maria Taglioni and Antonio Guerra. A two-act version with scenery by W. Griève and again with Taglioni in the title role was premièred at Her Majesty's Theatre, London, June 18, 1840. *Le Pas de l'Ombre,* a version of this ballet, was given in June, 1844, at Taglioni's farewell performance in Paris. *L'Ombre* (The Shade, or Spirit) is the ghost of a lady who has been murdered. She is mourned by her lover and returns to dance with him.

On My Mother's Side. Solo by Charles Weidman; music: Lionel Nowak; costumes: Charles Weidman. First prod.: N.Y., Dec. 26, 1940. A set of six portraits from Weidman's own family, all characters introduced by a chorus speaking prose-poetry written especially for the dance.

On Stage! Ballet in 1 act; chor.: Michael Kidd; commissioned music: Norman dello Joio; book: Michael and Mary Kidd; décor: Oliver Smith; costumes: Alvin Colt. First prod.: Ballet (now American Ballet) Theatre, Boston, Mass., Oct. 4, 1945; N.Y. première: Metropolitan Opera House, Oct. 9, 1945, with Michael Kidd (Handyman), Janet Reed (Girl), Nora Kaye (Princess), John Kriza (Hero). Alicia Alonso assumed the role of the Girl the following year. The shy Girl who has failed an audition is cheered by the Handyman who himself dreams of being a dancer. She dances so beautifully for him when she does not realize she is being observed that she is immediately engaged. This is Kidd's only ballet, the majority of his work being executed for musical comedy and films.

Ondine. Ballet in 3 acts; chor.: Frederick Ashton; music: Hans Werner Henze; décor: Lisa de Nobili. First prod.: Royal Ballet, Royal Opera House, Covent Garden, London, Oct. 27, 1958, with Margot Fonteyn (Ondine), Michael Somes (Palemon), Julia Farron (Berthe), Alexander Grant (Tirrenio). Ashton simplified the very complicated Perrot-Cerito scenario but retained the outline of the story. Ondine lures the nobleman Palemon away from his betrothed, Berthe; but Berthe wins him back and Ondine returns to the sea protected by Tirrenio, King of the Waters, who causes a great storm to arise. On the wedding day of Palemon and Berthe Ondine returns and Palemon kisses her, though he knows this means death, and she bears him away to live with her forever beneath the waves. Ondine is probably Fonteyn's greatest creation. Other versions using the Henze score are by Alan Carter for Munich Opera House, Jan. 25, 1959, and Tatiana Gsovska for Städtische Oper, West Berlin, Sept. 22, 1959.

Ondine, ou La Naiade. Ballet in 6 scenes; chor. and book: Jules Perrot and Fanny Cerito; music: Cesare Pugni; décor: W. Griève. First prod.: Her Majesty's Theatre, London, June 22, 1843, with Cerito in the title role and Perrot as the fisherman; St. Petersburg première: Feb. 11, 1851, under the title *The Naiad and the Fisherman,* with Carlotta Grisi, at Peterhof, July 23, 1851, at a Gala Performance for Grand Duchess Olga

Nikolaevna. Matteo the fisherman is betrothed to Giannina and is to marry her on the morrow when Ondine, a Naiad who has fallen in love with him, rises from the sea. Although she is warned by Hydrola, Queen of the Waters, of the danger of falling in love with a mortal Ondine succeeds in luring Giannina under the water and takes her place. Unable to live on land she is about to die when Hydrola restores Giannina to her lover and bears Ondine back to the sea. The ballet was famous for the "Shadow" dance when Ondine sees her shadow for the first time.

One in Five. Ballet in 1 act; chor.: Ray Powell; music: an arrangement of polkas and waltzes by Josef and Johann Strauss; décor: Derek Rencher. First prod.: Sunday Ballet Club, June 12, 1960, with Deanne Bergsma, Lawrence Ruffell, John Sale, Christopher Newton, Derek Rencher. Taken into the repertoire of Western Theatre Ballet with Hazel Merry in the lead; also in the repertoires of National Ballet of Canada, Australian Ballet, and Metropolitan Opera Ballet Studio, N.Y. The lively antics of a group of clowns, one of whom is a girl.

One-Night Stand. A town or city in which only one performance is given by a touring company; also the performance itself.

One-Step. A ballroom dance in 2/4 time introduced by Vernon and Irene Castle; a variation of foxtrot, also called the Castle Walk.

Opera-Ballet. Term originally applied to the type of ballet produced by Jean Philippe Rameau (1683–1764), later to ballets used as background for opera (*Don Giovanni,* 1787); now refers to ballets inserted in opera, often with no apparent justification.

Opéra Comique. One of the three National Lyric theatres of France, the others being l'Opéra and Comédie Française, all under the direction of a single General Administrator (director), who in 1967 was composer Georges Auric (appointed 1962).

Opera Lengths. Long hose usually sewn on to briefs, occasionally worn by female dancers in place of tights.

Operetta. See MUSICAL COMEDY.

Ophelia. Modern dance solo; chor.: Jean Erdman; music: John Cage; costume and set: Zenia Cage. First prod.: N.Y., Dec. 28, 1945.

Opus 34. Ballet in 2 scenes; chor. and book: George Balanchine; music: Arnold Schoenberg's *Begleitungsmusik zu einer Lichtspielszene* (Musical Accompaniment to a Motion Picture Scene); décor: Jean Rosenthal; costumes (for second scene): Esteban Francés. First prod.: New York City Ballet, City Center, N.Y., Jan. 19, 1954, with Diana Adams, Patricia Wilde, Nicholas Magallanes, Francisco Moncion (first scene); Tanaquil LeClercq and Herbert Bliss (second scene). The music was played through twice to accommodate the action. The first scene is abstract though suggestive of total destruction, the dancers in white tights and leotards forming shapeless, crawling heaps which finally collapse. For the musical repeat the scene starts as a kind of dual operation with surgeons and nurses bending over the two figures on operating tables. When these figures, apparently now corpses, slide from the tables, they begin a macabre dance in which both are finally engulfed by a viscous-like wave which drags the girl down while bearing the man upward. The use of the same music for two entirely unrelated, complete works, reduces to absurdity the idea that music and dance actually have any relation one to the other.

Orchesis. A Greek word meaning the art of dance, particularly the art of dance in a Greek chorus. The word was adopted by Margaret N. H'Doubler as a name for college dance clubs, an idea which she originated and developed. Orchesis played an important part in developing interest in dance in universities and colleges in the U.S.

Orchesographie. Book written by Thoinot Arbeau in 1588. A treatise in dialogue form on the history and nature of the dance, it is the most important surviving record of the dance of the 16th century. It includes the positions and describes various dances of the period. The book was first translated into English by Cyril W. Beaumont (London, 1925), and later by Mary Stewart Evans (N.Y., 1948).

O'Reilly, Sheilah, dancer, b. Bexley, England, 1931. Studied dance with Kathleen Danetree, Judith Espinosa, and at Sadler's Wells Ballet School. Joined Sadler's Wells Theatre Ballet at its inception (1946); remained until shortly after the company's U.S. tour (1951–52) when a foot injury brought about a premature retirement. She danced Waltz (*Les Sylphides*), Milkmaid (*Façade*), The Girl (*Mardi Gras*), title role (*Khadra*), and others.

Orff, Carl, German composer, b. Munich, 1895. Studied at the Academy of Music, Munich; composition with Heinrich Kaminski. In his compositions for the stage he prefers themes of the Middle Ages and antiquity. His best-known and most often used dance composition is his *Trionfi-Tryptichon: Carmina Burana* (1936), *Catulli Carmina* (1943), and *Trionfi di Afrodite* (1950–51). Kurt Jooss choreographed *Catulli Carmina* (Düsseldorf, 1955); Heinz Rosen did all three parts (Munich, 1959 and 1960); John Butler staged *Carmina Burana* (N.Y., 1959 and 1960), and *Catulli Carmina* for the Caramoor Festival, N.Y. (1964). Norman Walker staged this work (under the same title), premièred July 6, 1965 at Jacob's Pillow Dance Festival with Cora Cahan, the choreographer, and Robert Powell heading the cast.

Oriental Dance.

BY LA MERI.

In the Eastern world the dance is far more an integral part of living than it is in the West. Dance is an expression of worship as well as a highly-developed, royally patronized stage art. It is an expression so communal that even the children play games connected with dance.

Technically speaking the Oriental dance puts the burden of interpretation on the upper-body. Generally the hands play the most important role and each country has its characteristic style. The patake or flat hand of India has its prototype in all the countries of the East, but one is never identical with the other. The hands alone indicate the country of origin of the dance. Shoulders and neck are also important, both rhythmically and expressively, while the face has a hundred delicate shadings not always obvious to the Western observer. In the lower body, the dance accompaniment is developed. In some countries bells are used to accentuate the rhythmic understructure. Spread knees are invariably seen only in masculine types of dance. The costume, technique, story, often the routine itself, is traditional.

BURMESE—Burmese music and dance grew out of primitive religious rituals. With the passage of centuries both India and China influenced local styles and techniques. Unlike those of Java and Indo-China, the Burmese dance-drama is not based on the two great epics of India—the *Ramayana* and the *Mahabharata*—and hence shows no "fighting dance" although love scenes are depicted.

Early non-Buddhistic dances were those offered to the thirty-seven nats (spirits) by women mediums who performed in a trance to invoke them. These dances still survive, together with later Buddhistic pageantry, in the folk festivals. The Burmese is gay by nature and his festivals are filled with laughter, even street water fights and dances of animal mimicry.

After the fall of the kingdom of Pagan (A.D. 1287), pageants on the life of Buddha became popular. A little later clowns were introduced into the miracle plays to supply the comedy relief so dear to a laughter-loving people. The professional dancers who took part in these plays were usually men, but they drew their technique from the style of the nat mediums. Dancing became so popular that presently the drama was used only as an interlude to the dance.

When the Burmese conquered Siam (1767) they adopted the Siamese play together with its tradition. The base of Siamese acting technique is a gesture language, less elaborate than the Hindu but equally rigid.

After 1780, the Burmese drama again asserted itself over foreign importations. The villain became the comic, and here, of all Eastern theatres, the woman character had an active, rather than a passive role—for women have always been held the equals of men in Burma. Soon the dancer-actor gave the play only as a side issue to the singing and dancing. By 1885 the drama had declined in favor of the song and dance. At the time of the annexation of Burma as a province of the Indian Empire, matinee idols were Sein-Kadon and U Po Sein, both of whom were already using scenery and devices inspired by touring French and English companies. U Po Sein, who by 1912 had considerably raised the prestige of actors, is still the outstanding actor-dancer of his country.

Since the actors were originally spirit-dancers who before the performance made offerings to the thirty-seven nats, the first dance—the curtain-raiser—was a dance to the nats. Today this invocation has survived in the dance of the "posture girls" who perform at the opening of the drama.

The Burmese dance is characterized by an out-curving backbone and bent knees. Deep waist bends figure in both masculine and feminine techniques, with the head drooping toward the floor. Though the hands are subtle and pliable, few set poses are used. The face and general character are gay and smiling.

JAVANESE—Wayang Wong—the Javanese dance-drama. The Hindus arrived in Java during the second century. In the 9th century, theatre and dance flourished along with religion and architecture; the great temple of Borobudur is decorated with scenes from the Natya Sastra (see HINDU DANCE). King Dharmawanga then translated the Indian epic poem, the *Mahabharata;* during the 11th century Kawi wrote a play taken from this poem, *Arjunawawaha* (The Nuptials of Arjun), the earliest known lakon, or theatre-piece. Stylization of the technique began about 1200 and the Golden Age is considered to be 1350–1439. About 1900 the brother of the Sultan of Djokjakarta formed the Krida Beksa Wirama (Society of Music and Dance) for which technique and rules were established by Prince Souryadnigrat, who thus crystallized the dance-drama in its present form.

Historically, the Wayang Topeng (anciently called Raket) developed first, employing masked actors; it was used for magic and ancestor-worship. Then came the Wayang Poerwa, the shadow-play (sometimes Wayang Kulit or Wayang Gedog) and after it, marionettes made of leather, Wayang Klitik or Wayang Kroutjil. From these, which could be used in profile only, grew the wooden marionettes (Wayang Golek) with the operator (dalang) speaking for his dolls. The forms of Wayang in which the actors were puppets, or humans with masks, are considered to be more mysterious, profound, and abstract. The next stage of development was the Topeng Dalang, or Topeng Barangan, in which the operator spoke the lines and the masked actor portrayed them. These forms—all still in existence—

combined to produce the Wayang Wong, the most popular Javanese dance-drama.

In a play (Ringit Tyang), the Wayang Wong presents the human, unmasked actor. The appropriate actor lifts an arm to indicate that he is supposed to be speaking, while the dalang reads the lines. Dancing is incidental and consists of pokok or combat dances and miraga or decorative dances. The plays last many hours, even days. The technique, depending on the suppleness of the body, is a smooth even flow of movement, somewhat as in a slow-motion film. The aim is to soothe, not arouse; a well-acted Wayang Wong is as sedative as a drug. The subject matter of the plays is from the *Ramayana* and the *Mahabharata*. Choreography is arranged and altered only by members of the royal household. There are five different styles of technique: of the women; of the lyric hero (djoged allus); of the dramatic hero (djoged kasar); of the demons; and of the giants. The clown has no fixed technique; he alone may ad lib. There are three types of women dancers: the Srimpis, young girls of royal blood who dance in groups of four; the Badayas, who are attached to the court, and dance in groups of nine; the Ronggengs, or professional dancers. The latter are not recognized by the Krida Beksa Wirama, save that recently they have been granted the privilege of using the Badaya repertoire.

There are two centers of dance-drama in Java today, Soerakarta (Solo) and Djokjakarta; the ancient kingdom of Mataram thus dividing in 1775. Besides the contrasts in technical detail and style (Djokja is faster and more energetic), in Djokja men take women's roles. In Solo women take men's roles and painted moustaches are worn. In Djokja, the education of the actor-dancer is supposedly more scientific. The dalang reads the tales in the classical text. The actors are attached to the court, and the drama eclipses both music and speech. There is, however, more liberty in the choice of music. In Solo, the dalang improvises his tale-telling, but only classical music is used. It was the court of Solo that first revived the dance with the mask; it also first developed the Wayang Wong as it is performed today.

The Wayang Wong is the most perfectly finished theatre-piece in the world. It has been protected by the most cultured people of Java since its birth. All its movements, expressions, and presentations are rigidly orthodox. The dance is an integral part of the life of the Oriental, more important to his spiritual life than anything in the western mode of existence, save perhaps church to the very devout. The dance-drama is a composite presentation of the race history, actual and legendary. It was born as a ritual of worship, and at all times has retained this flavor. It is a spiritual exaltation in which actor and audience alike participate. The watcher is there not to be amused, but to learn and to worship. Even the foreigner feels the impact of this profound faith, as he might on entering a temple whose gods are strange to him.

Javanese dancing is far more difficult than it appears. The characteristic body-line is a rigidly-straight back (doubtless, taken from the puppet play) from which the head and limbs move in steady legato spiraling movements infrequently accented with a slight staccato rhythm.

JAPANESE—The origin of the Japanese dance is said to be the mimic steps which Ame-no-Iwato offered to the Sun goddess. Certain dances of the pre-historic era exist today in festival dances of the Kume-mai type. But the art of dance and drama have undoubtedly been much influenced by the Chinese and Indian dramatic arts. Gagaku, meaning noble and elegant music, is also the name of the Japanese Imperial Household Musicians and Dancers and the style of their music. A dance performance of Gagaku is called Bugaku, a term meaning dance and music. (For a more detailed explanation of these terms see GAGAKU in this volume.)

The Noh drama is a development of Bugaku and as Bugaku it belongs to the palace and the religious shrine. Dengaku is a form of folk dance-drama which grew up contemporaneously with the Noh of the palace. Like Dengaku, the Shosagota originated among the plain people, but has become a refined and beautiful spectacle—as is Kabuki, which is also of humble origin.

The Kabuki drama is a modernization of the Noh and has a more general appeal, for though its character remains purely Japanese and the technique is based on that of the Noh, the play moves at an exciting pace unknown in the majestic Noh. Nihonbuyo (classic dances) are nearly all a part of the Kabuki theatre. The repertoire is limited and steps and costumes are traditional. The dances are long and solo passages are generally excerpts from full ballets (Komoro-Kisen), or incidental dances of the hero and heroine of a drama (Fuji-Musune or Funa Benkei).

(For a fuller exposition see KABUKI in this volume.)

Nihonbuyo is divided into three classes: mai, odori, and shosa (or furi). Mai is slow and dignified; odori is light and gay; shosa, or furi, is dramatic or pantomimic. Mai (which is aristocratic) and odori (which is popular) are both pure dance—that is, without pantomimic meaning.

Pantomime in the classic dance is divided into direct and indirect expression. Direct is that which uses the whole or any part of the body. A butterfly might be expressed with the sleeves of a kimono or with a fan. With the indirect method the dancer would seek to catch the butterfly. In the first or direct technique the butterfly itself is mimed; in the second or indirect, action is directed toward the butterfly.

Properties are much used by the Japanese dancer. A fan can become in his expressive hands a variety of things—a drinking bowl, a falling leaf, a rising moon. Parasols, branches of flowers, tambourines, spears, and even the tenegui (towel) are used with great skill and beauty. The sleeves of the kimono are an endless source of air design and mime.

There is a marked difference of technique between men and women. Besides the natural difference in strength and delicacy, male technique demands spread knees and deep pliés. By contrast the Japanese geisha is trained to dance while holding a card between her knees, and evenness of gait is learned by carrying a pitcher of water on the head.

The Japanese is the best preserved of all eastern dances. Its tradition is alive and the art with its adjuncts—music, costume, and stage design—are well patronized.

The Noh drama is presented in all its rich tradition at definite intervals and for a sophisticated public. The Kabuki drama, housed in its own theatre, performs nightly with an all male cast. In the big Takarazuka theatre performances are given by an all female cast to full houses, offering traditional Kabuki ballets as well as western musical-comedy numbers in Japanese. (For a fuller exposition of TAKARAZUKA see that entry.) During the past few years Kabuki drama and dance-drama, Gagaku, and Takarazuka have performed in the United States.

INDO-CHINA—The native origins of the dance-drama of Siam and Cambodia have been practically obliterated by the influence of Hindu dramaturgy which began during the Hindu expansion (A.D. 800). In Indo-China, Chinese and Indian cultures met, but the Chinese was weaker than the Indian and so today one sees in the dances of Indo-China little of the Far East save the lines of the costumes. Both Siam and Cambodia adopted the two great epics of India—the *Ramayana* and the *Mahabharata*—as the sources for their own dance-dramas, although Siam has been less complete in its adoption than Cambodia. The Siamese stresses action rather than description in the presentation of the *Ramayana* and mixes most democratically, professional actors with lords and ladies of the court. The best Cambodian dancers are attached to the court and educated by the Crown.

In the eastern theatre there is no stage setting as we understand the term. The ballet is presented in the Hall of the Dance before the palace or temple—a noble "backdrop" for a noble art.

As has been indicated, the costumes are somewhat Chinese in line. Pointed caps on the shoulders and, sometimes, the hips, give a pagoda-like line. The prachadee headdresses, too, rise in tiers to a long point, rather like a temple's crest. The whole costume is encrusted with gems and gold embroidery. Masks are sometimes worn by the villainous characters.

The characteristic body-line is a rigidly-straight backbone, bent knees, and up-pointing toes. The seemingly double-jointed elbows turn inside-out and the supple wrists turn back again at something more than right-angles. The fingers curve far back and the few mudras (hand movements) are clear and clean-cut, with the thumb brought forward. "Flying" is executed with bent-knees and flat foot as contrasted with the Javanese "flying" on half-toe and straight knees. The salutation anjali curves the fingers outward instead of folding them flatly together as in Indian and Javanese dance. Other details, too numerous to mention, differentiate completely the style of this eastern dance from its chronological forebears and geographical neighbors.

BALI—Possibly in Bali, more than anywhere else in the East, the dance-drama has remained as the most important function in daily living. Birth, marriage, and death, temple festival, and village fête call for the appearance of the actor-dancers in performances which last throughout the night.

The legendary origin of the Balinese dance is attributed to Indra, the old Hindu god of the heavens. But there is little of Hinduism in the style. Scholars agree that the actual dances are the result of primitive rituals of the people themselves. Today, however, Balinese dance is essentially for exhibition and not communal.

In Java the dancers are of and in the court; in Bali the dancers are the peasants and so the dance is vigorously active. This does not imply that the dancers are untrained. On the contrary, many years of tireless effort and exercise go into the execution of the many traditional dances of Bali.

The best-known and most beautiful dance-type is the Legong, a pantomime-dance performed by two young girls wearing gold-encrusted gowns and flower-bedecked headdresses, each carrying a fluttering fan. Movements are lightning quick and combine at once moving brows, neck, shoulders, elbows, wrists, fingers, knees and feet. The backbone line is mercilessly cambré, i.e. bending back or to the side from the waist, and the knees are bent.

A popular and supposedly modern translation of the Legong is the Djoged in which one girl dances in the Legong type and boys of the audience, enticed by her, come into the ring to dance with her. The Sang Byang is the Legong dance performed by dancers while in a trance.

The Kebiyar is another well-known dance of the traditional repertoire. It is entirely modern, its creator, Mario, until his recent death, being its foremost teacher. It is a dance not unlike the Legong in movement, save that it has great virility of style and line and three-fourths of it is performed sitting down.

The shadow-plays of Bali are much like those of Java whence it is supposed they came. Stories of the *Ramayana* and *Mahabharata* are rendered by a dalang, while leather puppets act behind a white screen.

The dance-drama (also here called Wayang Wong) deals in plots taken from the two Indian epics, with dedori (Balinese nymphs) instead of Hindu apsarases dancing around the hero, Arjuna.

The Topeng is another form of dance-drama in which only two or three actors play all the parts, changing masks to do so. Material for the plays is drawn from Balinese political history both actual and legendary.

The romantic history of Bali is preserved in the *Ardja,* a sort of erotic opera in which princesses and princes of incredible beauty dance and sing to each other.

Not to be overlooked are the Baris and the Ketjak. Both performed by men, the former are ritualistic dances executed with weapons, while the latter are choral dances of distinct rhythmic pattern.

CHINA—There is very little existing documentation on the ancient classical dance of China. Some fragments dating from the Tang dynasty (A.D. 618–907) are all that remain. What we know of the Chinese classic dance today is due largely to the studies and artistry of one man—the actor-dancer Mei Lan-fang (1894–1943).

Dr. Mei spent a lifetime in piecing together scattered fragments to re-create the long-dead Chinese dance. Those who have intensively studied the theatre-art of other Eastern lands are convinced that the authorized technique now used in the Chinese classical dance is but a tithe of a far greater repertoire of steps and gestures. But if the classic dance as one sees it today seems limited, what remains has the quality of absolute purity. Each step, each gesture, each subtle turn of the head is from a technique which dates back over a thousand years.

Most of the technique of the Chinese classic dance has been preserved in the Chinese drama—a drama which today has less dancing than any Eastern theatre.

Masculine and feminine techniques are rigidly divided, the spread knees of the man being the most obvious example. In the Chinese theatre each character-type has a certain hand-posture of his own. For example, strong spread fingers are used only by the "shen" (male characters); "helpless" hands only by "tan" (female characters).

Within the tan roles there are seven different types: Lao-tan (dignified old woman), chini (virtuous woman), hua-tan (soubrette), kuei-men-tan (young maiden), tao-ma-tan (military woman), ch'an-tan (comedienne), tsai-tan (wicked woman). Each of these types has traditional movements of hands, sleeves, and feet which must be used. The technique of the "rippling water sleeves"—the three feet of white silk sewn into the mang or Teih-tzu sleeve—is a difficult and delicate art. There are more than a hundred movements with appropriate pantomimic meanings ranging from indifference to running.

By tradition, the color of costume indicates the character of the wearer (yellow—royal; red—honorable; white—young; black—straight-forward and brusque, etc.). Chronology is disregarded in combining costumes—the heroine may wear a costume of the Yang Kwei-fei period and play to a hero in relatively modern dress. Color in face-painting is also indicative of character (yellow—craftiness; red—loyalty; white—wickedness; black—simplicity).

Properties are used often and elegantly. Pheasant feathers require a special technique for handling; a cup and pitcher can become an excuse for graceful acrobatics; a horse-whip and sword are means of accentuating the beauty of a line in space.

The characteristic back in Chinese dance is plumb-line straight; the tan (female) steps are small and unobtrusive; some waist movements are used. The head is never quite still and the delicate shadow of emotion plays continually across the dreamy face.

Original Ballet Russe. See BALLET RUSSE DE MONTE CARLO.

Orlando, Mariane, Swedish ballerina, b. Stockholm, 1934; m. Knut Jonsson. Studied at the Royal Swedish Ballet School; also with Lilian Karina and at the Sadler's Wells (now Royal) Ballet School, London. Accepted into the Royal Swedish Ballet in 1948; ballerina in 1953, the youngest ever to secure that title in Sweden. Made her debut as ballerina in the double role of Odette-Odile in the

Mariane Orlando, Swedish ballerina, as Giselle, Act 1.

full-length *Swan Lake* the same year. Was invited to dance in the Soviet Union in 1959; went to Leningrad in 1960 to study at the Leningrad Kirov School. Took leave of absence (1961–62) to be guest artist with the American Ballet Theatre. She excels in dramatic roles such as *Medea* and had a triumph when she created the role of Hagar in *Pillar of Fire,* staged by Antony Tudor for the Royal Swedish Ballet (Dec. 30, 1962).

Orlikovsky, Vaslav, Russian dancer and ballet master, b. Kharkov, 1921. Among his teachers were Vadim Sulima and Vladimir Preobrajensky. Danced in Kharkov, Tbilisi, Prague, and Lvov (Poland) with European touring company directed by Antonina Tumkovskaya. Ballet master, Russian Classic Ballet in Munich (1950); Oberhausen (1952–54); Municipal Theatre, Basel (since 1955). As a dancer his repertoire includes principal roles in *The Sleeping Beauty, Swan Lake, Fountain of Bakhchisarai, Le Corsaire, Peer Gynt, Petrouchka, Harlequin.* Has revived a number of classic ballets of the Russian repertoire and choreographed several new works, among them *Peer Gynt, The Black Corsaire, Vienna Tales.* Staged a new version of *The Sleeping Beauty* for the Vienna State Opera Ballet (May 4 and 8, 1963) with Irina Kolpakova and Vladilen Semenov of the Kirov Ballet as guest artists with the resident company. Staged *Peer Gynt* for London's Festival Ballet (1963). Choreographed and co-directed with Raymundo de Larrain *Cinderella* staged to the Sergei Prokofiev music and premièred Dec. 4, 1963, as part of the International Dance Festival, Théâtre des Champs-Elysées, Paris. Became ballet master of the Vienna State Opera Ballet, without relinquishing his Basel post (fall, 1966).

Orphée. Choreographic drama in 1 act, 8 scenes; chor.: Maurice Béjart; electronic music: Pierre Henry; decor: Rudolf Kufner. First prod.: Liège Opera, Belgium, Sept. 17, 1958, with Maurice Béjart (Orphée) and Michèle Seigneuret (Shadow). An Orpheus in blue jeans in a world full of symbols.

Orpheus. Ballet; chor.: George Balanchine; music: Igor Stravinsky; décor and costumes: Isamu Noguchi. First prod.: Ballet Society, N.Y. City Center, Apr. 28, 1948, with a cast headed by Nicholas Magallanes (title role), Maria Tallchief (Eurydice), Francisco Moncion (Dark Angel), Herbert Bliss (Apollo). The classic Orpheus myth presented with unusual choreographic eloquence. Orpheus was one of the ballets presented on the opening night, Oct. 11, 1948, of the first season of the New York City Ballet when Ballet Society assumed this name for its performing company.

Orpheus and Eurydice. Ballet in 2 acts,

4 scenes; chor.: Ninette de Valois; music: Christoph Willibald Gluck, from the opera; book: after Ranieri di Calzabigi's libretto for the Gluck opera; décor: Sophie Fedorovitch. First prod.: Sadler's Wells (now Royal) Ballet, New Theatre, London, May 28, 1941, with Pamela May (Eurydice), Robert Helpmann (Orpheus), Margot Fonteyn (Amor), Mary Honer (Leader of the Furies). The Greek legend as told in the Gluck opera, with Amor leading Orpheus through Hades to the Elysian Fields to be reunited with his wife Eurydice, only to lose her again when he succumbs to her pleading to look at her before they have regained the upper world. Two singers in the orchestra pit sang the key arias.

Osato, Sono, dancer and actress, b. Omaha, Neb., 1919, of Japanese-Irish parentage. Studied dance with Adolph Bolm and Berenice Holmes in Chicago, and with Lubov Egorova in Paris. Joined the Col. de Basil Ballets Russes de Monte Carlo (1934) where she rose to soloist rank, creating one of the Nymphs in *Protée,* Barman's Assistant (*Union Pacific*), Siren (David Lichine's *Prodigal Son*). Joined Ballet (now American Ballet) Theatre (1940–42), creating Rosaline (Tudor's *Romeo and Juliet*), Lover-in-Experience (*Pillar of Fire*), and dancing solo roles. Featured dancer, *One Touch of Venus* (1943); co-starred with Nancy Walker, *On the Town* (1944); danced in *Ballet Ballads* (John Latouche–Jerome Moross) for Experimental Theater, 1949. Has appeared on Agnes de Mille television programs, but is now virtually retired.

Sono Osato, in the musical One Touch of Venus.

Osipenko, Alla, Peoples' Artist of the RSFSR, Soviet ballerina, b. 1932. Graduated from the Leningrad ballet school and was accepted into the Kirov Theatre (1950) a year before Agrippina Vaganova's death and is, together with Irina Kolpakova, one of the last ballerinas trained by the great teacher. She has a beautiful long line, grace, elevation, and a strong classic technique. In her first season with the Kirov Ballet she danced the Lilac Fairy in *The Sleeping Beauty* and Queen of the Ball in *The Bronze Horseman*. She achieved official ballerina status when she danced her first Odette-Odile in *Swan Lake* and Nikia in *La Bayadère* (1954). She showed unexpected versatility when she created the Mistress of the Copper Mountain in *The Stone Flower,* a role which demands plastic expressiveness and almost serpentine agility. In 1959 she shared with Kolpakova in the creation of the role of the Beloved in *Coast of Hope,* giving the more powerful and energetic interpretation. In 1961 she added Sarie in *Path of Thunder* to her roles in modern ballet. She first danced outside the Soviet Union in 1956 when she appeared on loan from the Kirov with the Stanislavsky-Nemirovich-Danchenko ballet in Paris. She again danced in Paris and later in London with the Kirov Ballet (1961).

Ostergaard, Solveig, soloist of the Royal Danish Ballet, b. 1939. Entered the company's school in 1947; accepted into the company in 1957; made soloist in 1962. Dances leading roles in *Don Quixote* pas de deux, *Symphony in C, Miss Julie, The Moon Reindeer, Conservatoriet, Napoli, Harlequinade, Festa, Peter and the Wolf, The Whims of Cupid and the Ballet Master, Cyrano de Bergerac, Graduation Ball, Solitaire, Les Victoires de l'Amour,* and others. Made an excellent impression during the U.S. tour of the Royal Danish Ballet Sept. 29–Dec. 19, 1965, especially with her dancing of Swanilda in *Coppélia* and one of the two leading ladies in *Napoli,* Act 3.

Oswald, Genevieve, curator of the Dance Collection of the New York Public Library, b. Buffalo, N.Y. Educated at Sacred Heart Academy; Univ. of North Carolina Woman's College, with a major in music composition; graduate work at Juilliard School of Music and Columbia Univ. With the exception of one year of concertizing as a lyric soprano, has worked in the Dance Collection since finishing undergraduate college work. Won the Capezio Award (1956) for her achievements as curator of the Collection. Her utmost dedication and hard work have resulted in the advancement of the Collection from a part of the Music Division to a separate Division of the Library (1964).

Otegui, Alberto, Argentine painter and scenic designer, b. La Plata, Argentina, 1913. Graduate of Escuela de Bellas Artes, Univ. of La Plata. Professor of Scenic Design at his alma mater and the Conservatorio de la Provincia de Buenos Aires; Director of Scenic Department of Teatro Argentino de La Plata (1948–60). He was responsible for most of the décors of ballets presented during those years. His work was exhibited at the Bienal of São Paulo, Brazil. He has also worked in television, films, and the legitimate theatre.

Otero, Decio, Brazilian dancer, b. Belo Horizonte, Brazil. Studied with Carlos Leite. Made his debut with Ballet de Minas Gerais, dancing in *Le Spectre de la Rose.* Joined Teatro Municipal, Rio de Janeiro (1955), creating first roles in *Yara* (1960) and *Amazon Symphony* (1961). Also member of Ballet Rio de Janeiro. Received Municipal Award as Best Dancer of 1960.

Othello. Ballet in 4 acts; chor. and book: Vakhtang Chabukiani; music: Alexei Machavariani; décor: Simon Virsaladze. First prod.: Paliashvili Theatre of Opera and Ballet, Tbilisi, Georgia, Nov. 29, 1957, with Vakhtang Chabukiani (Othello), Vera Zigvadze (Desdemona). On Mar. 24, 1960, it was first performed with the same choreography and Chabukiani in the title role at the Kirov Theatre, Leningrad. While closely following the story and spirit of Shakespeare's play, Chabukiani introduced some scenes the content of which is only referred to in the play; thus the first act starts with Desdemona's escape from her father's home and the scene in which Othello tells his life story is enacted in brief flashback scenes.

Oukrainsky, Serge (Leonides Orlay de Carva), dancer, choreographer, teacher, b. Odessa, Russia, American citizen since 1928. Educated in Paris; began his stage career as a mime in French Musical Festival at Théâtre du Châtelet, Paris (1911). Came to U.S. as a member of Anna Pavlova's company (1913), with which he remained as soloist and partner to Pavlova until 1915. Between 1915 and 1927 was leading dancer, choreographer, and director of the Chicago Opera Ballet. Established with Andreas Pavley a school in Chicago (1917) out of which grew the Pavley-Oukrainsky Ballet, the official ballet of the Chicago Opera (1921–22) which toured widely in U.S., Mexico, Cuba, and South America until 1927. Ballet master of Los Angeles and San Francisco operas (1927–30). Formed Serge Oukrainsky Ballet (1931) after the death of Pavley. Has been teaching in Hollywood since 1934 where he has also choreographed for motion pictures. Author of *My Two Years with Anna Pavlova* (1940).

Ouvert. In ballet, open position (e.g. 2nd and 4th positions of the feet) or movement (e.g. sissonne ouverte in which the raised leg is not closed behind the forward leg after the spring as it is in sissonne fermé).

Ovation. Prolonged and intense applause, very often at the first entrance of a favorite dancer upon the stage, also following a variation or pas de deux, or at the end of the ballet. An ovation often "stops the show."

Owl and the Pussycat, The. Ballet in 1 act; chor.: Gillian Lynne; commissioned music: Dudley Moore; décor: Kenneth Rowell. First prod.: Western Theatre Ballet, Sunday Ballet Club, June 17, 1962, with Clover Roope (Pussycat), Peter Cazalet (Owl). The libretto was based on Edward Lear's poem of the same name about the fowl and feline who went to sea in a beautiful peagreen boat. The ballet was first given on Eurovision from Brussels, Belgium, Apr. 29, 1962.

Ozaï. Ballet in 2 acts, 6 scenes; chor. and book: Jean Coralli; music: Casimir Gide; décor: Pierre Ciceri. First prod.: Théâtre de l'Académie Royale de Musique, Paris, Apr. 26, 1847, with Adeline Plunkett (Ozaï), H. Desplaces (de Surville), Elie (de Bougainville). This ballet, inspired by the voyages of the French explorer de Bougainville, was of interest because of its introduction of folk dances into ballet.

Paean. Ballet in 1 act; chor.: Tatiana Gsovska; music: Remi Gassmann and Oscar Sala. First prod.: Municipal (now German) Opera, West Berlin, May 29, 1960, with soloists Gisela Deege, Klaus Beelitz, Jurgen Feindt, Manfred Taubert, Rudolf Holz. This was a dance étude on an electronically produced theme which, without actual dramatic action, depicted the curve of a human life.

Paganini. Ballet in 1 act, 3 scenes; chor.: Michel Fokine; music: Sergei Rachmaninov's *Rhapsody on a Theme of Paganini* (for piano and orchestra); book: Rachmaninov and Fokine; décor: Sergei Soudeikine. First prod.: Col. de Basil's Ballet Russe, Royal Opera House, Covent Garden, London, June 30, 1939, with Dmitri Rostoff (Paganini), Irina Baronova (Divine Genius), Tatiana Riabouchinska (Florentine Beauty), Tamara Grigorieva (Guile), Paul Petroff (Florentine Youth). The story is based upon the legends surrounding the famous violin virtuoso who, it was said, had sold himself to the Devil. Here Guile, Scandal, Gossip, and Envy torment him; a horde of imitators mock him; but finally his Divine Genius puts them all to rout and bears him off to an immortal life with his precious violin. The Florentine Beauty dances to the magic of his guitar playing during an interlude of calm.

Paganini. Ballet in 1 act and 7 scenes; chor. and book: Leonid Lavrovsky; music: Sergei Rachmaninov's *Rhapsody on a Theme of Paganini* (for piano, and orchestra); décor: Vadim Ryndin. First prod.: Bolshoi Theatre, Moscow, Apr. 7, 1960, with Yaroslav Sekh in the title role. This is an original version having nothing in common with the Michel Fokine ballet of the same name. In this version Paganini is shown in the ecstasy of creation, inspired by his Muse. The role of Paganini is not mimed, but danced.

Paganini, Niccolo (1782–1840), Italian violinist and composer. His life was the basis for the ballet *Paganini* by Michel Fokine (1939) to Sergei Rachmaninov's *Rhapsody on a Theme of Paganini*. Vincenzo Tommasini used various themes of Paganini for *The Devil's Holiday* (Frederick Ashton, 1939). Antonia Cobos used his "Perpetual Motion" (Perpetuum Mobile) for *The Mute Wife*.

Pagava, Ethéry, French dancer, b. Paris, 1932, of Georgian parentage. A pupil of Lubov Egorova, she appeared as a child in the early performances of the Roland Petit and Janine Charrat groups. In 1945 she became a soloist in Les Ballets des Champs-Elysées, having a great success as the little acrobat in Roland Petit's *Les Forains*. In 1946 she danced Ganymède in

Les Amours de Jupiter, by the same choreographer. In 1948 she joined the Grand Ballet du Marquis de Cuevas, with which company she danced the Sleepwalker in George Balanchine's *Night Shadow* and Juliet in George Skibine's *Tragedy in Verona* (1950). Currently free-lancing.

Page, Annette, English dancer, b. Manchester, 1932; m. Ronald Hynd. Studied at Sadler's Wells School from 1945; entered Sadler's Wells Theatre Ballet (1950); promoted to soloist (1954). Transferred to Sadler's Wells (now Royal) Ballet (1955); ballerina since 1959. Her roles include title role and *Peasant* pas de deux (*Giselle*), Aurora and *Blue Bird* pas de deux (*The Sleeping Beauty*), Odette-Odile (*Swan Lake*), The Lady (*The Lady and the Fool*), Lise (*La Fille Mal Gardée*), The Suicide (*Miracle in the Gorbals*), and others. Guest artist, National Ballet, Ireland (1960); member of Margot Fonteyn's concert tour, Australia (1962).

Page, Ruth, contemporary dancer, choreographer, director, b. Indianapolis, Ind.; m. Thomas Hart Fisher. Began professional studies at twelve, later studying with Adolph Bolm and Enrico Cecchetti. Accompanied Anna Pavlova on South American tour (one year); created title role in *The Birthday of the Infanta* (1919), Chicago; danced at Coliseum, London, with Bolm; next two years in Music Box Revue. Première danseuse, Chicago Allied Arts (1924–27); also with Diaghilev Ballets Russes (1925); Municipal Opera Company, Buenos Aires (1925); Metropolitan Opera Ballet, N.Y. (1926–28); toured Orient with small group (1928); gave series of "American Dances," Moscow (1930); solo dances throughout U.S. (1930–35); toured U.S. and Orient with Harald Kreutzberg (1932–34). Première danseuse and ballet director, Chicago Grand Opera Company (1934–37); toured with Bentley Stone (1935–36); toured with Page-Stone Ballet Company (founded 1938); gave seasons of solo programs (1941–45). She has choreographed many ballets, both alone and with Stone for the Page-Stone company; also re-staged *Frankie and Johnny* (1945), *The Bells* (1946), and *Billy Sunday* (1948) for Ballet Russe de Monte Carlo, all of which were originally choreographed for the Page-Stone company. Director of Chicago Opera Ballet (1944–47). Took a group of dancers, including José Limón and his company, to Paris for a season of Les Ballets Américains at Théâtre des Champs-Elysées (1950); the following year choreographed *Revanche* and *Impromptu au Bois* for Les Ballets des Champs-Elysées. Staged *Vilia* (the revised version was subsequently titled *The Merry Widow*) for London's Festival Ballet (1953), *Minnie Moustache* for Théâtre Gaîté Lyrique, Paris (1954). In 1955 she staged *The Merry Widow, Susanna and the Barber* (based on Rossini's opera *The Barber of Seville*), and *El Amor Brujo* during the Nov. season of the Chicago Lyric Opera. This was the beginning of her Chicago Opera Ballet which, as Ruth Page Ballets, played a N.Y. season at the Broadway Theatre, Dec., 1955 (with Alicia Markova as guest artist in the title

Ruth Page, American dancer, choreographer.

role of *The Merry Widow*). It has subsequently played annual seasons in Chicago and toured the U.S. Ruth Page has choreographed for this company a number of ballets based on famous operas, using the music and following the story line as closely as possible. The first of these was *Revanche,* based on *Il Trovatore,* which she staged for her company as well as that of Les Ballets des Champs-Elysées. This was followed by *The Merry Widow, Susanna and the Barber, Camille* (1957), *Die Fledermaus* (1958), *Carmen* (1959). She has also choreographed *Pygmalion,* a pas de trois to music from von Suppe's opera *Pygmalion and Galatea* (1961), and in a quite different vein *Concertino pour Trois,* to an original score by the French composer Marius Constant (1960). In addition to her work with the Chicago Opera Ballet, she has also been responsible for the ballets in the operas presented during the Chicago Lyric Opera seasons since 1954. In Sept., 1966, the Chicago Opera Ballet was renamed Ruth Page's International Ballet for the company's tours, but retained its former name for the performances with the Chicago Opera Co.

Page-Stone Ballet Company, founded in 1938 by Ruth Page and Bentley Stone; disbanded in 1941 when the two founders decided to continue their careers separately. Toured over four thousand miles in its first season, giving about forty performances. First American ballet company to tour South America (1940). The company was later known as the Chicago Opera Ballet when it performed in the presentations of the Lyric Opera and ultimately developed into Ruth Page's Chicago Opera Ballet. Its repertoire included *An American Pattern, Guns and Castanets, Americans in Paris, Scrapbook, Frankie and Johnny,* choreographed jointly by Page and Stone; *Hear Ye! Hear Ye!, La Guiablesse, Gold Standard, Love Song, Iberian Monotone, The Bells, Billy Sunday,* by Ruth Page.

Pageant. 1. Originally the portable stage used in English miracle plays. 2. Type of English drama, usually an allegory, performed in procession to celebrate some important historical event or the visit of a sovereign, etc. 3. Spectacular theatrical display or exhibition.

Pages of Life. Ballet in 1 act; chor. and book: Leonid Lavrovsky; music: Andrei Balanchivadze; décor: Valery Dorrer. First prod.: Bolshoi Theatre, Moscow, Nov. 19, 1961, with Raisa Struchkova (Tamara), Maris Liepa (Georgi), Yuri Zhdanov (Andrei). A short ballet about love, friendship, and patriotism during World War II. The action takes place in Soviet Georgia.

Paige, Brydon, Canadian dancer, b. Vancouver, B.C., of English-Scottish parents. Began his dance studies with Kay Armstrong in Vancouver; had his first stage experience dancing at the Canadian Ballet Festivals and in the summer Theater under the Stars. Joined Les Grands Ballets Canadiens as a charter member (1953). A versatile character dancer, his range extends from the Moor in *Petrouchka,* von Rothbart in *Swan Lake,* and the Devil in *Night on a Bare Mountain,* to the Stranger in *Sea Gallows* and Il Dottore in the *Commedia dell'arte Farces* (Ludmilla Chiriaeff).

Palace. Ballet in 1 act; chor.: Gerald Arpino, with a pas de deux by Robert Joffrey; music: Rebekah Harkness; décor: Robert Fletcher. First prod.: Robert Joffrey Ballet, Kirov Theatre, Leningrad, Oct. 15, 1963, with Brunilda Ruiz, Lisa Bradley, Lone Isaksen, Marie Paquet, Paul Sutherland, Lawrence Rhodes, Nels Jorgensen, Finis Jhung, Robert Vickrey, and company. Excerpts from *Palace* had a world première at the White House, Washington, D.C., Oct. 1, 1963, on the occasion of a state dinner and entertainment given by President and Mrs. Kennedy in honor of Emperor Haile Selassie of Ethiopia. A divertissement which affectionately spoofs the kind of dance offered at the famous Palace Theatre during the 1920's, the numbers include "Bathing Beauties," "Darling of Old Broadway" (in the manner of a Marilyn Miller specialty), "Whiz Bangs" (a Charleston), "The Toppers" (top hats, tails, and taps), a dance in the Loie Fuller manner, and so on.

Palais de Cristal, Le. Ballet in 4 movements; chor.: George Balanchine; music: Georges Bizet's Symphony in C; décor: Leonor Fini. First prod.: Paris Opéra Ballet, Paris Opéra, July 28, 1947, with Tamara Toumanova, Lycette Darsonval, Micheline Bardin, Madeleine Lafon, Jacqueline Moreau, Denise Bourgeois, Alexandre Kalioujny, Michel Renault, Max Bozzoni, Roger Ritz. Balanchine staged this ballet as *Symphony in C* for Ballet Society the following year.

Palmer, Winthrop (née Bushnell), writer, b. New York City, 1899. A graduate of Barnard College, Columbia Univ., she also studied at New School of Social Research, N.Y., Kenyon College, Gambier, Ohio and Ecole Française des Hautes Etudes, Paris. She founded Dance Players Company (1941), and wrote the scenario for *Man from Midian* (based on a work by Darius Milhaud) for which Stefan Wolpe wrote the music and Eugene Loring created the choreography, also dancing the title role. Author of *Theatrical Dancing in America: The Development of the Ballet from 1900* (N.Y., 1945); also the story *Rosemary and the Planet* on which the off-Broadway musical *Miss Emily Adams* was based (1960). She was an editor of *Dance News* between 1948 and 1951 for which she reviewed the modern dance. She is a well known poet, and is currently Associate Professor of English and Fine Arts at C. W. Post College of Long Island Univ. She received an honorary degree of Doctor of Literature from Long Island Univ. in 1956.

Paltenghi, David (1919–1961), English dancer and choreographer; b. Christchurch, England, of an English mother and Swiss-Italian father; d. Windsor, England. Studied ballet with Antony Tudor and Marie Rambert. Joined Tudor's London Ballet (1939) and remained when it amalgamated with Ballet Rambert (1940). Created the Young Nobleman in Andrée Howard's *La Fête Etrange* (London Ballet, 1940). Joined Sadler's Wells Ballet (1941) as leading dancer. He was an exceptionally fine partner in the classic repertoire and a strong actor in character ballets. Among his creations were one of the Brothers in *Comus* (1942), King in *Hamlet* (1942), and Official in *Miracle in the Gorbals* (1944), all by Robert Helpmann. After leaving the company (1947), he re-joined Ballet Rambert as dancer and choreographer (*Eve of St. Agnes, Scherzi della Sorte,* and others). He also appeared in a number of films which featured dance and choreographed dance sequences for Marlene Dietrich (*Stage Fright*), Violetta Elvin (*Queen of Spades*), Yvonne de Carlo (*Hotel Sahara*). Retired as a dancer (1951) after appearing in Gene Kelly's film *Invitation to the Dance*. During his last years he was a successful director of "shorts" both for films and television, specializing in dance arrangements for television commercials.

Palucca, Gret, contemporary German dancer born 1902. Studied with Mary Wigman and was a member of the Wigman Company. She later gave performances as a solo dancer and with her own group. She reached the height of her performing career in the late 1920's through the middle 1930's. She established her own school in Dresden in 1925 at which she still teaches. As is the case with most German modern dancers, very little factual biographical material is available. John Martin, however, attending the Third German Dance Congress in Munich, July, 1930, for *The New York Times,* wrote as follows about Gret Palucca in a Sunday article (July 20): "Palucca, who is said to rival Wigman herself in popularity, appeared with a small group in seven concert numbers, all very abstract and very simple. After the hectic writhing and contorting of the programs which made up the bulk of the Congress . . . she came like a breath of Spring, albeit a very consciously vernal Spring. Palucca, it must be admitted, in spite of many good points, has fallen into mannerisms, physical and mental. These, of course, her girls imitate with some success . . . In composition she is utterly unimaginative, but she has a feeling for form, which is something to be deeply grateful for. In selecting a theme for her dance, Palucca takes the simplest conceivable movement; this she develops exclusively through several patterns—and there is the dance. Her technique, however, is tremendous, and is not exhibited for its own sake at any time. She is never a virtuoso, though she is well able to be. There is a charm of manner, a lightness of spirit, a lyrical lift, that make a rift in the heaviness of the Teutonic atmosphere; and though it is a studied change, it is apparently no less welcome to the native audience than to the 'Ausländer.' "

Panader, Carmen, Argentine ballerina, b. Buenos Aires, 1933. Studied dance with Esmée Bulnes, Yekaterina de Galantha, Michel Borovski, and Roberto Giachero. Joined the ballet company of Teatro Argentino de La Plata, Argentina (1949); designated ballerina (1953). Her repertoire includes *Apollon Musagète, Pas de Quatre, Swan Lake, Falarka, Tango, Les Sylphides, Romeo and Juliet* (chor.: Giachero), *Concierto Coreográfico* (chor.: Grigorieva), *Orpheus, Carnaval, Le Spectre de la Rose,* and others. Joined the Grand Ballet du Marquis de Cuevas (1954), but returned to Teatro Argentino (1955); joined the Opera Ballet in Stuttgart as guest artist (1958). At present she is dancing in Europe as guest artist with various companies.

Panaieff, Michel, dancer, choreographer, teacher, b. Novgorod, Russia, 1913. Studied dance at Royal Opera, Belgrade; State Theatre, Zurich; and with Nicholas Legat, Lubov Egorova; School of American Ballet, N.Y., etc. Made his debut in Royal Opera, Belgrade, becoming first dancer after two years; danced in Switzerland; soloist, René Blum Ballet; Ballet Russe de Monte Carlo; soloist, Original Ballet Russe (1940–41). He danced leading roles in *Swan Lake, Coppélia, Don Juan, L'Epreuve d'Amour, Les Sylphides,* etc. Also danced in films; with San Francisco Opera, Civic Light Opera, and Ballet Musicale group for which he staged dances. Has his own school and performing group (Los Angeles Civic Ballet). Choreographs for films and appears from time to time in straight acting roles such as *The Prize* and *Seven Days in May* (both 1963).

Panamerica. An evening of ballet to music by Latin-American composers and with choreography by George Balanchine, Gloria Contreras, Jacques d'Amboise, Francisco Moncion, and John Taras, premièred by New York City Ballet, City Center, N.Y., Jan. 20, 1960. The program was intended as a salute to Pan-American friendship. Nine composers and seven choreographers were originally announced, but the Peruvian composer Andrés Sas withdrew, as did the two choreographers Todd Bolender and Lew Christensen. A basic set with individual additions and changes was designed by David Hays and costumes were by Barbara Karinska and Esteban Francés. Three works were by Balanchine: *Preludios Para Percusión* (Luis Escobar, Colombia) danced by Patricia Wilde and Erik Bruhn; *Sinfonía No. 5 for String Orchestra* (Carlos Chavez, Mexico, who conducted his own composition), with Diana Adams, Nicholas Magallanes, Francisco Moncion, Jillana, Arthur Mitchell, Roland Vazquez, Sallie Wilson; and *Danzas Sinfónicas* (Julian Orbon, Cuba), with Maria Tallchief and Arthur

Mitchell, Conrad Ludlow, Edward Villella. Gloria Contreras, principal choreographer at Las Belles Artes, Mexico City, contributed two works: *Serenata Concertante*—2nd, 3rd, and 4th Movements (Juan Orrego Salas, Chile), with Allegra Kent and Jonathan Watts; and *Ocho Por Radio* (Silvestre Revueltas, Mexico), with Jillana, Arthur Mitchell, Deni Lamont, Roland Vazquez. The remaining works were *Choros No. 7* (Heitor Villa-Lobos, Brazil), by Francisco Moncion with Violette Verdy and Roy Tobias, *Sinfonía No. 2 for String Orchestra*—2nd Movement (Hector Tosar, Uruguay), by Jacques d'Amboise with Violette Verdy and Erik Bruhn; and *Variaciones Concertantes* (Alberto Ginastera, Argentina), by John Taras with Violette Verdy, Patricia Wilde, Edward Villella. Only the last named ballet survived, subsequently performed as *Tender Night*. It is in the repertoire of the Colón, Buenos Aires, Argentina, under its original title.

Panicker, Chathunni, Indian dancer and teacher, b. Kerala, India, of a famous family of Kathakali actors. Taught from childhood by the Guru of Kathakali, Katambur Gopalan Nair; began taking part in performances from age fourteen. Five years later he formed his own small group dedicated to preserving the traditional Kathakali art. Joined Mrinalini Sarabhai as her partner (1945); since 1948 has been Guru of Kathakali in her dance academy, Darpana, and leading male dancer of the company of the same name. In addition to the traditional Kathakali dance dramas, he dances in works created by Mrinalini Sarabhai, his most famous role being the name part in *Manushya* (Man). Holds the Veera-Shrinkhala, the highest award for Kathakali.

Pantalon (or Pantaloon), one of the stock characters of commedia dell'arte; an old-man type, usually a silly, fearful merchant who meddles in politics. Michel Fokine used this character in his ballet *Carnaval.*

Pantomime, Ballet, a part of stage movement the aim of which is to develop the action of the ballet. The ballet uses two kinds of pantomime: the conventional gesture, i.e. artificial or symbolic, invented for the purpose of ballet and imitative of nature; and the natural, or expressive gesture, borrowed from life. A good example of gestures in the first category is the pointing of the index finger of the right hand to the first joint of the ring finger of the left hand where the wedding ring is usually worn, to indicate wedding, married, husband, wife, etc. Pantomime as practiced in ballet has two forms: rhythmic, when the design of the pantomimic movement is conditioned by the rhythm and melody of the musical accompaniment; and non-rhythmic when the rhythm and melody of the musical accompaniment does not bind the dancer in his pantomimic movement. Jean Georges Noverre called rhythmic pantomime the recitative of ballet. In modern dance mimed action and pantomime are giving way to the expressive dance which advances the action of the ballet through dance rather than through separate pantomime. Remnants of classic ballet pantomime, especially conventional pantomime, are still to be found in certain scenes of such ballets as *Swan Lake, Giselle, Coppélia, La Fille Mal Gardée,* and *The Nutcracker,* which contains an excellent and well-staged example of straight ballet pantomime, very close indeed to the original St. Petersburg version. It is the entrance of Clara (or Masha) and the former Nutcracker (now the Prince) at the beginning of Act. 2. He relates the episode of the war between the Mice and Lead Soldiers, and describes the manner in which Clara (or Masha) saved his life. The quality of performance of this brief pantomime came as no surprise to the audience, because the choreographer of the present version is George Balanchine, who often played this role (the character was then called the Messenger) at the Maryinsky Theatre while still a student at the Imperial Ballet School.

Papagaio do Moleque (The Kid's Parrot). Ballet in 1 act; chor.: Vaslav Veltchek; music: Heitor Villa-Lobos; book and costumes: Gilberto Trompowsky; décor: Fernando Pamplona. First prod.: Teatro Municipal, Rio de Janeiro, Brazil, 1952, with a large cast headed by Dennis Gray (the Kid) and Beatriz Consuelo (the Parrot). The plot deals with a "moleque" (a Negro street urchin) who loses his kite. It comes back to him in the form of a green parrot. The word "papagaio" means both toy and the bird.

Paquita. Ballet in 2 acts, 3 scenes; chor.: Joseph Mazilier; music: Edward Deldevez; book: Paul Foucher and Joseph Mazilier; décor: Philastre, Cambon, Diéterle, Séchan, Despléchin. First prod.: Théâtre de l'Académie Royale de Musique, Paris, Apr. 1, 1846, with Carlotta Grisi and Lucien Petipa; London première: Theatre Royal, Drury Lane, June 3, 1846, with Grisi in title role; St. Petersburg première: Bolshoi Theatre, Sept., 1847, with revisions by Marius Petipa and music by Leon Minkus (interpolated numbers by Deldevez). *Paquita* is still in the repertoire of Russian ballet companies. A one-act version was staged by Alexandra Danilova for Ballet Russe de Monte Carlo and premièred Sept. 20, 1949, Metropolitan Opera House, N.Y., with Danilova dancing the title role, partnered by Oleg Tupine. Costumes were by Castillo and the set was the one designed by Eugene Berman for Frederick Ashton's *Devil's Holiday* (1939). The "ballet-Spanish" style pas de trois from *Paquita* remains a popular divertissement, a version staged by George Balanchine being in the repertoire of New York City Ballet. Paquita, a dancer in a Spanish Gypsy encampment, falls in love with Lucien, son of Comte d'Hervilly, a French general, but the difference in their stations makes their union impossible. After foiling the conspiracy of her Gypsy master and the local Governor to overthrow the French, she discovers by accident that she is actually the daughter of a nobleman and she and Lucien are happily united.

Par Terre (also called à terre), in ballet, steps performed on the floor as distinguished from movements performed in the air; steps which do not require jumping.

Parade. Ballet in 1 act, chor.: Leonide Massine; music: Eric Satie; book: Jean Cocteau; décor, curtain and costumes: Pablo Picasso. First prod.: Diaghilev Ballets Russes, Théâtre du Châtelet, Paris, May 18, 1917, with Lydia Lopoukhova, Leonide Massine, Leon Woicikowski, Nicholas Zverev. The theme of the ballet was the parade of circus performers who march through a town to attract customers to their performance and are later shown in the circus arena. The importance of the ballet lay in the creators of the various elements of the ballet and the personalities of the performers.

Paris Opéra Ballet, the French national ballet company attached to the Théâtre National de l'Opéra which, with the Opéra Comique, form the National Lyric Theatres. It is an outgrowth of l'Académie Royale de Musique, founded in 1671, which became the Théâtre National de l'Opéra in 1871. Since 1671 when the first opera-ballet, *Pomone,* was staged, there has been a continuous history of ballet at the Opéra. Jean Baptiste Lully became director of l'Académie Royale de Musique in 1672. Among the prominent ballet masters of the Académie, and later the Théâtre National, have been Charles Louis Beauchamps, Louis Pécourt, Jean B. Lany, Gaetano and Auguste Vestris, Maximilien and Pierre Gardel, Filippo Taglioni, Joseph Mazilier, Arthur Saint-Léon, and during the present century, Leo Staats, Albert Aveline, Serge Lifar, George Skibine, and Michel Descombey (since 1962). The Paris Opéra Ballet was the acknowledged leader of ballet in Western Europe during the eighteenth and first half of the nineteenth centuries. In the eighteenth century its dancers included

Marie Camargo, Marie Sallé, Madeleine Guimard, Louis Dupré, the Vestris, the Gardels, and Louis Duport. Among its choreographers were Jean Georges Noverre and Jean Dauberval. The great Romantic period ballets, *La Sylphide* and *Giselle,* were premièred at the Paris Opéra. All the great dancers of the period, among them Maria Taglioni, Fanny Elssler, Carlotta Grisi, Fanny Cerito, Jules Perrot, Lucien Petipa, and Louis Mérante danced there. The decline of the Paris Opéra Ballet began in the latter part of the nineteenth century and continued into the early years of the twentieth. Its revival is generally attributed to Jacques Rouché, director of the Paris Opéra (and Opéra Comique) from 1914 to 1944, who engaged Michel Fokine, Anna Pavlova, Olga Spessivtzeva, and Bronislava Nijinska as guest artists and appointed Serge Lifar as director of the Paris Opéra Ballet (1929). Although Lifar's ballets have rarely enjoyed a success when presented away from the Opéra, he was more than anyone else responsible for the revival of interest in the Opéra Ballet after the low repute into which it had fallen by the 1920's. He remained (except for an absence from 1944 to 1947) as director until 1958 when he was succeeded by George Skibine. During his tenure the leading dancers included Solange Schwarz, Micheline Bardin, Lycette Darsonval, Yvette Chauvire, Nina Vyroubova, Madeleine Lafon, Liane Daydé, Christiane Vaussard, Claude Bessy, Marjorie Tallchief, Lifar, Serge Peretti, Alexandre Kalioujny, Michel Renault, Jean-Paul Andreani, Youly Algaroff, Peter Van Dijk, Skibine, Max Bozzoni. Other prominent French dancers who began their careers with Lifar at the Opéra but achieved success as independent artists include Jean Babilée, Roland Petit, Renée Jeanmaire and others. During Skibine's regime as director of the Paris Opéra Ballet, Claire Motte and Attilio Labis came into prominence as leading dancers. The company has danced in N.Y. (1948), London (1954), and Moscow (1958). The ballet school attached to the Paris Opéra was established in 1713. Current director is Yvette Chauviré, appointed in the fall of 1963. The present director of the National Lyric Theatres is the composer Georges Auric.

Park, Merle, South African dancer, b. Salisbury, Rhodesia, 1937. Studied with Betty Lamb and at Elmhurst School, England. Joined Sadler's Wells (now Royal) Ballet (1954); soloist (1958). Danced in Rhodesia with fellow-countryman Gary Burne (1956). Roles include Lise (*La Fille Mal Gardée*), Swanilda (*Coppélia*), *Blue Bird* pas de deux, Aurora (*The Sleeping Beauty*). One of the Royal Ballet's Juliets in Kenneth MacMillan's *Romeo and Juliet;* played the Bride in the 1965 revival of *A Wedding Bouquet;* created one of soloist parts in *Laurentia* Pas de Six (all 1965).

Parkinson, Georgina, English dancer, b. Brighton, 1938; m. photographer Roy Round. Studied at Sadler's Wells Ballet School; entered Royal Ballet (1957); soloist (1959). Attracted attention when she danced Odette in *Swan Lake* at the Royal Ballet School performance, Mar., 1960. Her roles include title role (Andrée Howard's *La Belle Dame Sans Merci*), Crystal Fountain Fairy (*The Sleeping Beauty*), Lykanion (*Daphnis and Chloë*), Gypsy (*The Two Pigeons*), leads in *Diversions, Ballabile, Symphony,* and others. La Garçonne in Bronislava Nijinska's *Les Biches,* revived for the Royal Ballet (1964), has given Parkinson her finest role to date.

Parks, Carolyn (Carolyn Buchman), contemporary American teacher, b. Alamosa, Colo; m. Richard Parks. Studied ballet with Lillian Cushing, Michel Fokine, Luigi Albertieri, Lubov Egorova (Paris), Nicholas Legat (London). Began her career during the depression, dancing in *Mlle. Modiste* and in the ballet of the

Georgina Parkinson, ballerina of The Royal Ballet (British) in Les Biches.

Roxy Theatre, N.Y. In 1932 went to Paris with Maria Gambarelli's ballet at Les Ambassadeurs, replacing Gambarelli as soloist. Toured Europe in a Mistinguette revue and organized Carolyn Buchman Ballet (1933), touring Europe and South America. Returned to the U.S. (1936), dancing in *The Great Waltz,* then retired as a dancer to attend Mills College, Oakland, Calif. Began teaching after World War II in San Francisco. Founded the Bay Area Ballet Company (1957) with Leona Norman and Vern Nerden, one of the first regional companies on the West Coast, which has since been renamed the Pacific Ballet. Has choreographed several ballets for this group. Has twice visited Moscow and Leningrad to study teaching methods, the first time at the invitation of the U.S.S.R. Minister of Culture. Has written many articles including "Toe Shoes—When?" "The Academic Approach to Ballet," "Transatlantic Consultation," the last named a collaboration with Celia Sparger on the subject of ballet and anatomy.

Parlic, Dimitri, Yugoslav dancer and choreographer, b. Salonika, Greece, 1919. Studied with Natalia Boskovic, Yelena Poliakova, Tatiana Gsovska, Olga Preobrajenska. Joined Belgrade National Ballet (1938); promoted to principal dancer (1941); became choreographer (1949). His choreographic works include *Gingerbread Heart, Coppélia, Orpheus* (Stravinsky); *Macedonian Tale* (Gligor Smokvarski), the first ballet on a Macedonian theme, for the Skoplje Ballet company; *Chinese Tale* (Kresimir Baranovic), *Symphony in C* (Bizet), *El Amor Brujo, La Reine des Iles* (Maurice Thiriet), *The Miraculous Mandarin,* and others. Most of the above ballets have been staged for the Belgrade National Ballet, but Parlic also staged them for other theatres, among them the Vienna State Opera Ballet, where he was ballet master and choreographer (1958–61). He has also worked in Germany and Greece and was ballet master and choreographer of the Rome Teatro dell'Opera (1963–66). Staged the full-length *Swan Lake* at Bregenz on the Bodensee (Austria). Now free-lancing.

Parnel, Ruth, Yugoslav classic ballerina, b. Belgrade, 1928. Pupil of Mile Jovanovic and Nina Kirsanova. Joined Belgrade National Ballet (1941); promoted to ballerina (1946). Dances all classic ballets as well as several modern ones in the repertoire of the company, among them *Romeo and Juliet* (Prokofiev), *Symphony in C* (Bizet), *Chinese Tale* (Kresimir Baranovic), *The Goldfish* (Mihovil Logar), all choreographed by Dimitri Parlic.

Partita. Ballet in 1 act; chor.: Clover Roope; music: Johann Sebastian Bach's *Partita No. 1;* costumes: Michael Baldwin. First prod.: Western Theatre Ballet, Theatre Royal, Bristol, June 28, 1962, with Brenda Last, Hazel Merry, Gail Donaldson, Peter Cazalet, Victor Maynard. A themeless ballet.

Pas, in ballet, 1. a step. This word usually precedes the name of a step, as for instance pas de bourrée, pas de chat, pas de ciseaux, pas glissé, etc. In ballet technique, pas is considered a step in which there is a shift of weight from one foot to the other. A step in which there is no shift of weight is called temps, literally meaning time, as for instance, temps lié, temps de cuisse, etc. 2. Pas is used instead of the word dance, to designate a dance sequence or a scene in the ballet, as, for instance, pas seul (a solo dance), pas de deux (a dance for two), pas d'action (an action scene), pas caractère (a character dance), etc.

Pas Allé, in ballet, a walking step, the whole foot put down easily, not toe first forcefully as in pas marché.

Pas Couru, in ballet, a running step. See Couru.

Pas d'Action, in the classic ballet pas d'action was a pantomime scene inserted into the ballet between dances for the purpose of furthering the plot. Excellent examples of pas d'action are to be found in *Giselle* (particularly Act 1), *La Fille Mal Gardée,* and *Coppélia.* In the Russian Imperial Theatre pas d'action had a different meaning. It was a dance scene which helped to develop the plot, to move the action. A brilliant example is the so-called Rose Adagio of *The Sleeping Beauty* (Act 1) when Princess Aurora is being wooed by the four exotic Princes on her sixteenth birthday. The original libretto of 1890 labeled the scene Grand Pas d'Action. The pas de deux in what is now called Act 3 of *Swan Lake* (the so-called *Black Swan* pas de deux), also carried the appellation of Pas d'Action, according to the original program of the Maryinsky Theatre.

Pas de Basque, a ballet step named after the French province of Basque. It is the basic step for the mazurka. It is done in three counts. Technique: start 5th pos. R ft. front; with a rond de jambe à terre bring R ft. to 2nd pos. and put weight on it; slide L ft. through 1st pos. to 4th pos. front; slide R ft. behind L into 5th pos. Pas de basque may also be done going back, sauté (Giselle's first dance with the corps de ballet in *Giselle,* Act 1, begins with three ballonnés followed by pas de basque sauté; she later repeats this with Albrecht), and en tournant.

Pas de Bourrée, in ballet, a short, even, walking step by which the dancer makes progress on the stage in any given direction. In this step the movement begins with the back foot if the dancer moves forward, and with the front foot if the dancer moves backward. The name of this step has no connection with the pre-classic dance called Bourrée. Pas de bourrée may be done in innumerable ways, with or without change of feet—dessous, dessus, couru, en tournant, etc.

Pas de Chat, in ballet, a cat-like step. Technique: start in 5th pos., R ft. back; raise R leg, knee well bent; jump upward off L ft. and bend L knee; land first on R ft.; bring L ft. to 5th pos. in front. Russian (Vaganova) technique makes this a much bigger jumping step, as follows: start in 5th pos., R ft. back; throw the R leg, half-bent, back, with a demi-plié on the L ft. Push off with the L ft., throwing the L leg, half-bent, back to meet the right one. Land on R ft. first, the L ft. passing it into 4th pos. (may also be finished in 5th pos.). At the moment when both feet are in the air, the body bends backward.

Pas de Cheval, in ballet, a step resembling the pawing movement of a horse. Technique: start in 5th pos., R ft. front; lift R leg with a pawing movement, R knee bent and brought high; straighten R leg to 4th pos. ouvert; bring L ft. down to 5th pos. front.

Pas de Deux. 1. A dance for two people. 2. In the classic ballet, a choreographic poem in three parts: (a) adagio, which is danced by the ballerina and her partner, essentially a dance of love; (b) variations, i.e., solos by the male dancer and the ballerina; (c) coda, in which both dancers alternate and then dance together, finishing the composition. Pas de deux is a characteristic part of the classic ballet; the contemporary ballet seldom follows the definite structure of the classic pas de deux. Excellent examples of the pas de deux are to be found in *Swan Lake* (the Swan Queen and the Prince), *Sleeping Beauty* (the Blue Birds), *Giselle* (Giselle and Albrecht, Act 2), *Coppélia* (Swanilda and Franz, Act 3).

Pas de Deux. See TCHAIKOVSKY PAS DE DEUX.

Pas de Deux and Divertissement. Ballet in 1 act; chor.: George Balanchine; music: Léo Delibes (from his ballets *Sylvia, La Source,* and *Naïla*); costumes: Barbara Karinska. First prod.: Jan. 14, 1965, with Melissa Hayden and André Prokovsky in the pas de deux and finale and Suki Schorer leading a small corps de ballet in the divertissement. This is actually Balanchine's *Sylvia Pas de Deux,* with some additions, surrounded by a divertissement.

Pas de Dieux. Ballet in 1 act; chor.: Gene Kelly; music: George Gershwin's Piano Concerto in F; décor: André François. First prod.: Paris Opéra Ballet, July 6, 1960, with Claude Bessy, Attilio Labis, Michel Descombey. Greek gods and goddesses disport to jazz rhythms on modern French furniture. With this ballet Kelly became the first American-born choreographer to create a ballet for the Paris Opéra. He was decorated with the Legion of Honor (Chevalier) after the première.

Pas de Dix. Ballet in 1 act; chor.: George Balanchine; music: Alexander Glazounov's last act divertissement from *Raymonda;* costumes: Esteban Francés. First prod.: New York City Ballet, City Center, N.Y., Nov. 9, 1955, with Maria Tallchief, André Eglevsky, and Barbara Fallis, Constance Garfield, Jane Mason, Barbara Walczak, Shaun O'Brien, Roy Tobias, Roland Vasquez, Jonathan Watts. The last act divertissement of Marius Petipa's *Raymonda,* re-choreographed in a series of dazzling ensembles, soli, and pas de deux. The pas de deux for Jane Mason and Barbara Walczak was later dropped. *Pas de Dix* is also in the repertoire of the Robert Joffrey Ballet.

Pas de Quatre. Ballet divertissement; chor.: Jules Perrot; music: Cesare Pugni. First prod.: Her Majesty's Theatre, London, July 12, 1845, with Maria Taglioni, Carlotta Grisi, Fanny Cerito, Lucile Grahn. It was a great achievement for Benjamin Lumley, director of the theatre, to get the four greatest ballerinas of the period to dance together, and the resulting ballet was a huge success. It was revived at the same theatre in 1847 with Carolina Rosati taking the place of Lucile Grahn.

Pas de Quatre. Ballet; chor.: Keith Lester, a reconstruction of Perrot's famous *Le Pas de Quatre* (1845); music: Cesare Pugni, arr. and orch. by Lucas Leighton; costumes after Chalon. Prod.: Markova-Dolin Company (1936) with Molly Lake, Diana Gould, Kathleen Crofton, Prudence Hyman. Staged by Keith Lester for ballet (now American Ballet) Theatre, Royal Opera House, Covent Garden, London, Aug. 26, 1946; N.Y. première: Broadway Theatre, Oct. 8, 1946, with Alicia Alonso (Taglioni), Nora Kaye (Grisi), Barbara Fallis (Grahn), Lucia Chase (Cerito).

Pas de Quatre, Le. Ballet; chor.: Anton Dolin, a reconstruction of Perrot's famous *Pas de Quatre* (1845); music: *Cesare Pugni,* transcribed by Lucas Leighton, orch. by Paul Bowles; inspired by the famous lithograph of A. E. Chalon. First prod.: Ballet (now American Ballet) Theatre, Majestic Theatre, N.Y., Feb. 16, 1941, with Nana Gollner (Taglioni), Nina Stroganova (Grahn), Alicia Alonso (Grisi), Katherine Sergava (Cerito). Ballet Theatre presented this ballet with several casts, but one of the most outstanding was seen the following season (Nov., 1941) at the 44th Street Theatre, N.Y.: Alicia Markova (Taglioni), Irina Baronova (Grahn), Nora Kaye (Grisi), Annabelle Lyon (Cerito). Staged by Dolin for Ballet Russe de Monte Carlo, Metropolitan Opera House, N.Y., Sept. 18, 1948, with Mia Slavenska (Grisi), Alicia Markova (Taglioni), Nathalie Krassovska (Grahn), Alexandra Danilova (Cerito), probably the most notable cast the ballet has had since it has been reconstructed. Revived by London's Festival Ballet, Monte Carlo, May 21, 1961, with Alicia Markova, Tatiana Riabouchinska, Paula Hinton, Noel Rossana.

Pas des Déesses. Ballet in 1 act; chor.: Robert Joffrey; music: an arrangement by H. Hardy of music by John Field. First prod.: YM-YWHA, N.Y., May 29, 1954, with Lillian Wellein (Taglioni), Barbara Gray (Grahn), Jacquetta Kieth (Cerito), Michael Lland (Saint-Léon). An evocation of the Romantic period and, specifically, of the occasion which the lithograph by Jacques Bouvier immortalizes. The subject, if subject there truly can be said to be, is the Judgment of Paris, with the male dancer (as Paris) firmly refusing to choose between his goddesses. Joffrey staged this, with minor revisions for Ballet Rambert (Beryl Goldwyn, Noreen Sopwith, Patricia Dyer, Norman Dixon; June 30, 1955), and for a Ballet Theatre Workshop program (1956). It remains in the repertoire of the Robert Joffrey Ballet.

Pas de Trois (Glinka), chor.: George Balanchine; music: ballet music from Mikhail Glinka's *Russlan and Ludmila;* costumes: Barbara Karinska. First prod.: New York City Ballet, City Center, N.Y., Mar. 1, 1955, with Melissa Hayden, Patricia Wilde, and André Eglevsky. A brilliant companion piece to the same choreographer's *Pas de Trois* to music by Leon Minkus. For convenience's sake the two were billed as *Pas de Trois* (Minkus) and *Pas de Trois* (Glinka).

Pas de Trois (Minkus), chor.: George Balanchine; music: Leon Minkus from *Paquita;* costumes: Barbara Karinska. First prod.: New York City Ballet at City Center, N.Y., Feb. 18, 1951, with Maria Tallchief, Nora Kaye, André Eglevsky. A show-stopping pas de trois, and Eglevsky's first creation with the company he had just joined; famous for the series of cabrioles in which Eglevsky appeared to hang in the air for several seconds. Balanchine staged a rather different version for Grand Ballet du Marquis de Cuevas (1948).

Pas Marché, in ballet, steps taken forward with small développé and foot well arched and placed with toe down first.

Passacaglia (also Passacaille), a French court dance done in the court of Louis XIV. It was a slow dance in 3/4 time. Main movements were long glissés with arms held to sides.

Passacaglia. Ballet; chor.: Aurel Milloss; music: Johann Sebastian Bach's Passacaglia and Fugue in C minor; décor and costumes: Candido Portinari. First prod.: Ballet do IV Centenário, Teatro Municipal, Rio de Janeiro, 1954, with a cast headed by Edith Pudelko, Ady Addor, Neyde Rossi, Eduardo Sucena, Juan Giuliano, Ricardo Abellan. An abstract ballet described by Milloss as a "Choreographic Hymn."

Passacaglia in C Minor, modern group dance; chor.: Doris Humphrey; music: Johann Sebastian Bach. First prod.: Bennington College, Vt., Aug., 1938.

Passé, in ballet, an auxiliary movement which transfers the leg from one position to another; also the position in which the toe of one foot brushes the knee of the supporting leg.

Passepied, French dance, 17th century. It is a form of branle in 3/4 time.

Passo d'Addio, a tradition at Teatro alla Scala, Milan, by which graduating pupils of the ballet school are presented in a special performance which marks their farewell to the school. Passo d'Addio can be roughly translated as the Farewell Dance. It should not be confused with the debut of the dancer, which is quite a separate event, preceding or following the Passo d'Addio.

Pastorale. Ballet in 1 act; chor.: Francisco Moncion; music: Charles Turner; décor: David Hays; costumes: Ruth Sobotka. First prod.: New York City Ballet, City Center, N.Y., Feb. 14, 1957, with Allegra Kent, Francisco Moncion, Roy Tobias. For a few brief moments a blind boy hopes that his loneliness may be assuaged by the girl who did not at first realize that he was blind. But she cannot bring herself to accept the responsibilities their relationship entails and returns to her friends, while he is left alone once more. The ballet is also in the repertoire of the Robert Joffrey Ballet with Gerald Arpino as the boy.

Pastorela. Ballet-opera in 1 act; chor.: Lew Christensen; music: Paul Bowles; book: José Martinez, based on Mexican Christmas-play *Los Pastores;* décor and costumes: Alvin Colt. First prod.: The American Ballet, Municipal Theatre, Rio de Janeiro, Brazil, July, 1941; U.S. première: Ballet Society, Hunter Playhouse, N.Y., Jan. 13 and 14, 1947, with Jacques d'Amboise (St. Michael), Lew Christensen (St. Lucifer), Fred Danieli (Indian), Paul d'Amboise (Hermit), Luis Lopez (Boy), Beatrice Tompkins (Cook).

Path of Thunder, The. Ballet in 3 acts; chor.: Konstantin Sergeyev; music: Kara Karayev; book: Yuri Slonimsky, after the novel by South African author Peter Abrahams; décor: Valery Dorrer. First prod.: Kirov Theatre, Leningrad, Dec. 31, 1957, with Natalia Dudinskaya (Sarie) and Konstantin Sergeyev (Lenny). A story of love between a white girl and a colored boy, who are killed by the white people because they dare to oppose their customs. First performed at the Bolshoi Theatre with the same choreography and décor, June 27, 1959.

Patin, Jacques, French artist who designed the setting and costumes for *Ballet Comique de la Reine.*

Patineurs, Les. Ballet in 1 act; chor.: Frederick Ashton; music: Giacomo Meyerbeer, from his operas *Le Prophète* and *L'Etoile du Nord;* décor: William Chappell. First prod.: Vic-Wells (later Sadler's Wells, now Royal) Ballet, Sadler's Wells Theatre, London, Feb. 16, 1937, with Harold Turner, Margot Fonteyn, Mary Honer, Elizabeth Miller, Pamela May, June Brae. Harold Turner's Blue Skater was the outstanding piece of virtuoso male dancing in British ballet at that time. Other notable Blue Skaters are Brian Shaw and Graham Usher. Mary Honer contributed the brilliant series of fouettés subsequently performed as alternating singles and doubles by Rowena Jackson. Ashton staged *Les Patineurs* for Ballet (now American Ballet) Theatre in décor by Cecil Beaton, premièred at Broadway Theatre, N.Y., Oct. 2, 1946, with John Kriza (Green Skater in this version), Nora Kaye and Hugh Laing (White Skaters). The ballet is a divertissement made up of movements associated with ice skating and ends with the Blue Skater alone on the stage executing pirouettes à la seconde as the curtain falls.

Mimi Paul, ballerina of The New York City Ballet, in Swan Lake.

Paul, Mimi, dancer, b. Nashville, Tenn., 1943. Studied with Lisa Gardiner, Mary Day, and Frederic Franklin at Washington (D.C.) School of Ballet; summer of 1954 with Boris Kniaseff in Lausanne, Switzerland. Won National Society of Arts and Letters scholarship; also Ford Foundation Scholarship for study at School of American Ballet, N.Y. (both 1960). Danced with Washington (D.C.) Ballet (see REGIONAL BALLET) (1955–60), dancing title role in *The Chinese Nightingale* (1957) and Mary Day's *Ondine* (1959), dancing the latter when company appeared at Jacob's Pillow Dance Festival (1960). Joined New York City Ballet (1961); danced first solo roles: 2nd movement (*Symphony in C*), Symphony Section (*Episodes*), 5th and 6th Waltzes (*La Valse*), leader of the Pas de Neuf (George Balanchine's *Swan Lake,* Act 2), all in 1962. First leading role: alternate to Allegra Kent in Bugaku (Mar., 1963). Created Variation I in the Pas d'Action of George Balanchine's *Don Quixote* (Act 2). M. Michael Avedon (1967).

Pavanne (Pavin, Panicin), 17th-cent. dance, name derived either from town of Padua or from Pavo meaning peacock. It is probably the latter as ladies swept their trains in this dance in the manner of a peacock parading his tail. There were many curtsies, retreats, and advances in the Pavanne, and the lady rested her hand on back of man's. Poses were held and the style was dignified and aloof. The dance was set in 2/4 time. It was most popular in Italy, France, and Spain.

Pavillon d'Armide, Le. Ballet in 3 scenes; chor.: Michel Fokine; music: Nicholas Tcherepnine; book and décor: Alexandre Benois. First prod.: Maryinsky Theatre, St. Petersburg, Nov. 25, 1907, with Anna Pavlova in title role, Paul Gerdt, Vaslav Nijinsky. It was based on a short story by Théophile Gautier. Fokine had choreographed one scene of the ballet, "The Animated Gobelins," for the Annual Pupils' Performance at the Imperial School, Apr. 28, 1907, after which the director of the Imperial Theatres invited him to stage the full-length ballet. Serge Diaghilev included it on the opening night program of his Ballets Russes at the Théâtre du Châtelet, Paris, May 19, 1909, with Tamara Karsavina and Nijinsky in the principal roles.

Pavley, Andreas (Andres Van Dorph de Weyer) (1892–1931), dancer, director, b. Batavia, Java, of Dutch origin. Left Java at age of seven and began to study dance in The Hague, Holland, at age thirteen. Also studied with Ivan Clustine for two years and with Emile Jacques Dalcroze in Geneva for eighteen months. When only seventeen staged Beethoven's *Prometheus* in Amsterdam with one hundred performers. With the collaboration of the painter Arild Rosenkrantz staged *The Gate of Life,* to music from Beethoven's piano sonatas, at the Savoy Theatre, London (1912). Toured with Anna Pavlova's company in the U.S. (1913–15). His association with Serge Oukrainsky began in 1916 when they presented a James Whitcomb Riley Festival in Indianapolis with some students, one of whom was Ruth Page. Made guest star appearances with the Chicago Opera; founded the Pavley-Oukrainsky Ballet in Chicago which provided the ballets for the Chicago opera seasons and toured U.S., Mexico, Cuba, and South America. All the ballets in the repertoire were choreographed by the two directors. When Oukrainsky accepted the position of ballet master of the Chicago Opera in 1926, Pavley continued to tour with the Pavley-Oukrainsky Ballet and gave a season at the Théâtre de l'Etoile, Paris. Toured with Oukrainsky in Videballeton, which combined motion pictures and dancers (1927), principal dancers being Iva Kitchell, Lisan Kay, Vera Elisius, Viola Schermont, Angeles Campana. Gave solo performances and toured company in vaudeville (1929–30). Pavley died on the day the contract was signed for himself, Oukrainsky, and four of their dancers to appear at the Paris Opéra, June 26, 1931.

Pavlova, Anna (1881–1931).

Anna Pavlova, the greatest ballet dancer of the first third of the 20th century and a prima ballerina of the Maryinsky Theatre, was born on January 3rd, 1881, in St. Petersburg, the daughter of a peasant and a laundress. A premature child, she was frail and often ill.

In 1891 Pavlova was accepted into the Imperial School of Ballet and despite her physical weakness became an outstanding student both in dancing and in academic subjects. From her first years in the School she drew the attention of her teachers, Paul Gerdt and Christian Johannson, who prophesied a brilliant future for her.

She first appeared on the stage of the Maryinsky Theatre—while still a student in the School—in the "Pas des Aimées" from *The Daughter of Pharaoh,* at a benefit performance in honor of Christian Johannson. Upon her graduation from the School in 1899, she was accepted into the ballet company as a coryphée. In 1902 she was promoted to second soloist, and in 1903 to first soloist. In 1905 she became ballerina, and a year later, after a performance of *Swan Lake,* prima ballerina. In 1909 Pavlova celebrated her tenth anniversary as an artist of the Imperial Theatre with a performance of *La Bayadère.*

During her ten years at the Maryinsky Theatre, Pavlova danced, among other ballets: *Harlequinade, The Magic Flute, The Seasons, Don Quixote, Giselle* (The Queen of the Wilis and Giselle), *Le Corsaire, Paquita, Raymonda, La Source, Esmeralda, The Sleeping Beauty,* and *The Talisman.*

Beginning in 1907 Pavlova received leaves of absence to appear outside Russia. Her first tour, during which she was partnered by Adolph Bolm, took her to Stockholm, Copenhagen, Prague, and Berlin. The following year she danced in Leipzig, Prague, and Vienna with Bolm and

Nicholas Legat as partners. In 1909 she appeared with the Diaghilev Ballets Russes company during its Paris season at Théâtre Châtelet, and later danced with Mikhail Mordkin in Milan, Madrid, Brussels, Prague, Vienna, Berlin, and at the Paris Opéra. It was here that Otto Kahn, then director of the New York Metropolitan Opera, saw Pavlova and Mordkin and signed them for a month's season at the Metropolitan. They opened in New York in January, 1910.

In April of that year Pavlova made her debut in London. She appeared at the Palace Theatre, partnered by Mordkin. Eugenie Eduardova, Alexander Monakhov, and a group of eight supporting dancers formed the company. In 1911 Pavlova again appeared at the Palace Theatre in London, made a long U.S. tour, and in October once again danced in London, this time with the Diaghilev company.

In 1912 Pavlova bought the famous Ivy House in Hampstead, London, which became her permanent residence.

In the years 1910 to 1913 Pavlova appeared every season on the stage of the Maryinsky Theatre, dancing one or two months during the year. In 1913 she resigned from the Maryinsky Theatre and left Russia, never to return.

The declaration of the First World War found Pavlova in Berlin. She managed to get to England via Belgium. After a short time in London she assembled a company and came to the United States. She spent all the war years traveling in North and South America and returned to Europe nearly five years after her departure.

During the next eleven years Pavlova traveled virtually all over the world, dancing in every country in Europe (with the exception of Russia) and in the United States, Canada, Cuba, Costa Rica, Panama, Ecuador, Peru, Chile, Argentina, Uruguay, Puerto Rico, Brazil, Venezuela, Mexico, Japan, China, the Philippines, Malay States, Burma, India, Egypt, South Africa, Australia, New Zealand, and Java.

Among Pavlova's partners at the Imperial Theatre were Michel Fokine, Paul Gerdt, Samuel Andrianoff, Nicholas Legat. In the Diaghilev company she danced with Michel Fokine, Nijinsky, and Theodore Kosloff. In her own company she was partnered by Adolph Bolm, Nicholas Legat, Mikhail Mordkin, Laurent Novikov, Vladimir Tikhomirov, Alexandre Volinine, Pierre Vladimirov. Outstanding female dancers in her company were Hilda Butsova and Muriel Stuart.

Pavlova died on January 23, 1931, at The Hague, Holland, of double pneumonia. Her body was taken to England and cremated at the Golders Green Crematorium, where her ashes rest in an urn.

Pavlova was married to Victor Dandré (1870–1944).

Many books have been written about Pavlova the artist. None presented a clearer characterization of Pavlova than Cyril W. Beaumont in his little volume, *Anna Pavlova* (London, 1932). He wrote:

"All her dancing was distinguished by its grace, airiness, and absence of visible effort. It was sincere, refined, marked by a vivid sense of style-atmosphere, and a genuine and deeply felt reverence for the poetry of movement. She never permitted her dancing to become exaggerated; and even in her most ecstatic moments she retained complete control over her mind and body . . .

"She was first and last a great individual artist, a complete unity in herself, who had the supreme power of not only being able to breathe into a dance her own flame-like spirit, but, no matter how many times she had danced it before, to invest it with an air of spontaneity, novelty, and freshness, as though it had but just been born. She was something more than a great artist-dancer. She made her features speak and her body sing."

At the beginning of her career as a bal-

Anna Pavlova

lerina Pavlova had been a most enthusiastic follower of Michel Fokine's principles. Staunch supporters of the academic ballet considered her, along with Fokine, an artistic revolutionary. Pavlova reached the culmination of her unparalleled career during the subsequent period, which marked the advent of the modern ballet. Yet Pavlova did not participate in this historic moment. Her association with the Diaghilev Ballets Russes was short-lived and of little consequence to her and to ballet. In her independent work she paid little heed to what ballet, personified by Fokine and Diaghilev, was trying to do.

Many of the dances in Pavlova's vast repertoire were variations from old classic ballets with their quota of music by Pugni and Minkus, and special numbers of which her famous *Gavotte* to Paul Lincke's "Glow Worm" was representative. It is true that Pavlova danced also to the music of Chopin (*Chopiniana*), Saint-Saëns (*The Dying Swan*), Liszt (*Les Préludes*) and a few other outstanding composers, but they were in the minority and were not characteristic of her repertoire. Most of the décor and costumes of her ballets were equally undistinguished.

Pavlova was very conservative, actually reactionary, in her choice of choreography, music, décor, and subject matter of her ballets. She gravitated toward traditionalism in everything connected with ballet. As the new ballet was progressing and opening new vistas, she seemed content to remain with the form and standard she had accepted.

That Pavlova, in spite of all this, achieved an unprecedented success is due only to her genius. She was great because she was Pavlova: the sum total of a divine gift, an active mind, a perfect body, superb craftsmanship.

Her genius was as intangible as the artistic legacy she left behind her. What remains of Pavlova today is not a movement in art, a tendency in the ballet, or even a series of dances, but something less concrete, yet possibly even more valuable.

Pavlova's service to the ballet is inestimable. In twenty years of touring she danced in every part of the world. She must have traveled some 500,000 miles and given thousands of performances witnessed by millions of people. To all these people Pavlova brought a little happiness. To the majority of them Pavlova was the first contact with ballet, an art form of which they had never heard until her advent. To others she remained the only ballet dancer they had ever seen. To thousands she was a spark that ignited their imaginations, an ideal they chose to pursue.

Ballet companies today point with pride to their tours in America and Europe. However, it must not be forgotten that it was Pavlova who opened the world to ballet, that it was she who found and cultivated audiences for contemporary ballet companies. It was Pavlova who inspired youngsters to take up ballet as a career or hobby, and thus created the most valuable asset any theatrical art can hope to acquire —an active, participating audience.

Contemporaries of Pavlova attempted to change the content and form of ballet, tried and succeeded in directing its destinies—all within the sphere of ballet itself. Pavlova took the ballet, a concrete form, and moved it in time and space. She took it from the aristocratic Imperial Theatres of Russia and the resplendent opera houses of Western European capitals and gave it to the people, in cities and towns, villages and colonies. She danced wherever there was a stage—in theatres and music halls, high school auditoriums and movie houses.

From the point of view of the history of modern ballet Pavlova's role is not commensurate with her greatness as an artist. Had Pavlova's approach persisted rather than those of Fokine and Diaghilev, ballet could have died with Pavlova, as did her ballets. Yet Pavlova did not die an artistic pauper. She may have taken her art with her, but she left behind a legacy which still does, and for years to come, will feed the spirit and inspiration of dance-lovers all over the world.

Conservative or modern, reactionary or revolutionary, Pavlova—the artist and dancer—will always serve as an example to follow, an ideal to be pursued and emulated.

Pécourt, Louis (also spelled Pécour) (1655–1729), French dancer who danced leading roles in Jean Baptiste Lully's and Pierre Beauchamp's ballets. After Beauchamp left the Opéra, Pécourt arranged the choreography for a number of ballets and composed dances for Louis XIV. He has also been credited with being the actual author of Feuillet's *Chorégraphie*. He made his first appearance at the Opéra in 1672 in the ballet *Cadmus* and was demi-caractère in style. He was noted for precision, grace, and lightness. Personally he was a very acceptable man and mixed in the best society of the time.

Peer Gynt. Ballet in 3 acts, 10 scenes; chor.: Vaslav Orlikovsky; music: Edvard Grieg's incidental music for *Peer Gynt, Holberg Suite,* some of his songs and Norwegian dances; book: from the play *Peer Gynt* by Henrik Ibsen; décor: Edward Delany; costumes: Yvonne Lloyd. First prod.: London's Festival Ballet, Opera House, Monte Carlo, Apr. 13, 1963, with John Gilpin (Peer Gynt), Irène Skorik (Solveig), Marilyn Burr (Ingrid), Vassili Trunoff (Bridegroom), Angela Bishop (Aase), Irina Borovska (The Green One), Olga Ferri (Anitra); London première: Festival Hall, July 15, 1963. Karl Musil and David Adams also danced the title role, with Marilyn Jones alternating with Burr as Ingrid, Gaye Fulton with Skorik as Solveig, and Genia Melikova with Borovska as The Green One. The famous play, treated more lightly in accordance with the Grieg music but depicting the key scenes: Peer's dreams of glory and the crown he will offer his mother; his seduction of Ingrid; capture by the Trolls; his briefly successful career as a rich business man until Anitra steals everything from him; the scene in the madhouse; Peer's return to Norway, first to comfort the dying Aase and then to return to Solveig, who has waited so faithfully for him. Orlikovsky had previously staged a production of *Peer Gynt* in Basel, Switzerland (1950), for the Klassisches Russisches Ballett which he headed at the time.

Penché, in ballet, leaning forward, as arabesque penchée (in the *Giselle* Act 2 pas de deux, Giselle is supported by Albrecht as she does an arabesque penchée, after which he turns her slowly in a promenade).

Penitente, El. Modern trio dance; chor.: Martha Graham; music: Louis Horst; setting: Arch Lauterer; costumes: Edythe Gilfond. First prod.: Bennington, Vt., Aug. 11, 1940.

Penna, Nilson, Brazilian artist, designer, dance critic, b. Belem, Brazil, 1916. Graduated from the National School of Fine Arts, Rio de Janeiro; studied dramatic art and acted in several local companies; studied dance with Maryla Gremo, Vaslav Veltchek, and Tatiana Leskova. Made his debut as dancer in Ballet da Juventude (1949). He has designed scenery and costumes for almost all the local stage companies and won awards in 1949, 1953, 1954, and 1958 for his work; scholarship (1951–52) to study at Ecole des Arts, Paris; to U.S. (1955) on a Dept. of State Grant to study and observe the American theatre. Designed décor and costumes for *Aurora's Wedding* and *Coppélia* (Tatiana Leskova's Ballet Society); *Consolation* (Ballet da Juventude); *Abstract Composition* (Teatro Municipal); *Valse Triste* (Ballet Nina Verchinina), *O Garatuja* (Ballet Rio de Janeiro). Artistic director for Ballet Rio de Janeiro (1961–62). Currently assistant to dance section of Brazil's Culture Council in which capacity he was largely responsible for organizing the dance festival held in the Univ. of the State of Parana, Curitiba, which was attended by teachers and pupils from all over Brazil (1962). Writes occasionally on dance for *Jornal do Brasil.*

Pennsylvania Ballet, one of the professional companies brought into being under the Ford Foundation Grant (Dec. 1963). Its director Barbara Weisberger had been director of a regional company in Wilkes-Barre, Pa., and founded a school in Philadelphia about a year prior to the announcement of the grant with the idea of developing a resident company. The company did, in fact, give a single private performance in Philadelphia in the summer of 1963. Its first performance following the announcement of the grant was Apr. 19, 1964, in the Irvine Auditorium of the Univ. of Pennsylvania, since when it has had an annual subscription series in that auditorium. The repertoire during these early years has been mainly borrowed from New York City Ballet, principally George Balanchine's works, with guest artists from the same company. The full-length *Sleeping Beauty* with considerable emendations both to the story and choreography was staged by Heinz Poll and presented Nov. 26 and 27, 1965, at the Academy of Music, Phila. Guest artist Melissa Hayden was Aurora, partnered at the première by the company's young leading male dancer Alexei Yudenich, and by the company's ballet master Robert Rodham at the second. Pennsylvania Ballet's first tour in the Phila. area was in the spring of 1966. On Aug. 1, 1966, the Ford Foundation announced a further grant (on a matching basis) of $450,000. The 1966–67 season at the Academy of Music opened Oct. 21 with John Butler's *Carmina Burana* (its first performance by an American ballet company), Balanchine's *Donizetti Variations,* and Robert Rodham's *Trio* (music: Jacques Ibert). This performance marked the company's official move to the Academy of Music for a number of weekend performances a year. In Nov., 1966, it appeared at the Harper Theatre (Chicago) Dance Festival.

Percussive Movement, in modern dance, a type of movement used particularly in the early works of Martha Graham, and characteristic of much of her technique. The term is similar in meaning to "staccato," the implication being that the original force with which the movement is begun is intended to carry it beyond what is actually seen. Angular movements, with straight lines and angles as their conclusions, can be percussive; but percussive movements also end in unrealized curves or circles, the force behind these movements being so strong that the spectator's eye will see beyond what has actually been given. The original attack, which the word percussive suggests, is similar to the accent given to the beginning of a musical phrase and is not necessarily more obvious.

Peretti, Serge, French dancer, ballet master, teacher. Studied in the school of the Paris Opéra ballet. He was the first male to receive the title étoile (1941), formerly given only to female dancers. He danced in most of the important ballets presented at the Opéra between World Wars I and II, notably *The Creatures of Prometheus, Salade, La Vie de Polichinelle, Chevalier et la Damoiselle, Joan de Zarissa,* and *Le Tambourin* by Jean Philippe Rameau, his greatest role. Became ballet master in 1944; mounted *The Call of the Mountain* (1945) and retired from the stage shortly after. Now teaches in the Paris Opéra ballet school.

Performing Arts, School of, New York City, is the only high school of its kind in the U.S. and probably in the world. A dual-purpose school, as part of the New York City Board of Education school system it offers free professional training in dance, music, and drama, as well as the usual high school educational programs.

Under the leadership of Dr. Franklin J. Keller, Principal of the Metropolitan Vocational High School, and with the assistance of the late Mrs. Samuel A. Lewisohn, Chairman of the Advisory Commission on the Performing Arts, the School began in 1939 as a course in vocational music at the Metropolitan Vocational High School. In 1941 a course of vocational dramatics was added on an experimental basis within the Speech Dept. of the school. After a period of evaluation, the Board of Education approved the vocational music course as a regular department in the curriculum of the Vocational High School (1943). Later, courses in music and dance were offered to the drama students. In early 1948 the New York City Board of Estimates and the Board of Education approved the establishment of the School of Performing Arts as an Annex (division) of the Metropolitan Vocational High School. The new school was moved into a building formerly occupied by P.S. 67 on West 46th Street. The move permitted the remodeling of the old building's gymnasium into studio space and with it the opening of the Dance Dept. in Sept. of that year for which prospective students had been auditioned in Jan. Students of Performing Arts School work twice as hard as students in regular high school, who study only academic subjects. Their school day is equally divided between academic and vocational subjects; thus they complete their academic high school course in half the regular time. The dance curriculum includes ballet technique, modern dance technique, and, among the theoretical courses, dance history, ballet and modern dance survey (dealing with late history and current events), rhythmic analysis (music as applied to dance), dance notation, and some workshop classes in related subjects. During the first three years all students are required to take ballet and modern dance technique; in the senior year they major in one or the other technique. In addition to the chairmen of the departments and their faculties, each department has an Advisory Commission whose function it is to advise the respective chairmen and faculties on various subjects dealing with the educational aspect of the department, to participate in the annual auditions of aspirants desiring to join the school, assist at the evaluation of the success (or lack of it) of the graduating students during the so-called senior project. The present Chairman of the Dance Department is Dr. Rachael Dunaven Yocom. The present Advisory Commission on Dance includes Anatole Chujoy, Martha Graham, Martha Hill, Hanya Holm, Lydia Joel, Nora Kaye, Lincoln Kirstein, José Limón, John Martin, Zachary Solov, Clive Barnes, Walter Terry. The present Chairman of the full Advisory Commission on the Performing Arts is Mrs. Howard S. Cullman. The function of Performing Arts School is not to create artists, but rather to prepare competent craftsmen. That it is successful in fulfilling this function is demonstrated by the fact that each year a high percentage of graduates find employment soon after graduation and that several students each year begin to work, usually in Broadway musicals and television, in their senior year. Qute a number of graduates continue their education in colleges, usually those having a proper dance department. In Sept., 1962, the School of Performing Arts merged with the High School of Music and Art, in anticipation of sharing quarters in a new building in the area of Lincoln Center for the Performing Arts. Mr. Louis K. Wechsler is the present Principal of both schools, and School of Performing Arts is officially an Annex of the High School of Music and Art.

Péri, La. Ballet in 2 acts, 3 scenes; chor.: Jean Coralli; music: Norbert Burgmüller; book: Théophile Gautier and Jean Coralli; décor: Séchan, Dieterle, Depléchin (Act 1); Philastre, Cambon (Act 2); costumes: Marilhat and Paul Lormier. First prod.: Théâtre de l'Académie Royale de Musique, Paris, July 17, 1843, with Lucien

Petipa (Achmet) and Carlotta Grisi (The Péri); London première: Sept. 30, 1843, Theatre Royal, Drury Lane, with the same principals; St. Petersburg première: Feb. 1, 1844, with Yelena Andreanova in the title role. Coralli's *La Péri* is a long and complicated ballet which fascinated Parisians and Londoners nearly as much as *Giselle* had less than two years earlier. The plot deals with harems, slaves, odalisques, eunuchs, etc., a Pasha, the hero Achmet, and the Péri, who also disguises herself as Leila, a favorite of the Pasha. The plot is as involved as a good detective story, but everything ends happily with the Péri and Achmet united in heaven.

Péri, La. Ballet in 1 act; chor.: Frederick Ashton; music: Paul Dukas's tone poem of that name; décor: Ivor Hitchens; costumes: André Levasseur. First prod.: Sadler's Wells (now Royal) Ballet, Royal Opera House, Covent Garden, London, Feb. 15, 1956, with Margot Fonteyn (La Péri), Michael Somes (Iskender). Iskender, looking for the flower of immortality, finds it in the hands of the Peri who guards the gates of Paradise. She wakes as he tries to take it from her and lures it back with her dancing. As she disappears he realizes he must face the fate of all mortals. Like the music, *La Péri* is described as a "poème dansée." Ashton's first version was for himself and Alicia Markova in costumes by William Chappell, premièred Feb. 16, 1931, at Mercury Theatre in the earliest days of Ballet Rambert. Frank Staff subsequently staged another version, Mar. 13, 1938, at the Mercury, in décor by Nadia Benois, for himself and Deborah Dering.

Periodicals, Dance (England). Currently there are three monthly magazines in England concerned with theatrical dance of which the oldest-established is the *Dancing Times* (which see). *Ballet Today,* founded Mar.–Apr., 1946, by P. W. Manchester and edited by her until Apr. 1951, continues under the editorship of Mrs. Estelle Herf. *Dance and Dancers,* founded 1950, was edited by Peter Williams with Clive Barnes as executive editor. The latter left (fall, 1965) to become dance critic of *The N.Y. Times* and was succeeded by John Percival as associate editor. A fourth magazine, *Ballet,* edited by Richard Buckle, brought out two issues (July and Oct., 1939); publication was discontinued for the duration of World War II. It resumed publication for the period from Jan., 1946 to Oct., 1952, ceasing publication with that issue.

Periodicals, Dance (U.S.). Virtually the only serious and sustained attempt at a dance publication before 1925 was the *Denishawn Magazine* published by Ruth St. Denis and Ted Shawn when their company and school were nationally active.

In 1925 Harry Moss, who had been publishing a small ballroom dancers' periodical in N.Y., sold it to Macfadden Publications, Inc. That organization retitled it *Dancelovers Magazine,* enlarged it, and gave it national newsstand distribution. It was intended for the general public and had a strong fan approach.

In 1926 the magazine was radically changed: it became *Dance Magazine,* first under the editorship of Vera Caspary (1926–27), then W. Adolphe Roberts (1927), and Paul Milton (1928–29). *Dance Magazine* was, properly speaking, the first publication to give monthly coverage to the various phases of dance, to publish articles by virtually all available authorities, dancers, teachers, etc. Although it had an advertising billing and a circulation greater than any other dance publication in America, either before or after its time (the circulation fluctuated between thirty and fifty thousand), it fell victim to the Depression in 1932. With the fall of *Dance Magazine,* dance publications in general forsook any attempt to appeal to the general public and confined themselves to the dance profession and to that small segment of the public which have more than just a passing interest in dance.

In 1927 Ruth Eleanor Howard had founded in Los Angeles *The American Dancer,* which at first devoted itself chiefly to the West Coast activities. After *Dance Magazine* closed, *The American Dancer* moved to N.Y. early in 1933. Ruth Howard remained its publisher; Paul Milton became its editor. In the ensuing three years it had the field to itself, except for the *Dance Observer*.

Dance Observer was founded in N.Y. in 1933 by Louis Horst, a composer and pianist as well as author and instructor, and at the time musical director for Martha Graham and her group. He was a strong and outspoken devotee of modern dance and its practitioners, from professional dancers to the physical education teachers who taught the modern dance discipline in colleges and their students. His aim in publishing the *Dance Observer* was to reflect the development and activities of modern dance in the U.S. and to act as a deterrent to the spread of ballet in this country, which he and nearly everyone who was interested in modern dance considered an encroachment on their province. As time passed, the schism between modern dance and ballet narrowed so that by the mid-1940's it was barely noticeable. Founder and editor Louis Horst died in Jan., 1964. Predictably, the *Dance Observer* ceased publication with the last issue he edited: Jan., 1964.

In 1936 Paul Milton left *The American Dancer* and with a group of other dance writers, including Anatole Chujoy, established a new magazine entitled *Dance*. The new publication devoted more space to the professional dance than the *American Dancer,* and modern dance, almost entirely neglected by the older magazine, found considerable reflection in *Dance*. Shortly after establishing *Dance,* the same group began to publish the *Young Dancer*. Edited by Rosalie Livingston, *Young Dancer* was devoted entirely to the interests of the young dance students. Almost from the very beginning, both *Dance* and *Young Dancer* suffered from lack of capital.

After three and a half years the publishers were forced to sell both magazines. The purchaser was Richard Davis, then publisher of ballet souvenir programs. *Young Dancer* was discontinued soon after the purchase. In 1941 Davis sold *Dance* to Rudolph Orthwine, who also bought *The American Dancer* from Ruth Howard. The new publisher, who owned an excellent printing plant, combined both magazines under the title *Dance,* which he continues to publish. Milton and Chujoy left *Dance* when it was sold to Mr. Orthwine.

During the years 1937–40 Lucille Marsh published several issues of a small pamphlet-size magazine entitled *Dance Digest*. Subsequently she discontinued her publication and joined *Dance* as editor, a position she held until Dec., 1944.

In May, 1938, Dorothi Bock Pierre and Mary Jane Hungerford founded in Hollywood a magazine entitled *Educational Dance,* with Dorothi Bock Pierre as editor and Mary Jane Hungerford, Esther Pease, and Patricia Parmelee as associate editors. The objective of the magazine was to deal with all aspects of the dance in the educational field. It was circulated among physical educators and dance teachers in colleges, high and grade schools, and in libraries in the U.S. and abroad. *Educational Dance* was discontinued after the Aug.–Sept. issue of 1942.

In 1941 Michael Herman, a prominent N.Y. teacher of folk dancing, established a pamphlet-size magazine entitled *The Folk Dancer,* dedicated, as the title implies, to the folk dance. The magazine does not appear regularly.

In Jan., 1942, appeared the first issue of a new type of dance publication, *Dance Index,* edited by Lincoln Kirstein, Paul Magriel, and Baird Hastings, and published by Dance Index–Ballet Caravan, Inc. The stated purpose of *Dance Index* was to make an attempt to provide an historical and critical basis for judging the present and future of dancing. It fulfilled this purpose with a high degree of excellence. With a few exceptions, each issue of the magazine was a monograph, either on one subject or by one writer. It accepted no advertising and was sold only by subscription. By its very nature it appealed to a limited group of people with a deep interest in dance and therefore could never be made self-supporting. With an increased activity of Ballet Society and later the New York City Ballet, Lincoln Kirstein could not afford the time or expense of continued publication, and *Dance Index* was discontinued after the fall, 1948, issue (vol. 8, no. 6). The last editors of the magazine were Marian Eames and Lincoln Kirstein.

In Nov., 1942, a quite different type of dance publication made its appearance, *Dance News,* edited and published by Anatole Chujoy. In distinction from the generally accepted characteristics of dance publications, i.e. contents and format, *Dance News* is published in the form of a tabloid newspaper and occupies itself mostly with current events in all fields of the theatrical dance. With a string of correspondents in the U.S. and abroad, it presents monthly a comprehensive picture of dance activity the world over, including news, photographic coverage, reviews, articles on topical subjects, and illustrations. Although edited primarily for the dance profession, it is widely read by the general public interested in dance. Its circulation is international. Anatole Chujoy continues as editor and P. W. Manchester is managing editor.

Dance Perspectives, a quarterly, was founded in the autumn of 1958 by A. J. Pishl (Editor), Selma Jeanne Cohen (Associate Editor) and Sheppard Black (Assistant Editor). It is continuing, in the direction of *Dance Index,* but is more catholic in the selection of its material. Appropriately enough, the first issue (dated Winter, 1959), was a monograph by Lincoln Kirstein: "What Ballet Is About; an American Glossary and a Portfolio of Photographs of the New York City Ballet by Martha Swope." The quarterly is very handsomely designed. In Jan., 1963, the publishers issued a "bonus" (free to subscribers) almanac, *Dance 62,* which did not go on general sale. It contained a number of articles on topics of current interest with photographs, mostly by Martha Swope, and drawings by Karl Leabo, art editor of the publication and designer of *Dance 62*. With issue No. 21 (Spring, 1965) editor Selma Jeanne Cohen purchased *Dance Perspectives* from Sheppard Black. She continues as editor.

Peripheral Movements. See EUKINETICS.

Perkins, Dorothy Burrows, teacher, b. Princeton, Mo., 1884. Her teachers included Michel Fokine and Enrico Cecchetti. She also studied the Dalcroze system of Eurythmics in N.Y. and Paris. She opened a dance studio in Kansas City, Mo., and became one of the great pioneering American teachers, placing special emphasis on rhythmics and posture before ballet training. Among many pupils who went on to become famous in the dance and theatre are Rosella Hightower, Rabana Hasburgh, Peggy Cornell, Annette Van Dyke, Marian Calahan, Jane Everett, Donald Cook, Shirley Weaver. She is now semi-retired.

Perottet, Philippe, Australian dancer, choreographer, ballet master, b. Melbourne, 1921. Studied with Edouard Borovansky, Gordon Hamilton, Thadeo Slavinsky, Vera Volkova, George Gontcharov, Andrew Hardie. After service in the Royal Australian Air Force (1941–46), principal dancer and choreographer, Australian Ballet Society, Melbourne (1946). Came to England (1947); danced with International Ballet (1947–48), becoming soloist; later with London's Festival Ballet (1952–53). Currently ballet master for Sadler's Wells Opera.

Perrot, Jules Joseph (1810–1892), famous dancer and choreographer. A pupil of Auguste Vestris and Salvatore Vigano, he was born in Lyon, in June, 1810. He began his career as a circus pantomimist and clown, danced in provincial French theatres and later moved to Paris. In May, 1830, he made his debut at the Opéra and his very first performance created a sensation. Théophile Gautier called him "the greatest dancer of our times."

Perrot shared his first balletic victories with Maria Taglioni. His success grew with every performance and this success was an obstacle for the famous ballerina. After a few seasons she refused to dance with him. As a result, the doors of the Opéra became closed to Perrot (1835). Guest performances through Western Europe gradually drew Perrot into choreographic work, his first efforts being mostly divertissement numbers. Toward the end of 1840 Perrot was already a famous choreographer. His ballets *The Naiad and the Fisherman, Catarina, Esmeralda,* and *La Filleule des Fées* were famous throughout Europe.

In Naples he met the then unknown young dancer Carlotta Grisi, took her to Paris and later married her. Grisi made a successful debut at the Renaissance Theatre and was invited to join the Opéra. Perrot returned to the Opéra, but on the heels and in the service of Grisi. For himself he was unable to secure an engagement, although he was promised that he might stage a ballet.

On the strength of this promise he began rehearsing with Grisi without waiting for an official invitation. According to the Danish choreographer August Bournonville, who had been a classmate of Perrot's in Vestris' school, the following episode took place: "I personally witnessed Perrot coach Carlotta Grisi in fragments from the principal part of some ballet with the idea of using it in *Giselle*."

It was not, however, to the interest of the theatre to engage Perrot. The competition was not to the liking of the staff choreographer, Jean Coralli, very glad though he was at the same time to have Perrot work on the production of *Giselle*. Then began the love affair between Grisi and Gautier, a situation that made Perrot's presence at the Opéra impossible. His wife used her maiden name of Grisi for the posters and all Perrot's dreams went up in smoke. A few days later the première of *Giselle* brought unprecedented fame to Coralli, who declared himself the sole choreographer of the ballet.

Brought up on the examples of the Romantic theatre with its stormy passions and dramatic collisions, Perrot attempted to embody in the dance strong and dramatic situations. From his circus days he evolved the idea of rhythmic pantomime and a technique of simple yet telling stage situations. Jean Georges Noverre's traditions as realized in the brilliant productions of his pupils, Charles Didelot and Jean Dauberval, became an organic element in the creative power of Perrot, the leading ideas in his choreographic conception.

Some of the principal creations of Perrot are not at all peculiar to the Romantic ballet in its generally accepted sense. The overwhelming majority of his ballets have a realistic story, such as *Catarina, Esmeralda, Gazelda, Marco Bomba, Le Corsaire, The Wilful Wife,* and *Faust*.

In 1848 Perrot, in search of steady work, arrived in St. Petersburg. He was accepted into the Imperial Theatre and worked there from that year to 1859 (except for a short interval) as dancer, choreographer and artistic leader, producing nearly twenty ballets. But by 1859 Perrot with his democratic inclinations began to be a burden to the direction of the Imperial Theatres, and he was forced to leave.

He returned to his native France and did not immediately realize the changes which had taken place in Western Europe during his absence. He made several attempts to revive his former fame by showing his best works in France and in Milan, but was not successful.

He retired to a solitary, provincial, far-off French village. Although strong and full of vigor, he urged on death, idly whiling away his time in fishing. From time to time his few friends came to see him, or young ballerinas who wished to go through the parts of *Esmeralda* with him paid him an occasional visit. He, the rival of Maria Taglioni was, like her, unhappy in his old age. Bournonville in his memoirs speaks bitterly about the painful life of Perrot in his declining years. By the time of his death, he and most of his ideas had already been forgotten. (For a full biography and appreciation of Jules Perrot see "Jules Perrot," by Yury Slonimsky, trans. by Anatole Chujoy, with an Epilogomena by George Chaffee, *Dance Index,* Dec., 1945.)

Perry, Charlotte L., contemporary American teacher and director. B.A., Smith College; graduate courses at Parsons School of Fine Arts, N.Y. Univ., Columbia Univ., N.Y. School for Social Work. Studied drama with Marie Ouspenskaya, Erwin Piscator, Sanford Meissner, John Gassner, Sondheimer, and Sundgaard, working in the professional theatre for six years. Former director of drama, Bank Street Teacher Training School, Rosemary Junior College; guest instructor, N.Y. Univ. (1946), Hunter College (1947). Currently director of drama, Lenox School for Girls; co-owner and co-director, Perry-Mansfield Camps; director of Theatre School, Perry-Mansfield School of the Theatre and Dance, Steamboat Springs, Colo. Author of articles on drama and of children's plays. In the spring of 1963, Charlotte Perry and Portia Mansfield announced that they had made a gift of the Perry-Mansfield School and School of the Theatre and Dance to Stephens College, Columbia, Mo. Beginning with the summer of 1964, Stephens College took over the operation of camps and school. Charlotte Perry and Portia Mansfield continue to direct the activities and the instructional program and Dr. Melvin Davidson, Chairman of the Division of Arts at Stephens, is Chairman of the College Program and Director of the Theatre School. See also PORTIA MANSFIELD.

Persephone. Modern dance work; chor. and costumes: Pearl Lang; music: Meyer Kupferman. First prod.: Pearl Lang Dance Company, Hunter College Playhouse, N.Y., Feb. 17, 1957, with Pearl Lang (Persephone), David Lober (Pluto), Bruce Marks (Mercury), Karen Kanner (Demeter), and supporting dancers. The work was retitled *Persephone* (1963), the original title having been *Falls the Shadow Between.* Pearl Lang staged it for Nederlands National Ballet and it was premièred June 15, 1963, during the Holland Festival. A choreographic rendering of the myth of Persephone, the daughter of Zeus and Demeter. She was abducted by Pluto, the king of the underworld, to be his wife, but was permitted to return to the earth every spring.

Persephone. "Melodrame" in 3 scenes; chor.: Frederick Ashton; music: Igor Stravinsky; book: Stravinsky and André Gide; décor: Nico Ghika. First prod.: Royal Ballet, Royal Opera House, Covent Garden, London, Dec. 12, 1962, with Svetlana Beriosova (Persephone), Keith Rosson (Pluto), Alexander Grant (Mercury), Gerd Larsen (Demeter), Derek Rencher (Demophoon). Kurt Jooss staged the first Stravinsky *Persephone* for Ida Rubinstein (1934). It is seldom performed as Stravinsky and Gide devised it because of the difficulty of finding a dancer who can also speak the Gide poem. Vera Zorina is well known in the U.S. for her interpretation in concert performances and, in the summer of 1962, appeared in Thomas Andrew's staging of the complete work for the Santa Fé (N.Mex.) Opera. The work is a re-telling of the Persephone legend. Ashton's production was in homage of Stravinsky on his eightieth birthday, part of the world-wide celebrations of that event.

Perugini, Giulio, Italian dancer and ballet master, b. 1927, Rome. Studied at the ballet school of Teatro dell'Opera, Rome, under Ettori Caorsi, Teresa Bataggi; became premier danseur of Teatro alla Scala, Milan (1949). Since 1959 has been ballet master of that theatre. His roles included the Princes in *Cinderella, Swan Lake* (Act 2), and *The Nutcracker;* Joseph in *The Legend of Joseph,* and others.

Perugini, Mark E. (1876–1948), English writer on dance. His books, especially *The Art of Ballet* (1915) and *A Pageant of the Dance and Ballet* (1935), were important contributions to the scant literature on the subject. He was the husband of Ruby Ginner, an outstanding London teacher of the Greek dance and pantomime.

Peter and the Wolf. Ballet in 1 act; chor.: Adolph Bolm; music and book: Serge Prokofiev; décor and costumes: Lucinda Ballard. First prod.: Ballet Theatre, Center Theatre, N.Y., Jan. 13, 1940, with Eugene Loring (Peter), William Dollar (the Wolf), Viola Essen (Bird), Karen Conrad (Duck), Nina Stroganova (Cat). Elizabeth West staged a version of *Peter and the Wolf* for Western Theatre Ballet (1957). The music carries with it a narration about the little boy Peter, who (with the aid of his friends—the Cat and the Bird) captures a Wolf, in spite of the warnings of his Grandfather to keep safely behind his own fence.

Peter and the Wolf. Ballet in 1 act; chor.: Frank Staff; music and book: Serge Prokofiev; décor and costumes: Guy Sheppard. First prod.: Ballet Rambert, Arts Theatre, Cambridge, May 1, 1940, with Helen Ashley (Peter), Leo Kersley (the Wolf), Celia Franca (Bird), Sally Gilmour (Duck), Walter Gore (Cat). Helen Ashley was actually Marie Rambert's daughter, Lulu Dukes.

Peters, Kurt, German ballet critic and writer, b. Hamburg, 1915. Editor-Publisher of the magazine *Das Tanzarchiv* (German Periodical for Dance Art and Folklore), Köln. Founder and director of the International Library and Collection of the same title and of the Tanzarchiv book publishing house, specializing in dance textbooks and pedagogical books. President, Society of Friends of Dance Art and the Work Circle for the Preservation and Research of the German Folk Dance. Studied ballet with Mariska Rudolph, formerly of the Royal Budapest Opera, and with Alexandra Fedorova-Fokine when she was ballet mistress of the Riga (Latvia) Opera Ballet.

Petersen, Kirsten, soloist of the Royal Danish Ballet, b. 1936. Entered the company's school (1943). Accepted into the company (1952); made soloist (1957). Dances leading roles in *Romeo and Juliet, Concerto Barocco, Apollo, Graduation Ball, Le Spectre de la Rose, Les Sylphides, Serenade, Miss Julie, Blood Wedding, Carmen, Harlequinade, Conservatoriet, Etudes, The Lady from the Sea, Napoli,* and others.

Petipa, Jean Antoine (1796–1855), choreographer, dancer and teacher, father of Lucien and Marius Petipa. Born in Paris, he began his artistic career in Marseilles. Danced in Paris and Brussels, where he remained twelve years. Later worked as choreographer in Bordeaux and Madrid. Also appeared as guest artist in the U.S. In 1848 became instructor at the Russian Imperial Ballet School where, being considered an outstanding teacher, he worked until his death.

Petipa, Lucien, French dancer and choreographer, b. Marseilles, 1815, d. Versailles, 1898. Son of Jean Antoine Petipa and brother of Marius Petipa. Studied with his father and made his debut in Brussels where his father was ballet master. Made his debut at Paris Opéra (1840), partnering Fanny Elssler in *La Sylphide.* One of the outstanding dancers of his time he created the role of Albrecht in *Giselle* and also created the leading male roles in *La Jolie Fille de Gand, La Péri,* and other ballets of the Romantic period, frequently as partner to Carlotta Grisi. Choreographed *Sakountala* (1858); became maître de ballet of Paris Opéra (1865), for which company he choreographed *Namouna* (1882), to music by Edouard Lalo.

Petipa, Marie (née Sourovshchikova) (1836–1882), Russian dancer, first wife of Marius Petipa. His favorite dancer when he was teaching in the Imperial School, St. Petersburg, she and Petipa were married upon her graduation from the school (1854). She was famous for her character dancing. Her most famous dance, performed en travesti, was *The Little Moujik,* which Petipa created for her. They were separated in 1867.

Petipa, Marie (1857–1930), Russian dancer, daughter of Marius Petipa and his wife, Marie Sourovshchikova Petipa. Trained in the Imperial School, St. Petersburg, she made her debut at the Maryinsky Theatre (1875). One of the leading dancers of her time, she created the role of the Lilac Fairy in her father's *The Sleeping Beauty.*

Petipa, Marius (1819–1910), choreographer and dancer of the Russian Imperial Ballet. The "father of the classic ballet" was born in Marseilles, the son of the French dancer and teacher Jean Petipa. He made his debut in Nantes, France (1838); danced at the Paris Opéra with Fanny Elssler (1841); left Paris the next year for a more profitable engagement in Bordeaux, where he remained three years, later dancing in Spain. In 1847 the St. Petersburg Imperial Theatre signed a contract with Petipa for one year. Petipa went to St. Petersburg and remained there to the end of his days. He made his debut in St. Petersburg in the ballet *Paquita,* which he revived. In 1854 he married a pupil in the graduating class of the Imperial School, Maria Sourovshchikova. The same year he became instructor in the school and raised the standard of choreographic education in Russia to new heights. Petipa was considered an excellent dancer and partner. He was a good actor and his acting, stage manners, and pantomime were considered an example for generations of ballet dancers. In 1858 Petipa staged his first original ballet for the Imperial Theatre, *A Marriage During Regency;* in 1859 he staged *The Paris Market* and *The Blue Dahlia.* During the years 1859 and 1860 Petipa and his wife, on leave of absence, made a tour of European capitals. In 1862 he was appointed choreographer-in-chief, replacing Jules Perrot. The appointment came as a result of the enormous success of his ballet *The Daughter of Pharaoh.* Petipa is considered one of the greatest choreographers of all time. To his talent as chore-

Marius Petipa, the father of the classic ballet.

ographer he added exhaustive research in the subject matter of the ballets he was staging, making careful and detailed preparations for each production. He prepared minute plans for the composers and painters with whom he worked, and always considered that choreography proper took precedence over all other artistic expressions which were part of ballet, such as music, décor, and libretto. Petipa clarified and formulated the classic ballet as we know it today. In the nearly fifty years of his work as choreographer at the Imperial Theatre, he created more than sixty full-evening ballets, as well as innumerable short ballets and dance numbers. Under the artistic direction of Petipa the Russian ballet produced its greatest names and to this day the ballet in Soviet Russia is based largely on the repertoire of Petipa's productions. Among his greatest ballets are *Don Quixote, Camargo, La Bayadère, The Talisman, The Sleeping Beauty, Bluebeard, Raymonda, The Seasons, Harlequinade.* Among the ballets he restaged for the Imperial Theatre were *Paquita, Giselle, Le Corsaire, Coppélia, La Sylphide, Swan Lake* (Acts 1 and 3), *The Humpbacked Horse.* Petipa retired from the Imperial Theatre in 1903, as a result of the failure of his ballet *The Magic Mirror.* For a detailed biography of Petipa by Yuri Slonimsky, trans. from the Russian by Anatole Chujoy, see *Dance Index* (May–June, 1947); see also *Russian Ballet Master: The Memoirs of Marius Petipa,* ed. by Lillian Moore, trans. from the Russian by Helen Wittaker (N.Y., 1958); also "The Petipa Family in Europe and America," by Lillian Moore, *Dance Index* (May, 1942).

Petit, Roland, contemporary French dancer and choreographer, b. Villemomble, France, 1924; m. Renée Jeanmaire. Studied dance with Gustave Ricaux at Paris Opéra; became a member of the corps de ballet (1939). First important role was as Carmelo in *L'Amour Sorcier* (1943). During World War II gave some concert performances with Janine Charrat and began to choreograph, his first successes being at the Salle Pleyel, Paris, with *Orphée, Rêve d'Amour.* Jean Cocteau and Christian Bérard gave him artistic support. Left Paris Opéra in 1944, presenting Soirées de la Danse at Théâtre Sarah Bernhardt with Irène Lidova. His first major success was *Les Forains,* presented at Théâtre des Champs-Elysées, Mar. 2, 1945, with the financial assistance of his father, Edmond Petit. From 1945 to 1947 was choreographer, ballet master, and principal dancer of Ballets des Champs-Elysées, which he founded with Boris Kochno. Among his ballets of this period are *Le Rendez-vous, La Fiancée du Diable, Les Amours de Jupiter, Le Jeune Homme et la Mort, Treize Danses, Le Bal des Blanchisseuses.* After three years, Petit broke with the company and founded Les Ballets de Paris de Roland Petit (1948) which had its initial season at the Théâtre Marigny. For the première of *Les Demoiselles de la Nuit* (May 21, 1948), he invited Margot Fonteyn to appear, thereby ensuring one of those "tout Paris" openings so dear to Parisians. *L'Oeuf à la Coque, Carmen,* and *La Croqueuse de Diamants* also belong to this period. Toured U.S. and Europe; worked in Hollywood (1952), choreographing the Danny Kaye film *Hans Christian Andersen,* in which he also danced with Renée Jeanmaire. Re-organized Ballets de Paris de Roland Petit (1953), creating *Le Loup, Deuil en 24 Heures, Ciné-Bijou, Lady in the Ice.* This group also toured Europe and U.S. His flair for the theatre was shown in his Revue des Ballets de Paris for Jeanmaire, but he reverted to ballet with a season in Feb., 1958 at the Alhambra Theatre, Paris (*La Dame dans la Lune, Contre-Pointe, Rose des Vents*). A N.Y. season and short U.S. tour followed. Presented *Cyrano de Bergerac* at the Alhambra Theatre (1959), a full-evening ballet which also played in Brussels and London. Presented his wife as a music hall star in a show called simply

Zizi, her nick-name. Petit has not choreographed an outstanding work since 1953, but is currently preparing himself for a return to serious choreography at the Paris Opéra. For companies other than his own he has staged *Ballabile* (1950) for Sadler's Wells (now Royal) Ballet, and *La Chaloupée* for the Royal Danish Ballet (1961), for which company he has also staged his *Carmen* and *Cyrano de Bergerac*. The film *Black Tights* (1960, released in U.S. in 1962) consisted of four Petit ballets: *La Croqueuse de Diamants, Cyrano de Bergerac, Deuil en 24 Heures* (re-titled *A Merry Mourning*), and *Carmen*. In 1962 and 1963 he was commissioned by the Fine Arts Department to present seasons of ballet at the Chaillot Theatre, known as Festival Populaire du Ballet.

Petits Rats (lit., little rats), the name given to the children of the Paris Opéra Ballet school.

Petits Riens, Les. Ballet by Jean Georges Noverre, set to music by Wolfgang Amadeus Mozart, first produced in Paris (1778). The ballet was staged at the Old Vic Theatre, London, by Ninette de Valois (1928) and for Ballet Rambert at the Mercury Theatre by Frederick Ashton (1928). Ruth Page also staged *Les Petits Riens* for Ballet for America (1946).

Petits Tours, in ballet, a generic term for short, fast turns by which the dancer progresses in a straight line or in a circle. Most often used are coupé, piqué, déboulé. A series of such turns done in a circle around the stage is called manège; done in a straight line it is called chainé.

Petroff, Paul (Paul Eilif Wilhelm Petersen), contemporary dancer, teacher, b. Elsinore, Denmark; m. Nana Gollner. Studied dance with Katja Lindhart in Copenhagen and made his debut in concert performances with Violet Fischer in Denmark (1930). Premier danseur Col. de Basil's Ballet Russe and Original Ballet Russe (1932–43), dancing a large repertoire and creating Paolo Malatesta (*Francesca da Rimini*), Florentine Youth (*Paganini*), among others. He excelled particularly as a partner in classic roles. Principal dancer with Ballet (now American Ballet) Theatre (1943–45); season with International Ballet, in London and on tour in England (1947). Since 1948 has undertaken occasional tours with Nana Gollner in South America and U.S., but now mainly teaches in California.

Petrouchka. Ballet in 4 scenes; chor.: Michel Fokine; music: Igor Stravinsky; book: Igor Stravinsky and Alexandre Benois; décor: Alexandre Benois. First prod.: Diaghilev Ballets Russes, Théâtre du Châtelet, Paris, June 13, 1911, with Vaslav Nijinsky (Petrouchka), Tamara Karsavina (Ballerina), Alexandre Orlov (Moor), Enrico Cecchetti (Charlatan). Considered one of Fokine's greatest masterpieces and possibly Nijinsky's greatest role, *Petrouchka* has been in the repertoire of most major ballet companies. Fokine re-staged it for the Original Ballet Russe, N.Y., Nov. 21, 1940, with Yurek Lazowski (Petrouchka), Tamara Toumanova (Ballerina), Alberto Alonso (Moor), Marian Ladré (Charlatan); for Ballet (now American Ballet) Theatre, N.Y., Oct. 8, 1942, with Irina Baronova, Lazowski, Richard Reed (Moor), Simon Semenoff (Charlatan). Apart from Nijinsky some of the names most frequently associated with the title role are Leonide Massine, Leon Woicikowski, Stanislas Idzikowski, Yurek Shabelevsky, and Borge Ralov (in the version staged by Fokine for Royal Danish Ballet). More recently Nicholas Beriosoff staged *Petrouchka* for London's Festival Ballet (1950), with Anton Dolin (an outstanding Moor in the final Diaghilev years) in the title role. Serge Grigoriev revived it for Royal Ballet, Royal Opera House, Covent Garden, London, Mar. 26, 1957, with Alexander Grant (Petrouchka), Margot Fonteyn (Ballerina), Peter Clegg (Moor). Petrouchka, the Ballerina, and the Moor are three puppets displayed at fairs by the Charlatan. In the great square of St. Petersburg they dance for the populace. But Petrouchka is in love with the Ballerina who entices him only to have the jealous, stupid Moor punish poor Petrouchka. They run through the square and the Moor kills Petrouchka, making off with the Ballerina. The horrified onlookers call for the policeman, but the Charlatan, returning to find the square in an uproar over the terrible event, picks up the dead body and shows that it is only sawdust after all. As everyone leaves, the Charlatan drags the body away but, just as he is about to disappear, the tormented soul of Petrouchka rises from behind the puppets' booth and curses him.

Phaedra. Modern dance work; chor.: Martha Graham; music: Robert Starer; décor: Isamu Noguchi; costumes: Martha Graham. First prod.: Martha Graham and Dance Company, Broadway Theatre, N.Y., Mar. 4, 1962, with Martha Graham (Phaedra), Paul Taylor (Theseus), Bertram Ross (Hippolytus), Ethel Winter (Aphrodite), Helen McGehee (Artemis). This legend of Phaedra and her love for her stepson Hippolytus continues the long line of Graham re-creations of the mighty Greek myths.

Phèdre. Ballet in 1 act; chor.: Serge Lifar; décor and book: Jean Cocteau, a choreographic tragedy based on the Greek legend; music: Georges Auric. First prod.: Paris Opéra, Paris Opéra Ballet, June 14, 1950, with Tamara Toumanova (Phèdre), Serge Lifar (Hippolyte), Lycette Darsonval (Oenone), Liane Daydé (Aricie), Roger Ritz (Thesée). The ballet follows the famous story in a formal style, which is largely mime. A little stage, at the back of the stage proper opens its curtains from time to time to show, in tableau form, the progress of the drama.

Philadelphia Ballet, The. See LITTLEFIELD BALLET.

Philippart, Nathalie, French dancer, b. Bordeaux, France; m. Jean Babilée. Pupil of Lubov Egorova. Started her professional career in Soirées de la Danse organized by Irène Lidova (1944). Leading dancer with Ballets des Champs-Elysées (1945–48), dancing *Jeu de Cartes* (Queen of Spades), *Déjeuner sur l'Herbe, La Sylphide* (Effie), *Les Amours de Jupiter* (Danae), and (her greatest role) the Girl in *Le Jeune Homme et la Mort.* Danced Psyche in *Amour et son Amour* (Jean Babilée's first ballet, 1948). Guest artist with her husband, Jean Babilée, when he danced with American Ballet Theatre (1951).

Phillips, Ailne, English dancer and teacher, b. Londonderry, Northern Ireland, 1905. Studied with Lydia Kyasht, Margaret Craske, Ninette de Valois. Première danseuse and ballet mistress, Carl Rosa Opera Company until 1931. Joined Vic-Wells (later Sadler's Wells, now Royal) Ballet as soloist (1932–37), dancing in *Les Sylphides, Les Rendez-vous,* and many ballets in the early repertoire of that company. Principal, Sadler's Wells School (1940); personal assistant to Ninette de Valois, head teacher of dancing and repetiteur, Sadler's Wells Ballet (1946). In Turkey mounted ballets for Ankara State Opera Ballet Company (1960). Currently personal assistant to director of Royal Ballet and professor of dancing to that company.

Photographers, Dance (England). Ballet photography in England is a flourishing art and only a few names can be included out of many. Pioneers in the profession were J. W. Debenham (d. 1958) who photographed the early days of the Vic-Wells and Sadler's Wells companies, and Gordon Anthony (b. 1902), a half-brother of Ninette de Valois, whose published books include *Ballet Russe de*

Monte Carlo, Alicia Markova, Leonide Massine, Robert Helpmann, and *The Sadler's Wells Ballet.* He gave up photography in 1953. Later photographers have included Baron (Baron Nahum, 1906–56) whose published works include *Baron at the Ballet, Baron Encore,* and *Ballet Finale;* Anthony Crickmay; Mike Davis, whose books include *Mike Davis at the Royal Ballet,* and *Ballet in Camera,* and who directed the film *Background to Ballet;* Peggy Delius; Zoe Dominic, who accompanied the Royal Ballet to the U.S.S.R. as official photographer (1961); Felix (Hookham) Fonteyn, brother of Margot Fonteyn; Angus McBean; Edward Mandinian; Houston Rogers (b. 1902), a theatre photographer who has specialized in ballet and opera photography since 1950; Roy Round; Merlyn Severn, a pioneer of ballet in performance photography whose books include *Ballet in Action* and *The Sadler's Wells Ballet at Covent Garden;* Tunbridge-Sidgwick; G. B. L. Wilson; Paul Wilson; Roger Wood, whose books include *Katherine Dunham* (text by Richard Buckle), *The Sadler's Wells Ballet at the Royal Opera House, New York City Ballet In Action* (text by P. W. Manchester).

Photographers, Dance (U.S.). Although it cannot be said that there are photographers in the U.S., or anywhere else for that matter, who devote themselves entirely to dance, there is an appreciable number of excellent photographers who specialize in dance along with other theatrical forms and occasionally with fashion. Generally, a photographer specializing in dance is one who is also interested in dance as an art form. As to their fields of work, photographers can be divided into studio, studio-and-location, and location categories. [These fields are indicated by the initials (s), (sl) and (l) after the names of the photographers.] The divisions are of course not absolute, i.e. a studio photographer may go out on location once in a while and a location photographer may prefer to work in his studio. Within these limitations the following, in alphabetical order, are the best known practitioners: Chris Alexander (sl), N.Y.; Radford Bascome (sl), N.Y.; Marcus Blechman (s), N.Y.; Constantine (sl), Los Angeles; Arnold Eagle (sl), N.Y.; Fred Fehl (l), N.Y.; Paul Himmel (s), N.Y.; Marthe Krueger (sl), N.Y.; Louis Mélançon (sl), official photographer Metropolitan Opera House, N.Y.; Jack Mitchell (sl), N.Y.; Maurice Seymour (s), N.Y.; Wayne J. Shilkret (l), N.Y.; Vladimir Sladon (sl), N.Y.; Robert Sosenko (sl), N.Y.; William Stone (sl), N.Y.; Martha Swope (sl), official photographer, New York City Ballet, N.Y. Several photographers have had books of their photos published, among them: Constantine (*Souvenirs de Ballet,* San Diego, Calif., 1946); Maurice Seymour (*Seymour on Ballet,* N.Y., 1947; *Ballet Portraits,* N.Y., 1952); Paul Himmel (*Ballet in Action,* text by Walter Terry, N.Y., 1954); Albert E. Kahn (*Days With Ulanova,* photos and text, N.Y., 1962); Jack Mitchell (*An American Dance Portfolio,* N.Y., 1964); Martha Swope (*Murka,* a book about George Balanchine's cat with text by Tanaquil LeClercq, N.Y., 1964; by LeRoy Leatherman, *Martha Graham; Portrait of the Lady as an Artist,* N.Y., 1966). In addition, Miss Swope's photographs illustrate the souvenir programs of the New York City Ballet.

Photography, Amateur Dance.

Seasoned dance photographers have worked out for themselves a couple of rules to which amateur dance photographers might adhere. These rules ensure minimal friction with the management, stagehands and audience, yet permit them to take as many pictures as they desire. The first rule is to obtain permission to photograph from the management; the second is never to take pictures from an orchestra seat. The amateur photographer should buy a seat in a box or a place in standing room. At the Metropolitan Opera House, for example, the third or fourth box of the first tier is an excellent location. Since the seats in the boxes are not numbered, it is advisable to come to the theatre early in order to get the most conveniently placed chair or a choice standing room spot. The best location for a standee is about one-quarter of the distance away from the stage; at other theatres the ideal location is the first row center of the balcony.

When taking pictures from the sides of a theatre the photographer loses about twenty percent of the stage arena, but is compensated by an unobstructed view of the rest of the stage. He must be careful in selecting sides, so as not to miss important dancing or action. The fear that the described locations are too far from the stage is unwarranted because the somewhat greater distance from the stage permits the photographer more leeway in focusing and exposure. The professional photographer knows that the farther the object is from the camera, the greater is the depth of focus and the lower the speed necessary to freeze movement. The falling off of the size of the image is not too great a disadvantage, considering the opportunities gained.

Good stage shots are very difficult to take. All the odds are against you: you are restricted in your movements, the light is bad, you have no control over your subjects, you cannot focus properly. If you are a balletomane-photographer, however, these odds and a dozen others will offer no discouragement. However, the following hints on the technique of dance photography are of proven value to the amateur as well as the professional.

Don't attempt to shoot stage pictures unless your camera is equipped with at least an f:2.8 lens; if you are the fortunate possessor of a still faster lens, you have an advantage. Use the fastest film available for your camera and don't worry about grain; it is more satisfying to get a grainy negative than none at all, and fine-grain development takes care of much of the grain. Divide mentally all dance productions into three categories of lighting: strong, medium, and dark. Shoot most pictures at 1/50 of a second, at f:3.5 or 2.8 in strong light; at f:2.8 or 2 in medium light; and at f:1.5 or not at all in dark light. All this applies, obviously, to slow movements and poses. Fast movements must be shot at much faster speeds. Never attempt to shoot pictures of a production you are seeing the first time.

Dance photography is subject to a few tricks which amateurs learn through experience:

If you ask a dancer how long she can hold a pose on toe, she will tell you anything from a second to a minute. Actually, she seldom holds it longer than 1/10, perhaps 1/5, of a second. Either she freezes up, destroying all suggestion of freedom and spontaneity, or she begins to wobble. There are exceptions, of course, but we are speaking of the average dancer. There is one single moment at which the step culminates into a pose; this moment, depending on the pose, may last from 1/300 to 1/5 of a second. To determine this moment is one of the most important of the photographer's jobs, but to anticipate the moment, to foresee it a split second before it arrives is still more important. The recognition and the anticipation of the right moment determines the success of your picture.

The amateur photographer will find it necessary to develop an even acuter sense of anticipation when attempting to photograph movements, particularly turns and leaps. Only one-quarter of a complete turn is of any use to the photographer—that is the quarter during which the dancer faces directly front. In a single turn this position appears twice: once when the dancer begins the turn and once when she finishes it. Neither one of them is any good for a picture. One must learn to photograph the preparation or the termination, not the turn proper. To photograph multiple turns try to catch the beginning of the second or third turn, or (and this can be done only off stage), station yourself in back of the dancer and catch her on the second quarter of the turn when she faces the camera. Turns on toe are very fast and should be shot at 1/300 of a second or faster—lens, film, and lights permitting.

The most exciting pictures are those of dancers in the air—jumps and leaps. More than any step, a properly executed and well defined leap depicts the kinesthetic beauty of dance, especially of ballet. Every leap, every straight jump, has a peak: it is the moment when the ascending movement has just stopped and the descending one has not yet begun. Again, in order to catch a leap at its peak one must anticipate it. When one sees it, it is generally too late to shoot. Pictures of dancers in the air should be shot from a low angle; this adds elevation to the dancer's jump and makes for a more dramatic picture. 1/250 is the slowest speed ever successfully used to shoot dancers in the air.

Not all people in dance are agreed on the value of amateur, candid photographs of dancers. Most dancers and spectators feel that the amateur photographer performs a definite service to dance when he catches the fleeting moments of a dance composition. Others are of the opinion that candid photographs of dancers are worse than none at all. Lincoln Kirstein in his *Blast at Ballet* (N.Y., 1938) says the following:

"The candid camera in the hands of most news-photographers and the average eager amateur, is the worst liar in the photographic family. Under the guise of an objective and frank reporter, the candid-camera distorts, alters, and ultimately destroys the very dances it pretends to document. In the first place, the candid operator has usually to stand in the wings, on one side of the stage. At best, if placed in a prompter's box, he is too near to include the whole stage-picture, and from his seat he is too far away. Hence, nearly every shot is an angle-shot to start with, snapped from a place where no one in the audience has ever seen the ballet, and from where the choreographer never intended it to have been seen. If a considerable number of candid shots could be reproduced in sequence, an approximation of a record of motion might possibly be obtained. By a considerable number I mean fifty, not twenty. But lacking this, the ballet snapshot is usually seized out of its legitimate context, to accentuate an accidental if spectacular leap, or some astonishing motion only effective in a camera print, but which has little or no connection with the ballet as it is seen by an audience in the intended procedure of its performance."

Picasso, Pablo Ruiz, Spanish painter, b. Málaga, 1881, resident of France. He designed décor and costumes for the following ballets: *Parade* (1917), *The Three-Cornered Hat* (1919), *Pulcinella* (1920), *Cuadro Flamenco* (1921), and the drop curtain for *Le Train Bleu* (1924), all for the Diaghilev Ballets Russes; Mercure (1924), for Les Soirées de Paris; a drop curtain for *Les Rendez-vous* (1946), for Ballets des Champs-Elysées. Picasso's first wife, Olga Khokhlova, was a dancer with the Diaghilev company and a sister of ballerina Vera Nemtchinova.

Picnic At Tintagel. Ballet in 1 act, 3 scenes; chor.: Frederick Ashton; music: Arnold Bax's *The Garden of Fand;* book: Frederick Ashton; décor: Cecil Beaton. First prod.: New York City Ballet, City Center, N.Y., Feb. 28, 1952, with Diana Adams (Wife-Iseult), Jacques d'Amboise (Lover-Tristram), Robert Barnett (Caretaker-Merlin), Francisco Moncion (Husband-King Mark). Some Edwardian picnickers amid the ruins of King Arthur's castle are transported back in time to relive the Tristram and Iseult legend. Jacques d'Amboise danced his first leading role in this ballet.

Pied (Fr.), foot.

Pied Piper, The. Ballet in 1 act; chor.: Jerome Robbins; music: Aaron Copland's Clarinet Concerto. First prod.: New York City Ballet, City Center, N.Y., Dec. 4, 1951, with Janet Reed, Diana Adams, Tanaquil LeClercq, Jillana, Nicholas Magallanes, Roy Tobias, Todd Bolender, Herbert Bliss, Jerome Robbins, and almost the entire company. The stage was open to its back wall and the dancers wore a miscellaneous collection of practice costumes. The player of the clarinet at one side of the stage acted as the Pied Piper to whose tune they had to dance themselves into exhaustion. Although no one realized it at the time, *The Pied Piper* was the ballet which started Robbins in the direction of modern jazz which subsequently led to the creation of his company, Ballets: U.S.A., with its specialized repertoire.

Piège de Lumière. Ballet in 1 act, 3 scenes; chor.: John Taras; music: Jean-Michel Damase; book: Philippe Hériat; décor: Felix Labisse; costumes: André Levasseur. First prod.: Grand Ballet du Marquis de Cuevas, Théâtre de l'Empire, Paris, Dec. 23, 1952, with Rosella Hightower (Morphide), Serge Golovine (Iphias), Vladimir Skouratoff (Prisoner). This is probably Taras's best work and was one of the most successful productions of the Grand Ballet. The story is of escaped convicts in a tropical forest attempting to capture the exotic butterflies. One of the youngest prisoners seeks to take possession of the marvelous Morphide, but the male butterfly, an Iphias, in his efforts to save her, covers the prisoner with his pollen so that he becomes mad and believes that he has been transformed into an Iphias. Taras revived the work for the New York City Ballet, premièred Oct. 1, 1964, at the N.Y. State Theater, Lincoln Center, with Maria Tallchief, Arthur Mitchell, and André Prokovsky in the principal roles.

Pierre, Dorothi Bock, contemporary writer and journalist, b. Chicago, Ill. She began her professional career as a dancer, appearing in musical comedy and in concert performances; was also a soloist with the Michel Fokine Ballet for two years. Gave a series of lectures on the History of Dance at Univ. of Oregon (1933), and since then has written many articles on dance, lectured on dance and drama, and acted as press and public relations director for many organizations, including Ballet Russe de Monte Carlo, Hurok Attractions, Inc., American Ballet Theatre, etc. She is also publicity director for the Greek Theatre Association, Los Angeles, and Hollywood Bowl Association.

Pierrot, one of the stock characters of commedia dell'arte, a fool with white face wearing a white costume with long, loose sleeves and a conical hat over a black skull cap, a romantic but pathetic character. Pierrot was a popular character in ballets of the 19th century and in the famous mime plays of the two Jean-Caspard Debureaus, father and son (whose tradition survives in today's pantomimist, Marcel Marceau). He is one of the characters in Michel Fokine's *Carnaval,* and there are five of him in Ray Powell's *One in Five.* He is the principal character in the mime plays of the Tivoli Pantomime Theatre, Copenhagen.

Pillar of Fire. Ballet in 1 act; chor. and book: Antony Tudor; music: Arnold Schönberg's *Verklärte Nacht;* décor: Jo Mielziner. First prod.: Ballet (now American Ballet) Theatre, Metropolitan Opera House, N.Y., Apr. 8, 1942, with Nora Kaye (Hagar), Lucia Chase (Eldest Sister), Annabelle Lyon (Youngest Sister), Antony Tudor (Friend), Hugh Laing (Young Man from the House Opposite). *Pillar of Fire* follows the idea of a poem by Richard Dehmel which inspired Schönberg's composition. Hagar, fearing that she has lost the love of her Friend to her frivolous Youngest Sister, and seeing in the Eldest Sister the spinster which she herself must become, gives herself to a dissolute young man, but later finds peace in the gentle and understanding love of the Friend. The setting is a small town at the turn of the century. *Pillar of Fire* raised Nora Kaye to the rank of ballerina and her name is inextricably linked with the ballet. Tudor did not stage this work for any other company until Dec. 30, 1962, when it was presented by the Royal Swedish Ballet with Mariane Orlando (Hagar), Conny Borg (Young Man from the House Opposite), Verner Klavsen (Friend). Antony Tudor revived the work for the American Ballet Theatre's Jan.–Feb., 1966, season at the N.Y. State Theatre, when Sallie Wilson and Veronika Mlakar danced Hagar, Bruce Marks the Young Man, and Gayle Young the Friend. The same cast also danced the ballet during the tour of the Soviet Union (summer, 1966).

Pineapple Poll. Ballet in 1 act, 3 scenes; chor.: John Cranko; music: Arthur Sullivan (from the Gilbert and Sullivan operas *The Mikado, Trial by Jury, The Sorcerer, Patience, The Gondoliers, Cox and Box, Pirates of Penzance, Ruddigore, Princess Ida, Yeomen of the Guard,* and a brief excerpt from Sullivan's orchestral work *Overtura di Ballo*), arr. by Charles Mackerras; décor: Osbert Lancaster. First prod.: Sadler's Wells Theatre Ballet at Sadler's Wells Theatre, London, Mar. 13, 1951, with Elaine Fifield (Poll), David Blair (Captain Belaye), David Poole (Jasper). Freely based on W.S. Gilbert's poem, "The Bumboat Woman's Story" (from his *Bab Ballads*), the story tells how Captain Belaye was so irresistible that all the ladies of Portsmouth deserted their sailor husbands, taking their places as members of Belaye's crew, only to find that Captain Belaye was married that morning. Poll is consoled by the faithful potboy, Jasper. Copyright on the Sullivan music for the Gilbert and Sullivan operas expired in 1951 and Cranko was first in the dance field to use the music (which is now in public domain). The ballet is also in the repertoire of the National Ballet of Canada and the Australian Ballet.

Piper, John, English artist and designer, b. 1903. His designs for ballet, both décor and costumes, include *The Quest* (1943), *Job* (second version, 1948), *The Shadow* (1953), all for Sadler's Wells (now Royal) Ballet; *Sea Change* (1949), *Harlequin in April* (1951), both for Sadler's Wells Theatre Ballet; *The Prince of the Pagodas* (décor only, 1957), for the Royal Ballet.

Piqué, in ballet, the movement of stepping directly onto point of supporting foot. The working leg may be in a variety of poses.

Pirouette, in ballet, a turn on one foot, the motive power for which is supplied by a swing of the arm. Multiple pirouettes from the impetus of the original swing of the arm are part of the technical equipment of the virtuoso male dancer. Three or (rarely) four pirouettes on toe are the equivalent for a girl though, when supported by a partner, she can execute many more. The many varieties of pirouette include: pirouette en dehors (turn in the direction of the working leg, and the pirouette most usually performed); pirouette en dedans (turn in the direction of the supporting leg); pirouette sur le cou-de-pied (turn with the working leg at the ankle of the other leg), and others. They can be performed in place, en manège, and chaîné. A pirouette in the air is called tour en l'air. A grande pirouette begins like a simple pirouette, but continues with a series of turns on one foot, the other leg being raised to form an angle of 90°.

Pistolets. See AILES DE PIGEON.

Pistoni, Mario, Italian dancer, b. Rome, 1932. Studied at the ballet school of Teatro dell'Opera, Rome. Became soloist of Teatro alla Scala, Milan (1951), and subsequently premier danseur. His repertoire includes all the classic and romantic ballets, among them *Cinderella, The Nutcracker, Ballet Imperial, Allegro Brillante, La Sylphide, Giselle, Les Sylphides,* and others.

Place in the Desert, A. Ballet in 1 act; chor. and book: Norman Morrice; music: Carlos Surinach's *David and Bathsheba* (originally composed for John Butler's work of that name for CBS television); décor: Ralph Koltai. First prod.: Ballet Rambert, Sadler's Wells Theatre, London, July 25, 1961, with John Chesworth (Village Elder), Gillian Martlew (His Daughter), Kenneth Bannerman (His Heir), Norman Morrice (Company Agent). The conflict between tribal traditions and western engineering, combined with the love of the European engineer for the tribesman's daughter, which leads to a violent struggle between the engineer and the girl's brother.

Placide, Mme. See DOUVILLIER, SUZANNE THEODORE.

Plaisted, Ronald, contemporary English dancer, b. Newport, Monmouthshire; m. Patricia Thorogood. Joined Sadler's Wells Theatre Ballet (1946); became member of Sadler's Wells (now Royal) Ballet (1948) and is currently a soloist. Dances Spanish Dance (*Swan Lake*), Mother Simone (*La Fille Mal Gardée*), and others.

Planets, The. Ballet in 1 act, 4 scenes; chor.: Antony Tudor; music: Gustav Holst's score of that name; décor: Hugh Stevenson. First prod.: Ballet Rambert, Mercury Theatre, London, Oct. 28, 1934, with Pearl Argyle and William Chappell (Mortals born under Venus), Maude Lloyd (the Planet Venus), Hugh Laing (Mortal born under Mars), Diana Gould (the Planet Mars), Kyra Nijinsky (Mortal born under Neptune), Antony Tudor (the Planet Neptune). A fourth section (performed third in the order) was added for London Ballet, Toynbee Hall, London, Jan. 23, 1939, with Peggy van Praagh (Mortal born under Mercury), Guy Massey (the Planet Mercury). This version was first given by Ballet Rambert, June 20, 1940, Arts Theatre, London, when Frank Staff danced the Planet Mercury. The ballet, usually considered Tudor's first major work, was in four separate sections, each section being choreographed in accordance with the supposed astrological significance of the various planets. The ballet was Kyra Nijinsky's (Vaslav Nijinsky's daughter) introduction to England as a dancer.

Planets, The. Ballet in 7 scenes; chor.: Erich Walter; music: Gustav Holst; décor: Heinrich Wendel; costumes: Xenia Chris. First prod.: Vienna State Opera, Nov. 22, 1961, with Christl Zimmerl (Venus), Willy Dirtl (Mars), Karl Musil (Neptune), Paul Vondrak (Mercury). The music and choreography express, in an "esoteric astrology," the dispositions and influences of the Planets upon the nature and fate of men.

Platoff, Marc. See PLATT, MARC.

Platt, Marc (Marcel Le Plat), dancer, choreographer, director, b. Seattle, Wash., 1915. Studied dance at Cornish School and with Mary Ann Wells. After playing stock with Seattle Repertory Playhouse, joined Col. de Basil's Ballets Russes de Monte Carlo under the name of Marc Platoff and quickly rose from corps de ballet to create Old Shepherd (*Symphonie Fantastique,* 1936), Gianciotto Malatesta (*Francesca da Rimini*), King Dodon (*Coq d'Or,* both in 1937). Joined the Massine–Blum Ballet Russe de Monte Carlo as soloist (1938–42), creating Devil (*Devil's Holiday*), Sacher Masoch (*Bacchanale*), Leader of the Black Group (*Rouge et Noir*), and others; also danced Officer (*Gaîté Parisienne*), Hilarion (*Giselle*), Spirit of Creation (*Seventh Symphony*), etc. Featured dancer in original cast of *Oklahoma!* (1943) from which time he has used the name Marc Platt. Acted and

Marc Platt, dancer, actor, director of Ballet of Radio City Music Hall, N.Y.

danced in many Hollywood motion pictures, particularly noteworthy being *Tonight and Every Night,* in which his "Dictator's" dance remains a highlight in movie choreography and performance, and *Seven Brides for Seven Brothers* in which he was one of the redheaded brothers. Acted and danced in summer stock on West Coast. Became Director of the Ballet and producer at Radio City Music Hall, N.Y. (1962).

Playford, John, author of *The English Dancing Master,* published in 1651 in England. The complete title of this collection of 104 social dances is: *The English Dancing Master: or, Plaine and easie rules for the Dancing of Country Dances, with the tunes to each dance.*

Pleasant, Richard (1909–1961), ballet director and publicity man, b. Denver, Colo. Educated at Princeton Univ., from which he was graduated an architect. After several years in Hollywood as an artists' representative he came to N.Y. as manager of the Mordkin Ballet during its 1937–38 season. Out of this company he and Lucia Chase, then a ballerina of the company, organized the American Ballet Theatre which gave its first performances in 1940. It was largely due to his insistence that Antony Tudor was brought over from England as choreographer. Pleasant resigned his position as the company director after its second season (1941). During World War II he served in the U.S. Army. After tours in the cavalry and artillery he was transferred to Special Services with the rank of captain. His assignment was the overseeing of the entertainment of troops overseas. In 1949 he joined Isadora Bennett in her public relations firm which helped to present many modern dance attractions on and off Broadway. From 1954 to 1958 he was manager of the McCarter Theatre on the Princeton Univ. campus. He died July 5, 1961, of uremic poisoning.

Pleiades of Blasis. The name given to six pupils of Carlo Blasis who all became well known dancers during the middle part of the 19th century. They were Marietta Baderna, Augusta Domenichettis, Flora Fabbri, Amalia Ferraris, Sofia Fuoco, Carolina Granzini.

Pleshcheev, Alexander (1858–1945), Russian journalist, critic, and historian of ballet. Author of monumental Russian volume *Nash Balet* (Our Ballet), published in 1892 and 1899. Left Russia in 1918 and settled in Paris, where he published several small works on the ballet in the Russian language.

Plié, in ballet, bending the knees. Grand plié designates a deep bend, raising heels from floor to achieve full position; demi-plié, bending the knees as far as they can go without lifting the heels from the floor. It has been said that the entire technique of ballet consists in knowing when and how to do a plié. Plié is a very important exercise for the dancer in class and one of the most important parts of ballet technique. Plié is inherent in all turns and jumps; upon its proper execution depends the effectiveness of most ballet steps.

Plisetskaya, Maya, Peoples' Artist of the U.S.S.R., Soviet prima ballerina, b. 1925. Entered Bolshoi School in 1934 and was graduated from it in 1943 (class of Yelizaveta Gerdt). She attracted attention when she was eleven and twelve years old, respectively, dancing the Breadcrumb Fairy in *The Sleeping Beauty* and Pussy in *Baby Stork*. After her performance of the Grand Pas from *Paquita* (1941), two years before graduation, it became obvious that the school possessed a budding ballerina. Owing to wartime conditions, Plisetskaya performed many solo parts in the Bolshoi repertoire before her graduation so that her transition into the company (1943) was hardly perceptible. She never danced in the corps de ballet and in her first official season at the Bolshoi Theatre she had already performed more than twenty important roles in ballets and in opera divertissements. During that first season she was fortunate to be able to study in the classe de perfection of Professor Agrippina Vaganova, then working for one year in Moscow, and to rehearse with her the Mazurka in *Chopiniana,* the Lilac Fairy in *The Sleeping Beauty,* and Masha in *The Nutcracker*. In 1945 she passed her ballerina examination by dancing the title role in Leonid Lavrovsky's new version of *Raymonda*. In Apr., 1947, she danced Odette-Odile in *Swan Lake* for the first time, with extraordinary success. Her beautiful arms as Odette and the brilliance of her technique as Odile, coupled with a deep insight into the dual nature of the character, brought her immediate recognition, and Odette-Odile remains her greatest role. She soon added Aurora (*The Sleeping Beauty*), Myrtha (*Giselle*), and the Tzar-Maiden (*The Humpbacked Horse*) to her repertoire. In Soviet ballets her greatest roles are the Bird-Maiden (*Shurale*), Zarema (*The Fountain of Bakhchisarai*) and the heroic title role in *Laurencia* which Vakhtang Chabukiani staged for the Bolshoi (1956). More recent successes are Aegina (*Spartacus*) and the Mistress of the Copper Mountain (*The Stone Flower*). Plisetskaya has an extraordinary ability to make her body act as an obedient instrument to convey whatever plastic style and image she is portraying. Her musicality and phrasing are extraordinary. Her constant search for perfection has led her into new avenues. She worked on the role of Juliet in *Romeo and Juliet* for more than five years before she danced it, with great success, for the first time Dec. 28, 1961, creating a new portrayal—individual and utterly different from the original Juliet of Galina Ulanova. Plisetskaya is a niece of Asaf and

Maya Plisetskaya, prima ballerina of The Moscow Bolshoi Ballet.

Sulamith Messerer. She is married to the talented young composer Rodin Shchedrin, and dances the Tzar-Maiden to his new score for *The Humpbacked Horse* (1960), and a Russian dance in his opera *Not by Love Alone* (1961). She has danced in India, Czechoslovakia, Hungary, Germany, U.S., Canada, and France, where she had an overwhelming success as guest artist with the Paris Opéra in the autumn of 1961, and again in 1964. She was prima ballerina of the Bolshoi Ballet when the company danced in the U.S. on its third American tour (Apr.–June, 1966).

Plucis, Harijs, dancer, teacher, ballet master, b. Riga, Latvia, 1900. Graduated from the Latvian National Ballet School in Riga, Latvia, and in 1920 was engaged by the Riga National Opera, quickly becoming the company's first male dancer. His roles included the leading male roles in *Swan Lake, Raymonda, Coppélia, Don Quixote, The Sleeping Beauty, Les Sylphides,* as well as leads in national ballets such as *Ilga, Scaramouche, Milas Uzvara, Staburags,* and others. Studied with Nicholas Legat in Paris (1927); joined the Ida Rubinstein company (1928). Returned to Riga (1931) and founded its State Ballet School (1932), and was its director and principal teacher until 1944. Engaged as ballet master of Sadler's Wells (now Royal) Ballet (1947); remained until 1956. Between 1957 and Aug., 1961, was professor of dancing at the Zurich (Switzerland) Ballet Academy. Since Sept. 1, 1961, is head of the school and professor of dance at the Vienna State Opera House Ballet School; also gives class to the Vienna State Opera Ballet company.

Poe, Edgar Allan (1809–1849), American poet and short story writer whose famous poem *The Bells* is the basis for Ruth Page's ballet of the same namc. *The Masque of the Red Death* by Poe was also used for a ballet produced in Russia to music by Nicholas Tcherepnine.

Pointe, in ballet, the toe. The position of the foot in which there is a continuous straight line from the toe on which the dancer stands, through the instep, ankle, knee, and hip. The position of half-toe is called demi-pointe. The dance on pointe is characteristic of ballet, since of all forms of the theatrical dance only ballet uses it. In ballet, only women dance on pointes.

Poker Game. See CARD PARTY.

Polajenko, Nicholas, American dancer b. New York City, 1932, of Russian parents; m. Daphne Dale. A pupil of Ludmila Shollar and Anatole Vilzak, he began his professional career as guest artist with the Ottawa Ballet Company (Mar. 12, 1947), dancing the Prince in *The Nutcracker* and *Les Sylphides* with *Svetlana Beriosova,* who was also making her debut in this performance. A year later he left for Europe to join the Metropolitan Ballet in London. Later that year he transferred to Ballets des Champs-Elysées, continued with Roland Petit's Ballets de Paris as soloist, and went with that company to the U.S. (1950). Due to the dissolution of the company in the U.S., he remained in N.Y. and danced with the ballet of the Metropolitan Opera. After his return to Europe he joined London's Festival Ballet for the season 1954–55. From 1956 to 1962 he was a principal dancer of the Ballet International of the Marquis de Cuevas. After the Marquis' death and the eventual dissolution of his company, Polajenko free-lanced, then joined the troupe organized by George Skibine. Joined the Harkness Ballet as guest artist for the 1964–65 season.

Polka, a Bohemian folk dance in 2/4 time which originated in the 1830's and became popular in all countries of Central and Eastern Europe; often danced as a ballroom dance.

Polka-Mazurka, a Polish variation of the polka, in 3/4 time, danced as a ballroom dance in countries of Eastern Europe.

Polonaise, Polish dance first recorded about 1645. It is a marched dance of dignity, originally a warriors' triumphal march, into which women partners were later introduced. The polonaise has often been used in classic as well as contemporary ballets, e.g. *Swan Lake, The Sleeping Beauty, The Fountain of Bakhchisarai,* George Balanchine's *Night Shadow,* and *Theme and Variations.*

Polovetsian Dances. See PRINCE IGOR.

Ponomaryov, Vladimir (1892–1951), Honored Artist of the RSFSR, leading Soviet male teacher. Ponomaryov was graduated from the ballet school of the former Maryinsky Theatre in 1910, though he appeared on the stage earlier, having played The Nutcracker in the ballet of that name in 1909. He danced with the Diaghilev Ballets Russes (1911, 1912); became premier danseur of the Maryinsky (1912), and by 1913 already had a leading position among the male dancers of the company, dancing a large repertoire. His importance in the history of Russian ballet lies in his teaching, which he began in 1913. After the revolution he became the leading Leningrad teacher for male dancers, his pupils including Pyotr Gusev, Alexander Yermolayev, Vakhtang Chabukiani, Konstantin Sergeyev, Nicolai Zubkovsky, among others. The choreographers Leonid Lavrovsky and Rostislav Zakharov were also his pupils. From 1919 until his death Ponomaryov also conducted a classe de perfection for male dancers at the Kirov Theatre. He choreographed several ballets and revived *La Sylphide* with new choreography in 1922.

Poole, David, South African dancer, choreographer, teacher, b. Cape Town, 1925. Studied at Cape Town Ballet School, Sadler's Wells Ballet School (1947), joining Sadler's Wells Theatre Ballet the same year and becoming principal dancer. He danced a large repertoire and was a notably fine dancer-actor, creating The Beast (*Beauty and the Beast*), Jasper (*Pineapple Poll*), Leonardo (*Blood Wedding*), leading role in Kenneth MacMillan's *Danses Concertantes;* also dancing Prince (*Swan Lake,* Act 2), male dancer (*Les Sylphides*), Master of Tregennis (*The Haunted Ballroom*), Pierrot (*Carnaval*), and others. With Ballet Rambert (1956), where he added Albrecht in *Giselle* to his repertoire. Danced with the Edinburgh International Ballet at the 1958 Edinburgh Festival. Has taught for Kurt Jooss at the Folkwangschule, Essen, Germany. Currently teacher, producer, and choreographer, Cape Town Univ. Ballet.

Popova, Nina, dancer and teacher, b. Novorossisk, Russia, 1922. Educated in Paris; studied dance with Olga Preobrajenska, Lubov Egorova, and others; and with Anatole Vilzak, Anatole Oboukhov, Igor Schwezoff in N.Y. Made her debut with Ballet de la Jeunesse in Paris and London (a company organized in 1937 by Egorova) and was a soloist with *Original Ballet Russe* (1939–41), dancing Competition Dance (*Graduation Ball*), Fairy solo in *Aurora's Wedding,* and others; soloist with Ballet (now American Ballet) Theatre (1941–42), creating Bathing Girl (*Aleko*); Ballet Russe de Monte Carlo (1943, 1947), her roles including the Can-Can Leader (*Gaîté Parisienne*), First Hand (*Le Beau Danube*), and others. Appeared in several musicals; danced a season with Ballet Alicia Alonso in Cuba; appeared in television shows, including "Your Show of Shows," of which she was a regular member. Joined the faculty of School of Performing Arts, N.Y. (1954) and, except for a two year period during which she taught ballet in Mexico City and staged and revived the classic repertoire for local companies, has been teaching at the school ever since. She has also been assistant choreographer for the Broadway musical *Girls Against the Boys* (1959) and in 1960 staged and choreographed an original musical comedy at the Birmingham Southern College, Ala.

Port de Bras, in ballet, movement of the arms.

Portefaix, Loulou, Swedish dancer, b. ca. 1935. Entered Royal Swedish Ballet School (1943); accepted into the company (1953). Studied in London at the Royal Ballet School and with Anna Northcote, and in Paris with Lubov Egorova. Among her roles are Lilac Fairy, (*The Sleeping Beauty*), Odette-Odile (*Swan Lake*), and Persephone in Birgit Aakesson's *Sisyphus.*

Porter, Cole (1892–1964), American composer. He wrote the score for the ballet *Within the Quota,* staged by Jean Börlin (Paris, 1923), and a number of musical comedies.

Pose, any motionless moment in a dance; an assumed posture, a position held for any length of time, as differentiated from movement or step; poses in ballet include attitude, arabesque, etc.

Posé, in ballet a poising of the body, made by stepping, with the knee straight, on to the pointe or half-pointe; a ballet step "held," such as an arabesque posé, for instance.

Positions of Feet. In ballet there are five positions of the feet: 1st pos., the balls of both feet are completely turned out, the heels touch and form a single straight line; 2nd pos., the balls of both feet are also on one line, but there is a distance of about twelve inches between the heels; 3rd pos., one foot is in front of the other, the heel of each foot touching the middle of the other foot; 4th pos., the toe of one foot is directly in front of the heel of the other, the feet are parallel and one short step apart; 5th pos., both feet touch so that the toe of one foot reaches the heel of the other.

Poulenc, Francis (1899–1963), French composer, b. Paris. Member of the group, "Les Six," and one of the five composers for Jean Börlin's *Les Mariés de la Tour Eiffel* (Ballets Suédois, 1921). Wrote the music for many other ballets, among them *Les Biches* (Bronislava Nijinska, Diaghilev Ballets Russes, 1924), *Aubade* (the original Nijinska version, 1929; also used by George Balanchine, 1934), *Les Animaux Modèles* (Paris Opéra, 1942). His music has often been used for dance works, one of the best known being *Les Masques* (Frederick Ashton for Ballet Rambert, 1933) to his Trio for Piano, Oboe and Bassoon; others being Walter Gore's *Paris-Soir* (1939) and *Hoops* (1953), both to piano pieces, the *Hoops* score being orchestrated by Leighton Lucas. Todd Bolender used his Sextet for Wind Instruments and Piano for a short-lived work, *The Masquers* (1957).

Poulsen, Ulla, Danish ballerina, b. Copenhagen, 1905. A graduate of the Royal Danish Ballet School, she became principal dancer of the Royal Danish Ballet in 1924. Toured France, Germany, and the Scandinavian countries (1927–33). Awarded the Danish decoration "Ingenio et Arte" (1934). Retired in 1939.

Powell, Ray (Needham), English dancer and choreographer, b. Hitchin, Herts, 1925. Studied at Sadler's Wells School (1941); joined Sadler's Wells (now Royal) Ballet (1942) where, except for Army service (1944–48), he remained untill the fall of 1962 when he obtained a leave of absence to join Australian Ballet Company as ballet master for the 1962–63 season. He was ranking soloist and assistant ballet master with Royal Ballet, his many character roles including Carabosse (*The Sleeping Beauty*), Czardas and Tutor (*Swan Lake*), Red King (*Checkmate*), Gravedigger (*Hamlet*); creations include Bootface (Royal Ballet's staging of *The Lady and the Fool*), Punchinello (*Veneziana*), and others. His ballet *One in Five,* first staged for the Sunday Ballet Club, is in the repertoire of Western Theatre Ballet, National Ballet of Canada, Illinois Ballet (Chicago), and Australian Ballet. Other works are *Sweet Echo* (1953) and *A Fool's Tale* (1961).

Powell, Robert, American modern dancer, b. Hawaii, 1941. Graduated from School of Performing Arts, N.Y. (1958), joining Martha Graham company of which he is currently a leading member, creating important roles in *Acrobats of God, A Look at Lightning, Secular Games,* and *Circe,* among others, and dancing in most of the repertoire. Has also danced with the companies of May O'Donnell, José Limón, Norman Walker, Donald McKayle. Has appeared frequently on television. Danced several seasons with New York City Opera Ballet, and appeared at Jacob's Pillow, the Empire State and Boston Festivals, and at Festival of Two Worlds, Spoleto.

Prairie. Ballet in 4 movements; chor.: Eugene Loring; music: Norman Dello Joio; book: based on Carl Sandburg's poem; décor: James Stewart Morcom; costumes: Felipe Fiocca. First prod.: Dance Players, National Theatre, N.Y., Apr. 21, 1942, with a cast headed by Janet Reed, Bobbie Howell, Freda Flier, Lew Christensen, Eugene Loring.

Preisser, Suse, German dancer, b. Leipzig. Studied in the ballet schools of Leipzig and Milan. Soloist in Leipzig, Weimar, Berlin, dancing principal roles in *Swan Lake, Firebird, Petrouchka, Pelléas and Mélisande, Turandot, Abraxas, The Sleeping Beauty, L'Indifférent, Agon, Ondine.* At present soloist of the Städtische Oper, West Berlin; also has her own school.

Preludes, Les. Abstract ballet in 3 movements; chor.: Vaslav Veltchek; music: Francisco Mignone's *Preludes.* First prod.: Ballet Rio de Janeiro, Teatro Municipal, Rio de Janeiro, Brazil, 1956, with Alice Colino, Ismael Guiser, Dalal Achcar, Arthur Ferreira, Miriam Guimarães, Yellê Bittencourt.

Première, the presentation of a dance production for the first time. American première, for instance, is the first presentation of a dance production in America; world première is the first presentation anywhere.

Première Classique. Ballet in 1 act; chor.: Eric Hyrst; music: excerpts from Peter Tchaikovsky's *Swan Lake* which are usually omitted from contemporary productions; décor: Alexis Chiriaeff; costumes: Claudette Picard. First prod.: Les Grands Ballets Canadiens, Comédie Canadienne Theatre, Montreal, with Eva von Gencsy, Milenka Niderlova, Veronique Landory, Eric Hyrst, as soloists (1959). A themeless ballet presented in the manner of the last act divertissement of a late 19th century classic ballet.

Premier Danseur, the first, or principal male dancer of a ballet company (compare ballerina).

Première Danseuse, in ballet, the French term for ballerina, next in rank below danseuse étoile.

Preobrajenska, Olga, prima ballerina of the St. Petersburg Imperial Ballet, b. St. Petersburg, 1871, d. Paris, 1962. Graduated from the Imperial School (1889). One of the greatest dancers of her time, she particularly excelled in *Coppélia, La Fille Mal Gardée, Paquita, The Nutcracker, Esmeralda, The Fairy Doll, Talisman, The Sleeping Beauty, Raymonda, The Seasons, Harlequinade, Don Quixote, Giselle, Le Corsaire, La Sylphide.* In her twenty-five years on the Imperial stage she danced more than seven hundred times and gained recognition and praise from public, press, management, and colleagues alike, receiving two gold medals from the Ministry of the Court. During that period

The late Olga Preobrajenska with Dame Margot Fonteyn, who used to fly from London to Paris several times a year to study with the great teacher. (Photo ca. *1956)*

she also made guest appearances at La Scala, Milan (1904), Paris Opéra (1909), Royal Opera House, Covent Garden, London (1910). From 1917 to 1921 she taught in the State School of Ballet, Petrograd. Resigning her post she settled in Paris where she also taught (1923–60). Among her pupils were Irina Baronova, Tamara Toumanova, Igor Youskevitch, George Skibine, and later Serge Golovine, Milorad Miskovitch, as well as countless other dancers who studied with her to learn the secrets of style.

Preparation, in ballet, a preparatory pose taken to give impetus to a step, as 4th pos. plié for pirouettes.

Presages, Les. Ballet in 4 parts; chor. and book: Leonide Massine; music: Peter Tchaikovsky; décor and costumes: André Masson. First prod.: Col. de Basil's Ballet Russe, Théâtre de Monte Carlo, April 13, 1933, with Nina Verchinina (Action), Irina Baronova (Passion), Tatiana Riabouchinska (Frivolity), David Lichine (the Hero), Leon Woicikowski (Fate). This ballet, set to Tchaikovsky's Fifth Symphony, was Massine's first symphonic ballet. The underlying idea of the ballet is man's triumph over adversity.

Prévost, Françoise (1680–1741), leading dancer in Paris in her era. Besides grace, quickness, lightness, and precision she was known for her dramatic ability and mime. In 1708 she appeared with Blondy in a ballet given by the Duchesse de Maine, based on a tragic episode in Corneille's *Les Horaces.* Mlle. Prévost succeeded Mlle. Subligny as première danseuse at the Opéra. She taught at the Académie Royale and when she retired (1730) she was replaced by her students Marie Camargo and Marie Sallé.

Price Family of Denmark. A famous dynasty of dancers founded by James Price (b. London, 1761, d. Copenhagen, 1805), a circus rider and member of a pantomime troupe, who settled in Copenhagen and became director of Vesterbros Morkabsteater. His granddaughter, Juliette Price (1831–1906), most famous of the Prices, was a favorite pupil of August Bournonville and created the roles of Hilda in *Et Folkesagn* and Rosa in *Flower Festival at Genzano,* among others. Juliette's brother, Valdemar Price (1836–1908), also became a leading dancer in the Royal Theatre, Copenhagen. A grandniece of Juliette and Valdemar Price, Ellen Price created the title role in Hans Beck's *The Little Mermaid* (1909) and is the model for the famous Little Mermaid statue at Langelinie. Other well-known members of the Price family were Sophie, sister of Juliette; Amalie and Carl (cousins); and another cousin, Julius, who danced at the Vienna Opera and became court ballet master and professor at the conservatory.

Primitive Mysteries. Modern group dance; chor.: Martha Graham; music: Louis Horst; costumes: Martha Graham. First prod.: Craig Theatre, N.Y., Feb. 2, 1931.

Primus, Pearl, contemporary American dancer, b. Trinidad, British West Indies, 1919; m. Percival Borde. Ph.D. in Anthropology, Columbia Univ., N.Y. Made her N.Y. debut at YMHA (1943) and gave her first solo performance at Hunter College the following year. She has since given many performances of West Indian, African, and primitive dance both authentic and choreographed in the idiom. She has also choreographed Negro spirituals; other works are *Yanvaloo, Study in Nothing, Strange Fruit, Shouters of Sobo, The Negro Speaks of Rivers, Afro-Haitian Playdance, African Ceremonial Te Moana, Earth Theatre* (this last an evening of dance devised by herself with Percival Borde). Awarded a Julius Rosenwald Fellowship to make a survey of native dances of Africa (1948). On her return (1951) she presented many performances based on these dances and rituals. Delegate from the American Society on African Culture to the second World Congress of African Artists and Writers held in Rome (1959). In Oct., 1959, she left to spend six months in Liberia at the invitation of the Liberian government. There she became first director of a new performing arts center for which she instituted a program designed to preserve the native dance and other arts to which it is related. In 1962, the Rebekah Harkness Foundation sponsored a tour in Africa of Pearl Primus, Percival Borde, and a company of dancers at which time they also recorded native dances and music of the various African countries they visited.

Prince Goudal's Festival. Ballet in 1 act; chor.: Boris Romanov; music: Anton Rubinstein; décor: Mstislav Doboujinsky. American première: Ballet International, International Theatre, N.Y., Nov. 16, 1944, with Viola Essen and André Eglevsky in leading roles. The ballet was first given by Romanov's Romantic Theatre in Berlin in the early 1920's. A Caucasian prince is holding a festival in honor of his wife. The ballet was mostly an effective divertissement to music culled from Rubinstein's opera *Demon* and some short works not further identified. Doboujinsky's magnificent décor and costumes were used in 1951 by the Marquis de Cuevas company for George Skibine's ballet *The Prisoner of the Caucasus.*

Prince Igor. Ballet in 1 act; chor.: Michel Fokine; music: Alexander Borodin; décor: Nicholas Roerich. First prod.: Diaghilev Ballets Russes, Théâtre du Châtelet, Paris, May 18, 1909, with Sophie Fedorova (Polovetsian Girl), Yelena Smirnova (Polovetsian Woman), Adolph Bolm (Polovetsian Chief). The Polovetzian dances were revived by Serge Grigoriev and Lubov Tchernicheva for the Royal Ballet, Mar. 24, 1965, at the annual Royal Ballet Benevolent Fund Gala, with Rudolf Nureyev as the Warrior Chief. Staged by Fokine to the ballet music from the second act of the opera *Prince Igor,* its correct title is actually *Polovetsian Dances from Prince Igor.* This work is or has been in the repertoire of ballet companies all over the world. There is no story—just a display of magnificently savage dance, more or less in the Tartar folk idiom.

Prince of the Pagodas. Ballet in 3 acts; chor. and book: John Cranko; commissioned music: Benjamin Britten; décor: John Piper; costumes: Desmond Heeley; lighting: William Bundy. First prod.: Royal Ballet at Royal Opera House, Covent Garden, London, Jan. 1, 1957, with Svetlana Beriosova (Princess Belle Rose), *Julia Farron* (Princess Belle Epine), David Blair (Salamander Prince), Leslie Edwards (Emperor of the Middle Kingdom), Ray Powell (Dwarf), Anya Linden

(Moon), Maryon Lane and Brian Shaw (Fire). The wicked Princess Belle Epine tricks her father and his favorite daughter, Belle Rose, out of the kingdom. The Prince, bewitched as a salamander until Belle Rose expresses her love for him, vanquishes Belle Epine, restores the Emperor to his throne, and wins the hand of Belle Rose. This happy consummation is celebrated with a typical classic ballet last act divertissement. *Prince of the Pagodas* was the first evening-length British ballet to have its own commissioned score, and Britten himself conducted the first performance. It was also the first Western ballet to show the influence of the Bolshoi Ballet (which had appeared in London for the first time in 1956). Alan Carter choreographed a version in décor by Fabius Gugel at Munich State Opera, Mar. 17, 1958.

Princess Aurora. The name given to the Ballet (now American Ballet) Theatre's version of the last act of *The Sleeping Beauty,* usually known as Aurora's Wedding. Anton Dolin staged *Princess Aurora* for Ballet Theatre and it was given for the first time at the 44th Street Theatre, N.Y., Nov. 26, 1941, with Irina Baronova in the title role, partnered by Dolin. Ballerinas who danced Aurora in this production have been Alicia Markova, Alicia Alonso, Nora Kaye, Nana Gollner, and others. A divertissement of the same name was staged by Serge Lifar for the Paris Opéra Ballet, May 12, 1948, with Yvette Chauviré in the title role.

Prism. Modern dance work; chor.: Alwin Nikolais; music: Alan Hovhaness, George Antheil, and electronic tape; color design: George Constant. First prod.: Henry Street Playhouse Dance Company, Henry Street Playhouse, N.Y., Dec. 27, 1956, with Gladys Bailin, Phyllis Lamhut, Coral Martindale, Beverly Schmidt, Murray Louis, Bill Frank. With its strange, invented titles—"Tridem," "Pradomen," "Glaasch," et al., this is perhaps the definitive product of Alwin Nikolais' experimentations in dance, color, light, sound, and shapes.

Prisoner of the Caucasus. Ballet in 1 act, 3 scenes; chor.: George Skibine; music: Aram Khachaturian, from his ballet Gayané; décor: Mstislav Doboujinsky. First prod.: Grand Ballet du Marquis de Cuevas, Théâtre de l'Empire, Paris, Dec. 4, 1951, with Marjorie Tallchief and the choreographer in principal roles. Based on Alexander Pushkin's poem of the same name, the story tells of a Russian officer taken prisoner by the Circassians who is rescued by a Circassian girl. She helps him to escape and then stabs herself, having lost her lover and betrayed her country. The second scene, set in the Circassian camp, contains an exciting set of warrior dances. An earlier version was staged by Leonid Lavrovsky to music by Boris Asafiev at the Maly Theatre, Leningrad (1938).

Prisoners, The. Ballet in 1 act; chor.: Peter Darrell; music: Béla Bartók's Music for Celesta, Percussian and Strings; décor: Barry Kay. First prod.: Western Theatre Ballet, Dartington Hall, Devon, June 24, 1957, with Suzanne Muşitz (Madeleine), Erling Sunde (Christophe), Barry Salt (Baudin). Two escaped convicts find shelter in the home of the wife of one. She falls in love with the other (Baudin) and persuades him to kill her husband. She then confines him to her house and he realizes that he has simply exchanged one prison for another.

Prodigal Son, The. Ballet in 1 act, 3 scenes; chor.: George Balanchine; music: Serge Prokofiev; book: Boris Kochno; décor: Georges Rouault. First prod.: Diaghilev Ballets Russes, Théâtre Sarah Bernhardt, Paris, May 21, 1929, with Serge Lifar (Prodigal Son), Felia Doubrovska (Siren), Michael Fedorov (Father), Leon Woicikowski and Anton Dolin (Servants to the Prodigal Son); revived by Balanchine for New York City Ballet, Feb. 23, 1950, City Center, N.Y., with Jerome Robbins (Prodigal Son), Maria Tallchief (Siren), Michael Arshansky (Father), Frank Hobi and Herbert Bliss (Servants to the Prodigal Son). At this revival the Rouault décor was not available, being in the possession of Col. de Basil. Balanchine discovered Marc Chagall's floorcloth for the *Firebird* which was not being used by New York City Ballet and this was repainted in an approximation of the Rouault colors. When the company went to Europe in the summer of 1950, it was possible to have the original backcloth reproduced. Francisco Moncion, Hugh Laing, and Edward Villella have all triumphed in the title role, as have Yvonne Mounsey and Diana Adams as the Siren. Balanchine's re-telling in dance of one of the most famous and moving of all biblical parables is one of the masterworks of twentieth century ballet. David Lichine staged a new version to the Prokofiev music for Original Ballet Russe (1939) with himself in the title role and Sono Osato as the Siren.

Prodigal Son, The. Ballet in 2 acts, 6 scenes; chor. and book: Kurt Jooss; music: Fritz (Frederic) A. Cohen; décor and costumes: Hein Heckroth. First prod.: Folkwang Tanzbühne, Amsterdam, Holland, Oct. 6, 1933; re-staged by Jooss with new décor and costumes by Dimitri Bouchene and presented by Jooss Ballet, Bristol, England, Oct. 1939.

Prodigal Son, The. Ballet in 4 scenes; chor.: Ivo Cramér; music: Hugo Alfvén; décor: Rune Linstrom. First prod.: Royal Swedish Ballet, 1957, with Bjorn Holmgren (Prodigal Son), Teddy Rhodin (the False Prophet), Elsa-Marianne von Rosen (the Arabian Queen), Julius Mengarelli (Father), Anne-Marie Lagerborg (Mother). The ballet is inspired by the primitive paintings by the farmers in the province of Dalarna in which personalities of the Bible, wearing the garb of the late 18th and early 19th centuries, are often depicted as participating in the everyday life of the farmers, thus ingeniously invoking the Scriptures' help in solving their homely problems.

Prokhorova, Violetta. See ELVIN, VIOLETTA.

Prokofiev, Sergei (1891–1953), Russian composer. He wrote several scores specifically for ballets, and some of his other compositions were arranged for use as ballet scores. Some ballets devised to Prokofiev scores are: *Chout* and *Pas d'Acier* (Diaghilev Ballet Russes, 1927); *Prodigal Son* (George Balanchine, 1929; David Lichine, 1939); *Sur le Borysthène* (Serge Lifar, 1932. Shortly before the première was announced the direction of the Opéra decided that the Paris public would not be able to pronounce the word Dniepr in the original title *On the Dniepr* suggested by the composer, and the title was changed to *Sur le Borysthène,* Borysthenes being the ancient Greek name of the

Sergei Prokofiev, composer of music to The Prodigal Son, Romeo and Juliet, Cinderella, The Stone Flower, Peter and the Wolf, et al.

Ukrainian river); *Romeo and Juliet* (Leonid Lavrovsky, Leningrad Kirov Ballet, 1940; another version with some new mise-en-scènes, Moscow Bolshoi Ballet, 1946; Frederick Ashton, Royal Danish Ballet, 1955); *Cinderella* (Rostislav Zakharov, Bolshoi Ballet, 1945; Konstantin Sergeyev, Kirov Ballet, 1946; Frederick Ashton, Sadler's Wells [now Royal] Ballet, 1948). Antony Tudor used Prokofiev's *Classical Symphony* and first movement of the Third Piano Concerto for *Gala Performance* (1938). The score of *Peter and the Wolf* has been used by many choreographers, among them Adolph Bolm and Frank Staff (both 1940). Michel Fokine used the suite *Lieutenant Kije* for the ballet *Russian Soldier* (Ballet Theatre, 1941). Prokofiev's last ballet composition was *The Stone Flower*. It was first presented at the Moscow Bolshoi in 1954 with choreography by Lavrovsky, which was superseded in 1957 by a production by Yuri Grigorovich at the Kirov, and in 1959 at the Bolshoi.

André Prokovsky, principal dancer, late of The N.Y. City Ballet.

Prokovsky, André (family name Pokrovsky), dancer, b. Paris, 1939, of Russian parentage. Studied ballet with Lubov Egorova, Nora Kiss, Serge Peretti, Nicholas Zverev. Won a silver medal for his dancing at the World Festival of Youth in Moscow (1947). Made his professional debut with the Comédie-Française (1954). Danced in Janine Charrat's company (1955); with Roland Petit (1956); joined London's Festival Ballet (1957), becoming a leading dancer. Premier danseur, Ballet International du Marquis de Cuevas from 1960 until its final performances in 1962. Joined New York City Ballet as a leading soloist (spring season, 1963), making his debut Mar. 12, in the first movement of *Symphony in C*. Since that time he has undertaken a large repertoire, among his ballets being *Swan Lake* (Act 2), *Allegro Brillante, Gounod Symphony, Stars and Stripes* (pas de deux and finale), *Raymonda Variations,* and others; created leading roles in *The Chase* (Jacques d'Amboise, 1963), *Piège de Lumière, Irish Fantasy* (d'Amboise, 1964). Toured with a group called Stars of French Ballet, headed by Rosella Hightower and Liane Daydé (Feb.–Apr. 1964). Resigned from N.Y.C. Ballet in 1966.

Prologue. Modern dance work; chor.: Sophie Maslow; music: excerpts from Carl Orff's *Carmina Burana* and a fragment from Manuel de Falla's Harpsichord Concerto; costumes: Domingo Rodriguez. First prod.: Sophie Maslow and Company, YM–YWHA, N.Y., Apr. 12, 1959, with Andora Hodgin, Billie Kirpich, Muriel Mannings, Miriam Pandor, Marvin Gordon, Gene McDonald, Sheldon Ossosky. The introduction to Boccaccio's *Decameron* in dance. Ladies and gentlemen of the Florentine court flee from the city when a plague strikes to seek diversion in the country, but death is not to be denied.

Promenade, in ballet, term used to

designate slow turn of the body on the whole foot in adagio movements; also, in pas de deux when the partner circles the ballerina as he slowly turns her in a pose such as arabesque or attitude; similar movement in modern dance.

Promenade. Ballet in 1 act; chor.: Ninette de Valois; music: Josef Haydn, selected by Edwin Evans from various symphonies and piano sonatas and orch. by Gordon Jacob; décor: Hugh Stevenson. First prod.: Sadler's Wells (now Royal) Ballet, King's Theatre, Edinburgh, Oct. 25, 1943, with Gordon Hamilton, Margot Fonteyn (Beryl Grey subsequently danced the role), Pauline Clayden, Moira Shearer, Alexis Rassine, Ray Powell in leading roles. The ballet is a divertissement about people one might find in a park on a summer's day. Evans said of the music that it was "a short stroll through the works of Haydn."

Promenade Position, in ballroom dance, a couple in closed position moving sideways to the left, with the side of the foot leading.

Promethée. Ballet in 1 act; chor.: Maurice Béjart; music: Maurica Ohana; book: Pierre Rhallys; décor: Bernard Daydé. First prod.: Ballet 1956 of Milorad Miskovitch for Lyon Festival, June, 1956, with Miskovitch, Claire Sombert, and Veronika Mlakar. Based on the legend of Prometheus bringing fire to the world, Béjart gives a typically modern slant to the legend, aided by the striking décor of Daydé.

Prometheus (The Creations of Prometheus). Ballet in two acts; chor. and book: Salvatore Vigano; music: Ludwig van Beethoven, composed at the suggestion of the choreographer and to his libretto. First prod.: Vienna, Mar. 28, 1801, under the German title *Die Geschöpfe des Prometheus,* with Cassentini and the choreographer in the principal parts. In 1813 Vigano revived *Prometheus* at Teatro alla Scala, Milan, where he had become ballet master in 1812. For this production he elaborated on his libretto and changed the two-act original version into six-acts, set to additional music of other composers. This was not an exceptional practice of Vigano. According to Cyril W. Beaumont (*Complete Book of Ballets*): "The music of Vigano's ballets is rarely, if ever, by one composer. The score of a ballet consists of a skillful piecing together of airs drawn from the work of such composers as Haydn, Mozart, Beethoven, Rossini, and Spontini, interpolated with portions written by contemporary composers of another grade." Beethoven's score for *Prometheus* has been used by a number of choreographers, among them Serge Lifar (1929), Ninette de Valois (1936), Aurel Milloss (1940).

Prospect Before Us, The. Ballet in 7 scenes; chor. and book: Ninette de Valois; music: symphonies and sonatas of the 18th century composer William Boyce, arr. by Constant Lambert; décor: Roger Furse. First prod.: Vic-Wells (later Sadler's Wells, now Royal) Ballet, Sadler's Wells Theatre, London, July 4, 1940, with Robert Helpmann (Mr. O'Reilly), Claude Newman (Mr. Taylor), Pamela May (Mademoiselle Theodore), Frederick Ashton (Monsieur Noverre), Ursula Moreton (Madame Noverre), Alan Carter (Monsieur Didelot), John Hart (Monsieur Vestris), Mary Honer (Street Dancer), Margaret Dale (Cupid). The scenario is freely adapted from John Ebers' *Seven Years of the King's Theatre,* published in 1828, and gets its title from the Thomas Rowlandson (1756–1827) print of the same name. The Furse sets and dropcloth are in the Rowlandson manner. The story tells of two rival theatre managers, each trying to steal the other's company of dancers when their theatres burn down in turn. In the final scene, O'Reilly is delighted to relinquish the burden of management and takes to the bottle in a dance which became one of Helpmann's most famous humorous essays. A feature of *The Prospect Before Us* was a charming "ballet within a ballet," arranged by de Valois in the early 18th century manner. When Sadler's Wells Theatre Ballet revived this work, Stanley Holden had a great success in the Helpmann role.

Protée. Ballet in 1 act; chor.: David Lichine; music: Claude Debussy's *Danse Sacrée et Danse Profane;* book: Henry Clifford and Lichine; décor: Giorgio di Chirico. First prod.: Original Ballet Russe, Covent Garden Royal Opera House, London, July 5, 1938, with Lichine in the title role. The plot of the ballet derives from popular myth about the sea god who was able to change his form at will. The Teatro Colón, Buenos Aires, has its own version of this ballet.

Prothalamion. Ballet in 1 act; chor.: Brian Macdonald; music: Frederick Delius's *Walk to the Paradise Garden,* intermezzo from *A Village Romeo and Juliet;* décor: Robert Prevost. First prod.: School of Fine Arts, Banff, Alberta, Canada, Aug., 1961, with Annamarie and David Holmes. Went into the repertoire of Royal Winnipeg Ballet, Mar., 1962, with the same dancers. A hymn to marriage, inspired by John Milton's poem of the same name. It was created for Annamarie and David Holmes and dedicated by the choreographer to the memory of his wife, Olivia Wyatt, who died in 1959. Under the title *Hymn* it was staged for the Norwegian Ballet, Oslo, in the spring of 1963, with Hanne Thorstenson and Palle Damm. The Leningrad Kirov Ballet invited Macdonald to stage it for its repertoire.

Public Library, New York. See Dance Collection, The New York Public Library.

Pugni, Cesare (1802–1870), composer of ballet music, b. Genoa. Educated at the Milan Conservatory of Music. While in Milan he composed music for the ballets *Macbeth, The Kenilworth Castle, The Siege of Calais.* In Paris he was director of the Paganini Institute and composed *The Devil's Fiddle, The Marquitante, The Marble Maiden,* and *Stella.* The chief defect of this unquestionably gifted composer was the fact that he always worked in a great hurry and usually on specific order, hence the crudeness of his music. He composed especially for Maria Taglioni, Fanny Elssler, and Carlotta Grisi, and was forced to satisfy his customers. He went to St. Petersburg in 1851 from London, where he had been staff composer of ballet music at the Royal Covent Garden Opera House. In Russia he was staff composer at the Imperial Ballet and during his nineteen years there composed thirty-five ballets and a great number of individual dances. Among his outstanding compositions were *Esmeralda, The Humpbacked Horse, Daughter of Pharaoh, Catarina, Armide, Le Corsaire, Pas de Quatre, Paquerette, Faust, King Candaule.* As a composer his total output numbered three hundred and twelve ballets, ten operas, and forty Masses.

Pulcinella. Ballet in 1 act; chor.: Leonide Massine; music: Igor Stravinsky-Giambattista Pergolesi; curtain, décor and costumes: Pablo Picasso. First prod.: Diaghilev Ballets Russes, Théâtre National de l'Opéra, Paris, May 15, 1920, with Leonide Massine in title role, Tamara Karsavina (Pimpinella), Vera Nemtchinova, Lubov Tchernicheva, Enrico Cecchetti, Stanislas Idzikowski, Sigmund Novak, Nicholas Zverev. Pulcinella is one of the characters in commedia dell'arte. The ballet was inspired by an old Italian comedy *The Four Pulcinellas* (ca. 1700). Leon Woicikowski was excellent in the title role, and he revived the ballet (called *Les Deux Polichinelles*) for his company at the Coliseum, London (1935).

Punch and the Child. Ballet in 3 scenes;

chor.: Fred Danieli; music: Richard Arnell; décor, costumes, and masks: Horace Armistead. First prod.: Ballet Society, N.Y. City Center, Nov. 12, 1947, with a cast headed by Herbert Bliss (Father and Punch), Beatrice Tompkins (Mother and Judy), Gisella Caccialanza (Fishwife and Polly), Lew Christensen (Puppeteer and Devil), Charles Laskey (Street Cleaner and Constable), Judith Kursch (Child). A Child attracted by a Punch and Judy show succeeds in getting into the booth and participates in the performance. The Child associates the characters of the show with the people who surround her. Thus Punch becomes her Father, Judy her Mother, the Puppeteer the Devil, etc.

Punch and the Judy. Modern group dance; chor.: Martha Graham; music: Robert McBride; spoken text selected by Martha Graham; décor: Arch Lauterer; costumes: Charlotte Trowbridge. First prod.: Bennington College, Vt., Aug. 10, 1941.

Puppenfee, Die (The Fairy Doll). One of the most successful one-act ballets of the late 19th and early 20th century. Its success is to be credited to the simplest of ballet stories and its tuneful music. Its first production took place at the Vienna Hofoper on Oct. 4 (other sources have it as Apr. 10), 1888, with choreography by Josef Hassreiter; music by Josef Bayer; book by Franz Gaul and the choreographer; décor by Anton Brioschi. Other productions of note include the Munich Opera House (1895), in which Heinrich Kröller appeared in a solo part. In 1905 the ballet was staged at the London Empire Theatre with Adeline Genée in the title role and with choreography by Katti Lanner. This production was little more than a divertissement based, more or less, on the original Hassreiter choreography. In 1906 Nicholas Legat staged the ballet at the Maryinsky Theatre, St. Petersburg. In the early 1920's Ivan Clustine revived it for Anna Pavlova, the première taking place at the 44th Street Theatre, N.Y. The plot of *Die Puppenfee* concerns a number of dolls who come to life at night in the toyshop in which they are on display.

Pure Dance. See ABSTRACT DANCE.

Pushkin, Alexander (1799–1837), great Russian poet, playwright, and balletomane. Some of his works have been used as scenarios for ballets. Soviet ballet companies have produced his *Prisoner of the Caucasus, The Fountain of Bakhchisarai, Mistress into Maid, The Bronze Horseman.* The earliest version of *The Prisoner of the Caucasus* was that of Charles Didelot (1823). George Skibine also choreographed it for Grand Ballet du Marquis de Cuevas (1951). *Le Coq d'Or,* the opera and ballet, is based on Pushkin's folk tale-poem. Leonide Massine's Aleko is based on his narrative poem *The Gypsies.*

Pygmalion. Ballet; chor.: Marie Sallé. First prod.: Covent Garden, London, Feb. 14, 1734. Sallé appeared as Galatea and it was in this ballet that she danced in a simple muslin costume, omitting pannier, skirt, bodice, and all the other vestments that hampered the dancers of that time. She also wore her hair loose and without any kind of ornaments.

Qarrtsiluni. Ballet in 1 act; chor.: Harald Lander; book: Knudaage Riisager and Lander; music: Riisager; décor: Svend Johansen. First performed by the Royal Danish Ballet in 1942 in Copenhagen. The title of the ballet is a magic word of the Greenland Eskimos which expresses the people's longing for the arrival of spring after the long northern winter and which, primitive Eskimos believe, has the power to hasten the arrival of spring. Lander staged *Qarrtsiluni* to Riisager's music, originally written as a suite inspired by the legend of the magic word which the famous Danish explorer Knud Rasmussen brought back from his travels in Greenland. Niels Bjørn Larsen created the role of the drummer-dancer-magician who eventually makes the sun appear and dispel the winter.

Quadrille. 1. Type of American square dance in which four couples, arranged in a square, participate and perform the steps in couples. Traditionally there are five parts in a quadrille, but often in the U.S. some figures are combined. See SQUARE DANCE. 2. Group ballroom dance popular in Europe at end of 18th and in the 19th centuries. 3. Division in the ranks of dancers in the Paris Opéra ballet, equivalent to corps de ballet.

Quaternaria, German saltarello consisting of two steps and a reprise with a beat between.

Quatre Saisons, Les. Ballet in 1 act; chor. and book: Jules Perrot. First prod.: Her Majesty's Theatre, London, June 13, 1848, with Fanny Cerito, Carlotta Grisi, Carolina Rosati, Marie Taglioni (niece of the great Maria Taglioni) as Spring, Summer, Autumn, Winter, respectively. A new version of this ballet, founded on Lucien Petipa's ballet divertissement in the opera *The Sicilian Vespers* by Giuseppe Verdi, was produced at Her Majesty's Theatre, May 16, 1856. Amina Boschetti, the Italian ballerina, made her London debut in this ballet in the role of Winter. The ballet was little more than a divertissement for four ballerinas and a large corps de ballet, a production which was called a grand pas in the French and Russian ballet. According to contemporary sources Perrot outdid himself in devising dances for the ballerinas and groups from the corps, as well as for the full corps. Chronologically, *Les Quatre Saisons* was probably the last ballet of the Romantic period.

Quatrième (lit., fourth), in ballet, fourth position; also used to imply specifically fourth position front or back in the air, as grande quatrième devant or grande quatrième derrière.

Quatrième Concert Royal (Fourth Royal Concert). Ballet in 1 act; chor.: Ludmilla Chiriaeff; music: selected from François Couperin; décor: Mark Negin;

costumes: Josephine Boss. First prod.: Les Grands Ballets Canadiens, Comédie Canadienne Théâtre, Montreal Jan. 18, 1962, with Milenka Niderlova, Andrée Millaire, Brydon Paige, Vincent Warren, and an ensemble of four girls and four men. A glimpse of the court dances of France during the reign of Louis XIV.

Quest. Modern group dance; chor.: Charles Weidman; music: Norman Lloyd; costumes: Charles Weidman. First prod.: Aug. 1936, Bennington, Vt.

Quest, The. Ballet in 5 scenes; chor.: Frederick Ashton; commissioned music: William Walton; book: Doris Langley Moore, after Spenser's *Faerie Queene;* décor: John Piper. First prod.: Sadler's Wells (now Royal) Ballet, New Theatre, London, Apr. 6, 1943, with Margot Fonteyn (Una, personifying Truth), Robert Helpmann (St. George, personifying Holiness), Leslie Edwards (Archimago, personifying Hypocrisy), Celia Franca (Female Servant, transformed into Una), Beryl Grey (Duessa, personifying Falsehood), Franklin White, David Paltenghi, Alexis Rassine (Three Knights, Sansfoy, Sansjoy, Sansloy), Moira Shearer (Pride, as Queen). The triumph of St. George over the forces of Evil and his reunion with Una after he has been deceived by the evil magician. The episode of the Seven Deadly Sins, in which Moira Shearer (Pride) had an important dance as the Queen of a corrupt kingdom, was one of this dancer's earliest successes. Frederick Ashton obtained special leave from the Royal Air Force to create this ballet.

Quick, in ballroom dancing, half of the average length of time required to make one walking step; ballroom dance teachers divide dance rhythms into combinations of slow and quick, two quick counts equalling one slow count.

Quinault, Philippe, (1635–1688), French poet. The son of a baker, he became valet de chambre to Louis XIV. He was soon writing verse and in 1672 wrote the book for his first ballet, *Les Fêtes de l'Amour et de Bacchus,* for which he had the collaboration of Molière, Bensserade, and Perigny. In 1681 he wrote the book for *Le Triomphe de l'Amour.* He was connected with the Opéra for twenty-four years in which time he wrote most of the libretti for *Lully's* operas and ballets. He was a member of the Académie and was decorated with the order of St. Michel.

Rabovsky, Istvan. See KOVACH AND RABOVSKY.

Raccourci, in ballet, the shortening or foreshortening of a bent leg, a position in which toe of working leg touches knee of supporting leg, as in passé. A good example of raccourci in a contemporary ballet is the male dancer's final jump through the window in *Le Spectre de la Rose;* it is a grand jeté raccourci.

Rachmaninoff, Sergei Vassilievitch (1873–1943), Russian pianist and composer. His *Rhapsody on a Theme of Paganini* is the music used for the ballet *Paganini* (Michel Fokine, 1939; Leonid Lavrovsky, 1960).

Radice, Attilia, Italian ballerina, b. 1913. Entered the ballet school of Teatro alla Scala, Milan, in 1923. Became prima ballerina of La Scala and later of Teatro dell'Opera, Rome. She has been director of the Ballet School of the Rome Opera since 1958, appointed to that position upon the death of Teresa Bataggi.

Radio City Music Hall, one of the largest theatres in the world (seating capacity: 6,200). Opened in New York City, Dec. 27, 1932, by Samuel L. Rothafel (Roxy) as a music hall, it became within a few weeks (Jan., 1933) a theatre for motion pictures and stage shows. It has every kind of mechanical device for securing stage effects. Its corps de ballet and its precision dancers, the Rockettes, are a feature attraction. Leon Leonidoff, Senior Producer, supervises all stage productions and Russell Markert is Director of Rockettes and Producer. Each often produces his own show. Florence Rogge was Director of the Corps de Ballet and Associate Producer for 20 years. She was succeeded by her assistant, Margaret Sande (1952) who occupied the position until 1962, when Marc Platt took over the staging of all ballet numbers. Many famous dancers have been guest artists with the ballet. The Music Hall Ballet is the only resident ballet company in U.S. which performs fifty-two weeks a year.

Radunsky, Alexander, Honored Artist of the RSFSR, Honored Art Worker of the RSFSR, Soviet mime and choreographer, b. 1912. Entered the Bolshoi School in 1924, having already studied in private ballet studios. Graduated from the school into the company (1930). He is an outstanding actor-mime. During his first season in the Bolshoi company (1930–31) he received his first important role of *Don Quixote* in the ballet of that title and since then has created a great number of mimetic roles in which he has no peer, one of the most outstanding being Lord Capulet in *Romeo and Juliet.* He has choreographed several ballets, among them *Baby Stork* (with N. Popko and L. Pospekhin, 1937); *Svetlana* (music: D. Klebanov, 1939) and *Crimson Sails* (music: V. Yurovsky, 1942), both of these in collaboration with the same choreographers. Radunsky collaborated with Asaf Messerer on the current Bolshoi version of *Swan Lake* (1956). He choreographed a new version of *The Humpbacked Horse* to music by Rodion Shchedrin (1960). Radunsky also acted as ballet master of the Bolshoi, rehearsing with the leading dancers the dramatic aspects of their roles. His own latest role was that of the old Georgian in the Leonid Lavrovsky–Andrei Balanchivadze ballet *Pages of Life* (1961). Radunsky retired from the Bolshoi Theatre in 1962 and joined the Song and Dance Ensemble of the Soviet Army as chief choreographer.

Rainbow Round My Shoulder. Modern dance work; chor.: Donald McKayle; music: traditional prison songs of the South for male choir and guitarist, arr. by Robert de Cormier and Milt Okun. First prod.: Donald McKayle Dance Company, YM–YWHA, N.Y., May 10, 1959, with Donald McKayle, Mary Hinkson, Al de Sio, Jay Fletcher, Charles Moore, Harold Pierson, Jaime Rogers, Gus Trikonis. The prison songs translated into action—savage, desperate and full of longing—with Mary Hinkson as the wife and sweetheart of the prisoners' imaginings, culminating in the tragic finality of "Another Man Done Gone." Leon Bibb led the male choir, with John Stauber as guitarist.

Rake's Progress, The. Ballet in 6 scenes; chor.: Ninette de Valois; music and book: Gavin Gordon; décor: Rex Whistler. First prod.: Vic-Wells (later Sadler's Wells, now Royal) Ballet, Sadler's Wells Theatre, London, May 20, 1935, with Walter Gore (The Rake), Alicia Markova (Betrayed Girl), Ailne Phillips (Her Mother), Ursula Moreton (Dancer), Joy Newton (Street Singer), Harold Turner (Music Master). The theme of the ballet is based on the series of paintings by the English artist William Hogarth (1697–1764). The Rake, who leaves the country for London upon inheriting a fortune, quickly becomes the prey of anyone who can persuade him to part with his money in the process of becoming a gentleman. Gambling brings about his final ruin and he ends in an asylum amongst the poor lunatics who at that time were a public spectacle. Only the girl he betrayed still has pity for him and he dies in her arms. Robert Helpmann succeeded Gore as the Rake and it became one of his greatest roles. Harold Turner was also outstanding and Stanley Holden gave a remarkable performance in the revival by Sadler's Wells Theatre Ballet. *The Rake's Progress,* a milestone in the history of British ballet, made a deep impression when the Royal Ballet toured in the Soviet Union, where the Russians were quick to appreciate the dramatic truth of the action and the accuracy of its period feeling.

Rall, Tommy, dancer, actor, singer, b. Kansas City, Mo., 1929. Studied dance principally with David Lichine and Carmalita Maracci in Los Angeles, Anatole Oboukhov in N.Y.; dramatics with Jack Kosslyn and Herbert Berghof; singing with S. Robert, E. Schofield, R. Smolover. Started dancing at age of four and had his first professional engagement in vaudeville at age eight (1938). After small dancing roles in films (1941), joined Ballet (now American Ballet) Theatre and was a leading soloist (1944–47). Danced roles in *Interplay, Fancy Free, Helen of Troy* (Paris), *Blue Bird* pas de deux, and *Les Patineurs* (in which he created the role of the Green Skater); and others. Appeared in the Broadway musicals *Look Ma, I'm Dancin', Small Wonder, Miss Liberty, Call Me Madam.* Choreographed the Faye Emerson Television Show (1951–52 season), then went to Europe to appear in Gene Kelly's film *Invitation to the Dance.* Eight Hollywood films followed, the most important being *Seven Brides for Seven*

Brothers, Kiss Me, Kate, My Sister Eileen, and *The Second Greatest Sex.* Returned to Broadway in 1959 to act and dance a leading role in *Juno,* a musical based on Sean O'Casey's *Juno and the Paycock,* for which he received the Outer Critics Circle Award for best supporting actor. Returned to American Ballet Theatre for its 20th anniversary season at Metropolitan Opera House (1960), dancing in *Dialogues* (Serenade for Seven) and *Pillar of Fire* (Young Man from the House Opposite). The same summer received a scholarship to study operatic singing at Tanglewood Music Festival, Mass., and made his opera debut the following year singing and dancing the title role in Massenet's *Juggler of Notre Dame* with the New England Opera Theatre, Boston, Mass., under Boris Goldovsky. His acting, singing, and dancing role as the young Sahbra in the musical *Milk and Honey* (1961–62) elevated him to stardom on Broadway.

Ralov, Borge, Danish dancer, b. Copenhagen, 1908. Pupil of the Royal Danish Ballet School; graduated into the company (1927); solo dancer (1933); first solo dancer (1942), when he was officially named premier danseur, the first and only Danish male dancer to have this designation (see DENMARK, BALLET IN). Danced a wide repertoire of standard classics, Bournonville ballets and new works (being an especially striking Petrouchka), and frequently partnered Margot Lander. Has been teaching in the ballet school since 1945 and also rehearses some of the repertoire. Retired as a dancer in 1957. Choreographed *Enken I Spejlet* (The Widow in the Mirror, 1934), *Twelve for the Mail Coach* (1942), *The Courtesan* (1953).

Ralov, Kirsten, soloist of the Royal Danish Ballet, b. near Vienna, Austria, 1922; m. Fredbjørn Bjørnsson. Entered the company school (1929); accepted into the company (1940); made soloist (1942). Danced leading roles in *Sorcerer's Apprentice, Kermessen i Brügge, Petrouchka, Aurora's Wedding, Et Folkesagn, Symphony in C, Swan Lake, Blomsterfesten i Genzano, Le Beau Danube,* and others. Choreographed *Kameliadamen* (1960). Stopped dancing after her farewell performance as the Ballerina in *Petrouchka,* May 24, 1962, during the Royal Danish Ballet Festival. An expert in the Bournonville style, she is now devoting herself to assisting at rehearsals. Knight of the Order of Dannebrog since 1953.

Rambert, Dame Marie (Miriam Rambam, also called Rambach; Mrs. Ashley Dukes), Polish born English teacher, producer, director, b. Warsaw, 1888. She studied with Jacques Dalcroze and was one of his most promising pupils. When Serge Diaghilev saw a demonstration of Dalcroze pupils (1913) he was so impressed that he asked Dalcroze to recommend one of his pupils to instruct his company, Rambert was suggested. Vaslav Nijinsky was proud that his ballets *The Afternoon of a Faun* and *The Rite of Spring* reflected her training. Rambert became interested in ballet and studied with Enrico Cecchetti, becoming a member of the corps de ballet of the Diaghilev Ballets Russes. She established her own school in London (1920) and has since played a major part in fostering English ballet. By the middle 1920's her pupils were giving recitals which soon led to the founding of the Ballet Club at the little Mercury Theatre (1930), which became the first permanent English company and school. With Ninette de Valois she was responsible for the Camargo Society (1930). Though Mme. Rambert is not a choreographer herself, she has a talent for discovering, training, and developing the talents of others. Among the many young choreographers who received their start under her tutelage and created their early works for Ballet Rambert are Frederick (now Sir Frederick) Ashton, Antony Tudor, Andrée Howard, Frank Staff, Walter Gore, Norman Morrice. All of these were,

Dame Marie Rambert, "mother" of British Ballet.

or are, also dancers. Among the dancers she discovered are Pearl Argyle, Diana Gould, Elisabeth Schooling, Prudence Hyman, Maude Lloyd, Celia Franca, Sally Gilmour, Lucette Aldous, Harold Turner, Leo Kersley. Designers who owe much to Rambert include the late Sophie Fedorovitch and Hugh Stevenson, William Chappell (who was also one of her dancers in the early days), and many others. Marie Rambert was awarded the C.B.E. (Commander of the Order of the British Empire, 1954), the Legion of Honor (1957), and was subsequently made a D.B.E. (Dame of the Order of the British Empire, 1962).

Rameau, Pierre, French dancing teacher. He wrote *The Dancing Master* (1725), our best source of knowledge of 18th century dance, containing precepts of dance and engravings of various postures. Though principally a guide to social dancing, it had considerable effect on theatrical dance and used great stage dancers as models of perfection of form. Rameau states that since dancing adds grace and mitigates defects of body, it is useful and everyone should be skilled in it. He discusses posture and emphasizes the importance of the five absolute positions, attributed to Beauchamp by Rameau, but mentioned in Thoinot Arbeau's *Orchesography* (1588).

Rao, Shanta, Indian dancer, b. Mangalore, 1930. Studied the Art of Bharata Natya with Minkaisunderam Pillai; Kathakali with Ramuni Menon; Mohini Attam with Krishnan Pannicker. The last named style had almost died out when she rescued it from oblivion by her public performances. She has done this also with Bhama Sutram, the ritual dance of a little-known cult of worshippers of Satyabhama. She toured Europe and the U.S. in solo performances (1955); toured with her company of dancers and musicians in the U.S. (1957), returning with appearances at the Jacob's Pillow Dance Festival, followed by another tour (1963).

Rapp, Richard, contemporary American dancer, b. Milwaukee, Wis. Studied dance with Adele Artinian, Ann Barzel, School of American Ballet, N.Y., joining New York City Ballet in 1958; promoted to soloist (1961). Dances a large repertoire including roles in *Agon, Arcade, Donizetti Variations,* and others. Created title role in George Balanchine's production of *Don Quixote,* N.Y. State Theater, Lincoln Center (May 28, 1965).

Rasch, Ellen, Swedish ballerina, b. 1920. Studied at the Royal Danish Ballet School and with Boris Kniaseff; accepted into the company (1939); designated ballerina (1946). Guest artist with several French companies. Danced the title role in the film *Firebird,* choreographed by Maurice Béjart. Retired upon a final performance of *Giselle* in the version staged by Antony Tudor (1962).

Rassine, Alexis, dancer, b. Lithuania, 1919, of Russian parents. Raised in Cape Town, South Africa, where he began to study ballet; continued with Olga Preobrajenska in Paris, Vera Volkova and Stanislas Idzikowski in London. Made his professional debut in French revue *Bal Tabarin.* Member, Ballets Trois Arts (England, 1939–42); soloist, Anglo-Polish Ballet and, briefly, with Ballet Rambert. Joined Sadler's Wells (now Royal) Ballet (1942), becoming a premier danseur. Danced Albrecht (*Giselle*), *Blue Bird* pas de deux (*The Sleeping Beauty*), Franz (*Coppélia*), title role (*Le Spectre de la Rose*), and others; created Pas de Trois (*Promenade*), Sansloy (*The Quest*), Lover (*Miracle in the Gorbals*), Spirit of the Earth (*Homage to the Queen*), and others. Toured South Africa with Nadia Nerina (1952, 1955). Partnered Yvette Chauviré at Covent Garden (1958).

Ravel, Maurice (1875–1937), French composer of the ballets *Daphnis and Chloë* (Michel Fokine, Diaghilev Ballets Russes, 1912), *Bolero* (Bronislava Nijinska, Ida Rubinstein company, 1928), and *La Valse* (the same, 1929). Among the many subsequent versions of *Daphnis and Chloë* the outstanding one is that of Frederick Ashton for the Royal Ballet (1951). *Bolero* was used by Ruth Page under the title *Iberian Monotone* (1934). George Balanchine staged a ballet, *La Valse,* using this composition and Ravel's *Valses Nobles et Sentimentales* for the New York City Ballet (1951). Frederick Ashton also staged a version of *La Valse* at Teatro alla Scala, Milan (1958), and subsequently restaged it for the Royal Ballet (1959). Ashton used *Valses Nobles et Sentimentales* for a 1933 ballet, *Valentine's Eve,* for Ballet Rambert. Walter Gore used the same music for *Valse Finale,* later called *Les Valses,* and finally *Valses Sentimentales,* also for Ballet Rambert (1938). Ashton again used this music for an entirely new version staged under the title of the music for Sadler's Wells Theatre Ballet (1947). Ravel's *Pavane pour une Infante Défunte* has been used by various choreographers, notably Kurt Jooss; the composer's Introduction and Allegro and Alborado del Gracioso make the score for Andrée Howard's *The Mermaid.* His opera ballet *The Spellbound Child* was produced by Ballet Society (1946) with choreography by George Balanchine. It was staged by Dr. Frederic Cohen for the Juilliard Opera Theater (1957) when Doris Humphrey choreographed the movements and dances for the dancers of Juilliard Dance Theater, who appeared with the singers. *The Spellbound Child* under its original French title, *L'Enfant et les Sortilèges,* was first produced by the Serge Diaghilev Ballets Russes in 1925.

Rayet, Jacqueline, contemporary French ballerina, b. Paris. Entered Paris Opéra School as a "petit rat" at age nine. Promoted to première danseuse étoile (1961). Dances principal roles in *Firebird* (the Princess in Serge Lifar's version), *Daphnis and Chloë, Les Noces Fantastiques* (Oceanide), *Palais de Cristal,* among others. Has also created principal roles in *Symphonie Inachevée* and *Peau de Chagrin.* Guest ballerina, Hamburg, Germany (1961), where she danced *Romeo and Juliet, Pelléas and Mélisande,* George Balanchine's *Serenade.*

Raymonda. Ballet in 3 acts, 4 scenes; chor.: Marius Petipa; music: Alexander Glazounov; book: Lydia Pashkova and Marius Petipa; décor: Allegri, Ivanov, Lambini. First prod.: Maryinsky Theatre, St. Petersburg, Jan. 19, 1898, with Pierina Legnani in title role. This ballet was revived by Alexandra Danilova and George Balanchine for Ballet Russe de Monte Carlo, with décor and costumes by Alexandre Benois. First prod.: New York City Center, March 12, 1946, with Alexandra Danilova in title role. Raymonda, a beautiful young noble lady is in love with her fiancé Jean de Brienne; however, Abderahman, a Saracen knight, is in love with Raymonda and plans to abduct her. With the help of the White Lady, a Spirit of the Protectress of Raymonda's family, Abderahman is thwarted in his ambition and is killed in single combat with de Brienne. The famous *Grand Pas Hongrois* occurs in Act 3, the marriage celebration of Raymonda and Jean de Brienne. See also RAYMONDA VARIATIONS.

Raymonda Variations (original title: *Valses et Variations*). Ballet in 1 act; chor.: George Balanchine; music: from Alexander Glazounov's *Raymonda;* décor: Horace Armistead (his back cloth for *Lilac Garden*); costumes: Barbara Karinska. First prod.: New York City Ballet, City Center, N.Y., Dec. 7, 1961, with Patricia Wilde, Jacques d'Amboise, and Victoria Simon, Suki Schorer, Gloria Govrin, Carol Sumner, Patricia Neary. This abstract ballet opens with an ensemble waltz, a pas de deux for ballerina and premier danseur, nine variations for the dancers named, a coda and finale.

Recital, a dance performance given by one performer. In the U.S. the term is often loosely applied to a performance given by several dancers (which should be called a concert) and to a performance given by the pupils of a school.

Recreational Dance, a term coined by John Martin, former dance critic of the *N.Y. Times* and author, to include forms of the ballroom, folk, etc., dance in which the spectator is also a participant. Says Martin in his *Introduction to the Dance* (N.Y., 1939): "It [the recreational dance] is play in perhaps the least rationalized form practicable for social use, and in it, if we see it in its essential nature, we are able to find release for many of our repressions and return to the arbitrary disciplines of the social scheme refreshed and healthy of mind."

Red Flower, The (formerly *The Red Poppy*). Ballet in 3 acts; chor.: Vasily Tikhomirov and Lev Lashchilin; music: Reingold Glière; book: Mikhail Kurilko and Tikhomirov; décor: Kurilko. First prod.: Bolshoi Theatre, Moscow, June 14, 1927, under the title *The Red Poppy,* with Yekaterina Geltzer (Tao Hoa), Alexei Bulgakov (Captain). In 1949 Leonid Lavrovsky produced a new version of the ballet with Galina Ulanova as Tao Hoa. A considerably changed version of the ballet was also produced by Lavrovsky under the new title and first presented at the Bolshoi Theatre, Nov. 24, 1957. It retained, however, some of the best dances of the original production. Yet another version under the title *The Red Flower,* with new choreography by Alexei Andreyev, was staged at the Kirov Theatre, Leningrad, May 2, 1958. Under its original title, *The Red Poppy,* was the first "revolutionary" ballet produced in the Soviet Union. Tao Hoa, a Chinese dancer, meets a Soviet captain whose ship has brought grain as a present from the Soviet trade unions. Lie Shang-Foo, Tao Hoa's manager, plots with his European bosses against the Soviet captain, attempting to make Tao Hoa hand him a cup of poisoned tea, which she refuses to do. Lie Shang-Foo shoots at the captain while trying to escape during an uprising of the people and Tao Hoa, shielding the captain with her body, dies with the red flower in her hands, a symbol of his love.

Red Poppy, The. See RED FLOWER, THE.

Redowa, a variety of polka.

Reed, Janet, dancer, ballet mistress, b. Tolo, Oregon, 1916; m. Branson Erskine. Studied dance with local teachers but principally with Willam Christensen in Portland and in San Francisco. Première danseuse of San Francisco Opera Ballet (1937), dancing Swanilda (*Coppélia*) and Odette-Odile in the first full-length version of *Swan Lake* staged by an American company. Arrived in N.Y. in 1942 and after a season with Dance Players, creating leading roles in *Prairie, Man from Midian, Jinx, Sacramento,* and dancing leads in *City Portrait* and *Billy the Kid,* joined Ballet (now American Ballet) Theatre. For this company she created Second Girl

(*Fancy Free*), Blues pas de deux (*Interplay*), Girl (*On Stage!*), and others, also dancing in *Billy the Kid, Gala Performance, Judgment of Paris, Pillar of Fire, Graduation Ball,* etc. Retired temporarily in 1946 at the birth of her first child, then appeared in the Broadway musical *Look Ma, I'm Dancin'* (1947–48). Returned briefly to American Ballet Theatre before joining New York City Ballet (1949). Her many important creations included leader of Fête Polonaise movement (*Bourrée Fantasque,* 1949), one of the leading roles in *Pied Piper* (1951), Rich Girl (New York City Ballet's revival of *Filling Station,* 1953), 2nd movement (*Western Symphony,* 1954), Countess (*The Unicorn, the Gorgon and the Manticore,* 1957), and others. She also danced leading roles in *Mother Goose Suite, Serenade, Symphony in C, Con Amore,* etc. Her final creation, before retiring altogether as a dancer, was Peaches in *Creation of the World,* originally given as part of *Jazz Concert* (Dec. 7, 1960). Ballet mistress of New York City Ballet (1959–64). Teaching ballet at Bard College since 1965.

Reel, 1. a lively dance usually in 4/4 time for two or more couples, common both in Scotland and Ireland (the Highland Fling is a variant); 2. the second part of the three-part Virginia Reel.

Regional Ballet, the term for the non-professional companies attached to a school, or schools, and to the movement which has resulted in these companies. Many of the individual groups include the word "civic" in their titles. This does not mean official support from the town, but that the company performs a service for its city or region. The regional ballet movement had been quietly growing for years but the various groups worked mainly in isolation, unaware that there were many of them. This was changed in 1956 when the first Regional Ballet Festival was held in Atlanta, Ga. It was the result of a project suggested to Dorothy Alexander, artistic director of the Atlanta Civic Ballet, by Anatole Chujoy. He had attended several of the festivals held in Canada and believed that a festival along similar lines would focus attention on an important development in the cultural life of America and would also give the directors of the various groups the opportunity of seeing each other's works, exchanging views, and discussing problems.

Five companies appeared at this first Festival. So great was the enthusiasm that a Southeastern Regional Ballet Festival Assoc. was formed which has since grown to well over 20 companies. Festivals have been held each year since 1956: Birmingham, Miami (twice), Atlanta (with Southern Ballet of Atlanta as host company), Louisville, Orlando (twice), Jacksonville, Nashville, Memphis (where the 10th anniversary of the regional ballet festivals was celebrated in 1965), and with Miami projected for a third festival in 1967.

In 1958 a similar Festival Assoc. was formed in the Northeast, Scranton and Wilkes-Barre sharing the first festival in 1959, followed by Erie, Dayton, Schenectady, Detroit, Ottawa (Canada), Washington, D.C., and with Wabash (Ind.) projected for 1967. A third Southwestern Regional Ballet Festival Assoc. held its first festival in Austin, Tex. in 1963, followed by Houston (1964), Dallas (1965), Forth Worth (1966), and with Wichita Falls projected for 1967. The Pacific Western Regional Ballet Festival Assoc. held its first festival in Sacramento in 1966, with Laguna Beach projected for 1967.

All the Associations have greatly increased their membership since their formation so that currently there are between 70 and 80 groups which now belong to one or another of the four Associations. There are probably at least twice that number of companies which remain outside the Associations despite all benefit accrued to the companies from the public awareness of the movement which has grown because of the Festivals. A condition of joining an Association is that the company must be incorporated as a non-profit organization. It must also have given at least one public performance before a paid audience (not a school recital) within a year previous to applying for membership. For convenience in identifying the status of a company it is now accepted that only those companies which belong to a Regional Ballet Festival Association are called "regional" companies.

All regional ballet companies are non-professional and are not designed to take the place of professional companies. They are a means of promoting, maintaining, and increasing interest in ballet in towns which professional companies visit rarely or not at all. Above all, however, performances by regional companies give serious students of dance (of which there are some in every school, although they are not in the majority) a chance to perform in public under conditions very similar to those which apply in the professional theatre. It is becoming increasingly a preparation for a professional career, but it also provides an outlet for those students who, while receiving great pleasure from dancing, do not wish to make it a career.

Some companies do not give more than one major performance a year, others present several. As the movement grows these companies are invited to travel to neighboring towns, to perform for school children in public schools, and to expand in directions not even dreamed of before the Festivals induced a general awareness of the existence of these companies.

Regisseur, Regisseur-General, a stage manager, a person who has direct supervision over the presentation and the responsibility for the smooth running of a ballet performance. In the Diaghilev Ballets Russes and later in the Ballet Russe de Monte Carlo the regisseur-general also performed the duties of ballet master.

Regner, Otto Friedrich (1913–63) celebrated German ballet critic and writer. From 1960 until his death he was feature editor of the Frankfurter *Algemeine Zeitung.* His books include *Das Balletbuch* (1954) and *Balletführer* (1956). Wrote libretto to the ballet *Pigeon Flight,* choreographed by Alan Carter, music by Otto-Erich Schilling (1955). Contributed numerous articles to magazines and newspapers.

Reich, George, American dancer and choreographer, working in Paris. Has his own company *Ballet Ho,* which tours the music halls. Was a leading dancer with Ballets de Paris de Roland Petit (1953). His style is a mixture of ballet, modern jazz, and acrobatic. Appeared in the film *La Garçonne.*

Reid, Rex, contemporary Australian dancer and choreographer, b. Adelaide. Studied at Sadler's Wells (now Royal) Ballet School with Stanislas Idzikowski, and others. Joined Original Ballet Russe and returned with them to Australia (1938). Returned to Europe, where he danced with International Ballet, Ballet Rambert, and Grand Ballet de Monte Carlo. Again returned to Australia with Ballet Rambert and, with Joyce Graeme, created National Theatre Ballet Company in Melbourne, acting as assistant director, choreographer, and principal dancer. His ballet *Corroboree* is based on an Australian theme. To Rio de Janeiro (1954) to work with Aurel Milloss. Currently directing his own school in Melbourne. Choreographed *Melbourne Cup* for the Australian Ballet (1962).

Reiman, Elise, contemporary dancer and teacher, b. Terre Haute, Ind. Studied ballet with Adolph Bolm, School of American Ballet, N.Y. Created role of Calliope in Apollon Musagète (Bolm, 1928). Soloist, American Ballet (1935–36). Has appeared in musical comedies, films, on television, and with Ballet Society (1946–48), for which company she created roles in *The Four Temperaments, The Spellbound Child, Divertimento, The Minotaur, Highland Fling,* and other ballets. Now retired from dancing, but continues to teach.

Reinholm, Gert, leading German dancer, b. Chemnitz. Studied with Lizzie Maudrik, Lulu von Sachnowsky (at the Eugenia Edouardova School, Berlin), Tatiana Gsovska, Michel Borowski, Esmée Bulnes. Made his debut as soloist at the State Opera, Berlin, in *Daphnis and Chloë* (1946). Has danced with the State Opera, Berlin (1946–50); Teatro Colón, Buenos Aires (1952); Municipal (now German) Opera, Berlin (since 1954); Berliner Ballett (1955). Toured in South America with Irina Borowska; in Germany with Liena Gsovsky and Edel von Rothe under the title Dance Trio of the State Opera; recitals with Natasha Trofimova; toured with Yvette Chauviré in South America, Portugal, France. Received Prix des Nations in Paris as Best Dancer of 1961. Principal roles are Daphnis in *Daphnis and Chloë, Saint Francis, Le Spectre de la Rose, The Afternoon of a Faun,* Romeo in *Romeo and Juliet* (Prokofiev), *Prometheus,* Prince in *Sleeping Beauty, Hamlet* (Blacher), *Apollon Musagète,* Prince in *Swan Lake,* Knight in *The Lady and the Unicorn, Orpheus* (Liszt).

Reisinger, Julius, choreographer of the first version of *Swan Lake* (Moscow, 1877). He is a rather contemptible figure in the history of the classic ballet because in the opinion of his contemporaries and critics and, later, historians, it is on him more than on anyone else that the onus rests for the failure of the first production of *Swan Lake.* There is no information available on the dates and places of Reisinger's birth and death or, for that matter, on his activities prior to and following his stay in Moscow. He was brought to Moscow from Austria by the Direction of the Moscow Bolshoi Theatre in 1871 to stage the ballet *The Magic Slipper* (Cinderella), with a libretto by the chief machinist and stage designer of the Bolshoi, K. F. Valtz, and music by Wilhelm K. Mühldörfer, at the time second conductor of the Cologne Opera House. The Direction of the Bolshoi had commissioned Peter Tchaikovsky to write the score of the ballet the year before. Tchaikovsky composed a first draft and delivered it to the Direction but never heard from them again. The mystery of the reason for the cancellation of the commission, if a formal cancellation ever took place, is explained (in part at least) by the fact that Valtz had commissioned Mühldörfer, apparently in the name of the Direction of the Bolshoi, to compose the music, and that Julius Reisinger arrived in Moscow with his own plans for the production. *The Magic Slipper* was presented in late 1871. According to Yuri Slonimsky in his book *P. I. Tchaikovsky and the Ballet Theatre of His Time* (Moscow, 1956), the ballet was, ". . . an example of the Parisian style: a meaningless fairy-tale, which depended for its success on tricks, splendor of décor, lighting effects, machinery, etc." D. I. Moukhin, the historian of the Bolshoi Theatre, wrote about *The Magic Slipper* in his as yet unpublished *History of the Moscow Ballet:* "Reisinger turned out to be a very poor ballet master. The ballerinas choreographed their own variations and the other dances were staged collectively." The contemporary Moscow newspapers, without exception, had a poor opinion of the choreographer. In 1875, the year that Tchaikovsky began to work on the score of *Swan Lake,* Reisinger was appointed choreographer of the ballet. The Theatrical Almanac of that year wrote: "The ballet master [of *Swan Lake*] is the talentless Mr. Reisinger." All this, however, did not deter the Direction of the Theatre from keeping Reisinger on their rolls for over nine years. As is generally known, Reisinger considered Tchaikovsky's music undanceable and cut the score any way he pleased, paying little attention to the composer's protests. He also permitted the ballerina Pelagie (Pelaguëia) Karpakova to interpolate into the new ballet variations and music from other ballets she had danced. Reisinger considered himself a master of the character dance, hence he introduced various character dances into the third act, which he saw as a formal costume-ball spectacle. The critic of the famous Moscow newspaper *Russkiye Vedomosti* wrote about the première of the ballet: "Reisinger displayed, if not an art appropriate to his speciality, a wonderful talent for staging gymnastic exercises instead of dances. The corps de ballet executed a military 'mark time,' waving their arms like windmills, and the soloists jumped around the stage with gymnastic steps. More animated were the character dances in the third act, but these dances were not 'composed' by Reisinger but simply borrowed from other ballets. The 'Russian' dance was most probably the fruit of Reisinger's own fantasy, because only a German could consider the pirouettes which Mme. Karpakova was forced to execute, a Russian dance." There could be no doubt that Reisinger was no match to Tchaikovsky in talent, taste, musicality, education, background, or by any other criterion. But in order to keep a proper perspective on the situation, it must be remembered that the period in the history of the Bolshoi was, in the words of Yuri Slonimsky, "full of Reisingers." Tchaikovsky was the first great Russian composer to write a ballet, and *Swan Lake* was the first ballet he wrote.

Relevé, in ballet, rising with a small spring to pointe or demi-pointe from position in which whole foot is on the floor.

Remington, Barbara, Canadian dancer, b. Windsor, Ont., 1936. Studied with Sandra Severo, Detroit, and was a member of Severo Ballet, a regional company. Studied at School of American Ballet, N.Y., and Ballet Theatre School; also in England at Royal Ballet School (1956–58), joining the company (1959). Currently soloist, dancing Lilac Fairy (*The Sleeping Beauty*), The Wife (*The Invitation*), White pas de deux (*Les Patineurs*), Fairy Godmother (*Cinderella*), and others. Before joining Royal Ballet she had danced with American Ballet Theatre (1958), and Robert Joffrey Ballet (1959). Rejoined the American Ballet Theatre (summer, 1964), but left it again for the City Center Joffrey Ballet (1966).

Reminiscence. Ballet in 1 act; chor.: George Balanchine; music: Benjamin Godard, arr. and orch. by Henry Brand; décor and costumes: Serge Soudeikine. First prod.: The American Ballet, Adelphi Theatre, N.Y., Mar. 1, 1935, with a cast headed by Holly Howard, Elise Reiman, William Dollar. A divertissement of classic dances to new music which reminded Balanchine and part of the spectators of the ballets upon which he grew up in St. Petersburg.

Renard, Le (The Fox). Ballet-burlesque in 1 act for dancers and singers; chor.: George Balanchine; music and book: Igor Stravinsky; English-language version: Harvey Officer; décor: Esteban Francés. First American prod.: Ballet Society, Hunter College Playhouse, N.Y., Jan. 13 and 14, 1947, with Lew Christensen (Rooster), Fred Danieli (Cat), John Taras (Ram), and Todd Bolender in title role. The simple plot is a fable about a Rooster who by his ingenuity and despite some dangerous moments gets the better of the sly and avaricious Fox. The music for the ballet was composed in 1916 and the ballet was originally produced by the Diaghilev Ballets Russes with choreography by Bronislava Nijinska (1922). It was revived by the same company with new choreography by Serge Lifar (1929). This was the final production before the company disintegrated following the death of Serge Diaghilev, shortly after the production. In the Lifar production the roles taken by the dancers were doubled by acrobats. In 1927, Fedor Lopoukhov staged *Renard* (under the title *A Tale about the Fox, the Rooster, the Cat and the Ram*) at the State Academic Theatre of Opera and Ballet, Leningrad (now the Kirov Theatre). Alfred Rodrigues staged a version, in décor by Arthur Boyd, for Western Theatre Ballet, Empire Theatre, Edinburgh, Sept. 4, 1961, commissioned by Edinburgh Festival Society, with Suzanne Musitz, Dennis Griffith, Oliver Symons, Peter Cazalet.

Renault, Michel, French dancer, b. 1927. Began dance studies at age twelve under Gustave Ricaux and Serge Peretti at Paris Opéra. At eighteen became the youngest premier danseur étoile in the history of the Opéra. His creations include *Les Mirages* (1947), George Balanchine's *Le Palais de Cristal* (3rd movement, with Micheline Bardin, 1947), *Nauteos* (1954), and many others. Took over many of Serge Lifar's roles in the ballets *Le Chevalier et la Demoiselle, Guignol et Pandor, Salade,* and *Giselle* (1957). Was one of the two leading male dancers (Alexandre Kalioujny was the other) in Harald Lander's *Etudes,* staged for the Paris Opéra (1952). Left the Paris Opéra in 1959 and now makes guest artist appearances partnering Liane Daydé, with whom he has toured in France, South America, Soviet Russia. They first danced in Moscow while still members of the Paris Opéra company (1958).

Michel Renault, late premier danseur of the Paris Opéra Ballet.

Rencher, Derek, English dancer and designer, b. Birmingham, 1935. Studied at Royal College of Art, London; ballet with Barbara Vernon and John Gregory. Currently soloist with Royal Ballet. Roles include White pas de deux (*Les Patineurs*), King Florestan XXIV (*The Sleeping Beauty*), Benno and Master of Ceremonies (*Swan Lake*), Duke of Courland (*Giselle*), Orion (*Sylvia*), Bridegroom (*La Fête Etrange*), and others. His creations include Demophoon (*Persephone*), Aegisthus (*Elektra*), and others. His designs include Ray Powell's *One in Five* (1960) and *A Fool's Tale* (1961), both for the Sunday Ballet Club. Created Lysander in Frederick Ashton's *The Dream* (1964), and Paris in Kenneth MacMillan's *Romeo and Juliet* (1965).

Rencontre, La (Oedipus and the Sphinx. Ballet in 1 act; chor.: David Lichine; music: Henri Sauguet; book: Boris Kochno; décor: Christian Bérard. First prod.: Ballet des Champs-Elysées, Théâtre des Champs-Elysées, Paris, Nov. 8, 1948, with Leslie Caron (Sphinx) and Jean Babilée (Oedipus). The encounter of Oedipus and the Sphinx and his answering of the riddles. The sensations of the ballet were the circus-like trapeze on which the Sphinx lay, high above the floor of the stage and around which Babilée bounded, and the final plunge downward of the Sphinx, dangling by one foot from the rope ladder. Leslie Caron, then only sixteen years old, was a sensation in this ballet. As *The Sphinx* it was briefly in the repertoire of Ballet (now American Ballet) Theatre, premièred Apr. 21, 1955, at Metropolitan Opera

House, N.Y., with Nora Kaye and Igor Youskevitch.

Rendezvous, Les. Ballet in 1 act; chor.: Frederick Ashton; music: Constant Lambert's arrangement of music by François Auber (*L'Enfant Prodigue*); décor: William Chappell. First prod.: Sadler's Wells (now Royal) Ballet, Sadler's Wells Theatre, London, Dec. 5, 1933, with Alicia Markova, Stanislas Idzikowski, Ninette de Valois, Robert Helpmann. A suite of dances linked by the idea of young couples meeting, flirting, and parting in a public park. Margot Fonteyn and Harold Turner later took over the Markova and Idzikowski roles. The ballet has had several different décors, all designed by Chappell. It was staged for Sadler's Wells Theatre Ballet Dec. 26, 1947, with Elaine Fifield and Michael Boulton, and when this company was combined with the Royal Ballet at Royal Opera House, Covent Garden, became part of the entire repertoire.

Rendez-vous Manqué, Le. See BROKEN DATE.

René, Natalia (Roslavleva), Soviet ballet critic and historian, b. Kiev, 1907. Graduated from Univ. of Moscow (English Philology); studied ballet at Lunacharsky Choreographic Technicum, Moscow, and privately with Vera Mosolova; modern dance with Vera Maya and Lyudmila Alexeyeva. After general journalistic career, began writing on ballet in 1943. Author of the books *Maya Plisetskaya* (1956), *English Ballet* (1959), *Beryozka* (1960); collaborated on *The Bolshoi Theatre* (1958) and *Agrippina Vaganova* (1958), part of which consists of letters exchanged between the author and Vaganova, who was a personal friend. Collaborated on preparation of the Russian edition of the Fokine memoirs (1962). Author of numerous articles on ballet in leading Soviet magazines, also *Big Soviet Encyclopedia, Theatre Encyclopedia, Children's Encyclopedia, Enciclopedia dello Spettacolo, Dance Encyclopedia.* Under pen-name of Natalia Roslavleva wrote on Soviet ballet for *Ballet Today* in London (1946–50). Currently writes for *The Dancing Times* and *Dance and Dancers* (both London); also lectures on ballet. President, Ballet Section, U.S.S.R.–Great Britain Friendship Society.

Renversé, in ballet, a turn using the following technique: start 5th pos., R ft. front; relevé onto L pointe or demi-pointe and do a grand rond de jambe with R leg, rotating R leg at waist height in hip socket from front to side and then in back; place R ft. in 5th pos. in back and, as it is lowered, détourné on both pointes to R.

Repertoire (or repertory), list of ballets or dance numbers in a ballet or dance company with which the company is familiar, in which it is rehearsed, and for which it has the necessary décor, costumes, music, etc., so that the ballets can be given at any time.

Répétition, in ballet, a rehearsal.

Respighi, Ottorino (1879–1936), Italian composer. He arranged *Antiche Danze ed Arie* (Antique Dances and Airs), music which Agnes de Mille used for her ballet *Three Virgins and a Devil* (1941). He orchestrated music by Rossini for *La Boutique Fantasque,* a ballet by Leonide Massine (1919). Michael Somes also used the *Antique Dances and Airs* for his only ballet, *Summer Interlude* (1950). Robert Helpmann's *The Birds* (1942) was set to Respighi's suite *The Birds,* composed for the Aristophanes play of that name. The American modern dancer Vol Quitzow has composed a solo, *The Emperor in Command,* which he dances to "Pines of the Appian Way" from *Pines of Rome.*

Retombé, in ballet, falling back to original position.

Revanche (Revenge). Ballet in prologue and 4 scenes; chor.: Ruth Page; music: Giuseppe Verdi (from *Il Trovatore*); libretto: Nicholas Remisov and Page; décor: Antoni Clavé. First prod.: Ballets des Champs-Elysées, Théâtre de l'Empire, Paris, Oct. 17, 1951, with Sonia Arova (Azucena), Jacqueline Moreau (Leonora), Vladimir Skouratoff (Manrico), Gérard Ohn (Count di Luna). The story follows closely the complicated plot of the famous opera. Chicago Opera Ballet (then called Ruth Page Ballets) gave *Revanche* its American première at Civic Opera House, Chicago, Nov. 26, 1955, again with Arova, and Alicia Markova (Leonora), Oleg Briansky (Manrico), Bentley Stone (Count di Luna).

Revelations. Modern dance work; chor.: Alvin Ailey; music: traditional Negro music. First prod.: Alvin Ailey Dance Theatre, YM–YWHA, N.Y., Jan. 31, 1960. The work progresses through songs of sorrow, repentance, and hope, to spirituals, ring shouts, and song sermons in which dancers and singers alike burst into joyous affirmation of faith in salvation.

Revenge. See REVANCHE.

Révérence, in ballet, a bow, a curtsey; a position with one toe extended front, supporting leg in demi-plié, body leaning forward, arms croisé.

Revitt, Peter, artist, caricaturist, b. Northampton, England, 1916. Trained as a stage designer, spent many years drawing in ballet classes, mostly School of Russian Ballet (Nicholas Legat method). His book of caricatures *Ballet Guyed,* published in 1948 after some of his caricatures had appeared in the English magazine Ballet Today, led to his illustrating the Leo-Kersley-Janet Sinclair *A Dictionary of Ballet Terms* (London, 1952) and *Mime* (Joan Lawson, London, 1952). Co-author with Joan Lawson of *Dressing for the Ballet* (London, 1958); illustrated Celia Sparger's *Ballet Physique* (London, 1958); G. B. L. Wilson's *A Dictionary of Ballet* (Penguin Books, 1958); and Lawson's *Classical Ballet* (London, 1960). Has illustrated articles by Tamara Karsavina on ballet technique in the London *Dancing Times.*

Revue, theatrical production having no plot or story, made up of musical numbers (dances and songs) and sketches. Some of the best known revues have been *Cochran's Revue* (England), *Chauve-Souris* (Russia and France), *Ziegfeld's Follies, Earl Carroll's Vanities* (U.S.). See also MUSICAL COMEDY and OPERETTA.

Rhapsody in Blue. Ballet in 1 act; chor.: Nina Verchinina; music: George Gershwin; décor and costumes: Mario Conde. First prod.: Ballet Universidade de Cuyo, Mendoza, Argentina, 1952; revived in 1954 for Teatro Municipal, Rio de Janeiro, Brazil, with a cast headed by Tamara Capeller and David Dupré (Sweethearts), Nina Verchinina (Femme Fatale). In later season Tatiana Leskova danced the Femme Fatale in an excellent impersonation of Marlene Dietrich. The ballet is a cinematic love triangle set in N.Y. in the 1920's.

Rhodes, Lawrence, American dancer, b. Mount Hope, West Va., 1939. Studied dance with Violette Armand, Detroit. His first professional engagement was in corps de ballet of Ballet Russe de Monte Carlo. Joined Robert Joffrey Ballet (1960) and has created many leading roles, among them the Acrobat (Gerald Arpino's *Incubus*), male lead (Brian Macdonald's *Time Out of Mind*), and leads in Arpino's *Partita for Four,* and *Palace,* among others. He has made several guest appearances with the Ballet de Camara, Mexico City. He is one of the few dancers outside Denmark to have mastered the Bournonville style and technique, which he displays in the Robert Joffrey Ballet's pre-

Lawrence Rhodes, a principal dancer of the Harkness Ballet.

sentation of the *Flower Festival at Genzano* pas de deux. Joined the Harkness Ballet (1964).

Rhodin, Teddy, Swedish dancer, b. Stockholm, 1919. Pupil of the Royal Swedish Ballet School; accepted into the company (1937); made premier danseur (1942). Choreographed for operas and television. Retired at the end of the 1963–64 season, dancing three of his best roles —Jean (*Miss Julie*), Prince (*Swan Lake,* Act 2), and Peruvian (*Gaîté Parisienne*) —at a Gala Performance, May 21, 1964.

Rhumba, erroneous spelling of rumba.

Rhythm, is "the skeleton of music," according to Richard Wagner. *The Music Lovers' Encyclopedia* calls rhythm, "the arrangement of accented and unaccented, and of long and short sounds . . ." which follows a certain pattern. Rhythm is the conception which binds dance to music.

Riabouchinska, Tatiana, ballerina, b. Moscow, Russia, 1917; m. David Lichine. Studied dance with Olga Preobrajenska. Made her debut with Nikita Balieff's *Chauve-Souris* revue in Paris when she was only fifteen. One of the three original "baby ballerinas" (with Irina Baronova and Tamara Toumanova) in Col. de Basil's Ballets Russes de Monte Carlo (1932–41), creating Frivolity (*Les Présages*), Daughter (*Le Beau Danube*), Child (*Jeaux d'Enfants*), Florentine Beauty (*Paganini*), Junior Girl (*Graduation Ball*), title roles in *Coq d'Or* and *Cinderella;* dancing Prelude (*Les Sylphides*), *Blue Bird* pas de deux (*Aurora's Wedding*), Columbine (*Carnaval*), and others. Has been guest artist with American Ballet Theatre, London's Festival Ballet, Grand Ballet du Marquis de Cuevas, Les Ballets des Champs-Elysées; also

Tatiana Riabouchinska, one of the three original "baby ballerinas."

danced in musicals. Currently teaching in Calif.

Riabynkina, Yelena, Soviet ballerina, b. 1941. Daughter of Alla Zabel, a former member of the Bolshoi company, Riabynkina is currently the youngest ballerina of the Bolshoi Ballet. She entered the school in 1950 and was graduated from it in 1959. She had a most unusual debut. At the time when most of the Bolshoi ballerinas were touring the U.S., Riabynkina was entrusted with the role of Odette-Odile in *Swan Lake* while technically still a pupil. She danced it with great success for the first time June 7, 1959, breaking a record both in the history of the school and the theatre. From Vera Vassilieva, her teacher for five years, she acquired grace and a strong technique. Since graduating into the company she has worked with Yelizaveta Gerdt, who has passed on to her her famous plasticity of arms and nobility of manner. She has a very good line, musicality, taste, and good extensions although she lacks natural elevation and is a somewhat terre à terre dancer. Among her roles are Queen of the Ball (*The Bronze Horseman*), Needle-Fish (*Sadko*), Pas de Trois (*Swan Lake*), Queen of the Dryads (*Don Quixote*), title role in *Raymonda,* Tzar-Maiden (*The Humpbacked Horse*), and for the 1961–62 season Kitri (*Don Quixote*) and Phyrgia (*Spartacus*). She has danced in Austria, Poland, Denmark, Norway, Hungary, Finland, China, and the U.S.

Ricarda, Ana, dancer and choreographer, b. San Francisco; m. English artist Anthony Stubbing, 1963. Studied with Minnie Hawke in Washington, D.C.; Vincenzo Celli and Pierre Vladimiroff in N.Y.; with Vicente Escudero and Argentina in Europe. She danced with the Markova-Dolin Company, joining the Grand Ballet du Marquis de Cuevas as ballerina in 1949. Among the ballets she choreographed for that company were *Del Amor y de la Muerte, Dona Ines de Castro, La Tertulia,* and *Chanson de l'Eternelle Tristesse.*

Rich, John (ca. 1692–1761), founder of Covent Garden Theatre. Son of Christopher Rich, he inherited the Lincoln's Inn Fields Theatre from his father. He brought many French and Italian dancers to London and many Harlequin plays in which he himself often played Arlequin. He is credited with founding the English Harlequinade and producing the first pantomimes in London. Among the dancers he brought to London were Marie Sallé, Jean-Georges Noverre, and La Barberina.

Richards, Dianne, South African dancer, b. Northern Rhodesia, 1934. Studied with Marjorie Sturman. Joined London's Festival Ballet (1951); promoted to soloist (1955); ballerina (1959). Roles include Sugar Plum Fairy (David Lichine's *The Nutcracker*), *Harlequinade* pas de deux, Barbara Allen (*The Witch Boy*), title role (*The Snow Maiden*), Carlotta Grisi (*Pas de Quatre*), Queen of the Wilis (*Giselle*), and others. Guest ballerina with American Ballet Theatre, making her debut as Caroline in *Lilac Garden* in Washington, D.C., Feb. 20, 1963. Returned as full member of that company, with ballerina status (fall, 1963). Remained with the company until early 1964.

Richardson, Philip J. S. (1875–1963), English editor and writer, b. Winthrop, Notts. Educated at Beaumont College and University College School. In partnership with the late T. M. Middleton founded *The Dancing Times* (London, 1910). He edited this magazine, which was turned into a limited company with himself as principal shareholder, until 1957 when he appointed A. H. Franks as his successor. Co-founder, Association of Operatic Dancing of Great Britain (1920), now called The Royal Academy of Dancing, of which he was for many years Honorary Secretary and Vice-President; inaugurated series of Dancers Circle Dinners to bring together members of the profession (1920); between 1919 and 1930 organized ten Sunshine Matinees in aid of blind babies at which, at one time or another, most of the leading European dancers of the day appeared; co-founder (with Arnold L. Haskell) of The Camargo Society (1929); founded the Official Board of Ballroom Dancing (1929) and was its chairman until 1959 when he was succeeded by A. H. Franks and was created life-president; also president of the International Council of Ballroom Dancing. Joint editor (with Haskell) of *Who's Who in Dancing* (1932); co-author (with Victor Silvester) of *The Art of the Ballroom* (1936); author of *A History of English Ballroom Dancing from 1910 to 1945* (1946), *Social Dances of the Nineteenth Century* (1960), and numerous articles on the dance for magazines and newspapers. Received the prize of the Ministry of Arts of France (1931); awarded the O.B.E. (Order of the British Empire) and created Knight of Dannebrog (both 1952).

Riegger, Wallingford (1885–1961), American composer. Wrote scores for *New Dance, Theatre Piece, With My Red Fires* (Doris Humphrey); *Chronicle* (Martha Graham); *The Pilgrim's Progress* (Erick Hawkins). Co-composer of Hanya Holm's *Trend* (with Edgar Varèse) and Charles Weidman's *Candide* (with Genevieve Pitot).

Rieti, Vittorio, composer, b. Alexandria, Egypt, 1898. Graduate Bocconi Univ., Milan, Italy. Studied music with Giuseppe Frugatta and Ottorino Respighi. Composed and/or arr. and orch. the following ballet scores: for George Balanchine—*Barabau* (1925), *Le Bal* (1929), Diaghilev Ballets Russes; *Waltz Academy* (1944); Ballet Theatre; *Night Shadow* (*Sonnàmbula*) (1946), Ballet Russe de Monte Carlo; *Triumph of Bacchus and Ariadne* (1948), Ballet Society; *Native Dancers* (1959), New York City Ballet; for Serge Lifar *David Triumphant* (1935), Paris Opéra; for Antonia Cobos *The Mute Wife* (1944), Ballet International, N.Y.

Rietstap, Ine, Dutch dancer, b. The Hague, Holland, 1929. Began her training with Mascha ter Weeme and later studied with Angela Bayley and Job Leerink. Passed all R.A.D. exams in London, where she studied with Lydia Kyasht, Anna Northcote, Stanislas Idzikowski, but principally with Phyllis Bedells. Also worked in Paris with Nora Kiss. Soloist, Ballet der Lage Landen (1948–58); at present soloist with the Scapino Ballet. Among her roles in Ballet de Lage Landen were Odette in *Swan Lake* (Act 2); Dawn variation in *Coppélia* (Act 3); all three female parts in *Les Sylphides;* Snow Queen in *The Nutcracker; Peasant* pas de deux in *Giselle; Le Spectre de la Rose;* Maiden in *Death and the Maiden* (Andrée Howard). Soloist in *Kaleidoscope* (Walter Gore); Summer in *Stagioni* (Jack Carter); the Girl in Blue (Carter); The Girl in *Kennismaking* (Nettie van der Valk); leading part in *Sonatina* (Pieter van der Sloot). In Scapino Ballet she dances the leading part in *Springtime* (Alexandra Danilova); Swanilda in *Coppélia* (Act 2); Princess in *Princess and the Pea* (Jan Rebel); Infanta in *Birthday of the Infanta* (Rebel); The Woman in the Shadow (Karel Poons). She has translated Kay Ambrose's book *Beginners, Please* into Dutch and has written a chapter on ballet history in *Dance and Ballet,* a pocket book edited by Hans Snoek.

Rigaudon, a dance originating in Provence in 1485 and deriving its name from a dancing master in Marseilles. It was in common time (4/4 measure) and singing accompanied the dancing. The two dancers danced side by side but did not hold hands.

Rimsky-Korsakov, Nicholas Andreievitch (1844–1908), Russian composer. Michel Fokine used his music for the ballets *Schéhérazade* (1910), *Le Coq d'Or* (1914), *Igrouchki* (1921); Leonide Massine used his *Capriccio Espagnol* for his ballet of the same name (1939).

Rinaldo and Armida. Ballet in 1 act; chor.: Frederick Ashton; commissioned music: Malcolm Arnold; décor: Peter Rice. First prod.: Sadler's Wells (now Royal) Ballet, Royal Opera House, Covent Garden, London, Jan. 6, 1955, with Svetlana Beriosova (Armida), Michael Somes (Rinaldo), Julia Farron (Sibilla), Ronald Hynd (Gandolfo). Based on the Torquato Tasso poem, Armida is under the spell of a sorceress who uses her to lure men to their deaths. Armida must not respond herself or she will die; but when Rinaldo finds himself in the magic garden, she falls in love with him and saves his life by giving him the kiss which is her own death sentence.

Rios, Consuelo, Brazilian dancer and teacher, b. Vitoria. Arrived in Rio de Janeiro in 1943 to study at National School of Physical Education, from which she was graduated as teacher. Began to study dance (1944) under Anna Volkova; later studied with Tatiana Leskova, Tamara Grigorieva, Igor Schwezoff. Made her debut with Ballet da Juventude (1947); danced with Ballet Society (1948–49). Began to teach (1950), first on her own, then at Ballet da Juventude (1951); Ballet Society Academy (1952–60). Ballet mistress, Ballet do Rio de Janeiro (1959–61). Currently ballet teacher at ballet school of Teatro Municipal. She has also studied under Katherine Dunham (1950) and at the classe de perfection of Lubov Egorova in Paris (1954, 1958).

Ripman, Olive, English dancer and teacher, b. Teddington, Middlesex, 1886. Studied at Wordsworth Academy and later with well-known specialists. Formerly principal of the Ripman School in London; now co-director, Arts Educational Trust, London and Tring, Herts. Originator of formation ballroom dancing. Retired from teaching in 1965.

Rite of Spring, The. Ballet in 2 scenes; chor.: Vaslav Nijinsky; music: Igor Stravinsky; book: Nicholas Roerich and Stravinsky; décor: Roerich. First prod.: Diaghilev Ballets Russes, Théâtre des Champs-Elysées, Paris, May 29, 1913, with Maria Piltz as the Chosen Maiden. The ballet raised a storm of protest and was given only six times. Was revived and re-staged by Leonide Massine for the same company (1920), with Lydia Sokolova. This latter version, again with revisions by the choreographer, in collaboration with Martha Graham, was given in Philadelphia, Apr. 11, 1930, under the auspices of the League of Composers. Massine has also staged the ballet for Royal Swedish Ballet, Stockholm, May 30, 1956. In 1957 Mary Wigman staged her version for the Berlin Festival. Maurice Béjart has also choreographed *The Rite of Spring*, premièred at the Théâtre Royal de la Monnaie, Brussels, Dec., 1959. England's Royal Ballet premièred Kenneth MacMillan's version in décor by Sidney Nolan at Royal Opera House, Covent Garden, May 8, 1962, with Monica Mason as the Chosen Maiden; U.S. première: Metropolitan Opera House, N.Y., May 8, 1963. The two scenes are Adoration of the Earth and The Sacrifice. A primitive people gather for a ritual blessing of the earth in preparation for the coming spring; a maiden is chosen for the sacrifice, having first been worshiped by the people as a living goddess. On June 29, 1964, the Bolshoi Ballet, Moscow, produced the ballet, choreographed by a husband-and-wife team of the company's young dancers, Vladimir Vasilyov (not to be confused with Vassiliev) and Natalia Kasatkina. It was a fresh, exciting ballet, which was given a ten-minute standing ovation. The ballet was barred from the Soviet stage until the present time. The choreographers have another ballet to their credit, *Vanini Vanini,* staged in 1962.

Rites. Ballet in 1 act; chor.: Birgit Aakesson; music: Ingvar Lidholm; book: Erik Lindegren; décor and costumes: Lennart Rhode. First prod.: Royal Swedish Ballet, 1960, with Bjorn Holmgren, Yvonne Brosset, Loulou Portefaix, Mario Mengarelli, and Lilavati in the principal roles. The poet Lindegren's story is a balletic exposition of what he considers to be "the horrible truth"—that for mankind there is no way out: cruelty is permanent and so is power and the victim. The eternal phenomenon is the Young Man, the idealist.

Ritmo Jondo (Deep Rhythm). Modern dance work; chor.: Doris Humphrey; music: Carlos Surinach, based on Spanish gypsy songs and dances; décor: Jean Rosenthal. First prod.: José Limón Dance Company, Alvin Theatre, N.Y., during the season of American dance presented by B. de Rothschild Foundation, Apr. 15, 1953, with José Limón, Pauline Koner, Betty Jones, Ruth Currier, Lucas Hoving, Lavinia Nielsen, Ray Harrison, Charles Czarny, Crandall Diehl. A devastating and witty comment on the relationship between the sexes, with the men having it all their own way.

Rivera, Chita (Conchita del Rivero), American dancer, b. Washington, D.C., 1933; m. Tony Mordente. Graduate of Taft High School. Studied ballet at the School of American Ballet, N.Y. Her very successful career progresses mainly in musicals, for which she has a special flair. Her first job out of the ensemble was in *Call Me Madam,* in which she was one of the principal dancers. She then appeared in *Guys and Dolls* and *Can Can,* both choreographed by Michael Kidd. *Shoestring Revue,* staged by Dania Krupska, offered her her first singing and acting part. Then came *Seventh Heaven* (Fifi), choreographed by Peter Gennaro; *Mr. Wonderful* (Rita Romano), choreographed by Jack Donahue. She reached the pinnacle of her young career in the Arthur Laurents–Leonard Bernstein–Jerome Robbins musical *West Side Story* (1957), where she acted, sang, and danced the part of Anita. She repeated her demanding role in the subsequent London production. In 1960 she created the role of Rose Grant in *Bye Bye, Birdie,* directed and choreographed by Gower Champion; later repeated it in the London production. In the summer of 1964 she was rehearsing the part of Athena in the musical *Zenda* with Jack Cole choreographing. Danced the leading role of Anyanka, gypsy princess, in musical *Bajour* (fall, 1964); principal role in London production of *Sweet Charity* (fall, 1966). She is a frequent guest on television; among the shows in which she appeared are those of Garry Moore, Ed Sullivan, Arthur Godfrey, Dinah Shore, Judy Garland, Sid Caesar, Imogene Coca. She has also danced in a London Palladium television show.

Road of the Phoebe Snow, The. Modern dance work; chor.: Talley Beatty; music: arr. from Duke Ellington and Billy Strayhorn; lighting: Nichola Cernovich. First prod.: YM–YWHA, N.Y., Nov. 28, 1959, with Candace Caldwell, Georgia Collins, Joan Peters, Joann Gore, Barbara Gordon, Tommy Johnson, Herman Howell, Ernest Parham, Jerome Jeffery. An electrifying piece of jazz dance involving love and violence and taking place, as the title claims and the lighting suggests, by the railway tracks on the edge of a city. The title is taken from an early Lackawanna Railroad run. This was the first work to be financed by a grant from the Lena Robbins Foundation. See FOUNDATIONS, PHILANTHROPIC.

Jerome Robbins, dancer, choreographer.

Robbins, Jerome, choreographer and dancer, b. New York City, 1918. Studied with Antony Tudor, Eugene Loring, Ella Daganova, Helene Platova, New Dance League (modern), Helene Veola (Spanish), Nimura (Oriental), Alyce Bentley, Sonya Robbins (interpretive); also studied piano, violin, acting, etc. Member, Gluck Sandor-Felicia Sorel Dance Center (1937); danced in musicals (1938–40). Member, Ballet Theatre (1940–48), working up from corps de ballet to soloist, creating roles in *Romeo and Juliet, Helen of Troy, Bluebeard, Aleko,* and dancing title role in *Petrouchka*. Choreographed *Fancy Free, Interplay, Facsimile* for Ballet Theatre. Choreographed *The Guests, Age of Anxiety, Jones Beach* (with George Balanchine), *The Cage, Pied Piper, Ballade, Afternoon of a Faun, Fanfare, Quartet, The Concert* for New York City Ballet, of which he was Associate Artistic Director from 1949 to 1963. Formed own company, Ballets: U.S.A. (1958), creating for it *New York Export: Opus Jazz, Moves,* and *Events*. Choreographed and directed numerous musicals, among them *On the Town, Miss Liberty, The King and I, Peter Pan, West Side Story, Gypsy*. Has also directed plays, among them *Oh Dad, Poor Dad, Mama's Hung You in the Closet and I'm Feelin' So Sad*. Has also worked with dancers in Israel. In 1958 established the Lena Robbins Foundation (in memory of his mother) to assist young choreographers in bringing their work to the attention of the public. In Apr., 1962, Robbins won two Oscars: one for the direction of *West Side Story* and the other for his choreography in the same film. This was the first time the category of choreography was included in the nominations. He directed and choreographed for *Fiddler on the Roof,* (1964) a musical based on *Tevye, the Milkman* by Sholem Aleichem. On Nov. 3, 1964, the choreographer was awarded the rank of Chevalier de l'Ordre des Arts et Lettres by the French government. The decoration was presented to him at the Cultural Department of the French Embassy in N.Y. On March 30, 1965, the American Ballet Theatre presented Robbins' version of *Les Noces* (Stravinsky) which became the most exciting ballet in the company's 25th anniversary season. The American Concert Choir was the choral group for the performance and Leonard Bernstein conducted the on-stage choir, percussionists, and the four pianists. On May 16, 1966, the National Council on the Arts allocated $300,000 for a project proposed by Robbins, The American Lyric Theatre Workshop.

Robbins, Lena, Foundation. See FOUNDATIONS, PHILANTHROPIC.

Robin Hood Dell, an amphitheatre in Fairmount Park, Philadelphia, Pa., seating 6500, in which summer concerts have been given since 1930. Ballet groups have often been presented there.

Robinson, Bill ("Bojangles") (1878–1949), American tap dancer. Began tap dancing when a boy; was discovered while working in a beer garden between engagements in vaudeville, and quickly rose to fame. Has danced in most of the leading theatres and night clubs in U.S. Appeared in several moving pictures (*The Little Colonel, The Littlest Rebel, Rebecca of Sunnybrook Farm,* and others). Was featured in the Broadway and N.Y. World's Fair production of *The Hot Mikado*. So great was his fame as a tap dancer that on his sixtieth year in show business (Apr. 29, 1946) N.Y.'s Mayor William O'Dwyer proclaimed the day "Bill Robinson Day," and presented the dancer with a plaque in recognition of his contribution to show business.

Rochon, Roger, Canadian dancer, b. Montreal. Studied dance in London, Paris, and N.Y. Danced with the Ballet Concert Group of Ottawa (1951–52). Did considerable television work in Montreal and Toronto before joining Les Grands Ballets Canadiens (1953). As soloist his roles include, among others, Dr. Coppelius (*Coppélia*), Mother Simone (*La Fille Mal Gardée*), leading male role in Eric Hyrst's *Labyrinthe, Trianon* pas de deux (with Veronique Landory), Baron (Ludmilla Chiriaeff's *Camille*), one of the dancers of the pas de trois in *Sea Gallows*.

Rockefeller Foundation. See FOUNDATIONS, PHILANTHROPIC.

Rockettes, a famous group of precision dancers at Radio City Music Hall, N.Y. They were assembled and trained by Russell Markert, director of the troupe. Forerunners of Rockettes were the Roxiettes, also trained by Mr. Markert, a precision line at the Roxy Theatre, N.Y., demolished in 1963. The Rockettes have been subsequently trained and directed by the late Gene Snyder.

Rode, Lizzie, dancer of the Royal Danish Ballet, b. Copenhagen, 1933. Entered the company's school (1940); accepted into the company (1952). Leading roles in *La Jeunesse, La Sylphide, Kermessen i Brügge, Vision, Miss Julie, Medea, Blood Wedding, The Shadow, Graduation Ball,* and others. Choreographed *Ballet in D* (1961).

Rodeo, or The Courting at Burnt Ranch. Ballet in 2 scenes; chor. and book: Agnes de Mille; music: Aaron Copland; décor: Oliver Smith; costumes: Kermit Love. First prod.: Ballet Russe de Monte Carlo, Metropolitan Opera House, N.Y., Oct. 16, 1942, with Casimir Kokitch (Head Wrangler), Frederic Franklin (Champion Roper), Agnes de Mille (Cowgirl), Milada Mladova (Rancher's Daughter). After de Mille's guest appearances her role was taken by Lubov Roudenko who later was succeeded by Dorothy Etheridge. *Rodeo* introduced a novelty in ballet, an interlude consisting of a running square dance to the clapping of hands (of orchestra and dancers) and a caller. As the subtitle of the ballet reads, the plot of the ballet deals with courting. The courters are the cowhands, especially the Head Wrangler and the Champion Roper. The courted—almost any female around the ranch—not excluding the "Eastern" visitors from Kansas City. The only exception is the Cowgirl. She can ride and rope and do almost anything the boys can do and yet no one even attempts to court her. When everyone is dancing on Saturday night and she is not, the Cowgirl realizes that she is wearing bluejeans and boots while the other girls are dressed to kill. Unnoticed she runs to her room and returns dressed in a dainty frock, with a ribbon in her hair, just as the Eastern girls have. The dancing stops for a moment as she enters and the Head Wrangler and the Champion Roper are at her feet; she is the happiest girl on the floor.

Rodham, Robert, dancer, choreographer, b. Pittston, Pa., 1939. Studied with Barbara Weisberger, E. Virginia Williams, and at School of American Ballet, N.Y., on a Ford Foundation Scholarship. Became member of New York City Ballet (1960); promoted to soloist (1963), dancing in *Agon, La Valse, Allegro Brillante, Arcade, Pas de Dix,* and others. Most important role to date is that of Puck in *A Midsummer Night's Dream.* Staged George Balanchine's *Pas de Dix* for the Pennsylvania Ballet (1963) when he was also ballet master of that company. His first ballet, *Ballade,* to music by Chopin, was staged at the Fifth Northeast Regional Ballet Festival, Detroit, (1963), danced by Wilkes-Barre Ballet.

Rodrigues, Alfred, South African dancer and choreographer, b. Cape Town, 1921; m. Julia Farron. Began dance training with Cape Town Univ. Ballet Club. Joined Sadler's Wells (now Royal) Ballet (1947) shortly after his arrival in London (1946), where he studied with Vera Volkova. His roles included King Florestan (*The Sleeping Beauty*), Pan (*Daphnis and Chloë*), which he created, and others. Choreographed *Ile des Sirènes* for the Margot Fonteyn-Robert Helpmann touring group (1950) which was briefly in the repertoire of Sadler's Wells Theatre Ballet (1952). Also for the latter company he created *Blood Wedding* (1953) and *Café des Sports* (1954). His ballets for the Royal Ballet include *The Miraculous Mandarin* (1956) and *Jabez and the Devil* (based on Stephen Vincent Benet's *Devil and Daniel Webster,* 1961). He staged Prokofiev's *Romeo and Juliet* in Verona, Italy (1955); *The Nutcracker* and Prokofiev's *Cinderella* for Teatro alla Scala, Milan (1957). Maître de ballet, Sadler's Wells Ballet (1953–55). Choreographs mainly for musicals.

Rodriguez, Rodolfo, premier danseur, b. Buenos Aires, 1935. Studied dance with Michel Borovski, Amalia Lozano, Otto Werberg, Yekaterina de Galantha. Joined corps de ballet of Teatro Colón, Buenos Aires, Argentina (1954); became soloist; premier danseur (1957). Has danced *Swan Lake, Giselle, Apollon Musagète, Coppélia, Aurora's Wedding, El Junco, Don Quixote, Black Swan, The Three-Cornered Hat* (chor. Margaret Wallman), *Capriccio Espagnol,* and others. At present, on leave from Teatro Colón, he is premier danseur of Ballet de Cuba and partner of Alicia Alonso.

Roerich, Nicholas (1874–1947), Russian painter and designer. He designed the décor for Alexander Borodin's *Prince Igor,* the "Polovetzian Dances" from which were staged by Michel Fokine (1909), and for Stravinky's ballet *The Rite of Spring* (chor.: Vaslav Nijinsky, 1913).

Roger de Coverly, an old English country-dance, somewhat like the Virginia Reel; named after Addison's novel, *Sir Roger de Coverly.*

Rogers, Ginger (Virginia McMath), dancer and motion picture actress, b. Independence, Mo. Appeared on Broadway in musicals *Top Speed* and *Girl Crazy.* Later launched a successful career in motion pictures when she and Fred Astaire sang and danced in what had been intended as secondary roles in *Flying Down to Rio* (1933). This was followed by a long series of Hollywood musicals, the partnership continuing through *The Gay Divorcee, Roberta, Top Hat, Follow the Fleet, Swing Time, Shall We Dance?, Carefree, The Story of Vernon and Irene Castle,* and (after a lapse of several years) *The Berkeleys of Broadway.* After the partnership broke up, Ginger Rogers continued a successful film career in straight acting roles, winning an Academy Award for *Kitty Foyle.* She has also appeared in summer stock and on Broadway, taking over the title role from Carol Channing in *"Hello, Dolly!"* (1964).

Rogge, Florence, choreographer and ballet producer, b. Detroit, Mich., 1904; m. J. J. Dickman. Studied dance with

Theodore Smith, Theodore Koslov, Nicholas Legat, Luigi Albertieri, Michio Ito, Konstantin Kobeleff, and Margaret Wallmann. Taught dance in Toronto, Canada, and N.Y. Soloist and choreographer, Roxy Theatre, N.Y., for four years; choreographer and producer, Radio City Music Hall from its opening (1932) until her retirement (Sept. 24, 1952). Some of her ballets, such as Ravel's *Bolero, Rhapsody in Blue, Undersea Ballet,* and *White Ballet,* have been frequently revived by her successors.

Roje, Ana, ballerina, teacher, b. Split, Yugoslavia, 1909. Studed ballet in the state ballet schools in Zagreb and Belgrade, and then for four years in London with Nicholas Legat who taught her his own pedagogical methods. After his death (1937), she remained for one year helping his wife, Nadine Nicolaeva Legat, to carry on his school. At this time she won three prizes at the International Concourse de la Danse in Paris. Joined Ballet Russe de Monte Carlo (1938), dancing, teaching, and coaching the company, including the leading dancers; left to join Col. de Basil's Original Ballet Russe for its Australian tour. When World War II broke out, she was on holiday in Yugoslavia and remained there for ten years establishing (with Oskar Harmos) ballet companies in Split and Zagreb of which she was prima ballerina, teacher, and choreographer. The Zagreb company was the first outside Russia to stage the Soviet ballets *Fountain of Bakhchisarai* and *Romeo and Juliet*. For her dancing in these ballets (as Maria and Juliet, respectively), she was awarded the Order of the Republic (Honored Artist of Yugoslav Republic). Was later appointed Professor of Ballet Art at State Conservatory of Music and Drama in Yugoslavia. Between 1950 and 1953 she divided her time between Yugoslavia and England, where she taught. In 1953 she and Harmos established the International Ballet School in Split, Yugoslavia, which trains foreign as well as local students. Since 1954 she has divided her time between Yugoslavia and the U.S. (mainly N.Y. and Boston) and since 1959 has organized, danced in, and staged the annual Bermuda Ballet Festival. Currently teaching in her own school, Boston, Mass., during the season and in Bermuda during the summer.

Romanoff, Dimitri, dancer, ballet master, regisseur, b. Tzaritzin, Russia, 1907, now an American citizen; m. Francesca Giugni. Educated in Japan and San Francisco; studied piano; ballet with Theodore Koslov, Adolph Bolm, Mikhail Mordkin, Michel Fokine. Made his professional debut as partner to Nini Theilade in the film of *A Midsummer Night's Dream* (1935); toured in concert performances with her and was principal dancer of San Francisco Opera Ballet under Bolm; with Mikhail Mordkin Ballet (1937–39); joined Ballet (now American Ballet) Theatre for its initial season at Center Theatre, N.Y., (1940), and has

Dimitri Romanoff, dancer, regisseur of the American Ballet Theatre.

remained ever since, being appointed regisseur (1946). Was ballet master of Netherlands Opera Ballet, Amsterdam, (1958–59 season), staging the classic repertoire. As a dancer his roles included King Bobiche (*Bluebeard*), Hilarion (*Giselle*), Menelaus (*Helen of Troy*), and others. He created Friar Laurence (Antony Tudor's *Romeo and Juliet*), and others. Also teaches.

Romanov, Boris (1891–1957), Russian-born choreographer. Graduated from the St. Petersburg Imperial Maryinsky Ballet School (1909). While an artist of the Maryinsky Theatre, he also danced with the Diaghilev Ballets Russes (1910–14), for which he choreographed the *Tragedy of Salomé* (1912); also staged the dances in Igor Stravinsky's opera *The Nightingale* for the Paris Opéra (1913). Made his debut as choreographer at the Maryinsky Theatre with dances in the opera *Treason* (1914); from then on through 1917 staged dances in eighteen operas. In 1917 choreographed *Andalusiana* for the Theatre of Musical Drama in Petrograd. Left Russia in 1921 and founded in Germany the Romantic Theatre, a travelling troupe which danced nearly five years in Germany, France, Spain, and England. In 1925 became choreographer of Teatro alla Scala, Milan; subsequently choreographed for the Colón Theatre, Buenos Aires; Teatro del Opera, Rome; Teatro Reggia, Turin; Metropolitan Opera House, N.Y. (seasons 1938 through 1941–42; 1945–46 through 1949–50). He also staged ballets for Ballet International (1944), Ballet for America, and Foxhole Ballet (1946), Ballet Russe de Monte Carlo (1956). During the summers when he was free from his theatre work he taught at the School of Ballet Repertory, N.Y. His second wife, Eugenia Romanov, survived him. His first wife, Yelena Smirnova, a former ballerina of the Maryinsky Theatre, died in Buenos Aires while appearing as guest artist at the Colón (1935).

Boris Romanov, dancer, choreographer, one-time director of the Romantic Theatre Ballet.

Romanova, Maria (1886–1954), Honored Art Worker of the RSFSR, Soviet teacher. Mother of Galina Ulanova. Married to Sergei Ulanov (1881–1950), regisseur of the Kirov Ballet. Graduated into the corps de ballet from the theatre school in 1903. Danced abroad with Anna Pavlova's company (1911). Was soloist in the former Maryinsky Ballet until 1924. Taught in the Leningrad Ballet School from 1917 and at the School of Russian Ballet founded by Akim Volynsky. The first teacher of Ulanova and Vera Volkova, she passed on to her pupils her own qualities of softness and musicality, and played an important role in the development of her daughter, whom she taught for five years.

Romantic Ballet, both a style in ballet and a period in the history of ballet, and in neither case is it in opposition to classic ballet. A ballet can be Romantic in subject matter and classic in structure and execution. In style, the Romantic ballet is a department of the classic ballet. In period, the Romantic ballet bears the same essential characteristics as the other art forms of the Romantic period. The basic characteristic of the Romantic period was the desire to liberate the arts from the conventions and traditions of the neo-classic style. The essential characteristic of the Romantic ballet was the exposition of events, the treatment of subject matter on two planes; the plane of reality or, as it was often referred to, the bitter reality, and the fantastic plane or, the beautiful dream.

From this premise originated the basic theme of the romanticists: the never-ending struggle between the actual and the ideal, between the flesh and the spirit; the never-ending struggle in which bitter reality triumphs tragically over the beautiful dream.

In literature, painting, and music the Romantic period was a progressive development; in ballet it was little short of a revolution. Everything underwent a change. The subject matter of the pre-Romantic ballet—its mythological, heroic and pastoral themes—gave way to dramatic love themes, fairy tales, folk legends. The dance itself was all but transformed. For the first time in the history of dance the ballerina rose on her toes, manifesting outwardly the yearning of her time for greater heights, for closer proximity to the ideal, for lesser contact with the earth, the symbol of reality. Along with it appeared a change in the general pattern of the ballet dance: the technique was enriched with new steps, with greater deftness of their execution. Ballet moved further in its defiance of the laws of gravity and balance, laws which were holding the human body so realistically close to earth, so far away from the ideal, dream world. The woman began to reign supreme in ballet; she became both the main object and the main subject of the new Romantic lyricism. The theatricalized court costume was abandoned in favor of a more or less standardized dress for the female dancer—the tarlatan tunic, or tutu as it is often called, flesh colored tights, and specially designed soft, heelless slippers. Attention was beginning to be paid to the artistic value of music and décor used in ballet.

These changes were very significant. The Romantic dance brought forth new choreographic designs not known to the pre-Romantic ballet. In the simplicity of lines, poses, and movements there began to be noticed the great force of choreographic arrangements of lyric movements, expressing the disappointments in the realities of life, and the hopes in the ideal, in dreams which bid the human being to a higher life, to his everlasting spirit, to his all-conquering love.

It is doubtful whether the Romantic ballet could have achieved its significance if Théophile Gautier, one of the leaders of the Romantic movement, had not taken such an active part in it. Filippo Taglioni, who staged the ballets for his great daughter Maria Taglioni, was a skillful choreographer. However, his education and cultural background were not sufficient to make him realize the significance of his own time, much less prepare him for leadership in this period. He sensed rather than understood the Romantic movement. He was an apt craftsman and little more.

Théophile Gautier, though an outsider to ballet, was a writer and a poet of great talent, a true representative of the movement which embraced all that was talented in European art. Gautier, more than any person in the Romantic period, was the right man to create the masterpiece which would serve as an example of the Romantic ballet even to us, one hundred and twenty-five years after its creation. This masterpiece was *Giselle,* produced in 1841. The Romantic period in ballet began before the first performance of *Giselle,* and *Giselle* was not the first ballet to reflect the characteristics of the Romantic period. This honor belongs to *La Sylphide,* staged in 1832 for Maria Taglioni by her father. Four years later, Taglioni danced another Romantic ballet, *La Fille du Danube*. These compositions were more or less preliminary experiments, stepping stones leading to the full realization of the Romantic ballet which came nine years later with the production of *Giselle.*

Romanticism, a movement started about 1830 in France in an attempt to break away from classic forms and to express individuality and personal sentiments. In music Hector Berlioz, Frédéric Chopin, Franz Liszt, Franz Schubert, Robert Schumann, Carl Maria von Weber, and Richard Wagner were among the leaders of this movement. The dance also felt the effects of this movement and *La Sylphide,* produced by Filippo Taglioni for his daughter (1832), ushered in the Romantic age in ballet. This marked a change from the old ballet based on mythological subjects to ballet with an ethereal, fairylike quality, one which Maria Taglioni personified. At the same time the costume of dancers was changed from the Empire dress to the now-familiar long, or Romantic, tutu, designed by Eugène Lamy for *La Sylphide.* One of the best known ballets of the Romantic school is *Giselle* (Jean Coralli, 1841). *Swan Lake* by Marius Petipa and Lev Ivanov (1895) and *Les Sylphides* by Michel Fokine (1909) are examples of neo-romanticism.

Romeo and Juliet. It is not surprising that of all Shakespeare's plays this is the one that has most attracted choreographers since Vincenzo Galeotti staged his version for the Royal Danish Ballet, Copenhagen, Feb. 4, 1811, to music by Claus Schall. Peter Tchaikovsky's *Romeo and Juliet Fantasy Overture* has been the music most often used, some of the versions to this music being Serge Lifar's for Nouveau Ballet de Monte Carlo (1946) and for Paris Opéra (1949); Birger Bartholin for Royal Danish Ballet (1950), a restaging of his original version for Ballet de la Jeunesse, Paris (1937); George Skibine for Grand Ballet du Marquis de Cuevas (1950), under the title *Tragedy at Verona;* Oleg Briansky for Tamara Toumanova and himself (1955). Bronislava Nijinska's *Romeo and Juliet* for the Diaghilev Ballets Russes (1926) had a commissioned score by Constant Lambert. The ballet was not about Shakespeare's lovers but about two dancers (Tamara Karsavina and Serge Lifar) who elope while rehearsing a ballet on the theme of Romeo and Juliet. See also SHAKESPEARE PLAYS, BALLETS BASED ON.

Romeo and Juliet. Ballet in 3 acts, 13 scenes, with a prologue and epilogue; chor.: Leonid Lavrovsky; music: Sergei Prokofiev; book: Lavrovsky, Prokofiev, and Sergei Radlov, after Shakespeare's tragedy; décor: Pyotr Williams. First prod.: Kirov Theatre, Leningrad, Jan. 11, 1940, with Galina Ulanova (Juliet), Konstantin Sergeyev (Romeo), Andrei Lopukhov (Mercutio), Sergei Koren (Tybalt). The ballet closely follows Shakespeare's plot and the spirit of the tragedy, its scenes being a translation of the plot into a choreographic idiom. Restaged by the choreographer with some changes for the ballet of the Bolshoi Theatre, Moscow (1946). For more recent productions see entries below.

Romeo and Juliet. Ballet in 1 act; chor. and book: Antony Tudor; music: Frederick Delius ("Walk to the Paradise Garden," from his opera *A Village Romeo and Juliet; Brigg Fair; Eventyr; Over the Hills and Far Away*), arr. by Antal Dorati; décor: Eugene Berman. First prod.: Ballet (now American Ballet) Theatre, Metropolitan Opera House, N.Y., Apr. 6, 1943, with Alicia Markova (Juliet), Hugh Laing (Romeo), Nicholas Orlov (Mercutio), Antony Tudor (Tybalt). The ballet was unfinished at this performance and was given in full for the first time on Apr. 10. Nora Kaye and Alicia Alonso have also danced Juliet and John Kriza succeeded Hugh Laing as Romeo. The story is based on the play by Shakespeare. Staged by Tudor for Royal

Swedish Ballet, Dec. 30, 1962, with Berit Skold and Conny Borg in the title roles.

Romeo and Juliet. Ballet in 3 acts; chor.: Frederick Ashton; music: Sergei Prokofiev; décor: Peter Rice. First prod.: Royal Danish Ballet, Royal Theatre, Copenhagen, May 19, 1955, with Mona Vangsaa (Juliet), Henning Kronstam (Romeo), Frank Schaufuss (Mercutio), Niels Bjorn Larsen (Tybalt). Other versions to this score have been choreographed by Dmitri Parlic for the Belgrade Opera (1948); Margarita Froman for the Zagreb Opera (1949); Serge Lifar for the Paris Opéra (1955); John Cranko for Wuerttemberg State Opera Ballet, Stuttgart, Germany (1962); Kenneth MacMillan for the Royal Ballet, England (1965).

Romeo and Juliet. Ballet in 3 acts; chor.: Kenneth MacMillan; music: Serge Prokofiev; décor: Nicholas Georgiadis. First perf.: Royal Ballet, Royal Opera House, Covent Garden, London, Feb. 9, 1965, with Margot Fonteyn (Juliet), Rudolf Nureyev (Romeo), David Blair (Mercutio), Desmond Doyle (Tybalt), Anthony Dowell (Benvolio), Gerd Larsen (Nurse), Ronald Hynd (Friar Laurence), Julia Farron (Lady Capulet), Michael Somes (Capulet), Derek Rencher (Paris). MacMillan's version is centered on the fate of the two young lovers, rather than on the life and mores of the citizens, nobles, whores, and partisans of both houses, not directly related to the tragedy. This is, of course, as compared with the two other great productions of the ballet: Leonid Lavrovsky's for the Moscow Bolshoi, and Frederick Ashton's for the Royal Danish Ballet. Following Fonteyn and Nureyev, Lynn Seymour and Christopher Gable, Merle Park and Donald MacLeary, Antoinette Sibley and Anthony Dowell danced the title roles. Fonteyn and Nureyev danced the N.Y. première, Metropolitan Opera House, Apr. 21, 1965, and were followed by the other three pairs in the course of the season.

Rond de Jambe, a circular movement of the leg. Variants in ballet: 1. Rond de jambe à terre: describe circle on floor with working leg, either en dedans or en dehors. 2. Rond de jambe en l'air: with working leg in demi-seconde, describe an inward or outward circle, using leg from knee to toe only. Toe touches calf and returns to demi-seconde. Rond de jambe en l'air can also be done in grande seconde, toe touching knee as it comes inward. 3. Grand rond de jambe: lift leg to grande quatrième devant, carry it to grande seconde, then to grande quatrième derrière and place in 5th pos. back. It can also be started in back and done en dedans. 4. Rond de jambe en tournant: see FOUETTÉ EN TOURNANT.

Rooms. Modern dance work; chor.: Anna Sokolow; music: Kenyon Hopkins. First prod.: YM–YWHA, N.Y., Feb. 24, 1955, with Beatrice Seckler, Eve Beck, Donald McKayle, Jeff Duncan, Jack Moore, Sandra Pine, Judith Coy, Paul Sanasardo. The theme is the aloneness of the human spirit and especially the frightening anonymity of loneliness in a great city. Anna Sokolow has also staged *Rooms* for the Nederlands Dans Theater.

Rooney, Pat (1880–1962), dancer, b. New York City. His parents, Mr. and Mrs. Patrick James Rooney, were also in show business. His father decided on a vaudeville career after losing his first fight and his first wrestling match. Pat Rooney had his first vaudeville engagement when he was eleven and appeared in his first musical, *In Atlantic City,* in 1897. From then on he had a continuous career in vaudeville, night clubs, musical comedy, and the legitimate theatre, movies, and later, radio and television. He was possibly the last, and one of the best, of the soft-shoe dancers, his most famous number being a waltz-clog to *The Daughter of Rosie O'Grady* (which he originated at the Palace Theatre, 1919). His last Broadway appearance was in the musical *Guys and Dolls,* which opened in 1950 and ran for three years, and in which he played the role of the slum missionary, Arvide Abernathy.

Roope, Clover, English dancer, choreographer, b. Bristol, 1937. Studied at Royal Ballet School; entered Sadler's Wells Theatre Ballet (1956); transferred to Royal Ballet as junior soloist (1957). Her repertoire included Polka (*Façade*), Lovers (*Veneziana*), Pas de Trois (*La Fête Etrange*), Red Riding-hood (*The Sleeping Beauty*), and others. Her first choreography was *Le Farçeur* for Sunday Ballet Club (1958). After a season as choreographer at the Bristol Old Vic she joined Western Theatre Ballet (1960) as dancer and choreographer, where she danced Columbine (*Le Carnaval*), the Girl (*One in Five*), one of the eight dancers (Walter Gore's *Street Games*), Pussycat (*The Owl and the Pussycat*), Girl (Kenneth MacMillan's *Valse Excentrique*), and others. Choreographed and staged Gluck's *Orfeo and Euridice* (1961); Bach's *Partita, Rencontre Imprevu,* both in 1962 for Western Theatre Ballet. Made her N.Y. debut in Helen McGehee's *After Possession,* Kaufmann Auditorium of the YM-YWHA, Apr. 11, 1965. Choreographer-in-residence, Jacob's Pillow (1965), staging work for the student dancers and dancing Beauty in John Cranko's *Beauty and the Beast* with Christopher Layall.

Roos, Nel (Neeltje Roos), dancer, teacher, writer, b. Ridderkerk, Holland, 1914. Studied modern dance with Corrie Hartung, Kurt Jooss, Mary Wigman, Rosalia Chladek, Sigurd Leeder, Yvonne Georgi; ballet with Nora Kiss, Madame Rousanne Sarkissian, and Olga Preobrajenska in Paris. Began giving solo performances—1940; soloist and teaching assistant, Yvonne Georgi Company (1942–47); ballet mistress, Amsterdam Opera Ballet (1947); toured with partner throughout Europe (1947–48). Opened her own school in Amsterdam (1948); taught ballet and modern dance at Camp Norfleet, Burlington, Vt. (1954–61); choreographer-in-residence, Jacob's Pillow (1960–61). Appointed director of the city-owned Rotterdam Dance Academy (1961, 1965–66); is on the board of the Nederlands Nationaal Ballet; president of Board of State Examinations and member of State Scholarship Board. Netherlands correspondent to *Dance News* (since 1960); contributor to *Dance Encyclopedia.*

Root of an Unfocus. Modern dance solo; chor.: Merce Cunningham; music: John Cage; costume: Merce Cunningham. First prod.: N.Y., Apr. 1944. An early solo which foreshadowed the style the choreographer has since developed, both in his own solos and in his group works.

Roots of the Blues, The. Modern dance work; chor.: Alvin Ailey; music: traditional, for singer, guitar, double bass, and percussion. First prod.: Boston Arts Festival, June 9, 1961, with Carmen de Lavallade and Alvin Ailey. An exploration in dance and music of the origin and meaning of one aspect of Negro music.

Rosario (Rosario Perez), Spanish dancer, b. Seville, 1920. Studied under Realito; with her cousin Antonio made her debut in Liège, Belgium (1928); then travelled with him for fifteen years as the team Rosario and Antonio. When the partnership came to an end in 1953 she formed her own company, with Roberto Iglesias as her partner, and began touring (1954). Iglesias subsequently resigned to form his own group.

Rosati, Carolina (1827–1905), Italian-born ballerina of the Paris Opéra during the latter years of the Romantic period, particularly noted for her dancing in *Giselle* and *Esmeralda.* Was guest-ballerina of the St. Petersburg Imperial Theatre where she created the principal role in Marius Petipa's *Pharaoh's Daughter.* In 1847 she replaced Lucile Grahn in Jules

Perrot's *Pas de Quatre* in London. Created the role of Medora in *Le Corsaire* (1856); also principal roles in *La Somnambule* (1857) and *Marco Spada* (1857).

Rosay, Madeleine (Magdalena Rosenzveig), Brazilian dancer, teacher, choreographer, b. Rio de Janeiro. Began dance study (1932) at ballet school of Teatro Municipal under Maria Olenewa. Made her debut eight months later in the opera ballet *O Guarany*. Became the first classic ballerina born and developed in Brazil (1937). Danced principal roles in *Chopiniana, Petrouchka, Le Spectre de la Rose, Uirapuru, Les Deux Pigeons, Imbapara, Daphnis and Chloë, Slavonika, The Nutcracker, The Dying Swan,* and others. Resigned from Teatro Municipal in 1945; a year later received a scholarship at the School of American Ballet, N.Y., and studied there under Felia Doubrovska, Muriel Stuart, and Anatole Oboukhoff. Returned to Rio as actress-star in the Brazilian film *Darling Susanna.* After some free-lance dancing and teaching, returned to Teatro Municipal (1948) as assistant choreographer. In the season 1951–52 danced on U.S. television. In the summer 1953 danced with her own group in Petropolis. Later that year choreographed her most important work, *Mancenilha,* for Teatro Municipal. Also choreographed *Carnet du Bal* (Tchaikovsky), *Juca Mulato* (Lorenzo Fernandez), *Children's Games* (Martinez Grau), *Concerto* (Mendelssohn), *Rumanian Rhapsody* (Enesco), as well as many short recital numbers. Since 1959, she has been director and principal teacher of the Teatro Municipal Ballet School.

Rosen, Elsa-Marianne von. See VON ROSEN, ELSA-MARIANNE.

Rosen, Heinz, German choreographer and ballet master, b. Hannover. Pupil of Rudolf van Laban, Kurt Jooss, Victor Gsovsky. Member of Ballets Jooss during its world tours. Collaborated with Jean Cocteau on *The Lady and the Unicorn,* presented in Munich (1953), as well as in Berlin, Paris, Buenos Aires, U.S. Other ballets include *L'Indifférent, Visions en Masques, Bourgeois Gentilhomme;* revisions and revivals of *The Legend of Joseph, Joan von Zarissa, Danza, La Tragedia di Orfeo, La Buffonata,* for the Bavarian State Opera (since 1959). Simultaneously stage director for operas, dramas, and musicals.

Rosenthal, Jean, lighting and production designer and consultant, b. New York City, 1912. Received her theatre education at Neighborhood Playhouse (1928–30) and Yale Drama School (1931–34). Technical director W.P.A. Federal Theatre (1936); lighting and production manager for Mercury Theatre Productions (1937–39); for New York City Opera productions of *Wozzeck, Bluebeard, Cenerentola, Falstaff, Hansel and Gretel, The Trial* (1945–51); lighting and production designer for all New York City Ballet productions between 1946 (when it was still Ballet Society) and 1957; for Martha Graham's works since 1938; American Shakespeare Festival Theatre since 1954; Dallas Civic Opera since 1957; lighting designer for Jerome Robbins' Ballets: U.S.A. (1959–60); on Broadway for musicals such as *Jamaica, West Side Story, Sound of Music,* and many others; and plays including *Dark at the Top of the Stairs, Becket, A Taste of Honey, Night of the Iguana,* and others. Was theatre consultant for the stage renovations of Carnegie Hall (1956) and on the Restoration Committee of Philadelphia Academy of Music the same year; theatre consultant of Juilliard School of Music since 1959; lighting consultant, Los Angeles Music Center and Pan American Passenger Terminal, N.Y. International Airport. President since 1937 of Theatre Production Service, theatre consultants and supply services.

Bertram Ross, as "Sun" in Martha Graham's Canticle for Innocent Comedians.

Ross, Bertram, contemporary American modern dancer. First attracted attention in the title role of Nina Fonaroff's *Lazarus* (1952); shortly thereafter joined the Martha Graham company, becoming its leading male dancer and dancing almost all the principal male roles, usually as her partner. He danced in such works as *Letter to the World, Appalachian Spring,* and *Night Journey;* created *Canticle for Innocent Comedians* (For Sun, for Moon, for Death, 1952), *Seraphic Dialogue* (St. Michael, 1955), *Embattled Garden* (Adam, 1958), *Clytemnestra* (Agamemnon and Orestes, 1958), *Acrobats of God* (1960), *Alcestis* (Thanatos, 1960), *Samson Agonistes* (Samson the Dedicated, 1961), *A Look at Lightning* (1962), *Phaedra* (Hippolytus, 1962), and others. Also teaches at the Graham school. Made his debut as choreographer Mar. 11, 1965, at the Kaufmann Auditorium of the YM–YWHA, N.Y. with a program of three works: *Triangle, Breakup,* and an untitled one.

Ross, Herbert, American dancer and choreographer, b. Brooklyn, N.Y., 1926; m. Nora Kaye. Studied ballet with Helene Platova, Caird Leslie; modern dance with Doris Humphrey. His first ballet, *Caprichos,* staged for a Choreographers' Workshop program (1949) was taken into the repertoire of Ballet (now American Ballet) Theatre. For the same company he choreographed *The Thief Who Loved a Ghost* (1951). Choreographed for television and musicals including *A Tree Grows in Brooklyn, The Gay Life, I Can Get It For You Wholesale, Tovarich, Anyone Can Whistle,* and others. For Ballet Theatre Previews he choreographed *The Maids* (based on Jean Genet's play) and *Paean* (1957); also *Ovid Metamorphosis* (1958). *Paean* was taken into the American Ballet Theatre repertoire. Also for this company he choreographed *Concerto* (to Peter Tchaikovsky's Violin Concerto, Sept. 16, 1958), *Tristan* (music from Wagner's *Tristan and Isolde,* Sept. 23, 1958), *Dialogues* (to Leonard Bernstein's *Serenade for Violin Solo, Strings and Percussion,* Apr. 26, 1960). Choreographed *Angel Head* (1959) and *Toccata for Percussion* (Carlos Chavez, 1960) at Festival of Two Worlds, Spoleto; formed a company known as Ballet of Two Worlds which toured in Europe in summer and fall of 1960 and appeared at the Berlin Festival when he premièred a choreographic version of *The Dybbuk.* With the exception of *Caprichos,* his ballets have not survived their initial seasons. Since 1960 Ross has been specializing in choreography for musical comedies, assisted by his wife. He also directs musicals in the U.S. and Europe.

Rossana, Noel, Scottish dancer, b. East Kilbride, 1931. Studied at the Cone-Ripman School. An original member of London's Festival Ballet, becoming soloist and dancing a large repertoire.

Rosson, Keith, English dancer, b. Birmingham, 1937. Studied at Priory School, Birmingham (1951–53); Sadler's Wells

School (1953); entering Sadler's Wells (now Royal) Ballet (1955) where he is currently soloist. First attracted public attention with his creation of the Cockerel (*La Fille Mal Gardée,* 1960). Also dances Moor (*Petrouchka*), Etiocles (*Antigone*), male dancer (*Les Sylphides*), Prince Florimund (*The Sleeping Beauty*), Pluto—also a creation (Frederick Ashton's *Persephone*), and others. Created von Rothbart in *Swan Lake* (1963); one of the Athletes in the revival of *Les Biches* (1964); leader of the Mandolin Dance in Kenneth MacMillan's *Romeo and Juliet* (1965).

Rothschild, Bethsabee de, Foundation. See FOUNDATIONS, PHILANTHROPIC.

Rouault, Georges (1871–1958), great French painter of a mystical mind who often devoted himself to Biblical subjects. His single work for ballet was the décor and costumes for *The Prodigal Son* (Prokofiev-Balanchine) for the Diaghilev Ballets Russes (1929). The sets and costumes are now the property of the New York City Ballet in whose repertoire the ballet is still being performed.

Rouché, Jacques (1862–1957), director of the Paris Opéra (1914–44). During his administration he raised the ballet of the Opéra to the highest level since the Romantic period, often using his personal finances to achieve this end. In 1929 after the death of Serge Diaghilev, he invited George Balanchine to become ballet master of the Opéra. When Balanchine was taken ill and had to leave the position Rouché, at the suggestion of Balanchine, invited Serge Lifar to fill the post.

Rouge et Noir. Ballet in 4 movements; chor.: Leonide Massine; music: Dimitri Shostakovitch's Symphony No. 1; book: Leonide Massine; décor and costumes: Henri Matisse. First prod.: Ballet Russe de Monte Carlo, Théâtre de Monte Carlo, May 11, 1939, with Alicia Markova, Igor Youskevitch, Nathalie Krassovska, Frederic Franklin, Michel Panaieff, Marc Platoff in principal roles; N.Y. première: Metropolitan Opera House, Oct. 28, 1939. An abstract symphonic ballet having no definite plot.

Round Dance, any of the social dances such as the waltz or foxtrot danced by couples; a term used to distinguish this type of dancing from the square dance. See BALLROOM DANCES.

Roundelay, a folk dance performed in a circle, generally by dancers who hold hands to form the circle; found in dances of many nations, such as the Russian Khorovod, the Romanian Hora, the German Reigen, etc.

Rousanne, Madame (Rousanne Sarkissian), teacher, b. Baku (now Azerbaijan), 1894, d. Paris, 1958. Of Russian-Armenian parentage, she studied law in Moscow. Began studying ballet too late (in the middle 1920's) to become a really good dancer. Her only public performances were a few as a character dancer. Her teachers were principally Vera Trefilova, Ivan Clustine, and Alexandre Volinine in Paris, where she herself taught from 1928 until only a few days before her death. Most of the best-known dancers of the day studied with her at one time or another. Despite her limited stage experience, Mme. Rousanne was an outstanding teacher, on the level of the famous Russian former ballerinas teaching at that time in Paris.

Rowell, Kenneth, Australian artist and designer, b. Melbourne, 1922. Studied at Royal Melbourne Technical College. His designs (décor and costumes) for ballets include *Alice in Wonderland* (London's Festival Ballet, 1953); *Hoops* (1951) and *Crucifix* (1953) (Walter Gore Ballet); *Carte Blanche* (Sadler's Wells Theatre Ballet, 1953); *Winter Night* (1948); *Variations on a Theme,* and *Laiderette* (both 1954) (Ballet Rambert); Kenneth MacMillan's *Le Baiser de la Fée* (Royal Ballet, 1960); *Musical Chairs* (1959), *The Owl and the Pussycat* (1962) (Western Theatre Ballet).

Royal Academy of Dancing, The (R.A.D.), founded Dec. 31, 1920, as the Association of Operatic Dancing of Great Britain, with Mme. Adeline Genée as president, a committee consisting of Tamara Karsavina, Phyllis Bedells, Edouard Espinosa, and Mr. P. J. S. Richardson as treasurer-secretary. The title was changed by Royal Command to The Royal Academy of Dancing (1935) and the academy was granted a charter by King George V. Its headquarters are in London. The objects of the R.A.D. are to improve the standard of ballet dancing and to advance the art of the dance throughout Great Britain and the British Commonwealth. It is a non-profit organization established to promote the correct teaching of classic ballet and Greek dance and to preserve national dances. It established the syllabi and now regulates the curricula of dance schools and their examinations, awards scholarships to talented students, gives special lectures and post-graduate courses, grants scholarships to train and develop choreographers. R.A.D. scholarships include the Leverhulme (£500), the Sir James Nott (£500), the four Overseas (South Africa, New Zealand, and two to Australia: £200 each). In addition to the courses and examinations given in Great Britain, examinations are held and scholarships granted to members in South Africa, Australia, New Zealand, and Canada. In recent years examiners have annually visited the U.S. where a number of teachers follow the R.A.D. syllabi. The R.A.D. also emphasizes the value of dance in education and physical education for children who are not studying the dance professionally but take it as part of their general education. The R.A.D. Production Club was formed to give actual stage experience to those interested in ballet. There is also a three year Teachers' Training Course specifically designed for students not desirous of becoming professional dancers but wishing to teach. The course includes, in addition to ballet technique, dance history, anatomy, biology, pre-classic and national dances, music, French, pantomime, Dalcroze eurythmics, etc. The Royal Academy of Dancing established the Queen Elizabeth II Coronation Award in 1954 and each year this is presented for outstanding work for British ballet. The recipients (to 1964) have been Dame Ninette de Valois, Tamara Karsavina, Dame Marie Rambert, Anton Dolin, Phyllis Bedells, Robert Helpmann, Ursula Moreton, Cyril W. Beaumont, Philip J. S. Richardson (posthumously), and Kathleen Gordon, director of Royal Academy of Dancing. Dame Adeline Genée retired as President in 1954 and was succeeded by Dame Margot Fonteyn. The Royal Academy Gazette, official publication of the organization, is published quarterly.

Royal Ballet, The, the major British ballet company, based since 1946 at the Royal Opera House, Covent Garden. This company became the Royal Ballet under a Royal Charter dated Oct. 31, 1956, having previously made its fame as the Sadler's Wells Ballet, with its "junior partner" (from 1946), the Sadler's Wells Theatre Ballet. The company was directed by Dame Ninette de Valois, its founder, until the end of the 1962–63 season when she retired. Sir Frederick Ashton, until that time associate director and principal choreographer of the company, succeeded her. Assistant directors are Michael Somes, John Hart, and John Field, the latter in charge of the touring section.

The origins of the Royal Ballet may be best traced back to the Academy of Choreographic Art, a school founded by de Valois in 1926 in London. This group of dancers sometimes gave performances and de Valois, who had arranged with Lillian Baylis of the Old Vic Theatre to produce dances for the plays there, persuaded her in 1928 to accept an occasional ballet as a curtain raiser. A school of ballet was started at the newly opened Sadler's Wells Theatre in Jan., 1931, and the first full evening of ballet under de Valois' direction at the Old Vic was on May 5, 1931. The program was *Les Petits Riens, Danse Sacrée et Danse Profane, Hommage Aux Belles Viennoises, The Jackdaw and the Pigeons, Faust Scène de Ballet, Bach Suite, The Faun,* and a Spanish solo by Anton Dolin. The dancers were de Valois, Beatrice Appleyard, Ursula Moreton, Joy Newton, Sheila McCarthy, and Freda Bamford. Anton Dolin, Leslie French, and Stanley Judson were guest artists, and Constant Lambert conducted.

This success encouraged Lillian Baylis to allow fortnightly ballet performances to be interspersed through the opera and drama repertoire from 1931 on. Constant Lambert joined de Valois as musical director and conductor, a position he held until 1948 (three years before his death). The early repertoire was mainly choreographed by de Valois herself, but in 1933 a guest ballet, *Les Rendez-vous,* was produced by Frederick Ashton, who had studied both with Marie Rambert and at the Academy of Choreographic Art. Shortly afterwards he became attached to the Vic-Wells Ballet, beginning a series of choreographic successes. De Valois also continued to choreograph, although her output declined after 1938.

The Vic-Wells' first ballerina was Alicia Markova, who joined them in 1932, dancing *Swan Lake* (Act 2) with Anton Dolin. Lydia Lopoukhova made a guest appearance in 1933 in *Coppélia,* when a young Australian dancer made his London debut in the corps de ballet—Robert Helpmann. Nine months later he had the chance to dance Dolin's part of Satan in the ex-Camargo Society ballet *Job,* and his success established him as a future premier danseur. This was his position at the Wells from 1934 until his resignation in 1950. In Jan., 1934, Markova danced with Anton Dolin in *Giselle,* with Stanley Judson in *The Nutcracker,* and in Nov. of the same year in the full-length *Swan Lake.* The revival of all these classical ballets was in the hands of Nicolas Sergeyev.

In 1935 *Rio Grande* (another Camargo Society ballet) was revived with a fifteen-year-old dancer in Markova's role of the Creole Girl—Margot Fonteyn. She had previously made an impression in the mime part of Young Tregennis in *The Haunted Ballroom.* Markova left the Wells that year and from then on Margot Fonteyn was groomed for the prima ballerina position. She is still, as Dame Margot Fonteyn, guest artist and undisputed star of the Royal Ballet.

Other dancers, however, were making their names with the Vic-Wells Ballet: Pamela May, June Brae, Elizabeth Miller, Mary Honer, Harold Turner, William Chappell, and Michael Somes, whose first created leading role was in *Horoscope* (1938). Pre–World War II choreographic successes included *The Haunted Ballroom* (1934), *The Rake's Progress* (1935), and *Checkmate* (1937) by de Valois; *Apparitions* (1935), *Nocturne* (1936), *Les Patineurs* and *A Wedding Bouquet* (1937), and *Horoscope* (1938) by Ashton.

The war sent the Sadler's Wells Ballet on tour—Sadler's Wells Theatre was requisitioned in 1940. However, they found a West End home in London at the New Theatre and, for one season, the Princes. These were years of intensive activity: at one time they were giving nine performances a week (three on Saturdays). These were also years of danger: a British Council tour of Holland had coincided with the German invasion and while the company escaped with their lives they lost scenery, costumes, and scores for some of their most successful ballets. But these were years of great success, artistically speaking. From 1939 to 1946, apart from the full-length classical ballets, their repertoire included (in addition to ballets mentioned above) Ashton's *Dante Sonata* (1940) and *The Wanderer* (1941); de Valois' *The Prospect Before Us* (1940) and *Orpheus and Eurydice* (1941); and

Helpmann's (a new choreographer) *Comus* (1942), *Hamlet* (1942), and *Miracle in the Gorbals* (1944).

The end of the war saw tremendous changes for the company. On Feb. 26, 1946, their London home became the Royal Opera House, Covent Garden. Ashton returned from his service with the R.A.F. and began his post-war choreographic work with *Symphonic Variations* (1946). Leonide Massine was invited to revive *Le Tricorne, La Boutique Fantasque,* and *Mam'zelle Angot.* New choreographers emerged in the persons of John Cranko, Kenneth MacMillan, and Alfred Rodrigues. Andrée Howard, well-known with the Ballet Rambert, whose ballet *Le Festin de L'Araignée* for the company in 1943 had not been successful, made more impact with post-war works such as *A Mirror for Witches* and *Veneziana.* George Balanchine revived *Ballet Imperial* in 1950, the year Roland Petit produced *Ballabile.* The company in the earlier seasons was led by Fonteyn and Helpmann and principal dancers included Pamela May, Beryl Grey, Moira Shearer, Violetta Elvin, Michael Somes, John Hart, Alexis Rassine, and John Field.

On Apr. 6, 1946, a second company was launched at the Sadler's Wells Theatre, the Sadler's Wells Opera (later Theatre) Ballet, with the aim of developing dancers and choreographers for later promotion to the senior company. It was remarkably successful and had a distinct character of its own. Royal Ballet principals today who worked with the Sadler's Wells Theatre Ballet include Svetlana Beriosova, Maryon Lane, Annette Page, David Blair, Stanley Holden, Donald MacLeary, Nadia Nerina (a guest artist since the end of 1965–66 season), and others.

The year 1956 marked the greatest alteration in the company's history, due to the awarding of the Royal Charter: both companies became the Royal Ballet and the school, which had been expanded in 1947 to include a general education curriculum under the direction of Arnold Haskell, became the Royal Ballet School. The present Royal Ballet, administered by governors and a council, is divided into the company primarily based on the Royal Opera House and the touring section. Dancers are occasionally interchanged and some ballets are in both repertoires, but the individual character of each company is, on the whole, preserved. The Opera House company, led by Dame Margot Fonteyn (now a guest artist), lists its principals alphabetically for the 1966–67 season as follows: Svetlana Beriosova, David Blair, Anthony Dowell, Desmond Doyle, Leslie Edwards, Christopher Gable, Alexander Grant, Stanley Holden, Ronald Hynd, Maryon Lane, Gerd Larsen, Donald MacLeary, Annette Page, Merle Park, Georgina Parkinson, Keith Rosson, Brian Shaw, Antoinette Sibley, Graham Usher. Doreen Wells heads the touring section with David Wall as principal male dancer. Guest artists at Covent Garden have included Alicia Markova, Alexandra Danilova, Yvette Chauviré, Sonia Arova, Melissa Hayden, Carla Fracci, Violette Verdy, Anton Dolin, Leonide Massine, Frederic Franklin, Erik Bruhn, Rudolf Nureyev, Flemming Flindt, Attilio Labis.

Kenneth MacMillan was resident choreographer through the 1965–66 season. Among his ballets were *Danses Concertantes* (1955), *Solitaire* (1956), *The Invitation* (1956), *Le Baiser de le Fée* (1960), *Diversions* (1961), *The Rite of Spring* (1962), *Symphony* (1963), *Images of Love* (1964), *Romeo and Juliet* (Prokofiev, 1965), and *Song of the Earth* (Mahler's *Das Lied von der Erde,* 1966). Ashton's trend towards the full-length ballet which began with *Cinderella* (1948) was crowned by his production of *Ondine* (1958) and *La Fille Mal Gardée* (1960). Since becoming director of the company he has choreographed only two short works, *Monotones I* (1965) and *Monotones II* (1966), both to music by Erik Satie. He invited Bronislava Nijinska to revive her two best known ballets for the company: *Les Biches* (Dec. 2, 1964) and

Les Noces (Mar. 23, 1966), Balanchine's *Ballet Imperial* was revived (1964), while *Serenade* was danced by the Royal Ballet for the first time at a Gala Performance (May 7, 1964), and *Apollo* (Nov. 16, 1966) was premièred under its French title *Apollon Musagète.*

The Royal Ballet has toured extensively abroad since its triumphant 1949 appearance in the U.S., including four weeks in the Soviet Union (1961). The touring section, with Margot Fonteyn as guest artist, danced *Raymonda* in a version staged by Nureyev at the Spoleto Festival of Two Worlds (1964). This is now in the touring section's regular repertoire.

The Royal Ballet School has for the last few years given an annual matinee at Covent Garden, and this is a much-appreciated opportunity to see the developing talent available for the future.

Royal Danish Ballet. See DENMARK, BALLET IN.

Royal Swedish Ballet. See SWEDISH BALLET.

Royal Winnipeg Ballet, Canada's oldest ballet company, grew out of the school and Ballet Club established in Winnipeg in 1938 by Gweneth Lloyd and Betty Farrally. Its first public performance, as the Winnipeg Ballet, was given in 1939. This company played host to the first Canadian Ballet Festival (1948), thus establishing the Regional Ballet Festival movement which later spread to the U.S. The Winnipeg Ballet became a professional company in 1949, dancing a command performance before the then Princess Elizabeth (now H.M. Queen Elizabeth II) and Prince Philip, Duke of Edinburgh, in 1951. The company was granted the title Royal Winnipeg Ballet in 1953, following the second visit to Canada of Queen Elizabeth, becoming the first British company to earn this right (Sadler's Wells Ballet did not become the Royal Ballet until 1956). In 1954 Winnipeg's disastrous fire completely destroyed the company's entire physical assets and it was not able to perform again until 1956 when Ruthanna Boris was appointed artistic director and choreographer. She staged *Le Jazz Hot, Pasticcio, Roundelay,* and *The Comedians* between 1956 and 1959 when she was replaced for a season by Benjamin Harkarvy. When Gweneth Lloyd retired as founder-director in 1958, Arnold Spohr was appointed director. Like Canada's other two professional companies, Royal Winnipeg Ballet receives a grant from the Canada Council, its first being in 1957. In addition to excerpts from the standard classic repertoire —*Swan Lake, The Nutcracker, The Sleeping Beauty,* and *Don Quixote,* the company has built up a repertoire of its own ballets which includes *Shadow on the Prairie* (the first ballet with an indigenously Canadian theme), *Romance, Finishing School, Concerto* (all by Gweneth Lloyd); *The Darkling, Les Whoops-de-Do, Aimez-vous Bach?* (Brian Macdonald); *Grasslands, Brave Song* (Robert Moulton); *Ballet Premier, E Minor, Intermede, Hansel and Gretel* (Arnold Spohr); *Variations for a Lonely Theme, Un et Un Font Deux* (Michel Conte); *Ballet Three* (Don Gillies); *Bitter Weird* and *The Rehearsal* (Agnes de Mille), and others. Leading dancers include Sonia Taverner, Marina Katronis, Richard Rutherford, Fredric Strobel, James Clouser, and others. Brian Macdonald was officially appointed choreographer in the spring of 1964. In the summer of that year the company made its U.S. debut in Boston and later danced at Jacob's Pillow Dance Festival, Lee, Mass., appearing for two weeks in July. The company also danced three performances at the Long Island Festival of L.I. Arts Center, Inc. (Aug. 1, 2, 1964). S. Hurok signed the company for a U.S. tour (fall, 1965). In 1966 Brian Macdonald choreographed *Rose Latulippe* for the company, a ballet based on a French-Canadian legend (mus.: Harry Freedman; décor: Robert Prevost). This, the first full-length Canadian ballet, was premièred

Aug. 16, with Annette Wiedersheim, a guest artist from the Royal Swedish Ballet and the choreographer's wife as Rose.

Royale, in ballet, the first elaboration of a changement de pieds into an entrechat, made by a beating of the calves of the legs when first jumping up, then changing the feet before landing. The term was coined for Louis XIV who is said to have performed this step instead of an entrechat-quatre, which he could not master (also called changement battu).

Royalties, compensation paid to choreographers, composers, and authors of libretti for the use of their work in dance productions. Usually the choreographer and composer are paid a flat sum for setting a ballet and a certain amount agreed upon for each performance of the ballet. Often a company will guarantee the choreographer a definite number of performances during a given season. A choreographer for a musical comedy is usually paid a royalty based on the gross box-office receipts, generally 1 per cent.

Rozanova, Berta (Bertha Rosenblat), Brazilian dancer, b. Santos. Began her dance studies at the ballet school of Teatro Municipal, Rio de Janeiro, under Maria Olenewa (1938); later worked with Yuco Lindberg and Igor Schwezoff. Made her debut during Vaslav Veltchek's season (1943); promoted to soloist (1945), dancing roles in *Eternal Struggle, Les Sylphides, First Ball, Moonlight Sonata.* Joined Ballet da Juventude at its formation and danced in its 1947 season at Teatro Fenix. After the company was disbanded, danced in some shows and revues and with Ballet Society in 1948. Returned to Teatro Municipal (1950) as first dancer in *Aurora's Wedding, Les Sylphides, Giselle, Eternal Struggle, Pas de Quatre, Masquerade, Mancenilha, Salamanca do Jarau.* Joined Ballet do IV Centenario (1954). Went to France (1955) to dance and study with Rousanne Sarkissian, Nora Kiss, Boris Kniaseff; danced with Ballets France-Espagne de José Torres in France and Africa. Returned to Rio and Teatro Municipal (1956), reassuming her place and roles, among them *Capriccio Espagnol, Le Beau Danube, A Dancing Tragedy, Romeo and Juliet, Walpurgis Night, The Nutcracker, La Bayadère* pas de deux, and the full-length *Swan Lake.* Promoted to prima ballerina in 1959; the same year was chosen best dancer of the year. Rozanova has her own ballet school, dances weekly on television programs, and has taken leave of absence from Teatro Municipal to dance with the new company of Brazil's Ballet Foundation.

Ruanova, María, Argentine ballerina and teacher, b. Buenos Aires, 1912. Studied dance with Yelena Smirnova, Boris Romanov, and Bronislava Nijinska. Joined Teatro Colón ballet company (1926). In 1931, while still a soloist, was chosen by Michel Fokine to replace Olga Spessivtzeva in *Firebird, Carnaval,* and other ballets. Was named ballerina in 1932. Her repertoire included *Usher, Georgia, Les Sylphides, The Sleeping Beauty, Swan Lake, Coppélia, Bolero, The Three-Cornered Hat, Capriccio Espagnol, Joan von Zarissa, Hamlet, Daphnis and Chloë, Aubade, La Péri.* In 1934 she danced with Serge Lifar in *Prometheus, Le Spectre de la Rose,* and the *Blue Bird* pas de deux. She was engaged as ballerina of the René Blum Ballets Russes de Monte Carlo (1936) with which company she toured Europe and Africa. In London during the performances in celebration of the coronation of George VI, she danced in the premières of Fokine's *Don Juan* and *L'Epreuve d'Amour.* In 1956 she retired from Teatro Colón and joined for a short period the Grand Ballet du Marquis de Cuevas as ballerina and ballet mistress. At present she teaches the Advanced Division at the Escuela Nacional de Danzas, Buenos Aires.

Rubinstein, Anton (1829–1894), famous Russian pianist and composer. Composed several operas of which *The Demon* (1875) is best known, and one ballet, *The Vine* (1883), in 3 acts and 5 scenes with a libretto by Paul Taglioni. It was never presented in full in Russia, but Michel Fokine staged one act in Apr., 1906, for a charity performance.

Rubinstein, Ida (1885–1960), dancer and actress, b. St. Petersburg (now Leningrad), of Russian-Jewish parentage. She came from a rich family, who made it possible for her to cultivate an interest in ballet in her youth and to support ballet in her early womanhood. In the early years of the century she was taking private lessons with Michel Fokine and made her debut in a private performance of *Salomé* (1909), choreographed for her by Fokine. Public performances of *Salomé* were forbidden by the censor because of the scantiness of Miss Rubinstein's costumes. Her professional debut was made in Paris in 1909 in the first season of the Diaghilev Ballets Russes. She danced the title role of Fokine's ballet *Cléopâtre,* the other members of the cast being Anna Pavlova, Vaslav Nijinsky, and the choreographer. In 1910 she danced Zobeide in Fokine's *Schéhérazade* and in other ballets created by Fokine, among them *Bolero* (the music for which she commissioned from Maurice Ravel) and the same composer's *La Valse.* In 1911 she commissioned from Claude Debussy the score for Gabriele D'Annunzio's mystery play for soloists, chorus, and orchestra, *The Martyrdom of Saint Sebastian,* in which she played the title role.

She remained with the Diaghilev company until 1915 and some time later organized her own company, for which Bronislava Nijinska choreographed several ballets, among them *La Bien Aimée, La Valse, Bolero* (a new version), *Le Baiser de la Fée, La Princess Cygne,* and several others. Leonide Massine also staged ballets for her. Rubinstein lavishly supported choreographers, composers, and painters, often the greatest artists of her time. Her last appearance was in Paris in 1928 in the title role of *Orphée* by Roger Ducasse, which she mimed with great success. She retired in 1930 to Vence, on the French Riviera, where she lived in elegant seclusion and where she died at seventy-five.

Rues, Marga, German dancer and ballet mistress, b. Neisse, 1926. Among her teachers were Rudolf Kölling, Else Hellwig, Lotte Wernicke, Günther Hess, Victor Gsovsky, Lula von Sachnowsky, Leonid Gonta. Studied modern jazz in the U.S. Made her debut in *Princess of Tragant.* Member of the company at the State Opera and Operetta Company in Berlin, West Germany. Principal roles in *El Amor Brujo, Boutique Fantasque, Hungarian Dances* (Kodaly); also interpolated dances in classic and modern operettas. Ballet mistress of the State Operetta, Munich, for which she staged *Die Fledermaus, Fanny Elssler,* and others.

Ruins and Visions. Modern dance work; chor.: Doris Humphrey; music: Benjamin Britten String Quartet; décor: Paul Trautvetter; costumes: Pauline Lawrence. First prod.: José Limón Dance Company, 6th American Dance Festival, Connecticut College, New London, Aug. 20, 1953, with José Limón, Pauline Koner, Lucas Hoving, Lavina Nielsen, and members of the company; N.Y. première: Juilliard Concert Hall, Jan. 30, 1954. The title stems from Stephen Spender's book of poems of that name and the inspiration for the series of brief, interlocking scenes comes from quotations. A sense of doom permeates the stage, and this is the link that holds the seemingly unrelated scenes together—from the opening equivocal relationship between a mother and son, through the acted-out tragedy of an actor and actress which becomes a reality, to the final chaos of war.

Brunilda Ruiz, ballerina of the Harkness Ballet.

Ruiz, Brunilda, American dancer, b. Puerto Rico, 1936; m. John Wilson. Trained at School of Performing Arts, N.Y.; joined Robert Joffrey Ballet upon graduation (with honors). Has been with the company on all its tours, and for most of its between-season engagements, on television, with New York City Opera, etc. Created the only woman's role in Gerald Arpino's *Ropes;* danced the ballerina in George Balanchine's *Raymonda* Pas de Dix in the Robert Joffrey Ballet repertoire, a leading nightmare spirit in Arpino's *Incubus,* and many others. Joined the Harkness Ballet (spring, 1964).

Runanin, Boris, dancer, choreographer, b. Nis, Yugoslavia, 1917; Belgrade Univ. (two years); graduate (violin), Conservatory of Music and Academy of Dramatics, Belgrade. Studied dance with Helen D. Poliakova (1924–37); later with Lubov Egorova, Olga Preobrajenska in Paris; Pierre Vladimirov, Anatole Oboukhov, Anatole Vilzak, and others in N.Y. After several years with Belgrade Operetta and Belgrade Opera Ballet joined Original Ballet Russe (soloist, 1937–41); Ballet (now American Ballet) Theatre (1941–43). Created Head Mistress (*Graduation Ball*), Count Oscar (*Bluebeard*), among other roles. Served in U.S. Army (1943–46), after which he joined the cast of the musical *Oklahoma!* as featured dancer, subsequently dancing in a number of musicals. Currently working in television.

Running Set, type of American square dance performed by any even number of couples arranged in a circle. The dancers at times break off into small sets of two couples each for some of the steps, and at times dance in one large circle. This type of square dance has been especially popular in the south of the U.S., particularly in Kentucky and Tennessee. Agnes de Mille used a running set in her ballet *Rodeo* (1942). See SQUARE DANCE.

Russell, Francia, dancer, b. Los Angeles, Calif., 1938; m. Kent Stowell. Studied ballet with Iris de Luce in San Francisco; Mathilda Kschessinska in Paris; Vera Volkova in London; School of American Ballet and Ballet Theatre School, N.Y. Made her debut with William Dollar's group of dancers (1955). Joined New York City Ballet (1956); appointed soloist (1960). Her roles included Polyhymnia (*Apollo*), Pas de Deux (*Pied Piper*), Harp (*Fanfare*), Leader 2nd Campaign (*Stars and Stripes*), 4th movement (*Symphony in C*), leading roles in *Agon, Divertimento No. 15,* and *Four Temperaments.* Created Princess of West Indies (*Figure in the Carpet*). Resigned from N.Y.C. Ballet

(1961) and joined Jerome Robbins' Ballets: U.S.A. for its European tour that summer and subsequent N.Y. season. Returned to the New York City Ballet the following year. Currently assistant ballet mistress, rehearsing the company and staging Balanchine ballets for European companies. In Oct., 1966, after maternity leave and the birth of her first child, Christopher, left for Germany to stage Hindemith's *Four Temperaments* (Düsseldorf) and Tchaikovsky's *Allegro Brillante* (Köln).

Russian School of Ballet, a development in ballet style of the Italian and French schools. In his book *The Story of the Russian School* (London, 1932), the famous artist of the St. Petersburg Imperial Theatre Nicholas Legat says the following about the substance of the style of ballet which is known as the Russian School: "The secret of the development of Russian dancing lay in the fact that we learnt from everybody and adapted what we learnt to ourselves. We copied, borrowed from, and emulated every source that gave us inspiration, and then, working on our acquired knowledge and lending it the stamp of the Russian national genius, we moulded it into the eclectic art of the Russian ballet. . . . Christian Johannson always used to say to me: 'The Russian school is the French school, only the French have forgotten it.' . . . Though the Russian school first derived its technique from France, it had already acquired by the middle of the last century an international aspect through the influential personalities of Johannson and my father and through guest performers from many parts of Europe . . . and their influence gave a powerful impetus to the growing art of ballet at the time. . . . The only male dancer of the Italian group was Enrico Cecchetti. He was about forty-five years of age when he came to Russia, and at the height of his career, but too old to modify his school of tours de force or round out his dexterity with the dignity and poise which were then the outstanding attributes of the Russian school. . . . We found that they (the Italian dancers) had a school all their own, which was distinguished by remarkable dexterity and sensational brilliance. Their tours, their pirouettes, their fouettés, were all superior to our own. Their manners, on the other hand, often lacked grace . . . taste was sacrificed to effect and dexterity. . . . We readily acknowledged their technical superiority, and promptly set about to imitate, adapt, and ultimately to excel their technique. . . . Without embarking in this limited space on an analysis of the two systems, it may be said briefly that the differences lie, firstly in principle, and secondly in taste. One of the principles of the Russian school is that of balanced training; the Italians, on the contrary, permitted a great deal of onesidedness for the sake of superficial effect. Enrico Cecchetti, for example, though a brilliant pirouettist, could only do pirouettes and tours en l'air in one direction. . . . A series of double tours in alternate directions, often done by our dancers, was beyond him. Our dancers eventually did seven or eight pirouettes habitually in their solos, but they did them in either direction at will. . . . We rejected a number of easy effects obtained at the cost of beauty and grace, and we avoided those faults of épaulement and carriage which are always marked in the Italian school. To the untrained eye these differences may appear insignificant. But it was our refusal to sacrifice aesthetics to effect, combined with our success in adopting and adapting Italian technique, that enabled us in the generation that followed the arrival of the Italians in Russia to produce the greatest dancers of the past four decades." The principles of the Russian School outlined by Nicholas Legat are still being followed by the State Schools in the Soviet Union as well as by most professional schools in America and Europe. See also Soviet Ballet.

Russian Soldier. Ballet in four scenes; chor. and book: Michel Fokine; music: Sergei Prokofiev; décor and costumes: Mstislav Doboujinsky. First prod.: Ballet Theatre, Metropolitan Opera House, N.Y., Apr. 6, 1942, with Yurek Lazowski in title role. Set to the symphonic suite *Lieutenant Kije* and dedicated to the gallant Russian soldiers of World War II, the ballet told the life story of a simple Russian soldier, as it is remembered by him as he is dying on the battle field. It was an imaginative work of the great master which, however, did not please the critics or arouse the audience's interest. This was the last fully completed work of Fokine. Alexander Lapauri and Olga Tarasova used the same music for their ballet *Lieutenant Kije,* produced in 1963 for the Bolshoi Theatre, Moscow.

Russian Tea Room, a restaurant on West 57th Street, N.Y., established in 1932, which is the favorite gathering place of ballet dancers, choreographers, managers, writers, and others, at meal-times and especially after performances, when the fine points of a new ballet or a new ballerina may be discussed by the cognoscenti. On occasion important dance business is transacted at a table. It is not quite so resplendent (or expensive) as the famous Cubat's in St. Petersburg of pre-revolutionary years, but it serves much the same purpose in democratic N.Y.

Rutherford, Richard, American dancer, b. Augusta, Ga. Studied dance at Ballet Theatre School, with Edward Caton, Fernand Nault, Robert Joffrey, and Benjamin Harkarvy. Since joining the Royal Winnipeg Ballet (1958) as his first professional job, has appeared in a large repertoire. His leading roles include, among others, pas de trois from *Swan Lake* (Act 1), *Blue Bird* pas de deux, Green Boy (Ruthanna Boris' *The Comedians*), Dancing Master (*Finishing School*), Medicine Man (*Brave Song*), Flute (*A Court Occasion*). Among roles created by him are Hansel (Arnold Spohr's Hansel and Gretel), title role in *The Little Emperor* (James Clouser), and a leading role in Clouser's *Recurrence.* He also made many television appearances and danced in *Pajama Game, Carousel, Damn Yankees,* and *Brigadoon* in summer stock at the Rainbow Stage.

Ruth Page's International Ballet. See Chicago Opera Ballet, Ruth Page's.

S

Sabline, Oleg, dancer, choreographer, teacher, b. Berlin, Germany, 1925, of Russian origin; m. Tania Karina. Educated in Paris; studied dance with Nicolas Kremnev, Olga Preobrajenska, Lubov Egorova, Alexandre Volinine, Gustave Ricaux. Danced with Grand Ballet de Monte Carlo (1947–48), l'Opéra Comique Ballet (1948–50); soloist, Grand Ballet du Marquis de Cuevas (1950–56), his repertoire including *Polovetsian Dances from Prince Igor, Prisoner of the Caucasus, Les Sylphides, Le Beau Danube* (Dandy), the classic pas de deux, and repertoire. Came to U.S. (1958), since then he has appeared with his own group Ballet Concertante, at Jacob's Pillow, Brooklyn College, etc. Currently devotes most of his time to teaching.

Sachs, Curt (1881–1959), German-born musicologist and dance historian. Left Germany in 1933 at the rise of Hitler; lived for some time in Paris and London, then settled in U.S. where he was appointed Professor of Music at the Graduate School of Liberal Arts, N.Y. Univ. and Music Consultant to the N.Y. Public Library. Author of the standard volume *Eine Weltgeschichte des Tanzes* (1933) which was translated into English by Bessie Schönberg and published as *A World History of Dance* (1937).

Sacre du Printemps, Le. See Rite of Spring, The

Saddler, Donald, dancer, choreographer, b. Van Nuys, Calif., 1920. Studied dance with Carmalita Maracci, Anton Dolin, Antony Tudor; dramatics with Beno Schneider. Made his debut in 1938 with group in California. Member, Ballet (now American Ballet) Theatre (1939–43), returning in 1946 after war service, his roles including Alias (*Billy the Kid*), title role (*Bluebeard*), Benno (*Swan Lake*), adagio (*Les Patineurs*), and others. Choreographed a number of musicals in Italy, one of which *Tobia la Candida Spia* was awarded the Maschera d'Argento (Silver Mask). His first Broadway musical was *Wonderful Town* starring Rosalind Russell for which he received the Antoinette Perry Award for choreography. Since then he has been responsible for *John Murray Anderson's Almanac, Shangri-La, Milk and Honey, Sophie.* Choreographed the London production of *Wonderful Town* and another musical *When in Rome.* Choreographed for three motion pictures, all starring Doris Day: *April in Paris* (also starring Ray Bolger), *By the Light of the Silvery Moon,* and *Young at Heart.* Choreographed for three seasons for the "Bell Telephone Hour" on television; has also choreographed for the "Perry Como Show" and for Rome television. Directed the State Fair Musicals in Dallas, Tex. for two seasons; Carousel Theatre, Framingham, Mass. for one season; and the Greek Theatre, Los Angeles production of *Wonderful Town* with Carol Channing.

Choreographed ballets based upon Tennessee Williams' short play *This Property is Condemned* and Sherwood Anderson's *Winesburg, Ohio* (both with music by Genevieve Pitot). The latter was premiered at the 1958 Jacob's Pillow Dance Festival. Staged the dances for *To Broadway with Love,* the musical created for the Music Hall of the N.Y. World's Fair (1964–65). In the summer of 1964 joined the Harkness Ballet as assistant to artistic director George Skibine. Choreographed *Koshare,* a ballet on American Indian folklore for the Harkness Ballet (1966). Since July 1967, associate director of the company.

Sadler's Wells Ballet. See ROYAL BALLET (Britain).

Sadler's Wells Opera Ballet, name by which Sadler's Wells Theatre Ballet was known for its first season (1946). See ROYAL BALLET (Britain).

Sadler's Wells School. See ROYAL BALLET SCHOOL.

Sadler's Wells Theatre Ballet. See ROYAL BALLET.

Sadoff, Simon, conductor, pianist, b. Hoboken, N.J., 1919. B.A. (1940) Montclair State Teachers College, N.J.; studied music at Mannes Music School, N.Y., piano with Edward Stevermann, conducting with Leon Barzin. Solo pianist with American Ballet for its five month tour of South America (1941) and has been intermittently connected with the New York City Ballet organization ever since as pianist and conductor (1952, 1958 for the company's tour of Japan, Australia, Philippines, 1962 in Europe, Soviet Union). His long association with the José Limón Company began in 1948 as pianist and since 1949 as conductor; arranged the Henry Purcell music for Limón's *The Moor's Pavane* (1949). Conductor for Martha Graham Company's European tour (1954). Has given many piano recitals and appeared as soloist with orchestras; pianist and conductor of Broadway and off-Broadway theatres; conducts for films and television; musical coordinator for annual American Dance Festival at Connecticut College. In the 1963–64 season associate conductor of the New York City Ballet.

Sa'Earp, Elenita, Brazilian teacher and choreographer, b. S. Paulo. Came to Rio de Janeiro to study at the National School of Physical Education, from which she was graduated as professor. In 1943 had classes with Yat Malmgren; in 1955 studied under Mary Wigman, Rosalia Chladek, Sigurd Leeder, Anna Sokolow, and Harald Kreutzberg in Zurich. Since 1941 she is professor of dance at the Univ. of Brazil. In 1951 she visited the U.S., giving lecture-demonstrations in colleges. In 1954 she formed Grupo de Dança Contemporânea. The company has presented many performances, some sponsored by the Rio Museum of Modern Art.

Sager, Peggy, New Zealand dancer, b. Auckland, N.Z.; m. Paul Hammond. Studied locally, then with Helène Kirsova in Australia (1942), dancing in her company. Joined Borovansky Ballet (1946). Went to England in 1947 where she was leading soloist with Metropolitan Ballet. Danced in the film *The Red Shoes* and later at Théâtre Royal de la Monnaie, Brussels. Rejoined Borovansky Ballet in 1950 and remained with the company until 1955.

Sailor's Return, The. Ballet in 2 acts (prologue, 4 scenes, epilogue); chor. and décor: Andrée Howard; commissioned music: Arthur Oldham; book: based on the short novel by David Garnett. First prod.: Ballet Rambert, Sadler's Wells Theatre, London, June 2, 1947, with Sally Gilmour (Tulip), Walter Gore (William, the Sailor), Frank Staff (Sailor's Brother), John Gilpin (Rabbit-catcher). The sailor returns to his native English village with his little African bride Tulip. Her sweetness and innocence enchant at first but the narrow prejudices of a small community bring inevitable tragedy.

St. Denis, Ruth (1877–).

BY WALTER TERRY.

Often referred to as the First Lady of the American Dance and familiarly known by the entire dance and theatre world as "Miss Ruth," Ruth St. Denis has had an active career in the theatre for more than half a century. Born in 1877 on a New Jersey farm of an inventor father and a physician mother, Ruth Dennis began to dance and to "play" theatre when she was little more than a baby. Her temperament and great respect for the theatre became apparent early in her life when, as a student at Dwight L. Moody's Seminary, she berated this gentleman for his attacks on the theatre, called him "a narrow-minded old bigot," and fled home.

Before her debut as a creative dance artist, Miss St. Denis had a checkered career. She was a cloak model, a "skirt dancer," a participant in a six-day bicycle race at Madison Square Garden (she came in sixth), an actress (it was David Belasco who added the St. to her name and removed an "n"), and even a toe dancer. She had had practically no ballet training and states that she studied only three times with Maria Bonfanti (ballerina of *The Black Crook*), learned three of the classic five positions and was tossed out of class.

In 1904, while playing with Mrs. Leslie Carter in David Belasco's production of *Du Barry,* she determined upon her new career. Whatever inarticulate longings she had experienced, whatever tentative plans had been germinating in her mind, all came to a sudden head one day in Buffalo when she saw a cigarette poster advertising a brand of Egyptian cigarettes. The picture of the serene goddess Isis somehow symbolized the form, the substance, and the quality which the young dancer-actress had been seeking. For the remainder of the *Du Barry* tour, she turned every spare moment to the business of research and composition, but the estimated expense of staging *Egypta* discouraged her so thoroughly that she decided to create a less opulent Hindu dance production. Back in N.Y., she read everything she could find on India, met as many Hindus as possible, and emerged with the ballet *Radha,* which actually cost her almost as much as *Egypta* would have required. In 1906 *Radha* was presented at N.Y.'s Hudson Theater for a group of managers, later at a "smoking concert," then in vaudeville. Finally, back at the Hudson Theater on Mar. 22, 1906, it was featured in a complete dance program which also offered *The Incense* and *The Cobras.* Success was instantaneous, further performances followed, and in July of the same year St. Denis departed for what was to become a triumphal tour of Europe.

For three years she remained abroad, dancing in England, Scotland, France, Germany, Austria-Hungary, Italy, and Belgium. The *Nautch* and the *Yogi* were added to the program. Although she met with great success everywhere (except in the English provinces), Germany was the nation which took her to its heart. If she had so desired, Germany could have become her home and a theatre would have been built especially for her. However, she returned to America in 1909 and under the management of Henry B. Harris produced the long postponed *Egypta.* There followed coast-to-coast tours, vaudeville engagements and further dance works, among them the Japanese ballet *O-Mika.*

In 1914 Ted Shawn became her partner and, following their marriage on Aug. 13 of that year, Denishawn was founded. During the period of America's participation in World War I, while her husband was in the U.S. Army, she directed the Denishawn School, performed for soldiers, sold war bonds, and managed to fit money-

Ruth St. Denis in The Black and Gold Sari.

raising vaudeville tours into her schedule. With the return of peace, Shawn rejoined her and the Denishawn activities, both educational and performing, continued almost unbroken until the separation of St. Denis and Shawn at the end of their 1931–32 season. After the separation St. Denis continued to run Denishawn House in N.Y., but the expenses were too great and she was finally forced to give it up. Succeeding seasons found her in semi-retirement, busy with religious dances staged sometimes for churches but more often for small audiences who supported her Society of Spiritual Arts.

Together with La Meri she opened the School of Natya in N.Y. in 1940, thus renewing her active participation in Oriental dance. In addition to studio performances, she revived in 1941 the program which had launched her career and presented it at her husband's Jacob's Pillow Dance Festival with a resounding success which was later repeated in N.Y. and on tour. In the ensuing years—into the 1960's—she combined her activities in dance and religion with projects aimed at recording her solos on film. Thus, in 1960 and 1961, she returned to Adelphi College (where she had originally established the dance department) to head the dance section of a new department dedicated to the arts and religion. At the same time she sought means to continue the filming of her repertory and succeeded in having sound movies made of several of her major works.

Continuing an active career into her mid-eighties, she traveled from headquarters in Hollywood to perform, teach, film and lecture in New York and on tour. In 1961 she appeared as narrator and dancer in her *Incense* for the Boston Arts Festival's tenth anniversary program. The occasion marked the fifty-fifth anniversary of her first appearance in Boston in a solo she had performed at her Boston debut.

In 1963 she toured the U.S. (at eighty-five) as narrator in the same program, "America Dances," and as a dancer in *Incense.* These activities, together with frequent television appearances, kept her before a public which had seen her dance for seventy years.

Miss St. Denis has written, in addition to numerous magazine articles, a book of poems and her autobiography, *Ruth St. Denis: An Unfinished Life* (N.Y., Harper & Bros., 1939).

Saint Francis. Ballet in 5 scenes; chor.: Leonide Massine; music: Paul Hindemith; book: Hindemith and Massine; décor and costumes: Pavel Tchelitchev. First prod.: (as *Noblissima Visione*) Ballet Russe de Monte Carlo, Theatre Royal, Drury Lane, London, July 21, 1938, with Leonide Massine in the title role, Jeannette Lauret, Lubov Rostova, Nini Theilade, Frederic Franklin, Simon Semenov in leading parts. The ballet is a poetical vision of the life of the gentle saint.

Saint-Léon, (Charles Victor) Arthur Michel, famous French choreographer, dancer, and violinist, b. about 1815, (the exact year of his birth has never been established), d. 1870. Son of the ballet master of the Würtemberg Ducal Theatre, Stuttgart, he began his career at the age of fourteen in Munich, where he danced and played the violin. In 1833 he began a European tour which was to last until 1859. In Milan he met the celebrated ballerina Fanny Cerito whom he married. They continued to tour Europe together with great success. In 1847 he staged his first ballet *La Fille de Marbre* for Cerito's debut in Paris. The ballet was a huge success and led to the production of some sixteen of his ballets and divertissements for the Paris Opéra, among them *La Vivandière,* and *Le Violon du Diable* (in which Saint-Léon played a violin solo). In 1850 Saint-Léon and Cerito separated, and in 1859 the choreographer made his debut as ballet master of the

Imperial Theatre in St. Petersburg with Saltarella. Subsequently he staged in Russia *Graziella* (1860), *Mariquita, or the Pearl of Seville* (1860), *Metheor* (1861), *The Nymphs and the Satyr* (1861), *Theolinda* (1862), *Fiammetta* (1864), *The Humpbacked Horse* (1864), *The Goldfish* (1867), and others. It is interesting that Saint-Léon, a Frenchman, was the first to produce a ballet on a Russian theme *The Humpbacked Horse.* In Paris he staged among other ballets *La Source* to Delibes' music (1866) revived as *The Lily* (1869), and his most famous ballet *Coppélia* (1870). Saint-Léon staged ballets in all major European cities except Milan. He always wanted to be, but never was, engaged by La Scala, Milan. Traveling as guest choreographer from city to city, Saint-Léon generally staged the same ballets under different titles; thus, the ballet which was called *Nemea* in Paris became *Fiametta* in St. Petersburg and *Salamander* in Moscow. Saint-Léon attempted to introduce several novelties into his ballets but was not successful. In *La Fille de Marbre,* for instance, he wanted to have a singing chorus in addition to the corps de ballet and a separate principal singing role but he was overruled by the director of the St. Petersburg Theatre. Saint-Léon was not an outstanding dancer and his round shoulders and stooping figure were added handicaps to his dancing career. It is for this reason, probably, that he became a choreographer comparatively early in his life. His ambition and egomania were notorious. He considered himself an unsurpassed choreographer and could not stand criticism. Often biased and jealous of the success of others, he tried to keep down those who could possibly become his rivals. As a result he never commanded the love or respect of his colleagues. In addition to his ballets Saint-Léon left a treatise *La Sténochoregraphie ou l'art d'ecrire promptement la danse,* published in 1852. In it he made an attempt to evolve a system of dance notation. Saint-Léon left St. Petersburg in 1867 after the failure of his ballet *The Goldfish.* He became ballet master of the Paris Opéra, a post he held until his death.

St. Petersburg, capital of Russia until 1921, built by Peter the Great. In 1914 after the outbreak of World War I, Czar Nicholas II changed its name to Petrograd because the name St. Petersburg was of German origin. In 1924 after the death of Lenin, the Soviet Government changed the name to Leningrad.

Saint-Saëns, Charles Camille (1835–1921), French composer of the suite *Carnival of Animals* from which Michel Fokine used the music of "Le Cygne" for the dance *The Dying Swan* created for Anna Pavlova (1905). The Bacchanale from Saint-Saëns' *Samson and Delilah* is a well-known dance composition. Andrée Howard used Carnival of Animals for her ballet of the same name (1943).

Saisons, Les. Ballet in 1 act, 4 scenes; chor. and book: Marius Petipa; music: Alexander Glazounov; décor: Lambini; costumes: Ponomaryov. First prod.: Hermitage Theatre, St. Petersburg, Feb. 23, 1900. Each of the four scenes of the ballet depicts a season, beginning with winter. Only the last scene, autumn, was worthy of the music to which it was danced. That scene, the Bacchanale, is quite often used as a separate number by ballet companies and teams of dancers. It was one of the favorite numbers in the repertoire of Anna Pavlova company, especially when it was danced by Pavlova and Mikhail Mordkin.

Sakharov (Zuckerman), Alexandre, dancer, b. Mariupol, Russia, 1886, d. 1963. Went to Paris to study painting but after seeing Sarah Bernhardt in *L'Aiglon* discovered what he called, "the magic of movement," and decided to become a dancer. After studying dance in Munich he made his debut in that city (1911) in a series of solo recitals. In Berlin, which was his next performance date, he met Clothidle von Derp, a featured dancer in several productions of Max Reinhardt. They were married and became for many years the best known German team of concert dancers. As they continued working together they developed a highly individual style which Sakharov called "abstract mime." This name notwithstanding, most of their compositions had definite themes often charged with strong emotions. His artistically most successful compositions were in the style of the Renaissance. He designed all the costumes for his wife and himself and they contributed much to the success of the dancers. They toured Europe innumerable times and frequently visited South America. After World War II they settled in Rome where they opened a dance school, still continuing their tours. They gave their final performance in 1953 in Paris and since then have devoted themselves to teaching in Rome.

Sale, John, English dancer, b. 1934. Studied at Royal Ballet School; currently soloist, Royal Ballet. Roles include Blue Skater (*Les Patineurs*), Bluebird, Puss in Boots (*The Sleeping Beauty*), "Peasant" pas de deux (*Giselle*) and others.

Salem Shore. Modern dance solo; chor.: Martha Graham; music Paul Nordoff; spoken text read by Merce Cunningham; artistic collaboration: Arch Lauterer; costumes: Edythe Gilfond. First prod.: N.Y., Dec. 26, 1943.

Sallé, Marie (1707–1756), one of the most prominent dancers of her time, was the daughter of a tumbler. She was taught dancing at a very early age and made her debut in 1718 at the St. Laurent's Fair in an opéra-comique by Lesaye titled *La Princesse Carisme.* She toured in fairs, etc., for some years and in 1721 appeared for the first time in the Opéra in Paris in *Les Fêtes Venitiènnes.* She became a pupil of Françoise Prévost at the Academie Royale, but the jealousy of the older danseuse kept her from advancing rapidly. In 1725 John Rich took her to London where she first appeared in *Love's Last Shift* in an entr'acte divertissement with her brother. Later she danced in *Les Caractères de la Danse.* She stayed in London for two years and then returned to Paris where she danced at the Opéra in *Les Amours des Dieux.* She danced a solo entrée but for the next few months was in the corps de ballet. In about a year however she was recognized as a dancer of great talent and was cast in leading parts. The rivalry with Camargo which became a feature of both dancers' careers began at this time. During the next few years Sallé alternated her appearances between Paris and London. She was a woman of recognized intellect and numbered people such as Voltaire, Jean-Georges Noverre and David Garrick among her friends. She was a reformer in the dance and had a chance to demonstrate the validity of her ideas in London in 1734 when she appeared as Galatea in her own production of *Pygmalion.* She discarded the cumbersome dress of the day and danced in a muslin costume, her hair down and unornamented. This was in line with her belief that dance should be natural and expressive. Later in that year, Sallé appeared in a prologue to Handel's *Pastor Fido.* She took the part of Terpsichore and danced and mimed to singing. Other ballets in which Sallé appeared were *L'Enlèvement de Proserpine, Apollon and Daphne, Bacchus and Ariadne.* She also danced in a revival of *The Beggar's Opera.* Sallé appeared often in pas de deux as it gave her opportunity for expressive byplay rather than the virtuosity favored by her rival Camargo. Among her partners was the dancer David Dumoulin, and she often danced with her brother. Sallé retired in 1740 and many of her reforms were adopted by her successors. She was championed by reformer Noverre who agreed with her precepts. As a dancer she was loved for her naturalness, grace, and lack of affectation; as a woman she was known for her intelligence and virtue.

Salamanca do Jaraú. Ballet in 7 scenes; chor.: Tatiana Leskova; music: Luiz Cosme; book: Luiz Cosme, based on a folk tale by Simões Lopes Neto; décor and costumes: Tomás Santa Rosa. First prod.: Tony Seitz Ballet Group, Porto Alegre, Brazil, 1945; revived 1952 with Berta Rozanova, Arthur Ferreira, Johnny Franklin, Pita Lopes, Inez Litowski, Julia Rodrigues, David Dupré, Dennis Gray, Yellê Bittencourt in the principal roles. According to an old legend of the southern state of Rio Grande do Sul, Brazil, Salamanca do Jaraú is an enchanted cavern where Santão, a heretical sacristan and his beloved Teniguá, a Moorish princess, are held prisoners. Only when a human being decides to enter the cave and pass the seven dreadful tests will the sorcery end. A daring gaucho, the fearless Blau Nunes, led by the magician Boi Barroso and fascinated by the vision of the Princess, decides to save the two imprisoned lovers. He passes the tests and thus breaks the spell. The two prisoners appear in the images of a young gaucho and a charming metisse and leave together. Blau Nunes remains longing for the beautiful princess he could not possess.

Salon Mexico, El. Modern group dance; chor.: Doris Humphrey; music: Aaron Copland. First prod.: N.Y., Mar. 11, 1943.

Saltarello, a lively Italian court dance of the 15th century in 3/4 or 6/8 time, akin to the tarantella but consisting in the main of little jumps, danced in a great variety of figures. It was also danced in Spain where it was known as alta danza (high dance). Another form of saltarello was closer to the galliard and was most popular in Rome where it was danced by couples. The lady's part included much play of arms. According to G. B. L. Wilson, in the 16th century it was also an after-dance in triple time to the passamezzo, a dance popular at the time in England, France and Germany. It was performed in 2/4 time to an air sung by the dancers.

Salvioni, Guglielmina (1842– ?), Italian dancer who became première danseuse of the Paris Opéra (1864–67) and was the first interpreter of the role of Naïla in the ballet *La Source,* choreographed by Arthur Saint-Léon (1866).

Samba, a ballroom dance of Brazilian origin in 4/4 time. It has a syncopated rhythm of long *quick,* short quick, *slow,* and is the bridge between the dignified forms of ballroom dances and jitterbug.

Samson Agonistes. Modern dance work; chor. and costumes: Martha Graham; music: Robert Starer; décor: Rouben Ter-Arutunian. First prod.: Martha Graham Dance Company, 54th St. Theatre, N.Y., Apr. 16, 1961, under its original title *Visionary Recital,* with Bertram Ross (The Dedicated), Paul Taylor (The Destroyer), Dan Wagoner (The Tempter) as the three aspects of Samson; Martha Graham (The Awakener), Matt Turney (The Betrayer), Akiko Kanda (The Seducer) as the three aspects of Delilah. A considerably revised version under its present title was presented Mar. 7, 1962, at Broadway Theatre, N.Y., with Mary Hinkson as The Awakener and Helen McGehee The Seducer. The program note (in part) reads: "Along the corridors of memory walk images of love, hate, desire, despair, calculated cruelty and shame. . . . There are three aspects of Samson, a man blinded by his own strength and reborn through his vision."

Samtsova, Galina (Galina Ursuliak), Russian dancer, ballerina with National Ballet of Canada, b. Stalingrad, 1937. Trained at the Kiev Choreography School and graduated into the Kiev Opera and Ballet Theatre after dancing the Wedding Scene from *Laurencia* for her graduation exercise. Her roles in Kiev included *Swan Lake* pas de trois, *Le Corsaire* pas de trois, Queen of the Wilis (*Giselle*), *Snowflake* pas de deux (*Song of the Forest*), and others. Married a Canadian engineer of Russian extraction and joined National Ballet of Canada (1961). Made her U.S. debut in *Blue Bird* and *Black Swan* pas de deux at the 1961 Jacob's Pillow Dance Festival. Created title role in the Vaslav Orlikovsky-Raymundo de Larrain *Cinderella,* International Dance Festival, Théâtre des Champs-Elysées, Paris (Dec. 4, 1963). Currently (1966) with London's Festival Ballet.

San Francisco Ballet, organized by Willam Christensen (winter season, 1937–38) with a group of dancers who had been appearing in the San Francisco Opera ballets. During its first season the company made a short tour with a repertory of ballets by Christensen. Upon its return it became the official ballet of the San Francisco Opera. In the following years Willam Christensen staged many new ballets and revivals for the company including a three-act version of *Coppélia* and a full-length *Swan Lake* (the first produced in the U.S.). Among the soloists who danced with the company in the 1940's were Janet Reed, Lew, Harold, and Willam Christensen, Harold Lang, James Starbuck. In the fall of 1951 Willam Christensen left San Francisco, and Lew Christensen became director of the company. He inaugurated an artistic exchange policy with the New York City Ballet thereafter staging some of his works for that company and obtaining some of the works of George Balanchine for his own. In 1957 the San Francisco Ballet toured the Far East (being the first American ballet company to do so) under the auspices of the U.S. State Department. In 1958 it toured Latin America and the following year went to the Middle East and North Africa. Among the most popular ballets staged by Lew Christensen for the company in the 1950's were *Con Amore* and *The Nutcracker.* Among the soloists in this decade were Jocelyn Vollmar, Sally Bailey, Conrad Ludlow, Christiane Bering, Nancy Johnson, Roderick Drew and Thatcher Clarke. Though an independent group, the company has been sponsored at various times by the San Francisco Civic Ballet Association and the San Francisco Ballet Guild. The company maintains its own school.

Sanasardo, Paul, dancer, choreographer, director, b. Chicago, Ill., 1928. After graduating from the Art Institute of Chicago (1952) partnered Erika Thimey in her Dance Theatre performances in Washington (1953–54). Danced with Anna Sokolow Company in the 1955 American Dance Festival at the ANTA Theatre, N.Y., appearing in *Rooms* (in the role he created), *Lyric Suite* and *Poem.* Appeared the same year in the Broadway production of Sean O'Casey's play *Red Roses for Me.* Member, N.Y. City Opera Ballet (1956); guest artist, Pearl Lang's company since 1957, dancing the Father (*Rites*), Pluto (*Falls the Shadow Between*), creating Don Muerte (*Apasionada*), and also dancing in *Shirah, And Joy Is My Witness,* and *Legend.* Also, since 1957 co-director with Donya Feuer of the Paul Sanasardo–Donya Feuer Dance Company. Between them they have choreographed and danced *In View of God* (1959), *Laughter After All* (1960), *Pictures in Our House, Excursion for Miracles* (1961). Has also appeared in many television programs.

Sand, Inge, soloist of the Royal Danish Ballet, b. Copenhagen, 1928. Entered the company's school in 1935; also studied in Paris, London, and N.Y. Designated soloist in 1950. Joined Original Ballet Russe in England for the season 1951–52. During summer vacations organized a group of dancers from the Danish company to tour Europe, the U.S., and South America (1955, 1961). Leading roles in *Le Beau Danube, Sorcerer's Apprentice, Aurora's*

Wedding, Swan Lake, Symphony in C, Concertette, Night Shadow, Vivaldi Concerto, Coppélia, Serenade, Lunefulde Lucinda, Graduation Ball, The Burrow, Carmen, Pas de Quatre, and others. Awarded the Danish decoration Knight of the Order of Dannebrog.

Sandberg, Willy, Swedish dancer, b. 1929. Entered Royal Swedish Ballet School in 1939; studied also with Lilian Karina. Accepted into the company in 1947; promoted to premier danseur in 1955. Among his roles are Jason (*Medea*), Jean (*Miss Julie*), the Peruvian (*Gaîté Parisienne*), and others.

Sandbrook, June, English dancer, b. Birmingham, 1938. Trained at Ballet Rambert School (1953–55); joined Ballet Rambert (1958), promoted to soloist later that year. Dances title role (*La Sylphide*), Sleepwalker (*Night Shadow*), Maiden (*Death and the Maiden*), and others, created Daughter (*Hazana*), one of the leading roles (*Conflicts*), among others.

Sanders, Dick (Dirk), Dutch dancer, b. Java. Studied with Kurt Jooss (1950–52) before settling in Paris. His techniques include both modern dance and classic ballet. Danced in the U.S. with Ballets de Paris de Roland Petit (1958), having the leading male role in *La Dame de la Lune*. Also danced on television in U.S. with Mary Martin. Choreographed *Récréation* for Maurice Béjart's company; *L'Echelle* for Milorad Miskovitch's Ballets '56; *L'Emprise,* a pas de deux for himself and Claire Sombert, for the 1957 Enghien Festival; and *Maratona di Danza* (Dance Marathon) (libretto: Luchino Visconti; music: Hans Werner Henze) for the 1957 Berlin Festival. Danced with Renée Jeanmaire in *La Croqueuse de Diamants* in the film *Black Tights* (1960), rcleased in U.S. 1962. Staged the dances for the musical comedy *Loin de Rueuil* (1961). Currently dancing in Europe.

Sanders, Job, dancer, choreographer, b. Amsterdam, Holland, 1929. Studied with Alexander Gavrilov and at School of American Ballet, N.Y. Made his debut with Ballet Society; danced in musical *Carousel;* then four years with Ballet Russe de Monte Carlo where his roles included Favorite Slave (*Schéhérazade*), *Blue Bird* pas de deux, Doctor (*Mute Wife*), pas de trois (*Ballet Imperial*), male leads in *Concerto Barocco* and *Paquita,* and others. Also danced with American Ballet Theatre, Man She Must Marry (*Lilac Garden*), Tybalt (*Romeo and Juliet*), General and pas de deux (*Graduation Ball*), and others; two seasons with Ruth Page's Chicago Opera Ballet; two with Nora Kovach and Istvan Rabovsky, choreographing *Holberg Suite, España, Troubador* (solo). Danced in Europe and Israel for two years with American Festival Ballet, one year with Netherlands Ballet. Currently with Netherlands Dance Theatre as first dancer and choreographer dancing title role in John Butler's *Hadrian,* Tancredi (*The Duel*), *Don Quixote* pas de deux. His choreographic works include *L'Heure Bleue* (1956) for Alexandra Danilova's group; *Contretemps* (1956), Robert Joffrey Ballet, both with music by Gabriel Fauré; *El Viaje* (Heitor Villa-Lobos) and *The Taming* (Paul Creston), both 1962 for Netherlands Dance Theatre; *The Ragpicker* (Alban Berg), 1963 for Nederlands Dans Theater, and others. *The Taming* was danced by Sonia Arova and Glen Tetley at Jacob's Pillow Dance Festival (1962).

Sangalli, Rita (1851–1909), Italian ballerina. A pupil of Augusto Hus, she danced in Italy, London, and N.Y., where she created the principal role in the extravaganza *The Black Crook* (1886). Made her debut at the Paris Opéra in *La Source* (Delibes-Minkus-Saint-Léon) in 1872; later created roles in *Sylvia* (1876), *Yedda* (1879), and *Namouna* (1882) at the Opéra. Sangalli and Salvioni, who created the role of Naïla in *La Source,* had different variations set to different music which created a confusion when the music to *La Source* was published with double variations for the ballerina. Sangalli married Baron de Saint-Pierre in 1876.

Sanina, Mira, Yugoslav dancer, b. Zagreb, 1922. Studied with Kurt Jooss and Mile Jovanovic. Character ballerina of the Belgrade National Ballet since 1945. Dances principal roles in *The Ballad of a Medieval Love* (F. Lhotka–Mlakar), *Legend of Ohrid* (Hristic–Froman), *The Gingerbread Heart* (Baranovic–Parlic), *Bolero* (Ravel–Boris Romanov), *El Amor Brujo* (de Falla–Parlic), *Devil in the Village* (F. Lhotka–Mlakar), and others.

Santestevan, María, Argentine dancer, b. Morón, Argentina, 1933. Studied dance with Esmée Bulnes. Joined the corps de ballet of Teatro Colón at the age of thirteen. In 1948 joined Teatro Argentino de La Plata, Argentina, as corps de ballet dancer; became première danseuse in 1955. In 1957 was engaged as soloist by Grand Ballet du Marquis de Cuevas; became ballerina in 1959. Left that company the same year to join the Stuttgart Opera Ballet as ballerina. Her repertoire includes *Chopin Concerto, La Boutique Fantasque, Romeo and Juliet,* all with choreography by Roberto Giachero; *Black Swan* pas de deux, *l'Amour et son Destin* (chor. Lifar), *Narcissus* (chor. Serge Golovine), *The Sleeping Beauty, Le Beau Danube,* and others.

Sarabande (in Span., La Zarabanda), a dance of Moorish origin which came from Spain in the 12th century. The name comes from an Arabic word meaning noise. Originally it was danced in groups to the accompaniment of bells and castanets. It was wild in manner and only women participated. In France the sarabande became more subdued and was danced as a solo by either a man or woman. It was in 3/4 time and chief step consisted of a quick shift from toe-out to toe-in, characteristic movement of oriental dancing; the rest was slow glides.

Sarabande. Modern dance solo; chor.: Martha Graham; music: Lehman Engel; costume: Martha Graham. First prod.: Guild Theatre, N.Y., Feb. 18, 1934.

Sarabhai, Mrinalini, Indian dancer, choreographer, teacher, director, b. Madras, 1923. Began her training as a child with Sri Muthukumaran Pillai in Manarkoil; later with Sri Ellappa, Sri Chokkalingam Pillai, and particularly with Meenakshi Sundaram Pillai in the purest forms of Bharata Natyam of which she is today one of the foremost exponents. Made her debut in Madras (1939), and was partner to Ram Gopal there, in Bangalore, and Calcutta. Later studied the dances of Java, acting and stage tech-

Mrinalini Sarabhai, outstanding Indian dancer and choreographer.

nique at the American Academy of Dramatic Art, N.Y., and on her return to India studied Kathakali dance with Sri Kunju Kurup. Founded Darpana, an academy of dance, drama, and music in Ahmedabad (1948) and since 1949 her Darpana Dance Company headed by herself and Chathunni Panicker has traveled extensively in Europe, South America, and the Far East, in addition to India. Sarabhai gave several lecture-demonstrations in the U.S. in 1961, including two at Asia House, N.Y., and in 1963 was invited by the Institute of Advanced Studies in the Theatre to direct an Indian play *Vasavadatta,* translated from the Sanskrit and performed by American actors. In addition to the traditional dances and dance-dramas of India which she performs with her company, she has created many original works using the techniques of Kathakali, Bharata Natyam, Manipuri, and Kuchipudi, of which possibly the most famous is Manushya (Man), the life cycle from birth to death. Her awards include the title Natya Kala Kovida and the Veera-Shrinkhala for her contributions to Bharata Natyam and Kathakali respectively and the medal and diploma of the Archives Internationales de la Danse, Paris.

Sargasso. Ballet in 1 act; chor.: Glen Tetley; score: Ernst Krenek's *Symphonic Elegy* (In Memoriam Anton Webern); décor and lighting: Rouben Ter-Arutunian. First prod.: American Ballet Theatre, N.Y. State Theater, Mar. 24, 1965, with Sallie Wilson, Bruce Marks, Richard Zelens. A woman at the midpoint of her life stands trapped by the weed-sea of dreams and unfulfilled relationships. Tetley had previously staged this ballet for the Nederlands Dans Theater.

Sarkissian, Rousanne. See ROUSANNE, MADAME.

Sartorio, Angiola, dancer, choreographer, teacher, b. Rome, Italy, 1903; U.S. citizen since 1945. Studied music and painting with Dalcroze; dance with Rudolf von Laban, Kurt Jooss, Lubov Egorova; also studied national dances. Member, Ballets Jooss for four years. Choreographer, Rome Opera (1932); Max Reinhardt's *A Midsummer Night's Dream* (1933); Maggio Musicale Fiorentino (1933–38). Taught in Florence (1934–38). Came to U.S. 1939 and established own school and summer dance school in California after teaching at Jacob's Pillow, with Katherine Dunham in N.Y., etc.

Satie, Erik (1866–1925), French composer. His works, though seldom performed, have had considerable influence on the present generation of avant-garde composers. His first ballet score was *Parade* (Leonide Massine, 1917). He later composed, also for the Diaghilev Ballets Russes, *Jack in the Box* (1926). He composed *Relâche* for Ballets Suédois (1924) and *Mercure* and *Premier Amour* (based on his *Trois Morceaux en Forme de Poire*) for the Soirées de Paris (1924). Andrée Howard later used his *Mercure* for *Croquis de Mercure* (Ballet Rambert, 1938) and Merce Cunningham used *Trois Morceaux* for his *Septet*.

Sauguet, Henri, French composer, b. Bordeaux, 1901. Has composed many ballets since his first, *Les Roses* (Leonide Massine) for Les Soirées de Paris (1924). Among his most important works are *La Chatte* (George Balanchine, 1927), for the Diaghilev Ballets Russes, *La Nuit* (Massine, for a Charles B. Cochran revue, London, 1930), *Fastes* (Balanchine, Les Ballets, 1933), *Les Forains* (Roland Petit, Ballets des Champs-Elysées, 1945), *Les Mirages* (Serge Lifar, Paris Opéra, 1947), *La Rencontre, ou Oedipe et le Sphinx* (David Lichine, Ballets des Champs-Elysées, 1948), *La Dame aux Camelias* (Tatiana Gsovska, Paris Opéra, 1959).

Saut, in ballet, a jump.

Saut de Basque, in ballet, a jumped step done while turning, a variant of pas de basque. Technique: Start 5th pos., R ft. back; step to side on R ft., turning body to R and swinging L leg to grande quatrième devant ouverte; complete the turn to R with a jeté onto L ft., bringing R toe to L knee; finish facing front, weight on L fondu. Arms are usually in 5th pos. en haut at the apex of the jump.

Sauté, in ballet, a jumping step, such as échappé sauté.

Scala, Teatro alla, opera house in Milan, Italy. Opened in 1778 and produced five ballets the first season. Permanent Imperial Dancing Academy connected with it opened 1812 under impressario Benedetto Ricci. Its greatest period began with Carlo Blasis (1837) and lasted through most of the 19th century. At this time it had the greatest influence on classic dance. Enrico Cecchetti was one of its famous ballet masters. Among recent directors of the school have been Cia Fornaroli (1929–1933), Vera Volkova (1950–52), and since then Esmé Bulnes. The company has no permanent choreographer. Its repertoire includes many of the classics and George Balanchine, Leonide Massine, and Frederick Ashton have recently staged ballets there. Soloists in the late 1950's and 1960's have included Olga Amati, Luciana Novarro, Vera Colombo, Carla Fracci, Ugo Dell'Ara, Giulio Perugini, Mario Pistoni.

Scandinaviske Ballet, Den (The Scandinavian Ballet), company established by Swedish ballerina Elsa-Marianne von Rosen and her husband, writer and impresario Allan Fridericia, and sponsored by Riksteatern of Sweden and the Andelsteatret of Denmark. The first performance was given in Växjö, Sweden, in Feb., 1960. The company toured Sweden and Denmark and also gave performances in Germany. It presented two different programs: 1. *Irene Holm* (von Rosen); *La Sylphide* (August Bournonville); *Truffaldino* (Ivo Cramér); and 2. *Teenagers* (von Rosen); *The Feast in Albano* (Bournonville); *Romantic Suite* (Cramér). Principal dancers included von Rosen, Ulla Paulson, Lone Isaksen, Tyyne Talvo, Marianne Fröijdh, Margarethe Brock-Nielsen, Svend Bunch, Björn Treville. Guest artists were Vladimir Skouratov, Christopher Lyall, and Leo Guerard. The company was disbanded after two tours (autumn, 1961).

Scapino Ballet. See HOLLAND, DANCE IN; SNOEK, HANS.

Scarecrow, The. Symbolic ballet in 2 scenes; chor.: Tatiana Leskova; music: Francisco Mignone (at first called Impressões Sinfonicas, it was written for the ballet and was inspired by two paintings of Candido Portinari); book: Vera Pacheco Jordão; décor and costumes: Tomás Santa Rosa. First prod.: Teatro Municipal, Rio de Janeiro, 1954, with a cast headed by Arthur Ferreira, Dennis Gray, David Dupré. A group of children obey the call of Destiny. They return later in search of their lost innocence. The author of the book had hoped that the ballet would be produced by George Balanchine for the American Ballet Caravan on its South American tour in 1941, but touring conditions made this impracticable.

Scarlatti, Domenico (1685–1757), Italian composer. His music has been used by Leonide Massine for *The Good-Humored Ladies* (1917), by Eugene Loring for *Harlequin for President* (1936), and by Albert Aveline for *Elvire.*

Scènes de Ballet. Ballet in 1 act; chor.: Frederick Ashton; music: Igor Stravinsky; décor: André Beaurepaire. First prod.: Sadler's Wells (now Royal) Ballet, Royal Opera House, Covent Garden, London, Feb. 11, 1948, with a cast headed by Margot Fonteyn and Michael Somes. The music, *Scènes de Ballet,* was originally composed by Stravinsky for Billy Rose's revue *Seven Lively Arts,* the ballet for which was staged by Anton Dolin and presented at the Ziegfeld Theatre, N.Y. (1944–45), with Dolin and Alicia Markova in the principal roles. Moira Shearer, Beryl Grey, Nadia Nerina, Brian Shaw, and David Blair are some of the dancers who have led the Ashton version. David Dupré choreographed a version for a workshop program at Teatro Municipal, Rio de Janeiro (1961).

Schachteli, Werner, German stage designer, b. 1934. Studied in Kiel, Hamburg, and Paris. Among ballets he has designed are *The Miraculous Mandarin* (Munich, 1955); *Black Sun, Undine* (Berlin, 1959); *The Red Cloak, Goyescas* (Frankfurt a/M, 1961); *Lady and the Fool, Catalysis, Antigone* (Stuttgart, 1961).

Schang, Frederick, artists' manager, b. New York City, 1893. Bachelor of Literature, Columbia Univ. (1915). Began his career in 1917 as advance man for the Diaghilev Ballets Russes. For 44 years he was an artists' manager connected with the Metropolitan Musical Bureau (F. C. Coppicus, proprietor); Coppicus & Schang, Division of Columbia Artists Management, Inc.; and later Schang, Doulens & Wright, Division of the same company. Former president and board chairman of Columbia Artists Management, Inc., he is still a member of the board of directors. Associated in the management of many dancers and dance companies, including two U.S. tours of Ballet Russe de Monte Carlo; other companies and artists he has represented include La Argentina, Lisa and Margot Duncan, Angna Enters, Rosario and Antonio, Paul Draper, Mata and Hari, Kurt Jooss and his Ballet Jooss, Takarazuka Dance Company, (World's Fair, N.Y.C., 1939–40), Devi-Dja, Carmalita Maracci, Dancers of Bali, Royal Danish Ballet, Ximinez & Vargas, and others. Decorated by the Danish and Swedish governments; Ridder (Knight) of Dannebrog—first class, and Order of Vaso, respectively.

Schanne, Margrethe, soloist of the Royal Danish Ballet, b. Copenhagen, 1921. Accepted into the company's school in 1930. Joined the company in 1941; made soloist in 1943. Guest artist, Ballets des Champs-Elysées (1946) and Marquis de Cuevas International Ballet (1955). Appeared at the Nervi Festival (1957); toured South Africa (1958); danced in Rome (1961). Was chosen as model for the Danish postage stamp first issued in 1959 in time for the Royal Danish Ballet and Music Festival. She appears there in a grand jeté from the ballet *La Sylphide.* The stamp is issued every year in time for the Festival (May 15–31). Danced leading roles in *Le Spectre de la Rose, Les Sylphides, Den Detroniserede Løventaemmer, La Sylphide, Drømmebilleder, Petrouchka, Swan Lake, Drift, Giselle, Symphony in C, Night Shadow, Pas de Quatre, The Sleeping Beauty, Harlequinade, Medea, Kameliadamen,* and others. Awarded Danish

Royal Danish ballerina Margrethe Schanne with premier danseur Borge Ralov in Giselle.

decoration Knight of the Order of Dannebrog (1953). The Royal Danish Ballet brought her to the U.S. to dance during the N.Y. engagement (Nov. 23–Dec. 19, 1965) in *La Sylphide,* a ballet in which she made an unforgettable impression. She made her farewell as a dancer with the Royal Danish Ballet dancing the title role in *La Sylphide* at the 1966 Royal Danish Ballet and Music Festival. Continues to teach and coach young dancers in roles which she made her own during her distinguished career.

Schaufuss, Frank, soloist of the Royal Danish Ballet, b. Copenhagen, 1921; m. Mona Vangsaa. Entered the company's school in 1930; studied also in Paris and London; made soloist in 1949. Served as ballet master, 1956–59. Guest artist with Marquis de Cuevas International Ballet. Dances principal roles in *Swan Lake, Le Beau Danube, Graduation Ball, Romeo and Juliet, Les Sylphides, The Nutcracker, The Shadow, and others.* Choreographed *Idolon* (1952), *Feber* (1957), *Opus 13* (1959). Awarded Danish decoration Knight of the Order of Dannebrog.

Scheepers, Martin, dancer, b. Arnhem, Holland, 1933. Studied ballet in Holland with Yvonne Georgi, Françoise Adret; in London with Kathleen Crofton; in Paris with Serge Lifar, Victor Gsovsky, Nora Kiss. Began his professional career with Amsterdam Opera Ballet (1948) and returned as soloist (1951) after intervening seasons with Ballets des Champs-Elysées and London's Festival Ballet; promoted to premier danseur (1952), dancing both the classic and demi-caractère repertoire. Partnered Yvette Chauviré in the Amsterdam productions of *Swan Lake* and *Giselle;* leading dancer with Milorad Miskovitch's company (1958); danced in Roland Petit's *Cyrano de Bergerac* in Paris and London (1959); soloist with American Ballet Theatre since 1960.

Schéhérazade. Ballet in 1 act; chor.: Michel Fokine; music: Nicholas Rimsky-Korsakov; book: Alexandre Benois; décor and costumes: Léon Bakst. First prod.: *Diaghilev Ballets Russes,* Théâtre National de l'Opéra, Paris, June 4, 1910, with Ida Rubinstein (Zobeide), Vaslav Nijinsky (Favorite Slave), Enrico Cecchetti (Chief Eunuch) in main roles. When first given the ballet created a sensation because of its voluptuousness. It was criticized by some musical authorities who claimed Fokine's use of the symphonic poem was not what the composer had intended. The role of Zobeide, not a dancing one, was created to display Rubinstein's beauty and ability as a mime. Tamara Karsavina played this role in London and later Lubov Tchernicheva was very successful in it. The ballet has been revived at various times and was most popular during World War II in the U.S. Its popularity decreased after the war and it is now rarely presented. The plot of *Schéhérazade* is taken from the Introduction of *The One Thousand and One Nights* and deals with the infidelity of the wife and concubines of Shah Sharyar when he and his brother Shah-Zeman absent themselves from the palace on the pretense of a hunt. Bakst's décor and costumes are still considered among the finest of the Diaghilev period.

Schermerhorn, Kenneth D., conductor and musical director, b. Schenectady, N.Y., 1929; m. Lupe Serrano. Graduated with highest honors, New England Conservatory of Music (1950). Studied conducting with Leonard Bernstein; composition with Ben Weber. Conductor and musical director, American Ballet Theatre (since 1957). Has been guest conductor Ballet Russe de Monte Carlo, José Limón Dance Company, and at various ballet festivals. Assistant conductor, N.Y. Philharmonic Orchestra (1959–60); guest conductor, Philadelphia Orchestra, Baltimore Symphony, St. Louis Symphony, N.Y. Philharmonic, and others. Musical director, New Jersey Symphony. Recipient of Serge

Koussevitsky Memorial Award, Elizabeth Sprague Coolidge Medal, Harriet Cohen International Award.

Schiafino, Carlos, premier danseur of Teatro Colón, Buenos Aires, b. Buenos Aires, 1932. Studied dance at the Teatro Colón school with Michel Borovski, Esmée Bulnes, Maria Ruanova and Amalia Lozano. Became soloist of Teatro Colón in 1955, dancing in most ballets. In 1958 was chosen by Antony Tudor to create the title role in *The Legend of Joseph.* In 1961 he became premier danseur and added to his repertoire *Annabel Lee* and *Concerto* (both by Skibine), and *Concierto Coreográfico* by Tamara Grigorieva. The same year was invited by the Provincial Government of Cordoba, Argentina, to form Ballet Oficial de la Provincia de Cordoba with which he appears as guest artist, while remaining premier danseur of Teatro Colón.

Schlagobers. Ballet in 2 acts; chor.: Heinrich Kröller; book and music: Richard Strauss; décor and costumes: Ada Nigrin. First prod.: Operntheater, Vienna, May 9, 1924. Tilly Losch made her first solo appearance in this ballet. Schlagober is the name of a very popular Viennese pastry covered with whipped cream. The ballet has a very complicated scenario which must have delighted Viennese children. The basic plot is the dream of a little boy who had eaten too much pastry at his confirmation party and had become ill. His dream is populated by cakes, pastries, chocolates, candies, etc. Adults and non-Viennese are rather amused that a composer of the stature of Richard Strauss should have written not only the music but the story as well.

Schmidt, Beverly, American modern dancer, b. Chicago, Ill. B.A., Roosevelt Univ.; M.A., Sarah Lawrence College, where she studied dance with Bessie Schoenberg. She has also studied with Sybil Shearer, Hanya Holm, Oliver Kostock, at New Dance Group Studio, with Merce Cunningham and others. Since 1951 has studied with Alwin Nikolais being a leading member of his Henry Street Playhouse Company and dancing in most of his works. Received a Fulbright Scholarship in 1957 to study for a year with Mary Wigman in Berlin and was the recipient of the first Freda Miller Award for Choreography (1961) for her group number *Pindaric.* Began choreography in 1951 and has presented a number of works, both solos and for groups, usually at Henry St. Playhouse. Solos include *Black Traveler, Rite, Six Miniatures, Premonitions,* and others; group works include *Crest, Pindaric, Prelude to a Masked Event,* and others. She also teaches.

Schönberg, Arnold (1874–1951), eminent composer and theoretician. Some of his music has been used by American choreographers with a great deal of understanding and with artistic and popular success. Outstanding among them are his string sextet *Verklaerte Nacht* which Antony Tudor used for his ballet *Pillar of Fire* (1942); *Pierrot Lunaire* (op. 21) a musical setting to the twenty-one poems of Albert Giraud describing the haunting longings of a moon-stricken Pierrot for his native city of Bergamo which several choreographers, among them Eleanor King, Robert Joffrey, Glen Tetley, have choreographed in their own styles; and *Begleitungsmusik zu einer Lichtspielszene* (Musical Accompaniment to a Motion Picture Scene) which was used by George Balanchine for his ballet *Opus 34* for the New York City Ballet (1954). The "Dance Around the Golden Calf" from his opera *Moses and Aaron* is often used by Central European choreographers as a separate number. Paul Taylor's *Fibers* is set to his Five Pieces for Orchestra, op. 16.

Schooling, Elisabeth, English dancer, b. London, 1918. Studied with Marie Rambert and was one of the first members of the Ballet Club, later Ballet Rambert, becoming a principal dancer and dancing an enormous repertoire including many creations. Some of her best known roles were Hebe (Antony Tudor's *Descent of Hebe*), Venus (*Judgment of Paris*), Presque Classique—creation (*Czernyana*), The Chatelaine (*La Fête Etrange*). Also danced in Agnes de Mille's *Three Virgins and a Devil* (Palace Theatre, London, 1936), *Tales of Hoffmann* (Strand Theatre, London, 1942), *The Glass Slipper* (St. James's Theatre, 1940).

Schoop, Trudi, Swiss dancer and comedienne who organized her Trudi Schoop Comic Ballet in 1931 and in 1932 won the second prize at the choreographic competition sponsored by Archives Internationales de la Danse in Paris with her composition *Fridolin* (Kurt Jooss' *The Green Table* won first prize). From 1937–39 toured Europe and U.S. with *Fridolin, Want Ads, The Blonde Marie, Hurray for Love*. Schoop disbanded her company at the beginning of World War II. Reassembled (1946) and toured U.S. and Canada (1947) with a full-evening production called *Barbara*. Now retired.

Schorer, Suki (Suzanne), contemporary dancer, b. Cambridge, Mass. Graduated from high school *cum laude* and attended Univ. of California, Berkeley. Studied ballet at San Francisco Ballet School and became a member of the company, dancing the first Clara in Lew Christensen's revised version of *The Nutcracker*. In 1953 danced in a production of John Milton's *Comus* in Florence, Italy. After touring Orient, South America, and Middle East with San Francisco Ballet (1959) joined New York City Ballet; promoted to soloist (1963). Dances a large repertoire including 3rd movement (*Symphony in C*), Blackamoor (*La Sonnàmbula*); created variations in *Donizetti Variations* and *Raymonda Variations,* leading Fairy (*A Midsummer Night's Dream*). Created Pierrette in George Balanchine's *Harlequinade* and pas de deux Mauresque (with John Prinz) in Balanchine's *Don Quixote*. Married Dr. William Chick, Nov. 4, 1965 in New York.

Suki Schorer, soloist of The New York City Ballet with Denis Lamont in Harlequinade.

Schottelius, Renate (Renate Schottelius de Rosenberg), modern dancer, choreographer, teacher, b. Flensburg, Germany, 1921. Modern and ballet dance training at Städtische Oper, Berlin (1930–35); ballet for one year at Conservatorio Nacional, Buenos Aires, Argentina (1936). Studied modern dance for five years with Miriam Winslow, Buenos Aires (1945–49), during which period she was soloist, assistant teacher, and choreographer for Ballet Winslow, touring all over Argentina. From 1945 on also gave solo performances in Argentina, Uruguay, Peru, Amsterdam (Holland), Krefeld (Germany), and N.Y. (U.S.) While in New York (1953–54) studied modern dance with José Limón, and Hanya Holm, choreography with Doris Humphrey and Louis Horst, and Labanotation at Dance Notation Bureau. Formed her own company (1955), performing in Argentina, Brazil, Uruguay; also appeared on television in Argentina and Holland. Toured Germany, Holland and France with partner Juan Carlos Bellini (1959). Also teaches and is a member of the dance jury both for the Teatro Colón and the Fonda Nacional de las Artes, Buenos Aires. Since Sept., 1966 guest artist in residence at the Boston Conservatory of Music.

Schottische, a social dance popular in England and on the European continent in 1840's and 1850's; was also used as a stage dance. The correct name of the dance is actually scottish but for some reason the German Schottische is more often used. The French call it Ecassaise.

Schrifttanz. See LABAN DANCE NOTATION SYSTEM.

Schubert, Franz (1797–1828), Austrian composer. His music was used for part of Bronislava Nijinska's ballet *Beloved* (1928), for *Errante* (George Balanchine, 1933), *Death and the Maiden* (Andrée Howard, 1937; Erich Walter, 1964), *The Wanderer* (Frederick Ashton, 1941). His Symphony No. 7 was used by Leonide Massine for his ballet *Labyrinth* (1941). John Taras used his music for *Camille* (1946), and *Fantasy* (Fantasy for Piano Duet, op. 103, orch. by Felix Mottl).

Schubert, Lia, dancer and teacher, b. Vienna, 1926. Studied ballet at the Zagreb opera; came to Paris in 1938 and worked under Olga Preobrajenska, Lubov Egorova, Victor Gsovsky, Nora Kiss, and the Conservatoire Nationale de Paris. She danced with the Marseille and Lille opera ballets and free-lanced for a few years before being engaged by the Malmö (Sweden) Municipal Theatre. In 1953 she opened her own school in Stockholm, organized the Ballet Academy and has been its artistic director since 1957. Choreographed works for recitals and television in Stockholm.

Schuhplattltanz, a Bavarian folk dance. It was used by George Balanchine as a basis for the character dance in Scene II of *Le Baiser de la Fée.*

Schuman, Dr. William Howard, American composer, b. New York, 1910. President, Juilliard School of Music, N.Y. (1945–61). President and director, Lincoln Center for the Performing Arts, N.Y. (since Jan. 1, 1962). His compositions for dance include *Undertow* (Antony Tudor, Ballet Theatre (1945); *Night Journey* (1947), *Voyage, Judith* (1950) (all for Martha Graham).

Schumann, Robert (1810–1856), German composer. His music was used for the ballets *Le Carnaval* (1910) and its sequel *Papillons* (1912), both by Michel Fokine. His *Etudes Symphoniques* is the score for Igor Schwezoff's *The Eternal Struggle* and Ludmilla Chiriaeff's *Etude* is set to Schumann's *Scenes of Childhood.* Antony Tudor also used this music for a ballet which has on several occasions been danced by students of the dance department of the Juilliard School of Music at their annual performances.

Schurman, Nona, American modern dancer and teacher, b. Oxford, Nova Scotia, Canada. Graduate of McGill University and Conservatory of Music, Montreal, with special studies in French, cello, voice, stagecraft and playwriting. Studied modern dance at Sheffler Studio. Member of the Humphrey-Weidman Company (1939–43); production assistant, Roxy Theatre, N.Y. (1945); U.S.O. Camp Shows (ETO) (1946); director, Luening Opera, Columbia Univ. (1947); Audition Winner, YM–YWHA, N.Y. (1942); appeared with own company (1949). As a teacher she has been on the New Dance Group Studio faculty since 1938 and is vice-president of the Group and director of its Young Concert Dancers; on the YM–YWHA dance faculty since 1949; has taught summer sessions at Bennington

College and Connecticut College; taught at High School of Performing Arts, N.Y., and has her own studio in N.Y.

Schwarz, Solange, French ballerina, b. 1910. Educated at the school of the Opéra, Paris. After dancing several years with the Opéra Comique (where her two sisters were also dancers) she was ballerina of the Opéra Ballet until Oct., 1944, dancing both character and classic roles, among them *Coppélia* (perhaps her best role), *Les Sylphides, Entre deux Ronds,* and others. Appeared with the Opera Ballet at Covent Garden Royal Opera House at the coronation of King George VI of England. Guest artist, Ballets des Champs-Elysées (1946), dancing *La Forêt, Concert de Danses,* and others, première danseuse étoile Grand Ballet de Monte Carlo (1947). Now semi-retired.

Schwezoff, Igor, dancer, choreographer, teacher, b. St. Petersburg, Russia, 1904. Professional training, Technicum of Ballet, Academic Theatre (now Kirov) of Leningrad. Soloist, Academic Theatre of Ukraine (1926); in revues in Harbin, China (1930–31). Soloist, Ballet Russe de Monte Carlo (1931); first dancer, Teatro Colón, Buenos Aires (1931), dancing *Prince Igor, Carnaval, Firebird,* and others; soloist with Bronislava Nijinska's company at Opéra Comique, Paris, and on tour in Italy and south of France (1932). First dancer and assistant choreographer, Monte Carlo opera season (1936–37); taught in London (1937–39); soloist Original Ballet Russe (1939–40); choreographer, New Opera Company, N.Y. (1941); served in U.S. Army (1942–43). Director of Ballet, choreographer, and dancer at Municipal Theatre, Rio de Janeiro (1945), staging *Swan Lake, Les Sylphides,* and his own ballets, *Eternal Struggle, Red Poppy,* and others; also staged opera ballets. Choreographer, N.Y. City Opera (1946). In 1947 organized the Ballet da Juventude, Rio de Janeiro, staging standard works as well as his own. Opened his own studio in N.Y. (1949) and organized his own company (1953) (with Lupe Serrano as ballerina) which toured in South America with a repertoire of his ballets, including *Eternal Struggle,* Beethoven's *Moonlight Sonata, Masquerade, Nocturne,* and others. With brief absences taught at Ballet Theatre School (1956–62). Has written numerous articles published in Holland, England, Australia, U.S., and Brazil, and is author of *Borzoi,* an autobiography for which he received a literary prize of $1,000 (London, 1935); also published in U.S. under title *Russian Somersault* (N.Y., 1936), and in Sweden and Germany.

Scotch Symphony. Ballet in 3 movements; chor.: George Balanchine; music: Felix Mendelssohn's Symphony in A minor (The "Scotch") excluding the first movement; décor: Horace Armistead. First prod.: New York City Ballet, City Center, N.Y., Nov. 11, 1952, with Maria Tallchief, Patricia Wilde, André Eglevsky, Michael Maule, Frank Hobi. Although themeless the middle section hints at Romantic ballet with a supernatural creature who is found, lost, and found again by a human lover. The work opens with a brilliant pastiche of Scottish dancing translated into ballet.

Scott, David, British dancer, b. Colombo, Ceylon, 1928. Qualified as an engineer, he took up dance training at the age of nineteen, studying with Nora Fearn in Sunderland, England, and then in London at the Espinosa School, Anna Severskaya (Northcote), and Stanislas Idzikowski. Danced with Original Ballet Russe (1951); joined London's Festival Ballet (1952); promoted to soloist (1956). Roles include, among others, male dancer (*Les Sylphides*), Siegfried (*Swan Lake,* Act 2), Romeo (Oleg Briansky's *Romeo and Juliet*), Sugar Plum Fairy's Cavalier (*The Nutcracker*), one of the four dancers in Anton Dolin's *Variations for Four.* Joined National Ballet of Canada (1959), dancing Captain Belaye (*Pineapple Poll*), Florestan pas de trois (*Aurora's Wedding*), Groom (*Antic Spring*), Duke (*Offenbach in the Underworld*), and others.

Scott, Margaret, South African dancer, b. Johannesburg, 1922. Studied with Ivy Conmee (Johannesburg), Sadlers' Wells School, Marie Rambert. Member, Sadler's Wells Ballet for eighteen months; then joined Ballet Rambert where she danced Swan Queen (*Swan Lake,* Act 2), Italian and French ballerinas (*Gala Performance*), Elder Sister (*The Fugitive*), Minerva (*Judgment of Paris*); created Hen (Andrée Howard's *The Carnival of Animals*), and others. Collaborated with Rex Reid and Joyce Graeme in founding Australian National Theatre Ballet Company. Is now married to eminent Australian doctor Derek Denton.

Scott, Marion, modern dancer, choreographer, b. Chicago Ill., 1922. Studied modern dance with Martha Graham, Doris Humphrey, Charles Weidman, Frances Allis, Louis Horst; ballet with Vecheslav Swoboda, Maria Yurieva Swoboda, Adolph Bolm, Sonia Woicikowska. Danced with Martha Graham's group in Bennington Festival of the Arts (1941); member of the Humphrey-Weidman Company (1943–44), being in the original casts of *Inquest, Partita, Daddy Was a Fireman, The Heart Remembers;* assistant teacher for Doris Humphrey, Dance Center of YM–YWHA, N.Y. (1944–49). Was an Auditions Winner, presenting her work Mar. 7, 1948, at the YM–YWHA. Between 1947 and 1953 presented a number of her works for performances sponsored by Choreographers' Workshop. Her *Afflicted Children* based on the Salem witch trials, originally presented in a Choreographers' Workshop program in 1953, was shown that summer at Jacob's Pillow Dance Festival. Taught modern dance at High School of Performing Arts, N.Y. (1955–56); was a founding member of Contemporary Dance Productions (1956) and has presented a number of her own works, both solo and group, on their programs. Since 1960 has also been a member of Helen Tamiris–Daniel Nagrin Dance Company and an assistant to Helen Tamiris. Member of the board of directors of Contemporary Dance, Inc.

Marion Scott, modern dancer, choreographer, cofounder of Contemporary Dance Productions.

Scuola di Ballo. Ballet in 1 act; chor.: Leonide Massine; music: Luigi Boccherini, arr. by Jean Françaix; book: Leonide Massine; décor and costumes: Comte Etienne de Beaumont. First prod.: Comte Etienne de Beaumont (1924) at his Soirées de Paris; Col. de Basil's Ballet Russe, Théâtre de Monte Carlo, Apr. 25, 1933, with Irina Baronova, Eugenia Delarova, Tatiana Riabouchinska, André Eglevsky, Leonide Massine, Yurek Shabelevski, Leon Woicikowski in leading parts. The ballet was based on an eighteenth century Italian comedy by Carlo Goldoni.

Sea Change. Ballet in 1 act; chor.: John Cranko; music: Jan Sibelius (*En Saga*); décor: John Piper. First prod.: Sadler's

Wells Theatre Ballet, Gaiety Theatre, Dublin, July 18, 1949. London première: Sadler's Wells Theatre, Sept. 27, 1949, with Sheila O'Reilly, Michael Hogan, Jane Shore, Hans Zullig. An impression of life in a fishing community. This was Cranko's first important work.

Sea Gallows. Ballet in 1 act; chor.: Eric Hyrst; music: Michel Perrault; décor: Alexis Chiriaeff; costumes: Claudette Picard. First prod.: Les Grands Ballets Canadiens, Comédie Canadienne Théâtre, Montreal, Apr. 16, 1959, with Milenka Niderlova (The Young Girl), Brydon Paige (The Stranger), John Stanzel (The Fiddler), Marcel Fugère (The Priest). A young girl unknowingly falls in love with and marries a stranger who a year previously had murdered her lover. When she discovers this she resolves to kill the stranger but, in luring him to a cliff, she herself falls and drags him with her.

Seasons, The. Ballet in 1 act; chor.: Merce Cunningham; music: John Cage; décor and costumes: Isamu Noguchi. First prod.: Ballet Society, Ziegfeld Theatre, N.Y., May 18, 1947, with a cast headed by Merce Cunningham, Beatrice Tompkins, Tanaquil LeClercq, Gisella Caccialanza. An avant-garde work of the choreographer who at the time had recently left the Martha Graham company where he had been a principal male dancer. It was an amusing work rather than an important or even interesting one. This was John Cage's first composition for a large orchestra and Isamu Noguchi's first décor for a ballet company.

Sebastian. Ballet in 3 scenes; chor.: Edward Caton; music and book: Gian-Carlo Menotti; décor: Oliver Smith; costumes: Milena. First prod.: Ballet International, International Theatre, N.Y., Oct. 31, 1944, with Francisco Moncion (Sebastian), Viola Essen (Courtesan), Kari Karnakoski (Prince). Revived for Original Ballet Russe, Metropolitan Opera House, N.Y., Oct. 13, 1946, with Moncion in his original role, Rosella Hightower (Courtesan), George Skibine (Prince); revived for Grand Ballet de Monte Carlo (summer, 1947), with Skibine as Sebastian. The ballet is set in 17th century Venice. The Moorish slave Sebastian secretly loves the Courtesan who is loved by the Prince. The two sisters of the Prince attempt to kill the Courtesan by witchcraft, stabbing her wax replica over which they have placed one of her veils. But Sebastian, learning of their plot, takes the place of the image and is stabbed to death. A single performance of an entirely new version by Agnes de Mille was presented by American Ballet Theatre, N.Y., in a workshop performance May 27, 1957, with Lupe Serrano and John Kriza as the Courtesan and Sebastian. John Butler staged his own version for Nederlands Dans Theater, premièred Oct. 22, 1963 and for the Harkness Ballet in 1967.

Seckler, Beatrice, American modern dancer, b. Brooklyn, N.Y. Graduate of Hunter College, N.Y. Began her professional training with Michio Ito (1927–29), Oriental and interpretive; Angel Cansino (1929–30), Spanish; Yeichi Nimura (1930–31), Oriental; Doris Humphrey and Charles Weidman (from 1935) modern; Nenette Charisse (1948–50), ballet. Joined the Doris Humphrey–Charles Weidman company for its first long tour (1935) and remained until 1942 creating solo role in *Variations and Conclusions* from Humphrey's *New Dance,* the Instigator (*Lynchtown*) and Agnes (*Flickers*), both by Weidman. Featured dancer at Roxy Theatre, N.Y. (1942–45); toured with José Limón and Dorothy Bird (1945–46). Since 1948 has been a faculty member of New Dance Group Studio, N.Y., teaching Humphrey-Weidman technique and has continued to make guest appearances in works by Sophie Maslow and Anna Sokolow. Notable creations during this period were her roles in Sokolow's *Lyric Suite* and *Rooms.* Has also danced in off-Broadway productions, at Madison

Square Garden's annual Festival of Lights (1960–61), and on television.

Seconde, in ballet, second position.

Secular Games. Modern dance work in 3 movements; chor.: Martha Graham; music: Robert Starer's *Concerto à Tre;* set and lighting: Jean Rosenthal (properties sculptured by Marion Kinsella). First prod.: Martha Graham Dance Company, 15th American Dance Festival, New London, Conn., Aug. 17, 1962, with Robert Powell, David Wood, Richard Kuch, Richard Gain, Clive Thompson, Dudley Williams, Peter Randazzo, Helen McGehee, Lois Schlossberg, Juliet Fisher. An abstract work, the three movements being titled: Play with thought—on a Socratic island, for the seven male dancers; Play with dream—on a Utopian island; and Play—on any island.

Sedova, Julia, Russian ballerina, b. St. Petersburg, 1880. Made her debut at the Maryinsky Theatre after graduating from its ballet school (1898). Her graduating class was considered one of the most talented since the beginning of the school. It included such dancers as Lubov Egorova, Sedova, Michel Fokine, and Mikhail Oboukhov, among others. She was making excellent progress on the stage when in 1910 Nicholas Sergeyev, at the time chief regisseur of the Ballet, developed an animosity toward her and continued to persecute her to such an extent that she resigned from the Imperial Theatres (1911). After guest appearances in Europe and America she returned to St. Petersburg (1914) and petitioned to be reinstated so that she could stay long enough in the Maryinsky to earn her pension. She was reinstated despite the interference of Sergeyev. She remained at the Maryinsky until 1916 when she retired on a pension. Soon after the revolution she moved to France and is still teaching in Nice.

Segall, Bernardo, pianist, composer, b. Campinas, Brazil, 1911. Studied piano with José Klimas and A. Cantu in Brazil and with Alexander Siloti (1927–39) in N.Y.; composition with Lazare Saminsky (1930–38). Made his N.Y. debut with a recital in Town Hall (1936) since when he has given many performances both solo and with orchestras all over the U.S., South America, and Europe. Composed the scores for Jean Erdman's *Sea Deep* and *People and Ghosts;* Sophie Maslow's *The Wall* and for Valerie Bettis's *Desperate Heart* (1943) and *As I Lay Dying* (1948), *Domino Furioso* (1949), *The Golden Round* (1955). Has also composed scores for Tennessee Williams' play *Camino Real,* William Saroyan's *The Cave Dwellers,* and several scores for motion pictures, one of which (*Hope Is Eternal,* 1954) won the Punta Del Lesta Award.

Seguidilla, a Spanish dance which has many varieties and derivatives in every Hispanic country and province. Broadly speaking it is based on pas de basque which is called in Spanish paso de Vasco. See SPANISH DANCE.

Seigneuret, Michèle, French dancer, b. Paris, 1934. Studied with Jeanne Schwarz. Made her debut in 1953 with Ballets de l'Etoile de Maurice Béjart and was the first interpreter of principal roles in most of his ballets. Received the René Blum Award in 1956.

Sekh, Yaroslav, Honored Artist of the RSFSR, Soviet character dancer, b. in a Carpathian village (Ukraine), 1930. Sekh is one of the few dancers who did not go through the full course of ballet education. In 1944 he entered the railroad vocational school at Lvov where he took part in an amateur dancing group and in 1946 was seen accidentally by one of the dancers of the Lvov Opera who advised him to join the ballet school there. After two years he was accepted into the Lvov ballet company and danced at the opera house successfully (1948–49). He was then helped by the Ukrainian writer Yaroslav Galan to enter the Bolshoi School, Moscow, where he began his studies in 1949 and graduated with honors into the Bolshoi Ballet in 1951, becoming an outstanding character soloist in his first season. He made his debut in the mazurka in *Swan Lake* and later in the season performed the Spanish dance in the same ballet and the brilliant Panaderos in *Raymonda*. He is, however, much more than a character soloist as he has shown in such roles as Mercutio (*Romeo and Juliet*), Espada (*Don Quixote*), Georgi (*Gayané*), Dying Slave (*Spartacus*). His greatest achievement to date is the title role in Leonid Lavrovsky's *Paganini* which he created.

Selina. Ballet in 1 act; chor.: Andrée Howard; music: arr. by Guy Warrack from the following Rossini operas: *William Tell, The Lady of the Lake, Cenerentola, Count Orie;* the ballet beginning and ending with the Serenata from his *Soirées Musicales;* décor and libretto: Peter Williams. First prod.: Sadler's Wells Theatre Ballet, Sadler's Wells Theatre, London, Nov. 16, 1948, with Elaine Fifield (Selina), Hans Zullig (The Poet), Stanley Holden (Agnes, a Witch), Pirmin Trecu (The Brother). A satire on Romantic Ballet with magic bracelets, spells cast by a very incompetent witch, and true love conquering all. It was the first ballet to reveal fully the great comic gifts of Stanley Holden.

Selling, Caj, Swedish dancer, b. 1935. Studied with Lilian Karina, Olga Preobrajenska, Mme. Rousanne Sarkissian and Anna Northcote. Was engaged by the Royal Swedish Ballet in 1954 and continued to study at the Royal School under Mary Skeaping and Albert Kozlovsky. In 1956 was awarded a Fellowship by the King of Sweden. Partner of ballerina Mariane Orlando with whom he danced in the Soviet Union in 1958. Was promoted to premier danseur in 1959 and went to Leningrad that year to study at the ballet school of the Kirov Theatre for two months. Later that year partnered Beryl Grey at the Royal Opera House, Covent Garden, London, for two months as guest artist with Royal (British) Ballet. He dances the principal male roles in *Swan Lake, The Sleeping Beauty, Giselle, Miss Julie, The Moon Reindeer.* He took leave of absence with Mariane Orlando for the season 1961–62 to be guest artist with the American Ballet Theatre. Guest artist for the inaugural (1962–63) season of the Australian Ballet. Returned to American Ballet Theatre beginning of 1964 before returning to the Royal Swedish Ballet. Guest artist, Australian Ballet (1964).

Semenoff, Simon, b. Liepaja, Latvia, 1908. Studied with Alexandra Fedorova, Asaf Messerer, Vasili Tikhomirov (Latvia), Max Reinhardt (Berlin), Olga Preobrajenska, Lubov Egorova (Paris), Michel Fokine (U.S.). Made his debut as soloist, Riga (Latvia) National Opera (1922–30); Max Reinhardt's productions (Vienna and Paris, 1930); between 1937 and 1945 appeared with Leon Woicikowski's company, René Blum's Ballet Russe de Monte Carlo, Ballet Russe de Monte Carlo, Ballet (now American Ballet) Theatre, Ballet International. Among his roles were Slave, Saracen (*Raymonda*), Dr. Coppelius (*Coppélia*), Charlatan (*Petrouchka*), Chief Eunuch (*Schéhérazade*), Mother Simone (*La Fille Mal Gardée*), Menelaus (*Helen of Troy*), Hilarion (*Giselle*), and others. Has choreographed *Memories* (1944), *Gift of the Magi* (Ballet Theatre, 1945; San Francisco Ballet, 1949; London's Festival Ballet, Monte Carlo, 1956), *Rhapsody, Debut, Hebrew Chant* (1957). Opened his own school in Santa Monica, Calif. (1947) and presented his Ballet Vignettes on the Don Lee television show (1948–49) which won an award. Opened his own school in Stamford, Conn. (1954). Appeared as guest artist with Ballet Russe de Monte

Carlo (*Schéhérazade, Coppélia,* and Katisha in *The Mikado*) and with Ballet Theatre (*Bluebeard* and *Petrouchka*). Since 1958 has been coordinator and interpreter for foreign companies and individual artists with Hurok Attractions, Inc.

Semenov, Nicholas, Russian dancer. Member, corps de ballet of the Bolshoi Ballet, Moscow. Joined the Diaghilev Ballets Russes company in 1909. In the series of misunderstandings between Serge Diaghilev and Michel Fokine he sided consistently with Fokine, thus gaining favor with the choreographer. In 1912 he was appointed assistant to the regisseur Serge Grigorieff in charge, more or less, of the Fokine ballets. In 1925 he came to the U.S. and settled in Cleveland, Ohio, where he eventually opened a school. The low state of ballet in the U.S. at the time and especially the first flowering of the modern dance had such a strong emotional effect on Semenov that in 1932 he committed suicide "as a protest against the ugliness of the modern dance." Semenov's unnecessary martyrdom was the result of a chain of circumstances, not the least important of which was insufficient enrollment in his school, his meagre English, his lack of comprehension of life in America, and the fact that he was not gifted as a teacher.

Semyonov, Victor (1893–1942), Honored Artist of the RSFSR, premier danseur and Soviet teacher. Graduated from the Ballet School into the Maryinsky company in 1912 and by 1917 was a premier danseur. He possessed a very strong technique and extraordinary elevation. In style he was a true danseur noble, his one weakness being poor miming. His best known partners were Olga Spessivtseva and Marina Semyonova, his wife and namesake. He retired from the stage in 1931 and was transferred to Moscow to teach at the Bolshoi School. He was its principal teacher until his death training such ballerinas as Olga Lepeshinskaya and Sophia Golovkina.

Semyonov, Vladilen, Soviet premier dancer, b. Kuibyshev on the Volga, 1932. His given name is an abbreviation of Vladimir Lenin. His parents moved to Leningrad and in 1950 he was graduated from the Leningrad (Kirov) Ballet School where he was a pupil of Vladimir Ponomaryov, joining the Kirov company as a soloist and rising to his present position as leading classic male dancer. With his long legs, excellent figure and very clean and precise technique, Semyonov is a perfect cavalier for the ballerina. His first great success came in 1955 when his Romeo in *Romeo and Juliet* showed him to be an excellent actor as well as a fine dancer. Among his other fine roles are Albrecht (*Giselle*) which he first danced as partner to Alla Shelest, Siegfried (*Swan Lake*), Prince Desiré and the Blue Bird (*The Sleeping Beauty*), Prince (*The Nutcracker*), Vaslav (*The Fountain of Bakhchisarai*). Semyonov has danced in France, England, U.S., Germany, Poland, Finland, Canada, Roumania, Yugoslavia, Czechoslovakia, Hungary, Latin America, United Arab Republic (Egypt), and Lebanon. He is married to ballerina Irina Kolpakova.

Semyonova, Marina, Peoples' Artist of the RSFSR, Soviet ballerina and teacher, b. 1908. Semyonova was the first ballerina of Soviet ballet and the first great dancer trained by Agrippina Vaganova. She entered the Leningrad ballet school in 1919 and was graduated from it in 1925. While still a pupil she was given responsible roles and for her graduation performance danced the Nymph of the Stream in Leo Delibes' *La Source* which Vaganova had revived especially for her. She made her debut in the Kirov company as Aurora in *The Sleeping Beauty,* reaching ballerina status during her first season. Technical difficulties did not exist for the young ballerina but particularly attractive were the majestic quality of her dancing and her wonderful line. She excelled in broad, sweeping leaps and statuesque poses. Her first dramatic role was Nikia in *La Bayadère* taught her by Vaganova. Her greatest role was Odette-Odile in *Swan Lake*. Much of Semyonova's experience has become part of Soviet ballet and was made use of by all the ballerinas who came after her. Her personal greatness, however, remains unsurpassed. She was transferred to the Moscow Bolshoi Theatre as prima ballerina in 1930 dancing *Swan Lake, The Sleeping Beauty, La Bayadère, Esmeralda,* and many ballets created by Soviet choreographers among them Rostislav Zakharov's *The Prisoner of the Caucasus* (Pauline), *Mistress into Maid* (Lisa), *Flames of Paris* (Mireille de Poitiers), *Taras Bulba* (Pannochka, the Polish princess), and the title role in *Cinderella.* In 1935–36 she danced *Giselle* at the Paris Opéra with Serge Lifar. She retired from the stage in 1952 and retired completely from dancing in 1955. She began teaching as early as 1925 and is at present a coach for dancers in the Bolshoi Ballet and an instructor at the Moscow Choreographic School, formerly the ballet school of the Bolshoi Theatre. Her first husband's family name was also Semyonov. Yekaterina Axenova, her daughter by her third marriage, is a member of the Bolshoi Ballet.

Sentimental Colloquy. Ballet in 1 act; chor.: André Eglevsky; music: Paul Bowles; décor and costumes: Salvador Dali. First prod.: Ballet International, International Theatre, N.Y., Oct. 30, 1944, with André Eglevsky and Marie Jeanne in principal parts. It is based on a poem by Paul Verlaine. Revived for Grand Ballet de Monte Carlo with Eglevsky and Rosella Hightower (1948).

Septet. Modern dance work; chor.: Merce Cunningham; music: Erik Satie's *Trois Morceaux en Forme de Poire*. First N.Y. prod.: Theater de Lys, Dec. 29, 1953, with Merce Cunningham, Carolyn Brown and company. A suite of dances to match, underline and sometimes contradict the Satie music.

Sequence Dancing, a term used in England to describe those ballroom dances in which the steps have to be taken in a certain definite order as a consequence of which all couples are always making the same movement at the same time. The Veleta is the most popular of this kind of dancing throughout the country but there are today several hundreds of sequence dances and competitions are held every year to discover yet further new dances. Today this form of sequence dancing has injected new life into the genuine old-time dances which came back into great popularity at the end of World War II.

Seraphic Dialogue. Modern dance work; chor.: Martha Graham; music: Norman Dello Joio; décor: Isamu Noguchi. First prod.: Martha Graham Dance Company, ANTA Theatre, N.Y., May 8, 1955, with Linda Margolies (later Linda Hodes), Patricia Birsh, Mary Hinkson, Matt Turney, as aspects of St. Joan, and Bertram Ross (St. Michael). At the moment of her canonization as she is received at the gate of Heaven into the communion of saints, Joan (Linda Margolies) sees herself as Maid, Warrior, and Martyr. This work was originally a long solo for Martha Graham. See Triumph of St. Joan.

Serenade. Ballet in 4 movements; chor.: George Balanchine; music: Peter Tchaikovsky's Serenade for String Orchestra in C major, with the 3rd and 4th movements transposed; costumes: Jean Lurçat. First prod.: American Ballet, Adelphi Theatre, N.Y., Mar. 1, 1935, with Kathryn Mullowney and Heidi Vosseler in leading parts. Alvin Colt designed costumes for the American Ballet's tour in South America (1941) when Marie Jeanne had the leading woman's role. It was danced for the first time by New York City Ballet on Oct. 18 of that year with Marie Jeanne, Pat McBride, Herbert Bliss and Nicholas Magallanes. The women's roles in this ballet have been danced by as many as five, or as few as two, sharing the solo passages almost interchangeably. Costumes since 1948 are by Barbara Karinska. Balanchine staged *Serenade* for Ballet Russe de Monte Carlo (in the Lurçat costumes) at Metropolitan Opera House, N.Y., Oct. 17, 1940, with Igor Youskevitch, Frederic Franklin, and Marie Jeanne (as guest artist), her role being danced subsequently by Alexandra Danilova. Balanchine also staged this ballet for Paris Opéra Ballet (1947) and Royal Danish Ballet (1957). In 1960 *Serenade* was staged at Teatro alla Scala, Milan, and for the Netherlands Ballet and Royal Swedish Ballet. On May 7, 1964, the Royal Ballet, London, premièred *Serenade* at a Gala Performance. Although plotless there is a deep, though unexplained, emotional content in the relationship between the two women and the man in the final movement.

Sergava, Katherine, contemporary dancer; b. Tiflis, Russia. Studied dance with Mathilda Kchessinska, Michel Fokine, Lydia Kyasht, Julieta Mendes; acting with Zhilinsky of Moscow Art Theatre, Michel St. Denis of London Theatre Studio. Soloist, Mordkin Ballet (1938), Ballet (now American Ballet) Theatre (1940–41), Original Ballet Russe (1941), her roles including Prelude (*Les Sylphides*), Cerito (*Pas de Quatre*), Venus (*Judgment of Paris*), and others. Featured dancer in the musical *Oklahoma!* (1947–48). Took over the Lotte Lenya role in the long-running (five years) Theatre de Lys revival of Kurt Weill's *Three-Penny Opera.*

Sergeyev, Konstantin, Peoples' Artist of the U.S.S.R., Soviet premier danseur and choreographer, b. 1910. Currently artistic director of the Kirov Ballet. He joined the evening classes of the Leningrad Ballet School in 1924 while still at a regular academic school and was graduated in 1928, being a pupil of Victor Semyonov. He became premier danseur of a traveling ballet company founded by Iosif Kchessinski (brother of Mathilda Kchessinska) dancing all the classic roles including Siegfried in *Swan Lake* and Albrecht in *Giselle* when he was only eighteen. In the two years he spent with this company Sergeyev acquired considerable experience and a good technique. In 1929 he passed the entrance examinations to the Ballet School of the former Maryinsky Theatre (then called Choreographic Technicum) and was graduated into the company in 1930, making his debut as

Konstantin Sergeyev, dancer, choreographer, artistic director of the Leningrad Kirov Ballet, as Albrecht in Giselle.

the Young Coolie in *The Red Poppy* (Act 1). In the autumn of that year he officially became a member of the Leningrad Academic Theatre of Opera and Ballet as the theatre was then called and by the end of his first season danced his first *Swan Lake,* becoming one of best Siegfrieds in the company's history. He quickly achieved the position of premier danseur noble and became partner of Galina Ulanova. In addition to a complete repertoire of the classic ballets he created, among others, Vaslav (*The Fountain of Bakhchisarai,* 1934), Lucien (*Lost Illusions,* 1935), Koloman (*Raymonda,* new version, 1938), Romeo (*Romeo and Juliet,* 1940), Ostap and Andrei (*Taras Bulba,* 1941 and 1955 versions, respectively), Armen (*Gayané,* 1942), Prince (*Cinderella,* his own 1946 version), Yevgeny (*The Bronze Horseman,* 1949), Aly-Batyr (*Shurale,* 1951), Lenny (*Path of Thunder,* his own ballet, 1957). As a choreographer Sergeyev carried out important revivals of the Petipa ballets *Raymonda* (1948), *Swan Lake* (1950), *The Sleeping Beauty* with some changes in the mise-en-scènes (1952), in addition to his version of *Cinderella* and *Path of Thunder.* Besides being a virtuoso dancer he is an excellent actor. He was artistic director of the Kirov Ballet (1951–56) and reassumed the position in Apr., 1960. He is married to ballerina Natalia Dudinskaya whom he has partnered constantly since Ulanova left the Kirov company for Moscow's Bolshoi. He danced with his wife in China, Berlin, Warsaw, Czechoslovakia, Hungary, United Arab Republic (Egypt). In 1958 he visited Denmark and in 1961 he was in Paris, London, and the U.S. with the Kirov Ballet in his capacity of artistic director. He danced *Giselle* with British ballerina Nadia Nerina at the Kirov Theatre in the winter of 1960–61.

Sergeyev, Nicholas, ballet master, former dancer and regisseur-general of the Maryinsky Theatre, b. St. Petersburg, 1876, d. Nice, 1951. Was graduated from the St. Petersburg Imperial School of Ballet in 1894; promoted to first dancer and regisseur in 1904; became regisseur-general in 1914. Soviet sources have very little that is flattering to say about Sergeyev. In the two-volume *Materials on the History of Russian Ballet* (Materialy po Istorii Russkogo Baleta, Leningrad, 1939) Sergeyev is accused of exercising an alleged destructive influence on the St. Petersburg Ballet from 1906 when he became a virtual dictator of the ballet until 1917, when he resigned following the revolution. He left Russia in 1918. How much truth there is in these accusations is difficult to establish. The fact remains that outside Russia and especially in England Sergeyev did more than any other ballet master or dancer to preserve the classic ballet. The list of classic ballets which he revived and staged for various companies (with the aid of his volumes of detailed notes which he took with him when he left Russia) includes some of the great ballets produced in Russia during the second half of the 19th century, among them: *Tre Sleeping Beauty* for the Diaghilev Ballets Russes (1921), Sadler's Wells (now Royal) Ballet (1939), International Ballet, (1948); *Swan Lake* for Sadler's Wells Ballet (1934, 1943), International Ballet (1947); *Giselle* for Sadler's Wells Ballet (1935), Ballet Russe de Monte Carlo (1938), International Ballet (1948); *The Nutcracker* for Sadler's Wells Ballet (1934); *Coppélia* (a two-act version) for Sadler's Wells Ballet (1933), and with the third act added (1940), Ballet Russe de Monte Carlo (1938), International Ballet (1947). In Coppélia the *Hymen* pas de deux, the male variation, much of the Swanilda-Franz pas de deux, and the finale of Act 3 were arranged by Sergeyev himself.

Serpent's Heart. See CAVE OF THE HEART.

Serrano, Lupe (Guadalupe Serrano), ballerina, b. Santiago, Chile, 1930; m.

Lupe Serrano, ballerina of the American Ballet Theatre in the Don Quixote *pas de deux.*

Kenneth Schermerhorn. Studied dance with Nelsy Dambre (Mexico City) and Igor Schwezoff and Antony Tudor (N.Y.). She made her first stage appearance in Chile, aged four, and her professional debut, aged thirteen, with the Ballet of Mexico City. Made three-month tour of Central America with Ballet Alicia Alonso (1949); appeared with Ballet Nelsy Dambre and Academy of Mexican Dance in Mexico City (1949–51); toured U.S., Canada, and Venezuela as soloist with Ballet Russe de Monte Carlo (1949–51). Appeared in weekly television show in Mexico City (1952–53) for which she received an award in 1953; toured Colombia and Ecuador with Igor Schwezoff's Ballet Concerts (1953). Joined American Ballet Theatre (1953) of which she is currently prima ballerina dancing Swan Queen (*Swan Lake,* Act 2), Giselle and Queen of the Wilis (*Giselle*), *Black Swan, Nutcracker* and *Don Quixote* pas de deux, ballerina (*Theme and Variations*), Clorinda (*The Combat*), Mazurka and Pas de Deux (*Les Sylphides*), ballerina (*Etudes*), Lise (*La Fille Mal Gardée*), and others. Created the leading roles in Birgit Cullberg's *Lady from the Sea,* and *Moon Reindeer* for this company, among other roles. She was a great success when the company appeared in Russia in 1960, her *Don Quixote* variation having to be repeated on numerous occasions. She was guest ballerina with the Metropolitan Opera Ballet for the 1958–59 season, has danced in many television shows in N.Y. and Canada, and has made several appearances as guest artist with civic ballet companies, and with symphony orchestras. Went on maternity leave in early spring of 1963; daughter Erica was born Dec. 29, 1963. Rejoined the company for the 25th Anniversary Season, March 16–Apr. 11, 1965, dancing a brilliant *Giselle,* and *Black Swan, Don Quixote* and *Esmeralda* pas de deux.

Serrano, Mercedes (Mrs. Wasil Tupin), Argentine dancer, b. Jujuy, Argentina, 1930. Graduate of the ballet school of Teatro Colón where she studied with Esmée Bulnes and Michel Borovski; in Paris she studied with Lubov Egorova. Joined the corps de ballet of Teatro Colón; became soloist in 1950. Was soloist with the Grand Ballet du Marquis de Cuevas, 1956–59. Rejoined Teatro Colón, 1960.

Sert, José Maria (1876–1947), Spanish painter. First non-Russian designer employed by Serge Diaghilev. For the Diaghilev Ballets Russes Sert designed *Legend of Joseph* (1914), *Las Meninas* (1916), *Le Astuzzie Feminile* (1920), and *Cimarosiana* (1924).

Sevastianov, German, b. Moscow, 1906; m. Irina Baronova (later divorced). Educated at Russian Officers Training School, Moscow; University of Ljubljana, Yugoslavia. Executive secretary, Col. de Basil's Ballet Russe (1934–37); managing director, Educational Ballets, Ltd. and

Covent Garden Russian Ballet (1938–39), the successors to the Basil company; promotion manager, Hurok Attractions, Inc. (1940); Managing Director, Ballet (now American Ballet) Theatre (1941–43). After serving in U.S. Army (1943–46) Sevastianov did not renew his connections with ballet. Was naturalized as an American citizen under the name of Gerry Severn. Presently in import-export business, Europe.

Seven Deadly Sins. Ballet in 1 act; chor.: George Balanchine; music: Kurt Weill; book: Berthold Brecht. First prod.: Les Ballets 1933, Théâtre des Champs-Elysées, June 7, 1933, with Tilly Losch and Lotte Lenya as Anna-Anna. Berthold Brecht and Kurt Weill imagined life in America as they saw it from the despair and disillusion of Berlin in the days immediately preceding Hitler. Anna, the singer, and Anna, the dancer, are one and the same person pursuing a life that encounters the seven deadly sins in succession and leads them back to the little home where they began. Balanchine choreographed an entirely new version for New York City Ballet, premièred at City Center, N.Y., Dec. 4, 1958, again with Lotte Lenya but with Allegra Kent in the Tilly Losch role now called Anna-Anna. Décor was by Rouben Ter-Arutunian and he and Balanchine brilliantly recreated the atmosphere of the 1920's. The new English translation of Brecht's libretto was by W. H. Auden and Chester Kallman. Harald Lander staged a version for the Royal Danish Ballet in 1936 and Birgit Cullberg staged another version with Margareta Kjellberg and Kari Sylwan as the singing and dancing Anna-Anna for special performances in Stockholm's open air theatre in August, 1963.

Seven Sins, The. Ballet in 1 act; chor.: Tatiana Leskova; music: Maurice Ravel (*La Valse*); book, décor, and costumes: Thamar de Letay. First prod.: Teatro Municipal, Rio de Janeiro, Brazil, 1954, with Arthur Ferreira, Johnny Franklin, Ruth Lima, Diclea Ferreira, Helga Loreida, Sandra Dieken, Cecilia Wainstok, Arlette Saraiva. A ballet of symbols and atmosphere but without a definite plot.

Seventh Symphony. Ballet in 4 movements; chor.: Leonide Massine; music: Ludwig van Beethoven; book: Massine; décor and costumes: Christian Bérard. First prod.: Ballet Russe de Monte Carlo, Théâtre de Monte Carlo, May 5, 1938, with Alicia Markova, Jeannette Lauret, Nini Theilade, Frederic Franklin, Igor Youskevitch in the main roles. The movements were given the titles: The Creation, The Earth, The Sky, and The Bacchanale and Destruction, so that each movement, though complete in itself, had a linking idea.

Seventh Symphony. Ballet in 1 act, 2 scenes; chor. and book: Igor Belsky; music: 1st movement of Dmitri Shostakovich's Seventh ("Leningrad") Symphony; décor: Mikhail Gordon. First prod.: Kirov Theatre, Leningrad, Apr. 14, 1961, with Yuri Solovyov (Youth) and Alla Sizova (Girl). It is a ballet without a definite plot about youth and its heroic resistance to the enemy invasion inspired by the siege of Leningrad. The form of movement is closer to modern dance than to ballet.

Severn, Gerry. See SEVASTIANOV, GERMAN.

Severo, Raul, Uruguayan dancer, b. Montevideo, 1929. Began to study dance at S.O.D.R.E. ballet school, Montevideo, under Violete Lopes Lomba; later with Esmée Bulnes, Boris Kniaseff, and Vassili Lambrinos in Buenos Aires, Argentina; Tamara Grigorieva in Montevideo; Aurel Milloss in S. Paulo, Brazil. Made his debut with Kniasev Ballet (1948); soloist, Vasili Lambrinos company (1951); Teatro S.O.D.R.E. (1952); Ballet of IV Century, S. Paulo (1953–55); Teatro Municipal, Rio de Janeiro (1956); Ballet Cultura Artistica, S. Paulo (1957); Teatro S.O.D.R.E. under Yurek Shebelevski (1958); Ballet Rio de Janeiro (1960). Dances principal roles in most ballets of the repertoire of his present company, Ballet Rio de Janeiro. Has also danced on television.

Severskaya, Anna (Stafford-Northcote), contemporary English dancer and teacher. Studied with May Hare and Euphan Maclaren, Margaret Craske, Nicholas Legat, Olga Preobrajenska. Made her debut at twelve as First Fairy in *A Midsummer Night's Dream*. Danced with Henriette Fuller Dancers, Oumansky Ballet, Levitoff-Dandré Ballets Russes (1934), Ballet Russes de Paris, Col. de Basil's Ballet Russe de Monte Carlo. At outbreak of World War II started teaching for London Ballet Guild. Has had own studio since 1941.

Sevillana, a Spanish dance of many varieties and derivatives, closely related to Seguidilla; as a matter of fact the seguidilla is called sevillana in Andalusia, the sevillana being Seville's arrangement of seguidilla. See SPANISH DANCE.

Seymour, Lynn (Springbett), Canadian dancer, b. Wainwright, Canada, 1939; m. photographer Colin Jones. Studied in Vancouver, B.C., with Jepson and Svetlanoff and first attracted attention when she danced at the 1953 Canadian Ballet Festival (see REGIONAL BALLET). Went to England to study at Sadler's Wells (now Royal) Ballet School (1954); danced with Covent Garden Opera Ballet (1956); joined Royal Ballet (1957); created soloist (1958) and is currently principal dancer. Has danced the ballerina roles in the classic repertoire and created a number of important roles, the first of which, the Young Lover in *The Burrow,* gave promise of the great dramatic talents which have already established her as one of the foremost dancer-actresses of the day.

Lynn Seymour, Canadian-born ballerina in Swan Lake, *Act 3.*

Other creations are The Bride (Kenneth MacMillan's *Le Baiser de la Fée,* her first creation of a major leading part), The Girl (*The Invitation*), The Girl (*Les Deux Pigeons*). Kenneth MacMillan created the role of Juliet (*Romeo and Juliet*) on her, although Margot Fonteyn danced the première (Feb. 9, 1965). At the end of the 1965–66 season left the company to join the Berlin (West) State Opera Ballet in order to continue her artistic collaboration with Kenneth MacMillan.

Shabelevski, Yurek, Polish dancer, b. Warsaw, 1911. Attended the Government Ballet School of the Wielki (Grand) Opera House, Warsaw, and later studied with Bronislava Nijinska. He danced with the Ida Rubinstein company in Paris and on tour (1928); soloist, Col. de Basil's Ballet Russe de Monte Carlo (1932–39) where he created roles in *Jeux d'Enfants, Scuola di Ballo, Choreartium, Symphonie Fantastique,* and danced principal roles in *La Boutique Fantasque* (Snob), *Le Beau Danube* (Dandy), and *Polovetsian Dances* *from Prince Igor*. In 1940 he was guest artist with Ballet Theatre. After dancing for a short while with a small troupe organized by himself in the U.S., he left for South America where he currently lives.

Shadow, The. Ballet in 1 act; chor. and book: John Cranko; music: Ernst von Dohnanyi's Suite for Orchestra in F minor; décor: John Piper. First prod.: Sadler's Wells (now Royal) Ballet, Royal Opera House, Covent Garden, London, Mar. 3, 1953, with Philip Chatfield (The Youth), Svetlana Beriosova (Romantic Love), Rosemary Lindsay (Young Girl), Bryan Ashbridge (The Shadow). The Youth, beset by fears symbolized by the Shadow, is unable to accept love until he realizes that when confronted boldly the fears crumble and disappear.

Shadow of the Wind. Ballet in six episodes; chor. and book: Antony Tudor, based on poems of the eighth century Chinese poet Li Po; music: Gustav Mahler's song cycle *Das Lied von der Erde* (Song of the Earth); décor: Jo Mielziner. First prod.: Ballet (now American Ballet) Theatre, Metropolitan Opera House, N.Y., Apr. 14, 1948, with Alicia Alonso, Nana Gollner, Muriel Bentley, Igor Youskevitch, Hugh Laing; singers Robert Bernauer and Louise Bernhardt. The ballet was in six episodes: "Six Idlers of the Bamboo Valley," "The Abandoned Wife," "My Lord Summons Me," "The Lotus Gatherers," "Conversation with Winepot," "Poem of the Guitar." Although the ballet was not a success it has a certain historic importance in that it was Tudor's last work for Ballet Theatre until, as guest choreographer, he staged *Offenbach in the Underworld* (1956).

Shadow on the Prairie. Ballet in 1 act; chor. and book: Gweneth Lloyd; music: Robert Fleming (an idea adapted from the old English song "The Mistletoe Bough"); décor: John Graham; costumes: Stewart McKay. First prod.: Winnipeg (now Royal Winnipeg) Ballet, The Playhouse, Winnipeg, Oct. 30, 1952, with Carlu Carter and Gordon Wales. Set in the days of the Selkirk settlers and depicting many traditional customs familiar in the west of Canada, the story is of a young bride coming from the gentler countryside of Europe to the savage winter of the prairies. Unable to bear the loneliness, she creeps for comfort into the old chest containing her wedding gown and is smothered.

Shag. See JITTERBUG.

Shakespeare's plays, Ballets based on. The plays of Shakespeare have offered inspiration to many choreographers, both the literary-minded and those whose imaginations could not create ballet librettos of their own. The following is a listing of ballets on Shakespearean themes produced between the years 1808 and 1964. Unavoidably incomplete, the listing is a careful compilation from sources available at the time of the preparation of this volume. The titles are arranged in alphabetical order with the productions listed chronologically.

ANTONY AND CLEOPATRA

1808 (*Amour d'Antoine et de Cléopâtre*) Jean Aumer; music: Rudolphe Kreutzer; Paris.

HAMLET

1934 Bronislava Nijinska; to the Franz Liszt symphonic poem *Hamlet;* her own company and the Paris Opéra. (Nijinska danced Hamlet and Ruth Chanova Ophelia.)

1942 Robert Helpmann; to Peter Tchaikovsky's Fantaisie Overture; Sadler's Wells Ballet Company, London.

1954 Tatiana Gsovska; to a Boris Blacher score; Berliner Ballett, Berlin.

MERRY WIVES OF WINDSOR

1942 Vladimir Bourmeister and Ivan Kurilov; to a score by V. Oransky; Stanislavsky–Nemirovitch-Danchenko Theatre, Moscow.

MIDSUMMER NIGHT'S DREAM, A

1906 Michel Fokine; to Felix Mendelssohn's Incidental Music; Maryinsky Theatre, St. Petersburg.

1924 (*Les Elfes*) Michel Fokine; to Felix Mendelssohn's music; Fokine Ballet Company, Metropolitan Opera House, N.Y.

1925 (Dances in the play) Michel Fokine; Royal Theatre, Drury Lane, London.

1933 (*Nocturne*) David Lichine; to music of the fairies' episodes only; Ballet Russe de Monte Carlo. (Lichine's first ballet.)

1961 George Balanchine; to the incidental music Felix Mendelssohn composed for the several productions of the *Dream,* among them op. 60 and 61, *Die Erste Walpurgis Nacht,* and the concert overture "Die Schöne Melusine," and other orchestral pieces closely related in style to the basic work; New York City Ballet, City Center, N.Y.

1964 (*The Dream*) Frederick Ashton; to the incidental music by Felix Mendelssohn arr. by John Lanchbery; Royal Ballet, London.

OTHELLO

1818 Salvatore Vigano; to a score by Alessandro Sanquirico; Milan.

1949 (*The Moor's Pavane*) José Limón; to an arrangement of Henry Purcell's music; American Dance Festival, New London, Conn.

1955 (*The Moor of Venice*), Erika Hanka; to a score by Boris Blacher; Vienna State Opera, Vienna.

1957 Vakhtang Chabukiani; music: A. Machavariani; Tbilisi State Opera Ballet.

ROMEO AND JULIET

1811 Vincenzo Galeotti, to a score by Claus Schall; Danish Royal Ballet, Copenhagen.

1926 Bronislava Nijinska; to a score by Constant Lambert; Diaghilev Ballets Russes, Monte Carlo, Monaco.

1939 Guyla Harangozo; to the Peter Tchaikovsky Overture; National Opera Ballet, Budapest, Hungary.

1940 Leonid Lavrovsky; to the Sergei Prokofiev score; Ballet of the Kirov Theatre, Leningrad. (Revived for the Ballet of the Bolshoi Theatre, Moscow, 1946.)

1943 Antony Tudor; to a selection from the compositions of Frederick Delius, including "Walk to the Paradise Garden" from *A Village Romeo and Juliet, Brigg Fair, Eventyr, Over the Hills and Far Away;* Ballet Theatre, Metropolitan Opera House, N.Y.

1946 Serge Lifar; to the Peter Tchaikovsky Overture; Nouveau Ballet de Monte Carlo, Monte Carlo, Monaco.

1948 Dmitri Parlic; to the Prokofiev score; Belgrade Opera Ballet, Yugoslavia.

1949 Margarita Froman; to the Prokofiev score; Zagreb Opera Ballet, Yugoslavia.

1949 Serge Lifar; to the Peter Tchaikovsky Overture; Paris Opéra Ballet.

1950 (*Tragedy in Verona*) George Skibine; to the Peter Tchaikovsky Overture; Grand Ballet du Marquis de Cuevas.

1955 Frederick Ashton; to the Prokofiev score; Royal Danish Ballet, Copenhagen.

1955 George Skibine; to the Berlioz dramatic symphony for the Grand Ballet du Marquis de Cuevas, Paris. (For a special performance in the Cour Carrée of the Louvre.)

1955 Serge Lifar; to the Prokofiev

score; Paris Opéra Ballet.

1959 John Cranko; to the Prokofiev score; Teatro alla Scala Ballet, Milan.

1963 John Cranko; to the Prokofiev score; Württemberg State Opera Ballet, Stuttgart.

1964 John Cranko; to the Prokofiev score; National Ballet of Canada. (The Stuttgart production.)

TWELFTH NIGHT

1942 Andrée Howard; to an arrangement of Edvard Grieg's melodies, among them the *Holberg Suite;* The International Ballet, London.

Shankar, Uday, contemporary Hindu dancer, b. Udayapur, ca. 1902. With his father he produced native Hindu plays and ballets with such success that Anna Pavlova requested his help in producing her ballet *Radha-Krishna* in which he also danced. It was at her urging that he seriously considered dance as a career. After successful recitals in London, Vienna, Berlin, Budapest, and Geneva he returned to India and organized his own company with which he toured the U.S. (1931). Backed by American and British sponsors he founded a center of research in India (1938) for ancient dances, costumes, etc., as well as for teaching dance. Although continuing to tour he has spent more and more time at this Art Center. There was a ten year lapse between his last two U.S. tours (1952, 1962). Despite the fact that his last appearance on stage showed him much less of a dancer, his command of the stage and his radiant presence were as striking as ever. In his 1962 tour his wife Amala was his leading dancer and his son Ravi was the composer of all the original music; his daughter-in-law Rakshmi was the leading vocalist. Though never claiming complete authenticity in his own choreography, he has been responsible more than any other Indian dancer for arousing interest in the West in the richness of Indian dance.

Uday Shankar, the great Indian dancer and choreographer with his wife and partner, Amala.

Sharaff, Irene, outstanding American designer. Studied at N.Y. School of Fine and Applied Arts, Art Students League of N.Y., Grande Chaumière, Paris. Has designed costumes and décor for many ballets, musicals, and motion pictures since she attracted attention with her costumes for the Leonide Massine ballet *Union Pacific* (1934). Other ballets include *Card Game* (décor and costumes, American Ballet Theatre, 1937), *Interplay* (both American Ballet Theatre and N.Y.C. Ballet), *Afternoon of a Faun* (décor), *The Concert, Fanfare* (décor and costumes), all for N.Y.C. Ballet. Some of the musicals for which she designed costumes are *On Your Toes, Boys from Syracuse, Star and Garter, A Tree Grows in Brooklyn, The King and I, West Side Story, Flower Drum Song;* motion pictures include, among others, *An American in Paris, Call Me Madam, Guys and Dolls, Brigadoon, The King and I, Porgy and Bess, Can-Can, West Side Story,* and Elizabeth Taylor's costumes for *Cleopatra.* She has won three "Oscars" for her costume designs in *The King and I, An American in Paris,* and *West Side Story.*

Sharp, Cecil (1859–1924), founder of the English Folk Dance Society (1911). Almost singlehanded he revived the all but obsolete national dances which without the lifetime of care and research he devoted to the subject would by now have disappeared completely. He was first attracted to folk dancing when watching the Morris Dancers in Headington, Oxford (1899). Cecil Sharp House in London is the headquarters of the folk dance movement in England and there are various centers in other parts of the country. He also was a collector of folk music, including folk songs and dances of America.

Shaw, Brian (Earnshaw), English dancer, b. Huddersfield, 1928. Studied locally with Mary Shaw and at Sadler's Wells Ballet School (from 1942), entering company (1944). Except for Army service (1946–48) has remained with the company ever since and is currently a principal dancer of the Royal Ballet excelling in the virtuoso demi-caractère roles of the classic repertoire, especially Blue Bird (*The Sleeping Beauty*), pas de trois (*Swan Lake*), Peasant pas de deux (*Giselle*). He also dances roles in the modern repertoire where brilliance of technique is required such as the Blue Skater (*Les Patineurs*), male lead (*Les Rendez-vous*), Water (*Homage to the Queen*). Creations include one of the three male dancers (*Symphonic Variations*), Lover (*Bonne-Bouche*), one of the seven male dancers (*Birthday Offering*), Battista (Royal Ballet's staging of *The Good-Humored Ladies*), and others. Accompanied Margot Fonteyn on her Australasian tour (1962). Created one of the two male parts in the Frederick Ashton pas de quatre, which takes the place of the original pas de trois in the 1963 Royal Ballet version of *Swan Lake.*

Ted Shawn.

Shawn, Ted (1891–   ).

BY WALTER TERRY.

The dancer-choreographer Ted Shawn was born in Kansas City, Mo., Oct. 21, 1891, but grew up in Denver, Colo. He entered the University of Denver in order to study for the ministry, but while at college he was stricken with diphtheria and, due to an overdose of serum, was left partially paralyzed for slightly more than a year. Body exercises necessary to his recovery soon became of more than therapeutic concern to him. By the time he was able to walk again he had determined to forsake his theological studies and make dance his career. By working in a lumber camp, doing stenographic work, and earning money at other temporary jobs, he was able to afford dance lessons, studios, and opportunities for experimentation. After a period of study with Hazel Wallack, a teacher of ballet, he moved to Los Angeles where he opened a dance school. Joining forces with Norma Gould, he made one of the earliest dance motion pictures, *Dance of the Ages.*

The season of 1913–1914 found him on a coast-to-coast tour which terminated in N.Y. Here he met Ruth St. Denis, became her partner almost immediately, and married her Aug. 13, 1914. Together they founded the Denishawn schools and the Denishawn dancers.

Shawn's particular contributions to American dancing, both as an independent artist and as co-director of Denishawn, include the establishment of the dance technique which he considered necessary to the development of male dancing, the use of American thematic material (aboriginal, folk, and popular), the employment of non-doggerel music and the commissioning of music especially for dancing, the creation of dances suitable for church services, the introduction of ethnic dance forms into American dance training, and the formation of an all-male company of dancers which did much to assuage American prejudice against men dancers.

Because of his own size (over six feet tall and weighing about 175 pounds), he found himself unsuited to ballet and assumed that many other American men interested in dance would meet similar difficulties; therefore, he created a dance technique built primarily upon essentially masculine actions. In his dances he used themes of the American Indian, the early American pioneer, the Spanish conquistador, the American Negro, the American folk dancer, and the contemporary American seaman, farmer, laborer, politician, and artist. Ignoring traditional ballet music, he danced to Scriabin, Satie, Honegger, Vaughan Williams, Bach, Beethoven, and Mozart. Among the composers he commissioned to write music expressly for dance was Anis Fuleihan.

In 1917 he danced an entire church service at the International Church in San Francisco and continued to present religious dances not only in theatres but for other religious organizations from that time on. At Denishawn school and its branches, he set forth a teaching system which included primitive dance, ballet, Oriental dance, and other dance forms as they came within his range of experience. This teaching area continued to widen steadily to the end of Denishawn itself when, during its final season, he introduced the modern German dance to Denishawn students through Margarete Wallmann.

With the formation of his men's group in 1933, he embarked on a seven-year campaign to re-establish in the minds of Americans the right of men to dance.

With the disbanding of the men dancers, at a time when Shawn felt that their purpose had been realized, he sold his farm-headquarters (Jacob's Pillow, at Lee, Mass.) to a corporation and was engaged by that corporation to direct a summer dance school and festival over a five-year period, which terminated in the fall of 1946 at the close of the summer season. He returned as director in the summer of 1948.

In the ensuing years, he built the Jacob's Pillow Dance Festival into a dance center of international renown, presenting programs which sought to give equal opportunity to ballet, modern, and ethnic forms, to newcomers as well as to established stars, to new creations and to experimental works. In the Pillow's first two decades as a festival center, Shawn presided over the premières of more than one hundred new dances, some solos but others major productions. As impresario, he has introduced to American audiences ten leading dancers of the Royal Danish Ballet (and, subsequently, other Royal Danish Ballet units), the National Ballet of Canada, the Celtic Ballet of Scotland, England's Ballet Rambert, and other major companies and soloists. Although continuing to dance into the 1960's, his public performances became less frequent as he passed his seventieth birthday. He concentrated more and more effort on the direction of the ever-growing festival and its related "University of Dance." His occasional performances, however, were not limited to re-creations of his most noted solos but also included new roles in new works created for him by Myra Kinch such as *Sundered Majesty* (based on *King Lear*), *The Bajour, Sound of Darkness,* and *A Waltz Is a Waltz, Is a Waltz.* In addition to performances at Jacob's Pillow, he danced from time to time in major cities and universities. Two tours followed the establishment of Jacob's Pillow: his solo tour of Australia in 1947 (in which he gave more than fifty solo concerts in five cities) and, in 1952, with the touring company of the Jacob's Pillow Dance Festival for which he was both leading dancer and narrator. His own choreographies included *Minuet for Drums, The Dreams of Jacob,* and *The Song of Songs,* all large-scale productions. In the field of Spanish dance, he performed a leading role in La Meri's staging of *El Amor Brujo.*

Shawn has created an incredible number of dance works, ballets, ensembles, trios, duets, and solos for his own companies, for Denishawn, for vaudeville units, and for students. His ballet creations include *Xochitl, Cuadro Flamenco, The Feather of the Dawn,* and *Job.* His personal dance solos include *Invocation to the Thunderbird, Gnossienne, Flamenco Dances, Death of Adonis, Mevlevi Dervish, Cosmic Dances of Shiva, Prometheus Bound, The Divine Idiot, Four American Folk Dances, St. Francis,* and many solos extracted from Denishawn ballets and programs for the men's group. For his ensemble of men dancers, he composed divertissement programs and three full-length works, *O Libertad, Dance of the Ages,* and *The Dome.* Among his many special performances was the creation of the role of Orpheus in *Orpheus Dionysius* at the Munich Dance Congress (1930). Among his published works are the following books: *Ruth St. Denis: Pioneer and Prophet; Gods Who Dance; The American Ballet; Fundamentals of a Dance Education; Dance We Must; How Beautiful Upon the Mountain; Every Little Movement; 33 Years of American Dance;* and *One Thousand and One Night Stands.*

During World War I he served in the U.S. Army, first as an enlisted man, later as an officer. Ted Shawn has been honored with the degree of Master of Physical Education from Springfield College, the Capezio Dance Award (1957), and the Knighthood in the Order of Dannebrog, conferred upon him by King Frederick IX of Denmark (1957).

Sheafe, Alfonso Josephs (1874–1956), American writer, collector and former ballet instructor. Devoted his life to research and writing on dance. He was probably best known for his translation of Friedrich Albert Zorn's *Grammar of the Art of Dancing* from the German, editing and publishing it in two editions (Boston 1905, 1920). In his youth Mr. Sheafe established and conducted several dance schools in New England and N.Y. He had a large collection of books on dance and according to his friends upon his death was about to publish an extensive dictionary of the dance which is now in typescript form in the Dance Collection of the New York Public Library. He had also completed two other books on dance before he died.

Shearer, Moira (Shearer King), Scottish ballerina and actress, b. Dunfermline, 1926; m. Ludovic Kennedy. Studied with Nicholas Legat, Sadler's Wells (now Royal) Ballet School in London; Olga Preobrajenska in Paris. Member, International Ballet at its inception (1941); Sadler's Wells Ballet of which company she was ballerina (1944–52). She came into prominence when Frederick Ashton gave her an important role as Pride in *The Quest* (1943). Her repertoire included *Swan Lake, The Sleeping Beauty, Giselle, Coppélia;* she created pas de trois (*Promenade*), Lover (*Miracle in the Gorbals*), Butterfly (*The Spider's Banquet*), one of the three ballerinas (*Symphonic Variations*), Young Wife (*Don Juan*), title role (Frederick Ashton's *Cinderella*); also danced White Skater (*Les Patineurs*), bal-

Moira Shearer, ballerina of the Sadler's Wells Ballet and motion-picture star, most famous for The Red Shoes, *her first film.*

lerina (*Scènes de Ballet*), first ballerina (*Ballet Imperial*), Julia (*A Wedding Bouquet*), and others. She was the star of the motion picture *The Red Shoes* (1948) which probably created more interest in ballet among the lay public than any other single event in the modern history of ballet and followed this with the film version of *The Tales Of Hoffmann* (1950). Other films in which she acted and danced include *The Story of Three Loves* (made in Hollywood), *The Man Who Loved Redheads.* She danced the role of Roxanne in Roland Petit's *Cyrano de Bergerac* in the film *Black Tights* (released 1961). She has returned as guest artist with the Royal Ballet and also appeared earlier as guest artist with Roland Petit's Ballets de Paris. She appeared as Titania in *A Midsummer Night's Dream* with Robert Helpmann as Oberon at the 1954 Edinburgh Festival of Music and Drama. The play with choreography by Helpmann was later brought to the United States by impresario S. Hurok. The American première took place at the Metropolitan Opera House, Sept. 21 and was followed by a coast-to-coast tour. In straight plays, Shearer was outstanding in the title role of George Bernard Shaw's *Major Barbara* which she played both at the Bristol Old Vic and the original Old Vic in London, among other roles.

Shearer, Sybil, contemporary modern dancer, b. Toronto, Canada. Studied in France and England; also at Skidmore and Bennington Colleges in U.S. Soloist in the Humphrey-Weidman Company. Assistant to Agnes de Mille for *Three Virgins and a Devil* (the part of the Devil being worked out on her), and *Drums Sound in Hackensack* (the first ballet choreographed by someone outside the Jooss Ballet itself), both in 1941. Received the year's Dance Award given by John Martin of the *New York Times* for the most promising debut performance of a solo choreographer (1942). Made her headquarters in Chicago the following year and began an association with Helen Morrison who has designed and lit the stage for all her performances since that time. She has continued to appear almost annually in the N.Y. area and has also appeared in many other major cities and at colleges in the East and Midwest. From the beginning she thought of dance in a cyclic form, each dance being linked to its predecessor or the one following it. At first the cycles were short as *In the Field, In the Cool of the Garden, In a Vacuum,* or as in *Prologue, You Can't Eat Your Cake, As the Twig Is Bent, Spreading Like Wildfire, Time and Tide.* As time went on the cycles became longer and in her first Carnegie Hall solo performance (Apr. 24, 1949) the entire afternoon was occupied by a single abstract cycle, each dance having only a number and belonging in its set place in the cycle. This was followed by *Once Upon a Time* (Great Northern Theatre, Chicago, May 25, 1951), *Shades Before Mars* (Academy of Music, Brooklyn, Nov. 11, 1953), a second full-length abstract cycle (Academy of

Sybil Shearer, American modern dancer and choreographer.

Music, Brooklyn, Nov. 9, 1955). In 1959 she formed the Sybil Shearer Company, with Helen Morrison as director, and converted the Winnetka Community Theatre into a theatre for dance where full evening works with herself and her group have been *Within This Thicket* (Nov. 3, 1959), and *Fables and Proverbs* (Apr. 11, 1961). In May, 1962 she was appointed artist in residence at National College of Education, Evanston, Ill., where she continues to present her works in the college theatre. Among her new works are *Reflections in the Puddle Are Mine,* premièred April 9, 1963, and *In Place of Opinions,* Nov. 13, 1965. She is one of the great individualists of American modern dance who has created a style uniquely her own which is yet constantly changing and developing. In 1956 the British Film Institute requested for its dance film library a film of her solo dances (chiefly those performed at her Carnegie Hall recitals).

Sheina, Svetlana, Honored Artist of the RSFSR, Soviet dancer, b. 1918. Ballerina of the Leningrad Maly (Little) Opera House where for more than twenty years she performed all the leading roles of its repertoire after graduating with honors from the Leningrad ballet school in 1938 (class of Agrippina Vaganova). She was married to choreographer Boris Fenster (1916–1960).

Shelest, Alla, Peoples' Artist of the RSFSR, Soviet ballerina, b. 1919. Entered the Leningrad ballet school in 1927, was graduated from it in 1937 (class of Agrippina Vaganova). Vaganova entrusted her with responsible roles while she was still in the school. Her first important role with the Kirov company was that of the Girl-Swan in the Vaganova version of *Swan Lake* (1938–39). She is an extremely sensitive artist and one of the most interesting dancers of the Kirov Theatre, being at her best in such dramatic roles as Zarema (*The Fountain of Bakhchisarai*), Nikia (*La Bayadère*), Juliet (*Romeo and Juliet*), *Giselle* and *Laurencia.* Shelest's technique is completely subordinated to the creation of an image but she is a fine classic dancer and her Myrtha in *Giselle,* her Lilac Fairy and Aurora in *The Sleeping Beauty* are particularly notable for their sense of style and grand manner. Among her other roles are Yekaterina (*The Stone Flower*), Bird-Girl (*Shurale*), Tzar-Maiden (*The Humpbacked Horse*). She still occasionally dances in the Kirov company but now mainly coaches young dancers of the company in their roles and acts as rehearsal ballet mistress.

Shields, David, English dancer, b. Brentwood, Essex, 1935. Became a scholarship student of Sadler's Wells (now Royal) Ballet School in 1950 and danced with the company at Royal Opera House, Covent Garden, while still a student. Joined Sadler's Wells Theatre Ballet in 1952; in corps de ballet for three years; rising to soloist, then principal soloist. Danced Lover (*Blood Wedding*), Captain Belaye (*Pineapple Poll*), Hilarion (*Giselle*), Fencing Master and Mad Violinist (*The Rake's Progress*), Hussar (*Lady and the Fool*), Florestan (*Carnaval*), Spanish Dance (*The Nutcracker,* Act 2). Transferred to Royal Ballet as soloist in 1956 dancing Pas de Six and Spanish Dance (*Swan Lake*), King of the North (*Prince of the Pagodas*), Pas de Deux (*Noctambules*), Leading Coachman (*Petrouchka*), one of the seven male dancers (*Birthday Offering*). Joined Royal Winnipeg Ballet for the Royal Command Performance in July, 1959. Became a principal dancer, dancing a large repertoire, and ballet master. Has done much television work in Canada and in England. Left the Winnipeg Ballet to appear in a revival of *Brigadoon* at the N.Y. City Center, June, 1962. Currently free-lancing.

Shirah. Modern dance work; chor. and costumes: Pearl Lang; music: Alan Hovhaness' Concerto for Viola and Strings, composed for the occasion. First prod.: 13th American Dance Festival, Connecticut College, New London, Aug. 19, 1960, with Pearl Lang, Patricia Christopher, Bruce Marks, Dale Sehnert, Paul Berensohn, and students of the Connecticut College Summer School of Dance. N.Y. première: Hunter College Playhouse, Jan. 5, 1962, with Pearl Lang, Patricia Christopher, Norman Walker, Koert Stuyf, and group. Created as a memorial to Margaret Lloyd, *Shirah* (Hebrew for "song") is an affirmation of the belief in eternal life.

Shollar, Ludmila, former artist of the St. Petersburg Imperial Ballet, teacher, b. St. Petersburg, Russia; m. Anatole Vilzak. Graduated from the Imperial School (1906) as a pupil of Michel Fokine and Enrico Cecchetti. Began to dance solo roles shortly after being taken into the company of the Maryinsky Theatre. She was the original Estrella when Fokine staged *Carnaval* at the Pavlova Hall (St. Petersburg, 1910). From 1910 to 1914 she divided her time between the Maryinsky and the Diaghilev Ballets Russes. She created one of the Odalisques in *Schéhérazade,* one of the Gypsies and one of the Street Dancers in *Petrouchka,* and one of the two girls (the other was Tamara Karsavina) in Vaslav Nijinsky's *Jeux* (1913). In World War I she became a Russian Army (Red Cross) nurse, worked in the front lines, was wounded, and decorated with the medal of St. George. She returned to the Maryinsky Theatre in 1917, remaining until 1921 when she rejoined the Diaghilev company for its London season of *The Sleeping Beauty* in which she danced the White Cat on opening night and later Princess Florine in the *Blue Bird* pas de deux. Subsequently was a member of the Ida Rubinstein company in Paris, Karsavina-Vilzak company in London, and Bronislava Nijinska's company in Paris and on tour. Came to New York in 1935 where she taught until 1963. Many of the outstanding dancers of the day studied with her and she was particularly noted for her coaching in the classic variations. In the fall of 1963 she and her husband moved to Washington, D.C. where they taught at the Washington School of Ballet until the summer of 1965, when they left to join the San Francisco Ballet School.

Shooting of Dan McGrew, The. Ballet in 1 act; chor. and book: Gweneth Lloyd, based on the poem by Robert Service; music: Eric Wild, an arrangement of traditional drinking songs; décor: Joseph Chrabas; costumes: David Yeddeau. First prod.: Winnipeg (now Royal Winnipeg) Ballet, The Playhouse, Winnipeg, May 2, 1950, with Jean McKenzie, Lillian Lewis, Arnold Spohr, and Roger Fisher. A lively spoof of what might have happened on that famous night when "a bunch of the boys were whooping it up in the Malamute Saloon."

Shostakovitch, Dimitri, outstanding Soviet composer, b. St. Petersburg, 1906. His ballet compositions, few of which had a popular success mainly because of their mediocre plots, include *The Golden Age* (1930), *The Bolt* (1931), *The Bright Stream* (1935). Leonide Massine used his

Symphony No. 1, composed in 1936, for the ballet *Rouge et Noir* (1939), known in France as *L'Etrange Farandole.* Kirov Theatre's young choreographer Igor Belsky used the first movement of Shostakovitch's Symphony No. 7 (the "Leningrad") for a work reflecting the war between the Nazi and the Soviet forces during World War II. In 1963 Kenneth MacMillan created *Symphony* for the Royal Ballet to the music Massine had previously used for *Rouge et Noir.* The latter ballet had never been seen in London due to World War II.

Show Girl, a girl in a revue or musical comedy who generally does not dance or sing in the chorus, but whose beauty of face and figure and ability to wear elaborate costumes is supposed to lend glamour to the production, to "dress up the stage." The show girl reached her height of popularity during the time Florenz Ziegfeld set the style for musical productions (1907–1932). Ziegfeld, born in 1867 in Chicago, began his career by managing the bands of the Chicago World's Fair of 1893. He arrived in New York about 1897 with his first wife, Anna Held, and succeeded in placing her in a musical production. In 1907, with the aid of Charles B. Dillingham and Abraham L. Erlanger, the great theatrical impresarios of the first quarter of this century, he produced the first *Ziegfeld Follies;* he continued to produce new editions of the *Follies,* as well as other extravagant musical shows, until his death in 1932. The Shuberts, in association with Ziegfeld's second wife, Billie Burke, continued to produce the *Follies* for a few years longer. At present the importance of the show girl has diminished, and very few producers employ girls who do not dance, sing, or speak lines. Big Broadway night clubs catering to a transient clientele still use show girls, but even here their use is declining.

Shtay, (or sté), in ballet, a corruption of the term jeté, now infrequently used. Shtay over (jeté over), for instance, was a jeté en tournant.

Shurale. Ballet in 3 acts and 4 scenes; chor. and book: Leonid Yacobson (from the Tartar folk tales by the Tartar writer Faizie); music: Farid Yarullin; décor: A. Ptushko, L. Milchin, I. Vano. First prod.: Kirov Theatre, Leningrad, June 28, 1950, with Natalia Dudinskaya (Suimbike, the Bird-Girl), Konstantin Sergeyev (Ali-Batyr). On Jan. 20, 1955, the ballet had its first performance at the Filial of the Bolshoi Theatre, Moscow, and on Dec. 22, 1960, at the Bolshoi Theatre, Moscow. The ballet was originally intended for production at the Tartar Festival of Art which was to have taken place in Moscow in 1941, but owing to war conditions it was not shown until 1950 when Leonid Yacobson choreographed an augmented version in Leningrad. It is the story of the Bird-Girl Suimbike, the hunter Ali-Batyr, and the wood spirit Shurale who steals Suimbike's wings and prevents her from flying away. Suimbike falls in love with Ali-Batyr and stays with his people.

Shurr, Gertrude, contemporary American modern dancer, teacher, b. Riga, Latvia. B.A., San Francisco State College (1940); M.S. Univ. of Oregon (1941); studied dance at Denishawn, and with Doris Humphrey, Charles Weidman, Martha Graham. Member, Denishawn group (1925–27); first Humphrey-Weidman Concert Company (1927–29); Martha Graham's company (1930–38). Has taught extensively in schools and colleges and is co-founder and director with May O'Donnell of a N.Y. studio of dance. Is also dance consultant and teacher of modern dance at the N.Y. High School of Performing Arts and dance director of the annual summer Utah State Univ.'s Opportunity Theatre and Dance Workshop.

Sibelius, Jan, Finnish composer (1865–1957). Although he composed only one work for ballet, *The Black Swan* (Alexander Saxelin, Royal Danish Ballet, Copenhagen, 1947), his music is frequently used by choreographers, particularly English choreographers, among them Frederick Ashton (*Lady of Shalott,* 1931: piano pieces from op. 75, 76 and 85); Walter Gore (*Confessional,* 1941: "Death of Mélisande" from the *Pelléas Suite; Antonia:* tone poem *The Bard,* incidental music for *The Tempest,* "Festivo" from *Scènes Historiques*); Celia Franca (*Khadra,* 1946: *Belshazzar's Feast*); John Cranko (*Sea Legend, En Saga*). Sibelius' "Valse Triste" is a standard number used by solo dancers and occasionally groups, and *The Swan of Tuonela* has also been used by many choreographers.

Sibley, Antoinette, English dancer, b. Bromley, 1939; m. Michael Somes. Studied at Arts Educational School until 1949; then Royal Ballet School entering the company 1956, soloist 1959, principal 1960. Repertoire includes the ballerina roles in the classic ballets and *Blue Bird* pas de deux (*The Sleeping Beauty*), first ballerina (*Ballet Imperial*), Columbine (*Harlequin in April*), Mary Stone, her first major created role (Alfred Rodrigues' *Jabez and the Devil*), ballerina (*Les Rendez-vous*), Lise (*La Fille Mal Gardée*), Peasant pas de deux (*Giselle*), Mariucca (creation in the Royal Ballet's staging of *The Good-Humored Ladies*). Created Titania in *The Dream* (1964); one of the Juliets in Kenneth MacMillan's *Romeo and Juliet* (1965). She was also one of the three soloists in the Royal Ballet's *Laurentia* pas de six.

Antoinette Sibley as Titania with Anthony Dowell (Oberon) and Alexander Grant (Bottom) in Sir Frederick Ashton's The Dream.

Siciliana, pastoral dance in 6/8 or 12/8 time originating among the peasants of Sicily.

Sickle, or sickling, in ballet, a technical fault in which the foot is turned over, either inwards or outwards, from the ankle, thus breaking the line of the leg.

Sifnios, Dusanka (also called Duska), Yugoslav ballerina, b. Skoplje, 1934. Studied under Nina Kirsanova, Leonid Lavrovsky, and later at the Royal Ballet School (London). Prima ballerina of the Belgrade National Ballet, the Miskovitch Ballet (1960), and the same year Ballet Européen directed by Leonide Massine. Often dances with European ballet companies on leave of absence from Belgrade. The outstanding roles in the repertoire of her home company include *Giselle, The Miraculous Mandarin* (the Girl), *La Reine des Iles* (title role; music: Maurice Thiriet), *The Devil in the Village* (chor.: the Mlakars; music.: F. Lhotka), *Orpheus* (Eurydice; chor.: Parlic; music: Stravinsky), Juliet in *Romeo and Juliet* (chor.: Parlic; music: Prokofiev), *Coppélia* (Swanilda, chor.: Parlic), and others.

Simon, Victoria, dancer, b. New York City, 1939. Dance training at High School of Performing Arts, N.Y., winning a dance award upon graduation; School of American Ballet; American Ballet Center; Ballet Theatre School. When only fourteen danced a Candy Cane in New York City Ballet's première of George Balanchine's *The Nutcracker* (1954). A regular member of New York City Ballet since 1958; officially promoted to soloist, 1963. Her first important solo role was the First Variation (*Raymonda Variations,* Dec. 7, 1961); also danced the third waltz variation with William Weslow in the revival of *La Valse.* Other roles include Blackamoor and Pastorale interludes in *La Sonnàmbula,* Pas de Quatre and Pas de Neuf (Balanchine's *Swan Lake,* Act 2), 2nd Variation (*Raymonda Variations*), a solo role in *Donizetti Variations,* and others. Staged *Donizetti Variations* for the City Center Joffrey Ballet (Sept., 1966).

Simone, Kirsten, ballerina of the Royal Danish Ballet, b. Copenhagen, 1934. Entered the company's school, 1947; accepted into the company, 1952; promoted to soloist, 1956. Danced leading roles in *Et Folkesagn, The Nutcracker* (Sugar Plum Fairy), *Night Shadow, Konservatoriet, La Sylphide, Apollo, The Sleeping Beauty* (Aurora), *Harlequinade, Miss Julie, Carmen, Blood Wedding, Cyrano de Bergerac, Medea, Don Quixote* pas de deux, *Les Sylphides, Dances Concertantes, Pas de Quatre, Napoli,* and others. During the 1965 U.S. tour of the Royal Danish Ballet, Kirsten Simon has quite obviously reached the position of prima ballerina. While the company was performing in New York, Nov. 23–Dec. 19, she received the news that King Frederick IX of Denmark had conferred upon her the Order

Kirsten Simone (Julie) with Erik Bruhn (Jean) in Birgit Cullberg's Miss Julie, *at the Royal Danish Ballet.*

of Dannebrog, thus making her the youngest knight of the Order.

Simple Symphony. Ballet in 1 act, 4 movements; chor.: Walter Gore; music: Benjamin Britten's symphony of the same title; décor: Ronald Wilson. First prod.: Ballet Rambert, Theatre Royal, Bristol, Nov. 29, 1944, with Sally Gilmour and Walter Gore. Though plotless, the dances have an amusingly nautical flavor, matching the music whose themes are all taken from old sea shanties. William Dollar choreographed a version for Le Théâtre d'Art du Ballet (1961).

Sinfonia Clasica. Ballet in 4 movements; chor.: Tamara Grigorieva; music: Serge Prokofiev's *Classical Symphony;* décor: Edgar de Santo; costumes: Alejandro Degai. First prod.: Teatro Argentino de La Plata (Argentina), 1957, with Carmen Panader. An abstract ballet.

Sirènes, Les. Ballet in 1 act; chor.: Frederick Ashton; commissioned music: Lord Berners; décor: Cecil Beaton. First prod.: Sadler's Wells (now Royal) Ballet, Royal Opera House, Covent Garden, London, Nov. 12, 1946, with Margot Fonteyn (La Bolero), Robert Helpmann (Tenor), Frederick Ashton (King Heart), Beryl Grey (Countess Kitty), Michael Somes (Captain Vavasour). An Edwardian romp at a French plage, chiefly notable because Helpmann made his entrance in a balloon (after the première when Ashton did so) and sang an aria, thus becoming the first premier danseur to sing on an operatic stage.

Si-Sol, in ballet, a corruption of the term sissonne.

Sissonne, a ballet step. Technique: Sissonne en avant fermée—Start 5th pos., R ft. front; demi-plié and bound upward and forward off both feet, opening legs wide in an open 4th pos.; land on R ft. and an instant later put L ft. down in 5th pos. in back. When L ft. is not put down, the figure is called sissonne ouverte. Sissonne may also be done to the side (opening legs in 2nd pos. en l'air), to the back, battue, en tournant, etc. Sissonne is often confused with ciseaux.

Sisyphus. Ballet in 1 act; chor.: Birgit Aakesson and Kaare Gundersen; music: Karl-Birger Blomdahl; décor and costumes: Tor Horlin. First prod.: Royal Swedish Ballet, 1957, with the choreographer (who was later succeeded by Mariane Orlando), and Bjorn Holmgren, Mario Mengarelli, Teddy Rhodin, and Viveka Ljung. The story of the ballet was inspired by the well-known Greek myth and is in a very formal, stylized idiom.

Sitwells, The, famous English literary family and patrons of the arts, Dame Edith, Sir Osbert and Sacheverell. Sacheverell Sitwell wrote the book for *The Triumph of Neptune,* one of George Balanchine's ballets for the Diaghilev Ballets Russes (1926) and was the author of *Romantic Ballet,* a book dealing with 19th century lithographs of famous dancers. Dame Edith's poem *Façade* was set to music by William Walton which later became the score for Frederick Ashton's first important ballet of the same title. The Sitwells were patrons of Walton in his early years, their support enabling him to pursue his career as a composer.

Six, Les, a group of six young composers in France who after World War I were fervent exponents of modern music. This group included Darius Milhaud, Georges Auric, Arthur Honegger, Francis Poulenc, Germaine Tailleferre, and Louis Durey. All except Durey wrote music for various ballets.

Sizova, Alla, Soviet ballerina, b. Moscow, 1939. Sizova is the youngest ballerina of the Kirov Ballet. She entered the Leningrad ballet school in 1949 and first attracted attention while still at school during a nation-wide contest of ballet schools held in Moscow in 1958 when she danced the pas de deux from *Le Corsaire* with the assurance of a ballerina. She was graduated into the Kirov company the same year but had actually made her debut a year earlier when she performed the important part of the Queen of the Dryads in the vision scene of *Don Quixote*. In addition to her strong technique and good line, she has great warmth and radiance. Among her roles are Princess Florine in the *Blue Bird* pas de deux (*The Sleeping Beauty*), Masha (*The Nutcracker*), Myrtha, and the interpolated pas de deux (*Giselle*), Nikia (*La Bayadère*), Katerina (*The Stone Flower*). She also created the part of the Girl in *Seventh Symphony*. She danced her first Aurora in *The Sleeping Beauty* with great success when the Kirov Ballet was appearing in London (1961), and later the same year danced it for the second time at the Metropolitan Opera House, N.Y., on her 22nd birthday with equal success.

Skeaping, Mary, English choreographer, teacher, and ballet director, b. Woodford. Studied ballet with Laurent Novikov, Enrico Cecchetti, Vera Trefilova, Lubov Egorova, Margaret Craske; music at Royal College of Music, London. She toured with several companies, among them that of Anna Pavlova (1925–31) and Nemtchinova-Dolin. When the Second World War broke out she was on tour in South Africa. She was afraid to sail under war conditions and remained in South Africa where she found employment as ballet teacher and gave occasional dance recitals.

English choreographer and ballet director, Mary Skeaping, shown with a Chinese wind instrument.

In 1947 she directed the ballet sequences in the film *The Little Ballerina*. She was ballet mistress of the Sadler's Wells (now Royal) Ballet at the Royal Opera House, Covent Garden (1948–51). Has produced many classic ballets in many countries of Europe and in the U.S. Made her debut in Stockholm as a producer with the full-length *Swan Lake*, based on the St. Petersburg Maryinsky Theatre version, for the Royal Swedish Ballet (1953). Returned to Stockholm as director of the Royal Swedish Ballet in the autumn of 1953. In addition to *Swan Lake*, she mounted for this company *Giselle* (1953), *The Sleeping Beauty* (1955), *Les Sylphides*, and *Spectre de la Rose* (1957). She is also a specialist in mounting historical ballets and has done valuable work at the Drottningholm Court Theatre outside Stockholm, where she staged *Cupid Out of His Humour* (1956) to music by Henry Purcell, based on a libretto of an 18th century Swedish court ballet, in original rococo settings. The ballet was given on the occasion of the visit of Queen Elizabeth II to Sweden and was retained in the repertoire. Was made a Member of the Order of the British Empire (1958); was awarded the Swedish Order of Vasa in 1961. She returned to Stockholm in 1964, after several trips to South America where she lectured, taught and held examinations for the Cecchetti Society (London). She recreated for the summer 1965 season at the Drottningholm Theatre the seventeenth-century ballet *Atis and Camilla*. She continued research in court ballet and earliest forms of ballet technique. In the autumn she began rehearsals of a revival of her production of *The Sleeping Beauty* for the Royal Swedish Ballet, premièred Oct. 28, 1965.

George Skibine, dancer, choreographer, artistic director.

Skibine, George, dancer, choreographer, b. Yasnaia Poliana, Russia, 1920. His father Boris was a dancer with the Diaghilev Ballets Russes. Studied at Lycée Albert de Mun, Nogent-sur-Marne, France. Pupil of Olga Preobrajenska, Lubov Egorova, Anatole Vilzak, Anatole Oboukhov, Serge Lifar. First professional appearance at the Bal Tabarin in Paris, dancing the Can-Can. Was engaged by Leonide Massine for the newly formed Ballets de Monte Carlo (1938), directed by René Blum, creating the Deer in *Seventh Symphony.* Joined Original Ballet Russe (1940) for its Australian tour. Joined Ballet Theatre as soloist (1941), dancing *Les Sylphides, Bluebeard* (Sapphire), *La Fille Mal Gardée* (Colin), *Aleko,* and others. His career was interrupted by World War II. He served in the First U.S. Army Combat Intelligence (1942–45), rising to the rank of top sergeant and being decorated with the Bronze Star, five campaign medals, two Bronze Arrowheads. After demobilization he almost gave up the idea of a career in ballet and was working as interpreter and secretary to a N.Y. picture dealer, when impresario S. Hurok persuaded him to return as a member of the Markova-Dolin group. Joined Grand Ballet du Marquis de Cuevas (1947), repertoire including *Les Biches, Del Amor y de la Muerte, Sebastian, Night Shadow, Giselle, Dona Ines de Castro,* and others. Began his career as choreographer with *Tragedy in Verona* (1948), followed by *Annabel Lee* (1951), *Prisoner of the Caucasus* (1951), *Idylle* (1954), and *Romeo and Juliet* (Hector Berlioz) for the special performances in the Cour Carrée of the Louvre (1955). Toured in U.S. with Ruth Page's Chicago Opera Ballet, dancing in *Merry Widow, Camille, Revenge* (1956), prior to taking up position as premier danseur étoile of the Paris Opéra Ballet. His wife, Marjorie Tallchief, whom he had married in 1947, joined him at the same time as première danseuse étoile. Danced in *Giselle* (Albrecht), *Firebird* (Ivan in Serge Lifar's version), *Phèdre* (Hippolyte), *Suite en Blanc,* and others. Became ballet master of Paris Opéra (1958). Choreographed *Concerto* (André Jolivet, Opéra Comique, 1958), *Isoline* (1958), *Atlantide* (1958), *Daphnis and Chloë* (1959), *Facheuses Rencontres* (1959), *Conte Cruel* (1959), *Pastorale* (1961). The last named was staged for the state visit of President and Mrs. Kennedy to Paris, the performance in the theatre at Versailles being attended by Mrs. Kennedy. Staged Hindemith's *Metamorphoses* and *Concerto* in Buenos Aires (1961). Resigned from Paris Opéra as ballet master (1962) but remained as guest artist and choreographer. In the spring, 1964, joined the newly created Harkness Ballet as choreographer and artistic director. Resigned in 1966.

Sköld, Berit, Swedish dancer, b. Stockholm, 1939. She entered the Royal Swedish Ballet School in 1948; accepted into the company in 1956; promoted to soloist in 1960. Also studied with Lilian Karina. Shares with Gerd Andersson the role of the Princess of the Copper Mountain in the Royal Swedish Ballet's production of *The Stone Flower;* also dances title role in *Lady from the Sea;* created Juliet in Antony Tudor's staging of his *Romeo and Juliet* for Royal Swedish Ballet, Dec. 1962.

Skorik, Irène, French dancer, b. Paris, 1928, of Russian mother and French father. Educated high school; studied music; dance under Carlotta Zambelli, Olga Preobrajenska, Victor Gsovsky, Yves Brieux. Ballerina, Ballets des Champs-Elysées (1945–50), creating roles in *Jeu de Cartes, La Fiancée du Diable, La Sylphide* (Victor Gsovsky's reconstruction of the Filippo Taglioni original), *Le Peintre et son Modèle,* and others. Ballerina, Munich State Opera Ballet for several years (from 1950), dancing principal roles in *Hamlet, Cinderella, La Sylphide, Chemin de Lumière, Swan Lake, Giselle.* Has been guest ballerina with many companies including Tatiana Gsovska's Berlin Ballett, Strasbourg Opera, Milorad Miskovitch's companies (1957–60), Netherlands Ballet. Ballerina, Basel (Switzerland) opera (1961–62), dancing *Daphnis and Chloë, Prince of the Pagodas,* and the Soviet ballet *Stone Flower* with choreography by Vaslav Orlikovsky. Guest artist, London's Festival Ballet (1963).

Skouratoff, Vladimir, contemporary French dancer, of Russian parentage. Pupil of Olga Preobrajenska, Boris Kniaseff, and others. First major engagement with Nouveau Ballet de Monte Carlo (1946), partnering Renée Jeanmaire in *Aubade* (Serge Lifar–Francis Poulenc). Soloist, Original Ballet Russe du Col. de Basil (1947); premier danseur, Ballets de Paris de Roland Petit (1947), creating *Que le Diable l'Emporte* and dancing principal roles in *L'Oeuf à la Coque, Etudes Symphoniques, La Femme et son Ombre* (Janine Charrat). Danced a season with Ballets des Champs-Elysées (1951). Joined Grand Ballet du Marquis de Cuevas (1952), dancing in *Tertulia, Piège de Lumière, Duo,* classic pas de deux, and almost the entire repertoire. After leaving the Cuevas company created one of the leading roles in Françoise Sagan's *Rendez-vous Manqué* (John Taras, Monte Carlo, 1958). During last few years has been guest artist with London's Festival Ballet, Nice Opera, Royal Swedish Ballet, and others.

Slansk (pronounced Slonsk), Polish State Folk Ballet, founded in 1954 by Stanislaw Hadyna, who is still its director. The entire company both sings and dances. Choreographer is Elwira Kaminska, who leaves the source material almost intact. The company has toured all over Europe and Russia as well as its own country. It visited the U.S. and Canada (1959), appearing at City Center, N.Y., Nov. 3–22.

Slavenska, Mia (Mia Corak), ballerina, choreographer, teacher, b. Slavenski-Brod, Yugoslavia, 1916; m. Kurt Neumann. Studied for seven years at the Royal Academy of Music, Zagreb. Dance training in Zagreb, Vienna, Paris (Bronislava Nijinska), N.Y. (Vincenzo Celli). She was a child prodigy, making her debut at the Zagreb National Opera House in 1921. Engaged by the company of the Zagreb National Opera (1923), became soloist (1931), and prima ballerina (1933). Made concert tours of Europe and North Africa (1936) and won first Prize at the Dance Olympiad, Berlin, and Plaque d'Honneur, France, the same year. Was the ballerina in the motion picture *La Mort du Cygne* (titled *Ballerina* in the U.S., 1937). Ballerina, Massine-Blum Bal-

Mia Slavenska, Yugoslav-born ballerina, choreographer, teacher, in Giselle, *Act 1.*

let Russe de Monte Carlo (1938–42); formed her own Slavenska Ballet Variante in Hollywood and toured in U.S., Canada, South America (1947–52). Formed the Slavenska-Franklin Ballet (1952), its best known production being *A Streetcar Named Desire,* choreographed by Valerie Bettis and based on the Tennessee Williams' play, with Slavenska in the role of Blanche. This company toured U.S., Canada, and Japan (1953). Prima ballerina, Metropolitan Opera Ballet (1955–56). She has worked extensively with regional companies in Louisville, Ky. and Fort Worth, Tex., and danced many times at Jacob's Pillow Dance Festival, Boston Arts Festival, and in summer productions of operas and operettas. She staged a number of ballets for her own company but is best known for her virtuoso technique in such roles as *Giselle,* Swanilda (*Coppélia*), Odette (*Swan Lake*), Grisi, Taglioni, and Cerito, all of which she danced at different times in *Pas de Quatre,* and the various classic pas de deux. Currently teaches in N.Y.

Sleeping Beauty, The. Ballet in 3 acts, 5 scenes; chor. and book: Marius Petipa; music: Peter Tchaikovsky; décor: Ivan Vsevolojsky. First prod.: Maryinsky Theatre, St. Petersburg, Jan. 15, 1890, with Carlotta Brianza (Princess Aurora), Paul Gerdt (Prince Charming), Enrico Cecchetti (Carabosse), Marie Petipa (Lilac Fairy), Cecchetti and Barbara Nikitina (*Blue Bird* pas de deux). The ballet was based on Perrault's fairy tale. Revived for the Diaghilev Ballets Russes by Nicholas Sergeyev, one-time regisseur-general of the Maryinsky, under the title *The Sleeping Princess;* chor.: Petipa and Bronislava Nijinska; décor: Léon Bakst; Alhambra Theatre, London, Nov. 2, 1921, with Olga Spessivtzeva (Aurora), Pierre Vladimiroff (Prince Charming), Carlotta Brianza in her last stage appearance (Carabosse), Lydia Lopoukhova (Lilac Fairy), Stanislas Idzikowski and Lopoukhova (*Blue Bird* pas de deux). Others in the cast opening night were Felia Doubrovska, Lubov Egorova, Bronislava Nijinska, Ludmila Shollar, Vera Nemtchinova, Lydia Sokolova, Lubov Tchernicheva, Tadeo Slavinsky, Anatole Vilzak, Leon Woicikowski, Nicholas Zverev. In subsequent performances Egorova, Lopoukhova, and Vera Trefilova danced the title role; Nijinska alternated with Lopoukhova as the Lilac Fairy. On Jan. 5, 1922, Cecchetti celebrated fifty years of his stage career in principal parts by taking his original role of Carabosse. This version of *The Sleeping Beauty* followed Petipa's with but minor changes: a few of the original dance numbers were omitted and several borrowed from Tchaikovsky's *The Nutcracker* (the Porcelain Princesses and the Mandarin danced to "Danse Chinois"; the Lilac Fairy danced the Sugar Plum Fairy variation as arranged by Lev Ivanov; and there was a Schéhérazade episode to the "Danse Arabe"). The Three Ivans staged by Nijinska was set to the music which originally was the coda to the last act pas de deux for Aurora and the Prince. Although this production ran for over 100 performances it was a financial disaster for Diaghilev, aggravated when most of the scenery and costumes were ruined by dampness while in storage. A divertissement from the last act of *The Sleeping Beauty* titled *Aurora's Wedding* was presented May 18, 1922, at the Paris Opéra with Trefilova and Vladimiroff as Aurora and the Prince. The dancers wore new costumes designed by Nathalie Gontcharova or the costumes designed by Bakst for *Le Pavillon d'Armide.* In this version, which was later in the repertoire of Col. de Basil's Ballets Russes de Monte Carlo, the Sugar Plum variation, danced in *The Sleeping Princess* by the Lilac Fairy, became the variation for Aurora. In the de Basil production, Alexandra Danilova, Irina Baronova, and Tamara Toumanova were all notable for their interpretation of Aurora. Anton Dolin staged another one-act version *Princess Aurora;* first prod. by Ballet (now American Ballet) Theatre,

Final scene of Aurora's Wedding *in the Col. de Basil's Ballet Russe de Monte Carlo production. In center: Alexandra Danilova (Aurora) and Paul Petrov (Prince).*

44th Street Theatre, N.Y., Nov. 26, 1941, with Baronova and Dolin in the leads. Subsequently Alicia Markova alternated with Baronova and later Alicia Alonso, Nora Kaye, and Nana Gollner all danced Aurora. The full-length Petipa ballet, still under the title of *The Sleeping Princess,* was staged for the Vic-Wells (later Sadler's Wells, now Royal) Ballet by Sergeyev, décor by Nadia Benois, Sadler's Wells Theatre, London, with Margot Fonteyn (Aurora), Robert Helpmann (Prince Charming), John Greenwood (Carabosse), June Brae (Lilac Fairy), Mary Honer and Harold Turner (*Blue Bird* pas de deux). The ballet, once again called *The Sleeping Beauty,* but entirely re-staged in décor by Oliver Messel, was the production with which the then Sadler's Wells Ballet re-opened the Royal Opera House, Covent Garden, London, after World War II, Feb. 20, 1946, with Margot Fonteyn (Aurora), Robert Helpmann (Carabosse and Prince Florimund—not Prince Charming as in the Diaghilev production), Beryl Grey (Lilac Fairy), Pamela May and Alexis Rassine (*Blue Bird* pas de deux). Frederick Ashton choreographed a new Garland Waltz for Act 1 and a new Florestan and his Sisters for Act 3, in which act also Ninette de Valois choreographed a new Three Ivans. It was with this production that Sadler's Wells Ballet made its U.S. debut at the Metropolitan Opera House, Oct. 9, 1949. Since 1946 there has been a long and distinguished line of Royal Ballet Auroras, among them Beryl Grey, Violetta Elvin, Pamela May, Moira Shearer, Nadia Nerina, Anya Linden, Annette Page, Svetlana Beriosova, Antoinette Sibley. Brian Shaw's Blue Bird is also a classic performance. Sergeyev also staged the full-length work, once more as *The Sleeping Princess,* for International Ballet in May, 1948, with Mona Inglesby (Aurora), Ernest Hewitt (Prince Florimund), Herida May (Lilac Fairy). Costumes and décor were by Prince A. Chervachidze and Hein Heckroth. Ninette de Valois and Peggy van Praagh staged *The Sleeping Beauty* in décor by André Delfau for the Royal Danish Ballet in 1957. Mary Skeaping staged it for the Royal Swedish Ballet, basing it on the 1939 Sadler's Wells production. In the U.S.S.R. the Kirov Ballet has a magnificent version based on the Petipa original with revisions by Konstantin Sergeyev. This version keeps the Petipa Gold, Silver, Diamond, and Sapphire variations in Act 3, the music of which (since Diaghilev) has been associated with the Florestan and his Sisters pas de trois. When the Kirov Ballet first danced in the U.S. (1961), Alla Sizova, Irina Kolpakova, and Ninel Kurgapkina were seen as Aurora. Interestingly enough, the Bolshoi Ballet of Moscow does not at present have a *Sleeping Beauty* in its repertoire. In the U.S. two attempts were made to revive a more or less complete version of the ballet (Mikhail Mordkin, 1936; Catherine Littlefield, 1937), but they did not remain long in the repertoire. Yet another short version of the last act was staged as *Divertissement* by Serge Lifar for the Paris Opéra Ballet, May 12, 1948, with Yvette Chauviré as Aurora. The *Blue Bird* pas de deux, one of the most famous of the classic pas de deux, is often given as a separate divertissement.

Sleeping Princess, The. The name used by Serge Diaghilev for his Ballets Russes revival of *The Sleeping Beauty* at the Alhambra Theatre, London, 1921. The story goes that he changed the title because the piquante Lydia Lopoukhova was the first of his Auroras and, fascinating and delightful as she was, could not strictly be called a beauty. When Sadler's Wells Ballet presented this ballet for the first time in 1939 the Diaghilev title was used, but the 1946 production reverted to the original. See SLEEPING BEAUTY, THE.

Slonimsky, Yuri, M.A., Soviet ballet historian, critic, and author of many ballet librettos, b. 1902. Educated at the Law School, Univ. of Petrograd and the Institute for History of Arts (Theatre Division). Developed an interest in ballet in his youth. Began to write ballet criticism in 1919. In 1922 he translated some of Jean-Georges Noverre's *Letters* from the French. He published small but important monographs on *Giselle* (1926) and *La Sylphide* (1927). His next important work *Masters of the Ballet of the XIXth Century* (1937) brought him wide recognition and he became known to ballet scholars all over the world, particularly after Anatole Chujoy translated into English the essays on Marius Petipa, Jules Perrot, and Lev Ivanov. In the 1930's Slonimsky took an active part in the activities of the Leningrad and Moscow ballet schools, lecturing on the history of ballet and editing publications such as the handsome volume *Klassiki Choreographii* (The Classics of Choreography) published by the Leningrad ballet school in 1937, for which he also wrote essays on Carlo Blasis and August Bournonville; and *Reminiscences of a Balletmaster* by Adam Gluszkowski, published by the Moscow Bolshoi school in 1940. Slonimsky wrote the introductory article, "Birth of the Moscow Ballet" and prepared the entire Gluszkowski manuscript for publication. More recently Slonimsky has written two outstanding books: *Tchaikovsky and the Ballet Theatre of his Times* (1956) and a biography of Charles Didelot (1958), the latter the result of thirty years of study, containing a wealth of little-known or heretofore unpublished material. For the Didelot biography the Paris Université de la Danse awarded him a Doctorate in Arts Honoris Causae. In 1956 the Foreign Language Publishing House in Moscow published in English his *Bolshoi Theatre Ballet* of which a second revised and enlarged edition is now in preparation. Slonimsky has lectured at the Choreographers' Faculty of the Moscow Theatre Institute and the Ballet Instruction Faculty of the Leningrad Conservatory. For many years he was senior staff worker of the Leningrad Scientific Research Institute of Theatre, Music and Cinema, retiring for reasons of health in 1961. The importance of his role in Soviet ballet scholarship is that he was the first to bring a sound scientific grounding to the study of ballet. In addition he actively participated in the development of Soviet choreography since many Soviet ballets were created on the basis of his librettos, the most important being *Youth* (1949); *Seven Beauties* (chor.: Pyotr Gusev; music: Kara Karayev, 1952); *Path of Thunder* (1957); *Coast of Hope* (1959). From 1957 until it ceased publication with the 1963 ed., he contributed regularly to *The Ballet Annual* (London) on Soviet Ballet. In 1962 he edited the Soviet (Russian-language) edition of Michel Fokine's memoirs under the title *Against the Tide*.

Slow, in ballroom dancing the average length of time required to make one walking step; ballroom dance teachers divide rhythms into combinations of slow and quick, two quick counts equaling one slow count.

Smallens, Alexander, Russian-American conductor, b. 1889. At one time conductor of the Anna Pavlova company, he settled in N.Y., for many years conducting the summer concerts at Lewissohn Stadium. In 1940 he was engaged as principal conductor of the newly-organized Ballet (now American Ballet) Theatre. In 1944 he assumed the same post with the International Ballet of the Marquis de Cuevas for the company's inaugural N.Y. season at the International Theatre. In 1947 he was appointed musical director and chief conductor of Radio City Music Hall, a post he held for a number of years.

Smirnova, Yelena (1888–1935), ballerina of the St. Petersburg Imperial Theatre. Graduated 1906 from the St. Petersburg Imperial School of Ballet in 1906. Among her ballet roles were principal parts in *Coppélia, The Sleeping Beauty, Don Quixote*. She married Boris Romanov and left Russia with him in 1920. She died in Buenos Aires while guest artist at the Teatro Colón.

Smith, Felix, dancer, b. Wichita, Kansas, 1935; m. Elisabeth Carroll. Began dance training at age eight with Nico Charisse in Hollywood, Calif.; then studied with Maria Kedrina in Santa Barbara, Adolph Bolm, Eugene Loring. Began his professional career in 1952 with dance roles in a number of motion pictures including *5,000 Fingers of Doctor T., Oklahoma!, Seven Brides for Seven Brothers,* and others. Danced in Los Angeles Civic Light Opera productions and with Eugene Loring's Dance Players in Hollywood (1952–53) before joining American Ballet Theatre at the end of that year for its 1954 tour. His career was interrupted by two years with the U.S. Army in Korea (1958–60) during which time he earned an Army test credit for first year college and a scholarship at the Far East Extension University of Maryland. Returned to American Ballet Theatre (1960) and was promoted to soloist the following year, his repertoire including Pat Garrett (*Billy the Kid*), Head Wrangler (*Rodeo*), Drummer (*Graduation Ball*), Count Oscar (*Bluebeard*), solo male dancer (*Theme and Variations*), and others. With his wife joined Robert Joffrey Ballet prior to its Near Eastern tour (1962); joined the Harkness Ballet in 1964.

Smith, George Washington (1820?–1899), American dancer. Smith made his debut in Philadelphia in 1838. When Fanny Elssler came to the U.S. (1840) Smith joined her company and began to take lessons with James Sylvain, Elssler's partner. He later became the partner of Mary Ann Lee and partnered her in the first U.S. performance of *Giselle,* Jan. 1, 1846, in Boston. For a period ballet master for Lola Montez. In 1859 became principal dancer of the Ronzani Ballet, which included Cesare and Pia Cecchetti and their seven-year-old son, Enrico. In the early 1880's Smith opened a dance school in Philadelphia which flourished. For detailed information on George Washington Smith see Lillian Moore's monograph, "George Washington Smith," *Dance Index,* June–Aug., 1945.

Smith, Lois, Canadian ballerina, b. Vancouver; m. David Adams. Studied dance with Mara McBirney, Eugene Loring, and others. Prima ballerina, National Ballet of Canada since its inception (1951). Dances all the major classic roles: Odette-Odile (*Swan Lake*), Snow Queen and Sugar Plum Fairy (*The Nutcracker*), *Giselle,* Swanilda (*Coppélia*), as well as the modern repertoire, notably Antony Tudor's *Dark Elegies* and *Jardin aux Lilas* (Caroline). Created Electra in Grant Strate's *House of Atreus* (Jan. 13, 1964).

Smith, Oliver, co-director of American Ballet Theatre since 1945; theatrical designer and producer, b. Waupawn, Wisc., 1918; B.A. Pennsylvania State Univ. Designer of the ballets *Rodeo, Fancy Free, On Stage!, Fall River Legend, Facsimile, Les Noces,* and others. Has also designed many musicals of which a few of the best known are *On The Town, Brigadoon, High Button Shoes, Gentlemen Prefer Blondes, My Fair Lady, West Side Story, Sound of Music, Camelot;* a number of plays including *Becket* and *Auntie Mame;* the operas *La Traviata* and *Martha* (Metropolitan Opera), *The Harvest* (Chicago Lyric Opera), *The Tender Land* (N.Y. City Opera); the motion pictures *The Band Wagon, Oklahoma!, Guys and Dolls* (nominated for an Academy Award), *Porgy and Bess.* He has received a number of awards for his designs for the theatre including four Donaldson Awards, five Antoinette Perry Awards, Sam Shubert Award, four Critics' Awards, and has had an exhibition of his designs at the Museum of the City of N.Y. Designed the scenery for the American Ballet Theatre's production of Stravinsky's *Les Noces* (1965), choreographed by Jerome Robbins.

Snijders, Ronald (Jacobus), b. Alkmaar, Holland, 1937. Danced for several years with the Nederlands Ballet, interrupted by a period of study in England. Returned to the Nederlands Ballet as soloist and now (1964) occupies this position in Het Nationaal Ballet where his repertoire includes *Etudes* (Harald Lander), *The Prisoner of the Caucasus* (George Skibine), *Suite en Blanc* (Serge Lifar), *Graduation Ball* (David Lichine), and others.

Snoek, Hans (Johanna R. de Vries-Snoek), Dutch dancer and choreographer, b. Geertruidenberg, The Netherlands. Dance education with Kurt Jooss and Sigurd Leeder. In 1945 was choreographer of and soloist in first ballet after the Liberation, *On Free Feet.* Founder and artistic director of Scapino Ballet, a professional troupe performing for children. Her ballets for Scapino include *The Cricket and the Ant, The Magic Flute, Once Upon a Time, The Golden Swan,* and others. She also staged dances in Shakespeare plays as well as the first ballet for Netherland's television, *Village Without Men.* In 1951 married television pioneer Erik de Vries. Ballet teacher of Netherlands' Royal Princesses (1950–57). Author of *Dance and Ballet* (Querido, 1959); Director Scapino Ballet School and Academy; member, Board of Federation of Professional Artists Unions; member, International Theatre Institute and other cultural organizations. Visited North, Central and South America in 1956 and choreographed *Tia Pamchita* in San José, Costa Rica. Awarded Knight of the Order of Orange-Nassau (1960). Visited U.S. with the Scapino Troupe (Christmas, 1963) when the company appeared at Philharmonic Hall, Lincoln Center, N.Y.

Snow Maiden, The. Ballet in 3 acts; chor.: Vladimir Bourmeister; music: Peter Tchaikovsky's Symphony No. 1 in G minor, op. 13, 1st and 2nd movements, and his incidental music for Ostrovsky's fairy play *Spring Tale;* décor: Yuri Pimenov and Gennady Epishin. First prod.: London's Festival Ballet, Festival Hall, London, July 17, 1961, with Belinda Wright (Snow Maiden), Marilyn Burr (Kupava), Oleg Briansky (Mizgir). Irina Borowska also danced Snow Maiden with great success. The libretto was adapted by Bourmeister from Alexander Ostrovsky's fairy play on which the well-known Rimsky-Korsakov opera is based. The Snow Maiden, who is an elemental, lives only with the cold of winter and disappears with the warmth of spring. She falls in love with a mortal, but spring takes her away from him. Bronislava Nijinska choreographed a ballet of the same name and same theme to music by Alexander Glazounov, libretto by Sergei J. Denham, décor by Boris Aronson for Ballet Russe de Monte Carlo; première: Metropolitan Opera House, N.Y., Oct. 12, 1924, with Alexandra Danilova (Spring), Nathalie Krassovska (Snow Maiden), Igor Youskevitch (the Shepherd), Frederic Franklin in leading roles.

Social Dancing, History of.

BY ANNE BARZEL.

Social dancing began as soon as Man developed a pattern of gregarious living. Modern ballroom dance has its roots in the religious ritual, the funeral, the wooing, initiation and war dances of primitive times. However, a history of ballroom dances may arbitrarily start with those that were danced by couples and had no pantomimic themes.

Though they were not born full-blown, we find a large number of social dances were in existence in 16th century Europe. These were the basse danse and branle, the bourée, pavane, canaries, galliarde, tordion, courante, and volta. There were scores of branles named either according to locality or with a picturesque connotation, such as "Branle des Lavandieres" (washerwomen's) or "Branle des Sabots" (clog dance). In Germany various forms of the Landler were danced, and in Spain there were the zarabanda, chaconne, pasacalle, and folia. Most of these were danced by couples in a procession or ring and they were, for the most part, lively.

Dances of the 17th century were in a more sedate vein. To the previous century's dances were added the allemande, sarabande, passepied, rigaudon, and gavotte. In England country dances in many forms were popular. The minuet, which was to be the dominant dance in the next century, was first danced in the 1600's. Square formations were added to the ring.

The English country dance found its way to France and as the contradanse was one of the mainstays of the 18th century ballroom. It included chains and sets and led to the quadrille with its many figures. The cotillon, polonaise, galop, and mazurka followed.

The leading dances of the 19th century were in the quadrille form. The cotillon, lancers, and German were most fashionable. These dances, requiring a constant changing of partners, predicated the social customs and etiquette of the day when balls were not public affairs and participants knew each other well or had been properly introduced. The keynote of the cotillon was variety and just a listing of the names of a few figures (of which there were literally hundreds) gives an idea of the range. There were, as part of a single cotillon: Presentation, Rounds of Three, Serpent, The Trap, The Bridge, Hungarian Change, Double Windmill, The Graces, Star and Circle, Eccentric Columns, Thread the Needle, Gliding Line, The Oracle, The Candle, The Fan, The Turning Hat, The Butterfly, The Sphinx, et al. Many figures used accessories, such as fans, kerchiefs or tiny bouquets, and favors or prizes were given.

This period also saw dances called caledonians and the circassian circle. The polka, first introduced circa 1840, was a dance that waned and was revived a number of times. Other dances of this time were the redowa, varsosienne, polka-mazurka, and schottische.

Stemming from the 16th century volta was the waltz which spread like a contagion and, in many forms, has dominated the ballroom floor for over a hundred years.

Beginning with the second decade of the 20th century, the ballroom dance has been influenced by the syncopated popular music of America. The change in manners and the truly public character of the ballroom has dictated the individualistic type of dance in which each couple dances its own steps and patterns, with no relationship to any other couples on the floor. The foxtrot, one-step, two-step, and waltz are the basic standbys, but variations on them have been innumerable and there have been many additions.

The cakewalk, turkey-trot, grizzly bear, and bunny hug of the first decades of the century were followed by the shimmy, the toddle, and the Charleston. The Big Apple of the 1930's had its roots in the barn dance. The improvisation of swing music gave birth to the jitterbug, the most spectacular and individualistic of ballroom dances of the 1940's.

South American dances have been danced in the ballrooms of two continents since the Argentine tango was imported to Paris circa 1912. This was followed by the Brazilian Maxixe. The Cuban rumba found its way north around 1930. The conga, samba, mambo, meringue, cha-cha-cha, and other Latin American dances are danced in the ballrooms of North America, and, indeed, throughout the world.

In the late 1950's came rock-and-roll, a dance based on a heavy monotonous beat in which partners faced one another but seldom touched. This dance was the province of adolescents. A dance that began with the young and in the early 1960's spread rapidly to madcaps of all ages was the twist. Based on uninhibited gyrations, the basic step was a twisting of one hip while the other leg remained limp. Partners were often taken, but each dancer improvised on his own. New dances in this category are being invented at a rapid pace, and discarded just as rapidly by the adolescents who form the majority of their practitioners.

Söderman, Jackie, dancer, choreographer, director, b. Gothenburg, Sweden, 1927. Studied ballet with Lubov Egorova, Olga Preobrajenska, Albert Kozlovsky, Harold Turner. Member, Storm Teatern ballet group (1945); ballet master (1953–55). Director of operettas and musicals since 1955. Has choreographed ballets for Swedish television and Parkteateatern (open air theatre) in Stockholm. Continues to make public appearances as a dancer and was guest artist with the Norwegian Ballet (1961).

Soft Shoe Dance, a form of tap dance performed in shoes with soft soles and without metal taps. Ray Bolger was probably the most outstanding practitioner of the soft shoe dance in the present generation.

Soirée Musicale. Ballet in 1 act; chor.: Antony Tudor; music: Rossini-Benjamin Britten suite *Soirées Musicales;* décor: Hugh Stevenson. First prod.: Cecchetti Society matinee, Palladium, London, Nov.

26, 1938; London Ballet, Dec. 12, 1938, at Toynbee Hall; Ballet Rambert, June 21, 1940, Arts Theatre, London. The original cast included: Gerd Larsen and Hugh Laing (Canzonetta), Maude Lloyd and Antony Tudor (Tirolese), Peggy van Praagh (Bolero), Monica Boam, and Guy Massey (Tarantella). Innumerable Ballet Rambert dancers have performed this divertissement since its original production. Peggy van Praagh staged it for the Robert Joffrey Ballet in 1959.

Soirées de Paris, Les, a short ballet season (May 17–June 30, 1924) organized by Count Etienne de Beaumont at the Théâtre de la Cigale, Paris. Leonide Massine was the choreographer of the works presented and several of Serge Diaghilev's artists designed the décors. The season had a strong snob appeal since most of the participants belonged to the avant-garde of their professions and the engagement itself was obviously a transitory event which would have no repetition in the future. The program included *Romeo and Juliet* in a version staged by Jean Cocteau, a theatrical production which defied classification (décor: Jean Hugo); *Mercure* (music: Erik Satie; décor: Pablo Picasso); *Salade* (music: Darius Milhaud; décor: Georges Braque); *Le Beau Danube* (music: Johann Strauss; décor: Vladimir Polunin, after Guys); *Gigue* (décor: André Derain); and *Scuola di Ballo* (music: Luigi Boccherini; décor: Count Beaumont).

Sokolova, Eugenie (1854–1926), Russian ballerina and teacher. Graduated from the St. Petersburg Imperial School of Ballet in 1869 and accepted into the St. Petersburg Maryinsky Ballet. Retired from the stage in 1886 and later became an outstanding teacher, exerting a strong influence on the development of nearly all Russian ballerinas and premiers danseurs of the first decade of the 20th century. Among her pupils were Anna Pavlova, Tamara Karsavina, Olga Spessivtzeva, Vera Trefilova, and others.

Sokolova, Lydia (Hilda Munnings), English ballerina, b. Wanstead, 1896. Studied dance at Stedman's Academy, London, and made her first appearance at the Royal Court Theatre in a school performance (1909). Her professional debut was in the corps de ballet of *Alice in Wonderland* (Christmas, 1910). After a few private lessons with Mikhail Mordkin when he was appearing in London with Anna Pavlova, he engaged her to join his Imperial Russian Ballet group for a U.S. tour (1911). Joined the Diaghilev Ballets Russes (1913), becoming principal character dancer and having the distinction of being the first English dancer to be accepted into the company. She created Kikimora (*Contes Russes*), Tarantella Dancer (*La Boutique Fantasque*), Friend (*Les Matelots*), Goddess (*Triumph of Neptune*). She also danced the Miller's Wife (*The Three-Cornered Hat*), Columbine, Papillon (*Carnaval*), Ballerina (*Petrouchka*), Chloë (*Daphnis and Chloë*), Hostess (*Les Biches*), Cherry Blossom Fairy, Red Riding Hood in the 1921 revival of *The Sleeping Beauty,* and many others. Her greatest role was the Chosen Maiden in Leonide Massine's revival of *Le Sacre du Printemps.* Except for the break during World War I and periods of absence due to illness, she was with the company until Diaghilev's death in 1929. Her memoirs, *Dancing for Diaghilev* (1961), are not only valuable as the story of an entire ballet era but as a personal and very human picture of a Diaghilev very different from the character portrayed by Romola Nijinsky, Michel Fokine, Serge Lifar, and others. Sokolova retired after the death of Diaghilev and the disbanding of his company. Returned briefly to dance during the London season of Leon Woicikowski's company (1935). Currently living in England where she teaches and coaches. Returned briefly to the stage for the Royal Ballet's revival of *The Good-Humored Ladies* (premièred

July 11, 1962), recreating Guiseppina Cecchetti's original role of the Marquise Silvestra.

Sokolow, Anna, American modern dancer, choreographer, teacher, b. Hartford, Conn., 1915, of Polish parents. Began to study dance at age ten with Blanche Talmud; later with Martha Graham and Louis Horst at the Neighborhood Playhouse, then located on Grand Street. Studied ballet with Margaret Curtis at Metropolitan Opera Ballet School. Began performing with Playhouse Children's Theatre; member, Martha Graham's company (1930–39), teaching concurrently at Neighborhood Playhouse as assistant to Horst. Formed her own dance group (1934) and from that time gave performances of her own compositions, both solos and group works. Invited by Ministry of Fine Arts of Mexico to give performances in Mexico City for six weeks, she remained almost a year and formed the first modern dance group in Mexico (1939). For the following nine years she spent about six months a year in Mexico training dancers, some of whom have become leading choreographers. From this period date some of her notable solos: *Lament for the Death of a Bullfighter, Mexican Retablo, Kadisch, Mama Beautiful,* etc.; also a number of group works created for the Ballet de Bellas Artes: *El Renacujo Paseador* (Silvestre Revueltas), *Antigona* (Carlos Chavez), and others. On a visit to Mexico in 1953 she created *Lyric Suite* (Alban Berg) which she staged for her group in N.Y. the following year. During these periodical visits to Mexico she also choreographed for the opera at the Bellas Artes and for films. She returned in 1961 to teach and stage *Opus '60* (Teo Macero), *Dreams* (Anton von Webern), and *Musical Offering* (Bach) for Bellas Artes. In the U.S. her own company, re-formed in 1954 by which time she no longer was dancing herself, has given performances at intervals of her works, including *Rooms* (Kenyon Hopkins, 1955); *Poem* (to Scriabine's "Poème d'Extase"), *Le Grand Spectacle* (Teo Macero) both in 1956; *Metamorphosis* (based on the short story by Franz Kafka, 1957); *Opus '58* (Macero, 1958); *Dreams* (Webern, 1961). Received a grant from the Lena Robbins Foundation to stage a two-week season at the off-Broadway York Theatre beginning Dec. 26, 1958. Staged *Rooms* and *Opus '58* for Nederlands Danse Theater (1959). She has choreographed for the Broadway theatre other than musicals, for television, and for New York City Opera (1956). Went to Israel for the first time in 1953, invited by the American Fund for Israel Institutions, to teach the newly formed Inbal company. Returned the following year and almost every year subsequently. In the spring of 1962, with financial support from the Rebekah Harkness, Lena Robbins, and America-Israel Cultural Foundations, she went to Israel to organize a performing group of ten actor-dancers. In addition to her activities as choreographer in U.S. and abroad, she also teaches.

Anna Sokolow, American modern dancer, choreographer and teacher.

Soleares, a Spanish flamenco dance now seldom performed, but which, with Alegrias, is said to be the origin of all flamenco dances. See SPANISH DANCE.

Soliloquy. Modern dance solo; chor.: Merce Cunningham; music: John Cage; costume: Merce Cunningham. First prod.: Hunter College Playhouse, N.Y., Jan. 9, 1945. One of Cunningham's early solo dances marked by contrast between a remarkable technique and an apparent (though not actual) improvization of movement patterns.

Solitaire. Ballet in 1 act; chor.: Kenneth MacMillan; music: Malcolm Arnold's two suites comprising *Eight English Dances,* and a specially composed "Sarabande" and "Polka"; décor: Desmond Heeley. First prod.: Sadler's Wells Theatre Ballet, Sadler's Wells Theatre, London, June 7, 1956, with Margaret Hill, Sara Neil, Donald Britton. A ballet with an idea rather than a plot in which a lonely girl imagines herself joining in the joyous play of the young people around her, but essentially she always remains alone. Royal Ballet took it into its repertoire Mar. 14, 1958; Royal Danish Ballet also staged a version.

Soloist, a member of a ballet company who does solo parts and dances alone, with a partner, or in groups of not more than four. Thus the four dancers who dance the pas de quatre of the little swans in *Swan Lake* are considered soloists. A soloist may be, but is not always, a ballerina or a premier danseur. The official position of a soloist (called soliste) in Russian Imperial companies was between that of ballerina (or premier danseur) and coryphée or (coryphé).

Solov, Zachary, dancer, choreographer, director, b. Philadelphia, Pa., 1923. Studied ballet with Catherine Littlefield and made his debut with her company at Robin Hood Dell at the age of fourteen, although he had been appearing as an entertainer on a Sunday radio show from the time he was ten. After touring the U.S. and Canada with the Littlefield company, he joined American Ballet for its South American tour under the auspices of the U.S. Office for Coordination of Commercial and Cultural Relations Between the American Republics (1941), and later for the New Opera Company season in N.Y. Danced leading roles with Eugene Loring's *Dance Players* and when it was disbanded appeared briefly with the resident dance troupe of the Roxy Theatre. Following four years in the U.S. Army during which time he choreographed and danced in thirty-five Army revues in the U.S. and India, he joined Ballet (now American Ballet) Theatre as soloist (1946–49), followed by a season as leading dancer in the Broadway musical *Along Fifth Avenue.* Appointed choreographer of the Metropolitan Opera Ballet (1951) and for his work in opera ballets became the recipient of the first Capezio Dance Award. Between 1951 and 1958 he was ballet master as well as choreographer at the Met and for the 1959–60 season was guest choreographer. He choreographed *Mlle. Fifi* for Alexandra Danilova (1953), re-staging it for London's Festival Ballet as *La Jarte,* and *The Golden Apple* for the Ballet Sextette Company—Maria Tallchief, Melissa Hayden, Nora Kaye, Patricia Wilde, André Eglevsky, Hugh Laing (1954). Over this period he choreographed thirty ballets for operas and also staged two ballets presented before short operas: *Vittorio* (1955), in which he danced the title role

Zachary Solov, dancer, ballet master, choreographer.

with Mia Slavenska as guest ballerina, and *Soirée,* with Mary Ellen Moylan and Oleg Briansky in the leading roles (1956). He has also staged frequently for television, industrial shows, and summer theatres. In 1960 and 1961 his own Zachary Solov Ballet Ensemble toured in a repertoire of his ballets. In the season 1963–64 he rejoined the Metropolitan Opera Ballet as choreographer; in the season 1965–66 he staged anew the dances in *La Périchole* and *Samson et Dalila.* The Metropolitan also used his choreography in the revivals of *Don Giovanni* and *Rigoletto.* His summers are often devoted to choreographing musicals in the U.S. and Canada.

Solovyov, Yuri, Soviet dancer, b. 1940. Entered the Leningrad Ballet School in 1949; graduated in 1958 (class of Boris Shavrov). He soon attracted attention by the softness and charm of his dancing, the strength of his technique, and his readiness for hard work. He was soon given the opportunity to dance the *Blue Bird* pas de deux in *The Sleeping Beauty* and is considered the best performer of this role in the Kirov Ballet. Since graduating into the company he has performed many other responsible roles, among them Andrei (*Taras Bulba*), the interpolated pas de deux (*Giselle*), pas de trois (*Swan Lake*), Danila (*The Stone Flower*), Frondozo (*Laurencia*). In 1961 he created the principal role of the Youth in Igor Belsky's *Seventh Symphony.* He is now a leading soloist with the Kirov. On tour in London, the U.S., and Canada he danced leading roles ranging over the entire repertoire, including Siegfried in *Swan Lake* and *Prince Desiré* in *The Sleeping Beauty,* always with extraordinary success. He is married to dancer Tatiana Legat, granddaughter of Nicholas Legat by his first marriage to Antonina Chumakova.

Sombert, Claire, French dancer, b. Courbevoie, 1935. A pupil of Yves Brieux, she made her first professional appearance in Switzerland (1950). Soloist, Ballets Janine Charrat (1951), with Ballets de Paris de Roland Petit (1953), in which company she danced principal roles in *Le Loup* (the young Gypsy) and *Deuil en 24 Heures* (in N.Y.). One of the principal dancers in the Gene Kelly motion picture *Invitation to the Dance* (1956). Ballerina, Ballets Jean Babilée (1956), dancing *Balance à Trois, Le Jeune Homme et la Mort,* and others. Danced with Milorad Miskovitch's company at Lyons Festival (1956), creating a leading role in *Promethée;* danced Lisa in Serge Lifar's *Queen of Spades,* Monte Carlo (1960). Was one of the stars of Anton Dolin's International Stars season in London (1961) and the same year danced at the Royal Academy of Dancing Gala organized by Margot Fonteyn, at Drury Lane Theatre. She was one of the several dancers who assumed the title role in Raymundo de Larrain's *Cinderella* (1963–64). Partnered by Michel Bruel she toured the U.S. with Victor Borge; also appeared with Bruel in several pas de deux at the Dance Festival sponsored by the Rebekah Harkness Foundation at the open-air Delacorte Theatre, Central Park, N.Y. (Sept., 1966).

French ballerina, Claire Sombert.

Sombreros. Ballet in 1 act; chor.: Leon Danielian; music: Mexican folk tunes, arr. by Ivan Boutnikov; costumes: William Cecil, executed by Karinska. First prod.: Ballet Russe de Monte Carlo, Carter Barron Amphitheatre, Washington, D.C., June, 1956; N.Y. première: Metropolitan Opera House, Apr. 26, 1957, with Irina Borowska, Deni Lamont, and group. Leon Danielian's first ballet, a charming pastiche of Mexican folk dances adapted into ballet idiom with the wispy (but sufficient) theme of boy getting girl and immediately changing from subservient lover to all-conquering male.

Somers, Harry, Canadian composer, b. Toronto, Ontario, 1925. Studied composition under John Weinzweig at Royal Conservatory of Music of Toronto, and in Paris with Darius Milhaud (1949–50). Composed scores for *Fisherman and His Soul* and *Ballad,* both for National Ballet of Canada. Commissioned by the Koussevitsky Foundation to write a work for the 1959 Inter-American Music Festival; wrote the incidental music for *A Midsummer Night's Dream* at the Stratford (Ontario) Shakespeare Festival (1960). The same year received Canada Council Senior Arts Fellowship to study and compose in France. His compositions have been commissioned in Canada, the U.S., and other countries.

Somes, Michael, premier danseur, director, b. Horsley, England, 1917; m. Deirdre Dixon (d. 1959); Antoinette Sibley (1964). Studied with Miss Blott at Weston-super-Mare and with Edouard Espinosa. Became first boy to win a scholarship to the Sadler's Wells Ballet School (1934). Joined the company as a member of the corps de ballet, attracting public attention with his ballon and great jump in *Les Patineurs* and as Guy in *A Wedding Bouquet* (both 1937). Created his first leading role as the Young Man (*Horoscope,* 1938), following this with Pan (*Cupid and Psyche*), Monseigneur

Michael Somes, premier danseur of the Royal Ballet and its assistant director.

(*Harlequin in the Street*), Bridegroom (*The Wise Virgins*), Leader, Children of Light (*Dante Sonata*), Young Lover (*The Wanderer*), and dancing many roles in the repertoire of that time. After service in World War II, during which he sustained a severe injury in an accident, he returned to the company (1945). He created Florestan when the company reopened the Royal Opera House, Covent Garden with *The Sleeping Beauty* (1946) and one of the three male dancers in Frederick Ashton's *Symphonic Variations* the same season. Succeeded Robert Helpmann as Margot Fonteyn's partner (1950) although he had already partnered her and the other ballerinas of the company in the full-length *Swan Lake, Giselle, The Sleeping Beauty,* and others. Between 1951 and 1961 he created Prince (*Cinderella*), Daphnis (*Daphnis and Chloë*), Caricaturist (*Mam'zelle Angot*), Aminta (*Sylvia*), Iskender (*La Péri*), Rinaldo (*Rinaldo and Armida*), Ivan Tsarevitch (Royal Ballet's production of *The Firebird*), title role (*Tiresias*), Palemon (*Ondine*), Creon (*Antigone*), leading male role in *Ballet Imperial, Scènes de Ballet, Homage to the Queen, Birthday Offering.* He also danced many other roles including Stranger (*Miracle in the Gorbals*), title role (*Hamlet*), and others. He retired from dancing roles in 1961, but continues to appear in pantomime and acting roles. In 1963 he played the Father in *Marguerite and Armand.* He was noted for his handsome and quietly commanding presence. He was created a C.B.E. (Commander of the Order of the British Empire) in 1959. Currently assistant director Royal Ballet. His only ballet, *Summer Interlude,* was staged for Sadler's Wells Theatre Ballet in 1950. Created Capulet in Kenneth MacMillan's *Romeo and Juliet* (1965).

Sommerkamp, Helga, German dancer, b. Berlin. Studied with Tatiana Gsovska and Gustav Blank. Has danced with the State Opera, Berlin (1948–56); Municipal Theatre, Basel (1956–57); Berliner Ballett, including South American tour (1958); prima ballerina, Municipal Theatre, Frankfurt a/M (1959–61). Dances principal roles in *Sleeping Beauty, Swan Lake, Cinderella, Lady of the Camelias, Peer Gynt* (Solveig). Makes frequent television appearances.

Son, the Cuban name for the ballroom form of rumba.

Sonate à Trois. Ballet in 1 act; chor.: Maurice Béjart; music: Béla Bartók's Sonata for 2 pianos and percussion; décor: Bert. First prod.: Théâtre Marigny, Paris, June 19, 1957, with Michèle Seigneuret, Tania Bari, and Béjart. Béjart then staged it for Western Theatre Ballet (in association with Théâtre Royale de la Monnaie, Brussels), Sadler's Wells Theatre, London, Apr. 22, 1960, with Hazel Merry, Sylvia Wellman, and Laverne Meyer; it was then taken into the Western Theatre Ballet's general repertoire. *Sonate à Trois* was one of the ballets presented by this company when it made its U.S. debut at the 1963 Jacob's Pillow Dance Festival. It is adapted from the existentialist play *Huis Clos* (No Exit) by Jean-Paul Sartre, and Béjart originally used the play's title for his ballet. The man and the two women discover that hell is an eternity of being alone together in an ever-lighted room.

Song of the Turning World. Modern dance work; chor. and costumes: Jean Erdman; music: Beethoven's Great Fugue in B flat. First prod.: Jean Erdman and company, Brooklyn Academy of Music, N.Y., Dec. 9, 1953, with Jean Erdman, Barbara Casper, Kate Clyne, Mimi Kirk, Irene Loren, Remy Charlip, William Ligon. An abstract dance which follows the musical line.

Songes, Les. See DREAMS.

Songs Remembered. Modern dance work; chor.: Jack Moore; music: Alban Berg's *Songs with Piano and Orchestra.* First prod.: 13th American Dance Festival, Connecticut College, New London, Aug. 20, 1960, with Jack Moore and Nancy Lewis; N.Y. première: YM–YWHA, Dec. 18, 1960, presented by Contemporary Dance Productions. A looking backward at youth and love, joy and sorrow.

Sonnàmbula, La. See NIGHT SHADOW.

Sorcerer's Apprentice, The. A symphonic scherzo by Paul Dukas, the music of which Michel Fokine used for his ballet of the same title (1916). The sorcerer's apprentice, left to his own devices, remembers the magic word that sets the broom carrying water for him, but then cannot remember the word which will stop the broom.

Sorcerer's Apprentice, The. Ballet in 1 act; chor.: Maryla Gremo; music: Paul Dukas; book based on the ballad by Goethe; décor: Fernando Pamplona. First prod.: Teatro Municipal, Rio de Janeiro, 1959, with a cast headed by Arthur Ferreira and Dennis Gray, alternating with Edmundo Carijó and Albert Ribeiro. The plot is the same as in the citation above. The Royal Danish Ballet staged a version by Harald Lander (1940) which provided Margot Lander as the Broom with one of her most successful roles.

Sorell, Walter, American writer and lecturer, b. Vienna, Austria, 1905; educated at Univ. of Vienna and Columbia Univ. (Master of Fine Arts); U.S. citizen since 1945. On faculty of Columbia Univ., The New School for Social Research, Connecticut College School of Dance, and others. Editorial Board, *Dance Observer* (final issue Jan. 1964). Contributor to many magazines and to "Voice of America" (radio programs to foreign countries). Edited *The Dance Has Many Faces* (1951, 1957, rev. ed. 1966); author of essay on dance in *The Hebrew Impact on Western Civilization* (1951). His plays include *Isadora Duncan,* produced by N.B.C.; listed in *Best Short Plays, 1952–53; Everyman Today,* produced by Union Theological Seminary and the Phoenix Theatre, 1958; C.B.S. Television, 1958; also several television plays, some related to dance; *Egypt Hill,* a play about a Negro dancer in 2 acts. Translator, *Mary Wigman: Die Sprache des Tanzes* (*The Language of Dance*).

Sorley Walker, Kathrine, contemporary writer on ballet, b. Aberdeen, Scotland. Educated at King's College, London Univ. (both London); Bonn Univ., Germany; Univ. of Besançon, France. Contributor to *The Dancing Times, The Stage, The Daily Telegraph,* and other periodicals; ballet critic, *Playgoer* (1946–51). Hon. Archivist Ballet Guild Archives (subsequently London Archives of the Dance). Contributor to *Enciclopedia dello Spettacolo* (Italy). Author of *Brief for Ballet* (1947), *Robert Helpmann* (Theatre World Monograph, 1957), *Eyes on the Ballet* (1962, 1965). Member of the Critics' Circle, London. London Editor, *Dance Encyclopedia* (1967).

Soubresaut, in ballet, a jump in 5th pos. in place. Technique: Start in 5th pos., R ft. front; demi-plié and jump upward off both feet, keeping feet in 5th pos.; land on both feet in 5th pos., R ft. still in front; the body is arched while in the air.

Soudeikine, Serge (1882–1946), Russian-American painter. Designed décor and costumes for the ballets *The Fairy Doll* (for Anna Pavlova), *Giselle, La Fille Mal Gardée, The Goldfish, Voices of Spring* (Mordkin Ballet), *Reminiscence* (George Balanchine, 1935), *Paganini* (Michel Fokine, 1939). He was also designer for the *Chauve-Souris,* Paris (1920); Metropolitan Opera House (*Les Noces, Petrouchka,* etc.) (1922); for motion picture *Today We Live;* for musical *Porgy and Bess,* among others.

Source, La. Ballet in 3 acts, 4 scenes; chor.: Arthur Saint-Léon; music: Leon Minkus (first and last scenes), Léo Delibes (two middle scenes); book: Charles Nuitter and Saint-Léon. Décor: Désplechin, Lavastre, Rube, Chapéron. First prod.: Théâtre Impérial de l'Opéra, Paris, Nov. 12, 1866, with Guglielmina Salvioni and Louis Mérante in the leading roles of Naïla and Djémil. Its first performance in St. Petersburg, Dec. 8 (Dec. 21 new style), 1902, was at a benefit for Olga Preobrajenska. Agrippina Vaganova choreographed a new version and danced the role of Naïla at her farewell benefit Jan. 13 (new style), 1916. The story is the typical complicated nonsense of the period with a Persian setting. Djémil the huntsman is in love with Nouredda. He saves the magic flower which gives life to Naïla, Spirit of the Spring, and through this action is later able to save Nouredda from the advances of the Khan. Nouredda, however, does not love him and when he begs Naïla to bestow on her (Nouredda) the flower which will change her coldness, she (Naïla) does so out of her own love for Djémil, though knowing it will bring about her death. Eugénie Fiocre was the first Nouredda and was painted in the role by Edgar Dégas. The role of Naïla had been intended for Adele Grantzova but she did not dance it until the following year when it became one of her greatest successes.

Sous-Sous, in ballet, a temps levé done from 5th pos. into 5th pos. while moving with a small jump forward, to the side, or back. A relevé onto pointes in 5th pos., drawing pointes to a close 5th pos., is often called this, but is not a sous-sous.

Soutenu, in ballet, a sustained or drawn-out movement.

South Africa, Ballet in. The most important activity in South Africa has derived from two Cape Town groups: the University Ballet Company and the Cape Town Ballet Club. The former is directed by Dulcie Howes who studied with a notable South African teacher, Helen Webb. In 1934 Dulcie Howes founded the University Ballet School and Company, producing ballets at the Little Theatre and the City Hall. The Cape Town Ballet Club was formed by Cecily Robinson and Yvonne Blake (formerly with the Ballets de Monte Carlo). It has, among other things, staged the first versions in S. Africa of ballets from the international repertoire. The University Ballet Company pioneered in touring from 1941. This gave rise to the Johannesburg and Pretoria Festival Ballet Societies developed from the schools run by Marjorie Sturman and Poppy Frames. Faith de Villiers has also produced ballets; Dorothy McNair helped to form a University Ballet Club in Natal; Eileen Keegan (who taught Nadia Nerina) has a flourishing school in Durban. Many South African dancers have become well known overseas and some have now returned to work at home, among them David Poole who is now teacher, producer, and choreographer for Cape Town University Ballet. South African dancers and choreographers of international reputation include Nadia Nerina, Alexis Rassine, Alfred Rodrigues, John Cranko, Desmond Doyle, Patricia Miller, Maryon Lane, Vyvyan Lorrayne, Deanne Bergsma, and others. However, South Africa has now limited the number of dancers who will be allowed to leave the country for study and possible absorption into English or other companies.

Souvenirs. Ballet in 1 act; chor. and book: Todd Bolender; music: Samuel Barber; décor: Rouben Ter-Arutunian. First prod.: New York City Ballet, City Center, N.Y., Nov. 15, 1955, with Irene Larsson (Vamp), Carolyn George (Young Girl). The Palm Court of a resort hotel is the scene for some laughs at the expense of the tango teas and other extravagances of pre-World War I era. There is a little wistfulness along the way when the lonely Young Girl—a wallflower—daydreams about being irresistible to all the young men. The ballet concludes with a Mack Sennett beach chase finale.

Soviet Ballet.

BY NATALIA ROSLAVLEVA.

Soviet ballet is inseparable from the history of ballet in Russia. The Soviet ballet is a national Russian ballet because it preserves its national traditions and its great heritage. But, being firmly implanted in the best achievements of the past and treasuring the wealth of its classical legacy, Soviet ballet represents a new, higher stage in the development of the Russian School. Agrippina Vaganova, one of the greatest ballet teachers of all time, began the preface to her book *Fundamentals of the Classic Dance* (1934) thus: "We carefully preserve the classical dance, but I think that should Didelot, Taglioni-père, Perrot—in other words those who developed it in Russia—rise from their graves they would not recognize their offspring. Time does its work. Everything becomes perfected." And a little further on, Vaganova explained the reason for the constant perfecting of her method: "At present an impetuous forward drive is an inevitability. We are moving together with the tempo of life."

Vaganova speaks here of the classical dance proper. The broad sweeping movements of the Russian school, inherited directly from the Russian national dance with its graceful and expressive movements of the entire body, have been developed to the point where they have become the hallmark of Soviet choreography. The strong and buoyant technique of Soviet dancers characterizes entire companies which are trained according to a uniform method worked out by the Soviet school of ballet instruction. Not only has the classical dance broadened technically but it has also acquired new significance and new ways of application. One of its most important features is that it has become multi-national; not only may ballet now be found in all the constituent republics of the Soviet Union, many new, sometimes newly-discovered dances have been introduced into Soviet ballets, expanding the somewhat limited range of the academic character dances. In the national republics many ballets have been choreographed in the idiom of the local folk dance. This has resulted in the fusion of traditional ballet pas with new folk dance steps, ensuring the continuous expansion of the ballet vocabulary.

To dance music instead of merely dancing *to* music is an old principle of the Russian school. In Soviet ballet this principle, once evident only in the works of the greatest dancers, is taught to the youngest pupils in all ballet schools until it becomes second nature. Music and its emotional meaning dominate the Soviet style of dancing and, consequently, the choreography.

The corps de ballet is expected to meet these requirements. The corps de ballet as a whole and its individual dancers are equal members of the company, fully realizing the meaning and aim of the ballet and of each part, however small. Conventional mimetic gestures have been abandoned on the Soviet stage; only expressive mime, corresponding to the requirements of the Stanislavsky system of living the role, is permissible in any ballet, old or new.

Soviet ballets always carry a deep and serious idea, expressed through the medium of dance and mime. The dramatic content, usually conceived by a talented dramatist (several of them, such as Yuri Slonimsky and Nicolai Volkov, specialize in ballet librettos), aims at elevating the spectator to a higher moral plane instead of merely entertaining him. The Soviet school of choreography chooses themes of noble passions and feelings, of heroic deeds and poetic love. The ballets of the 1930's—*The Fountain of Bakhchisarai, Romeo and Juliet, Flames of Paris, Laurencia,* and *Heart of the Hills* are typical examples.

New choreographers are eagerly seeking for new dance idioms and fresh imagery capable of conveying contemporaneous themes, but in their work the young choreographers are supported by all the previous experience of Soviet ballet. Moreover, the famous ballets of the 1930's by bringing recognition to Soviet choreographers for the serious artistic values of their creations, gave them the right to stand side by side with artists working in other media. Their aim was the portrayal of living characters through dance closely related to the content of the music. For their part, Soviet composers have done much to enrich ballet music by providing colorful, meaningful images in scores composed according to symphonic principles.

Soviet ballet has preserved the best from the classical heritage so that it can continue serving as a source of inspiration for both the choreographer and the spectator. However, in accordance with the demands of the contemporary theatre, classical works such as *Swan Lake, The Sleeping Beauty, Giselle,* have been given a new lease on life in Soviet ballet. While all the most valuable scenes and dances have been preserved, the set gestures of conventional pantomime have been dispensed with since the 1920's. Greater dramatic tension, a sensitive feeling for the music, excellent dancing and acting have given new touches to old works and raised the Russian ballet to a higher level.

New choreographic styles as well as magnificent opera houses with large ballet companies have appeared in many republics of the Soviet Union that previously had little acquaintance with classical ballet. There is an Opera and Ballet Theatre in each of the fifteen constituent republics of the Soviet Union, and in the most important autonomous republics (such as the Karelian and the Buryat autonomous republics within the Russian Federation). In many cities of the Russian Federation (RSFSR) and the Ukraine—in Perm, Sverdlovsk, Novosibirsk (a city in Western Siberia), Saratov, Kharkov, Donetz, Lvov, Odessa—there are also resident ballet companies in opera houses, some new, some old. It is natural that the ballet companies of the Bolshoi (Moscow) and Kirov (Leningrad) theatres serve as lodestars for the rest of Soviet ballet, with respect to repertoire and standards of performance.

Altogether there are 34 ballet companies in 31 cities of the Soviet Union. Moscow and Leningrad each have two opera and ballet theatres—the Bolshoi and Stanislavsky and Nemirovich-Danchenko in Moscow, and the Kirov and the Maly Operny (the Little Opera House, formerly the Mikhailovsky Theatre) in Leningrad. There are many beautiful new buildings, such as the Novosibirsk Opera, which prides itself on being the largest in the country, or the reconstructed and enlarged one at Perm. There are also older opera houses in the baroque style in traditionally music-loving towns such as Odessa. The Novosibirsk ballet company numbers 120 dancers; the small companies in some of the more distant opera houses number 45–47. In addition, many towns have operetta theatres which also employ a resident ballet company. Some towns have a rather unusual type of musico-dramatic theatre which present light opera, operetta, and ballet divertissements. The most interesting is the Vanemuine Theatre in Tartu, Estonia, where each member of the company is expected to sing, act, and dance, depending on whether the current production is an opera, drama, or ballet.

With such a great and ever-growing demand for talent, the ballet schools of the Soviet Union are insufficient in number to supply fully-trained dancers to all the theatres throughout the vast country. It therefore happens that in the provinces one finds fairly good dancers trained in amateur dance groups, or by studios opened in many theatres, or by occasional private teachers. In every good opera house, on the other hand, the nucleus of the ballet company has invariably been trained at one of the State Ballet Schools and thus serves as an example to be followed by the rest of the company. At Novosibirsk the company is constantly being replenished from its own school; the same applies to Perm where the school was founded during World War II by evacuated Leningrad dancers. In the opinion of many, this company holds third place in the country, after Leningrad and Moscow.

In Tsarist Russia there were three established ballet schools—in St. Petersburg, Moscow, and Warsaw (when Poland belonged to Russia). Today there are twenty State Choreographic Schools in the Soviet Union, thirteen with complete nine-year ballet and general education curricula. The rest have varying periods of study but the most customary is six years. All over the country boys and girls study ballet in many amateur ballet groups and often find their way to the professional stage.

Children are accepted by the full-course State Ballet (Choreographic) Schools at the age of ten, after three years in a secondary, academic school. The remaining seven years of the general education syllabus, emphasizing the history of the arts and music, is given during the nine years of professional training at the ballet school. Besides classic dance the ballet syllabus includes the study of character dancing, historical dance, supported adagio (a separate subject in senior classes), and mime. All the schools comply with a general program issued by the Arts School Department of the Ministry of Culture, but provision is made for schools in the national republics to pay greater attention to study of local national dances. Russian folk dance is taught as a separate subject at the Moscow school by a leading soloist of the Piatnitsky Choir dance group.

Pupils of the State Ballet Schools, beginning with the first year of study, take part in ballet performances of the theatre to which the school is attached, thus forming a direct link with the theatre at a very early age.

A unique college of higher ballet education, the only one of its kind in the world, exists in Moscow. It is the Ballet Faculty of the State Institute of Theatre Art. At present it has two divisions: choreographic and pedagogical. Only students with full ballet education and some theatrical experience are accepted. Critics and historians of ballet are educated in the Theatre History Department of the same Institute. The first graduates of the Choreographic Department are already directing ballet companies in opera houses at Alma-Ata, Ulan-Ude, Kazan, Perm, Cheliabinsk, Gorky, and other cities.

The present goal of all Soviet ballet is to create works on contemporary themes. It was the consensus expressed emphatically at a nation-wide choreographic conference held in Moscow in Feb., 1960, that it is of paramount importance not to lose in the process of innovation the great traditions of the Russian school with its highly expressive acting and its approach to ballet as a story interpreted through the medium of the dance set to a score built along symphonic lines. There are no serious differences between Soviet choreographers on this matter. However, the latest works of gifted Leningrad choreographers Igor Belsky and Yuri Grigorovich are more "modern" and show an inclination to do away with independent mime scenes; instead the entire action is expressed through dance integrated with mime.

Leonid Lavrovsky's latest works in Moscow—entirely new versions of Rachmaninov's *Paganini* and Bartók's *Miraculous Mandarin*—while much more modern in idiom than his earlier works, show a tendency toward greater dramatic expression. They are also more sustained and mature than the creations of the young Leningraders. The difference in style is not to be interpreted as a sign of rivalry between Moscow and Leningrad, but of healthy creative competition out of which the best achievements will be merged in an eloquent new style of Soviet choreography. It goes without saying that the quest for a plastic image of Soviet contemporary life should be based by all choreographers, young and old, first and foremost on the study of life around them. It is not surprising that unexpected successes in this connection have come from amateur dance groups which work in the very midst of life. These amateur ballet theatres, such as the People's Ballet Theatre of Dniepropetrovsk and the amateur choreographic studio at the Hammer and Sickle plant in Moscow, often perform on a level that is almost professional.

There is hardly a company in the U.S.S.R. that is not working on a ballet with a contemporary theme. Yuri Grigorovich, after experimenting in the modern idiom with two fairy tales, *The Stone Flower* and *Legend of Love,* is collaborating with composer Dmitri Shostakovich on *The Irkutsk Story,* after a successful play of that title by A. Arbusov on a contemporary industrial theme with moving human interest. The Bolshoi Theatre also has on its production schedule a new ballet on a contemporary Soviet theme, for which Alexei Yermolayev received a second prize in a recent contest.

The ultimate goal of Soviet ballet is the creation of a contemporary production equal in its artistic impact to the finest of classical masterpieces. This goal cannot be reached overnight, but Soviet choreographers are working assiduously to find the correct solution to this problem.

There was a time when Soviet ballet was known elsewhere in the world only by its reputation, spread by word of mouth and through a few films. The genius of Galina Ulanova was known outside the U.S.S.R. long before she appeared before any foreign audience (when Ulanova retired as dancer in 1962 to devote herself to teaching and coaching young ballerinas in their roles, Maya Plisetskaya became prima ballerina). Today, however, Soviet companies have danced in London, Paris, New York, Brussels, Montreal, Tokyo, and Peking; groups of Soviet dancers have also performed in Africa, Australia, and South America. The Bolshoi Ballet had the distinction of closing the old Metropolitan Opera House with the final performance of the N.Y. season (Apr. 19–May 8, 1966).

Spanish Dance.

BY LA MERI.

The Spanish dance is considered by many authorities to be one of the finest of the Occidental choreographic arts, ranking with ballet and contemporary dance in purity of line and emotional impact. It antedates other European dance-arts by several centuries (there exist in Spain today choreographies dating from the Hellenic supremacy in the Mediterranean, 550 B.C.). By the time Rome became the ruling Western empire, "Las Andaluces delicias" (dancing girls from Cadiz) were already recognized artists.

The invasion of southern Spain by the Moors in the early 700's left a strong mark on both music and dance in Andalucia. What the non-Iberic world loosely calls Spanish Dancing is, oftener than not, pure Andalucian.

Under the rule of the Caliphs, music and dance was a form of social entertainment performed in the palace. During the reign of Ferdinand and Isabella (1479–1516) the Spanish drama was born and through it dancing was introduced to the theatre. At the same time, choreography found its way into the church, where traces of it still remain, notably in Sevilla and Toledo. The Sarabande, Pavane, Passecalle, and other court dances also belong to this choreographic epoch.

Before two centuries had passed, Spain rocked to the rhythm of the Fandango, the Bolero, the Cachucha, and the Seguidillas Manchegas. From the Seguidillas Manchegas grew the beloved Sevillana which is today considered the national dance.

The choreography of Spain is of four distinct styles: regional, flamenco, school, and renaissance. The regional dance includes all the colorful communal dances of the forty-three provinces: the Jota of Aragon, the Sardana of Cataluna, the Danza Prima of Asturia, the thirty airy dances of the Basques, the Seguidillas of Castile, the Jota of Valencia, the Sevillanas of Andalucia, and literally hundreds of others. Each is characterized by tuneful and typical music and by elaborate traditional costumes. The choreography ranges from solos and duets through squares and rounds. These dances are beautiful and complete when performed in their native setting. However, transplanted to the stage by an artist such as Argentinita (Encarnacion Lopez) they become the charming vehicle for a character sketch as racially typical as their own region.

The baile flamenco was originated by the Gypsies in southern Spain. Many ethnologists believe the flamenco to be of

Indian origin, to which ancient Persian chronicles testify. It is written that in their migrations these wandering Indians mixed with both the Phoenicians and the Egyptians. Gypsies living in Spain today feel they are descended from the Moors—although the typical tribal names of Maya and Amaya are of Sanskrit origin. Today there are more than forty thousand Gypsies in Spain. Until the end of the 18th century they were an outcast people, hounded by both the law and the public. Within the last half-century the world has acknowledged them as the creators of an original and poignantly beautiful art. The largest Gypsy quarters in Spain are El Albaicin in Granada and La Triana in Sevilla. The Granada Gypsy calls himself a "gitano" and lives, more often than not, in a cave hollowed out in the Sacro-Monte (Sacred Mountain). The Sevillian Gypsy calls himself a "flamenco" and lives in a spotlessly whitewashed adobe house. The repertoire of Gypsy dances is limited in name only, since the performer improvises within a traditional form according to his mood, accompanied by an expert guitarist and encouraged by his fellows who take part in the dance by clapping, stamping, and shouting in rhythmic accompaniment. Rhythm-forms of flamenco dances are: Alegrias, Soleares, Bulerias, Farruca, Zapateado, Tango, Zambra, and Seguiriyas.

The school dance is one which is learned in a dancing school, more often than not a stylized "routine" of a folk expression. One of the earliest of the school dances was the Bolero. It is said that Cerezo, a ballet dancer at the court in 1790, used the folk Bolero as a base and wove into it all the intricacies then known of the French ballet. The Seguidillas of La Mancha was adopted as a school dance, as was the Malaguena and the Jota of Valencia. In Andalucia many school dances had their origin in the Sevillanas—the Peteneras, Las Manchegas, El Ole, Las Panaderos, El Vito, and a host of others. In the early part of the 19th century the school dance reached its height. A few masters of classical dance—of whom Otero was the dean—created any number of routines whose steps began to include the heel-work of the Gypsy. Today the school dance is almost a period-piece, its place having been taken by the new dance-art of Spain.

The renaissance or neo-Spanish dance has grown up in the past forty-five years, beginning twenty years (according to Otero) after its decadence had set in. A great art is never the product of a single artist, but of the temper of the folk, the times, and the corollary arts. A new aspect of an art, long gestating, is often brought to its first flower by an isolated genius. In the case of the concert dance of Spain, Argentina (Antonia Merce, 1890–1936) was that genius. It was she who first set the old school dance to the classical compositions of Albeniz, de Falla, Turina, and other great Iberian composers.

Within a quarter of a century the Spanish dance has been accepted as an art form, technically and artistically sufficient unto itself. Many ballets have been composed to be expressed solely through the crystallized technique of the Spanish dance of which the best known are *El Amor Brujo* and *The Three-Cornered Hat,* both composed by de Falla. Each of the styles has contributed color, line, and emotion to the enrichment of this new art form.

The Spanish dance possesses a comprehensive technique and an exhaustive terminology, but to the average audience it is the castanets and heel-work which typify the art form. However, it is necessary to dispel the misconceptions which have risen around these elements.

Castanets are Spanish but not flamenco. Many Gypsy men consider their usage effeminate. This instrument, whose origin has been lost, requires far more artistry than the average listener may believe. Good castanets, which are rare as well as expensive, are tuned; the right is 1/3 of a tone higher than the left. Three to four months of daily practice (one to two hours) will give the student a relative control, but artistry on this instrument as on any other is the result of years of application coupled with an inherent musical ability.

Heel-work (taconeo) is exclusively Gypsy and doubtless stems from the floor-contact work of the Near and Middle East. The three basic sounds (i.e. the striking of the half-toe, the striking of the heel, and the striking of the full sole) are capable of producing endless varieties of tone and rhythmic combination. Any non-flamenco dance which uses heel-work is called "agitanado."

The steps and typical combinations of Spanish dance have acquired authenticity through long usage. Many steps draw their names from the dances in which they appear: Sevillanas, Malaguenas, Seguidillas, etc. Aside from the steps, the character of the Spanish dance lies in the carriage of head, torso, and arms, and in the projection of the emotional quality of the Iberian—the pride, the sensuality, the "rhythm in the veins"—all the psychological earmarks which contribute to the greatest dance of the Occident.

Sparemblek, Milko, dancer and choreographer, b. Yugoslavia, 1928. Educated through high school. Studied ballet at school of Zagreb Opera with Ana Roje. Soloist, Zagreb Opera (1949–53). Arrived in Paris in 1953 and studied with Olga Preobrajenska, Serge Peretti. Soloist, Les Ballets Janine Charrat (1954–56); Milorad Miskovitch's Ballet de Paris (1956–58); with Ludmilla Tcherina (1958–61). First choreographer, *L'Echelle* (The Ladder), in collaboration with Dirk Sanders for the Miskovitch company (1957), followed by *Quatuor* (music: Raffaello de Banfield, 1957), *Heros et son Miroir* (1960), also for Miskovitch. Other works include *Les Amants de Teruel* (Ludmilla Tcherina Ballet, 1958), Monteverdi's *Orfeo* (Brussels Opera, 1960), *Climats* (Brussels Opera, 1961). He dances in many of his own ballets; appeared as dancer and actor in the film of *Les Amants de Teruel* (1961). Succeeded Maurice Béjart as director and choreographer of the Brussels Opera Ballet, Théâtre Royal de la Monnaie (season (1963–64) while Béjart was on leave of absence.

Spartacus. Ballet in 4 acts; chor.: Leonide Yacobson; music: Aram Khachaturian; book: Nicolai Volkov; décor: Valentina Khodasevich. First prod.: Kirov Theatre, Leningrad, Dec. 27, 1956, with Askold Makarov (Spartacus) and Inna Zubkovskaya (Phrygia). Volkov's libretto follows ancient authors, particularly Plutarch, rather than the popular novel of the same name by the Italian author Giovanniolli. According to the plot of Volkov's libretto, Spartacus and his followers are betrayed by the courtesan Aegina who is enamored of Spartacus's friend Harmodius. One of the principal scenes is the gladiators' circus in Rome. A version of the same ballet by Igor Moiseyev with décor by Alexander Konstantinovsky was first performed March 11, 1958, at the Bolshoi Theatre but is no longer in its repertoire. Yacobson choreographed a new version of his production shortened to three acts in the spring of 1962. This version had its N.Y. première at the Metropolitan Opera House, Sept. 12, 1962, with Dmitri Begak (Spartacus) and Maya Plisetskaya (Phrygia). Students from several N.Y. ballet studios were used as supernumeraries in the triumphal procession and orgy scenes.

Specialty, more properly, specialty dance, a solo or duet executed by solo dancers in a musical. Generally speaking, a specialty is a dance prepared by the dancers themselves as opposed to a dance staged by the choreographer of the musical.

Spectacular Dance, a term coined by

John Martin, author and former dance critic of *The New York Times,* to include ballet and the dance in musical comedies, revues, etc.

Spectre de la Rose, Le. Ballet in 1 act; chor.: Michel Fokine; music: Carl Maria von Weber; book: J. L. Vaudoyer; décor and costumes: Léon Bakst. First prod.: Diaghilev Ballets Russes, Théâtre de Monte Carlo, Apr. 19, 1911, with Tamara Karsavina and Vaslav Nijinsky. This ballet, suggested by a poem of Théophile Gautier and set to Weber's "Invitation to the Dance," was created to set off Nijinsky's unusual elevation in contrast to the poetic dream-like quality of the young girl. It was so enthusiastically received that at one performance at the Paris Opéra, the whole ballet was repeated for an encore. A Young Girl returns from a ball with a rose in her hand. Tired, she sits down in a chair, falls asleep and dreams that the specter of the rose is dancing with her. When the specter disappears through a window, she awakens, still under the spell of her dream. It is a well-composed little ballet. Its great popularity is due to the consummate artistry of Karsavina and Nijinsky, its first performers. Their artistry has not been matched in the 56 years since the ballet's première, although nearly all great (and not so great) ballerinas and premiers danseurs of this generation attempt the ballet.

Spellbound Child, The (L'Enfant et les Sortilèges). Opera-ballet in 2 parts; chor.: George Balanchine; music: Maurice Ravel; poem: Colette (Mme. Colette Willy); décor and costumes: Aline Bernstein. First prod.: Ballet Society, Central H.S. of Needle Trades, N.Y., Nov. 26, 1946. The dancers included Gisella Caccialanza, Georgia Hiden, Elise Reiman, Beatrice Tompkins, Paul d'Amboise, William Dollar, John Scancarella. Ravel's opera for children, which Balanchine transformed into an opera-ballet, was given with the singers in the pit and the dancers on stage. Twelve-year old Joseph Connolly sang and acted the role of the Child. It was a magical entertainment despite the fact that it was given on a most primitive and unsuitable stage. The slight but amusing plot deals with a child about whom everyday objects are transformed by magic into animated figures. The figures' action and the Child's sung or spoken reaction to them furnish the plot.

Spessivtzeva, Olga, outstanding Russian ballerina, b. 1895. Graduated from the ballet school of the Imperial Maryinsky Theatre in 1913, a classmate of Felia Doubrovska. After graduation she was accepted into the Maryinsky Ballet and in 1918 promoted to ballerina. In the next five years of her association with the Maryinsky she danced the principal roles in *Esmeralda, Giselle, Chopiniana* (*Les Sylphides*), *The Nutcracker, Paquita, Le Corsaire, Bayaderka, The Sleeping Beauty, The Daughter of Pharaoh, Don Quixote,* and *Swan Lake,* a number of ballets seldom, if ever, matched by any other ballerina.

Spessivtzeva was probably the greatest Romantic ballerina of her generation. Her consummate artistry did not induce her to neglect her technique, as often happens. In 1916, while still a soloist, she took leave of absence to join the Diaghilev Ballets Russes on its U.S. tour during which she danced *Le Spectre de la Rose* with Vaslav Nijinsky. She returned to the Maryinsky in 1917. In 1921, now a full-fledged ballerina, she was again invited to join the Diaghilev Ballet, this time to dance Aurora in the London production of the full-length *Sleeping Beauty* (called there *The Sleeping Princess*), which opened Nov. 2 at the Alhambra Theatre. Her Prince Charming was Pierre Vladimirov. She remained with the company as long as the ballet was being performed and returned to Russia in 1922.

She left Russia never to return in 1923 and joined the Teatro Colón, Buenos

Olga Spessivtzeva, great Russian ballerina, with Anatole Vilzak in Swan Lake, *Act 2, in Dandré-Levitov company (1934–35).*

Aires, Argentina. In 1924 she joined the Paris Opéra and remained there, with short intervals, until 1932. In 1927 she danced the title role in George Balanchine's *La Chatte* and a few other ballets in the Diaghilev company. She danced again with that company in its final London season in 1929, when her great success was *Swan Lake* (Act 2) with Serge Lifar. In 1931 she was elevated to première danseuse étoile of the Paris Opéra Ballet, but remained there only through the spring of 1932. Later that year she once again went to Teatro Colón, where Michel Fokine was ballet master, and danced there for six months. In the autumn of 1934 she became ballerina of the Victor Dandré–Alexander Levitov company (formerly the Anna Pavlova company) for the Australian tour where she was partnered by Anatole Vilzak. She gave her last performance during a brief engagement in Buenos Aires. Her eventual serious illness could have been predicted, for signs of her depression began to manifest themselves during the last Australian tour.

Spessivtzeva moved to the U.S. in 1939. In 1943 she suffered a nervous breakdown and was placed in a hospital for mental cases where she remained until Feb., 1963. With the help of several friends, among them Felia Doubrovska, Anton Dolin, and Dale Edward Fern, she was discharged from the hospital and settled on the Tolstoy Farm, Valley Cottage, Rockland County, N.Y., a Russian settlement maintained by the Tolstoy Foundation and headed by Mme. Alexandra Tolstoy, daughter of the great Russian writer Leo Tolstoy.

Spider's Banquet, The. Ballet in 1 act; chor.: Andrée Howard; music: Albert Roussel, composed for the original work, *Les Festin de l'Araignee;* décor: Michael Ayrton. First prod.: Sadler's Wells (now Royal) Ballet, New Theatre, London, June 20, 1944, with Celia Franca as the Spider. Andrée Howard used the same theme as the original ballet-pantomime by Gilbert de Voisins: a Spider waits in her web for her prey—ants, a pair of praying mantises, and a mayfly.

Split, acrobatic version of a grand écart; a movement in which the body is lowered to the floor with one leg stretched out straight in front, the other in back, at right angles to the torso.

Spohr, Arnold, Canadian dancer, choreographer, director of Royal Winnipeg Ballet, b. Rhein, Saskatchewan. Studied dance in London, receiving the advanced certificate and solo seal of the Royal Academy of Dancing; also studied in N.Y. and Hollywood. Joined Winnipeg (now Royal Winnipeg) Ballet (1947) and was leading male dancer until 1954, dancing a large repertoire including *Les Sylphides, Shooting of Dan McGrew,* and leads in his own ballets, *Ballet Premier* and *Intermede* (1951), among others. During 1955 he was choreographer and dancer for Canadian Broadcasting Corporation television. During the Christmas season (1956–57), he partnered Alicia Markova in the children's play *Where the Rainbow Ends,* at the Coliseum Theatre, London. He was appointed director of the Royal Winnipeg Ballet in Mar., 1958; choreographed *E Minor* in 1959. He is an accomplished pianist and taught piano between 1948 and 1953 in addition to dancing with the Winnipeg company.

Spotting, the movement of the head during fast turns sur place or traveling, where the eyes of the dancer fix on an immobile spot in the classroom, rehearsal hall, or auditorium, as the case may be, while the body is turning. The head makes the turn quicker than the body and the eyes return to the same spot, thus diminishing the possibility of dizziness. In traveling turns the dancer spots on a fixed point in the direction of the movement, thus helping himself to stay "on course."

Sprain. See ACCIDENTS.

Spring Tale, A. Ballet in 4 scenes; chor. and book: Kurt Jooss; music: Fritz Cohen; costumes: Hein Heckroth. First prod.: Jooss Ballet, Shakespeare Memorial Theatre, Stratford-on-Avon, Feb. 2, 1939, with Ulla Soederbaum, Hans Züllig, Noelle de Mosa, Elsa Kahl, Rolf Alexander, Hans Gansert. The ballet is a fairy tale.

Spurgeon, Jack, English dancer and teacher, b. London, 1918; m. Joan Tucker. Studied with Italia Conti, Nicholas Legat, Olga Preobrajenska, Anton Dolin, Anna Severskaya. Appeared as dancer in musicals in London (1927–34); member, Leon Woicikowski Ballet (1934); soloist, Ballet de Monte Carlo (1936); principal dancer, Polish National Ballet (as Jan Spur) (1938); Trois Arts Ballet (1939). War service (1940–45). Principal dancer, International Ballet (1945–49); then toured in England, Pakistan and India (1950–51). Season with Original Ballet Russe (1951). Co-principal with Joan Tucker of The Academy of Ballet, Edinburgh, begun in 1954 under the title The Stage School of Dancing.

Square Dance, any type of American folk dance in which an even number of couples participate, arranged so that they form a square, as in the square set and quadrille, or in two lines facing each other as in the longway set, or in a circle as in the running set. The term square dance is used for any type of dance that is not performed by individual couples; round dance for any type of dance that is performed by individual couples. The square dance is made up of many figures which are called out by the caller. Square dances have always been popular in rural districts of the U.S.; they have also been increasing in popularity in cities since the early 1930's. Most of these dances were originally brought to the U.S. from England.

Square Dance. Ballet in 1 act; chor.: George Balanchine; music: excerpts from Arcangelo Corelli's Suite for Strings and from several concerti grossi by Antonio Vivaldi; caller: Elisha C. Keeler. First prod.: New York City Ballet, City Center, N.Y., Nov. 21, 1957, with Patricia Wilde, Nicholas Magallanes and ensemble. Classical ballet enchaînements, performed in practice costume in square dance formations, with the caller and the string orchestra on stage. This ballet is also in the repertoire of the Robert Joffrey Ballet.

Square Set, type of American square dance in which four couples participate. At the start of the dance, the four couples are so arranged that they form a square with opposite couples facing each other. See SQUARE DANCE.

Staats, Leo (1877–1952), ballet master and dancer, pupil of Louis Mérante. His career was closely connected with Paris Opéra where he made his debut at age ten and choreographed his first ballet when only sixteen. As a dancer he appeared in many ballets, notably *Javotte* (1909). As choreographer he staged and revived many works. Artistic director of Theatre des Arts, 1910–14. Returned to Opéra, 1915, choreographing *Cydalise et le Chèvre-Pied* (1923), among others. Also worked for music halls, revues, private companies, and taught in his own studio until his death.

Staff, Frank, choreographer and dancer, b. Kimberly, South Africa, 1918, of English father and Irish mother. Studied ballet in Capetown with Helen Webb and Maude Lloyd; in London (1933) with Marie Rambert, Antony Tudor. Danced with Ballet Rambert (1933–45), except for seasons with Vic-Wells (later Sadler's Wells, now Royal) Ballet (1934–35 and 1938–39), and briefly with London Ballet. For Ballet Rambert he created Julien, the Boy (*Fête Etrange*), and others, and danced a large repertoire including the Faun (*Afternoon of a Faun*), Lover (*Lilac Garden*), *Blue Bird* pas de deux, Harlequin (*Carnaval*) and many others. For the Vic-Wells Ballet he created the Hornblower (*The Rake's Progress*) and Cupid in Frederick Ashton's *Cupid and Psyche* (1939), among others. His first choreography was for Ballet Rambert: *The Tartans* (1938). He later created a number of works, best known of which are *Czernyana* (1939), *Enigma Variations*, and *Peter and the Wolf*, both 1940. He also choreographed *The Lovers' Gallery* (1947) and *Fanciulla delle Rose* (1948) for Metropolitan Ballet. Currently working in South Africa.

Stage Dance Council (Great Britain), an organization founded in 1959 largely for the purpose of achieving reasonable unity in the syllabi of stage dance competitions. The Council is also in process of promoting standardized descriptions of various British national dances including the Sailor's Hornpipe, the Highland Fling, and the Sword Dance, among others. Membership comprises: Allied Dancing Association, British Association of Teachers of Dancing, Dance Teachers' Association, International Dancing Masters' Association, National Association of Teachers of Dancing, Northern Counties Dance Teachers' Association, Scottish Dance Teachers' Alliance, United Kingdom Alliance, and the British Ballet Organization.

Stahl, Steffy, dance educator, b. Vienna, 1919. Her studies include piano and musical education with private teachers; anatomy and physiology at the Univ. of Vienna; dance with Gertrud Bodenweiser. Since 1938 she has headed the educational dance program incorporated into the obligatory school curriculum of kindergarten and primary state schools in Venezuela. This has included the training of hundreds of teachers to carry out her work in areas outside Caracas, where she teaches at the municipal and national schools. Her system, which teaches the child to coordinate cerebral messages with muscular movements, has proved valuable in other mental fields and a notable help in the general assimilation of studies, quite apart from its creative value as dance. For her services she has been awarded the Condecoracion Orden Francisco de Miranda by the Venezuelan Government (1950).

Stahle, Anna Greta, Swedish writer, journalist, critic, b. Stockholm, 1913. Graduate of the Univ. of Stockholm (history, literature, French and German languages). Dance, theatre, and motion picture critic of Swedish newspaper *Dagens Nyheter* since 1951; Scandinavian correspondent of *Dance News* since 1955. Has written articles on dance for *Ballet Annual, Dance Perspectives,* and other publications; contributor to *Dance Encyclopedia.*

Stanislavsky and Nemirovich-Danchenko Lyric Theatre, Ballet Company of.

Known popularly as the Nemirovich-Danchenko Ballet or, outside the Soviet Union, as the Stanislavsky Ballet, this second ballet company of Moscow grew out of the Art Ballet founded in 1929 by Victorina Krieger. The Art Ballet looked upon its members as dancing actors or dancer-actors. Such artistic principles had much in common with those of the Moscow Art Theatre. One of its illustrious founders, Vladimir Nemirovich-Danchenko founded, as an offshoot of the main theatre, a Musical Studio which later grew into a Lyric Theatre bearing his name. In 1933 he invited Victorina Krieger's group (drawn mostly from graduates of the Lunacharsky Theatre Technicum—choreographic division) to join his theatre. Among them were Vladimir Bourmeister, Alexander Klein, Marra Sorokina, Nicolai Kholfin. This Lyric Theatre later merged with the Opera Studio founded by Konstantin Stanislavsky, also as an offshoot of the Moscow Art Theatre, and thus acquired the names of its joint founders. The company headed first by Victorina Krieger and later by Vladimir Bourmeister was guided by the method of Stanislavsky and Nemirovich-Danchenko, while seeking a special choreographic form for its application. One of its first successful productions was a new version of *La Fille Mal Gardée* with the Peter Ludwig Hertel music, but an entirely new libretto entitled *The Rivals,* and choreography by Nicolai Kholfin and Pavel Markov (1933). Then followed *The Gypsies,* choreography by Kholfin, music by Sergei Vasilenko (1937), *Christmas Eve* (Fedor Lopukhov—Boris Asafiev, 1938), *Straussiana* (Bourmeister, 1941), *Merry Wives of Windsor* (Bourmeister and Ivan Kurilov —V. Oransky, 1942), *Lola* (Bourmeister —Vasilenko, 1943), new versions of *Schéhérazade* (1944) and *Carnaval* (1946) both by Bourmeister, *Francesca da Rimini* (Kholfin—Asafiev, 1947), a new version of *Esmeralda* by Bourmeister (1948) and, above all, the outstanding production of *Swan Lake* staged by Bourmeister in 1953. Except for the second act which follows the Lev Ivanov choreography and the Riccardo Drigo arrangement of the score, the Bourmeister version has entirely new choreography arranged to the original 1875 Tchaikovsky manuscript music. Among the company's other choreographers are Alexei Chichinadze (*Daughter of Castilia,* 1955; *Wood Fairy,* 1960), Nina Grishina (new version of *Le Corsaire,* 1959), and Igor Smirnov (a version of the ballet *Masquerade* on the theme of the Lermontov drama, to music by the young composer Mikhail Laputin, 1961). The company danced in Paris in 1956 at the Théâtre du Châtelet. Vladimir Bourmeister after a two-year leave of absence is again chief choreographer of the company.

Star System, the system by which a ballet company is built around one or several famous dancers whose presence in the company is apt to attract spectators and thus guarantee a financial success. Most impresarios, directors of ballet companies, and managers favor the star system for obvious reasons. Dancers within the company are generally against the star system because they feel that under it their chances for advancement are limited. Another frequent and valid complaint is that regular members of the company are called on to dance principal parts on the road, especially at one-night stands, but are not given an opportunity to dance these parts in New York and other metropolitan centers and thus are deprived of showing themselves to larger audiences and, especially, to critics.

Starbuck, James, dancer, choreographer, b. Denver, Colo. Studied dance with Raoul Pause, Adolph Bolm, Edward Caton, Vincenzo Celli, Willam Christensen, Martha Graham, Vera Nemtchinova, Anatole Oboukhov, Anatole Vilzak, and others. Started his career as a juvenile actor and as dancer with a concert group, Ballet Moderne. Principal dancer, San Francisco

Opera Ballet (1935–38); member, Ballet Russe de Monte Carlo (1938–44), rising to soloist rank. After dancing in the musical *Song of Norway* (1944), he appeared in a number of musicals, both dancing and acting, and staged the summer shows at Camp Tamiment, Pa. (1945–48). Since then his principal and most successful work has been in television as choreographer for some of the best known series, including the now-legendary "Your Show of Shows," starring Sid Caesar and Imogene Coca (1951–54) which developed out of the preceding "Admiral Broadway Revue" (1949), and "Saturday Night Revue" (1950). With these shows he introduced the concept of a group of dancers who appeared weekly in specially arranged numbers. His satires on ballet classics in which he frequently appeared as partner to Imogene Coca were hilarious in themselves but created an interest in ballet among the millions of regular viewers which made it possible for him to invite artists like Alicia Markova, Mia Slavenska, Maria Tallchief, and others to appear in excerpts from the classic ballets or in numbers especially arranged for them. After "Your Show of Shows" came to a close, he went to Hollywood to create the dances for Danny Kaye's *The Court Jester* (1954–55). Since then has choreographed for innumerable "television specials," night club acts, commercial shows, staged the dances for the 1958 musical *Oh Captain!* (in which Alexandra Danilova did a number which stopped the show); was choreographer and associate producer of *A Thurber Carnival* (1960), and since 1961 has staged "Sing Along With Mitch," the weekly television show. Has found time to create ballets, including *Le Pont* (1956) and *Mal de Siècle* (1958), both for Grand Ballet du Marquis de Cuevas, and *The Comedians* (Kabalevsky) for Ballet Russe de Monte Carlo's 25th Anniversary season (1961–62). Continues to work in television.

Starer, Robert, composer, b. Vienna, Austria, 1924. Studied at the State Academy of Music, Vienna; the Jerusalem Conservatory, Israel; Juilliard School of Music, N.Y. Has written many orchestral works, chamber music, works for chorus, piano, and songs, over 70 of which have been published. His compositions for dance include *Masque* (Nina Fonaroff, 1949); *Indeterminate Figure* (Daniel Nagrin, 1957); *The Story of Esther* (Anna Sokolow, C.B.S. Television, 1960); *The Dybbuk* (Herbert Ross, premièred at Berlin Festival, 1960); Samson Agonistes (1961), *Phaedra,* and *Secular Games* (1962), all for Martha Graham; *Brief Dynasty* (John Butler, C.B.S. Television, 1962), *Hadreanus* (John Butler, Nederlands Danse Theater, 1962). He was one of the eight composers who wrote variations on William Schuman's theme for José Limón's *Performance,* specially created for dance students of the Juilliard School of Music and presented Apr. 14, 1961. He is on the faculty of the Juilliard School of Music.

Stars and Stripes. Ballet in 5 campaigns; chor.: George Balanchine; music: John Philip Sousa's "Corcoran Cadets," "Thunder and Gladiator," "Rifle Regiment," "Liberty Bell," "El Capitan," and "Stars and Stripes Forever," adapted and orchestrated by Hershy Kay; décor: David Hays; costumes: Barbara Karinska. First prod.: New York City Ballet, City Center, N.Y., with Allegra Kent (1st Campaign), Robert Barnett (2nd Campaign), Diana Adams (3rd Campaign), Melissa Hayden and Jacques d'Amboise (4th Campaign pas de deux). The 5th Campaign was for the entire company. A brilliant piece of quasi-military nonsense. The 3rd Campaign was later omitted as being too much like (but inferior to) the 1st. The ballet is dedicated to the memory of Fiorello H. La Guardia, N.Y.'s beloved mayor (1933–1945).

Stepanoff, Vladimir (1866–1896), Russian dancer of the St. Petersburg Imperial

Ballet. Author of a dance notation system which he published in Paris in 1892 under the title *Alphabet des Mouvements du Corps Humain; essai d'enregistrement des mouvements du corps humain au moyen des signes musicaux*. In 1893 his system, after a thorough examination by a committee of dancers and choreographers, was included in the curriculum of the St. Petersburg Imperial School of Ballet. In 1895 he was sent to Moscow to introduce his system to the artists and teachers of the Bolshoi Theatre. After his death in Moscow his notation system fell into neglect and has not been used since.

Steuart, Douglas (Tom Douglas), Scottish dancer, b. Rosyth, 1927. Studied with Marjorie Middleton and at Sadler's Wells (now Royal) Ballet School, then entering the company. Also danced with Metropolitan Ballet, returning to Sadler's Wells where he is now a soloist with the Royal Ballet. His roles include Pas de Trois (*Les Rendez-vous*), Puss in Boots (*The Sleeping Beauty*), Spanish Dance (*Swan Lake*), Foxtrot (*Façade*), and others.

Stevenson, Hugh (1910–1956), English designer. Among the many ballets for which he designed the décor and costumes are *Unbowed* (his first, chor. Sara Patrick, 1932), *Pavane pour une Infante Defunte* (Antony Tudor, 1933), *The Planets* (1934), *Lilac Garden* (1936), *Gallant Assembly*—in which he also appeared (Antony Tudor, 1938), *Soirée Musicale* and *Gala Performance* (1938), *Pas des Déesses* (Keith Lester, 1939), *Flamenco* (Elsa Brunelleschi, 1943), *The Fugitive* (Andrée Howard, 1944), *Giselle* (Ballet Rambert, 1945). He designed the first full-length version of *Swan Lake* for Vic-Wells (later Sadler's Wells, now Royal) Ballet and later their productions of *Gods Go a'Begging* and *Promenade*. For Sadler's Wells Theatre Ballet he designed *Mardi Gras* and John Cranko's *Pastorale*. His last works for ballet were *Giselle* and David Lichine's *Symphonic Impressions* for London's Festival Ballet.

Still Point, The. Ballet in 1 act; chor.: Todd Bolender; music: Claude Debussy's String Quartet (first 3 movements), transcribed for orchestra by Frank Black. First prod.: New York City Ballet, City Center, N.Y., Mar. 13, 1956, with Melissa Hayden, Jacques d'Amboise, and Irene Larsson, Jillana, Roy Tobias, John Mandia. A young girl moves from the fears and uncertainties of adolescence to the secure happiness of mature love. The first version of this ballet was choreographed by Bolender for the Dance Drama Company, a modern dance group headed by Emily Frankel and Mark Ryder and premièred Aug. 3, 1955 at Jacob's Pillow Dance Festival, Lee, Mass., with Frankel and Ryder in the leading roles.

Stjepan (also called Stepan), **Zlatica,** Yugoslav dancer, b. Zagreb, 1929. Studied in Yugoslavia under Margarita Froman and in Paris under Olga Preobrajenska and Serge Peretti. Joined the Zagreb National Ballet in 1946; promoted to ballerina in 1950. Dances the classic as well as the modern repertoire of her company.

Stone, Bentley, contemporary dancer, teacher, choreographer, b. Plankinton, S.D. Studied dance with Margaret Severn, G. M. Caskey (Milwaukee), Luigi Albertieri, Laurent Novikoff, Marie Rambert. Began his career in musicals, among them *The Black Crook* (Hoboken, N.J., 1929). Concerts with Margaret Severn; soloist, Chicago Civic Opera Ballet (1930–32); premier danseur, Chicago Grand Opera Ballet (1933), Opera Intime (1934); premier danseur and ballet director, Century of Progress Ballet (1934); premier danseur and co-choreographer, Chicago City Opera (1935–37), Ballet Rambert (1937), Page-Stone Ballet (1938–41); guest artist, Ballet Russe de Monte Carlo (1945). With the U.S. Air Corps (1942–45). Danced principal roles in *Spectre de la Rose, Les Sylphides, Swan*

Lake, Death and the Maiden, Frankie and Johnny, Guns and Castanets, and others. He has choreographed some twenty-five ballets, among them *Les Preludes* (Liszt); *Rhapsody in Blue* (Gershwin, 1934); *Mercure* (Satie); *Casey at the Bat* (Aborn, 1939); *Les Enfants Perdus* (Ravel, 1951); *The Wall* (Auber, 1956); *Les Biches* (Poulenc, 1961); and in collaboration with Ruth Page: *An American in Paris, Frankie and Johnny, Guns and Castanets, Scrapbook, Zephyr and Flora,* and others. Currently teaching at the Stone-Camryn School, Chicago, and dancing as guest artist with Ruth Page's Chicago Opera Ballet.

Stone Flower. Ballet in 3 acts, music: Sergei Prokofiev; libretto: Mira Mendelssohn–Prokofieva (wife of the composer) and Leonid Lavrovsky, inspired by the story *The Malachite Casket* by Pavel Bazhov, based on Ural Mountain folk-tales. First produced at the Moscow Bolshoi Theatre, 1954, with choreography by Lavrovsky, with Galina Ulanova, Maya Plisetskaya, Vladimir Preobrazhensky, and Alexei Yermolaev in the principal roles. The work did not have a success and was soon taken out of the repertoire. On April 25, 1957, Yuri Grigorovich staged his own version of the *Stone Flower* at the Leningrad Kirov Theatre which was acclaimed by audience and press alike. Two years later Lavrovsky produced the new version of the ballet in Moscow (March 7, 1959). N.Y. saw this version during the first U.S. tour of the Bolshoi Ballet in the spring of 1959 (premièred May 5) with Maya Plisetskaya alternating with Nina Timofeyeva, as Mistress of the Copper Mountain; Vladimir Vasiliev, as Danila, the stone-cutter who is working on the creation of a stone flower which he hopes will be his great work of art; Marina Kondratieva alternating with Yekaterina Maximova as Katerina, the girl with whom Danila is in love and who loves Danila; Vladimir Levashev as the evil bailiff who attempts to carry away Katerina and is stopped by the Mistress of the Copper Mountain who causes the earth to swallow him up (the most effective scene in the entire ballet). Soviet choreographers, dancers and critics consider the *Stone Flower* one of the greatest of contemporary ballets. To Western eyes the ballet is rather old-fashioned and padded with over-long character numbers. Prokofiev's score is not in a class with his *Prodigal Son, Romeo and Juliet,* or *Cinderella.*

Stoneham, Jean, British ballerina, b. Edinburgh, Scotland, 1929. Began her ballet studies with June Roper in Vancouver, B.C., at age nine; later studied with Louisa Macdonald and Nesta Toumine in Ottawa, dancing with the latter's Classical Ballet Concert Group of Ottawa. She became the first Canadian dancer to dance *Giselle* (partnered by Vladimir Dokoudovsky) at a command performance at which the Canadian Governor General Viscount Alexander and Lady Alexander were present (1948). Joined the Winnipeg (now Royal Winnipeg) Ballet (1951), dancing leading roles in both its classic and modern repertoire and also making many television appearances until retiring upon her marriage (1953).

Stop the Show, a phrase used when a dancer or number evokes applause of such intensity and duration (an ovation) that the show cannot continue for minutes. Alexandra Danilova has been known to stop the show with her mere entrance in a ballet closely associated with her, such as *Gaîté Parisienne.*

Story of Mankind. Modern dance work; chor.: Doris Humphrey; music: Lionel Nowak; costumes: Pauline Lawrence. First prod.: Belasco Theatre, N.Y., Jan. 5, 1947, with Beatrice Seckler and José Limón. Pauline Koner also frequently danced the woman's role. Based on a New Yorker magazine cartoon by Carl Rose, the *Story of Mankind* shows man and his mate scrambling their way from the paleolithic to the penthouse age, with a glance at the modes and manners of the periods on the way, and finishing back where they started as a newspaper announces the splitting of the atom.

Strain. See ACCIDENTS.

Strate, Grant, Canadian dancer and choreographer, b. Cardston, Alberta, 1927. B.A. and L.L.B., Univ. of Alberta. Studied modern dance with Laine Mets, Edmonton, Alberta; ballet with Celia Franca and Betty Oliphant, National Ballet School of Canada. Joined the newly founded National Ballet of Canada as dancer in 1951 and in 1958 was made assistant to artistic director Celia Franca. His ballets include *The Fisherman and His Soul, The Willow* (music: Arthur Foote, 1957), *Ballad, Antic Spring, House of Atreus,* and *Patterns,* the last-named choreographed for the National Ballet School and performed May 10, 1962, at Hart House Theatre, Toronto (music: Carl Maria von Weber). Received a Canada Council grant for study in U.S. and Europe (1962); taught at Juilliard School of Music (N.Y.) Dance Department, beg. Dec., 1962. Choreographed for Juilliard Dance Ensemble *House of Atreus* to the String Quartet No. 2 of Alberto Ginastera (Apr. 5, 1963). Completely revised version with a commissioned score by Harry Somers was premièred by National Ballet of Canada in Ottawa, Jan. 13, 1964, with Lois Smith (Electra), Jacqueline Ivings (Clytemnestra), Earl Kraul (Orestes), David Adams (Agamemnon). Took three months' leave of absence from National Ballet of Canada (Dec. 1965–Feb. 1966) for study in Europe. The Royal Flemish Opera Ballet, Antwerp, Belgium, commissioned a ballet from him for presentation in the spring of 1966.

Strauss, Johann, Jr. (1825–1899), Austrian composer known as "The Waltz King." He composed several hundred waltzes and innumerable polkas. Many choreographers have used his music in various arrangements to make a complete score, the most prominent examples being Leonide Massine's *Le Beau Danube* and David Lichine's *Graduation Ball.* His best-known light opera *Die Fledermaus* (The Bat; also known in U.S. as *Rosalinda*) is the basis of a ballet by Ruth Page. George Balanchine used the overture to *The Bat* for a ballet of the same title (1936).

Strauss, Richard (1864–1949), German composer. Composed the music for *The Legend of Joseph,* choreographed by Michel Fokine for the Diaghilev Ballets Russes (1914); and *Schlagobers,* choreographed by Heinrich Kröller for the Vienna State Opera Ballet (1924). His music for the dance interludes in Molière's *Bourgeois Gentilhomme* was used for a separate ballet choreographed by George Balanchine for Ballet Russe de Monte Carlo (Monte Carlo, 1932), and later for a new version (N.Y., 1944). Soviet choreographer Leonid Yacobson used his *Til Eulenspiegel* music for a one-act ballet staged for the graduation performance of the Leningrad School (1933), his first major work. Balanchine also used *Til Eulenspiegel's Merry Pranks* for his ballet *Tyl Ulenspiegel* (1951) for the New York City Ballet. This music has been used for ballet by both Vaslav Nijinsky and Jean Babilée. Antony Tudor used his *Burleska* for *Dim Lustre* (Ballet Theatre, 1943; revived for the N.Y. City Ballet, 1964). Frederick Ashton used the tone poem *Don Juan* for a ballet on the same subject, using the same title, for the Sadler's Wells Ballet (1948).

Strawbridge, Edwin, dancer, choreographer, actor, children's theatre director, b. York, Penna., d. New York City, Oct. 29, 1957. Studied at Academy of Dramatic Arts, N.Y. Appeared with Adolph Bolm's Ballet Intime, with Littlefield Ballet, and as premier danseur with Ravinia Opera Company. For many years toured U.S. for the Junior Programs organization, presenting theatre and dance performances for children.

Strobel, Fredric, American dancer, b. Chicago, 1936. After studying dance in Chicago with Elisa Stigler, Bernice Holmes and Robert Lunnon, came to N.Y. to study at the School of American Ballet, Ballet Theatre School, and with Robert Joffrey. At fourteen toured Fair Shows in the U.S. and Canada with Dorothy Hild and in N.Y. danced at Radio City Music Hall. Has been a soloist with Royal Winnipeg Ballet for several years, excluding an interim season with Ruth Page's Chicago Opera Ballet. Dances both classic and modern roles and created roles in *Twisted Heart* (Benjamin Harkarvy), *E Minor, Chinese Nightingale* (Heino Heiden), *A Court Occasion.* Has done much television work in Canada and summer stock at Winnipeg's Rainbow Stage.

Stroganova, Nina (Nina Rigmor Strom), dancer, teacher, b. Copenhagen; m. Vladimir Dokoudovsky. Studied ballet with Jenny Moller and teachers from the Royal Danish Ballet; later with Olga Preobrajenska in Paris; Ludmila Shollar, Anatole Vilzak, Bronislava Nijinska, Mikhail Mordkin, Vladimir Dokoudovsky in N.Y. Ballerina, Opéra Comique, Paris (1936); Mordkin Ballet, N.Y. (1937); Ballet Russe de Monte Carlo (1937); Ballet (now American Ballet) Theatre (1940); Original Ballet Russe (1942–47), and in its final European season after the death of Col. de Basil (1951–52). Her repertoire included *Swan Lake, Les Sylphides, Le Spectre de la Rose, Les Présages* (Frivolity and Passion), *Le Beau Danube, Giselle* (Queen of the Wilis and Giselle), *Pas de Quatre* (Lucile Grahn), and others. She was guest ballerina with the Royal Danish Ballet in 1950 when she was presented with a medal from members of the company and Danish balletomanes as the first Danish dancer trained outside the Royal Theatre to appear with the company. Appeared with her husband and their own ballet group at Jacob's Pillow Dance Festival (1956). Since 1947 has been teaching in N.Y.

Strolka, Egbert, German dancer, b. Berlin, 1935. Studied with Gustav Blank and Lotte Sevelin. Has danced with Municipal (now German) Opera, West Berlin (1953–56); Municipal Theatre, Wuppertal (1956–59); guest artist thereafter. Has made guest appearances in Wiesbaden, Vienna, Bregenz, Bonn, Heidelberg, and at the Berlin Festival. Principal roles include those in *The Sleeping Beauty, Peter and the Wolf, Jeu des Cartes. The Song of the Nightingale, The Miraculous Mandarin,* and others. Also makes frequent television appearances.

Struchkova, Raisa, Peoples' Artist of the U.S.S.R., Soviet ballerina, b. 1925; m. Alexander Lapauri. Entered the Bolshoi Ballet School in 1935, and was graduated in 1944. While only in her third year she created the role of the Baby Stork in the ballet of that name (1937–38). In 1941 she danced with great success in a concert of fifth- and sixth-year pupils, performing the choreographic étude *Spring* to music by Grieg. For her graduation performance she danced both the White and the Black Swan pas de deux from *Swan Lake.* The grace and lightness of her dancing and her strong technique were already evident. Her first major role with the Bolshoi Ballet was Lise in *La Fille Mal Gardée* and year by year since then she has added to her repertoire *Cinderella,* Maria (*The Fountain of Bakhchisarai*), Parasha (*The Bronze Horseman*), Jeanne (*Flames of Paris*), Odette-Odile (*Swan Lake*), Aurora (*The Sleeping Beauty*), Tao Hoa (*The Red Flower*), Juliet (*Romeo and Juliet*), Katerina (*The Stone Flower*), *Fadette,* Pascuala (*Laurencia*), Aisha (*Gayané*). As the Bacchante in "Walpurgis Night" from *Faust,* which she first danced in 1955, she had a chance to demonstrate her exceptional technique in

Raisa Struchkova, ballerina of the Moscow Bolshoi Ballet, with husband-partner Alexander Lapauri in spectacular Moszkowski Waltz.

semi-acrobatic pas de deux with difficult aerial lifts. She excels in this particular style and the *Moszkowski Waltz* which she performs with her husband and partner, Alexander Lapauri, is a stunning feat of virtuosity. She has appeared with him in more than fifteen countries including England, France, North and South America. She has also travelled much in the Soviet Union, where she is a great popular favorite.

Stuart, Muriel (Muriel Mary Stuart Popper), dancer and teacher, b. London, 1903. Studied dance with Anna Pavlova at Ivy House, London from age eight; also with Ivan Clustine, Enrico Cecchetti, Uday Shankar, Harald Kreutzberg, Martha Graham, Carmalita Maracci; dance composition with Louis Horst. Soloist, Pavlova company (1916–26). Opened school in San Francisco (1927); ballet mistress and soloist, Chicago Civic Opera (1930); opened school in Los Angeles (1931). On the faculty of School of American Ballet, N.Y., since 1934. Author of *The Classic Ballet: Basic Technique and Terminology* (N.Y., 1952).

Subligny, Marie (1666–1736), one of the first women dancers at the Paris Opéra. She succeeded Mlle. Lafontaine as première danseuse. When Subligny went to London for an engagement she took with her a letter of introduction to philosopher John Locke.

Suite en Blanc. Ballet in 1 act; chor.: Serge Lifar; music: Edouard Lalo (*Namouna,* 1882). First prod.: Paris Opéra Ballet, Paris Opéra, July 23, 1943, with Yvette Chauviré, Solange Schwarz, Lycette Darsonval, Serge Lifar, Roger Ritz, Roger Fenonjois. This was Lifar's first themeless ballet, danced in practice costumes, with the girls in simple white tutus, and without scenery. Lifar re-staged it with certain changes for Nouveau Ballet de Monte Carlo (1946) when it was retitled *Noir et Blanc.* It remained in the repertoire when the company was taken over by the Marquis de Cuevas.

Sujet, in French ballet, a term indicating a soloist. French ballet companies, particularly the companies at the National Opera Houses, are divided into: élèves (apprentice dancers), quadrille (corps de ballet), coryphés and coryphées (junior soloists), sujets (soloists), premières danseuses (ballerinas), premiers danseurs, étoiles (prima ballerinas and first male dancers). The designation corps de ballet in France applies to the company of dancers as a whole.

Sulich, Vasili, ballet dancer, b. Puscice, Yugoslavia, 1929. Studied with Ana Roje, Boris Kniaseff, and subsequently with nearly all the great Paris teachers. Began his career with the National Ballet of Zagreb (1946–49). Subsequently danced as soloist with a number of European ballet companies, among them those of Janine Charrat (1956–59), Milorad Miskovitch (1956), Ballets de Paris de Roland Petit, and Ludmilla Tcherina (both in 1959). Among his creations are roles in *Promethée* (Maurice Béjart, 1956), *L'Echelle* (Dick Sanders, 1956), *Pelléas et Mélisande* (George Skibine, 1957). Appeared at the Nervi Festival (1960) and later that summer danced with Massine's Ballet Européens at the Edinburgh International Festival of Music and Drama. In 1961 he staged the dance part (forty-minute prologue) in Jean Cocteau's *Oedipus and the Sphinx* to Maurice Thiriet's music for the Lyon Opéra. Sulich visited the U.S. in 1962 and upon his return to Europe he choreographed the same production for the Geneva Opera House. In May, 1963, he choreographed the "Bacchanal" in *Samson and Delilah* for Teatro Colón, Buenos Aires, Argentina. In 1964 he came to N.Y. with the Folies Bergère to dance with ballerina Lianne Montevecchi. While in N.Y. he was given a scholarship by Martha Graham to study in her school. He also took daily ballet lessons. Returned to Geneva to choreograph the dances in Mozart's *Idomineo* to be performed by the Serge Golovine company at the Opera House (1964).

Summer Day, A. Ballet in 1 act; chor.: Janine Charrat; music: Werner Egk; book: Paul Strecker; décor: Lothar Schenk von Trapp. First prod.: Städtische Oper, Berlin (West), Jan. 22, 1950. Unrestrained summertime gaiety in a girls' boarding school. The ballet is the middle part of a ballet trilogy by the painter Paul Strecker (1898–1950), whose first part is *The First Ball* and the third, *Chiarina.*

Summer Interlude. Ballet in 1 act; chor. and book: Michael Somes; music: Ottorio Respighi's arrangement of *Ancient Airs and Dances;* décor: Sophie Fedorovitch. First prod.: Sadler's Wells Theatre Ballet, Sadler's Wells Theatre, London, Mar. 28, 1950, with Patricia Miller (The Girl), Elaine Fifield (The Bathing Belle), Pirmin Trecu (The Boy), David Blair (The Young Man). The sophisticated Young Man is momentarily fascinated by the simplicity of the Young Girl, but the Bathing Belle easily wins him back. The Boy, who loves the Girl, seems at the end to be left with no one. This is Michael Somes' only ballet (1965).

Sumner, Carol, dancer, b. Brooklyn, N.Y., 1940. Began dance studies at age thirteen with Eileen O'Connor; continued at School of American Ballet, N.Y., and became an apprentice member of New York City Ballet after three years' study at the school. Became a regular member of the company after a few months; promoted to soloist (1963). Her many roles include Sacred Love (*Les Illuminations*), Marzipan Shepherdess (George Balanchine's *The Nutcracker*), leader of 1st Regiment (*Stars and Stripes*), 1st Pas de Trois (*Agon*), Prince's Bride (George Balanchine's *The Firebird*), 3rd Waltz (*La Valse*), Young Girl (*Souvenirs*). Creations include 4th Variation (*Raymonda Variations*), 2nd Couple (with Robert Rodham, *Fantasy*).

Sunday Ballet Club, a London performing club founded in 1958 which stages ballets by new choreographers at occasional Sunday evening performances. Choreographers whose works have been seen at these performances include Ray Powell, Clover Roope, Gillian Lynne, Peter Darrell. A number of ballets presented by the Club are now in the repertoires of several ballet companies, particularly Western Theatre Ballet.

Sundered Majesty. Modern dance work;

chor.: Myra Kinch; music: Manuel Galea; décor: John Christian. First prod.: Jacob's Pillow Dance Festival, Lee, Mass., 1955, by Myra Kinch and company with Ted Shawn as guest artist in the role of Lear, Myra Kinch (Cordelia), William Milié (Fool), Maxine Bacon (Goneril), Ella Lukk (Regan); N.Y. première: Brooklyn Academy of Music, Dec. 10, 1955. Shakespeare's King Lear seen at the moment of his madness in the storm when the vision of his children appears to him, the Fool in this context being the sinister introducer of his hallucinations.

Sur Place, literally, in place; in ballet, a step executed without moving from the place where the dancer is standing, such as fouettés sur place—a series of fouettés done on the same spot, without traveling.

Surinach, Carlos, composer, b. Barcelona, Spain, 1915. Studied piano, theory, harmony, counterpoint, composition, and orchestration at the Municipal Conservatory of Barcelona; later at the piano "oberklasse" of the Robert Schumann Conservatory, Düsseldorf; the class for conductors at the Hochschule, Cologne, with Prof. Eugen Papst. Admitted with a citation of "special distinction" to the Preussische Akademie der Kuenste, Berlin, under Prof. Max Trapp. His first important engagements were as conductor of the Barcelona Philharmonic Orchestra (1944) and as one of the conductors of the Gran Teatro del Liceo Opera House in that city. Moved to Paris (1947), appearing as guest conductor of the Lamoureux Orchestra, the Orchestre Nationale, and Radio-symphonique. Made frequent guest appearances with European orchestras, often conducting his own works. Has lived in N.Y. since 1951, now principally composing. One of his first important commissions came from the Bethsabee de Rothschild Foundation (1952) for the score which became the Doris Humphrey work *Ritmo Jondo*. Other scores for dance works include *Embattled Garden* and *Acrobats of God* for Martha Graham, and *Apasionada* for Pearl Lang. He wrote the score for *David and Bath-Sheba* for C.B.S. television, choreographed by John Butler (1960). The following year Norman Morrice used this music for *A Place in the Desert,* produced for the Ballet Rambert. Morrice also used Surinach's *Tientos* and *Doppio Concertino* as the score for *Hazana*. John Butler used his *Concertino for Piano, Strings and Cymbals* for *La Sibila* premièred at the Spoleto Festival of Two Worlds (1959). Surinach has transcribed for orchestra seven sections of the Albeniz piano suite *Iberia* to complete the set begun by Enrique Fernandez Arbos, who transcribed five. The famous Spanish dancer-choreographer Antonio has used this for his work *Cordoba,* premièred May 1, 1960, at the Gran Teatro del Liceo, Barcelona. Alvin Ailey's ballet *Feast of Ashes,* based on the Lorca play *The House of Bernarda Alba,* in the repertoire of the Robert Joffrey Ballet, used Surinach's *Doppio Concertino* and a section of *Ritmo Jondo* not used in the Humphrey work, the composer creating several minutes of music to bridge the two scores (1962). Was commissioned by the Harkness Ballet (1966) to compose the score for a ballet by Salvador Dali entitled *Space Unlimited* for which Dali had both written the story and designed the décor. Brian Macdonald was invited to choreograph the work. Was awarded the Arnold Bax Society Medal for non-Commonwealth Composers given annually by the Harriet Cohen International Music Awards (London).

Suspension. Modern dance work; chor.: May O'Donnell; music: Ray Green's *Music for Piano and Percussion*. First prod.: May O'Donnell Dance Company, YM-YWHA, N.Y., Apr. 6, 1952. The inspiration comes from T. S. Eliot's ". . . at the still point of the turning world—there the dance is." The work is themeless, notable for the sense of timelessness achieved by the curving sweep of the movement and the sustained balances.

Sutherland, Paul, American dancer, b. Louisville, Ky., 1935; m. Marie Paquet. Early dance studies with Ross Hancock. Before joining the Robert Joffrey Ballet (1958) he danced with American Ballet Theatre, Royal Winnipeg Ballet, and William Dollar's Concert Group. Between seasons with the Joffrey company he and his wife danced with American Ballet Theatre on its 1960 tour of Europe. He dances a large repertoire including the following creations: Gerald Arpino's *Partita for Four* and *Sea Shadow;* The Bridegroom in Alvin Ailey's *Feast of Ashes;* Brian Macdonald's *Les Caprices;* Robert Joffrey's *Gamelan.* Has appeared on television shows including "Omnibus," and others. Re-joined American Ballet Theatre in the summer of 1964 and is currently (1966) a principal dancer.

Svetlov, Valerian (Ivchenko) (1860–1934), outstanding Russian ballet critic, writer, editor. He wrote innumerable articles on the ballet in Russian and French. Outside Russia he is known principally for his monumental volume *Le Ballet Contemporain* (1911), published simultaneously in Russian and French. Left Russia in 1917 and settled in Paris. Was married to ballerina Vera Trefilova.

French-born ballerina Marina Svetlova of the original Ballet Russe, the Metropolitan Opera Ballet, and her own group (1944–58).

Svetlova, Marina (Yvette von Hartmann), ballerina, b. Paris, France, of Russian parents, 1922; U.S. citizen since 1947. Studied with Vera Trefilova, Lubov Egorova, Olga Preobrajenska, Anatole Vilzak, Edward Caton, Victor Gsovsky. Made her debut in Leonide Massine's *Amphion* for Ida Rubinstein's company at the Paris Opéra (1931). Soloist, Original Ballet Russe (1939–41), dancing leading roles in *Paganini, Les Sylphides, Aurora's Wedding,* and others; Ballet (now American Ballet) Theatre (spring season, 1943); première danseuse, Metropolitan Opera Ballet (1943–50); première danseuse, N.Y. City Center Opera (1951–52). Since 1944 she has had her own group which annually tours the U.S. and Canada and has at various times toured in Central and South America, India, Greece, Israel, and in Europe. She has also been guest ballerina with European ballet companies. Since 1958 has also conducted a summer school at an art center in Vermont.

Swan, Paul, dancer, b. Nebraska, ca.

1889. Known in the 1920's as "the most beautiful man in the world," he was largely self-taught. He gave recitals in Paris and London, and was the founder and director of the School of the Aesthetic Ideal, N.Y. In his later years he gave weekly Sunday night programs in Studio 90, Carnegie Hall, where he also exhibited his paintings and sculptures.

Swan Lake. Ballet in prologue and 3 acts (today often described as ballet in 4 acts); chor.: original version, Julius Reisinger; music: Peter Tchaikovsky; book: V. P. Begitcheff and Vasily Geltzer (father of Yekaterina Geltzer, famous ballerina); décor: Shangin, Valtz, and Groppius. First prod.: Bolshoi Theatre, Moscow, Feb. 20, 1877 (old style), Mar. 4 (new style), with Pauline Karpakova as Odette-Odile and Gillert II as Siegfried. Both Reisinger and Karpakova took many liberties with the score: changed the sequence of dances, omitted some numbers, added some from other ballets. The resulting production, though not very successful, remained in the Moscow repertoire as long as the scenery lasted. The Danish ballet master of the Bolshoi Ballet, Emil Hansen, revived it in 1880 and 1882 with no more success than the original. Tchaikovsky died believing that his score for *Swan Lake* was a complete failure. A second version choreographed by Marius Petipa (1st and 3rd acts) and Lev Ivanov (2nd and 4th acts), in décor by Botcharov and Levogt, was staged at the Maryinsky Theatre, St. Petersburg, Jan. 27, 1895, with Pierina Legnani as Odette-Odile and Paul Gerdt as Siegfried. It was immediately successful and has never been out of the repertoire since. Petipa outlined the entire ballet and staged the numbers for Acts 1 and 3, while Ivanov was responsible for the lyrical, romantic tenderness of the two "white acts." In 1911 Alexander Gorsky re-staged this version with some changes (notably in the introduction of the Jester) for the Bolshoi Theatre, Moscow, and it is this version the Russian companies today follow. (See also entry SWAN LAKE, chor.: Vladimir Bourmeister.) The one-act *Swan Lake* (Act 2) versions danced by most companies everywhere are based on the *Swan Lake* staged from the St. Petersburg version by Anatole Vilzak for Diaghilev Ballets Russes. George Balanchine staged it in his own choreography, retaining the famous pas de quatre of the Little Swans for New York City Ballet (1951) with Maria Tallchief and André Eglevsky in the leading roles and with Patricia Wilde and Yvonne Mounsey heading a pas de trois and pas de neuf, respectively, of Balanchine's creation. Outstanding Swan Queens in the one-act version have been Olga Spessivtseva (for the Diaghilev Ballets Russes—she danced the full-length version in Russia), Alexandra Danilova, Alicia Markova, Irina Baronova, Tamara Toumanova, Nana Gollner, Alicia Alonso, among others. The Ballroom scene (Act 3) was revived in the U.S. under the title *The Magic Swan* by Alexandra Fedorova for Ballet Russe de Monte Carlo (1941). In it Tamara Toumanova wore a black tutu, which is the origin of the title *Black Swan* pas de deux. Vic-Wells (later Sadler's Wells, now Royal) Ballet revived the complete version staged by Nicholas Sergeyev, which followed the St. Petersburg production, at Sadler's Wells Theatre, London, Nov. 24, 1934, in décor by Hugh Stevenson, with Alicia Markova as Odette-Odile and Robert Helpmann as Siegfried. It was entirely re-staged by this company at the New Theatre, London, Sept. 7, 1943, in décor by Leslie Hurry with Margot Fonteyn and Robert Helpmann. Hurry re-designed an enlarged version for the company at Royal Opera House, Covent Garden, Dec. 18, 1952, with Beryl Grey and John Field heading the cast on that occasion. The Royal Ballet ballerinas who have danced the dual role are Pamela May, Moira Shearer, Violetta Elvin, Nadia Nerina, Svetlana Beriosova, Antoinette Sibley, among others; Michael Somes, John Hart, Bryan Ashbridge, Philip Chatfield, Desmond

Doyle, David Blair, Ronald Hynd, are some of the Siegfrieds. Sir Frederick Ashton re-choreographed parts of the 1963 production of the ballet (Prologue, pas de douze to the Waltz in Act 1; pas de quatre in place of the original pas de trois; entry of the Brides in the ballroom scene and general dance; and Act 4). The ballet as a whole was staged by Robert Helpmann. In Russia, Marina Semyonova, Galina Ulanova, Maya Plisetskaya, Nina Timofeyeva, among others, are noted interpreters of what is probably the most exacting role in ballet. Constantin Sergeyev, Vladimir Preobrajensky, Nicolai Fadeyechev, Vladilen Semenov, are outstanding Soviet Siegfrieds. Other full-length versions have been those of the International Ballet, staged by Sergeyev in décor by William Chappell and premièred at the Adelphi Theatre, London, Mar. 18, 1947, with Mona Inglesby and Jack Spurgeon; the production staged by Mary Skeaping, largely following the St. Petersburg version, for the Royal Swedish Ballet (1953) with Mariane Orlando and Teddy Rhodin. British choreographer Jack Carter staged a full-length version, using the original 1877 score exactly as it was composed, for the Teatro Colón, Buenos Aires, May 28, 1963, when different dancers were the Odette and the Odile (Norma Fontenla and Esmeralda Agoglia), with Enrique Lommi as Siegfried.

The story of the full-length version is as follows: Prince Siegfried, merry-making with his friends on the occasion of his birthday, is told by his mother that he must now choose a bride and that he must make his choice at a great ball when the eligible princesses will be displayed for that purpose. He goes into the forest to hunt wild swans, where he meets the beautiful Swan Queen, Odette, under the spell of the magician Rothbart. Only at night can she resume her human shape. She tells Siegfried that only when a man loves her to the exclusion of all other women will the spell of the magician be broken. Siegfried swears eternal love before she is drawn away by the magician. Siegfried, still dreaming of Odette, rejects the brides who dance before him at the ball. Then the magician enters in disguise, bringing with him his beauteous daughter Odile who has assumed the appearance of Odette. Delighted, Siegfried dances with her and declares that she and she alone will be his bride. Immediately he has sworn this oath von Rothbart and Odile disappear, Siegfried sees the despairing Odette at the window and realizes he has been tricked. Rushing back to the lake he finds Odette about to kill herself. Together they defy the magician, after which Odette, and then Siegfried, plunge into the lake. This breaks the spell, the magician dies, and Odette and Siegfried live happily ever after in the kingdom beneath the lake where life and love are eternal. In the Soviet version, Siegfried defeats the magician in combat, the spell is broken as his great owl wings are torn away, and the living Odette and Siegfried are united. When only Act 2 is given, it is a matter of the director's choice as to whether von Rothbart strikes Siegfried down by his magic or Siegfried is left to watch as the Swan Queen and the other enchanted princesses float back across the lake. Robert Helpmann's introduction of the idea that the Swan Queen flies across the sky at the end has been retained by the Royal Ballet and is followed by some other companies. It does away with the often wobbly passage across the back cloth of the wooden Swans which frequently ruins what should be a romantic moment.

Swan Lake. Ballet in 4 acts with a prologue; chor.: Vladimir Bourmeister (1st, 3rd, and 4th acts) and after Lev Ivanov (2nd act); music: Peter Tchaikovsky; book: Vladimir Begichev and Vassily Geltzer; décor: Anatole Lushin. First performed in this version at the Stanislavsky and Nemirovich-Danchenko Lyric Theatre, Moscow, Apr. 24, 1953, with Violetta Bovt (Odette-Odile) and Oleg Chichinadze (Siegfried). In his version of *Swan*

Lake, Bourmeister used the original Tchaikovsky score of 1877, with the exception of Act 2, which he left intact with Ivanov's choreography (revived by Pyotr Gusev) and Riccardo Drigo's interpolations of other Tchaikovsky numbers and arrangement of the score. Bourmeister's version begins with a prologue wherein the princess, Odette, is turned into a swan by the evil magician while gathering flowers at a lakeside. In Act 3 the entire divertissement is conceived as sorcery of the evil magician. The ballet ends with the overflowing of the lake in a great flood as originally envisioned by Tchaikovsky. Odette throws herself into the lake in order to save Siegfried. The force of her love breaks the spell. The Bourmeister *Swan Lake* was the great success of the Stanislavsky Ballet's appearance at the Châtelet Theatre, Paris (1956). In 1960 Bourmeister staged it for the Paris Opéra, with Josette Amiel and Peter van Dijk dancing Odette-Odile and Siegfried at its première, Dec. 21.

Swan of Tuonela, The. Ballet in 1 act; chor. and book: Dennis Gray; music: Jean Sibelius; décor and costumes: Mario Conde. First prod.: Teatro Municipal, Rio de Janeiro, 1956, with Ady Addor (The Swan), Johnny Franklin (Troubadour, Helga Loreida (The Princess). The plot is based on the Finnish epic *Kalevala* of which "The Swan of Tuonela" is a part. Tuonela is the Finnish conception of Hades. The Swan glides in the black river which surrounds it. With the help of the Swan, the Troubadour saves the Princess from Tuonela.

Sweden, Ballet in.

BY ANNA GRETA STÅHLE.

Ballet originally came to Sweden as entertainment for the Royal family and court. The French ballet master Antoine de Beaulieu was engaged to create a court ballet after the French pattern. The first ballet performance in Sweden took place in 1638, and was followed by many others to celebrate important events such as royal weddings and military victories. The first professional dancers came to Sweden when King Gustav III founded an opera in Stockholm in 1773. Again a French ballet master was engaged. Louis Gallodier of the Paris Opéra assembled twenty-four dancers, most of them French but some Swedish. This troupe danced in the first production, the opera *Thétis and Pélée,* a very successful debut.

The ensemble grew and in ten years included seventy-two members. The first years the leading dancers were all French, but soon Swedish artists developed enough skill to be promoted to soloists. Interest in ballet grew and performances and dancers were often described in contemporary letters and memoirs. King Gustav loved the theatre and even appeared on the stage himself. He wrote dramas and operas and created a distinctive "Gustavian style" that has influenced Swedish literature and theatre ever since. It is significant that his own court theatre at the Drottningholm Palace has been preserved to show posterity an eighteenth century theatre complete with its stage machinery, settings, and costumes.

Under Gallodier the ballet had been pre-Noverre, but it underwent a significant change when Antoine Bournonville, a pupil of Noverre, was added to the ensemble in 1781 as a dancer and choreographer. He staged several ballets of great charm, among them *Les Meuniers Provençaux* (1785) and *Les Pêcheurs* (1789). Another French dancer and choreographer of importance was Marcadet.

The king appreciated his dancers so much that the ballerina, Madame du Tillet, earned a higher salary than the leading singer. The king encouraged the dancers to perfect their art and gave scholarships to the most talented to go to Paris and study under the best teachers. He sent the Stockholm-born Charles Didelot to Paris and paid for his studies for several years, but received very little reward in return for his generosity. Didelot returned as premier danseur in 1786 but left again in 1789 to begin an international career.

The Royal Swedish Ballet continued its ties with France for several decades after Gustav's time. Most of the ballet masters were French and ballets which were successful at the Paris Opéra were often staged in Stockholm soon after. *Giselle* was danced by the Royal Swedish Ballet in 1845; the original score is still in the library.

A great personality among the leading artists was Filippo Taglioni who was premier danseur during 1803–1804 and acted as ballet master in 1818. He married Sophia Karsten, daughter of a Swedish opera singer, and their daughter Maria was born in Stockholm. During his short tenure as ballet master, he staged two of his own ballets and, what was more important, redesigned the costumes to make real elevation possible. Maria Taglioni did not return to her native city until 1841 when she danced a suite from *La Sylphide* and *Le Lac des Fées* and created such a Taglioni fever that the Opera management considered giving her an apartment in the theatre, so violent was the enthusiasm whenever she left the stage door.

Maria Taglioni deprived the Royal Swedish Ballet of its most promising premier danseur, 24-year-old Christian Johansson. He was her partner in *Le Lac des Fées* and she realized immediately how great a dancer he was. She persuaded him to leave Sweden and follow her to Russia. Christian Johansson had been trained in the Royal Swedish Ballet school and the theatre had sent him to Copenhagen for further study under August Bournonville. Back in Stockholm he had been premier danseur from 1837 to 1841. In St. Petersburg he very soon took up teaching and played a most important role in the training of generations of Russian dancers.

The Royal Swedish Ballet acquired its first native ballet master, Anders Selinder, in 1833. Selinder can in many ways be compared with August Bournonville: he had the same ambition to create a national repertoire and also introduced the Romantic ballet to Sweden. None of his own ballets about elves, sylphides, or roses have been preserved, but one of his creations, a folk dance arrangement, is still performed. Selinder studied Swedish folk dances and used them in several ballets. He arranged a series of lovely dances for a folklore musical play, *Värmlänningarna* (People of Värmland) in 1846. The play is still a great favorite and by tradition is given at Christmas by the Royal Theatre. The national movement to revive the old folk dances had begun at the turn of the century, but it was Selinder's collection of dances, taught by a former member of the Royal Swedish Ballet, that formed its basis. Without Anders Selinder most of these dances would have been lost.

August Bournonville was guest choreographer several times with the Royal Swedish Ballet and many of his ballets were given. However, around 1860 there was a definite decline in the ballet. The management turned to opera and had little understanding of the dance as an art. However, the few dancers the Royal Theatre retained were fairly well trained.

At the beginning of the twentieth century the public in Stockholm enjoyed several dance events. Isadora Duncan gave a recital in 1906 and was a great inspiration to the artistic world, and in 1908 Anna Pavlova gave her first dance performance outside Russia. She was received with enormous enthusiasm and awarded a Litteris et Artibus medal by the king. She has described how silent masses of people gathered in front of her hotel waiting to show their gratitude. She was very touched by the reception in Stockholm which encouraged her to continue touring.

Since there was a public for dance artists, the time finally came when the Royal Swedish Ballet was allowed to give it valuable programs.

In 1913 Michel and Vera Fokine were invited as guest artists. Fokine staged some of his ballets which were presented with himself and his wife in the main roles, supported by Swedish artists. Like all gifted choreographers, he spotted potential talents among the very young, gave them their first parts and encouraged them to further studies. Three of these youngsters became internationally known: Jenny Hasselqvist, Carina Ari, and Jean Börlin. All three studied under Fokine while he was in Denmark. Jenny Hasselqvist was the ballerina of Les Ballets Suédois and appeared as dancer and actress in several famous Swedish silent films. Carina Ari also became a ballerina of Les Ballets Suédois, but eventually remained in Paris. She became ballet mistress of the Opéra Comique, and danced with Serge Lifar at the Paris Opéra. Les Ballets Suédois was a company formed by balletomane Rolf de Maré. It acquired several of the Royal Swedish Ballet's best artists. The principal dancer and choreographer during the company's existence (1920–25) was Jean Börlin.

Fokine returned several times to Stockholm, each visit resulting in a momentary renaissance of the ballet. But it was very difficult for the small Swedish ensemble to maintain its standards. There was no artistic tradition and no organization upon which to rely. Still the situation was far better than it had been before Fokine's first visit. Some quite charming ballets from the repertoire of Les Ballets Suédois were introduced by Börlin. In 1928 the Pole Jan Cieplinski, who was engaged as ballet master, staged some of the classics. He was succeeded in 1931 by Julian Algo who was really more a modern than a classic dancer. Algo was a pupil of Rudolf von Laban at the time of his most exciting experiments.

Algo staged "after" Fokine, Massine, and Nijinska, but he also staged his own ballets in an expressionistic style. In 1940 the Finnish choreographer George Gué was invited to Stockholm. He was at his best in lyrical ballets; his *Concerto* to music by Chopin was regarded as his finest work. He also reproduced Fokine and Petipa ballets with varying results. The dancers were not trained as a professional troupe of today; the theatre was satisfied if they were capable of appearing in operas and gave an occasional evening of ballet. There was talent and personality among the dancers, but very few technicians. Gué, who often arranged dances for operettas, avoided the difficult steps and replaced them with theatrical effects and glittering décor. Ballet in the 'Forties was very much of a show.

The discriminating public in Stockholm found ballet at the Royal Theatre in bad taste and turned its attention to groups of young dancers outside the Royal Swedish Ballet. Kurt Jooss visited Sweden several times; the public also knew Mary Wigman quite well. Each year brought interesting dance personalities to Stockholm, such as Harald Kreutzberg and Alexander von Swain. When Birgit Cullberg and Ivo Cramér formed their own groups it was a national answer to a modern dance movement that was already familiar. These two young artists had the cultural background and contemporary ideas that the old ballet lacked. They were witty and idealistic, they had a fine feeling for décor, music, and literature. Their performances received an enormous response from the public.

Leading dancers at the Royal Swedish Ballet during the period between World Wars I and II were Lisa Steier, Ebon Strandin, Sven Tropp, Otto Thoresen, Valborg Franchi (who for many years taught the children's classes), Elly Holmberg, Cissi Olsson, Brita Appelgren, Teodora Lagerborg, Carl Gustaf Kruuse, and Teddy Rhodin.

The first steps toward reforming the Royal Swedish Ballet were taken in 1950 when Antony Tudor came as director of the ballet. The Latvians Nina and Albert Kozlovsky were engaged as teachers for the children. They introduced the Vaganova system into the school. Tudor stayed only a year, but during that time staged

Giselle and his own works *Lilac Garden* and *Gala Performance*. He gave the company proper training and was a great inspiration to all the dancers.

Mary Skeaping introduced herself to Stockholm in 1953 with a full-length *Swan Lake* based on the Nicholas Sergeyev version. The performance was an immediate success with the public and had a stimulating effect on the dancers. In 1954 the Royal Theatre asked her to accept the post of ballet director and try to bring the company up to an international level. She encountered many difficulties. The Royal Swedish Ballet was not really a company in its own right; it served most of the time as an opera ballet. It had no repertoire. Ballets were staged and danced for a time, then were dropped and forgotten. Ballet performances were very irregular because the opera always received primary consideration.

Fortunately, Mary Skeaping had had a rich experience with ballet companies in many parts of the world, and she recognized what had to be done. She built a solid repertoire of classical works. She let the artists alternate in leading roles to give them as much experience as possible. The dancers responded enthusiastically and developed their technique. Among her productions for the Royal Swedish Ballet, *Giselle* and *The Sleeping Beauty* should be mentioned. Both are very complete versions, as true to the originals as possible. She also tried to encourage Swedish choreographers and to keep their works in the repertoire.

It is the modern national repertoire that has given the Royal Swedish Ballet a personality. In the 'Fifties the Royal Theatre commissioned ballets from three Swedish choreographers. The pioneer among them was Birgit Cullberg. Her masterpiece, *Miss Julie*, was such a success in 1950 when it was first danced on a tour by Riksteatern, that it was brought straight to the Royal Theatre. With *Miss Julie* came the young ballerina Elsa-Marianne von Rosen, at the time a free-lance dancer. The theatre engaged her as premiere danseuse and for a long time Birgit Cullberg created roles specifically for her. Later von Rosen shared the ballerina roles in all the classics. Cullberg stayed as resident choreographer with the company until 1957 and soon afterwards her international career began.

By 1961 the Royal Swedish Ballet had danced a dozen ballets by Cullberg, including *Miss Julie, Medea, Oscar's Ball,* the Swedish fairy tale ballet *Ungersvennen och de Sex Prinsessorna* (The Young Man and the Six Princesses), *Pas de Coq, Romeo and Juliet, The Three Musketeers, Serenade, Moon Reindeer, Lady from the Sea, Odysseus,* and *Eden.*

Ivo Cramér added two works to the repertoire: *The Prodigal Son* (1957) and *The Linden Tree* (1958). *The Prodigal Son* has been one of the company's special treasures. The modern dancer Birgit Åkesson was inspired to create works for the company; her ballets, *Sisyphus, The Minotaur,* and *Rites,* to commissioned scores by Sweden's modern composers Karl-Birger Blomdahl and Ingvar Lidholm, have aroused great interest.

Leonide Massine, Antony Tudor and George Balanchine are all represented in the current repertoire of the Royal Swedish Ballet. The leading dancers of the last decade have been Bjorn Holmgren, Mariane Orlando, Caj Selling, Ellen Rasch, Gunnel Lindgren, Gerd Andersson, Verner Klavsen, Loulou Portefaix, Yvonne Brosset, and the youngest: Berit Sköld, Conny Berg, Kari Sylwan, and Nils Wingvist.

Since the Second World War Sweden has had a succession of distinguished visitors: New York City Ballet, Grand Ballet du Marquis de Cuevas, London's Festival Ballet, Jerome Robbins' Ballets: U.S.A., the Peking Opera, and the Japanese Kabuki company, the Indians Ram Gopal and Mrinalini Sarabhai. The Royal Swedish Ballet has toured abroad. The Swedish dancers have appeared in Berlin (1953), Nervi, Italy (1956), Edinburgh

Festival (1957), Seville (1958), Paris (1959), East Germany and China (1960).

Swedish Dance Theatre, founded in 1946 by Birgit Cullberg and Ivo Cramér with a group of dancers, mostly pupils of Kurt Jooss. Repertory included ballets by the two founders. The troupe toured Sweden, Norway, Denmark, Holland, Belgium, and Czechoslovakia. It was disbanded in 1947.

Sweeney Todd. Ballet in 1 act; chor.: John Cranko; commissioned music: Malcolm Arnold; décor: Alix Stone. First prod.: Royal Ballet, Stratford-on-Avon, Dec. 10, 1959, with Donald Britton (The Demon Barber), Elizabeth Anderton (Johanna), Desmond Doyle (Mark). The theme follows the famous Victorian melodrama of the *Demon Barber of Fleet Street* whose victims ended up as meat pies until the gory doings were exposed by the honest sailor, Mark.

Swinson, Cyril (1910–1962), English writer on ballet, editor and publisher of books on ballet. Joined publishing house A. & C. Black (1927); returned there after army service in India in World War II. Took over and built up A. & C. Black's outstanding list of ballet books. His own publications include *Façade and Other Early Ballets of Frederick Ashton; Three Fokine Ballets; The Nutcracker* (monographs published under the pseudonym of Joseph Sandon); *Ballet for Boys and Girls* (1952, called *The Ballet* in its American edition, written under the pseudonym of Hugh Fisher); *The Story of the Sadler's Wells Ballet* (1954); *The Sadler's Wells Theatre Ballet* (1956); *Guidebook to the Ballet* (1961, in the "Teach Yourself" series of the English Universities Press). Edited *Dancers of Today* series (fifteen titles) and *Dancers and Critics* (1950); on editorial board of the *Ballet Annual.*

Swoboda, Maria (Yurieva), former dancer, now teacher, b. St. Petersburg; m. Vecheslav Swoboda. Studied dance with Lydia Nelidova in Moscow and entered Bolshoi Theatre, Moscow, at age fifteen. Left Russia after revolution in 1917 and danced with group organized by her and her husband through the Balkans, France, Germany, Italy. Both came to U.S. as ballerina and premier danseur of Chicago Civic Opera Company; made several tours of U.S. Opened N.Y. school (1937) and after the death of Swoboda (1948) continued until 1954, when the school became the company school of Ballet Russe de Monte Carlo with herself as head teacher.

Swoboda, Vecheslav (1892–1948), dancer and teacher, b. Moscow; m. Maria Yurieva. Graduated into the Moscow Bolshoi Theatre from the School at age sixteen, later becoming soloist. Made concert tours through Russia with Yekaterina Geltzer; appeared in over fifty Russian films. Danced with Diaghilev Ballets Russes in Paris and London; also with Ida Rubinstein in Paris. Toured Europe with his and his wife's group. Came to U.S. with his wife as ballet master and first dancer of Chicago Civic Opera Company; made several tours of U.S. One-time official instructor of Ballet Russe de Monte Carlo. Established school in N.Y. (1937) where he taught until his death.

Sword Dance, originated from the Spartan Pyrrhic dance and the Roman Troy-Game. The Sword Dance was done in Nuremberg in 1350 and later was often part of the court ballet when mock battles were staged between Summer and Winter, etc. The Scottish Sword Dance developed from this.

Sylphide, La. Ballet in two acts; chor.: Filippo Taglioni; music: Jean Schneitzhoeffer; book: Adolphe Nourrit; décor: P. L. C. Ciceri; costumes: Eugène Lami. First prod.: Théâtre de l'Académie Royale de Music, March 12, 1832, with the choreographer's daughter Maria Taglioni, for whom the ballet was created, in the title role. This was the work which inaugurated the Romantic era in ballet. The subject matter of the ballet is typical of the Romantic period: the juxtaposition of the mortal with the supernatural. The plot of *La Sylphide* deals with James, a Scots peasant about to marry a peasant girl, Effie. A Sylphide, however, is in love with James and on his wedding day she makes herself visible to him, whereupon he, in turn, falls in love with her. Leaving his bride-to-be, relatives and wedding guests behind, he escapes with the Sylphide. He, a simple mortal, soon realizes that he will have difficulties in trying to keep the flying Sylphide by his side. While the Sylphide is flying around with her friends, the sylphs, James sees Old Madge, a sorceress in whom he confides his troubles. The sorceress offers him a magic scarf and tells him to tie it around the Sylphide's waist; this will make her wings drop off and she will be unable to fly. After the departure of the sorceress, the Sylphide flies in. James ties the scarf around her waist, the wings drop off, and she falls to the ground as if stricken by a mortal blow. The sylphs appear from all sides and surround the Sylphide, who dies in their arms. James in deep sorrow kneels beside her. The sylphs lift the body of the Sylphide and carry her away from the stricken James. The costume which Eugène Lami designed for Maria Taglioni and the sylphs—tight-fitting bodice, leaving bare the shoulders and neck, with the white tarlatan, muslin, or silk, many-layered skirt reaching between the knee and the ankle, became the standard costume (the Romantic tutu) of the female dancer in the Romantic ballets. Another significance of the ballet is that Maria Taglioni was supposed to have actually danced *La Sylphide* on her toes as understood in ballet now, and not on a high half-toe. Following the Paris première, the ballet was performed by Taglioni at Covent Garden, London, July 28, 1832; the Bolshoi Theatre, St. Petersburg, Sept. 6–18, 1837; Teatro alla Scala, Milan, May 29, 1841. The ballet is still being performed by several European ballet companies. The Royal Danish Ballet performs *La Sylphide* to different music and with different choreography in a version also in the repertoire of American Ballet Theatre.

Sylphide, La (Sylfiden). Romantic ballet in 2 acts; chor.: August Bournonville; music: Hermann von Løvenskjold. First prod.: Royal Danish Ballet, Copenhagen, 1836. Bournonville saw Filippo Taglioni's *La Sylphide* in Paris (1834) and staged it with his own choreography to new music for his favorite pupil, Lucile Grahn, with himself as James. The ballet has been in the repertoire of the Danish company ever since. From time to time it has been somewhat revised by Harald Lander. Lander also staged this version for the Grand Ballet du Marquis de Cuevas (1953), with Rosella Hightower and Serge Golovine; for Teatro alla Scala, Milan, with Carla Fracci and Mario Pistoni (1962); for the Nederlands Nationaal Ballet, with Sonja van Beers and Ben de Rochemont (1963). Harald Lander's production in décor by Robert O'Hearn, with additional music by Edgar Cosma, was also staged for American Ballet Theatre; première: San Antonio, Texas, Nov. 11, 1964, with Toni Lander (La Sylphide) and Royes Fernandez (James); N.Y. première: Mar. 18, 1965, with the same dancers. Elsa-Marianne von Rosen staged the Bournonville version with additions by Ellen Price de Plane, a recognized authority on Bournonville choreography in Denmark, for Ballet Rambert, Sadler's Wells Theatre, London, July 20, 1960, in décor by Robin and Christopher Ironside, with von Rosen in the title role, Flemming Flindt (James), Gillian Martlew (Madge), Shirley Dixon (Effie). In order to avoid confusion with *Les Sylphides,* Ballet Rambert always uses the title *The Sylphide.*

Sylphides, Les. Ballet in 1 act; chor.: Michel Fokine; music: Frédéric Chopin (Nocturne in A flat, op. 32, No. 2; Waltz in G flat, op. 70, No. 1; Mazurka in C, op. 67, No. 3; Mazurka in D, op. 33, No. 2; Prelude in A, op. 28, No. 7; Waltz in C sharp minor, op. 64, No. 2; Waltz in F flat, op. 18, No. 1); décor: Alexandre Benois. Alexander Glazounov orchestrated the Chopin pieces for the original production and there have been many orchestrations since: Nicholas Tcherepnine, Igor Stravinsky, Anatole Liadov, and, most recently, Sir Malcolm Sargent for the Royal Ballet (1963). Kurt-Heinz Stolze, musical director of the Stuttgart State Opera Ballet also introduced some piano solos into the score (1963). The ballet, under the title *Chopiniana,* was originally presented at a charity performance for the Society for the Prevention of Cruelty to Children at the Maryinsky Theatre, St. Petersburg, Mar. 8, 1908, with Olga Preobrajenska, Anna Pavlova, Tamara Karsavina, Vera Fokina, and Vaslav Nijinsky. At this performance it opened with a Polonaise, which was danced by a number of couples in Polish costumes. The Nocturne came next. It showed the composer in the monastery on Majorca tortured by visions of dead monks until he is rescued by his Muse. The Mazurka was the scene of a Polish wedding. It ended with a Tarantella, danced by Vera Fokina and an ensemble. The ballet was staged for the Serge Diaghilev Ballets Russes in the form we know today and premièred at the Théâtre du Châtelet, Paris, June 2, 1909, with Pavlova (Mazurka), Nijinsky (Mazurka—male solo), Karsavina (Waltz), Alexandra Baldina (Prelude), Pavlova and Nijinsky (Waltz pas de deux). The titles *Les Sylphides* was suggested by the costumes, the long Romantic tutu first worn by Maria Taglioni in the ballet *La Sylphide* (Filippo Taglioni, 1832). *Les Sylphides* is purely a Romantic ballet without a story, one of the loveliest and most poetic. It is in the repertoire of almost every major and several minor ballet companies with a greater or lesser degree of authenticity. Fokine staged it for the Royal Danish Ballet under the original title of *Chopiniana* (1925) to avoid confusion with the Bournonville ballet *La Sylphide* (Sylfiden). He also revived it for René Blum's Ballet de Monte Carlo (1936) and Ballet (now American Ballet) Theatre (1940). Though each company has its own scenery, the costumes are always Romantic tutus, with the male dancer in white tights and black jacket over a long-sleeved white blouse. The original wig of long blond hair curling to the shoulders is no longer used. In the Soviet Union the ballet remains in the repertoire of the state ballet companies under the title *Chopiniana,* with the "Polonaise Militaire" played as an overture and with the male dancer performing his variation to the Mazurka Op. 33, No. 3, a change which Fokine made when he returned to Russia to work and teach at the Maryinsky between 1914 and 1917, and which he retained in the version he staged for René Blum.

Sylvia. Ballet in 3 acts; chor.: Frederick Ashton; music: Léo Delibes; décor: Robin and Christopher Ironside. First prod.: Sadler's Wells (now Royal) Ballet, Royal Opera House, Covent Garden, London, Sept. 3, 1952, with Margot Fonteyn (Sylvia), Michael Somes (Aminta), John Hart (Orion), Julia Farron (Goddess Diana), Alexander Grant (Eros). Frederick Ashton followed, with simplifications, the story of the original Jules Barbier and Baron de Reinach scenario for the Louis Mérante ballet. Sylvia, a votaress of Diana, is accidentally struck with an arrow from the bow of Eros when she has angrily confronted the shepherd, Aminta, and wounded him after he has surprised her during her dance celebrating the glories of the chase. Orion, the dark huntsman, captures Sylvia but she is rescued by Eros and reunited with Aminta. Diana, at first angry at losing the nymph dedicated to her service, yields when reminded that she too once loved a shepherd. Nadia Nerina, Beryl Grey, Violetta Elvin were other Sylvias. After being out of the repertoire for several years, it was revived in 1963 with Doreen Wells and Christopher Gable as Sylvia and Aminta. Melissa Hayden and Flemming Flindt danced these roles as guest artists with the Royal Ballet (June, 1963).

Sylvia, ou La Nymphe de Diane. Ballet in 3 acts, 4 scenes; chor.: Louis Mérante; music: Léo Delibes; book: Jules Barbier and Baron de Reinach; décor: Chéret, Rubé, Chaperon; costumes: Eugene Lacoste. First prod.: Théâtre de l'Opéra, Paris, June 14, 1876, with Rita Sangalli (Sylvia), Louis Mérante (Shepherd). There have been several revivals, among them those by Léo Staats (1919), Serge Lifar (1941), and Albert Aveline (1946). The first Russian production was at the Maly Theatre, St. Petersburg, 1891, for the ballerina Adelina Rossi, choreographed by ballet master M. Saracco. Serge Diaghilev resigned from the staff of the Imperial Theatre as a result of difficulties put in his way when he projected *Sylvia* for the Maryinsky Theatre. It was staged for the Maryinsky, however, Dec. 15, 1901, as a benefit for Olga Preobrajenska. Choreography was by Lev Ivanov (who died before the ballet was completed) and Paul Gerdt. This version, staged by Samuel Adrianov, was revived May 17, 1916, for Tamara Karsavina. A one-act version arranged by C. Wilhelm and Fred Farren was given at the Empire Theatre, London, May 18, 1911, with Lydia Kyasht in the title role. George Balanchine arranged one of his most brilliant pas de deux to the Act 3 pas de deux music (including the famous "Pizzicato Polka"), premièred at City Center, N.Y., Dec. 1, 1951, with Maria Tallchief and Nicholas Magallanes. André Eglevsky later danced the male part and Patricia Wilde and Melissa Hayden have taken Tallchief's role. See also SYLVIA (chor.: Frederick Ashton).

Sylwan, Kari, Swedish dancer, b. 1940. Pupil of Lilian Karina since 1952. Engaged by the Royal Swedish Ballet in 1959. Made her solo dance debut as Ellida in Birgit Cullberg's *Lady from the Sea;* danced Eve in the same choreographer's *Eden;* also the Italian Ballerina in Antony Tudor's *Gala Performance* (all in 1961). Since 1962 also dances title role in *Miss Julie.* Joined Birgit Cullberg's new dance company which is part of the Stockholm City Theatre (1966). Visited U.S. (summer, 1966) mainly to study in the N.Y. school of Martha Graham.

Symons, Oliver, English dancer, b. London, England, 1936; m. Hazel Merry. Dance training at Sadler's Wells (now Royal Ballet) School. Made his debut with Sadler's Wells Ballet (1954). After two years in the Royal Air Force joined Sadler's Wells Opera Ballet. Joined Western Theatre Ballet upon its formation (1957), creating roles in *Non Stop, The Prisoners,* Alfred Rodrigues' *Le Renard* (Goat), *Street Games, One in Five,* Maurice Béjart's *Sacre du Printemps,* and others. Also dances *Nutcracker* pas de deux, Pantalon (*Carnaval*), etc. Appears on television, in films, pantomimes, revues, and musicals.

Symphonic Ballet, a term used in the 1930's and early 1940's to designate the type of work popularized by Leonide Massine in such ballets as *Les Présages* and *Choreartium.* These ballets, choreographed to full symphonies, had no plot or subject other than the mood of the music or the program indicated by the composer. The forms of the choreography were very closely correlated with the forms of the music. This distinguished the genre from the ballets later choreographed to symphonies by George Balanchine, who used the music with more technical freedom, though still reflecting its atmosphere and moods in the dance.

Symphonic Variations. Ballet in 3 movements; chor.: Frederick Ashton; music: César Franck's *Symphonic Variations* for piano and orchestra; décor: Sophie Fedorovitch. First prod.: Sadler's Wells (now Royal) Ballet, Royal Opera House, Covent Garden, London, Apr. 24, 1946, with Margot Fonteyn, Pamela May, Moira Shearer, Michael Somes, Henry Danton, Brian Shaw. This themeless ballet for six dancers has become one of the great classics of the British repertoire.

Symphonie Concertante. Abstract ballet in 4 movements; chor.: George Balanchine; music: Wolfgang Amadeus Mozart (Symphonie Concertante in E flat; K 364); décor and costumes: James Stewart Morcom. First prod.: Ballet Society, City Center, N.Y., Nov. 12, 1947, with a cast headed by Maria Tallchief, Tanaquil LeClercq, Todd Bolender. Currently in the repertoire of the New York City Ballet. Prior to this, the official première, the ballet was presented Nov. 5, 1945, at Carnegie Hall, N.Y., on a program called "Adventure in Ballet," by pupils of the School of American Ballet.

Symphonie Fantastique. Ballet in 5 scenes; chor.: Leonide Massine; music and book: Hector Berlioz; décor and costumes: Christian Bérard. First prod.: Col. de Basil's Ballet Russe, Royal Opera House, Covent Garden, London, July 24, 1936, with Leonide Massine (Young Musician), Tamara Toumanova (The Beloved), Nina Verchinina, Paul Petroff, Marc Platoff, Yurek Shabelevski, George Zoritch. Berlioz's music bears the sub-title, "Episodes de la vie d'un artiste." The plot followed to a certain extent the program set for the symphony by the composer. Thematically and visually it was probably Massine's greatest achievement among his symphonic ballets.

Symphonie pour un Homme Seul (Symphony for a Lonely Man). Ballet in 1 act; chor.: Maurice Béjart; music: an electronic score by Pierre Schaeffer and Pierre Henry. First prod.: Ballets de l'Étoile, Théâtre d l'Étoile, Paris, Aug. 3, 1955, with Michèle Seigneuret, Maurice Béjart, and corps de ballet. This was the first Béjart ballet in a style which has since become typical of his work. Though there is no story there is the theme of man as prisoner: of himself, of a woman, of "the others," prisoners of all the pressures of modern life. The hanging ropes on an otherwise bare stage are the symbols of his attempts to escape. Part of this score was used by Merce Cunningham for one of his "choreography by chance" works (*Collage,* 1952) and was the first musique concrète heard in the U.S.

Symphony. Ballet in 4 movements; chor.: Kenneth MacMillan; music: Dimitri Shostakovitch's Symphony No. 1; décor: Yolanda Sonnabend. First prod.: Royal Ballet at Royal Opera House, Covent Garden, London, Feb. 15, 1963, with Antoinette Sibley, Georgina Parkinson, Donald Macleary, Desmond Doyle, and corps de ballet. Though without an explicit plot, the four dancers suggest an interrelationship which changes as the ballet progresses. The role created by Antoinette Sibley was intended for Lynn Seymour, who missed the première due to illness but who danced in subsequent performances.

Symphony for Fun. Ballet in 1 act; chor.: Michael Charnley; music: Don Gillis' Symphony No. 5½; décor: Tom Lingwood. First prod.: London's Festival Ballet, Festival Hall, London, Sept. 1, 1952, with Noel Rossana, Anita Landa, John Gilpin. A gay ballet in the jive manner about youngsters enjoying themselves.

Symphony in C. Abstract ballet in 4 movements; chor.: George Balanchine; music: Georges Bizet's Symphony in C. First prod.: Ballet Society at City Center, N.Y., Mar. 22, 1948, with Maria Tallchief and Nicholas Magallanes (1st movement, Allegro Vivo), Tanaquil LeClercq and Francisco Moncion (2nd movement, Adagio), Beatrice Tompkins and Herbert Bliss (3rd movement, Allegro Vivace), Elise Reiman and Lew Christensen (4th movement, Allegro Vivace). Originally staged in 1947 as *Le Palais de Cristal* for the Paris Opéra Ballet, *Symphony in C* was presented in its American version in simple white tutus for the girls and practice costumes for the men. Themeless, each movement is led by a pair of dancers, all four pairs participating in the final movement with the full ensemble. When Ballet Society changed the name of its performing company to New York City Ballet and gave its first season under its new name in the fall of 1948, George Balanchine himself conducted the first performance of *Symphony in C,* Nov. 8, 1948. It is also in the repertoire of Royal Danish Ballet, Royal Swedish Ballet, and the Nederlands Ballet. See HOLLAND, DANCE IN.

Szilard, Paul, dancer, choreographer, impresario, b. Budapest, Hungary, 1919. A piano major of the Budapest Academy of Music, he studied solfeggio with Béla Bartók. Studied ballet with V. G. Trojanoff in Budapest, and with Olga Preobrajenska, Mme. Rousanne, Alexandre Volinine, Lubov Egorova in Paris; Stanislas Idzikowski in London. His career as a dancer was interrupted in 1941 when he was war-stranded for four years in the Philippines, but the experience he then gained in forming a company of which he was dancer, teacher, choreographer, producer, and business manager led to his present career as impresario-producer. As such he has brought Dancers of Bali to the U.S., toured in the Orient with his own ballet company of which Nora Kaye, Colette Marchand, Sonia Arova, Milorad Miskovitch were the stars (1954), managed the Far East–Australian tours of New York City Ballet (1958). He arranges all tours for Theatre d'Art du Ballet, as well as musical attractions.

Tablet. Modern dance work; chor.: Paul Taylor; music: David Hollister; costumes and masks: Ellsworth Kelly. First prod.: Festival of Two Worlds, Spoleto, Italy, 1960, for which it was commissioned, with Akiko Kanda and Paul Taylor; N.Y. première: Jan. 14, 1961, with Pina Bausch and Dan Wagoner. A series of poses such as are found on Babylonian tablets given choreographic continuity, seeming to show the formal development of a courtship.

Taconeo, the heel work in the Spanish flamenco dance. See SPANISH DANCE.

Taglioni, Filippo (1778–1871), Italian dancer and choreographer, father of Maria and Paul Taglioni. After making his debut at Pisa (1794) he was premier danseur at Florence, Venice, Paris, and ballet master and dancer at Stockholm (1803). He produced the ballets *The Reception of a Young Nymph at the Court of Terpsichore* in which Maria Taglioni made her debut, Vienna (June 10, 1822); *Joko* (1826); *Le Dieu et la Bayadère* (1830); *Nathalie, ou La Laitière Suisse* (1831); *La Sylphide,* his most famous ballet and the one which opened a new epoch in ballet—the Romantic ballet (1832); *La Fille du Danube* (1836); *La Gitana* (1838); *L'Ombre* (1839), and others. See also ROMANTIC BALLET.

Taglioni, Maria (1804–1884), Italian ballerina of the Romantic period, b. Stockholm. Her father was the choreographer and dancer Filippo Taglioni; her mother was a daughter of the famous Swedish-born actor Karsten (or Carstain). Maria Taglioni made her debut at the Hoftheater, Vienna, in *La Réception d'une Jeune Nymphe à la Cour de Terpsichore* (1822), a ballet specially staged for the occasion by her father. Another great dancer of the period, Fanny Elssler, appeared in the corps of this ballet. Following the Vienna debut Taglioni appeared in Germany, Italy, and France. In 1827 she made her debut at the Paris Opéra but met with an indifferent reception. She continued to dance there and on Mar. 12, 1832, created the title role in a new ballet called *La Sylphide,* achieving a success which echoed throughout Europe. She came to London and became the idol of the city. *La Sylphide* was the first ballet of the Romantic movement in choreography and inaugurated a new era. It also marked the introduction of a new costume for ballet dancers designed by Eugène Lami for Taglioni—a tight-fitting bodice leaving the neck and shoulders bare, bell-shaped skirt reaching mid-way between the knee and the ankle made of a light, white material, and pale pink tights and satin shoes. Taglioni is often credited with having been the first dancer to rise

Maria Taglioni, great ballerina of the Romantic period. (Drawing by Léon Noël, 1833.)

on her toes (pointes). Although the precise time of the introduction of toe dancing in ballet has never been established, it is reasonably definite that there were ballerinas before Taglioni who danced on their toes (see also TOE DANCE). Taglioni's shoes were not blocked, support being given by the darning of the toe of the shoe.

Taglioni exercised a great influence upon ballet. She freed it from the lingering remnants of affectation, the artificial and stilted style of the 18th century. Her art invested ballet with a hitherto unknown quality of spirituality, emphasized by her technique, her prodigious elevation, and her ability to seemingly remain in the air at the highest point of ascent before descending. The ballets in which Taglioni achieved her principal successes were *La Sylphide* and *La Fille du Danube*. In 1832 Taglioni married Count Gilbert de Voisins, but the marriage did not prove successful and ended in a separation (1835). From Sept., 1834, Taglioni had to contend with a serious artistic rival in the person of Fanny Elssler who made her debut at the Paris Opéra at that time. Feeling that her dictatorial reign at the Opéra had received a setback with the debut of Elssler, Taglioni accepted a very profitable three-year contract from the St. Petersburg Imperial Theatre (1837–39). After the expiration of the contract Taglioni returned to Western Europe where she continued to dance with great success until her retirement (1848). She settled on her estate near Venice, but toward the end of her life went bankrupt and was forced to teach dancing in London and Paris. She died in Marseilles, France. (For a full biography and appreciation of Taglioni see André Levinson's *Marie Taglioni*, trans. from the French by Cyril W. Beaumont [London, 1930].)

Taglioni, Marie Paul (1830–1891), dancer, daughter of Paul and Amalie Galtser Taglioni, and niece of the great Maria Taglioni, with whom she is often confused. Appeared at Her Majesty's Theatre, London (1847–49), as soloist in *Thea, Fiorita,* and *Electra.* Was prima ballerina of the Berlin State Opera (1848–65), appearing in her father's ballets *Flick and Flock, Satanella, Metamorphoses,* and others. Made guest appearances in Vienna and other principal cities of the continent. Retired upon her marriage to Prince Joseph Windisch-Grätz (1866).

Taglioni, Paul (1808–1884), Italian dancer and choreographer, son of Filippo, brother of Maria Taglioni, and father of Marie Paul Taglioni. He produced many ballets which were successful in their time, among them *Coralia, or The Inconstant Knight* (1847), *Thea, or The Flower Fairy* (1847), *Winter Pastimes, or The Skaters* (1849), *The Metamorphosis* (1850), all in Berlin.

Taglioni, Salvatore (1790–1868), Italian dancer and choreographer, brother of

Filippo Taglioni. Was principal dancer and ballet master at Naples for half a century. In the 1830's he choreographed there, among other ballets, his own version of *La Sylphide*. This was one of the three versions which were subsequently given at Teatro alla Scala, Milan: Filippo's, Salvatore's, and—more than a century later—Bournonville-Lander's. Salvatore's daughter Louise Taglioni (1823–93) was a première danseuse at the Paris Opéra (1848–57). She danced in the U.S. in 1855 on leave of absence from the Opéra.

Takarazuka (pronounced tah-kah-rahz′ oo-kah), a popular Japanese all-girl dance troupe which takes its name from a town near Osaka, where the home of the company, the Takarazuka Grand Theatre, is located. The troupe was founded by Ichizo Kobayashi in 1914. It is common belief in Japan that Mr. Kobayashi created the Takarazuka company mainly to increase the number of passengers carried by the Kei-Han-Shin railroad of which he was president. This railroad connects Osaka and Kobi with Takarazuka and what had been a small village was developed into a big recreation park of which the Takarazuka Grand Theatre built in 1924 and seating 4,000 is a part. The park also includes a zoo, a botanical garden, an insect house, an aquarium, a movie theatre, restaurants, etc. The railroad has grown to such an extent that in 1957, the year of the death of Mr. Kobayashi, it carried 700,000 passengers daily.

Mr. Kobayashi began his project with the establishment of a school of dancing, singing, and acting in Takarazuka and invited into it the young and attractive daughters of the neighboring families. He introduced a strict discipline in the school and the subsequent companies, and the girls' reputations made them the idols of Japanese fans. The life of the Takarazuka girls is masked in mystery. They have all adopted stage names and their actual identities are never disclosed. They keep themselves aloof from others and are seldom seen with outsiders.

The full name of the Takarazuka company is Takarazuka Shodjo Kagueki Dan which, loosely translated, means Takarazuka Single (i.e. unmarried) Singing and Acting Company. The companies depend entirely on their school for replacements. The school accepts annually from fifty to sixty students, between the ages of fourteen and eighteen. The course of study is two years. Classes run six hours a day, of which three are spent on dance lessons (Japanese and Western), the rest on music, singing, and acting. The Takarazuka companies accept all graduates since there is a large turnover among the performers—most of it owing to marriages. A girl must leave the company as soon as she marries. Each of the companies also loses two to five girls a year to movies and a few to other theatres. This turnover is not considered unfortunate, as it helps to keep the companies young. The average age of the stars of the Takarazuka is about twenty-two.

Takarazuka companies danced in the U.S. at the Golden Gate International Exposition on Treasure Island, San Francisco; the N.Y. World's Fair (1939); also in 1959, on an extensive tour.

Tallchief, Maria, ballerina, b. Fairfax, Okla., 1925, of American Indian (Osage) descent, sister of Marjorie Tallchief; m. George Balanchine, Henry Paschen, Jr. Studied dance with Ernest Belcher, Bronislava Nijinska, George Balanchine, and at the School of American Ballet, N.Y. At first undecided as to whether her career was to lie with ballet or as a concert pianist, her appearance at the Hollywood Bowl dancing in Nijinska's *Chopin Concerto* when she was fifteen decided her future path. Joined Ballet Russe de Monte Carlo (1942–47), eventually becoming a soloist. Created Coquette (*Night Shadow*), role in *Danses Concertantes;* also danced in *Ballet Imperial, Serenade, Baiser de la Fée* (Fairy), *Gaîté Parisienne*

Maria Tallchief, outstanding American ballerina in a pas de deux, partnered by André Eglevsky.

(Can-Can Dancer), *Schéhérazade* (Zobeide). Guest artist with the Paris Opéra (summer, 1947), dancing in *Apollo, Serenade, Baiser de la Fée,* all staged by Balanchine. Joined Ballet Society (forerunner of New York City Ballet) (fall, 1947) and from that time until she left the company in late 1965 her career is part of the history of the New York City Ballet. Apart from a season with Ballet Russe de Monte Carlo (1954–55) and a maternity leave of absence (1958–59), she was the New York City Ballet's first ballerina, dancing with a sometimes incredible brilliance a large repertoire which included such creations as the title role in Balanchine's version of *Firebird, Sylvia Pas de Deux,* Eurydice (*Orpheus*), ballerina (*Scotch Symphony*), ballerina (*Pas de Dix*), Swan Queen (*Swan Lake,* Act 2, Balanchine version); Sugar Plum Fairy (*The Nutcracker,* Balanchine version), ballerina (*Allegro Brillante*), Terpsichore (*Apollo*), leading girl (*Divertimento*), and many others. Joined American Ballet Theatre (1960) and appeared with this company on its tour of the Soviet Union and later during its N.Y. season (1961) when she danced the title role in *Miss Julie,* ballerina (*Grand Pas-Glazounov*), and others. She has also been a guest artist with Ruth Page's Chicago Opera Ballet (1961), the Royal Danish Ballet (*Miss Julie, Don Quixote* pas de deux, 1961), and the Chicago Lyric Opera (1962 opera season). Has appeared many times on television. Returned to the New York City Ballet in Sept., 1963. Received the Capezio Dance Award for 1965 (Mar. 15). The citation read: "To Maria Tallchief. Her artistry which encompasses superb technical discipline, command of style and arresting individuality, is admired, respected and applauded around the world. Thus, as an American ballerina, she has brought luster to American ballet itself, contributing immeasurably in placing it on an equal esthetic footing with the ballet standards of those European cultures which first nurtured the art of ballet."

In Oct. 1965 she resigned from the New York City Ballet, stating that while she did not mind being listed in the alphabetical order in which the company lists its principal dancers and soloists, she did mind being given roles in alphabetical order (the letter T coming very nearly at the end of the alphabet). At the International Festival in the Théâtre des Champs-Elysées, Paris, that summer, Miss Tallchief and her partner Peter van Dyk won the "Best Lyrical Team" award. At present (1966) she is living in Chicago.

Tallchief, Marjorie, ballerina, b. Denver, Colo., 1927, of American Indian (Osage) descent, sister of Maria Tallchief; m. George Skibine (1947). Educated Beverly Hills High School, Calif. Studied ballet with Bronislava Nijinska and David Lichine in Calif. Joined Ballet Theatre (1944), dancing Queen of the Wilis in *Giselle,* Medusa in *Undertow, On Stage!, Graduation Ball,* and other roles. Ballerina, Grand Ballet de Monte Carlo (which became Grand Ballet du Marquis de Cuevas, 1947–56), dancing a large repertoire including *Les Biches, Brahms Variations, Aubade, Concerto Barocco, Night Shadow* (Coquette, 1948; Sleepwalker, 1949), *Annabel Lee, Prisoner of the Caucasus, Idylle,* and Skibine's production of Berlioz' *Romeo and Juliet* presented in the Cour Carrée of the Louvre (1955). Was invited to join the Paris Opéra Ballet as première danseuse étoile (1956). She accepted the position (1957), becoming the first American to have this designation other than as a guest artist. Her ballets included *The Firebird* (Lifar version), *Les Noces Fantastiques, Giselle;* created roles in *Conte Cruel* (1959), *Concerto* (1958), *Pastorale* (1961), among others. Toured the U.S. with Ruth Page's Chicago Opera Ballet (1956, 1958), creating title role in *Camille* (1958) and dancing *The Merry Widow* and *Revenge.* Danced in Skibine's staging of Hindemith's *Metamorphoses* and *Concerto* at the Colón, Buenos Aires, Argentina (Aug., 1961). Resigned with her husband from Paris Opéra (1962). Toured Europe with Skibine and small group; joined the Harkness Ballet as guest prima ballerina (summer, 1964); resigned at the end of the 1965–66 season to be able to spend some time with her children in N.Y.

Tally-Ho, or the Frail Quarry. Ballet in 1 act; chor. and book: Agnes de Mille; music: from Felix Mottl's ballet suite of music by Christoph Wilibald Gluck, arr. by Paul Nordoff; décor: Motley. First prod.: Ballet (now American Ballet) Theatre, Los An-

Marjorie Tallchief, talented American ballerina of the Grand Ballet du Marquis de Cuevas.

geles, Calif., Feb. 25, 1944; N.Y. première: Metropolitan Opera House, N.Y., Apr. 11, 1944, with Agnes de Mille (Wife), Hugh Laing (Genius-Husband), Anton Dolin (Prince), Lucia Chase (Innocent), Muriel Bentley (A Lady-No-Better-Than-She-Should-Be). A French (Louis XVI) park setting for the story of a genius-husband too engrossed in his books to notice that his wife is trying to arouse his jealousy by responding to the attentions of the Prince. Janet Reed later danced the Wife and John Kriza the Prince. Revived as *The Frail Quarry* (Agnes de Mille's original choice of title) by American Ballet Theatre, Apr. 2, 1965, with Carmen de Lavallade (Wife), Royes Fernandez (Husband), John Kriza (Prince).

Tamiris, Helen (Helen Becker) (1905–1966), dancer, choreographer, teacher, lecturer, director, b. New York City; m. Daniel Nagrin. Studied with Metropolitan Opera Ballet and with Michel Fokine. Danced three seasons at Met; toured South America as ballerina, Bracale Opera Company; specialty dancer, *Music Box Revue*. Made her concert debut at Little Theatre, N.Y. (1927). Introduced American folk and Negro spirituals at Salzburg Festival, Austria; also danced in Berlin and Paris. Appeared annually with own company in N.Y. (from 1930); was director and teacher of School of American Dance (1930–45); choreographer, Dance Project, N.Y. (1937–39). During the period (1930–45) she taught extensively outside her own school, including body movement for actors and directors and stage movement for directors, while continuing to perform alone and with her group, producing about 135 dance works. From 1945 she choreographed many musicals, revues, and films including *Up in Central Park* (1945); *Showboat, Annie Get Your Gun, Park Avenue* (all 1946); *Inside U.S.A.* (1948); *Touch and Go* (1949); *Great To Be Alive, Bless You All* (1950); *Flahooley, Just for You* (1952); *By the Beautiful Sea* (1954); *Fanny, Plain and*

Helen Tamiris, American modern dancer, choreographer and teacher.

Fancy (1955). Her choreography in *Touch and Go* won the Antoinette Perry Award ("Tony") for the best choreography of the season (1949). She returned to the modern dance performing field in 1957 with a number of group works, the most important being *Pioneer Memories* (1957), *Dance for Walt Whitman* (1958), *Memoir* (1959); with Daniel Nagrin as co-director and leading dancer formed the Tamiris-Nagrin Dance Co. (1960), her works for this group including *Women's Song* (1960), *Once Upon a Time* (1961), and others. Taught at Perry-Mansfield School of Theatre and Dance, Steamboat Springs, Colo. (1956–58). From 1957 to 1964 conducted the Tamiris-Nagrin Dance Workshop based in N.Y.C., with summer sessions in Maine; conducted summer workshops with Daniel Nagrin at C. W. Post College of Long Island Univ. (1962, 1963). Died of cancer in N.Y. (Aug. 4, 1966).

Tango. 1. Spirited Spanish flamenco dance with steps heavier and simpler than those of the Alegrias and Bulerias but with more scope for floor designs (see SPANISH DANCE). 2. Ballroom dance of Latin American origin in 4/4 time. Its basic rhythm is *slow,* slow, *quick*-quick, slow, in two measures of music.

Tanzarchiv, Das, German language monthly magazine for dance art and folklore, established in 1953 by Kurt Peters in Hamburg. The magazine covers the dance in Germany and Austria and also publishes articles reflecting the dance in other European countries, England, and occasionally the U.S. It is connected with the International Library and Collection. Peters is the editor-publisher of the magazine and curator of the library. Moved to Cologne in 1966.

Tap Dance, a type of dance characterized by the rapid tapping of the toes and heels on the floor, generally done in shoes fitted with cleats or metal plates (known as taps) to emphasize the beats. When this type of dance is done in soft-soled shoes without metal or wooden cleats it is called soft shoe dance.

Taqueterie, in ballet, a generic term for sharp steps on pointes, such as piqués, pas de bourrée, emboités, etc. The term is derived from the French word taquet, meaning peg.

Tarantella, Italian folk dance. There are two theories about the origin of the name. One links it with the town of Taranto where the dance supposedly originated; the other traces the name to tarantula, because the dance was said to have been used as a cure for the bite of the tarantula spider. It is danced either by two girls or a girl and a man (it is considered unlucky to dance it alone). Good examples of the use of the tarantella in ballet are to be found in *Swan Lake,* Act 3 (Petipa, and—in the Royal Ballet version —Frederick Ashton), *Napoli* (Bournonville), *La Boutique Fantasque* (Massine). George Balanchine created a pas de deux, *Tarantella,* to Louis Gottschalk's *Grand Tarantelle,* reconstructed and orchestrated by Hershy Kay, an outstanding example of the traditional dance translated into ballet. It was premièred at City Center, N.Y., Jan. 7, 1964, with Patricia McBride and Edward Villella.

Taras, John, dancer, choreographer, ballet master, b. New York City, 1919. Studied ballet with Michel Fokine, Anatole Vilzak, Ludmila Shollar, Elisabeth Anderson-Ivantzova, School of American Ballet, and others. Early career in musicals. Member, American Ballet Caravan (N.Y. World's Fair, 1940); Littlefield Ballet (season, 1940–41); American Ballet (South American tour, 1941); Ballet (now American Ballet) Theatre (1942–46) which he entered as a member of the corps de ballet, progressing to the positions of soloist and ballet master, and for which company he staged his first ballet, *Graziana* (1945). This was followed by a *Tchaikovsky Waltz* for the Markova-Dolin group, and *Camille* to music of Schubert arr. and orch. by Vittorio Rieti for Original Ballet Russe (both 1946). Choreographed *The Minotaur* to a score by Elliott Carter for Ballet Society; staged world première of *The Mother of Us All,* Columbia Univ.; joined Original Ballet Russe as dancer and ballet master for European tour (all 1947). Choreographed *Designs With Strings* for Metropolitan Ballet (1948); *Persephone* for San Francisco Ballet; joined the Grand Ballet du Marquis de Cuevas as ballet master (also in 1948). From then until 1959 he was associated with the Cuevas company except for a break between 1952 and 1955 and another between 1956 and 1958. His ballets for this company include *Elégie* and *Fête Polonaise* (1948), *Bal des Jeunes Filles* (1950), *Tarasiana* (1951), *Cordelia, Nuit d'Eté, Scherzo* and his most important work to date, *Piège de Lumière* (1952); collaborated on the staging of the Berlioz *Romeo and Juliet* in the Cour Carrée of the Louvre and the dances for the Gluck opera *Orfeo ed Euridice* at the Aix-en-Provence Festival (1955); collaborated on *Voyage Vers L'Amour* (1958) especially staged for the Brussels World's Fair. Returned to N.Y. in 1959 to revive (and to dance the role of the Baron in) George Balanchine's *Night Shadow* (*La Sonnàmbula*) for New York City Ballet; joined the company as assistant to Balanchine, a position he currently occupies. Choreographed for the company *Variaciones Concertantes* (later called *Tender Night*) and *Ebony Concerto* (1960), *Arcade,* and *Fantasy* (1963). He staged his *Piège de Lumière* for the New York City Ballet (1964), created *Shadow'd Ground,* a ballet with photographic projections by John Braden (1965), and staged his own version of *Jeux* to the Claude Debussy score (1966). The original short-lived version was choreographed by Vaslav Nijinsky (Paris, 1913). His *La Guirlande de Campra,* created for a Gala Benefit performance (Apr. 19, 1966) at the New York State Theater, had its first performance in the regular repertoire of the New York City Ballet on Dec. 1, 1966. He also staged *Variaciones Concertantes* for the Teatro Colón, Buenos Aires, and the National Ballet of Chile, sponsored by the U.S. State Dept. During his periods away from the Cuevas company he staged *L'Opéra de Quat' Sous* (The Three-Penny Opera) in Paris, arranged the dances for the operas *Mireille* and *Don Giovanni* at the Aix-en-Provence Festival, choreographed Stravinsky's *Scènes de Ballet* for the Nederlands Ballet (see HOLLAND, DANCE IN), and arranged dances for the Christmas children's play *Where the Rainbow Ends,* London (between 1952 and 1955). Choreographed *Fanfare for a Prince,* for the Monte Carlo Opera on the occasion of Prince Rainier's marriage, as well as *Entre Cour et Jardin* (later called *Le Rideau Rouge*), and *Suite New-Yorkaise.* Choreographed *Les Griffes* for Les Ballets '56; arranged dances for Rameau's opera *Platée* and Mozart's *Le Nozze di Figaro* at Aix-en-Provence Festival (all 1956). Organized *Le Ballet de Pâques* (Ballet for Easter) at Monte Carlo

Opera, choreographing *Le Fôret Romantique, Soirée Musicale, Les Baladins;* choreographed the first and third acts of Françoise Sagan's ballet *Le Rendezvous Manqué* (all 1957). He has staged *Designs With Strings* for a number of other companies, including Ballet Theatre (1949); Grand Ballet du Marquis de Cuevas (1949, under the title *Dessins pour le Six*); Royal Danish Ballet (1953) for whom he also staged *Night Shadow;* Nederlands Ballet (1954), André Eglevsky's Petit Ballet (1960), National Ballet of Chile (1960). A number of his other works have been staged for several companies.

Taras Bulba. Ballet in 4 acts, 11 scenes; chor.: Boris Fenster; music: Vasily Solovyov-Syedoy; book: Semyon Kaplan, after Nicolai Gogol's novel of the same name; décor: Alexander Konstantinovsky. First prod.: Kirov Theatre, Leningrad, June 28, 1955, with Mikhail Mikhailov (Taras), Askold Makarov (Ostap), Konstantin Sergeyev (Andrei), Alla Shelest (Oksana), Natalia Dudinskaya (Pannochka). An epic story of the life of the Zaporozhye cossacks and their fight against Polish invaders of the Ukraine. Taras Bulba kills his son Andrei when he learns that, having fallen in love with the Polish Pannochka, he has gone over to the enemy's side. His other son, Ostap, is captured by the enemy and executed before his father's eyes. The first version of this ballet, with choreography by Fedor Lopukhov and décor by Vadim Ryndin, was premièred at the Kirov, Dec. 12, 1940. Another version, with choreography by Rostislav Zakharov and décor by A. Petritsky, was staged at the Bolshoi Theatre, Moscow, Mar. 26, 1941.

Tarasov, Ivan (1878–1954), Russian dancer and teacher, b. Moscow; m. Norwegian dancer Margit Leerass. A graduate of the Moscow Imperial School of Ballet and dancer for thirteen years of the Bolshoi Ballet, Moscow. He left the company to join the Diaghilev Ballets Russes, with which company he came to the U.S. (1916). He did not return with the company to Europe but remained in the U.S. to dance and to teach. He danced mostly in vaudeville and in 1925 was in charge of the ballet at the Rivoli Theatre, N.Y. He began teaching at the school of Theodore Koslov and later opened his own school. He taught flashy steps to vaudevillians, musical comedy and revue specialty dancers. He was a frequent teacher at dance teachers associations' conventions. Retired from teaching ca. 1940. Died in Monrovia, Calif. His son Nicolai Tarasov is an artist of the Bolshoi Ballet.

Tarasov, Nicolai, Honored Artist of the RSFSR, Soviet dancer, professor, b. 1902. Son of Ivan Tarasov, artist of the Imperial Ballet, Moscow. Entered the ballet division of the Bolshoi Theatre school, 1913 and was graduated in 1920. He considers himself a pupil of Nicholas Legat who taught in Moscow (1919–20) and exerted a great influence on the young dancer who at an early stage became interested in teaching. Tarasov was one of the leading dancers of the Bolshoi company in the 1920's but his importance in Soviet ballet is connected with his teaching activities rather than his dancing. He started teaching privately immediately following graduation and since 1923 has taught at the Bolshoi School, having particular success with boys' classes. He is a theoretician as well as a fine teacher and has the official title of Professor at the State Theatre Institute (Choreographers' Faculty). Coauthor (with V. Moritz and A. Chekrygin) of a textbook *Method of Classical Training* (1940).

Tashamira (Vera Milcinovic), contemporary dancer, b. Zagreb, Yugoslavia. Studied ballet; Dalcroze Eurythmics; modern dance with Rudolf von Laban. Made her American debut with a solo recital at Music Box Theatre, N.Y.; later danced in musicals, gave many solo recitals and lecture-demonstrations and inaugurated Folk Dances of Many Nations, New School

Yugoslav-born modern dancer Tashamira, now resident in New York.

for Social Research, N.Y. Toured South America (1947–48) with her solo program. Has retired from the stage.

Taubert, Manfred, German dancer and choreographer, b. Berlin, 1935. Studied at the ballet school of the Deutsches Opernhaus, Berlin with Tatiana Gsovska and Lena Gsovska. Soloist, Municipal (now German) Opera, Berlin. Dances principal roles in *The Sleeping Beauty, Swan Lake, The Moor of Venice, Medea, Undine, Black Sun*. Has choreographed *Theme in Jazz* (Stan Kenton) and *Circe* (J. J. Johnson); a television ballet, *Salomé* (Florent Schmitt); also opera ballets.

Taverner, Sonia, English dancer, b. Byfleet, Surrey, 1936. Studied dance at Elmhurst Ballet School (1952–54), and at Sadler's Wells (now Royal) Ballet School (1954–55), winning scholarships to both schools. Was awarded the Adeline Genée Silver Medal of the Royal Academy of Dancing. Member, Sadler's Wells Ballet (1955–56); joined Royal Winnipeg Ballet (1956) where she is now a leading soloist. In the classic repertoire she dances Odile (*Swan Lake,* Act 3), Sugar Plum Fairy (*The Nutcracker*), Princess Aurora (*The Sleeping Beauty*), *Don Quixote* pas de deux. Her modern repertoire includes leading roles in *Chinese Nightingale* (Heino Heiden), *Ballet Premier, Concerto, Romance* (both Gweneth Lloyd), *Ballet Three* (Don Gillies), *Variations for a Lonely Theme, Brave Song, Pas de Dix* (George Balanchine), *A Court Occasion,* and others.

Taylor, Brenda, English dancer, b. London, 1934; m. Desmond Doyle. Studied at Sadler's Wells Ballet School from 1946; entered Sadler's Wells Ballet (1951); junior soloist (1955); senior soloist, Royal Ballet touring section (1959); retired (1961). Her roles included Aristocrat (*Mam'zelle Angot*), Lilac Fairy (*The Sleeping Beauty*), Queen of the Wilis (*Giselle*), Red Queen (*Checkmate*), Blanche (*Pineapple Poll*), and others.

Sonia Taverner and Fredric Strobel in Black Swan pas de deux.

Taylor, Jonathan, English dancer, b. Manchester, 1941; m. Ariette Taylor (née van Rossem). Began training in Manchester; then won a five-year scholarship to the Royal Academy of Dancing, London; also studied three years with Andrew Hardie, London. Member of the Nederlands Nationaal Ballet; then appeared at the Nervi Festival in the Leonide Massine season (1960). Joined Ballet Rambert (1961), dancing a wide variety of leading roles including Franz (*Coppélia*), Albrecht (*Giselle*), Espada, Gypsy (*Don Quixote*), Harlequin (*Night Shadow*), Agent (*A Place in the Desert*), and others; also creating Choreographer (*Conflicts*), The Man (*The Travellers*).

Taylor, Paul (Paul Bellville Taylor, Jr.), American modern dancer, b. Pittsburgh, Pa., 1930. He received a painting scholarship to Syracuse Univ. and later dance scholarships for Juilliard School of Music Dance Dept., Connecticut College School of Dance (summer), the Martha Graham School, and Metropolitan Opera Ballet School. Has had his own dance company since 1954 when one of his earliest works, *Three Epitaphs* to music by the Laneville-Johnson Union Brass Band, focused attention on him as an original and creative mind in the field of modern dance. Since then he has created many solo and group works, among them *The Least Flycatcher, Untitled Duet, Tropes* (1956), *The Tower, Seven New Dances* (1957), *Images and Reflections, Rebus* (1958), *Option, Meridian, Tablet* (1960), the last two being commissioned by the Festival to Two Worlds, Spoleto; *Fibers, Insects and Heroes, Junction* (1961), *Tracer,* premièred during the Théâtre des Nations Festival, Paris; *Aureole,* premièred at the American Dance Festival, Connecticut College; *Piece Period* (1962), *Scudorama* and *Party Mix* (1963), *The Red Room* (1964). Many of his works have commissioned scores: *Meridian* and *Images and Reflections* (Morton Feldman); *Tablet* and *Rebus* (David Hollister); *Seven New Dances* (John Cage); *Option* (Richard Maxfield); *Insects and Heroes* (John Herbert McDowell). From 1955 to 1961 he was also a leading soloist with Martha Graham's company, creating Aegisthus (*Clytemnestra*), Hercules (*Alcestis*), Antony (*One More Gaudy Night*), Samson the Destroyer (*Visionary Recital,* afterwards called *Samson Agonistes*), and also dancing Tiresias (*Night Journey*) and the Stranger (*Embattled Garden*). He was guest artist with New York City Ballet when George Balanchine created a special variation for him in *Episodes* (1959) which has never yet been performed without him. Guest choreographer for the Nederlands Ballet at Amsterdam Opera House (1960) creating *The White Salamander* to a commissioned score by Joop Stockkermans. He received the Critics' Award as best choreographer at the Théâtre des Nations Festival (1962); received fellowship for choreography from the John Simon Guggenheim Memorial Foundation (1961–62). Invited by Mexican Government to appear with his company

Paul Taylor with partner Bettie de Jong in Scudorama.

at the National Institute of Fine Arts, Mexico City, Jan., 1963. Toured Europe in 1964, again appearing at the Festival of Two Worlds, Spoleto, at which time he premièred *The Red Room,* to music by Gunther Schuller; its U.S. première was Aug. 7, 1964, during the second Long Island Arts Festival. With his company appeared in Paris and London in 1964; under the Cultural Exchange Program of the U.S. Dept. of State, he toured South America (1965), Europe, North Africa and the Near East (Jan.; July–Aug. 1966) (Feb., Mar. 1967). For his performances in Chile he received the Premio de la Critica award as the outstanding visiting company in 1965. During his appearances at the Holland Festival (July 4–15, 1966) he premièred *Orbs,* an hour-length work to the final quartets of Beethoven. Received the Capezio Dance Award for 1967.

Taylor, Valerie, English dancer, b. London, 1931. Studied with Phyllis Bedells, Margaret Clark, and on a Royal Academy of Dancing scholarship at Sadler's Wells Ballet School, becoming first head girl after it became a school for general education as well as ballet training. Entered Sadler's Wells (now Royal) Ballet (1948), becoming soloist (1953), and dancing Woodland Glades Fairy (*The Sleeping Beauty*), Miller's Wife (*The Three-Cornered Hat*), Queen of the Wilis (*Giselle*), Prayer (*Coppélia*), Tarantella (*La Boutique Fantasque*), and others.

Tchaikovsky, Peter (1840–1893), Russian composer of ballets *Swan Lake* (chor.: Julius Reisinger, 1877; Marius Petipa and Lev Ivanov, 1895), *The Sleeping Beauty* (Petipa, 1890), *The Nutcracker* (Ivanov, 1892). His music has been used for many ballets: *Serenade for Strings* for *Eros* (Michel Fokine, 1915), and for *Serenade* (George Balanchine, 1935); the symphonic poem *Francesca da Rimini* for a ballet of the same title (Fokine, 1915; David Lichine, 1937); Symphony No. 5 for *Les Présages* (Leonide Massine, 1933); *Mozartiana* for the ballet of the same name (Balanchine, 1933); Piano Concerto No. 2 in G major for *Ballet Imperial* (Balanchine, 1941); Trio in A Minor for *Aleko* (Massine, 1942) and *Designs with Strings* (John Taras, 1948); the symphonic poem *Hamlet* for a ballet of the same title (Robert Helpmann, 1942); Piano Concerto No. 1 in B♭ minor for *Ancient Russia* (Bronislava Nijinska, 1943); Suite No. 3 in G for *Theme and Variations* (Balanchine, 1947) and *Parures* (Anthony Burke, 1948); the single movement of his unfinished Piano Concerto No. 3 for *Allegro Brillante* (Balanchine, 1956); Violin Concerto for *Concerto* (Herbert Ross, 1958); some music from his original score for *Swan Lake,* hitherto never used, for Tchaikovsky *Pas de Deux* (Balanchine, 1960), and others. His fantasy-overture, *Romeo and Juliet,* has been used by countless choreographers, some of them being Serge Lifar, Birger Bartholin, George Skibine, Oleg Briansky. See also MARIUS PETIPA; HISTORY OF BALLET.

Tchaikovsky Foundation, The. See TSCHAIKOVSKY FOUNDATION, THE.

Tchaikovsky Pas de Deux. Chor.: George Balanchine; music: Peter Tchaikovsky; costumes: Barbara Karinska. First prod.: New York City Ballet, City Center, N.Y., Mar. 29, 1960, with Violette Verdy and Conrad Ludlow. A pas de deux arranged by Balanchine in a manner reminiscent of the Soviet "Highlight" pieces, but in his own style and taste. The music is hitherto unknown pas de deux written by Tchaikovsky for the 1877 production of *Swan Lake* but never used. It was intended for the pas de deux of Odile and Siegfried in Act 3. Because it was not published with the rest of the score it remained unknown to Marius Petipa and Lev Ivanov when they were preparing to stage the St. Petersburg version (1895) and they substituted music from Act 1 which became the famous *Black Swan* pas de deux. The music lay unnoticed in the Tchaikovsky Museum in Klin until it was brought to light by the efforts of the Tschaikovsky Foundation of N.Y. It has become one of the great show pieces for Violette Verdy and Edward Villella who danced it at the Royal Academy of Dancing Gala in London organized by Margot Fonteyn in 1962. Villella danced it again as guest artist with the Royal Danish Ballet (Jan. 11, 1963), teaching the ballerina role to Solveig Ostergaard. Violette Verdy staged it for the Royal Ballet and danced the first performance with David Blair at the Royal Opera House, Covent Garden, London (Mar. 16, 1964).

Tchelitchev, Pavel (1898–1957), Russian painter and stage designer who lived and worked in the U.S. (1934–51), becoming an American citizen. His talent and imagination made him one of modern art's most debated figures. Ballet occupied a predominant part of his imagination and some of his most exciting décors were done for ballet. He was a firm friend of George Balanchine and Lincoln Kirstein, active in building the American Ballet (1934–36), and exerted a strong influence on the development of the company. Among his work for produced ballets (he also designed a number of ballets which were never produced) are: *Ode* (Nicholas Nabokov–Leonide Massine, the Diaghilev Ballets Russes, 1928); *Errante* (Franz Schubert–George Balanchine, Les Ballets, 1933, Paris; American ballet, N.Y., 1935); *Orpheus* (Gluck–Balanchine, American Ballet, Metropolitan Opera House, N.Y., 1936); *Saint Francis* (known in Europe as *Nobilissima Visione*) (Hindemith–Massine, Ballet Russe de Monte Carlo, 1938); *Balustrade* (Stravinsky–Balanchine, Original Ballet Russe, 1941); *Apollon Musagète* (Stravinsky–Balanchine) and *Concerto* (Mozart–Balanchine, both at Teatro Colón, Buenos Aires, 1942). The Museum of Modern Art and the Gallery of Modern Art in N.Y. own some of his most brilliant paintings.

Tcherepnine, Alexander, Russian composer, b. St. Petersburg, 1899, now living in Paris. Son of Nicholas Tcherepnine. Composed scores for *Trepak* (Mordkin Ballet, 1937); *Déjeuner sur l'Herbe* (Roland Petit, Ballets des Champs-Elysées, 1945); *Chota Roustavelli* (Serge Lifar, Nouveaux Ballets de Monte Carlo, 1946); *La Femme et Son Ombre* (Janine Charrat, Ballets de Paris, 1948).

Tcherepnine, Nicholas (1873–1945), Russian composer and conductor. He wrote the scores for *Le Pavillon d'Armide,* choreographed by Michel Fokine for the Diaghilev Ballets Russes (1909); *Narcisse* by the same choreographer for the same company (1911); orchestrated Schumann's music for *Les Papillons* (1914); composed the ballets *The Goldfish* and *Dionysius* (Mordkin Ballet, 1937). He was the father of the composer Alexander Tcherepnine.

Tcherina, Ludmilla, French dancer, b. Paris, 1925, of Russian-French parentage. Trained with Blanche d'Alessandri, Ivan Clustine, Olga Preobrajenska. Danced as a child prodigy in concert performances. Ballerina, Monte Carlo Opera (1940–44). Made her Paris debut June 16, 1942, in Serge Lifar's *Romeo and Juliet* at the Salle Pleyel. Guest ballerina, Ballets des Champs-Elysées (1945), dancing *Les Forains, La Forêt.* Ballerina, Nouveau Ballet de Monte Carlo (directed by Eugene Grünberg and Serge Lifar, 1946), creating *A La Memoire d'un Heros, Mephisto Valse,* and others. Married dancer Edmond Audran who was killed in a car crash (1951). Appeared both as dancer and actress in Debussy's *Martyrdom of St. Sebastian* at the Paris Opéra (1957). Organized her own company which had its first season Feb., 1959, Théâtre Sarah Bernhardt, Paris. Repertoire including *Les Amants de Teruel,* written and directed by Raymond Rouleau, with choreography by Milko Sparemblek; also *Feu aux Poudres* (Paul Goubé). Appeared in

Soviet Russia (1960) on a concert tour and at Bolshoi Theatre in *Giselle*. Appeared at Fenice Theatre, Venice (summer, 1961) in Salvador Dali's ballet *Gala*, choreographed by Maurice Béjart. Has appeared in many films as dancer and actress, among them *The Red Shoes*, *Tales of Hoffmann*, *Oh, Rosalinda*, and ballet-film of *Les Amants de Teruel* (1961–62).

Tchernicheva, Lubov, Russian dancer, teacher, b. St. Petersburg, 1890; m. Serge Grigoriev, former dancer, regisseur of the Diaghilev Ballets Russes and regisseur-general of Col. de Basil's Ballet Russe. Graduated from the Imperial School of Ballet, St. Petersburg (1908); obtained leave of absence to dance with the Diaghilev Ballets Russes (1911); soon resigned from the Imperial Theatre (1912). A leading dancer with the Diaghilev company until his death (1929), she joined Col. de Basil's Ballet Russe (1932), remaining with the company when the split came (1937) and continuing with Original Ballet Russe, being ballet mistress in its final years. Her most famous roles were Zobéide (*Schéhérazade*), Miller's Wife (*The Three-Cornered Hat*), Thamar (*Thamar*), Constanza (*The Good-Humored Ladies*), and the title role in *Francesca da Rimini*, which she created. Currently living in London with her husband. Together they have re-staged *Firebird*, *Les Sylphides*, and *Petrouchka* from the Diaghilev repertoire for Sadler's Wells (now Royal) Ballet.

Teachers' Organizations (Britain), include the following: Royal Academy of Dancing, Imperial Society of Teachers of Dancing, Dance Teachers' Association, British Ballet Organization, Allied Dancing Association, Ltd., British Association of Teachers of Dancing, Institute of Teachers of Dance, International Dancing Masters' Association, The National Association of Teachers of Dancing, The United Kingdom Alliance of Professional Teachers of Dancing and Kindred Arts, The Scottish Dance Teachers' Alliance, The Northern Counties Dance Teachers' Association.

Teachers' Organizations (U.S.), have been in existence since the middle of the nineteenth century. Until 1884 almost all organizations were local. That year the American National Association of Masters of Dancing was founded and was the only national organization until the organization of International Association of Masters of Dancing (1894). In 1926 the two associations merged into Dancing Masters of America, the largest teachers' organization in U.S. with a membership of about one thousand and clubs or branches in many parts of the U.S. In 1912 the Chicago National Association of Dancing Masters was founded as a regional organization drawing its membership from the Mid-western states. In the late 1920's and early 1930's the organization spread its influence to the west and south and became in effect a national body with a membership of about eight hundred. Both organizations hold annual conventions and normal schools, usually at the end of July and beginning of August, to which teachers from all parts of the country come in quest of teaching material and technique classes in various phases of dance. Outstanding teachers are invited to instruct. Lectures on management are usually featured and business meetings and election of officers are held. Local clubs hold monthly meetings to which guest instructors are invited. A N.Y. group, organized in 1932 as Dancing Teachers Business Association, subsequently changed its name to Dance Educators of America. It was a local club of Dancing Masters of America from 1939 to 1947, when it became an independent national organization. It runs its own normal school and convention. Among the smaller organizations are the independent American Society of Teachers of Dancing, the N.Y. Society of Teachers of Dancing, and the Dance Teachers' Club of Boston.

Two teachers' organizations in the U.S. were built and function on different premises from the so-called "old line" societies listed above. These are the Cecchetti Council of America with headquarters in Detroit, and the National Dance Teachers Guild, Inc., based in N.Y. The Cecchetti Council of America, organized in 1939 and incorporated in 1951, is devoted to serious ballet teachers, particularly those who adhere to the Cecchetti method of ballet instruction, or wish to become acquainted with the system. The Council runs monthly meetings as well as a summer school for students and a seminar for teachers. The National Dance Teachers Guild, organized in 1956, leans toward the modern dance but includes ballet as one of the disciplines of teaching dance in their annual fall or winter conventions. The Guild makes excellent use of lectures on vital teaching subjects and panel discussions of topics of interest to teachers.

Teaching Dance in the U.S., History of.

BY ANNE BARZEL.

The teaching of dance in the U.S. began almost as soon as colonists settled. The first teacher on record was Francis Stepney who taught in Massachusetts in 1685. There were French and English dancing masters who taught in every colony. The subjects in the dance academies were ballroom dancing and etiquette. The academies also organized public and private dances.

The plantation owners of Virginia and the other southern colonies imported tutors (often bonded servants) to educate their children. Dancing masters from France were usually included.

Theatrical dancing was taught from late in the 18th century, when the French theatre in Charleston and traveling troupes made people conscious of this form of dance. Hornpipes, jigs, and harlequinades were taught to theatrical aspirants, usually by professional dancers such as James Byrnes and William Francis.

A number of fashionable academies that taught ballroom dancing were soon opened in the larger cities; representative schools were those of Pierre Tastel, Charleston (1791), and Lorenzo Papanti, Boston (1823).

When the ballet stars of Europe, such as Fanny Elssler, Paul and Amalie Taglioni, and Mlle. Hutin came to America, they found a number of ballet-trained dancers with whom to supplement their troupes. They had been trained by dancers like P. H. Hazard (French), and Charles Durang (American) who had schools in Philadelphia, and Mr. Conway (English) who had one in N.Y. The dancing taught included the technique prevalent at the academy of the Opéra in Paris. Many of the visiting dancers—Jules Martin, Mme. Lecomte, Pauline Desjardins—settled in America and opened dance schools. Elegant foot work and gracious manners were the chief subjects of study.

The Italian influence and style were felt with the visits of the Ronzani, Del Pol, and Morlacchi troupes in the middle of the 19th century. That century also saw a number of itinerant dancing masters whose lessons in the latest steps were often a side-line to the wares they were peddling.

Productions of *The Black Crook* and other spectacles that featured ballets in the last decades of the 19th century led to schools being opened by the retired ballerinas of these shows. Marie Bonfanti and Elizabetta Menzeli were among those who started schools. The music hall performers of the next decades as well as a number of non-professionals studied with them.

In the latter half of the 19th century a number of German dancing masters came to America. They taught ballroom dancing to children and adults, also drills and fancy dances. The school exhibition or recital was noteworthy because in it children from middle-class non-theatrical homes appeared in costumed dances. It was on an amateur basis, but it was the beginning of the recognition of theatrical dancing as respectable. The dance teacher was also becoming socially acceptable.

In the first decades of the 20th century Delsarte, the kindergarten movement, the development of physical education instruction, and the recognition of dancing as a form of physical exercise all encouraged the teaching of dance to pupils hoping for a professional career as dancers or teachers. Folk dancing found its way into the dance school. Diluted ballet, featuring character dances, found its way into the gymnasium. Albert Newman, Louis Chalif, and Dr. Luther Gulick were among the leaders in this movement which, among other things, resulted in the organization of the normal school, where practicing dance teachers could acquire training in, among other subjects, the methodology of teaching. The dance school was at this time not only accepted as reputable, but acknowledged as an educational force.

With the coming to America of the Anna Pavlova and Diaghilev companies, Adeline Genée and others in the early 20th century, ballet training of a more technical order was offered by teachers such as Luigi Albertieri, Mascagno, and Zanfretta. An influx of Russian dancers from the Imperial ballet companies came in the 1920's, most of whom taught. Among them, Michel Fokine, Mikhail Mordkin, Adolph Bolm, Alexis and Theodore Koslov, Ivan Tarasov, Konstantin Kobeleff, Anatole Bourman and others made the dance school an artistic and social necessity.

The Central European modern dance became popular in the late 1920's and 1930's. A number of teachers came to America to teach this form, often sponsored by physical education departments of colleges. The American modern dance developed and the schools of Martha Graham, Humphrey-Weidman, Hanya Holm and others spread it throughout the country. A new element entered the teaching field: the pupil not only was taught an art form, but an attempt was made to make him a creative artist.

In the middle 1930's and in the 1940's came the period of the thoroughly professional ballet school that trained students for the new opportunities which the ballet dancer had in the growing number of large and small companies and in musical shows. Technique was more exact and there was more emphasis on virtuosity. Led by the School of American Ballet, headed by George Balanchine and Lincoln Kirstein, schools developed more inclusive curricula and invited more varied faculties, including prominent dancers and choreographers such as Balanchine, Hilda Butsova, Edward Caton, Alexandra Danilova, Felia Doubrovska, Frederic Franklin, Anatole Oboukhov, Ludmila Shollar, Vecheslav Swoboda, Antony Tudor, Pierre Vladimirov, Maria Yurieva, and others.

Thousands of schools all over the U.S. reflected these developments. Some of the influence was directly through contact with the metropolitan schools, part came through the teachers' organizations which, though leaning to conservative and "useful" forms of dance, included new phases and movements in their "teaching material" courses offered at annual conventions and in normal schools.

From 1935 to 1960 many European-trained ballet dancers, for reasons of age or to avoid the rigors of touring, accepted positions in established schools or opened their own. They were well prepared for teaching both academically and artistically. This group was joined soon after World War II by youngish veterans of American and British training. As a result subtle changes took place in ballet classes, not only in the large cities but also in smaller cities and towns. Classwork began to be geared to the standards of ballet companies. Many schools became centers of civic and regional ballet groups on non- or semi-professional levels. Ballet teaching was itself reaching a new high. (For a detailed history of dance teaching in the U.S. see Ann Barzel's monograph, "European Dance Teachers in the United States," *Dance Index,* Apr.–May–June, 1944.)

Telyakovsky, Vladimir A. (1860–1924), the last director of the Russian Imperial Theatres, which he headed from 1901 to 1917 when he was relieved by the revolutionary government. A member of the high aristocracy, he was graduated from the Imperial Corps of Pages, the Cavalry Officers' School, and subsequently from the Academy of the General Staff. He served in one of the most exclusive cavalry guard regiments in Imperial Russia and retired in 1897 with the rank of colonel. He was an accomplished musician (pianist), having studied at a private conservatory of music while still in the service. He also took lessons in theory and composition from the well-known Russian composer Anatole Liadov. He began his administrative career as manager of the Moscow Imperial Theatres in 1898. In 1901 he was appointed director of all Imperial Theatres. The Imperial Theatres and especially the opera and ballet at the Maryinsky reached their apogée during his administration. His book, *Reminiscences,* published in Russian in 1924, furnishes an unexcelled account of the Imperial Theatres during the last twenty years of the old regime. Regrettably it has not been translated into English. Telyakovsky died in Leningrad soon after the publication of his book.

Tempest, Doreen, contemporary English dancer, teacher, b. London; m. Robert Lunnon. Trained at Sadler's Wells Ballet School (now Royal Ballet School) (1946–50), joining Sadler's Wells Theatre Ballet (1951). During her seven years with the company she danced leading roles in a large repertoire including *Swan Lake, Coppélia, Giselle, The Nutcracker, Les Sylphides, Les Patineurs, The Rake's Progress, Le Fête Etrange, Pineapple Poll, Lady and the Fool,* and others. Established residence in Chicago in 1957. Toured with Ruth Page's Chicago Opera Ballet as principal soloist (1957). She has taught in Chicago; was co-director (with Lunnon) of the Regional Ballet Ensemble of Chicago and leading dancer with the Allegro American Ballet Company. Left for London in 1966.

Temps, in ballet, a step or movement in which there is no transfer of weight from one foot to the other, as opposed to pas in which the weight shifts from one foot to the other. According to Cyril W. Beaumont, the relation of temps to pas is that of a syllable to a word; it is therefore a part of pas. A temps, however, may in itself contain more than one movement.

Temps de Cuisse, a ballet step. Technique: start in 5th pos., R ft. front; demi-plié on R leg while sliding L to 2nd pos. and then putting L ft. immediately in 5th pos. front, with fondu on both legs; jump off both feet, moving to R side and opening L leg to demi- or grande seconde pos. en l'air; land in 5th pos. plié, L ft. front. Temps de cuisse may also be done placing the foot back and without changing the feet.

Temps de Flêche, a ballet step. Technique: start 5th pos., R ft. front; step on R ft. and sweep L leg up in grand battement en avant; spring off R ft. throwing R leg upward in grand battement en avant, L leg passing it on the way down, and land on L; bring R ft. down to 5th pos. in front. Temps de flêche is also done bending the knee of the first leg that goes up so that it has the appearance of a bow, while the straight leg that passes it is the arrow. Temps de flêche may also be done lifting the legs in back.

Temps de Poisson, in ballet a step in which the body is supposed to resemble a fish. Technique: start 5th pos., R ft. front; spring upward and sideward off both feet, pressing calves of legs together, legs thrown to side and back, body curved sideward, L arm up in effacé pos.; land on R ft. Preparation for temps de poisson is usually assemblé dessus. The curve of the body resembles the curve of a fish in a leaping movement.

Temps Levé, a ballet step. Technique: from 1st pos. demi-plié, push off with the heels and with a little jump rise on the pointes; then lower into demi-plié. May also be done from 2nd and 5th positions. The last named is often called, but is not, a sous-sous.

Temps Lié, a ballet step. Technique: start 5th pos., R ft. front; with a demi-plié step forward to 4th pos. croisé; straighten knees and transfer weight to R ft., leaving L toe pointed in back. Temps lié may also be done changing the weight to the back foot, and in effacé.

Tender Night. See VARIACIONES CONCERTANTES.

Tendu in ballet, stretched, or held, as in battement tendu.

Tension-Relaxation, English translation of the German term Anspannung-Abspannung formulated by Rudolf von Laban. American modern dancers prefer the terms contraction-release, fall-recovery.

Ter-Arutunian, Rouben, scenery and costume designer, b. Tiflis, Soviet Georgia, 1920, of Armenian parentage. His parents moved to Paris when he was one year old, then to Berlin where he went to school. He studied for a career as concert pianist for a time. He attended Reimann Art School (1939–41) and took courses in the composition of film music at the Musik Hochschule (1941–42); concurrently attended Friedrich Wilhelm University (1941–43) and later the Univ. of Vienna (1944–45). Designed décor, costumes, and club interiors for U.S. Third Army Special Services in Germany (1945–47). Studied art in Paris (1947–50) at École des Beaux Arts, Atelier Souverbie, Académie Julian, Grande Chaumière. Emigrated to U.S. (1951) and has been a citizen since 1957. Since 1951 has been a television staff designer for many shows, including the Igor Stravinsky-George Balanchine *Noah and the Flood* (1962—commissioned to celebrate Stravinsky's eightieth birthday); designed décor and/or costumes for a number of Broadway shows, both musicals and plays. Designed the new Festival Stage for the American Shakespeare Festival, Stratford, Conn. (1956), which was retained until 1960 at which time another of his designs went into use until 1962. Designed décor and/or costumes for many opera productions, both in Europe and in U.S. His work for dance began in 1941 with costumes for the soloists of the Berlin State Opera Ballet. His first ballet designs in America were for New York City Ballet's *Souvenirs* (1955), followed by *Seven Deadly Sins* (1958) for the same company, *Masque of the Wild Man* (John Butler Dance Theater, Festival of Two Worlds, Spoleto, 1958), Paul Taylor's *Fibers* (1960), Martha Graham's *Samson Agonistes* (1961, décor only), San Francisco Ballet's *Swan Lake,* Glen Tetley's *Pierrot Lunaire* (1962), N.Y.C. Ballet's *Ballet Imperial* (1964, décor only). He received television's "Emmy" Award for best art direction for *Twelfth Night* (1957); Outer Circle Award for the best scenic designs for the off-Broadway *Who Was That Lady?* (1957); "Tony" Award for the best costume designs for the musical *Redhead* (1958). Designed new scenery, special effects and lighting for George Balanchine's revised production of *The Nutcracker* given for the first time at New York State Theater (Dec. 11, 1964); also décor for *Harlequinade* (1965). Designed Glen Tetley's *Sargasso* (Mar. 24, 1965) and *Ricercare* (Jan. 25, 1966), both for American Ballet Theatre.

Ter Weeme, Mascha, contemporary Dutch dancer and artistic director, b. Amsterdam. Professional training with Mary Wigman, Hellerau-Laxenburg, Yvonne Georgi, Igor Schwezoff, Victor Gsovsky, Leo Staats, Olga Preobrajenska. Soloist and assistant to Yvonne Georgi

(1936–44), then formed team with Antony Raedt to give recitals. Was artistic director of Het Ballet der Lage Landen (1947–59) and held the same position with Het Amsterdams Ballet (1959–61). Since Sept., 1961, he is head of the opera dept. of Het Nederlands Nationaal Ballet. See also HOLLAND, DANCE IN.

Teresa (Teresa Viera-Romero), Spanish dancer, b. New York City, 1929; m. Luisillo; later Werner Torkanowsky, musical conductor. Trained by Luisillo in Mexico and after appearing with him in Carmen Amaya's company, formed their own (1949). As the Teresa and Luisillo Ballet Español, the company toured all over the world, including U.S. (1954). When this company broke up in the mid-1950's, Teresa formed her own company with which she now tours.

Terpis, Max (Max Pfister) (1889–1958), Swiss dancer, ballet master, choreographer and theoretician of the dance. He originally studied architecture but at the age of twenty began to be interested in the dance, upon whose development in Germany he exercised a distinct influence. Some thirty years later he was to write: "The architect and the choreographer are brothers who aspire toward the realization of their ideas from the same spiritual sources and of similar aesthetic and formal principles." In 1921 Terpis moved to Germany where he studied in Dresden with Mary Wigman and later became ballet master of the Hannover Opera. From there he was called to Berlin where he was appointed ballet master of the State Opera to succeed Heinrich Kröller. With the advent of the Nazis in 1933 he was forced to leave the Opera. He opened his own school where hundreds of German dancers received their training. He returned to Switzerland in 1941 and through 1943 was ballet master of the Municipal Theatre, Basel. Author of *The Dance and the Dancer* (Zurich, 1946).

Terpsichore, the Muse of dance and choral singing, usually represented with a lyre, one of the nine Muses of Greek mythology; a character in George Balanchine's ballet *Apollo.*

Terre à Terre, in ballet, steps done on the ground; a dancer who lacks elevation is called a terre à terre dancer.

Terry, Walter, critic, lecturer, b. Brooklyn, N.Y., 1913. B.A. (drama major, music minor), Univ. of North Carolina. While at college he wrote for the university publications, directed and wrote plays for the Carolina Playmakers, and studied dance, being a principal dancer in the student dance company. Continued dance studies under various teachers in ballet, modern dance, ethnic, and other techniques, the program being planned for the functions of the critic, not as a performing career. Dance critic, Boston *Herald* (1936–39); dance critic and dance editor, N.Y. *Herald-Tribune* (1939–42); U.S. Armed Forces (with Army Air Corps, now Air Force, 1942–45) with three-year overseas duty in British West Africa (now Ghana), Belgian Congo (now Congo Republic), and Egypt. While in Cairo taught modern dance to thirty boys and girls at the American Univ., Cairo. Returned to the *Herald-Tribune* (1945) and when the *Herald Tribune* discontinued publication as a separate newspaper (Sept., 1966) Terry was invited to join the amalgamated afternoon paper *World-Journal-Tribune* in the same capacity. Author of *Invitation to Dance; Star Performance; The Story of the World's Great Ballerinas; Ballet in Action* (in collaboration with Paul Himmel, photographer); *The Dance in America; Ballet: A New Guide to the Liveliest Art* (paperback); *On Pointe: The Story of Dancers and Dancing on Toe,* and *Isadora Duncan, Her Life, Her Art, Her Legacy*. Has contributed chapters and/or essays to other books and encyclopedias, including *Dance Encyclopedia;*

articles in *Look, This Week, Kenyon Review, Theatre Arts, Think, Horizon, Pageant,* and others; also for foreign publications including the Sunday *Times,* London; formerly Dance Editor for the *Encyclopedia Britannica.* Has prepared scripts for the "Voice of America," the U.S. Information Agency, and others; has written scripts, selected dances and dancers, or served as dance consultant for various television shows; consultant for and participant in "A Time to Dance," a series produced by educational television under a Ford Foundation grant. In 1967 joined the *Saturday Review* as dance editor and critic.

Glen Tetley, modern dancer and choreographer.

Tetley, Glen, American modern dancer, b. Cleveland, Ohio, 1926. Began his dance training with a scholarship from Hanya Holm (1946) after completing pre-medical training at Franklin and Marshall College, Lancaster, Pa. under the Navy V-12 program and enrolling in Columbia Medical School. To facilitate his dance training he transferred to N.Y. Univ., graduating with a B.S. degree (1948). His professional career began with Hanya Holm's company (1946–51). He also acted as her assistant in the Broadway productions of *Ballet Ballads, Kiss Me, Kate,* and *Out of This World.* Studied ballet with Margaret Craske and Antony Tudor, beginning 1949. Danced with Melissa Hayden and Nicholas Magallanes in the world première of Gian-Carlo Menotti's opera, *Amahl and the Night Visitors* (NBC-TV, 1951) and has appeared in many subsequent Christmas performances. First dancer of New York City Opera (1952–54); returned for the 1959 season to dance in John Butler's production of Carl Orff's *Carmina Burana.* A leading member of John Butler's company for many years, he toured Europe in 1955 with his American Dance Theater and has appeared in many of Butler's televised works for "Omnibus," "Camera Three," "Adventure," and "Look Up and Live." Guest artist with Robert Joffrey Ballet (1956–57); member of Martha Graham Dance Company (1958), creating Serpent in *Embattled Garden.* Danced at the first two Festivals of Two Worlds, Spoleto (1958–59); played the mimed role of the Clarinetist in the television series "Play of the Week" production of Jean Anouilh's *Thieves' Carnival* (1960). Later the same year danced the show-stopping Irish slip-jig in the Broadway musical *Juno,* choreographed by Agnes de Mille. Joined American Ballet Theatre (Apr., 1960) for the Broadway season and tour of Europe and the Soviet Union, creating the Husband (*Lady from the Sea*) and also dancing the Sailor. His other roles included The Friend (*Pillar of Fire*), Lover (*Lilac Garden*), Jean (*Miss Julie*), title role (*Bluebeard*), Alias (*Billy the Kid*). Joined Jerome Robbins' Ballets: U.S.A. for its 1961 tour of Europe dancing Faun (*Afternoon of a Faun*), Husband (*The Concert*), Intruder (*The Cage*), one of the four principals (*Events*), pas de deux (*Moves*). Has also been guest artist with several modern dance companies, dancing with Pearl Lang at the première of *And Joy Is My Witness,* and being the first dancer to take over the role of the Friend (following Lucas Hoving) in José Limón's *The Moor's Pavane.* Presented his first program of his own choreography, N.Y. Fashion Institute of Technology, May 5 and 6, 1962: *Gleams in the Bone House* (Harold Shapero), *Birds of Sorrow* (Peter Hartman), *How Many Miles to Babylon* (Carlos Surinach), and *Pierrot Lunaire* (Arnold Schoenberg). Joined Nederlands Dans Theater as guest artist (fall, 1962) and has since remained as choreographer and dancer, staging *Pierrot Lunaire* and other ballets, dancing in John Butler's *Carmina Burana* and the title role of his *Hadrianus* (prem.: Nov. 29, 1962, Rotterdam), and others. His *Game of Noah,* premièred at The Hague (July 1, 1965) as part of the Holland Festival, was in the repertoire of the Robert Joffrey Ballet. American Ballet Theatre premièred his *Sargasso* (mus.: Ernst Krenek; décor: Rouben Ter-Arutunian; Mar. 24, 1965) at N.Y. State Theater with Sallie Wilson and Bruce Marks in the principal roles. The same company premièred his *Ricercare* (mus.: Mordecai Seter; décor: Ter-Arutunian; Jan. 25, 1966) at the same theatre with Mary Hinkson (guest artist) and Scott Douglas. *Mythical Hunters,* which he first staged for the Bathsheva Company of Israel, was premièred at the Hunter College Playhouse (mus.: Oedeon Partos; costumes: Anthony Binstead; Apr. 1, 1966). He danced the première with Carmen de Lavallade. His *Chronochromie* (to the Olivier Messaien score of that name) with Carmen de Lavallade and Ross Parkes was premièred at the Jacob's Pillow Dance Festival (July 5–9, 1966).

Thamar. Ballet in 1 act; chor.: Michel Fokine; music: Mily Balakirev's symphonic poem *Thamar;* book and décor: Léon Bakst. First prod.: Diaghilev Ballets Russes, Théâtre du Châtelet, Paris, May 20, 1912, with Tamara Karsavina in the title role and Adolph Bolm as the Prince. The plot of the ballet deals with Thamar, Queen of Georgia, who seduces a visiting prince and then stabs him dead, his body falling through an open panel into the swift waters of the river Terek. This dramatic ballet featured a passionate pas de deux of the Prince and Queen and many Caucasian dances. Revived by Col. de Basil's Ballets Russes de Monte Carlo, the new version appeared to have lost most of the fire of the original.

Theatre Authority, a voluntary organization of actors set up in New York to regulate benefit performances given by companies and individual performers. The organization collects a certain percentage of the proceeds for actors' charities in the cases where performers appear gratis.

Theatre d'Art du Ballet, Le, ballet company founded in 1957 by Anna Galina and Tatiana Piankova which since that date has traveled widely in Europe, South Africa, the Middle and Far East, and in the U.S. (1961). It has a repertoire of Michel Fokine ballets staged by his son Vitale Fokine: *Les Sylphides, Carnaval, Le Spectre de la Rose, The Adventures of Harlequin, Igrouchki;* modern works by Leonide Massine (*Ballade*), Janine Charrat (*Danseuses de l'Opéra*), William Dollar (*Francesca da Rimini, The Fountain of the Blind, Simple Symphony*), Edward Caton (*Trilogy*), etc. Anna Galina is ballerina, Bogdan Bulder, Roy Tobias, and Françoise Nef are among the leading dancers.

Theatre Piece. Modern group dance; chor.: Doris Humphrey (part of trilogy including *New Dance* and *With My Red Fires*); music: Wallingford Riegger; costumes: Pauline Lawrence. First prod.: N.Y., Jan. 19, 1936.

Theatrics. Modern dance work; chor.:

Valerie Bettis; music: Paul Benet; designer: Saul Bolasni. First prod.: Adelphi Theatre, N.Y., May 13, 1945.

Theilade, Nini, Danish dancer, b. Java, 1916, of Danish father and mother of Polish, German and Hindu descent. Studied dance as a child with her mother and in Denmark; later with Lubov Egorova, Paris. Leading dancer in Max Reinhardt theatrical productions. Soloist, Ballet Russe de Monte Carlo (1938–40), creating Poverty (*Saint Francis*), Venus (*Bacchanale*), Stream (*Seventh Symphony*), and dancing Prelude (*Les Sylphides*), Prayer (*Coppélia*), and other roles. Living in South America since 1940. Holds Order of Dannebrog presented by King of Denmark.

Theme and Variations. Ballet in 1 act; chor.: George Balanchine; music: Peter Tchaikovsky's Suite No. 3 in G; décor: Woodman Thompson. First prod.: Ballet (now American Ballet) Theatre, Richmond, Va., Sept. 27, 1947; N.Y. première, City Center, Nov. 26, 1947, with Alicia Alonso and Igor Youskevitch. An abstract classic ballet, the variations providing the musical basis for a magnificent series of pas, especially the male variation and the final polonaise for the whole company. The décor was lost in a fire when the company was touring in Europe (1958), and the ballet was given Sept. 17, 1958, at the Metropolitan Opera House, N.Y., in new costumes (against a cyclorama) by André Levasseur, with Violette Verdy and Royes Fernandez. The ballerina role is one of Lupe Serrano's great successes. *Theme and Variations* was briefly in the repertoire of New York City Ballet (premièred Feb. 5, 1960) with Violette Verdy and Edward Villella. Balanchine also revived the ballet for the Latin-American tour of the American Ballet Theatre.

Theodore, Mlle. (Marie Madeleine Crespé), b. Paris, 1760; m. Jean Dauberval, dancer and choreographer. Dauberval created the original choreography for *La Fille Mal Gardée* (1786) in which Mlle. Theodore created the role of Lise. She was a favorite dancer of Jean-Georges Noverre. She died in 1796.

There Is a Time (original title, Variations on a Theme). Modern dance work; chor.: José Limón; music: Norman dello Joio; costumes: Pauline Lawrence; commissioned by Juilliard School of Music for Festival of Modern Music. First prod.: José Limón Dance Company, Juilliard Concert Hall, N.Y., Apr. 20, 1956, with José Limón, Pauline Koner, Ruth Currier, Betty Jones, Lavina Nielsen, Lucas Hoving, and company. The theme derives from the Book of Ecclesiastes quotation, "To everything there is a season, and a time to every purpose under the heaven."

Thibon, Nanon, French dancer, b. Paris, 1944. A pupil of the Paris Opéra Ballet school, she entered the company and was promoted to première danseuse in 1963. Dances pas de trois (*Swan Lake*), 1st movement: "Scottish Dance" (*Scotch Symphony*), among other roles.

Thimey, Erika, contemporary dancer, choreographer, director, teacher, b. Itzhoe, Germany. Graduate of Mary Wigman School, Germany; studied in N.Y. with Hanya Holm, Doris Humphrey, Charles Weidman, member of the Martha Graham School faculty, and Connecticut College Summer School of Dance. First appeared professionally with Margaret Wallman Group in Europe, then gave solo performances in Europe and U.S. Dance partner to Jan Veen for six years. Head of Modern Dance Department Chicago's North Shore Conservatory (1932–38); director of Dance Group Howard University, Washington, D.C. (1943–53). Founded Dance Theatre of Washington, D.C. (1943), home of the Chamber Dance Group and the Children's Dance Theatre. The first is a group of five dancers who travel widely with a repertoire of modern dance works choreographed by Erika Thimey. Children's Dance Theatre tours all over the U.S. with a repertoire of works for performance to juvenile audiences.

Thistle, Lauretta (née Finlayson), contemporary Canadian writer and critic, b. Nova Scotia, Canada. B.A., Mount Allison Univ., Sackville, N.B. (first class honors in English). She also studied music at Mount Allison Conservatory, and later with private teachers. Music and ballet critic for *The Ottawa Citizen* since 1947, her writings on the dance, both professional and in its regional ballet aspects, have had a considerable influence on the course of ballet in Canada. Contributor to *Dance Encyclopedia;* Canadian correspondent for *Dance News* (since June, 1966).

Thomson, Virgil, composer, writer and music critic, b. Kansas City, Mo., 1896. His major work for dance is *Filling Station* (1938), which he wrote for Ballet Caravan. His *Acadian Songs and Dances* was used by George Balanchine for *Bayou,* choreographed for the New York City Ballet (1952). *Bayou* was not a success and was soon taken out of the repertoire. The music was used again by Ruthanna Boris for her ballet *Will o' the Wisp* for the same company (1953). Some of the composer's music for the film *Louisiana Story* was used by Robert Moulton for his ballet *Grasslands,* produced by the Royal Winnipeg Ballet, Winnipeg, Canada (1958).

Thousand Times Neigh, A. See FORD BALLET.

Three-Cornered Hat, The. Ballet in 1 act; chor.: Leonide Massine; music: Manuel de Falla; book: Martinez Sierra; décor: Pablo Picasso. First prod.: Diaghilev Ballets Russes, Alhambra Theatre, London, July 22, 1919, with Leonide Massine (Miller), Tamara Karsavina (Miller's Wife), Leon Woicikowski (Corregidor), Stanislas Idzikowski (Dandy). Lubov Tchernicheva was later an outstanding Miller's Wife. In the repertoire of Col. de Basil's Ballet Russe de Monte Carlo, with Massine and Tamara Toumanova as the Miller and Miller's Wife; Massine revived it for Ballet (now American Ballet) Theatre (1943) when he was with that company, and for Sadler's Wells (now Royal) Ballet (1947) when as guest artist he danced the Miller with Margot Fonteyn (later Violetta Elvin) as the Miller's Wife. Massine also staged the ballet for the Royal Swedish Ballet. The libretto is based on a 19th century play *El Sombrero de Tres Picos* by the Spanish poet Pedro Antonio de Alarcón. The Miller and his Wife are completely devoted to each other though not above pretending to flirt with others. The Corregidor has his bodyguard kidnap the Miller so that he can be alone with the beautiful Wife. She, however, pushes the Corregidor into the stream and runs for help. The Corregidor crawls out and puts on the Miller's dressing gown. His bodyguard comes back and mistaking him for the Miller pummels him unmercifully. The Miller, reunited with his wife, returns with the other villagers. They, too, set upon the unfortunate Corregidor and finally, in a general dance of triumph over hated authority, toss his effigy in a blanket. Highlights of *The Three-Cornered Hat* are the Miller's farucca, the fandango for the Miller's Wife, and the jota for the ensemble. Picasso's front curtain for this ballet which depicted onlookers at a bullfight watching the dragging out of a dead bull was lost in the early 1920's and never reproduced. It was discovered a few years ago in South America and now hangs in the bridge between the two rooms of The Four Seasons restaurant in N.Y.

Three Virgins and a Devil. Ballet in 1 act; chor.: Agnes de Mille; music: Ottorino Respighi's *Antiche Danze ed Arie;* book: Ramon Reed; décor: Arne Lundborg, after sketches by Sophie Harris; costumes: Motley. First prod.: Ballet

Theatre, Majestic Theatre, N.Y., Feb. 11, 1941, with Agnes de Mille (Priggish Virgin), Lucia Chase (Greedy Virgin), Annabelle Lyon (Lustful Virgin), Eugene Loring (Devil), Jerome Robbins (A Youth). Miss de Mille first set her ballet to music by Walford Hyden, Palace Theatre, London, 1934 as an item in a revue, with Greta Nissen, Elisabeth Schooling, M. Braithwaite, Stanislas Idzikowski. The new score by Respighi was a much happier choice. The Devil tempts two of the girls with promises of that which each is the least able to resist, but has to resort to a struggle to capture the Priggish Virgin. Jerome Robbins in one brief entry as A Youth carrying a rose scored his first major success as a dancer.

Threnody. Modern dance work; chor.: Mary Anthony; music: Benjamin Britten's *Sinfonia da Requiem;* décor: William Sherman. First prod.: Bennington College, Vt., Spring, 1956, by graduating students of the dance department, four of whom (Bette Shaler, Joy Gitlin, Paul Berensohn, John Starkweather) became members of Mary Anthony's dance company; N.Y. première: YM–YWHA, Dec. 1956, with Bette Shaler (Mother), Mary Anthony and Joy Gitlin (Daughters), Paul Berensohn, John Starkweather, Cameron McCosh (Sons). Based on J. M. Synge's one-act play *Riders to the Sea.* The Mother accepts the loss of her last son to the sea that has taken all the men-folk of her family.

Tights, close fitting garment covering the body from the waist down, including legs and feet, worn by dancers. For stage use tights are made of nylon (usually stretch nylon), silk, and (usually for modern dancers) wool; for classroom and rehearsal wool or cotton is used. Tights covering only legs and feet are called opera lengths. Tights worn by modern dancers usually leave the feet bare. See also MAILLOT.

Tikhomirov, Vassily (1876–1956), Peoples' Artist of the RSFSR, famous Soviet dancer and teacher, b. Moscow. He was connected with a brilliant period of the Russian ballet as a dancer and left an invaluable legacy as a teacher. He was placed in the Bolshoi School at the age of nine (1885) and was graduated from it when he was still a year under the age for entering the company (1891). He was therefore sent to the St. Petersburg school to study under Christian Johansson and Paul Gerdt, remaining for two years and becoming an outstanding premier danseur and teacher. On returning to Moscow he had a brilliant debut at the Bolshoi Theatre in an interpolated pas de deux with Lubov Roslavleva in the ballet *Robert and Bertram* which marked the beginning of a long and fruitful career as dancer, choreographer, and teacher at the Moscow Bolshoi Theatre and School. Great as he was as a dancer, he will be remembered in the history of the Moscow Ballet for the galaxy of dancers he trained and for the teaching methods which became the cornerstone of the Moscow school. Some of his pupils were Mikhail Mordkin, Alexander Volinine, Theodore and Alexis Koslov, Leonid Zhukov, Asaf Messerer and many others, all typical of his own manly and vigorous style. He also trained a long line of ballerinas including Alexandra Balashova, Xenia Makletzova, Victorina Kriger. His life-long partner and wife, Yekaterina Geltzer, prima ballerina assoluta of the Bolshoi, studied with him throughout her career (with the exception of two years in St. Petersburg when she studied under Christian Johansson). Tikhomirov became first teacher of the Bolshoi school in Sept. 1896, and was later named director of the school, resigning only because of ill health when he became permanently bedridden (1937). As a teacher Tikhomirov did much for the development of the Russian school and must be ranked among the greatest teachers of all time. He applied the fundamentals acquired from Gerdt and Johansson in his own way, developing a system that yielded excellent results. Outside Russia he danced in London at the Alhambra Theatre in Alexander Gorsky's *Dance Dream* (1911) and with Anna Pavlova (1914). In the classic ballets he was particularly impressive as Jean de Brienne (*Raymonda*) and Conrad (*Le Corsaire*). He created the role of Narr'Avas in Gorsky's *Salammbo* (1910) and of the Soviet Captain in his own version (with Lev Lashchilin) of *The Red Poppy* (1927). He also choreographed revivals of *La Bayadère* and *The Sleeping Beauty* (1924), re-choreographed the second act of *La Sylphide* (music by Jean Schneitzhoffer) on the occasion of the centenary of the Bolshoi Theatre (1925), and staged a new version of *Esmeralda* (1926). After the October, 1917, revolution Tikhomirov played an important role in the maintenance of the Moscow ballet school as a special institution for ballet instruction and, with Geltzer, did much to preserve the classic heritage. His great influence on Russian ballet and the contribution he made to it will be felt for many years to come. His first wife was Yekaterina Geltzer, his second Lydia Abrikosova, a member of the well-known family of Moscow patrons of art. Died in Moscow, 1956.

Til Eulenspiegel. Ballet in 1 act; chor.: Jean Babilée; music: Richard Strauss' *Til Eulenspiegel's Merry Pranks;* décor: Tom Keogh. First prod.: Ballets des Champs-Elysées, Théâtre des Champs-Elysées, Paris Nov. 9, 1949, with Babilée in the title role. The ballet, like the music, stems from the old Flemish legends of the mischievous Til, whose pranks in the market place and disrespect for those in authority finally bring him to the hangman's noose. Babilée repeated his creation in the original décor for Ballet Theatre at the Metropolitan Opera House, Sept. 25, 1951. The same title, music, and subject were used by Vaslav Nijinsky for his last ballet, in décor by Robert Edmond Jones. With Nijinsky in the title role this version was premièred at the Metropolitan Opera House, Oct. 23, 1916. See also TYL ULENSPIEGEL.

Timofeyeva, Nina, Honored Artist of the RSFSR, Soviet ballerina, b. 1935. Entered the Leningrad Ballet School in 1943 and was graduated from it in 1953 (class of Natalia Kamkova, a pupil of Agrippina Vaganova). Was accepted into the Kirov Ballet (1953) and remained there until 1955. Her debut in the role of Odette-Odile in *Swan Lake* (1954) placed her in the front rank of promising young ballerinas and led to an invitation to join the Bolshoi Ballet (1956). Her repertoire at the Bolshoi includes: Odette-Odile (*Swan Lake*), Kitri and Street Dancer (*Don Quixote*), title role (*Laurencia*), Mireille (*Flames of Paris*), Mistress of the Copper Mountain (*The Stone Flower*), title role (*Gayané*), Phrygia (*Spartacus*), Myrtha (*Giselle*), *Chopiniana,* Bacchante ("Walpurgis Night" from *Faust*), Girl (*The Night City*), and others. Timofeyeva excels in ballets of the classical repertoire, but her creation of the Girl in Leonid Lavrovsky's ballet *The Night City* to Béla Bartók's *The Miraculous Mandarin* score reveals her as a dancer capable of creating powerful characterizations in modern ballet. Timofeyeva first appeared abroad during the Bolshoi Ballet's season in London (1956) and since then she has danced in the U.S., Canada, Austria, France, Belgium, Poland, Japan, Finland, Holland, Rumania, and Germany. She is married to Gennady Rozhdestvensky, a Bolshoi Theatre conductor.

Tire-Bouchon, en (like a corkscrew), a position in ballet in which the working leg is raised to ninety degrees and bent in the knee; the toe of the raised leg pressed closely to the knee of the supporting leg. A pirouette in this position gives the impression of a corkscrew, hence the name.

Tiresias. Ballet in 3 scenes; chor.: Frederick Ashton; commissioned music:

Nina Timofeyeva, ballerina of the Moscow Bolshoi Ballet in Swan Lake, *Act 2.*

Constant Lambert; décor: Isabel Lambert. First prod.: Sadler's Wells (now Royal) Ballet, Royal Opera House, Covent Garden, July 9, 1951, with Margot Fonteyn and Michael Somes in the dual role of Tiresias. A re-telling of the Greek myth of the blind seer Tiresias. Metamorphosed into a woman when he kills the sacred snakes, he returns to his masculine form when he repeats the action. Asked by Hera and Zeus to decide their quarrel as to whether a man or a woman receives more pleasure in love, he is struck blind by Hera who is enraged when he says woman, but Zeus makes compensation by giving him the gift of prophecy.

Tivoli Pantomime Theatre, so called because it is situated in Copenhagen's famous amusement park, Tivoli Garden, was built by the Danish architect Vilhelm Dahlerup (1874), the same year he completed the construction of the Royal Danish Theatre, Copenhagen. The Pantomime Theatre has remained exactly the same since it was built. The theatre with its peacock curtain and open-air seats offers performances every afternoon in the old commedia dell'arte tradition and modern ballets every evening during the Tivoli season May 1st to Septemer 15th. Niels Bjorn Larsen, form. artistic director of the Royal Danish Ballet, is the director of the Tivoli Pantomime Theatre.

The history of the Theatre goes back further than its construction. When Georg Carstensen opened his Tivoli amusement park on Aug. 15, 1843, it contained a primitive theatre in Moorish style on the site of the present Theatre. Pantomime plays with Italian masked figures had been performed in Copenhagen for a long time, mainly by the Price family, descended from the English equestrian and circus artiste James Price, whose company was in high favor with the royal houses in Vienna, Stockholm, and Copenhagen. It was, however, in Denmark that commedia dell'arte took root. Guiseppe Casorti, a descendant of old Pasquale Casorti and his "Big Italian Company," was a highly talented Pagliacco, or Pierrot. He remained in Denmark and began the Casorti line of pantomime which since then has been an unbroken tradition of the Tivoli Pantomime Theatre. Thanks to Casorti and his successor in the Pierrot profession, John Adolph Price, the old pantomimes Harlequin Skeleton, Harlequin Statue, Harlequin Cook, experienced a renaissance as a popular form of entertainment of the open-air stage of the Theatre. There are four central figures in the pantomime: Pantalone, who through the ages has been changed into the Holberg-Molière burgher Cassander; Harlequin, the mischievous teaser; Columbine, dressed in a ballerina tutu; and Pierrot who, due primarily to the eminent Danish actor Niels Hendrik Volkersen (1820–1893), has undergone a gradual development by adapting national Danish characteristics. Over the years commedia dell'arte declined and details of the original plays were forgotten, but in the past several years every effort has been made to revive and renew the Casorti-Price-Volkersen tradition. The Tivoli Pantomime Theatre is playing a most important, even unique, part in this effort.

Tobias, Roy, contemporary dancer, teacher, b. Philadelphia. Began dance training at age fourteen; joined Ballet (now American Ballet) Theatre two years later. Played the on-stage piano for Michael Kidd's *On Stage!* Appeared in Broadway musicals *High Button Shoes, Carousel.* Danced one season with Grand Ballet du Marquis de Cuevas in Paris, returned to U.S. for further study at School of American Ballet, N.Y., joining Ballet Society at same time and remaining when it became New York City Ballet. In this company he rose to leading soloist dancing a large repertoire. Taught ballet in Japan (1961–63). Joined Le Théâtre d'Art du Ballet (1963) as a leading dancer. Returned to U.S. in 1966.

Toby, Harriet (Katzman) (1929–52), American dancer, b. Paris. Began dance studies with Alexandre Volinine at age eight, then in N.Y. with Ludmila Shollar, Anatole Vilzak, and at School of American Ballet. Made her debut (using her mother's maiden name) in the Markova-Dolin ballet in *The Seven Lively Arts* revue (1944). Joined Ballet Russe de Monte Carlo (1946), Roland Petit's Ballets de Paris (1948), and Grand Ballet du Marquis de Cuevas (1949), becoming a leading soloist. Some of her ballets were *Les Biches, Del Amor y de la Muerte, Concerto Barocco, Blue Bird* pas de deux. She was killed in an air crash at Nice when flying to join her company for a Brussels opening.

Toe Dance. Although it is not known who first danced on toe (sur les pointes), it was apparently practiced in London in the 1820's. There is a print of Fanny Bias on toe (1821), and in reviewing the debut of Vaque-Moulin (1829) the London *Times* remarked on her dancing "on the extremities of her feet." An earlier reference is in the Almanach of Teatro alla Scala, Milan (1827) in which an account of the ballet *Dircea,* presented at La Scala Mar. 28, 1826, with choreography by Louis Henry, includes a paragraph on Amalia Brugnoli, one of the great ballerinas of the early nineteenth century. This specifically states that, ". . . in dancing effectively on the tip of her foot, her steps, her attitudes, her movements assume a je ne sais quoi of airiness which astonishes and arouses admiration." Toe dancing, made possible by the introduction of reinforced shoes, permitted more brilliant pirouettes because of the smaller point of contact between the dancer and the floor, gave an appearance of lightness, and a more continuous line of flow of the body. The dancer appeared to rise from the ground and glide or flow across the stage. This was one of the features of romantic ballet. There is reasonably compelling evidence that Maria Taglioni danced *La Sylphide* (1832) on point. See also ROMANTIC BALLET and GISELLE.

Toe-Shoe, a slipper used by dancers who dance on toes. Toe-shoes are usually, but not always, made of silk and the toe of the shoe is reinforced with a box made of several layers of strong glue between layers of material. The invention of the toe-shoe dates back to a few years after the beginning of the dance on toe. The exact year has never been established, but it is generally considered that the toe dance began in the early 1820's. There are still a few pairs of Maria Taglioni's shoes in existence which show no reinforcement of any kind except for a little darning at the tips. Numerous lithographs and engravings of dancers of that period also indicate that they did not use boxed shoes. It is reasonable to believe that these dancers had strongly developed toes and could do some dancing on their toes in soft slippers with perhaps some darning of the tips of the shoes. Eventually dancers began to use more and more reinforcement until one of them or a shoemaker developed the idea of boxing the toe of the shoe with layers of glue. The fact that the shoes in the lithographs of the 1840's and 1850's do not appear to have the specific square boxed toes may be attributed to the desire of the artists to glamorize the dancer. In addition to the box, dancers all the world over continue to darn the tip of the toe-shoe to effect a better grip of the shoe on the floor.

Tombé (from the Fr., lit. fallen), in ballet, a step in which the dancer falls from one leg to the other, or from two feet to one, placing the weight heavily on the foot which moves and bending the knee on landing.

Tomin, Jorge (George Fostikoff), Argentine dancer, choreographer, and teacher, b. Kharkov, Russia, 1915, now an Argentine citizen. Studied dance with his mother Victoria Tomina and at the Conservatorio Nacional. In 1937 he partnered Olga Spessivtzeva in the *Blue Bird* pas de deux and *Elegie* at a performance in Argentina. In 1939 he joined the Original Ballet Russe for its U.S. tour. On his return to Buenos Aires he was engaged as premier danseur at Teatro Colón where he remained as dancer, choreographer, and ballet master. He has a vast repertoire of classic and demi-caractère roles. At present he revives ballets for Teatro Colón and teaches at its Escuela Superior de Arte. Works as choreographer in Tucuman, Rio Cuarto, Santa Fe.

Tommasini, Vincenzo (1880–1950), Italian composer; arranged music of Domenico Scarlatti for the ballet *The Good-Humored Ladies* (Leonide Massine) and music of Paganini for *Devil's Holiday* (Frederick Ashton).

Tompkins, Beatrice, dancer, teacher, b. New York City, 1918. Studied dance at School of American Ballet, N.Y. Joined Ballet Caravan (1939) and remained with this nucleus group which developed into Ballet Society and finally, New York City Ballet. She was an unusual and interesting dancer, mainly in character roles, creating Mother and Judy (*Punch and the Child*), one of the five girls (*Divertimento*), Third Movement (*Symphony in C*), Leader of the Furies (*Orpheus*), Bearded Lady (*Jinx*), End Man (*Cakewalk*), and others. Also danced seasons with San Francisco Ballet, Ballet Russe de Monte Carlo. Has danced in television programs and has appeared as an actress in summer stock and on television. Dancer, and later ballet mistress, with Robert Joffrey Ballet (1958–60), with which company she also danced seasons in the New York City Center Opera. Retired in 1963.

Tordion, a 16th century court dance derived from the galliard. Originally it was a lively dance and was used in black-face numbers. Even when it became a court dance it was brisk and was danced with feet close to the ground.

Torenbosch, Chris, Dutch dancer, b. Amsterdam, Holland, 1930. Studied dance with Françoise Adret of the Amsterdam Opera and with Darja Collin, Tatiana Tamarova, Roland Casenave. Joined the company in the Amsterdam Stadsschouwburg (1952) and has remained through its various changes, first under Françoise Adret, then Mascha Ter Weeme (1959–61) and currently under Sonia Gaskell as the Nederlands Nationaal Ballet (see HOLLAND, BALLET IN). Chiefly a character dancer, his large repertoire includes Janine Charrat's *Jeu de Cartes,* Alan Carter's *House of Shadows,* Jack Carter's *The Disenchanted,* Herbert Ross's *Caprichos,* David Lichine's *Graduation Ball,* Rudi van Dantzig's *Jungle.*

Totem. Modern dance work; chor., sound score and lighting: Alwin Nikolais; color design: George Constant. First prod.: Henry Street Playhouse, N.Y., Jan. 29, 1960, with Murray Louis, Gladys Bailin, Phyllis Lamhut, Arlene Laub, Beverly Schmidt, Dorothy Vislocky, and members of the Playhoue Dance Company. A series of rituals in the typical manner of this choreographer. The effect is that of watching a series of spells in which we sometimes see the casting of the spell and sometimes the result of the incantation. A very much revised version with several new sections was presented at Henry St. Playhouse, Feb. 1, 1962.

Totentanz. See DANCE MACABRE.

Tamara Toumanova, one of the original "baby ballerinas," in Swan Lake, *Act 2.*

Toumanova, Tamara, ballerina, b. 1919. Toumanova was born in a box-car when her parents were fleeing from the Russian revolution. Brought up in Paris, she studied there almost exclusively with Olga Preobrajenska. George Balanchine saw her there and engaged her for the Ballets Russes de Monte Carlo creating for her *Cotillon* and *Concurrence* (1932). After the first season she joined Les Ballets 1933 in which company Balanchine created for her *Les Songes.* After that company's Paris and London seasons she rejoined Ballets Russes (1934) where, with Irina Baronova and Tatiana Riabouchinska, she was one of the "baby ballerinas" of that period. She danced the title role in *Firebird,* Miller's Wife (*The Three-Cornered Hat*), Ballerina (*Petrouchka*), Swan Queen (*Swan Lake,* Act 2), Aurora (*Aurora's Wedding*), and many others and created The Beloved (*Symphonie Fantastique*). When the company split (1937) she went with Leonide Massine and became one of the ballerinas of Ballet Russe de Monte Carlo, at which time she added *Giselle* to her repertoire. Since 1938 she has danced on Broadway in the musical *Stars in Your Eyes,* appeared in motion pictures (*Days of Glory, Tonight We Sing*—in which she portrayed Anna Pavlova), and been guest ballerina with many companies, among them Ballet (now American Ballet) Theatre, Paris Opéra Ballet (for which she created *Phèdre* in the Cocteau-Lifar production), Grand Ballet du Marquis de Cuevas. In recent years has also given many concert performances, principally in South America and Europe, partnered mainly by Vladimir Oukhtomsky. Appeared in Alfred Hitchcock's film *The Torn Curtain* (1966).

Toumine, Nesta (née Williams), Canadian dancer, choreographer, teacher, and director of Classical Ballet Concert Group of Ottawa, Canada, b. England, 1912. Educated in Ottawa, to which city her family had emigrated. Her first dance studies as a child were with Gwendolyn Osborne (Ottawa) and Konstantin Kobelev (N.Y.). Later she studied with Nicholas Legat, Serafima Astafieva, and Margaret Craske in London; Olga Preobrajenska in Paris, and from time to time with Julia Sedova. Made her debut in Sir Oswald Stoll's production of *The Golden Toy* (1932), in dances staged by Ninette de Valois. Toured with Ballet Russe de Paris (1933–34) and with Ballet Russe de Monte Carlo (1934–41). Began teaching in Ottawa in 1945 and became director of the Classical Ballet Studio (1949), at the same time organizing a group of students which as Classical Ballet Company participated in five of the six Canadian Ballet Festivals. This group developed in 1958 into the Classical Ballet Concert Group of semi-professional dancers which receives official government recognition in the form of financial support from the Canada Council for performances outside Ottawa (see CANADA, DANCE IN). Classical Ballet Concert Group has performed at each of the Northeast (U.S.) Regional Ballet Festivals since their inception (1959 to date). Nesta Toumine has staged many of the standard classic and Michel Fokine ballets for her company including *Swan Lake* (Act 2), *The Nutcracker, Giselle, Coppélia, Les Sylphides, Les Elves, Le Spectre de la Rose, L'Epreuve d'Amour.* She has choreographed a number of original ballets, among them *David, Fadette, Fairy Doll, Faust Ballet Suite, Marie-Madeleine, Mozartiana, Shostakovich Ballet Suite, The Seasons, Les Valses.* In 1941 married artist and former dancer Sviatoslav Toumine who often designs décor and costumes for the company's ballets.

Tour, in ballet, a turn.

Tour de Role. See ALTERNATE.

Tour en l'Air, in ballet, a turn achieved with a jump off both feet; a pirouette in the air.

Tour Jeté, in ballet, a corruption of the term jeté en tournant, used in the U.S.

Trade Unions, Theatrical. Professional dancers appearing on stage, screen, or television belong to theatrical trade unions having jurisdiction in the respective fields. Dancers in ballet companies, modern groups, and opera ballets are covered by the American Guild of Musical Artists (AGMA). Actors Equity Association (commonly known as Equity) handles the affairs of dancers appearing in musical comedies, revues, and straight plays. Dancers appearing in motion pictures are under the jurisdiction of the Screen Actors Guild. The American Federation of Television and Radio Artists is the union of dancers appearing in television. Dancers appearing in vaudeville, circus, night clubs, and similar places are under the jurisdiction of the American Guild of Variety Artists (AGVA). A dancer need not belong to all of the unions to practice his profession. When he changes from one field of employment to another he obtains a transfer from one union to the other. He pays one initiation fee at the beginning of his career and one set of dues. In the case of prolonged unemployment the dancer obtains from his union an Honorable Withdrawal. If the unemployment lasts less than a full year he has to pay up his back dues for the elapsed time; if the unemployment period lasts more than a year he pays a $2.00 reinstatement fee. In September, 1964 the union signed a five-year basic agreement with the Metropolitan Opera, by which the dancers (and choristers) receive a weekly salary for 52 weeks a year. A similar, but two-year agreement, was signed by the union in October, 1964 with the New York City Ballet.

Tragedia di Orfeo, La. Ballet in 6 scenes; chor.: Heinz Rosen; music: Wilhelm Killmayer; book: Angelo Poliziano; décor: Helmut Jürgens; costumes: Charlotte Flemming. First prod.: State Opera Munich, June 9, 1961, with Heino Hallhuber (Orfeo) and Sonia Arova (Eurydice). The fate of Orpheus and Eurydice is dressed in the style of baroque art in the form of ballet chanté.

Tragedy of Fashion, A (or *The Scarlet Scissors*). Ballet in 1 act; chor.: Frederick Ashton; music: from Eugene Goossen's *Kaleidoscope;* décor: Sophie Fedorovitch. First prod.: Lyric Theatre, Hammersmith, June 15, 1926, as part of the revue *Riverside Nights,* with Frederick Ashton (Monsieur Duchic), Marie Rambert (Orchidée), Frances James and Elizabeth Vincent (Models). Of historical importance because this was Ashton's first ballet. The story was a variation of the legend that the great chef Vatel committed suicide when his fish course arrived late for King Louis XIV's dinner. Ashley Dukes (Mme. Rambert's husband) suggested that it was an amusing theme for a ballet. As it finally developed, the story became that of a couturier who stabbed himself with his scissors when his masterpiece did not please his richest client. This was Ashton's first ballet; it was also his first collaboration with Sophie Fedorovitch.

Tragic Exodus. Modern group dance; chor.: Hanya Holm; music: Vivian Fine. First prod.: N.Y., Feb. 19, 1939.

Trailine, Boris, French dancer of Russian parentage, b. Lemnos, Greece, 1921. Pupil of Julie Sedova (1934) and Ivan Clustine. Premier danseur of Ballets de Cannes (1941); danseur étoile with Nouveaux Ballets de Monte Carlo (1943), and later with Nouveau Ballet de Monte Carlo, directed by Eugène Grunberg and Serge Lifar (1946). Danced the classic repertoire and *Dramma per Musica, Chota Roustaveli, Night on Bald Mountain,* all with choreography by Lifar. Subsequently joined Grand Ballet de Monte Carlo (later called Grand Ballet du Marquis de Cuevas). Since 1948 has partnered such stars as Yvette Chauviré, Janine Charrat at guest appearances and Festivals, including Maggio Musicale Fiorentino and Salzburg Festival. Created role of the Knight in *La Dame à la Licorne* (Jean Cocteau—Heinz Rosen), Munich, 1953. On death of Alexandre Volinine (1955) he took over his Paris studio where he now teaches; also choreographs for television and some European festivals.

Trailine, Hélène, French ballerina; b. Bombas (Lorraine), 1928, of Russian parentage; sister of Boris Trailine; m. Juan Giuliano. Pupil of Julie Sedova (Cannes), and Lubov Egorova (Paris). Made her debut with Nouveau Ballet de Monte Carlo (1946). Danced leading roles in *Dramma Per Musica, Suite en Blanc, Chota Roustaveli,* and remained until 1948 by which time the company had become Grand Ballet de Monte Carlo (later du Marquis de Cuevas). Ballerina, Ballets des Champs-Elysées (1949–50); with Ballets Janine Charrat for several seasons between 1952 and 1959, dancing in Europe, the U.S., Central and South America. Has also danced with Ballet Milorad Miskovitch for special seasons and festival performances, creating a leading role in Maurice Béjart's *Haut Voltage* (1956). Was Demeter to Vera Zorina's Persephone in the Stravinsky work choreographed by Margaret Wallman for the Salzburg Festival (1955). Has frequently danced in ballets by Aurel Milloss at the Maggio Musicale Fiorentino; guest artist with Ballet Rambert (1956) dancing *Swan Lake* and classic pas de deux. Created leading role in Béjart's *Equilibre* for a season in Berlin and later in Paris; danced at Théâtre Royal de la Monnaie, Brussels. Guest ballerina with Ballet Russe de Monte Carlo in U.S. (1960–61, 1962), dancing the classic repertoire, pas de deux, and also Glove Seller (*Gaîté Parisienne*), Street Dancer (*Le Beau Danube*), and others.

Train Bleu, Le. Ballet in 1 act; chor.: Bronislava Nijinska; music: Darius Milhaud; book: Jean Cocteau; décor: Henri Laurens; costumes: Chanel; curtain: Pablo Picasso. First prod.: Diaghilev Ballets Russes, Théâtre des Champs-Elysées, Paris, June 20, 1924, with Bronislava Nijinska, Lydia Sokolova, Anton Dolin, Leon Woizikowski in principal roles. This ballet was created for Anton Dolin and is based on beach games and swimming, tennis, and golf movements.

Traitor, The. Modern dance work; chor.: José Limón; music: Gunther Schuller's *Symphony for Brasses;* décor: Paul Trautvetter; costumes: Pauline Lawrence. First prod.: José Limón Dance Company, Seventh American Dance Festival, Connecticut College, New London, Aug. 19, 1954, with José Limón (Traitor), Lucas Hoving (Leader) and Charles Szarny, Richard Fitz-Gerald, Michael Hollander, Alvin Schulman, Otis Bigelow, John Coyle. The re-telling in movement of the betrayal of Christ by Judas Iscariot. It was commissioned by the American Dance Festival.

Transcendence. Ballet in 1 act; chor.: George Balanchine; music: Franz Liszt's *Etudes d'éxécution transcendante,* orch. by George Antheil; book: Lincoln Kirstein; décor: Gaston Longchamp; costumes: Franklin Watkins. First prod.: The American Ballet, Adelphi Theatre, N.Y., Mar. 5, 1935 (after a performance Dec. 6, 1934, in Hartford, Conn., by the Producing Company of the School of American Ballet). One of the works presented on the second program of The American Ballet. Set in the epoch of Liszt and Paganini, the virtuoso instrumentalist hypnotizes the peasant girls and particularly one girl, who deserts her lover. Disguised as a monk the mysterious figure shows her a Witches' Sabbath, but her lover and his friends finally rescue her and bear him away. However, nothing can quench his indomitable energy and he returns under his three aspects of artist, priest, and man to lead the whole company in a wild Hungarian dance.

Travellers, The. Ballet in 1 act; chor.: Norman Morrice; commissioned music: Leonard Salzedo; décor and lighting: Ralph Koltai. First prod.: Ballet Rambert, Festival of Two Worlds, Spoleto, June 27, 1963, with Jonathan Taylor, Alan Cunliffe, Gayrie MacSween, Ariette Taylor, Peter Curtis in leading roles; London première: Sadler's Wells Theatre, July 18, 1963. The travellers are amused when on arrival at an airport they are met with a barrage of the usual instructions blared through a loudspeaker. But when they later seek to rejoin their aircraft, the instructions take on a sinister note; the travellers are trapped for no known reason. When one rebels, he is captured and returns to the group brainwashed. Another, breaking away from the horrors of unexplained detention, is shot. The curtain falls with a reminder that such episodes can take place anywhere, at any time.

Travesti (lit. disguised), in ballet, a female dancer wearing a man's costume and taking the part of male dancer, usually as a partner in a pas de deux or adagio; opera ballets often use female dancers en travesti. In the ballet of the Paris Opéra dancers en travesti are still being used, the role of Franz in *Coppélia* still being traditionally danced by a girl.

Trecu, Pirmin (Aldebaldetrecu), dancer, b. Zaraus, Spain (Basque Province), 1930. Was sent to England as a refugee during the Spanish Civil War. Entered Sadler's Wells School (1946); became a member of Sadler's Wells Theatre Ballet (1947), transferring to Sadler's Wells (now Royal) Ballet (1955) where he became a leading soloist. A leg injury brought his dancing career to a premature close and he gave his last performance Jan. 27, 1961, as the Boy in *La Fête Etrange,* probably his best role and one for which his strange and compelling personality was particularly suited. He is now Dance Director of the Parnasso School, Oporto (Lisbon) Opera House.

Trefilova, Vera (1875–1943), Russian ballerina. Graduated from the St. Petersburg Imperial School of Ballet (1894). Was accepted into the Maryinsky Theatre but due to intrigues and in spite of her talent, was kept in the back row of the corps de ballet for nearly two years. Because of this situation she was ready to give up her career, but Pierina Legnani, the prima ballerina of the Maryinsky Theatre at the time, took an interest in the young dancer, advised her to continue to work and promised to help her. A strict classic dancer with a virtuoso technique, she attracted the attention of the audience, the press and the Imperial Court. In 1904 she became a ballerina and her first ballerina role was Princess Aurora in *The Sleeping Beauty.* In 1906 she was promoted to prima ballerina. A year later she took a leave of absence to appear in Paris where she was received with acclaim. In 1910, still unable to cope with intrigues backstage at the Imperial Theatre, Trefilova resigned from the company. Her last appearance on the stage of the Maryinsky was in *Swan Lake.* For a few years she kept away from the theatre, but returned to the stage as a dramatic actress (1915), appearing at the Imperial Mikhailovsky Theatre in St. Petersburg. Trefilova left Russia in 1917 and settled in Paris where she opened a ballet studio. In 1921 Serge Diaghilev invited her to appear in her old role of Princess Aurora in his full-length revival of *The Sleeping Beauty* in London. She accepted the invitation and danced the role, taking turns with Lubov Egorova, Lydia Lopoukhova, and Olga Spessivtzeva. These performances proved to be the ballerina's last appearances on the stage. Vera Trefilova was married three times. Her first two husbands, A. I. Butler and N. V. Soloviev, died very early. Her third husband was Valerian Svetlov, the dean of Russian ballet critics and author of several books on ballet, among them *Le Ballet Contemporain* (1911), published in French and Russian. He died in Paris in 1934, as did Trefilova during the German Occupation (1943).

Trend. Modern group dance; chor.: Hanya Holm; music: Wallingford Riegger, with mechanical reproduction of Edgar Varèse's *Ionization;* and *Octandre;* setting: Arch Lauterer; costumes: Betty Joiner. First prod.: Bennington College, Aug., 1937. N.Y. première: Dec. 28, 1937, at Mecca Temple (now City Center). Louise Kloepper, Lucretia Wilson, Elizabeth Waters, Henrietta Greenhood (Eve Gentry) were among the principals. Hanya Holm's first major composition and a revolutionary work in its time. Its six parts were an expression of the rhythm of Western civilizations, the timeless creative forces persisting beneath the surface of contemporary existence with an awareness of the essential purposes of living finally emerging with a renewed affirmation.

Trepak, a Russian or more properly Ukrainian, folk dance performed by men. It is in 2/4 time and full of typical squatting steps alternating with big leaps. A famous example in ballet is the Russian dance in Lev Ivanov's *The Nutcracker* (Act 2).

Triadic Ballet. See ABSTRACT DANCE.

Tricorne, Le. See THREE-CORNERED HAT, THE.

Triomphe de L'Amour, Le. Ballet by Jean-Baptiste Lully, produced in St. Germain in 1681. It was the first ballet of the era in which women participated. They were ladies of the court, but when the ballet was repeated later at the Académie, professional dancers took part (including Mlle. Lafontaine, the first professional première danseuse. The libretto was written by Benserade and Quinault, and Berain designed the costumes and settings. Pécourt and Beauchamp danced in this ballet—Beauchamp as Mars and Pécourt performing several entrées. Harald Lander staged a new version for the Royal Danish Ballet (1962), using the music and libretto of the original.

Trisler, Joyce, American modern dancer, choreographer, teacher, b. Los Angeles, Calif., 1934; m. Charles Woodford. Attended Univ. of California at Los Angeles; graduate of Juilliard School of Music. Studied dance with Lester Horton, Carmalita Maracci, Antony Tudor, Hanya Holm, Robert Joffrey, Edward Caton. Member, Lester Horton Dance Theatre (1951–54), making her N.Y. debut with that company (1953). After moving permanently from California to N.Y. became a leading member of Juilliard Dance Theatre throughout its existence (1955–59), while giving performances with her own group occasionally. Combined with John Wilson (1960) in the Trisler-Wilson Company to perform at the YM–YWHA, various colleges, etc. Among her choreographic works are *Journey* (Charles Ives, 1958), *The Bewitched* and *Theatre Piece* (Arnold Schoenberg, both 1959), *Bronx Zoo Cantata* (1960), *Theatre Piece,* revised (Schoenberg-Ives), *Ecossaises* (Schubert), *Brandenburg Concerto* (Bach, both 1961). She has also choreographed for plays, operas, and operettas for special performances, and in summer stock. She is one of the foremost teachers of the Lester Horton technique of modern dance and has lectured widely. Was the recipient of an Alice Ditson Fund grant to choreograph *The Bewitched* and of an Elizabeth Talbot Fund grant to lecture at the Univ. of Chicago.

Joyce Trisler, American modern dancer.

Triumph of Bacchus and Ariadne, The. Ballet-cantata; chor.: George Balanchine; music: Vittorio Rieti; décor and costumes: Corrado Cagli. First prod.: Ballet Society, N.Y. City Center, Feb. 9, 1948, with the full cast of dancers headed by Nicholas Magallanes and Tanaquil LeClercq (title roles), Marie Jeanne, Herbert Bliss, Charles Laskey, Francisco Moncion, Pat McBride, Claudia Bell, and a choral assembly of forty singers. First performance by New York City Ballet (the name given by Ballet Society to its performing company later the same year), Nov. 1, 1948, with the same cast. The theme is taken from a Florentine carnival song written by Lorenzo de Medici (the Magnificent). The work consists of separate entrées each depicting mythological characters: Bacchus and Ariadne, Nymphs and Satyrs, Silenus and Midas, ending with a Bacchanale danced by all the characters and the ensemble.

Triumph of Neptune, The. Ballet in 2 acts, 6 scenes; chor.: George Balanchine; music: Lord Berners; book: Sacheverell Sitwell; décor and costumes: adapted from scenes and costumes for the Juvenile Drama as published by B. Pollack and H. J. Webb. First prod.: Diaghilev Ballets Russes, Lyceum Theatre, London, Dec. 3, 1926, with Alexandra Danilova, Vera Petrova, Lydia Sokolova, Lubov Tchernicheva, George Balanchine, Michael Fedorov, Stanislas Idzikowski, and Serge Lifar in leading roles.

Triumph of St. Joan. Modern dance solo; chor. and danced by Martha Graham; music: Norman Dello Joio, Columbia Auditorium, Louisville, Ky., Dec. 5 and 6, 1951. The work was commissioned by the Louisville Arts Council, played at these performances by the Louisville Symphony Orchestra, and danced by Martha Graham. Its New York première was at Juilliard Concert Hall, Apr. 22, 1952. It was later entirely re-choreographed as a group work titled *Seraphic Dialogue* (which see).

Trninic, Dusan, Yugoslav dancer, b. Belgrade, 1929. Studied with Nina Kirsanova and Olga Preobrajenska. Joined Belgrade National Ballet (1946); promoted to premier danseur (1948). Studied at the Royal Ballet School, London (1959). His repertoire includes *El Amor Brujo* (de Falla-Parlic), *La Reine des Iles* (Thiriet-Parlic), *Romeo and Juliet* (Prokofiev-Parlic), *The Devil in the Village* (Fran Lhotka–Pino and Pia Mlakar), *Orpheus* (Stravinsky-Parlic), *The Ballad of a Medieval Love* (Lhotka–the Mlakars), *Giselle* (Lavrovsky), *Coppélia, Symphony in C, Gingerbread Heart* (all by Parlic); Ancient Games (Richard Strauss–Pino and Pia Mlakar).

Trofimova, Natasha, contemporary German ballerina, b. Berlin, of Russian extraction. Studied dance with Eugenia Edouardova, Sabine Hess, Tatiana Gsovska, Victor Gsovsky. Made her debut in the title role in *Cinderella,* Scala Theatre, Berlin (1943). Prima ballerina, State Opera, Berlin (1946–51). Toured with the ballet *Abraxas* in the Helge Pavlinin company. Since 1951 prima ballerina of the State Opera Ballet, Munich. Appeared as guest artist State Opera Hamburg, Opera House Frankfurt a/M and Berliner Ballett. Dances principal roles in *Petrouchka, Romeo and Juliet, The Sleeping Beauty, Saint Francis, Hamlet, Joan von Zarissa, Tragedie de Salomé, Abraxas, Chinese Nightingale, The Miraculous Mandarin, The Legend of Joseph, Catulli Carmina, Danza, Gala Performance.*

Trowbridge, Charlotte, contemporary painter, b. Sacramento, Calif. Designed costumes for *Punch and the Judy* (Martha Graham); *Yanvaloo, Shouters of Sobo* (Pearl Primus); *Adolescence, Short Story* (Jane Dudley); *Adios* (William Bales); *Mozart's Gigue, Saturday Night, Yankee Bluebritches* (Erick Hawkins); *Totem Ancestor* (Merce Cunningham); *People and Ghosts* (Jean Erdman). She has also published a book, *Dance Drawings of Martha Graham* (1945).

Truitte, James, contemporary American modern dancer and teacher, b. Chicago, Ill. Intended to be a doctor and had a year of premedical study at Univ. of California at Los Angeles. Later concentrated on dance studies, first with Archie Savage, then with Janet Collins, Frances Allis, Carmalita Maracci, and from 1948 with Lester Horton, becoming a member of the Horton company (1950). His previous professional career had included touring with the national company of *Carmen Jones* (1945–47) and dancing in the Greek Theatre, Los Angeles, revival of the musical *Finian's Rainbow*. After Horton's death (1953), Truitte assumed most of the teaching responsibilities and remained with the company until 1959, choreographing a number of works. He danced in several motion pictures during this period, best known of which are *Carmen Jones* (1954) and *South Pacific* (1959). Was choreographic assistant to Horton for *South Sea Woman* (1952) and choreographer for *The Mole People* (1958) and *The Sins of Rachel Cade* (1959). Has appeared in leading night clubs and in many television shows. Currently teaching in N.Y. (since 1959) and performing with Geoffrey Holder, Joyce Trisler, John Wilson, and as a permanent leading member (and assistant to Alvin Ailey) of Alvin Ailey's Dance Theatre. Received a John Hay Whitney Fellowship (1959–60) to study Labanotation for the purpose of recording the technique vocabulary of the Lester Horton method.

Trumpet Concerto. Ballet in 1 act, 3 movements; chor.: George Balanchine; music: Josef Haydn's trumpet concerto; décor: Vivienne Kernot. First prod.: Sadler's Wells Theatre Ballet, Opera House, Manchester, Sept. 14, 1950; London première: Sadler's Wells Theatre, Sept. 19, with Svetlana Beriosova, and David Blair heading the company. Balanchine's only original ballet for a British company and, unfortunately, not one of his most distinguished.

Trunoff, Vassili, dancer and choreographer, b. Melbourne, Australia, 1929; m. Joan Potter. Studied with Edouard Borovansky; founder-member of Borovansky's first Australian Ballet (1943); principal dancer (1946). Soloist with Ballet Rambert (1947–48), joining the company on its Australian tour and coming to England with it. Played Judd in the musical *Oklahoma!* (1949–50) in Australia. Returned to Europe (1950), and joined Markova-Dolin company in which, when it became London's Festival Ballet, he was principal character dancer. Principal dancer with Borovansky Ballet in Australia (1954–58), rejoining London's Festival Ballet (1959). Roles include Chief Warrior (Polovetsian Dances from Prince Igor), Golden Slave (*Schéhérazade*), Vassili (*The Snow Maiden*), and others. Ballets he has choreographed include *Conflict* (Melbourne Ballet Guild, 1950), *Opus 2*, *Rossiniana* (in Adelaide).

Truscott, Anna, dancer, b. Orkney Isles, Scotland, 1940. Dance training at Legat School of Ballet, London, and at International School of Ballet (Ana Roje, Oskar Harmos), Split, Yugoslavia. Danced with the Yugoslav State Theatre Ballet, Split, her roles including Swanilda (*Coppélia*), Waltz, Pas de Deux, Mazurka (*Les Sylphides*), and others. Joined Ballet Rambert (1959) where she dances Ballerina from Moscow (*Gala Performance*), Episode in His Past (*Jardin aux Lilas*), Girl in Black (*Winter Night*), Queen of the Wilis (*Giselle*). Created Foreman's Wife (*Hazana*), among other roles.

Truyol, Antonio, premier danseur and choreographer, b. Buenos Aires, 1933. Studied dance at Teatro Colón ballet school with Gemma Castillo, Michel Borovski, and later with Aurel Milloss. Soloist, Teatro Colón; promoted to premier danseur in 1953. He is a demi-caractère dancer, excelling in pantomime. In 1959 he choreographed his first ballet for Teatro Colón, *Pavana Real* to music by Joaquin Rodrigo. He was appointed Director of the Colón ballet company (1960) and staged his second ballet, *Opus 34,* to music by Benjamin Britten. In 1961 received a grant to study choreography in the U.S. and Europe.

Tschaikovsky Foundation, The, N.Y., was started in the summer of 1945 as a repository for pre-Soviet Russian music and other pertinent matter. Its library is unique in that the collection comprises manuscripts, letters, documents, and varied source material which cannot be found elsewhere on this continent—material bearing not only on Tchaikovsky but other 19th century Russian composers as well. The ballet music division is particularly strong in that it contains copies of both orchestra and piano scores of ballets which Tchaikovsky borrowed from the libraries of the Bolshoi and Maryinsky theatres for study and reference during the composition of his own works. These ballets comprise the gamut of the classics. These items are supplemented by a miscellany of single collections of ballet material. Extensive files on ballet composers and data in individual ballets are maintained by the organization. The library, privately endowed, is for the purposes of research and consultation. Peter March is editor and administrative director.

Tucker, Gregory, contemporary American composer of the music for *Metropolitan Daily* (Hanya Holm), *Sea Bourne* (William Bales), *Saturday Night* (Erick Hawkins).

Tucker, Joan, English dancer and teacher, b. London, 1927; m. Jack Spurgeon. Studied with Joan Watts in Carshalton, and Phyllis Bedells, Anna Severskaya, and Nicholas Sergeyev. After one month in International Ballet School (1944), joined company, becoming soloist, dancing *Giselle,* Lilac Fairy (*The Sleeping Beauty*), Swanilda (*Coppélia*), Maria (*Twelfth Night*), and others. Toured in variety, danced in India and Pakistan, then joined Original Ballet Russe (1951), dancing Queen of Shemakhan (*Le Coq d'Or*), Frivolity (*Les Présages*). Opened school with her husband in Edinburgh (1954) under the name The Stage School of Dancing; now known as The Academy of Ballet.

Tudor, Antony, dancer, choreographer, teacher, b. London, 1909. Did not begin his dance studies until he was nineteen. Studied with Marie Rambert, Margaret Craske, Nicholas Legat, and others. Dancer and choreographer with the Ballet Club (which became Ballet Rambert) (1930–38), also dancing with the Vic-Wells (later Sadler's Wells, now Royal) Ballet (1933–35). His first ballet *Cross-garter'd,* based on the Malvolio-yellow stockings episode in *Twelfth Night* (1931), was followed by a number of others, notably his first important work *The Planets* (1934), *The Descent of Hebe* (1935), *Jardin aux Lilas* (1936), *Dark Elegies* (1937), *Judgment of Paris* (1938). Left Ballet Rambert (1938) to found London Ballet for which he choreographed *Soirée Musicale* and *Gala Performance* the same year. Also choreographed ballets for several operas and musical comedies and arranged the ballet in the play *The Happy Hypocrite* in which Vivien Leigh became an overnight sensation in London. Choreographer and dancer, Ballet (now American Ballet) Theatre since its inception (except for the season 1945–46), until he left the company to become director of the Ballet Theatre and Metropolitan Opera Ballet School (fall, 1950); remained director and head of the faculty when Ballet Theatre withdrew and the Met continued with its own school. During his years with Ballet Theatre he re-staged *Jardin aux Lilas* (renamed *Lilac Garden*), *Gala Performance, Judgment of Paris, Dark Elegies,* and choreographed *Pillar of Fire* (which brought immediate recognition to Nora Kaye as a great dramatic ballerina), *Romeo and Juliet, Dim Lustre, Shadow of the Wind,* and his final work for the company, *Nimbus* (1950). As a dancer he

Antony Tudor (center) rehearsing dancers of The New York City Ballet in his Dim Lustre.

had appeared in most of his own ballets in England and with Ballet Theatre re-created The Man She Must Marry (*Lilac Garden*), Cavalier for the Italian Ballerina (*Gala Performance*), Drunken Guest (*Judgment of Paris*), and his roles in *Dark Elegies.* He created the Friend (*Pillar of Fire*), Tybalt (*Romeo and Juliet*), one of the male roles in *Dim Lustre.* In ballets by other choreographers he created The Dummy (Eugene Loring's *The Great American Goof*), King Bobiche (*Bluebeard,* N.Y. première), Zemphira's Father (*Aleko*). For other than Ballet Theatre during that period he choreographed *Time Table* for Ballet Caravan (1941) and the dances in the musicals *Hollywood Pinafore* and *The Day Before Spring* (1945). Since taking up his position as head of the Metropolitan Opera Ballet School he has created few new works. *Lady of the Camellias* (Feb. 28, 1951) for New York City Ballet did little more than provide Diana Adams and Hugh Laing with new roles soon after they joined the company. For the same company he staged *La Gloire* (1952) which was also quickly dropped. *Offenbach in the Underworld* for National Ballet of Canada (1955) was more successful than his mounting of it for American Ballet Theatre (1956). Many of his ballets have, however, been most successfully presented by companies in Europe, notably Sweden and South America. He first went to Sweden in 1950 where *Gala Performance* has ever since been a regular part of the Royal Swedish Ballet repertoire, and in Dec., 1962, he staged *Pillar of Fire* and *Romeo and Juliet* for the company—the first time these ballets had ever been mounted for a company other than American Ballet Theatre. As a teacher at Juilliard School of Music Dance Department since its inception he also choreographs little works at the annual performances of the graduating class. It is generally agreed that if he never created another ballet his *Lilac Garden, Pillar of Fire, Romeo and Juliet,* would be sufficient to place him in the very front rank of choreographers. While retaining his positions with the Metropolitan Opera Ballet School and Juilliard he was appointed artistic director of the Royal Swedish Ballet in the fall of 1963, and in June, 1963, became one of an artistic council (the others being Birgit Cullberg and Birgit Aakesson) formed to direct the artistic policy of the company. His first original work for the Royal Swedish Ballet, and his first important work for many years, was *Echoes of Trumpets,* premièred Sept. 20, 1963. He resigned his position with the Royal Swedish Ballet in 1964.

Tugal, Dr. Pierre, French writer, b. Russia, 1895, d. Paris, 1964. Co-founder in 1931 (with Rolf de Maré) and curator of the Paris Archives Internationales de la Danse until its dissolution (1952). Doctor of Law, diploma in Social and Political Sciences. Devoted himself to literary and art research, specializing in the theatre and dance. Delegate to UNESCO. Author of many articles and several books on dance including *Initiation à la Danse* (1947) and *La Danse Classique Sans Maître* (with Lucien Legrand, 1956), and others. M. Tugal died in Paris, June 6, 1964, after a long illness.

Tupin, Wasil, Argentine dancer, b. Bulgaria, 1922; m. Mercedes Serrano. Studied in Paris with Lubov Egorova; later in Original Ballet Russe with Anatole Oboukhov and in Buenos Aires with Esmée Bulnes and Michel Borovski. Joined Original Ballet Russe as corps de ballet dancer (1939). Engaged by Teatro Colón, Buenos Aires, as premier danseur (1948); joined Grand Ballet du Marquis de Cuevas (1957); returned to Colón as guest artist (1960). In 1961 danced with Yvette Chauviré and Natalie Krassovska at Colón. His repertoire includes *Les Sylphides, Giselle, Swan Lake, Black Swan* pas de deux, *Concerto* (Skibine), *Metamorphosis, Gaîté Parisienne, Prince Igor, Choreartium, Aurora's Wedding,* and others.

Tupine, Oleg, dancer, b. on shipboard off Istanbul, Turkey, 1920, of Russian parents. Studied dance with Lubov Egorova (1935–38) and danced with her Ballets de la Jeunesse, Paris. Joined Original Ballet Russe (1938–47), creating Abel in David Lichine's *Cain and Abel,* the Sun in Vania Psota's *Yara,* and dancing leading classic roles. With Markova-Dolin Company (1947–48). Joined Ballet Russe de Monte Carlo until 1951, after which time he appeared with this company occasionally as guest artist. Danced principal roles in *Swan Lake* (Act 2), *Les Sylphides, Black Swan* and *Don Quixote* pas de deux, etc. After several years teaching in Los Angeles and performing with a group organized by himself and his former wife Natalia Clare (Conlon), he went to Washington, D.C. where he now teaches.

Turandot, Princess. Ballet in 2 acts; chor.: Tatiana Gsovska; music: Gottfried von Einem; book and décor: Luigi Malipiero. First prod.: State Opera Dresden, Feb. 5, 1944, with Evelyne Marek (Turandot) and Franz Karhanek (Kalaf). The cruel Turandot has agreed to marry the prince who solves the three riddles she asks (the answers: folly, foolishness, and love). Although Kalaf has fulfilled the condition, Turandot still resists him, but his unshakable true love conquers the indifference of her heart. The ballet was produced on several German stages, among them the Municipal Opera, Berlin, with choreography by Gustav Blank (1952) and at the State Opera, Munich, with choreography by Pino Mlakar (1954).

Turnbull, Julia, American ballerina, b. Montreal, Canada, June 18, 1822, d. Brooklyn, N.Y., Sept. 11, 1887. Julia Ann Turnbull came to the U.S. at the age of three when her father, an actor, accepted an engagement in Albany, N.Y. She played children's roles there and in N.Y. She studied dancing under the French ballerina Mme. LeComte and her brother, Jules Martin. She made her ballet debut as co-star with Mary Ann Lee in *The Sisters* at the Bowery Theatre, N.Y. (1839). During Fanny Elssler's tour of the U.S. (1840–42), she danced important roles in her company and continued her training under James Sylvain, Elssler's partner. Later she scored in *Giselle, Nathalie, or the Swiss Milkmaid,* and *Esmeralda,* being one of the first American dancers to undertake these demanding classical roles. From 1850 she also appeared in acting parts, although she continued to dance until her retirement in 1857.

Turner, Harold, English dancer and teacher, b. Manchester, 1909, d. London, 1962; m. Gerd Larsen. Studied dance in Manchester with Alfred Haines, in London with Marie Rambert. He became a principal dancer with Ballet Rambert in its early days, partnering Tamara Karsavina in *Le Spectre de la Rose* (1930), and dancing in most of the ballets of that period. Guest artist, Vic-Wells (later Sadler's Wells, now Royal) Ballet (1929–30); became a regular member in 1935, remaining as principal dancer (except for a brief period with International Ballet and war service in the mid-1940's) until he retired as a dancer in 1955, though continuing to make occasional guest appearances. He taught at the Royal Ballet School until his sudden death, July 2, 1962. He was returning to the stage to dance the role of the old Marquis in the revival of *The Good-Humored Ladies,* and died on his way to his dressing room following a rehearsal. He was the first virtuoso male dancer produced by British ballet, noted for his Blue Bird in *The Sleeping Beauty, Swan Lake* pas de trois, *Peasant* pas de deux (*Giselle*), and for his creations of the Blue Skater (*Les Patineurs*), Red Knight (*Checkmate*), Dancing Master and Man with a Rope (*The Rake's Progress*). He danced many other roles in the repertoire of the early Ballet Rambert and of the Royal Ballet. His name will always be associated with the pioneering days of ballet in Great Britain.

Turney, Matt, contemporary American modern dancer, b. Americus, Ga., married to Bob Teague, NBC–TV newscaster and sports commentator. Majored in dance at the Univ. of Wisconsin. Joined Martha Graham company in 1951 and between then and 1964 performed major roles during its N.Y. seasons and on its European and Asian tours. Among her creations for that company are one of the aspects of St. Joan (*Seraphic Dialogue*), Lilith (*Embattled Garden*), The Betrayer (*Samson Agonistes*), and the only woman's role in *A Look at Lightning.* Has also danced with the companies of Donald McKayle, Alvin Ailey, Paul Taylor, Pearl Lang, and has given many joint programs with Robert Cohan.

Turn-Out, the ability of the dancer to turn out his knees much farther than is usual in everyday life. The principle of the turn-out is based on the anatomical structure of the hip-joints. In normal positions the movements of the legs are limited by the structure of the joint between the pelvis and the hips. As the leg is drawn to the side the hip-neck meets the brim of the acetabulum and further movement is impossible. But if the leg is turned out, the big trochanter recedes and the brim of the acetabulum meets the flat side-surface of the hip-neck. This allows the dancer to extend the leg so that it forms an angle of ninety degrees or more with the other leg. The turn-out is not an aesthetic conception but an anatomical and technical necessity for the ballet dancer. It is the turn-out that makes the difference between a limited number of steps on one plane and the possibility of control of all dance movements in space.

Tutu, the standard ballet skirt made of several layers of tarlatan, occasionally of silk or nylon, or two of the three materials. The classic tutu reaches to somewhat above the knee or higher, the Romantic to halfway between the knee and the ankle in length. The Romantic tutu was introduced by Maria Taglioni in the ballet *La Sylphide* (1832). Ballet historians are not agreed on the name of the artist who designed the Romantic tutu; some consider him to have been Paul Lormier, others that it was Eugene Lami, still others think that it must have been M. du Faget. The classic tutu was introduced, probably in the 1880's, by the virtuoso Italian ballerinas who dominated the European stages at the time and who needed a short skirt to enable them to execute their difficult steps and to display their legs to the spectators. According to G.B.L. Wilson's *Dictionary of Ballet,* the word tutu is derived from the French child's word tu-tu (also cul-cul), meaning "bottom." Writes Mr. Wilson: "Semantically the word tutu thus relates to the panties to which the skirt is sewn on rather than to the skirt itself." Among Russian dancers a tutu is generally called "patchka," meaning a batch or a package and referring perhaps to the layers of material in a tutu.

Twelve Goddesses, The. Masque by Samuel Daniel and Inigo Jones given in 1604. It was presented by Queen Anne at Hampton Court in honor of the Spanish Ambassador.

Twist, The, a social dance phenomenon of the early 1960's. Its peculiarity was that partners never touched each other and could equally well be dancing by themselves. The movements, as the title suggests, were a twisting of feet, hips, and shoulders. Another oddity was that this dance, patently designed by and for teenagers, was taken up by the so-called café society and for this reason briefly commanded much publicity space in newspapers and periodicals.

Two Brothers. Ballet in 1 act; chor.: Norman Morrice; music: Ernst von Dohnanyi's String Quartet No. 2 in D flat, Op. 15; décor: Ralph Koltai. First prod.: Ballet Rambert, Marlowe Theatre, Canterbury, Aug. 14, 1958, with Gillian Martlew (The Girl), John Chesworth (Young Man), Norman Morrice (His Brother). This was Norman Morrice's first ballet and one of the few English ballets with a contemporary theme. The younger brother, beset by adolescent rebellions and yearnings he hardly understands, is bitterly jealous when he sees the happiness of his older brother and the girl he loves. Tension builds until he kills the older brother in a fight. The ballet was televised in its entirety by the British Broadcasting Corporation (1959) and was successfully performed at the Jacob's Pillow Dance Festival the same year.

Two Pigeons, The. Ballet in 3 acts; chor.: Louis Mérante; music: André Messager; décor: Rube, Chaperon, J. B. Lavastre; costumes: Bianchini. First prod.: Paris Opéra, Oct. 18, 1886, with Marie Sanlaville (en travesti) as Pepio and Rosita Mauri as Gourouli. This version was revived by Albert Aveline in 1952. The story is based on the La Fontaine fable, the "pigeons" being the two young lovers Gourouli and Pepio. Pepio is drawn away by what he imagines will be the fascinating life of a Gypsy. His sweetheart follows him and disguised as a Gypsy completely enchants him. However, the others rob him of all and he returns home, like the prodigal son, to be forgiven by the loving Gourouli. Frederick Ashton used the same music and story, in general, for his two-act ballet of the same name, premièred by the Royal Ballet, Royal Opera House, Covent Garden, London, Feb. 14, 1961, in décor by Jacques Dupont, with Lynn Seymour (The Young Girl), Christopher Gable (The Young Man), Elizabeth Anderton (The Gypsy), Robert Mead (Gypsy Chief). He also used two real white pigeons as symbols of the young lovers. In his version, however, the girl does not follow the boy (an artist in this production) in disguise, and he is momentarily fascinated by the Gypsy girl who has, however, a lover of her own in the Gypsy Chief. Merle Park also dances the Young Girl, Alexander Grant and Kenneth Mason the Young Man, Georgina Parkinson and Monica Mason the Gypsy.

Two-Step, a ballroom dance in 2/4 time which formed the basis for the foxtrot. The even rhythm of the original two-step (*quick*-quick, *slow*) gave way to the broken rhythm of the foxtrot. The terms two-step and foxtrot are interchangeable, but the former is seldom used in America today although it still prevails in Europe.

Tyl Ulenspiegel. Ballet in 2 scenes; chor.: George Balanchine; music: Richard Strauss's *Til Eulenspiegel's Merry Pranks;* décor: Esteban Francés. First prod.: New York City Ballet, City Center, New York, Nov. 14, 1951, with Jerome Robbins in the title role. A preliminary scene, mimed to drum rolls, shows the child King Philip of Spain opposing a child Tyl at a game across a table, the king playing with a ship, Tyl with a loaf of bread. As the ship forces the loaf off the gameboard, Strauss's music begins. The rest of the ballet shows Tyl's pranks directed against the hated Spanish dominion over the Netherlands. The ballet ends with the king and his retinue leaving the Netherlands in their ships. See also TIL EULENSPIEGEL.

Tyven, Gertrude (1924–1966), American dancer, teacher, b. Brooklyn, N.Y., of Finnish parentage; m. Eugene Slavin. Studied dance with Maria Yurieva and Vecheslav Swoboda. Member, Ballet Russe de Monte Carlo (1942–59), rising from corps de ballet to leading dancer and dancing a large repertoire including Can-Can Dancer (*Gaîté Parisienne*), Seamstress (*Le Beau Danube*), Dawn (*Coppélia*), and later Swan Queen (*Swan Lake,* Act 2), *Blue Bird, Black Swan, The Nutcracker, Don Quixote* pas de deux, and others. Until 1946 she danced under the name of Gertruda Svobodina as a tribute to her late teacher. Her sister, Sonja Taanila, was also a dancer with Ballet Russe de Monte Carlo. She retired from the stage soon after her marriage and taught ballet until her death.

U

Uboldi, Oscar, Argentine writer and lecturer, b. Buenos Aires, Argentina, 1925. Left the university to travel through Europe (1947–49), during which time he was in close contact with the artistic life, especially dance activities, of London, Paris, Brussels, and Rome. After a second trip to Europe (1950) he became dance critic of the magazine *Buenos Aires Musical,* a post he still holds. Has lectured widely on dance and at the request of Fondo Nacional de las Artes has collaborated on the dance section of the 1961 *Art Annual.* At present is working on cinema scripts on ballet and opera while continuing his other activities.

Ugarte, Floro M., composer and professor of music, b. Buenos Aires, Argentina, 1885. Technical Director and Member of the Board of Directors of Teatro Colón, Buenos Aires (1924–27). Former president of Sociedad Nacional de Musica; member of Comisión Nacional de Bellas Artes; professor of Conservatorio Nacional of Buenos Aires. Among his many compositions is the ballet *El Junco,* choreographed by Michel Borovski and premièred at Teatro Colón (1955).

Uirapurú. Ballet in 1 act; chor.: Aurel Milloss; music and book: Heitor Villa-Lobos; décor: Clovis Graciano. First prod.: Ballet do IV Centenario Teatro Municipal, Rio de Janeiro, Brazil, 1954, with Lia Marques (the Huntress), Juan Giuliano (Uirapurú), Eduardo Sucena (the Ugly Indian). One of the best known examples of Braziliana, this work had been staged in many versions by Vaslav Veltchek (1939, 1953), Eros Volusia (1943), Yuco Lindberg (1946), Carlos Leite (1959). In the silence of the tropical jungle Indian maidens try to hear the voice of Uirapurú, the bird of love and happiness. The love-hungry Ugly Indian imitates his singing, only to be rejected by the girls when they discover the deceit. Soon the real Uirapurú begins to sing and the beautiful Huntress shoots her arrow. The wounded bird falls to the ground and is transformed into the Handsome Indian. All the girls surround him to pay him homage and they dance together the dances of love. But the Ugly Indian, returned to take revenge, shoots the Handsome Indian, who, transformed again into a bird, disappears into the jungle. The only thing that remains for the Indian maidens, who dreamed of love, is the solitude of the forest.

Ulanova, Galina, Peoples' Artist of the U.S.S.R., Lenin Prize of 1957, Soviet prima ballerina assoluta, b. St. Petersburg, 1910. Daughter of Sergei Ulanov (1881–1950), dancer and regisseur of the

Galina Ulanova, the first Soviet prima ballerina assoluta, taking her final bow of the New York season of the Bolshoi Ballet in 1962, as The Dying Swan.

Maryinsky (later Kirov) Theatre, and Maria Romanova (1886–1954), dancer of the Maryinsky Theatre and teacher of the Leningrad Ballet School. Her mother was her first teacher at the Leningrad School, for five years, and Professor Agrippina Vaganova taught her for the remaining four. To the former she owes the softness and plasticity of her arms, and the wonderful placing and strength of her back to the latter. She was a tomboy at school and her first solo part was that of a boy in a wooden shoe dance interpolated in *La Fille Mal Gardée*. For her graduation performance, May 16, 1928, Ulanova danced the Waltz and Mazurka in *Chopiniana* and the Sugar Plum Fairy Variation from *The Nutcracker*. In *Chopiniana* the young dancer showed the fine nuances of phrasing that established from the outset her own style of dancing—simple, lyrical, extremely sincere and profound. In her first season at the Kirov Theatre she danced Princess Florine in the *Blue Bird* pas de deux as well as Aurora in *The Sleeping Beauty*. In her second season she danced Odette-Odile in *Swan Lake*. But the turning point in her development as a dancer came with her creation of Maria in *The Fountain of Bakhchisarai* (1934), a production which marks the beginning of the search for dramatically motivated action in Soviet ballet. Ulanova's creation of the role of the captive Polish princess was a pure image of great poetic beauty which has been unsurpassed by any other interpreter. Ulanova is the embodiment of the Soviet school of ballet, partly by training and partly because her creations have determined to a considerable extent the style and method of Soviet choreography and performing art. Ulanova dances music. She expressed this in an article, "Expressive Means of Ballet" (*Sovietskaya Muzika,* No. 4, 1955, p. 70), in which she wrote: "Dance is engendered by music and it is the dance, what may be called the movement of music, that makes it visible." Ulanova speaks in the same article of the necessity for the dancer to attain a cantilena quality. She herself possesses this evenly flowing quality to the utmost degree. The intellect plays a great role in her creations, and in her early youth she was greatly influenced in her general cultural development by the family of the well-known Leningrad dramatic actress Yelizaveta Tihmé, who was the Cleopatra in Michel Fokine's *Les Nuits d'Égypte* when it was produced in St. Petersburg.

Ulanova's second important stage of development as a consummate dancer-actress began with the role of Juliet in *Romeo and Juliet* (1940). All three of Sergei Prokofiev's ballets—*Romeo and Juliet, Cinderella,* and *The Stone Flower*—were composed with Ulanova in mind as the principal protagonist. She breathed new life into the century-old *Giselle,* making it into a great poem of love that is stronger than death. Although she ennobles the spectator by raising him to a higher spiritual plane, there is nothing done "out of inspiration" in her creations. She speaks in her "School of the Ballerina" of hard work, particularly of the "work of the mind," as she calls it.

Ulanova was evacuated to Tashkent and Perm at the beginning of World War II and danced in both cities. In 1944 she was transferred to the Bolshoi Ballet. She danced *Giselle* when it was revived in connection with the centenary of its first production in Russia, and re-created Juliet in a revival of *Romeo and Juliet* with some new mise-en-scène in 1946. She created the title role in the Bolshoi Theatre's *Cinderella* (1945), Katerina in Leonid Lavrovsky's *The Stone Flower* (1954), and Tao-Hoa in Lavrovsky's first version of *The Red Flower,* formerly known as *Red Poppy* (1949).

After 1959 she limited her appearances to occasional ones, without the formal obligation to dance a definite number of performances in a season. During the 1960–61 season she danced *Chopiniana* and *Fountain of Bakhchisarai* several times. Since 1959 Ulanova has also acted as ballet mistress of the Bolshoi Theatre, rehearsing *Giselle* with the young ballerina Yekaterina Maximova and passing on her great experience as dancer and actress to the younger generation.

Ulanova is married to Vadim Ryndin, principal designer of the Bolshoi. Her first marriage to Yuri Zavadsky, the well-known Russian stage director, ended in divorce.

Ulanova's great artistry became known in Europe and the U.S. before she ever actually danced outside the Soviet Union. Her first appearance outside Russia was at the Fourteenth Maggio Musicale Fiorentino (1951). She then danced with the Bolshoi Ballet in Berlin (1954), London (1956), Japan (1957), Paris (1958), U.S., and Canada (1959, 1962) and in the United Arab Republic (Egypt) (1961). She also headed the Hungarian tour of the Bolshoi Ballet as its artistic director (1961).

Ulanova's roles, in addition to those already mentioned, included Masha and the "Golden Waltz" (*The Nutcracker,* 1929 and 1934), the Young Communist Girl of the West (*The Golden Age,* 1930), Solveig (Fedor Lopukhov's *Ice Maiden,* 1931), Mireille de Poitiers (*Flames of Paris,* 1932), Tzar-Maiden (*The Humpbacked Horse,* 1932), Diana (Agrippina Vaganova's *Esmeralda,* 1935), Coralli (*Lost Illusions,* 1936), title role in Vassily Vainonen's new version of *Raymonda* (1938), Nikia (*La Bayadère,* 1941). In recital performances she also danced *The Dying Swan.* Ulanova visited the U.S. for the second time in 1962 as principal ballet mistress of the Bolshoi Ballet. She officially retired from the stage in 1962, but continues her association with the Bolshoi Ballet, mainly coaching young dancers in important roles. She is often invited to preside at ballet festivals and competitions in Eastern Europe and occasionally writes articles on ballet for the Soviet press. A number of books have been published in the Soviet Union about Ulanova. Albert E. Kahn wrote *Days With Ulanova* (N.Y., 1962), illustrated with some three hundred magnificent photographs taken by the author. The thousands of negatives shot by Kahn were presented to the Dance Collection of the N.Y. Public Library as a gift by Robert E. Dowling.

Ulbrich, Werner, German dancer, ballet master and choreographer, b. Dresden, 1928. Studied with Dore Hoyer and Gustave Blank. Soloist, Comic Opera Berlin (1951–56); ballet master, Municipal Theatre, Chemnitz (1954–56) and Opera Leipzig (1956–58); guest choreographer, Stuttgart and Hamburg (1959); ballet master, German Opera on the Rhein, Düsseldorf (since 1960). Made many study trips to the U.S., Soviet Union, Hungary, Bulgaria, Czechoslovakia. His choreographic works include *The Bridal Kerchief, The Haiduk Song, The Wooden Prince, Droit du Seigneur, Apollon Musagète, The Swan of Tuonela, The Four Temperaments, Bolero, Romeo and Juliet, Undine, Coppélia.*

Ullman, Chinita, pioneer of the modern dance in Brazil, dancer, choreographer, teacher, b. Porto Alegre, ca. 1908. Began dance studies at fifteen and was first Brazilian dancer to study with Mary Wigman. Made her professional debut with Tanzgruppe Mary Wigman and toured Europe with the troupe until 1927. Toured Europe, Argentina, and Brazil with the Italian dancer Carletto Thieben. Her debut in Rio de Janeiro (1931), presented by Cultura Artística, was considered a great event at the time. In 1932 she established her first school with Kitty Bodenheim in São Paulo, but continued to dance professionally in Brazil and Europe. Her last European tour was broken off in 1939, due to the beginning of World War II. During her career she choreographed all the works in which she appeared. Retired in 1954; she lives and occasionally teaches in São Paulo and continues to be a very important person in the Brazilian dance world.

Umbrella, The. Ballet in 1 act; chor.: Aurel Milloss; music: Francisco Mignone; book: Oswald de Andrade, Jr.; décor: Heitor dos Prazeres. First prod.: Ballet do VI Centenário, Teatro Municipal, Rio de Janeiro, 1954. A comedy-ballet in which an umbrella changes the lives of two flirtatious couples, very "carioca" in color, characters, and feeling.

Un et Un Font Deux (One and One Make Two). Ballet in 1 act; chor. and music: Michel Conte; décor: Jacques de Montjoye. First prod.: Montréal Théâtre Ballet, Montréal, Mar., 1957, with Tommy Scott (The Boy) and Sylvia Tysick (The Girl). A classroom flirtation treated in the tradition of the classic pas de deux, with an adagio, two variations and a coda, the ballet is now in the repertoire of the Royal Winnipeg Ballet, danced by David Shields and Sonia Taverner.

Understudy, a dancer who learns the role of another dancer so that he can execute it should the first dancer be prevented from dancing (because of illness, for instance). A dancer who alternates with another dancer in a given role is generally called an alternate.

Undertow. Ballet in prologue, 1 act and epilogue; chor. and book: Antony Tudor; music: William Schuman; décor: Raymond Breinin. First prod.: Ballet (now American Ballet) Theatre, Metropolitan Opera House, N.Y., Apr. 10, 1945, with Hugh Laing (The Transgressor), Nana Gollner (Medusa), Alicia Alonso (Ate), Diana Adams (Cybele), Lucia Chase (Polyhymnia), Patricia Barker (Aganippe), Shirley Eckl (Volupia), John Kriza (Pollox). In spite of the Greek names given by Tudor to his characters, this is a modern psychological ballet. The young man, who feels himself rejected by his parents, goes through several experiences which leave him more and more disillusioned and despairing until his hatred of women is climaxed by his murder of Medusa. This "psychological murder ballet" was suggested by the playwright John van Druten.

Unicorn, the Gorgon and the Manticore, The. A ballet fable; chor.: John Butler; music and libretto: Gian-Carlo Menotti (twelve madrigals with orchestral interludes); décor: Jean Rosenthal; costumes: Robert Fletcher. First prod.: New York City Ballet, City Center, N.Y., Jan. 15, 1957, with Nicholas Magallanes (Poet), Arthur Mitchell (Unicorn), Eugene Tanner (Gorgon), Richard Thomas (Manticore), Janet Reed (Countess), Roy Tobias (Count), and Wilma Curley, Lee Becker (première only, subsequently Barbara Milberg), John Mandia, Jonathan Watts. The creatures the Poet leads about the town are symbols of Youth, Manhood, and Old Age, but the townspeople who follow him, sheeplike, realize this only at his death. Previous to its N.Y. première the work was performed in the Coolidge Auditorium, Washington, D.C., Oct. 21, 1956, having been commissioned by the Elizabeth Sprague Coolidge Foundation in the Library of Congress. Musical groups frequently perform the work in other versions. England's Western Theatre Ballet premièred it at Theatre Royal, Bristol, June 28, 1962 (chor.: Peter Darrell; décor: Barry Kay; with Erling Sunde, Sylvia Wellman, Hazel Marry, Brenda Last). A previous version by Peter Darrell with Laverne Meyer as the Man in the Castle was premièred by New Opera Company, presented by Western Theatre Ballet, Sadler's Wells Theatre, July 22, 1958.

Union Pacific. Ballet in 4 scenes; chor.: Leonide Massine; music: Nicholas Nabokov; book: Archibald MacLeish; décor: Albert Johnson; costumes: Irene Sharaff. First prod.: Col. de Basil's Ballet Russe, Forrest Theatre, Philadelphia, Pa., Apr. 6, 1934, with a cast including Tamara Toumanova, Sono Osato, Eugenia Delarova, André Eglevsky, David Lichine, Leonide Massine. A choreographic treatment of an apocryphal episode in the building of the Union Pacific Railroad, involving Irish and Chinese workers, a Mexican barman, ladies of easy virtue, etc. Massine's Barman's dance was so sensational that it stopped the show.

Unions. See THEATRICAL TRADE UNIONS.

Usher. Ballet in 3 scenes, based on *The Fall of the House of Usher* by Edgar Allan Poe, adapted by Leonide Massine and Roberto Garcia Morillo; chor.: Leonide Massine; music: Roberto Garcia Morillo; décor: Armando Chiesa; costumes: Alvaro Duranona y Vedia. First prod.: Teatro Colón, Buenos Aires, Argentina, July 1, 1955, with Maria Ruanova (Madeleine), José Neglia (Roderick), Jorge Tomin (The Poet). Garcia Morillo's excellent score, which seems to emerge from Poe's tale to create the exact atmosphere, together with Neglia's inspired portrayal of Roderick Usher, make this ballet a work of great dramatic force.

Usher, Graham, English dancer, b. Beverley, E. Yorks, 1938. Studied at Sadler's Wells School (from 1949); entered Sadler's Wells (now Royal) Ballet (1955); promoted to soloist (1958); currently principal dancer. His roles include Blue Bird (*The Sleeping Beauty*), Pas de Trois (*Swan Lake*), Blue Skater (*Les Patineurs*), Colas (*La Fille Mal Gardée*), male dancer (*Les Sylphides*), *Don Quixote* pas de deux, and others. Created one of the two male parts in the Frederick Ashton pas de quatre, which takes the place of the original pas de trois in the 1963 Royal Ballet version of *Swan Lake.*

U.S.O. (United Service Organization), a voluntary service organization created in 1943 to furnish entertainment for U.S. troops in U.S. and overseas, establish clubs, supply sports equipment, etc. During World War II organizations like Ballet Russe de Monte Carlo and Ballet (now American Ballet) Theatre gave free performances for the military under the auspices of U.S.O. In addition, through U.S.O., managers of ballet companies and modern groups distributed thousands of free tickets to enlisted men and noncommissioned officers for performances in the U.S.

Uthoff, Ernst, contemporary dancer, teacher, choreographer, former head of Chilean National Ballet, Santiago, Chile, b. Düisburg. Studied under Kurt Jooss and Sigurd Leeder; joined the Jooss Ballet as soloist (1927), and later also became assistant ballet master. He came to America with the company in 1933 and stayed on with it through 1934, rejoining it in 1936 as soloist and ballet master. Among his roles were the Standard Bearer (*The Green Table*), the Libertine (*The Big City*), the Friend (*The Prodigal Son*), and other principal parts. Married Lola Botka, a soloist in the company. When the Jooss Ballet decided to return to Europe in 1942, Uthoff and his wife remained in Santiago, where they began teaching dance and later organized a company which subsequently became the Chilean National Ballet. Both the school and the company are part of the Instituto de Extensión Musical of the Univ. of Chile. Since the establishment of the school, Uthoff and Botka have trained a large group of dancers in the Jooss-Leeder movement style and technique. Kurt Jooss subsequently visited Santiago and revived for the company his *The Green Table, A Ball in Old Vienna,* and *Pavane* (1948).

Among Uthoff's works are *Juventud* (Handel), *Don Juan* (Gluck), *Petrouchka* (Stravinsky), *Carmina Burana* (Carl Orff), *Allotria.* Uthoff is assisted in the school by Lola Botka and Rudolf Pescht. The Chilean National Ballet made its first U.S. tour in the winter of 1964, managed by Columbia Artists Management, the same organization which had handled the Jooss Ballet some thirty years before. Ernst Uthoff's son Michael is a soloist in the City Center Joffrey Ballet.

Mr. and Mrs. Ernst Uthoff left their positions in Chile in 1966.

Vaganova, Agrippina (1879–1951), Peoples' Artist of the RSFSR, professor, ballerina, founder of the Soviet system of ballet education and one of the greatest masters of ballet of all time, b. and d. Leningrad. Daughter of an usher of the Maryinsky Theatre, Vaganova was placed in the Ballet School in 1889, graduating in 1897 (class of Paul Gerdt). Among her teachers were Lev Ivanov, Yekaterina Vazem, and Nicholas Legat. While not actually a pupil of Enrico Cecchetti, she gained much from observing his classes while in her last year at school and from watching Olga Preobrajenska who was his pupil. From all these she acquired a knowledge of several aspects of the classic school which she re-worked and blended into one whole, adding to them from her own experience and that of the young Soviet ballet until this formed what is now known as the Vaganova system.

As a dancer herself Vaganova was known as "queen of variations." In her time few male dancers could achieve soaring leaps and twinkling batterie. Due to Vaganova's teaching both have become characteristic of Soviet ballet.

Vaganova possessed neither good looks nor influential protectors so she was given the official status of ballerina only in 1915, one year before her retirement from the stage. Her roles included: Naïla (*La Source*), Odette-Odile (*Swan Lake*), the Mazurka (*Chopiniana*), Tzar-Maiden (*The Humpbacked Horse*), the Pearl (*Beautiful Pearl*), *Giselle,* and numerous solo roles. She retired in her prime and did not immediately start teaching since she did not see any particular demand for her knowledge or experience. However, after the revolution when there was a great demand for teachers and when a new type of choreographic school was being organized, Vaganova began working with great enthusiasm and energy. From 1919 to 1921 she taught at the School of Russian Ballet founded by Akim Volynsky, where Vera Volkova has benefited from her lessons. In 1921 she was invited to teach at the Leningrad Choreographic School (the former Maryinsky) and she soon became its leading teacher.

Her first pupils, Natalia Kamkova and Marina Semyonova, upon whom she created and tried out her method, were trained by her from their first to last year of study. Subsequently she taught classes only in the last two or three grades. Semyonova became an ideal embodiment of the Vaganova method. Her other favorite pupil was Natalia Dudinskaya. The last Kirov ballerina trained by her was Irina Kolpakova. Vaganova not only created a galaxy of ballerinas and leading soloists but exerted great influence on the style of male dancing in Soviet ballet and on the work of Soviet choreographers who were able to achieve more with dancers who had such complete command of their bodies.

Vaganova herself was ever growing,

Agrippina Vaganova, great Russian teacher and ballet mistress.

constantly borrowing from works of Soviet choreographers so as to keep her classes abreast of the times. Attempting a summing up of what was most important in the Vaganova method it should be said that there was nothing in it that could be isolated from the other elements in her system. Everything was subordinated to the main goal of bringing the human body into a state of harmony, achieved by the means of the complete coordination of all its members. However, the "Vaganova back" was the first thing that struck the eye in Vaganova-trained dancers. She brought her pupils into a state of complete stability (équilibre) but, while they were very firmly placed on the ground, the strength of their backs enabled them to take off at any moment and soar in the air, continuing to move and to maneuver their bodies during the flight. Vaganova treated the body as a harmonious living whole; above all she wanted the body to be alive, and treated it as a sculptor of ancient Greece, bringing out each pupil's assets while concealing her defects.

Vaganova influenced Soviet ballet education, not only because of her book *Fundamentals of the Classic Dance* (1934), which tells how to perform steps of classic ballet but does not sum up the main precepts of her system, nor because she taught for one year (1943) at the Bolshoi Theatre in Moscow, but because her method was accepted by all teachers as the one that summed up all that was best in the Russian School. Most of her pupils, particularly the early ones, have become teachers upon retiring—Semyonova, Kamkova, Galina Ulanova, and, more recently, the great Kirov prima ballerina Natalia Dudinskaya. Vaganova taught in the pedagogical departments (founded especially for training teachers) at the Leningrad Ballet School (1934–41) and at the Leningrad Conservatory (1946–51) where she occupied the chair of choreography and received the degree of professor.

Vaganova revived *Chopiniana* at the Kirov Theatre (1931), but her most important choreographic work was her original version of *Swan Lake* staged to a new libretto by Vladimir Dmitriev, with Galina Ulanova as the Swan Queen (1933). She also staged a new version of *Esmeralda* for her pupil Tatiana Vecheslova (1935). *Diana and Acteon,* a pas de deux from the second act divertissement, is still used as a pièce de resistance in concert programs. It was created for Ulanova and Vakhtang Chabukiani. She also choreographed many recital numbers, such as Mikhail Glinka's *Valse-Fantaisie* and a one-act ballet, *The Poet's Vision,* to music by A. Gladkovsky, produced on the occasion of her thirtieth anniversary in the theatre (1927).

An impressive volume of articles by her leading pupils and extracts from her memoirs and letters entitled *Agrippina Yakovlevna Vaganova* has been published (Iskusstvo, Leningrad-Moscow, 1958). Her *Fundamentals of the Classic Dance* was translated into English by Anatole Chujoy (1937). It has also been translated into Spanish, German, Czech, Hungarian, and Georgian (the last published in Tbilisi in a translation by her pupil, ballerina Yelena Gvaramadze).

The Leningrad Ballet School was named after Vaganova in 1957 and her bust was placed in the two-tiered Rehearsal Hall opposite that of Marius Petipa. In addition, a memorial plaque was placed on the house where she lived and a monument erected on her grave at Volkovo cemetery in Leningrad.

Vainonen, Vassily (1898–1964), Honored Artist of the RSFSR, Soviet choreographer. His mother, a widow with fourteen children, placed him in the school of the Maryinsky Theatre (now Kirov) in 1911. When he was graduated in 1919 it was called the Choreographic Technicum. He began his career in the corps de ballet of the Kirov company and rose to solo character parts during a period marked by experimentation and a search for novelty. Early in the 1920's Vainonen became connected with the Young Ballet (Molodoi Balet), a group very much influenced by the work of Fedor Lopukhov and Kasian Goleizovsky. Among his colleagues were Georgi Balanchivadze (George Balanchine), Leonid Lavrovsky, Alexei Yermolayev, and Olga Mungalova. Vainonen's first ventures into choreography were in the form of several dances done for recitals of this youthful group. His semi-acrobatic *Moszkowski Waltz* is still a popular concert number, particularly when performed by Raisa Struchkova and Alexander Lapauri of the Bolshoi Ballet. The Young Ballet disbanded in 1923 but came to life again in 1925 when its participants prepared several programs. Vainonen gradually abandoned dancing altogether and devoted himself entirely to choreography. His first important ballet, *Flames of Paris* (1932), marked a new stage in the development of Soviet ballet. While remaining firmly founded in classic ballet, Vainonen made wide use of national dances for the portrayal of his characters; for instance, Thérèse, the Basque girl (Nina Anisimova), became the first important ballerina role for a character dancer. Vainonen continued to use character dance, but always as a vehicle for conveying dramatic content, in such ballets as *Partisans Days* (1937), *Militza* (1947), *Mirandolina* (1949), and *Gayané* (1957). He also did a suite of Czech dances for the Smetana opera *The Bartered Bride* (1948). His version of *The Nutcracker* (1934) contains extremely difficult choreography as does the famous pas de deux for Jeanne and Jerome in *Flames of Paris.* Both show Vainonen as a master in inventing classic enchaînements and virtuoso variations. Of particular interest is his dance of the Snowflakes in *The Nutcracker* which, symphonic by its very nature, is considered one of the best corps de ballet ensembles in Soviet ballet. In his earlier period Vainonen created controversial works which did not stand the test of time, such as *The Golden Age* in collaboration with Leonid Yacobson and others (1930), and the new version of *Raymonda* (1938) in which the new story and action were in disharmony with Alexander Glazounov's music. In his mature years, Vainonen became an authority on the classic heritage. In 1950–51, he spent more than a year in Budapest, staging his *Flames of Paris* and *The Nutcracker* and doing much to assist in the revival and development of Hungarian ballet. In 1952–53 he was chief choreographer at the Novosibirsk Theatre of Opera and Ballet, choreographing an excellent production of *The Sleeping Beauty.* His *Nutcracker* was revived Dec. 29, 1961, at the newly-opened Kremlin Palace of Congresses, a magnificent stage given over to the Bolshoi Theatre. Vassily Vainonen died Mar. 22, 1964, of heart failure; he was survived by his widow, Klavdia Armashevskaya, former Kirov soloist, currently a ballet mistress at the Bolshoi Theatre.

Valse. See WALTZ.

Valse, La. Ballet in 1 act; chor.: George Balanchine; music: Maurice Ravel's *Valses Nobles et Sentimentales,* and *La Valse;* costumes: Barbara Karinska. First prod.: New York City Ballet at City Center, N.Y., Feb. 20, 1951, with Tanaquil LeClercq, Nicholas Magallanes, Francisco Moncion. The ballet is neo-Romantic and without a definite plot, but there is an air of doom which makes itself felt from the outset and throughout the slightly hectic gaiety of the first set of waltzes. The entry of the young girl at her first ball heightens and deepens the atmosphere to the moment when Death enters and forces her to dance with him to the inevitable end. After a lapse of nearly six years *La Valse* was revived May 1, 1962, with Patricia McBride in LeClercq's role; Magallanes and Moncion repeated their creations. The first production of a ballet to the music of *La Valse* was by Bronislava Nijinska in décor by Alexandre Benois for the Ida Rubinstein Company at the Opéra, Paris, May 23, 1929, with Rubinstein and Anatole Vilzak. The scene was a ball, taking place in a magnificent Third Empire ballroom. This version was rechoreographed by Michel Fokine and premièred June 25, 1931, also at the Opéra. Harald Lander choreographed a ballet to *La Valse* for the Royal Danish Ballet in 1940. Frederick Ashton staged another version in décor by André Levasseur for Teatro alla Scala, Milan, Feb. 1, 1958, which was revived by the Royal Ballet at Royal Opera House, Covent Garden, London, Mar. 10, 1959, but remained in the repertoire for a short time only.

Valses et Variations. See RAYMONDA VARIATIONS.

van Beers, Sonja, Dutch dancer, b. Arnhem, Holland, 1940. Began her career in Nederlands Ballet; now soloist with Het Nationaal Ballet, dancing principal roles in *Caprichos* (Herbert Ross), *Concerto Barocco* (Balanchine), *Designs for Six* (John Taras), *Four Temperaments; Jazz Nocturne, De Wille Salamander, Les Mirages, Othello, Les Présages* (Leonide Massine), *Serenade* (Balanchine), *Rencontre* (Lichine).

van Dantzig, Rudi, Dutch dancer and choreographer, b. Amsterdam, 1933. Studied at the academy of Sonia Gaskell and, in his words, "got an education for years in one afternoon, watching a demonstration class by Martha Graham and company in 1954." Made his debut with Miss Gaskell's Ballet Recital (1952–54); with Het Nederlands Ballet as dancer and choreographer (1954–59), staging *Night Island* (Debussy, 1954), *Time and Tide* (van Delden, 1955), *Mozart Symphony* (1956), *The Family* (Bartók's *The Miraculous Mandarin,* 1957), *Spring Concerto* (Gluck, 1958). With Het Nederlands Dans Theater (1959–60), staging *Giovinezza* (Vivaldi) and *Looking Back* (Schumann, 1959). In 1961 he staged *Jungle* for Het Nationaal Ballet, to electronic music by Henk Badings and in the same year received the Prix des Critics in Paris for the choreography of *Night Island.*

van de Weetering, Conrad, Dutch dancer, b. The Hague, 1929. Made his debut with the Nederlands Ballet; is now (1966) soloist and character dancer of Het Nationaal Ballet, dancing principal roles in *Caprichos* (Herbert Ross), *Francesca da Rimini* and *Graduation Ball* (Lichine), *The Prisoner of the Caucasus* (Skibine), *Contrasten* (Robert Kaesen), *Four Temperaments, Jungle* (Rudi Van Dantzig), and *The Miraculous Mandarin.* He is the author of the book *Morgen Dans Ik Beter* (I Shall Dance Better Tomorrow).

van der Sloot, Pieter, Dutch dancer and choreographer, b. Amsterdam, 1926. Studied with Igor Schwezoff, Yvonne Georgi, Vera Volkova, Lydia Kyasht, Olga

Preobrajenska, Elvira Roné, Gérard Mulys. Danced with Ballet Recital, Amsterdam Opera Ballet, Ballet der Lage Landen (all in Holland); Regent Ballet, London; Opera Ballet, Nice; Teatro Italiano del Balletto, Italy. Among his roles are Albrecht in *Giselle,* Siegfried in *Swan Lake,* Chief Warrior in *Prince Igor, Les Sylphides,* as well as those in modern ballets. His ballets include, among others, *The Wedding Bouquet* (1947), *Cagliostro* (1948), *Garden Party* (1950), *Achilles* (1954), *Peter and the Wolf* (1955), and the medieval passion play *Levate li occhi e resghardate* (1961). Currently Artistic Director (with Vittorio Rossi), first dancer and choreographer of Teatro Italiano de Balletto, founded in Rome (1955), the only Italian ballet company not connected with an opera house. The company has annual tours through the principal cities of Italy, as well as cities in Spain, Austria, and Switzerland, and appears in films and theatrical productions.

van der Valk, Nettie. See HOLLAND, DANCE IN.

van Dijk, Peter, German dancer of Dutch extraction, b. Bremen, Germany, 1929. Studied with Tatiana Gsovska, Boris Kniaseff, Serge Lifar. Soloist, Berlin Opera (1946–50); choreographer and soloist, Wiesbaden Opera (1952); principal dancer with Ballet de France de Janine Charrat (1952), creating principal male role in *Les Algues* (1953); engaged as premier danseur étoile of Paris Opéra (1955). Created leading roles in *Les Noces Fantastiques* (Lifar–Marcel Delannoy, 1955), *Chemin de Lumière* (Taras–Georges Auric, 1957), and danced in *Giselle, Swan Lake,* Harald Lander's *Etudes,* and others. Choreographer of *Pelléas and Mélisande* (to Schönberg's music, Wiesbaden, 1952), *Symphonie Inachevée, Peau de Chagrin* (Opéra Comique, Paris), *Romeo and Juliet* (Prokofiev, Hamburg Opera). Created Phlegmatic Variation in Balanchine's *Four Temperaments,* Dec. 18, 1963. Combined duties as an étoile of the Paris Opéra with guest appearances as dancer and choreographer with the Hamburg State Opera Ballet, of which latter organization he is now ballet director. He simplified the spelling of his family name to Van Dyk in 1965. Has become permanent choreographer and ballet master at the Hamburg Opera House. In the summer of 1965 appeared in Jacob's Pillow Dance Festival, dancing with Maria Tallchief. In November of that year, at the Third International Dance Festival in Paris, he danced with Miss Tallchief his *Poème,* "a ballet for two," to parts of Arnold Schönberg's *Verklärte Nacht,* choreographed for the occasion. They won the award, Best Lyrical Team.

van Lennep, Dr. William Bird, lecturer, writer, b. Philadelphia, 1906, d. Bay Head, N.J., 1962. Attended Phillips Exeter Academy and Princeton Univ.; graduated from Harvard Univ. (1929), from which institution he also received his doctorate (1934). Taught drama and theatrology (the scientific study of the theatre, as in historical research, etc.) in several universities, colleges, and conservatories, and was the author of many articles on the theatre. As Curator of the Harvard Theatre Collection (1940–60), he contributed much knowledge and interest toward the enlargement of the Dance Department of the Collection with books as well as with iconographic material.

van Manen, Hans, Dutch dancer and choreographer, b. Amsterdam, 1932. Danced under Sonia Gaskell (1952–53); soloist, Netherland's Opera Ballet under Françoise Adret (1953–58); guest artist and choreographer with the same company (1958–59); with Roland Petit company (1959–60). Joined Nederlands Dans Theater (1960) of which he has been artistic director and choreographer since 1961. Among his ballets are *Intermezzo* (Honneger), *Mouvements Sym-*

phoniques (Haydn), *Moon in the Trapeze* (Britten), *Klaar Af* (Duke Ellington), *Concertino* (Blacher), *Eurydice* (Geza Frid). Has also staged for television since 1958.

Peggy van Praagh, British dancer and ballet mistress; now director of the Australian Ballet.

van Praagh, Peggy, English dancer, ballet mistress, director, teacher, b. London, 1910. Studied dance with Aimée Phipps, Margaret Craske, Lydia Sokolova, Vera Volkova; mime with Tamara Karsavina; modern dance with Gertrud Bodenweiser and Agnes de Mille. Soloist, Ballet Rambert (1933–38); principal dancer, Antony Tudor's *London Ballet* (1938), creating Episode in His Past (*Lilac Garden*), Bolero (*Soirée Musicale*), Russian Ballerina (*Gala Performance*), Mortal Under Mercury (*The Planets*), *Dark Elegies.* She also danced Chatelaine–the Bride (*La Fête Etrange*), Venus (*Judgment of Paris*), Caroline (*Lilac Garden*), among many others. Inaugurated Lunch-Hour Ballet at Arts Theatre in wartime London, 1940. Joined Sadler's Wells (now Royal) Ballet as principal dancer (1941), dancing Swanilda (*Coppélia*), Blue Girl (*Les Patineurs*), and others. Appointed ballet mistress of the newly-formed Sadler's Wells Theatre Ballet (1946), becoming its assistant director (1951–55). Ballet producer for British Broadcasting Corporation Television (1949–58). Since 1955 has mounted ballets from the British repertoire in Munich, the Scandinavian countries, for the National Ballet of Canada, and has staged *Soirée Musicale* for the Robert Joffrey Ballet. On the death of Edouard Borovansky she was invited to take over the artistic direction of his company in Australia (1960). After a season, during which she was guest teacher of the Ballet International du Marquis de Cuevas (1961), she was again invited to direct the re-constituted Australian Ballet, and became its first artistic director (from 1963). She has been an Examiner and Member of London Committee of the Cecchetti Society since 1935 and has taught for the Cecchetti Council of America during its summer seminars. Author of *How I Became a Dancer* (1954); *The Art of Choreography* (with Peter Brinson, 1963). In the 1966 Birthday Honors, Queen Elizabeth II created her a Commander of the Order of the British Empire (C.B.E.).

van Tuyl, Marian, dancer, teacher, lecturer, editor, b. Michigan, 1907. A.B., Univ. of Michigan. Began dance training at age five with lessons in Duncan dance technique and Dalcroze eurythmics; five years at Bennington School of Dance (Fellow, 1938); work and study in N.Y. with Martha Graham, Louis Horst, Hanya Holm, Doris Humphrey; also studied ballet in Chicago and San Francisco. Instructor in Dance, Univ. of Chicago (1928–38); choreographer and leading dancer, Van Tuyl Dance Group (1933–47); director of dance department, Mills College, Oakland, Calif. (1938–47); lecturer and teacher of choreography, Mills College (1950–56). Made two experimental films with Sidney Peterson: *Horror Dream* and *Clinic of Stumble.* Has toured widely as dancer, teacher and lecturer, conducting master classes and special courses at many universities and colleges. Editor of *Impulse, the Annual of Contemporary Dance* (1951 to date), Impulse Publications, Inc., and *Modern Dance Forms in Relation to the Other Modern Arts* (Louis Horst and Carroll Russell, 1961).

van Vechten, Carl (1880–1964), journalist, writer, b. Cedar Rapids, Iowa, 1880. Ph. D., Univ. of Chicago. Assistant music critic, *N.Y. Times* (1906–07, 1910–13); Paris correspondent, *N.Y. Times* (1908–09); drama critic, *N.Y. Press* (1913–14). His criticisms of dance in various books and publications helped to popularize dance in U.S. and are important sources of information on the period. Among his books are: *Music After the Great War* (1915), *Interpreters and Interpretations* (1917), *The Merry-Go-Round, Music of Spain* (1918), *Sacred and Profane Memories* (1932), and several novels. Contributed musical biographies to *Century Dictionary* (rev. ed., 1911); founded collections of art, music, and books. His numerous photographs of dancers comprise the Fania Marinoff Collection of Dance Photographs by Carl Van Vechten, an integral part of the Dance Collection, The New York Public Library. A collection of his dance criticisms published in *Dance Index* (Sept.–Nov., 1942) is an important contribution to the history of dance in the U.S. He died in his sleep Dec. 21, 1964, in N.Y.

Carl van Vechten, writer, journalist.

van Wilgenburg, Margot, b. Laren, Holland. Studied with Gertrud Leistikow, Kurt Jooss, Sonia Gaskell; in Paris with Lubov Egorova, Nora Kiss; in London with Marie Rambert, Vera Volkova. Danced with The Ballet Studio, under Sonia Gaskell (1945); The Scapino Ballet (1948–50); the Netherlands Opera Ballet (1950–59); ballet mistress with the Amsterdam Ballet (1959–61), Het Nationaal Ballet (from 1961). Qualified teacher of Benesh Dance Notation. See also HOLLAND, DANCE IN.

Vance, Norma (Norma Kaplan) (1927–56), dancer, b. New York City, d. in a private plane crash, Apr. 15, 1956. Studied at Professional Children's School; dance studies with Swoboda-Yurieva, N.Y. Appeared in musicals; member, Mia Slavenska's group (1944–45); soloist Ballet (now American Ballet) Theatre from 1946, dancing Youngest Sister (*Pillar of Fire*), French Ballerina (*Gala Performance*), Prelude (*Les Sylphides*), and others. Danced under name of Vaslavina until fall, 1946.

Vangsaa, Mona, ballerina of the Royal Danish Ballet, b. Copenhagen, 1920; m. Frank Schaufuss. Entered the company's school in 1926; also studied in Paris and London. Accepted into the company in 1938; became soloist in 1942. Has made guest appearances in London, Berlin, and Stockholm. Her repertoire includes leading roles in *Drømmebilleder, Bolero, Conservatoriet, Swan Lake, Napoli, Giselle,*

Le Beau Danube, Symphonie Fantastique, La Valse, The Sleeping Beauty, Romeo and Juliet, Kermessen i Brügge, Graduation Ball, Symphony in C, Night Shadow, The Moon Reindeer, Vision, Harlequinade. Has choreographed *Et Nodablad* (Charlottenburg Opera, 1957), *Spektrum* (1958). Resigned from company in the spring of 1962. Awarded the decoration Knight of the Order of Dannebrog.

Vargas, Manolo, Mexican dancer, b. Mexico. Trained as a dancer from childhood, his mother, Maria Aranda, having had a school of dance. Was with Argentinita for several years and after her death (1945) became leading dancer with the company formed by her sister, Pilar Lopez. Left in 1955 to form with Roberto Ximenez, also a leading dancer with the company, their own Ximenez-Vargas Ballet Español.

Variaciones Concertantes. Ballet in 1 scene; chor.: John Taras; music: Alberto Ginastera; décor and costumes: Horacio Butler. World première Jan. 20, 1960 by the New York City Ballet at the N.Y. City Center as part of the Pan American program. Was later called *Tender Night.* May 25, 1960 Taras produced the ballet at Teatro Colón, Buenos Aires, Argentina, with Esmeralda Agoglia, Olga Perri, José Neglia, and augmented corps de ballet.

Variation, in ballet: 1. The second part of a classic pas de deux, following the adagio. 2. Any solo performed in a ballet; also a solo dance in a divertissement. The often-used expression "solo variation" is therefore redundant.

Variations for Four. Ballet in 1 act; chor.: Anton Dolin; commissioned music: Marguerite Keogh; costumes: Tom Lingwood. First prod.: London's Festival Ballet, Festival Hall, London, Sept. 5, 1957, with John Gilpin, Flemming Flindt, Louis Godfrey, André Prokovsky. A divertissement for four male dancers which Dolin also staged for American Ballet Theatre, Metropolitan Opera House, N.Y., Sept. 25, 1958, with Erik Bruhn, Royes Fernandez, Scott Douglas, John Kriza.

Variations on a Lonely Theme. Ballet in 1 act; chor.: Michel Conte; music: Brahms' *Variations on a Theme by Haydn;* décor: Claude Jasmin; costumes: Jacques de Montjoye. First prod.: Royal Winnipeg Ballet, Playhouse Theatre, Winnipeg, Mar. 18, 1960, with David Shields (Theme), Marilyn Young (Woman), Sonia Taverner (Witch). Set in the Middle Ages, the ballet is a choreographic interpretation of the music. A lonely boy (the Theme) tries to find companionship among various people with whom he comes in contact but finds nobody cares about him. The encounters are only variations of his loneliness and he is destined to finish as solitarily as he started.

Variety, British term for vaudeville; continental Europe uses "variété."

Varsoviana (It.), **Varsovienne** (Fr.), in Poland, a slow dance in 3/4 time having an accented down-beat in alternate measures.

Vassiliev, Vladimir, Soviet dancer, b. 1940. Entered Bolshoi Theatre School in 1939 and was graduated in 1958 (class of Mikhail Gabovich). In his first season with the Bolshoi company (1958–59) he was given the important leading role of Danila in *The Stone Flower* and danced it in the U.S. and Canada (1959). He is strong and virile, excelling in roles requiring characterization. He is particularly good as such Russian heroes as Danila and as Ivan in the new version of *The Humpbacked Horse,* which he created (1960). He also dances Ali-Batyr (*Shurale*), Lukash (*Song of the Woods*), the Faun (*Walpurgis Night* from *Faust*), Andrei (*Pages of Life*). He is married to classmate and partner Yekaterina Maximova.

Vaussard, Christiane, French ballerina, b. Neuilly sur Seine, 1923. Began ballet studies under Carlotta Zambelli at Paris Opéra school (1933); promoted to première danseuse (1945), and subsequently première danseuse étoile (1947). Her repertoire includes *Giselle, Coppélia, Les Deux Pigeons, Soir de Fête, Serenade* (Balanchine), *Le Baiser de la Fée, Isoline,* and creations in *La Symphonie Fantastique* (Leonide Massine, 1957), *Le Chevalier Errant* (1950), *Variations* (1953), the Princess in Serge Lifar's *Firebird* (1954), *Pas de Quatre* (1960).

Vecheslova, Tatiana, Honored Art Worker of the RSFSR, Honored Artist of the RSFSR, Soviet ballerina and teacher, b. 1910; m. dancer Sviatoslav Kuznetzov (later divorced). Daughter of former dancer and Kirov Ballet teacher Yevgenia Snietkova (1882–1961), she comes from an old theatrical family connected for many generations with the Maryinsky Theatre. She entered the Petrograd School in 1919, graduating in 1928 (class of Agrippina Vaganova). Galina Ulanova's classmate and school friend, she was considered among the most promising pupils of her class. If later Ulanova became the greater dancer of the two and was the one to attain international fame, Vecheslova nevertheless occupied for over twenty-five years a prominent ballerina position in the Kirov Ballet. She developed particularly as a dancer-actress in the 1930's during the period of dramatic ballets. Her greatest role was that of *Esmeralda* which she first danced in 1931 in the old version when the ballerina Yelena Lucom was suddenly taken ill. In 1931 Vecheslova toured the U.S. with Vakhtang Chabukiani, the first Soviet dancers to do so. When Vaganova staged a new version of *Esmeralda* in 1935, Vecheslova created the title role with great dramatic impact. She also created Zarema (*Fountain of Bakhchisarai*), Florine (*Lost Illusions*), Manije (*Heart of the Hills*), Pascuala (*Laurencia*), and Noune (*Gayané*). Vecheslova retired from dancing in 1953 and is now ballet mistress of the Kirov, passing on her great experience as dancer-actress to young artists. Between 1952–54 she was director of the Leningrad school. Her biography *Ya Ballerina* (I am a Ballerina) was published by Iskusstvo, Leningrad & Moscow.

Veen, Jan (Hans Wiener), dancer, choreographer, teacher, b. Vienna, Austria, 1908. Studied with Rudolf von Laban, Mary Wigman, Emile Jaques Dalcroze; also corrective gymnastics, Mensendieck technique. Studied piano and harmony in Vienna. Soloist, Yvonne Georgi Ballet (1925–26); solo tour in the Orient (1926–28) when he established a school in Shanghai. Arrived in U.S. (1928) under the auspices of S. Hurok who presented him in solo performances as the first European modern dancer on Broadway. Created his own ballets with Boston Symphony "Pops" under Arthur Fiedler (1931–41); Boston Civic Symphony (1942–45). Founded Dance Department of Boston Conservatory of Music (1944) of which he was director. The Conservatory awards a Bachelor of Fine Arts Degree to dance majors. Also founder and artistic director of Boston Dance Theatre (from 1948). Has taught and lectured in universities in the U.S. and given master classes in West Berlin, Vienna, and Athens. Has choreographed over one hundred and fifty solo and group works (performing in many of them), including works for which he commissioned scores, such as *The Incredible Flutist* (Walter Piston, 1938), *Hudson River Legend* (Joseph Wagner, 1942), *Narragansett Bay* (Daniel Pinkham, 1946), *Aftermath—Is There Survival?* (Alan Hovhaness, 1950). Has published articles on dance in various periodicals. Died 1967 in Boston.

Veltchek, Vaslav, Czech choreographer and ballet master, b. Prague, Czechoslovakia, ca. 1896; Brazilian citizen. Studied at ballet school of the National Theatre of Prague and later with Nicholas Legat in Paris. Made his debut at Narodne Divadlo, Prague (1914). First dancer and choreographer, Ljubliana Opera, Yugoslavia (1918–24); Marinetti's Teatro Futurista; Opéra Comique, Paris (1928); partner of La Argentina, dancing Carmelo in *El Amor Brujo* (1929). Choreographed for the René Clair movie, *Le Million* (1932); ballet master, Théâtre Châtelet, Paris (1933–38); choreographer for International Exposition, Paris (1937); guest choreographer for Teatro Municipal, Rio de Janeiro, Brazil (1939); organized ballet school and first corps de ballet in São Paulo (1940–42); ballet master and choreographer, Teatro Municipal, Rio de Janeiro (1943). Formed, directed, and presented Conjunto Coreografico Brasileiro (1944–50) with his pupils, his most important work in Brazil. Again ballet master of Teatro Municipal (1948); guest choreographer, same theatre (1952–53); ballet master and choreographer, Teatro S.O.D.R.E., Montevideo, Uruguay (1953–54); taught and lectured on dance throughout Brazil (1956–58). Ballet master, National Ballet of Venezuela (1959); teacher in Madrid (1960). Currently ballet master, Teatro S.O.D.R.E. His Brazilian ballets include: *Uirapurú* (Villa-Lobos), *Leilão* (Mignone), *Ball in the Country* (José Siqueira), *Sinho do Bonfim* (Camargo Guarnieri), *Batucage* (Mignone), *Streetcorner Waltzes* (Mignone), *Three Sisters* (Frutuoso Viana), *Siesta* (Nepomuceno), *The Kid's Parrot* (Villa-Lobos), *Preludes* (Mignone).

Veneziana. Ballet in 1 act; chor.: Andrée Howard; music: excerpts from operas of Gaetano Donizetti, mainly *La Favorita* and *Don Sebastian,* arr. by Denis ApIvor; décor: Sophie Fedorovitch. First prod.: Sadler's Wells (now Royal) Ballet, Royal Opera House, Covent Garden, London, Apr. 9, 1953, with cast headed by Violetta Elvin (La Favorita), Ray Powell (Punchinello). A divertissement ballet, the dances strung together on the idea of a masked ball in Venice. This was Sophie Fedorovitch's last décor for the ballet, unfinished due to her death.

Venieris, Calliope (Calliope Venieris d'Alexandre), Brazilian dancer, b. Athens, Greece. Came to Brazil (1942), as a war refugee. Began dance study under Edy Vasconcellos (1950); also studied with Gertrude Wolff and Renée Toso Wells at the Teatro Municipal ballet school. After graduation studied with Nina Verchinina, William Dollar, Igor Schwezoff, Serge Peretti, Lilian Arlen. Made her debut at Teatro Municipal (1955). Joined American Ballet Theatre in U.S. (1956). Transferred to Grand Ballet du Marquis de Cuevas (1957) in France, becoming soloist (1960). Joined Hamburg Opera Ballet (1961) as ballerina dancing, among others, *Les Sylphides, La Valse, Pas de Dix, The Four Temperaments.*

Ventana, La (The Window). Ballet in 1 act; chor.: August Bournonville; music: Hans Christian Lumbye. First prod.: Royal Danish Ballet, Copenhagen, 1854. Revised by the choreographer in 1856. This ballet, one of Bournonville's shortest, is Spanish-flavored. Its action revolves about an old theatre trick—a mirror dance in which the reflection is performed by another dancer.

Verchinina, Nina (Nina Verchinina de Beausacq), contemporary Russian dancer, teacher and choreographer, b. Moscow, brought up in Shanghai (China) and Paris. Studied dance with Olga Preobrajenska and Bronislava Nijinska. Later studied the Rudolf von Laban method, thus developing a special style of her own, a blend of the classic and modern schools. Made her debut with Ida Rubinstein company (1929). With Ballet Russe de Monte Carlo (1933–37), creating roles specially designed for her style in Leonide Massine's *Les Présages* and *Choreartium* (1933) and *Symphonie Fantastique* (1936), also dancing a number of other ballets in the reper-

Nina Verchinina, dancer, choreographer, ballet mistress, director.

toire. Guest choreographer, San Francisco Opera Ballet (1937–38); Original Ballet Russe (1939–41); guest choreographer, Havana (Cuba) Opera Ballet (1942–45); re-joined Original Ballet Russe (1946); ballet mistress, Teatro Municipal, Rio de Janeiro (1946–47); again joined Original Ballet Russe (1948). Toured Spain with her own dance group (1949). Guest choreographer, Buenos Aires (1950); Teatro Argentino de La Plata (1952); ballet mistress and choreographer, Mendoza, creating the Ballet Universidade de Cuyo (1951–54); to Rio de Janeiro as choreographer for Casino Copacabana (1954); guest choreographer, Teatro Municipal, (1954–55); formed and presented in Rio and on a South American tour her Ballet Nina Verchinina (1957); choreographer, Ballet Rio de Janeiro (1960). Currently teaching in her studio at Copacabana and working with her company, Ballet Nina Verchinina. Has choreographed *Pastoral Symphony* (Handel), *The Quest* (Bach), *Valse Triste* (Sibelius), *Gay Youth* (Schubert), *Narcise* (Ravel), *Suite Choregraphique* (Gounod), *Rhapsody in Blue* (Gershwin), *Redemption* (Max Steiner), *Matices* (Bach), *Slavonika* (Smetana), *El Amor Brujo* (Falla), *Salomé* (Richard Strauss), *Tahina Can* (Villa-Lobos), *Zuimaaluti* (Claudio Santoro).

Verdon, Gwen (Gwyneth Verdon), musical comedy dancer, singer, actress, b. Culver City, Calif., 1925, of French-Irish descent; m. Bob Fosse. Began her dance studies with her mother, a Denishawn dancer, at a very early age and later studied many kinds of dance including Spanish with the Cansinos, ballet with Ernest Belcher and Carmalita Maracci. While still in her early 'teens she was performing with Aida Broadbent's group on the West Coast. From 1947 worked principally with Jack Cole in night club acts, Roxy Theatre, N.Y., etc. Was his assistant for the Broadway musical *Magdalena* (1949) and continued with him as assistant, also dancing and acting small parts in a number of movies, the best known being *The Merry Widow, Gentlemen Prefer Blondes, Farmer Takes a Wife.* After another brief appearance on Broadway in the revue *Alive and Kicking* (1950), she choreographed her only film *Mississippi Gambler* (1951), then taught in Hollywood (1951–52). She suddenly sprang into prominence in the Cole Porter musical, *Can-Can* (1953) for which Michael Kidd choreographed dances which made her an overnight sensation. Her performance won her the "Tony" (Antoinette Perry) Award as best supporting actress, a Daniel Blum Theatre Award for outstanding performance, and two Donaldson Awards for best supporting actress and dancer. Since that time she has been a reigning queen of American musical comedy, starring in *Damn Yankees* (1955–56), for which she won a "Tony" for top musical star, *New Girl in Town* (1956–57), and *Redhead* (1958–60 on Broadway and on the national tour), for both of which she also won "Tonies." She starred in the film *Damn Yankees* (1959). She has made guest appearances on most of the important television shows (those of Dinah Shore, Garry Moore, Danny Kaye, Perry Como, and others). In 1966 was featured in Broadway musical *Sweet Charity.*

Violette Verdy, French-born American ballerina, in Cullberg's Miss Julie.

Verdy, Violette (Nelly Guillerm), contemporary French dancer, b. Pont L'Abbé-Lambour, Brittany, France; m. Colin Clark. Studied dance with her mother, Victor Gsovsky, and Mme. Rousanne. A child prodigy, she made her debut (under her own name) as the girl acrobat in *Les Forains* with Les Ballets des Champs-Élysées (1945), remaining with that company until 1949. She changed her name when she starred in the French motion picture *Ballerina,* made in 1949–50. Danced seasons with Ballets de Paris de Roland Petit between 1950 and 1956, her best known creation being the Bride in *Le Loup.* Also danced several seasons with London's Festival Ballet including its U.S. tour (1954); has been guest artist with Ballet Rambert and at Teatro alla Scala, Milan. Leading dancer with American Ballet Theatre (1957–58) creating the title role in its production of *Miss Julie.* Joined New York City Ballet as a principal dancer (1958) making her debut Nov. 25 in *Divertimento No. 15* and *Symphony in C* (1st Movement). Subsequent ballets included *Stars and Stripes, Con Amore, Apollo, Western Symphony,* and others; creations included *Medea* (Creusa), *Figure in the Carpet, Liebeslieder Walzer, Episodes, A Midsummer Night's Dream* (Act 2), *Tchaikovsky Pas de Deux,* and others. Guest artist with Royal Ballet in Feb. and Mar. 1964, dancing *The Sleeping Beauty,* first ballerina *Ballet Imperial,* and *Tchaikovsky Pas de Deux* (with David Blair), also staging the last named work for the company. Due to a foot injury refrained from dancing for nearly a year. Returned to the N.Y. City Ballet in 1966. Is often invited to teach master classes at regional ballet festivals and at teachers' conventions and conferences.

Vernon, Barbara, English dancer and teacher, b. Hampton in Arden, 1918; m. John Gregory. Studied with Stella Crabtree, Nicholas Legat, Mathilda Kchessinska, Tamara Karsavina. With Monte Carlo Opera Ballet (1938–39); soloist, Ballet Russe de Monte Carlo, Anglo-Polish Ballet, Jay Pomeroy's Russian Ballet, London Ballet. First classically trained dancer to dance with Ballets Jooss. In partnership with John Gregory opened School of Russian Ballet in Chelsea, London (1949). Ballerina, ballet mistress and principal teacher, Harlequin Ballet, since 1959.

Véron, Dr. Louis-Désiré (1798–1867), Director of the Paris Opéra from 1831 to 1835, during the period of the first flowering of the Romantic ballet. It was during his regime that Filippo Taglioni produced the ballet *La Sylphide* (1832), thus launching both his daughter Maria Taglioni and the Romantic era in ballet. He was a clever man and a crafty diplomat, qualities needed to run the Opéra and keep more or less content, if not happy, such temperamental and ambitious dancers as Maria Taglioni and Fanny Elssler. He knew how to conduct intrigues, both big and little, involving hundreds of well-placed supporters. His negotiations to engage Elssler for the Opéra as competition to the somewhat older Taglioni, who had become impossible to control, could not have been made more exciting by a fiction writer. He resigned to turn to journalism and founded the influential *Revue de Paris* and revived *Le Constitutionnel.*

Verstegen, Aart, Dutch dancer and choreographer, b. Rotterdam, 1920. Has been studying ballet since 1936, his first teachers being Els Keezer and Sonia Gaskell. Danced as soloist with Jooss Ballet (1947–48); Metropolitan Ballet, London (1948–49); Ny Norsk Ballet, Oslo (1949–51); Opernhaus Düsseldorf, Germany (1951–53); Nederlands Ballet, The Hague (1953–59), Nederlands Dans Theater (from 1959 on). Danced most principal roles in the above companies. Currently co-director with Carel Birnie of Nederlands Dans Theater, as well as dancer and choreographer. See also HOLLAND, BALLET IN.

Vertes, Marcel (1895–1961), painter, b. Budapest, Hungary, d. Paris. Divided his time between Paris and N.Y. from 1935. Designed the décor for Michel Fokine's *Bluebeard* (1941), David Lichine's *Helen of Troy* (1943), Bronislava Nijinska's *Brahms Variations* (1944). His costumes and set designs for the film *Moulin Rouge* won him two "Oscars." Wrote an illustrated autobiography *Amandes Vertes* (Green Almonds).

Vesco, Eleonore, German dancer, b. Berlin. Pupil of Tatiana Gsovska and Gustav Blank. Made her debut in 1947. First soloist of the State Opera Berlin. Appeared as guest artist in Dresden, Leipzig, Göttingen, and other cities. Her principal roles include *The Sleeping Beauty, Cinderella, Apollo and Daphne, Don Quixote, Gayané, New Odyssey, Swan Lake.*

Vestri, Gaetano Apollo Baldassare (1825–1862), son of Gaetan Vestris.

Vestris, Armand (1787–1825), French dancer and choreographer. Made his debut at the Paris Opéra in 1800 when both his father Auguste Vestris and his grandfather Gaetan appeared on the stage with him; made his London debut in 1809. Choreographer, King's Theatre, London (1813–16). Married actress Lucia Elisabeth Bartolozzi who became famous as Mme. Vestris. Choreographer and ballet master in Vienna intermittently from about 1813 until his death.

Vestris, Auguste (1760–1842) (full name Marie August Vestris, also known as Vestr'Allard), b. Paris, the son of Gaetan Vestris and his mistress, dancer Marie Allard. He was taught dancing by his father who called himself "Le Dieu de la Danse." Auguste Vestris made his debut at the Paris Opéra at the age of twelve in a divertissement called *Cinquantaine* in which he performed a chaconne. In 1773 he appeared as Eros in *Endymion.* He remained as first dancer at the Opéra for thirty-six years. With success he became more and more conceited and arrogant, but his talent was so great that the directors of the Opéra suffered his bad manners. In spite of his short stature he was a danseur noble who moved with grace and precision. He had great style and added virtuosity to the ballet of his day. His elevation was tremendous and his entrechats and pirouettes brilliant. In 1795 he married a dancer, Anne Catherine Augier. Like his father before him, Auguste Vestris was the greatest male dancer of his time. He was also a great teacher, numbering among his pupils Fanny Elssler, Charles Didelot, Jules Perrot, and others.

Vestris, Auguste Armand, son of the more famous Auguste Vestris, he danced at the Opéra for a short time (ca. 1800).

Vestris, Charles (1797– ?), cousin and pupil of Auguste Vestris. Made his debut at the Paris Opéra (1809), later became first dancer at San Carlo Theatre, Naples, where he married ballerina Caroline Maria Ronzi, subsequently known as Ronzi-Vestris. Both Charles Vestris and his wife danced in the U.S. with enormous success (1828–29).

Vestris, Gaetan (1729–1808), one of the greatest dancers of the Paris Opéra. Born in Florence, Italy, son of Thomas Vestris, he was of a theatrical family of Italian origin. He studied dancing under Dupré at the Royal Academy, Paris, which he entered in 1748. He became a soloist in 1751 and maître de ballet in 1761. He was also dancing master to Louis XVI. From 1770 to 1776 he composed ballets. During the holidays from the Opéra, Vestris visited Stuttgart where Jean Georges Noverre was working out some of his famous reforms and he danced there and worked with Noverre. In Stuttgart he met and married Anne Heinel, noted dancer (1752). Vestris' dancing was noted for its elegance and he was considered to be a fine mime. In 1772 in the ballet *Castor et Pollux* he discarded the mask, then part of every performer's costume, and astonished the audience with the effectiveness of his mime. Though illiterate and conceited he was known as the greatest male dancer of his time and he influenced male dancing of the next century. Marie Allard, his mistress, was mother of his son, the brilliant dancer Auguste Vestris.

Vestris, Thérèse (1726–1808), French dancer, sister of Gaetan Vestris. After dancing in Dresden and Florence, went to Paris where she made her debut at the Opéra in 1751, dancing there until her retirement in 1766. She often danced with her brother Gaetan and shone in his reflected glory.

Victorica, Victoria Garcia, Argentine writer on dance, b. Buenos Aires, 1922; m. Vladimir Irman. Educated privately and studied dance. Her interest in ballet began with the visit of the Ballet Russe de Monte Carlo to Argentina (1940). Director of the Boris Kniaseff Ballet Company during Kniaseff's sojourn in Argentina. Author of the monumental volume *The Original Ballet Russe in Latin America; Dance News* correspondent in Argentina since 1949; contributor to *Dance Encyclopedia.*

Vic-Wells Ballet. See ROYAL BALLET (British).

Salvatore Vigano, for whom Beethoven composed Prometheus, *his only ballet score.*

Vigano, Salvatore (1769–1821), dancer, choreographer, teacher, b. Naples of a family of dancers; nephew of the composer Luigi Boccherini. As a youth Vigano was more interested in literature and music than in dance, but gradually he turned to the latter. He made his debut in Rome in a woman's role. With an uncle he went to Madrid to take part in a festival and while there married an Austrian dancer known as Maria Medina. He also met Dauberval who invited Vigano to accompany him to London. No doubt this acquaintance increased Vigano's interest in the dance, especially in choreography. He returned to dance in Venice (1790) and produced his first ballet there the following year. With his wife he visited Vienna (1793–95) and toured Central Europe with great success. After a short while in Italy (1798), they returned to Vienna where they lived until 1803. Vigano was producing ballets during this time. After becoming estranged from his wife he produced ballets in Milan, Padua, Venice, returning to Milan as ballet master at Teatro alla Scala (1812). His ballets were very dramatic; his music often a clever use of the works of several composers, or even composed by himself if he could not find what he wanted. Beethoven composed *Prometheus* especially for Vigano's ballet (1801). Of his more than forty ballets the best known were *Gli Strelizzi* (1809), *Dedalo* (1813), *Otello* (1818), *La Vestale* (1818), *I Titani* (1819).

Vigarani, Carlo (1622–1713), architect and artist who designed sets and machinery for many of Jean Baptiste Lully's ballets. An Italian, he came to France in 1659 to design a theatre for Cardinal Jules Mazarin, chief minister of Louis XIV.

Vilia. Operette dansée; chor.: Ruth Page; music: Franz Lehàr's *The Merry Widow,* arr. and orch. by Isaac van Grove; décor: Georges Wakhevitch. First prod.: London's Festival Ballet, Palace Theatre, Manchester, Apr. 30, 1953, with Nathalie Krassovska (The Merry Widow), Oleg Briansky (Danilo), Anton Dolin (Baron Popoff); London première: Festival Hall, July 20, 1953, with Daphne Dale in Krassovska's role. This was Ruth Page's first version of *The Merry Widow* which she afterwards staged for her Chicago Opera Ballet, in décor by Rolf Gerard. The later version has been a staple part of the Chicago Opera Ballet repertoire for many years. The title of *Vilia,* after one of the most famous songs in the operetta, was due to copyright problems over the original title.

Village I Knew, The. Modern dance work; chor.: Sophie Maslow; music: Samuel Matlowsky's *Festival* and traditional Hebrew music arr. by Gregory Tucker; costumes: Eileen Holding. First prod.: New Dance Group, American Dance Festival, Connecticut College, New London, Aug. 18, 1950, with Jane Dudley, Muriel Manings, Sophie Maslow, Anneliese Widman, Ronnie Aul, William Bales, Irving Burton, Donald McKayle, and others. One long section, the part known as "Festival," was presented at the 1949 American Dance Festival. The program note says simply: "In Czarist times Jewish communities were frequently uprooted by the authorities and the people driven from their homes." *The Village I Knew* depicts a series of scenes culminating in the despairing, hopeless flight of people once again made homeless.

Villa-Lobos, Heitor (1890–1959), Brazilian composer and conductor. His many compositions have been used by dancers in Latin America and the U.S., specifically his several *Bachianas Brasileiras* (e.g. Louis Johnson's *Lament* and Job Sanders' *Bachianas Brasileiras,* both to the No. 5); *Dolorosa, Incantation, Two Primitive Canticles, Offering* (all Martha Graham); *Rude Poem* (Doris Humphrey); *Coros No. 7* (Francisco Moncion). Other of his scores were used by José Limón for his *Emperor Jones,* by Bentley Stone for his *In My Back Yard,* and by Maurice Béjart for his *l'Étranger.* Among the compositions written by Villa-Lobos specifically for dance are *Uirapuru, Danses Africaines, Danses des Indiens Métis du Bresil,* and *Mandu-Carara.*

Villanelle, lit. a pastoral poem or dance tune. As a dance (ca. 1580) it was rustic and gay in 3/4 time. The name comes from "vilano" meaning a peasant.

Villella, Edward, American dancer, b. Long Island, N.Y., 1936; m. Janet Greschler. Began his dance training at ten at School of American Ballet; one year at N.Y. High School of Performing Arts concurrently. He stopped training at age fifteen and did not resume for four years, then returned to School of American Ballet. His general education included

New York City Ballet's premier danseur Edward Villella as The Prodigal Son.

four years at Maritime College, from which he graduated with a B.S. in Maritime Transportation. Joined New York City Ballet for its 1957 winter season, his first solo role being the Faun in Jerome Robbins' *Afternoon of a Faun* (Dec. 21, 1957). He was soon dancing a large repertoire including *Interplay, Symphony in C* (3rd Movement), *Western Symphony, Stars and Stripes, Agon* (succeeding Todd Bolender), and others. On Jan. 16, 1960, he gave his first performance in the title role of *The Prodigal Son,* his greatest achievement to date. Among his creations are Harlequin (*La Sonnàmbula*), Entry of the French Ambassador (*Figure in the Carpet*), Sweep (*Creation of the World*), *Electronics,* Oberon (*A Midsummer Night's Dream*), First Couple—with Patricia McBride (*Fantasy*), *Tarantella* pas de deux (1964), and others (all for the New York City Ballet). Made his N.Y. debut as actor-dancer when he played Harry Beaton in the City Center Light Opera Company's revival of *Brigadoon* (summer, 1962). Danced in London for the first time later the same year when he and Violette Verdy had a great success in the *Tchaikovsky Pas de Deux* which they danced at the Royal Academy of Dancing Gala Performance organized annually by Dame Margot Fonteyn. In Dec., 1962, and Jan., 1963, danced the same work as guest artist with the Royal Danish Ballet, Copenhagen. He has made a number of very successful television appearances.

Vilzak, Anatole, dancer, teacher, b. St. Petersburg, Russia; m. Ludmila Shollar. He is a graduate of the Imperial Ballet School of the Maryinsky Theatre (1915) where he was a pupil of Michel Fokine. He was promoted to premier danseur three years after entering the company, partnering Mathilda Kchessinska, Vera Trefilova, Tamara Karsavina, Olga Spessivtseva, and other leading ballerinas of the day in the entire classic repertoire. Left Russia (1921) and joined the Diaghilev Ballets Russes as premier danseur. His outstanding roles for this company included Bova Korolevich (*Contes Russes*), Favorite Slave (*Schéhérazade*), male role (*Les Sylphides*), Prince (*Swan Lake*). He and Shollar staged the shortened version of *Swan Lake* for the Diaghilev company, the second act becoming the basis of the subsequent one-act versions in the repertoires of most present-day companies. Later joined Ida Rubinstein's company, creating the leading male roles in *La Bien-Aimée* and *Bolero* (1928), *La Valse* (1929), and others. He then formed a company with Shollar and Karsavina which appeared in London. Joined the State Opera House in Riga, Latvia, as premier danseur, ballet master, and choreographer. Joined René Blum's Ballet Russe de Monte Carlo for which he created the title role in Fokine's *Don Juan* (1936), also dancing Harlequin (*Carnaval*), Polovetsian Chief (*Prince Igor*), etc. Premier danseur, Metropolitan Opera House, N.Y. (1936–37), when George Balanchine was choreographer; then joined faculty of School of American Ballet. Established the Vilzak-Shollar School in 1940, left in 1946 for Europe, returning a year later. Taught at the Ballet Russe de Monte Carlo School, N.Y., Washington

School of Ballet, and in September, 1965 joined the San Francisco Ballet School.

Violon du Diable, Le. Ballet in 2 acts, 6 scenes; chor. and book: Arthur Saint-Léon; music: Cesare Pugni. First prod.: Théâtre de l'Opéra, Paris, Jan. 19, 1849, with Fanny Cerito and Saint-Léon. A very long and very complicated ballet, the plot is a lighthearted variation on the theme of *Faust.* There are two magic violins in the ballet: one of the devil and another of an angel. It is the angel's violin which finally wins the heroine for the hero, the devil having to retire in defeat. Saint-Léon not only staged the ballet and danced the role of the hero Urbain, a celebrated violinist, but he also played the violin and, according to contemporary sources, played it very well.

Virginia Reel, a type of longway set (square dance) popular in U.S. in which any even number of couples may participate. Arranged in two lines with partners facing each other, the head and foot couples perform the figures in the first part; both lines participate in the second part, which is a reel, and in the third part, a march which brings the head couple to the foot of the line. Thus each time the steps are repeated, a new couple takes part. This is continued until all couples have taken part in the figures.

Vision of Marguerite. Ballet in 1 act; chor.: Frederick Ashton; music: Franz Liszt's *Mephisto Valse;* décor: James Bailey. First prod.: London's Festival Ballet, Festival Hall, London, Apr. 3, 1952, with Belinda Wright, John Gilpin, and Oleg Briansky. A complete re-working of Ashton's *Mephisto Valse* using the same music and story.

Visionary Recital. See SAMSON AGONISTES.

Vladimiroff, Pierre, dancer, teacher, b. St. Petersburg, Russia, 1893; m. Felia Doubrovska. Graduated from the Imperial Ballet School of the Maryinsky Theatre (1911); became premier danseur (1915), his repertoire including *Carnaval, Paquita, Chopiniana, Giselle, Raymonda, Harlequinade,* and others. Danced with Diaghilev Ballets Russes (1912, 1914). Resigned from the Maryinsky Theatre and left Russia (1918). Again danced with the Diaghilev company and was the Prince in the famous 1921 revival of *The Sleeping Beauty* (called *The Sleeping Princess* at that time). Joined the Anna Pavlova company (1928) as her partner and premier danseur, remaining until her death (1931). Came to U.S. to join the faculty of the School of American Ballet (1934) where he continues to teach.

Vlassi, Christiane, contemporary French ballerina, b. Paris; m. Attilio Labis. Graduated from the school of the Paris Opéra Ballet into the company, where she rose from the corps de ballet to première danseuse and was nominated an étoile in the fall of 1963. Dances Odette-Odile in *Swan Lake* (Vladimir Bourmeister version), and leading roles in *Suite en Blanc, Les Sylphides, Palais de Cristal* and others. Made her U.S. debut at the Jacob's Pillow Dance Festival (1963).

Vodehnal, Andrea, American dancer, b. Oak Park, Ill., 1938; m. Eugene Collins. Studied with Alexander Kotchetovsky, Ballet Russe de Monte Carlo School of Ballet, School of American Ballet, N.Y., Tatiana Semenova (Houston, Tex.); received scholarship given by Allied Arts of Houston for study with Alexandra Danilova (1953). Entered Ballet Russe de Monte Carlo (1957), becoming soloist (1961). Her repertoire included *Swan Lake, Les Sylphides, Ballet Imperial, Giselle* (Queen of the Wilis), etc., and she has created roles in *Tribute* (chor. Frederic Franklin) and *España* (chor. Leon Danielian). Ballerina with American Festival Ballet for one season (1962). Joined National Ballet, Washington, D.C. at its

Andrea Vodehnal, ballerina of the National Ballet of Washington.

inception (1962), dancing ballerina roles in *Swan Lake* (Act 2), *Les Sylphides, Coppélia, Tribute, Homage au Ballet* (chor.: Franklin), *Early Voyagers* (chor.: Valerie Bettis), the last two being creations, and also creating the Wife in *Con Amore* and a leading role in *Serenade* in National Ballet's productions of these works.

Volé, in ballet, a "flown" movement, such as brisé volé.

Volinine, Alexandre (1882–1955), dancer, teacher, b. Moscow, Russia. Graduated from the Imperial School of the Bolshoi Theatre, Moscow (1901), and became premier danseur of the Bolshoi Ballet after two years, dancing all the leading male roles of the classic repertoire. Danced with Diaghilev Ballets Russes for its Paris season at the Châtelet Theatre (1910), partnering Yekaterina Geltzer. Also danced with Geltzer at the Winter Garden, Berlin, and Metropolitan Opera House, N.Y. (1911). Toured England, Australia, and U.S. with Adeline Genée (1912, 1913). Toured the world as partner to Anna Pavlova (1914–26) and on his retirement opened a school in Paris with Tamara d'Erlanger. Some of his best known pupils were Madeleine Lafon, André Eglevsky, David Lichine, Tatiana Riabouchinska, Jean Babilée, and Leslie Caron, among others. Staged *Giselle* for the Royal Danish Ballet, Copenhagen (1946). He also wrote a series of articles under the title *My Dance of Life* for the American magazine *The Dance* (1930).

Volkonsky, Prince Serge (1860–1937), director of the Russian Imperial Theatres (1899–1902). An erudite, cultured, and liberal man, he encouraged Michel Fokine to become a choreographer. A follower of Dalcroze, he made attempts to reform the system of dance training at the Maryinsky Theatre School, St. Petersburg, but did not succeed, due to opposition from artists, teachers, and the court. He was forced to leave the post of director following an incident with Mathilda Kchessinska, then all-powerful ballerina of the Imperial Ballet at the Maryinsky Theatre. Left Russia after the revolution of 1917. Wrote a number of books on theatrical subjects in Russian and French; lectured in U.S. on religious and philosophical subjects (1896). Died in Hot Springs, Va., U.S.

Volkov, Boris (Boris Baskakov), dancer, teacher, choreographer, b. Tula, Russia, 1902. Studied dance with Jan-Janowicz Domaratski-Novakowski, Moscow State Ballet. First character dancer, Opera House, Baku (1916–18); danced with Moscow State Ballet School; first character dancer, Mordkin Ballet, Moscow (1922). Toured with Moscow State Ballet through Siberia (1924); dancer and choreographer, Carlton Cafe, Shanghai (fall, 1924). After dancing in Far East he arrived in U.S. (1927) and became a leading member of Adolph Bolm Ballet (1928). Directed ballet at Uptown Theatre, Toronto, Canada (1929), then opened own studio in Toronto (1930). Formed his own group, the Volkov Dancers, which represented

Canada at XIIth Olympiad, Berlin (1936). Staged ice shows (1932–41), ballets for Opera Guild of Toronto (1937, 1939), and organized his Volkov Canadian Ballet which gave its first performance in Toronto, May, 1939. Currently heads his school and directs his company in Toronto.

Volkov Canadian Ballet, group organized by Boris Volkov in Toronto, Canada, as a development of the annual recitals given by students of his school. Gave its first performance in Toronto, May, 1939, and has since performed in various theatres and concert halls in Toronto and as guest artists with the Toronto Philharmonic Orchestra and Toronto Opera. Volkov is choreographer of the entire repertoire which includes a version of *The Nutcracker, Tuonela* (Jan Sibelius), *Moonlight Sonata* (Beethoven), *Classical Symphony* (Prokofiev), and many others. Melissa Hayden (Mildred Herman) is an alumna of the Volkov School and Ballet.

Volkova, Vera, contemporary ballet teacher, b. St. Petersburg, Russia; m. English painter Hugh Williams. Began dance training with Maria Romanova (mother of Galina Ulanova) and later with Agrippina Vaganova, when Vaganova first began to develop her theories of training. Made her debut in Russia but left soon after the revolution, living for several years in China where she danced with George Goncharov, a former colleague. After a brief period with International Ballet (1941), she began teaching in London (1943) and before long her studio attracted dancers, not only from the English companies, but from all the major visiting companies. Spent several months as teacher to the company at Teatro alla Scala, Milan (1950). Teacher and artistic adviser to the Royal Danish Ballet since 1952. Guest instructor, Harkness Ballet at Watch Hill, R.I. (summers, 1964, 1965). Toured the U.S. with the Royal Danish Ballet as artistic adviser and instructor (winter, 1966). Continues teaching the company at the Royal Theatre, Copenhagen. Is a naturalized British subject.

Vera Volkova instructing a class of the Harkness Ballet dancers.

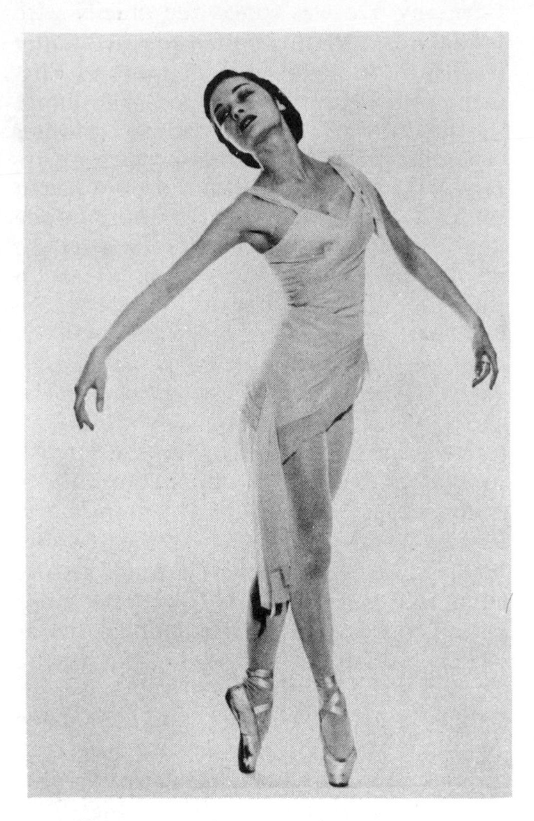

Vollmar, Jocelyn, contemporary American dancer, b. San Francisco, Calif. Studied ballet with the Christensen brothers at the San Francisco Ballet School, joining the company in 1943 and rising first to soloist and subsequently to ballerina (1947). Danced two seasons with New York City Ballet as leading soloist and one season with Ballet Theatre (1948–49). Joined Grand Ballet du Marquis de Cuevas (1950), remaining for three and one-half years; prima ballerina Australian Ballet of Edouard Borovansky (1954–56). Rejoined San Francisco Ballet, first as guest artist for its three State Dept. tours and then permanently as ballerina. She dances the whole classic repertoire and many Lew Christensen ballets, creating the title role in his *Lady of Shalott* (1958). Has choreographed works for the summer workshop programs of the company. Two books of her poems have been published, *Preludes* (1959) and *Arabesques* (1966).

Volta, a 16th century dance originating as a peasant dance in Provence. The name comes from "volta" meaning turning. The dance was in triple time and consisted of two steps and a leap. It was very popular in England where in one form the gentleman lifted the lady high in the air. The modern waltz is derived from the volta.

Volynsky, Akim Lvovitch (Flekser) (1863–1926), Russian literary critic, art specialist, and author. Well educated and erudite, he was head and shoulders above his contemporaries. His greatest work was a monumental volume on Leonardo da Vinci which brought him an honorary citizenship of the city of Milan, Italy. He was an ardent balletomane and wrote ballet criticisms for St. Petersburg newspapers and magazines which the dancers themselves often found difficult to understand. During the first years after the revolution he headed a private "Russian Choreographic School." His most important work on ballet is *Kniga Likovanii* (The Book of Exultations), published in Petrograd in 1923. It was an attempt to formulate a philosophy of the ballet dance. The book has not been translated into English except for one chapter, "The Verticality and the Dance on Toe," which appeared in *Dance News* (Oct., 1943) in a translation by Anatole Chujoy.

von Derp, Clotilde. See SAKHAROFF, ALEXANDRE.

Vondrak, Paul, Austrian dancer, b. Vienna, 1939. Studied with his father Ewald Vondrak, a former soloist of the Vienna State Opera Ballet, and at the ballet school of the Vienna State Opera. Was accepted into the company (1953); promoted to soloist (1957). Dances leading roles in *Swan Lake, La Boutique Fantasque, Symphony in C, Giselle, Hotel Sacher,* the various pas de deux, and others.

von Einem, Gottfried, Austrian composer, b. Bern, Switzerland, 1918. A pupil of Boris Blacher, von Einem is a neo-Romantic whose ballets have received a wider acceptance than his orchestral works. His compositions for ballet include, among others, *Princess Turandot* (Tatiana Gsovska, 1944); *Rondo of the Golden Calf* (1952), *Medusa* (1957), both for Erika Hanka; *Pas de Coeur, Glück, Tod und Traum, Ballade* (all for Yvonne Georgi). Many Central European ballet companies have produced these works subsequent to their premières.

von Gencsy, Eva, contemporary Hungarian ballerina, b. Budapest. Entered Russian Ballet Academy, Budapest, at ten; later won a scholarship to Salzburg, Austria, where she began her professional career as soloist at the Opera House (1945). Emigrated to Canada (1948) and joined the Winnipeg (now Royal Winnipeg) Ballet, becoming its ballerina. One of her outstanding roles with this company was The Lady Known as Lou in *The Shooting of Dan McGrew*. Joined Les Grands Ballets Canadiens (1954), performing chiefly on television during its first years. Her roles with this company included Odile (*Swan Lake*, Act 3), Swanilda (*Coppélia*), Ballerina (*Petrouchka*), and many of the original works by Ludmilla Chiriaeff and Eric Hyrst. In recent years she has become interested in modern and jazz works by such choreographers as Michel Conte and Brian Macdonald, and now works mainly on television in Montreal, with occasional guest appearances with Les Grands Ballet Canadiens.

von Laban, Rudolf (1879–1958), teacher and theorist, b. Bratislava, Slovakia. Devised a new system of dance that greatly affected the European modern dance and, to a lesser extent, the ballet. He studied painting in Munich and dancing in Paris. Laban was appointed director of the Allied State Theatres in Berlin (1930) and choreographed large productions for "movement choirs" throughout Germany. He was concerned chiefly with plastic rhythm, the supremacy of motion for its own sake. Mary Wigman and Kurt Jooss are his two best-known pupils. Through Jooss and Sigurd Leeder Laban's ideas were reflected in the Jooss dance group. Laban's work in Germany was really the groundwork for the modern dance and his influence has been felt by all modern dancers in the U.S. as well as in Europe. It is possible that Laban was the philosopher who researched and formulated the principles while Jooss, with his sense of theatre, systematized these principles. Together they analyzed the coordination of mind, nerves, and muscles, and codified these laws of physical expression (see EUKINETICS). During World War II Laban organized a system for teaching corrective exercises to factory workers in England. His last years were spent in Surrey where, with Lisa Ullman, he conducted his Art of Movement Studio. Laban also invented a system of Dance Notation, which he published under the

Rudolf von Laban, theoretician of dance and of all human movement and inventor of a dance notation system.

title *Kinetographie Laban* (1928). Laban married twice; his second wife was dancer Maja Lenares. His daughter, Juana de Laban, teaches dance in the U.S. on the university level.

von Rosen, Elsa-Marianne, Swedish ballerina and choreographer, b. 1927; m. Danish writer and impresario Allan Fridericia. Studied with Vera Alexandrova, Albert Kozlovsky, Jenny Hasselqvist; was a guest pupil at the Royal Danish Ballet School (1945–47). Made her debut in recitals; was later a member of Ballet Russe de Monte Carlo (1947); soloist at the Oscars Theatre in Stockholm. With her husband formed The Swedish Ballet (1950) for which Birgit Cullberg choreographed the first versions of *Miss Julie* and *Medea,* in both of which Elsa-Marianne von Rosen created the title roles. This company danced in Sweden and in London, England. Ballerina of the Royal Swedish Ballet (1951–59), dancing all the great classic roles as well as leading parts in ballets by Birgit Cullberg, Ivó Cramér and Leonide Massine. Formed her own company, Skandinaviska Baletten (Scandinavian Ballet) in 1960 and toured Sweden, Denmark, and Germany. The company was disbanded in the autumn of 1961. Staged and danced title role in August Bournonville's *La Sylphide* for her own company and for Ballet Rambert (1960). Her own ballets include *Irene Holm* and *Teenagers* (Scandinavian Ballet); *Prometheus,* to the Beethoven score (Royal Swedish Ballet); again *Irene Holm* and *The Virgin Spring* (Royal Danish Ballet, 1964), and several works for Danish television.

Elsa-Marianne von Rosen, Scandinavian ballerina, creator of the title roles in Cullberg's Miss Julie *and* Medea. *Shown here in* La Sylphide.

Vsevolojsky, Ivan (1835–1909), director of the Russian Imperial Theatres (1881–99), playwright and painter. His costume designs were used for some twenty-five ballets, among them *The Sleeping Beauty, Cinderella, The Nutcracker, La Fille Mal Gardée, The Seasons, Esmeralda, Raymonda.* He was the author of the book for *The Sleeping Beauty.* He exercised a strong influence upon Marius Petipa and guided him toward his most successful productions, especially *The Sleeping Beauty* and *Raymonda.* His manner of running the Imperial Theatres was that of a courtier rather than an administrator of public theatres. He considered himself a marquis of the court of Louis XIV and the Imperial Theatres the property of the court (which they actually were). He directed the Theatres for the entertainment of the Imperial family. Vsevolojsky is credited with establishing a unity of style in the production of ballets, demanding and achieving a harmony of dance, music, and décor. He also originated the so-called "production council," composed of the author of the book, the composer, designer, and choreographer of a ballet, as a preliminary to the actual staging of a ballet.

Vyroubova, Nina, French ballerina of Russian parentage, b. Gourzouv (Crimea), U.S.S.R., 1921. Educated at the Lycée Jules Perry, Paris. Began studying ballet with her mother, who was a teacher, later with Vera Trefilova, Olga Preobrajenska, Victor Gsovsky, Boris Kniaseff, Lubov Egorova, Serge Lifar, Nicholas Zverev, Yves Brieux. Appeared in Soirées de la Danse organized by Irène Lidova (1944), dancing with Roland Petit in *Giselle* and *Nightingale and the Rose.* Created the principal role in Roland Petit's *Les Forains* (1945). Her first major success was in the title role of *La Sylphide,* re-created by Victor Gsovsky after Filippo Taglioni's original ballet of 1832, for Les Ballets des Champs-Élysées (1946). Première danseuse étoile of the Paris Opéra (1949–56), one of the few dancers trained outside the theatre to hold this position. Her repertoire included the classic ballets, as well as *Blanche Neige, Firebird* (Lifar version), and *Les Noces Fantastiques,* among others. Left the Opéra to become ballerina with Grand Ballet du Marquis de Cuevas (1957–61), dancing *Giselle, Swan Lake, L'Amour et son Destin,* and others; was one of the Auroras in the Marquis' final production, *The Sleeping Beauty.* Since the death of Cuevas she has been guest ballerina with various companies such as Ballet Russe de Monte Carlo (1961–62 U.S. tour) and the ballet of the Colón Theatre, Buenos Aires, Argentina (May–June, 1964). Her performance in the title role in *Giselle* won the Prix Pavlova of the Institut Chorégraphique de Paris (1957). At present dancing and teaching in France.

W

Wagner, Richard (1813–1883), German composer. The overture and "Bacchanale" from his opera *Tannhäuser* were used by Leonide Massine for his ballet *Bacchanale* (1939). Massine also used parts of *Tristan und Isolde* for the music for *Mad Tristan* (1944). *Cain and Abel* (David Lichine, 1946) is set to excerpts from *Siegfried.*

Wakhevitch, Georges, French stage designer of Russian parentage, b. 1907. He has designed many ballets including *Le Jeune Homme et la Mort* (Ballets des Champs-Elysées, 1946), *La Croqueuse de Diamants* (Ballets de Paris de Roland Petit, 1950), *Le Combat* (American Ballet Theatre, 1952), Ruth Page's *Vilia* (London's Festival Ballet, 1953), *Hymn to Beauty* (Leonide Massine, Teatro Municipal, Rio de Janeiro, 1955); for the Paris Opéra ballet: "Le Turc Généreux" scene in *Les Indes Galantes* (1952), Serge Lifar's *Firebird* (1954), Lifar's *Romeo and Juliet* (1955); for the Vienna Statsoper: *The Moor of Venice* (Hanka–Blacher, 1955), *Giselle* (Hamilton–Adam, 1955), *Joan von Zarissa* (Hanka–Egk, 1957), *Hotel Sacher* (Hanka, 1957), and others.

Waldteufel, Emil (1837–1915), French composer. During his lifetime he wrote several hundred very successful waltzes and other dance compositions.

Walker, Norman, dancer, choreographer, teacher, b. New York City, 1934. Graduate of the N.Y. School of Performing Arts (drama major), City College, N.Y. He studied modern dance with May O'Donnell, Gertrude Shurr, and at the Martha Graham School; ballet with Valentina Pereyaslavec, Robert Joffrey. Made his debut as a dancer with the May O'Donnell company (1953) and became leading male dancer (1955). During his service in the U.S. Army was featured dancer in Army shows (1957–59). Formed his own company which made its debut at the YM–YWHA, N.Y. (1960) and appeared at Jacob's Pillow Dance Festival (1961, 62, 67). A teacher at School of Performing Arts since 1956 (with time out for army service), his first dance work *Four Cantos,* to music by Vivaldi, was for a student performance (1956). He also staged this work for the regional company, Garden State Ballet, N.J. (1961). Some of his other works are *Crossed Encounter* (Brahms, 1960), *Baroque Concerto* (Vivaldi, 1960), *Splendors and Obscurities* (Alan Hovhaness, 1961). Has choreographed and danced leading roles in musicals staged for the Summer Dance Festivals at Utah State Univ., and for television. Made an auspicious television debut with *Reflections,* to Norman Dello Joio's *Variations,* created for the first of the WCBS–TV series "Repertoire Work-

Norman Walker with partner Cora Cahan and Marilyn Liebman (left) in his Baroque Concerto.

shop," Jan. 2, 1963. Toured with Walter Terry's America Dances company (spring, 1963); appeared with his company at Utah State Univ. (summer, 1963, 1964); choreographed Carl Orff's *Trionfo di Afrodite* (summer, 1964). Has appeared as guest artist with partner Cora Cahan with N.Y. Philharmonic, the Shreveport (La.), and the New Orleans (La.) Symphony Orchestras. In addition to performing and choreographing, he continues to teach.

Walkowitz, Abraham (1880-1965), Russian-born American painter. He was a prolific and important member of the N.Y. avant-garde movement in the 1920's and a co-founder and one-time director of the Society of Independent Artists. He is represented in several museums and in a number of private collections and has been exhibited widely in the U.S. and Europe. His special fame in the dance world rests upon his drawing and water colors of Isadora Duncan, of whom he must have made virtually thousands of sketches. He wrote a small book illustrated with his drawings, *Duncan and Her Dances.* Duncan is reputed to have said to him: "Walkowitz, you have written my biography in lines without words." In 1943–44 a group of some one hundred American artists individually painted and exhibited Walkowitz's portraits. *Life Magazine* (Feb. 21, 1944) devoted a four-page spread to color reproductions of many of these portraits and to the story about this extraordinary occasion.

Wallman, Margaret, contemporary Austrian choreographer, ballet mistress, opera director. Member of the Diaghilev Ballets Russes and ballet mistress of the Vienna State Opera Ballet until 1929. Taught in N.Y. (1929–32) and staged dances for Hollywood films; became ballet mistress at Colón Theatre, Buenos Aires, Argentina. In 1952 went to Teatro alla Scala, Milan, as choreographer, her works for that company including *Legend of Joseph* (Richard Strauss). She is also a notable director of operas which she has staged in many of the world's great opera houses, including the Metropolitan Opera House, N.Y. (1964–66).

Walter, Erich, German dancer and choreographer, b. Fürth, Bavaria, 1927. Studied with Olympiada Alperova. Performed in Nuremberg (1946–50), Göttingen (1950–51), Wiesbaden (1951–53); ballet master and choreographer, Wuppertal (1953–64). Choreographed *Four Seasons* (Vivaldi), *Baiser de la Fée, Orpheus, Pulcinella, Apollon Musagète, Jeu des Cartes, Nightingale, Firebird* (all by Stravinsky), *Duel, L'Orfeo* (Monteverdi), *Pelléas and Mélisande* (Schönberg), *Daphnis and Chloë* (Ravel), *Marsyas* (Luigi Dellapicola), *White Rose* (Wolfgang Fortner), *The Miraculous Mandarin* (Bartók), *The Planets* (Gustav Holst). For his final performance in Wuppertal, Jan. 30, 1964, he staged *Scènes de Ballet* (Stravinsky), *Our Lady's Juggler* to an electronic score by Konrad Boehmer, and *Death and the Maiden* (Schubert's String Quartet No. 6 in D minor). Appointed director of Düsseldorf Opera Ballet (fall, 1964). Guest choreographer in Berlin, Salzburg, Stuttgart.

Walton, Sir William, British composer, b. Oldham, Lancs, 1902. At age ten was a pupil of Christ Church Cathedral school, Oxford, later studied music at Oxford with Sir Hugh Allen and E. J. Dent, but is mostly self-trained. His *Façade,* a setting of poems by Edith Sitwell, became the musical basis for Frederick Ashton's first major ballet (1922). His only original composition for ballet is Ashton's *The Quest* (1943). A short orchestral piece *Siesta,* was used by Ashton for a pas de deux (1936). Walton made an arrangement and orchestrated music by J. S. Bach for Ashton's *The Wise Virgins* (1940). John Taras used his *Music for Children* for *Devoirs des Vacances* (Ballets des Champs-Élysées, 1949). An early overture, *Portsmouth Point,* was played as an interlude during the Diaghilev Ballets Russes London season of 1926 and subsequently.

Waltz. 1. Basic dance in the classic and romantic ballets, most often used for large ensembles. Marius Petipa was celebrated as a choreographer to waltz music, as witness his waltzes in *The Sleeping Beauty* (Garland Dance, Act 1); in *Swan Lake* (Acts 1 and 3); in *Raymonda;* in *Bayaderka* (Act 4), and others. Other great waltzes in ballet are "The Waltz of the Flowers" (called in Russia the "Golden Waltz"); in *The Nutcracker* (Act 2); in *Swan Lake* (Act 2, both by Lev Ivanov); in *Giselle* (Act 1, Jean Coralli). In modern ballet the waltz is often used for pas de deux as in *Les Sylphides* (Fokine); *Le Beau Danube, Gaîté Parisienne* (both by Massine); *La Valse* (George Balanchine), and others. 2. Ballroom dance in 3/4 time, of which there are two basic variations: the faster Viennese waltz, in which couples turn in circles in one direction, and the slower Boston (originated in America), in which the couples turn in circles in several directions. A further variation of the Boston Waltz is the Hesitation, introduced by Vernon and Irene Castle. The basic form of the waltz—turns—remains in all its variations and modifications.

Waltz Is a Waltz Is a Waltz, A. Modern dance work; chor.: Myra Kinch; music: Strauss waltzes, arr. by Manuel Galea; décor: John Christian. First prod.: Jacob's Pillow Dance Festival, Lee, Mass., Aug. 27, 1960, with Myra Kinch, Ted Shawn, Shirley Jensen, Alonso Castro. A bracelet belonging to a genteel young lady (Shirley Jensen) is stolen in rapid succession by the other disreputable characters but is returned to her in the end.

Waltz-Scherzo. Pas de deux; chor.: George Balanchine; music: Peter Tchaikovsky's Op. 34 for violin and orchestra; costumes: Barbara Karinska. First prod.: New York City Ballet, City Center, New York, Sept. 9, 1958, with Patricia Wilde and André Eglevsky. Dropped from the repertoire in 1959, it was revived Jan. 9, 1964, in a considerably revised version and danced by Patricia Wilde and Jacques d'Amboise. It is a brief lyrico-romantic pas de deux. The original version contained no lifts, but a few were incorporated into the revival.

Wanderer, The. Ballet in four movements; chor. and book: Frederick Ashton; music: Franz Schubert's "Wanderer" Fantasie; décor: Graham Sutherland. First prod.: Sadler's Wells (now Royal) Ballet, New Theatre, London, Jan. 27, 1941, with Robert Helpmann in the title role and Margot Fonteyn, Pamela May, and Michael Somes in other leading parts. There is no story but the protagonist is a Wanderer in his imagination, reliving his experiences of life, its loves, failures, and triumphs. George Balanchine used the same music for his ballet *Errante,* originally staged for *Les Ballets 1933* and revived for the American Ballet (1935).

War Between Men and Women, The. Modern dance work; chor.: Charles Weidman; music: Peter Tchaikovsky's Symphony No. 6 in B minor (the "Pathétique"). First prod.: Charles Weidman Theatre Dance Company, YM–YWHA, New York, Apr. 25, 1954, with Charles Weidman and Lila Lewis as husband and wife. The famous series of James Thurber drawings brought to life on the stage but given an un-Thurberish sentimental ending as the warring couple are reconciled by their child. The unlikely but (in this case) hilariously suitable accompaniment of Tchaikovsky's most famous symphony added to the success of Weidman's choreography.

Wardrobe, collective term for all the costumes used by a ballet or other company for its repertoire.

Wardrobe Mistress, person responsible for the wardrobe—in charge of its appearance, cleaning, pressing, and repairing, having necessary costumes ready for each production, seeing that all costumes are packed for tours, etc.

Warm-Up, in modern dance the term given to the group of exercises executed by dancers prior to rehearsal or performance. For the modern dancer the floorwork would normally be done first, followed by other exercises at the barre. The dancer's warm-up serves him in exactly the same way a warm-up serves any athlete who goes through certain preliminary, simple exercises before actual competition. By so doing, the dancer and the athlete prevent injury to the muscles and tendons which would otherwise be insufficiently limber to withstand sudden or extreme usage such as is possible after these parts of the body have been used and conditioned.

Watts, Jonathan (John Leech), dancer, b. Cheyenne, Wyo., 1933; m. Dianne Consoer. A graduate of High School of Performing Arts, N.Y., he studied ballet mainly with Robert Joffrey there and at Joffrey's school; modern dance with Gertrude Shurr and May O'Donnell. Appeared in Joffrey's first program of choreographic works and has frequently been guest artist since with the Robert Joffrey Ballet. Joined New York City Ballet (1954), subsequently being promoted to junior soloist (1957), then to principal soloist (1959). His creations include leading roles in *Agon, Episodes* (1st movement), *Liebeslieder Walzer, Don Sebastian Variations,* and others; also danced a large repertoire including Sugar Plum Fairy Cavalier (*The Nutcracker*), Prince (*Swan Lake,* Act 2), 1st and 2nd movements (*Symphony in C*), 1st movement (*Western Symphony*), *Gounod Symphony, Divertimento No. 15, Pas de Dix,* Sanguinic variation (*Four Temperaments*), and others. Rejoined Robert Joffrey Ballet for its 1962–63 tour of Europe and the Near East (1962), after dancing with New York City Ballet in Europe and Soviet Union. Following tour with Robert Joffrey Ballet, joined Australian Ballet (1962–63) as guest artist. His roles with Robert Joffrey Ballet included Saint-Léon

(*Pas des Déesses*), Colin (*La Fille Mal Gardée*), *Flower Festival at Genzano* pas de deux, *Pas de Dix,* and others; with Australian Ballet he danced Siegfried in full-length *Swan Lake,* Franz in *Coppélia.* Returned to N.Y. (summer, 1963) and devoted some time to teaching ballet. In July 1965 he joined the Cologne (Germany) Opera Ballet as premier danseur. His wife also signed. Both dancers are also instructors at the company's ballet school.

Weaver, John (1673–1760).

BY GEORGE CHAFFEE.

Once famous as a dancing master, theatrical dancer, choreographer, ballet master, teacher, and author, John Weaver is consistently remembered only in histories in the field of drama and music. Ballet histories seldom so much as mention his name, and then only as teacher and writer. Outside dance literature Weaver achieved a left-handed fame as "the Father of English Pantomime." The son of a dancing master of the same name, Weaver was born in Shrewsbury, England (July 21, 1673), and was the most prominent figure in the English School of dance and ballet which flourished in London and the provinces in Restoration-Augustan times (1660–1760). His immediate forerunners as dancer-choreographers were men such as Luke Channel and Josias Priest (choreographer for the Henry Purcell "operas"). His noted contemporaries were Shaw, Isaac, Coverley, Siris, John Essex, Kellom Tomlinson, and John Thurmond. His favorite ballerina, who created the principal roles in his ballets, was the lovely and gifted Hester Santlow (Mrs. Barton Booth). As a professional dancer, Weaver rarely assumed "noble" roles. Demi-caractère or comic parts were his forte. He was noted, particularly in later years, as Clown in the English pantomime, a then-new theatrical genre actually built around dance, which soon spread its influence across the Channel. It was destined to enjoy enduring popularity in England. Weaver was featured dancer and choreographer-ballet-master at either Drury Lane or Lincoln's Inn Fields theatres from 1700 to 1736. In his later years he lived in Shrewsbury where, admired, respected and beloved, he taught and produced ballets until his death at the age of eighty-seven (Sept. 24, 1760). John Weaver's fame in dance history is (or should be) as the first producer of pantomime ballets, in the classic sense of the term—the "ballet d'action"—long before the days of Hilverding (1710–1768), Noverre (1727–1809), and Angiolini (1731–1803). Weaver's first pantomime ballet was a burlesque work, "after the manner of the Modern Italians," but unlike their pieces completely without dialogue. This was *The Tavern Bilkers,* first danced at Drury Lane on Oct. 23, 1702 (revived 1715–16; 1732–33). During the 1716–17 season at Drury Lane, Weaver produced his first "serious" large scale work, *The Loves of Mars and Venus,* "A Dramatic Entertainment of Dancing," with Louis Dupré, Sr. as Mars; Hester Santlow, the first English ballerina of note, as Venus; himself as Vulcan; and 23 other dancers. This work, in six scenes (a camp, Venus' boudoir, Vulcan's workshop, a garden, etc.) has always been regarded as a milestone in the annals of the London stage and also as the immediate springboard for a different species of mixed entertainment, the English pantomime. The program-libretto of the show is also a manifesto. It leaves no doubt as to the nature of Weaver's undertaking, the ideas that inspired it, and the precise character of the production. Published in London in 1717 it is by many years the first known formal libretto of a ballet d'action and the first of a number of similar works that Weaver staged in London from 1717 to 1733.

John Weaver is the most eminent writer on the art of dance in English literature previous to the 20th century. Besides his ballet libretti, which he himself wrote, he published the following works (all in London): *Orchesography* (first English rendering of Raoul Anger Feuillet's *Chorégraphie*), 1706; 2nd edition of same, ca. 1716; *A Small Treatise of Time and Cadence in Dancing* (eight pages of text and four of choreographic notation) 1706; *The Union, a New Dance Compos'd by Mr. Isaac . . . and writt down in Characters by John Weaver* (engraved by H. Hulsbergh, the only known signed example of Weaver's own choreographic writing of isolated dances), 1707; *An Essay towards an History of Dancing,* 1712; *Anatomical and Mechanical Lectures upon Dancing,* 1721 (according to Curt Sachs' *World History of the Dance,* N.Y., 1937, "The first attempt to base dancing and dance instruction on the knowledge of the body"); *History of Mimes and Pantomimes,* 1728.

For further information on Weaver and dance in London in his generation see *Dictionary of National Biographies* (English); Grove's *Dictionary of Music and Musicians;* Allardyce Nicoll's *History of Restoration* (also, *Early 18th Century*) *Drama;* and Emmet Langdon Avery, *Dancing and Pantomime on the English Stage, 1700–1737,* in University of Chicago *Studies in Philology,* vol. 33, no. 3, pp. 417–53, 1934.

Web, The. Ballet in 1 act; chor.: Laverne Meyer; music: Anton von Webern's String Quartet Op. 5; décor: Diana Dewes. First prod.: Western Theatre Ballet, Elmhurst Studio Theatre, Camberley, Surrey, England, Sept. 4, 1962, with Gail Donaldson and Simon Mottram. A young man prevents a girl from committing suicide and finds himself entangled in her emotional problems.

Weber, Carl Maria von (1786–1828), German composer. Michel Fokine set his ballet *Le Spectre de la Rose* (1911) to Weber's "Invitation to the Dance." Leonide Massine used a selection of his music for his ballet *Vienna—1814* (1940). Massine used "straight" Weber after Paul Hindemith had been commissioned to write the score (which was his *Symphonic Metamorphosis on Themes of Carl Maria von Weber,* arranged and orchestrated from the 1st, 3rd, and 4th movements of Weber's Piano Music for Four Hands). George Balanchine later used the Hindemith score for *Metamorphoses* (1952). Balanchine also arranged a short-lived *Pas de Deux Romantique* (1950) to Weber's *Concertino for Clarinet.*

Webster, Sir David, General Administrator of the Royal Opera House, Covent Garden, London, since 1946; b. 1903. Educated at Holt School, Liverpool and Oxford Universities. Chairman Liverpool Philharmonic Society, Ltd. (1940–45); attached to the Ministry of Supply Ordnance Factories (1942–44); Administrator of the Covent Garden Preliminary Committee (1944–46); Governor and Treasurer Royal Ballet School since 1955; Governor of the Royal Ballet since 1957. Sir David shared with Dame Ninette de Valois, Director of the Royal Ballet until her retirement in 1963, the responsibility for and the credit of building the Royal Ballet (formerly Sadler's Wells Ballet) into an international organization of the highest caliber, which has no peer in Western Europe. It is also due to Sir David to a great extent that American ballet companies have been invited to dance at the Royal Opera House: Ballet Theatre (1946, 1950, 1953), and New York City Ballet (1950, 1952). In an informal way this is in exchange for the nine visits of the Royal Ballet to the United States between 1949 and 1967, managed here by impresario S. Hurok. He also negotiated the first visit of the Bolshoi Ballet to the Royal Opera House (1956), which paved the way for its tour of the U.S. (1959), also managed by S. Hurok.

Wedding Bouquet, A. Ballet in 1 act; chor.: Frederick Ashton; music, décor, book (with verses by Gertrude Stein): Lord Berners. First prod.: Vic-Wells (later Sadler's Wells, now Royal) Ballet, Sadler's Wells Theatre, London, Apr. 27, 1937, with Mary Honer (Bride), Robert Helpmann (Groom), Margot Fonteyn (Julia), June Brea (Josephine), Julia Farron (Pepe the dog), Ninette de Valois (Webster, a maid), and with Pamela May, Elizabeth Miller, Molly Brown, Jill Gregory, William Chappell, Harold Turner, Michael Somes, Leslie Edwards, Claude Newman, in parts which the motion pictures of today would call "cameos." At first the verses by Stein were chanted on stage by a chorus, but later they were spoken by Constant Lambert with tremendous point and humor, with a few devastating interpolations of his own. The verses are entirely nonsensical but, when put together with the actions which sometimes matched and sometimes are diametrically opposed to the words, a mad kind of plot emerges about a wedding in provincial France in the early 1900's: a bridegroom whose former love embarrassingly turns up to harass him, a bridesmaid who drinks a little too much, and a Mexican hairless dog (the then-tiny Julia Farron) who aspires to be a ballerina. *A Wedding Bouquet* was revived by Sadler's Wells Ballet at Royal Opera House, Covent Garden, Feb. 17, 1949, with Margaret Dale as the Bride, Moira Shearer as Julia, and Helpmann as devastating as ever as the Bridegroom. It was one of the ballets presented at the twenty-first anniversary performance of Sadler's Wells Ballet at Sadler's Wells Theatre, May 15, 1950 (by a miscalculation it was actually the 20th not the 21st), when as many of the original cast as possible returned and Dame Ninette again danced Webster (her final stage appearance), though not this time on point. Dutch choreographer Pieter van der Sloot has staged this ballet in Holland (1947). Revived in 1965 for the U.S. tour with Alexander Grant, alternating with Stanley Holden (Bridegroom), Merle Park (Bride), Monica Mason (Webster), Annette Page (Julia), Deanne Bergsma (Josephine), with Robert Helpmann as Narrator.

Wedding Present, The. Ballet in 1 act; chor.: Peter Darrell; music: Béla Bartók's Piano Concerto No. 3; décor: Judith Wood. First prod.: Western Theatre Ballet, Empire Theatre, Sunderland, England, Apr. 19, 1962, with Laverne Meyer, Brenda Last, Sylvia Wellman, Victor Maynard. The effect of an earlier homosexual relationship on a young man's marriage.

Wedding Procession in Hardanger (Brudenfaerden in Hardanger). Ballet in 2 acts by August Bournonville; music: Holger Simon Paulli. First prod.: Royal Danish Ballet, Copenhagen, 1853. The action takes place alternately on the farms Vold and Heja and at the Hardanger Fjord. After a trip to Norway the choreographer, full of admiration for what he had seen, created this ballet based on Norwegian folkways.

Weidman, Charles, dancer, choreographer, teacher, b. Lincoln, Neb., 1901. Studied with Eleanor Frampton (Lincoln); also at Denishawn and with Theodore Koslov (Calif.). First professional experience was in vaudeville (*Xochitl*) with Martha Graham. Member of the Denishawn company eight years, touring U.S., England, the Orient (1925). Established school and concert company with Doris Humphrey (1927) and during this period (which lasted until 1945) created many works, some of the best known being *And Daddy Was a Fireman, Atavisms* of which the episode *Lynch Town* is still occasionally performed, and *Flickers,* a satire on silent movies. He also staged dances in musicals, including *Americana, I'd Rather Be Right, As Thousands Cheer, School for Husbands, Sing Out Sweet Land;* also staged dances for the dance team of Harrison-Fisher, and others. Established his own school in 1945 and his own dance group in 1948 in which year he created his most famous work, *Fables Of Our Time,* based on some of the James Thurber fables. Another Thurber work, *The War Between Men and Women* was created in 1954.

Charles Weidman, American modern dance pioneer, still dancing and teaching.

During the late 1950's he spent much time on the West Coast, mainly teaching; then returned to N.Y. to establish with artist Mikhail Santaro the Expression of Two Arts Theatre where they present performances in which the dance shares importance with music, painting, and sculpture. Weidman continues to teach, conducting courses and giving master classes in many colleges in the U.S. Some of the best known modern dancers of the day have been his pupils, among them José Limón, Sybil Shearer, Eleanor King, William Bales, Jack Cole.

Weill, Kurt, composer, b. Dessau, Germany, 1900, d. New York, 1950; m. Lotte Lenya. Studied composition with Engelbert Humperdinck. Became internationally famous with his *Dreigroschenoper* (The Three-Penny Opera) (1928), a modern treatment of John Gay's *Beggar's Opera.* Antony Tudor used parts of this music for *Judgment of Paris.* Composed the music for George Balanchine's *Seven Deadly Sins* created for Les Ballets 1933. Balanchine staged an entirely new version for New York City Ballet in 1958. Weill came to the U.S. in 1935 and wrote the music for a number of Broadway musicals, among them *Knickerbocker Holiday, Lady in the Dark, One Touch of Venus, Street Scene, Lost in the Stars.* He became an American citizen in 1943.

Welch, Garth, Australian dancer. Began his career in musicals at seventeen; then joined the Borovansky Ballet as corps de ballet member, rising to principal dancer. Borovansky awarded him a scholarship in 1959 to enable him to study abroad. After ten months he returned to the company. The Australian Ballet Foundation awarded him a second scholarship in 1961. Danced with the Ballet International du Marquis de Cuevas as soloist, later becoming a leading dancer. Joined Australian Ballet as principal dancer for its 1962–63 season.

Wells, Doreen, English dancer, b. London, 1937. Studied at Bush-Davies School. Entered Sadler's Wells Theatre Ballet (1955), Royal Ballet (1956). Currently ballerina, touring section of Royal Ballet. Repertoire includes Aurora (*The Sleeping Beauty*), *Giselle,* Odette-Odile (*Swan Lake*), Swanilda (*Coppélia*), The Girl (*The Two Pigeons*), The Girl (*The Invitation*), *Don Quixote* pas de deux, Lise (*La Fille Mal Gardée*), and others. Danced the title role in *Raymonda* (staged by Rudolf Nureyev) at the Spoleto Festival to Two Worlds (1964), taking over at a few hours' notice the role which had been intended for Margot Fonteyn who had been obliged to return suddenly to England. U.S. debut April 26, 1967 as Aurora.

Wendel, Heinrich, German stage designer and regisseur, b. Bremen, 1915. Close collaborator of the choreographer Erich Walter in many productions, among them *Apollon Musagète, Jeu de Cartes, White Rose* (Fortner), *Boulevard Solitude* (Henze), *Flamingos* (Fortner), *Verklärte Nacht* (Schönberg), *L'Orfeo* (Monteverdi), and others. Designer of the guest performances of the Wuppertal Teams (Berlin, 1957), Salzburg Festival (1959, 1960); Festivals in Stuttgart (1960), Vienna (1960, 1961).

Werner, Margot, dancer, b. Salzburg, Austria, 1937. Studied with Hanna Kammer and Derra de Moroda (Salzburg). Danced at Salzburg Landestheater (1952–55); since 1955 at State Opera, Munich. Principal roles are Belle Epine (*Prince of the Pagodas*), The Wife of Potiphar (*The Legend of Joseph*), Isabeau (*Joan von Zarissa*), and others.

Weslow, William, dancer, b. Seattle, Wash., 1925. Studied with Mary Ann Wells, Seattle, Wash.; Edward Caton, Anatole Vilzak, George Balanchine, Vera Nemtchinova, Igor Schwezoff (N.Y.). Danced in a number of musicals including *Call Me Madam, Wonderful Town, Girl in Pink Tights, Plain and Fancy.* Was a dancer in the television show "Your Hit Parade" for a year, and has appeared in many other television programs including those of Agnes de Mille for "Omnibus." Soloist at Radio City Music Hall; later a soloist with American Ballet Theatre. Now a member of New York City Ballet, he was promoted to soloist in 1959, dancing Sailor (*Con Amore*), Tea—Chinese Dance (*The Nutcracker*), Blackamoor (*La Sonnàmbula*), and appearing in many of the plotless Balanchine ballets.

West, Elizabeth (1927–1962), English dancer, choreographer, director, b. Alassio, Italy. Studied ballet with Edouard Espinosa, Muriel Carpenter, Bristol School of Dancing; stagecraft at Bristol Old Vic Theatre School. Assistant stage manager for Bristol Old Vic (1946), then embarked on career of acting, stage management, chorus dancing in musicals, choreography in television, Christmas pantomimes, musicals (including the very successful *Salad Days,* 1954); choreographer for Bristol Old Vic and Shakespeare Memorial Theatre, Stratford-on-Avon. Co-founder with Peter Darrell and artistic director of Western Theatre Ballet (1957) in which year she choreographed *Pulcinella* and *Peter and the Wolf* for the company, then concentrated on the administrative side. Killed in an Alpine accident near the Matterhorn, Sept. 28, 1962.

Western Symphony. Ballet in 4 movements; chor.: George Balanchine; music: Hershy Kay (based on American folk themes); décor: John Boyt; costumes: Barbara Karinska. First prod.: New York City Ballet, City Center, New York, Sept. 7, 1954, with Diana Adams and Herbert Bliss (1st movement), Janet Reed and Nicholas Magallanes (2nd movement), Patricia Wilde and André Eglevsky (3rd movement), Tanaquil LeClercq and Jacques d'Amboise (4th movement). Melissa Hayden succeeded Janet Reed in the 2nd movement, and Diana Adams has been as successful in the 4th movement as in the 1st. The music, though entirely based on Western songs and orchestrated with bar piano and folk-fiddling interpolations, keeps to the symphonic form: Allegro (choreographed in the form of a square dance), Adagio, Scherzo, and Rondo. Balanchine is said to have had as a program the idea of a troupe of French Can-Can dancers finding themselves in a Western town at the time of the Gold Rush, but the ballet itself does not carry this out. First performed in practice costumes, décor and costumes were added Feb. 27, 1955.

Western Theatre Ballet, an English ballet company which gave its first performance at the Theatre Royal, Bristol, June 18, 1956. By summer, 1957, the company was able to undertake a tour of the West Country (Devon, Cornwall, etc.) under the artistic direction of Elizabeth West and Peter Darrell with a repertoire of five ballets: *The Prisoners, Pulcinella, Peter and the Wolf, Celeste and Celestina,* and *Tableaux Vivants.* The company was headed by Peter Darrell, Suzanne Musitz, Brenda Last, Anna Paskevskaya, Jean Cebron. The company has since toured in Belgium, Holland, Italy, and Spain, as well as in Great Britain, appearing for short seasons in London. Helped by an Arts Council grant, this has become one of the liveliest and most interesting of the small companies in existence. After Elizabeth West met her death in an accident in Switzerland (fall, 1962), the company continued under the direction of Peter Darrell, who is now also principal choreographer. Other choreographers whose works are in the repertoire include Elizabeth West, Clover Roope, Ray Powell, Gillian Lynne, Meriel Evans, Walter Gore, Laverne Meyer. Tamara Karsavina staged a revival of Michel Fokine's *Carnaval* for the company. Recent ballets include Darrell's *A Wedding Present,* Laverne Meyer's *The Web, Partita, The Owl and the Pussycat, One in Five,* and others. The company made its U.S. debut at the Jacob's Pillow Dance Festival (1963).

Whistler, Rex (1905–1944), English artist and designer, killed in action in Normandy during World War II. His designs for ballet included décor and costumes for *The Rake's Progress* (1935), *The Wise Virgins* (1940), *Le Spectre de la Rose* (1944) all for Sadler's Wells (now Royal) Ballet; and *Everyman* (1943) for International Ballet.

White, Franklin, English dancer, lecturer, b. Shoreham, Kent, 1924. Studied with Marie Rambert (1935–39); later with Peggy van Praagh, Vera Volkova. Made his debut with Ballet Rambert partnering Sally Gilmour in the *Aurora* pas de deux. Joined Sadler's Wells (now Royal) Ballet (1942). Was promoted to senior soloist and principal character mime, his repertoire including Kostchei (*Firebird*), Dr. Coppelius (*Coppélia*), Hilarion (*Giselle*), Tutor (*Swan Lake*), Carabosse (*The Sleeping Beauty*), and others; also such creations as Government Official (*Mam'zelle Angot*), Notary (*La Fille Mal Gardée*), etc. Taught mime and make-up at Royal Ballet School. Has lectured and taught widely in England and abroad. Author of *The Sadler's Wells Ballet Goes Abroad* (1951). Now director of the Vancouver (B.C.) Ballet (since summer, 1966).

White, Onna, contemporary dancer, choreographer, b. Nova Scotia, Canada, now American citizen; m. actor Larry Douglas. Made her professional debut with San Francisco Opera Ballet; N.Y. debut in *Finian's Rainbow.* Michael Kidd, its choreographer, took her to London when he staged *Finian's Rainbow* there. Was also his assistant on *Guys and Dolls.* Arranged dance for television and night club acts and was choreographer of musicals for two seasons (including *Fanny*) at N.Y. City Center. Established herself as one of Broadway's leading choreographers in musicals with *The Music Man* (1957), followed by *Hot Spot, Half a Sixpence* (1965), and others. Choreographer for the film version of *Bye Bye, Birdie.*

White Fawn, The, a theatrical extravaganza which had its première Jan. 20, 1868, at Niblo's Garden, N.Y. It was produced by William Wheatley, the producer of *The Black Crook,* a week after the latter closed its sixteen-month run. The play *The White Fawn* was as ridiculous as *The Black Crook:* a princess is changed into a white fawn by day, becoming a woman at night. Good and evil fairies contend over the fate of the princess and the good fairies win in the end. The chief attraction in *The White Fawn* was the ballet headed by Maria Bonfanti, who had also headed the ballet in *The Black Crook*. The most beautiful scene, according to contemporary reports, was one called "The Enchanted Lake." *The White Fawn* was a very successful production, but could not approach *The Black Crook* either in public acclaim or in financial rewards.

White Rose, The. Ballet in 2 scenes; chor.: Jens Keith; music: Wolfgang Fortner; book: Oscar Wilde (*The Birthday of the Infanta*); décor: Paul Seltenhammer. First prod.: Municipal Opera, Berlin, Apr. 28, 1951, with Suse Preisser (Infanta), Erwin Bredow (Dwarf), Rainer Köchermann (Vision). At the performance in honor of the Infanta the Dwarf also offers his dance. In contrast to the formal court dances, he dances straight from his inner emotions—jealousy, love, hope, grief, and joy speak out of his movements. The Infanta is enraptured and throws him a white rose which he passionately kisses. In a dream he sees himself as a magnificent young man dancing with the princess. When he awakens and wants to draw near her, she repulses him and points out to him his likeness in the mirror. Full of horror and despair, he falls dead.

Whoops-de-Doo, Les. Ballet in 1 act; chor.: Brian Macdonald; music: Don Gillies (*Portrait of a Frontier Town*); décor: Ted Korol. First prod.: Royal Winnipeg Ballet, Flin Flon Community Centre, Flin Flon, Manitoba, Oct., 1959, with Marina Katronis, David Shields, Virginia Wakelyn, Robert Lee Jones, Marilyn Young, James Clouser. A whoop-up dedicated to the misalliance of classic dance and the Western myth. A rowdy and outrageous romp designed to continue the tradition created by Gweneth Lloyd and the Royal Winnipeg Ballet in *The Shooting of Dan McGrew*.

Wied, Karl Viktor Prinz Zu (Prince Carl Victor Wied), b. Potsdam, Germany, 1913. Attended high school and universities in Germany and in 1936 received degree of Doctor of Jurisprudence. While living in Rumania during World War II, he was drafted into the German army (1942). After the war, part of which he spent as a prisoner of war, he settled in Munich and became a free-lance journalist, writer, and lecturer, mainly on ballet. His book *Königinnen Des Balletts* (Queens of the Ballet) (Munich, 1961), included biographies and evaluations of eleven ballerinas, beginning with Camargo and ending with Margot Fonteyn, thus spanning two hundred years of European ballet. He is president of the Gesellschaft der Freunde des Balletts (Society of the Friends of the Ballet), Munich.

Wiesenthal (sisters), **Grete, Elsa and Berta,** Austrian dancers of the first decade of the 20th century. Though trained at the school of the Vienna Royal Opera Ballet, they proceeded to develop their own Viennese style of dance. For many years they gave performances in Austria and abroad featuring graceful movements and poses, eye-catching costumes, and melodious music (usually waltzes, but occasionally also polkas and galops). They enjoyed a huge following wherever they appeared. In a period of "Sturm und Drang" in the dance —Isadora Duncan, Michel Fokine, Anna Pavlova, Vaslav Nijinsky, Serge Diaghilev —the emergence of the Wiesenthal sisters signified the introduction of a new element into the classic ballet of opera houses of Central Europe in a rather unexpected manner; that is, not in the sense of any planned reform, but in the charm and gracefulness of the sisters who enchanted everyone, while in other parts of Europe the principles of Duncan and Fokine were subjects of lively discussion. In a way the emergence of the Wiesenthal sisters also signified a new victory of the waltz which was celebrating its resurgence in this manner. The Wiesenthal style is not dead even at this writing (1967), at least not in Vienna. The style, perhaps in just a little more sophisticated form, is being kept alive in the dance department of the Vienna Academy of Music and Performing Arts. A course in Wiesenthal Technique is part of the Academy's curriculum, along with ballet, the modern dance, forms of folk dance, etc.

Wigman, Mary, German dancer, b. Hanover, 1886. Studied with Emile Jaques-Dalcroze and later with Rudolf von Laban, becoming his assistant in 1914. Her own personality survived both Dalcroze and Laban, and she composed her own works, some danced without music, others with only percussion accompaniment. She created *The Seven Dances of Life* (1918), thus beginning her public career on the concert stage. In 1920 she founded the Mary Wigman Central Institute in Dresden to train dancers and experiment in choreography. She toured frequently with her own group, making her first appearance in London in 1928 and in the U.S. in 1930. During World War II, she taught in Leipzig as a virtual prisoner of the Nazis. In 1950 she opened a school in West Berlin, where she continued to choreograph works such as *Le Sacre du Printemps* for the 1957 Berlin Festival. Wigman's early works—predominantly tense, introspective, and sombre—caused her to be considered the originator of modern dance in Europe. She has had a decided influence on contemporary dancers. In the U.S., Hanya Holm is an outstanding pupil of Wigman.

Mary Wigman, dancer, choreographer, teacher, originator of the modern dance in Europe.

Wilde, Patricia (Patricia White), dancer, b. Ottawa, Canada, 1930; m. George Bardyguine. Studied ballet with Miss G. Osborne, Ottawa; later with Dorothie Littlefield in Philadelphia, and at School of American Ballet, N.Y. After appearing with Ballet International in its first season (1944–45), she joined Ballet Russe de Monte Carlo (1945–49), having leading roles in *Concerto Barocco, Rodeo,* and *Pas de Quatre* (with Alexandra Danilova, Mia Slavenska, and Alicia Markova). She was guest artist with Ballets de Paris de Roland Petit (1950); guest ballerina, Metropolitan Ballet, for Holland tour and London season (1949–50). Joined New York City Ballet (1950) and danced a large repertoire of George Balanchine ballets, creating principal roles in many works including *Swan Lake* (leading the pas de trois specially created by Balanchine for his version of Act 2 of this ballet), *Caracole* (afterwards called *Divertimento No. 15*), *Scotch Symphony* (1st movement), *Western Symphony* (3rd movement), *Glinka Pas de Trois* (with Melissa Hayden and André Eglevsky), *Square*

Patricia Wilde, director of the Harkness School of Dance.

Dance, Waltz-Scherzo, Native Dancers, Raymonda Variations, and others. She is noted for the clean brilliance of her style, her speed, and her magnificent jump. She makes occasional guest appearances for special performances in the U.S., Canada, Puerto Rico, and the Caribbean Islands, usually with symphony orchestras, and has appeared on television in U.S. and abroad. Has choreographed for herself and a small group for the N.Y. Philharmonic "Promenade" concerts (1964, 1965). In October 1965 the dancer was engaged as head of the Dance Department of the Harkness House for Ballet Arts. She was to establish curriculum for the trainees and scholarship students, supervise the school, organize appearances of groups from the school in educational and other institutions.

Wilis (or Willis), in Western-Slavic and Eastern-German legends, the spirits of betrothed girls who have died as a result of their being jilted by faithless lovers. They came out to dance at night and led the faithless ones to their deaths by making them dance until they fell dead of exhaustion. See also GISELLE, ROMANTIC BALLET.

Willard, Helen Delano, museum curator, b. Chicago, Ill., 1905. Educated at Oberlin College; B.A., Univ. of Wisconsin; graduate study at Columbia Univ. Assistant Curator of Drawings, Fogg Art Museum, Harvard Univ., for thirteen years; in the Print Department, Museum of Fine Arts, Boston, for two years. When Dr. William B. Van Lennep retired from the curatorship of the Harvard Theatre Collection due to ill health, she took over the administration of the department (July 1, 1960) and continued as curator after his death. Organized and arranged a special exhibition on the Romantic Ballet displayed in the Houghton Library (summer, 1966), in honor of the publication of Edwin Binney's *Les Ballets de Théophile Gautier* and Ivor Guest's *The Romantic Ballet in Paris.*

William the Jew of Pesaro (Guglielmo Ebreo), Italian dancing master born sometime before 1440. He taught social dancing at various princely and ducal courts of Northern Italy in the second half of the 15th century. He wrote in Latin a book entitled *De Pratica seu Arte Tripudii* (The Practice or Art of the Dance) in which he outlined the qualifications necessary for a dancer—among them musicality, memory, style, or manners—and described in detail the many dances which he composed. Because of the historical importance of his work, William is often referred to as the first choreographer. The manuscript of his book is in the Bibliothèque Nationale, Paris, and bears a dedication to Galeazzo-Maria Sforza (1444–1476), Duke of Milan. More about William may be found in Otto Kinkeldy's *A Jewish Dancing Master of the Renaissance: Guglielmo Ebreo.*

Williams, Peter, English editor and writer on ballet, ballet designer, b. Burton Joyce, Notts., 1914. Assistant editor, *Ballet* (1948–50); ballet critic, *Daily Mail* (1950–53). Founded *Dance and Dancers,* Jan., 1950, of which he is still editor. Lectured extensively in 1959. Gives annual course on ballet design at Slade School of University College, London. Member, Advisory Committee of the Arts Council (1961). His designs for ballet include *Designs with Strings, Prince Igor,* and other works for Metropolitan Ballet (1947–49); *Selina* (for which he also wrote the book) for Sadler's Wells Theatre Ballet (1948). Designed and wrote book for *Paseo,* staged by Luisillo's Spanish Dance Theatre (1962). Member of the Critics' Circle, London.

Williams, Dr. Ralph Vaughan, O.M. (Order of Merit) (1872–1958), English composer whose "Masque for Dancing," *Job* (composed in 1927), became the score for the first major English ballet. He also wrote the music for Ninette de Valois' short ballet *The Picnic* (later called *The Faun*) given at the Old Vic as a curtain raiser to the opera *Rigoletto* (1929). He was one of the original patrons of The Camargo Society for which *Job* was first staged. In 1953 on his eightieth birthday, the Royal Ballet gave a special performance of *Job* in his honor.

Williams, Stanley, soloist and instructor of the Royal Danish Ballet, b. Chappel, England, 1925. Raised and educated in Denmark, he studied at the school of the Royal Danish Ballet and also in Paris; accepted into the company (1943); became solo dancer (1949). Teacher in the school since 1950. Guest artist in Iceland (1947), Brussels, and Stockholm (1948); ballet master and leading dancer with George Kirsta's Ballet Comique in England (1953–54). Guest teacher at School of American Ballet, also giving class to New York City Ballet company (1960–61, 1961–62). His repertoire in Denmark included leading roles in *Far From Denmark, La Sylphide* (second male solo in first act, and also James), *Napoli, Concerto Barocco, Konservatoriet,* Frederick Ashton's *Romeo and Juliet* (Mercutio), *Coppélia* (Dr. Coppelius), and others. He is a Ridder (Knight) of Dannebrog. Since fall of 1964 he has been on the faculty of the School of American Ballet, N.Y.

Williamson, Audrey, English critic and author, b. Thornton Heath, England, 1918. Ballet critic, *Theatre World* (1942–47), *Tribune* (1948–53); contributor to such publications as *The Dancing Times, Musical America, Theatre Arts, The Observer,* and others; lecturer at London City Literary Institute for two years; N.Y. correspondent (opera and ballet) the *London Times* (1961–62), *Manchester Guardian* (1962). Author of *Contemporary Ballet* (London and N.Y., 1946); *Ballet Renaissance* (London, 1948); *The Art of Ballet* (London, 1950; rev. ed. London and N.Y., 1953); *Ballet of Three Decades* (London and N.Y., 1958). Has also written books on drama and opera.

Wilson, G. B. L., engineer, museum curator, writer, editor, b. Kew Gardens, England. Educated at St. Paul's School, London, and Corpus Christi College, Cambridge (M.A. Honors). Assistant Keeper of the Science Museum, London, since 1954. His interest in ballet goes back to the 1930's. Founder and chairman of The Association of Ballet Clubs since 1947; assistant editor, *The Ballet Annual* (since 1948). His *Dictionary of Ballet* (London, 1957) has been sold out; making the publication of an enlarged and revised edition in hard cover necessary (1961). The volume has also been translated and published in Italy. Contributed several articles to the *Enciclopedia dello Spettacolo* (Rome, 1960). Edits the monthly "Off Stage" feature in the London *Dancing Times*. Is a member of the Grand Council of the Royal Academy of Dancing and honorary curator of the British Theatre Museum Association. Is also a ballet photographer since 1941. As an engineer he is on the editorial committee of the Newcomen Society, wrote the article on locks for the 1961 *Encyclopedia Britannica,* and a chapter, "Technical Gains During the Nineteenth Century," for the *UNESCO History of the Cultural and Scientific Development of Mankind* (Neuchatel, 1961). Lectures both on ballet and history of engineering.

Wilson, John, American dancer, singer, musician, b. Los Angeles, 1927; m. Brunilda Ruiz. A singing and composition major in college, he also studied music for a year in Geneva, Switzerland. Had his early dance training with Katherine Dunham in N.Y. Made three transcontinental tours with Hariette Ann Gray as dancer, singer, composer, and pianist. Has also given a number of solo performances, with his own group and with Joyce Trisler at the YM–YWHA and Henry Street Playhouse, N.Y. He is on the faculty of the Juilliard School of Music. Was with the Robert Joffrey Ballet on its first tour in 1956 and has remained (with brief absences) since that time as dancer and, at times, as pianist. In the summer of 1964 joined the newly organized Harkness Ballet, with which his wife is a principal dancer.

Wilson, Sallie, American dancer, b. Fort Worth, Texas, 1932; m. Ali Pourfarrokh. Began dance training with the late Dorothy Colter Edwards (Fort Worth, 1945); from 1948 studied in N.Y., mainly with Margaret Craske and Antony Tudor, but also with Edward Caton. Joined Ballet (now American Ballet) Theatre (1949); Metropolitan Opera Ballet (1950–55). Rejoined American Ballet Theatre (1955); elevated to soloist (1957); first soloist (1960); ballerina (1962). Her first solo roles included Lover-in-Experience (*Pillar of Fire*), Rosaline (*Romeo and Juliet*), Lilac Fairy (*Princess Aurora*), and others. As soloist she danced the Waltz (*Les Sylphides*), Myrtha (*Giselle*), Juno (*Judgment of Paris*), created the role of Kristin (the cook) in American Ballet Theatre's staging of *Miss Julie*. As first soloist alternated Waltz and Mazurka (*Les Sylphides*), Boulotte (*Bluebeard*), Young Mother (*Fall River Legend*), alternated third and fourth variations in *Grand Pas Glazounov;* created Blues role in Dania Krupska's *Pointes on Jazz*. Since being promoted to ballerina she has danced Mazurka and pas de deux (*Les Sylphides*), ballerina role (*Theme and Variations*), Russian Ballerina (*Gala Performance*), Maja (*Caprichos*). During the period between 1958 and 1960 when American Ballet Theatre was not functioning, she joined New York City Ballet and danced Queen (*The Cage*), 3rd movement (*Symphony in C*), 3rd movement (*Western Symphony*), Second Regiment (*Stars and Stripes*), Harp (*Fanfare*), and others, and created Queen Elizabeth in *Episodes* (Part I, chor.: Martha Graham). She has danced many times at Jacob's Pillow and made guest appearances with St. Louis Municipal Light Opera, etc. Returned to the American Ballet Theatre in the summer of 1964.

Sallie Wilson, ballerina of the American Ballet Theatre.

Her spectacular rise as ballerina began during the 25th anniversary season of the American Ballet Theatre (Mar.–Apr., 1965) when she danced three ballerina roles in one month: Glen Tetley's *Sargasso,* Lizzie Borden in Agnes de Mille's *Fall River Legend,* Myrtha in *Giselle.* She also made an excellent impression as the Mother of the Groom in Jerome Robbins' *Les Noces.* On Jan. 20, 1966, came her crowning achievement, the role of Hagar in Antony Tudor's *Pillar of Fire,* the ballet that had made a star of Nora Kaye twenty years earlier.

Wind in the Mountains, The. Ballet in 1 act; chor.: Agnes de Mille; commissioned score: Laurence Rosenthal, based largely on early American songs and folk tunes; décor and lighting: Jean Rosenthal; costumes: Stanley Simmons. First prod.: American Ballet Theatre, N.Y. State Theater, Mar. 17, 1965, with Joseph Carow (Pathfinder), Gayle Young (Young Man), Karen Krych (Young Woman), Judith Lerner (Diversion), William Glassman (Stranger), Eliot Feld, and Ted Kivitt (Two Skaters). Subtitled "A Country Calendar," the cycle of the seasons allows for a series of country dances in suitable moods which link together a slender story of young love going temporarily astray with the intrusion of the stranger from the city, but working out happily for everyone in the end.

Windows. Group dance in 5 scenes with prologue and epilogue: Bedtime Story, Alone, Hep Session, Triad, The Spirit Moves; chor.: Hanya Holm; music: Freda Miller. First prod.: Aug. 7, 1946, Colorado College, Colo.

Winnipeg Ballet. See ROYAL WINNIPEG BALLET.

Winslow, Miriam, contemporary American dancer, choreographer, teacher. b. Beverly, Mass. Professional training at Denishawn School (Boston and N.Y.), Wigman School (Dresden); Spanish dance with Otero (Spain), and others. Had school in Boston (1929–35). Soloist, Ted Shawn Company (summer, 1932); partnership with Foster Fitz-Simons (1935–42), touring U.S., Canada, and South America as soloist. Gave dance concerts with symphony orchestras (1934–42). Has choreographed all her own dances since 1934. In 1943 settled in Buenos Aires, Argentina, where she founded her own group for which she choreographed and of which she was principal dancer. After some eighteen years she discontinued her group and now devotes her time to choreography for other groups, lectures and lecture-demonstrations and occasional private teaching and coaching assignments.

Winter, Ethel, contemporary American modern dancer, choreographer, teacher, b. Wrentham, Mass. She is a graduate of Bennington College, Vt., where she studied dance, and a student of Martha Graham, becoming a member of the Graham company in the late 1940's. Since that time she has danced a large repertoire of important roles. She has the distinction of having been chosen by Martha Graham to re-create two of her great early roles: *Herodiade* at a Juilliard Concert Hall program honoring Paul Hindemith (Mar. 15, 1963), and the solo *Frontier* for the Louis Horst Memorial Program, American Dance Festival, New London (1964). Her own dance works include a solo, *En Dolor* (Manuel de Falla), *Suite of Three* (Joseph Liebling), *Night Forest* (Eugene Lester), *The Magic Mirror* (Arthur Murphy), *Fun and Fancy* (Paul Bowles). In Nov. 1964, she created the role of Leah in Sophie Maslow's ballet *The Dybbuk,* based on An-sky's play of the same title.

Winter Night. Ballet in 1 act; chor.: Walter Gore; music: Rachmaninov's Piano Concerto No. 2 in C minor; décor: Kenneth Rowell. First prod.: Ballet Rambert, Princess Theatre, Melbourne, Australia, Nov. 19, 1948, with Sally Gilmour, Paula Hinton, Walter Gore. A dance allegory for a man and two women: "Life consists of meeting and parting." The man discards an old love for a new and the first learns to accept the situation.

Witch Boy, The. Ballet in 1 act, 3 scenes; chor.: Jack Carter; commissioned music: Leonard Salzedo; décor: Norman McDowell. First prod.: Ballet der Lage Landen, Amsterdam, May 24, 1956, with Norman McDowell, Angela Bayley; staged for London's Festival Ballet, Nov. 27, 1957, with John Gilpin, Anita Landa. The scenario is freely based on the "Ballad of Barbara Allen" with a different ending. The girl falls in love with the Witch Boy. The villagers, suspicious of his strangeness, kill him; but he is immediately re-born.

With My Red Fires. Group dance; chor.: Doris Humphrey (part of the trilogy including *Theatre Piece* and *New Dance*); music: Wallingford Riegger; costumes: Pauline Lawrence. First prod.: Aug. 13, 1936, Bennington College, Vt.

Woizikowska, Sonia, dancer and teacher, b. London, England, 1919. Daughter of Leon Woizikowski and Helene Antonova, both at that time members of Diaghilev Ballets Russes. Educated in France; studied ballet with Lubov Egorova, Carlotta Brianza (Paris); Ludmila Shollar, Anatole Vilzak (N.Y.); and others. Began her career in her father's company; soloist, Original Ballet Russe (1938), dancing Frivolity (*Les Présages*), Can-Can (*La Boutique Fantasque*), Waltz (*Les Sylphides*), and others. Came to U.S. as star of Polish Ballet, appearing at the N.Y. World's Fair (1939) and then touring in Europe. Soloist with Ballet (now American Ballet) Theatre (1940); Ballet Russe de Monte Carlo (three years), dancing Seamstress (*Le Beau Danube*), Fiancée (*Saratoga*), Queen of Spades (*Poker Game*), and others. During World War II gave many performances in camps, hospitals, etc. for U.S.O.; followed this with two years in the national company of *Oklahoma!* as the Girl Who Falls Down. Currently teaching in N.Y.

Woizikowski, Leon, Polish dancer, ballet master, teacher, b. Warsaw, 1897. Was with the Diaghilev Ballets Russes (1915–29) and subsequently with Ballet Russe de Monte Carlo. Organized his own company and danced with it in several continental European countries and England (1935–36). Returned to Poland where he became ballet master and teacher at the New Theatre, Warsaw. He left for London to revive *Petrouchka* (1958) and *Schéhérazade* (1959) for London's Festival Ballet. Was ballet master for Leonide Massine's Ballets Européens of Nervi (1959),

Leon Woizikowski as the Tatterdemalion in Balanchine's Concurrence.

for London's Festival Ballet (1961), and for the Opera Ballet at Köln, Germany. Woizikowski was considered one of the most outstanding character dancers of his generation. He excelled as the Polovetzian chief in *Prince Igor,* Petrouchka, Niccolo in *The Good-Humored Ladies,* the Corregidor in *The Three-Cornered Hat,* the Conductor of the dance in *Cotillon,* the Tatterdemalion in *Concurrence,* and many other roles.

Wood, Roger. See PHOTOGRAPHERS, DANCE (ENGLAND).

Wooden Prince, The. Ballet in one act; music: Béla Bartók; chor.: Otto Zöblich; book: Béla Balazs, based on an old Hungarian fairy tale; décor: Count Bánffy. First prod.: Royal Opera House, Budapest, May 12, 1917. The plot deals with a Prince in love with a bewitched Princess, who is enamored of a Wooden Prince, and a Good Fairy who does what good fairies usually do in ballets. In 1939 the Budapest Opera invited Gyala Harangozó to stage a new production of the ballet, in which the choreographer also danced the title role. Other productions include Dore Hoyer's, Hamburg Staatsoper (ca. 1945); Herbert Freund's for the Municipal Stages, Frankfurt a/M (1959); Hans Macke's for the Municipal Theatre, Zürich (1958).

World of Art. See MIR ISSKOUSTVA.

WPA Dance Project. See DANCE PROJECT.

Wright, Belinda, English dancer, b. Southport, Lancs, 1929; m. Jelko Yuresha. Studied with Dorothea Halliwell locally; also with Olga Préobrajenska (Paris), Kathleen Crofton (London). Joined Ballet Rambert (1945), dancing her first Swan Queen (*Swan Lake,* Act 2) when only sixteen. Joined Ballets de Paris de Roland Petit (1949); London's Festival Ballet (fall, 1951); ballerina, Grand Ballet du Marquis de Cuevas (1954). Rejoined Festival Ballet as prima ballerina (1955–57); danced at Festival of Basel, Switzerland (1959), then rejoined Festival Ballet until 1962. Made a concert tour of South Africa with Anton Dolin and John Gilpin (1960) and has frequently appeared on television in England and Holland. Currently free-lancing as a guest

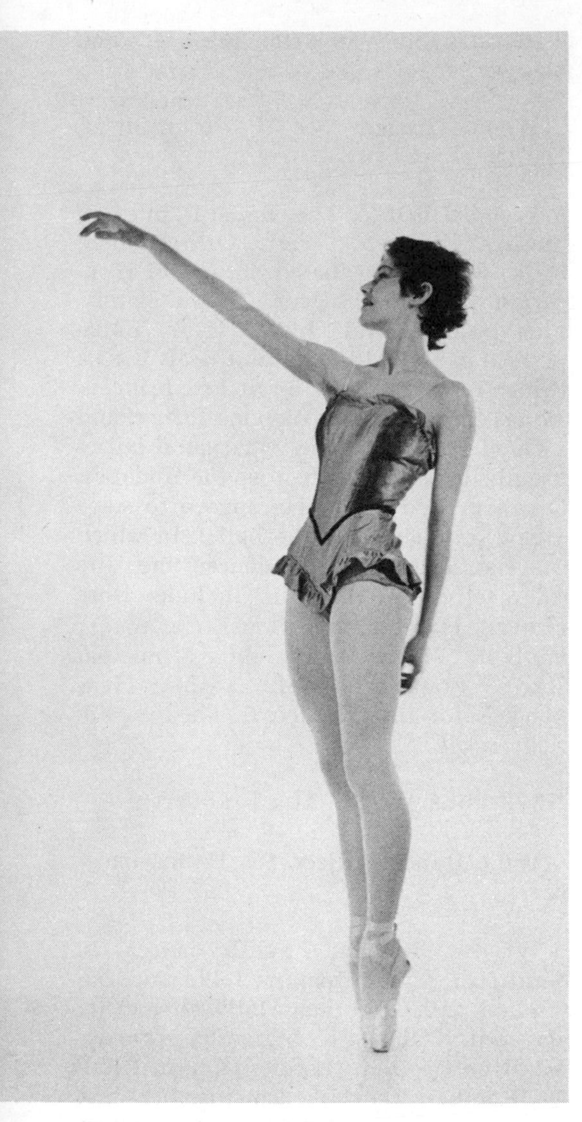

English ballerina Belinda Wright in the ballet Impressions.

artist. Her creations include Fleur de Lis (*Esmeralda*), Marguerite (*Vision of Marguerite*), Alice (*Alice in Wonderland*—Festival Ballet, 1953), Snow Maiden (*The Snow Maiden*), Swanilda (Festival Ballet's *Coppélia*), Sugar Plum Fairy (*The Nutcracker*), title role (*Giselle*), and others.

Wright, Peter, English dancer, choreographer, ballet master, b. London, 1926; m. Sonya Hana. Studied with Kurt Jooss (member of Ballet Jooss, 1945–46, 1951–52), Vera Volkova, Peggy van Praagh. Danced with Metropolitan Ballet (1947); St. James' Ballet (1948); soloist, Sadler's Wells Theatre Ballet (1949–51, 1952–55); assistant ballet master for the company (1955). His repertoire included Captain Belaye (*Pineapple Poll*), The Beast (*Beauty and the Beast*), Moondog (*The Lady and the Fool*), Leonardo (*Blood Wedding*), and others. Dancer and assistant dance director, Edinburgh International Ballet (1958), for which he choreographed *The Great Peacock.* Teacher at Royal Ballet School (1957–59). Has danced in musicals, been ballet master for British Broadcasting Corporation television productions. Has choreographed for the Old Vic Theatre, Sadler's Wells Opera, Covent Garden Opera, Royal Ballet (*A Blue Rose*), Western Theatre Ballet (*Musical Chairs,* 1959). Currently ballet master, Württemberg Staatstheater Ballett, Stuttgart.

Wyman, Lilla Viles (1859–1944), teacher, b. Waltham, Mass. Her father, John Viles, taught dance before and after the Civil War; his daughter Lilla and son Frank Thornton Viles were his assistants in his later years. For over sixty years under her married name she taught dance in Boston, coaching and staging the early Vincent Club shows which were presented (with men barred) in the drawing rooms of Proper Bostonians. She was also a member of the famous women's orchestra The Fadettes (as pianist). Presented the May Festivals (known as Mrs. Wm. S. Butler's May Festivals) at Mechanics Building for many years. She taught, coached, and started on his way to stardom the famous female impersonator of the early 1900's, Julian Eltinge. She studied extensively in N.Y. and Europe, to which she travelled almost every summer of her life. Was a member of the Imperial Society in London, and founder and first president

(1914) of the Dance Teachers Club of Boston. She wrote a dance primer (now out of print) *Let's Dance,* and had a rare collection of dance books, including many first editions, which she left to the Boston Public Library. She was one of America's real pioneer teachers in an era when very few were qualified.

Ximenez, Roberto, Mexican dancer and choreographer, b. Mexico City. Has a degree in Business Administration, Milton Academy, Mexico; is a Doctor of Economic Sciences, Univ. of Mexico; Doctor of Education in Dance (drama, lighting, painting, designing, music, languages) of the Palace of Fine Arts, Mexico. Leading dancer with the Ballet Español de Pilar Lopez (1948–55). Left with Manolo Vargas, also a leading dancer with the same company, to form the Ximenez-Vargas Ballet Español. He has taught Mexican folklore dances to Leonide Massine and Encarnacion Lopez (Argentinita). Has been decorated by the governments of Mexico and Denmark.

Ximenez-Vargas Ballet Español, Spanish dance company formed in 1955 by Roberto Ximenez and Manolo Vargas who up to that time had been leading dancers with the Pilar Lopez company. After touring successfully in Europe, they made a triumphant U.S. debut with a single performance at the YMHA, N.Y., Mar. 3, 1958 (a second request performance being hastily added Mar. 6), and were a sensation at the Jacob's Pillow Dance Festival in the summer of the same year. They have since successfully toured the U.S., Europe, and South America. In addition to traditional Spanish dance, Ximenez and Vargas perform unusual folklore dances of Mexico and South America.

Ximenez-Vargas Ballet Español; soloists Roberto Ximenez, Maria Gloria, Manolo Vargas.

Yacobson, Leonid, Honored Art Worker of the RSFSR, Soviet choreographer, b. 1904. Yacobson joined the Evening Courses of the Leningrad Ballet School in 1923, along with Konstantin Sergeyev, Vakhtang Chabukiani, Sergei Koren, and other talented youths who thus were given a chance to receive ballet training despite their being past the entrance age to the ballet school of the Kirov Theatre. Having shown good progress he was transferred to the main (daytime) department in 1925 and was graduated from it in 1926. At the Kirov Theatre he danced grotesque and demi-caractère roles. He became interested in choreography at a very early stage in his training and his first dances were staged for fellow-pupils. His first important work was a one-act ballet to Richard Strauss's *Til Eulenspiegel,* with a libretto written jointly with Yevgeny Mravinsky (who later became a famous conductor). It was danced at the 1933 graduation performance of the Leningrad School. Yacobson's methods of stage directing and choreography were new and daring for that time. While well grounded in classic technique he used a freer form of movement in his choreography from the beginning. He had shown this already in 1930 when he was one of the four choreographers of the controversial ballet *The Golden Age,* for which he created most of the second act dances. He choreographed a very difficult, semi-acrobatic dance for Galina Ulanova and four cavaliers, of whom he was one. In the following years he choreographed many dance numbers performed at recitals of which the best known—*The Bird and the Hunter* and *The Blind Girl* —are still very popular. He was also very interested in plastique as a form of movement and this led him to choreograph several dances for the Isadora Duncan Studio in Moscow which several of her pupils maintained until 1949. In 1941 Yacobson choreographed his first major work *Shurale.* He worked on it in Kazan for the Festival of Tartar Art in Moscow, but war prevented performance. He re-created it in 1950 for the Kirov Theatre and in 1955 for the Bolshoi Filial. In 1952 he choreographed another three-act ballet for the Maly (Little) Opera House in Leningrad, *Solveig,* to music by Edvard Grieg arranged by Boris Asafiev and Yevgeny Kornblit. He created *Spartacus* for the Kirov Ballet (1956), using no pointe work and deliberately introducing turned-in positions borrowed from antique bas-reliefs and statues, following in this quest for authenticity the precepts of Michel Fokine. A production of this work on a larger scale for performance on the huge new stage of the Kremlin Palace of Congresses was staged in 1962. Yacobson is married to Irina Pevsner, character soloist of the Kirov Ballet.

Yankee Clipper. Ballet in 1 act, 15 scenes; chor.: Eugene Loring; music: Paul Bowles; book: Lincoln Kirstein; costumes:

Charles Rain. First prod.: Ballet Caravan, Town Hall, Saybrook, Conn., July 12, 1937, with Loring in leading role. The cycle of a sailor's life in the mid-nineteenth century from the farewell as he sails from a New England port, through adventures on board and wherever his ship sails the Orient, the South Seas, Africa—to the return and farewell again. *Yankee Clipper* belongs to the period of Kirstein's interest in Americana and its themes as subjects for contemporary American ballet.

Yara. Ballet in 3 scenes; chor.: Harald Lander; music: Heitor Villa-Lobos (*Bachianas* No. 4 and No. 7); idea and argument: Circe Amado; décor: Fernando Pamplona; costumes: Kalma Murtinho. First prod.: Teatro Municipal, Rio de Janeiro, Brazil, 1960. A dramatic ballet based on the old Brazilian legend about Yara, the siren of rivers and ponds.

Yazvinsky, Jan (Ivan), Russian dancer, b. 1892. He graduated from the Moscow School in 1910 and entered the Moscow Imperial Theatre. Early in his career he joined the Diaghilev Ballets Russes after the dissolution of which he danced with other European ballet companies. Created the Mandarin (*L'Epreuve d'Amour,* 1936). Regisseur-general, Ballet Russe de Monte Carlo (1938–44). Taught in N.Y. until his retirement in 1960.

Yenakieva, Juliana, dancer, choreographer, teacher, b. Vienna, Austria, ca. 1918, of Russian parents. Educated in Paris; began studying dance with Olga Preobrajenska. Won first prize in Archives Internationales de la Danse contest in Paris (1932), and Grand Prix Championnat du Monde at Salle Wagram (1933). Has appeared with Col. de Basil's Original Ballet Russe and many other companies, and has toured widely. Guest ballerina with Teatro Municipal, Rio de Janeiro, Brazil (1939, 1945). Has appeared in revues, motion pictures, and on television. Now teaches in her own two schools in Rio de Janeiro.

Yermolayev, Alexei, Peoples' Artist of the RSFSR, Soviet premier danseur, b. 1910. Yermolayev was the first male dancer to develop the heroic manner of dancing which contributed to the style of the Soviet school that was growing in the 1920's. Like Vakhtang Chabukiani, Asaf Messerer, Mikhail Gabovich, and a few others, he did not begin his ballet training as a child, but in spite of this achieved extraordinary virtuosity. Only at the age of fourteen (1924) did he enter the former Maryinsky ballet school. In two years he was graduated with honors (class of Vladimir Ponomaryov). He was a sensation at the graduation performance when he danced Vayu, God of the Wind, from the old ballet *The Talisman.* In the Kirov company he danced leading roles of the classic repertoire and in 1930 was transferred to the Bolshoi Theatre where he danced more than twenty important roles, developing his dramatic gifts so that he became an outstanding dancer-actor as well as a virtuoso. His Tybalt (*Romeo and Juliet*), Yevgeny (*The Bronze Horseman*), Li Shan-Foo (*The Red Flower,* formerly known as *Red Poppy*) and Albrecht (*Giselle*) are all unforgettable. He retired from the stage in 1959 and devoted himself to fostering and developing the dramatic abilities of the leading Bolshoi dancers. In 1961 he began teaching the graduating male class of the Bolshoi school and immediately attracted attention by the originality of his method and the superb quality of his teaching. He also teaches a male class of company dancers. He is the author of several librettos for ballets and in 1939 choreographed *The Nightingale,* to music by M. Kroshner, for the Minsk Opera Ballet.

Yevdokimov, Gleb, Soviet dancer, b. Moscow, 1923. Entered the Bolshoi school in 1932, graduating in 1941. Due to wartime conditions, part of the company was evacuated and he began receiving important solo roles before his actual graduation. He has always been a dancer of impeccable technique, and his clean-cut beats can only be compared to those of Danish dancers trained in the Bournonville tradition. His short stature prevented him from becoming a great danseur noble and he became an outstanding virtuoso instead, excelling as the Blue Bird (*The Sleeping Beauty*), in the *Peasant* pas de deux (*Giselle*), pas de trois (*Swan Lake*), and in demi-caractère roles requiring considerable powers of characterization, such as Nur-Ali (*Fountain of Bakhchisarai*). On June 24, 1962, Yevdokimov gave his last performance at the Bolshoi, dancing the pas de trois in *Swan Lake*, retiring as a dancer after twenty years' service. He continues, however, to teach one of the male classes, and since 1960 has also taught in the Bolshoi school, passing on to his pupils his excellent technique.

YMHA. See YOUNG MEN'S & YOUNG WOMEN'S HEBREW ASSOCIATION.

Yocom, Dr. Rachael Dunaven, educator, administrator, author, photographer, b. Corvallis, Ore., 1916. B.A., Willamette Univ., Salem, Ore.; M.A. Univ. of Ore., Eugene; Ph.D., New York Univ., N.Y.; member of Pi Lambda Theta Honor Society; received the Delta Psi Kappa Research Award (1951). Instructor in Dance and Physical Education, Salem (Ore.) High School (1937–41). Associate Professor and Director of Physical Education and Dance, College of Idaho (1941–42). Director of Physical Education and Dance, Utah State Univ., Logan (1942–46), and is still its eastern representative and dance administrator of its special summer course. Research Fellow (1946–47) and Instructor, New York Univ. (1947–52). Chairman, Dance Department, School of Performing Arts, N.Y. since 1959. Author of (with H. B. Hunsaker) *Individual Sports for Men and Women* (1940); (with Gertrude Shurr) *Modern Dance Techniques and Teaching* (1946); (with Dr. L. A. Larson) *Measurements and Evaluation in Physical, Health and Recreation Education* (1950). Has also been a freelance writer, song writer, and photographer in education and dance.

Young, Marilyn, Canadian dancer, b. Winnipeg, Manitoba, 1936. Began dance studies at Canadian School of Ballet, Winnipeg, later studying in N.Y. with Robert Joffrey, School of American Ballet, Ballet Theatre School. Joined Winnipeg (now Royal Winnipeg) Ballet at the age of fifteen making her debut in *The Nutcracker* pas de deux and advancing to the rank of soloist. Has been with the company since 1952, creating the Girl (*The Darkling*), Floozie (James Moulton's *Grasslands*), Yellow Girl (Ruthanna Boris' *The Comedians*), Pas de Deux (*Variations for a Lonely Theme*), leading female role in Arnold Spohr's *E Minor.*

Marilyn Young, partnered by David Schields in The Darkling.

Has danced on Canadian Broadcasting Corporation television, at the summer Theatre Under the Stars, Vancouver (1954, 1955, 1957), and Winnipeg's Rainbow Stage (1956, 1958). Danced as guest artist with the Royal Winnipeg Ballet during their U.S. engagement (summer, 1964).

Young Men's & Young Women's Hebrew Association, the famous 92nd Street "Y" which, as part of its Educational Department, organized a center for modern dance and dance theatre in 1937. Its activities include technique classes at all levels, lectures, conferences (including an annual Conference of Creative Teaching of Dance), and performances. There is a special department for the teaching of Israeli dance, and the Merry-Go-Rounders (the performing group for children) was founded at the "Y." Most of the modern dancers of the day have appeared in the Kaufmann Concert Hall, presenting themselves in solo recitals or with their groups. Such famous performers and companies as Pauline Koner, Paul Draper, Ximenez-Vargas Ballet Español, Shanta Rao, Iva Kitchell, Valerie Bettis, Pearl Lang, Donald McKayle have performed there and, in the early days: Rosario and Antonio, Argentinita, Martha Graham, José Limón, Doris Humphrey, Charles Weidman, Sybil Shearer and many others. For several years annual auditions were held for young dancers, the winners presenting their works in special performance, but this practice was discontinued in the early 1950's. Dance groups from Barnard, Bennett College, Vassar, Bennington, Cornell, Smith, and others have appeared there, but Bennington alone has continued to make this an annual event. The organization also sponsors forums and lectures in dance, among them several series by dance critic Walter Terry with famous guest artists. Dr. William Kolodney is head of the Educational Department, and it is through his interest that dance has become as important a part of the Kaufmann Concert Hall presentations as the poetry readings, chamber music concerts, and other projects.

Youshkevitch, Nina, contemporary dancer, teacher, b. Russia. Studied dance with Olga Preobrajenska, Lubov Egorova, Leo Staats in Paris. Ballerina, René Blum's Ballets Russes (Australia, 1937); Polish National Ballet (Europe and N.Y. World's Fair, 1939). Leading dancer, Metropolitan Opera Ballet, N.Y. (1942–44); guest artist in full length *The Sleeping Beauty* with San Francisco Opera Ballet (1945). At present instructor in dance at Wayne State College (Wayne, Neb.).

Youskevitch, Igor, premier danseur and teacher, b. Moscow, 1912, U.S. citizen since 1944; m. Anna Scarpova. His family moved to Belgrade, Yugoslavia (1920), to escape the revolution. From early years he was interested in athletics and participated in many athletic events. Was a member of the famous athletic organization Sokol. Was invited to become partner of Yugoslav dancer Xenia Grunt (1932) and after a year of intensive ballet lessons and rehearsals gave performances with her in Paris (1933). Remained in Paris and studied with Olga Preobrajenska for two years. Member, Bronislava Nijinska's Les Ballets de Paris (1934). Leon Woizikowski's company (1935), remaining with group for its Australian tour under Col. de Basil (1937); joined the Massine-Blum Ballet Russe de Monte Carlo as premier danseur in 1938, remaining until 1944. Created the Officer (*Gaîté Parisienne*), the god (*Seventh Symphony,* 3rd movement), the Man (*Rouge et Noir*), and danced the classic roles. Served in U.S. Navy (1944–45). Guest artist, Leonide Massine's Ballet Russe Highlights (1946). Joined Ballet (now American Ballet) Theatre (fall, 1946) and remained until spring, 1955. His partnership with Alicia Alonso in the classic ballets, especially *Giselle,* was internationally famous and his reputation as one of the great premiers danseurs classique of the century was es-

Igor Youskevitch, outstanding classic dancer, seen here in his variation of Swan Lake, *Act 3.*

tablished over that period. He created the leading male role in *Theme and Variations,* Stanley (*A Streetcar Named Desire,* Ballet Theatre production), and others; danced Romeo (Antony Tudor's *Romeo and Juliet*), Paris (*Helen of Troy*), Prince (*Swan Lake,* Act 2), and the great classic pas de deux. Rejoined Ballet Russe de Monte Carlo, fall of 1955, creating the Knight (*The Lady and the Unicorn*), Harlequin (Boris Romanoff's *Harlequinade*). After 1957 he appeared with this company only as guest artist, leaving permanently in 1962. Between 1948 and 1959 he appeared with Alicia Alonso in special performances with symphony orchestras, and with her company Ballet Alicia Alonso in South America and in Cuba. Although virtually retired as a dancer, he danced in the ballet in the Metropolitan Opera House production of *Adriana Lecouvreur* (1963). Currently teaching in his own school and also directing a semi-professional company.

Youth. Ballet in 4 acts, 6 scenes; chor.: Boris Fenster; music: Mikhail Chulaki; book: Yuri Slonimsky; décor: Tatiana Bruni. First prod.: Maly (Little) Opera House, Leningrad, Dec. 9, 1949. A story of the Civil War and friends who grow up together with the times. The action takes place in a small Ukrainian town in the years immediately after the revolution and partly follows the novel *How Steel Was Tempered* by Nicolai Ostrovsky.

Yugoslavia, Dance in. The first ballet performance ever seen in Yugoslavia was given in the Croatian National Theatre in Zagreb, Mar. 3, 1892. It was Joseph Bayer's *Die Puppenfee.* It was performed by actors, not ballet dancers, for the simple reason that at the time there were no ballet dancers in Yugoslavia. Two years later, under the direction of Stjepan Miletic, the Zagreb Theatre had a ballet master: Otokar Bartic, who some years later taught and danced at the Metropolitan Opera, N.Y.; a ballerina, Emma Grondone, of Milan; Luisa and Achille Viscusi as soloists; and a corps de ballet of twelve. On May 1, 1895, they appeared in *Coppélia.* The second great event in the history of the Yugoslav Ballet came in Jan. 1897, when a full-size company danced its first *Giselle.* In 1898 the company appeared in two original works on Croatian themes—*Jela,* to music by B. Adamovic, and *At the Plitvica Lakes* (in two acts), to music by S. Albini.

Of the ten ballet companies presently attached to opera houses in Yugoslavia, six were founded during the period between the two World Wars: in Belgrade, Zagreb, Ljubljana, Osijek, Rijeka, and Split. The other four—in Sarajevo, Skoplje, Maribor, and Novi Sad—were established after World War II. From the beginning there were perhaps a dozen people who contributed more than anyone else to the founding and guiding of most of the ballet companies. Among these were Margarita Froman, who helped establish both the Zagreb and the Belgrade companies and danced, taught, choreographed, and acted as ballet mistress for more than a quarter of a century; Natalia Boskovic, the first prima ballerina of the Belgrade ballet; Yelena Poliakova, dancer, ballet mistress, and teacher; Nina Kirsanova, ballerina of the Belgrade ballet and later teacher. In the middle 1930's Russian names begin to give way to Yugoslav, both of dancers and choreographers, and ballets on Yugoslav themes begin to assume places in the repertoire alongside works from the repertoire of Russian and Western European theatres. Thus, Margarita Froman staged the first national ballet, *The Gingerbread Heart,* to music by Kresimir Baranovic in 1927. In 1938 Pino and Pia Mlakar produced another native ballet, *The Devil in the Village,* to music by Fran Lhotka. Since Yugoslav ballet companies did not perform during the German occupation, the country had to wait until 1947 for the production of Stevan Hristic's four-act *The Legend of Okhrid,* choreographed by Froman. An-

A group from Yugoslav folk dance ensemble Tanec, which made a very successful U.S. tour.

other gifted choreographer and dancer of the period was Dimitri Parlic who staged a number of ballets, mainly of the standard repertoire. Other talented teachers, dancers, and choreographers were Ana Roje and Oskar Harmos. Outstanding Yugoslav dancers of a later period include Dusan Trninic, Mira Sanina, Ruth Parnel, Dusanka Sifnios, Visnja Dordevic, Zlatica Stjepan, Sonja Kastl, Vera Markovic, Milko Sparemblek, Nenad Lhotka (choreographer and dancer), Mile Jovanovic (dancer, teacher, and ballet master), Milica Jovanovic, Bojana Peric, Boris Radak, Katarina Obradovic, Ljljana Dulovic, and several others. In addition to the ballet companies, Yugoslavia has three professional folk dance companies: Kolo of Belgrade, Lado of Zagreb, and Tanec of Skoplje (Macedonia). Of these, Tanec and Kolo have toured the U.S. under S. Hurok's management.

A number of Yugoslav and Yugoslav-trained dancers have achieved high standing in Western European and American dance companies, among them Milorad

Miskovitch, who dances in first-rate companies and for a time had an ensemble of his own; Veronika Mlakar, a scion of the Mlakar family who has danced with Roland Petit's Ballets de Paris, Jerome Robbins' Ballets: U.S.A., Ruth Page's Chicago Opera Ballet, and the Munich State Opera Ballet (where she created the role of the Unicorn in the Jean Cocteau—Heinz Rosen *The Lady and the Unicorn*); she is now (1967) ballerina of American Ballet Theatre, dancing *Pillar of Fire, Giselle,* et al.; Jelko Yuresha, now with the Royal Ballet (British); Vassili Sulich, an outstanding dancer with several European companies, including Leonide Massine's Ballet Européen; Miljenko Vikic, Vesna Butorac, Aleksej Judenic, Stane Leben, Damir Novak, Durdica Ludvig; choreographers-dancers Sonja Kastl and Nevenka Bidjin; choreographer Dimitri Parlic who has staged ballets in many countries and who was choreographer and ballet master of the Vienna State Opera (1958–61). Dancers of a somewhat older generation, most of whom are now teaching in the U.S. are Margarita Froman, Natalia Boskovic, Mia Slavenska, Casimir Kokich, Sonja Dragomanovic, and others. In a separate category is Herci Munitich who with her husband Myles Marsden heads the State Ballet of Rhode Island, and Boris Runanin, who is a television specialist.

Yuresha, Jelko, Yugoslav dancer, b. Zagreb, 1937; m. English dancer, Belinda Wright, 1961. Studied at Ana Roje's International School of Ballet, Split, Yugoslavia; at the Legat School and with Kathleen Crofton, London. Made his debut in Yugoslavia (1954). Soloist, Yugoslav National Ballet, Split (1958). Guest artist, Bermuda Ballet Week, Irish National Ballet (1958), principal dancer, Festival of Basle (1959); guest artist Bermuda Ballet Season (1959, 1960). Joined London's Festival Ballet, Jan., 1960. His roles included *Les Sylphides, The Snow Maiden* (Leil), *Romeo and Juliet* (Romeo), *The Nutcracker* (Prince). Left Festival Ballet (autumn, 1962) to join the Royal Ballet (British).

Yurieva, Maria. See SWOBODA, MARIA.

Yuriko (Yuriko Kikuchi), modern dancer and teacher, b. San Jose, Calif. Educated in Japan. Began her dance career with recitals and a tour of the Orient with Konami Ishii Dance Co. of Tokyo (1930–37). Returned to this country (1937) and between that year and 1941 was a member of Dorothy S. Lyndall's Junior Dance Group in Los Angeles. Received a scholarship to the Martha Graham School in Feb., 1944, and joined her company in May, remaining to date, and dancing many roles including the creations Moon (*Canticle for Innocent Comedians*), Eve (*Embattled Garden*), Iphigenia (*Clytemnestra*). Since 1949 has also given solo performances, and in Nov., 1960, presented her first major program, with a group, at the Phoenix The-

Yuriko and Bertram Ross in Martha Graham's Canticle for Innocent Comedians.

atre, N.Y. Danced Eliza in Jerome Robbins' famous "The Small House of Uncle Thomas" in the Rodgers and Hammerstein musical *The King and I* (1951–54), which she repeated in the motion picture (1955); was the featured soloist in another Rodgers and Hammerstein musical, *Flower Drum Song* (1958–60). Appears in frequent performances as a soloist or with her group and occasionally with the Martha Graham company. Teaches at the Martha Graham School of Contemporary Dance, N.Y., Rochester Univ., and Brooklyn College. Presented a program of works, all choreographed to the music of Alan Hovhaness, Feb. 21, 1965, at the Kaufmann Auditorium of the YM–YWHA, N.Y., and repeated it in 1966.

Zakharov, Rostislav, Peoples' Artist of the RSFSR, professor, Soviet choreographer, b. 1907. Zakharov entered the Leningrad Ballet School in 1920 and was graduated from it in 1925 (class of Vladimir Ponomaryov). His first engagements were in Kharkov and Kiev. He remained in Kiev until 1929 and made his debut as a choreographer arranging a dance in a dramatized version of Victor Hugo's *Esmeralda.* In Kiev he choreographed his first ballet *The Sailor's Dream,* for which he also wrote the libretto and danced the role of the Captain. In the summer of 1929 he was invited to work as a choreographer in Saratov and Astrakhan for the theatres of operetta and ballet. Here he staged dances in many operettas and choreographed his first major ballet, *Don Quixote,* to the Leon Minkus music. Having decided to become a choreographer, he entered the Leningrad Institute of Scenic Art (Dept. of Dramatic Production), as at that time there was no special school for the training of choreographers. Graduating in 1932, Zakharov was sent for further advancement to the Kirov Theatre where he began as assistant director of operas and, the same year, staged the Persian dances in Mussorgsky's opera *Khovanshchina.* By 1934 he was considered one of the most promising choreographers of the Kirov Theatre and was entrusted with the production of *The Fountain of Bakhchisarai.* It is his most important ballet to date and has been staged in many countries, including Finland and Japan. He used the fundamentals of the Stanislavsky method in this production, applying them to ballet for the first time.

Zakharov's next creations, *Lost Illusions* (1936) and *The Prisoner of the Caucasus* (1938), were dramatic ballets in which the attention to motivation of action and dramatic expressiveness interfered at times with the purely choreographic elements. But in the general development of Soviet choreography this period of dramatic ballets was very important and the principles of deep content and motivated action laid down at that time have grown to be the cornerstone of contemporary Soviet ballet. Subsequently the dramatic contents became completely integrated with the danced action. Already in *The Bronze Horseman* (1949) the story was told mainly through the medium of classic dance with the exception of the magnificent scene of the St. Petersburg flood of 1824, in the staging of which Zakharov revealed his great gifts and knowledge as a theatrical director.

His remarkable production talents were also exploited in the staging of operas. He directed the revival of Mikhail Glinka's *Russlan and Ludmila* (1937); and *Carmen* (1953), choreographing the dances in both.

He was the first choreographer of Sergei Prokofiev's *Cinderella* at the Bolshoi Theatre (1945). All his life he has been interested in creating ballets after Pushkin's poems and the Pushkin theme remains the main subject of his work. In addition to *The Fountain of Bakhchisarai, The Prisoner of the Caucasus,* and *The Bronze Horseman,* he staged a fourth Pushkin ballet, *Mistress into Maid* (1946). Between 1936 and 1939 Zakharov was artistic director of the Bolshoi Ballet and between 1946 and 1949 he headed the Bolshoi Ballet School. He was one of the most active founders of the Choreographers' Faculty of the Theatre Institute, Moscow, which since its establishment in 1946 has trained numerous young choreographers now working in companies all over the country. Zakharov headed the Chair of Choreography and was given the title of Professor. In 1954 he published *The Choreographer's Art,* a book in which he analyzed in detail the art of making a ballet as a vehicle for the evocation of human thoughts and emotions. He also paid much attention to the relation between music and dance. In the appendix of the book are the detailed choreographic scenarios written by Zakharov for his ballets.

He is married to Maria Smirnova, former soloist of the Kiev Ballet. His son Vladimir is a soloist of the Bolshoi Ballet.

Zambelli, Carlotta, Italian ballerina, b. Milan, 1877. She studied at the Milan Conservatory and danced at Teatro alla Scala. She made her debut at the Paris Opéra in 1894. Promoted soon after to the rank of étoile, she succeeded Rosita Mauri as the Snow Fairy in *La Maladetta.* She was a precise technician and an elegant dancer, two qualities one did not often find in French dancers of the period. Her repertoire included *La Korrigane, Namouna, Les Deux Pigeons, Sylvia, Coppélia, Cydalise et le Chevre-Pied.* She was invited as guest artist to the Maryinsky Theatre, St. Petersburg (1901), the last foreign ballerina to appear on the Imperial stage. After her retirement from the stage she began teaching at the ballet school of the Paris Opéra (1927). The French Government named her Officer of the Legion d'Honneur (1956).

Zambra, a Spanish flamenco dance of direct Moorish origin, performed exclusively by women. See SPANISH DANCE.

Zapateado, a Spanish flamenco dance consisting almost entirely of heel work; it is essentially a man's dance and is usually danced without musical accompaniment. See SPANISH DANCE.

Zarabanda. See SARABANDE.

Zhdanov, Yuri, Honored Artist of the RSFSR, premier danseur of the Bolshoi Ballet, Moscow, b. 1925. At twelve he danced in amateur groups appearing in workers' clubs and Palaces of Culture. At thirteen he was accepted into the Experimental Six-Year Department of the Bolshoi School established to provide classical dance education for those children (preferably boys) who missed entering school at the proper age of ten. In spite of not benefiting from the full nine-year course, Zhdanov was graduated in 1944 (class of Nicolai Tarasov), attracting attention at the graduation performance in the pas de deux from *La Fille Mal Gardée.* He began receiving important roles soon after entering the Bolshoi company, the first being Vaslav in *The Fountain of Bakhchisarai.* In 1951 he danced Yevgeny in the Bolshoi production of *The Bronze Horseman,* becoming Galina Ulanova's partner the same year. This had the greatest possible influence on the young dancer's artistic outlook and approach to characterization. He has said of his work with Ulanova: "Ulanova not only becomes completely transformed herself on the stage, but she transforms her partner as well." With this help from the great ballerina, Zhdanov created a romantic Romeo in *Romeo and Juliet.* He also danced Albrecht with Ulanova in *Giselle* and Ma Li-chen in *The Red Flower* (formerly

Red Poppy) to her Tao-Hoa. Among his other roles are Prince Desiré in *The Sleeping Beauty* and the Actor in *Flames of Paris*. He is a good landscape painter and his range of interests is wide. His wife Ariadna is a scientist. He has danced in many foreign countries including France, England, and the U.S. Now retired.

Zhukov, Leonid (1892–1951), Russian dancer. He was graduated from the Bolshoi Ballet School, Moscow (1909), and accepted into the Bolshoi company. He was an outstanding premier danseur, both in classic and demi-caractère roles, in the style of Mikhail Mordkin. He followed Mordkin in a number of roles, among them the older dancer's famous *Italian Beggar*. A product of Alexander Gorsky and Vassily Tikhomirov, he danced in almost all of Gorsky's productions, including his re-workings of the great classics. He was the favorite partner of ballerinas Yekaterina Geltzer, Vera Karalli, Elisabeth Anderson-Ivantzova and his wife, Maria Reisen.

Ziegfeld, Florenz. See under SHOW GIRL.

Zimmerl, Christl, Austrian dancer, b. Vienna, 1939. Studied at the ballet school of the Vienna State Opera and with Victor Gsovsky, Nora Kiss, Anton Dolin, Derra de Moroda; also with teachers of the Royal Ballet School, London. Accepted into the ballet company of the Vienna State Opera (1953); promoted to soloist (1956). Her many roles include Desdemona (*The Moor of Venice*), title role in *Medusa* (both by Erika Hanka), title role in *Ruth, Agon* (both by Yvonne Georgi), Myrtha (*Giselle*), Elvira (*Don Juan*), Florence (*Joan von Zarissa*), title role (*Die Puppenfee*), *Symphony in C*, Prelude (*Les Sylphides*), Venus (*Planets*), Lilac Fairy (Vaslav Orlikovsky's version of *The Sleeping Beauty*), Aurel Milloss' *Estro Arguto* and *Estro Barbarico*, Ninette de Valois's *Checkmate*, Leonide Massine's *The Three-Cornered Hat*. On Oct. 19, 1964, she danced Odette-Odile to Karl Musil's Prince Siegfried in Rudolf Nureyev's version of the full-length *Swan Lake*, staged for the Vienna State Opera Ballet (following Dame Margot Fonteyn in the role) with great success. She appears in television programs in Austria and Germany.

Christl Zimmerl, ballerina of the Vienna State Opera Ballet in Erika Hanka's Medusa.

Zlocha, Erika, Austrian dancer, b. Vienna, 1939. Studied at the ballet school of the Vienna State Opera and during summers after graduation (1953), with Mathilda Kchessinska, Olga Preobrajenska, Victor Gsovsky, Nora Kiss, Leon Woizikowski. Accepted into the Vienna State Opera Ballet (1953); promoted to soloist (1957). Received fifth prize in the International Ballet Competition, Rio de Janeiro (1961). Her roles include *Symphonie Classique, Peasant* pas de deux

(Act 1), and title role (*Giselle*), Divertissement (*The Sleeping Beauty*), *The Legend of Joseph,* Gretchen (*Abraxas*), Pas de Trois (*Swan Lake*), *Les Sylphides,* Divertissement (*The Nutcracker*), *Catulli Carmina, Joan von Zarissa, Hotel Sacher, Rondo of the Golden Calf, Homeric Symphony,* Street Dancer (*Petrouchka*), *Symphony in C, Die Puppenfee, Evolutions, Agon, Dreams* (music: Benjamin Britten), Juliet (*Romeo and Juliet*), *Turandot, The Seasons* (music: Berger), *Eine Kleine Nachtmusick, White Rose, Planets,* as well as pas de deux and pas de trois. Solo performances include: *Fanny Elssler,* on the occasion of the 150th anniversary of the birth of the ballerina, at the Vienna Opera House (1960). Has made television appearances in Austria and Germany; guest appearances with the Vienna State Opera Ballet on tour.

Zolan, Miro, dancer, b. Prague, Czechoslovakia; m. Sandra Vane. Studied with Olga Preobrajenska and Lubov Egorova in Paris; Vera Volkova in London. Joined International Ballet (1947); to Australia with Ballet Rambert (1948). Returned to Australia to dance with Borovansky's Australian Ballet (1951–52). Soloist, Sadler's Wells Theatre Ballet (1953–57); ballet master, Royal Winnipeg Ballet (1957–59); also in Teheran, Iran (1960).

Zompakos, Stanley, dancer, b. New York City, 1925. Studied dancing at School of American Ballet, N.Y. Member, New Opera Company (1942), and American Concert Ballet (1943). Appeared in the musicals *The Merry Widow, Song of Norway,* and others. Soloist, Ballet Russe de Monte Carlo (1945–48), dancing the Gigue (*Mozartiana*), Athlete (*Le Beau Danube*), Officer (*Gaîté Parisienne*), Page (*Cirque de Deux*), and others. Currently teaching ballet.

Zorina, Vera (Eva Brigitta Hartwig), contemporary ballerina, actress, b. Berlin, Germany, of Norwegian parents; U.S. citizen since 1943. Studied dance with Eugenie Eduardova in Germany; later with Victor Gsovsky and Nicholas Legat. Professional debut in Max Reinhardt's production of *A Midsummer Night's Dream* (First Fairy) and *Tales of Hoffmann.* She was Anton Dolin's partner in the play *Ballerina* (London, 1933) while still in her mid-teens. First soloist, Ballet Russe de Monte Carlo (1934–36), dancing Can-Can (*La Boutique Fantasque*), Street Dancer (*Le Beau Danube*), Action (*Les Présages*), and others. Star of musicals *On Your Toes* (London, 1936), *I Married an Angel* (1938), *Louisiana Purchase* (1940), all in N.Y., and in the films *Goldwyn Follies* (1937), *On Your Toes, Star Spangled Rhythm,* and others. Guest ballerina with Ballet (now American Ballet) Theatre, dancing the title role in *Helen of Troy,* Terpsichore in *Apollo,* and others (1943); danced and acted Ariel in Shakespeare's

Vera Zorina as guest ballerina with the Ballet Theatre in Fokine's Helen of Troy.

The Tempest (1944–45). Her first marriage to George Balanchine ended in divorce; her second husband is Goddard Lieberson, president of the Columbia Record Company. Since Jan., 1948, when she spoke the lines of the title part in Arthur Honegger's dramatic oratorio *Joan of Arc at the Stake* with the N.Y. Philharmonic Symphony Orchestra at Carnegie Hall, she has had great success in this specialized career as narrator-performer in similar works, including Stravinsky's *Perséphone,* Milhaud's *Les Choëphores,* Debussy's *The Martyrdom of St. Sebastian,* et al.

Zoritch, George, contemporary American dancer, b. Moscow, ca. 1919. Educated in Kovno, Lithuania, where, at the age of eleven, he began to study ballet at the Opera ballet school. Two years later went to Paris to study with Olga Preobrajenska and a year after that became a member of Ida Rubinstein's company (1933). Joined Col. de Basil's Ballet Russes (1936) and in his first season created the Young Shepherd (*Symphonie Fantastique*) and the Poet (*Jardin Public*), both by Leonide Massine. Joined the Massine-Blum Ballet Russe de Monte Carlo (1938), his repertoire including Baron (*Gaîté Parisienne*), Mercury (*Seventh Symphony*), the male roles in *Les Sylphides, Afternoon of a Faun, Le Spectre de la Rose,* and others. In 1943 danced and acted the juvenile lead in the musical *Early to Bed,* later appearing in *Rhapsody, The Merry Widow,* and others, and in several Hollywood motion pictures, among them *Night and Day, Escape Me Never, The Unfinished Dance, Look for the Silver Lining.* In 1944 he danced with Marquis de Cuevas' International Ballet in N.Y. After appearing in the Olsen and Johnson Broadway show *Pardon Our French,* he returned to ballet, re-joining Grand Ballet du Marquis de Cuevas in Paris and touring Europe and South America as premier danseur, dancing lead roles in *Swan Lake, Ines de Castro, Tragedy in Verona, Night Shadow, Prisoner of the Caucasus,* and the classic pas de deux. Toured with Anna Magnani in a musical revue in Italy (1954) and the same year played eight weeks at Radio City Music Hall. Has been guest artist with various South American ballet companies. Appeared also in concert performances, before returning for three further seasons with de Cuevas. Re-joined Ballet Russe de Monte Carlo (1957), dancing a large repertoire including Albrecht (*Giselle*), Baron (*Gaîté Parisienne*), Siegfried (*Swan Lake*), and Franz (*Coppélia*). Danced at many summer festivals in Europe and several times at Jacob's Pillow. Since 1961 has also toured on many occasions with Marina Svetlova. Does a great deal of teaching throughout the country and has staged several works for regional ballet companies. Opened ballet studio in West Hollywood in Sept., 1964.

George Zoritch, premier danseur classique, shown here in the principal role of Afternoon of a Faun.

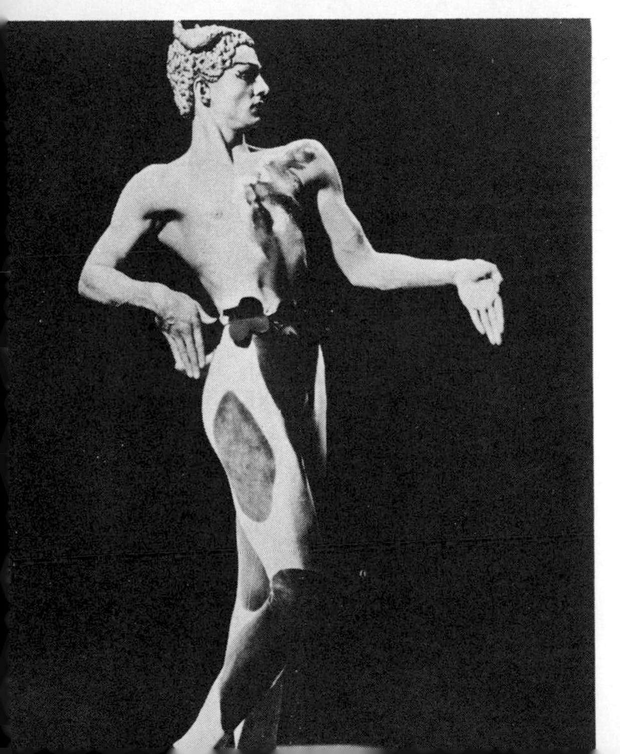

Zorn, Friedrich-Albert, 19th century dance teacher. Studied with Otto Stoige at the Univ. of Koenigsberg and with Bernard Klemm in Leipzig. He was instrumental in forming the German Academy of the Art of Teaching Dance (1873). He also devised a system of dance notation and wrote *Grammatik der Tanzkunst* (Grammar of the Art of Dance) (Leipzig, 1887), which was translated into English by Alfonso Josephs Sheafe and published in Boston (1905, 1920). A piano score of music for the various exercises and some of the short dances described and notated are included in the volume.

Zubkovskaya, Inna, Peoples' Artist of the RSFSR, Soviet ballerina, b. 1923. Zubkovskaya was born in Moscow and graduated from the Bolshoi Theatre in the same class with Violetta Elvin (Prokhorova) (1941). World War II began within two months of her graduation and she was evacuated to Perm, to which city the Kirov Theatre was also evacuated. She joined that company at a time when it was unprecedented for a graduate of the Moscow school to dance in the Kirov company. She easily blended her style with that of the Kirov whose restrained and noble academism suited her own cold, sparkling brilliance. She soon began dancing leading roles, her repertoire including Maria (*The Fountain of Bakhchisarai*), Bird-Girl (*Shurale*), Nikia (*La Bayadère*), Mistress of the Copper Mountain (*The Stone Flower*), Odette-Odile (*Swan Lake*), Lilac Fairy (*The Sleeping Beauty*), Kitri (*Don Quixote*), *Esmeralda*. She created Phrygia in *Spartacus* (1956). Although she is predominantly a lyrical classic dancer she has performed with success a variety of roles of an entirely different kind. In 1961 she created (alternating with Olga Moiseyeva) the role of Mekhmene-Banu in *Legend of Love*. Her first husband was Nicolai Zubkovsky; her second husband is Sviatoslav Kuznetzov of the Kirov Ballet. She had danced in England, U.S., France, Iceland, Hungary, Yugoslavia, Czechoslovakia, and Germany.

Zubkovsky, Nicolai, Honored Artist of the RSFSR, Soviet dancer, b. 1911. Zubkovsky was graduated from the Leningrad Ballet School in 1931 and danced for three years in the Kirov Theatre. He possessed an exceptional ballon and virtuoso technique but due to his short stature was unable to dance danseur noble roles, but excelled in demi-caractère parts. In 1934 he joined the ballet company of the Maly Operny (Little Opera) Theatre of Leningrad with which he was connected even while he was still dancing in the Kirov company. At the Maly he was able to perform parts which gave him the chance to develop his outstanding gifts as an actor. Among his best roles were Harlequin in Fedor Lopoukhov's version of *The Millions of Harlequin* (1933), The Classical Dancer (*Bright Stream,* 1935), Colin (*La Fille Mal Gardée*), André and René in *Fadette,* and especially Truffaldino in *The False Bridegroom,* Boris Fenster's ballet based on Goldoni's *Servitóre di due Padroni* (The Servant of Two Masters), which Zubkovsky created in 1946. He was married to Inna Zubkovskaya, ballerina of the Kirov Theatre, but they were subsequently divorced. He retired from active dancing in 1959.

Zucchi, Virginia (1847–1930), famous Italian ballerina, b. Parma. A pupil of Carlo Blasis, she began her career in the corps de ballet. She became ballerina in Padua, her first ballet being *Brahma.* Appeared as guest artist in Rome, Naples, Madrid, Milan, Turin, Berlin, Paris, and London. In 1885 she went to St. Petersburg as ballerina in a summer theatre (called Abandon Sorrow), where she appeared in the ballet *A Trip to the Moon.* So successful was she in this ballet that the Russian Court ordered the director of the Imperial Theatres to engage her as guest ballerina for the Maryinsky Theatre. She danced there from 1885 to 1892, appearing in all important ballets such as *The Daughter of Pharaoh, Coppélia, Paquita, La Fille Mal Gardée, Esmeralda,* and others. Zucchi was the first ballerina to bring to Russia an example of the forceful and brilliant Italian technique, as differentiated from the graceful and soft French technique prevalent at the Russian Imperial Theatre until then. In a way she created a revolution in the Russian ballet, forcing the school to adapt a more rigorous system of training. In addition to her brilliant technique she had an extraordinary command of pantomime. According to a contemporary critic (Konstantin Skalkovsky), Zucchi's talent lay ". . . in her gift to dance lightly, gaily, elegantly, with a soul and fire, apparently without the slightest effort, and at the same time originally, daringly, gracefully, coquettishly and charmingly." Leaving Russia, Zucchi continued to dance for several years in the capitals of Western Europe and then opened a ballet school in Monte Carlo, where she taught until her last days.

Zuimaaluti. Ballet in 1 act; chor.: Nina Verchinina; music: Cláudio Santoro's Fifth Symphony; book: Manuel Bandeira, inspired by the poem *Toada do Pai-do-Mato* by Mário de Andrade; décor: Roberto Burle-Marx. First prod.: Ballet Rio de Janeiro, Teatro Municipal, Brazil, 1960, with a cast headed by Elza Garcia Galvez (Zuimaaluti), and Arthur Ferreira (Pai-do-Mato). A ballet based on a Brazilian legend which tells of the Indian girl Zuimaaluti who unwittingly joins in the dances of the daughters of Pai-do-Mato, the Father of the Woods, and becomes their companion forever. The modern choreography of Verchinina includes suggestions of native Brazilian dances.

Zullig, Hans, dancer, choreographer, teacher, b. Rorschach, Switzerland, 1914. Studied at Jooss-Leeder School, Essen, Germany, and Dartington Hall, Devon, England (1931–35); Spanish dance with Juan Martinez, Paris (1933). A member of Ballets Jooss, he was a leading dancer from 1935 until the company was disbanded. He created unforgettable portraits of the Young Workman (*Big City*), Young Soldier (*The Green Table*), Mysterious Companion (Kurt Jooss' *Prodigal Son*). His repertoire also included Marquis (*Ballade*), Admirer (*A Ball in Old Vienna*), Armando (*Company at the Manor*), Philippe (*Chronica*), Prince (*A Spring Tale*), and others. Choreographed *Le Bosquet* (1945), in which he danced the leading male role, and *Fantaisie* (1951). Soloist with Sadler's Wells Theatre Ballet (1948–49) creating the Poet (*Selina*). Rejoined Jooss in Essen, teaching in the school and dancing with the company until 1953. Now teaching in Switzerland.

Zverev, Nicholas (ca. 1897–1965), dancer, ballet master, teacher, b. Moscow. Joined the Diaghilev Ballets Russes (1915) and soon became a soloist. His first important solo role was the Acrobat in *Parade* (1917). He also danced Nijinsky's role, the Favorite Slave, in *Schéhérazade* (1921). In Jan., 1926, he and Vera Nemtchinova left the company in Monte Carlo without preliminary notice to fulfill an engagement in London, thus severing their connection with Diaghilev. After their marriage, he and Nemtchinova danced with various companies from 1926 to 1936. They were later divorced. He joined René Blum's Ballet de Monte Carlo as character dancer (1936), remaining with the company until 1945, during which time he also served as ballet master. He revived *Petrouchka* (1948), *Prince Igor* (1949), *Schéhérazade* (1951), and *Le Spectre de la Rose* (1954) for the Paris Opéra. Died in an old people's home in St.-Raphael, France.

PHOTO CREDITS

Derek Allen (London)–331
Kjell Andersson–147
Baron (London)–323, 827
Radford Bascome–185, 976
Isadora Bennett Collection (N.Y.)–459, 468
Paul Berger (Paris)–317
Ingemar Berling–834
Rudolph Betz (Munich)–51
Marcus Blechman–437, 479, 685, 794, 810, 890
Anatole Bourman–186
Bruno of Hollywood–593
Campbell & Chipman (Winnipeg)–893, 979
A. Castro–943
Consolidated Concerts Collection (N.Y.)–134
Constantine (California)–475, 836, 912
S. F. Cristof–206
Dance Collection of the Performing Arts, N.Y. Public Library–614, 885
Dance News, N.Y.–11, 67, 121, 275, 282, 298, 445, 520, 552, 585 (DN Collection), 642, 672, 726 (DN Collection), 755, 774, 828, 835, 859 (DN Collection), 934 (DN Collection), 963, 967
Eileen Darby–601
Frederika Davis–131
del Rote (Trieste)–16
Dominic (London)–820, 938
Engberg–553
S. Enkelman (Berlin)–195
Fayer (Vienna)–157
Muriel Francis Collection–648
Zachary Freyman–917
Grands Ballets Canadiens Collection–198
Peter Gravina Collection–788
Hama (Vienna)–118, 681
Annemarie Heinrich–352, 893
Constance Hope Collection (N.Y.)–395
Hurok Attractions Collection–62, 491, 515, 532, 624, 636, 831, 983
Studio Iris (Paris)–973
Knutson (Colorado)–471
Murray Korman–154
Dr. H. von Kuffner–327, 521
Serge Lido (Paris)–13, 49, 73, 128, 193, 310, 501, 632, 742, 746, 762, 847, 889
Studio Lipnitzki–575
George Platt Lynes–564, 638
Angus McBean (London)–295
Louis Mélançon–319, 846
Metro-Goldwyn-Mayer–523
Metropolitan Musical Bureau Collection–334, 511
Jack Mitchell (N.Y.)–9, 65, 194, 270, 279, 311, 313, 348, 476, 534, 554, 587, 616, 635, 654, 658, 765, 770, 816, 818, 894, 903, 951, 957, 971
Mydtskov (Copenhagen)–522, 547, 607, 804, 832, 954
Walter Owen–6, 15, 537, 604, 669, 968
Carolyn Parks Collection–76
Pimentel Collection (Brussels)–125
Robbins Brothers (N.Y.)–135
Housten Rogers–707
Romaine–75, 508
Roy Round–974
Oscar Savro (Rome)–273
Leif Schröder (Sundbyberg)–239
Seeberger (Paris)–272
Maurice Seymour (N.Y.)–115, 145, 149, 165, 222, 266, 267, 306, 386, 412, 455, 492, 563, 574, 619, 621, 700, 773, 871, 944, 990
Hemendra Shah (India)–801
Wayne Shilkret–624
Noah Sirota–188
Stephan–52
Sune Sondahl (Stockholm)–1
Soichi Sunami–199
Martha Swope–57, 77, 143, 247, 348, 418, 421, 448, 524, 528, 606, 608, 615, 617, 628, 633, 674, 712, 807, 848, 868, 921, 927, 939, 948
Arthur Todd–392
Alfredo Valente–538, 887, 989
Vandamm Studios–696

ABOUT THE AUTHORS

ANATOLE CHUJOY has been the editor and publisher of *Dance News*—the bible of the dance world—since 1942 when he founded it. He is the author of the following books: *Ballet; The Symphonic Ballet; The New York City Ballet*. He edited *Fokine, Memoirs of a Ballet Master,* and translated Agrippina Vaganova's textbook, *Fundamentals of the Classic Dance.* He has also contributed to various dictionaries.

P. W. MANCHESTER has been Managing Editor of *Dance News* since 1951. Previously she had lived and worked in her native England where she was ballet critic for *Theatre World* and later assistant general manager of *Ballet Rambert,* England's oldest ballet company. She also founded and edited *Ballet Today,* a monthly magazine. She is the author of *Vic-Wells: A Ballet Progress* and co-author (with the late Iris Morley) of *The Rose and the Star,* both published in England. She is New York dance critic of the *Christian Science Monitor* and a contributor to various dictionaries, encyclopedias and magazines here and in England.